OXFORD EU LAW LIBRARY

Series Editors: *David Anderson, QC*
Barrister at Brick Court Chambers and
Visiting Professor of Law at King's College London.
Piet Eeckhout, Professor of Law at King's College London,
and Director of the College's Institute of European Law.

EU EMPLOYMENT LAW

Fourth Edition

OXFORD EUROPEAN UNION LAW LIBRARY

The aim of this series is to publish important and original studies of the various branches of EC and EU law. Each work provides a clear, concise, and critical exposition of the law in its social, economic, and political context, at a level which will interest the advanced student, the practitioner, the academic, and government and community officials. Formerly the Oxford European Community Law Library.

EU External Relations Law
Second edition
Piet Eeckhout

EU Justice and Home Affairs Law
Third edition
Steve Peers

The European Union and its Court of Justice
Second edition
Anthony Arnull

The General Principles of EU Law
Third edition
Takis Tridimas

EC Company Law
Vanessa Edwards

Goyder's EC Competition Law
Fifth edition
Joanna Goyder and Albertina
Albors-Llorens

EC Agriculture Law
Second edition
J.A. Usher

Intellectual Property Rights in EU Law
Vol 1: Free Movement and Competition Law
David T. Keeling

EC Customs Law
Second edition
Timothy Lyons, QC

Directives in EC Law
Second edition
Sacha Prechal

The Law of Money
and Financial
Services in the EU
Second edition
J.A. Usher

Workers, Establishment,
and Services in the
European Union
Robin C.A. White

EC Common
Fisheries Policy
Robin Churchill, Daniel Owen

EC Securities
Regulation
Second edition
Niamh Moloney

EU Anti-Discrimination Law
Second edition
Evelyn Ellis and Philippa Watson

EU EMPLOYMENT LAW

Fourth Edition

CATHERINE BARNARD

OXFORD

UNIVERSITY PRESS

OXFORD
UNIVERSITY PRESS

Great Clarendon Street, Oxford, OX2 6DP,
United Kingdom

Oxford University Press is a department of the University of Oxford.
It furthers the University's objective of excellence in research, scholarship,
and education by publishing worldwide. Oxford is a registered trade mark of
Oxford University Press in the UK and in certain other countries

First Edition published in 2006
Fourth Edition published in 2012

Impression: 1

British Library Cataloguing in Publication Data
Data available

Library of Congress Cataloging in Publication Data
Library of Congress Control Number: 2012940351

Printed in Great Britain by
CPI Group (UK) Ltd, Croydon, CR0 4YY

ISBN 978–0–19–969291–0 (Hbk)
ISBN 978–0–19–969292–7 (Pbk)

SERIES EDITORS' FOREWORD

From its conception, the European Economic Community has been struggling with questions about the need for a veritable European social policy, and the role it should play. This excellent book, now in its 4th edition, is no less than a full, next to definitive account of the law which has been created, over many decades, to shape at least some kind of EU social policy. It goes by the name of EU Employment Law, but a moment's browsing will show that that is by no means a narrow concept. It is indeed remarkable how wide-ranging the subject-matter of this book is, including as it does: the law on migrant workers; equality law; health and safety and working conditions; employee rights on the restructuring of enterprises; and collective labour law. And these are only the general parts, which in turn contain more specific chapters.

Professor Barnard does not confine her clear and comprehensive analysis to the legislation which the EU has adopted, and to the case law to which the Treaty provisions and the legislation have given rise. Her approach is richly contextual, and pays great attention to the history of EU social policy. The book also brings to the fore the inherent tension in this policy, between labour deregulation and harmonization. It further exemplifies the strong links between some of the EU's main ventures—the internal market and economic and monetary union—and EU social policy.

What is truly remarkable for the EU law generalist, is the number of EU law core concepts and *causes célèbres* which come under the banner of EU employment law. To mention just a few, the book talks about *Van Duyn* and *Defrenne*; about subsidiarity and the reach of the EU Charter of Fundamental Rights; about *Viking* and *Laval*; about market access, the principle of equality, and positive discrimination; about *Barber* and the *Working Time Directive Case*; about the Open Method of Coordination (OMC); and about most of the case law on remedies in national courts. Invariably, Professor Barnard offers trenchant and insightful analyses, of great relevance to both the practitioner working in the field and to the academic with an interest in EU law, employment law, or both.

This fourth edition is most welcome, in light of the many important developments in this field, in recent years. For one, the EU Charter of Fundamental Rights has entered into force, and it contains an important Solidarity title, listing a number of social rights which are already becoming a presence in the case law. The *Viking/Laval* saga has exposed the scope for tension between the internal market freedoms and fundamental labour rights—something of a clash between EU law titans. Those and many other developments are carefully dissected and critically commented. But Professor Barnard goes further, and bravely puts the most recent life of EU employment law in the context of the ongoing financial crisis. Her carefully argued defence of social *rights*, in the face of attempts to make progress by means of the OMC and of austerity responses to the crisis, puts the icing on the cake of this marvellous fourth edition.

Piet Eeckhout
David Anderson
April 2012

PREFACE

Any book about the employment law of the European Union must consider the rules—both hard and soft—which regulate the relationship between individuals and their employer, and between worker representatives and employers. However, in order to understand EU employment law, the regulation in this field needs to be considered against the broader backcloth of national employment laws and collective agreements, of employment policy (measures to protect and promote employment), and of social policy. Traditionally, 'social' policy refers to measures which come under the broad umbrella of the welfare state, such as housing, healthcare, education, social security, and social assistance. However, in the EU context, social policy has often been considered as broadly synonymous with employment law: the relevant Title in the Treaty (Title X) is headed social policy and the relevant chapter (Chapter 1) is entitled 'Social provisions' even though their content, especially in the early days, was broadly employment related. Thus, there is an inevitable bleeding and mixing of concepts.[1] It is with the area of social policy concerned with employment law, both individual and collective, that this book is concerned, and not with social law and policy as more broadly understood.

Within the field of employment law—and policy—this book considers both the law-making process and the rules which result. It also analyses the (now extensive) case law of the Court of Justice of the European Union (CJEU) which has, at times, been creative and imaginative in constructing a distinctive body of European social law, but at other times the Court has appeared conservative and even destructive of the national employment law on which it has to draw for much of foundations of EU employment law. This book does not examine the individual employment laws of the Member States, although it does draw on examples from certain jurisdictions—particularly the UK, the system with which I am most familiar—to give examples of not only how the EU rules have been implemented by the Member States but also how aspects of EU law are informed by, and derived from, national employment laws.

Since the last edition of this book was published in early 2006, the law has changed substantially. In particular, the Lisbon Treaty has come into force giving legal effect to the Charter of Fundamental Rights, the EU2020 strategy has replaced the less than successful Lisbon strategy, and the seismic decisions of *Viking*[2] and *Laval*[3] and their progeny have been handed down by the CJEU. Meanwhile Europe has experienced the worst financial crisis since the 1930s and the Euro has been brought to the brink of collapse. As Chapter 3 will demonstrate, this has direct and indirect consequences for employment law.

---

[1] See further N. Countouris, 'European Social Law as an Autonomous Legal Discipline' (2009) 28 *YEL* 95.

[2] Case C–438/05 *Viking Line ABP* v. *The International Transport Workers' Federation, the Finnish Seaman's Union* [2007] ECR I–10779.

[3] Case C–341/05 *Laval un Partneri Ltd* v. *Svenska Byggnadsarbetareförbundet* [2007] ECR I–11767.

The fourth edition of this book broadly retains the structure of the previous edition. It is divided into six parts. The first Part is introductory, intended to give an overview of the development of social policy by the EU and the various approaches to rule making. In particular, Chapter 1 considers the Union's stumbling progress towards developing 'social policy', or more particularly 'employment law' at EU level. It considers the rationale for such a policy and the pressures which operate to constrain its development. Chapter 2 examines how these pressures shape the law-making process in the field of (hard) EU employment law, while Chapter 3 considers the Employment Title, the Lisbon/EU2020 strategy, and soft law-making in the social field together with a consideration of the effects of the financial crisis on employment law.

The remainder of the book focuses on the substantive law. Part II looks at the position of migrant workers. Chapter 4 considers the rights of migrant workers, primarily under Article 45 TFEU. Since the question of personal scope has become such an important issue in EU employment law, this Chapter uses the discussion of 'who is a worker' for the purposes of Article 45 as the basis of a broader consideration about the personal scope of EU employment law. A new Chapter 5 considers how the internal market has had an impact on national labour law. In particular, it examines the effects of Article 49 TFEU on freedom of establishment and Article 56 TFEU on national laws which permit strike action. Thus the main—but not the exclusive—focus of this Chapter is on the decisions in *Viking* and *Laval* and the Commission's response in the form of the proposed Monti II Regulation and the proposed enforcement Directive.[4]

Part III considers one of the major pillars of EU employment law: equality and non-discrimination. After an introduction (Chapter 6) considering how the law has evolved in this field and an explanation of the key principles, the following Chapters go on to examine equal pay (Chapter 7), equal treatment (Chapter 8), family friendly policies (Chapter 9), and equal treatment in respect of social security and pensions (Chapter 10). Part IV then looks at health and safety (Chapter 11) and working conditions (Chapter 12), while Part V considers employee rights on the restructuring of enterprises, in particular transfers of undertakings (Chapter 13), and collective redundancies and employee rights on the insolvency of the employer (Chapter 14). Finally, Part VI examines the more 'collective' aspect of labour law: Chapter 15 looks at worker representation, particularly through information and consultation, and Chapter 16 examines freedom of association, collective bargaining, and industrial action.

One major issue has bedevilled the writing of this edition: Treaty (re)numbering. Even prior to Lisbon, the renumbering of the Treaties was a particular problem in the social field because, in effect, it happened twice: once when the Social Policy Agreement (SPA) was incorporated into the Treaty of Rome at Amsterdam in 1997 and again when the whole Treaty was renumbered, also at Amsterdam. Thus, for example, the health and safety legal basis Article 118a EEC became Article 118, then Article 137 EC, and is now Article 153 TFEU. Confusingly, Article 3 SPA became Article 118a at Amsterdam, and then Article 138 EC, and is now Article 154 TFEU. The working practice I have

---

[4] COM(2012) 130 and 131 respectively.

adopted is that, when talking historically, I have used the original EEC or EC numbers followed by the Lisbon numbers, where appropriate. Otherwise, I have used the Lisbon numbers throughout even in respect of cases decided under the Rome or Amsterdam numberings to avoid (even greater) confusion. At times the result is not very satisfactory. I have also converted most references from 'Community' to 'Union', except in the case of the *Community* Social Charter 1989 and the 'classic *Community* method'.

Many people have been extremely generous with their time and patience in the completion of this book. The first three editions benefited from the advice of Jon Clark, Nicholas Emiliou, Andrew Fielding, Lorraine Fletcher, Rosa Greaves, Bob Hepple, Clive Lewis, Roy Lewis, Tonia Novitz, and Christine Warry. For this edition I have benefited greatly from chatting with Louise Merrett about the intricacies of the formation of the under-8s' defence in football and the Rome I Regulation; from Sarah Hansen's assistance with addressing the renumbering; from regular meetings and lively discussions with Sjoerd Feenstra, usually about *Viking* and *Laval*; and from my participation in the Commission funded European Labour Law Network. Alex Flach at OUP has been enthusiastic, patient, and supportive. Zoë Organ, Ceri Warner, and Matthew Humphrys have worked wonders on the text. Domestically, I have been (generally) grateful for the distraction of my three troops—large, medium, and small—while enjoying the love and support of their commander-in-chief.

Catherine Barnard
Trinity College
31 January 2012

SUMMARY TABLE OF CONTENTS

PART VI COLLECTIVE LABOUR LAW

CONTENTS

PART I INTRODUCTION

PART II MIGRANT WORKERS

PART IV HEALTH AND SAFETY AND WORKING CONDITIONS

PART V EMPLOYEE RIGHTS ON RESTRUCTURING ENTERPRISES

PART VI COLLECTIVE LABOUR LAW

TABLE OF CASES AND EUROPEAN
COMMUNITY DECISIONS

GENERAL COURT

United States of America

EFTA Court

TABLE OF LEGISLATION

PROPOSED EUROPEAN UNION DIRECTIVES

National Legislation

Canada

Denmark

LIST OF FIGURES

LIST OF TABLES AND BOXES

PART I

INTRODUCTION

1

THE EVOLUTION OF EU 'SOCIAL' POLICY

A. INTRODUCTION

Social policy has long been viewed as the poor relation in the integration process. The near total absence of any provision for social matters in the original EEC Treaty eventually precipitated one of the most profound debates affecting the development of the European Union: should the Union have a social face and, if so, what form should it take and at what level should it be provided? The principal aim of this chapter is to trace the evolution of Union social policy[1] and to consider the forces and principles driving this development. It will be seen that the creation of a European social policy has been by no means linear: phases of great activity have been matched by lengthy phases of inertia. It will also be seen that while there is now an identifiable body of EU law which can loosely be described as 'labour' or 'social' policy, its coverage is far from comprehensive, and it certainly does not represent a replication of national social policy on the EU stage. The justifications for establishing a European social policy have also varied over time, and the legislative techniques for achieving these objectives have been the subject of a dramatic evolution. Chapter 1 focuses on the development of EU 'social' policy and the justification for its existence; Chapters 2 and 3 examine the different legislative and governance techniques.

---

[1] For more detail, see, e.g., B. Bercusson, *European Labour Law* (Cambridge, CUP, 2009); R. Blanpain, *European Labour Law* 12th edn (Kluwer, 2010); J. Kenner, *EU Employment Law: from Rome to Amsterdam and Beyond* (Hart Publishing, Oxford, 2003); R. Nielsen and E. Szyszczak, *The Social Dimension of the European Community* 2nd edn (Handelshøjskolens Forlag, Copenhagen, 1997); M. Shanks, *The European Social Policy Today and Tomorrow* (Pergamon, Oxford, 1977); P. Teague, *The European Community, the Social Dimension, Labour Market Policies for 1992* (Kogan Page, London, 1989) esp. ch. 4; P. Watson, *EU Social and Employment Law* (OUP, Oxford, 2009).

B. THE DEVELOPMENT OF EU SOCIAL POLICY BY THE UNION INSTITUTIONS

1. THE TREATY OF ROME

1.1. The social provisions

The basic thrust of the Treaty of Rome was economic: to create a common market consisting of free movement of products (goods and services) and production factors (labour and capital).[2] Although the Treaty of Rome did contain a Title on Social Policy, its provisions were largely exhortatory and conferred little by way of direct rights on citizens.[3] This was illustrated by Article 117 EEC (new and amended Article 151 TFEU), which provided: 'Member States agree upon the need to promote improved working conditions and an improved standard of living for workers, so as to make possible their harmonisation while the improvement is being maintained'. Similarly, Article 118 EEC (new and amended Article 156 TFEU) failed to provide legally enforceable rights. It entrusted the Commission with the task of promoting 'close cooperation between the Member States and [facilitating] the coordination of their action in all social policy fields', particularly in matters relating to employment, labour law and working conditions, basic and advanced vocational training, social security, prevention of occupational accidents and diseases, occupational hygiene, the right of association, and collective bargaining between employers and workers. The limited scope of this provision was highlighted in *Germany, UK and Others* v. *Commission*[4] where the Court ruled that the Article gave the Commission procedural powers only to set up consultations within the subjects covered. It could not be used to impose on Member States results to be achieved, nor could it prevent Member States from taking measures at national level.

The other social provisions found in the Social Title were similarly limited in scope. Article 121 EEC (new but wholly revised Article 160 TFEU) permitted the Council to assign to the Commission tasks in connection with the 'implementation of common measures', in particular as regards social security for migrant workers; Article 122 EEC (Article 161 TFEU) required the Commission to include a separate chapter on 'social developments' in its annual report to the European Parliament,[5] and Article 128 EEC (new and amended Article 166 TFEU) required the Council to 'lay down general principles' for implementing a common vocational training policy. The only provision which might have contained some substance was Article 119 EEC (Article 157 TFEU) on equal pay for men and women; and even that obligation was addressed to the Member States and not to individual employers.

---

[2] Arts. 2 and 3 EEC.

[3] W. Hallstein, *Europe in the Making* (1972), 119, cited in P. Watson, 'The Community Social Charter' (1991) 28 *CMLRev.* 37, 39.

[4] Joined Cases 281/85, 283/85, 285/85, 287/85 *Germany, UK and Others* v. *Commission* [1987] ECR 3203.

[5] The Parliament may also request the Commission to draw up reports on any particular problems relating to social conditions.

1.2. The influence of the Ohlin and Spaak reports

This raises the question why a Title headed 'Social Policy' should contain so little of substance. The answer lay in part with the original objectives of the European Union, which was conceived as the European *Economic* Community. The view was that economic integration—the removal of artificial obstacles to the free movement of labour, goods, and capital—would in time ensure the optimum allocation of resources throughout the Union, the optimum rate of economic growth and thus an optimum social system,[6] which would lead, according to the Preamble, to the 'constant improvement of the living and working conditions of their peoples'. This approach was spelled out in Article 117 EEC (Article 153 TFEU) which provided that Member States believed that an improvement in working conditions 'will *ensue* not only from the functioning of the Common Market . . . but also . . . from the approximation of provisions laid down by law, regulation or administrative action'.[7] This statement represented a victory for the classic neo-liberal market tradition: there was no need for a European-level social dimension because high social standards were 'rewards' for efficiency.[8]

The highly influential Spaak report,[9] drawn up by the foreign ministers prior to the signing of the Treaty of Rome, had also envisaged only limited action in the social field to ensure the functioning of the Common Market. It rejected the idea of trying to harmonize the fundamental conditions of the national economy—its natural resources, its level of productivity, the significance of public burdens—considering that any harmonization might be the result of, as opposed to a condition precedent to, the operation of the Common Market and the economic forces which it released. Spaak relied heavily on the earlier Ohlin report of ILO experts.[10] This report had argued for the transnational harmonization of social policy in some areas, such as equal pay, but, invoking the economic theory of comparative advantage, rejected a general role for harmonization of social policy. It argued that differences in nominal wage costs between countries did not, in themselves, pose an obstacle to economic integration because what mattered was unit labour costs, taking into account the relationship between nominal costs and productivity. Because higher costs tended to accompany higher productivity, differences between countries were less than they seemed. This explained why there was no need for harmonization.

Ohlin also suggested that the system of national exchange rates, which could be expected to reflect general prices and productivity levels within states, would cancel out the apparent advantage of low-wage states, so avoiding a race to the bottom—the phenomenon of standards of social protection either being depressed in states with higher standards or at least prevented from rising, by increased competition from states with substantially lower social standards. Consequently, Ohlin argued that the market itself would ensure that conditions of competition were not distorted. The strength of

---

[6] M. Shanks, 'Introductory Article: The Social Policy of the European Community' (1977) 14 *CMLRev.* 14.

[7] Emphasis added.

[8] See further T. Hervey, *European Social Law and Policy* (Longman, Harlow, 1998) 7.

[9] Rapport des Chefs de Délèlgations, Comité Intergouvernemental, 21 April 1956, 19–20, 60–1.

[10] International Labour Office, 'Social Aspects of European Economic Cooperation' (1956) 74 *International Labour Review* 99.

this argument and its influence on the debate about the function of EU social policy is considered below.

Although opposed to general intervention in the social sphere, the Spaak committee did say that action should be taken to correct or eliminate the effect of specific distortions which advantage or disadvantage certain branches of activity. By way of example, the authors cited a list of areas including working conditions of labour such as the relationship between the salaries of men and women, working time, overtime and paid holidays, and different policies relating to credit. This suggested that the Union should act in these fields only.

However, later commentators suggested that the Spaak committee's views were not as clearly reflected in the final version of the Treaty as might have been the case,[11] perhaps because the relevant provisions were drafted only at the end of a crucial conversation between the French and German Prime Ministers.[12] At the time of the Treaty negotiations there were important differences in the scope and content of social legislation in force in the states concerned. France, in particular, had a number of rules which favoured workers, including legislation on equal pay for men and women, and rules permitting French workers longer paid holidays than in other states. French workers were also entitled to overtime pay after fewer hours of work at basic rates than elsewhere. This raised concerns that the additional costs borne by French industry would make French goods uncompetitive in the Common Market. Consequently, the French argued that an elimination of gross distortions of competition was not enough, and that it would be necessary to assimilate the entire labour and social legislation of the Member States, so as to achieve a parity of wages and social costs. The Germans, however, were strongly committed to keeping to a minimum government interference in the area of wages and prices. The resulting compromise was reflected in the Treaty's social policy provisions. Articles 117 and 118 EEC (new and amended Articles 151 and 156 TFEU) on the need to improve working conditions and cooperation between states, even if textually broad, were legally shallow, reflecting the German preference for laissez-faire.[13] Article 119 EEC (Article 157 TFEU) on equal pay and Article 120 EEC (Article 158 TFEU) on paid holiday schemes and the third protocol on 'Certain Provisions Relating to France' on working hours and overtime,[14] by contrast, were specific

---

[11] O. Kahn-Freund, 'Labour Law and Social Security', in E. Stein and T. Nicholson (eds.), *American Enterprise in the European Common Market: A Legal Profile* (University of Michigan Law School, Ann Arbor, 1960) 300. See C. Barnard, 'The Economic Objectives of Article 119', in T. Hervey and D. O'Keeffe (eds.), *Sex Equality Law in the European Union* (Wiley, Chichester, 1996).

[12] Kahn-Freund, above n. 11, citing M. Katzenstein, *Der Arbeitnehmer in der Europäischen Wirtschaftsgemeinschaft* (1957) 31 *Betriebs-Berater* 1081.

[13] M. Forman, 'The Equal Pay Principle under Community Law' (1982) 1 *LIEI* 17.

[14] This provided that the Commission was to authorize France to take protective measures where the establishment of the Common Market did not result, by the end of the first stage, in the basic number of hours beyond which overtime was paid and the average rate of additional payment for overtime industry corresponding to the average obtaining in France in 1956. It does not seem that France has called upon this safeguard clause: M. Budiner, *Le Droit de la femme l'Égalité de salaire et la Convention No. 100 de l'organisation internationale du travail* (Librairie Générale de Droit et de Jurisprudence, Paris, 1975).

provisions designed to protect French industry.[15] This was the sort of intervention envisaged by Spaak and Ohlin.

While light on traditional social policy measures, the original Treaty did contain more detailed provisions in respect of free movement of persons. According to the Spaak report,[16] free movement of labour was crucial to social prosperity. By allowing workers to move to find available work, they would go from areas where labour was cheap and plentiful to areas where there was demand. It was hoped that free circulation of labour would facilitate an equalization in the terms and conditions of competition.[17] To achieve this goal, Articles 48–66 EEC (Articles 45–62 TFEU) were introduced into the Treaty to remove obstacles to the free movement of persons, and complemented by Article 123 EEC (Article 162 TFEU) establishing the European Social Fund, designed to make the employment of workers easier and to increase their geographic and occupational mobility.[18] Article 51 EEC (Article 58 TFEU) provided a basis for EU regulation in the social security field, based on a policy of co-ordination and not harmonization. The provisions on free movement of persons are considered in detail in Chapters 4 and 5 of this book.

In conclusion, the absence of a clearly identifiable Union social policy can be explained by the fact that generally Member States believed that social policy, and labour law in particular, lay at the very heart of national sovereignty,[19] and viewed it as an important vehicle to preserve 'the integrity and political stability of their respective political regimes'.[20] Thus, at a time of unprecedented activity at national level with workers gaining new legal rights and welfare benefits, there was little pressure for harmonization at European level. However, this decision to give precedence to economic over social objectives was to have serious ramifications in years to come. By decoupling two policies (economic policy and social policy) traditionally inter-linked at national level, and by giving primacy to economic policy, social policy has inevitably been downgraded. And, as decisions of the Court of Justice have shown,[21] in the absence of an express constitutional imperative to take social matters into account, economic policies such as free trade and free competition, read in conjunction with the doctrines of supremacy and direct effect, risked seriously destabilizing national social systems.

---

[15] According to the French Advocate General Dutheillet de Lamothe in Case 80/70 *Defrenne (No. 1)* v. *SABENA* [1971] ECR 445, 'It appears to be France which took the initiative, but the article [157] necessitated quite long negotiations'. However, the content of Art. 157 TFEU was strongly influenced by ILO Convention No. 100 on equal pay. See C. Hoskyns, *Integrating Gender* (Verso, London, 1996).

[16] Rapport des Chefs de Délégations, Comité Intergouvernemental, 21 April 1956, 19–20, 60–1.

[17] Ibid., 78.

[18] There was also a social dimension to the Common Agricultural Policy Art. 39 TFEU (ex 33 EC) in the form of grants from the European Agricultural Guidance and Guarantee Fund (EAGGF).

[19] G. Ross, 'Assessing the Delors' Era and Social Policy', in S. Leibfried and P. Pierson (eds.), *European Social Policy: Between Fragmentation and Integration* (Brookings Institution, Washington DC, 1995) 360.

[20] W. Streeck, 'Neo-voluntarism: A New Social Policy Regime' (1995) 1 *ELJ* 31.

[21] See in particular the cases discussed in Ch. 5.

That said, the Commission noted in its *First General Report on the Activities of the Community* in 1958[22] that '[i]t [the Commission] bears particular responsibilities in this field [of social policy] and intends to neglect no sphere in which it may prove possible to "promote close cooperation"'. With remarkable prescience, the Commission observed that '[i]t is convinced that in the future the [Union] will be judged by a large part of public opinion on the basis of its direct and indirect successes in the social field'.[23] The Commission also noted that the reference in the Preamble of the Treaty to 'both economic and *social* progress' and to 'constantly improving the living and working conditions of their peoples' made it clear that 'the objectives of a social character are placed on the same footing as those of an economic character',[24] albeit that 'the legal framework of the [Union's] action in the social field is less rigid'.[25] These words neatly encapsulate the tension originally surrounding social policy at European level: the desire, especially in the Commission, to develop an EU social policy but the absence, at least until recently, of a clear legal basis on which to do so.

2. A CHANGE OF DIRECTION

2.1. The 1970s and legislative activity

Non-intervention in the social field did not last. On the eve of the accession of three new Member States in 1973, the heads of government meeting in Paris issued a communiqué, stating that the Member States:

> ...emphasised that vigorous action in the social sphere is to them just as important as achieving Economic and Monetary Union. They consider it absolutely necessary to secure an increasing share by both sides of industry in the [Union's] economic and social decisions.[26]

This change of approach can be explained in part by reference to the social unrest in Western Europe in 1968,[27] and in part by an economic recession in Europe following the twin oil shocks of the 1970s. The feeling was that the Union required a human face to persuade its citizens that the social consequences of growth were being effectively tackled and that the Union was more than a device enabling business to exploit the Common Market.[28] Failure to have taken action at this time might have jeopardized the whole process of economic integration. Thus, the early 1970s was the first time when it was realized that the growth-based, neo-liberal ideology was not actually delivering on its promises and that a social dimension was necessary to address the problems faced by the 'losers'—both individuals and companies—suffering from the consequences of European economic integration; and that social policy measures were now necessary to maintain and support the established social order.

---

[22] 17 September 1958. The Social Affairs Council did not even meet between 1964 and 1966, see Hervey, above, n. 8, 16.
[23] Para. 103.   [24] Para. 102.   [25] Para. 103.   [26] EC Bull. 10/1972, paras. 6 and 19.
[27] M. Wise and R. Gibb, *Single Market to Social Europe* (Longman, Harlow, 1993) 144.
[28] Shanks, at n. 1, 378.

In response, the Commission drew up an Action Programme[29] containing three objectives: the attainment of full and better employment in the Union; the improvement of living and working conditions; and increased involvement of management and labour in the economic and social decisions of the Union and of workers in the life of the undertaking. This Action Programme precipitated a phase of remarkable legislative activity. Directives were adopted in the field of sex discrimination,[30] and the whole field of sex equality assumed a new importance as a result of judgments by the Court in the *Defrenne* cases.[31] An Action Programme and a number of Directives were adopted in the field of health and safety and, in the face of rising unemployment, measures were taken to ease the impact of mass redundancies,[32] the transfer of undertakings,[33] and insolvent employers.[34] At the same time, the European Regional Development Fund[35] was introduced in order to address the problems of socio-economic convergence in the Union.

Although this legislation appeared quite extensive, it was in fact confined to certain areas of employment law, as strictly understood, and not to the broader social sphere as originally envisaged by the 1972 communiqué. Further, this legislation had to be adopted under the general Treaty bases, Articles 100 and 235 EEC (Articles 115 and 352 TFEU), both requiring the unanimous agreement of all the Member States. This ensured the Member States retained control over the supranational regulation of employment rights.

2.2. The early 1980s: stagnation

By the start of the 1980s, enthusiasm for developing a European social policy began to wane. The new Conservative government in the UK, led by Margaret Thatcher, insisted on strict limits to the growth of Union social policy, and, in particular, it was fundamentally opposed to the notion that workers' participation had an essential role in the management of change, thereby stymieing the adoption of two important Directives: the Fifth Directive on Company Structure and the draft Vredling Directive on information and consultation of employees.[36] The UK strongly advocated deregulation of the labour markets in order to ensure maximum flexibility of the workforce, in line with the American model, and argued for the need to adapt to new technology and the necessity of reducing the burden of regulation on business in order to enable business to compete in a global market.[37] This view represented a strong form of the neo-liberal market tradition. Put simply, the Thatcherite view was that society comprised individuals, each of whom could compete within the marketplace: no further state intervention, especially in the social field was either necessary or desirable.[38] This philosophy ran into direct

---

[29] OJ [1974] C13/1.
[30] Dir. 75/117 on equal pay (OJ [1975] L45/19), Dir. 76/207 on equal treatment (OJ [1976] L39/40) and Dir. 79/7 on equal treatment in social security (OJ [1979] L6/24).
[31] Case 80/70 *Defrenne (No. 1)* v. *Belgian State* [1971] ECR 445, Case 43/75 *Defrenne (No. 2)* v. *SABENA* [1976] ECR 455 and Case 149/77 *Defrenne (No. 3)* v. *SABENA* [1978] ECR 1365. See further Ch. 6.
[32] Dir. 75/129/EEC (OJ [1975] L48/29).   [33] Dir. 77/187/EEC (OJ [1977] L61/27).
[34] Dir. 80/987/EEC (OJ [1980] L283/23).   [35] Reg. 724/75 (OJ [1975] L73/8).
[36] See further Ch. 15.   [37] See e.g. *Employment: the Challenge to the Nation*, Cmnd 9474.
[38] Hervey, above, n. 8, 7.

conflict with the regulatory stance adopted by the Commission. While the Commission recognized the need for a flexible and adaptable workforce, it did not equate flexibility with deregulation and it refused to renege on its commitment to safeguarding the rights of employees.[39] However, since at that stage, all social policy measures required unanimity in Council the UK was able to veto any proposals to which it objected.[40]

Stagnation in the social field reflected a wider malaise with the Union. Disillusion with the tenets of Union policy and wranglings over budgetary contributions brought the Union legislative process shuddering almost to a halt. The arrival of Jacques Delors as President of the Commission, and his proposal for a Single Market to be completed by 1992, represented, at least in the medium term, an end to this period of inertia.

3. THE SINGLE MARKET AND THE COMMUNITY SOCIAL CHARTER 1989

3.1. The Single European Act 1986

The Single European Act 1986 (SEA) and the Single Market programme breathed new life into the idea that liberalization of trade would lead to economies of scale and economic growth from which the greatest number of Union citizens would benefit. The Cecchini report on the costs of non-Europe emphasized the importance of the Single Market programme in terms of its implications for 'very substantial job creation'.[41] This was really the only recognition of the social consequences of the Single Market. Although the idea of adding a social dimension to the internal market programme had been discussed, particularly by the European Parliament, the Single European Act in fact made few concessions to those who had argued for greater social competence for the Union. The Union did, however, commit itself to strengthening economic and social cohesion (Article 130a EEC (Article 174 TFEU)), with the aim of reducing disparities between the levels of development of the various regions and the backwardness of the least favoured regions, including rural areas, and to developing the 'dialogue between management and labour at European level', institutionalizing the so-called social dialogue (Article 118b EEC (new and amended Article 155 TFEU)). Otherwise, Article 8a EEC (Article 26 TFEU), setting the deadline of 31 December 1992 for the completion of the internal market programme, was concerned only with the realization of the four freedoms (goods, workers, services, and capital) and made no mention of social policy.

For practical purposes, perhaps the most significant innovation for social policy introduced by the SEA was the extension of qualified majority voting to measures adopted in the field of health and safety of workers by Article 118a EEC (new and amended Article 153 TFEU), although matters 'relating to the rights and interests of employed persons'

---

[39] See further B. Hepple, 'The Crisis in EEC Labour Law' (1987) 16 *ILJ* 77, 81.

[40] Union legislation on sex equality and health and safety was, however, adopted in this period. This can be explained in part by the fact that UK legislation already guaranteed fairly substantial protection in these fields.

[41] P. Cecchini, *The European Challenge: 1992, the Benefits of a Single Market* (Gower, Aldershot, 1988) XIX.

(Article 100a(2) EEC (Article 114(2) TFEU)) still required the unanimous agreement of Council. Article 118a(2) EEC gave the Council the power to adopt minimum standards directives which allowed Member States to maintain or introduce 'more stringent measures for the protection of working conditions compatible with this Treaty' (Article 118a(3) EEC).[42] These provisions represented an important shift in thinking. First, they demonstrated that the Union would not harmonize all labour standards but merely set a floor of basic rights. Secondly, they viewed the 'protection' of labour as a value in its own right, and a value which the Union should have a role in preserving.

The true significance of Article 118a EEC only became apparent as the British hostility to the Union's social policy became ever more firmly entrenched: Article 118a EEC provided the Commission with a way of circumventing the UK's veto. Article 118a EEC therefore offered the EU the opportunity to construct a larger 'social' Europe, providing a bulwark against the dismantling of national labour law,[43] at a time when certain Member States (notably the UK) were pursuing a deregulatory agenda. As a result, Article 118a EEC provided the legal basis for the successful adoption of important Directives on Working Time,[44] Pregnant Workers,[45] and Young Workers.[46]

The lack of a true social dimension to the SEA did, however, prompt some concern that the ambitious Single Market programme would not succeed unless it had the support of the Union citizens. This concern was combined with the realization that the Single Market programme would also produce negative consequences for employees: as the European market opened up, uncompetitive firms would go out of business and large companies might relocate to areas of Europe where social costs were lower. In both cases unemployment would result. For these reasons Jacques Delors set out his plans for 'L'Espace Social Européen',[47] arguing that:

> The creation of a vast economic area, based on the market and business cooperation, is inconceivable—I would say unattainable—without some harmonisation of social legislation. Our ultimate aim must be the creation of a European social area.[48]

Delors's vision coincided with growing pressure for the establishment of a people's Europe designed to give the 'individual citizen a clearer perception of the dimension and the existence of the [Union]'[49]—in other words a recognition that 'Europe exists for its citizens, and not the other way round'.[50]

---

[42] These provisions are considered further in Ch. 2.

[43] M. Poiares Maduro, 'Europe's Social Self: "The Sickness unto Death"', in J. Shaw (ed.), *Social Law and Policy in an Evolving European Union* (Hart Publishing, Oxford, 2000).

[44] Council Dir. 93/104/EC (OJ [1993] L307/18).

[45] Council Dir. 92/85/EEC (OJ [1992] L348/1).

[46] Council Dir. 94/33/EC (OJ [1994] L216/12).

[47] This is not a new concept: the French government had been talking in these terms since 1981. See further, R. Vandamme, 'De la Politique Social à l'Espace Social Européen (1983) *Revue du Marché Commun* 562. Mitterand had issued a memorandum to Council on the creation of a European Social Area.

[48] EC Bull. 2/1986, 12.

[49] The Adonnino Report, *A People's Europe: Reports from the ad hoc Committee*, Bull. Supp. 7/1985, 14. See further Commission, *Towards a People's Europe*, European File 3/86.

[50] President of the Council, 14 July 1993, cited in Commission, *A Citizen's Europe* (Brussels, 1993) 9.

These statements demonstrated a growing recognition that social and economic conditions were not in fact divisible and that economic efficiency had to be balanced by welfare objectives to 'humanize' the market, for reasons of fairness and distributive justice.[51] This is sometimes described as the market-correcting or the social justice approach to social policy. As Hervey points out, this model is based on notions of solidarity, a position which views social welfare as a collective activity rather than the responsibility of individuals, and social citizenship, the normative claim that egalitarian provision of welfare needs is superior to individual neo-liberal provision.[52]

3.2. The Community Social Charter 1989 and the Social Charter Action Programme

The social dimension of the internal market took more concrete form with the signing of the Community Charter of Fundamental Social Rights, by all the Member States except Britain, during the Strasbourg summit in 1989. Although the European Parliament was most anxious that the Charter be incorporated into Union law by means of a binding instrument,[53] in the event it was adopted merely as, in the words of the Preamble, a 'solemn proclamation of fundamental social rights'. It therefore had no free-standing legal effect[54] (albeit it has been invoked by the Court of Justice as an interpretative tool[55]). The absence of legal effect, combined with concerns about its content,[56] attracted adverse comment in some quarters. Vogel-Polsky described it variously as a 'bitter failure' and putting 'non-decision into a concrete form';[57] and Metall called it 'a non-binding wish list' full of 'rubber formulations' and loopholes that were 'not worth the paper on which it was printed'.[58] Silvia explained the Charter's failings by reference first, to British intransigence within the Council, combined with a willingness on the part of the other governments to take advantage of the UK's position; and second, to the failure by the European Trade Union movement either to raise convincingly the spectre of social unrest if it was dissatisfied or to promise electoral benefits to ministers if they adopted more radical social policy proposals.[59]

In one sense the Charter is not a radical document: its Preamble still contains an endorsement of the old philosophies, that the completion of the internal market is the 'most effective means of creating employment and ensuring maximum well being in the

---

[51] Hervey, at n. 8, 10.   [52] Ibid.   [53] See OJ [1991] C96/61 and OJ [1989] C120/5.

[54] Cf. A. Riley, 'The European Social Charter and Community Law' (1989) 14 *ELRev*. 80 and the reply by M. Gould, 'The European Social Charter and Community Law. A Comment' (1989) 14 *ELRev*. 80. AG Jacobs confirmed that the Charter was not legally binding: Case C–67/96 *Albany International BV* v. *Stichting Bedrijfspensioenfonds Textielindustrie* [1999] ECR I–5751, para. 137.

[55] See, e.g. Joined Cases C–397/01 to C–403/01 *Pfeiffer* v. *Deutches Rotes Kreuz* [2004] ECR I–8835, para. 91.

[56] See esp. B. Bercusson, 'The European Community's Charter of Fundamental Social Rights of Workers' (1990) 53 *MLR* 624; P. Watson, 'The Community Social Charter' (1991) 28 *CMLRev*. 37; S. Silvia, 'The Social Charter of the European Community: A Defeat for European Labor' (1990–91) 44 *Industrial and Labour Relations Review* 626.

[57] 'What Future is there for a Social Europe Following the Strasbourg Summit?' (1990) 19 *ILJ* 65.

[58] German Metal Workers' Union, quoted in Silvia, above, n. 56.

[59] Silva, above, n. 56, 640. See further A. Jacobs, 'Social Europe in Delay' (1990) 6 *IJCLLIR* 26, 35.

[Union]', earlier references to combating *un*employment having been removed. Earlier drafts of the Charter had also talked of improvements in the social field for *citizens*. The final version specified that the Charter gave rights only to *workers*.[60] This suggests that the concept of a European social area had been abandoned for the present; and that the social aspect of the internal market had been substituted in its place. On the other hand, the Charter does contain 26 rights which Member States have the responsibility to guarantee and it does recognize that the 'same importance' be attached to the social aspects as to the economic aspects of the European Union which must be 'developed in a balanced manner'.

The rights contained in the Social Charter 1989 were to be implemented through the Social Charter Action Programme[61] and any measures adopted were to be based on the EEC Treaty and therefore binding on the UK. The Action Programme put forward by the Commission, when its power, prestige and entrepreneurialism may have been at its highest point, proposed that 47 different instruments be submitted by 1 January 1993. However, of these 47 proposals there were only 17 Directives,[62] of which 10 dealt with narrow health and safety matters, such as safety of the workplace,[63] safety of work equipment,[64] safety of VDUs,[65] and manual handling of loads.[66] This contrasted unfavourably with the proposals for almost 300 Directives submitted as part of the White Paper for Completing the Internal Market.[67] Nevertheless, the Action Programme led to the enactment of important pieces of social legislation aimed at protecting individual workers, including Directives on proof of the employment contract,[68] posted workers,[69] and, taking advantage of the new legal basis, Article 118a EEC, the Commission also managed to secure the adoption of Directives on pregnant workers,[70] working time,[71] and young workers.[72] The Action Programme also led to the enactment of some soft law measures, such as the Commission Recommendation on Sexual Harassment,[73] which softened up the legislature towards enacting a hard law measure in the field sometime later.[74]

Although the Directives adopted under the Social Charter Action Programme focused principally on individual rights, the Social Charter itself contained a strong endorsement of collective rights, including freedom of association,[75] the right to negotiate and conclude collective agreements,[76] possibly resulting in 'contractual relations',

---

[60] See Bercusson, above, n. 56, 626.   [61] COM(89) 568 final Brussels, 29 November 1989.

[62] Social Europe 1/90, Commission of the European Communities (Brussels, 1990) contains the full text of the Social Charter, the Action Programme, background material and comments. Reports on the progress of the implementation of the Action Programme can be found in COM(91) 511 final, summarized in ISEC/B1/92, and E. Szyszczak (1992) 21 *ILJ* 149, ISEC/B25/93 COM(93) 668 final.

[63] Council Dir. 89/654/EEC (OJ [1989] L393/1).   [64] Council Dir. 89/655/EEC (OJ [1989] L393/13).

[65] Council Dir. 90/270/EEC (OJ [1991] L156/14).   [66] Council Dir. 90/269/EEC (OJ [1990] L156/9).

[67] COM(85) 310 final.   [68] Council Dir. 91/533/EEC (OJ [1991] L288/32).

[69] Council Dir. 96/71/EC (OJ [1997] L18/1).   [70] Council Dir. 92/85/EEC (OJ [1992] L348/1).

[71] Council Dir. 93/104/EC (OJ [1993] L307/18).   [72] Council Dir. 94/33/EC (OJ [1994] L216/12).

[73] Commission Recommendation 92/131/EEC on the protection and dignity of men and women at work (OJ [1992] L49/1).

[74] The prohibition against sexual harassment is now contained in Art. 2(2)(a) of the Sex Equality Dir. 2006/54 (OJ [2006] L204/23).

[75] Art. 11.   [76] Art. 12.

and the right to resort to collective action in the event of a conflict of interests, including the right to strike.[77] These rights have not, however, been reflected in any legislation, although the role of collective bargaining was given a considerable boost by the Treaty on European Union agreed at Maastricht (see later in this chapter).

The Social Charter Action Programme and the resulting Directives represented the high point for what is referred to as Union social policy but what, in reality, amounts to employment law—and an eclectic body of employment law at that. As Freedland has pointed out, it was concerned with equal pay and equal treatment between men and women, rather than with discrimination in employment generally (although this is now changing); with collective dismissals and acquired rights on transfer of undertakings, rather than with the termination of employment more generally; with particulars of the terms of the contract, rather than the terms themselves; with consultation of worker representatives on certain issues, rather than with collective representation and workers' organizations as a whole; and with working time and health and safety, rather than with the quality of working conditions more generally.[78]

4. THE TREATY ON EUROPEAN UNION 1992

4.1. Introduction

By the early 1990s, the Union had to come to terms with three main trends in economic and industrial relations, common across virtually all Member States.[79] The first concerned the structural transformation of the economy, involving the internationalization of corporate structures and the sectoral redistribution of the labour force away from agriculture and traditional industries to services, particularly private services. The second trend concerned the economic crises leading to recessions in the early 1980s and again in the early 1990s. These were accompanied by relatively high levels of unemployment and, with some exceptions, relatively low levels of inflation. At the same time there were increasing problems of industrial adjustment, mismatches between the supply and demand for skills, and as Rhodes points out, a more general failure of west European welfare states to respond to the challenges of post-industrial economic development.[80] The third trend was the change in the political climate in the 1980s, reflected in a general move to the right in national government policy-making together with a shift in the economic balance of power away from employees and trade unions and towards employers and managers. Employment relations were characterized by greater flexibility in recruitment, deployment, and rewards, and the decentralization of

---

[77] Art. 13.

[78] M. Freedland, 'Employment Policy', in *European Community Labour Law: Principles and Perspectives. Liber Amicorum Lord Wedderburn of Charlton*, eds. P. Davies, A. Lyon-Caen, S. Sciarra, and S. Simitis (Clarendon, Oxford, 1996), 278–9.

[79] See C. Barnard, J. Clark, and R. Lewis, *The Exercise of Individual Employment Rights in the Member States* (Department of Employment, 1995).

[80] M. Rhodes, 'Employment Policy: Between Efficacy and Experimentation' in H. Wallace, W. Wallace, and M. Pollack (eds.), *Policy Making in the European Union* (OUP, Oxford, 2005) 281.

decision-making, mainly through collective bargaining but also increasingly through the exercise of managerial prerogative.

The conclusion of the Treaty on European Union, with its significant amendments to the Treaty of Rome,[81] represented the EU's response to these changes. The desire to combat unemployment and encourage non-inflationary growth were now placed at the forefront of the Union's agenda. Article 2 EC (repealed and replaced in substance by Article 3 TEU) said that the Union's tasks would be to promote throughout the Union 'sustainable and non-inflationary growth respecting...a high level of employment and of social protection, the raising of the standard of living and quality of life, and economic and social cohesion and solidarity among Member States'. In order to achieve these objectives the Union was given some additional activities, listed in Article 3(i) and (p) EC, as amended by Maastricht, which talked of 'a policy in the social sphere comprising a European Social Fund', 'the strengthening of economic and social cohesion' and 'a contribution to education and training of quality'.[82] The Edinburgh European Council helped to provide the financial support necessary to achieve these objectives. Agreement was reached to increase the Union's own resources from 1.2 per cent of GDP in 1993 to 1.27 per cent by 1999 in order to precipitate a 'big bang effect'[83] to achieve growth.

These new tasks and activities were reflected in the relabelling of the social policy title as 'Social policy, education, vocational training and youth'. Articles 123–128 EEC on the European Social Fund were combined (Articles 123–125 EC (Articles 162–164 TFEU)) and Articles 126 and 127 EEC (Article 149 and 150 EC (Articles 165 and 166 TFEU)) formed a new chapter covering education, vocational training, and youth, where the Union was given new, but closely circumscribed, competence. The question of competence was brought into sharp focus by the inclusion of Article 3b EEC (Article 5 EC (Article 5 TEU)) where, for the first time, the Treaty recognized the doctrine of attribution of powers, the principle of subsidiarity (with the presumption that Member States should act, unless the action could be better achieved by the Union), and proportionality.[84]

4.2. The Social Chapter

For our purposes the most significant change introduced by the Maastricht Treaty concerned social policy. It was originally proposed that Articles 117–122 EEC be amended to expand the EU's social competence but this idea met with stubborn resistance from the UK. In order to secure the UK's agreement to the Treaty on European Union as a whole, it was agreed to remove these changes from the main body of the Treaty and place them in a separate Protocol and Agreement (the Social Policy Agreement (SPA) and the Social Policy Protocol (SPP), together referred to as the Social Chapter) which

---

[81] See generally, A. Lo Faro, 'EC Social Policy and 1993: The Dark Side of European Integration' (1992) 14 *Comparative Labour Law Journal* 1, esp. 27ff.

[82] Art. 3(j), (k) and (q) EC, respectively.

[83] J. Kenner, 'Economic and Social Cohesion: The Rocky Road Ahead' [1994] *LIEI* 1.

[84] These principles are considered further in Ch. 2.

would not apply to the UK. In what was the first clear example of a two-speed Europe,[85] the UK secured an opt-out from the Social Chapter as well as from the provisions on economic and monetary union (EMU).

At the time, there was much debate about the legal status of this opt-out. The prevailing view[86] was that the Protocol was an agreement by the 12 Member States that only 11 were to be bound by the new social provisions.[87] According to Article 51 TEU, protocols annexed to the Treaties form an integral part of the Treaties. The Protocol on social policy was therefore part of the Maastricht Treaty and thus part of Union law. Similarly, since the Protocol provided that the agreement on social policy was annexed to the Protocol, which in turn was annexed to the Treaty, the Agreement also formed part of Union law. Nevertheless, this view was not without its critics[88] who argued variously that the Social Chapter constituted an intergovernmental agreement or that the Agreement on social policy was not part of the Protocol on social policy but was an independent arrangement made between the 11.[89] The debate was effectively settled in favour of the Social Chapter being part of Union law when the Court was prepared to rule in *UEAPME*[90] on the legality of the Parental Leave Directive adopted under the Social Chapter.

As far as substance is concerned, the SPA was significant for three reasons. First, it both broadened the scope of Union competence in the social field as well as increasing the areas in which measures could be taken by qualified majority vote.[91] Thus, measures concerning working conditions, information and consultation of workers, equality between men and women with regard to labour market opportunities and treatment at work, and the integration of those excluded from the labour market could be adopted by qualified majority vote.[92] In addition, the Council of Ministers could adopt, by unanimity, measures in the area of social security and social protection of workers,

---

[85]   See generally, B. Towers, 'Two Speed Ahead: Social Europe and the UK after Maastricht' (1992) 23 *IRJ* 83; J. Shaw, 'Twin-track Social Europe—The Inside Track', in D. O'Keeffe and P. Twomey (eds.), *Legal Issues of the Maastricht Treaty* (Wiley, Chichester, 1994) 295. Such 'flexibility' was consititutionalized at Amsterdam. C.D. Ehlermann, 'Differentiation Flexibility, Closer Cooperation: the New "Provisions of the Amsterdam Treaty"' (1998) 4 *ELJ* 246, 247.

[86]   P. Watson, 'Social Policy After Maastricht' (1993) 31 *CMLRev.* 481, 488, *Maastricht and Social Policy—Part Two*, *EIRR* 239, 19, E. Whiteford, 'Social Policy after Maastricht' (1993) 18 *ELRev.* 202.

[87]   The Social Protocol opens with the statement that 'THE HIGH CONTRACTING PARTIES [the twelve], NOTING that eleven Member State…wish to continue along the path laid down in the 1989 Social Charter; that they have adopted among themselves an agreement to this end'.

[88]   M. Weiss, 'The Significance of Maastricht for European Social Policy' (1992) 8 *IJCLLIR* 3; C. Barnard, 'A Social Policy for Europe: Politicians 1 Lawyers 0' (1992) 8 *IJCLLIR* 15; E. Vogel-Polsky, *Evaluation of the Social Provisions of the Treaty on European Union*, Report prepared for the Committee on Social Affairs, Employment and the Working Environment of the European Parliament, DOC EN\CM\202155, cited in Watson, previously, at n. 86, 481, 491. See further the submissions made in *R v. Secretary of State for Foreign and Commonwealth Affairs, ex parte Lord Rees Mogg* [1993] 3 CMLR 101.

[89]   Cf. Watson, previously, at n. 86, 481, 491–4 and Whiteford, above, n. 86, 203–4.

[90]   Case T–135/96 *UEAPME* v. *Council* [1998] ECR II–2335, considered further in Ch. 2.

[91]   As amended to take account of the UK's absence (44 votes out of a possible 66 needed). Now the ordinary legislative procedure is applied (see further Ch. 2).

[92]   Art. 2(1) and (2) SPA (Art. 153(1) and (2) TFEU).

protection of workers when their employment contract is terminated, representation and collective defence of the interests of workers and employers, and the inclusion of co-determination and conditions of employment for legally resident third country nationals (Article 2(3) SPA (Article 153 TFEU)). However, Article 2(6) SPA (Article 153(5) TFEU) expressly provided that '[t]he provisions of this Article shall not apply to pay,[93] the right of association, the right to strike or the right to impose lock-outs'.[94]

The second reason for the SPA's significance lay in the greater role it envisaged for the Social Partners (representatives of management and labour): not only would they be consulted both on the possible direction of Union action and on the content of the envisaged proposal,[95] but they could, if they chose, also negotiate collective agreements[96] which could be given *erga omnes* effects by a Council 'decision'.[97] The details of this collective approach to legislation or 'law by collective agreement' are considered in Chapter 2. For the present it is sufficient to note two points. First, these new provisions were the direct result of the 'Val Duchesse' social dialogue between the intersectoral (cross-industry) Social Partners (UNICE (now BusinessEurope) and CEEP on the employers' side and ETUC on the workers' side) which started in 1985.[98] On 31 October 1991 these Social Partners reached an agreement which, to the surprise of its proponents, was inserted almost *verbatim* into Articles 3 and 4 SPA (Articles 154 and 155 TFEU). Thus, for the first time in the social field *private* agents could make public policy.[99] Second, this bipartite social dialogue highlights the multi-faceted and paradoxical nature of the principle of subsidiarity. Although the Social Partners are negotiating (a form of 'horizontal' subsidiarity), they are doing so at European level at a time when decentralized collective bargaining is the trend in many states.[100]

The third reason for the SPA's significance was more intangible: the inclusion of a more substantial provisions on social policy helped to rebalance the disequilibrium

---

[93] Pay is excluded because generally fixing of wage levels falls within the contractual freedom of the social partners at national level and within the relevant competence of the Member States: Case C–307/05 *Del Cerro Alonso* v. *Osakidetza-Servicio Vasco de salud* [2007] ECR I-7109, para. 40.

[94] This provision, as a derogation from Art. 153(1)–(4) TFEU, must be interpreted strictly: Joined Cases C–395/08 and C–396/08 *INPS* v. *Bruno* [2010] ECR I-000, para. 36. The Court also suggested that the reference to 'pay' here covered measures such as 'the equivalence of all or some of the constituent parts of pay and/or the level of pay in the Member States or the setting of a minimum guaranteed wage' (para. 37). And even in these areas excluded from EU competence, the Member States and the social partners must exercise their competence consistently with EU law including respecting the principle of non-discrimination (para. 39).

[95] Art. 3(2) and (3) SPA (Art. 154(1) and (2) TFEU).

[96] Art. 4(1) (Art. 155(1) TFEU). See generally B. Bercusson, 'Maastricht—a Fundamental Change in European Labour Law' (1992) 23 *IRJ* 177 and 'The Dynamic of European Labour Law after Maastricht' (1994) 23 *ILJ* 1.

[97] Art. 4(2) SPA (Art. 155(2) TFEU). The term 'decision' is not used in the sense of Art. 288 TFEU but has been interpreted to mean any legally binding act, in particular, Directives.

[98] This is considered further in Ch. 16.

[99] D. Obradovic, 'Accountability of Interest Groups in the Union Law-Making Process' in P. Craig and C. Harlow (eds.), *Lawmaking in the European Union* (Kluwer, Deventer, 1998) 355.

[100] E.g., in the UK, most leading firms have abandoned industry-wide agreements and moved towards single employer bargaining. P. Edwards *et al.*, 'Great Britain: From Partial Collectivism to Neoliberalism to Where?' in A. Ferner and R. Hyman (eds.), *Changing Industrial Relations in Europe* (Blackwell, Oxford, 1998).

inherent in the original Treaty of Rome between the economic and social dimension of the (newly named) European Union. This reorientation of the Treaty was reinforced by the inclusion in (what is now) Article 20 TFEU of the title of 'Union citizen' for those holding the nationality of one of the Member States. While many were disappointed by the paucity of rights expressly conferred on Union citizens,[101] Article 20(2) TFEU allows Union citizens to enjoy rights (but also duties) drawn from across the Treaties, including most obviously the social provisions, and now, the Charter, while Article 21(1) TFEU grants EU citizens the right to move to other Member States and reside there subject to the limitations and conditions laid down in the Treaties.

4.3. Economic and monetary union

From an economic perspective, the establishment of a timetable for the creation of economic and monetary union (EMU) was by far the most significant component of the Treaty on European Union. While, at first sight, the provisions of EMU had no direct impact on either national or European social policy, its indirect effect was potentially vast—as has been borne out by the eurozone crisis. On the positive side, it was believed that the creation of a single currency would lead to currency stability which in turn would be good for the economy and for jobs. On the negative side, the constraints imposed by EMU on national government expenditure inevitably had (or at least should have had) an effect on the ability of national governments to control their own social policies. In particular, the budgetary restrictions imposed by the convergence criteria of the euro and the Stability and Growth Pact[102] (should have) prevented any systematic policy of public investment, and the existence of the single currency and its management by the European Central Bank prevented national governments from pulling any monetary or interest rate levers to promote national competitiveness.[103] Further, the absence of any employment criteria among the convergence criteria for accession to the EMU highlighted the continued dissonance between the economic and social aspects of the European Union.

The introduction of EMU was significant for another reason: the new method of governance it put in place to ensure that Member States conducted their economic policies in accordance with both the objectives of Union law based on broad economic guidelines laid down by the European Council to steer Member State policies, combined

---

[101] See M. Everson, 'The Legacy of the Market Citizen' in J. Shaw and G. Moore (eds.), *New Legal Dynamics of European Union* (OUP, Oxford, 1995). Full details on the effect of the citizenship provisions can be found in C. Barnard, *The Substantive Law of the European Union: The Four Freedoms* 3rd edn (Oxford, OUP, 2010), ch. 12.

[102] This includes Resolution of the European Council on the Stability and Growth Pact Amsterdam, 17 June 1997 (OJ [1997] C236/1); Council Regulation (EC) No 1466/97 of 7 July 1997 on the strengthening of the surveillance of budgetary positions and the surveillance and coordination of economic policies (OJ [1997] L209/1, as amended, and Council Regulation (EC) No 1467/97 of 7 July 1997 on speeding up and clarifying the implementation of the excessive deficit procedure (OJ [1997] L 209/6). The Stability and Growth Pact (SGP) is considered further in Ch. 3.

[103] V. Hatzopoulos, 'A (More) Social Europe: A Political Crossroad or a Legal One-Way? Dialogues between Luxembourg and Lisbon' (2005) 42 *CMLRev.* 1599, 1600.

with multilateral surveillance. Using this new type of soft law,[104] which combined an intergovernmental approach dominated by the Council and the Commission, political monitoring at the highest level, clear procedures, and iterative processes,[105] the EU was able to link Union and national action while leaving states with a considerable discretion as to how to manage their own policies. This methodology subsequently provided the template for Union action in other areas, notably employment, in the Amsterdam Treaty.[106]

5. FROM MAASTRICHT TO AMSTERDAM

With the Social Charter Action Programme 1989 nearing its natural conclusion and now armed with the new Social Chapter, the Commission began to examine the future direction of Union social policy in the light of the changing trends in economic and industrial relations, focusing especially on the serious levels of unemployment and the implications of EMU. Its response was to issue a White Paper on Growth, Competitiveness and Employment,[107] and a Green Paper on European Social Policy,[108] leading to a White Paper on Social Policy, putting forward specific proposals.[109] The striking feature of these three documents was the emphasis placed on social goals, such as the promotion of high levels of employment and the elimination of social exclusion, and the move away from harmonization of social rights to a greater reliance on convergence, technocratic support, and soft law.[110]

The Growth White Paper, issued by DGXV (now DG Internal Market), saw the issues of growth, competitiveness, and employment as interrelated and said that the 1992 programme, while successful in its own terms, had generated 'jobless growth'. To address the EU's problem of high levels of unemployment, it put forward a package of proposals with a potent mix of deregulation (making labour markets more flexible), infrastructure investment (especially developing trans-European networks), and active labour market measures (such as the investment in training). As we shall see, this prescription continues to underpin the Union's recent concentration on raising the levels of employment.

---

[104] D. Hodson and I. Meyer, 'The Open Method as a New Mode of Governance: the Case of Soft Economic Policy Coordination' (2001) 39 *JCMS* 719 and 'Soft Law and Sanctions: Economic Policy Coordination and Reform of the Stability and Growth Pact' (2004) 11 *JEPP* 798.

[105] S. Borrás and Jacobsson, 'The Open Method of Coordination and New Governance Patterns in the EU' (2004) 11 *JEPP* 185, 188.

[106] Presidency Conclusions, Extraordinary European Council Meeting on Employment, Luxembourg, 20 and 21 November 1997, para. 3 said that the Employment Guidelines would draw 'directly on the experience built up in the multilateral surveillance of economic policies'.

[107] Bull. Supp. 6/93.

[108] COM(93) 551, 17 November 1993 and ECOSOC's response 94/C148/10. See B. Kuper, 'The Green and White Papers of the European Union: The Apparent Goal of Reduced Social Benefits' (1994) 4 *Journal of European Social Policy* 129, and J. Kenner, 'European Social Policy—New Directions' (1994) 10 *IJCLLIR* 56.

[109] COM(94) 333, 27 July 1994.

[110] H. Cullen and D. Campbell, 'The Future of Social Policy-Making in the EU', in Craig and Harlow (eds.), above, n. 99, 263.

Meanwhile, the Green and White Papers on Social Policy, issued by DGV (now DG Empl, the Employment, Social Affairs and Inclusion Directorate General) concentrated more on consensus building, based on shared values to create a European social model. The Commission said that the SPA provided a new basis for Union action which it intended to use 'to ensure a dynamic social dimension of the Union'.[111] However, recognizing that the UK would not be bound by any measure adopted on such a basis, the Commission noted the 'strong desire of all Member States to proceed as twelve wherever possible' and hoped that 'Union social policy action will in future once again be founded on a single legal framework'.[112] This was achieved when the Labour government came to power in the UK in May 1997. One of the first steps taken by the new government was to agree to sign-up to—or opt back into—the Social Chapter.[113] This raised the question of how the UK would be bound by the legislation which had already been adopted under the Social Chapter. In fact, during the five years of the UK opt-out only four Directives had been adopted under the Social Chapter[114] (on European Works Councils,[115] Parental Leave,[116] Part-time Work,[117] and Burden of Proof[118]). Thus, despite the 11 Member States' avowed intention of continuing 'along the path laid down in the 1989 Social Charter',[119] they did so with little enthusiasm in the absence of the UK. In fact, the extension of these four measures to the UK when it decided to sign up to the Social Chapter in 1997 did not prove difficult: they were re-adopted under the legal bases provided for by the Treaty and the UK was set new deadlines by which to implement the measures.

6. THE AMSTERDAM TREATY

6.1. The Social Title

With the UK's decision to opt back into the Social Chapter, the Amsterdam IGC agreed to amend the chapter on social policy, incorporating both Articles 117–121 EEC and the SPA, into the EC Treaty, in a new section entitled 'The Union and the Citizen'.[120] The

---

[111] COM(94) 333, 13.

[112] COM(94) 333, 13. See further the Commission's Communication concerning the application of the SPA: COM(93) 600.

[113] See C. Barnard, 'The United Kingdom, the "Social Chapter" and the Amsterdam Treaty' (1997) 26 *ILJ* 275. The UK also signed up to the Social Charter 1989 at the same time.

[114] C. McGlynn, 'An Exercise in Futility: The Practical Effects of the Social Policy Opt-out' (1998) 49 *NILQ* 60.

[115] Council Dir. 94/95/EC (OJ [1994] L254/64), as amended by Council Dir. 97/74/EC (OJ [1998] L10/22); consolidated legislation (OJ [1998] L10/20).

[116] Council Dir. 96/34/EC (OJ [1996] L145/4), as amended by Council Dir. 97/75 (OJ [1998] L10/24).

[117] Council Dir. 97/81/EC (OJ [1998] L14/9), as amended by Council Dir. 98/23/EC (OJ [1998] L131/10; consolidated legislation (OJ [1998] L131/13).

[118] Council Dir. 97/80/EC (OJ [1997] L14/16), as amended by Council Dir. 98/52/EC (OJ [1998] L205/66).

[119] Opening words of the Preamble to the SPP.

[120] The social provisions were then renumbered twice: the first time to reflect the incorporation of the SPA into the Treaty and then the whole Social Chapter was renumbered again as part of the global renumbering which occurred at Amsterdam. This second renumbering is reflected in the equivalence tables.

IGC also agreed three substantive changes to the text of the new Chapter on Social Provisions. First, Article 117 EEC (Article 151 TFEU) was significantly revised to include, among other things, an express reference to 'fundamental social rights such as those set out in the European Social Charter signed at Turin on 18 October 1961[121] and in the 1989 Community Charter of Fundamental Social Rights'. While the (11) Member States had, in the SPA agreed at Maastricht, referred to their wish to 'implement the 1989 Social Charter on the basis of the *aquis communautaire*', the reference to the 1961 Social Charter adopted by the Council of Europe is new, although the Court had already referred to it as a source of fundamental rights in various cases.[122] The importance of Article 117 EEC (Article 151 TFEU) had already been emphasized by the Court in *Sloman*[123] where it said that the objectives of Article 117 EEC, although in the nature of a programme, constituted an important aid for the interpretation of other provisions of the Treaty and of secondary legislation on the social field.

The second change was that the co-operation procedure was replaced with the co-decision procedure (now the ordinary legislative procedure). Further, the European Parliament and the Council were given powers to 'adopt measures designed to encourage co-operation between Member States through initiatives aimed at improving knowledge, developing exchanges of information and best practices, promoting innovative approaches and evaluating experiences in order to combat social exclusion'. This is a Treaty recognition of OMC-style processes which are considered in more detail in Chapter 3.

The third change concerned the importance of equality between men and women. The significance of this principle was reinforced by its inclusion in Article 2 EC (repealed and replaced in substance by Article 3 TEU) as one of the tasks of the Union and as one of the activities of the Union in Article 3 EC. Article 3 (Article 8 TFEU) mainstreams gender equality. It provides that '[i]n all the activities, the [Union] shall aim to eliminate inequalities, and to promote equality, between men and women'. Perhaps more importantly, Article 119 EEC (Article 157 TFEU) on equal pay was amended for the first time since 1957. In particular, Article 157(3) TFEU finally provides an express legal basis for the Council to adopt measures, again in accordance with the ordinary legislative procedure, 'to ensure the application of the principle of equal opportunities and equal treatment of men and women in matters of employment and occupation, including the principle of equal pay for equal work or work of equal value'. There is, however, some overlap between Article 157(3) TFEU and Article 153(1) TFEU which allows for Union action in the field of 'equality between men and women with regard to labour market opportunities and treatment at work'.[124] The other striking change to Article 119

---

[121] The content of this Charter was drawn on in e.g. Joined Cases C–395/08 and C–396/08 *INPS* v. *Bruno* [2010] ECR I–000, para. 31 to guide the interpretation of the Part-time Work Dir. 97/81 considered in Ch. 9.

[122] Case 149/77 *Defrenne (No. 3)* [1978] ECR 1365, para. 28; Case 126/86 *Zaera* v. *Instituto Nacional de la Securidad Social* [1987] ECR 3697, para. 14.

[123] Joined Cases C–72/91 and C–73/91 *Sloman Neptun* v. *Bodo Ziesemer* [1993] ECR I–887, para. 26.

[124] Given that the legislative procedures are the same under each Article, the overlap is not perhaps of great significance.

EEC can be found in the paragraph 4 (now Article 157(4) TFEU) which recognizes the principle of positive action, first introduced by Article 6(3) SPA.[125] The importance of these developments will be considered in Chapters 6–8.

6.2. The Employment Title

The other significant development at Amsterdam was the inclusion of a new Title on Employment,[126] introduced largely as a result of pressure from France and the Scandinavian countries. A new task for the Union of 'a high level of employment and of social protection' was added to Article 2 EC (repealed and replaced in substance by Article 3 TEU) and the objective of a 'high level of employment' was mainstreamed (i.e. 'taken into consideration in the formulation and implementation of Union policies and activities') by Article 147(2) TFEU.[127] Article 147 TFEU, the key provision of the new Title, provides that:

> Member States and the Union shall, in accordance with the Title, work towards developing a co-ordinated strategy for employment and particularly for promoting a skilled, trained and adaptable workforce and labour markets responsive to economic change with a view to achieving the objectives defined in Article 3 TEU.

Although it appears from Article 145 TFEU that action is to be jointly conducted by Member States and the Union, the principal actors are, according to the Treaties, the Member States. Article 146 TFEU requires the Member States to co-ordinate their policies for the promotion of employment (which is to be regarded as an issue of 'common concern')[128] within the Council, in a way consistent with the broad economic guidelines laid down within the framework of EMU, which are issued annually by the Council as part of the process of ensuring economic stability and convergence.[129] The European Council must also draw up guidelines according to Article 148 TFEU which the Member States are obliged to take into account in their employment policies. Under Article 149 TFEU the Council may adopt incentive measures designed to encourage co-operation between Member States.[130]

This annual cycle of policy formation, policy implementation, and policy monitoring was formally launched at Luxembourg in November 1997 and became known as the European Employment Strategy (EES). The EES highlighted a shift in emphasis in the EU from measures protecting those in employment, to addressing the high levels of unemployment in Europe. This was a direct response to the growing crisis faced by many west European states of 'welfare without work': expensive social welfare programmes unsupported by high levels of employment which risked putting eurozone countries in breach of the budgetary commitments laid down by EMU. Furthermore, as

[125] See L. Betten and V. Shrubsall, 'The Concept of Positive Sex Discrimination in Community Law—Before and After the Treaty of Amsterdam' (1998) 14 *IJCLLIR* 65.
[126] For a full consideration of this subject, see D. Ashiagbor, *The European Employment Strategy* (OUP, Oxford, 2006).
[127] See further Art. 9 TFEU.   [128] Art. 146(2) TFEU.   [129] Art. 146(1) TFEU.
[130] The decision-making mechanism under the Employment Title is considered in more detail in Ch. 3.

we saw above, traditional national tools for addressing high levels of unemployment—monetary and fiscal policy—could no longer be used as a result of the constraints imposed by the Stability and Growth Pact. Thus the EES replaced the focus on demand side policies with the adoption of *supply* side policies, stimulating productivity through the creation of a favourable business environment, shorn of much red tape, and improving the quality of the workforce.[131]

The inclusion of the Employment Title amounted to a recognition by the eurozone states—largely overlooked at Maastricht—of the increased inter-dependencies between EU economic policy and national social policy. As Trubek and Trubek put it,[132] so long as national markets are relatively closed and national budgets relatively independent, social policy is basically a domestic concern. But once nations create a common currency and join in a Single Market, then social policy in one country becomes relevant to other nations. Thus, the constraints and interdependencies generated by EMU pointed to the need for some form of transnational policy co-ordination in the field of employment: the Employment Title was the EU's response.

For Szyszczak, the Amsterdam Treaty represented the culmination and implementation of the Commission's attempts during the 1990s, through its soft law discourse on social policy, to create a better mix between economic and social policies.[133] However, given the acute political sensitivities involved (the Member States have long viewed job creation as lying at the heart of national sovereignty), a new method of policy-making was needed to be developed which would stimulate job creation without threatening national social, employment, and economic policies. This new approach, found in Articles 145–149 TFEU, is modelled in part on the strategy which had been adopted in respect of EMU,[134] based on the Commission proposing (non-binding) guidelines which the Member States are obliged to take into account in their national action plans (NAPs), now renamed national reform programmes (NRPs). Thus, in terms of regulatory technique, this new approach focused less on providing rights for individual employees and more on the co-ordination of employment policies, focusing in particular on active labour market policies such as training, work practice, and lifelong learning. At Lisbon this new method of governance was given a name: the Open Method of Co-ordination (OMC).

7. THE LISBON AND EU2020 STRATEGIES

At the Lisbon summit in March 2000[135] the Union set itself a new and ambitious strategic goal 'to become the most competitive and dynamic knowledge-based economy in the world capable of sustainable economic growth with more and better jobs and greater social cohesion'.[136] The strategy had three, mutually interdependent limbs: an economic

---

[131] Hatzopoulos, previous, n. 103, 1600.

[132] 'Hard and Soft Law in the Construction of Social Europe: the Role of the Open Method of Coordination' (2005) 11 *ELJ* 343, 345.

[133] 'The New Paradigm for Social Policy: A Virtuous Circle' (2001) 38 *CMLRev.* 1125, 1134.

[134] See further Ch. 3.   [135] Presidency Conclusions, 24 March 2000.   [136] Para. 5.

limb (making the EU more competitive while sustaining a stable economy), an environmental limb (especially sustainable development), and a social limb (modernizing the European social model, investing in people, and combating social exclusion). This strategy was designed to enable the Union to regain 'the conditions for *full employment*' (not just a high level of employment as laid down by Article 9 TFEU), and 'strengthening regional cohesion in the European Union'. This is to be achieved by 'improving existing processes, introducing a new open method of coordination at all levels coupled with a stronger guiding and coordinating role for the European Council'.[137] The Presidency Conclusions describe the Open Method of Co-ordination (OMC) as the means of spreading best practice and achieving greater convergence towards the EU's main goals by helping Member States develop their own policies.[138] Implementation of OMC involves tools such as indicators and benchmarks as well as the exchange of experiences, peer reviews and the dissemination of good practice. In particular, the Lisbon and subsequently Stockholm European Council set the EU the objective of reaching an overall employment rate of 70 per cent by 2010, an employment rate of over 60 per cent for women and an employment rate among older men and women (55–64) of 50 per cent.[139] However, in its 2005 mid-term review of the Lisbon strategy, the Brussels European Council recognized that there were significant delays in reaching these targets, and in the Lisbon relaunch no reference is made to the 2010 deadline. By the time of the EU2020 strategy,[140] adopted in 2010 to replace the Lisbon strategy, the deadlines had disappeared altogether but the targets, although fewer in number, remain. EU2020 set new objectives of smart growth, sustainable growth, and inclusive growth, the latter being the direct descendant of the modernizing social policy limb of the Lisbon Strategy.

Given the importance of these developments, they are considered in detail in Chapter 3. For the purposes of this chapter, the Lisbon/EU2020 strategies were significant for five reasons. First, as Hatzopoulos points out,[141] they were the next 'big' project for the EU, after the completion of the internal market (1992), EMU (1999), and enlargement (2003–5), but, unlike the previous projects, the Lisbon/EU2020 had a determinedly social aspect.

Secondly, the regulatory techniques used to achieve these objectives shifted from an exclusive focus on traditional command and control regulation, adopted under the

---

[137] Para. 7. The Commission's social policy agenda goes further. The Commission says that it does not 'seek to harmonise social policies. It seeks to work towards common European objectives and increase coordination of social policies in the context of the internal market and the single currency' (COM(2000)379, 7).

[138] Lisbon European Council, 23 and 24 March 2000, para. 37. See further the definition of OMC offered in the Final Report of Working Group XI on Social Europe: 'It is a new form of coordination of national policies consisting of the Member States, at their own initiative or at the initiative of the Commission, defining collectively, within the respect of national and regional diversities, objectives and indicators in a specific area, and allowing those Member States, on the basis of national reports, to improve their knowledge, to develop exchanges of information, views, expertise and practices, and to promote, further to agreed objectives, innovative approaches which could possibly lead to guidelines or recommendations'.

[139] Stockholm European Council, 23 and 24 March 2001, para. 9.

[140] COM(2010) 2020.   [141] At, n. 103, 1628 and 1630.

classic Community Method based on harmonization, towards a new mode of governance based on co-ordination of action by the states under the direction of the European Union (particularly the European Council, the Council of Ministers, and the Commission).[142] To give a concrete example, in the field of equal opportunities, the emphasis is no longer exclusively on the enactment of equality Directives, although this is still taking place,[143] but Member States are now required also to look at issues ranging from the organization of work, childcare, tax, and benefit structures to school curricula and careers advice.[144] Thus, in areas where law has proved to be a rather blunt instrument to bring about social change, the Union has focused on different regulatory techniques to achieve its objectives. With the advent of enlargement—the arrival of 12 new Member States with very diverse legal and industrial relations traditions—the change in approach has proved particularly significant.

Thirdly, the Lisbon/EU2020 approach was intended to improve the legitimacy of governance within the European Union by involving a wider range of social actors, including not only the Social Partners but also civil society more generally. Fourthly, as we have already noted, the principal emphasis of Union social policy has changed from employment protection (giving rights to those already in work) to employment creation (getting people into employment). Thus employment is seen as the key to citizenship, 'guaranteeing equal opportunities for all' and enabling the 'full participation of citizens in economic, cultural and social life and realising their potential'.[145]

The need for individuals to be given opportunities to help themselves rather than relying on the state was reflected in the two key documents on the future of social policy 'Opportunities, Access and Solidarity: towards a new social vision for 21st century Europe' of 2007[146] and 'Renewed Social Agenda: Opportunities, Access and Solidarity'[147] published in 2008. The striking feature of these documents is the recognition 'that whereas society cannot guarantee equal *outcomes* for its citizens, it must become much more resolute in fostering equal *opportunities*...The central ambition is to achieve a wider distribution of "life chances" to allow everyone in the EU to have *access* to the resources, services, conditions and capabilities in order to turn the theoretical equality of opportunities and active citizenship into a meaningful reality'.[148] The addition of 'solidarity' into the mix provides a social justice counterweight to the potentially neo-liberal direction that an agenda based purely on access and opportunities might lead the EU.

Fifthly, not only does the Lisbon strategy aim at more jobs but it also requires those jobs to be 'better'.[149] A key element of this is the so-called 'flexicurity agenda' which, according to the Commission, 'promotes a combination of flexible labour markets and

---

[142] Despite the perceived novelty of this approach, the Treaty of Rome had always envisaged co-ordination as the principal regulatory approach, as Art. 118 EEC (Art. 156 TFEU) made clear.

[143] See, esp. Chs 6–10.

[144] E. Szyszczak, 'The New Paradigm for Social Policy: A Virtuous Circle' (2001) 38 *CMLRev.* 1125, 1144.

[145] Dir. 2000/78 establishing a general framework for equal treatment in employment and occupation (OJ [2000] L303/16), ninth preambular paragraph.

[146] COM(2007) 726.   [147] COM (2008) 412.   [148] COM (2007) 726, 6.

[149] Lisbon European Council Presidency Conclusions, paras. 28–30.

26INTRODUCTION

adequate security'.[150] It says flexicurity is not about deregulation, giving employers freedom to dissolve their responsibilities towards the employee and to give them little security. Instead, flexicurity is about bringing people into good jobs and developing their talents. This, says the Commission, is the way to 'maintain and improve competitiveness whilst reinforcing the European social model'. The European Social Models (sic), it says, are based on 'social protection, social cohesion and solidarity'.[151] So, in this brave new world of employment policy, the most vulnerable are not to be left behind: the principle of solidarity will be used to ensure that states continue to provide a safety net for them.

8. THE NICE TREATY

Article 137 EC (now Article 153 TFEU) was amended again by the Treaty of Nice. Most of the changes were cosmetic and involved a restructuring and tidying up of the Article. However, one substantive change was made: in line with the increasing focus on OMC methodology, greater prominence was given to this approach. While Article 137(1) EC (Article 153(1) TFEU) lists the fields in which the Union must 'support and complement the activities of the Member States', with two new areas specified—social inclusion and the modernization of social protection systems—Article 137(2) EC (Article 153(2) TFEU) then details how this might be achieved. Part (a) provides that the Council may 'adopt measures designed to encourage cooperation between Member States...excluding any harmonisation of the laws and regulations of the Member States'; the power to adopt Directives appears only in part (b). In addition, the Treaty of Nice amended Article 144 EC (Article 160 TFEU) to empower the Council to establish a Social Protection Committee with advisory status to promote cooperation on social protection between Member States and with the Commission. It, too, is to use OMC techniques including 'promoting exchanges of information, experience and good practice'.

From the perspective of this book, by far the most significant development at Nice was the adoption of the Charter of Fundamental Rights. As the European Council explained, 'Protection of fundamental rights is a founding principle of the Union and an indispensable prerequisite for her legitimacy'. The final Charter, agreed at Nice, contained, in a single document, civil and political economic and social rights based on, variously, the European Convention on Human Rights, the Community Social Charter 1989, and the Council of Europe's Social Charter 1961, as well as the constitutional traditions common to the Member States. The Charter was intended to codify—and act as a showcase for—existing rights. It was not intended to create new rights.[152] Although not initially legally binding, it was nevertheless regularly referred to in the pre-Lisbon

---

[150] This is considered further in Ch. 3.
[151] <http://eur-lex.europa.eu/LexUriServ/LexUriServ.do?uri=COM:2007:0359:FIN:EN:PDF> p. 7 (last accessed 24 January 2010).
[152] See further the Preamble to the Protocol: 'WHEREAS the Charter reaffirms the rights, freedoms and principles recognised in the Union and makes those rights more visible, but does not create new rights or principles'.

period by the Advocates-General, the General Court, and, latterly, by the Court of Justice to reinforce the interpretation of existing provisions of EU law.[153] The significance of the Charter is considered below.

9. THE LISBON TREATY

9.1. The changes

In the field of social policy, as narrowly defined, the Lisbon Treaty had little direct impact. Some minor tweaking was introduced (for example, reference to management and labour became references to the Social Partners whose role was expressly recognized in Article 152 TFEU) but otherwise the inclusion of the Title on social policy into Part Three of the Treaty meant that these provisions were not subject to careful scrutiny by the original Convention and by the Lisbon IGC.[154]

However, as we shall see in subsequent chapters, by giving the Charter of Fundamental Rights the same legal value as the Treaties the Lisbon Treaty has made a significant impact in the field of social policy more generally. In addition, the Lisbon Treaty gave social policy a more prominent role in the values of the Union. For example pluralism, non-discrimination, tolerance, justice, solidarity, and equality between women and men are expressly identified as values of the EU in Article 2 TEU. More noteworthy, is the description in Article 3(3) TEU of the objectives of the EU: the Union shall 'work for the sustainable development of Europe based on balanced economic growth and price stability, a highly competitive social market economy,[155] aiming at full employment and social progress, and a high level of protection and improvement of the quality of the environment'. This emphasizes the links between the social and economic provisions of the Treaty, a link which the Amsterdam Treaty had begun to identify. Moreover, at the request of the French the 'neo-liberal' objective of creating a system of undistorted competition was relegated to an annex. In fact this seems to have made little difference to the Court.[156] New mainstreaming provisions were also introduced, in

---

[153] See e.g. Case C–540/03 *Parliament v. Council (Family reunification)* [2006] ECR I–5769; Case C–303/05 *Advocaten voor de Wereld* [2007] ECR I–3633; Case C–305/05 *Ordre des barreaux francophones et germanophone and Others* [2007] ECR I–5305; Joined Cases C–402/05P and C–415/05P *Kadi and Al Barakaat International* [2008] ECR I–6351.

[154] Indeed, originally there was no working group at all on 'Social Europe': C. Joerges and F. Rödl, '"Social Market Economy" as Europe's Social Model?' EUI Working Paper Law No. 2004/8, 21. For further details, see P. Syrpis, 'The Treaty of Lisbon: Much Ado...But About What?' (2008) 37 *ILJ* 219.

[155] For a discussion of this term, see Joerges and Rödl, ibid., 19 who argue that 'this concept contained an ordoliberal basis which was complemented by social and societal policies, whose aims and instruments were supposed to reply on market mechanisms'. According to Working Group XI on Social Europe (CONV 516/1/03 REV 1, para. 17), the objectives should refer to 'social market economy' to underline the link between the economic and social development and the efforts made to ensure greater coherence between economic and social policies.

[156] Case C–52/09 *Konkurrensverket v. TeliaSonera Sverige AB* [2011] ECR I–000, para. 20; 'it must be observed at the outset that Article 3(3) TEU states that the European Union is to establish an internal market, which, in accordance with Protocol No 27 on the internal market and competition, annexed to the Treaty of Lisbon (OJ 2010 C 83, p. 309), is to include a system ensuring that competition is not distorted'.

particular Article 9 TFEU requiring the Union to take into account 'the promotion of a high level of employment, the guarantee of adequate social protection, the fight against social exclusion…'.

9.2. The Charter

(a) Introduction

The EU Charter 2000 was greeted with brickbats and bouquets. The bouquets come largely from interest groups who see it both as an important way of reigning in the excesses of the EU as its competence expands to areas as diverse as immigration, asylum, and police cooperation, and as a potentially dynamic tool to challenge existing EU law.[157] The brickbats come from the 'awkward squad' states with a dominant Eurosceptic press (UK, Poland, and the Czech Republic) which (incorrectly) see the Charter as bringing in 'new laws which would destroy jobs'[158] and affecting 'policies on abortion, immigration and public services and forc[ing] an end to the ban on secondary picketing in industrial disputes'.[159] As a result, when negotiating the IGC mandate for the Lisbon Treaty, one of the UK government's 'red lines' was to protect the UK from the consequences of the change of status of the Charter of Fundamental Rights.[160] The principal and most public demonstration of this desire was the adoption of what became Protocol 30 on the application of Charter of Fundamental Rights of the European Union to Poland and to the UK, referred to, in the (incorrect) short-hand, as the 'opt-out'. Given the importance of the Charter throughout this book, some attention will now be devoted to its provisions, its scope, and Protocol 30.

(b) Rights and principles

The legal position of the Charter was changed by the Lisbon Treaty. Article 6(1) TEU says the Charter has the 'same legal value as the Treaties'. In other words, it forms part of the primary law of the EU, with the result that its provisions have legal effect and can be enforced before the European Court of Justice, as well as before the national courts when Union law issues are at stake. This has given rise to a number of concerns, especially in the UK.

The first concern relates to the fact that the Charter includes social and economic rights in the same document as civil and political rights.[161] This is unusual in international human rights instruments. Generally, the two groups of rights are placed in separate documents due to the (contested) argument that while civil and political rights are

---

[157] An early example of this was the—ultimately unsuccessful—challenge to the British government's refusal to ban the export of sodium thiopental to the US, a widely used anaesthetic but one which the state of Tennessee used to render the prisoner unconscious before putting him to death by lethal injection: *R (on the application of Zagorski and Baze) v. Secretary of State for Business, Innovation and Skills* [2010] EWHC 3110 (Admin).

[158] J. Lyons, 'EU Traitor', *The News of the World*, 24 June 2007.

[159] 'How Brussels will get its way', *Sunday Express*, 21 October 2007.

[160] As Tony Blair then British Prime Minster, said to the Liaison Committee of the 18 June 2007 (reported in the House of Commons' European Scrutiny Committee's 35th Report, para. 52): 'First we will not accept a treaty that allows the charter of fundamental rights to change UK law in any way…'.

[161] See Lord Goldsmith, 'A Charter of Rights, Freedoms and Principles' (2001) 38 *CMLRev.* 1201, 1212.

essentially negative and so do not require state resources, economic and social rights are positive and do. While the UK is prepared to accept that traditional civil and political rights are *rights* (e.g. Article 2 'Everyone has the right to life', Article 11 'Everyone has the right to freedom of expression'), it is concerned about the potential budgetary implications of the economic and social rights. It is particularly worried about the implications of the Solidarity Title (where the economic and social rights are predominantly located), in particular Article 28 on the right to strike. The UK has therefore argued that the economic and social rights are not actually 'rights' but 'principles' which are not intended to be justiciable (i.e. they cannot be relied on directly before the courts). The UK secured an amendment to the Charter at the time of the Constitutional Treaty to make this clear: as Article 52(5) now puts it, the provisions of the Charter containing principles 'may be implemented by legislative and executive acts' of the Union and the Member States when implementing Union law. Such provisions 'shall be judicially cognisable only in the interpretation of such acts and in the ruling on their legality'. In other words principles will not be directly effective in the national courts.

However, the stumbling block remains that the Charter does not identify which provisions contain rights, and which principles. The revised explanations accompanying the Charter—'drawn up as a way of providing guidance in the interpretation of this Charter' and which must be 'given due regard by the court of the Union and of the Member States'[162]—were intended to address this problem. They give examples of principles, drawn from the Solidarity Title of the Charter, including Article 25 on the rights of the elderly ('The Union *recognises and respects* the rights of the elderly to lead a life of dignity and independence and to participate in social and cultural life'), Article 26 on the integration of persons with disabilities, and Article 37 on environmental protection.

Confusingly, the explanations also state that some articles may contain elements of rights and principles, such as Article 23 on equality between men and women, Article 33 on family and professional life, and Article 34 on social security and social assistance (Articles 33 and 34 are in the Solidarity Title). Therefore, this suggests that some social and economic rights will not be mere principles but may in fact give rise to justiciable rights,[163] a view confirmed by the (pre-Lisbon) decision of the Court of Justice in *Viking*.[164] As we shall see later, concerns that the Solidarity Title might include rights, and not just principles, influenced the drafting of the UK/Poland Protocol No. 30. Before considering the Protocol, we need to consider the scope of application of the Charter.

(c) To whom/what does the Charter apply?

Article 51(1) of the Charter says the Charter applies firstly to the institutions, bodies, offices, and agencies of the Union, with due regard for the principle of subsidiarity.

---

[162] Article 52(7) of the Charter.
[163] See, e.g. Article 31 'Every worker has the right to working conditions which respect his or her health, safety and dignity'.
[164] Case C–438/05 *Viking* [2008] ECR I–10889.

It also applies to the Member States but only when they are implementing Union law, a point emphasized by the Czech Republic in its (non-binding) Declaration on the Charter. This says: 'The Czech Republic stresses that [the Charter's] provisions are addressed to the Member States only when they are implementing Union law, and not when they are adopting and implementing national law independently from Union law'.[165] In other words, purely national issues will not be affected by the Charter.[166]

The meaning of Article 51(1) is—to an extent—clarified in the explanations:[167] Article 51 'seeks to establish clearly that the Charter applies *primarily* to the institutions and bodies of the Union, in compliance with the principle of subsidiarity'.[168] The institutions include the European Court of Justice. This raises the tantalizing prospect that the Charter, drafted primarily to govern vertical relationships (individual v. EU, individual v. Member State), might acquire some quasi-horizontal or indirect effect (individual v. individual)[169] through judicial interpretation (see e.g. *Kücükdeveci*[170]). *Kücükdeveci*, a case concerning a private sector employer discriminating against his employee on the grounds of age, also appears to suggest that general principles of law may have some form of horizontal effect, at least in so far as they can be used to disapply conflicting provisions of national law, and, as Article 6(3) TEU makes clear, fundamental rights are general principles of law.[171] The general principles may thus be broader in their field of application than the Charter.

The significance of the fact that the actions of the EU institutions are subject to review under the Charter has already been felt. In *Schecke*[172] the Court used the Charter to strike down an EU Regulation (requiring individuals to agree that, in order to receive money from EU agricultural funds, their name, address and the amounts they receive had to be recorded on a publicly accessible website) for its incompatibility with an individual's fundamental right to privacy, in part because the Council and Commission had failed to consider whether there were any less restrictive alternatives to achieve the objective of transparency.

---

[165] Declaration 53, first paragraph. See further new Art. 4(1) TEU and Art. 5(2) second sentence.

[166] Despite the attacks on the wholly internal rule led by AG Sharpston in Case C–212/06 *Government of the French Community and Walloon Government* v. *Flemish Government* [2007] ECR I–1683 and Case C–34/09 *Gerardo Ruiz Zambrano*, Opinion of 30 September 2010, the Court does not seem prepared to use the Charter to reverse the rule: Case C–339/10 *Estov* v. *Ministerski savet na Republika Bulgaria*, Order of 12 November 2010.

[167] Explanations relating to the Charter of Fundamental Rights (OJ [2007] C303/17).

[168] Emphasis added. The institutions already consider themselves bound by the Charter: Commission Communication, *Compliance with the Charter of Fundamental Rights in Commission Legislative Proposals*, COM(2005) 172. See further House of Lords EU Select Committee: *Human Rights Proofing EU Legislation*, 16th Report of Session 2005–06, HL Paper 67.

[169] See P. Craig, *The Lisbon Treaty: Law, Politics and Treaty Reform* (OUP, Oxford, 2010) who also points out that analogous reasoning could equally apply to national courts since they are part of the Member States: Case C–224/01 *Köbler* [2003] ECR I–10239.

[170] Case C–555/07 *Kücükdeveci* v. *Swedex GmbH & Co. KG* [2010] ECR I–000, para. 22 considered further in Ch. 6.

[171] See e.g. Case 29/69 *Stauder* [1969] ECR 419; Case 11/70 *Internationale Handelsgesellschaft mbH* v. *Einfuhr und Vorratsstelle für Getreide und Futtermittel* [1970] ECR 1125, para. 4.

[172] Case C–92/09 and C–93/09 *Volker und Markus Schecke GbR* v. *Land Hessen; Hartmut Eifert* v. *Land Hessen*, judgment of 9 November 2010.

While the Charter applies 'primarily' to the EU institutions, it also applies to the Member States but, apparently, only when 'implementing' EU law. This has prompted some controversy: according to the case law of the Court, general principles of law (which include fundamental rights) apply when Member States implement (*Wachauf*[173]), derogate (*ERT*[174]), and, more generally, act within the scope of (*Annibaldi*[175]) EU law. Does this mean that the Charter is limiting the earlier case law? The general view is not, not least because the explanations add: 'As regards the Member States, it follows unambiguously from the case-law of the Court of Justice that the requirement to respect fundamental rights defined in the context of the Union is only binding on the Member States when they act in the scope of Union law' (citing the very cases *Wachauf, ERT*, and *Annibaldi*).[176] If the Charter is meant to be a clarification of the existing law, then the term 'implementing' would also cover the two broader uses.[177] And even if the Charter applies only to Member States when implementing EU law, in the narrow sense, this may not matter as much as would first appears due to the continued role of general principles of European Union law; principles first developed by the Court and now given Treaty recognition, which will apply whenever Union law is engaged.

(d) Does the Charter expand the EU's competence?

During its drafting, a number of states were concerned about the Charter being used as a Trojan horse to expand the EU's competence to legislate. The horizontal provisions found in Title VII of the Charter try to reassure those Member States. The second sentence of Article 51(1) provides that the Union institutions and the Member Sates must 'respect the rights, observe the principles and promote the application thereof in accordance with their respective powers and respecting the limits of the powers of the Union as conferred on it in the Treaties'. In addition, Article 51(2) provides that the Charter 'does not extend the field of application of Union law beyond the powers of the Union or establish any new power or task for the Union, or modify powers and tasks as defined in the Treaties'.[178] This careful ring-fencing of competence in Title VII of the Charter must have satisfied the UK since there is no reference to it in Protocol No.30.

(e) The non-opt-out opt-out

The original intention behind Protocol 30 was to 'clarify the application of the Charter'.[179] It was therefore meant to be a document which all the Member States could sign up to.

---

[173] Case 5/88 *Wachauf* [1989] ECR 2609.   [174] Case C–260/89 *ERT* [1991] ECR I–2925.

[175] Case C–309/96 *Annibaldi* [1997] ECR I–7493.

[176] The explanation adds: 'Of course this rule, as enshrined in this Charter, applies to the central authorities as well as to regional or local bodies, and to public organisations, when they are implementing Union law'.

[177] Although it is not expressly discussed, the Court had no hesitation in applying the Charter to a situation of derogation in Case C–578/08 *Chakroun* v. *Minister van Buitenlandse Zaken* [2010] ECR I–000. The British courts have taken a similar view: *R (on the application of Zagorski and Baze) v. Secretary of State for Business, Innovation and Skills* [2010] EWHC 3110 (Admin), per Lloyd Jones J, para. 70.

[178] See further Art. 6(1) TEU and Declaration 1 of the Final Act of the Treaty of Lisbon'.

[179] Protocol 30, 8th Preamble. See further, W. Belling, 'The Legal Effects of the so-called opt-out from the Charter of Fundamental Rights' (2012) 18 *ELJ* 251.

In the event, only Poland and the UK agreed to it. The Protocol thus promptly assumed the look of an 'opt-out', a view reinforced by the British Prime Minster's statement in Parliament: 'It is absolutely clear that we have an opt-out from both the charter and judicial and home affairs'.[180] Yet, if Protocol 30 is compared with other genuine 'opt-outs', such as the UK/Denmark opt-out from EMU, it looks nothing like it. So what does Protocol 30 do?

First, it clarifies existing provisions, as Article 1(1) shows:

> The Charter *does not extend* the ability of the Court of Justice of the European Union, or any court or tribunal of Poland or of the United Kingdom, to find that the laws, regulations or administrative provisions, practices or action of Poland or of the United Kingdom are inconsistent with the fundamental rights, freedoms and principles that it reaffirms.[181]

This provision, when read in conjunction with the Preamble ('Whereas the Charter reaffirms the rights freedoms and principles recognised by the Union and makes those rights more visible, but does not create new rights or principles'), appears to suggest that since the Charter is simply a reaffirmation of the previous law, it will apply to the UK and Poland. In other words, to the extent that the Charter is merely a restatement of the existing law, then the Protocol is not an opt-out and the Charter will apply to the UK/Poland. This view is reinforced by the existence of Article 1(2) of the Protocol (see further) as well as the fact that Article 2 of the Protocol provides that '[t]o the extent that a provision of the Charter refers to national laws and practices, it shall only apply to Poland or the United Kingdom to the extent that the rights or principles that it contains are recognised in the law or practices of Poland or of the United Kingdom'. Both Article 1(2) and 2 proceed on the assumption that the Charter will apply to the UK and Poland.[182]

The fact that the Protocol is not an opt-out is further confirmed in public statements made first by the Labour, and now by the Coalition, government. For example, in its evidence to the House of Lords Select Committee, the Department of Work and Pensions' (DWP) said: 'The UK Protocol does not constitute an "opt-out". It puts beyond doubt the legal position that nothing in the Charter creates any new rights, or extends the ability of any court to strike down UK law'.[183] More significantly, the UK's lawyers told the Court of Appeal in *Saaedi*[184] in 2010 that:

> the Secretary of State accepts, in principle, that fundamental rights set out in the Charter can be relied on as against the UK, and submits that [Cranston J, the first instance judge]

---

[180] <http://www.publications.parliament.uk/pa/cm200607/cmhansrd/cm070625/debtext/70625-0006.htm> (last accessed 22 December 2010).

[181] Emphasis added.

[182] I am grateful to Paul Craig for this point.

[183] House of Lords EU Select Committee, *The Treaty of Lisbon: An Impact Assessment*, 10th Report, 2007–8, HL Paper 62, para. 5.86.

[184] [2010] EWCA Civ 990, para. 8. A question on the effect of the Protocol has now been referred to the Court of Justice in Case C–411/10 *NS* which was joined with a case from Ireland, C–493/10 *ME* [2011] ECR I-000. The Court considered that in the context of deporting a failed asylum seeker, the Charter applied to the UK.

erred in holding otherwise.... The purpose of the Charter protocol is not to prevent the Charter from applying to the United Kingdom, but to explain its effect.

All this seems pretty conclusive: Protocol 30 is not apparently an opt-out and the Court in *Saaedi* appears to proceed on this basis.

But is there any wriggle room for the UK/Poland to argue that *in extremis*, Protocol 30 does provide an opt-out? For the purposes of this book, the answer may be yes, at least in context of Article 1(2) of the Protocol. This says:

> In particular, and for the avoidance of doubt, nothing in Title IV of the Charter creates justiciable rights applicable to Poland or the United Kingdom except in so far as Poland or the United Kingdom has provided for such rights in its national law.

Article 1(2) therefore appears to refer back to the rights/principles dichotomy discussed above. The Article makes clear that the provisions in Title IV, the Solidarity Title of the Charter, contain principles and not rights—and principles, as Article 52(5) of the Charter makes clear, are not justiciable. But Article 1(2) appears to leave open the door to the possibility of the UK/Poland having an opt-out from any provisions in Title IV which might be considered, in the future, to contain rights, rather than principles. However, even if the UK and Poland do enjoy a limited opt-out, litigants will still be able to resort back to relying on the general principles of law to enforce their fundamental social rights.

As we shall see in the following chapters, the Charter is already being felt in individual cases. In the long run, however, the Charter's greatest importance may lie in the fact that, in the social field at least, it will help provide some counterweight to the neoliberal orientation of the Treaties, providing the Court with a firmer foundation to reconcile social and economic rights. For the other Union institutions and the Member States, the Charter will provide a stark reminder of the EU's social rights agenda at a time when aspects of the EES have a deregulatory edge[185] and states, deprived of the traditional tools for managing their economies, might look to removing social rights as a way of gaining a competitive advantage.[185A]

C. THE NATURE AND PURPOSE OF EU SOCIAL POLICY

1. THE EUROPEAN SOCIAL MODEL

It is clear from the description above that the evolution of EU social policy has been spasmodic with the resulting rules representing a patchwork of European social regulation rather than a fully fledged social policy with welfare institutions and cradle-to-grave protection.[186] It makes no provision for what is generally agreed to be

---

[185] B. Hepple, *Rights at Work* (Sweet & Maxwell, London, 2005) 36–7.

[185A] See Case C-128/12 Sindicato dos Bancários do Norte.

[186] This section develops the arguments in C. Barnard, 'EU "Social" Policy: from Employment Law to Labour Market Reform', in P. Craig and G. de Búrca (eds.), *The Evolution of EU Law* (OUP, Oxford, 2011).

the central core of social policy: social insurance, public assistance, health and welfare services, education, and housing policy.[187] There is also no evidence of the creation of a European welfare state to replace the national welfare states: the EU has
neither the competence nor the budget for it.[188] However, the existing body of
EU regulation is often referred to as 'European social policy' and various institutions
talk of the European Social Model.[189] For example, in its White Paper on Social
Policy[190] the Commission said that the 'European Social Model' is based around
certain shared values:

> These include democracy and individual rights, free collective bargaining, the market
> economy, equality of opportunity for all and social welfare and solidarity. These values... are
> held together by the conviction that economic and social progress must go hand in hand.
> Competitiveness and solidarity have both been taken into account in building a successful
> Europe for the future.

Six years later, at the Nice European Council, the heads of state said:[191]

> The European social model has developed over the last forty years through a substantial
> [Union] acquis... It now includes essential texts in numerous areas: free movement of
> workers, gender equality at work, health and safety of workers, working and employment
> conditions and, more recently, the fight against all forms of discrimination.

The Council continued that this social model also includes the agreements between the
Social Partners in the law-making process, the Luxembourg EES, and the open method
of co-ordination on the subject of social exclusion and greater co-operation in the field
of social protection.[192]

The Final Report of the Constitutional Treaty's Working Group XI on Social Europe
offered its own view.[193] It said that 'the European social model is based on good economic performance, competitiveness, a high level of social protection and education
and social dialogue'. It also noted that the European social model allows for a diversity
of approaches in order to achieve shared European values and objectives and that this
diversity should be treated as an asset and a source of strength.[194]

The common features of these descriptions are first, that there is no single concept of
a European social model, that it is based on some shared values but a diversity of means
for achieving this, and that the success of this social model is tied up with good economic performance; second, the European social model is based on *high* standards

---

[187] G. Majone, 'The European Community: Between Social Policy and Regulation' (1993) 31 *JCMS* 153, 158.
However, the TFEU does contain a Title on education, vocational training, youth, and sport and Titles on
culture, public health, and consumer protection. The cases on health testing of staff at the institutions also
demonstrate some awareness of the wider dimension of social policy. See e.g. Case C–404/92 P *Commission v.
X* [1994] ECR I–4737.

[188] P. Teague, 'Deliberative Governance and EU Social Policy' (2001) 7 *EJIR* 7, 21.

[189] See N. Adnett and S. Hardy, *The European Social Model: Modernisation or Evolution* (Edward Elgar,
Cheltenham, 2005); M. Poiares Maduro, 'European Constitutionalism and Three Models of Social Europe' in
M. Hesselink, *The Politics of a European Civil Code* (Kluwer, The Hague, 2006). This issue is considered further
in Ch. 3.   [190] COM(94) 333, para. 3.

[191] Para. 12.   [192] Para. 11.   [193] CONV 516/1/03.   [194] Para. 17.

(such as a high level of social protection) and quality,[195] rather than a low quality, low skilled workforce; and third, all the institutions mention an eclectic range of policies grouped together under the broad banner of European social policy. Finally, and perhaps most importantly, all of the EU institutions recognize that there is such a thing as European Union social model which builds on but is, in many respects, separate from the social model found in the Member States. This raises the fundamental question as to why the EU, a transnational body with limited competence, has a European social model that it wishes to call its own. This question has bedevilled the Union since its inception.

2. MARKET MAKING v. MARKET CORRECTING

2.1. Introduction

Traditionally, at national level, social policy is viewed as serving a social justice/social cohesion or a *market-correcting*[196] function. In Marshall's words, social policy involves the use of 'political power to supersede, supplement or modify operations of the economic system in order to achieve results which the economic system would not achieve on its own, . . . guided by values other than those determined by market forces.'[197] These values include the need to redistribute income and resources in order to promote social inclusion and cohesion, thereby ensuring political stability. As we shall see, elements of this logic, given renewed vigour by the advent of European Union citizenship, can be detected in the development of EU social legislation.

On the other hand, as Streeck has observed, 'Economic governance through fragmented sovereignty and international relations is more suited to *market making* by way of negative integration and efficiency enhancing regulation than to institution building and redistributive intervention, or market distortion.'[198] Thus Streeck argues that the Treaty of Rome charged the Union with:

> developing *a new kind of social policy*, one concerned with *market making rather than market correcting*, aimed at creating an integrated European labour market and enabling it to function efficiently, rather than with correcting its outcomes in line with political standards of social justice.

In other words, the existing body of EU employment-related social policy represents regulation in support of a free or common market to ensure, in the words of Article 116 TFEU, that the conditions of competition are not distorted. This has been the most influential of the justifications for social policy. The market-making thesis comprises two limbs: first, the creation of a 'European-wide labour market',[199] by removing

---

[195] See, e.g. Commission Communication, 'Employment and Social Policies: a framework for investing in quality' (COM(2001) 313, 5).

[196] W. Streeck, 'From Market Making to State Building? Reflections on the Political Economy of European Social Policy', in Leibfried and Pierson (eds.), above, n. 19, 399.

[197] T. H. Marshall, *Social Policy* (Hutchinson, London, 1975) 15.   [198] Streeck, above, n. 20, 34.

[199] Streeck, above, n. 196, 397.

obstacles to the mobility of workers,[200] and secondly, removing distortions to competition by, on the one hand, seeking to harmonize costs on firms and, on the other, preventing social dumping by firms and a race to the bottom by States.

The clearest example of the market-making thesis can be found with the inclusion of Article 157 TFEU on equal pay. As we have seen, much of the debate between the French and German governments prior to the signing of the Treaty of Rome revolved around economic interests (concerns about loss of competitiveness on the part of France) rather than the social interests of the workers in the EU (although the drafting of Article 157 was inspired by ILO Convention No. 100).[201] The French were particularly concerned about discriminatory pay rates resulting from collective agreements in Italy. At that time France had one of the smallest differentials between the salaries of male and female employees (7 per cent compared with 20–40 per cent in the Netherlands and in Italy).[202] This risked placing those parts of French industry employing a very large female workforce, such as textiles and electrical construction, in a weaker competitive position than identical or similar industries in other Member States employing a largely female workforce at much lower salaries.[203]

Consequently, Article 157 TFEU was originally included in the EEC Treaty to impose parity of costs on the Member States and to prevent such destructive competition.[204] This point was noted, albeit somewhat obliquely, by the French Advocate General Dutheillet de Lamothe in *Defrenne (No. 1)*,[205] the first case to consider the application of Article 157 TFEU. Advancing the market-making thesis, he said that although Article 157 had a social objective it also had an economic objective,

> for in creating an obstacle to any attempt at 'social dumping' by means of the use of female labour less well paid than male labour, it helped to achieve one of the fundamental objectives of the common market, the establishment of a system ensuring that 'competition is not distorted'.

---

[200] Considered further in Ch. 4.

[201] C. Hoskyns, *Integrating Gender: Women, Law and Politics in the European Union* (Verso, London, 1996) Ch. 3.

[202] M. Budiner, *Le Droit de la femme a l'Egalité de salaire et la Convention No. 100 de l'organisation internationale du travail* (Librairie Générale de Droit et de Jurisprudence, Paris, 1975), citing E. Sullerot, *L'emploi des femmes et ses problèmes dans les Etats Membres de la Communauté Européene* (CEC, 1972) 177. See generally Barnard, previously, at n. 11.

[203] Budiner, previously, at n. 202, citing Jean-Jacques Ribas, 'L'Egalité des salaires feminins et masculins dans la Communauté Economique européene' (novembre 1966), *Droit Social*, para. 1, and P. Clair, 'L'article 119 du Traité de Rome. Le Principe de l'Egalisation des salaires masculins et feminins dans la CEE' (mars 1968), *Droit Social*, 150. In addition, France had ratified ILO Convention No. 100 by Law No. 52–1309 of 10 December 1952 (Journal Officiel, 11 décembre 1952). By 1957 the Convention had also been ratified by Belgium, France, Germany, and Italy, but not by Luxembourg and the Netherlands. (Luxembourg ratified the Convention in 1967 and the Netherlands in 1971.)

[204] See further Ch. 6.

[205] Case 80/70 [1971] ECR 445. In Case 69/80 *Worringham and Humphreys* v. *Lloyds Bank* [1981] ECR 767 Advocate General Warner again referred back to Advocate General Dutheillet de Lamothe's statement in *Defrenne (No. 1)* that the first purpose of Art. 157 TFEU was to 'avoid a situation in which undertakings established in Member States with advanced legislation on the equal treatment of men and women suffer a competitive disadvantage as compared with undertakings established in Member States that have not eliminated discrimination against female workers as regards pay'.

He continued: 'This explains why Article [157 TFEU] is of a different character from the articles which precede it in the chapter of the Treaty devoted to social provisions'.

It would therefore seem that the social provisions of the Treaties respond above all to the fear that unless employment costs are harmonized, economic integration will lead to competition to the detriment of countries whose social legislation is more advanced. However, the Court, pursuing in Streeck's words its own 'distinctive integrationist agenda',[206] has recognized the market-correcting, as well as market-making, dimension of the 'social' provisions. In its landmark judgment in *Defrenne (No. 2)*[207] the Court said:

> Article [157] pursues a double aim. *First*,...the aim of Article [157] is to avoid a situation in which undertakings established in states which have actually implemented the principle of equal pay suffer a competitive disadvantage in intra-[Union] competition as compared with undertakings established in states which have not yet eliminated discrimination against women workers as regards pay.

Having recognized the economic purpose of Article 157 TFEU, the Court then continued:

> *Second*, this provision forms part of the social objectives of the [Union], which is not merely an economic union, but is at the same time intended, by common action to ensure social progress and seek the constant improvement of living and working conditions of their peoples... This double aim, which is at once economic and social, shows that the principle of equal pay forms part of the foundations of the [Union].

The Court again recognized the dual purpose of the Union's social provisions in *Commission* v. *UK*.[208] It said that in the Directives on Collective Redundancies and Acquired Rights[209] 'the [Union] legislature intended both to ensure comparable protection for workers' rights in the different Member States and to harmonise the costs which such protective rules entail for [Union] undertakings'.[210] Further, the legislation of the 1970s cannot be explained solely in terms of harmonization of costs. Measures such as those on sex equality, transfers of undertakings, collective redundancies, and insolvency suggested a project of market correcting as well as market making for Union social policy.[211]

It therefore seems that the Union has seen social policy in terms of a dichotomy combining a market-led conception of employment regulation, with some recognition of the market-correcting or social function of such regulation. This prompts Freedland to suggest that the evolution of EU employment law has always depended on the possibility of legitimating it in economic policy terms as well as social policy terms. He argues that this is a possibility which is made all the more attainable by the fact that the proponents of economic policy have felt the need to lay claim to a social legitimation.[212]

---

[206] Streeck, previous, n. 20, 39.
[207] Case 43/75 [1976] ECR 455. This was emphasized in Case C–50/96 *Deutsche Telekom* v. *Schröder* [2000] ECR I–743, paras. 53–5.
[208] Case C–382/92 *Commission* v. *UK* [1994] ECR I–2435 and Case C–383/92 [1994] ECR I-2479.
[209] Originally Directives 75/129/EEC (OJ [1975] L48/29) and 77/187/EEC (OJ [1977] L61/27), respectively considered in detail in Chs. 13 and 14.
[210] Para. 15.   [211] Streeck, above, n. 20, 399.   [212] Freedland, above, n. 78, 287.

2.2. The market-making thesis examined

The effect of the EU rules on free movement of goods, persons, services and capital is to place the different national systems into competition because those individuals or companies not satisfied with the political/legal/social environment in which they find themselves are free to move to another Member State which has a regime which suits them better.[213] This freedom for individuals/capital to move has the effect of forcing the national systems to compete to produce the best rules to attract (or retain) valuable assets (capital and labour). This is known as competitive federalism or regulatory competition.[214]

For competitive federalism to function, two conditions need to be satisfied. First, the *federal* (central) authorities must lay down and enforce the rules giving goods, persons, and capital freedom to exit one Member State and enter another. Second, the *states* (the decentralized authorities) must remain free to regulate the production of goods and the qualifications of people according to their own standards, enabling regulators to respond to the competition. The outcome of this process of regulatory competition should be to produce optimal, efficient, and innovative legislation (a race to the top) because state officials vie with one another to create increasingly attractive economic circumstances for their citizens, knowing that their re-election depends upon their success.

Yet, in order to ensure successful regulatory competition, certain conditions must be satisfied.[215] For example, there must be full mobility of people and resources at little or no cost; migrants must have full knowledge of each jurisdiction's revenue and expenditure patterns; and there must be a wide choice of destination jurisdictions to enable the citizens to be able to make meaningful decisions about migration. In reality these conditions are never met. For individuals the likelihood of exit is slim because they are unlikely to leave their own jurisdiction for linguistic, cultural, financial, or personal reasons; and capital (direct investment in business operations) is unlikely to leave unless a variety of factors (market proximity, transport costs, infrastructure levels, labour costs, and productivity levels) justify the move. Even if these conditions could be met, state legislation is often insufficiently responsive to the needs of its consumers.[216] This creates the risk that the type of regulatory competition which emerges is undesirable: it does not lead to a race to the top but a race to the bottom.[217]

The following example demonstrates this. The UK knows that in practice workers are less mobile than capital and so it decides to gain a competitive advantage by reducing

---

[213] Some of this section is taken from C. Barnard, *The Substantive Law of the European Union: The Four Freedoms* (OUP, Oxford, 2010).

[214] This is based on Tiebout's famous 'pure theory' of fiscal federalism: C. Tiebout, 'A pure theory of local expenditure' (1956) 64/5 *Journal of Political Economy* 416. For further details see C. Barnard and S. Deakin, 'Market Access and Regulatory Competition', in C. Barnard and J. Scott (eds.), *The Law of the Single European Market: Unpacking the Premises* (Hart Publishing, Oxford, 2002).

[215] For the literature on the economics of federalism, see Tiebout, previous, n. 214; F. Easterbrook, 'Antitrust and the Economics of Federalism' (1983) 26 *Journal of Law and Economics* 23, 34.

[216] J. Sun and J. Pelkmans, 'Regulatory Competition in the Single Market' (1995) 33 *JCMS* 67, 84.

[217] This is sometimes referred to as the 'Delaware effect': W. Cary, 'Federalism and Corporate Law: Reflections Upon Delaware' (1974) 83 *Yale Law Journal* 663.

employment protection. While such a strategy might have short-term benefits (e.g. job creation or at least job retention) it undermines longer-term interests of the citizenry as a whole (e.g. lower quality jobs and inferior working environments). Nevertheless, faced with such deregulation by the UK, Poland—which risks losing capital and thus jobs to the UK—relaxes its own standards. The UK responds by lowering its standards still further and a race to the bottom ensues where the UK and Poland are competing on the basis of low standards.

While there is much controversy about the likelihood of EU states actually engaging in a full-blown race to the bottom,[218] and to what extent it is actually going on in practice,[219] there is a perception that so long as states remain free to regulate or, more likely deregulate, their social standards it may happen. These concerns were brought into sharp focus by the highly publicized Hoover affair. Hoover decided to close its factory in Longvic, near Dijon, with the loss of 600 out of 700 jobs, and to transfer its activities to the Cambuslang plant, near Glasgow in Scotland, resulting in the recruitment of 400 workers on 24-month fixed-term contracts.[220] This followed the conclusion of a collective agreement between management and the British Amalgamated Engineering and Electrical Union (AEEU) providing for improved flexibility of labour, new working patterns, a no-strike deal, and a pay freeze. At the same time Rockwell Graphic systems announced that 110 jobs were to be lost out of 272 at its Nantes plant with production being relocated to Preston in England. The French blamed the deregulatory agenda adopted by the British Conservative government between 1979 and 1997. Martine Aubry, the French Minister for labour, and the French Prime Minister both said that Hoover's decision constituted 'social dumping'.[221]

---

[218] C. Barnard, 'Social Dumping Revisited: Lessons from Delaware' (2000) 25 *ELRev.* 57. However, despite the rhetoric there is in fact little evidence of the states being engaged in an active policy of deregulation of labour standards for the purpose of gaining a competitive edge, a point noted by the OECD which said 'there is no compelling evidence that "social dumping" has occurred so far in OECD countries' (OECD, 'Labour Standards and Economic Integration', in *Employment Outlook 1994* (OECD, 1994) 138). Schonfield has added: 'The dangers of "social dumping" have been exaggerated with only isolated examples of competitive undercutting of pay and conditions by firms exploiting labour cost differences between countries' (reported by Taylor, 'Wage Bargaining diversification under EU Single Market', *Financial Times*, 7 April 1997). On the other hand, he noted that there was evidence from Germany that companies are increasingly using the possibility of relocation as a bargaining counter to achieve changes in working practices at home. See e.g. the concessions made by German workers at Bosch and Daimler Benz because of threats of relocating to new plants abroad (see 'Can Europe compete?', *Financial Times*, 28 February 1994).

[219] P. De Grauwe, 'Let's Stop being Gloomy about Europe', *CEPS Working Paper no, 293, May 2008.*

[220] See *EIRR* 230, 16.

[221] *EIRR* 230, 16. John Major, the then British Prime Minister, is reported as saying in response: 'France can complain all it likes. If investors and business choose to come to Britain rather than pay the costs of socialism in France, let them call it "social dumping". I call it dumping socialism' (*Financial Times*, 6 March 1993). Such concerns also underpinned much of the criticism levelled at the Commission's first draft of the services Directive (COM(2004) 2). Trade unions feared that it would allow a firm to establish itself in State A (with lower labour standards) and then provide services in State B (with higher standards but with which the firm's workforce would not have to comply). In order to combat this perception, the Presidency Conclusions of the Brussels European Council of 22–23 March 2005, para. 2 expressly said: 'The internal market of services has to be fully operational while preserving the European social model'. This Directive is considered further in Ch. 5.

'Social dumping' is the term used to describe a variety of practices by both Member States and employers. In essence it concerns behaviour designed to give a competitive advantage to companies due to low labour standards[222] rather than productivity. Companies that move in response to a deliberate lowering of standards by the state are said to be engaged in social dumping. This in turn might precipitate a race to the bottom, with Member States competing to deregulate to attract capital or at least to retain existing capital.[223] Social dumping inevitably leads to calls for transnational social legislation to prevent this race to the bottom. In its White Paper on Social Policy[224] the Commission relied on this rhetoric to justify the enactment of Union social legislation:

> the establishment of a framework of basic minimum standards, which the Commission started some years ago, provides a bulwark against using low social standards as an instrument of unfair economic competition and protection against reducing social standards to gain competitiveness, and is also an expression of the political will to maintain the momentum of social progress.[225]

However, some argue that such legislation would be inefficient[226] and would have the effect of killing the poorer states with kindness,[227] depriving them of their comparative advantage—their cheaper workforce—and their vehicle for improvement. In other words by requiring the southern and eastern European states to apply the full gamut of EU social legislation serves to reinforce the already advantageous position enjoyed by the Northern European states when in fact the evidence of capital flight to the East is not borne out by the research. For example, in its publication 'Enlargement, two years after: an economic evaluation', [228] the Commission notes that the evidence indicates that foreign direct investment (FDI) flows to the new Member States, while relevant for the recipient countries, have in fact been only a minor part of overall FDI outflows of the EU-15: within the latter, in 2004 the share of outflows to new Member States was 4 per cent against a corresponding share of 53 per cent for outflows to other Member States in the EU-15 and a 12 per cent share for flows to the US. The Commission also says that a large part of the FDI by the EU-15 in the new Member States, particularly in the services sector where most of FDI is invested, has occurred in the context of privatization programmes

---

[222] See further B. Hepple, 'New Approaches to International Labour Regulation' (1997) 26 *ILJ* 353, 355 and, more generally, *Labour Laws and Global Trade* (Hart Publishing, Oxford, 2005). Cf now the position of countries in receipt of a bail-out considered in Chapter 3.

[223] See further the Commission's Green Paper on European Social Policy (COM(93)551, 7) which describes social dumping as 'the gaining of unfair competitive advantage within the [Union] through unacceptably low social standards'.

[224] COM(94) 333, 27 July 1994.

[225] Ibid., Introduction, para. 19. See further COM(94) 333, Ch. III, para. 1 and the Commission's Green Paper on European Social Policy (COM(93) 551, 46) where it said that '...a commitment to high social standards and to the promotion of social progress forms an integral part of the [TEU]. A "negative" competitiveness between Member States would lead to social dumping, to the undermining of the consensus making process...and to danger for the acceptability of the Union'.

[226] See e.g. D. Fischel, 'The "Race to the Bottom" revisited—Reflections on Recent Developments in Delaware's Corporation Law' (1982) 31 *Northwestern University Law Review* 913.

[227] *The Economist*, 23 June 1990, 17.

[228] <http://ec.europa.eu/economy_finance/publications/publication7548_en.pdf> (last accessed 12 March 2012).

to capture fast-growing markets and does not involve the substitution of activities previously carried out in the home country.

3. THE NEW APPROACH: ACTIVE LABOUR MARKET POLICIES

Others argue that the debate about social dumping in the EU misses the point: the
challenge to northern European employers/producers comes not from within the EU
but from outside, especially from South East Asia and China.[229] This has forced the
EU to think hard about what sort of European social model it wishes to have: one
based on low wages and low skills or one based on higher wages and high skills. As we
have already seen, the Union institutions have opted for the high skills model. Thus,
the focus of the European Union's attention dating from around the time of the
Amsterdam Treaty is on flexibility for firms combined with security for workers—so-
called 'flexicurity' (considered earlier in this chapter). More specifically, the Commission thinks that 'the flexible firm could offer a sound basis for fundamental
organisational renewal built on high skill, high productivity, high quality, good environmental management—and good wages'.[230] In other words, the EU is breaking away
from the rather sterile market-making/market-correcting dichotomy to see social
rights no longer as merely a beneficial consequence of growth but as an integral part
of realizing that growth.[231] This view is supported by Sen's capability approach[232]
which has been translated by lawyers to mean that:

> Social rights are the foundation of a market order which is based on extensive mobilisation
> of resources and the widest division of labour which are compatible with a given society's
> initial endowments in terms of human and physical resources.[233]

Deakin and Browne illustrate the value of the capability approach by using the example of laws prohibiting the dismissal of a pregnant woman.[234] While a conventional
economic analysis would view the introduction of such a law as imposing costs on
employers who might be discouraged from employing women of child-bearing age

---

[229] 'Relocation of Production and Industrial Relations' (6 February 2006): <http://www.eurofound.europa.
eu/eiro/2005/11/study/tn0511101s.htm> (last accessed 12 March 2012).

[230] See, e.g. Commission's Green Paper, *Partnership for a New Organisation of Work*, COM(97) 127 final,
para. 24.

[231] See the Commission Communication, 'Modernising and Improving Social Protection in the EU'
COM(97) 102 and the follow-up 'A Concerted Strategy for Modernising Social Protection' COM(99) 347. This
theme is considered further in Ch. 3.

[232] See, e.g., *Commodities and Capabilities* (North-Holland, Deventer, 1985) and *Development as Freedom*
(OUP, Oxford, 1999).

[233] S. Deakin and J. Browne, 'Social Rights and Market Order: Adapting the Capability Approach' in
J. Kenner and T. Hervey (eds.), *Economic and Social Rights under the EU Charter of Fundametnal Rights* (Hart
Publishing, Oxford, 2003), 42. More generally, see S. Deakin and F. Wilkinson, *The Law of the Labour Market:
Industrialization, Employment, and Legal Evolution* (OUP, Oxford, 2005) and S. Deakin, 'The "Capability"
Concept and the Evolution of European Social Policy', in M. Dougan and E. Spaventa, *Social Welfare and EU
Law* (Hart Publishing, Oxford, 2005).

[234] Ibid., 35–6.

who would then eventually become deskilled, a capability approach would view the situation rather differently. In addition to remedying the injustice which would otherwise affect individuals who are dismissed for being pregnant, such a law has the potential to alter incentive structures to encourage women employees to seek out, and employers to provide training for, jobs involving relation-specific skills. Deakin and Browne conclude that pregnancy protection laws can be seen as a form of institutional support for individual capabilities: they provide the conditions under which the freedom for women workers to enter the labour market becomes more than merely formal; it becomes a substantive freedom. Thus, relying on Sen's capability arguments (which were, in turn, referred to in the Commission Social Vision paper of 2007, considered earlier), they argue that social rights have a value not just in themselves, a fact which the Court has recognized in cases such as *Deutsche Post*[235] and *Albany*,[236] but in terms of their pro-competitive effect, in the sense of encouraging enterprises to invest in human capital and avoiding the destructive social effects of low wage competition.[237]

Although social rights, particularly when viewed in terms of their capacity to enhance capability, have a value in the new approach to EU social policy, the core of the capabilities approach lies with the idea of encouraging active economic participation in the labour market[238] by ensuring that employees possess the new skills that are required in a knowledge-based society. Thus, much emphasis is placed on training workers and providing them with incentives to enable them to acquire sufficient skills both to enter the workforce and then to adapt themselves to the changing demands of the workplace in years to come. In this way employers will gain the flexibility necessary to enable them to compete; individuals will attain higher standards of living; and national welfare systems will be able to afford to continue providing high levels of protection to those in need which are funded by contributions made by those in employment. Given the importance of this 'third way' to the success of the EU economy, it is considered in more detail in Chapter 3.

4. THE LEGISLATIVE IMPACT

The choice of thesis that shapes EU social policy has implications for regulation. If a pure *market-correcting* vision of social policy were accepted, this would point to the need for a comprehensive social policy at EU level, replacing national diversity with uniformity, and imposing EU homogeneity on long-standing national policy regimes and institutional arrangements. By contrast, if a pure *market-making* conception of EU social policy prevailed, this would suggest that the EU should enact social policy only where there is a risk that conditions of competition are distorted

---

[235] Joined Cases C–270/97 and C–271/97 *Deutsche Post* v. *Sievers and Schrage* [2000] ECR I–929, para. 57.
[236] Case C–67/96 *Albany* [1999] ECR I–5751.
[237] Ibid., 42.
[238] 'The New Paradigm for Social Policy: A Virtuous Circle?' (2001) 38 *CMLRev.* 1125, 1125.

or where there is a transnational interest at stake (e.g. the regulation of transnational companies where national regulation would prove ineffective unless co-ordinated). This model would envisage significantly less EU-level legislation in terms of volume but nevertheless when such legislation is enacted it would need to be set at the highest level to ensure that standards in the highest regulated state were not undercut.

Neither outcome is palatable to the Member States with their diverse industrial relations traditions and strong desire to preserve their national social systems. Nor would such uniformity be desirable or optimal: uniformity would replace diversity and the freedom to experiment would be removed. As we shall see in Chapter 2, the legislative approach actually adopted conforms to neither stereotype: most EU legislation sets minimum standards (to avoid the worst excesses of race to the bottom, imagined or real), giving Member States the freedom to improve upon those standards in their own system, thereby preserving some regulatory diversity. The question of whether the Union should act in a particular field, and why (the subsidiarity question), has received only cursory attention from the courts, thereby avoiding difficult judgments about the nature of EU social policy.

If, however, the goal of European social policy is, in fact, about active labour market polices then a traditional legislative approach cannot provide the answer. As Kilpatrick points out, states have always had employment polices aimed at activities such as vocational training and income replacement in periods of employment or underemployment.[239] Such policies have never typically been associated with a hard law 'command and control model' but have relied instead on spending money and the creation of guidelines and indicators in attempts to steer national policies.[240] It should therefore come as no surprise that employment policies at EU level rely on the same kind of tools as used at national level. Traditional legislation is not a suitable tool to achieve the objectives of full employment. Moreover, the EU has limited direct control over national employment policies. As we have seen at Amsterdam and then in the Lisbon Strategy, it has therefore developed a different regulatory technique, the Open Method of Co-ordination (OMC), which commits Member States to work together towards common goals (such as full employment) without seeking to harmonize their diverse policy regimes and institutional arrangements. Some commentators see this as the 'third way' for EU social policy between 'regulatory competition and harmonization, an alternative to both intergovernmentalism and supranationalism, which may open up a sustainable path between a fragmented Europe and a European super state'.[241] Whether OMC is capable of delivering on such promise will be considered in Chapter 3.

---

[239] 'New EU Employment Governance and Constitutionalism' in G. De Búrca and J. Scott (eds.), *Law and New Governance in the EU and US* (Hart Publishing, Oxford, 2006).

[240] Ibid.

[241] J. Zeitlin, 'Introduction: The Open Method of Coordination in Question' in J. Zeitlin and P. Pochet with Magnusson (eds.), *The Open Method of Coordination in Action: The European Employment and Social Inclusion Strategies* (PIE Peter Lang, 2005).

D. CONCLUSIONS

It would seem that the development of the Union's 'social' policy has in the past been constrained—perhaps fatally[242]—by the need to operate within a framework which is both economic and social. This has led, on the one hand, to some inconsistent decisions by the Court concerning the interface between Union law on market integration and national law and, on the other, to a patchwork of Union social legislation aimed at both harmonization and minimum standards. Of course, national social policy faces similar dilemmas but the dichotomy is brought into sharper focus in the Union context due to its original economic objectives and to the lack of the underpinnings of a welfare state. On the other hand, the absence of any 'social' policy in the EU would have caused a serious legitimacy crisis. The piecemeal European social model which has been created, however awkwardly, through a mix of legislation (both hard and soft) and judicial decisions, provides the bridge between the economic aspect of the Treaty (job creation) and the social dimension of the Treaty (politics of social inclusion, solidarity, and citizenship) and a step towards the creation of a European 'civil society'.[243] This has gone some way to rebutting allegations of the EU's 'social deficit'.

The Amsterdam Treaty and Lisbon/EU2020 strategies have brought about a seismic shift in EU social policy as it moves from being focused solely on a rights-based agenda, where the EU legislates for employment rights, towards employment policies with a new method of governance based on guidelines, benchmarking, targets, National Reform Programmes, and recommendations. While much has been written about the newness of the governance techniques adopted in this area, it is important to view these developments in context. OMC does not mean throwing the legislative baby out with the bath-water; rather, OMC and legislation serve different functions. While OMC tools are particularly suited to the area of employment or labour market *policy* (i.e. job creation and combating unemployment), legislation (hard law) is more suited for the creation of employment *rights* intended to protect workers. What is new is that employment policy has now become an EU objective and not just a national one; that social justice at EU level is no longer conceived of simply in terms of creating ad hoc rights for those

---

[242] See, e.g., the problems generated by the Commission in the case of atypical workers noted by S. Deakin and F. Wilkinson ('Rights vs Efficiency? The Economic Case for Transnational Labour Standards' (1994) 23 *ILJ* 289, 302–3). In the Explanatory Memorandum accompanying its proposals for a draft Directive on atypical work the Commission said that 'relative cost differences resulting from different kinds of rules on different types of employment relationships,...may provide comparative advantages which constitute veritable distortions of competition' (COM(90) 228). However, the Commission's arguments were weakened by its attempts to suggest that while harmonization of indirect wage costs resulting from social security taxation and employment regulation should take place, harmonization of direct costs (rules governing wages and salaries) was unnecessary because 'differences in productivity levels attenuate these differences in unit labour costs to a considerable degree'. Such a distinction has little merit from either an economic or a legal standpoint and it had the effect of rejecting the very argument put forward in 1957 for the adoption of Art. 157 TFEU.

[243] See Opinion of the Economic and Social Committee, 'The Role and Contribution of Civil Society Organisations in the Building of Europe' (OJ [1999] L329/30), 32.

who are already economically active (workers) but extends to removing obstacles to labour market participation for socially excluded groups;[244] and that there is greater and more deliberate synergy between the classic Union method and new governance tools, notably OMC. Chapter 2 examines the traditional legislative route for the creation of employment rights while Chapter 3 examines the creation of employment policy through the EES and the Lisbon/EU2020 Strategy. As we shall see, stereotypes about the governance tools used to achieve the different results soon break down, with hard law in the employment rights field being characterized by diversity and soft law in the employment policy field being buttressed by some hard(ish) rules, leading to the emergence of an increasingly sophisticated, hybrid regime. The question remains: does it work?

So far this chapter has told a fairly positive story about the evolution of social policy at EU level—the creation of ever more rights for individuals by the EU legislature and the largely pro-worker interpretation of those rights by the Court of Justice. Albeit somewhat eclectic, the EU definitely has a social face which relies in part on EU level rights and in part on the maintenance of social rights at national level. However, that very social dimension, so painfully crafted, is facing two serious threats from the EU itself. The first is from the Treaty provisions on free movement: does national labour law interfere with the free movement of workers, freedom of establishment, and freedom to provide services? These issues were brought into sharp focus by the decisions in a series of cases beginning with *Viking*[245] and *Laval*.[246] These cases are discussed in detail in Chapters 4 and 5. The second major challenge to EU labour law comes from the EU's reponse to the eurozone crisis, which is considered in Chapter 3. First, however, we turn to consider the law-making process.

---

[244] Ibid.
[245] Case C–438/05 *Viking Line ABP* v. *The International Transport Workers' Federation, the Finnish Seaman's Union* [2007] ECR I–10779.
[246] Case C–341/05 *Laval un Partneri Ltd* v. *Svenska Byggnadsarbetareförbundet* [2007] ECR I–11767.

2

(HARD) LAW-MAKING IN THE FIELD OF SOCIAL POLICY

A. INTRODUCTION

While the Treaties themselves laid down substantive rights in the field of equal pay, the main body of EU employment law has taken the form of secondary legislation, primarily Directives. Most of this hard law has been adopted via the classic 'Community' method[1] where the Commission proposes legislative measures and the Council and European Parliament adopt them.[2] According to the stereotype, such traditional top-down, command and control regulation results in mandates that are 'relatively specific and uniform, hierarchically determined, static and substantive'.[3] When compared with the Open Method of Co-ordination (considered in Chapter 3) which uses 'soft law' techniques including (non-binding) objectives and guidelines, the legislation to be discussed in this chapter certainly does have a 'hard' edge, creating obligations on states and, once implemented, on employers, which are enforceable in national courts. However, the very different legal, social and industrial relations cultures in the Member States have forced the European Union to be experimental and flexible in the social field, even when adopting 'hard' law. This chapter begins by examining the traditional route to legislation and considers the way in which the EU has attempted to reconcile the goal of setting common Union standards with the need to accommodate diversity at national level. It then considers the innovative method of law-making introduced by the Maastricht Treaty—of legislating by collective agreement, primarily by the cross-industry (interprofessional or intersectoral) Social Partners but also by the sectoral Social Partners.

---

[1] J. Scott and D. Trubek, 'Mind the Gap: Law and New Approaches to Governance in the European Union' (2002) 8 *ELJ* 1.

[2] Governance White Paper COM(2001) 428, 8.

[3] J. Mosher, 'Open Method of Coordination: Functional and Political Origins' (2000) 13 *ECSA Rev.* 6, 6.

B. ADOPTING UNION SOCIAL LEGISLATION

1. INTRODUCTION

In order for the Union to legislate in a particular field it must have the competence to act. The Union must also consider whether it is the most appropriate body to act (the subsidiarity question) and, if it is, whether the action it takes is proportionate. In the social field, a further question needs to be considered: what form should that action take: hard law or soft; and are there other ways of reconciling flexibility with uniformity? We shall consider these issues in turn.

2. COMPETENCE

2.1. The nature of the EU's competence to act

The European Union enjoys no general competence to enact legislation: it has only specific competences or enumerated powers given to it by the Member States in the Treaties. As Article 5(2) TEU makes clear, '… the Union shall act only within the limits of the competences conferred upon it by the Member States in the Treaties to attain the objectives set out therein'.[4] These powers may be specific, as in the case of Article 153 TFEU (ex 137 EC) concerning measures in the field of, *inter alia*, health and safety and working conditions, or more general, as in the case of Articles 114, 115, and 352 TFEU (ex 95, 94, and 308 EC) concerning measures for the attainment of the common market and internal market.[5] Where the Union has *per se* exclusive competence in a specific area, only the Union may legislate and adopt legally binding acts.[6] Member States cannot act in that field, irrespective of whether the Union itself has acted.[7] The corollary of this is where the Member States have not conferred power to act on the Union, the Member States retain legal competence.[8]

---

[4] See A. Dashwood, 'The Limits of European Community Powers' (1996) 21 *ELRev*. 113.

[5] Art. 115 TFEU (measures which directly affect the establishment or functioning of the Common Market) was used to adopt the three Directives in the late 1970s: on restructuring of enterprises (Dir. 75/129 (OJ [1975] L48/29)); on collective redundancies (now Dir. 98/59 (OJ [1998] L225/16)); Dir. 77/187 on transfers of undertakings (OJ [1977] L61/126) now replaced by Dir. 2001/23 (OJ [2001] L82/16), and Dir. 80/987 (OJ [1980] L283/23). Dir. 75/117 on equal pay (OJ [1975] L45/19) was also adopted on the basis of Art. 115 TFEU. Dir. 76/207 on equal treatment in respect of access to employment (OJ [1976] L39/40) and Dir. 79/7 on equal treatment in matters of social security (OJ [1979 L6/24) were adopted on the basis of Art. 352 TFEU (action by the Union to attain one of the objectives of the Union where the Treaty has not provided the necessary powers). Dirs. 86/378 (OJ [1986] L225/40) and 86/613 (OJ [1986] L359/56) on equality in occupational social security and of the self-employed respectively were based on both Arts. 115 and 352 TFEU. Both legal bases require unanimous voting in Council.

[6] Art. 2(1) TFEU.

[7] See e.g. in the context of Art. 207 TFEU (ex 133 EC) *Opinion 1/75* [1975] ECR 1355 and Case 41/76 *Donckerwolke* v. *Procureur de la République* [1976] ECR 1921.

[8] Art. 4(1) TEU and Art. 5(2) TEU.

Between these two extremes lie areas where the Union and the Member States have shared competence. This means that until the Union acts in these fields a Member State may act,[9] provided it does so within the limits set by the Treaties relating to, for example, free movement of goods and persons under Articles 34, 45, 49, and 56 TFEU (ex 28, 39, 43, and 49 EC), non-discrimination on the grounds of nationality under Article 18 TFEU (ex 12 EC), and the obligation of co-operation with the Union under Article 4(3) TEU (ex 10 EC). Thus, in the social field, in the absence of Union action, Member States remain free to legislate provided that their social legislation does not, for example, discriminate against other EU nationals. In other words, concurrence still implies the supremacy of Union norms. However, if, by reason of the scale and effects of the measure needed,[10] the Union decides it should act, it can convert a field of concurrent competence into a field of exclusive competence for the Union.[11] This is described in American constitutional law as the doctrine of 'preemption'.[12]

While the attribution of competence to the Union has great significance, both internally and externally,[13] the original EEC Treaty did not identify those areas which fall within the exclusive competence of either the Union or the Member States, or those areas which fall within the concurrent competence of the Member States and the Union. We know, because the Maastricht Treaty told us, that in the field of social policy the Union has no competence, at least under Article 153 TFEU,[14] to legislate in respect of pay, the right to strike, or the right to impose lock-outs (Article 153(5) TFEU). Subsequently, the Lisbon Treaty addressed years of uncertainty by identifying 'social policy for the aspects defined in this Treaty' as an area of shared competence.[15] Employment policies, by contrast, are subject merely to 'coordination'.[16] Therefore, there is shared competence in respect of both Article 114(2) TFEU concerning 'the rights and interests of employed persons' introduced into the Treaty by the Single European Act (SEA) and the areas listed in Article 153 TFEU. The predecessor provision to Article 153 TFEU was Article 137 EC; its predecessor was Article 118a EEC, included in the Treaty of

---

[9] Art. 2(2) TFEU.

[10] The principle of subsidiarity set out in Art. 5(3) TEU is considered further.

[11] If the Union acts again in this field the principle of subsidiarity does not, at least according to the theory, apply.

[12] See, e.g. S. Weatherill, 'Beyond Preemption? Shared Competence and Constitutional Change in the European Community', in D. O'Keeffe and P. Twomey (eds.), *Legal Issues of the Maastricht Treaty* (Chancery, Chichester, 1994).

[13] Where the Union has internal competence it also has authority to enter into international commitments necessary to attain this objective, even in the absence of express provision to that effect: Joined Cases 3, 4 and 6/76 *Kramer and Others* [1976] ECR 1279 and *Opinion 2/91* [1993] ECR I-1061.

[14] See G. Brinkman, 'Lawmaking under the Social Chapter of Maastricht', in P. Craig and C. Harlow (eds.), *Lawmaking in the EU* (Kluwer, Deventer, 1998) 244, who suggests that this does not preclude other legal bases from being used, a view confirmed by Final Report of Working Group XI on Social Europe CONV 516/1/03, para. 28 and Case C–14/04 *Abdelkader Dellas and Others* v. *Premier Ministre and Others* [2005] ECR I–10253, para. 39. The Monti II proposal on the exercise of the right to take collective action within the context of the freedom of establishment and the freedom to provide services (COM(2012) 130) (discussed in Ch. 5) has been proposed under Art. 352 TFEU.

[15] Art. 4(2)(b) TFEU.   [16] Art. 5(2) TFEU.

Rome by the SEA 1986. Prior to the Social Policy Agreement being incorporated into the Treaty at Amsterdam in 1997, Article 118a EEC was the only express legal basis included in the Social Title of the Treaty of Rome. Given that a number of important pieces of Union legislation were adopted under Article 118a EEC (as it then was) it deserves some attention in its own right before we consider Article 153 TFEU in detail.

2.2. Article 118a EEC

(a) The scope of the competence

Article 118a(1) EEC provided that 'Member States shall pay particular attention to encouraging improvements, especially in the working environment, as regards health and safety of workers'. The post-Nice modified version talks in Article 153(1)(a) TFEU of 'improvements in particular of the working environment to protect workers' health and safety'. Article 118a(2) EEC then added that the Council, acting by a qualified majority vote,[17] was to adopt Directives laying down '*minimum requirements* for gradual implementation' (emphasis added) to help achieve the objective laid down in Article 118a(l) EEC. According to Article 118a(3) EEC, Member States were free to maintain or introduce 'more stringent measures for the protection of working conditions'.[18]

The nature of the then Community's competence in respect of social policy was considered by the Court in *Opinion 2/91*[19] concerning ILO Convention No. 170 on safety in the use of chemicals at work. During the negotiations leading up to the agreement of this Convention, the Commission argued that the subject-matter of the Convention fell within the exclusive competence of the Union. This was disputed by some Member States and the matter was considered by the Court under what is now the Article 218(11) TFEU procedure. The Court began by noting that the area covered by the Convention fell within the Title on Social Policy. Referring to Article 118a EEC, it said that the Union 'enjoys an internal legislative competence in the area of social policy'.[20] It continued that since the subject-matter of Convention No. 170 coincided with that of several Directives adopted under Article 118a EEC,[21] the Convention fell within the Union's area of competence. The Court then distinguished between two situations. On the one hand, it said that in the areas where the Union had laid down only minimum requirements and those standards were inferior to those set by the ILO, the Member States had competence under Article 118a(3) EEC to adopt more stringent measures.[22] On the

---

[17] At Maastricht this was amended to the co-operation procedure contained in Art. 252 EC.

[18] See further Case C–14/04 *Abdelkader Dellas and Others* v. *Premier Ministre and Others* [2005] ECR I–10253, para. 51, considered further in Ch. 12.

[19] [1993] ECR I–1061. See N. Emiliou, 'Towards a Clearer Demarcation Line? The Division of External Relations Power between the Community and the Member States' (1994) 19 *ELRev.* 76.

[20] Para. 40.   [21] See further Ch. 11.

[22] Para. 18. The Court dismissed the argument made by the Commission that it could be difficult to determine whether one specific measure was more favourable to a worker than another. The Court said that such difficulties could not constitute a basis for exclusive competence.

other hand, the Court said that in those areas where the Union had harmonized rules, for example, relating to classification, packaging, and labelling of dangerous substances and preparations,[23] the Union alone had competence.

The ILO Convention also contained provisions about implementation, making express reference to consultation with the Social Partners. The Court said that insofar as it had been established that the substantive provisions of the Convention came within the Union's sphere of competence, the Union was also competent to undertake commitments for putting those provisions into effect. It recognized that 'as [Union] law stands at present, social policy and in particular co-operation between the two sides of industry are matters which fall predominantly within the competence of the Member States'[24] but, pointing to Article 118b EEC (now significantly amended by Article 155 TFEU) which provided that the Commission shall endeavour to develop a dialogue between management and labour at European level,[25] it said these matters had not been 'withdrawn entirely from the competence of the [Union]'. It added that where the subject-matter of an agreement fell in part within the competence of the Union and in part within the competence of the Member States, there had to be a close association between the two, particularly because, unlike the Member States, the Union had only observer status at the ILO and so could not itself conclude an ILO Convention.[26]

(b) The legislative procedure

The legal basis of a measure not only confers the Union with the power to act but it also sets out the legislative procedure by which the measure must be adopted, be it simple consultation with the European Parliament and unanimous voting[27] (as is the case with Article 114(2) TFEU concerning 'the rights and interests of employed persons', which appears to refer back[28] to the procedure in Article 115 TFEU), or now, more usually, the ordinary legislative procedure[29] under Article 294 TFEU. When Article 118a EEC was introduced by the SEA in 1986, the choice of legal basis became a political football: the Commission, in an attempt to circumvent the UK's blocking power, made extensive use of Article 118a EEC (in preference to say, Article 100a(2) EEC (new Article 114(2)

[23] Dir. 67/548/EEC (OJ/SE [1967] 234), as amended and Dir. 88/379/EEC (OJ [1988] L187/14).

[24] Para. 30.

[25] Para. 31. Cf. Case C–67/96 *Albany International BV* v. *Stichting Bedrijfspensioenfonds Textielindustrie* [1999] ECR I-5751, considered further in Ch. 16.

[26] Paras. 36–7.

[27] The Lisbon Treaty termed this the 'special legislative procedure': Art. 289(2) TFEU.

[28] In the original EEC Treaty there was only one legal basis in this area, Article 100 EEC which required unanimous voting. The SEA 1986 introduced Article 100a which provided for qualified majority voting in respect of measures which have as their object the establishment and functioning of the internal market. Article 100a(2) EEC contained an exception for, *inter alia*, rules relating to the 'rights and interests of employed persons'. It was therefore thought that, for measures adopted under this provision, the procedure defaulted back to the basic position as set out in Article 100 EEC. This position remained through the Amsterdam and Nice Treaty amendments. However, at Lisbon the ordinary legislative procedure became the basic position and the order of Articles 100 EEC (now Article 115 TFEU) and 100a EEC (now Article 114 TFEU) were reversed. Nevertheless, given the history, it is likely that Article 114(2) TFEU still refers to the procedure in Article 115 TFEU.

[29] Art. 289(1) TFEU. This used to be called the co-decision procedure.

TFEU) on the rights and interest of employed persons) since Article 118a EEC provided for qualified majority, as opposed to unanimous, voting.

The Commission's strategy was eventually challenged in *UK v. Council (Working Time)*.[30] The Working Time Directive 93/104/EC[31] (now Directive 2003/88) was adopted under Article 118a EEC, with the UK abstaining in the final vote. The UK then challenged the choice of legal basis under Article 263 TFEU (ex 230 EC) arguing, *inter alia*, that since the organization of working time envisaged by the Directive was intended to achieve both job creation and social policy objectives, recourse should have been had to Article 115 TFEU or to Article 352 TFEU, both requiring unanimity in Council. It also argued that on a proper interpretation, Article 118a EEC (new Article 153 TFEU) had to be read in conjunction with Article 100a(2) EEC (new Article 114(2) TFEU) concerning the rights and interests of employed persons and required a unanimous vote.

The Court rejected these arguments. It said that since Article 118a EEC appeared in the section dealing with social provisions it related only to measures concerning the health and safety of workers.[32] The Court reasoned that it therefore constituted a more specific rule than Articles 100 and 100a EEC (new Articles 115 and 114 TFEU respectively), an interpretation confirmed by the fact that the provisions of these general legal bases were to apply 'save where otherwise provided in this Treaty'.[33]

The UK also argued that the link between health and safety (as narrowly understood under English law) and working time was too tenuous. However, the Advocate General pointed out that under Danish law the term 'working environment' (*arbejdsmiljø*) in Article 118a(1) EEC was a very broad one, not limited to classic measures relating to safety and health at work in the strict sense, but included 'measures concerning working hours, psychological factors, the way work is performed, training in hygiene and safety, and the protection of young workers and worker representation with regard to security against dismissal or any other attempt to undermine their working conditions'.[34] The Court, without referring to the Danish origins of Article 118a EEC, also favoured a broad approach to health and safety. It pointed to the World Health Organization's definition of health as 'a state of complete psychic, mental and social well being that does not merely consist of an absence of disease or infirmity'.[35] As a result it was able to conclude that 'where *the principal aim* of the measure in question is the protection of the health and safety of workers, Article 118a [EEC] must be used, albeit such a measure

---

[30] Case C-84/94 *UK v. Council (Working Time)* [1996] ECR I-5755. See generally, *The ECJ's Working Time Judgment: The Social Market Vindicated*, CELS Occasional Paper No. 2, 1997; L. Waddington, 'Towards a Healthier and More Secure European Social Policy' (1997) 4 *Maastricht Journal of European and Comparative Law* 83.

[31] OJ [1993] L307/18. See Ch. 12 for further details of the Directive.

[32] Case C-84/94 *UK v. Council (Working Time)* [1996] ECR I-5755, para. 12.

[33] Ibid. An approach favouring a specific basis in preference to a general legal basis is consistent with the Court's earlier jurisprudence, esp. the *Tariff Preference* case (Case 45/86 *Commission v. Council* [1987] ECR I-1493) concerning Arts. 207 and 352 TFEU.

[34] Para. 42. It is worth considering the extent to which the revised wording in Art. 153(1)(a) TFEU would now permit such a broad reading.

[35] Para. 15.

may have ancillary effects on the establishment and functioning of the internal market'.[36]

The Court then examined whether the Directive was correctly based on Article 118a EEC. Noting that the Directive was a social policy measure and not a general measure relating to job creation and reducing unemployment, the Court said that health and safety was the essential objective of the Directive,[37] albeit that it might affect employment as well, and therefore the Directive was properly adopted on the basis of Article 118a EEC. The Court did, however, annul Article 5(2) of the Directive which provided that the minimum weekly rest period 'shall in principle include Sunday'. The Court said that the 'Council has failed to explain why Sunday as a weekly rest day, is more closely connected with health and safety of workers than any other day of the week'.[38] As a result, the provision 'which is severable from the other provisions of the Directive', had to be annulled.[39]

The outcome of the decision is unsurprising and served to reinforce Article 118a EEC as an autonomous legal basis for social policy measures, thereby preserving the rather fragile 'social' policy which was being constructed by the Union, with the Commission at the helm. In this respect, the judgment can be seen as political. This helps to explain why, on the one hand, the Court was content with relying on 'self-justifying proclamations' in the Preamble as the basis of making the link between working time and health and safety,[40] and, on the other, why the Court failed to give a thorough examination of the scientific evidence produced and failed to consider the impact of the numerous exceptions and derogations to the Directive on the overall health and safety objective.[41]

2.3. Article 153 TFEU

(a) The competence

The Maastricht Social Policy Agreement (SPA) substantially amended Article 118a EEC in respect of the then 11 Member States and extended the areas to which qualified majority voting applied. It also introduced express new areas of competence to which unanimous voting applied. These changes were incorporated into the Treaty at Amsterdam with minor revisions in what became Article 137 EC. The Nice Treaty significantly amended and reorganized Article 137 EC. The TFEU reproduces the Nice version of Article 137 EC unamended and renumbered in Article 153 TFEU. Thus, according to Article 153(1) and (2) TFEU, the Union now has competence to adopt, by the ordinary legislative procedure under Article 294 TFEU (which includes *qualified majority voting*), after consulting the Economic and Social Committee and the

---

[36] Para. 22. This approach confirms that adopted by the Court in e.g. the *Waste Directive* case (Case C–155/91 *Commission v. Council* [1993] ECR I–939) and Case C–271/94 *Parliament v. Council* [1996] ECR I–1705.

[37] Para. 30.   [38] Para. 37.   [39] Ibid.

[40] J. Kenner, 'A Distinctive Legal Base for Social Policy? The Court of Justice Answers a "Delicate Question"' (1997) 22 *ELRev*. 579, 584.

[41] E. Ellis (1997) 34 *CMLRev*. 1049, 1057. See further Ch. 12.

Committee of the Regions, minimum standards Directives, supporting and complementing the activities of the Member States, concerning:

a. improvements in particular of the working environment to protect workers'
   health and safety;

b. working conditions;

e. the information and consultation of workers;

h. the integration of persons excluded from the labour market without prejudice to
   Article 166 TFEU on vocational training;

i. equality between men and women with regard to labour market opportunities
   and treatment at work.

The Nice Treaty added two further areas for EU competence:

j. the combating of social exclusion;

k. the modernization of social protection systems without prejudice to point (c)
   which refers the EU's competence in respect of social security and social protection of workers which must be decided by unanimous vote (see further).

The Council also has the power to adopt minimum standards Directives by *unanimous*
vote in accordance with the special legislative procedure, again after consulting the
European Parliament and the relevant Committees, in the fields of:

c. social security and social protection of workers;[42]

d. protection of workers where their employment contract is terminated;

f. representation and collective defence of the interests of workers and employers,
   including co-determination, subject to paragraph 5 (which provides that the
   'provisions of this Article shall not apply to pay, the right of association, the right
   to strike and the right to impose lock-outs');

g. conditions of employment for third country nationals legally residing in Union
   territory.[43]

The Treaty envisages that not only can legislative acts be adopted but OMC methodologies can also be used. The European Parliament and the Council:

may adopt measures designed to encourage cooperation between Member States through
initiatives aimed at improving knowledge, developing exchanges of information and best

---

[42] In an attempt to ring-fence social security from the incursion of European Union law still further, the
Treaty of Nice also adds that the provisions adopted pursuant to Article 153 TFEU 'shall not affect the right of
Member States to define the fundamental principles of their social security systems and must not significantly
affect the financial equilibrium thereof' (Article 153(4) TFEU first indent).

[43] According to Art. 153(2) TFEU, the Council, acting unanimously on a proposal from the Commission,
and after consulting the European Parliament, can decide to render the ordinary legislative procedure
applicable to the areas currently decided by unanimity with the exception of the fields of social security and
social protection of workers.

practices, promoting innovative approaches and evaluating experiences, excluding any harmonisation of the laws and regulations of the Member States...

The use of these OMC methodologies is identified in Article 153(2)(a) TFEU, and the possibility of adopting directives placed in Article 153(2)(b) TFEU. The Nice Treaty reversed the order prescribed by the Amsterdam Treaty (which had the use of legislation in (a) and OMC in (b)), thus suggesting that OMC is now the preferred way forward in respect of all the fields of social activity.

(b) The general limits on the scope of the EU's competence

Article 153 TFEU envisages two limits on the EU's exercise of its competence. First, in all cases, the Directives must avoid imposing administrative, financial and legal constraints which would hold back the creation and development of small and medium-sized enterprises (Article 153(2)(b) TFEU).[44] The importance of this provision (or at least its predecessor in Article 118a(2), paragraph 2 EEC) was recognized by the Court in *Kirsammer-Hack*[45] where, in the context of national legislation exempting part-time workers from the protection against unfair dismissal, the Court ruled that such legislation formed part of a series of measures 'intended to alleviate the constraints burdening small businesses which play an essential role in economic development and the creation of employment within the [Union]'.[46] The Court also indicated that these undertakings could be 'the subject of special economic measures'.[47] Thus, the Court suggested that the national law, albeit indirectly discriminatory on the grounds of sex, could be justified on the basis of the 'need to alleviate the constraints weighing on small businesses'.[48]

The second limit laid down by Article 153(2)(b) TFEU is that the EU can adopt minimum standards directives only 'for gradual implementation, having regard to the conditions and technical rules obtaining in each of the Member States'. This is the direct successor to Article 118a(2) and (3) EEC. So when the Council adopts a measure setting minimum requirements under Article 153(2) TFEU, Member States remain free to maintain or introduce more stringent protective measures compatible with the Treaty.[49] In the *Working Time* case[50] the Court said that the phrase 'minimum requirements' in Article 118a(2) EEC (now Article 153(2) TFEU) did not limit Union action 'to the lowest common denominator, or even the lowest level of protection established by the Member States'.[51] It meant that Member States were free to adopt more stringent measures than those resulting from Union law,[52]

---

[44] This does not, mean, however, according to the first declaration appended to the Social Policy Agreement, that when laying down minimum requirements for the protection of health and safety there is an intention to discriminate 'in a manner unjustified by the circumstances' against employees in small and medium-sized enterprises.

[45] Case C–189/91 *Kirsammer-Hack* v. *Sidal* [1993] ECR I–6185.   [46] Para. 33.

[47] Para. 34.   [48] Second concluding paragraph.   [49] Art. 153(4) TFEU, second indent.

[50] Case C–84/94 *UK* v. *Council* [1996] ECR I–5755.   [51] Para. 56.

[52] See further *Opinion 2/91* [1993] ECR I–1061, para. 16, and Case C–2/97 *Società Italiana Petroli SpA* v. *Borsana* [1998] ECR I–8597.

high as that might be.[53] The Advocate General also strongly rejected the contention that 'the [Union] cannot take action except on the basis of the lowest common denominator, or at the lowest possible level'. He said that this was diametrically opposed to the very conception of Union law where Union action has never been geared towards levelling down, in particular because Article 2 EC (now 3 TEU) referred to 'harmonious development', and to a 'high degree of convergence', 'to a high level of employment and of social protection'.[54] The function of minimum standards Directives is considered further.

3. SUBSIDIARITY AND PROPORTIONALITY

If the Union does have (non-exclusive) competence to legislate, it must then consider the application of the principle of subsidiarity. Article 5(3) TEU (ex 5(2) EC)[55] requires that Union action should be taken 'only if and insofar as the objectives of the proposed action cannot be sufficiently achieved by the Member States, either at central level or at regional and local level, but can rather, by reason of the scale and effects of the proposed action, be better achieved at Union level'.[56] This is a decentralized or bottom-up approach to subsidiarity, where the presumption is that it is the Member States that should act. Article 5(4) TEU then adds that 'the content and form of Union action shall not exceed what is necessary to achieve the objectives of the Treaties' (the principle of proportionality). Read together, Article 5(3) and (4) TEU mean that in areas such as social policy the Union can take action only if the tests of effectiveness and scale are satisfied and any measure taken is proportionate. The Commission has phrased this rather differently.[57] It says that three questions must be answered:

- What is the Union dimension of the problem?

- What is the most effective solution given the means available to the Union and the Member States?

- What is the real added value of common action compared with isolated action by the Member States?[58]

---

[53] Para. 56. As E. Szyszczak notes in 'The New Parameters of European Labour Law', in D. O'Keeffe and P. Twomey (eds.), *Legal Issues of the Amsterdam Treaty* (Hart Publishing, Oxford, 1999), such high principles do not always rule the day in practice. E.g. the UK was responsible for watering down the content of the Pregnant Workers' Directive 92/85/EEC (OJ [1992] L348/1) to such an extent that the Italian government abstained, claiming that the level of protection was too low for it to accept.

[54] Para. 54.

[55] See further Protocols 1 and 2 added by the Lisbon Treaty. For a full discussion, see M. Dougan, 'The Treaty of Lisbon 2007: Winning Minds, Not Hearts' (2008) 45 *CMLRev*. 617.

[56] See generally, A. Toth, 'A Legal Analysis of Subsidiarity', in D. O'Keeffe and P. Twomey (eds.), *Legal Issues of the Maastricht Treaty* (Chancery, London, 1994). See as well the essays by J. Steiner and N. Emiliou in the same volume; and N. Emiliou, 'Subsidiarity: An Effective Barrier Against "the Enterprises of Ambition"' (1992) 17 *ELRev*. 383.

[57] *Commission Report to the European Council on the adaptation of Community legislation to the subsidiarity principle* COM(93) 545 final, 1. See further SEC(92) 1990, 27 October 1992.

[58] See, in addition, the Commission White Paper COM(94) 333, 11. The Preamble to the Community Social Charter 1989 makes clear that the implementation of social rights must respect the principle of subsidiarity, i.e. 'responsibility for the initiatives to be taken...lies with the Member States or their constituent parts and, *within the limits of its powers*, with the European [Union]' (emphasis added).

It continues that 'the intensity of the action should leave the Member States all possible room for manoeuvre in its implementation. Subsidiarity requires [Union] legislation to be limited to what is essential'.

The application of the principle of subsidiarity to employment issues raises particularly difficult questions. First, what is the most effective level? Is it EU level, national level, or perhaps regional, district, sectoral, enterprise, or plant level? Secondly, who should make the decisions—the EU institutions, national or regional authorities, the Social Partners, or the individual manager? Thirdly, what type of measures should be taken—normative measures such as directly applicable regulations, Directives which confer some discretion on Member States as to their manner of implementation, soft law measures such as recommendations and opinions, collective agreements, or now OMC? And if Directives are the chosen method, to what extent should they be exhaustive harmonization measures or merely minimum harmonization?[59]

The subsidiarity question also raises a further, particularly contested issue: what is the appropriate extent of the Union action? Different views exist as to precisely when the Union should act in the social field.[60] The first view advocates a positive and active role for the Union, regarding the Union as having a duty of care for the social well-being of its citizens as much as the furtherance of their collective economic interests within the framework of a single integrated market. This would justify wide-ranging action by the Union. The second view sees the Union as being primarily concerned with economic matters and therefore as being competent to act in the social field only to the extent necessary to prevent distortions of competition arising out of divergences in production costs between Member States due to differences in national social standards, levels of health and safety protection, and other similar matters. This would suggest only limited action at EU level, a view which commands less support now that the creation of a 'social market economy' is one of the objectives of the Union. The third view claims that the Union should act in the social field only where it can add value: i.e. where there is a transnational element to the problem. The fourth view says that the Union should not act since there is no firm evidence on the incidence of differing social standards upon production costs. This last view is not supported by the legislation adopted to date but elements of the first three views have influenced Union action.

The question of subsidiarity was broached, albeit rather hesitantly, in *Working Time*[61] where the UK alleged that Directive 93/104 (now Directive 2003/88) infringed the principles of subsidiarity and proportionality. Advocate General Léger dismissed the UK's arguments. Distinguishing between subsidiarity and proportionality, he said:

> The two principles operate in turn, at two different levels of [Union] action. The first (subsidiarity) determines whether [Union] action is to be set in motion, whereas the second (proportionality) defines its scope. Hence the question of competence is dissociated from

---

[59] For a discussion of the differences between these terms, see C. Barnard, *The Substantive Law of the EU: the Four Freedoms* (OUP, Oxford, 2010) Ch. 18.

[60] P. Watson, 'The Community Social Charter' (1991) 28 *CMLRev.* 37, 40.

[61] Case C–84/94 *UK* v. *Council* [1996] ECR I–5755.

that of exercise.'[62] In other words, the principle of subsidiarity comes into play before the [Union] takes action, whilst the principle of proportionality comes into play after such action has been taken.[63]

He then said that in so far as harmonization is an objective of the Directive, it was difficult to criticize the measures adopted by the Council. He said it would be illusory to expect the Member States alone to achieve the harmonization envisaged since it necessarily involved supranational action.[64]

The Court also rejected the argument of non-compliance with the principle of subsidiarity, saying:

> Once the Council has found that it is necessary to improve the existing level of protection as regards the health and safety of workers and to harmonise the conditions in this area while maintaining the improvements made, achievement of that objective through the imposition of minimum requirements necessarily presupposes [Union] wide action.[65]

Thus, the Court was prepared to accept without question the Council's assertion that harmonization was necessary. Starting from this premise, the Court was able to conclude that harmonization 'necessarily presupposes [Union] wide action', thereby reinforcing a centralized, top-down approach to subsidiarity.

The Court then examined the application of the principle of proportionality, looking to see whether the means which the Union institution employed were suitable for the purpose of achieving the desired objective and whether they went beyond what was necessary to achieve it. Rejecting the plea,[66] the Court said:

> As to the judicial review of these conditions, however, the Council must be allowed a wide discretion in an area which, as here, involves the legislature in making social policy choices and requires it to carry out complex assessments. Judicial review of the exercise of that discretion must therefore be limited to examining whether it has been vitiated by a manifest error or misuse of powers, or whether the institution concerned has manifestly exceeded the limits of its discretion.[67]

It therefore seems that the Court has clipped the wings of Articles 5(3) and (4) TEU and restricted judicial review to the rare case of manifest abuse.

4. THE FORM OF LEGISLATION: DIVERSITY AND FLEXIBILITY

4.1. Introduction

The principle of subsidiarity applies not only to the level at which legislation is enacted but also to the form which it takes. This is particularly significant in the labour law context where the national systems are characterized, at least in the EU-15, by their wide

---

[62] Citing K. Lenaerts and P. Van Ypersele, 'Le principe de subsidiarité et son contexte: étude de l'article 3B du traité CE' (1994) 1–2 Cahiers de droit Européen 3, para. 100.
[63] Para. 126.   [64] Paras. 130–1.   [65] Para. 47.
[66] Para. 57, citing Case C–426/93 Germany v. Council [1995] ECR I–3723, para. 42.   [67] Para. 58.

diversity. Prior to the enlargement of the EU in 2004, three main systems of legal regula-tion of industrial relations could be found in the EU:[68] the Romano-Germanic system, the Anglo-Irish system, and the Nordic system.

The hallmark of the Romano-Germanic system, found in countries such as Belgium, France, Germany, Greece, Italy, Luxembourg, and the Netherlands, is that the state has a central and active role in industrial relations and workers' rights are provided by both constitutional provision and comprehensive labour market regulation. In addition, in states such as Belgium, France, and Germany, collective agreements can be extended to all workers and employers. Trade union density also tends to be lower in these countries than elsewhere, and falling—in France, for example, trade union membership declined from around 20 per cent in the mid-1970s to below 10 per cent today.[69] The Romano-Germanic system is also characterized by comprehensive legislation governing various areas of working conditions such as the length of the working day, rest periods, and employee representation. Since the Union was numerically dominated by those Mem-ber States from the highly regulated Romano-Germanic tradition, in the past this has provided the model for much EU legislation on employment rights.

The main feature of the Anglo-Irish system was the limited role played by the state in industrial relations (sometimes known as voluntarism or collective laissez-faire). For example, collective agreements apply solely to the parties involved; they are not legally

Table 2.1 Crude Union density rates

1. over 90% in Finland;
2. 80%–89% in Belgium and Sweden;
3. 70%–79% in Denmark and Norway;
4. 60%–69% in Italy;
5. 50%–59% in Cyprus, Luxembourg and Malta;
6. 40%–49% in Romania;
7. 30%–39% in Austria, Ireland and Slovenia;
8. 20%–29% in Bulgaria, the Czech Republic, Germany, Greece, Hungary, the Netherlands, Portugal and the UK;
9. 10%–19% in Latvia, Poland, Slovakia and Spain;
10. below 10% in Estonia and Lithuania.

Source: European Industrial Relations Observatory, Trade Union Membership 2003–2008 (2009) <http://www.eurofound.europa.eu/eiro/studies/tn0904019s/tn0904019s.htm> (last accessed 26 December 2011).

---

[68] The following discussion draws on Commission, *Comparative Study on Rules Governing Working Conditions in the Member States—a Synopsis* SEC(89) 1137, 30 June 1989, 10 and J. Due, J. Madsen, and C. Jensen, 'The Social Dimension: Convergence or Diversification of IR in the Single European Market' (1991) 22 *IRJ* 85, 90–1. See further B. Fitzpatrick, 'Community Social Law After Maastricht' (1992) 21 *ILJ* 199, 209–13.

[69] France is excluded from Table 2.1 because the crude data were not available: <http://www.eurofound.europa.eu/eiro/studies/tn0904019s/tn0904019s.htm> (last accessed 12 March 2012).

binding, nor can they be extended to the entire workforce by administrative act. Neither the individual nor the collective relationship is subject to extensive legal regulation, especially when compared with the Romano-Germanic system, despite a trend towards legislative intervention over the last four decades. Consequently, the Anglo-Irish system is characterized by the lack of comprehensive coverage of either collective agreements or legislation and it is the contract of employment which forms the cornerstone of the employment relationship.

In the Nordic system the state also assumes a relatively limited role in industrial relations. However, the functional equivalent to a legislative framework is provided by a series of corporatist labour market collective agreements, including a permanent basic agreement which is seldom challenged or amended. The state participates only when asked to do so by the parties, and there is very limited general legislative regulation. However, as a result of high levels of unionization which is characteristic of the Nordic system, the vast majority of workers are covered by collective agreements (see Table 2.1). The Nordic model has in recent years attracted considerable interest in the EU, since it combines high levels of unionization, high public spending and high tax rates with a knowledge economy and flexicurity. But, as we shall see in Chapter 5, this model is also under threat from the opening up of the services market.

However, as Rhodes points out, the different systems of labour market regulation belie a more complex reality.[70] While employers in Germany, the Netherlands, Belgium, and the Nordic countries are heavily constrained by hiring, dismissal and contract regulation, they enjoy more in-firm flexibility due to high levels of skills and consensual workplace rule setting. By contrast, employers in the UK and Ireland enjoy higher levels of internal and external flexibility but have a less skilled workforce which constrains adjustment capacities. Employers in southern states (Italy, Greece, Portugal, and Spain) experience the worst of both worlds: they have enjoyed neither flexibility nor consensus due to tightly constraining, state legislated labour regulations and this is combined with adversarial industrial relations. Enlargement has added a further model to the mix: state intervention, akin to that of the southern countries, is combined with weak levels of unionization (see Table 2.1) and firm-level representation of the Anglo-Irish group.[71]

4.2. The EU's response: the need for flexibility

Many commentators make much of the diversity[72] of industrial relations systems in the Member States and the dangers of simply identifying what is successful in one state and bolting it onto the structures in other states where different political and industrial

---

[70] M. Rhodes, 'Employment Policy: Between Efficacy and Experimentation' in H. Wallace, W. Wallace, and M. Pollack (eds.), *Policy Making in the European Union* (OUP, Oxford, 2005) 281.

[71] Ibid.

[72] See e.g. R. Hyman, 'Industrial Relations in Europe: Theory and Practice' (1995) 1 *EJIR* 17, 35, but cf. P. Marginson and K. Sisson, 'European Collective Bargaining: A Virtual Prospect?' (1998) 36 *JCMS* 505, 509, and L. Hansen, J. Madsen, and C. Jensen, 'The Complex Reality of Convergence and Diversification in European Industrial Relations Systems' (1997) 3 *EJIR* 357.

relations cultures exist.[73] On the other hand, other commentators have advised caution in suggesting that characteristics of employee relations policies are necessarily predetermined to be culturally specific.[74] Nevertheless, the different national approaches to the regulation of labour standards have forced the Union to be creative and flexible about its legislation.[75] This flexibility takes a number of forms, which we shall now consider.[76]

(a) The use of Directives

First, there has been flexibility in the forms of legislative instrument. Regulations, seen by many as the epitome of uniformity, have never been used to set EU employment standards. The principal regulatory vehicle has been Directives which, by their very nature, allow for a degree of flexibility in the way in which EU norms manifest themselves in the Member States. This flexibility is increased in three ways: first, by the use of framework Directives which lay down certain core standards but the detail of their operation is left to be determined by the Member States and/or the Social Partners;[77] secondly, through the use of Directives aimed at partial harmonization;[78] and thirdly, through the use of Directives setting minimum standards which Member States are free to improve upon.[79]

This practice of adopting minimum standards Directives was endorsed by the Council Resolution on Certain Aspects for a European Union Social Policy.[80] It points out:

> Minimum standards constitute an appropriate instrument for achieving economic and social convergence gradually while respecting the economic capabilities of the individual Member States. They also meet the expectations of workers in the European Union and calm fears about social dismantling and social dumping in the Union.[81]

---

[73] For his seminal analysis, see O. Kahn-Freund, 'On the Uses and Misuses of Comparative Law' (1974) 37 *MLR* 1. For a practical example of the problems experienced with comparative work, see the Supiot report, *Transformation of Labour and Future of Labour Law in Europe*, June 1998, published as A. Supiot, *Beyond Employment: Changes in Work and the Future of Labour Law in Europe* (OUP, Oxford, 2001).

[74] J. Bridgeford and J. Stirling, 'Britain in a Social Europe: Industrial Relations and 1992' (1991) 22 *IRJ* 263, 263.

[75] See generally, G. Falkner *et al.*, *Complying with Europe: EU Harmonisation and Soft Law in the Member States* (CUP, Cambridge, 2005).

[76] This section draws on C. Barnard, 'Flexibility and Social Policy', in G. De Búrca and J. Scott (eds.), *Flexible Governance in the EU* (Hart Publishing, Oxford, 2000).

[77] See e.g. the Framework Directive on Health and Safety 89/391 (OJ [1989] L183/9), considered further in Ch. 11 and the Parental Leave Dir. 96/34/EC (OJ [1996] L145/4) now repealed and replaced by Council Dir. 2010/18/EU (OJ [2010] L68/13), considered further in Ch. 9.

[78] Dir. 2001/23/EC on transfers of undertakings (OJ [2001] L82/16) and Dir. 98/59/EC on collective redundancies (OJ [1998] L225/16) provide a good example of this. While these Directives provide a core of rights, such as the right for the transferor's employees to enjoy the same terms and conditions when transferred to the transferee, the detail of those rights and key definitions, e.g. the meaning of terms 'dismissal' and 'worker representatives', are left to be determined by national law. See further Chs. 13 and 14.

[79] See Arts. 153(2)(b) and (4) TFEU.

[80] Council Resolution of 6 December 1994 on certain aspects for a European Union Social Policy: a contribution to economic and social convergence in the Union (OJ [1994] C368/6).

[81] Para. 10.

The Resolution continues that the Council is convinced that a 'comprehensive legislative programme' is not necessary but rather it requires 'agreement on specific fields of
action in order to build up the core of minimum social standards gradually in a pragmatic and flexible manner'.[82] The resolution then provides a framework for Union social
legislation. Union legislative acts must:[83]

- take account of the situation in all Member States when each individual measure is adopted
  and neither overstretch any one Member State nor force it to dismantle social rights;

- avoid going into undue detail but concentrate on basic, binding principles and leave the
  development and transposition to the Member States individually and, where this is in
  accordance with national traditions, to the two sides of industry;[84]

- be flexible enough and confine themselves to provisions which can be incorporated into
  the various national systems;

- include clauses which allow the two sides of industry room for manoeuvre on collective
  agreements;

- contain review clauses so that they can be corrected in the light of practical experience.

Stressing the diversity of the national systems, the Resolution says that 'unification of
national systems in general by means of rigorous approximation of laws [is] an unsuitable direction to follow as it would also reduce the chances of the disadvantaged regions
in the competition for location'.[85] The Resolution advocates instead 'gradual convergence of systems—with due regard for economic strength of the Member State—by
means of alignment of national goals'.[86]

From the perspective of the market-making/market-correcting debate considered
in Chapter 1, minimum standards Directives help to square a particularly difficult
circle: the Directives occupy the field in respect of the minimum standards but above
those minima they promote a space for states to experiment and develop diverse
national solutions. The minima thus represent a 'floor of rights', allowing Member
States to improve upon their provisions but generally preventing 'downwards' derogation.[87] Thus, minimum standards Directives may operate to induce individual
states to enter into a 'race to the top' when they would otherwise have had an incentive

---

[82] Para. 11.   [83] Para. 17.

[84] See further the Commission's Green Paper, *Partnership for a New Organisation of Work* (COM(97)127)
which talks of 'the likely development of labour law and industrial relations from rigid and compulsory systems
of statutory regulations to more open and flexible legal frameworks' (para. 44). This raises 'fundamental
questions concerning the balance of regulatory powers between public authorities (legislation) and the social
partners (collective bargaining) and between the social partners and individual employees (individual
employment contracts) which may well mean greater scope for derogations from legislative standards through
not just collective agreements but also individual contracts of employment (para. 43).

[85] Para. 18.   [86] Para. 19.

[87] Most of the social Directives are minimum harmonization Directives and some Directives also contain a
'Non-regression clause': see e.g. Art. 16 of Council Dir. 94/33/EC (OJ [1994] L216/12) '...as long as the
minimum requirements provided for by this Directive are complied with, the implementation of this Directive
shall not constitute valid grounds for reducing the general level of protection afforded to young people'. See S.
Peers, 'Non-regression clauses: The Fig Leaf has Fallen' (2010) 39 *ILJ* 436.

to compete on the basis of the withdrawal of protective standards (the 'race to the bottom').

(b) The use of soft law measures

Another consequence of this desire for flexibility in the form of legislative instruments has been the increasing use of soft law measures. Most of the EU legislation adopted under the 1974 and 1989 Social Action Programmes was legally binding, hard law.[88] By contrast, the Action Programmes from 1995 onwards,[89] have been characterized by their heavy reliance on soft law measures[90] which are persuasive rather than coercive in nature.[91] This shift had already been flagged up by the conclusions of the Edinburgh Council of 1992 on the implementation of Article 5 EC on the principle of subsidiarity[92] which said that 'Non-binding measures such as recommendations should be preferred where appropriate. Consideration should also be given where appropriate to the use of voluntary codes of conduct'.[93] The Commission endorsed this view, suggesting that recourse to the most binding instruments should be had only as a last resort.[94]

Soft law measures have also formed the principal legislative vehicle under the Employment Title. Presidency Conclusions, Commission Communications, annual reports, and even the Employment Guidelines[95] all fall into the category of soft law: they are no more than methods of Union guidance or rules which create an expectation that the conduct of Member States will be in conformity with them (the Open Method of Coordination (OMC)), but without any accompanying legal obligation.[96] This, Kenner

---

[88] See generally F. Beveridge and S. Nott, 'A Hard Look at Soft Law', in Craig and Harlow, previous, at n. 14; L. Senden, *Soft Law in European Community Law* (Hart Publishing, Oxford, 2004).

[89] See e.g. COM(95) 134; COM(98) 259; COM(2000) 379; COM(2005) 33.

[90] See e.g. the Council Resolution on the promotion of equal opportunities through action by the Structural Funds (94/C 231/01 (OJ [1994] C231/1); Council Recommendation on the balanced participation of men and women in the decision-making process (96/C694/EC (OJ [1996] C319/11)) and Resolution of the Council and of the Representatives of the governments of the Member States 94/C 368/02 on equal participation by women in an employment intensive economic growth strategy in the EU (OJ [1994] C368/2), considered in more detail in Ch. 6.

[91] See additionally F. Snyder, 'Soft Law and Institutional Practice in the European Community', EUI Working Paper, Law No. 93/5, J. Klabbers, 'Informal Instruments before the European Court of Justice' (1994) 31 *CMLRev.* 997 and J. Kenner, 'EC Labour Law: The Softly, Softly Approach' (1995) 11 *IJCLLIR* 307.

[92] EC Bull. 12/1992, 25–6, Council Conclusions II, Guidelines, 3rd para., point 3.

[93] See generally S. Sciarra, 'Social Values and the Multiple Sources of European Social Law' (1995) 1 *ELJ* 60, esp. 78–9 and E. Whiteford, 'W(h)ither Social Policy', in J. Shaw and G. More (eds.), *New Legal Dynamics of European Union* (Clarendon, Oxford, 1995).

[94] SEC(92) 1990 final. L. Cram, *Policy Making in the EU: Conceptual Lenses and the Integration Process* (Routledge, London, 1997) describes the Commission as a 'purposeful opportunist' in that it uses soft law measures among others to 'soften-up' the Member States, paving the way for the Commission's preferred course of action should a 'policy window' open up.

[95] See e.g. Council Resolution of 15 December 1997 on the 1998 Employment Guidelines (OJ [1998] C30/1). Cf. Council Dec. 2000/228/EC on guidelines for Member States' Employment Policies for the Year 2000 (OJ [2000] L72/15).

[96] J. Kenner, 'The EC Employment Title and the "Third Way": Making Soft Law Work' (1999) 15 *IJCLLIR* 33, 57–8.

notes, has certain advantages. The flexibility of soft law allows the Union institutions to stimulate European integration by building on and around existing Treaty objectives without directly creating legal obligations. They are a kind of informal law-making by exhortation.[97] OMC is considered in detail in Chapter 3.

(c) 'Internal flexibility'

Flexibility is not confined to the form of the legislative instruments. Increasingly flexibility manifests itself within a Directive. This can be described as 'internal flexibility'. Two examples illustrate this. First, Article 13 of the original European Works Councils Directive 94/45/EC[98] provided that where an agreement covering the entire workforce was already in existence by 22 September 1996,[99] the date by which the Directive had to be implemented, the substantive obligations contained in the Directive did not apply. By the September 1996 deadline, 386 such agreements had been signed,[100] including 58 signed by British companies at a time when the UK had secured an opt-out from the Social Chapter.[101] In a similar vein, Article 5 of the Framework Directive 2002/14[102] for informing and consulting employees provides that where information and consultation agreements between management and labour already exist they can contain provisions different to those laid down in the Directive provided that they respect the general principles laid down in Article 1 which include an obligation on the two sides working together in a 'spirit of cooperation'.

The second example of internal flexibility can be found in provisions allowing Member States more time to implement certain more controversial Directives. For example, according to Article 17(1)(b) of the Young Workers Directive 94/33/EC the UK could 'refrain from implementing' certain provisions on working time and night work for a period of four years.[103] The Working Time Directive 2003/88[104] (originally 93/104/EC[105]) not only provided for the possibility of an individual opt-out from Article 6 on the maximum 48-hour working week (subject to review)[106] but it also permitted the states to delay the implementation of the four weeks' paid annual leave contained in Article 7.[107] These flexibility provisions were introduced largely for the benefit of the UK where the legacy of collective laissez-faire meant that the state has traditionally abstained from regulating key aspects of the employment relationship, notably pay and working time,

---

[97] Ibid.

[98] OJ [1994] L254/64. This has now been repealed and replaced by the recast Dir. 2009/38/EC (OJ [2009] L122/28).

[99] 15 December 1999 for the UK: Art. 3(1) of Dir. 97/74/EC (OJ [1998] L10/22). The effect of Art. 13 agreements have been maintained by Art. 14 of Dir. 2009/38/EC.

[100] See P. Marginson *et al.*, *Negotiating European Works Councils: an Analysis of Agreements under Article 13*, European Foundation of Living and Working Conditions, EF9839. A particularly high incidence of such agreements can be found in Norway, see H. Knudsen and N. Bruun, 'European Works Councils in the Nordic Countries: An Opportunity and a Challenge for Trade Unionism' (1998) 4 *EJIR* 131.

[101] See Ch. 1 for further details.   [102] OJ [2002] L80/29 considered further in Ch. 13.

[103] OJ [1994] L216/12. See further the transitional provisions in Art. 10 of Dir. 2002/14.

[104] OJ [2003] L299/9.   [105] OJ [1993] L307/18.

[106] Art. 18(1)(b)(i), now Art. 22(1) of Dir. 2003/88. This remains one of the most controversial features of the Directive.

[107] Art. 18(1)(b)(ii), now Art. 22(2) of Dir. 2003/88.

leaving these issues to be negotiated collectively. These two Directives (on Working Time and Young Workers) therefore represented a cultural clash between the Romano-Germanic countries, with their history of centralized regulation of issues such as working time, and the abstentionist Anglo-Saxon tradition.

A further accommodation of the Anglo-Saxon tradition can be found in the substantial role for the Social Partners envisaged by the Working Time Directive. It provided that not only could the 'social partners' implement the Directive,[108] but 'collective agreements or agreements between the two sides of industry' could be used in setting certain standards, such as the duration and terms on which a rest break can be taken,[109] and derogating from those standards.[110] Thus, the Working Time Directive provides a further example of internal flexibility by introducing a new set of actors: the Social Partners can negotiate for better standards and—contrary to the general Continental legal tradition[111]—for worse. This is one example of 'controlled' or 'negotiated' flexibility'[112] and it is seen by the Commission as the likely future for the development of labour law and industrial relations. In its Green Paper on *Partnership for a New Organisation of Work*[113] the Commission talked of a move from 'rigid and compulsory systems of statutory regulations to more open and flexible legal frameworks... [paving] the way for a new balance of regulatory powers between the State and the social partners'.

(d) Negotiated flexibility

The possibility introduced by the Maastricht Social Chapter for negotiated European-level collective agreements concluded by the European Social Partners provides a further example of the phenomenon of flexibility in 'hard' law.[114] Once negotiated, these agreements can be extended to cover all workers by means of a 'decision'.[115] These agreements take controlled flexibility one stage further: it is the interprofessional (or sectoral) European-level Social Partners who are negotiating a framework collective agreement which in turn provides space for the national (interprofessional or sectoral) or subnational (enterprise or plant) level social partners to act. This process also demonstrates a form of subsidiarity—not just in the vertical sense envisaged by Article 5(3) TEU (Member State or Union level) but in the horizontal or multi-layered sense that different tasks can be assigned to different actors.[116] As the Council Resolution on certain aspects for a European Union Social Policy explains, the Social Partners are 'as a rule closer to social

---

[108] The details of this procedure are considered further in Section C.   [109] Art. 4.

[110] Art. 17.

[111] B. Wedderburn, 'Collective Bargaining at European Level: the Inderogability Problem' (1992) 21 *ILJ* 245.

[112] This is also described as 'centrally-coordinated' regulation (A. Ferner and R. Hyman, *Changing Industrial Relations in Europe* (Blackwell, Oxford, 1998) xvi). See further Art. 5(2) of Dir. 2001/23 (OJ [2001] L82/16).

[113] COM(1997) 128, para. 44.

[114] See further in Section C. The background to the adoption of this procedure is considered further in Ch. 16.

[115] This has been interpreted to mean any legally binding instrument, including a Directive.

[116] S. Sciarra, 'Collective Agreements in the Hierarchy of European Community Sources', in P. Davies *et al.* (eds.), *European Community Labour Law: Principles and Perspectives* (OUP, Oxford, 1996) 203.

reality and to social problems'.[117] This raises the fundamental question, who are the Social Partners? Are they truly representative? This will be considered in the next section. For the present it is sufficient to note that the Union now has a twin-track approach to legislation: on the one hand legislative, following the usual channels, and on the other, collective, based on collective bargaining between the Social Partners.[118] This latter approach has been described by Streeck as 'neo-voluntarism', putting the will of those affected by a rule, and the 'voluntary' agreements negotiated between them, above the will or potential will of the legislature.[119]However, as we shall see with the benefit of years of experience, the results of this collective route are less impressive.[119A]

5. CONCLUSIONS

The discussion so far demonstrates the lengths the Union legislature has gone to—over many years—to ensure that the social legislation adopted is flexible and adaptable. Far from employing a detailed regulatory approach, which both the market-making and market-correcting theses might support, the Union has generally adopted legislation which provides a steer to the Member States or the Social Partners to negotiate solutions suitable to their own national systems, with the minima laid down by the Directive as a back up. This prompts some commentators to describe Union social legislation as a form of 'reflexive harmonisation', by analogy with the idea of reflexive law.[120] The essence of reflexive law is the acknowledgement that regulatory interventions are most likely to be successful when they seek to achieve their ends not by direct prescription, but by inducing 'second-order effects' on the part of social actors.[121] In other words, reflexive law aims to 'couple' external regulation with self-regulatory processes:[122] the law underpins and encourages autonomous processes of adjustment, in particular by supporting mechanisms of group representation and participation, rather than by intervening to impose particular distributive outcomes.[123] We see this with Directives which allow Member States to act above the minimum standards or allow other actors such as trade unions and employers to make qualified exceptions to limits on working time or similar labour standards.

---

[117] OJ [1994] C368/6, II.3. See further e.g. Recital 9 of the Parental Leave Dir. 96/34/EEC (OJ [1996] L145/4).

[118] B. Bercusson, 'The Dynamic of European Labour Law after Maastricht' (1994) 23 *ILJ* 1; J. Shaw, 'Twin-track Social Europe—the Inside Track' in D. O'Keeffe and P. Twomey (eds.), *Legal Issues of the Maastricht Treaty* (Wiley Chancery, Chichester, 1994).

[119] W. Streeck, 'Competitive Solidarity: Rethinking the 'European Social Model' *MPIfG Working Paper* 99/8 and W. Streeck, 'Neo-voluntarism: A New European Social Policy Regime' (1995) 1 *ELJ* 31. See further C. Jensen, 'Neo-functionalist Theories and the Development of European Social and Labour Market Policy' (2000) 38 *JCMS* 71, 90.

[119A] S. Clauwaert, '2011: 20 years of European interprofessional social dialogue; (2011) 17 *Transfer* 169, 172.

[120] See generally, G. Teubner, *Law as an Autopoietic System* (Oxford, Blackwell, 1993); R. Rogowski and T. Wilthagen (eds.), *Reflexive Labour Law* (Kluwer, Deventer, 1994).

[121] See C. Barnard and S. Deakin, '"Negative" and "Positive" Harmonisation of Labor Law in the European Union' (2002) 8 *Columbia Journal of European Law* 389.

[122] Ibid., 408.   [123] Ibid.

Reflexive law also implies an important difference in the way in which the law responds to market failures: it does not seek to 'perfect' the market, in the sense of reproducing the outcome which parties would have arrived at in the absence of transaction costs, because it is understood that information problems facing courts and legislatures make the process of identifying an optimal bargaining solution extremely hazardous.[124] Rather, reflexive law concentrates on the value of the process of discovery or adaptation instead of focusing on the achievement of optimal states of distribution. This is done by giving states a number of options for implementation as well as by allowing for the possibility that existing, self-regulatory mechanisms can be used to comply with EU-wide standards. In these ways, far from suppressing regulatory innovation, harmonization aims to stimulate it.

Of course, not all Union law conforms to this ideal: some Directives—particularly the older Directives adopted under the traditional route to legislation—more closely mirror the traditional command and control model than others. On the other hand, the Directives adopted under the collective route to legislation do approach the reflexive law model. In the next section we consider the legislative process applied under the two routes.

C. THE LEGISLATIVE PROCESS

1. INTRODUCTION

Whether Union social legislation is to be adopted via the legislative or the collective route the Commission retains the power of initiative for submitting proposals (see Figure 2.1). Before doing so it must consult the Social Partners on the possible direction of Union action.[125]

2. CONSULTATION OF MANAGEMENT AND LABOUR

Article 154(1) TFEU (ex 138(1) EC) provides that the Commission has the task of promoting the consultation of management and labour at Union level. It must also take any relevant measures to facilitate their dialogue by ensuring balanced support for the parties. This provision was intended to replace the weaker obligation 'to endeavour to develop the dialogue' contained in the original Article 118b EEC. The Commission considers that it can be more active under Article 154(1) TFEU than under Article 118b EEC by providing three types of support: the organization of meetings; support for joint studies or working groups; and technical assistance necessary to underpin the dialogue.[126]

---

[124] Ibid., 409.   [125] Art. 154(2) TFEU. For further details of this process, see Brinkman, above, n. 14.
[126] COM(93) 600, para. 12.

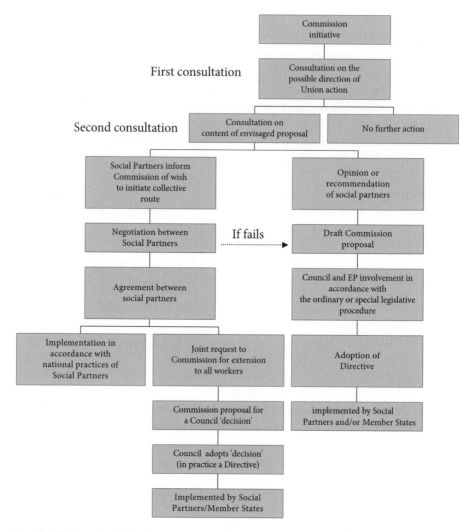

Fig. 2.1. The Legislative Process.
Source: COM(93) 600, 43 with updates.

The Treaty offers no guidance as to which organizations should be consulted. As a result, in a Communication of 1993[127] the Commission set out a number of criteria to identify those representatives of management and labour whose representativity[128] entitled them to be consulted. The criteria applied are:

- the associations must be cross-industry or relate to specific sectors or categories and be organized at European level;

---

[127] COM(93) 600, para. 24. This list only applies to the consultation stage provided for by Art. 154(2) and (3) TFEU, see Case T–135/96 *Union Européenne de l'Artisanat et des Petites et Moyennes Entreprises' (UEAPME)* v. *Council and Commission* [1998] ECR II–2335, para. 77.

[128] See Case T–135/96 *UEAPME* [1998] ECR II–2335, para. 72.

- the associations must consist of organizations which are themselves 'an integral and recognized part of Member State social partner structures', have the capacity to negotiate agreements and be representative of all Member States 'as far as possible'; and

- the associations must have adequate structures to ensure their effective participation in the consultation process.[129]

Despite much disagreement,[130] these criteria were confirmed by the Commission in 1998.[131] The Social Partner organizations which currently comply with these criteria fall into five categories and cover about 50 organizations:[132]

- general cross industry organizations (the trade union body ETUC,[133] the employers' organization BusinessEurope (formerly UNICE[134]), and the public sector employers' association CEEP[135]);

- cross-industry organizations representing certain categories of workers or undertakings (UEAPME,[136] CEC,[137] and Eurocadres);

- specific organizations (the association of European Chambers of Commerce and Industry, EUROCHAMBRES);

- sectoral organizations representing employers such as the Community of European Railways (CCFE), and the Association of European Airlines (AEA);

- European trade union organizations such as European Transport Workers' Federation (ETF).

Consultation for the purposes of legislation occurs at two stages. First, *before submitting proposals* in the social policy field, the Commission must consult management and

---

[129] This list is a slimmed down version of the criteria proposed by ETUC, CEEP, and UNICE (now Business Europe) (*Social Europe* 95/2, 164). The European Parliament proposed that two further criteria be added: that eligible organizations are composed of groups representing employers or workers with membership that is voluntary at both national and European level; and that they have a mandate from their members to represent them in the context of the Union social dialogue and can demonstrate their representativeness: Report A3–0269/94, PE 207.928—fin, cited in COM(96) 448, para. 62. ECOSOC proposed that the criteria should also include the capacity to negotiate for and bind national structures: Opinion 94/C397/17, paras. 2.1.12 and 2.1.15 (OJ [1994] C397/43).

[130] See e.g. the responses to the Commission's Communication concerning the Development of the Social Dialogue at Community Level: COM(96) 448.

[131] COM(98) 322.

[132] Annex II of Commission's Communication COM(93)—600. An updated list of those organizations satisfying the criteria is found in Annex I of COM(98) 322 and a further revised list is found in Annex I of COM(2002) 341. The ICL-IST, the Institute of Labour Sciences at the Catholic University of Louvain, carried out research for the Commission in order to enable it to assess the representativeness of the European Social Partner organizations until 2005. Subsequently the task was taken on by the EuroFound: <http://www.eurofound.europa.eu/areas/industrialrelations/dictionary/definitions/representativenessofeuropeansectoralsocialpartnerorganisations.htm> (last accessed 12 March 2012).

[133] European Trade Union Confederation.

[134] Union of Industrial and Employers' Confederations of Europe.

[135] European Centre of Enterprises with Public Participation and of Enterprises of General Economic Interest.

[136] Union Européenne de l'Artisanat et des Petites et Moyennes Entreprises.

[137] Confédération Européene des Cadres (higher white-collar employees and managerial employees).

labour about the possible direction of Union action.[138] If, after such consultation, due to last no longer than six weeks,[139] the Commission considers that Union action is advisable, the second stage of consultation is triggered. This requires the Commission to consult management and labour *on the content of the envisaged proposal*.[140] The Social Partners then have a choice. One possibility is for them to forward to the Commission an opinion or a recommendation within six weeks.[141] Any measure proposed will then follow the usual legislative route outlined in Section 3. The other possibility, provided by Article 154(4) TFEU, is for management and labour to inform the Commission of their wish to initiate the process to negotiate Union-level agreements provided for in Article 155 TFEU (ex 139 EC). This is considered in Section 4.

3. THE LEGISLATIVE ROUTE

If management and labour do not inform the Commission of their wish to negotiate collectively, the measure follows the legislative route. Depending on the subject-matter,[142] a Directive will be adopted either by the ordinary or special legislative procedure. Once adopted, Article 153(3) TFEU provides the Member States with the possibility of entrusting the Social Partners, at their joint request, with the implementation of any Directives. This possibility had already been introduced in Directives in the early 1990s.[143] This is a further example of 'internal' flexibility: it allows the general language of the Directive to be adapted to local conditions, especially at company or plant level. However, the buck stops with the Member States. According to Article 153(3) TFEU, second indent, Member States must take 'any necessary measure enabling it at any time to be in a position to guarantee the results imposed by that directive'. This may include, as in Belgium, the passing of a Royal Decree which gives *erga omnes* effect to a collective agreement.[144] Thus, despite the autonomy of the Social Partners, Member States do

---

[138] Art. 154(2) TFEU. It also proposes to continue to consult all European or national organizations which might be affected by the Union's social policy. This confirms previous practice (COM(93) 600, para. 22).

[139] COM(93) 600, 19. Despite some criticisms that the six-week time limit was too short, the Commission has decided to maintain it so as not to put the effectiveness of the process at risk, but may apply it flexibly depending on the nature and complexity of the subject-matter (COM(98) 322, 9).

[140] Art. 154(3) TFEU.

[141] Ibid. It seems that there is no obligation on the Commission to take into account the recommendation or opinion issued by management and labour.

[142] See Art. 153(1) and (2) TFEU.

[143] See e.g. Dir. 91/533/EC on conditions applicable to the contract of employment (OJ [1991] L288/32), Dir. 92/56 on collective redundancies (OJ [1992] L255/63) and the Working Time Dir. 93/104/EC (OJ [1993] L307/18). This corresponds to the implementation requirements of the ILO (Convention Nos 100, 101, 106, 111, 171, 172) and the Council of Europe (Art. 35(1) of the European Social Charter).

[144] In a case decided before the Maastricht Treaty changes were adopted, the Court considered that Belgium had adequately implemented the Directive on collective dismissals when a collective agreement had been extended *erga omnes* by legislative instruments: Case 215/83 *Commission* v. *Belgium* [1985] ECR 1039, discussed in A. Adinolfi, 'The Implementation of Social Policy Directives through Collective Agreements?' (1988) 25 *CMLRev.* 291. Art. 153(3) TFEU was introduced to meet the Court's earlier criticisms of implementation of Directives by collective agreements: see e.g. Case 1/81 *Commission* v. *Italy* [1982] ECR 2133, considered further in Ch. 14.

retain the ultimate responsibility of ensuring that all workers are afforded the full protection of the Directive, especially in the case where the workers are not union members, where the sector is not covered by a collective agreement, or where the agreement
does not fully guarantee the principle laid down in the Directive.[145]

4. THE COLLECTIVE ROUTE

4.1. Negotiation

The collective route constitutes the second limb of this twin-track approach to Union
social legislation. The Social Partners at Union level negotiate agreements which are
then extended to all workers by Council 'decision'. The collective route is triggered
when, at the second stage of the consultation process,[146] the Social Partners inform the
Commission that they would like to negotiate Union-level agreements. If they do this
they have nine months,[147] or longer with the agreement of the Commission,[148] to enter
into 'a dialogue' at 'Union level [which] may lead to *contractual relations*, including
agreements'.[149] There is no indication as to what constitutes an agreement, nor what is
considered a suitable subject-matter of the agreement.[150] The Commission's Communication simply says that the question of whether an agreement between Social Partners
constitutes a sufficient basis for the Commission to suspend its legislative action will
have to be examined on a case-by-case basis.[151]

The Commission's view about who should negotiate has changed over the years. In its
first Communication the Commission said that 'the social partners concerned will be
those that agree to negotiate with each other'.[152] Such agreement is entirely in the hands
of the different organizations. Subsequently, the Commission said that the Social
Partners can develop 'their own dialogue and negotiating structures'.[153] The Commission continued:

> …it is up to the social partners who sits at the negotiating table and it is up to them to come
> to the necessary compromises. The respect of the right of any social partner to choose its
> negotiating counterpart is a key element of the autonomy of the social partners.[154]

---

[145] Case C–187/98 *Commission* v. *Greece* [1999] ECR I–7713, para. 47. See further Case 143/83 *Commission*
v. *Denmark* [1985] ECR 427, para. 8.

[146] COM(93) 600, para. 29, although ECOSOC has suggested that it might occur after the first stage of
consultation.

[147] Art. 154(4) TFEU.   [148] Ibid.

[149] Art. 155(1) TFEU, emphasis added. 'Contractual relations' is a translation of the French term *relations
contractuelles* which means relations based on agreement. It has been suggested that the addition of the phrase
'including agreements' serves to emphasize that legally binding contracts are only one potential outcome. B.
Hepple, *European Social Dialogue—Alibi or Opportunity* (IER, London, 1993) 23.

[150] The Commission has, however, made clear that certain matters are not appropriate for negotiations such
as the Burden of Proof in Sex Discrimination cases (COM(93) 600, para. 67).

[151] COM(93) 600, para. 30.   [152] COM(93) 600, para. 31.

[153] COM(98) 322, 12.   [154] Ibid.

However, particularly following the *UEAPME* decision (considered below),[155] the Commission has become more concerned about the question of the representativity of those negotiating (i.e. whether those affected by an agreement have been represented). It therefore says that the question of representativeness must be examined on a case-by-case basis, as the conditions will vary depending on the subject-matter under negotiation. The Commission examines whether those involved in the negotiation have a genuine interest in the matter and can demonstrate significant representation in the domain concerned.[156] To date, in the interests of efficient bargaining, negotiation over agreements which apply generally to all employment relationships[157] has been conducted by the established general cross-industry organizations (ETUC, UNICE (now BusinessEurope), CEEP)[158] 'based on principles of autonomy and mutual recognition of the negotiation parties'.[159] The Commission has said that these three organizations fulfil its own criteria of representativeness.[160] However, subsequently three other cross-industry organizations have become involved (UEAPME, Eurocadres, and CEC) (see Box 2.1).

Box 2.1 The six cross-industry organizations involved in European social dialogue

1. **European Trade Union Confederation (ETUC)** represents workers across the industries at European level. Set up in 1973, the ETUC includes 82 national organizations from 36 European countries (among them all the EU countries) and 11 European industry federations, with some 60 million members. In the context of European social dialogue, the ETUC executive committee can adopt decisions supported by 2/3 of its members. The 11 federations include the majority of European branch trade unions, which allows for some coordination across sectors.

2. **Confederation of European Business (BUSINESSEUROPE, formerly UNICE)** (1958) is the largest European employers' organization in terms of economic coverage. It includes 41 employers' associations from 35 European countries (among them all the EU countries) and represents its members' economic and industrial interests at European level. BUSINESSEUROPE represents some 20 million businesses in Europe. Decisions (including in the field of social dialogue) are taken by the council of presidents, voting unanimously.

---

[155] Case T–135/96 *UEAPME* [1998] ECR II–2335.   [156] COM(96) 448, para. 71.

[157] Sectoral agreements have also been negotiated by European sectoral organizations. These are considered further.

[158] These three cross-sector organizations have long enjoyed a favoured position through the social dialogue steering group and have therefore developed a 'substantial body of experience' COM(93) 600, para. 25, confirmed in COM(96) 448 and COM(98) 322.

[159] COM(98) 322, 13. See Case T-135/96 *UEAPME* [1998] ECR II–2335, para. 79, 'it is the representatives of management and labour concerned, and not the Commission which have charge of the negotiation stage properly so-called'. See generally, M. Peruzzi, *L'autonomia nel dialogo sociale europeo* (Bologna, Il Mulino, 2011).

[160] COM(96) 26 final, para. 14.

3. **European Centre of Employers and Enterprises providing Public services (CEEP)** (1961) is an employers' association for public-sector entities, networked businesses (e.g. local transport, post offices, energy, water, ports) and, in some countries, local authorities. The CEEP has national sections in 17 European countries and permanent links with its member businesses. CEEP decisions are taken by the general assembly.

4. **European Association of Craft, Small and Medium Sized Enterprises (UEAPME)** (1979) is the employer's organization representing the interests of European crafts, trades and small businesses at EU level. UEAPME numbers 44 member organizations (from 26 European countries) including national cross-sectoral SME federations, European branch federations and other associate members supporting small businesses. According to its own figures, UEAPME represents 11 million businesses employing 50 million people across Europe. In December 1998, UEAPME reached an agreement with BUSINESSEUROPE allowing it to take part in European social dialogue.

5. **Eurocadres** is the council of professional and managerial staff in Europe representing all branches of industry, public and private services and administrative departments. It gathers 46 organizations from 46 European countries. It is associated with the ETUC and has more than 5 million staff in membership.

6. **European Confederation of Executives and Managerial Staff (CEC)** is a professional organization but is independent of the ETUC. It represents European branch federations and 17 national organizations uniting some 1.5 million executives and professionals in 14 EU countries.

The two professional and managerial organizations (EUROCADRES and CEC) signed a cooperation agreement in 2000, establishing a liaison committee through which they take part in European social dialogue. They are represented in the ETUC employees' delegation.

Source: <http://ec.europa.eu/social/main.jsp?catId=479&langId=en> (last accessed 27 December 2011).

As the Commission explains, if employers and workers decide to enter into negotiations on an issue, each side prepares a negotiation mandate (which must be approved by the respective decision-making bodies) and appoints a negotiating team. An independent mediator presides over the meetings. The results of negotiations are adopted by the Social Dialogue Committee (SDC)[161] and approved by the signatories' decision-making bodies. The SDC is usually responsible for following up the implementation of negotiated agreements.

---

[161] Set up in 1992, the SDC is the main body for bipartite social dialogue at European level. It comprises 64 members (32 employers, 32 workers) either from European secretariats or national organizations.

4.2. Implementation

(a) Via national or subnational collective agreements: autonomous agreements

Once an EU-wide collective agreement is reached, Article 155(2) TFEU provides two methods for its implementation. First, an agreement can be implemented 'in accordance with the procedures and practices specific to management and labour and the Member States'—so-called autonomous agreements. The second declaration appended to the Maastricht Social Policy Agreement (SPA) explains that this means 'developing, by collective bargaining according to the rules of each Member State, the content of the agreements'. However, the declaration continues that this does not imply any obligation on the Member States 'to apply the agreements directly or to work out rules for their transposition, nor any obligation to amend national legislation in force to facilitate their implementation'. In other words, in the case of an EU-level agreement, there is no obligation to bargain on these matters at national level nor to ensure that it applies to all workers. As Hepple has argued, these provisions attach the social dialogue to the existing structures of collective bargaining and labour law in the Member States. These structures were never intended to take on a new hierarchy of EU-level obligations and, in many cases, are under compelling pressures to decentralize and become more flexible.[162]

The Telework Agreement of July 2002[163] was the first agreement to be implemented via this route.[164] This agreement defines the scope of telework and establishes a general European framework for teleworkers' conditions of employment. It aims to ensure that teleworkers are afforded a general level of protection equivalent to employees working on the employer's premises. The same approach was adopted in:

- the Social Partners' framework agreement on work-related stress,[165] the aim of which is to increase awareness and understanding of work-related stress among employers, workers, and their representatives, and draw their attention to signals that could indicate that workers are suffering from stress,

- the framework agreement on harassment and violence at work[166] which aims to increase the awareness and understanding of employers, workers, and their representatives of workplace harassment and violence and to provide employers, workers, and their representatives at all levels with an action-oriented framework to identify, prevent, and manage problems of harassment and violence at work.

---

[162] Hepple, above, n. 149, 31.

[163] <http://resourcecentre.etuc.org/Agreements-57.html> (last accessed 31 March 2012), considered in Ch. 9.

[164] For an assessment of the implementation, see T. Prosser, 'The Implementation of the Telework and Work Related Stress Agreements: European social dialogue through soft law?' (2011) 17 *EJIR* 245.

[165] <http://resourcecentre.etuc.org/Agreements-57.html> (last accessed 31 March 2012), considered in Ch.11. The Commission Communication 'Partnership for change in an enlarged Europe—Enhancing the contribution of European social dialogue' (COM(2004) 557) which, in Annex 2, also details other possible outcomes of the European social dialogue such as Process Oriented texts (frameworks of action, guidelines and codes of conduct, policy orientations), Joint Opinions and tools and procedural texts.

[166] Signed on 26 April 2007. See further the ETUC's interpretation guide: <http://www.etuc.org/a/4758> (last accessed 12 March 2012). For the state of play on the implementation, see <http://ec.europa.eu/employment_social/dsw/public/actRetrieveText.do?id=8861> (last accessed 28 December 2011).

The most recent of these autonomous agreements concerns inclusive labour markets. The aim of this agreement is to 'maximize the full potential of Europe's labour force and to increase employment rates and to improve job quality'.[167] This last agreement fits neatly alongside the EU's more general active labour market policy considered in Chapter 3.

In its 2004 Communication on the European Social dialogue, the Commission noted that it has a particular role to play if the autonomous agreement was the result of an Article 154 TFEU consultation because the Social Partners' decision to negotiate an agreement temporarily suspends the legislative process at Union level. The Commission also says that it will undertake its own monitoring of the agreement to assess the extent to which the agreement has actually contributed to the achievement of the Union's objectives and, where it considers the agreement wanting, it will consider proposing a legislative act. It also threatens to exercise its own right of initiative at any point, including during the implementation period, should it conclude that either management or labour are delaying the pursuit of Union objectives.

The three autonomous agreements have been supplemented by two 'frameworks of action', one on lifelong learning, the other on gender equality. In respect of the first, on action for the lifelong development of competences and qualifications, the Social Partners decided to implement it not via national or subnational collective agreements but (for the first time) via the Open Method of Co-ordination. The Social Partners agreed to monitor progress of the four agreed priorities[168] on an annual basis and evaluate the impact on both companies and workers though annual reports presented at the Tripartite Social Summit[169] taking place (usually) in March of each year before the Spring summits. This evaluation can, if necessary, lead to updating of the priorities identified.[170]

Some commentators express concern that the predominance of autonomous agreement and other process-oriented texts has diluted the role of the social partner directives, (see later in this chapter) as an instrument of European social policy-making.[171]

(b) Via a 'decision' of the Council

The alternative method for implementation envisaged by Article 155(2) TFEU is for management and labour jointly to request the Commission to propose that the Council adopt a 'decision' implementing the agreement in respect of matters covered by Article 153 TFEU.[172] This would give *erga omnes* effect, extending the collective agreement to all

---

[167] Agreement of 25 March 2010, <http://resourcecentre.etuc.org/Agreements-57.html> (last accessed 31 March 2012).

[168] (1) To identify and anticipate competences and qualifications needs; (2) to recognize and validate competences and qualifications; (3) to inform, support, and provide guidance; and (4) to mobilize resources.

[169] Council Dec. 2003/174/EC (OJ [2003] L70/31).

[170] EIRO, *Industrial relations developments in Europe 2004* (OPEC, Luxembourg, 2005) 5–6.

[171] B. Keller and S. Weber, 'Sectoral social dialogue at EU level: Problems and prospects of implementation' (2011) 17 *EJIR* 227, 239.

[172] The Social Partners are not obliged to do this. They could confine themselves to negotiating a single agreement producing effects *inter partes*, see Case T–135/96 *UEAPME* [1998] ECR II–2335, para. 45.

workers. The Council then follows the procedure set out in Article 153 (qualified majority vote except where the agreement contains one or more provisions relating to one of the areas for which unanimity is required in which case it must act unanimously).[173] The Social Partners had requested that in order to respect the autonomy of the Social Partners the Commission's proposal should follow the Social Partners' agreement 'as concluded' by them[174] but this requirement was deleted from the final version of the SPA.[175] While this appears to give the Commission the discretion to amend the agreement in its proposal to the Council, the Commission has never done so. In practice, the agreement has been annexed to the proposal to the Council, and the Commission considers that the Council has no opportunity to amend the agreement.[176] This seems to have been acknowledged by the Council: according to its legal service, while the Commission and Council could introduce rules for implementation or amend those agreed by management and labour, neither could amend the essence of the agreement.[177]

In making its proposals for a 'decision' by the Council, the Commission resumes control of the procedure.[178] In its capacity as guardian of the Treaties, the Commission considers the mandate of the social partners[179] and the 'legality' of each clause in the collective agreement in relation to Union law, and the provisions regarding SMEs set out in Article 153(2)(b) TFEU.[180] The Council, when taking its 'decision' must verify whether the Commission has fulfilled these obligations, otherwise it runs the risk of ratifying a procedural irregularity capable of vitiating the measure ultimately adopted by it.[181]

The use of the term 'decision' as the legal form by which the agreement is implemented is misleading. In Article 288 TFEU (ex 249 EC) a 'Decision' is defined as being 'binding in its entirety upon those to whom it is addressed'. Decisions are individual in nature and are addressed to undertakings, individuals, or Member States; they are not usually normative in the sense of creating generally applicable Union law. Therefore, the Commission has said that in this context the term 'decision' refers to one of the binding legislative instruments listed in Article 288 TFEU (Regulations, Directives, and Decisions) and that the Commission will choose the most appropriate measure.[182] In the case of the original Parental Leave Collective Agreement the Commission said that the

---

[173]   Art. 155(2) TFEU, second indent.

[174]   The October 1991 agreement had provided 'on a proposal from the Commission, with regard to the agreements *as they have been concluded*' (emphasis added): *Social Europe* 2/95, 149.

[175]   The Framework Agreement, as implemented by the Council Decision (Directive) is an integral component of that Directive: Case C–149/10 *Chatzi* v *Ipourgos Ikonomikon* [2010] ECR I–000, para. 44.

[176]   COM(93) 600, para. 38.

[177]   Opinion of 31 March 1994, Council Doc 6116/94, cited in Brinkman, above, n. 14.

[178]   Case T–135/96 *UEAPME* [1998] ECR II–2335, para. 84.

[179]   Confirmed by Case T–135/96 *UEAPME* [1998] ECR II–2335, para. 85.

[180]   COM(93) 600, para. 39. This assumption of power was contested by ECOSOC (Opinion 94/C 397/17 (OJ [1994] C397/40), cited in B. Bercusson, 'Democratic Legitimacy and European Labour Law' (1999) 28 *ILJ* 153, 162) on the grounds that the Commission has no discretion whether a collective agreement should be put to the Council.

[181]   Case T–135/96 *UEAPME* [1998] ECR II–2335, para. 87.

[182]   COM(96) 26 final, 7. See generally B. Bercusson and J. Van Dijk, 'The Implementation of the Protocol and Agreement on Social Policy of the Treaty on European Union' (1995) 11 *IJCLLIR* 3.

content of the agreement and its framework nature suggested that a Directive was the most appropriate legal form, based on what is now Article 153(1)(i) TFEU (equal opportunities for men and women on the labour market). It therefore seems that 'decision' in the context of Article 155(2) TFEU has a more general meaning. This is reflected in the German and Danish texts which use 'decide' as a verb rather than in the technical sense of a 'Decision'.[183]

The European Parliament has no formal role in this collectively negotiated legislation. For this reason, its attitude towards the corporatist pattern of interest representation is ambiguous. On the one hand, it sees the collective approach to legislating as a step towards greater involvement of citizens in policy formation.[184] It also recognizes that the lack of parliamentary involvement is common in those Member States where collective agreements are given *erga omnes* effect, usually by an *administrative* act.[185] Nevertheless, the absence of European Parliamentary involvement has prompted concerns by some MEPs about the possible 'democratic deficit' of a process where the Social Partners dictate social legislation from behind closed doors.[186] This criticism is all the more pertinent now that, following the Lisbon Treaty, the ordinary legislative procedure, giving the European Parliament powers of co-decision with the Council, has become the norm. Despite the wording of the Treaty, the Commission says that the Parliament will have the opportunity to see any proposed decision and deliver an opinion where necessary.[187] The Lisbon Treaty made this official: Article 155(2)TFEU provides that 'The European Parliament shall be informed' of agreements concluded at Union level.

4.3. The collective route to legislation in practice

(a) Introduction

When the collective route to legislation was introduced at Maastricht it was hoped that, by using the Social Partners as legislators, this would not only improve the legitimacy of EU legislation but would also make the resulting legislation sufficiently flexible to accommodate the diversity of European industrial relations. However, the first attempt to use the collective route was unsuccessful. It had been intended to break the deadlock over the proposals for requiring firms of a certain size to establish a European Works Council.[188] On 8 February 1994, in accordance with Article 154(3) TFEU, the Commis-

---

[183] Hepple, previous, at n. 149, 31 (*Beschluß* v. *Entscheidung*).

[184] D. Obradovic, 'Accountability of Interest Groups in the Union Lawmaking Process', in Craig and Harlow (eds.), previous, at n. 14, 363–4.

[185] See the agreement between management and labour of 31 October 1991, *Social Europe* 2/95, 148.

[186] See A3–0091/94 *Resolution on the New Social Dimension of the Treaty on European Union* (OJ [1994] C77/30). See Case T–135/96 *UEAPME* [1998] ECR II–2335, para. 89, considered further, and L. Betten, 'The Democratic Deficit of Participatory Democracy in Community Social Policy' (1998) 23 *ELRev*. 20. Parliament asked the Commission and the Council to conclude an institutional agreement in order to ensure the consultation and opinion of Parliament before the Council refuses to implement an agreement.

[187] COM(93) 600, para. 40.

[188] See e.g. COM(90) 581 final (OJ [1991] C39/10). For further details see Ch. 15.

sion initiated the second phase of the consultation process. By the deadline for the second phase of consultation, 30 March 1994, the Social Partners sent their views on the consultation document. However, the Social Partners failed to reach agreement on setting in motion the procedure provided for in Article 155 TFEU.[189] Because the Commission considered that a Union initiative on the information and consultation of workers was still warranted, it adopted a further proposal,[190] this time on the legislative footing of Article 153(2) TFEU. The measure, Directive 94/45, was adopted on 22 September 1994. The collective approach was, however, successful in the (less controversial) case of parental leave and it is this (original) Directive[191] that we shall now consider as an example of the collective route to legislation.

(b) Negotiating the Parental Leave Directive 96/34/EC

The Parental Leave agreement was reached against a background of further institutional failure. The Commission's proposal for a Council Directive on parental leave and leave for family reasons[192] had been discussed in the Council of Ministers on various occasions between 1985 and 1994 but the unanimity required by Article 115 TFEU, the Directive's proposed legal basis, was not obtained. As a result, the Commission decided to initiate the procedure under Article 154 TFEU. Seventeen employers' and workers' organizations informed the Commission of their views at the end of the first consultation period but it was the three established partners, UNICE (now BusinessEurope), CEEP, and the ETUC, which, on 5 July 1995, announced their intention of starting negotiations, with the assistance of an active conciliator appointed by the parties. A framework agreement laying down minimum requirements designed to facilitate the reconciliation of parental and professional responsibilities for working parents[193] was concluded by the Social Partners on 14 December 1995.

The matter was then placed in the hands of the Commission which proposed that the measure be adopted by a Directive. The Explanatory Memorandum accompanying the 'Proposal for a Council Directive on the framework agreement on parental leave concluded by UNICE, CEEP and the ETUC'[194] carefully details the Commission's application of its own 1993 Communication on how the process would work.[195] First, the Commission considered the representative status of the contracting parties and their mandate.[196] It said that since UNICE (BusinessEurope), CEEP, and ETUC had committed themselves to an 'autonomous and voluntary process' (the Val Duchesse dialogue) since 1985 they satisfied the criteria defined in the Commission's Communication,[197]

---

[189] For details of the Social Partners' 'talks about talks', see M. Gold and M. Hall, 'Statutory European Works Councils: the Final Countdown?' (1994) 25 *IRJ* 177, 179–82.

[190] COM(94) 134 final.

[191] Dir. 96/34/EC (OJ [1996] L145/4) now repealed and replaced by Council Dir. 2010/18/EU (OJ [2010] L68/13). See further Ch. 9.

[192] COM(83) 686 final.   [193] Clause 1(1).   [194] COM(96) 26 final.

[195] COM(93) 600. See now the Commission's drafting checklist for new generation Social Partner texts: Commission Communication 'Partnership for change in an enlarged Europe—Enhancing the contribution of European social dialogue' (COM(2004) 557), Annex 3.

[196] COM(96) 26 final.   [197] COM(93) 600, para. 24.

and so they were representative.[198] Second, the Commission considered the 'legality' of the clauses of the agreement. It found that none of the clauses contravened Union law even though the collective agreement contained a clause imposing obligations on the Member States to implement the Commission decision.[199]

The Commission's proposal for a Directive on parental leave contained two articles. The first provided that the parental leave agreement annexed to the Directive was made binding. The original proposal also contained two additional clauses concerning the principle of non-discrimination and sanctions but they were dropped from the final version. The collective agreement itself was placed in a separate annex. The Commission kept the Parliament informed about the various phases of consultation of the Social Partners and also forwarded the proposal to the Parliament and the Economic and Social Committee so that they could deliver their opinion to the Commission and Council. The Directive was adopted on 3 June 1996.

A similar approach was followed in the case of Part-time Work and Fixed-term Work,[200] the two other directives successfully adopted by the intersectoral social partners. It was also applied in respect of the sectoral agreements that have been negotiated, including the agreement on the organization of working time by seafarers which was negotiated under the collective route by the European Community Shipowners' Association (ECSA) and the Federation of Transport Workers' Unions (FST)[201] and extended by Directive 99/63/EC[202] to all seafarers on board every commercial seagoing ship registered in the territory of a Member State, and again in the agreement between the Association of European Airlines (AEA), European Region Airlines Association (ERA), International Air Carrier Association (IACA), European Cockpit Association (ECA), and European Transport Workers' Federation (ETF) on the working time of mobile workers in civil aviation.[203]

(c) A challenge to the legitimacy of the collective route

The UEAPME case

The successful outcome of the negotiations on parental leave was hailed by some as the birth of Euro-corporatism.[204] However, UEAPME, CEC, and EUROCOMMERCE criticized the monopoly created by the established Social Partners. This led UEAPME,

---

[198] The Commission forwarded the framework agreement to all of the organizations which it had previously consulted or informed.

[199] The Commission said that it followed from the second declaration annexed to the SPA that collective agreements were likely to create obligations for the Member States.

[200] Council Dir. 97/81/EC (OJ [1998] L14/9) as amended by Council Dir. 98/23/EC (OJ [1998] L131/10), and Council Dir. 99/70/EC (OJ [1999] L175/43), respectively. See A. Lo Faro, *Regulating Social Europe: Reality and Myth of Collective Bargaining in the EC Legal Order* (Hart Publishing, Oxford, 2000) Ch. 5; G. Falkner *et al*, *Complying with Europe: EU Harmonisation and Soft Law in the Member States* (CUP, Cambridge, 2005) Ch. 9.

[201] A European Industry Committee with ETUC affiliation: COM(98) 322, Annex 1.

[202] OJ [1999] L167/33.   [203] Council Dir. 2000/79/EC OJ [2000] L302/57.

[204] G. Falkner, 'The Maastricht Protocol on Social Policy: Theory and Practice' (1996) 6 JESP 1 and EU Social Policy in the 1990s: Towards a Corporatist Policy Community (Routledge, London, 1998).

representing small and medium-sized employers, to bring judicial review proceedings seeking the annulment of the Parental Leave agreement and/or Directive 96/34,[205] with respect to its application to small and medium-sized undertakings. The grounds of review advanced by UEAPME were breach of the principle of equality, breach of Articles 153(2), 154(3), and 155 TFEU, the principles of subsidiarity and proportionality, and the principle of *patere legem quam ipse fecisti* (every authority abides by its own rules).

However, before the General Court (GC) could consider the substantive grounds of challenge it had to examine whether UEAPME, a 'non-privileged applicant' (NPA), had *locus standi* to bring the claim. A literal reading of what is now Article 263 TFEU (ex 230 EC) suggested that UEAPME had no locus because, as the law stood at the time, natural or legal persons (NPAs) could 'institute proceedings against a decision addressed to that person or against a decision which, although in the form of a regulation or a decision addressed to another person, is of direct and individual concern to the former'. Thus, since the measure was a Directive and not a Decision or a Decision in the form of a Regulation it seemed as though UEAPME did not have *locus standi*. However, the GC reached a different conclusion. Taking into account its character and legal effects, rather than its form,[206] the GC agreed that Directive 96/34 was not a 'decision' but a general legislative measure.[207] Yet, the Court went on to find that, notwithstanding the legislative character of Directive 96/34, it might nevertheless be of direct and individual concern to UEAPME.[208]

The case therefore turned on the question of individual concern. The Court noted that such individual concern would be present where a measure affected an applicant in a special way 'by reason of certain attributes peculiar to them or by reason of circumstances which differentiate them from all other persons'.[209] UEAPME claimed that this was the case, by reference to the consultation procedures set out in Article 154 TFEU, as implemented by the Commission. It argued that, as it had been represented in the 'informal' consultation (as we have seen, it was explicitly listed in the Commission's Communication), its exclusion from the formal negotiation stage was unlawful. The GC did not agree. It said that the consultation stage was separate from the negotiation stage, and there was no general right of those consulted to take part in the negotiations under Articles 154(4) and 155 TFEU or an individual right to participate in negotiation of the framework agreement.[210]

---

[205] Case T–135/96 *UEAPME* [1998] ECR II–2335. In Case T–55/98 *UEAPME* v. *Council*, UEAPME started but then withdrew, on 14 January 1999, a challenge to the Directive on Part-time Work. For an early example of an unsuccessful claim of this sort, see Case 66/76 *CFDT* v. *Council* [1977] ECR 305. CFDT, the second largest trade union confederation, complained that it had not been included among the representative organizations designated to draw up lists of candidates for a consultative committee. The Court dismissed the application because the (then) ECSC Treaty did not empower claimants like CFDT to file such an application.

[206] See Case C–298/89 *Gibraltar* v. *EU Council* [1993] ECR I–3605.

[207] Case T–135/96 *UEAPME*, paras. 63–7.

[208] Applying Case C–358/89 *Extramet Industrie* v. *Council* [1991] ECR I–2501; Case C–309/89 *Codorniu* v. *Council* [1994] ECR I–1853.

[209] Para. 69; Case 25/62 *Plaumann* v. *Commission* [1963] ECR 95; Case C–309/89 *Codorniu* [1994] ECR I–1853.   [210] Para. 82.

However, the GC found that this in itself did not render the action inadmissible. The question was whether 'any right of the applicant has been infringed as the result of any failure on the part of either the Council or the Commission to fulfil their obligations under the [collective] procedure'.[211] The GC said that the Commission and Council were obliged, in carrying out their roles under Articles 154(4) and 155 TFEU, to act in conformity with the principles governing their action in the field of social policy.[212] In particular, the Commission was obliged by Article 154(1) TFEU to promote consultation of management and labour and facilitate dialogue by ensuring balanced support for the parties. This obligation was interpreted by the GC as imposing a duty on the Commission, when resuming control of the collective procedure at the joint request of the social partners under Article 155(2) TFEU, to examine the representativity of the signatories to agreements proposed for implementation at the Community level under Articles 154(4) and 155 TFEU, and a duty on the Council to verify whether the Commission had fulfilled this task. Both institutions had to ascertain whether 'having regard to the content of the agreement in question, the signatories, taken together are sufficiently representative'.

The GC noted that the Council and Commission's duty to examine the representativity of the signatories to agreements was particularly important in the case of the collective procedure from which, as we have seen, the European Parliament is excluded. It said that participation of the European Parliament in the Union legislative process reflects, at Union level, 'the fundamental democratic principle that the people must share in the exercise of power through a representative assembly'.[213] The Court pointed out that, in respect of measures adopted by the Council under the legislative route provided by Article 153 TFEU, the democratic legitimacy derives from the European Parliament's participation.[214] By contrast, in respect of measures adopted under the collective route (Articles 154(4) and 155 TFEU) the European Parliament is absent. In this case, the 'principle of democracy on which the Union is founded requires...that the participation of the people be otherwise ensured, in this instance through the parties representative of management and labour who concluded the agreement which is endowed by the Council...with a legislative foundation at [Union] level'.[215]

Thus, the autonomy of the social dialogue is subject to the scrutiny of the Commission, the Council, and ultimately the Court. The Court continued that where that degree of representativity was lacking the Commission and Council had to refuse to implement the agreement at Union level.[216] In such a case, the representatives of management and labour which were initially consulted by the Commission under Articles 154(2) and (3) TFEU but which were not parties to the agreement, and 'whose particular representation—again in relation to the content of the agreement—is necessary in order to

---

[211] Para. 83.   [212] Para. 85.
[213] Citing, inter alia, Cases C–300/89 Commission v. Council [1991] ECR I-2867, para. 20; Case 138/79 Roquette Frères v. Council [1980] ECR 333, para. 33.
[214] Para. 88.   [215] Para. 89.   [216] Para. 90.

raise the collective representativity[217] of the signatories to the required level, have the right to prevent the Commission and the Council from implementing the agreement at [Union] level by means of legislative instrument'.[218] Thus, even after a European collective agreement has been concluded it can be challenged by those organizations excluded from it on the grounds of the absence of sufficient collective representativity.

The GC went on to find that, in respect of the Framework Agreement on Parental Leave, the Commission and Council did indeed take sufficient account of the representativity of the parties.[219] Since the Agreement applied to all employment relationships, the signatories, in order to satisfy the requirement of sufficient collective representativity, had to be qualified to represent all categories of undertakings and workers at Union level. Since the signatories (ETUC, UNICE (BusinessEurope), and CEEP) were *general* cross-industry organizations with a general mandate, as distinct from cross-industry organizations representing *certain* categories of workers and undertakings with a specific mandate (the sub-group in which UEAPME was placed), they were sufficiently representative.[220] The GC also considered that the particular constituency which UEAPME claimed to represent—small and medium-sized undertakings—was adequately represented by UNICE which was a signatory party to the agreement. The fact that UEAPME represented more small and medium-sized undertakings than UNICE, and that CEEP represented only the interests of undertakings governed by public law, was not sufficient to require UEAPME's participation. UEAPME had failed to show that it was sufficiently different, in terms of its representativity, from all other organizations consulted by the Commission which were not part of the formal negotiation procedure.[221] Thus UEAPME was not individually concerned by Directive 96/34 by reason of certain attributes which were peculiar to it or by reason of a factual situation which differentiated it from all other persons, and so the GC found the action inadmissible.[222]

The legitimacy of governance by the social partners

The judgment in the *UEAPME* case raises general issues concerning the nature of governance and democratic processes in the EU.[223] As we have seen, it has been argued that the social dialogue, and the collective route to legislation in particular, help to legitimize the EU in the eyes of its citizens because it enhances democracy, not by conferring

---

[217] Bercusson, previous, at n. 180, argues that this is an inadequate translation of the original French 'une representativité *cumulée* suffisante'. He prefers the translation found earlier in para. 90 'the signatories, *taken together*, are sufficiently representative'. This interpretation might include collective organizations which in themselves are not sufficiently representative but, when taken together, attain that status.

[218] Para. 90.

[219] See Commission, *The European social dialogue, a force for innovation and change*, COM(2002) 341 on the Commission's continued awareness of the profound governance issues raised by the bipartite social dialogue and the need to keep representativity under review.

[220] Paras. 95 and 96.   [221] Para. 111.

[222] The appeal of Case C–316/98 *UEAPME* [1998] ECR II–2335 to the Court was removed from the Court's register on 2 February 1999.

[223] See K. Armstrong, 'Governance and the Single Market', in P. Craig and G. de Búrca (eds.), *The Evolution of EU Law* (OUP, Oxford, 1999); K. Armstrong, *The Problems and Paradoxes of EU Regulatory Reform* (Kogan Page, London, 1999); N. Bernard, *Multi-level Governance in the European Union* (Kluwer, The Hague, 2002).

ever wider powers on the European Parliament—quite the converse—but because, as the Court notes, it provides an alternative type of representative democracy. This is based, not on representatives elected by their constituencies on a territorial basis, but on representatives of management and labour selected on a functional basis. The GC has therefore effectively condoned the 'established' Social Partners of UNICE/Business Europe, CEEP, and the ETUC, thereby ensuring continuity of the social dialogue process begun under the Delors Presidency at the Val Duchesse talks of 1985. However, the GC did not take the opportunity to undertake a wider consideration of the representativity of the established Social Partners, especially in respect of those who are not members of a trade union at all.[224] Instead, it confined itself to imposing a minimal review requirement on the Commission and Council.

But are the Social Partners truly representative?[225] Bercusson argues that they are representative of the *interests* of their members, rather than the actual number of those members,[226] from whom they have a mandate to negotiate.[227] As far as the cross-industry (intersectoral) Social Partners are concerned, the ETUC changed its statutes in 1995 to mandate the ETUC to negotiate by qualified majority decisions with a view to strengthening and intensifying the bargaining capacity of the European-level association. In BusinessEurope a similar change occurred. If required, BusinessEurope can receive a mandate to negotiate but, unlike the ETUC, a consensus of all members is still required in the Council of Presidents for all decisions referring to the Social Chapter. As Keller and Sörries point out, this internal rule can constrain BusinessEurope's ability to enter into negotiations and to ratify more far-reaching agreements because it takes only one vetoing member to undermine any agreement. This also has the effect of neutralizing the shift to qualified majority voting elsewhere. As far as representativity is concerned, BusinessEurope is the most representative of all categories of private undertakings, although this is questioned by UEAPME.[228] However, in contrast with ETUC, Business Europe has no sectoral organization but only national umbrella associations as members. According to BusinessEurope, these sectoral interests are already represented within its national member federations which have sectoral members

---

[224] That said, in many systems, trade unions are accustomed to negotiating on behalf of members and non-members alike.

[225] See the Social Partners' Study of 1993, Doc No. V/6141/93/E. The main findings of the study can be found in COM(93) 600, Annex 3. The European Foundation conducts studies on the representativeness of the European Social Partner organizations: <http://www.eurofound.europa.eu/areas/industrialrelations/dictionary/definitions/representativeness.htm> (last accessed 3 April 2012).

[226] B. Bercusson, 'Democratic Legitimacy and European Labour Law' (1999) 28 *ILJ* 153, 159. See B. Wedderburn, 'Collective Bargaining or Legal Enactment: the 1999 Act and Union Recognition' (2000) 29 *ILJ* 1, 6. See E. Franssen and A. Jacobs, 'The Question of Representativity in the European Social Dialogue' (1998) 35 *CMLRev.* 1295, 1309 where they argue that 'it is essential to judge the representativeness of the totality of the signatory parties, not the representativeness of one single organisation'.

[227] This reflects the Parliament's proposed criteria for representativity listed in COM(96) 448, para. 62. The following draws on B. Keller and B. Sörries, 'The New Social Dialogue: Old Wine in New Bottles?' (1999) 9 *JESP* 110.

[228] However, since the *UEAPME* case, UNICE (now BusinessEurope) and UEAPME have concluded a co-operation agreement (12 November 1998) outlining 'the modalities of cooperation . . . in social dialogue and negotiation meetings'.

themselves, albeit that BusinessEurope has started to develop an informal network of sectoral business associations on a voluntary basis to keep its members informed. CEEP covers only public enterprises. This leaves other public employers, notably the civil service without representation.[229] The ETUC, by contrast, does represent the overwhelming majority of trade unions but some national trade union organizations are still not affiliated to the ETUC (see further Box 2.1).

Thus, while the picture is complicated, the established interprofessional Social Partners do seem to be more representative than the other organizations. But the representativity of the established Social Partners is likely to become more problematic if law-making in the social field expands under the Social Policy Title. For instance, it is difficult to see how BusinessEurope, CEEP, and the ETUC could represent the various concerns of those who might be affected by action to promote 'the integration of persons excluded from the labour market' (Article 153(1)(h) TFEU), a social policy matter covering issues far wider than those of classic labour law agreements which are traditionally the subject of social dialogue. Even in the more traditional labour law areas, as trade union membership continues to decline across the Member States (see Table 2.1), the extent to which trade unions actually represent 'the people', especially women, is questionable. There is a risk, as Betten suggests, that the social dialogue actually leads to a predominance of an interest group in creating rules.[230]

Given the problems of viewing the legitimacy of the social dialogue as being derived from representative democracy, other commentators have argued that the legitimacy of the social dialogue actually comes from the participatory model of democracy. At the heart of this model lies the idea that decisions are taken as close to the citizens as possible on subject matters of interest and relevance to the citizens. As Fredman puts it, the social dialogue is uniquely suited to the development of social policy because it is based on an intimate knowledge by the bargainers of the factual basis of issues discussed, and leads to a synthesis which is all the more effective because it carries with it the commitment of the two sides of industry.[231] Yet, this model is also problematic: as Fredman argues, there is the fundamental inequality of bargaining power between the two sides of the process and the use of bargaining could well entrench such inequalities leading to an unjustifiable concentration of power in the hands of management representatives legitimized under the cloak of Social Dialogue.[232] This prompts Obradovic to suggest that corporatism should supplement, but not supplant, representative democracy, by facilitating consultation and co-ordination between social interests and public bodies.[233]

---

[229] Franssen and Jacobs, above, n. 226, 1299.

[230] L. Betten, 'The Democratic Deficit of Participatory Democracy in Community Social Policy' (1998) 23 *ELRev*. 20.

[231] S. Fredman, 'Social Law in the European Union: the Impact of the Lawmaking Process', in Craig and Harlow (eds.), above, n. 14, 386, 410.   [232] Ibid.

[233] See previously, n. 184, citing P. Hirst, *Representative Democracy and its Limits* (Polity Press, Cambridge, 1990) 12.

However, Bercusson doubts the validity of viewing the collective route to legislation through a public law lens. He argues that although in *UEAPME* the GC opted for 'the EU constitutional law paradigm of democratic legitimacy' in its analysis of the social dialogue, the social dialogue should not be seen as a legislative process at all. With its roots in private law and industrial relations, he advocates that 'European labour law cannot afford to abandon national labour law systems'.[234] However, as Fredman notes, the nature of the sanctions available to the parties especially the unions in respect of European level collective bargaining is far weaker than at domestic level due to the absence of any economic pressure such as industrial action.[235] The only pressure to reach an agreement, especially on the employer's side, is the prospect that without an agreement the legislative initiative will return to the Union legislator which will lead, at least for employers, to inferior results (less flexibility and fewer derogations).[236] This has been described as 'bargaining in the shadow of the law'.[237] For these very reasons, the union representatives prefer the use of the law, with collective bargaining being used to top up the minimum standards provided by the law[238] since this may well produce superior results for their members.

4.4. Sectoral social dialogue

It therefore seems that the issues raised by *UEAPME* are to be resolved by the EU's legislative, rather than judicial, institutions. Szyszczak notes that the Commission has begun to address some of the problems of representativity by means of developing a sectoral strategy.[239] In its Communication on *Adapting and Promoting the Social Dialogue at Community Level*,[240] the Commission announced that it would set up a new framework for the sectoral social dialogue. This led to a Decision[241] on the establishment of new sectoral dialogue committees[242] which constitute the main forum for sectoral social dialogue (consultation, joint action, and negotiations). The committees are to be set up in all sectors which 'submit a joint request and are sufficiently well organized

---

[234] B. Bercusson, 'Democratic Legitimacy and European Labour Law' (1999) 28 *ILJ* 153, 165.

[235] Fredman, above, n. 231, 408.

[236] Fredman, above, n. 231, 409, Keller and Sörries, above, n. 227, 115, and H. Cullen and D. Campbell, 'The Future of Social Policy Making in the European Union', in *Lawmaking in the European Union* (Kluwer, The Hague, 1998) 272, citing G. Ross, *Jacques Delors and European Integration* (Cambridge, Polity Press, 1995) 150–1.

[237] B. Bercusson, 'Maastricht: a Fundamental Change in European Labour Law' (1992) 23 *IRJ* 177, 185.

[238] Fredman, above, n. 231, 409. They fear that the social dialogue will enable employers to 'avoid the unwelcome attentions of the European Commission and European Parliament and to engage in what will in effect be a social monologue with trade unions weakened by recession and structural changes in the economy'.

[239] Szyszczak, previously, at n. 53.

[240] COM(98) 332.

[241] Commission Decision 98/500/EC on the establishment of Sectoral Dialogue Committees promoting the Dialogue between the Social Partners at European level (OJ [1998] L225/27). On the future of the sectoral dialogue see B. Keller and B. Sörries, 'The Sectoral Social Dialogue and European Social Policy: More Fantasy, Fewer Facts' (1998) 4 *EJIR* 331, and 'Sectoral Social Dialogues: New Opportunities or Impasses?' (1999) 30 *IRJ* 330.

[242] Replacing existing Joint Committees on Maritime Transport, Civil Aviation, Inland Navigation, Road Transport, Railways, Telecoms, Agriculture, Sea Fishing, and Post.

with a meaningful European presence in line with the established criteria of representativeness'.[243] The committees are consulted on developments at Union level having social implications and must develop and promote the social dialogue at sectoral level.[244] A maximum of 50 people, representing the two sides of industry equally, can take part in the meetings of the Committees.[245] Although each committee, together with the Commission, is to establish its own rules of procedure[246] the Decision does specify that the committee must meet at least once a year[247] (the 'high level plenary meeting'),[248] and that the meeting is to be chaired by a representative of the employers' or employees' delegations or, at their joint request, by a representative of the Commission.[249] Where the Commission informs the Committee that a matter discussed is confidential, members of the committee are bound not to disclose any information acquired at the meetings of the secretariat.[250] Finally, the Decision provides that the Commission and the Social Partners are to review the functioning of the sectoral committee regularly.[251]

There are currently 40 sectoral social dialogue committees covering 145 million workers in the EU and including key sectors such as transport, energy, agriculture, construction, trade, fisheries, public services, metal, shipyards, and education.[252] While much of this dialogue has involved identifying relevant problem areas for the social dialogue and trying out common vocabulary, as well as agreeing guidelines and recommendations,[253] agreements on the organization of working time (maritime transport,[254] civil aviation,[255] and railways[256]) have been negotiated, as have agreements on preventing injuries and infections to healthcare workers from sharp objects such as needles,[257]

---

[243] COM(98) 332, 8 and Art. 1 of the Commission Decision 98/500/EC (OJ [1998] L225/27).
[244] Art. 2.   [245] Art. 3.   [246] Art. 5(1).   [247] Art. 5(3).
[248] There is to be reimbursement for a maximum of 15 representatives on each side.
[249] Art. 5(2).   [250] Art. 6.   [251] Art. 5(4).   [252] SEC(2010) 964.
[253] See e.g. recommendations on avoiding bogus self-employment in the construction sector, guidelines for promoting gender equality in local and regional government, a handbook for fishermen to help prevent accidents at sea, recommendations on better anticipating and managing restructuring in the textile industry. For details, see <http://ec.europa.eu/social/main.jsp?catId=480&langId=en> (last accessed 29 December 2011).
[254] Council Dir. 99/63 concerning the Agreement on the Organisation of Working Time of Seafarers concluded by ECSA and FST (OJ [1999] L167/33, corrected OJ [1999] L244/64), now amended by Council Dir. 2009/13/EC (OJ [2009] L124/30). An agreement has now been adopted on Inland Waterways: Memo/12/107.
[255] Dir. 2000/79 concerning the European Agreement on the Organisation of Working Time of Mobile Workers in Civil Aviation (OJ [2000] L302/57).
[256] On 18 September 1996 the Social Partners meeting in the Joint Committee on Rail Transport reached agreements on including all railway workers, whether mobile or non-mobile under Dir. 93/104. See additionally Council. Dir. 2005/47 on the Agreement of 27 January 2004 between the Community of European Railways (CER) and the European Transport Workers' Federation (ETF) on certain aspects of the working conditions of mobile workers engaged in interoperable cross-border services in the railway sector (OJ [2005] L195/15).
[257] Council Dir. 2010/32/EU (OJ [2010] L134/66). This was agreed by the European Hospital and Healthcare Employers' Association (HOSPEEM) and the European Federation of Public Service Unions (EPSU). For problems regarding turning the agreement into a Directive, see <http://register.consilium.europa.eu/pdf/en/10/st06/st06635.en10.pdf> (last accessed 30 December 2012). The European Biosafety Network (<http://www.europeanbiosafetynetwork.eu/>) was established following the adoption of the Sharps Directive to improve the safety of patients and healthcare and non-healthcare workers.

and on improving working conditions for maritime workers incorporating internation-ally-agreed standards into EU law.[258] The five agreements have been extended to all workers in the relevant sector by Directive.

In its Communication on Adapting and Promoting the Social Dialogue[259] the Com-mission noted that there was nothing in the SPA (as it then was) 'that limits possible sectoral negotiations thereunder, either as a complement to cross-industry agree-ments or establishing independent agreements limited to their sector concerned'. However, a potential problem may arise if the sectoral organizations were to negoti-ate a collective agreement in an area already covered by the intersectoral partners and then pass it on to the Commission for a Council decision. Generally, the Commission is positive about the sectoral dialogue's contribution to social progress and modern-izing industrial relations. The Commission notes that it intends to encourage the European and national sectoral social partners to make full use of their capacity to negotiate, to reinforce their administrative capacity and representativeness, and to create synergies between sectors.[260] However, the sectoral social dialogue has not led to transnational collective bargaining and genuine Europe wide industrial relations[261] and some suggest that, despite the formal institutional structures in place, the secto-ral social partners' voice remains weak.[262]

D. CONCLUSIONS

This chapter has focused on the 'hard' rules adopted by the European Union. As we have seen, in the social field, the hard rules are not as rigid as would first appear. By concentrating on Directives, especially framework Directives, the EU has allowed Member States to adapt EU requirements to national situations. The use of opt-outs and delayed implementation has allowed Member States to move at different speeds while ensuring that they keep moving in the same direction. Most radically, the collective route to legislation has allowed the Social Partners to negotiate collective agreements which become hard law. Thus social legislation has never conformed to the hard law stereotype.

Nevertheless, despite the flexibility already incorporated into the Directives, tradi-tional legislation was not seen as a suitable vehicle for responding to the structural problems presented by increasingly high levels of unemployment, an ageing popula-tion, and a rising number of people excluded from the labour market. Nor did the EU have clear competence to address these problems. This led the Portuguese Presidency

---

[258] Council Dir. 2009/13/EC implementing the agreement concluded by the European Community Shipowners' Associations (ECSA) and the European Transport Workers' Federation (ETF) on the Maritime Labour Convention, 2006 and amending Directive 1999/63/EC (OJ [2009] L124/30).

[259] COM(98) 322, 14.   [260] SEC(2010) 964.

[261] Keller and Weber, above n. 171, 239.

[262] E. Léonard, 'European Sectoral Social Dialogue: An Analytical Framework' (2008) *EJIR* 401, 416–17.

of the Council of Ministers in 2000 to look round for alternatives. Drawing inspiration from the OECD, and the Treaty-based procedures found in the Titles on Economic and Monetary Policy and Employment,[263] the Lisbon Presidency developed a new approach, the Open Method of Co-ordination. The Employment Title, the Lisbon and EU2020 Strategy and OMC form the subject of Chapter 3.

---

[263] M. Rodrigues, 'The Open Method of Coordination as a New Governance Tool' *Europa Europe* 2–3 (special issue, 'L'evoluzione della governance europea', ed. Mario Telò). Rome: Fondazione Istituto Gramsci available on the OMC website at Wisconsin: <http://www.eucenter.wisc.edu/OMC/index.htm>. Maria João Rodrigues was special adviser to the Portuguese Prime Minister at the time of Lisbon and co-ordinator of the Lisbon European Council.

3

THE EMPLOYMENT TITLE, THE LISBON AND EU2020 STRATEGIES, AND THE FINANCIAL CRISIS

A. INTRODUCTION

So far this book has focused on the development of employment rights and the legislative processes (either traditional or collective) used to adopt these rights. In essence such legislation has broadly drawn on the classic 'Community' method to produce binding rules enforceable by national courts. The Treaty of Amsterdam, which introduced the Employment Title into the Treaty, marked a sea change, moving away from giving rights to those in work in favour of addressing the high levels of unemployment across the European Union. This new focus was accompanied by a more voluntarist, intergovernmental form of governance based on the co-ordination of policy, the use of non-binding, flexible instruments and new techniques such as benchmarking. This new approach was given a formal title by the Lisbon European Council in March 2000—the Open Method of Co-ordination (OMC). OMC was to be one of the central means for achieving the Lisbon objective of making the EU the most competitive and dynamic knowledge-based economy in the world by 2010. The Lisbon European Council certainly did not anticipate the financial crash of 2008 and the crisis that followed, making this objective undeliverable. Nevertheless, the EU2020 strategy, adopted in March 2010 to replace the Lisbon strategy, continued in much the same vein, albeit with fewer objectives. The aim of this chapter is consider how the EU has set about trying to realize the Lisbon and EU2020 goals, to examine the interplay between the Lisbon/EU2020 strategy, the European Employment Strategy (EES), and the EU's economic strategy, and to consider how the EU's response to the crisis has an impact on national labour law.

B. THE EMPLOYMENT TITLE

1. INTRODUCTION

While there was much agreement as to the need to increase the employment rate, there was much less agreement as to how to bring it about. In the mid-1990s, there was an active debate about whether centralized expenditure should be used to stimulate demand, and thus employment, through investments in infrastructure and public works.[1] While this approach received some impetus from the 1993 White Paper on *Growth, Competitiveness and Employment*,[2] the Member States refused to countenance a significant increase in the Commission's budget. However, the importance of this White Paper lay in the policy mix it proposed, based on the centralized co-ordination of employment policies and its combination of a deregulatory agenda with active labour market measures.

This policy mix was essentially endorsed by the Essen summit in 1994. A number of the areas for intervention identified by the Essen Council were clearly deregulatory in character,[3] stressing the reduction of the 'tax wedge' of indirect labour costs and the need for greater flexibility in the utilization of labour. Others, however, assumed a more pro-active role for the state and were based on an agenda of restructuring public expenditure in favour of more active employment market policies (e.g. subsidies for training) and the need to strengthen structural policy objectives relating to those excluded from the labour market (women, young people, and the long-term unemployed).[4] From a procedural perspective, the approach agreed at Essen was also of longer-term interest. The Council laid down a monitoring procedure under which the Member States were required to report back on the steps they had taken. A benchmarking exercise was conducted to promote best practice, focusing on long-term unemployment, youth unemployment, and equal opportunities.

Essen therefore provided the template for the European Employment Strategy, and the Essen priorities were replicated in what became the Employment Guidelines. Most significantly, Essen showed to the Member States that it was possible to co-ordinate their activities at *European* level to achieve *national* objectives of reducing unemployment. The Essen policy agenda was taken further by the Florence Council of 1996 which endorsed a 'Confidence Pact' on employment put forward by the Commission, and by the Dublin Council of 1997 which issued a 'Declaration on Employment'. Together these steps paved the way for the adoption of the Employment Title at Amsterdam.

---

[1] C. Barnard and S. Deakin, 'A Year of Living Dangerously? EC Social Policy Rights, Employment Policy and EMU' (1998) 2 *IRJ European Annual Review* 117.

[2] EC Bull. Supp. 6/93.

[3] See S. Deakin and H. Reed, 'Between Social Policy and EMU: The New Employment Title of the EC Treaty', in J. Shaw (ed.), *Social Law and Policy in an Evolving European Union* (Hart Publishing, Oxford, 2000).

[4] E. Szyszczak, 'The New Paradigm for Social Policy: A Virtuous Circle' (2001) 38 *CMLRev.* 1125, 1136.

There were social and economic justifications for focusing on employment. The social justification, based on the contribution of employment towards social cohesion and personal dignity was emphasized in the Amsterdam European Council's Resolution on Growth and Employment:[5]

> This approach, coupled with stability based policies, provides the basis for an economy founded on principles of inclusion, solidarity, justice and a sustainable environment, and capable of benefiting all its citizens. Economic efficiency and social inclusion are complementary aspects of the more cohesive society that we all seek.

At the economic level, three arguments were made for lowering unemployment. First, by making productive use of unused labour stock this would lead to a significant reduction on the burdens experienced by national social security systems. As the Commission's Communication *Community Policies in Support of Employment* pointed out, if the performance of the three best Member States or of the US were taken as a benchmark, an additional 30 million or more people could be employed, raising EU employment from 150 million to 180 million, substantially improving public finances and making pension systems more sustainable.[6] This highlights the second argument: that an ageing population needs to be supported by higher employment. Third, high levels of employment are also important to close the gender gap between male and female employment rates.

2. THE TREATY PROVISIONS

2.1. The co-ordination of policy

Despite the fact that there had been little evaluation of the success of the Essen strategy,[7] its approach was a defining feature of the new Employment Title introduced by the Amsterdam Treaty.[8] According to the key provision of the new Title, Article 145 TFEU (ex 125 EC):

> Member States and the Union shall, in accordance with the Title, work towards developing a *coordinated strategy* for employment and particularly for promoting a skilled, trained and adaptable workforce and labour markets responsive to economic change with a view to achieving the objectives defined in Article 3 of the Treaty on European Union.[9]

Article 146 TFEU (ex 126 EC) makes clear that the principal actors are the Member States. They are required to co-ordinate their policies for the promotion of employment (which is to be regarded as an issue of 'common concern')[10] within the Council, but in a way consistent with the Broad Economic Guidelines (BEPG) laid down

---

[5] 97/C 236/02. See further Resolution of the European Council on the European Employment Pact, paras. 1, 3 and 4, June 1999.   [6] COM(99) 127.

[7] P. Pochet, 'The New Employment Chapter of the Amsterdam Treaty' (1999) 9 *JESP* 271, 275.

[8] See further M. Biagi, 'The Implementation of the Amsterdam Treaty with Regard to Employment: Coordination or Convergence?' (1998) 14 *IJCLLIR* 325.   [9] Emphasis added.

[10] Art. 146(2) TFEU.

within the framework of economic policy.[11] Thus, the Treaty appears to mandate the supremacy of the BEPGs over employment policy, a view which is supported by the harder sanctions available for the failure to comply with the chapter on Economic Policy.[12] However, in recognition of the diversity of social policy, the states must have regard to 'national practices related to the responsibilities of management and labour'.[13]

The (subsidiary) role of the Union is laid down by Article 147 TFEU (ex 127 EC) which calls on the Union to 'contribute to a high level of employment by encouraging cooperation between Member States and *by supporting* and, if necessary, complementing their action' after respecting 'the competence of the Member States'.[14] This provision is reminiscent of the circumscribed competence of the Union in the fields of education and vocational training (Articles 165 and 166 TFEU (ex 149 and 150 EC)), culture (Article 167 TFEU (ex 151 EC)), and public health (Article 168 TFEU (ex 152 EC)) where the Union is ostensibly given competence but has limited options as to how to exercise it. Together these provisions provide a good example of what Kenner describes as 'Third Way' thinking: the principal themes are those of shared responsibility between and within the Union and the Member States, and a decentralizing conception of subsidiarity in which the 'the [Union] enables and the Member States deliver'.[15]

2.2. The review process

(a) Drawing up of the Guidelines

The role of the Union is in fact less subsidiary than would first appear when the process laid down in Article 148 TFEU for monitoring and reporting on Member States' activities is considered. Each year the Council and Commission are to make a joint report on employment in the Union.[16] This is then considered at a European Council meeting which draws up its conclusions.[17] On the basis of these conclusions the Council, acting by qualified majority on a proposal from the Commission (after consulting the European Parliament, the Economic and Social Committee, the Committee of the Regions, and the Employment Committee (EMCO)), draws up Employment Guidelines which the Member States 'shall take into account in their employment policies'.[18] These Guidelines must also be consistent with the Broad Economic Guidelines issued in relation to EMU.[19] Since 2005 they have formed an integrated package.

---

[11] This point is reiterated in Article 148(2) TFEU (ex 128(2) EC).

[12] S. Ball, 'The European Employment Strategy: The Will but Not the Way?' (2001) 30 *ILJ* 353, 360 although she notes that the Cologne and subsequent European Councils have stressed the equal importance of both aspects of EU law and policy.

[13] Art. 146(2) TFEU.   [14] Emphasis added.

[15] J. Kenner, 'The EC Employment Title and the "Third Way": Making Soft Law Work' (1999) 15 *IJCLLIR* 33, 48.   [16] Art. 148(1) TFEU.

[17] Art. 148(1) TFEU.   [18] Art. 148(2) TFEU.   [19] Art. 121 TFEU (ex 99 EC).

(b) The role of EMCO

The Employment Committee (EMCO)[20] which the Council has to consult, consists of two nominees from each Member State and two from the Commission,[21] selected from among 'senior officials or experts possessing outstanding competence in the field of employment and labour market policy in the Member States'.[22] It has an 'advisory status' to promote co-ordination between Member States on employment and labour market policies.[23] Its tasks are to monitor employment policies both within the Member States and the Commission, and to formulate opinions at the request of the Commission or the Council or on its own initiative. It must also contribute to the preparation of the Employment Guidelines.[24] In fulfilling its mandate, the Employment Committee is obliged to consult the Social Partners[25] who are represented on the tripartite Standing Committee on Employment.[26] Only European-level Social Partners are now represented on the Standing Committee. EMCO was supposed to be a 'deliberative institution' located between the Commission and the Member States. In fact, it has continued to be driven by intergovernmental, interest-based bargaining rather than results-oriented, open deliberation.[27]

(c) National Action Plans/National Reform Programmes

Once the Employment Guidelines for a given year are adopted, Article 148(3) TFEU requires each Member State to make an annual report to the Council and the Commission on 'the principal measures taken to implement its employment policy in the light of the guidelines for employment'—the so-called National Action Plans (NAPs)[28] renamed in 2005 as National Reform Programmes (NRPs). In order to achieve greater coherence between the employment and economic strategies, the national reform programmes (NRP) are now published alongside the stability and convergence programmes (SCP) where Member States present and discuss their medium term budgetary strategies. These NRPs are considered by EMCO as part of a process of mutual surveillance and peer review. EMCO then reports to the Council which examines the employment policies of the Member States in the light of the Guidelines on employment. The Council (EPSCO—the Employment, Social Affairs, Health and Consumer Affairs Council) and Commission then submit a joint report to the European Council[29] on how far the

[20] Council Decision 2000/98/EC establishing the Employment Committee (OJ [2000] L29/21).
[21] Art. 150 TFEU (ex 130 EC).   [22] Art. 2 of Decision 2000/98.
[23] Art. 150 TFEU.   [24] Ibid.   [25] Art. 2 of Decision 2000/98.
[26] Council Decision 1999/207/EC (OJ [1999] L72/33) on reform of the Standing Committee on Employment and repealing Decision 70/352/EEC (OJ [1970] L273/25). The Preamble to Decision 2000/98/EC says that the Employment Committee should 'collaborate closely with the social partners, in particular with those represented in the Standing Committee on Employment'.
[27] M. Rhodes, 'Employment Policy: Between Efficacy and Experimentation' in H. Wallace, W. Wallace, and M. Pollack (eds.), Policy Making in the European Union (OUP, Oxford, 2005) 298.
[28] Communication from the Commission From Guidelines to Action: The National Action Plans for Employment, COM(98) 316.
[29] The report is drafted by the Commission which is then modified and/or endorsed by EPSCO.

Guidelines have been implemented.[30] The process, now renamed the European semester of policy co-ordination (discussed later), then starts all over again.

(d) The recommendation procedure

When making its examination of the NRPs, the Council may, acting by qualified majority on a recommendation from the Commission, 'make recommendations to Member States'.[31] This recommendation procedure is the main innovation in the Employment Title: if the Employment Guidelines are not being observed by a Member State, a recommendation can be issued which is, in effect, a warning for failure to comply with the Guidelines. A similar procedure can be found in monitoring the compliance with economic governance requirements and the Council recommendation on the NRP is published at the same time as the Council Opinion on the convergence programme.[32] However, under EMU as it then stood, a Member State which failed to observe warnings issued by the Council in relation to excessive levels of national debt and excessive budget deficits could be subject to a fine;[33] under the Employment Title the recommendation is without sanction. This recommendation process is supposed to form part of the 'naming and shaming' process. In practice, recommendations on the NRPs have been issued annually against all Member States since 1999 and the Member States have been involved in drafting the recommendation to be used against them, largely through their representatives in EMCO, with the result that the Commission's draft recommendations are considerably watered down and sensitive suggestions and wording are removed.

(e) Incentive measures

Not only can the Council issue recommendations, it can also act to 'adopt incentive measures designed to encourage co-operation between Member States and to support their action in the field of employment through initiatives aimed at developing exchanges of information and best practices, providing comparative analysis and advice as well as promoting innovative approaches and evaluating experiences, in particular by recourse to pilot projects' (Article 149 TFEU (ex 129 EC)). However, these limited measures 'shall not include harmonisation of the laws and regulations of the Member States'.

Two Declarations issued at the time of the adoption of the Amsterdam Treaty further limit the utility of Article 149 TFEU. The first sets limits to the validity, duration, and financing of measures under this Article and the second says that incentive measures may not be supported from the structural funds expenditure but from other areas of the Union budget where resources are insignificant compared to those available to the Social Fund. These restrictions were included at the insistence of the German and

---

[30] Art. 148(5) TFEU.

[31] Art. 148(4) TFEU. For examples of the most recent recommendations, see <http://ec.europa.eu/europe2020/reaching-the-goals/monitoring-progress/recommendations-2011/index_en.htm> (last accessed 3 April 2012).

[32] See e.g. <http://eur-lex.europa.eu/LexUriServ/LexUriServ.do?uri=OJ:C:2011:217:0012:0014:EN:PDF>.

[33] Art. 126(1) TFEU (ex 126 EC). The rules on fining defaulting Member States are to change in the 'fiscal compact' agreed in December 2011 (see later in this chapter).

British governments and illustrate again how the Member States resisted any significant expansion in the powers of the central Union organs to act as initiators of expenditure aimed at boosting job creation. Article 149 TFEU has, however, led to the launch of the peer-review procedure. Under this procedure, states hosted reviews of their own pro- grammes and visited programmes presented by other Member States. Initial assess- ments indicated that little learning was achieved, what was learnt was not passed on to the relevant decision makers, and there was little transfer of ideas.[34]

In 2007, the original Employment Incentive Measures[35] were regrouped under the Community Programme for Employment and Social Solidarity (PROGRESS).[36] The programme is now based on four specific Community Action Programmes which finance the implementation of the Social Policy Agenda as well as policies in relation to employment and working conditions.

(f) Assessment

Deakin and Reed suggest that the institutional framework put in place by the Employ- ment Title is facilitative rather than prescriptive.[37] Member States continue to have immediate control over their own employment policies which may well be highly diverse in terms of their approach and effects. Harmonizing laws are ruled out and, in their place, is a process of benchmarking, peer review, and multilateral surveillance.

This soft policy co-ordination apes the business oriented model of 'management by objective' aimed at delivering targets within a given timeframe. While targets are laud- able, businesses and government differ. Businesses need to concentrate on one princi- pal objective: the bottom line for their shareholders. By contrast, governments have multiple objectives to reconcile and there is a risk that, by focusing on the objectives in one field, this may have unintended consequences in another. These unintended conse- quences are magnified in a necessarily more wooden, rules-based environment such as EU level policy co-ordination, where Member States do not want/trust the Commis- sion to operate more discretionary rules.[38]

Academic commentators have also been critical of the Employment Title. For example, De la Porte *et al.*, question the effectiveness of the benchmarking methodol- ogy.[39] They note that it is difficult to reach agreement on common objectives and guidelines and, even once a benchmark is agreed, the means to pursue it may not be. Targets can also prove hostages to fortune; often they depend on external factors (e.g.

---

[34] B. Casey and M. Gold, 'Peer Review of Labour Market Programmes in the European Union: What Can Countries Really Learn from One Another?' (2005) 12 *JESP* 23.

[35] COM(2008) 328.

[36] EP and Council Dec. 1672/2006 establishing a Community Programme for Employment and Social Solidarity—PROGRESS (OJ [2006] OJ L 315/1).

[37] S. Deakin and H. Reed, 'Between Social Policy and EMU: the New Employment Title of the EC Treaty' in J. Shaw (ed.), *Social Law and Policy in an Evolving European Union* (Hart Publishing, Oxford, 2000).

[38] These comments are based on conversations with a Commission official to whom I am most grateful.

[39] C. De la Porte, P. Pochet, and G. Room, 'Social Benchmarking, Policy Making and New Governance in the EU' (2001) 11 *JESP* 291.

energy prices) over which governments have no control. Szyszczak doubts the legitimacy of the benchmarking exercise: its prioritization of some Union policies over
others and its choice of indicators and the creation of league tables—so central to the
naming and shaming process—is not an outcome envisaged by the Treaties.[40] More
fundamentally, Goetschy and Pochet[41] question the need for a joint approach, given
that unemployment had already been reduced in a number of states using different
methods. They also said that the choice of a 'diplomatic' type process involving Ecofin
(the Economic and Finance Council), EPSCO (the Social Affairs Council), and the
European Council was risky in terms of the consistency of diagnosis and solutions.
This process favours consensual solutions (such as vocational training) over possibly
more suitable but also more controversial solutions (such as reducing labour costs or
reducing working time).

3. THE LUXEMBOURG PROCESS

3.1. The Luxembourg Guidelines

Despite these concerns, the European Council decided to put the relevant provisions on
monitoring employment policy into effect before the Treaty of Amsterdam came into
force. This became known as the European Employment Strategy (EES).[42] At an extraordinary meeting of the European Council in Luxembourg in November 1997, the first
Guidelines outlining policy areas for 1998 were agreed by the Member States and
adopted by the Council of Ministers.[43] Developing the fields of action identified at
Essen, the (19) Guidelines centred on four main 'pillars' (see Table 3.1)[44] which were
intended to address 'the jobs gap, the skills gap, the participation gap and the gender
gap'.[45] So what were these pillars and what did they do?

First, the *employability* pillar focused on the prevention of long-term and youth
unemployment by means of vocational education and training[46] and active labour
market policies including the placement of young workers in work experience schemes
and the giving of subsidies to employers offering training.

Secondly, the *entrepreneurship* pillar attempted to make the process of business start-
ups more straightforward, and incorporated steps to revise regulations affecting small
businesses. Thirdly, the *adaptability* pillar encouraged negotiation over the improvement of productivity through the reorganization of working practices and production

---

[40] Previous, at n. 4, 1146.

[41] J. Goetschy and P. Pochet, 'The Treaty of Amsterdam: a New Approach to Social Affairs' (1997) 3
Transfer 607.

[42] <http://ec.europa.eu/social/main.jsp?catId=101&langId=en>.

[43] Council Resolution of 15 December 1997 on the 1998 Employment Guidelines (OJ [1998] C30/1). See
further D. Ashiagbor, *The European Employment Strategy: Labour Market Regulation and New Governance*
(OUP, Oxford, 2005) 74–85, on the influence of the OECD's Jobs Strategy on the EU's EES.

[44] See Barnard and Deakin, previous, at n. 1, 117.

[45] 'An interview with Padraig Flynn' (1998) 288 *European Industrial Relations Review* 20.

[46] See Resolution of the Council and Representatives of the Governments of the Member States on the
employment and social dimension of the information society (OJ [2000] C8/1).

Table 3.1 The Luxembourg Process: Employment Guidelines 1998

Pillars	Guidelines	Examples of activities and targets
I. Improving employability	Tackling youth unemployment	Within a period not exceeding five years:
		—every unemployed young person is offered a new start before reaching six months of unemployment (e.g. training, retraining, work practice)
		—unemployed adults to be offered a 'fresh start' before reaching 12 months of unemployment
	Transition from passive measures to active measures	To increase the numbers of unemployed who are offered training, each MS will fix a target of the average of the three most successful states and at least 20%
	Encouraging a partnership approach	Social Partners to conclude agreements to increase the possibilities for training, work experience, traineeships and equivalent
		MS and Social Partners to develop possibilities for lifelong training
	Easing the transition from school to work	MS to improve the quality of school to reduce substantially the number of young people who drop out from school early
		MS to ensure that they equip young people with greater ability to adapt to technological and economic changes
II. Developing entrepreneurship	Making it easier to start up and run businesses	Reduce significantly the overhead costs and administrative burdens for businesses, especially SMEs, particularly in relation to hiring workers
		Encourage the development of self-employment by removing obstacles (e.g. tax and social security) to setting up as self-employed or running small businesses
	Exploiting the opportunities for job creation	MS must investigate measures to exploit fully the possibilities for job creation at local level, especially concerning new activities not yet satisfied by the market
	Making the taxation system more employment friendly and reversing the long-term trend towards higher taxes and charges on labour[1]	MS to set a target for gradually reducing the overall tax burden and for reducing the fiscal pressure on labour and non-wage labour costs

(continued)

Table 3.1 Continued

Pillars	Guidelines	Examples of activities and targets
		MS to examine the advisability of reducing the rate of VAT on labour intensive services not exposed to cross-border competition[2]
III. Encouraging adaptability in businesses and their employees	Modernizing work organization	Social Partners to negotiate agreements to modernize work, including flexible working arrangements (e.g. annualized hours, reduction of working hours, reduction of working time, development of part-time work, lifelong training and career breaks) striking a balance between flexibility and security
		MS to look at the possibility of incorporating in its law more adaptable types of contracts
	Support adaptability in enterprises	Examine obstacles, especially tax obstacles, to investment in human resources
IV. Strengthening policies for equal opportunities	Tackling gender gaps	MS to reduce the gap in unemployment rates between women and men by actively supporting the increased employment of women and acting to reverse the under-representation of women in certain economic sectors and over-representation in others
	Reconciling work and family life	MS to implement the Directives on Parental Leave and Part-time Work
		MS to raise levels of access to care services where some needs are not met
	Facilitating return to work	MS to examine the means of gradually eliminating the obstacles to return to work for women and men
	Promoting the integration of people with disabilities into working life	MS to give special attention to the problems people with disabilities may encounter in participating in working life

MS = Member State

[1] These increased from 35% in 1980 to more than 42% in 1995.
[2] This has now become a permanent Directive: Council Dir. 2009/47/EC (OJ [2009] L116/18).

processes. The reduction and renegotiation of working time, the flexible implementation of labour standards, and information and consultation over training issues also came under this heading. Finally, the *equal opportunities* pillar concerned raising awareness of issues relating to gender equality in terms of equal access to work, family friendly policies, and the needs of people with disabilities.[47]

Some of the benchmarks set by the 1998 Guidelines were detailed and specific. For example, the second Guideline under the first pillar (employability) said that in order to increase significantly the number of persons benefiting from active measures (training) to improve their employability, Member States must fix a target 'of gradually achieving the average of the three most successful Member States, and at least 20 per cent'. However, in most areas the Guidelines lacked any quantitative target; their wording was vague and aspirational. For example, the fourth Guideline under the equal opportunities pillar merely provided that the Member States would give 'special attention to the problems people with disabilities may encounter in participating in working life'.

The need for quantitative targets and indicators was noted in the 1999 Guidelines which required Member States to develop reliable flow data on employment and unemployment, and to ensure that adequate and comparable data systems and procedures were available. Member States were also invited to 'set themselves national targets which could be quantified wherever possible and appropriate'.

3.2. Subsequent Guidelines

(a) 1999–2004 Guidelines

The substance of the 1999[48] and 2000[49] Guidelines largely repeated those of 1998, albeit that they placed greater emphasis on the need to exploit the job-creation potential of the services sector (especially information and communication technologies), on partnership—particularly with the Social Partners—at all levels (European, national, sectoral, local, and enterprise) and on promoting a labour market open to all, especially those with disabilities and ethnic minorities. The 1999 Guidelines also devoted more attention to the problems faced by women in gaining access to the employment market, in career development, and in reconciling professional and family life.

The 2001 Guidelines were drafted against the backdrop of the Lisbon strategy which had been launched in March 2000 (considered below). To the four pillars were added five 'horizontal objectives', contained in a so-called 'chapeau', designed to reorientate the EES towards the Lisbon strategy. These objectives included enhancing job opportunities and providing adequate incentives for all those willing to take up gainful employment with the aim of moving towards full employment and developing comprehensive and coherent strategies for lifelong learning with responsibility shared among public authorities, enterprises, the Social Partners, and individuals, with relevant contributions from civil society. The 2001 Guidelines also updated the existing Guidelines (e.g. 'easing the

---

[47] See generally the Commission's 'EQUAL' programme 2000–2008 and now use of the European Social Fund.
[48] Council Resolution on the 1999 Employment Guidelines (OJ [1999] C69/2).
[49] Council Dec. 2000/228/EC (OJ [2000] L72/15).

transition from school to work' became 'developing skills for the new labour market in the context of lifelong learning') as well as introducing new ones (e.g. 'active policies to develop job matching and to prevent and combat emerging bottlenecks').

At the Barcelona Spring Council in March 2002, the heads of state declared that 'The Luxembourg Employment Strategy has proved its worth' but noted that the Strategy had to be simplified with fewer guidelines and had to be aligned with the Lisbon deadline of 2010. The strategy also had to be streamlined with the other policy co-ordination processes,[50] with synchronized calendars for the adoption of the Broad Economic Policy Guidelines and the Employment Guidelines, and that both sets of Guidelines, together with the third policy co-ordination instrument, the internal market strategy, had to operate in a consistent way with a new, three-year perspective.[51]

As a result, the timetable of the EES was brought into line with the BEPGs, a three-year policy cycle was introduced, and the structure of the 2003 Employment Guidelines[52] was overhauled. The four pillars were dismantled in favour of three 'overrarching and interrelated objectives' of 'full employment, quality and productivity at work, and social cohesion and inclusion',[53] thus reflecting the Lisbon strategy's goals. These objectives were then fleshed out by 10 'result oriented' Guidelines, the so-called 'ten commandments' (as compared with the 20 or so Guidelines under the previous regime), which included, for example, active and preventative measures for the unemployed and inactive, job creation and entrepreneurship, addressing change, and promoting adaptability and mobility in the labour market.

Nevertheless, the 2003 Guidelines reflected the content of the original four pillars and accompanying Guidelines. Thus, there is emphasis on the need to encourage people into training and to update their skills, on the need to reduce burdens on business and to modernize work organization, but no reference to underemployability (setting out active policies to develop job matching and to combat emerging bottlenecks in the new European labour markets). There was also new emphasis on addressing regional disparities together with the need for economic migration from third countries, given the ageing and related skills gaps.

The 2003 Guidelines contained a greater number of specific targets e.g. 25 per cent of the long-term unemployed participating in an active measure in the form of training, work practice, etc. by 2010 with the aim of achieving the average of the three most advanced Member States; by 2010 at least 85 per cent of 22-year-olds in the EU should have completed upper secondary education. Some targets are more vague, e.g. a 'significant reduction' in each Member State in the unemployment gaps for people at a disadvantage and a 'significant reduction' in each Member State

---

[50] Commission Communication, *Taking Stock of Five Years of the European Employment Strategy*, COM(2002) 416.

[51] Council Dec. 2003/578/EC (OJ [2003] L127/13, preambular para. 6. See further Commission Communication, *Streamlining the Annual Economic and Employment Policy Coordination Cycles* (COM(2002) 487).

[52] Council Decision 2003/578/EC (OJ [2003] L197/13. See the influence of the Commission's Communication, *The future of the European Employment Strategy (EES). A strategy for full employment and better jobs for all* (COM(2003) 6).   [53] Annex, p. 17.

in the unemployment gaps between non-EU and EU nationals, according to national targets. The 2003 Guidelines also reduced the number of indicators from 99 in 2002 (35 key indicators and 64 context indicators) to 64 (39 key indicators and 25 context indicators).

The other striking feature of the 2003 Employment Guidelines was the greater emphasis they placed on 'good governance and partnership' in employment policies. A wide range of actors were to be involved: parliamentary bodies, both at European, national, and sub-national level, the Social Partners at national and European level, and other relevant actors, including 'operational services' which should 'deliver the employment policies in an efficient and effective way'. Member States were required to ensure transparency and cost-effectiveness in spending to implement the Employment Guidelines, while complying with the need for sound public finances in line with the Broad Economic Policy Guidelines. Reference is also expressly made to the potential contribution of the Union structural funds, especially the European Social Fund, to support the delivery of policies and to strengthen the institutional capacity in the field of employment.

(b) The 2005 Guidelines

Because the 2003 Employment Guidelines were intended to form part of a three-year policy cycle, they were applied without alteration during 2004.[54] However, following the intervention of the European Employment Taskforce, headed by Wim Kok, which carried out a detailed examination of employment-related policy challenges during 2003,[55] the emphasis for 2004 was on more forceful recommendations and a more effective peer review, rather than more changes to the Guidelines.[56] The relaunch of the Lisbon strategy in 2005[57] precipitated yet another overhaul of the Guidelines because the EU was not on course to achieve its Lisbon objectives.[58] These concerns were articulated more clearly at the Brussels Spring Council in 2004 where the heads of state noted that 'the pace of reform needs to be significantly stepped up if the 2010 targets are to be achieved'.[59] This was confirmed by Wim Kok's 2004 Report[60] which pressed the Member States and Social Partners to give 'urgent attention' to four particular structural challenges (adaptability of workers and enterprises to changing economic conditions and labour market demands; attracting more people into and remaining in the labour market and making work a real option for all; improving the quality of employment; and investing in human capital). More significantly, the Kok report emphasized the need to

---

[54] Council Dec. 2004/740/EC (OJ [2004] L326/45).

[55] Jobs, Jobs, Jobs. Creating More Employment in Europe, November 2003.

[56] Council Dec. 2004/740/EC (OJ [2004] L326/45), second preambular para.

[57] W. Kok, Facing the Challenge: The Lisbon Strategy for Growth and Employment. Report from the High Level Group chaired by Wim Kok (OPEC, Luxembourg, 2004). See further Presidency Conclusions, Brussels, 25–26 March 2004, para. 36.

[58] See e.g. Presidency Conclusions, Thessaloniki 19 and 20 June 2003, para. 48.

[59] Presidency Conclusions, Brussels, 25 and 26 March 2004, para. 7.

[60] Facing the Challenge: The Lisbon Strategy for Growth and Employment. Report from the High Level Group chaired by Wim Kok (OPEC, Luxembourg, 2004).

improve governance of the EES in order to encourage a broader ownership of the Lisbon strategy, not only in national governments but among civil society.

The Commission's own diagnosis of the failure of the Lisbon strategy to deliver was based on the fact that '[t]he overall Lisbon goals were right but the implementation was poor'.[61] Part of the problem seems to have been too many objectives and lack of focus.[62] More fundamentally, the problems also lay with the methodology: OMC was proving too unwieldy.[63] As the Commission pointed out, the Lisbon strategy contained 28 main objectives, 120 sub-objectives, 117 different indicators, and a reporting system which led 25 Member States to produce up to 300 annual reports: 'Nobody reads all of them'.[64] As a result, the Commission proposed a new programme entitled 'Working together for Growth and Jobs'[65] in which it identified 'new actions at European and national level which will help to see our Lisbon vision achieved', without attempting to rewrite the Lisbon strategy (or indeed the ambitious Lisbon targets).[66] This was endorsed by the Brussels European Council 2005 which said that the relaunch of the Lisbon process had two objectives: first, a refocusing on growth and jobs, and, secondly, effective ownership by improving governance procedures at both the European and national levels. This responded to the Commission's concern that responsibilities had been muddled between the Union and the Member States, with 'too many overlapping and bureaucratic reporting procedures and not enough political ownership'.[67]

The new programme was based on a three-year cycle which started in 2005.[68] The most significant change was that the relevant formations of the Council would adopt a package of 'integrated guidelines' consisting of both the Broad Economic Policy Guidelines (BEPGs), adopted by Ecofin, and Employment Guidelines (EGs), adopted by EPSCO based on a proposal by the Commission, thereby integrating macroeconomic, microeconomic, and employment policies into one instrument.[69] Both the Commission and the Member States then respond to these 'integrated guidelines'.[70] In the case of the *Member States*, they draw up 'national reform programmes' (replacing National Action Plans) in respect of the Employment Guidelines and the BEPGs. As a counterpart to the national programmes, the *Commission* presents a 'Community Lisbon programme' covering about 100 measures to be taken at Union level in the

---

[61] IP/05/130, 2 February 2005.

[62] Commission Communication, *Working Together for Growth and Jobs. A New Start for the Lisbon Strategy* COM(2005) 24.

[63] Kok report, see previous n. 57, 42: 'The open method of coordination has fallen far short of expectations'.

[64] This can now be found at: <http://www.euromove.org.uk/index.php?id=6507>.

[65] Communication to the Spring European Council, 'Working Together for Growth and Jobs—a new Start for the Lisbon Strategy' (COM(2005) 24).

[66] COM(2005) 24, 7.   [67] COM(2005) 24, 10.

[68] See Brussels European Council Presidency Conclusions, 22–23 March 2005, para. 39 and the greater detail in SEC(2005) 193.

[69] Ibid., para. (b). See Commission, *Delivering on Growth and Jobs: A New and Integrated Economic and Employment Co-ordination Cycle in the EU*, SEC (2005) 193.

[70] See Brussels European Council Presidency Conclusions, 22–23 March 2005, para. 39(c).

interests of growth and employment, taking account of the need for policy convergence.[71]

The new cycle began in April 2005 with the Commission submitting a proposal for integrated Guidelines for growth and jobs for the period 2005–2008.[72] Guidelines 1–6 related to macroeconomic issues, Guidelines 7–16 concerned microeconomic issues, and Guidelines 17–24 concerned employment issues (see Table 3.2). These Guidelines were then fleshed out by a Commission Recommendation on the BEPG in respect of macro- and microeconomic issues[73] and by a Council Decision in respect of the Employment Guidelines.[74]

The 2005 Employment Guidelines are based around three overarching objectives which mirror those expressed in the 2003 Guidelines (see Table 3.2), albeit amended to reflect the need for territorial as well as social cohesion. In addition, the 2005 Guidelines list a number of other objectives, such as implementing the European Youth Pact[75] and reducing employment gaps for people at a disadvantage. Like their 2003 counterparts, the 2005 Guidelines also emphasized the need for good governance using a wide range of actors and tools to achieve their objectives. The 2005 Guidelines were fleshed out by reference to a number of activities which draw on the activities listed in previous sets of Guidelines, albeit with a greater emphasis on a 'new inter-generational approach'. Guideline 17 contains the overall objective of the EES (full employment, productivity and quality of work, and social and territorial cohesion). This time, however, there are no targets or benchmarks attached.

Table 3.2 Integrated Guidelines for Growth and Jobs 2005–2008, Annex II, Brussels European Council Presidency Conclusions, 16–17 June 2005

Integrated guidelines for growth and jobs 2005–2008—Employment Guidelines

17.	Implement employment policies aimed at achieving full employment, improving quality and productivity at work, and strengthening social and territorial cohesion
18.	Promote a lifecycle approach to work
19.	Ensure inclusive labour markets, enhance work attractiveness, and make work pay for job seekers, including disadvantaged people and the inactive
20.	Improve matching of labour market needs
21.	Promote flexibility combined with employment security and reduce labour market segmentation, having due regard to the role of Social Partners
22.	Ensure employment-friendly labour costs developments and wage-setting mechanisms
23.	Expand and improve investment in human capital
24.	Adapt education and training systems in response to new skill requirements

---

[71] COM(2005) 330.   [72] COM(2005) 141.

[73] <http://ec.europa.eu/economy_finance/publications/publication6432_en.pdf> (last accessed 21 December 2011).

[74] Co. Dec. 2005/600/EC (OJ [2005] L205/21).   [75] COM(2005) 206, considered further in Ch. 12.

The only targets and benchmarks found are those contained in the 2003 Guidelines which have been consolidated and placed in a separate annex.[76] In July 2006 and 2007, as promised, the Council maintained the 2005 Guidelines.[77]

The EES was further reinforced by the 2007–2013 cohesion policy[78] which encourages Member States to submit National Strategic Reference Frameworks that promote growth and better jobs. These new developments address previous concerns that the EES was being undermined by its uncertain relation to macroeconomic policy and the scarcity of financial support for innovative developments. In addition, the Commission launched a mutual learning programme aimed at encouraging the exchange of good practice and the dissemination of the experiences with the EES and EU2020.[79]

(c) 2008 and 2010 Employment Guidelines

The 2008 Employment Guidelines[80] were based on the same eight integrated Guidelines as for 2005 (Table 3.2). The same three objectives were identified (full employment, improving productivity and quality at work, and strengthening economic, social, and territorial cohesion) but this time the EU required that action should be concentrated on three priorities which reflect the debate on flexicurity and employability (see heading 3.4 later in this chapter):

1. Attracting and retaining more people in employment, increasing labour supply and modernizing social protection systems (Guidelines 18–20).

2. Improving the adaptability of workers and enterprises (Guidelines 21–22).

3. Increasing investment in human capital through better education and skills (Guidelines 23 and 24).

The targets and benchmarks have been stripped down to eight:

1. That every unemployed person is offered a job, apprenticeship, additional training or other employability measure; in the case of young persons who have left school within no more than four months by 2010 and in the case of adults within no more than 12 months.

2. That 25 per cent of long-term unemployment should participate by 2010 in an active measure in the form of training, retraining, work practice, or other employability measure, with the aim of achieving the average of the three most advanced Member States.

3. That jobseekers throughout the EU are able to consult all job vacancies advertised through Member States' employment services.

4. An increase by five years, at EU level, of the effective average exit age from the labour market by 2010 compared to 2001.

---

[76] Council Dec. 2005/600/EC.
[77] Council Dec. 2006/544/EC (OJ [2006] L215/26); Council Dec. 2007/491/EC (OJ [2007] L183/25).
[78] COM(2006) 281.
[79] <http://www.mutual-learning-employment.net/> (last accessed 21 December 2011).
[80] Council Dec. 2008/618/EC (OJ [2008] L198/47).

5. The provision of childcare by 2010 to at least 90 per cent of children between three years old and the mandatory school age and at least 33 per cent of children under three years of age.

6. An EU average rate of no more than 10 per cent early school leavers.

7. At least 85 per cent of 22-year-olds in the EU should have completed upper secondary education by 2010.

8. That the EU average level of participation in lifelong learning should be at least 12.5 per cent of the adult working-age population (25 to 64 age group).

These Guidelines and targets were maintained for 2009[81] and should have been maintained for 2010. However, the financial crisis and the expiry of the Lisbon strategy precipitated a further rethink. There was still concern that the 24 Guidelines did not set clear enough priorities and the links between them could have been stronger. So they were replaced by the EU2020 Integrated Guidelines based on the EU2020 objectives and incorporating the EU2020 headline targets (see further Section C). There are now six Economic Guidelines and four Employment Guidelines. The four Employment Guidelines concern:[82]

1. Increasing labour market participation of women and men, reducing structural unemployment and promoting job quality.

2. Developing a skilled workforce responding to labour market needs and promoting lifelong learning.

3. Improving the quality and performance of education and training systems at all levels and increasing participation in tertiary or equivalent education.

4. Promoting social inclusion and combating poverty.

These Guidelines were maintained for 2011 and 2012.[83]

Thus, in a period of less than 15 years, the Guidelines have been revamped and revamped again. Their architecture has varied and with the years, they have slimmed down rather than fattened up, but the basic prescription remains essentially the same: greater labour market participation; more active labour market policies; modernizing social models; combating segmentation in the labour market; and greater flexicurity.

3.3. Assessment

The tension, long recognized, between deregulation as a means of achieving the flexibility necessary to help fight against unemployment, and the need for social rights[84] can be seen very clearly in the Luxembourg strategy. The deregulatory aspects of the

---

[81] Council Dec. 2009/536/EC (OJ [2009] L180/16).

[82] Council Dec. 2010/707/EU (OJ [2010] L308/46).

[83] Council Dec. 2011/308/EU (OJ [2011] L138/56) and Council Dec. 2012/238/EU (OJ [2012] L119/47).

[84] See S. Sciarra, 'The "Making" of EU Labour Law and the "Future" of Labour Lawyers' in C. Barnard *et al.* (eds.), *The Future of Labour Law: Liber Amicorum Sir Bob Hepple QC* (Hart Publishing, Oxford, 2004).

Employment Strategy was most obviously seen in the original entrepreneurship pillar and in aspects of the employability and adaptability pillars. On the other hand, the emphasis on social rights could be found in the equal opportunities pillar as well as in social policy more generally. While the pillars are long gone, that rather unhappy policy mix can still be seen in the 2010 Employment Guidelines. For example, under Guideline 7 the Council talks of Member States encouraging 'the right framework conditions for wage bargaining and labour cost development consistent with price stability and productivity trends'. This essentially means keeping a lid on pay rises, ensuring that they are in line with productivity. On the other hand, the same paragraph talks of 'gender equality including equal pay', and the integration into the labour market of young people, people with disabilities, legal migrants and other vulnerable groups'.

The Treaty of Amsterdam does not itself contain an obviously deregulatory agenda. Not only did the Treaty incorporate the Social Policy Agreement into the new Social Title in the EC Treaty (and now the TFEU), but Article 2 EC (now repealed but broadly replaced by Article 3 TEU) talked of 'a high level of employment *and* social protection' (emphasis added) and 'equality between men and women', as well as 'sustainable and non-inflationary growth, a high degree of competitiveness and convergence of economic performance'. Nor did the Lisbon Treaty envisage an overtly deregulatory agenda with its key reference to a 'social market economy'

Read together, the Treaties of Amsterdam and Lisbon and the Luxembourg strategy demonstrate the Union's attempts to find a 'third way' between the 'Anglo-Saxon' model of deregulation, low unemployment, and fewer welfare benefits, and the European model of job protection, high unemployment, and generous welfare provision. This third way was to create a new European employment model which would balance social protection, competitiveness, and welfare provision with sound finance.[85] The aim is to achieve competitiveness through creating highly productive workplaces, rather than combating unemployment through the creation of low-paid, low-productivity 'entry jobs'.[86] Thus, the emphasis is on flexibility for firms combined with security for workers. This is referred to in the jargon as 'flexicurity'. [87]

3.4. Flexicurity

'Flexicurity' is the theme found in a variety of Commission documents dating back to the mid-1990s,[88] the Commission's Communications and, for the first time, in the 1998 Employment Guidelines under the Adaptability Pillar. Most important is the Commission's

---

[85] See further J. Kenner, 'The EC Employment Title and the "Third Way": Making Soft Law Work' (1999) 15 *IJCLLIR* 33.

[86] Deakin and Reed, previous, at n. 37.

[87] See more generally J. Kenner, 'New Frontiers in EU Labour Law: From Flexicurity to Flex-security' in S. Currie and M. Dougan (eds.), *Fifty Years of the Treaty of Rome* (Oxford: Hart Publishing, 2009).

[88] Commission, *Partnership for a New Organisation of Work*, COM(97) 127 final; Commission, *Modernising and Improving Social Protection in the European Union* COM(97) 102 final. See further Commission Communication: A Concerted Action for Modernising Social Protection COM(99) 347; Council Conclusions on the strengthening of co-operation for modernizing and improving social protection (OJ [2000] C8/7); and Commission, *Modernising the Organisation of Work*, COM(98) 592.

Communication: *Towards Common Principles of Flexicurity: More and Better Jobs through Flexibility and Security.*[89] According to the Commission, 'Flexicurity promotes a combination of flexible labour markets and adequate security'. It says flexicurity is not about deregulation, giving employers freedom to dissolve their responsibilities towards the employee and to give them little security. Instead, flexicurity is about bringing people into good jobs and developing their talents. The Commission continues:[90]

> Flexibility, on the one hand, is about successful moves ('transitions') during one's life course: from school to work, from one job to another, between unemployment or inactivity and work, and from work to retirement. It is not limited to more freedom for companies to recruit or dismiss, and it does not imply that open-ended contracts are obsolete. It is about progress of workers into better jobs, 'upward mobility' and optimal development of talent. Flexibility is also about flexible work organisations, capable of quickly and effectively mastering new productive needs and skills, and about facilitating the combination of work and private responsibilities. Security, on the other hand, is more than just the security to maintain one's job: it is about equipping people with the skills that enable them to progress in their working lives, and helping them find new employment [i.e. from 'job security' to 'employment security']. It is also about adequate unemployment benefits to facilitate transitions. Finally, it encompasses training opportunities for all workers, especially the low skilled and older workers.

The Commission recognizes that delivering on flexicurity has four policy components:[91]

- *Flexible and reliable contractual arrangements* (from the perspective of the employer and the employee, of 'insiders' and 'outsiders') through modern labour laws, collective agreements and work organisation;
- *Comprehensive lifelong learning (LLL)* strategies to ensure the continual adaptability and employability of workers, particularly the most vulnerable;
- *Effective active labour market policies (ALMP)* that help people cope with rapid change, reduce unemployment spells and ease transitions to new jobs;
- *Modern social security systems* that provide adequate income support, encourage employment and facilitate labour market mobility. This includes broad coverage of social protection provisions (unemployment benefits, pensions and healthcare) that help people combine work with private and family responsibilities such as childcare.

For the purposes of this book it is the first limb ('flexible and reliable contractual arrangements') that is of most interest. In its earlier Green Paper, *Modernising labour law to meet the challenges of the 21st century*,[92] the Commission recognized that with changes in the nature of production, business needs workers on a variety of different contracts, with those on permanent contracts at the core but whose work is supplemented by those on atypical contracts (e.g. zero-hours, temporary, part-time, fixed-term, seasonal contracts). This creates a system of insiders, who often benefit from good employment protection legislation, and outsiders who have little or no employment protection. While for some people, such atypical contracts are a good way of getting into the labour market and on to standard contracts, for others they are a trap and they

---

[89] COM(2007) 359.   [90] COM(2007) 359, 4–5.   [91] COM(2007) 359, 12.   [92] COM(2006) 708.

remain in a succession of short-term, low quality jobs with inadequate social protection, leaving them in a vulnerable position. There is also a strong gender and intergenerational dimension to the risk of having a weaker position in the labour market: women, older, and also younger, workers engaged on non-standard contracts have fewer chances to improve their position in the labour market. Even the position of insiders might not be as good as would first appear: the very existence of high levels of employment protection legislation provide a disincentive to move from one job to another and this in turn may affect productivity.[93] Further, while high levels of employment protection legislation can encourage enterprises to invest in training and promotes loyalty and higher productivity of employees, it can also serve as a disincentive for employers to hire in the first place.

So what can be done to enable firms to enjoy this flexibility, particularly in terms of employment contracts, while at the same time giving some protection to those on atypical contracts. First, the Commission drew up eight flexicurity principles (see Table 3.3) to help Member States in establishing flexicurity strategies. Second, it identified some good practice from other Member States which other states might learn from. For example, it uses the UK as an example of a 'targeted approach' where employees, after a certain period of service enjoy full employment protection. By contrast workers enjoy less—but at least some—employment protection. The Commission also holds up Denmark as an example of a country which has achieved a lifecycle approach to work: Denmark enjoys 'light' employment protection legislation, intensive active labour market measures, and substantial investment in training as well as high unemployment benefits with strong conditionality.

Third, and inspired by these examples, the Commission identifies four 'flexicurity pathways': different prescriptions for different systems as to how to achieve the holy grail of marrying flexibility and security. For example, Pathway 1 'tackling contractual segmentation' is of interest to countries 'where the key challenge is segmented labour markets, with insiders and outsiders. This pathway would aim to distribute flexibility and security more evenly over the workforce. It would provide entry ports into employment for newcomers and it would promote their progress into better contractual arrangements'. So the Commission suggests that within *contractual arrangements*, this pathway would aim to improve the position of workers on fixed term contracts, agency work, on-call work, etc. It would ensure that adequate protection is offered to these workers, for example equal pay and a minimum number of working hours for on-call workers. Secondary employment conditions, such as coverage by occupational pension funds and access to training, would also apply to these workers. Legislation and collective agreements would limit consecutive use of non-standard contracts and promote timely progress into better contracts. A complementary approach would be to redesign the open-ended contract. In this option, workers would have an open-ended contract from the very beginning of the employment relationship with their employer and would no longer, as is now often the case, start with a series of fixed term or agency contracts. The

---

[93] COM(2006) 708, 8–9; COM(2007) 359, 5–6.

Table 3.3 Flexicurity principles

---

(1) Flexicurity involves flexible and reliable contractual arrangements (from the perspective of the employer and the employee, of insiders and outsiders); comprehensive lifelong learning strategies; effective active labour market policies; and modern social security systems. Its objective is to reinforce the implementation of the Growth and Jobs Strategy, create more and better jobs, and strengthen the European social models, by providing new forms of flexibility and security to increase adaptability, employment and social cohesion.

(2) Flexicurity implies a balance between rights and responsibilities for employers, workers, job seekers and public authorities.

(3) Flexicurity should be adapted to the specific circumstances, labour markets and industrial relations of the Member States. Flexicurity is not about one single labour market model or a single policy strategy.

(4) Flexicurity should reduce the divide between insiders and outsiders on the labour market. Current insiders need support to be prepared for and protected during job to job transitions. Current outsiders—including those out of work, where women, the young and migrants are over-represented—need easy entry points to work and stepping-stones to enable progress into stable contractual arrangements.

(5) Internal (within the enterprise) as well as external (from one enterprise to another) flexicurity should be promoted. Sufficient flexibility in recruitment and dismissal must be accompanied by secure transitions from job to job. Upward mobility needs to be facilitated, as well as between unemployment or inactivity and work. High-quality workplaces with capable leadership, good organization of work, and continuous upgrading of skills are part of the objectives of flexicurity. Social protection needs to support, not inhibit, mobility.

(6) Flexicurity should support gender equality by promoting equal access to quality employment for women and men, and by offering possibilities to reconcile work and family life as well as providing equal opportunities to migrants, young, disabled and older workers.

(7) Flexicurity requires a climate of trust and dialogue between public authorities and social partners, where all are prepared to take responsibility for change, and produce balanced policy packages.

(8) Flexicurity policies have budgetary costs and should be pursued also with a view to contribute to sound and financially sustainable budgetary policies. They should also aim at a fair distribution of costs and benefits, especially between businesses, individuals and public budgets, with particular attention to the specific situation of SMEs. At the same time, effective flexicurity policies can contribute to such an overall objective.

---

open-ended contract would be redesigned to include a progressive build-up of job protection (as in the UK). It would start with a basic level of job protection, and protection would build up progressively with job tenure, until 'full' protection was achieved. This 'tenure track approach' would guarantee automatic progress into better contractual conditions; the risk of getting 'stuck' in less protected contracts would thus be reduced. The pathway then also makes concrete suggestions in respect of lifelong learning, active labour market policies, and social security systems.

By contrast, pathway 4, 'Improving opportunities for benefit recipients and informally employed workers' is of 'interest to countries which have experienced substantive economic restructuring in the recent past, resulting in high numbers of people on long-term benefits with difficult perspectives of returning to the labour market. It would aim at improving opportunities for benefit recipients and shifting from informal to formal employment through development of effective active labour market policies and lifelong learning systems combined with an adequate level of unemployment benefits'. In these countries, traditional, often industrial, enterprises have been forced to make redundant large numbers of people. Unemployed workers receive benefits that are often designed as 'labour market exit benefits' rather than 'transition into new employment'. Investments in active labour market policies are limited and chances of finding new employment are low. New jobs often have low levels of protection, while some measures that apply to old jobs may be too restrictive. Many people have recourse to the informal economy.[94] Weak vocational training systems make it difficult for low skilled workers and young people without work experience to adjust to the requirements of the labour market. In respect of contractual arrangements, the pathway suggests that workers employed in emerging sectors of the economy, many of whom work on a fixed-term or on-call basis, are offered adequate levels of protection. Regularizing informal work could be made more attractive by improving informal workers' rights and providing access to professional training. Higher regularized employment would lead to increased tax revenues and social contributions. Transitions to formal employment would also require further reforms of labour taxation and business registration requirements, as well as strengthening of labour inspectorates and financial institutions combating informal work. Workers on open-ended contracts would benefit from increased investments in their training and early action in case of threatened redundancy.

Thus, the flexicurity narrative is presented in terms of a win-win situation:

> Flexibility internal to the enterprise not only promotes corporate productivity but also the quality of working life...Security for workers can also give benefits to the enterprise in the form of a more stable, versatile and motivated workforce.[95]

This was part of the bigger picture painted in the 1990s/early 2000s that saw social policy as an input into the productive process[96] and not a burden on it. As the

---

[94] In the *Modernisation of Labour Law* Green Paper (COM(2006) 708, 14, undeclared work is identified as a 'particularly worrying and enduring feature of today's labour markets...Being the main contributing factor to social dumping, it is responsible not only for the exploitation of workers but also for distortions to competition'.   [95] COM(98) 592, 3.

[96] See S. Deakin and F. Wilkinson, 'Rights vs Efficiency: the Economic Case for Transnational Labour Standards' (1994) 23 *ILJ* 289, 295–6.

Commission said in its White Paper on Social Policy 'the pursuit of high social standards should not be seen as a cost but also as a key element in the competitive formula';[97] and in the Medium Term Social Action Programme it talks of encouraging 'high labour standards as part of competitive Europe'.[98] However, some commentators are sceptical of claims that there is a genuine *quid pro quo* between flexibility for employers and security for workers. For example, Ball, writing about the original EES Guidelines, notes that the main thrust of the employability pillar is to place an onus on individuals to enhance their own value by learning new and higher skills, without any correlative obligation on employers to offer security of employment.[99]

It could therefore be argued that, through the EES, the EU is developing a new type of social citizenship, a citizenship which is no longer based merely on an eclectic range of social rights and social security[100] but one which requires an active involvement in the market.[101] For individuals—all individuals, young and old—this means equipping themselves with the necessary skills to make themselves more employable and then going out to find a job or moving between jobs as and when the need so arises. Yet while having a job is seen as an important means for integrating the socially excluded, the focus on employment risks creating another group of the socially excluded—those who cannot work or, for family reasons, do not wish to work.

C. THE LISBON AND EU2020 STRATEGIES

1. INTRODUCTION

On 23–24 March 2000 the European Council held a special meeting in Lisbon to agree a 'new strategic goal' for the Union in order to 'strengthen employment, economic reform and social cohesion as part of a knowledge-based economy'.[102] This strategic goal was for the Union to become 'the most competitive and dynamic knowledge based economy in the world, capable of sustainable economic growth with more and better jobs and greater social cohesion'.[103] The heads of state agreed that achieving the Lisbon goal required an overall strategy aimed at:

---

[97] COM(94) 333, introduction, para. 5.

[98] Social Europe 1/95, 9, 18, 19.

[99] See n. 12. For further discussion of—and a challenge to—the flexibility agenda, see G. Standing, *The Precariat: the New Dangerous Class* (Bloomsbury, London, 2011).

[100] Cf. the Supiot report, *Beyond Employment: Changes in Work and the Future of Labour Law in Europe* (OUP, Oxford, 2001) 228.

[101] The language of 'active citizenship' is used by the Commission in its Communication in European policies concerning youth: COM(2005) 206, 8.

[102] Lisbon Presidency Conclusions, 23 and 24 March 2000.   [103] Para. 5.

1. Preparing the transition to a knowledge-based economy and society by better policies for the information society and R&D, as well as stepping up the process of structural reform for competitiveness and innovation and by completing the internal market;

2. Modernising the European social model, investing in people, and combating social exclusion;

3. Sustaining the healthy economic outlook and favourable growth prospects by applying an appropriate macro-economic policy mix.[104]

As originally conceived, Lisbon was about harnessing the internal market strategy, the Broad Economic Policy Guidelines and the Employment Guidelines[105] to enable the Union to regain 'the conditions for *full employment*', not just a high level of employment as envisaged by Article 2 EC, the position now found in Article 3 TEU. Subsequently, the 2001 Göteborg European Council incorporated the environment as a further pillar to the strategy. The Lisbon strategy was revised in 2005 and replaced by EU2020 in June 2010.

The EU2020 strategy[106] had to respond to the economic crisis starting in the Autumn of 2008. This crisis revealed the extravagance of the targets prescribed by the Lisbon strategy: Europe was far from being the most dynamic knowledge-based economy in the world in 2010, quite the contrary. The crisis wiped out any gains in economic growth and job creation which had occurred over the previous decade—GDP fell by 4 per cent in 2009, industrial production dropped back to the levels of the 1990s, and 23 million people (10 per cent of the active population) were unemployed. Public finances were also severely affected, with deficits at 7 per cent of GDP on average and debt levels at over 80 per cent of GDP.[107]

These bald statistics tend to suggest that the Lisbon strategy was a failure:[108] the goals were too ambitious; there were too many targets; the Commission had no real powers to use against defaulting states; there was a lack of commitment by a number of states to the strategy, many of which saw it as a bureaucratic exercise which had little effect on their day-to-day government; and, at a time of the largest expansion of the European Union and major Treaty reform, insufficient attention was paid to realizing the Lisbon strategy and communicating and promoting its benefits. On the other hand, the shift in emphasis identified by the Lisbon strategy in fact has marked a more permanent and fundamental change in the EU's approach to workers: workers

---

[104] Ibid.

[105] Brussels Presidency Conclusions, 20 and 21 March 2003, para. 17.

[106] COM(2010) 2020.

[107] Commission Communication, Europe 2020. *A Strategy for Smart, Sustainable and Inclusive Growth*, COM(2010) 2020, 5.

[108] The Swedish prime minister, Frederick Reinfeldt, is reported as having recognized this: EurActiv, 'Sweden admits Lisbon Agenda "failure"', 3 June 2009, <http://www.euractiv.com/en/priorities/sweden-admits-lisbon-agenda-failure/article-182797> (last accessed 19 July 2010).

are no longer seen as (passive) beneficiaries of social rights. Instead they are viewed as having to take (active) responsibility for updating their skills and making themselves employable.

In other words, the Lisbon and European Employment strategies represented a shift in emphasis from the enactment of employment *law* (the body of rules directly concerned with the employment relationship) to the creation of employment *policy* (measures directly concerned with the creation and maintenance of employment, including measures concerned with training).[109] As Freedland observes, vocational training policy seems to lie within a relatively highly consensual area of convergence between economic policy and social policy (particularly if dressed up as education policy):[110] it has always been potentially difficult to deny the generally ameliorative nature of vocational training policy. On the other hand, while it may seem overridingly important to ensure that vocational training is provided for all groups in society, especially to the young, this may result in an under-awareness of, or under-concern with, the potential of vocational training arrangements to erode labour standards. Freedland therefore argues that there is a danger that an educational policy in favour of ever greater flexibility and adaptability in vocational training might be conducive to an over-ready endorsement of all forms and types of flexibility as a matter of employment policy.

2. THE AIMS

2.1. Introduction

The modernization agenda made concrete by the Lisbon strategy fed directly into the less ambitious Europe 2020 programme adopted in March 2010. It also puts forward three mutually reinforcing priorities:

1. *Smart growth*: developing an economy based on knowledge and innovation.

2. *Sustainable growth*: promoting a more resource efficient, greener and more competitive economy.

3. *Inclusive growth*: fostering a high-employment economy delivering social and territorial cohesion.

These three priorities are accompanied by five headline targets:

1. Seventy-five per cent of the 20–64-year-olds to be employed.

2. Three per cent of the EU's GDP (public and private combined) to be invested in R&D/innovation.

---

[109] See M. Freedland, 'Employment Policy', in P. Davies, A. Lyon-Caen, S. Sciarra, and S. Simitis (eds.), *European Community Labour Law: Principles and Perspectives. Liber Amicorum Lord Wedderburn of Charlton* (Clarendon, Oxford, 1996) 97.

[110] M. Freedland, 'Vocational Training in EC Law and Policy—Education, Employment or Welfare' (1996) 25 *ILJ* 110, 118–19.

3. The 20/20/20 climate/energy targets to be met.[111]
4. Reducing school drop-out rates below 10 per cent and at least 40 per cent of 30–34-year-olds completing third-level education.
5. At least 20 million fewer people in or at risk of poverty and social exclusion.[112]

And these targets are supported by 'seven flagship initiatives to catalyse progress under each priority theme'. We shall focus on the third priority, inclusive growth, which is directly relevant for the purposes of this chapter, and the flagship initiative, 'An agenda for new skills and jobs'.

2.2. Inclusive growth

(a) Introduction

The 'inclusive growth' priority is the direct descendant of the third limb of the Lisbon strategy of 'modernising the European social model' and the active labour market policies it envisaged. So, the Commission says that '[i]nclusive growth means empowering people through high levels of employment, investing in skills, fighting poverty and modernising labour markets, training and social protection systems' to help people anticipate and manage change, and build a cohesive society.[113] It continues: 'Implementing flexicurity principles and enabling people to acquire new skills to adapt to new conditions and potential career shifts will be key'. Further, in a reference to the principles underpinning its 2007[114] and 2008 Social Agenda communications,[115] the Commission says that inclusive growth is also about 'ensuring access and opportunities for all throughout the lifecycle'.[116]

(b) The Lisbon Strategy: Modernizing the European Social Model

The original Lisbon strategy required the 'European social model' to be modernized. According to the Lisbon Conclusions, it will come about by 'investing in people and building an active welfare state'.[117] Inspiration is drawn from the successful Nordic model,[118] which combines open markets and job flexibility with all the support employers need to restructure their workforce to meet changing demands. The Nordic approach is endorsed by strong trade unions because of the tripartite pact between employers, trade unions, and the state, and a generous system of social welfare to cushion the effect of change. High levels of public expenditure also produce highly educated school leavers

---

[111] I.e. greenhouse gas emissions 20 per cent (or even 30 per cent, if the conditions are right) lower than 1990; 20 per cent of energy from renewables; 20 per cent increase in energy efficiency.
[112] See further K. Armstrong, 'The Lisbon Agenda and Europe 2020: From Governance of Coordination to the Coordination of Governance', Queen Mary University of London, School of Law Legal Studies research paper No. 89/2011 who notes the paradox that the response to the crisis, particularly in the form of dramatic budget cuts, may well undermine the objectives of EU 2020.
[113] COM(2010) 2020, 16.
[114] *Opportunities, access and solidarity: towards a new social vision for 21st century Europe*, COM(2007) 726.
[115] *Renewed Social Agenda: Opportunities, Access and Solidarity*, COM(2008) 412.
[116] Ibid.   [117] Para. 24.
[118] See further Ch. 2. Cf 'Europe's banker talks tough. Draghi says Continent's Social Model is "Gone"', *Wall St. Jo.* 24 Feb. 2012.

and graduates and a good health service.[119] This has led to steady economic growth for over 50 years, low levels of inflation, and relatively low levels of unemployment (between 5 and 6 per cent).

The Lisbon strategy therefore identified four elements to this process of modernization: education and training; more and better jobs; modernizing social protection; and promoting social inclusion. For our purposes, it is the 'more and better jobs' category that is of particular importance. The Lisbon strategy looked to the Luxembourg process, as amended by the mid-term review,[120] to give substance to the goal of 'more and better jobs'. However, it recognized that the Luxembourg process needed to be better targeted. The heads of state then agreed at Lisbon to set employment rate targets for what would amount to 'full employment', something they had not managed at Luxembourg.[121] The targets were ambitious: 'raising the employment rate from an average of 61 per cent today to as close as possible to 70 per cent by 2010 and to increase the number of women in employment from an average of 51 per cent today to more than 60 per cent by 2010'. An additional target was added by the Stockholm European Council, namely increasing the average EU employment rate among older men and women (55–64) to 50 per cent by 2010.[122] These targets made for convenient round numbers (70 per cent/60 per cent/50 per cent) but proved overoptimistic except in the case of female employment where the figure currently stands at 63 per cent (although male employment stands at 76 per cent).[123]

While the Lisbon strategy focused on 'more' jobs, the question of 'better' jobs was left to be fleshed out by the Commission in its Social Policy Agenda adopted in June 2000. It said that 'growth is not an end in itself but essentially a means of achieving a better standard of living for all. Social policy underpins economic policy and employment has not only economic but also a social value'.[124] Against this backcloth, said the Commission, is the 'promotion of quality as the driving force for a thriving economy...quality of work, quality in industrial relations and quality of social policy'.[125] Quality of *work* includes better jobs and more ways of combining working life with personal life. It is based on 'high skills, fair labour standards and decent levels of occupational health and safety'.[126] Quality of *social policy* implies a high level of social protection, good social services, real opportunities for all and the guarantee of fundamental and social rights.[127] Quality of *industrial relations* is determined by the capacity to build consensus on both diagnosis and ways and means of taking forward the adaptation and modernization agenda.[128] The heads of state meeting at

---

[119] P. Toynbee, 'The most successful society the world has ever known: The Nordic model mixes welfare and economic success, but Sweden's Social Democrats are at a risk from a loss of confidence', *The Guardian*, 25 October 2005, 33; N. Watt, 'Europe's leaders look north, but has Sweden really got the best of both worlds? The next EU summit will highlight the Nordic model of steady growth and social protection as a solution to economic slumber', *The Guardian*, 5 January 2006, 20.

[120] See the Presidency Conclusions of the Barcelona European Council, 15–16 March 2002, para. 30.

[121] Cf. Commission Communication, 'Proposal for Guidelines for Member States Employment Policies 1998', COM(97) 497, Section I where the Commission proposed a target of increasing the employment rate from 60.4 per cent to 65 per cent thereby creating at least 12 million new jobs.

[122] Stockholm European Council, 23 and 24 March 2001, para. 9. In 2010 it was only 46 per cent (as compared with 62 per cent in the US and Japan: COM(2010) 2020, 5).

[123] COM(2010) 2020, 5.   [124] COM(2000) 379, 13.   [125] Ibid.

[126] Ibid.   [127] Ibid.   [128] COM(2000) 379, 14.

Nice in December 2000 agreed that '[q]uality of training, quality in work, quality of industrial relations and quality of social policy as a whole are essential factors if the European Union is to achieve the goals it has set itself regarding competitiveness and full employment'.[129] Thus, quality was seen as a 'key element' linking competitiveness and social cohesion which the Commission depicts in a diagram illustrating the virtuous circle linking economic, social, and employment policies in a mutually reinforcing manner.[130]

(c) EU2020: Inclusive growth

The 2020 document proposes a more limited set of targets than the Lisbon strategy, although these are still ambitious. These EU targets, which have to be translated into individualized national targets and trajectories, include 75 per cent of the population aged 20–64 to be employed (currently it is 69 per cent)—achieved by getting more people into work, especially women, the young, older and low-skilled people and legal migrants; 3 per cent of the EU's GDP to be invested in R&D; and the share of early school leavers to be under 10 per cent. These targets are interrelated. As the Commission notes, better educational levels help employability and progress in increasing the employment rate helps to reduce poverty. A greater capacity for research and development as well as innovation across all sectors of the economy, combined with increased resource efficiency, will improve competitiveness and foster job creation.

Under the heading 'Inclusive Growth—a high employment economy delivering economic, social and territorial cohesion', the Commission has two flagship initiatives, the first, and the most relevant for us, 'An Agenda for new skills and jobs'[131] aims 'to create conditions for modernising labour markets with a view to raising employment levels and ensuring the sustainability of our social models. This means empowering people through the acquisition of new skills to enable our current and future workforce to adapt to new conditions and potential career shifts, reduce unemployment and raise labour productivity'. The document then distinguishes between what can be done at EU level and at national level. At EU level, this includes: defining and implementing the second phase of the flexicurity agenda, together with European social partners; identifying ways to better manage economic transitions and to fight unemployment and raise activity rates; adapting the legislative framework, in line with 'smart' regulation principles, to evolving work patterns (e.g. working time, posting of workers) and new risks for health and safety at work; facilitating and promoting intra-EU labour mobility and better match labour supply with demand, with appropriate financial support from the structural funds, notably the European Social Fund (ESF); and strengthening the capacity of social partners and making full use of the problem-solving potential of the social dialogue at all levels (EU, national/regional, sectoral, company). At national level, Member States will need to do the following: implement their national pathways for flexicurity to reduce labour

---

[129] European Council's Social Policy Agenda, Annex I to the Nice Presidency Conclusions, para. 26.
[130] Communication entitled 'Employment and Social Policies: a Framework for investing in quality' COM(2001) 313.
[131] The other is the 'European Platform against Poverty'.

market segmentation and facilitate transitions as well as facilitating the reconciliation of work and family life; review and regularly monitor the efficiency of tax and benefit systems so as to make work pay with a particular focus on the low skilled, whilst removing measures that discourage self-employment; and promote new forms of work-life balance and active ageing policies and increase gender equality.

3. THE METHODS

3.1. Introduction

According to the Presidency Conclusions, implementing the Lisbon strategy was to be achieved in part by improving the existing processes (i.e. through the Broad Economic Policy Guidelines together with, for example, the Luxembourg EES processes, now synchronized in terms of calendars),[132] and in part through the 'new' approach, the so-called Open Method of Co-ordination[133] (OMC) together with corporate social responsibility (CSR). In its social Policy Agenda 2000, the Commission went further and emphasized that OMC was just one of a number of means by which the strategy would be realized,[134] a view endorsed by the Nice European Council.[135] The other methods were: legislation, adopted via the legislative or collective routes,[136] developing or adapting standards, social dialogue, and the structural funds, especially the European Social Funds. This policy mix has been followed in EU2020 albeit that the EU2020 document itself is less explicit about the means.

Thus, using Daintith's distinction,[137] the Commission envisages a mix of not only government by *imperium* (attaining objectives by commands—both hard and soft—backed by sanctions) and *dominium* (attaining objectives through the use of government wealth) but also governance by private actors (such as the social partners and corporations). In this section we shall examine three of the main means for achieving the Lisbon strategy: legislation and the social dialogue, CSR, and, most importantly, OMC.

3.2. Open Method of Co-ordination

(a) What is it?

The OMC is described as a 'means of spreading best practice and achieving greater convergence towards the main EU goals[138] through common targets and Guidelines for Member States, sometimes backed up by national action plans.'[139] It relies on regular

---

[132] Barcelona Presidency Conclusions, 15 and 16 March 2001, para. 49.
[133] Paras. 7 and 37.   [134] COM(2000) 379, para. 3.3
[135] Nice Presidency Conclusions, 7–9 December 2000, para. 28.
[136] See further Ch. 2.
[137] T. Daintith, 'The Techniques of Government', in J. Jowell and D. Oliver (eds.), *The Changing Constitution* 3rd edn (OUP, Oxford, 1994) 209.
[138] COM(2002) 629, para. 14.
[139] The European Governance White Paper (COM(2001) 428, 21).

monitoring of progress to meet those targets, allowing Member States to compare their efforts and learn from the experience of others.[140] In the specific context of the Lisbon strategy, the European Council explained that OMC means:[141]

- · fixing Guidelines for the Union combined with specific timetables for achieving the goals which they set in the short, medium, and long terms;

- establishing, where appropriate, quantitative and qualitative indicators and benchmarks against the best in the world and tailored to the needs of different Member States and sectors as a means of comparing best practice;

- translating these European Guidelines into national and regional policies by setting specific targets and adopting measures, taking into account national and regional differences;

- periodic monitoring, evaluation, and peer review organized as mutual learning processes.

Thus, the Lisbon European Council confirmed the EES (and the economic governance) methodology, gave it a new title, and extended it to other areas (e.g. social inclusion and pension reform (since 2001), information society/eEurope, enterprise promotion research, and innovation, education, and training).[142] However, there is no single 'OMC' methodology. As Belgian minister Frank Vandenbroucke vividly put it,[143] open co-ordination is not some kind of 'fixed recipe' that can be applied to whichever issue, but is instead 'a kind of cookbook that contains various recipes, lighter and heavier ones'.[144] OMC for policy areas such as the EES, BEPG, and social inclusion is of the 'heaviest' variety and the most fully institutionalized. In the case of the EES and the BEPG, it is also Treaty based and backed up by some law sanctions.[145]

    In the context of the EES and economic governance, OMC can be broken down into five component parts: (1) agreeing common objectives for the Union; (2) establishing common indictors as a means of comparing best practice and measuring progress; (3) translating the EU objectives into national/regional policies through the development of

---

[140] Ibid.   [141] Ibid.

[142] The Lisbon Treaty did not formally recognize 'OMC' as such. It did, however, in Art. 5(2) TFEU say that '[t]he Union shall take measures to ensure coordination of the employment policies of the Member States, in particular by defining guidelines for these policies'.

[143] He played a key part in launching the social inclusion and pensions processes during his country's presidency of the Council in 2001.

[144] Cited in J. Zeitlin, 'Introduction: The Open Method of Coordination in Question' in J. Zeitlin and P. Pochet with L. Magnusson (eds.), *The Open Method of Coordination in Action: The European Employment and Social Inclusion Strategies'* (PIE/Peter Lang, Brussels, 2005). See further Final report of Working Group XI on Social Europe, CONV 516/1/03, para. 39: 'An empirical approach has been used to develop and adapt this method to the specific characteristics of each field of action. The method is therefore applied in different ways to different areas, with an ad hoc procedure being worked out each time. That is why we sometimes speak of open methods of coordination, in the plural'.

[145] For a helpful catalogue of the differences between the OMC processes, see S. Borrás and K. Jacobsson, 'The Open Method of Coordination and New Governance Patterns in the EU' (2004) 11 *JEPP* 185, 193–4. For a full discussion, see C. Sabel and J. Zeitlin (eds.), *Experimentalist Governance in the European Union: Towards a New Architecture* (Oxford, OUP, 2010).

National Action Plans/National Reform Programmes; (4) publishing reports analysing and assessing the National Action Plans; and (5) establishing an EU Action Programme to promote policy co-operation and transactional exchange of learning and good practice.

In other areas, a 'lighter' approach is used involving only certain elements of the broader methodology such as scoreboards, peer review, and exchange of good practices. For example, in the field of education and training, bench-marking is the principal policy instrument,[146] referring to concrete targets for which it is possible to measure progress.[147]

(b) Perspectives on OMC

Borrás and Jacobssen argue that OMC perches on the fence between the 'Community method' and the international method. It coaxes Member States into co-ordinating their national public actions within a collectively decided framework, spreads widely into different policy areas, and cuts across the national-EU borders using persuasion but not coercion.[148] Rhodes describes it as heterarchical, adopting a 'new' problem-solving logic based on deliberation and policy learning.[149] Most commentators agree that it should increase democracy in the EU through the enhanced role for deliberation among policy makers and participation of a broad range of actors at different levels.[150]

Advocates of OMC therefore argue that it offers a 'third way' for European social policy between regulatory competition (with the risk of a race to the bottom) and har-monization (with the risk of ill-suited uniformity). According to the Commission,[151] OMC has greater visibility, encourages a strategic and integrated approach, puts a par-ticular issue in the mainstream, mobilizes all relevant actors, and encourages mutual learning. It can also be used in areas which are not so easily susceptible to regulation either because of the subject-matter (e.g. employment policy) or because of a lack of clear Union competence (e.g. education). It can sit alongside a legislative approach, in areas such as employment and social policy, or it can stand alone, adding 'value' at a European level where there is little scope for legislative solutions (e.g. work at a Euro-pean level defining future objectives for national education systems).[152]

On the other hand, detractors of OMC criticize the process on a number of levels: in terms of its legality in that it allows the EU to encroach into policy areas largely reserved for the Member States;[153] in terms of its governance techniques in that it is more opaque and unaccountable[154] than the classic 'Community' method;[155] in terms of substance,

---

[146] Communication from the Commission, 'European Benchmarks in Education and training: follow-up to the Lisbon European Council' (COM(2002) 629).

[147] Para. 20.   [148] See previously n. 145, 187.   [149] Rhodes, above, n. 27, 292.

[150] Although, for a sceptical view based on a case study taken from the Occupational Health and Safety sector, see S. Smismans, 'New Modes of Governance and the Participatory Myth', *European Governance Papers* (EUROGOV) No. N–06–01.

[151] <http://europa.eu.int/comm/employment_social/social_inclusion/index_en.htm> (no longer available on the web).   [152] Governance White Paper, COM(2001) 428, 22.

[153] E. Szyszczak, 'The New Paradigm for Social Policy: A Virtuous Circle' (2001) 38 *CMLRev.* 1125.

[154] C. De la Porte and P. Nanz, 'The OMC—a deliberative-democratic mode of governance? The cases of employment and pensions' (2004) 11 *JEPP* 267. As B. Hepple puts it (*Rights at Work* (Sweet & Maxwell, London, 2005) 32, the Employment Guidelines are phrased in 'the mumbo-jumbo of modern management speak'.

[155] Cf. the principles of good governance set out in the Commission's *White Paper on Governance* (COM(2001) 428).

in that the supremacy of the BEPGs constrain the free development of a social policy; and in terms of its outcomes, in that it is still dependent on Member State action. If or when states do not fulfil their commitments, the credibility of the process is undermined.

Others point out that OMC has led to a proliferation of national and Union reporting obligations[156] which may not translate into action, and an obsession with placings in league tables to the detriment of the quality of outcomes. This has led some to suggest that OMC in its present form amounts to little more than 'the European emperor's newest clothes, an exercise in symbolic politics where national governments repackage existing policies to demonstrate their apparent compliance with EU objectives'.[157]

3.3. Corporate social responsibility

While OMC was the principal 'new' mechanism introduced at Lisbon, the European Council at Lisbon and again in the EU2020, made a 'special appeal' to companies' corporate sense of social responsibility (CSR) regarding best practices on lifelong learning, work organization, equal opportunities, social inclusion, and sustainable development.[158] This led to a Green Paper on Promoting a European Framework for CSR, followed by a Council Resolution,[159] a follow-up Communication from the Commission,[160] and a further Council Resolution. CSR involves companies voluntarily taking on commitments which go beyond common regulatory and conventional requirements, 'to raise the standards of social development, environmental protection and respect for fundamental rights and embrace open governance, reconciling interests of various stake-holders in an overall approach of quality and sustainability'.[161] Implementation of CSR can be 'facilitated by the participation of workers and their representatives in a dialogue that promotes exchanges and constant adaptation'.[162] In this respect business is being encouraged to ape government, especially with the appeal to business to be more participatory and accountable in its decision-making.

From the perspective of this chapter, the CSR envisaged by the Commission is primarily internal to the enterprise: it relates to quality employment, life-long learning, information, consultation and participation of workers, equal opportunities, integration of people with disabilities, anticipation of industrial change, and restructuring.

---

[156] Commission, 'Working Together for Growth and Jobs. Next steps in implementing the revised Lisbon strategy' SEC(2005) 622/2, 5.

[157] See further F. Scharpf, 'Notes Towards a Theory of Multilevel Governing in Europe', MPIfg Discussion Paper 2000/5.

[158] <http://consilium.europa.eu/ueDocs/cms_Data/docs/pressData/en/ec/00100-r1.en0.htm>, para. 39 (last accessed 4 April 2012).

[159] Council Resolution on the follow-up to the Green Paper on corporate social responsibility 2002/C 86/03, [2002] OJ C86/3), para. 10.

[160] Commission Communication, *Corporate Social Responsibility: A Business Contribution to Sustainable Development* (COM(2002) 347).

[161] COM(2001) 366, 3 and 6.   [162] Ibid.

Social dialogue is seen as a powerful instrument to address employment-related issues.[163]

CSR 'fits' with OMC in that both are examples of new forms of governance which do not rely on top-down command and control-style regulation. CSR is about 'responsible self-regulation'.[164] Indeed, if a sufficient number of companies embrace CSR, the carrot is that it might become the alternative to traditional forms of regulation in the social field. As Anna Diamantopoulou, former Social Affairs Commissioner, pointed out,[165] globalization and advances in communications technology are making it increasingly hard 'for legislators to address social problems with the necessary flexibility and lightness of touch'. She adds that in many cases CSR and partnership will come to be seen as the 'preferred solution'. This theme was developed by the Commission in its policy on CSR published in October 2011[166] where it identified improving self-regulation and co-regulation processes (e.g. sector-wide codes of conduct on societal issues relevant to the sector in question) as a new area for policy action. It also says that it will present a legislative proposal on the transparency of the social and environmental information provided by companies in all sectors.

3.4. Legislation and the social dialogue

The remaining tools to achieve the Lisbon and EU2020 objectives are legislation and the social dialogue. The first two chapters of this book have already highlighted the patchwork of legislation adopted in the social field. In some areas, hard law plays an important role in helping to steer a broader policy agenda. Thus a Directive prohibiting age discrimination not only provides a concrete tool to help those who are discriminated against on the grounds of age but it also sends out a strong signal that a policy of active ageing is a genuine commitment. In this way legislation provides the cornerstone for a broader range of policy initiatives.

Furthermore, legislation, social dialogue, and OMC, far from being mutually exclusive, can be mutually enhancing. As the Commission noted in its Governance White Paper,[167] 'legislation is often only part of a broader solution combining formal rules with other non-binding tools such as recommendations, guidelines, or even self-regulation within a commonly agreed framework'.[168] Thus, the effectiveness of the Race Discrimination Directive 2000/43 has been enhanced by a wider range of supporting policy tools (such as networks of experts and an action plan), while the Member States are

---

[163] COM(2002) 347, 19.
[164] J. Hunt, 'The European Union: Promoting a Framework for Corporate Social Responsibility?' in F. Macmillan, *International Corporate Law Annual* (Hart Publishing, Oxford, 2003) 137.
[165] Cited in Hunt, ibid., 137.
[166] Commission Communication, *A renewed EU Strategy for 2011–2014 for Corporate Social Responsibility*, COM(2011) 681.
[167] COM(2001) 428, 20.
[168] See further COM(2001) 428, 21: 'In some areas, such as employment and social policy or immigration policy, [OMC] sits alongside the programme-based and legislative approach; in others [such as education], it adds value at a European level where there is little scope for legislative solutions'.

encouraged to promote dialogue with the social partners with a view to fostering equal treatment.[169]

Yet despite the Commission's commitment to use legislation to achieve the goals laid down in the European Social Policy Agenda, in fact the legislative cupboard has been rather bare. In its 2005 Communication on the European Social Agenda,[170] the Commission proposed the updating of the Directives 2001/23 on transfers of undertakings and 98/59 on collective redundancies, the revision of Directive 94/45 on European Works Councils (EWC), the consolidation of the various provisions on worker information and consultation, and the amendment of the regulations on the co-ordination of social security. The only area in which new (unspecified) measures were to be considered was in the field of diversity and non-discrimination. Six years later, only the EWC Directive has been recast.[171]

Thus, despite the protestations about the value of legislation, there is in fact a disequilibrium: OMC processes are in the ascendancy, replacing traditional rights at work with programmes which may well be destructive of national social rights, a problem now exacerbated by the EU's response to the financial crisis (see later in this chapter). With the potential removal of national social rights under the impetus of the EES, especially under what were the entrepreneurship, employability, and adaptability pillars of the EES, there are currently no concrete plans to restore those rights at EU level. Instead, the Commission puts its trust in the social dialogue which it promotes at cross-industry and sectoral levels, especially by strengthening its logistic and technical support.[172] This in turn raises the question of the importance of the Social Partners as key actors in the Lisbon/EU2020 strategies.

4. THE ACTORS

4.1. Introduction

We have already seen how a wide range of actors are to be harnessed to the yoke of reform. According to the Lisbon summit, the European Council is to take a 'pre-eminent guiding and coordinating role to ensure overall coherence', in particular through an additional meeting of the European Council, taking place in the spring, concerned solely with economic *and* social questions;[173] and the Council and the Commission must draw up reports, benchmarking best practice. For the Commission, soft co-ordination has not necessarily been a good thing: it has reinforced its think-tank role, at the expense of its role in hard policy (as we have seen there are few legislative initiatives in the pipeline), and this makes the Commission look weaker than the other institutions.[174]

---

[169] OJ [2000] L180/22. See G. de Búrca, 'EU Race Discrimination Law: a Hybrid Model' in G. de Búrca and J. Scott (eds.), *Law and New Governance in the EU and US* (Hart Publishing, Oxford, 2006) and Ch. 6 of this book for further details.

[170] COM(2005) 33.   [171] Dir. 2009/38/EC (OJ [2009] L122/28).

[172] Commission Communication, 'Partnership for change in an enlarged Europe—Enhancing the contribution of European social dialogue' COM(2004) 557. See additionally COM(2012) 173, 20–21.

[173] Paras. 35 and 36.   [174] Discussion with Commission official.

At national level, the Member States, regional and local authorities, companies through CSR, NGOs, and civil society more generally[175] all have a role to play. But prominent among these actors, under the Lisbon strategy but to a lesser extent under EU2020,[176] are the Social Partners, at European, national, and subnational levels.[177]

4.2. The Social Partners

As we saw in Chapter 2, the role of the Social Partners was formally recognized by the Maastricht Treaty when they were given the power to adopt collective agreements which could be given legislative effect. The Luxembourg EES also envisaged a major role for the Social Partners. The first set of Employment Guidelines made specific appeals to the interprofessional and sectoral Social Partners, at European and national level, to take new initiatives, especially under the adaptability and employability pillars. The Lisbon summit emphasized the need for the Social Partners to be more closely involved in 'drawing up, implementing and following up the appropriate guidelines',[178] focusing particularly on modernizing work organization[179] and equal opportunities. They were also to have a significant role in respect of lifelong learning,[180] and they were to be actively involved in this OMC, especially benchmarking best practices, 'using variable forms of partnership'.[181]

The Commission also envisages that the Social Partners will have a particular role in respect of modernizing and improving social protection systems and promoting social inclusion[182] and quality in industrial relations.[183] At Nice, the European Council recognized that in modernizing and deepening the European social model 'all due importance' had to be given to the social dialogue.[184] The Commission took up this theme again in its Communication, *The European social dialogue, a force for innovation and change*,[185] where it noted that the Social Partners are 'best placed to take up the fundamental challenge of [the Lisbon] strategy: the positive management of change which can reconcile the flexibility essential to businesses with the security needed by employ-

---

[175] Luxembourg Presidency Conclusions, 22 and 23 March 2005, para. 6; COM(2010) 2020, 28.

[176] The principal reference to the social partners can be found under the flagship initiative on new skills and jobs: 'To strengthen the capacity of social partners and make full use of the problem-solving potential of social dialogue at all levels (EU, national/regional, sectoral, company)'. COM(2010) 2020, 16.

[177] See, e.g., Commission Communication, *Social Policy Agenda* COM(2000) 379, 14; the Nice Presidency Conclusions, 7–9 December 2000, para. 27; the Commission's White Paper *European Governance* COM(2001) 428, 14; and Commission, *The European Social Dialogue, a force for innovation and change* COM(2002) 341, 7.

[178] Presidency Conclusions, Lisbon European Council, 23 and 24 March 2000, para. 28, a view reiterated by the Conclusions to the Feira European Council, 19–20 June 2000, para. 34. See, in particular, Horizontal objective C in Council Decision 2001/63/EC on Guidelines for Member States' Employment Policies for the year 2001 (OJ [2001] L22/18).

[179] See in particular the Adaptability pillar of the 2001 Employment Guidelines: Council Decision 2001/63/EC OJ [2001] L22/18 and Commission Communication, *Promoting core labour standards and improving social governance in the context of globalization* COM(2001) 416 final.

[180] Presidency Conclusions of Feira European Council, 19 and 20 June 2000, para. 33 and Annex I of the Nice Presidency Conclusions, paras. 15 and 11.

[181] Presidency Conclusions, Lisbon European Council, 23 and 24 March 2000, para. 38.

[182] COM(2000) 379, 20.   [183] COM(2000) 379, 23.

[184] Nice Presidency Conclusions, Dec. 2000 Annex I, para. 26.   [185] COM(2002) 341.

ees, particularly in the event of major restructuring.[186] These pronouncements were made in the late 1990s/early 2000s; the high-point of social dialogue.

The Tripartite Social Summit for Growth and Employment,[187] enables the troika (the Council presidency and the two subsequent presidencies), the Commission, and the Social Partners to meet to ensure greater consistency in tripartite concertation in four areas (macroeconomics, employment, social protection, and education and training). In respect of the macroeconomic dialogue, Article 1(6) of the Council Decision 2000/604 on the statutes and composition of the Economic Policy Committee says:[188]

> The Committee shall provide the framework within which the macroeconomic dialogue involving representatives of the Committee (including the European Central Bank), the Economic and Financial Committee, the Employment Committee, the Commission and social partners shall take place at technical level.

This has led the Commission to note that the EMU process and economic convergence have 'progressively made visible the importance of the role of the Social Partners, not only in influencing the local competitiveness and employment conditions, but also as a major player in the achievement of growth and an employment-friendly overall policy mix in the Euro zone and in the [Union]'.[189]

However, the Social Partners' involvement in such a dialogue may come at a price. The 1999 (and subsequent) Guidelines provide that '[f]or wage developments to contribute to an employment-friendly mix, the Social Partners should continue to pursue a responsible course and conclude wage agreements in Member States in line with the general principles set out in previous Broad Economic Policy Guidelines', namely:[190]

1. Nominal wage increases must be consistent with price stability.

2. Real wage increases in relation to labour productivity growth should take into account the need to strengthen and maintain the profitability of investment.

3. Wage agreements should take into account differentials in productivity levels according to qualifications, regions, and sectors.

As Deakin and Reed point out, the suggestion in the Council Resolution on growth and employment which accompanied the Stability and Growth Pact (SGP) (see later in this chapter) that the Social Partners should 'fully face their responsibilities within their respective sphere of activity',[191] coupled with the direction in the Broad Economic Guidelines that real wage levels should be pegged below increases in productivity so as to provide incentives for investment, indicate a role in suppressing wage growth which sits unhappily with the traditional role of trade unions.

---

[186] Ibid., 6.   [187] Established by Council Decision 2003/174/EC (OJ [2003] L70/31).

[188] Council Decision 2000/604/EC on the composition and the statutes of the Economic Policy Committee (OJ [2000] L257/28).

[189] Commission Communication, *Adapting and Promoting the Social Dialogue at Community Level* COM(98) 322, 4.

[190] Council Recommendation 99/570/EC (OJ [1999] L217/34).

[191] Resolution 97/C 236/02, para. 13.

Nevertheless, the importance of social dialogue as a mechanism for promoting the appropriate conditions for growth should not be underestimated; it is reflected in experiences at Member State level. Italy, Spain, and France, for example, have a long tradition of successful tripartite bargaining between government and the Social Partners over labour costs, flexibilization, and wage growth.[192] On the other hand, experience to date of social partner involvement in the various Lisbon processes has been patchy. De la Porte and Nanz note a lack of commitment to the strategy on the union side and a reluctance to become involved on the employers' side.[193] Even in respect of the NAPs/NRPs, the involvement of the Social Partners has varied significantly from state to state.[194]

4.3. The missing actors

Notable by their absence from the discussion so far is the Court of Justice and the European Parliament. To date, the Court of Justice has no specific role in OMC, due to the strong political logic of the methodology, although it may eventually have to rule on the legality of some of the procedural issues involved in the OMC process, as it was prepared to do in *Commission* v. *Council (SGP)*.[195] There, in the context of the excessive deficit procedure, the Court ruled that the Council could not depart from the rules laid down by the Treaty and in the SGP (see Section D). However, unlike soft law adopted under the classic 'Community' method—such as the recommendation on sexual harassment, which is subject to judicial interpretation[196] and once hardened into hard law, judicial enforceability—the soft law of the EES derives its regulatory strength from government powers or capacities.[197] As Kilpatrick puts it, OMC does not constitute a hard law opportunity manqué—rather, soft law in this regard is shorthand for 'different from law (in its classical conception)', not 'less than law'.[198]

If this interpretation is correct, then the role for the Court of Justice will always be residual. This then focuses attention on political accountability. Yet the European and national parliaments have also been marginalized in the OMC process. According to Article 148(2) TFEU the European Parliament is to be consulted in the drawing up of the Employment Guidelines (although it is not involved in any other OMC process) but experience over the first five years of the EES showed that

---

[192] See T. Treu, 'European Collective Bargaining Levels and the Competences of the Social Partners', in P. Davies, A. Lyon-Caen, S. Sciarra, and S. Simitis (eds.), *European Community Labour Law: Principles and Perspectives. Liber Amicorum Lord Wedderburn of Charlton* (Clarendon, Oxford, 1996) 179.

[193] 'The OMC—a deliberative-democratic mode of governance? The cases of employment and pension' (2004) 11 *JEPP* 267, 279.

[194] EIRO, 'Participation of Social Partners in the NAPs of the Employment Strategy (2002) <http://www.eurofound.europa.eu/eiro/2002/06/tfeature/es0206205t.htm> (last accessed 4 April 2012).

[195] Case C–27/04 [2004] ECR I–6649.

[196] Case 322/88 *Grimaldi* v. *Fonds des Maladies Professionnelles* [1989] ECR 4407.

[197] Borrás and Jacobsson, above n. 145, 188 and 199.

[198] 'New EU Employment Governance and Constitutionalism' in G. De Búrca and J. Scott (eds.), *Law and New Governance in the EU and US* (Hart Publishing, Oxford, 2006).

the European Parliament's role was marginal, in part due to the lack of time in the EES timetable for it to prepare its opinion.[199] The European Parliament itself has admitted that:[200]

> Many of the measures agreed at Lisbon were not legislative but intergovernmental, based on coordination and benchmarking among Member States, with the Commission and European Parliament in a bystanders' role.

Yet, the EU2020 confirms the pre-eminent role of the European Council which will have 'full ownership and be the focal point of the strategy'.[201]

The European Council also said that 'A more effective form of governance in the employment and social area than the open method of coordination, which failed to achieve some of its aims, is needed for the years to come' and that the Council and the Commission must 'involve Parliament fully in drawing up objectives, targets and indicators for the new economic and employment strategy, and also to give Parliament access to documents, meetings, and work on monitoring and reviewing progress'.[202] Yet the EU2020 strategy has not changed much. It talks of the European Parliament playing 'an important role in the strategy, not only in its capacity as a co-legislator, but also as a driving force for mobilising citizens and their national parliaments'. It concludes, rather lamely, that the Parliament could use its next meeting with the national parliaments 'to discuss its contribution to Europe 2020 and jointly communicate views to the Spring European Council'.[203]

The Lisbon Treaty has not changed this. Despite the generalizing of the ordinary legislative procedure by the Lisbon Treaty, this has not been extended to Article 148 TFEU, the legal basis for adopting the Employment Guidelines. The involvement of the Social Partners was hoped to fill this legitimacy gap but the commitment on paper to the participation of the Social Partners has often not manifested itself in practice. This has led some commentators to suggest that, on the one hand, the involvement of such a wide range of actors has actually blurred responsibility for economic and social policy, and, on the other, the absence of effective involvement by the social partners, the lack of involvement by the European Parliament, and the absence of judicial review, has meant that the EES and Lisbon strategies far from being open, heterarchical, and deliberative, are more closed, elitist, and less democratic than the classic 'Community' methods.[204]

[199] The 2003 reforms have helped to overcome this problem: Rhodes, above n. 27, 295.
[200] <http://www.europarl.europa.eu/sides/getDoc.do?type=IM-PRESS&reference=20070202BKG02682&language=EN#title1> (last accessed 19 July 2010).
[201] COM(2010) 2020, 4.
[202] <http://www.europarl.europa.eu/news/expert/infopress_page/048-73522-116-04-18-908-20100426IPR73482-26-04-2010-2010-false/default_en.htm> (last accessed 19 July 2010).
[203] COM(2010) 2020, 27.
[204] P. Syrpis, 'Legitimising European Governance: Taking Subsidiarity Seriously within the OMC', *EUI Working Papers*, Law 2002/10.

D. THE FINANCIAL CRISIS

1. INTRODUCTION

This plethora of guidelines, pacts, and strategies outlined in the previous sections failed to anticipate or, subsequently, address the financial crisis which started in 2008 and is still ongoing. For trade unions and for workers, the crisis has been devastating for jobs and has had a disproportionate effect on the young, especially in countries such as Spain. Yet, the EU's response to the crisis has also posed a threat to workers: EU or EU/IMF-sanctioned deregulation of employment rights at national level. In order to appreciate the impact of the crisis on labour law we need to understand, at least in outline, the crisis itself and the EU's response to it.[205] We then consider how the EU's response to the crisis has an impact on labour law.

2. THE CONTEXT

It is possible to identify three overlapping phases of the crisis. First came the financial crisis in 2008 where banks realized that, following the housing bubble and the general credit boom, they were holding too much toxic debt. They stopped lending to each other and to customers. This resulted in governments pumping large sums of money into the system to 'bail-out' the banks. The sovereign debt crisis of 2010 followed shortly afterwards. A number of states had run up large deficits and, worse, large debts, some brought about through bailing out the banks. Because the money markets were worried that some states might default they would lend to these states only at ever higher rates. This became unmanageable for Greece, Ireland, and Portugal and they had to be 'bailed out' (in fact given loans) by the EU Member States and the IMF in the case of Greece in 2010 (and again in 2012) and the EU and the IMF in the case of Ireland in 2010 and Portugal in 2011. But in order to be able to deliver on the major changes to fiscal policy demanded by the troika (the EU Commission, the European Central Bank, and the IMF) an effective government was needed. In Greece and Italy democratically elected governments were replaced by governments of technocrats in November 2011 and this precipitated a third phase of the crisis: a crisis of democracy.

The EU's response to the crisis has four limbs. First, in order to address the financial crisis there has been, and continues to be, financial reform. This includes setting up a European banking authority to oversee the banking sector and recapitalization of the banks. In addition, legislation has been adopted on: increasing the amounts of regulatory capital banks hold; addressing risky securitization operations; ensuring remuneration policies do not encourage excessive risk; and increasing the protection of citizens' bank deposits up to 100,000 euros. Legislation is in the pipeline concerning: reinforced

---

[205] The following section draws on C. Barnard, 'The Financial Crisis and the Euro Plus Pact: a Labour Lawyer's perspective' (2012) 41 *ILJ* 98.

rules on credit-rating agencies; transparency and market conduct on all trading plat-forms; and a strengthened framework to combat market abuse, including criminal sanctions and a European framework on bank resolution.

The second limb of the EU's response has focused on stabilizing the situation. This has involved establishing the European Financial Stabilisation Mechanism,[206] an emergency funding programme reliant upon funds raised on the financial markets and guaranteed by the European Commission, using the budget of the EU as collat-eral. In addition, a (temporary?) European Financial Stability Facility (EFSF) has been set up,[207] a special purpose vehicle financed by the members of the eurozone to help combat the sovereign debt crisis. This 440 billion euro fund was due to be replaced by the (permanent) European Stability Mechanism (ESM), a 500 billion euro fund, as of 2013; however this was brought forward to 2012 by the European Council in December 2011.[208] The ECB has also participated actively in stabilizing the bond markets by providing funding to banks. Other measures being debated in-clude the controversial financial transactions tax (the 'Tobin tax') and Eurobonds.[209] While Germany is opposed to the creation of Eurobonds, the UK's opposition to the Tobin tax was responsible in part for its refusal to agree to Treaty reform at the December 2011 European Council meeting (albeit that any such tax could have been blocked by the UK under the provision of Article 113 TFEU, the legal basis of the Tobin tax).

The third limb of the EU's response to the crisis has focused on improving eco-nomic governance. This limb is forward looking, intending to send a message to the markets that the crisis is now under control and that it will not repeated. The first change involved the adoption of the so-called 'European semester',[210] (see Figure 3.1) launched in 2011.[211] This requires much greater scrutiny of all Member State budgets prior to them being adopted. The Commission describes the stages in the following terms:[212]

— The new six-month cycle starts each year in January when the Commission publishes the Annual Growth Survey (AGS), to be discussed by Council forma-tions and the European Parliament ahead of the Spring meeting of the European Council in March.

---

[206] Regulation (EU) No 407/2010 of 11 May 2010 establishing a European financial stabilisation mechanism (OJ [2011] L 118/1).

[207] <http://www.efsf.europa.eu/attachments/20111019_efsf_framework_agreement_en.pdf> (last accessed 12 March 2012).

[208] An ESM Treaty has now been signed: <http://www.european-council.europa.eu/home-page/highlights/european-stability-mechanism-treaty-signed?lang=en> (last accessed 3 February 2012).

[209] See Commission Green Paper on the feasibility of introducing Stability Bonds: COM(2011) 818.

[210] <http://ec.europa.eu/europe2020/pdf/chart_en.pdf> (last accessed 12 March 2012).

[211] This was put on a legal footing by Reg. 1175/2011 (OJ [2011] L306/12). The process is started with the publication by the Commission of the Annual Growth Survey (AGS): see e.g. COM(2011) 11. Further details can be found at <http://ec.europa.eu/europe2020/reaching-the-goals/monitoring-progress/annual-growth-surveys/index_en.htm> (last accessed 4 April 2012).

[212] <http://ec.europa.eu/europe2020/pdf/m11_14.en.pdf> (last accessed 24 December 2011).

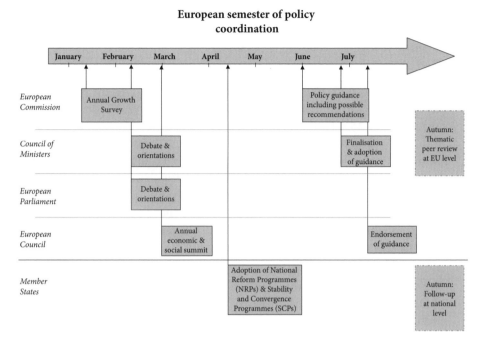

Fig. 3.1. The European semester.

Source: <http://ec.europa.eu/economy_finance/articles/euro/documents/com_367_european_semester_en.pdf>.

— At the Spring Council, Member States, essentially on the basis of the Annual Growth Survey, identify the main challenges facing the EU and give strategic advice on policies.

— Taking this guidance into account, the Member States will present and discuss their medium-term budgetary strategies through Stability and Convergence Programmes and, at the same time, draw up National Reform Programmes setting out the action they will undertake in areas such as employment, research, innovation, energy or social inclusion. These two documents are then sent in April to the European Commission for assessment.

— Based on the Commission's assessment, the Council will issue country-specific guidance by June and July and possible country-specific guidance to countries whose policies and budgets are out of line (for instance, if their plans are not realistic in terms of macroeconomic assumptions or they do not address the main challenges in terms of fiscal consolidation, competitiveness, imbalances, etc).

— Each July, the European Council and the Council of Ministers will provide policy advice before Member States finalise their draft budgets for the following year. Draft budgets are then sent by Governments to the national Parliaments, which continue to fully exercise their right to decide on budget.

This improved governance was reinforced by the adoption of the Euro Plus Pact (EPP) in March 2011 (see later). In addition, in the Autumn of 2011, the so-called 'six pack' regulations were adopted concerning fiscal and macro surveillance. Four measures have been adopted on fiscal surveillance:

1. A regulation introducing revisions to the *preventive* arm of the Stability and Growth Pact (SGP).[213] The SGP was first introduced in 1997. The preventive arm requires states to submit annual stability or convergence programmes, showing how they intend to achieve or safeguard sound fiscal positions in the medium term. The new rules guide Member States towards a country-specific, medium-term budgetary objective (MTO) in order to ensure public finance sustainability. They define a new 'expenditure benchmark' to help assess progress towards these MTOs which places a cap on the annual growth of public expenditure according to a medium-term rate of growth. These rules apply to states which are not in EDP (see later). Currently this is the case for Estonia, Finland, Luxembourg, and Sweden.[214]

2. A regulation introducing revisions to the *corrective* arm of the SGP.[215] The corrective arm of the SGP is the dissuasive part of the Pact. It governs the excessive deficit procedure (EDP) which is triggered by the deficit breaching the 3 per cent of GDP threshold of the Treaty. If it is decided that the deficit is excessive within the meaning of the Treaty, the Council issues recommendations to the Member State concerned to correct the excessive deficit and gives a time frame for doing so. The new rules place a greater emphasis on debt, rather than just deficit, which had been overlooked in the past: if the 60 per cent reference for the debt-to-GDP ratio is not respected, the Member State concerned will be put in excessive deficit procedure (even if its deficit is below 3 per cent), after taking into account all relevant factors and the impact of the economic cycle, so long as the gap between its debt level and the 60 per cent reference is not reduced by 1/20th annually (on average over three years). Transitional rules apply. Twenty-three Member States, including the UK, are currently in the EDP.

3. A new directive on national fiscal frameworks aimed at tightening up rules on data collection.[216] This is intended to address some of the problems revealed by the Greek financial crisis.

---

[213] Regulation (EU) No 1175/2011 of the European Parliament and of the Council of 16 November 2011 amending Council Regulation (EC) No 1466/97 on the strengthening of the surveillance of budgetary positions and the surveillance and coordination of economic policies (OJ [2011] L306 12).

[214] This summary is based on information in <http://europa.eu/rapid/pressReleasesAction.do?reference=MEMO/11/898&format=HTML&aged=0&language=EN&guiLanguage=en>.

[215] Council Regulation (EU) No 1177/2011 amending Regulation (EC) No 1467/97 on speeding up and clarifying the implementation of the excessive deficit procedure (OJ [2011] L306/33).

[216] Council Directive 2011/85/EU on requirements for budgetary frameworks of the Member States (OJ [2011] L306/41).

4. A new regulation on effective enforcement of budgetary surveillance.[217] This applies to the Eurozone countries only. Where Member States are in the EDP they must comply with a recommendation issued by the Council. While it has been possible for a state ultimately to be fined for non-compliance with the recommendation, this has never in fact happened despite numerous defaults. Now, where a euro area Member State does not respect its obligations, a financial sanction can be imposed by the Council on the basis of a Commission recommendation, unless a qualified majority of Member States vote against it (the so-called 'reverse qualified majority' voting procedure).

Two measures have been adopted on macro-surveillance:

1. A new regulation on prevention and correction of macro-economic imbalances such as housing bubbles.[218] This Regulation also has a preventive arm, whereby the Commission and the Council can adopt preventive recommendations under Article 121(2) TFEU at an early stage before the imbalances become large, and a corrective arm where an excessive imbalance procedure can be opened for a Member State. In this case, the Member State concerned will have to submit a corrective action plan with a clear roadmap and deadlines for implementing corrective action.[219]

2. A new regulation on effective enforcement of macroeconomic surveillance[220] which applies to the eurozone countries only. It has two elements. First, it 'consists of a two-step approach whereby an interest-bearing deposit can be imposed after one failure to comply with the recommended corrective action. After a second compliance failure, this interest-bearing deposit can be converted into a fine (up to 0.1 per cent of GDP)'.[221] Secondly, it provides for an 'early warning system'—an alert system based on an economic reading of a scoreboard consisting of a set of 10 indicators covering the major sources of macro-economic imbalances[222]—which can trigger 'in-depth studies which will do deep dive analyses to

---

[217] Regulation (EU) No 1173/2011 of the European Parliament and of the Council of 16 November 2011 on the effective enforcement of budgetary surveillance in the euro area (OJ [2011] L306/1).

[218] Regulation (EU) No 1176/2011 of the European Parliament and of the Council of 16 November 2011 on the prevention and correction of macroeconomic imbalances (OJ [2011] L306/25).

[219] <http://europa.eu/rapid/pressReleasesAction.do?reference=MEMO/11/898&format=HTML&aged=0& language=EN&guiLanguage=en> (last accessed 12 December 2011).

[220] Regulation (EU) No 1174/2011 of the European Parliament and of the Council of 16 November 2011 on enforcement measures to correct excessive macroeconomic imbalances in the euro area (OJ [2011] L306 8).

[221] <http://europa.eu/rapid/pressReleasesAction.do?reference=MEMO/11/898&format=HTML&aged=0& language=EN&guiLanguage=en> (last accessed 12 December 2011).

[222] The current planned scoreboard looks at e.g. three-year backward moving average of the current account balance as a per cent of GDP, with the a threshold of + 6 per cent of GDP and – 4 per cent of GDP; net international investment position as a per cent of GDP, with a threshold of – 35 per cent of GDP; three years percentage change in nominal unit labour cost, with thresholds of + 9 per cent for euro-area countries and + 12 per cent for non-euro-area countries; three-year backward moving average of unemployment rate, with the threshold of 10 per cent.

determine whether the potential imbalances identified in the early-warning system are benign or problematic'.[223]

In mid-November 2011 the Commission announced yet further reforms to economic
governance for eurozone states, 'the two-pack'. The first, a proposed Regulation strengthening surveillance of budgetary policies in the euro area Member States,[224] would require
countries to present their draft budgets at the same time each year and give the Commission the right to assess and, if necessary, issue an opinion on them as well as proposing
closer monitoring and reporting requirements for euro area countries in the EDP, to apply
on an on-going basis throughout the budgetary cycle. The second, a proposed Regulation
strengthening economic and fiscal surveillance of euro area countries facing or threatened with serious financial instability,[225] would ensure that the surveillance of these Member States under a financial assistance programme, or facing a serious threat of financial
instability, is robust, follows clear procedures, and is embedded in EU law.[226]

In their 'fiscal compact' of 9 December 2011, the EU-26 agreed to take the six and two
pack rules on board while also constitutionally enshrining a golden rule on balanced
budgets (the annual structural deficit must not exceed 0.5 per cent of nominal GDP).
The UK has refused to participate. This was followed up by an informal summit on 30
January 2012 where a new Treaty on Stability, Coordination and Governance in the
Economic and Monetary Union was finalized and agreed by all EU Member States
except the UK and the Czech Republic.[227]

The fourth limb of the EU's response to the crisis, and arguably the most important
from an employment point of view, are measures to facilitate growth. It is, however, the
least developed aspect of the EU's response. The monetarist argument is that a stable
economic policy creates the best environment for growth—hence the reforms to economic governance. Yet when this is accompanied by stringent austerity measures the
chance for growth is slim so long as workers are losing—or at risk of losing—their jobs.
The Commission cites the EU's 2020 strategy as a vehicle for delivering growth. Yet this
strategy is dependent on significant government expenditure which governments,
already encumbered by substantial debt, are not in a position to provide. Reforms to the
single market, as mandated by the (non-legally binding) Single Market Act 2011,[228] are
likely to achieve only limited amounts of growth and these in the longer term. So what
is left? The traditional tool for delivering speedy growth—devaluation of the currency—
is not available to Eurozone Member States. This puts labour law in the front line. It is

---

[223] <http://europa.eu/rapid/pressReleasesAction.do?reference=MEMO/11/898&format=HTML&aged=0&
language=EN&guiLanguage=en> (last accessed 12 December 2011).

[224] COM(2011) 821.

[225] COM(2011) 819.

[226] <http://europa.eu/rapid/pressReleasesAction.do?reference=IP/11/1381&format=HTML&aged=0&lang
uage=EN&guiLanguage=en> (last accessed 12 December 2011).

[227] <http://www.european-council.europa.eu/home-page/highlights/the-fiscal-compact-ready-to-be-
signed-(2)?lang=en> (last accessed 12 March 2012).

[228] COM(2011) 206. There are signs the Commission is taking the growth issue seriously: "*Towards a job
rich recovery*": COM(2012) 173.

one of the few areas over which Member States retain competence to regulate and, more realistically at present, to deregulate. The EU seems to be encouraging this view, first through the Euro Plus Pact (EPP) and second through the MoU.

3. THE IMPACT OF THE CRISIS ON LABOUR LAW

3.1. The Euro Plus Pact

(a) Background

The 'Euro Plus Pact' (EPP) was agreed at the European Council meeting of 24–25 March 2011.[229] The 'Plus' reflects the fact that the deal applies to not only the Eurozone states but also to Bulgaria, Denmark, Latvia, Lithuania, Poland, Romania (the same group of states which agreed unconditionally to the Fiscal Compact of the 9 December 2011). The other Member States (UK, Sweden, Hungary, and the Czech Republic) remain free to join. According to the European Council, the aim of the Pact is to 'further strengthen the economic pillar of EMU and achieve a new quality of economic policy coordination, with the objective of improving competitiveness and thereby leading to a higher degree of convergence reinforcing our social market economy'.

The EPP, the details of which are set out in Annex I of the European Council Conclusions, was adopted largely to placate the Germans who were bankrolling many of the changes and, in particular were being asked to accept the European Stability Mechanism (ESM), found in Annex II of the European Council Conclusions.

(b) What does the pact do?

Participating Member States agree to take all necessary measures to pursue the following objectives:

1. *Foster competitiveness*: The Pact provides: 'Progress will be assessed on the basis of wage and productivity developments and competitiveness adjustment needs. To assess whether wages are evolving in line with productivity, unit labour costs (ULC) will be monitored over a period of time, by comparing with developments in other euro area countries and in the main comparable trading partners. For each country, ULCs will be assessed for the economy as a whole and for each major sector (manufacturing; services; as well as tradable and non-tradable sectors).'

2. *Foster employment*: The Pact provides: 'A well-functioning labour market is key for the competitiveness of the euro area. Progress will be assessed on the basis of the following indicators: long term and youth unemployment rates, and labour participation rates.'

3. *Contribute further to the sustainability of public finances*: The Pact provides that in order to secure the full implementation of the SGP, the 'highest attention' will be paid to the 'sustainability of pensions, healthcare and social benefits'.

---

[229] <http://www.consilium.europa.eu/uedocs/cms_data/docs/pressdata/en/ec/120296.pdf> (last accessed 12 March 2012).

4. *Reinforce financial stability*: This covers maters such as putting in place national legislation for banking resolution, strict bank stress tests, and monitoring macro-financial stability and macroeconomic developments in the euro area.

The Pact therefore builds on existing instruments (e.g. EU2020, the European Semester, the Integrated Guidelines,[230] the SGP, and the new macroeconomic surveillance framework).[231] The Member States made their first commitments under the Pact in their Stability or Convergence Programmes and National Reform Programmes.[232] They are thus subject to the regular surveillance framework, with a strong central role for the Commission in the monitoring of the implementation of the commitments, and the involvement of all the relevant formations of the Council and the Eurogroup.

The Pact is upfront: it focuses 'primarily on areas that fall under national competence'. The crucial point about the Pact is that '[t]he selection of the specific policy measures to be implemented will remain the responsibility of each country, but the choice will be guided by considering in particular the issues mentioned above'. While many would recognize that this reflects the absence of EU competence to act and, in the most general terms, the principle of subsidiarity, the Realpolitik of this goes to the heart of the problems facing the EMU: there has been monetary union but no meaningful fiscal union. While states need to be more accountable for the economic decisions they take, it is still the states taking those decisions. From that point of view, the six-pack regulation is more prescriptive.

(c) Impact on labour law

As the brief outline of the four objectives of the Pact makes clear, three of the Pact's objectives have a direct impact on labour issues. The provisions under the 'Fostering competitiveness' objective were particularly contested. The Pact provides that each country will be responsible for the specific policy actions it chooses to foster competitiveness, but particular attention will be given to respecting national traditions of social dialogue and industrial relations, and measures to ensure costs developments in line with productivity, such as: (1) reviewing the wage setting arrangements, and, where necessary, the degree of centralization in the bargaining process, and the indexation mechanisms, while maintaining the autonomy of the social partners in the collective bargaining process; and (2) ensuring that wages settlements in the public sector support the competitiveness efforts in the private sector (bearing in mind the important signalling effect of public sector wages).

The proposed monitoring system for wage and productivity levels proved particularly controversial. The original German plan would have achieved this partly by forcing

---

[230] Namely the Council's recommendation on the broad guidelines for the economic policies of the Member States and the Union (2010 to 2014) and a decision on guidelines for the employment policies of the Member States. Together they form the 'integrated guidelines'.

[231] Ibid., p.14.

[232] <http://ec.europa.eu/economy_finance/economic_governance/sgp/convergence/programmes/2011_en.htm> (last accessed 24 December 2011).

countries to end the indexing of wages to inflation—a move strongly opposed by a number of Member States, in particular Belgium which feared this would undermine its social model.[233] However, the final version does not oblige countries to give up indexing but, if they do not, each government must implement other measures to ensure that wages develop in line with productivity. The original draft also talked of enhancing 'decentralisation in the bargaining process'.[234] This antagonized trade unions in those key countries with centralized bargaining processes such as Finland, the Netherlands, and Austria. Again, this has been diluted to 'where necessary' reviewing the degree of centralization in the bargaining process.

The second part of the Pact which impacts on labour comes under the heading 'fostering employment'. This provides that each country will be responsible for the specific policy actions it chooses to foster employment, but particular attention will be given to: (1) labour market reforms to promote 'flexicurity', reduce undeclared work, and increase labour participation; (2) life long learning; (3) tax reforms, such as lowering taxes on labour to make work pay while preserving overall tax revenues, and taking measures to facilitate the participation of second earners in the work force.

The third area where labour issues are directly affected comes under the heading enhancing the 'sustainability of public finances'. It provides that reforms necessary to ensure the sustainability and adequacy of pensions and social benefits could include: (1) aligning the pension system to the national demographic situation, e.g. by aligning the effective retirement age with life expectancy or by increasing participation rates; and (2) limiting early retirement schemes and using targeted incentives to employ older workers (notably in the age tranche above 55).

There was much concern in the earlier drafts of the pact that retirement ages would have to be raised. The final version is more vague. The new pension monitoring system would not force countries to raise retirement ages but it would develop indicators showing whether state pension schemes could be sustained under existing funding levels. Pension reform *could* include limiting early retirement schemes, but again this is less mandatory than in earlier drafts.

What can we make of these proposals? Although many feared that the Euro Plus Pact would be deregulatory, in fact the final version is more complex. As a product of many hands, it sought both to assuage the concerns of the Germans (who want more control over national expenditure) while at the same time supporting other states, such as

---

[233] P. Hollinger and P. Spiegel, 'Cracks over Franco-German Eurozone plan' *FT. com*, 4 February 2011. Cf. Council Recommendation 2011/C 209/01 on the NRP 2011 of Belgium and delivering a Council Opinion on the updated Stability program of Belgium 2011–14 (OJ [2011] L209/1) which identifies the 'system of wage bargaining and wage indexation' as a problem needing reform, a point reiterated in the Council Recommendation 2011/C 217/05 on the implementation of the broad guidelines for the economic policies of the Member States whose currency is the euro (OJ [2011] L209/1), para. 5.

[234] L. Phillips, 'Competitiveness pact "was never the blueprint people thought it was"' *EU Observer*, 11 March 2011.

Spain and Belgium, which are wedded to the maintenance of their national social systems. Hence the final Pact does create the space to recognize the diversity of the national
systems. One of the 'six pack' measures, the Macro-economic Surveillance Regulation
1176/2011, goes even further in recognizing the role for the national systems and, at the
behest of the European Parliament,[235] now contains a 'Monti' clause:[236]

> The application of this Regulation shall fully respect Article 152 TFEU and the recommen-
> dations issued under this Regulation shall respect national practices and institutions for
> wage formation. It shall take into account Article 28 of the Charter of Fundamental Rights
> of the European Union, and accordingly shall not affect the right to negotiate, conclude and
> enforce collective agreements and to take collective action in accordance with national law
> and practices.

(d) Effectiveness of the Pact

The Euro Plus Pact adds yet a further layer to the wedding cake of strategies to address
unemployment in Europe. It has been developed out of the same intergovernmental
methodology—i.e. European Council led. The elephant in the room has always been
the question of the effectiveness of this approach. As we have seen, the Member States'
commitments under the EPP have to be included in their Stability or Convergence
Programmes and their national reform programmes (SCP/NRP) as part of the European semester. While Member States did make reference to the commitments under the
EPP in their SCP/NRPs for 2011, the commitments of some states, such as Belgium,
were vague and lacked specifics, as the Council noted:[237] 'there is no information on the
measures to be taken in order to achieve the required objective on the fiscal side; nor
is there any information on how real wage growth or energy prices could be
controlled....'

Even with more precise commitments, can they be enforced successfully? Prodi *et al.*
think not. Writing about the Euro Plus Pact in the *FT*,[238] they say:

> The Franco-German proposal was also based on an intergovernmental model of peer pres-
> sure that has proved repeatedly ineffective. It lacks the discipline and impartial adjudica-
> tion to deliver results. Both the Lisbon strategy for growth and the stability and growth pact
> failed to live up to expectations, because Member States are reluctant to sanction each
> other.

The absence of any sanctions in the Pact suggests that its influence may be less than
would first appear and that the six-pack hard law measures may in fact prove to be

---

[235] A7-0183/3.

[236] Art. 1(3). See further Recital 25 which adds 'When the Council and the Commission apply this Regulation,
they should fully respect the role of national parliaments and social partners and respect differences in national
systems, such as the systems for wage formation'. See further Ch. 5.

[237] Council Recommendation 2011/C 209/01 on the NRP 2011 of Belgium and delivering a Council
Opinion on the updated Stability program of Belgium 2011–14 (OJ [2011] L209/1).

[238] G. Verhofstadt, J. Delors, and R. Prodi, 'Europe must plan a reform, not a pact', *Financial Times* 2 March
2011.

more significant. However, as the French and Germans demonstrated in the mid-2000s, Ecofin was prepared to suspend the excessive deficit procedure against France and Germany, even though their net borrowing exceeded 4 per cent of GDP.[239] And even when peer pressure is applied through the examination of each other's budgets, all Member States, at least in theory, have an equal say over the sins of the others: so Greece (Ireland, Italy and even Spain) will be checking on the performance of Germany (and vice versa) but it is not in these countries' interests to point out the speck in the German eye when they realize the existence of a plank in their own. It is easy to see how any peer review quickly becomes a paper tiger. In this way the Pact is significantly less robust than the semi-automatic sanctions envisaged in the six pack and reinforced by the Fiscal Compact.

3.2. The Memoranda of Understanding

Thus, despite fears raised by the EPP, in fact it probably presents a less direct threat to national labour law than would first appear. Much is left to the Member States to decide, and what started off as mandatory in early drafts became optional by the time it was finally agreed by the Member States. The EPP thus stands in stark contrast to the much more intrusive provisions in the Memoranda of Understanding (MoU) which those countries receiving a bail-out have signed. Space precludes a detailed analysis of these lengthy documents but two examples will suffice to make the point.

First, take the case of Ireland.[240] The Irish government committed itself in the MoU to cut its minimum wage (NMW) by a euro an hour. This decision was justified by the National Recovery Plan 2011–14[241] in the following terms:

Where a NMW is imposed at a level higher than the equilibrium wage rate, unemployment will result. Some workers will be willing to work for a wage lower than NMW but employers are restricted from providing these job opportunities. Other negative effects include:

1. Acting as a barrier for younger and less skilled workers to enter the labour force and take up jobs;

2. Preventing SME's from adjusting wage costs downward in order to maintain viability and improve competitiveness; and

3. Reducing the capacity of the services sector to generate additional activity and employment through lower prices for consumers.

---

[239] Ecofin's decision was, however, successfully challenged by the Commission: Case C–27/04 *Commission v. Council* [2004] ECR I–6649.

[240] See Implementing Decision 2011/77/EU (OJ [2011] L 30/34) on granting Union financial assistance to Ireland for a period of three years under the provisions of the Treaty and Regulation (EU) No 407/2010 of 11 May 2010 establishing a European financial stabilisation mechanism. The accompanying Memorandum of Understanding signed on 16 December 2010 and its first update lay down the economic policy conditions on the basis of which the financial assistance is granted. Implementing Decision 2011/77/EU was amended by Implementing Decision 2011/326/EU (OJ [2011] L 147/17) For a fuller discussion, see N. Bruun, 'Economic Governance of the EU Crisis and its Social Policy Implications' in N. Bruun et al. (eds), *The Lisbon Treaty and Social Europe* (Oxford, Hart Publishing, 2012).

[241] <http://budget.gov.ie/RecoveryPlan.aspx> (last accessed 11 December 2011).

In addition, collective agreements (properly known as Registered Employment Agreements or Employment Regulation Orders) in the agricultural, catering, construction, and electrical contracting sectors have also been repealed. As the National Recovery Plan states:

> Both types of agreements constitute another form of labour market rigidity by preventing wage levels from adjusting. This in turn affects the sustainability of existing jobs and may also prevent the creation of new jobs, particularly for younger people disproportionately affected by the employment crises who form part of the labour force for these sectors.[242]

While a number of these agreements had been around for over 50 years and could result in arbitrary geographical divisions,[243] the removal of the agreements affected some of the lowest paid workers. In recognition of this, the reduction in the minimum wage was reversed in the summer of 2011.

Secondly, there is Portugal.[244] Portugal voluntarily committed itself to a range of cuts in the employment field including a temporary suspension of thirteenth and fourteenth-month bonus salary payments for civil servants and pensioners who earn more than €1,000 a month. It also agreed, in the MoU, to implement a reform in the severance payments for new hires in line with a tripartite agreement of March 2011. This included aligning the severance payments of open-ended contracts with those of fixed-term contracts and reducing total severance payments for new open-ended contracts from 30 to 10 days per year of tenure (with 10 additional days to be paid by an employers' financed fund) with a cap of 12 months and elimination of the 3 months of pay irrespective of tenure and reducing total severance payments for fixed-term contracts from 36 to 10 days per year of tenure for contracts shorter than 6 months and from 24 to 10 days for longer contracts (with 10 additional days to be paid by an employers' financed fund).

The Government is also in the process of reforming the legislation on individual dismissals with a view to fighting labour market segmentation and increasing the use of open-ended contracts. In particular, it proposes making it possible to dismiss for reasons of the unsuitability of the worker (e.g. where a worker has not fulfilled 'specific delivery objectives and does not fulfil them, for reasons deriving exclusively from the workers' responsibility') even in cases where new technology or other changes to the workplace were not introduced (art. 373–380, 385 Labour Code). It also proposes removing strict LIFO (last in, first out) criteria in the case of redundancy, provided that the employer establishes relevant and non-discriminatory alternative criteria, and removing the obligation to attempt a transfer for a possible suitable position (art. 368, 375 Labour Code).

---

[242] Ibid., p. 37.

[243] See the Duffy/Walsh report commissioned by the Irish government in accordance with its commitment in the MoU to hold an independent review of the Framework REA and ERO agreements: <www.djei.ie/publications/employment/2011/Report_ERO_REA.pdf>.

[244] On 17 May 2011, the Council adopted Implementing Decision 2011/344/EU (OJ [2011] L159/88) to make available to Portugal medium-term financial assistance for a period of three years 2011–2014 in

To British eyes, these reforms are not radical. Nevertheless they go straight to the heart of the national labour law systems which, in turn, go to the core of national sovereignty. Furthermore, such reforms, together with the EU's own Council recommendations on the national reform programmes,[245] have created an expectation as to what Member States, who are in a state of crisis but not (yet) being bailed out, should do. The Italians have responded to this pressure. In Silvio Berlusconi's (in)famous letter to the heads of state meeting at the end of October 2011, he committed Italy to submitting the following additional measures: 'A reform of labour legislation (a) promoting greater readiness to take on employees and the efficiency requirements of business by means of, among other things, new rules governing dismissals for economic reasons in permanent employment contracts.'[246] However, even here the picture is not a straightforward story of deregulation. In the same paragraph he also talks about '(b) stricter conditions in the use of pseudo-sub contracting, given that such contracts are often used for workers formally classed as independent but essentially engaged as employees.'[247]

D. CONCLUSIONS

It is not clear whether some governments are using the crisis as a cover for reforms they had already intended to introduce. Certainly the economic benefits of deregulation are highly contested.[248] Nevertheless, the striking change that has occurred over the last year or so is the role of the EU towards employment protection. Traditionally, the EU has been seen as something of a bastion against deregulation at national level. Yet, now the EU—whether through the Council formations in the context of its recommendations on the integrated guidelines or at least the heads of state or government—has become responsible for the very deregulation it resisted for many years. Longer term, the EU may be responsible for precipitating a race-to-the-bottom: as we have seen Portuguese law is destined to become rather British.

However, while governments might be pushing for deregulation, this might not receive support from key constituencies. For example, in Italy provision was made for greater use of decentralized bargaining and, in particular, a reform of 2009 allowed for the possibility of 'opening clauses' (i.e. derogations from the sectoral wage agreed at

accordance with Council Regulation (EU) No 407/2010 of 11 May 2010 establishing a European financial stabilisation mechanism. The accompanying Memorandum of Understanding signed on the same day and its successive supplements lay down the economic policy conditions on the basis of which the financial assistance is disbursed. For a legal challenge and some of the changes, see the reference in Case C-128/12 Sindicatos dos Bancários do Norte.

[245] <http://ec.europa.eu/europe2020/reaching-the-goals/monitoring-progress/recommendations-2011/index_en.htm> (last accessed 4 April 2012).

[246] See the direct parallels between his letter and the Council recommendation 2011/C 215/02 of 12 July 2011 on the National Reform programme 2011 of Italy and delivering a Council opinion on the update Stability programme of Italy, 2011–14 (OJ [2011] L215/4), para. 2.

[247] <http://blogs.ft.com/brusselsblog/files/2011/11/BerlusconiLetter.pdf>.

[248] See e.g. <http://www.oecd.org/dataoecd/57/7/1868601.pdf>. Cf. <http://www.tuc.org.uk/extras/flexiblewiththetruth.pdf>.

national level by plant or firm level agreements); the trade unions resisted, the provision was generally not used, and it has now been dropped. Yet, despite some signs of resistance, the overall direction of travel is clear: labour law is on the menu. This point was underlined by President Sarkozy and Mrs Merkel in their joint letter to European Council President Herman Van Rompuy:[249] the 'Stability and Growth Union' should be based on a 'new common legal framework...allowing for faster progress in specific areas such as financial regulation [and] labour markets'.

The question remains whether the EPP and the other strategies are capable of delivering. The EU is dependent on the Member States co-operating and delivering substantively on their commitments and not just on paper. In fact, with the Lisbon strategy this 'voluminous churning of paper' has produced scant results,[250] in part because the Lisbon goals were both immensely (unrealistically?) ambitious and amorphous.

For states which have to implement these policies, and for commentators who observe and try to explain them, the Lisbon strategy in its various forms was like nailing blancmange to a wall. There was no obvious way of grasping what was actually required, just a sense that (lots of big) 'things have got to be done'. It would be unfair to say that the Lisbon relaunch and now the EU2020 strategy has the feeling of deckchairs being reorganized on the Titanic, but achieving the Lisbon goals does require the turning round of a large and unwieldy steamship. The crisis has given a renewed focus to the need for reform. It has also revealed the inherent tension in the EU2020 strategy: inclusive growth requires investment by the states at a time when money is very short. The question then is: to what extent is national labour law a victim of attempts to bring about reform?

*   *   *

As we know, some of the techniques deployed in the Lisbon strategy have been extended to the substantive areas of employment law which form the major preoccupation of this book. For those states where employment law is being deregulated,[251] the EU rules are increasingly becoming the floor below which national law cannot go. We begin by considering the rules on free movement of workers (Part II) and equality (Part III), both rights which have been found in the Treaty since its inception in 1957, before moving on to consider health and safety and working conditions (Part IV) and the rules on employees' rights when enterprises are restructured (Part V). We conclude by looking at the collective dimension to EU employment law, notably worker representation and collective action (Part VI).

---

[249] <http://blogs.ft.com/brusselsblog/2011/11/italian-monitoring-the-leaked-berlusconi-letter/#axzz1r2rxF8gP> (last accessed 4 April 2012).

[250] J. Gillingham, *Design for a New Europe* (CUP, Cambridge, 2006) 10.

[251] For a country-by-country analysis, see S. Clauwaert and I. Schömann, The crisis and national labour law reforms: a mapping exercise. <www.etui.org>.

PART II

MIGRANT WORKERS

4

FREE MOVEMENT OF WORKERS

A. INTRODUCTION

Free movement of workers, while one of the original four fundamental freedoms of the EU, has in fact been the Cinderella provision, with generally limited use being made of it by EU workers. That changed significantly with the 2004 enlargement of the Union when about 3.6 million workers migrated, primarily to the UK (about one third), to Spain (18 per cent), and to Ireland (10 per cent),[1] adding about 0.3 per cent to GDP of the EU as a whole. Their migration was mainly as workers under Article 45 TFEU (ex 39 EC), as self-employed under Article 49 TFEU (ex 43 EC), or as service providers under Article 56 TFEU (ex 49 EC). The focus of this chapter will be on the position of workers and the free movement rights they enjoy; specific issues concerning the establishment of natural persons (i.e. the self-employed) will be discussed and some reference to the provision of services—always in an employment context—will also be made. The rights of free movement are dependent on the individual, a national of a Member State, actually exercising the right of free movement. EU law does not apply to wholly internal situations.[2] Third country nationals (TCNs) who are workers enjoy a certain number of rights. These are considered in outline in Section E.

The principle of free movement was introduced to enable workers from states with high levels of *un*employment to move to states where employment levels were high. There they could find a job, probably benefit from higher wages than in their home state, and provide the skills needed by the host state.[3] Furthermore, the principle of non-discrimination meant that employers would select candidates based on merit and not nationality. At least, this was the theory. In practice, workers from the original Member States often preferred to stay (unemployed) in a state they were familiar with, in the company of family and friends. The Union addressed this problem by adopting a series

---

[1] Commission, *Five years of an enlarged EU: Economic achievements and challenges*, COM(2009) 79, 6.

[2] Case 175/78 *R* v. *Saunders* [1979] ECR 1129, para. 11.

[3] This is the experience with enlargement: see Commission (2009), above, n. 1. The Employment Guidelines continue to push labour mobility: see e.g. Dec. 2010/707/EU (OJ [2010] L308/46): Guideline 7 Increasing labour market participation of women and men, reducing structural unemployment and promoting job quality.

of measures giving rights not only to workers but also to their families in an attempt to encourage them to move as a unit. The legislature's approach has been reinforced by the Court which has been instrumental in helping secure this objective, first by removing obstacles which impeded free movement and then on finding ways to ensure that workers and their families became integrated into the host state. And with these developments came a change in perspective. Workers were no longer simply viewed as factors of production needed to fulfil the objectives of the common market. Now they were seen as EU citizens with rights enforceable against the host state. This perspective was reinforced by the inclusion of the provisions on Citizenship into the Treaty at Maastricht and now the adoption of the Citizens' Rights Directive (Directive 2004/38 (CRD)).[4] This chapter begins by examining who is a worker, who is a self-employed person, and who is a service provider, before considering the rights enjoyed, in particular by workers and their family members, and the limitations on those rights.

B. PERSONAL SCOPE

1. INTRODUCTION

The term 'worker' is the lynchpin to Article 45. Yet, the Treaties provide no definition of the concept. The term is also used in a number of Directives, such as the Working Time Directive 2003/88 and the Pregnant Workers Directive 92/85. Other Directives, such as the Transfer of Undertakings Directive 2001/23, use the term 'employee' albeit with reference back to national law.[5] As the nature of employment relationships has evolved, with increasing use of 'atypical' contracts (e.g. zero hours contracts, volunteer and intern relationships), the traditional divide between (dependent) employee and (independent) self-employed is breaking down. This is as much a problem for the EU as for the Member States when identifying the personal scope of the various measures. Since the Court has elaborated its thinking most extensively in the area of free movement of workers, we shall use this as an opportunity to discuss the question of personal scope more broadly. This is all the more justified by the fact that, in recent years, the Court has used the definition of 'workers' under Article 45 TFEU as a point of reference in determining the meaning of similar terms in other employment Directives.

2. THE TRADITIONAL DISTINCTION: EMPLOYEE V. SELF-EMPLOYED

As the Commission said in its Green Paper, *Modernising labour law to meet the challenges of the 21st century*:[5A]

---

[4] OJ [2004] L158/77.   [5] Art. 2(1)(d) of Dir. 2001/23.   [5A] COM(2006) 708.

The original purpose of labour law was to offset the inherent economic and social inequality within the employment relationship. From its origins, labour law has been concerned to establish employment status as the main factor around which entitlements would be developed. This traditional model reflects several key assumptions about employment status. It was assumed to involve i) permanent, full-time employment; ii) employment relationships regulated by labour law, with the contract of employment as the pivot; and iii) the presence of a single entity employer accountable for the obligations placed upon employers.

Because of this inherent inequality, labour law has protected the weaker party, the employee. By contrast, since, according to the theory at least, the self-employed are independent and thus not in this subordinate position they do not need the protection of labour law.

Traditionally, employees sell their labour while the self-employed sell a product—a product which may be produced as the result of their services. This distinction is reflected in the language used: contract *of* service (employees) and contract *for* services (self-employed). The classic distinction between employees and the self-employed is illustrated by the example of a chauffeur (employee) and a taxi driver (self-employed). The distinction between employees and the self-employed is well-known to all Member States. It is a distinction that the European Foundation also draws:

> A self-employed person is defined as an independent worker, who works independently of an employer, in contrast with an employee who is subordinate to and dependent on an employer.[6]

Taking the British case law by way of example, the classic test for distinguishing between employees and the self-employed concerns *control*—that the servant agrees that, in the performance of that service, he will be subject to the other's control in a sufficient degree to make that other master.[7] In other words, there is a degree of subordination. While this formulation might seem rather anachronistic and so has been subject to certain modifications (reflecting the changing nature of control from 'how to' to 'what to'[8]), the use of the control test has by no means died out.[9] In the absence of control, the individual is likely to be considered self-employed.

In other cases the courts have looked at the level of *integration* of the individual into the employer's business.[10] They have also examined the *economic reality* of the situation,[11] looking to see whether the provisions are consistent with it being a contract of service (e.g. does the employer have the power to select and dismiss, is the worker paid

---

[6] <http://www.eurofound.europa.eu/areas/industrialrelations/dictionary/definitions/selfemployedperson. htm> (last accessed 12 March 2012).

[7] *Ready Mixed Concrete (South East) Ltd* v. *Minister of Pensions and National Insurance* [1968] 2 QB 497, MacKenna J at 515; *Nethermere (St.Neots) Ltd* v. *Gardiner* [1984] ICR 612, Stephenson LJ, 623.

[8] See Viscount Simmonds in *Mersey Docks & Harbour Board* v. *Coggins & Griffiths Ltd* [1947] AC 1, 12.

[9] *Lane* v. *Shire Roofing* [1995] IRLR 493, 495 (Henry LJ).

[10] *Stevenson, Jordan & Harrison Ltd* v. *Macdonald & Evans* [1952] 1 TLR 101, 111.

[11] This includes looking 'beyond and beneath' the documents to what the parties said and did, both at the time when they were engaged and subsequently, including evidence as to how the relationship had been understood by them: *Raymond Franks* v. *Reuters Limited* [2003] IRLR 423, para. 12 (per Mummery LJ).

a wage or a lump sum, does the worker have to render exclusive service, or to work on the employer's premises; does the employer own the tools and the materials; does the employer bear the primary chance of profit or risk of loss; is the work an integral part of the business?).[12] This approach shows the extent to which the courts will not just look at one single factor but instead take a multiple or 'pragmatic' approach, weighing up all the factors for and against a contract of employment and determining on which side the scales will settle.[13]

However, the world has changed. As the Commission notes, rapid technological progress, increased competition stemming from globalization, changing consumer demand, and significant growth of the services sector have shown the need for increased flexibility. The emergence of just-in-time management, the shortening of the investment horizon for companies, the spread of information and communication technologies, and the increasing occurrence of demand shifts, have led businesses to organize themselves on a more flexible basis. This is reflected in variations to work organization, working hours, wages, and workforce size at different stages of the production cycle. These changes have created a demand for a wider variety of 'atypical' employment contracts:[14] for homeworkers,[15] agency workers,[16] zero-hours contract workers,[17] part-time and fixed-term workers, and seasonal workers. How can we tell whether they are employees? In British labour law one test seems to have taken precedence over the established tests to determine whether these atypical workers are employees: *mutuality of obligation.* This asks whether there is an obligation on the employer to provide work and a concomitant obligation on the individual to accept work offered. Only if such mutuality exists will the individual be an employee. In the absence of such mutuality the individual is likely to be self-employed.

This need to establish mutuality of obligation can be seen in *Carmichael.*[18] Carmichael was employed as a tour guide at a power station, working on a 'casual as required basis'. In order to claim particular employment rights she had to show she was an employee. The Employment Tribunal (the first tier court in employment matters) found that she was employed on a series of successive ad hoc contracts of service, or for services and that when she was not working as a guide the employee was under no contractual obligation to the power station. The House of Lords (the highest court in the UK) agreed. Lord Irvine of Lairg (then Lord Chancellor) said that there was no obligation on the power station to provide casual work nor on Carmichael to undertake it. For this reason, there would be an absence of 'that irreducible minimum of mutual obligation necessary to

---

[12] *Ready Mixed Concrete (South East) Ltd* v. *Minister of Pensions and National Insurance* [1968] 2 QB 497.

[13] I. Smith, *Industrial Law* (Butterworths, London, 2003).

[14] COM(2006) 708, 5. At p. 7 the Commission notes that the share of total employment taken up by those engaged on working arrangements differing from the standard contractual model as well as those in self-employment has increased since 2001 from over 36 per cent in 2001 to almost 40 per cent of the EU-25 workforce in 2005.

[15] *Nethermere (St.Neots) Ltd* v. *Taverna and Gardiner* [1984] IRLR 240.

[16] *Wickens* v. *Champion Employment Agency* [1984] ICR 365.

[17] *Clark* v. *Oxfordshire Health Authority* [1998] IRLR 125.

[18] *Carmichael* v. *National Power* [2000] IRLR 43.

create a contract of service' She therefore did not have a global contract of employment, although she might have been an employee during individual assignments.

3. DEPENDENT SELF-EMPLOYED

Individuals such as Carmichael find themselves in a particularly invidious position. They may well think of themselves as employees dependent on one particular employer but the courts find that they are not and so they may well be classed as self-employed *faute de mieux* and thus deprived of access to many employment rights (except possibly anti-discrimination law protection—see later). This is where the increasingly important and relatively new category of 'dependent self-employed' fits in. The existence of this category has been identified by the European Foundation:

> insofar as the concept of employee implies an element of economic dependence, in that employees are dependent for subsistence paid by the employer, self-employed workers may be little different, as no less dependent economically on their work for subsistence, though paid by their clients or customers.

The Commission, in its *Modernising Labour Law Green Paper*, also recognizes this category:[19]

> The concept of *'economically dependent work'* covers situations which fall between the two established concepts of subordinate employment and independent self-employment. These workers do not have a contract of employment. They may not be covered by labour law since they occupy a 'grey area' between labour law and commercial law. Although formally 'self-employed', they remain economically dependent on a single principal or client/ employer for their source of income.

In some systems such individuals might be considered 'workers'.[20] For example, in the UK the legal category of 'workers' covers not only employees but also individuals who undertake to do or perform 'personally any work or services for another party to the contract whose status is not by virtue of the contract that of a client or customer of any profession or business undertaking carried on by the individual'. Again the courts have been forced to produce criteria to identify this group of individuals. In *Byrne v. Baird*[21] the Employment Appeal tribunal (the second tier court) had to consider whether an individual working in the construction industry was a 'worker' for the purpose of claiming holiday pay under the Working Time Regulations which implement the Working Time Directive 2003/88. Mr Recorder Underhill QC recognized that, by giving rights to workers, the intention behind the Regulations was to create 'an intermediate class of

---

[19] COM(2006) 708 final, 11.

[20] Examples of 'employee-like' workers corresponding to the civil law notion of *'parasubordination'* in Italy and Germany. In Germany amendments to the Social Code introduced in 1999 to cover the social security status of economically dependent workers were subsequently modified in 2002: COM(2006) 708, 11. For a full analysis, see M. Freeland and N. Kountouris, *The Legal Construction of Personal Work Relations* (OUP, Oxford, 2011).

[21] [2002] IRLR 96.

protected worker, who is on the one hand not an employee but on the other hand cannot in some narrower sense be regarded as carrying on a business'.[22] He recognized that
workers enjoy protection because of their subordinate and dependent position vis-à-vis
their employers and for this reason the test for workers shared much in common with
the test for employee, including control and mutuality of obligation but with a lower
'pass-mark' so that cases which failed to reach the mark necessary to qualify for protection as employees might nevertheless be considered as workers.[23]

This analysis would seem to suggest that while the dependent self-employed should
benefit from being covered by much of labour law, the independent self-employed
(namely entrepreneurs who truly are in business on their own account) should not.
Such entrepreneurs are either individual contractors with a business of their own who
take the risks of losses and the chances of profits (e.g. a one-person business such as a
plumber) or individuals who do not have an identifiable business but who work as professionals for a large number of separate employers/clients (e.g. a consultant).[24]

These four different statuses are shown diagrammatically in Fig 4.1.

4. THE COURT OF JUSTICE'S CASE LAW ON WORKERS

The question, then, is how these national ideas of employee, worker and self-employed
are reflected at EU level in the case law of the Court of Justice of the European Union
(CJEU). The CJEU has had few opportunities to consider the definition of these key
terms in the context of the social policy Directives. There is, however, abundant case law
on the term 'worker' as used in Article 45 TFEU on the free movement of workers, a
term which the Court has insisted on giving a wide EU meaning.[25] In *Lawrie-Blum*[26] it

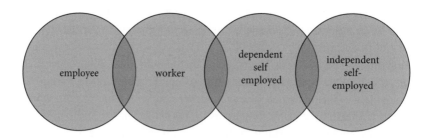

Fig. 4.1. Different employment statuses.

---

[22] Para. 17.   [23] Ibid.
[24] See e.g. S. Deakin and G. Morris, *Labour Law* (Hart Publishing, Oxford, 2009) 150.
[25] For criticism, see C. O'Brien, 'Social Blind spots and monocular policy making: The ECJ's migrant worker
model' (2009) 46 *CMLRev.* 1107.
[26] Case 66/85 [1986] ECR 2121, paras. 16–17.

said that the essential feature of an employment relationship is that 'for a certain period of time a person performs services for and under the direction of another person in return for which he receives remuneration'. The national court must decide whether a relationship of subordination exists.[27] The sphere of employment[28] and the nature of the legal relationship between employer and employee (whether or not it involves public law status or a private law contract)[29] are immaterial.

The Court has also required that a 'worker' be engaged in a 'genuine and effective' economic activity. While most activities satisfy this requirement[30]—including playing professional football,[31] being a prostitute,[32] doing an apprenticeship,[33] and other types of training[34]—this may not always be the case. For example, work as part of a community-based religion might not constitute an economic activity[35] nor might work not performed under 'normal' conditions (e.g. work undertaken as part of a drug rehabilitation programme[36]). The economic activity must also not be on 'such a small scale as to be purely marginal and ancillary'.[37] Although this hurdle might raise particular difficulties for part-time workers, the Court has generally found that they are still workers.[38]

This line of case law tends to suggest that the Court will favour a finding that an individual is a worker where possible, a view confirmed in *Vatsouras*.[39] The referring court had found that the 'brief minor' professional activity engaged in by Mr Vatsouras 'did not ensure him a livelihood'.[40] Nevertheless, the Court of Justice said that, 'independently of the limited amount of the remuneration and the short duration of the professional activity, it cannot be ruled out that that professional activity, following an overall assessment of the employment relationship, may be considered by the national authorities as real and genuine, thereby allowing its holder to be granted the status of "worker" within the meaning of Article [45 TFEU]'.[41]

---

[27] Case C-337/97 *Meeusen* v. *Hoofddirectie van de Informatie Beheer Groep* [1999] ECR I-3289, para. 15.

[28] Case 36/74 *Walrave and Koch* v. *Union Cycliste Internationale* [1974] ECR 1405, para. 21.

[29] Case 152/73 *Sotgiu* v. *Deutsche Bundespost* [1974] ECR 153, para. 5.

[30] See, e.g., Case 13/76 *Donà* v. *Mantero* [1976] ECR 1333, para. 12.

[31] Case C-415/93 *Union Royale Belge de Société de Football Association* v. *Bosman* [1995] ECR I-4921, para. 73.

[32] Case C-268/99 *Aldona Malgorzata Jany and others* v. *Staatssecretaris van Justitie* [2001] ECR I-8615, para. 33.

[33] Case C-188/00 *Kurz, née Yüce* v. *Land Baden-Württemberg* [2002] ECR I-10691.

[34] Case C-109/04 *Kranemann* v. *Land Nordrhein-Westfalen* [2005] ECR I-2421; Case C-10/05 *Mattern* v. *Mininstre du Travail et de l'emploi* [2006] ECR I-3145, para. 21.

[35] Cf. Case 196/87 *Steymann* v. *Staatssecretaris van Justitie* [1988] ECR 6159, para. 14.

[36] Case 344/87 *Bettray* v. *Staatssecretaris van Justitie* [1989] ECR 1621, para. 17. Cf. Case C-1/97 *Birden* v. *Stadtgemeinde Bremen* [1998] ECR I-7747, decided in the context of the EEC-Turkey Association Agreement, where a person employed under a job-creation scheme was considered a worker.

[37] See, e.g., Case C-357/89 *Raulin* v. *Minister van Onderwijs en Wetenschappen* [1992] ECR I-1027, para. 10.

[38] Case 53/81 *Levin* [1982] ECR 1035, para. 17.

[39] Joined Cases C-22/08 and 23/08 *Vatsouras* v. *Arbeitsgemeinschaft* [2009] ECR I-4585, para. 30.

[40] Para. 25.   [41] Para. 30.

The Court has also extended the definition of 'worker' to include those seeking work.[42] While the period allowed for work seekers to remain in the host state depends on the rules of that state, they must be given at least three months to look for work,[43] although if they are dependent on social security they may be asked to leave.[44] At the time of the decision in *Antonissen*[45] migrants in the UK could have six months to look for work[46] which the Court found to be compatible with Union law. If, at the end of the six-month period, work seekers can show that they have a genuine chance of being employed, they cannot be required to leave the host state. For this reason the Court said in *Commission* v. *Belgium*[47] that a Belgian law requiring a work seeker to leave the state automatically on the expiry of the three-month period breached Article 45 TFEU. Article 14(4)(b) CRD confirms this line of case law, making clear that Union citizen work seekers (and their family members) cannot be expelled so long as they can 'provide evidence that they are continuing to seek employment and that they have a genuine chance of being engaged'. No time limit is specified.

Article 7(3) CRD also makes provision for those Union citizens who are no longer employed as workers (or self-employed) to retain worker (or self-employed) status in four situations:

(a) Where the individual cannot work because that person is temporarily incapacitated through illness or accident.[48]

(b) Where the individual has become *involuntarily* unemployed after having been employed for more than one year, and has registered as a job seeker with the relevant employment office.

(c) Where the individual has become *involuntarily* unemployed after having completed a fixed-term contract of less than one year or after having become involuntarily unemployed during the first 12 months and after having registered as a job seeker with the relevant employment office. In this situation the status of worker can be retained for no less than six months.

(d) Where the individual embarks on vocational training. Unless the individual is involuntarily unemployed, the retention of the status of worker requires the training to be related to the previous employment.[49]

---

[42] Case C–85/96 *Martínez Sala* v. *Freistaat Bayern* [1998] ECR I–2691, para. 32; Case C–138/02 *Collins* v. *Secretary of State for Work and Pensions* [2003] ECR I–2703, para. 29.

[43] In certain circumstances work seekers are entitled to social security benefits for three months under Art. 64 of Regulation 883/04.

[44] Declaration of the Council accompanying Dir. 68/360 and Reg. 1612/68 ([1968] OJ Spec Ed Series I–475).

[45] Case C–292/89 *R* v. *IAT, ex p. Antonissen* [1991] ECR I–745, para. 21.

[46] Statement of Changes to the Immigration Rules (HC 169).

[47] Case C–344/95 *Commission* v. *Belgium* [1997] ECR I–1035, para. 18.

[48] Cf. Case C–43/99 *Leclere* [2001] ECR I–4265 considered at n. 189.

[49] Case 39/86 *Lair* [1988] ECR 3161 considered below at n. 210.

In designating these individuals as workers (or self-employed), the CRD confirms and extends the case law of the Court.[50] It also means that these deemed workers/self-employed enjoy full equality of treatment under Article 24(1) CRD, for at least six months in the case of work seekers satisfying the conditions in Article 7(3)(c) CRD, and are not subject to the derogation in Article 24(2) CRD.[51]

5. THE COURT OF JUSTICE'S CASE LAW ON THE SELF-EMPLOYED

While Article 45 TFEU concerns free movement of workers, Article 49 TFEU gives rights of free movement to those who are self-employed wishing to establish themselves. As with Article 45 TFEU, the Treaties do not define 'self-employed', but in *Jany*[52] the Court explained that, unlike workers, the self-employed work outside a relationship of subordination, they bear the risk for the success or failure of their employment, and they are paid directly and in full.[53] The case concerned Czech and Polish women working as prostitutes in the Netherlands.[54] They paid rent to the owner of the premises and received a monthly income (of between FL. 1,500 and 1,800) which they declared to the tax authorities. The Court considered them to be self-employed.[55] *Jany* therefore suggests that Article 49 TFEU permits individuals to engage in a wide range of economic activities in other Member States and still be considered self-employed. As the Court put it in *Barkoci and Malik*,[56] a self-employed person could conduct 'activities of an industrial or commercial character, activities of craftsmen, or activities of the professions of a Member State'.[57] If the self-employed work is performed only temporarily in another Member State then the individual provider is likely to fall in the scope of Article 56 TFEU.

Outside the free movement context, there has been no Court of Justice case law on the meaning of the phrase 'self-employed'. However, the significance of this classification

---

[50] See, e.g., Case C–35/97 *Commission* v. *France* [1998] ECR I–5325, para. 41; Case C–413/01 *Ninni-Orasche* [2003] ECR I–13187, para. 34.

[51] Joined Cases C–22/08 and 23/08 *Vatsouras* [2009] ECR I–4585, paras. 32–34.

[52] Case C–268/99 *Jany and others* v. *Staatssecretaris van Justitie* [2001] ECR I–8615.

[53] Paras. 34 and 70–1.

[54] The case was decided under the Europe Agreements but in this regard the Court said that the principles were the same as those under Art. 49 (para. 38).

[55] On the difficulties involved in distinguishing between employees and the self-employed, see Case C–161/07 *Commission* v. *Austria (self-certification)* [2008] ECR I–10671. Austrian legislation, introduced in the light of the EU's enlargement in 2004, required nationals of the eight new Member States to prove that they would not be working as employees (and thus excluded from the free movement of workers provisions under the transitional arrangements) by producing a certificate showing that, for example, they were the member of a partnership or a limited liability company. This enshrined a difference in treatment on the grounds of nationality which was prohibited, in principle, by Art. 49 TFEU.

[56] Case C–257/99 *R.* v. *Secretary of State for the Home Department, ex p. Barkoci and Malik* [2001] ECR I–6557, para. 50. This was in the context of Art. 45(3) of the Association Agreement which has wording 'similar or identical to' Art. 49 TFEU.

[57] See additionally Case C–55/94 *Gebhard* [1995] ECR I–4165, para. 23, 'all types of self-employed activity'.

should not be underestimated. In its *Modernisation of Labour Law* Green Paper[58] the Commission notes:

> Self-employment is also providing a means of coping with restructuring needs, reducing direct or indirect labour costs and managing resources more flexibly in response to unforeseen economic circumstances. It also reflects the business model of service-oriented business delivering completed projects to their customers. In many cases it reflects a free choice to work independently despite lower levels of social protection in exchange for more direct control over employment conditions and terms of remuneration. Self-employed workers in the EU-25 numbered over 31 million in 2005 or 15% of the total workforce[1]. Those who are self-employed on their own account and without employees constitute 10% of all workers in the EU-25.

6. LEARNING ACROSS THE PROVISIONS

In recent years the Court has drawn on its case law in the field of free movement to inform its interpretation of similar terms in other directives. For example, in *Union Syndicale Solidaires Isère*[59] the Court, citing the case law under Article 45, said that the concept of worker for the purposes of the Working Time Directive 2003/88:

> may not be interpreted differently according to the law of Member States but has an autonomous meaning specific to European Union law. The concept must be defined in accordance with objective criteria which distinguish the employment relationship by reference to the rights and duties of the persons concerned. The essential feature of an employment relationship, however, is that for a certain period of time a person performs services for and under the direction of another person in return for which he receives remuneration.

The decision in *Allonby*[60] highlights a further interesting phenomenon: the blurring of the distinction between employees and the dependent self-employed under EU law. The case concerned part-time teachers who used to be employed directly by a further education (FE) college but were told that they could continue working for the college only if they were engaged on a self-employed basis by an agency, ELS. The effect of these changes was to reduce Allonby's pay. She claimed that her rights to 'equal pay for male and female *workers*' under Article 157 TFEU had been infringed. The question for the Court was whether the lecturers were workers. The Court began by noting that the term 'worker' used in Article 157(1) TFEU had a broad, Union meaning.[61] Then, drawing on its free movement of workers case law under Article 45 TFEU, the Court said:[62]

---

[58] COM(2006) 708.
[59] See Case C–428/09 *Union Syndicale Solidaires Isère v. Premier Ministre* [2010] ECR I–000, para. 28.
[60] Case C–256/01 *Allonby v. Accrington & Rosendale College* [2004] ECR I–873.
[61] Para. 66.
[62] Case 66/85 *Lawrie-Blum* [1986] ECR 2121, para. 17, and Case C–85/96 *Martínez Sala* [1998] ECR I–2691, para. 32.

For the purposes of that provision [Article 157(1)], there must be considered as a worker a person who, for a certain period of time, performs services for and under the direction of another person in return for which he receives remuneration.

The Court said that '[i]t is clear from that definition that the authors of the Treaty did not intend that the term "worker", within the meaning of Article [157(1) TFEU], should include independent providers of services who are not in a relationship of subordination with the person who receives the services'.[63] However, the Court added the caveat that formal classification of a self-employed person under national law did not exclude the possibility that a person had to be classified as a worker within the meaning of Article 157(1) TFEU if her independence was 'merely notional, thereby disguising an employment relationship within the meaning of that article'. It said that it was necessary 'in particular to consider the extent of any limitation on their freedom to choose their timetable, and the place and content of their work'. It continued: 'The fact that no obligation is imposed on them to accept an assignment is of no consequence in that context'.[64] This suggests that, in the EU context, the UK's 'mutuality of obligation' requirement may be diminished in the light of the practical realities of the situation when EU employment rights are at stake.

Further, *Allonby* also suggests that the courts should be prepared to look behind the labels attached by the parties themselves to their relationship to see if the individual is in fact in a situation of dependence such as to merit the classification of an employment relationship, a point the Court confirmed in *Danosa*.[65] The case raised the question whether a member of a board of directors could be a worker for the purposes of the Pregnant Workers Directive. The Court said the fact that:[66]

Ms Danosa was a member of the Board of Directors of a capital company is not enough in itself to rule out the possibility that she was in a relationship of subordination to that company: it is necessary to consider the circumstances in which the Board Member was recruited; the nature of the duties entrusted to that person; the context in which those duties were performed; the scope of the person's powers and the extent to which he or she was supervised within the company; and the circumstances under which the person could be removed.

National courts have long looked at the reality of the situation. For example, the French Court de cassation said: 'the existence of an employment relationship does not depend on the will of the parties however they have expressed it, nor on the label which they give their agreement, but on the factual matrix within which the relevant labour services are carried out'.[67] The criminal chamber of the Court had previously said in 1985, in a case concerning workers who had been given the title of 'artisans' by their employer

---

[63] Para. 68. See further, in the context of free movement of workers, Case C–337/97 *Meeusen* [1999] ECR I–3289, para. 15.
[64] Citing Case C–357/89 *Raulin* [1992] ECR I–1027, paras. 9 and 10.
[65] Case C–232/09 *Danosa* v. *LKB Līzings SIA* [2010] ECR I–000.
[66] Para. 47.
[67] Soc., 19. décembre 2000; noted by A. Jeammaud [2001] *Droit Social* 227.

under agreements purporting to be 'sub-contracts', that the will of the parties 'is insufficient to remove from workers the social status that necessarily attaches to them by
virtue of the manner in which they carry out their tasks'.[68] The UK courts have also been
willing to look behind the label.[69] For example, in *Quinnen* v. *Hovells,*[70] where an
employer described a shop assistant as self-employed to avoid the relationship of
employer and employee and the complications that accompany that relationship, the
Employment Appeal Tribunal said that the applicant came within the scope of the
equality legislation because 'a contract for the personal execution of work or labour was
intended' and the personal scope of the legislation was broader than 'the ordinary connotation of employment, so as to include persons outside the master-servant
relationship'.

Quinnen v. *Hovells* alludes to another point which has attracted the Commission in
recent years: that different groups enjoy different rights. So, for example, in the UK
employees, the most narrowly defined group, enjoy the full gamut of employment protection legislation, albeit often after a period of service (e.g. two years' service in the case
of unfair dismissal and redundancy); *workers*, a more broadly defined group including
employees and the dependent self-employed, enjoy some employment rights, but a
reduced range (e.g. national minimum wage, working time); professionals, a still more
broadly defined group including employees and workers but also those providing personal service, enjoy a still further reduced number of rights but do benefit from the
anti-discrimination legislation. However, the genuinely self-employed benefit from no
employment rights at all. The Commission puts it in the following way:[71]

> The 'targeted approach' adopted in the UK to establishing differing rights and responsibili-
> ties in employment law for 'employees' and 'workers' is an example of how categories of
> vulnerable workers involved in complex employment relationships have been given mini-
> mum rights without an extension of the full range of labour law entitlements associated
> with standard work contracts. Anti-discrimination rights, health and safety protection,
> guarantees of minimum wage as well as safeguards for collective bargaining rights, have
> been selectively extended to economically dependent workers in several Member States.
> Other rights, particularly those relating to notice and dismissal, tend to be restricted to
> regular employees having completed a prescribed period of continuous employment.

This more nuanced approach is one that the EU has used itself. In the Commercial
Agents Directive 86/653/EEC,[72] which concerns the self-employed, the EU has chosen
to give basic employment protection to the agents including payment of remuneration;
conditions for the conversion of fixed-term contracts into contracts of indefinite duration; as well as compensation in the event of damage suffered due to the termination of
a contract.

---

[68] Crim., 20 octobre 1985, *Bull. crim.* No. 335.
[69] See, in particular, the Supreme Court in *Autoclenz* v. *Belcher* [2011] IRLR 820.
[70] [1984] IRLR 227.
[71] COM(2006) 708.   [72] OJ [1986] L382/17.

7. WHO IS THE EMPLOYER?

While considerable attention has now been paid in the case law to the identification of the individual who benefits from the EU rights, much less attention has been paid to the question as to who is the employer. While in many cases this may be obvious—the natural or legal person with whom the individual has a contract—in more complex arrangements (e.g. chains of sub-contracting) the identity of the employer is not always so obvious. There have been two responses to this problem. First, in some cases the Court is prepared to look at the reality of the situation, even if this means piercing the corporate veil. *Albron*[73] provides a good example of this. The employee had a contract with the parent company (Heineken) but he was assigned to work for a Heineken subsidiary. When the activities of the subsidiary were transferred to Albron, the Court said that the subsidiary was the transferor even though the contract was with the parent and so Directive 2001/23 on transfers of undertaking in principle applied. The Court said that the requirement under Article 3(1) of Directive 2001/23 that there be either an employment contract, or, in the alternative and thus as an equivalent, an employment relationship at the date of the transfer suggested that, in the mind of the Union legislature, a contractual link with the transferor was not required in all circumstances for employees to be able to benefit from the protection conferred by Directive 2001/23.[74] It continued that 'it is not apparent from Directive 2001/23 that the relationship between the employment contract and the employment relationship is one of subsidiarity and that, therefore, where there is a plurality of employers, the contractual employer must systematically be given greater weight.'[75]

The second response lies in deeming a particular person as taking responsibility for ensuring individuals benefit from employment rights even if they are not the employer in the legal sense. For example, as the Commission notes,[76] in extended chains of sub-contracting several Member States have made principal contractors responsible for the obligations of their sub-contractors under a system of joint and several liability. Such a system encourages principal contractors to monitor compliance with employment legislation on the part of their commercial partners. In *Wolff and Müller*[77] on the posting of workers such a system was considered to be an acceptable procedural means of safeguarding an entitlement to minimum rates of pay where this form of worker protection is necessary and proportional and in accord with the public interest. This approach is now reflected in the draft enforcement Directive on posted workers considered in Chapter 5.

---

[73] Case C–242/098 *Albron Catering* v. *FNV Bondgenoten and John Roest* [2010] ECR I–000.
[74] Para. 24.
[75] Para. 25.
[76] COM(2006) 708, 13.   [77] Case C–60/03 [2004] ECR I–9553.

C. THE RIGHTS CONFERRED ON WORKERS

1. THE TREATY PROVISIONS

1.1. The content

Having looked to see whether an individual is a worker, we turn now to see what rights workers enjoy. Article 45(1) TFEU provides that workers enjoy the right of free movement which, according to Article 45(2) TFEU, includes the abolition of any discrimination based on nationality between workers of the Member States, as regards employment, remuneration and other conditions of work and employment.[78] Article 45(3) TFEU then adds that free movement comprises the right to:

- accept offers of employment actually made,
- move freely within the territory of the Member States for this purpose,
- stay in the Member State for the purpose of the employment, and
- remain in the Member State after having been employed.[79]

In addition, the Court has recognized that workers have the right, derived directly from the Treaty, to leave their state of origin, to enter the territory of another Member State, and to reside and pursue an economic activity there,[80] rights now repeated in the CRD. A Member State can deny free movement on the grounds of public policy, public security, and public health.[81]

1.2. Direct effect

The rights contained in Articles 45, 49, and 56 TFEU are directly effective. In respect of Article 45 TFEU this was first acknowledged by the Court in *French Merchant Seamen*[82] and confirmed in *Van Duyn*[83] where the Court ruled that, despite the derogations to the principle of free movement contained in Article 45(3) TFEU, the provisions of Articles 45(1) and (2) TFEU imposed a sufficiently precise obligation to confer direct effect. The Court also ruled that Articles 49 and 56 TFEU were directly effective in *Reyners*[84] and *Van Binsbergen*[85] respectively. Applicants can rely on the direct effect of Articles 45, 49,

---

[78] Art. 45(2) TFEU. The following section draws on C. Barnard, *The Substantive Law of the European Union* (Oxford, OUP, 2010), Ch. 9.

[79] Art. 45(3) TFEU.

[80] Case C–363/89 *Roux v. Belgium* [1991] ECR I–273, para. 9; Case C–18/95 *Terhoeve v. Inspecteur van de Belastingdienst Particulieren* [1999] ECR I–345, para. 38.

[81] See e.g. Art. 45(3) TFEU and Articles 27–33 CRD. Since these provisions are rarely invoked against those exercising their rights to free movement as workers they will not be considered further in this chapter. More detail can be found in Ch. 13 of C. Barnard, *The Substantive Law of the EU: The Four Freedoms* 3rd edn (OUP, Oxford, 2010).

[82] Case 167/73 *Commission v. France* [1974] ECR 359, para. 41.

[83] Case 41/74 [1974] ECR 1337, para. 8.

[84] Case 2/74 [1974] ECR 631, para. 32.

[85] Case 33/74 *van Binsbergen v. Bestuur van de Bedrijfsvereniging voor de Metaalnijverheid* [1974] ECR 1299, para. 27.

and 56 TFEU[86] against both the host state (the more usual situation)[87] and the home state,[88] provided the situation is not wholly internal.

While in principle Treaty provisions can have both vertical and horizontal direct effect (and so can be relied on by an individual against both the state and a private body),[89] for many years it was not clear whether Articles 45, 49, and 56 TFEU had vertical and horizontal direct effect or only vertical direct effect. In *Walrave and Koch*[90] the Court suggested that the Treaty provisions had both: it said 'the rule on non-discrimination applies in judging *all legal relationships* in so far as these relationships, by reason either of the place they are entered into or the place where they take effect, can be located within the territory of the [Union]'. The Court also said that in addition to public authorities the ban on discrimination 'extends likewise to rules of any other nature aimed at collectively regulating gainful employment and services'.[91] Yet subsequent cases concerned action taken by public authorities[92] or professional regulatory bodies (e.g. the Bar Council,[93] the Italian football association,[94] or the International Cycling Union[95]) which suggested an extended form of vertical direct effect only.

However, in *Clean Car*[96] the Court provided a strong hint that the free movement of *workers* provisions had both vertical and horizontal direct effect, and this was subsequently confirmed in *Angonese*.[97] Applicants applying for jobs in a private bank had to produce a certificate of bilingualism issued by the local authority. The Court noted that since working conditions were governed not only by laws but also by agreements and other acts adopted by private persons, there would be inequality in the application of Article 45 TFEU if it applied only to acts of a public authority.[98] Drawing on the long-established case law interpreting Article 157 TFEU (ex 141 EC) on equal pay,[99] the Court then ruled that the prohibition of discrimination in Article 45 TFEU applied

---

[86] The applicants can be the workers, self-employed or service providers themselves or employers applying on their behalf: Case C–350/96 *Clean Car* [1998] ECR I–2521, para. 24.

[87] E.g., Case 41/74 *van Duyn* [1974] ECR 1337.

[88] This arises in cases concerning impediments to the 'export' of the worker, self-employed person or company, and service: e.g. Case C–384/93 *Alpine Investments* [1995] ECR I–1141, para. 30; Case C–107/94 *Asscher* [1996] ECR I–3089, para. 32; C–18/95 *Terhoeve* [1999] ECR I–345, para. 39; but also in cases about returners: e.g. Case C–19/92 *Kraus* [1993] ECR I–1663, para. 15.

[89] See e.g. Case 43/75 *Defrenne v. Sabena* [1976] ECR 455 concerning Art. 157 TFEU on equal pay but not goods (see Ch. 6).

[90] Case 36/74 [1974] ECR 1405, dispositif, emphasis added.

[91] Para. 17.

[92] See e.g. the Home Office in Case 41/74 *Van Duyn* [1974] ECR 1337 and local authorities in Case 197/84 *Steinhauser* v. *Ville de Biarritz* [1985] ECR 1819 and Case C–168/91 *Konstantinidis* v. *Stadt Altensteig-Standesamt* [1993] ECR I–1191.

[93] Case 71/76 *Thieffry* v. *Conseil de l'ordre des avocats de la cour de Paris* [1977] ECR 765; Case C–309/99 *Wouters* [2002] ECR I–1577, para. 120.

[94] Case 13/76 *Donà* [1976] ECR 1333.

[95] Case 36/74 *Walrave and Koch* [1974] ECR 1405.

[96] Case C–350/96 [1998] ECR I–2521, itself confirming the hint in Case C–415/93 *Bosman* [1995] ECR I–4921, para. 86.

[97] Case C–281/98 [2000] ECR I–4139.

[98] Para. 33.

[99] Esp. Case 43/75 *Defrenne* v. *Sabena* [1976] ECR 455, considered in Chs. 6 and 7.

both to agreements intended to regulate paid labour collectively and to contracts between individuals.[100] Therefore Article 45 TFEU had horizontal direct effect and so applied to private persons.[101] It is not clear whether this ruling can be extended to Article 49 TFEU on establishment and Article 56/57 TFEU on services. This is considered in more detail in Chapter 5.

2. THE SECONDARY LEGISLATION

2.1. Introduction

The details of the rights laid down by Article 45 TFEU were expanded by three secondary measures: Directive 68/360 on the rights of entry and residence, Regulation 1612/68 on the free movement of workers[102] (now Regulation 492/2011),[103] and Regulation 1251/70 on the right to remain. Directive 68/360,[104] Regulation 1251/70,[105] and two Union Directives on establishment and services,[106] including the provisions on family rights laid down in Articles 10 and 11 of Regulation 1612/68, have been replaced by a single Directive on Citizens' Rights (Directive 2004/38 (CRD)). This Directive applies to all citizens, not just to the economically active. At the heart of the CRD lies the basic idea that the rights enjoyed by the migrant increase the longer a person is resident in the host state. There are three different degrees of integration: (1) rights for those wishing to enter for up to three months;[107] (2) rights for those residing for up to five years;[108] and (3) rights for those residing for more than five years ('the right of permanent residence').[109] While the CRD will have a significant effect on the non-economically active and their family members, those who are economically active as workers or self-employed will enjoy the rights laid down in the Treaties and they enjoy these rights from day one. Most of the existing secondary legislation, as interpreted by the Court, will continue to apply to workers. Therefore, the existing legislation is discussed here together with reference to the changes introduced by the CRD where appropriate. However, the interface between the Treaty, the CRD, and Regulation 492/2011 is not always straightforward.

2.2. Access to employment and the right to equal treatment

(a) Introduction

Although Article 24 of the CRD lays down the general principle of equal treatment for all Union citizens, the detailed manifestation of this principle for *workers* is still spelt out in Regulation 492/2011 and it is likely that the Court will continue to refer to this Regulation when considering workers' cases. Regulation 492/2011 was designed both

---

[100] Para. 34.   [101] Para. 36.   [102] OJ [1968] L257/2.   [103] [2011] L141/1.
[104] OJ [1968] SE (II) L257/13/485.
[105] This was repealed by Commission Reg. 635/2006 (OJ [2006] L112/9).
[106] Dir. 73/148 (OJ [1973] L172/14) and Dir. 75/34 (OJ [1975] L14/10).
[107] Art. 6.   [108] Arts. 7–15.   [109] Arts. 16–18.

to facilitate the free movement of workers and their families as well as ensuring their integration into the community of the host state. When enacting the original Regulation 1612/68, the Council

> ... took into account, first, the importance for the worker, from a human point of view of having his entire family with him and, secondly, the importance, from all points of view, of the integration of the worker and his family into the host Member State without any difference in treatment in relation to nationals of that State.[110]

The consideration of Regulation 492/2011 falls into two parts: first, the right of *access* to a post on non-discriminatory terms (Title I), and second, the right to equal treatment while doing that job, i.e. non-discrimination in respect of *exercise* of Union rights (Title II).

(b) Equal treatment in respect of access to employment

Article 1 of Regulation 492/2011 reiterates the substance of Article 45 TFEU: any national of a Member State 'has the right to take up an activity as an employed person, and to pursue such activity, within the territory of another Member State', enjoying the same priority as a national. The worker may conclude and perform contracts of employment in accordance with the laws of the host state.[111] Any provisions which discriminate against foreign nationals or hinder foreign nationals from obtaining work are not permissible.[112]

(i) Direct discrimination

The prohibition against discrimination applies to both directly and indirectly discriminatory measures. Measures are directly discriminatory where the migrant worker is treated less favourably than the national worker. This was the case with the Italian law in *Commission* v. *Italy*[113] which provided that private security work could be carried out only by Italian security firms employing only Italian nationals. The '3 + 2 rule' in *Bosman*,[114] according to which football clubs could play no more than three foreign players and two 'acclimatised' players in any match, was also directly discriminatory. The Court, referring to the principle of non-discrimination contained in Article 45(2) TFEU and Article 4 of Regulation 492/2011, said that the principle applied to clauses contained in the regulations of sporting associations which restricted the rights of nationals of other Member States to take part, as professional players, in football matches. It continued that it was irrelevant that the clauses did not concern the employment of such players, on which there was no restriction, but the extent to which their clubs could field them

---

[110] Case C–249/86 *Commission* v. *Germany* [1989] ECR 1263, para. 11.

[111] Art. 2.

[112] Art. 3(1). Some examples listed in Art. 3(2) are: prescribing a special recruitment procedure for foreign nationals, restricting the advertising of vacancies in the press, and imposing additional requirements on applicants from other Member States of subjecting eligibility for employment to conditions of registration with employment offices.

[113] Case C–283/99 *Commission* v. *Italy* [2001] ECR I–4363.

[114] Case C–415/93 [1995] ECR I–4921. See further Case 13/76 *Donà and Mantero* [1976] ECR 1333.

in official matches. It said that in so far as participation in official matches was the essential purpose of a professional player's life, a rule which restricted that participation obviously also restricted the chances of employment of the player concerned. Such directly discriminatory measures breach both Article 45 TFEU (and the Regulation) and can be saved only by reference to one of the express derogations laid down by the Treaties or the secondary legislation. The express derogations cover public policy, public security and public health. The case law on the derogations has been codified in Article 27(2) CRD:

> 2. Measures taken on grounds of public policy or public security shall comply with the principle of proportionality and shall be based exclusively on the personal conduct of the individual concerned. Previous criminal convictions shall not in themselves constitute grounds for taking such measures.
>
> The personal conduct of the individual concerned must represent a genuine, present and sufficiently serious threat affecting one of the fundamental interests of society. Justifications that are isolated from the particulars of the case or that rely on considerations of general prevention shall not be accepted.

As the language suggests, this derogation is generally invoked by states refusing a migrant initial entry to the territory rather than by employers, whether public or private, justifying direct discrimination in respect of access or, as below, exercise of employment. Furthermore, as Article 27(1) makes clear, the provision cannot be used to serve economic ends. Therefore, any attempt by, say, a public authority to have a recruitment policy based on prioritizing jobs for nationals over migrants (as Gordon Brown, then British Prime Minister famously put it, 'British jobs for British workers'[115]), would be acting contrary to Article 27(1) CRD.

Regulation 492/2011 itself identifies and seeks to eliminate other directly discriminatory barriers on access to employment. For example, Article 4(1) provides that national provisions which restrict, by number or percentage, the employment of foreign nationals in any undertaking do not apply to nationals of the other Member States. Therefore in *Commission v. France*[116] the Court said that a French rule requiring a ratio of three French to one non-French seaman on a merchant ship contravened Article 4(1). Article 4(2) provides that if there is a requirement that an undertaking is subject to a minimum percentage of national workers being employed, nationals of the other Member States are counted as national workers. Article 6 provides that the engagement and recruitment of a worker must not depend on medical, vocational, or other criteria which are discriminatory on the grounds of nationality. However, it does permit the employer to require the migrant worker to take a vocational test when offering employment.

---

[115] Cf C. Barnard, '"British Jobs for British Workers": The Lindsey Oil Refinery Dispute and the Future of Local Labour Clauses in an Integrated EU Market' (2009) 38 *ILJ* 245.

[116] Case 167/73 *Commission v. France (French Merchant Seamen)* [1974] ECR 359. See further the '3 + 2 rule' in Case C–415/93 *Bosman* [1995] ECR I–4921.

(ii) Indirect discrimination

Indirect discrimination involves the elimination of requirements which, while apparently nationality-neutral on their face, have a greater impact or impose a greater burden on nationals of other Member States or have the effect of hindering the free movement of persons.[117] Thus, indirect discrimination focuses on the effect of a measure. This is recognized by Article 3(1) of Regulation 492/2011 which says that provisions laid down by national law will not apply where, 'though applicable irrespective of nationality, their exclusive or principal aim *or effect* is to keep nationals of other Member States away from employment offered'.[118] The Court also made this clear in *O'Flynn*:[119]

> Conditions imposed by national law must be regarded as indirectly discriminatory where, although applicable irrespective of nationality, they affect essentially migrant workers...or the great majority of those affected are migrant workers,...where they are indistinctly applicable but can be more easily satisfied by national workers than by migrant workers...or where there is a risk that they may operate to the particular detriment of migrant workers...

Indirectly discriminatory measures also breach Article 45 TFEU and the Regulation unless saved by one of the express derogations or objectively justified.[120] As the Court continued in *O'Flynn*:[121]

> It is otherwise only if those provisions are justified by objective considerations independent of the nationality of the workers concerned, and if they are proportionate to the legitimate aim pursued by national law.

From this we can see that, unless objectively justified and proportionate to its aim, the provision of national law must be regarded as indirectly discriminatory and contrary to Union law if it is *intrinsically liable* to affect migrant workers more than national workers and if there is *a risk* that it will place migrant workers at a particular disadvantage.[122] The Court added that it was not necessary to find that the measure did in practice affect a substantially higher proportion of migrant workers. It was sufficient that it was liable to have such an effect.[123]

Service requirements are often found to be indirectly discriminatory. This can be seen in *Scholz*[124] where a German woman applied for a job in Italy but the selection

---

[117] See e.g. Case C–175/88 *Biehl* v. *Admininstration des Contributions* [1990] ECR I–1779; Case C–111/91 *Commission* v. *Luxembourg* [1993] ECR I–817.

[118] Emphasis added.

[119] Case C–237/94 *O'Flynn* v. *Adjudication Officer* [1996] ECR I–2617, para. 18.

[120] See e.g. Case C–15/96 *Kalliope Schöning-Kougebetopoulou* v. *Freie und Hansestadt Hamburg* [1998] ECR I–47. See Case C–187/96 *Commission* v. *Greece* [1998] ECR I–1095; Case C–350/96 *Clean Car Autoservice* v. *Landeshauptmann von Wien* [1998] ECR I–2521.

[121] Para. 19.

[122] Para. 20. The fact that nationals may also be affected by the rule does not prevent the rule from being indirectly discriminatory, provided that the majority of those affected were non-nationals: Case C–281/98 *Roman Angonese* v. *Cassa di Risparmio di Bolzano* [2000] ECR I–4139, para. 41.

[123] Para. 21.

[124] Case C–419/92 *Scholz* v. *Opera Universitaria di Cagliari and Cinzia Porcedda* [1994] ECR I–505.

board refused to take into account her previous employment in Germany. The Court found this constituted unjustified indirect discrimination.[125] Language requirements are also indirectly discriminatory but they can usually be justified. This is expressly recognized by Article 3(1), paragraph 2 of Regulation 492/2011 which provides that the principle of equal treatment does not apply in respect of 'conditions relating to linguistic knowledge required by reason of the nature of the post to be filled'. This provision was successfully relied on by the Irish government in *Groener*[126] concerning a Dutch woman who was refused a permanent post at the design college in Dublin where she had been teaching because she did not speak Gaelic. Even though she did not need to use Gaelic for her work, the Court upheld the language requirement because it formed part of government policy to promote the use of the Irish language as a means of expressing national culture and identity.[127] It said that since education was important for the implementation of such a policy, with teachers playing an essential role, the requirement for teachers to have an adequate knowledge of the Irish language was compatible with Article 3(1), provided that the level of knowledge was not disproportionate to the objective pursued.[128] However, the Court did add that the Irish government could not require that the linguistic knowledge be acquired in Ireland.[129] *Angonese*[130] emphasized this point.

Angonese concerned a requirement imposed by a bank operating in Bolzano (the Italian and German speaking province of Italy), that admission to its recruitment competition was conditional on possession of a certificate of bilingualism. Because this certificate could be obtained only in Bolzano, Angonese, an Italian national who had studied in Austria, was not able to compete for a post working in the bank on the grounds that he lacked the Bolzano certificate, even though he submitted other evidence of his bilingualism.

The Court found the rule to be indirectly discriminatory[131] even though the requirement affected Italian nationals resident in other parts of Italy as well as nationals from other Member States. It said that since the majority of residents of the province of Bolzano were Italian nationals the obligation to obtain the certificate put nationals of other Member States at a disadvantage compared with residents of the province, making it difficult, if not impossible, for them to get jobs in Bolzano.[132] On the question of justification, the Court said that while the bank could justify requiring job applicants to have a certain level of linguistic knowledge (e.g. a diploma), the fact that it was impossible to show proof of this knowledge by any other means—in particular by equivalent qualifications from other Member States—was disproportionate[133] and so the bank's requirement breached Article 45 TFEU.

---

[125] Para. 11.   [126] Case 379/87 *Groener* v. *Minister for Education* [1989] ECR 3967.
[127] Paras. 18–19.   [128] Para. 21.   [129] Para. 23.   [130] Case C–281/98 [2000] ECR I–4139.
[131] The Court reasoned that 'in order for a measure to be treated as being discriminatory on grounds of nationality, it is not necessary for the measure to have the effect of putting at an advantage all the workers of one nationality or of putting at a disadvantage only workers who are nationals of other Member States, but not workers of the nationality in question' (para. 41).
[132] Para. 39.   [133] Para. 44.

(iii) Non-discrimination and measures which (substantially) impede market access

Non-discriminatory national measures which (substantially) impede access to the market also breach Article 45 TFEU and the Regulation unless objectively justified. This can be seen in *Bosman*.[134] Not only did Bosman object to the 3 + 2 rule but he also complained about the rules laid down by sporting associations under which a professional footballer who was a national of one Member State could not, on the expiry of his contract with a club, be employed by another, unless the latter club had paid to the former a transfer, training, or development fee. The rules were not discriminatory because they also applied to transfers between clubs belonging to different national associations within the same Member State and were similar to those governing transfers between clubs belonging to the same national association. Nevertheless, the Court found that the rules 'directly affect[ed] players' access to the employment market in other Member States'[135] and therefore constituted an unjustified 'obstacle to the freedom of movement of workers'.[136] They therefore breached Article 45 TFEU.

On the other hand, if the rule is non-discriminatory and does not affect market access, or if the effect of the national legislation is, as in *Graf*,[137] 'too uncertain and indirect . . . to be capable of being regarded as liable to hinder free movement for workers', then the measure does not breach Article 45 TFEU or the Regulation.[138] The facts of *Graf* were unusual. Graf, a German national, had worked for his Austrian employer for four years until he resigned to take up employment in Germany. Under Austrian law, a worker who had worked for the same employer for more than three years was entitled to severance compensation provided that he was dismissed (and did not just resign). Graf argued that this rule contravened Article 45 TFEU because the effect of the Austrian rule was that he lost the chance of being dismissed and so was unable to claim the severance payment.

The Court disagreed: the Austrian law was genuinely non-discriminatory and did not preclude or deter a worker from ending his contract of employment in order to take a job with another employer. The Court explained that the entitlement to unfair dismissal compensation was not dependent on the worker's choosing whether or not to stay with

---

[134] Case C–415/93 [1995] ECR I–4921.   [135] Para. 103.   [136] Para. 104.

[137] Case C–190/98 [2002] ECR I–493. See further Case C–285/01 *Burbaud* v. *Ministère de l'Emploi et de la Solidarité* [2003] ECR I–8219 where the Court said that the requirement of passing an exam in order to take up a post in the public service could not 'in itself be regarded as an obstacle' to free movement (para. 96). The national rule was therefore compatible with Union law (see further Case C–33/99 *Fahmi and Cerdeiro-Pinedo Amado* v. *Bestuur van de Sociale Verzekeringsbank* [2001] ECR I–2415, para. 43). Similarly, in Case C–542/08 *Barth* v. *Bundesministerium für Wissenschaft und Forschung* [2010] ECR I–3189, para. 39 the Court ruled that applying a three-year limitation period to claim a length of service increment which had been unlawfully denied to those working in non-Austrian universities, did not constitute, by itself, a restriction on the freedom of movement for workers within the meaning of Article 45 TFEU. The Court said: 'When that limitation period is applied, the application has an impact on the possibility of obtaining the special length-of-service increment for a period entirely in the past. It follows that it is not such as to preclude or deter a worker such as the applicant in the main proceedings from exercising his rights to freedom of movement for workers, because the possibility of obtaining that increment in respect of the past is not dependent on the worker's choosing to exercise those rights'.

[138] Paras. 24–5.

his current employer but on a future and hypothetical event (being dismissed). The Court concluded that such an event was too uncertain and indirect a possibility for legislation to be capable of being regarded as liable to hinder free movement for workers.[139] Thus, the Court considered that the event was too remote to be considered liable to affect free movement. Putting it another way, non-discriminatory measures which do not substantially hinder access to the market fall outside Article 45 TFEU.

Sometimes the Court abandons the discrimination analysis altogether and examines instead whether the national measure constitutes an 'obstacle to freedom of movement for workers' (the language used in *Bosman* and confirmed in *Terhoeve*)[140] or is 'liable to hamper or to render less attractive' the exercise of the rights to free movement (*Kraus*).[141] The yet more modern formulation can be found in *Casteels*:[142]

> all of the provisions of the FEU Treaty relating to the freedom of movement for persons are intended to facilitate the pursuit by European Union nationals of occupational activities of all kinds throughout the European Union, and preclude measures which might place such nationals at a disadvantage when they wish to pursue an economic activity in the territory of another Member State.

The significance of this shift away from the discrimination analysis can be seen on the facts of *Casteels*. Mr Casteels worked for BA from 1974 in various Member States. When he moved from Belgium to Germany under the relevant collective agreement no account was taken of his service to the company in the other Member States when determining the period for the acquisition of definitive entitlements to supplementary pensions benefits. The Court noted that the provisions of the collective agreement applied without distinction to all employees working in BA's establishments in Germany and did not differentiate on grounds of the nationality of the employees concerned. However, it continued that 'the fact nonetheless remains that that collective agreement has the effect of placing workers in Mr Casteels' situation, by reason of the fact they have exercised their right to free movement within the European Union, at a disadvantage in comparison with workers employed by BA who have not exercised such a right'.[143] The BA rule therefore constituted an 'obstacle to the freedom of movement for workers which is, in principle, prohibited by Article 45' unless it could be objectively justified (not on the facts).

(iv) Justification

As we have seen, indirectly discriminatory measures, non-discriminatory measures which substantially impede market access, and other rules which create an obstacle to free movement, in principle breach Article 45 TFEU. However, if the defendant Member State can objectively justify the measure and the steps taken are proportionate then the

---

[139] Para. 25.

[140] Case C-18/95 *Terhoeve* [1999] ECR I-345, para. 41; Case C-385/00 *F.W.L. de Groot* v. *Staatssecretaris van Financiën* [2002] ECR I-11819, para. 95.

[141] Case C-19/92 *Kraus* v. *Land Baden-Württemberg* [1993] ECR I-1663, para. 32; Case C-431/01 *Mertens* v. *Belgium* [2002] ECR I-7073, para. 37.

[142] Case C-379/09 *Casteels* v. *British Airways* [2011] ECR I-000, para. 21.   [143] Para. 23.

measure is lawful. Justifications recognized by the Court which are particularly relevant in the employment context include:

- prevention of social dumping[144] or unfair competition;[145]
- prevention of abuse of free movement of services[146] or Union law more generally;[147]
- avoiding disturbances on the labour market;[148]
- the survival of small and medium-sized undertakings and the maintenance of employment;[149]
- social protection of workers in respect of, for example, social security provision;[150]
- combatting illegal employment;[151] and
- protection of workers.[152]

The application of the Court's approach to justifications can be seen in *Bosman*. The justifications raised were that in view of the considerable social importance of sporting activities and in particular football in the Union, the aims of maintaining a balance between the clubs by preserving a certain degree of equality and uncertainty as to results, and of encouraging the recruitment and training of young players, had to be accepted as legitimate. However, while the Court in principle accepted the justification, it supported Bosman's contention that the application of the transfer rules was not an adequate means of maintaining financial and competitive balance in the world of football. Those rules neither precluded the richest clubs from securing the services of the best players nor prevented the availability of financial resources from being a decisive factor in competitive sport, thus considerably altering the balance between clubs.

The Court also accepted that the prospect of receiving transfer, development, or training fees was likely to encourage football clubs to seek new talent and train young players. However, it said that since it was impossible to predict the sporting future of young players with any certainty and because only a limited number of such players went on to play

---

[144] Case C–244/04 *Commission v. Germany* [2006] ECR I–885, para. 61; Case C–341/05 *Laval* [2007] ECR I–987, para. 103.

[145] Case C–60/03 *Wolff & Müller v. Pereira Félix* [2004] ECR I–9553, para. 41.

[146] Case C–244/04 *Commission v. Germany* [2006] ECR I–885, para. 38.

[147] Case C–147/03 *Commission v. Austria (higher education)* [2005] ECR I–5969, para. 70.

[148] Case C–445/03 *Commission v. Luxembourg* [2004] ECR I–10191, para. 38.

[149] Case C–464/05 *Geurts v. Administratie van de BTW* [2007] ECR I–9325, para. 26.

[150] Case C–255/04 *Commission v. France* [2006] ECR I–5251, para. 47.

[151] Ibid., para. 52.

[152] Case 279/80 *Criminal Proceedings against Webb* [1981] ECR 3305, para. 19; Joined Cases 62 & 63/81 *Seco v. EVI* [1982] ECR 223, para. 14. Subsequently in Case C–272/94 *Criminal Proceedings against Guiot* [1996] ECR I–1905, para. 16, the Court stressed the importance of the social protection of workers in the construction industry but this did not entail strike action to enforce terms and conditions of employment which exceed the exhaustive list in Art. 3(1) of the Posted Workers Dir. 96/71: Case C–341/05, *Laval un Partneri Ltd v Svenska Byggnadsarbetareförbundet* [2007] ECR I–987, para. 110.

professionally, those fees were by nature contingent and uncertain and were, in any event, unrelated to the actual cost borne by clubs of training both future professional players and those who would never play professionally. The prospect of receiving such fees could not therefore be either a decisive factor in encouraging recruitment and training of young players or an adequate means of financing such activities, particularly in the case of smaller clubs.

2.3. Equal treatment during the employment relationship

(a) Equal treatment in respect of the terms and conditions of employment

Title II of the Regulation 492/2011 concerns the exercise of employment. Article 7(1) states that a migrant worker must not be treated:

> ... differently from national workers in respect of any conditions of employment and work, in particular as regards remuneration, dismissal, and should he become unemployed, reinstatement or reemployment.[153]

Most of the case law concerns indirectly discriminatory measures. For example, in *Allué and Coonan*[154] an Italian law limited the duration of contracts of employment of foreign language assistants, without imposing the same limitation on other workers. Since only 25 per cent of foreign language assistants were Italian nationals, the law essentially concerned nationals of other Member States. It was indirectly discriminatory[155] and could not be justified.

As we have already seen in respect of access to employment, service requirements may be indirectly discriminatory. For example, in *Ugliola*[156] German law provided that a period spent performing military service in Germany had to be taken into account by an employer when calculating periods of service for the purposes of pay or other benefits but this requirement did not apply to military service carried out in other Member States. The Court found the rule to be indirectly discriminatory since it had a greater impact on non-Germans working in Germany who were more likely to have done their military service in their state of origin. Similarly, in *Schöning-Kougebetopoulou*[157] the Court found that a collective agreement (BAT) providing for promotion on grounds of seniority but which took no account of service performed in another Member State 'manifestly' worked to the detriment of migrant workers and so breached Article 45 TFEU.

---

[153] Art. 7(1) only applies to payments made by virtue of statutory or contracted obligations incumbent on the employer as a condition of employment: see Case C–315/94 *Peter de Vos v. Stadt Bielefeld* [1996] ECR I–1417.

[154] Case 33/88 *Allué and Coonan v. Università degli studi di Venezia* [1989] ECR 1591. See further Case 41/84 *Pinna v. Caisse d'allocations familiales de la Savoie* [1986] ECR 1 and Case C–272/92 *Spotti v. Freistaat Bayern* [1993] ECR I–5185.

[155] Para. 12.

[156] Case 15/69 *Württembergische Milchverwertung Südmilch AG v. Ugliola* [1969] ECR 363.

[157] Case C–15/96 [1998] ECR I–47. See further Case C–187/96 *Commission v. Greece* [1998] ECR I–1095; Case C–195/98 *Österreichischer Gewerkschaftsbund, Gewerkschaft öffentlicher Dienst v. Republik Österreich* [2000] ECR I–10497; Case C–27/91 *URSSAF v. Le Manoir* [1991] ECR I–5531 and Case C–419/92 *Scholz* [1994] ECR I–505.

Subsequently, in *Köbler*[158] the Court departed from the discrimination model in favour of the hindrance/obstacle approach in a case concerning a special length-of-service increment granted by Austria to professors who had worked in an Austrian university for at least 15 years. It said that such a regime was clearly 'likely to impede freedom of movement for workers'[159] because first, the regime operated to the detriment of migrant workers who were nationals of other Member States and secondly, it deterred freedom of movement for workers established in Austria by discouraging them from leaving the country to work in other Member States if this period of experience was not taken into account on their return to Austria.[160] The measure was therefore 'likely to constitute an obstacle to freedom of movement for workers'.[161]

Residence requirements are also likely to be indirectly discriminatory. So, in *Clean Car*[162] the Court found that an Austrian rule requiring business managers to be resident in Austria before they could work in Vienna breached Article 45 TFEU. It noted that the rule was liable to operate mainly to the detriment of nationals of other Member States since the majority of non-residents were foreigners.[163]

If the measure is indirectly discriminatory, then, as we saw above, the burden shifts to the Member State to justify the restriction and to show that the steps taken are proportionate. In *Clean Car*[164] Austria sought to justify the residence requirement on the grounds that the manager needed to be in a position to act effectively in the business, to be served with a notice of any fines imposed and to have those fines enforced against him. The Court rejected such justifications, ruling that the residence requirement was either inappropriate to achieve the aim pursued or went beyond what was necessary for that purpose.[165] It also noted that other less restrictive measures were available to achieve those objectives, such as serving a notice of the fines at the registered office of the company employing the manager. Austria could also ensure that the fines would be paid by requiring a guarantee in advance.

The Court adopted a similarly rigorous approach to justification of seniority requirements. In *Schöning-Kougebetopoulou*[166] the German government justified its rule on the grounds that it rewarded loyalty to the employer and motivated the employee by the prospect of improvement in his financial situation. The German government explained that the BAT covered not only the majority of German public institutions but also undertakings performing public interest tasks. For this very reason, the Court said that to take into account periods of employment completed with one of those institutions in determining seniority for the purposes of promotion could not, given the multiplicity of employers, be justified by the desire to reward employee loyalty. The system afforded employees covered by the BAT considerable mobility within a group of legally separate employers and therefore the discrimination could not be justified.

Where, as in *Schöning-Kougebetopoulou*, the Court finds that a clause from a collective agreement or contract discriminates against workers from other Member States,

---

[158] Case C–224/01 *Gerhard Köbler* v. *Republik Österreich* [2003] ECR I–10239.   [159] Para. 72.
[160] Paras. 73–4.   [161] Para. 77.   [162] Case C–350/96 [1998] ECR I–2521.   [163] Para. 29.
[164] Case C–350/96 [1998] ECR I–2521.   [165] Para. 34.   [166] Case C–15/96 [1998] ECR I–47.

Article 7(4) of Regulation 492/2011 provides that such clauses are null and void in so far as they lay down or authorize discriminatory conditions. Until the parties amend the agreement to eliminate the discrimination, the migrant workers enjoy the same rules as those which apply to nationals.[167]

(b) Equal treatment in respect of social and tax advantages

(i) Tax advantages

Article 7(2)[168] provides that a worker will enjoy the same social and tax advantages as national workers. As far as taxation is concerned,[169] most of the cases concern the situation of national rules which treat residents differently from non-residents. As we have already seen, discrimination on the grounds of residence can indirectly discriminate against migrants.[170] However, this presupposes that the circumstances of residents and non-residents are comparable. In *Schumacker*[171] the Court recognized that this might not always be the case since there are objective differences between the two situations: usually the state of residence grants taxpayers all the tax allowances relating to their personal and family circumstances because the state of residence is in the best position to assess the taxpayers' ability to pay tax since their personal and financial interests are centred there;[172] the same will not apply to non-residents. This distinction is recognized by international tax law and may justify the two situations being treated differently.

However, if, on the facts of the case, the situations of the resident and non-resident taxpayer can be considered comparable, then it would be discriminatory to treat the two situations differently. This is particularly so in the case of frontier workers such as Mr Schumacker,[173] a Belgian national who lived in Belgium with his family but worked in Germany. Because he was a non-resident worker his wages were subject to German income tax on a limited basis. This meant that he was denied certain benefits which were available to resident taxpayers. The Court ruled that a non-resident taxpayer who received all or almost all of his income in the state of employment was objectively in the same situation as a resident in that state who did the same work there. The discrimination arose because the non-resident taxpayer did not have his personal and family circumstances taken into account either in his state of residence (where he received no

---

[167] Case C–15/96 *Kalliope Schöning-Kougebetopoulou* [1998] ECR I–47, para. 33, applying by analogy the Art. 157 TFEU case law on equal pay: e.g. Case C–184/89 *Nimz* v. *Freie und Hansestadt Hamburg* [1991] ECR I–297, para. 18; Case C–33/89 *Kowalska* v. *Freie und Hansestadt Hamburg* [1990] ECR I–2591, para. 20. This is considered further in Ch. 7.

[168] For a detailed examination of this provision see D. O'Keefe, 'Equal Rights for Migrants: the Concept of Social Advantages in Article 7(2), Reg. 1612/68' (1985) 5 *YEL* 92.

[169] It has always been clear that direct taxation falls within the competence of the Member States. As the Court pointed out in Case C–246/89 *Commission* v. *UK* [1991] ECR I–4585, the powers retained by the Member States in respect of taxation, however, must be exercised consistently with Union law.

[170] Case C–175/88 *Biehl* v. *Administration des contributions du grand-duché de Luxembourg* [1990] ECR I–1779, para. 14.

[171] Case C–279/93 *Finanzamt Köln-Altstadt* v. *Schumacker* [1995] ECR I–225.

[172] Para. 32.

[173] Case C–279/93 [1995] ECR I–225. See additionally Case C–87/99 *Zurstrassen* v. *Administration des contributions directes* [2000] ECR I–3337.

income) or in his state of employment (where he was not resident).[174] Consequently, his overall tax burden was greater than that of the resident taxpayer.[175]

If discrimination can be shown, then the Court must consider whether it can be justified. In *Bachmann*[176] the Court recognized the 'need to preserve the cohesion of the tax system' as one such justification. The case concerned a Belgian law according to which the cost of life insurance premiums could not be deducted from taxable income where the premiums were paid in other Member States. This was because Belgium tax law gave the individual the choice of either having tax deducted on the premiums and then paying tax on future benefits or not having tax deducted on the premiums and then not paying tax on future benefits. If it deducted premiums paid in Germany, it would have no way of being able to tax future benefits also payable in Germany. For this reason the Belgian rules were justified because there was a 'direct link' between the right to deduct contributions and the taxation of sums payable by insurers under pension and life assurance contracts; and that preserving that link was necessary to safeguard the cohesion of the tax system.[177]

(ii) Social advantages

Article 7(2) requires social advantages to be provided on a non-discriminatory basis. In *Even*[178] the Court defined 'social advantages' broadly to include all benefits:[179]

> ...which, whether or not linked to a contract of employment, are generally granted to national workers primarily because of their objective status as workers *or by virtue of the mere fact of their residence on the national territory* and the extension of which to workers who are nationals of other Member States therefore seems suitable to *facilitate their mobility* within the [Union].

The concept of social advantage embraces benefits granted as of right[180] or on a discretionary basis[181] and those granted after employment has terminated (e.g. a pension).[182] It also covers benefits not directly linked to employment such as language rights,[183] death benefits,[184] rights for a dependent child to obtain finance for

---

[174] Para. 38.   [175] Para. 28.

[176] Case C–204/90 *Bachmann v. Belgian State* [1992] ECR I–249, para. 21, and Case C–300/90 *Commission v. Belgium* [1992] ECR I–305, para. 14.

[177] Paras. 21–3.

[178] Case 207/78 *Criminal Proceedings against Even* [1979] ECR 2019.

[179] Para. 22, emphasis added.

[180] See e.g. Case C–111/91 *Commission v. Luxembourg*; Case C–85/96 *Martínez Sala* [1998] ECR I–2691, para. 28.

[181] Case 65/81 *Reina v. Landeskreditbank Baden-Württemberg* [1982] ECR 33, para. 17.

[182] See e.g. Case C–57/96 *Meints v. Minister van Landbouw, Natuurbeheer en Visserij* [1997] ECR I–6689, para. 36 (payment to agricultural workers whose employment contracts are terminated); Case C–35/97 *Commission v. France* [1998] ECR I–5325 (supplementary retirement pension points).

[183] Case 137/84 *Criminal proceedings against Mutsch* [1985] ECR 2681, para. 18 (criminal proceedings in the defendant's own language).

[184] Case C–237/94 *O'Flynn* [1996] ECR I–2617 (social security payments to help cover the cost of burying a family member).

studies,[185] and rights to bring in unmarried companions.[186] These financial benefits are all intended to facilitate access to the labour market.[187]

The decision in *Even*, with its reference to 'residence on the national territory', showed that Article 7(2) applied not just to benefits granted by the host state to its workers[188] but also to its residents.[189] This meant that both migrant workers *and* their families who were legally resident could enjoy the social advantages offered by the home state.[190] The Court justified this development on the grounds that Article 7(2) was essential not only to encourage free movement of workers as well as their families (without whom the worker would be discouraged from moving)[191] but also to encourage their integration into the environment of the host state.[192] As the Court said in *Baumbast*,[193] the aim of Regulation 492/2011 on free movement of persons was 'for such freedom to be guaranteed in compliance with the principles of liberty and dignity, the best possible conditions for the integration of the [Union] worker's family in the society of the host Member State'.

However, there are some limits to the scope of Article 7(2). This can be seen in *Leclere*.[194] Leclere and his wife were Belgian. He was a frontier worker who lived in Belgium but worked in Luxembourg. After having an accident in Luxembourg the authorities there paid him an invalidity pension but when his wife subsequently had a child he was refused a childbirth allowance by the Luxembourg authorities on the grounds that he was not a worker. The Court upheld this decision. It said that as a former worker Leclere retained his status as worker in respect of the invalidity pension linked with his previous employment and so was protected against any discrimination affecting rights acquired during the former employment. On the other hand, since he was not currently engaged in an employment relationship, he could not claim *new* rights which had no links with his former occupation.[195]

If the benefit does constitute a social advantage, then it must be provided on a non-discriminatory basis. While most of the cases considered so far concern direct discrimination, the Court has also used Article 7(2) to prohibit unjustified indirect

---

[185] Case C–3/90 *Bernini* [1992] ECR I–1071; Case C–337/97 *Meeusen* [1999] ECR I–3289, para. 15.

[186] Case 59/85 *Netherlands* v. *Reed* [1986] ECR 1283, para. 28.

[187] Joined Cases C–22/08 and C–23/08 *Vatsouras* [2009] ECR I–4585, para. 45.

[188] This includes those who are not resident in the territory of the providing state: Case C–57 *Meints* [1997] ECR I–6689, para. 50; Case C–337/97 *Meeusen* [1999] ECR I–3289, para. 21.

[189] AG Jacobs in Case C–43/99 *Leclere and Deaconescu* v. *Caisse nationale des prestations familiales* [2001] ECR I–4265, para. 96. S. Peers, '"Social Advantages" and Discrimination in Employment: Case Law Confirmed and Clarified' (1997) 22 *ELRev*. 157, 164.

[190] Cf. the early decision in Case 76/72 *Michel S.* v. *Fonds national de reclassement social des handicapés* [1973] ECR 457, para. 9, where the Court limited social advantages to workers.

[191] See e.g. Case 94/84 *ONEM* v. *Deak* [1985] ECR 1873.

[192] See further Joined Cases 389 and 390/87 *Echternach* v. *Minister van Onderwijs en Wetenschappen* [1989] ECR 723; Case C–308/93 *Bestuur van de Sociale Verzekeringsbank* v. *Cabanis-Issarte* [1996] ECR I–2097.

[193] Case C–413/99 *Baumbast and R* v. *Secretary of State for the Home Department* [2002] ECR I–7091, para. 50.

[194] Case C–43/99 [2001] ECR I–4265.

[195] Para. 59.

discrimination.[196] For example, in *O'Flynn*[197] an Irish national resident in the UK applied to the British authorities for a payment to cover the costs of his son's funeral in Ireland. His application was refused on the grounds that the burial should have taken place in the UK. This requirement was found to be indirectly discriminatory and contrary to Article 7(2). However, the Court did say that the UK could limit the allowance to a lump sum or reasonable amount fixed by reference to the normal cost of a burial in the UK.

Increasingly problematic for Member States has been the Court's changing position on benefits for work-seekers. In *Collins*[198] the Court reversed a long line of case law, in view of the establishment of the status of citizenship of the Union, to rule that the principle of equal treatment in Article 45(2) TFEU now applied to benefits of a financial nature intended to facilitate access to employment in the labour market of a Member State. However, the Court did recognize that it was legitimate for a Member State to impose (indirectly discriminatory) conditions (e.g. a residence rule) on the grant of such an allowance in order 'to establish a real link between the job-seeker and the labour market of that State'.[199] The existence of such a link can be determined, in particular, by establishing that the person concerned has, for a reasonable period, in fact genuinely sought work in the Member State in question.[200]

The position has now been complicated by the CRD. Article 24(1) contains the general principle of equal treatment:

> Subject to such specific provisions as are expressly provided for in the Treaty and secondary law, all Union citizens residing on the basis of this Directive in the territory of the host Member State shall enjoy equal treatment with the nationals of that Member State within the scope of the Treaty. The benefit of this right shall be extended to family members who are not nationals of a Member State and who have the right of residence or permanent residence.

However, Article 24(2) contains a limitation:

> By way of derogation from paragraph 1, the host Member State shall not be obliged to confer entitlement to social assistance during the first three months of residence or, where appropriate, the longer period provided for in Article 14(4)(b), nor shall it be obliged, prior to acquisition of the right of permanent residence, to grant maintenance aid for studies, including vocational training, consisting in student grants or student loans to persons other than workers, self-employed persons, persons who retain such status and members of their families.

Thus, Article 24(2) establishes a derogation from the principle of equal treatment enjoyed by Union citizens—other than workers, self-employed persons, persons who retain such status, and members of their families—who reside within the territory of the

---

[196] See e.g. Case C–299/01 *Commission v. Luxembourg* [2002] ECR I–5899. See additionally Case C–111/91 *Commission v. Luxembourg* [1993] ECR I–817.
[197] Case C–237/94 [1996] ECR I–2617.
[198] Case C–138/02 *Collins* [2004] ECR I–2703, para. 63.
[199] Case C–224/98 *D'Hoop* [2002] ECR I–6191, para. 38.
[200] Case C–138/02 *Collins* [2004] ECR I–2703, para. 70.

host Member State. The exception will, however, apply to job seekers under Article 14(1)(b) for the longer period during which they have the right to reside there.[201] How does this fit with the case law on Article 7(2) of Regulation 492/2011? Well, if the individual started as a worker, then became involuntarily unemployed in the conditions laid down in, for example, Article 7(3)(c) he or she will retain the status of worker for no less than six months. In this situation, the Treaty, Article 24(1) CRD and Article 7(2) of Regulation 492/2011 will apply for those six months and the work seeker will enjoy the principle of equal treatment. If, on the other hand, the individual arrives in the host-state as a work seeker then he or she may be subject to the derogation in Article 24(2) CRD. However, the Court avoided some of the potential impact of Article 24(2) by saying in *Vatsouras* that '[b]enefits of a financial nature which, independently of their status under national law, are intended to facilitate access to the labour market cannot be regarded as constituting "social assistance" within the meaning of Article 24(2) of Directive 2004/38'.[202] This suggests that 'social assistance' is intended to protect individuals from destitution; 'social advantages' are aimed at labour market integration. The Article 24(2) derogation applies to the former only.

2.4. Equal treatment and vocational training

Article 7(3) provides that a worker shall 'have access to training in vocational schools and retraining centres' under the same conditions as national workers. In *Gravier*[203] the Court defined 'vocational training' broadly to include any form of education which prepares for a qualification or which provides the necessary training or skills for a particular profession, trade, or employment. In *Blaizot*[204] the Court confirmed that vocational training could be received at universities, except in the case of courses intended for students 'wishing to improve their general knowledge rather than prepare themselves for a particular occupation'.[205]

Access to training is one thing, payment for that training is another. In *Gravier* the Court said that since access to training was likely to promote free movement of persons by enabling them to obtain a qualification in the Member State where they intended to work,[206] the conditions of access to vocational training fell within the scope of the Treaty. Therefore, if a host state charged a registration fee to migrant students but not to its own students, it breached Article 18 TFEU.[207]

---

[201] Joined Cases C–22/08 and 23/08 *Vatsouras* [2009] ECR I–4585, paras. 34–5.

[202] Ibid, para. 45.

[203] Case 293/83 *Gravier* v. *Ville de Liège* [1985] ECR 593, para. 30. For background see K. Lenaerts, 'Education in European Community Law after "Maastricht"' (1994) 31 *CMLRev*. 7; J. Shaw, 'From the Margins to the Centre: Education and Training Law and Policy', in P. Craig and G. de Búrca (eds), *The Evolution of EU Law* (OUP, Oxford, 1999).

[204] Case 24/86 *Blaizot* v. *Université de Liège and Others* [1988] ECR 379.

[205] Paras. 19–20.   [206] Para. 24.   [207] Para. 26.

Gravier concerned fees and not maintenance grants. Maintenance grants can constitute 'social advantages' within the meaning of Article 7(2),[208] as *Matteucci*[209] shows. The case concerned the daughter of an Italian worker in Belgium who was educated in Belgium and then taught rhythmics. She applied for a scholarship, which was available on a bilateral (Belgium–Germany) basis, to study singing in Berlin but her application was rejected on the ground that she was not Belgian. The Court said that this was contrary to Article 7(2): a bilateral agreement reserving scholarships for nationals of the two Member States which were the parties to the agreement could not prevent the application of the principle of equality under Union law.

Mateucci's case was a strong one: she had lived and worked in Belgium all her life. But the case law on Article 7(2) is open to exploitation by those who do short-term casual work in another Member State and then claim entitlement to social advantages in the form of a grant for further study in the host state. The Court had to deal with this problem in two important cases, *Lair*[210] and *Brown*.[211] *Lair* concerned a French woman who had moved to Germany where she worked on a series of part-time contracts. Having decided to study for a languages degree at the University of Hanover, she sought a maintenance grant. The Court recognized that people who had previously pursued an effective and genuine activity in the host state could still be considered workers and so could receive a maintenance grant under Article 7(2) but on condition that there was a link between the previous occupational activity[212] and the studies.[213] However, in the case of a migrant worker becoming involuntarily unemployed no link between the studies and the occupational activity was required before a maintenance grant was awarded. This line of case law has been incorporated in Article 7(3)(d) CRD, which confirms that a Union citizen retains the status of worker or self-employed person if 'he/she embarks on vocational training. Unless he/she is involuntarily unemployed, the retention of the status of worker shall require the training to be related to the previous employment.' The status of worker means that the individual is entitled to equal treatment in respect of maintenance grants under Article 24(2) CRD. For those who are not economically active, they will enjoy equal treatment in respect of students' maintenance only when they are permanent residents (i.e. after five years' residence).

---

[208] Case C–3/90 *Bernini* [1992] ECR I–1071, para. 23, where the Court ruled that descendants of workers could rely on Art. 7(2) to obtain study finance under the same conditions as children of national workers. This also applies to non-resident children of migrant workers (Case C–337/97 *Meeusen* [1999] ECR I–3289, para. 25) but not to workers who have returned to their states of origin (Case C–33/99 *Fahini* [2001] ECR I–2415, para. 46).

[209] Case 235/87 *Matteucci* v. *Communauté française de Belgique* [1988] ECR 5589.

[210] Case 39/86 *Lair* v. *Universität Hannover* [1988] ECR 3161. See further Case C–357/90 *Raulin* [1992] ECR I–1027, para. 21.

[211] Case 197/86 *Brown* v. *Secretary of State for Scotland* [1988] ECR 3205.

[212] The host state cannot make the right to the same social advantages conditional upon a minimum period of prior occupational activity (Case 39/86 *Lair* [1988] ECR 3161, para. 44).

[213] If no link exists between the study and the previous occupational activities, the person does not retain the status of a migrant worker (Case C–357/89 *Raulin* [1992] ECR I–1027).

Brown concerned a student with dual French and British nationality who lived in France for many years but had a place at Cambridge University to read engineering. He was sponsored by Ferranti and worked for the company in the UK for eight months before starting his course. He then claimed that he was a worker and so was entitled to a grant from the British government under Article 7(2). However, the Court refused to recognize him as a worker, viewing his work for Ferranti as merely ancillary to his studies,[214] and so he could not claim a grant under Article 7(2). Nor could he rely on the general prohibition of discrimination in Article 18 TFEU to obtain a maintenance grant. The Court said that at that stage of development of Union law the assistance given to students for maintenance and training fell outside the scope of the Treaty for the purposes of Article 18 TFEU.[215] This latter aspect of the ruling in *Brown* has been reversed by *Bidar*[216] where the Court ruled that social assistance for a student 'whether in the form of a subsidised loan or a grant, intended to cover his maintenance costs'[217] fell within the scope of application of the Treaty. As a result, Bidar was therefore entitled to have the principle of non-discrimination on the grounds of nationality applied to him.[218] In *Förster*[219] the Court confirmed that the principle of equal treatment applied to maintenance grants but, relying on the derogation from the principle of equal treatment in Article 24(2) CRD (cited above), said that host states can require migrants to have five years' prior residence.

2.5. Equal treatment and other benefits

Equality is not confined to tax and social advantages and vocational training. Article 8(1) provides that migrant workers must also enjoy equality of treatment with nationals in respect of trade union membership and the exercise of rights related to trade union membership, 'including the right to vote and to be eligible for the administration or management posts of a trade union'.[220] Workers, however, may be excluded from taking part in the management of bodies governed by public law and from holding office governed by public law.[221]

Finally, Article 9 provides that workers must enjoy all the rights and benefits accorded to national workers in matters of housing, including ownership, and the right to put their names on housing lists in the region where they are employed. Therefore in

---

[214] Para. 27.   [215] Para. 18.

[216] Case C–209/03 *R (on the application of Danny Bidar)* v. *London Borough of Ealing, Secretary of State for Education and Skills* [2005] ECR I–2119.

[217] Para. 42.

[218] See M. Dougan, 'Fees, Grants, Loans and Dole Cheques: Who Covers the Costs of Migrant Education within the EU' (2005) *CMLRev.* 943.

[219] Case C–158/07 *Förster* v. *Hoofddirectie van de Informatie Beheer Groep* [2008] ECR I–8507.

[220] See further A. Evans, 'Development of European Community Law regarding the Trade Union Rights and Related Rights of Migrant Workers' (1979) 28 *ICLQ* 354. See additionally Case C–213/90 *Association de Soutien aux Travailleurs Immigrés* v. *Chambre des Employés Privés* [1991] ECR I–3507 and Case C–118/92 *Commission* v. *Luxembourg* [1994] ECR I–1891. In respect of Art. 10 of the EEC–Turkey Agreement which is interpreted in the same way as Art. 8 of Reg. 492/2011, cf. Case C–171/01 *Wählergruppe, 'Gemeinsam Zajedno/Birlikte Alternative und Grüne Gewerkschafter Innen/UG' and others* [2003] ECR I–4301.

[221] Art. 8.

Commission v. *Greece*[222] the Court found a Greek rule restricting a foreigner's right to own property in Greece breached the free movement rules since access to housing and ownership of property was the corollary of free movement.[223] Originally, Article 10(3) of Regulation 1612/68 provided that workers must have available for their family 'housing considered as normal for national workers in the region where he is employed'. According to *Diatta*,[224] the purpose of Article 10(3) was both to implement public policy and to protect public security by preventing immigrants from living in precarious conditions.[225] This rule has now been abolished and not replaced either by the CRD or by Regulation 492/2011.

2.6. Equal treatment and the right to work for family members

Article 23 CRD permits the Union citizen's family members who have the right of residence or the right of permanent residence to take up employment or self-employment in the host state (but not in any other state).[226] This provision broadly replicates Article 11 of Regulation 1612/68. Both Article 23 and the original Article 11 make clear that the right to work applies irrespective of the nationality of the family member.[227] Article 24(1) CRD provides that these family members must also enjoy equal treatment in respect of their own employment.

2.7. The right to permanent residence in the host Member State

The third 'tier' of residence rights is the right to permanent residence. There are two ways of acquiring permanent residence: (1) through five years' continuous legal residence; or (2) through a shorter period for those who were economically active either as a worker or as a self-employed person but who satisfy the conditions under old Regulation 1251/70[228] and Directive 75/34.[229] In both situations the Directive considers the migrants to be so assimilated into the host state that they are regarded and treated as nationals in all but name. This is a remarkable development. We shall examine the two situations in turn.

(a) Article 16: Five years' residence

Union citizens and their family members, including third country nationals' family members,[230] who have resided legally for a continuous period of five years in the host state, have the right of permanent residence there.[231] This right is not dependent on the Union citizen being a worker/self-employed person or having sufficient resources/medical insurance,[232]

---

[222] Case 305/87 *Commission* v. *Greece* [1989] ECR 1461.   [223] Para. 18.
[224] Case 267/83 [1985] ECR 567.   [225] Ibid., para. 10.
[226] Case C–10/05 *Mattern* v. *Ministre du travail et de l'Emploi* [2006] ECR I–000.
[227] Case 131/85 *Gül* v. *Regierungspräsident Düsseldorf* [1986] ECR 1573.
[228] On the right of workers to remain in the territory of the host state after having been employed there [1970] OJ L142/24.
[229] On the right of the self-employed to remain [1975] OJ L14/10.
[230] Art. 16(2).   [231] Art. 16(1).
[232] Ibid., second sentence.

albeit that in most cases[233] the migrant will have been a worker/self employed/student/ person of independent means/family member under Article 7 during the previous five years in order to accrue the five-year period of residence. The family members of a Union citizen to whom Article 12(2) (death/departure of the Union citizen) or Article 13(2) (divorce or equivalent) apply, who satisfy the conditions laid down in those Articles (e.g. the family members are workers/self-employed etc.), will also acquire the right of permanent residence after residing legally for a period of five consecutive years in the host state.[234]

Continuity of residence is not affected by temporary absences not exceeding a total of six months a year, or by absences of a longer duration for compulsory military service, or by one absence of a maximum of 12 consecutive months for important reasons such as pregnancy and childbirth, serious illness, study or vocational training, or a posting in another Member State or a third country.[235] On the other hand, continuity of residence is broken by any expulsion decision duly enforced against the person concerned.[236] Once acquired, the right of permanent residence is lost only through absence from the host Member State for a period exceeding two consecutive years.[237]

(b) Article 17: Other ways of acquiring permanent residence

While five years' residence is the usual way for acquiring a right to permanent residence, it is also possible for a migrant or their family members to acquire a right to permanent residence before they have completed a continuous period of five years' residence in the situations which were originally laid down in Regulation 1251/70[238] (and Directive 75/34). The Regulation made provision for workers and their family members to remain in a Member State after having been employed there. This regulation has now been repealed[239] and replaced by Article 17 CRD which maintains the existing acquis but changes the language from the 'right to remain' to the 'right of permanent residence'. Article 17(1) provides that workers and the self-employed have the right to permanent residence in three situations:

> (a) retirement at the pension age[240] or through early retirement, provided they have been employed in the host state for the preceding 12 months[241] and resided in the host state continuously for more than three years;

---

[233] Joined cases C-424/10 and C-425/10 Ziolkowski [2011] ECR I-000. Cf. also Art. 12(1) para. 2 which expressly requires EU national *family members* to be economically active/student/have sufficient resources before they acquire the right of permanent residence.

[234] Art. 18.

[235] Art. 16(3).

[236] Art. 21.

[237] Art. 16(4).

[238] [1970] OJ SE L142/24, 402.

[239] Commission Reg. 635/2006 (OJ [2006] L112/9). Dir. 75/34 was repealed by the CRD.

[240] If the law of the host state does not grant the right to an old-age pension to certain categories of self-employed persons, the age condition is deemed to have been met once the person has reached the age of 60.

[241] Periods of involuntary unemployment duly recorded by the relevant employment office, periods not worked for reasons not of the person's own making and absences from work or cessation of work due to illness or accident are to be regarded as periods of employment: Art. 17(1), para. 3.

(b) incapacity, provided they have resided for more than two years in the host state[242] and have ceased to work due to some permanent incapacity; or

(c) frontier workers, provided after three years of continuous employment and residence in the host State A, they work in an employed or self-employed capacity in State B, while retaining their residence in State A to which they return each day or at least once a week.

The conditions as to length of residence and employment in parts (a) and (b) do not apply if the worker/self-employed person's spouse or partner[243] is a national of the host state or has lost the nationality of the host state through marriage to the worker/self-employed person.[244]

The worker/self-employed person's family members residing with that person in the host state (irrespective of nationality) are also entitled to benefit from the reduced period of residence. According to Article 17, they too can enjoy permanent residence in the host state where either (1) the worker/self-employed person is entitled to permanent residence under Article 17(1);[245] or (2) under Article 17(4) the worker/self-employed person dies during his or her working life but before having acquired the right to permanent residence under 17(1) and:

(a) the worker/self-employed person had resided continuously in the host state for two years at the time of death; or

(b) the death resulted from an accident at work or occupational disease; or

(c) the surviving spouse lost the nationality of the host state through marriage to the worker/self-employed person.

In *Givane*[246] the Court showed that it will interpret these requirements strictly. Givane, a Portuguese national, worked in the UK as a chef for three years before going to India for 10 months. He then returned to the UK with his Indian wife and three children but died less than two years later. The Court upheld the British authorities' decision refusing Givane's family indefinite leave to remain on the grounds that Givane had not satisfied the requirements of what is now Article 17(4) which required him to have resided in the UK for the two years immediately preceding his death.[247] Such a literal reading of the requirement stands in stark contrast to the generous approach to the interpretation of other provisions of Union law based on the right to family life in cases such as *Carpenter*.[248] More striking still is the fact that the Court uses the integration argument to

---

[242] If the incapacity is due to an occupational accident or disease entitling the worker to a pension for which an institution of the state is entirely or partially responsible, then no condition to length of residence is imposed.

[243] Partner as defined in Art. 2(2)(b) CRD.

[244] Art. 17(2).

[245] Art. 17(3).

[246] Case C–257/00 *Givane and others* v. *Secretary of State for the Home Department* [2003] ECR I–345.

[247] Para. 46.

[248] Case C–60/00 *Mary Carpenter* v. *Secretary of State for the Home Department* [2002] ECR I–6279, para. 38. See additionally Case C–413/99 *Baumbast* [2002] ECR I–7091; Case C–459/99 *MRAX* [2002] ECR I–6591, paras. 53–61.

justify *excluding* Givane's family from the UK. It said that the two-year requirement was intended to establish a significant connection between the Member State and the worker and his family and 'to ensure a certain level of their integration in the society of that state'.[249]

In the case of those family members faced with the death or departure of the Union citizen in circumstances not covered by Article 17, and in the case of those family members faced with divorce or equivalent, they can acquire permanent residence only if they meet the requirements laid down in Article 7(1) (i.e. they must be workers/self-employed/persons of independent means/student/family member) and have resided legally for a period of five consecutive years in the territory of the host state.

D. EMPLOYMENT IN THE PUBLIC SERVICE

1. INTRODUCTION

So far we have been talking about workers' rights. We turn now to look at the derogations from those rights. Although the general derogations (public policy, public security, and public health) have little impact in practice on this area of law (since they apply to state—rather than employer—action), the specific derogation (employment in the public service) has had a much larger effect in practice. It has been traditional for Member States, as part of the exercise of their sovereignty,[250] to reserve certain public service jobs to their own nationals.[251] Article 45(4) TFEU provides that the principles of free movement of workers and non-discrimination on the ground of nationality do not apply to 'employment in the public service'. Articles 51 and 62 TFEU contain an equivalent provision in respect of establishment and services, albeit drafted in rather different terms. Article 51 TFEU says that '[t]he provisions of this chapter shall not apply ... to activities which in that State are connected, even occasionally, with the exercise of official authority'. The justification for the employment in the public service/exercise of official authority derogation is that particular posts presume a 'special relationship of allegiance to the State' and a 'reciprocity of rights and duties which form the foundation of the bond of nationality'.[252]

Because Articles 45(4), 51, and 62 TFEU represent further exceptions to fundamental freedoms they must also be narrowly construed,[253] with their scope limited to what is 'strictly necessary for safeguarding the interests of the State which that provision

---

[249] Para. 46.

[250] See Mancini AG in Case 307/84 *Commission* v. *France* [1986] ECR 1725, para. 2.

[251] For further details see G. Morris, S. Fredman, and J. Hayes, 'Free Movement and the Public Sector' (1990) 19 *ILJ* 20; C. Lenz, 'The Public Service in Article 48(4) EEC with Special Reference to the Law in England and in the Federal Republic of Germany' [1989] 15 *LIEI* 75.

[252] Case 149/79 *Commission* v. *Belgium* [1980] ECR 3881, para. 10. See further J. Handoll, 'Article 48(4) and Non-National Access to Public Employment' (1988) 13 *ELRev.* 223.

[253] Case 152/73 *Sotgiu* v. *Deutsche Bundespost* [1979] ECR 153, para. 4.

allows the Member States to protect'.[254] Therefore, in *Sotgiu*[255] the Court said that Article 45(4) TFEU applied only to conditions of access to employment; it did not authorize discriminatory conditions of employment once access had been granted. This meant that the German postal service could not rely on Article 45(4) TFEU to justify its refusal to pay Sotgiu, an Italian national, a separation allowance granted to German workers, on the ground that he was employed in the public service. The Court said that the fact that Sotgiu had been admitted to the service denied the existence of those interests which justified the derogation.

2. ARTICLE 45(4) TFEU

The Court has insisted on a Union definition of the phrase 'employment in the public service'.[256] In *Commission v. Belgium*[257] it explained that the jobs envisaged by Article 45(4) TFEU 'involve direct or indirect participation in the exercise of powers conferred by public law and duties designed to safeguard the interests of the State or of other public authorities'. The Court continued that these jobs are 'characteristic of specific activities of public service insofar as [they are] invested with the exercise of public power *and* the responsibility for safeguarding the general interests of the State'.[258] It is not clear whether these requirements are to be read cumulatively or disjunctively. A cumulative reading is consistent with the view that Article 45(4) TFEU must be interpreted restrictively; but support can be found in *Commission v. Italy*[259] for the argument that the requirements are to be read disjunctively.

The other question facing the Court is whether the phrase 'public service' requires an institutional or a functional approach. The *institutional* or organic approach, which is supported by the wording of Article 45(4) TFEU, views the institution and its personnel as a whole, regardless of the specific functions carried out by individuals within the organization. This approach would allow a Member State to reserve all jobs in a particular organization, such as the civil service, to nationals even where some of those jobs are of a purely administrative or technical nature and involve no tasks designed to safeguard the interests of the state. This approach has been favoured by states keen to reserve as many posts as possible for their own nationals.[260] By contrast, the *functional* approach looks at the work required of a particular post to see if it involves direct or indirect participation in the exercise of powers conferred by public law and duties designed to safeguard the interests of the state. The functional approach would allow Member States to reserve only certain posts to nationals.

---

[254] Case 225/85 *Commission v. Italy* [1987] ECR 2625.
[255] Case 152/73 [1979] ECR 153, para. 4.
[256] See, e.g., Case C–473/93 *Commission v. Luxembourg* [1996] ECR I–3207, para. 26.
[257] Case 149/79 [1982] ECR 1845, para. 7.
[258] Emphasis added.
[259] Case 225/85 [1987] ECR 2625, paras. 9–10.
[260] See the Belgian government's arguments in Case 149/79 *Commission v. Belgium* [1980] ECR 3881.

Consistent with the view that derogations are narrowly construed, the Court adopts the functional approach.[261] On a case-by-case basis, it examines the tasks and responsibilities inherent in the post[262] to see if they fulfil 'the very strict conditions'[263] of Article 45(4) TFEU rather than considering the nature of the legal relationship between the employee and the employing administration or the individual's job description.[264] This approach has led the Court to find that most jobs do not benefit from the Article 45(4) TFEU derogation. For example, it has said that the jobs of a teacher in a state school,[265] a state nurse,[266] a foreign-language assistant in a university,[267] various posts on the state railways,[268] a local government employee,[269] a trainee lawyer,[270] a seaman,[271] a job in research which did not involve sensitive research work,[272] and a post in the lower echelons of the civil service all did not constitute employment in the public service.[273] On the other hand, in the rather odd case of *Commission* v. *Belgium*[274] the Court found that local authority posts for architects, supervisors,[275] and night watchmen did fall within the Article 45(4) TFEU exception. Less controversially, it said in *Commission* v. *Italy*[276] that those involved in advising the state on scientific and technical questions were employed in the 'public service'.

While it is difficult to draw any clear principles from the case law, it seems that senior government jobs can be confined to nationals only, even though this may mean that Article 45(4) TFEU represents a barrier to promotion for non-nationals.[277] However, where the exercise of public law powers is purely marginal and ancillary to the principal function of the posts, then such jobs generally fall outside Article 45(4) TFEU. This is the view taken by the Commission in its Communication designed to eliminate restrictions in areas of the public sector[278] where it listed jobs in the public sector to which, in normal circumstances, Article 45(4) TFEU did not apply. These included public health-care services, employment in state educational institutions, research for non-military

[261] Case C–473/93 *Commission* v. *Luxembourg* [1996] ECR I–3207, para. 27.
[262] Case 149/79 *Commission* v. *Belgium* [1982] ECR 1845, para. 8; Case C–473/93 *Commission* v. *Luxembourg* [1996] ECR I–3207, para. 27.
[263] Case C–473/93 *Commission* v. *Luxembourg* [1996] ECR I–3207, para. 33.
[264] Case 152/73 *Sotgiu* [1974] ECR 153.
[265] Case 66/85 *Lawrie-Blum* [1986] ECR 2121; Case C–4/91 *Bleis* v. *Ministère de l'éducation nationale* [1991] ECR I–5627.
[266] Case 307/84 *Commission* v. *France* [1986] ECR 1725.
[267] Case 33/88 *Allué and Coonan* [1989] ECR 1591.
[268] Case 149/79 *Commission* v. *Belgium* [1982] ECR 1845.
[269] Case 149/79 *Commission* v. *Belgium* [1980] ECR 3881 and [1982] ECR 1845 (plumbers, carpenters, electricians, gardeners).
[270] Case C–109/04 *Kranemann* v. *Land Nordrhein-Westfalen* [2005] ECR I–2421, para. 19 where the Court made clear that the concept of employment in the public service did not encompass employment by a private natural or legal person, whatever the duties of the employee.
[271] Case C–37/93 *Commission* v. *Belgium* [1993] ECR I–6295.
[272] Case 225/85 *Commission* v. *Italy* [1987] ECR 2625.
[273] Case 66/85 *Lawrie-Blum* [1986] ECR 2121.
[274] Case 149/79 *Commission* v. *Belgium* [1982] ECR 1845, para. 8.
[275] Namely head technical office supervisor, principal supervisor, works supervisor, and stock controller.
[276] Case 225/85 *Commission* v. *Italy* [1987] ECR 2625, para. 9.
[277] Ibid., para. 10.   [278] 88/C 72/02.

purposes in public establishments, and public bodies responsible for administering public commercial services, including public transport, gas or electricity distribution, air or maritime navigation, post and telecommunications, and broadcasting. On the other hand, the Commission suggested that Article 45(4) TFEU would apply to the police and other forces of order, the armed forces, the judiciary, the tax authorities, and the diplomatic service.[279]

The Commission's approach was reflected in the Court's decisions in *Anker*[280] and the *Spanish Merchant Navy* case,[281] both decided on the same day. In *Anker* the Court upheld in principle a German law requiring the post of master of a fishing vessel flying the German flag to be German. Because the job entailed duties connected to the maintenance of safety and to the exercise of police powers, particularly in the case of danger on board, together with powers of investigation, coercion, and punishment, the Court said that the post entailed direct participation in the exercise of powers conferred by public law for the purposes of safeguarding the general interest of the state.[282] It added that even though masters were employed by private bodies this did not take the matter outside the scope of Article 45(4) TFEU because they were acting as 'representatives of public authority in the service of the general interests of the State'.[283] However, the Court emphasized that, to benefit from the Article 45(4) TFEU derogation, the powers had to be exercised on a regular basis and did not represent a 'very minor part of their activities'.[284] It therefore found that the post of master of small-scale deep-sea fishing vessels which involved skippering small boats with a small crew and participating in fishing and processing fish products did not benefit from the Article 45(4) TFEU derogation.[285] In the *Spanish Merchant Navy* case[286] the Court followed *Anker*, and found that the posts of master and chief mate in the Spanish merchant navy were also posts in which exercise of the duty of representing the flag state was in practice only occasional and so again did not benefit from the Article 45(4) TFEU derogation.[287]

The Commission followed up its Communication on public sector posts with enforcement proceedings against defaulting Member States. For example, Greece was condemned for maintaining posts for its own nationals in education, healthcare, the

---

[279] [1988] OJ C72/2, P. Watson, 'Free Movement of Workers: Recent Cases' (1989) 14 *ELRev.* 415. And even in respect of these sectors, the Commission has since tightened up its approach: COM(2002) 694, 19.

[280] Case C–47/02 *Albert Anker, Klaas Ras, Albertus Snoek v. Bundesrepublik Deutschland* [2003] ECR I–10447.

[281] Case C–405/01 *Colegio de Oficiales de la Marina Mercante Española v. Administración del Estado* [2003] ECR I–10391.

[282] Para. 61.

[283] Para. 62.

[284] Para. 63.

[285] Para. 64.

[286] Case C–405/01 *Colegio de Oficiales de la Marina Mercante Española v. Administración del Estado* [2003] ECR I–10391.

[287] Para. 45. See further Case C–89/07 *Commission v. France* [2008] ECR I–45: requirement of French nationality for access to the posts of master (captain) and officer (chief mate) on all vessels flying the French flag could not be justified under Article 45(4) TFEU. See further Case C–447/07 *Commission v. Italy* [2008] ECR I–125*; Case C–94/08 *Commission v. Spain* [2008] ECR I–160*.

utilities, public transport, post and telecommunications, radio and television broadcasting, the Athens opera, and municipal and local orchestras;[288] and Luxembourg was condemned for restricting posts in the public sectors of research, education, health, inland transport, post, telecommunications, and the utilities to its own nationals.[289] In the field of education, the Luxembourg government argued that teachers had to be Luxembourg nationals in order to 'transmit traditional values' and that, in view of the size of the country and its specific demographic situation, the nationality requirement was an essential condition for preserving Luxembourg's national identity. While recognizing that the preservation of the Member States' national identities was a legitimate aim, the Court said that the Luxembourg government's response was disproportionate. It argued that Luxembourg's interest could be effectively safeguarded otherwise than by a general exclusion of nationals from other Member States, in particular by imposing conditions relating to training, experience, and knowledge of the language.[290]

E. THIRD COUNTRY NATIONALS AND THE RIGHT TO WORK

1. INTRODUCTION

So far, we have focused on the rights of EU nationals to move to another Member State to work. The position of TCNs has only been relevant in so far as they are family members of the EU worker. However, there is a growing body of legislation which gives free-standing rights to TCNs who are legally present in the EU as well as rights of entry to the EU for specific groups. This is not mere altruism. Despite the currently high levels of unemployment, the EU is concerned about an ageing population, a skills gap, and losing competitiveness to the US.[291] The section that follows provides a brief outline of some of the employment rights conferred on TCNs by this legislation.[292]

2. FAMILY REUNIFICATION

For the past 20 years, family reunification has been one of the main sources of immigration to the EU.[293] The Family Reunification Directive 2003/86[294] was the first of two measures put forward by the Commission aimed at integrating TCNs into the com-

---

[288] Case C–290/94 *Commission v. Greece* [1996] ECR I–3285.

[289] Case C–473/93 *Commission v. Luxembourg* [1996] ECR I–3207. See additionally Case C–173/94 *Commission v. Belgium* [1996] ECR I–3265.

[290] Case C–473/93 *Commission v. Luxembourg* [1996] ECR I–3263, paras. 32–5.

[291] See e.g. Commission Communication: *The Hague Programme: ten priorities for the next five years. The Partnership for European renewal in the field of Freedom, Security and Justice* (COM(2005) 184).

[292] For full details, see S. Peers, *EU Justice and Home Affairs Law* 3rd edn (Oxford, OUP, 2011).

[293] COM(2008) 610, 3.

[294] [2003] OJ L251/12 adopted under Art. 63(3)(a) EC. The UK, Ireland, and Denmark are not taking part in this measure.

munity of the host state and ensuring fair treatment of TCNs. The Directive provides that a TCN ('the sponsor')[295] residing lawfully in the territory of a Member State, holding a residence permit issued by a Member State valid for a year or more, with reasonable prospects of obtaining the right of permanent residence, can apply for family reunification[296] (usually while the TCN family members are outside the territory).[297] The right to reunification is also dependent on evidence of the existence of 'normal' accommodation for a comparable family in the same region, sickness insurance for the TCN and the family members, and stable and regular resources which are higher than or equal to the level of resources which are sufficient to maintain the sponsor and the family members.

In order to ensure the integration of the family members the Directive allows Member States to require the TCN family members to comply with integration measures, such as attending language courses.[298] It also provides for family members to enjoy access to employment and self-employment,[299] education and vocational training[300] but not social security or social assistance. After five years the spouse and children who have reached majority have the right to an autonomous residence permit independent of that of the sponsor.[301]

3. RIGHTS OF LONG-TERM RESIDENTS

The Long Term Residents' Directive 2003/109[302] was the second measure proposed by the Commission in the name of integration.[303] The aim of this Directive is to establish a common status of long-term resident for those TCNs who have resided 'legally and continuously' for five years in the territory of the Member State concerned.[304] A long-term residence permit, valid for at least five years, will be granted where the TCN has adequate resources and sickness insurance.[305] It is automatically renewable on expiry.[306]

---

[295] The Directive therefore does not apply to non-migrant nationals wanting to be joined by TCN family members (e.g. a German living in Germany wanting to be joined by his Chinese wife). This situation is covered by national law.

[296] Art. 1. Under Art. 8 Member States may require the sponsor to have stayed lawfully in their territory for a period not exceeding two years. This provision was unsuccessfully challenged in Case C–540/03 *EP* v. *Council (Family Reunification Directive)* [2006] ECR I–5769.

[297] Art. 5(3).

[298] Art. 7(2).

[299] Art. 14(2) allows Member States to delay the exercise of employment/self-employment rights for up to 12 months.

[300] Art. 14(1).

[301] Art. 15(1).

[302] [2003] L16/44, adopted under Art. 63(3)(a) and (4) EC. The Directive does not apply to the UK, Ireland, and Denmark.

[303] COM (2001) 127.

[304] There is a long list of lawful residence in Art. 3(2) which will not entitle the TCN to long-term residence status: e.g. students, refugees, au-pairs.

[305] Cf. the CRD which does not impose the same obligations on EU citizens who have permanent residence.

[306] Art. 9 makes provision for the loss of long-term resident status including in the case of fraudulent acquisition of the status or absence from the territory for more than 12 consecutive months.

Member States can also require TCNs to comply with (unspecified) 'integration condi-tions',[307] before becoming long-term residents, tests which are usually reserved to grant-ing an individual citizenship of a state, not merely long-term residence status.

Long-term residents enjoy not only a secure residence but also equal treatment with nationals as regards a number of matters, including: access to employment (but not in respect of activities which entail even occasional involvement in the exercise of public authority or activities that are reserved to nationals under laws in force on 25 November 2003); education and training (including study grants);[308] recognition of diplomas; social protection and social assistance (including social security);[309] and access to goods and services. In addition, the long-term resident 'with reasonable prospects of obtain-ing the right of permanent residence' will also enjoy the right to family reunion under Directive 2003/86.[310] Both the Family Reunification Directive and the Directive on long-term residents are subject to derogations on the grounds of public policy, security, and health.

Long-term residents with a long-term resident permit (and their families) will also enjoy the rights of free movement to other Member States (i.e. secondary mobility). The Directive provides that long-term residents (and their families) can *reside* in (but makes no provision on entry to[311]) the territory of another Member State for more than three months if they are exercising an economic activity as an employed or self-employed person or studying there and have adequate resources and sickness insurance, or simply have adequate resources and sickness insurance.[312] This Directive demonstrates the increasing parallelism between the rights of legally resident TCNs and those of nation-als of the Member States who are citizens of the Union.

4. THE 'FIRST ADMISSIONS' DIRECTIVES

The two Directives considered so far—on family reunification and long term residence—focused on the integration of TCNs who had already been admitted to a Member State under *national* law. The Commission's other proposals have been concerned with manag-ing legal migration flows and in particular giving certain groups a right of *entry*—under Union law—to the Member States. The first, a proposed Directive on the conditions of entry and residence of TCNs for the purpose of paid employment and self-employed economic activities,[313] was seen as the 'cornerstone of immigration policy' and central to addressing the 'shortage of skilled labour in certain sectors of the labour market'.[314] It pro-vided for the grant of a renewable 'residence permit-worker' to a TCN, subject to certain

---

[307] Art. 5(2).   [308] Subject to limits in Art. 11(3).   [309] Although this can be limited: Art. 11(4).
[310] Art. 3(1).
[311] S. Bolaert-Souminen, 'Non-EU Nationals and Council Directive 2003/109/EC on the Status of Third Country Nationals who are Long-Term Residents: five paces forward and possibly three paces back' (2005) 42 *CMLRev.* 1011, 1030.
[312] For criticism of these provisions, see A. Kocharov, 'What intra-Community mobility for third country nationals' (2008) 33 *ELRev.* 913, 919.
[313] COM(2001) 386.   [314] Preambular paras. (3) and (6).

formalities, valid for three years, where a job vacancy could not be filled by an EU citizen or other TCNs already legally resident in the EU (the 'economic needs test' or 'Union preference' test). Such a permit would have allowed the TCN to enter into and reside in the territory of the issuing state, exercise the activities authorized by the permit, and enjoy equal treatment with nationals in a number of areas, including working conditions, recognition of qualifications, social security including health care, and access to goods and services.

Given that this proposal was merely a 'first step' in achieving a Union policy, it did not affect Member States' responsibility for deciding whether to admit economic migrants, taking into account the needs of their labour markets and their overall capacity to integrate the migrants, a point now enshrined in Article 79(5) TFEU.[315] Nevertheless, despite the professed importance of this Directive, it could not be agreed upon and the proposal was withdrawn.[316]

The Commission therefore focused on sectoral specific measures as part of its approach to managing economic migration.[317] It had already contemplated a measure, which became a Directive, on the conditions of entry and residence for TCNs for the purpose of studies, pupil exchange, vocational training, or voluntary service.[318] This measure is less market-oriented than the previous Directive because the stay of migrants covered by this Directive is temporary and is viewed as a form of 'mutual enrichment for the migrants who benefit directly from it, both for their country of origin and for the host country, while helping mutual familiarity between cultures'.[319] Despite these worthy words, the Directive does have a labour market dimension since, as the Commission notes, many Member States provide certain TCNs with the opportunity to remain after their training 'so as to remedy shortages of skilled manpower'.[320] This Directive requires those affected to have adequate resources and medical insurance. Students and unremunerated trainees can also have limited access to the employment market.

This measure was followed by Directive 2005/71 on a specific procedure for admitting third country nationals for the purposes of scientific research.[321] TCN researchers working with an approved research organization in the Member States are to be given a residence permit for a period of at least a year provided they have the relevant documentation and can show sufficient resources and medical insurance. Their family members can accompany them. The Directive does allow the researchers to teach for a certain

---

[315] 'This Article shall not affect the right of the Member States to determine volumes of admission of third-country nationals coming from third countries to their territory in order to seek work, whether employed or self-employed.'

[316] COM(2005) 462.

[317] See e.g. the Commission's Green Paper COM(2004) 811 and COM(2005) 669.

[318] Council Dir. 2004/114/EC ([2004] OJ L375/12) adopted on There is to be a proposal on the conditions of entry and residence for remunerated employees: COM(2005) 669. the basis of Art. 63(3)(a) and (4) EC. The UK, Ireland, and Denmark are not taking part in the Directive.

[319] COM(2002) 548, 2.

[320] COM(2002) 548, 3.

[321] [2005] OJ L289/15 adopted under Art. 63(3)(a) and (4) EC. Ireland has notified its wish to participate in this measure; the UK and Denmark are not participating.

number of hours and to enjoy equal treatment with Member State nationals in respect of terms and conditions of employment, dismissal, and social security.

The Directive also gives TCNs the right to carry out part of their research in another Member State. By allowing secondary mobility, the first admissions Directives mark a new step in the evolution of policy in respect of TCNs in that they give those covered by the Directives a secondary right of free movement. The rationale for this is competition rather than principle: the EU was losing out to the US in attracting the brightest and the best from third countries. Secondary mobility rights are seen as a pull factor to make the EU more attractive as a destination.[322]

The final and perhaps most important of the first admissions Directives is Directive 2009/50[323] on highly qualified workers (the so-called 'Blue Card Directive'). A TCN with a job offer for 'highly qualified' work (i.e. work requiring higher education qualifications or, where permitted by national law, five years' equivalent professional experience) in an EU Member State, with sickness insurance and who is not a threat to public policy, security, or health, must be issued with an EU blue card.[324] Member States do not, however, need to issue a blue card where, for example, the vacancy could be filled by a member of the national or Union workforce, where the Member State deems the volume of admission of TCNs is too high, or where the job is in a sector suffering from a lack of qualified workers in the country of origin (e.g. healthcare).[325] Once in possession of a blue card, the TCNs must do the work they came for the first two years; after that Member States 'may grant' the persons concerned equal treatment with nationals as regards access to highly qualified employment.[326] Blue card workers also enjoy equality in respect of a wider range of matters including working conditions, freedom of association, social security, and goods and services.[327] Finally, the Directive allows for secondary mobility. It prescribes the right of residence (but not entry) in the second Member State for TCN blue card holders and their family members[328] after 18 months of legal residence in the first Member State in order to undertake highly qualified employment.[329]

Complementing these three sectoral Directives is Council Directive 2011/98[330] on a single application procedure for a single permit for TCNs to reside and work in the

---

[322] S. Iglesias Sánchez, 'Free Movement of Third Country Nationals in the European Union? Main Features, Deficiencies and Challenges of the new Mobility Rights in the Area of Freedom, Security and Justice' (2009) 15 *ELJ* 791, 799; A. Kocharov, 'What Intra-Community Mobility for Third-country Workers?' (2008) 33 *ELRev.* 913, 915 who cites figures showing that the US attracts 55 per cent of all skilled migrants worldwide, while the EU attracts only 1/11th of that number.

[323] [2009] OJ L155/17 adopted under Article 63(3)(a) and (4) EC. The UK, Ireland, and Denmark are not taking part.

[324] Arts. 5 and 7.

[325] Arts. 6 and 8.

[326] Art. 12.

[327] Art. 15.

[328] Arts. 18 and 19.

[329] In addition, there is a proposal for a Directive on the conditions of entry and residence of TCNs for the purposes of seasonal employment (COM(2010) 379) and intra-corporate transfer (COM(2010) 378).

[330] OJ [2011] L343/1. The UK, Ireland, and Denmark are not participating.

territory of a Member State and on a common set of rights for TCNs legally residing in a Member State. There are thus two limbs to this 'horizontal' Directive. The first concerns those seeking to come to the EU to work. The Directive contains a single application procedure, resulting in a single permit to work and stay. No additional permits (e.g. work permits) can then be required.[331] The second limb of the Directive concerns those who are already legally residing in an EU Member State. Those legally working but not yet holding long-term resident status are to enjoy equal treatment in respect of employment related matters. However, the Directive makes no provision on admissions criteria.

So far we have concentrated on those who are legally present in the Member State. In respect of those illegally present, the most important measure from an employment perspective is Directive 2009/52[332] on minimum standards on sanctions against employers of illegally staying third-country nationals. This measure is seen as particularly important since the possibility of finding work is a pull factor for illegal immigration. Article 3(1) prohibits the employment of illegally staying TCNs. To that end, it obliges employers to require TCNs to hold a valid residence permit or authorization for their stay, to hold a copy of that document for inspection by the authorities, and to notify the authorities of the employment of TCNs. Article 5 requires sanctions for infringement of Article 3 to be 'effective, proportionate and dissuasive'. These sanctions must include 'financial sanction which shall increase in amount according to the number of illegally employed [TCNs]' and payments of the costs of return of illegally employed TCNs. Infringement is also to be a criminal offence when committed intentionally in certain circumstances.[333] In addition, employers must pay any outstanding remuneration to illegally employed TCNs. The agreed level of remuneration is presumed to be 'at least as high as the wage provided for by the applicable laws on minimum wages, by collective agreements or in accordance with established practice in the relevant occupational branches'.[334] Liability for these financial sanctions and back payments is also extended to the principal contractor in subcontracting situations. Finally, the Directive also requires Member States to take other measures against defaulting employers including excluding them from participating in public procurement contests for up to five years.[335]

---

[331] Posted third-country nationals are not covered by this Directive. According to the preamble, this should not prevent third-country nationals who are legally residing and working in a Member State and posted to another Member State from continuing to enjoy equal treatment with respect to nationals of the Member State of origin for the duration of their posting, in respect of those terms and conditions of employment which are not affected by the application of Directive 96/71/EC of the European Parliament and of the Council of 16 December 1996 concerning the posting of workers in the framework of the provision of services.

[332] [2009] OJ L168/24, proposed under Art. 63(3)(b) EC. The UK, Ireland, and Denmark are not taking part in this Directive.

[333] Art. 9.

[334] Art. 6(1). The Article also requires that the employer must pay any taxes and social security contributions as if the TCN had been legally employed.

[335] Art. 7.

F. CONCLUSIONS

Free movement of workers is the oldest labour right in the EU, the most elaborated but, at least prior to 2004, relatively little used. Various attempts to reinvigorate it have not enjoyed much success. The rights given to TCNs may, in the long term prove to be of greater practical significance. One growing area of importance, in legal terms if not in numerical terms, is posting of workers which is covered by Article 56 TFEU. Some of the issues which arise in this area overlap with Article 45 TFEU: what constitutes a breach, how can it be justified, is the measure proportionate? Yet, there is a major difference. Articles 45 (and 49) TFEU are premised on host state control of the individual; Articles 56 TFEU is premised on home state control. As the *Laval* litigation considered in the next chapter demonstrates, this raises economic, political, and legal problems.

5

LABOUR LAW AND THE INTERNAL MARKET

A. INTRODUCTION

The previous chapter suggested that the single market is good for workers: they can go, if they choose, to another Member State to seek employment, they enjoy equal treatment with national workers and, after five years, they enjoy rights of permanent residence. However, many, particularly in the trade union movement in the old Member States, are increasingly seeing the internal market as a threat to national labour law systems, not their salvation, and that the market making thesis outlined in Chapter 1, risks producing a 'race to the bottom', not to the top. The decisions in *Viking*,[1] *Laval*,[2] *Rüffert*,[3] and *Commission* v. *Luxembourg*[4] exacerbated these concerns. Section C considers these cases in detail, looks at their impact on national labour law systems and considers the Commission's response in the Monti II proposal,[5] and the proposed enforcement Directive[6] which is designed to 'improve, enhance and reinforce the way in which [the Posted Workers Directive 96/71 (PWD)] is implemented, applied and enforced in practice'. Section D then takes, as a case study, the example of public procurement which gives some indications as to how in fact national labour law and policy can be combined with the imperatives of the single market. First, however, Section B considers some early examples of the potential threat posed by the internal market to national labour law in the field of anti-trust (as broadly defined) and how the Court has responded to that challenge.

---

[1] Case C–438/05 *Viking Line ABP* v. *The International Transport Workers' Federation, the Finnish Seaman's Union* [2007] ECR I–10779.

[2] Case C–341/05 *Laval un Partneri Ltd* v. *Svenska Byggnadsarbetareförbundet* [2007] ECR I–11767.

[3] Case C–446/06 *Rüffert* v. *Land Niedersachsen* [2008] ECR I–1167.

[4] Case C–319/06 *Commission* v. *Luxembourg* [2009] ECR I–4323.

[5] COM(2012) 130.   [6] COM(2012) 131.

B. EU COMPETITION LAW MEETS NATIONAL LABOUR LAW

1. THE THREAT POSED TO LABOUR LAW

1.1. Introduction

The first hints that the single market may pose a threat to national systems of labour law rather than acting as their promoter, as Article 117 EEC had envisaged, came from competition law and the Court's apparent desire to focus entirely on the anti-trust perspective of the Treaty provisions. For example, in *Macrotron*[7] the Court held that the German Federal Employment Office (FEO) was not entitled to maintain its statutory monopoly over employment placement services. The Court said the FEO was abusing its dominant position contrary to Articles 102 and 106 TFEU (ex 82 and 86 EC) because the statutory service could not meet demand and tolerated private head-hunters, even though their activities were illegal. However, the Court made no reference to the social interest behind the German legislation: that private employment agencies might be tempted to concentrate on the most attractive job seekers, leaving aside the weaker prospects.[8]

Similarly, in *Porto di Genoa*[9] the Court said that Article 106 TFEU precluded national rules which conferred on an undertaking established in that state (but not individual dockers)[10] the exclusive right to organize dock work and required it to have recourse to a dock work company formed exclusively of national workers. Although the facts of *Porto di Genoa* were exceptional (the company was abusing its monopoly to demand payment for unrequested services, to offer selective reductions in prices, and by refusing to have recourse to modern technology), the most striking feature of the Court's judgment, as Deakin points out,[11] was the almost complete disregard shown for social arguments which could have been made in favour of the dock labour monopoly. In particular, no reference was made to the need to combat casualization of labour.

1.2. State aid

Subsequently it was the state aid rules that posed a challenge to national social legislation, as *Commission* v. *France*[12] demonstrated. The Commission decided that the finan-

---

[7] Case C–41/90 *Höfner and Elser* v. *Macroton* [1991] ECR I–1979; see additionally Case C–55/96 *Non-Contentious Proceedings brought by Job Centre Coop arl* [1997] ECR I–7140. See generally, G. Ricci, 'Il controverso rapporto fra principi comunitari della concorrenza e normative nazionali del lavoro il caso *Job Centre II*' (1998) 2 *Diritto delle relazioni industriali* 145.

[8] S. Sciarra, 'Part II: *Job Centre*: An Illustrative Example of Strategic Litigation', in S. Sciarra (ed.), *Labour Law in the Courts: National Judges and the European Court of Justice* (Hart Publishing, Oxford, 2001) 245.

[9] Case C–179/90 *Merci Convenzionali Porto di Genova* v. *Siderurgica Gabrielli* [1991] ECR I–5889. See Case C–163/96 *Criminal Proceedings against Silvano Raso* [1998] ECR I–533; Decision of the Commission 97/744/EC *Re Italian Ports Employment Policy: The Community* v. *Italy* [1998] 4 CMLR 73.

[10] Case C–22/98 *Criminal Proceedings against Bew, Verweire, Smeg and Adia Interim* [1999] ECR I–5665.

[11] S. Deakin, 'Labour Law as Market Regulation: the Economic Foundations of European Social Policy', in P. Davies, A. Lyon-Caen, S. Sciarra, and S. Simitis (eds.) *European Community Labour Law: Principles and Perspectives. Liber Amicorum Lord Wedderburn* (Oxford, Oxford University Press, 1996).

[12] Case C–241/94 *French Republic* v. *Commission* [1996] ECR I–4551. See further Case C–256/97 *Proceedings*

cial participation of the French Fonds National de l'Emploi (FNE), a state body, in
paying for measures included in the social plan drawn up by a company faced with large
scale redundancies, constituted a state aid contrary to Article 107(1) TFEU (ex 87(1)
EC) and therefore had to be notified to the Commission.[13] The Commission did, however, conclude that, in the event, the aid was not illegitimate, since it fell under an exception provided by Article 107(3)(c) TFEU (which allows aid where it is made 'to facilitate
the development of certain economic activities or of certain economic areas, where
such aid does not adversely affect trading conditions to an extent contrary to the common interest'). The French government challenged the Commission's initial finding
that the payment by FNE came under Article 107 TFEU at all, because, if correct, it
meant that France would have to notify all similar payments in future to the Commission. The Commission would then have the power to nullify them if the payments did
not, in its view (subject to review by the Court), fall under the relevant derogation.

Article 107(1) draws a distinction between measures of general application, which
are not aid, and subsidies payable to particular undertakings, which are. According to
Advocate General Jacobs in *Commission* v. *France*:

> . . . measures taken within the framework of employment policy are usually not state aid. How-
> ever, where public funds are used to reduce the salary costs of undertakings, either directly (for
> example by recruitment premiums) or indirectly (for example by reductions in fiscal or social
> charges), the distinction between state aid and general measure becomes less clear. The exist-
> ence of discretion serves to identify those financial measures promoting employment which are
> liable to distort competition and affect trade between Member States.

The Court followed this lead and concluded that since the French legislation gave the
administration some discretion in the amounts of subsidy which it could grant to a particular employer, this constituted a state aid. It therefore had to be notified and approved.

However, in *Kirsammer-Hack*[14] and *Viscido*[15] the Court found that national measures aimed at job creation, being of general application, were compatible with the

---

relating to *DMT* [1999] ECR I–3913. For an early example, see Case 173/73 *Italy* v. *Commission (textiles)* [1974]
ECR 709.

[13] See Case 203/82 *Commission* v. *Italy* [1983] ECR 2525: legislation reducing employer's sickness insurance
contributions by different amounts in respect of male and female employees indirectly benefited certain sectors
with more female employees and was declared contrary to Art. 107 TFEU.

[14] Case C–189/91 *Kirsammer Hack* v. *Sidal* [1993] ECR I–6185. See additionally Joined Cases C–72/91 and
C–73/91 *Sloman* [1993] ECR I–887, where the Court held that only benefits granted directly or indirectly out of
state resources were to be regarded as an aid. Consequently, a German system allowing employment contracts for
seamen not to be subject to German law did not constitute a state aid. This was confirmed in Case C–319/07 *3F*
v. *Commission* [2009] ECR I–5963 where the Court said a system such as that established by the DIS register,
which enables contracts of employment concluded with seafarers who are nationals of non-member countries
and have no permanent abode or residence in the Member State concerned to be subjected to working conditions
and rates of pay which are not covered by the law of that Member State and are considerably less favourable than
those applicable to seafarers who are nationals of that Member State, did not constitute state aid within the
meaning of Art. 107(1) TFEU. See A. Biondi and Rubini, 'EC State Aid Law and its Impact on National Social
Policies' in M. Dougan and E. Spaventa (eds.), *Social Welfare and EU Law* (Hart Publishing, Oxford, 2005).

[15] Joined Cases C–52/97, C–53/97 and C–54/97 *Viscido* v. *Ente Poste Italiane* [1998] ECR I–2629.

rules on state aid. In the first case the Court found that the exemption of small business from national unfair dismissal law did not constitute a state aid[16] and in the
second the Court ruled that a law exempting the Italian post office from the requirement that employees had to be appointed on indefinite contracts only also did not
constitute a state aid.

Subsequently, the Commission issued a Regulation on the application of Articles 107 and 108 TFEU (ex 87 and 88 EC) to state aid for employment.[17] Consistent
with the social inclusion objectives of the Luxembourg European Employment
Strategy and the Lisbon strategy, the Commission permitted states to provide aid
for the creation of employment, for the recruitment of disadvantaged and disabled
workers, or to cover the additional costs of employing disabled workers, provided
the conditions laid down in the Regulation were satisfied. In these circumstances,
the aid does not need to be notified to the Commission. The Court rejected Belgium's challenge to this Regulation in *Belgium* v. *Commission*.[18] In particular, the
Court noted that the Commission is required to ensure that Articles 107 and 108
TFEU are applied consistently with other provisions of the Treaty, including Article 147 TFEU (ex 127 EC) which requires the Union to contribute to a high level
of employment.[19] This Regulation expired in June 2008[20] and was replaced by
Commission Regulation 800/2008, the new General Block Exemption Regulation
(GBER) replacing the existing separate block exemption regulations.[21] This makes
provision for training aid and aid for disadvantaged and disabled workers as being
compatible with the common market under Article 107(3) TFEU and exempt from
the notification requirements under Article 108(3) TFEU. As the Commission
explains: 'The promotion of training and the recruitment of disadvantaged and
disabled workers, and compensation of additional costs for the employment of
disabled workers constitute a central objective of the economic and social policies
of the [Union] and of its Member States'. It continues: 'Training usually has positive externalities for society as a whole since it increases the pool of skilled workers from which other firms may draw, improves the competitiveness of [Union]
industry and plays an important role in the [Union] employment strategy'. Training is also:

---

[16] See further Dec. 2000/394/EC (OJ [2000] L150/50) where the Commission declared that reduction in
social security contributions granted to small and medium sized undertakings in Chioggia and Venice was
compatible with the state aid rules.

[17] Commission Reg. 2204/2002 (OJ [2002] L349/126) adopted under the powers laid down by Council Reg.
994/98 on the application of Arts. [107] and [108 TFEU] to certain categories of horizontal state aid (OJ [1998]
L142/1) See additionally Commission Communication on the criteria for the analysis of the compatibility of state
aid for the employment of disadvantaged and disabled workers (OJ [2009] C188/6).

[18] Case C–110/03 *Belgium* v. *Commission* [2005] ECR I–2801.

[19] Para. 66.

[20] C. Reg. 1976/2006 (OJ [2006] L368/85).

[21] The General Block Exemption Regulation (OJ [2008] L214/3).

...essential for the constitution, the acquisition and the diffusion of knowledge, a public good of primary importance. In view of the fact that undertakings in the [Union] generally under-invest in the training of their workers, especially when this training is general in nature and does not lead to an immediate and concrete advantage for the undertaking concerned, State aid can help to correct this market failure.[22]

2. THE COURT'S RESPONSE

2.1. Ring-fencing national law: *Albany*

The cases considered so far were mere skirmishes in advance of the main battle: did competition law apply to labour law and to collective agreements on wages and conditions in particular? This was the issue in *Albany*.[23] According to the Commission's submissions in the case, collective agreements are, by their very nature, restrictive of competition since generally employees cannot offer to work for a wage below the agreed minimum, and they affect trade between Member States.[24] Such agreements would thus be prohibited and void unless they satisfied the conditions in Article 101(3) TFEU.[25] The granting of such an exemption would be unlikely since that provision does not allow social objectives to be taken into account.[26] This result would occur despite the fact that 'there is international consensus on the legitimate and socially desirable character of collective bargaining'[27] which is to prevent employees from engaging in a 'race to the bottom' with regard to wages and working conditions.[28]

---

[22] Recitals 61 and 62.

[23] Case C–67/96 *Albany* [1999] ECR I–5751.

[24] Para. 175. AG Jacobs in *Albany* doubted this (para. 182). He said that collective agreements on wages, working time, or other working conditions, although they may restrict competition between employees, probably do not have an appreciable restrictive effect on competition between employers. As regards competition on the demand side of the labour market, normally each employer remains free to offer more advantageous conditions to his employees. As regards competition on the product or services markets on which the employers operate, first, agreements on wages or working conditions harmonize merely one of many production cost factors. Therefore only one aspect of competition is affected. Secondly, proximity to the market of the factor in issue is an important criterion for assessing appreciability. In the case of collective agreements on wages and working conditions, the final price of the products or services in question is influenced by many other factors before they reach the market. Thirdly, and perhaps most importantly, production factor costs are only apparently harmonized, because in economic terms labour, in contrast to raw materials, is not a homogeneous commodity. The fact that employees earn nominally the same wage does not mean that the real costs for their respective employers are identical. Real costs can be determined only when the employees' productivity is taken into account. Productivity is determined by many factors, e.g. professional skills, motivation, technological environment, and work organization. All those factors can be and are influenced by employers. That is precisely the task of efficient management of human resources. Thus, competition on labour as a cost factor is in fact strong.

[25] This is increasingly unlikely: see Commission Notice, *Guidelines on the application of Article 101(3) of the Treaty* OJ [2004] C101/97 where no reference was made to social (or environmental) considerations. Only economic considerations can be taken into account when deciding whether an agreement fulfils the conditions of Art. 101(3) TFEU.

[26] Para. 175. Cf. para. 193.   [27] Para. 164.   [28] Para. 178.

Collective agreements therefore present a conflict between the social and competition provisions of the Treaties. As Advocate General Jacobs pointed out,[29] the authors of
the Treaties either were not aware of the problem or could not agree on a solution[30] and
so the Treaties do not give clear guidance as to which policy should take priority. He
said that since both sets of rules were Treaty provisions of the same rank, one set of rules
should not take absolute precedence over the other and neither set of rules should be
emptied of its entire content. He therefore suggested the following reconciliation: since
the Treaty rules encouraging collective bargaining presuppose that collective agreements are in principle lawful, Article 101(1) TFEU could not have been intended to
apply to collective agreements between management and labour on core subjects such
as wages and other working conditions. Accordingly, such collective agreements should
enjoy automatic immunity from antitrust scrutiny.

He then proposed three conditions for ipso facto immunity: first, the agreement
must be made within the formal framework of collective bargaining between both sides
of industry. Unilateral co-ordination between employers unconnected with the collective bargaining process should not be automatically sheltered, whatever the subject of
the co-ordination may be.[31] Secondly, the agreement should be concluded in good faith.
In that context account must be taken of agreements which apparently deal with core
subjects of collective bargaining such as working time but which merely function as
cover for a serious restriction of competition between employers on their product markets. In those exceptional cases, too, competition authorities should be able to examine
the agreement in question.[32] Thirdly, the immunity extends only to those agreements
for which it is truly justified, i.e. that the collective agreement deals with the core subjects of collective bargaining, such as wages and working conditions, and does not
directly affect third parties or markets.

He suggested that the test should be 'whether the agreement merely modifies or
establishes rights and obligations within the labour relationship between employers
and employees or whether it goes beyond that and directly affects relations between
employers and third parties, such as clients, suppliers, competing employers, or consumers'. Because the latter types of agreement have potentially harmful effects on the
competitive process, they should be subject to antitrust scrutiny by the Commission or
other competent authorities, which would examine whether there was in fact an appreciable restriction of competition. If so, the Commission should, as the law stood then,
be able to balance the different interests involved and, where appropriate, grant an
exemption according to Article 101(3) TFEU.[33] He pointed out that both the Court and
the Commission had, on occasions, recognized the possibility of taking account of

---

[29] Para. 179.   [30] Ibid.   [31] Para. 191.   [32] Para. 192.

[33] The system is now based on *ex post* control rather than *ex ante* notification. So while, at the time of *Albany*
there was a system of notifications of individual agreements and exemptions, the system is now based on
directly applicable 'exception'. Unless an agreement falls within the scope of a Block Exemption Regulation,
parties must assess their agreements and decide whether they comply with the conditions in Article 101(3)
TFEU. If there is a complaint or a contractual dispute, then national courts may apply the conditions in Article
101(3) TFEU as may National Competition Authorities.

social grounds in particular by interpreting the conditions of Article 101(3) TFEU broadly so as to include concerns for employment.[34]

Thus, in Advocate General Jacobs' view, collective agreements concluded in (1) good faith on (2) core subjects (such as wages and working conditions) which do not (3) directly affect third markets and third parties, are not caught by Article 101(1) TFEU.[35] Agreements which do not satisfy one of these conditions are caught by Article 101(1) TFEU and will be subject to scrutiny (then) by the Commission under Article 101(3) TFEU if notified (now, by the national courts or competition authorities). This is very much the perspective of a competition lawyer.

The Court took a rather different, labour relations approach which offered greater respect to the autonomy of the Social Partners. It began by observing that the Union's activities include not only 'a system ensuring that competition in the internal market is not distorted'[36] but also 'a policy in the social sphere',[37] and that one of the Union's tasks is to promote a 'harmonious and balanced development of economic activities' and a 'high level of employment and social protection'.[38] It then pointed to the Commission's duties under Article 156 and Article 155 TFEU concerning collective bargaining and the role of the social dialogue under Articles 151, 155(1), and (2) TFEU[39] It continued:

> 59. It is beyond question that certain restrictions of competition are inherent in collective agreements between organisations representing employers and workers. However, the social policy objectives pursued by such agreements would be seriously undermined if management and labour were subject to Article [101(1) TFEU] when seeking jointly to adopt measures to improve conditions of work and employment.
>
> 60. It therefore follows from an interpretation of the provisions of the Treaty as a whole which is both effective and consistent that agreements concluded in the context of collective negotiations between management and labour in pursuit of such objectives must, by virtue of their nature and purpose, be regarded as falling outside the scope of Article [101(1) TFEU].

Thus, while the Advocate General thought that competition law applied in principle to collective agreements but that collective agreements did not fall within the prohibition in Article 101(1) TFEU so long as the three strict conditions were satisfied, the Court took the view that competition law did not apply at all provided that the collective agreement was aimed at improving working conditions.[40]

---

[34] Citing Case 26/76 *Metro* v. *Commission* [1977] ECR 1875, para. 43, Case 42/84 *Remia* v. *Commission* [1985] ECR 2545, para. 42; *Synthetic Fibres* (OJ [1984] L207/17), para. 37, and *Ford* v. *Volkswagen* (OJ [1993] L20/14), para. 23. However, cf. Commission Notice, *Guidelines on the application of Article 81(3) of the Treaty* OJ [2004] C101/97 considered above which refers only to economic considerations which can be taken into account when deciding whether an agreement satisfies Art. 101(3).

[35] Para. 194.

[36] Art. 3(g).

[37] Art. 3(j).

[38] Para. 54.

[39] Paras. 55–8.

[40] AG Fennelly in Case C–222/98 *Van der Woude* v. *Stichting Beatrixoord* [2000] ECR I–7111, para. 26 said that 'as an exception to the general field of application of Article [101 TFEU], the scope of the *Albany* exception should be narrowly construed'.

Albany itself concerned a collective agreement negotiated by representative organizations of employers and workers setting up a supplementary pension scheme, managed by a pension fund, to which affiliation was compulsory. The Dutch Minister of Employment had, on request of the Social Partners, made affiliation to the scheme compulsory for all workers in the sector. The Court said this guaranteed a certain level of pension to all workers in the sector which contributed directly to the improvement of one of the conditions of employment, namely their pay. Thus Article 101 TFEU did not apply.[41] As far as extending the collective agreement is concerned, as we have seen in Chapter 2, the possibility of giving *erga omnes* effect to a collective agreement exists in certain Member States and in the Union itself (through a 'decision' of the Council of Ministers).[42] This was recognized by the Court in *Albany*.[43] It said that since the collective agreement itself was not caught by Article 101(1) TFEU the Member State was free to extend it to all workers in the sector.[44] Similarly, in *Van der Woude* the Court said that a collective agreement establishing a health care insurance scheme contributed to improving the working conditions of employees, not only by ensuring that they have the necessary means to meet medical expenses but also by reducing the costs which, in the absence of a collective agreement, would have to be borne by the employees.[45] By reason of its nature and purpose, the agreement did not therefore fall within the scope of Article 101(1) TFEU.[46]

This solution—of ringfencing national labour law from the reach of EU internal market law—has been applied elsewhere. For example, it was used in the Services Directive 2006/123.[47] Article 1(6) provides that the Directive 'does not affect' labour law or social security legislation.[48] Article 1(7) contains a so-called 'Monti' clause:

---

[41] Paras. 63–4. See additionally Joined Cases C–115–7/97 *Brentjens Handelsonderneming BV* v. *Stichting Bedrijfspensioenfonds voor de Handel in Bouwmaterialen* [1999] ECR I–6025; Case C–219/97 *Maatschappij Drijvende Bokken BV* v. *Stichting Pensioenfonds voor de Vervoer- en Havenbedrijven* [1999] ECR I–6121. These cases are considered by S. Vousden, 'Albany, Market Law and Social Exclusion' (2000) 29 *ILJ* 181. See further Case C–222/98 *Van der Woude* v. *Stichting Beatrixoord* [2000] ECR I–7111 considered by S. Evju, 'Collective Agreements and Competition Law. The *Albany* puzzle and *Van der Woude*' (2001) 17 *IJCLLIR* 165.

[42] See further Ch. 2.

[43] Paras. 66 and 67.

[44] Para. 69. Although Art. 101 TFEU concerns only the behaviour of undertakings and not legislative or regulatory measures emanating from Member States, Member States are obliged under Art. 101 TFEU read in conjunction with Art. 4(3) TEU not to take or maintain in force legislation capable of eliminating the useful effect of the competition rules which apply to undertakings. This is not the case here. See further Case C–437/09 *AG2R Prévoyance* v. *Beaudout Père et Fils* [2011] ECR I–000.

[45] Para. 25.

[46] Para. 26.

[47] [2006] OJ L376/36. See further Art. 1(3) of Reg 1176/2011 on the prevention and correction of macroeconomic imbalances (OJ [2011] L306/25).

[48] A similar clause appears in the 53rd recital of the third postal liberalization Directive 2008/6/EC (OJ [2008] L52/3). The Groundhandling Directive 96/67 (OJ [1996] L272/36) is more robust. Article 18 provides: 'Without prejudice to the application of this Directive, and subject to the other provisions of [Union] law, Member States may take the necessary measures to ensure protection of the rights of workers and respect for the environment'.

This Directive does not affect the exercise of fundamental rights as recognised in the Member States and by [Union] law. Nor does it affect the right to negotiate, conclude and enforce collective agreements and to take industrial action in accordance with national law and practices which respect [Union] law.

2.2. The principle of solidarity

In more recent cases the Court has developed a new principle to help balance the EU competition rules with the needs of the national welfare state: the principle of solidarity.[49] Advocate General Fennelly defined solidarity in his opinion in *Sodemare*[50] as the 'inherently uncommercial act of involuntary subsidization of one social group by another'.[51] In the national system it has meant that national taxpayers pay their taxes to help look after their fellow nationals who need assistance. This sense of solidarity is derived in part from a shared nationality, in part from a shared sense of identity.

The Court started using the principle of solidarity in the early 1990s to protect certain social welfare schemes from EU competition law:[52] the Court says that where the activity is based on national solidarity, it is not an economic activity and therefore the body concerned cannot be classed as an undertaking to which Articles 101 and 102 TFEU (ex 81 and 82 EC) apply. This principle, when applied, indicates a certain supremacy for social protection over the Single Market.

The principle was first recognized in this context in *Poucet and Pistre*[53] where the Court held that certain French bodies administering the sickness and maternity insurance scheme for self-employed persons engaged in non-agricultural occupations and the basic pension scheme for skilled trades, were not to be classified as undertakings for the purpose of competition law. The schemes provided a basic pension.[54] Affiliation was compulsory. The pension scheme was a non-funded scheme: it operated on a redistributive basis with active members' contributions being directly used to finance the pensions of retired members; and the schemes had a social objective in that they were intended to provide cover for the beneficiaries against the risks of sickness or old age regardless of the individuals' financial status and state of health at the time of affiliation. The principle of solidarity was embodied in the *redistributive* nature of the pension

---

[49] T. Hervey, 'Social Solidarity: a Buttress against Internal Market Law?', in J. Shaw (ed.), *Social Law and Policy in an Evolving European Union* (Hart Publishing, Oxford, 2000). See further U. Neergaard, 'In Search of the Role of "Solidarity" in Primary Law and the Case Law of the European Court of Justice' in U. Neergaard, R. Nielsen, and L. Roseberrry (eds.), *The Role of Courts in Developing a European Social Model* (DJØF Publishing, Copenhagen, 2010) and more generally, G. De Búrca (ed.), *EU Law and the Welfare State: In Search of Solidarity* (OUP, Oxford, 2005).

[50] Case C–70/95 *Sodemare SA, Anni Azzurri Holding SpA and Anni Azzurri Rezzato Srl* v. *Regione Lombardia* [1997] ECR I–3395.

[51] Para. 29.

[52] For a fuller consideration of these developments, see C. Barnard, 'Solidarity and New Governance in the Field of Social Policy?' in G. De Búrca and J. Scott (eds.), *New Governance and Constitutionalism in Europe and the US* (Hart Publishing, Oxford, 2006).

[53] Joined Cases C–159/91 and C–160/91 *Poucet and Pistre* v. *AGF and Cancava* [1993] ECR I–637.

[54] These are helpfully summarized by AG Jacobs in his Opinion in Case C–67/96 *Albany* [1999] ECR I–5751, para. 317.

scheme: contributions paid by active workers served to finance the pensions of retired
workers. It was also reflected by the grant of pension rights where no contributions had
been made and of pension rights that were not proportional to the contributions paid.
Finally, there was solidarity between the various social security schemes, with those in
surplus contributing to the financing of those with structural difficulties. The Court
said:

> It follows that the social security schemes, as described, are based on a system of compul-
> sory contribution, which is indispensable for the application of the principle of solidarity
> and the financial equilibrium of those schemes.
> ... [O]rganisations involved in the management of the public social security system fulfil
> an exclusively social function. That activity is based on the principle of national solidarity
> and is entirely non-profit-making. The benefits paid are statutory benefits bearing no
> relation to the amount of the contribution. Accordingly, that activity is not an economic
> activity...

However, in *FFSA* (also known as *Coreva*)[55] the Court 'clarified' its case law. The case
concerned a French supplementary retirement scheme for self-employed farmers.[56]
The Court noted that in *FFSA* membership of the scheme was optional, that the scheme
operated in accordance with the principle of capitalization, rather than on a redistributive basis as in *Poucet*, and that the benefits to which it conferred entitlement depended
solely on the amount of contributions paid by the recipients and the financial results of
the investments made by the managing organization. It concluded that the managing
body therefore carried on an economic activity in competition with life assurance companies and so the Union competition rules, in particular Article 101 TFEU, applied. On
the question of solidarity the Court said that 'the principle of solidarity is extremely
limited in scope' and noted that while the scheme had solidaristic elements that was not
sufficient to take the scheme outside Article 101 TFEU.

The Court reached much the same conclusion in *Albany*,[57] another case involving a
capitalization scheme. It said that a pension fund charged with the management of a
supplementary pension scheme set up by a collective agreement to which affiliation was
compulsory by the public authorities for all workers in that sector, was an undertaking
within the meaning of Article 101 TFEU. However, it did say that the solidarity elements[58] justified the exclusive right of the fund to manage the supplementary scheme

[55] Case C-244/94 *Fédération Française des Sociététs d'Assurances* [1995] ECR I-4013 discussed by P. Laigre,
'L'intrusion du droit communautaire de la concurrence dans le champ de la protection sociale' [1996] *Droit
Social* 82.
[56] Case C-67/96 *Albany v. Stichting Bedrijfspensioenfonds Textielindustrie* [1999] ECR I-5751, para. 325.
This case is considered in more detail in Ch. 16.
[57] Case C-67/96 [1999] ECR I-5751, para. 87.
[58] The solidarity was reflected by the obligation to accept all workers without a prior medical examination,
the continuing accrual of pension rights despite exemption from contributions in the event of incapacity for
work, the discharge by the fund of arrears of contributions due from an employer in the event of the latter's
insolvency, and by the indexing of the amount of the pensions in order to maintain their value. The principle
of solidarity was also apparent from the absence of any equivalence, for individuals, between the contribution

under Article 106(2) TFEU (ex 86 EC) and so there was no breach of Articles 102 and 106(1) TFEU respectively.

Although the Court's initial enthusiasm for the principle of solidarity seemed to have rather cooled after *FFSA*, the principle was successfully invoked in *Sodemare*[59] to allow Italy to insist that only non-profit-making private operators could participate in the running of its social welfare system. The Italian rules did not breach Articles 49 and 54 TFEU (ex 43 and 48 EC) on freedom of establishment because, as the Court noted, the system of social welfare, whose implementation is in principle entrusted to the public authorities, is based on the principle of solidarity, as reflected by the fact that it is designed as a matter of priority to assist those who are in a state of need.[60] Thus, in *Sodemare* the Court used the principle of solidarity to reinforce its view that Union law is not just about unrestricted access for all economic operators to the market in other Member States.[61]

Since *Sodemare* the Court has carefully examined the facts of the individual cases to consider whether there is a sufficient degree of solidarity to justify a finding that the activity is not economic, so falling outside the scope of Union law, or insufficient solidarity and so Union law applies. For example, in *AOK*[62] the Court found that the sickness funds in the German statutory health insurance scheme were involved in the management of the social security system where they fulfilled 'an exclusively social function which is founded on the principle of national solidarity and is entirely non-profit-making'.[63] Since the funds were obliged by law to offer their members essentially identical benefits, irrespective of contributions; they were bound together in a type of union founded on the basis of solidarity which enabled an equalization of costs and risks between them; and they did not compete with one another or private institu-

paid, which was an average contribution not linked to risks, and pension rights, which were determined by reference to an average salary. Such solidarity made compulsory affiliation to the supplementary pension scheme essential. Otherwise, if 'good' risks left the scheme, the ensuing downward spiral would jeopardize its financial equilibrium (para. 75). This would increase the cost of pensions for workers, particularly those in small and medium-sized undertakings with older employees engaged in dangerous activities, to which the fund could no longer offer pensions at an acceptable cost (para. 108).

[59] Case C–70/95 *Sodemare* v. *Regione Lombardia* [1997] ECR I–3395.
[60] Para. 29.
[61] In the context of free movement of goods, cf. Case C–267/91 *Criminal proceedings against Keck and Mithouard* [1993] ECR I–6097.
[62] Joined Cases C–264/01, C–306/01, C–354/01 and C–355/01 *AOK Bundesverband, Bundesverband der Betriebskrankenkassen (BKK)* v. *Ichthyol-Gesellschaft Cordes, Hermani & Co.* [2004] ECR I–2493. See further Case C–218/00 *Cisal di Battistello Venanzio & C.Sas* v. *Istituto nazionale per l'assicurazione contro gli infortuni sul lavoro* [2002] ECR I–691 concerning compulsory insurance against accidents at work and occupational diseases; Case C–355/00 *Freskot AE* v. *Elliniko Dimosio* [2003] ECR I–5263; Case T–319/99 *FENIN* v. *Commission* [2003] ECR II–357 (concerning the bodies which run the Spanish national health system); Joined Cases C–266/04 to C–270/04 *Nazairdis* v. *Caisse nationale de l'orgaisation autonome d'assurance viellesse des travailleurs non salariés des professions industrielles et commerciales (Organic)* [2005] ECR I–9481, para. 54 (old age insurance schemes for self-employed persons in the craft sector). See S. Sciarra, 'Market Freedom and Fundamental Social Rights' in B. Hepple (ed.), *Social and Labour Rights in a Global Context* (CUP, Cambridge, 2002).
[63] Para. 51.

tions,[64] the Court considered they fell on the *Poucet and Pistre* side of the line and so their activity could not be regarded as economic in nature. On the other hand, in *Wouters*[65] the Court said that because a professional regulatory body such as the Bar of the Netherlands was neither fulfilling a social function based on the principle of solidarity nor exercising powers which were typically those of a public authority, it did engage in an economic activity and so was subject to Union law.

A further tactic used by the Court to shield national labour law from the full rigours of the internal market, at least in the context of the four freedoms, is recourse to the public interest requirements (sometimes referred to as objective justifications) which were discussed in Chapter 4. This was the approach adopted in *Viking* and *Laval* and will be considered below. Even here, solidarity has a role to play. For example, in *Kattner Stahlbau*[66] the Court recognized as a justification the obligation of solidarity which is 'characterised, in particular, by funding through contributions the amount of which is not strictly proportionate to the risks insured and by the granting of benefits the amount of which is not strictly proportionate to contributions'.

C. THE FOUR FREEDOMS MEET NATIONAL LABOUR LAW

1. INTRODUCTION

So far we have focused on the interplay between EU competition rules and national social policy. Is the situation the same when the EU's four freedoms come face to face with national social policy? The Court had to address this issue in the seminal 'Viking quartet' (*Viking, Laval, Rüffert* and *Commission* v. *Luxembourg*). There had been earlier challenges to national labour laws from the four freedoms but, when they came, they were deflected by the Court in various ways. For example, in some cases, the Court said that the effect of the national labour law rule on free movement was 'too uncertain and indirect'[67] or that it did not affect free movement at all.[68] In other cases, where the Court considered that EU law was engaged, it applied the principle of non-discrimination to ensure that no breach of EU law was found. An early example of this can be seen in *Commission* v. *France*:[69]

---

[64] Paras. 51–3.

[65] Case C–309/99 *Wouters, Savelbergh, Price Waterhouse Belastingadviseurs BV* v. *Algemene Raad van de Nederlandse Orde van Advocaten* [2002] ECR I–1577, para. 58. See additionally Case C–55/96 *Job Centre Coop. Arl* [1997] ECR I–7119.

[66] Case C–350/07 *Kattner Stahlbau GmbH* v. *Maschinenbau- und Metall- Berufsgenossenschaft* [2009] ECR I–1513, para. 87. See additionally Case C–192/05 *Tas-Hagen* v. *Raadskamer WUBO van de Pensioen- en Uitkeringsrad* [2006] ECR I–10451, paras 34–5.

[67] Case C–190/98 *Graf* [2002] ECR I–493.

[68] Case C–542/08 *Barth* [2010] ECR I–3189, para. 39. In the field of goods, see Case 155/80 *Oebel* [1991] ECR 1993 (nightwork in bakeries); Case C–312/89 *Union départementale des syndicats CGT de l'Aisne* v. *SIDEF Conforama, Société Arts et Meubles and Société Jima* [1991] ECR 997 (working on a Sunday).

[69] Case 167/73 [1974] ECR 354. para. 45.

The absolute nature of this prohibition [against discrimination], moreover, has the effect of not only allowing in each state equal access to employment to the nationals of other member states, but also, in accordance with the aim of Article [151 TFEU], of guaranteeing to the state's own nationals that they shall not suffer the unfavourable consequences which could result from the offer or acceptance by nationals of other Member States of conditions of employment or remuneration less advantageous than those obtaining under national law, since such acceptance is prohibited.

In other words, by applying the principle of equal treatment, the terms and conditions of employment of nationals of the host state would be protected against undercutting by migrants. The use of the non-discrimination approach, as the underlying test for the application of the free movement provisions, therefore effectively immunized national labour law from challenge under EU law. Provided national labour law rules were non-discriminatory they would be compatible with EU law. If they did discriminate either directly or indirectly, the discriminatory element had to be removed but the underlying rule remained intact.

However, the Court's embrace in the 1990s of the *Säger*[70] 'market access' approach (more recently referred to as the 'restrictions' approach), in place of the discrimination analysis, threatened to undermine the careful balance between the preservation of national labour law and EU rules on free movement, the balance foreseen by the original Treaty. While the non-discrimination model adopts a comparative approach looking to see how both nationals and migrants are treated (and only if there is a difference in treatment is there a potential illegality), the market access/restrictions approach considers the perspective of the out-of-state actor only. It asks whether the national rule hinders/restricts the ability of the out-of-state actor to gain access to the market or to exercise freedom of movement.

While there is a lively debate in the literature as to what precisely what the market access test means and how it should apply to rules which 'structure the market' such as labour law rules, rules on taxation, environmental laws, and so on,[71] the upshot of it is that national labour law rules potentially become liable to challenge as a restriction to free movement even where they are non-discriminatory. This can be seen in *Commission* v. *France (performing artists)*[72] where the Court said that French law which presumed artists had 'salaried status', resulting in them being subject to the social security scheme for employed workers, constituted a restriction on freedom to provide services.

---

[70] Case C–76/90 [1991] ECR I–4221, para. 12, Article 56 TFEU required '*not only* the elimination of all discrimination against a person providing services on the ground of his nationality *but also* the abolition of any restriction, even if it applies without distinction to national providers of services and to those of other Member States, when *it is liable to prohibit or otherwise impede* the activities of a provider of services established in another Member State where he lawfully provides similar services'.

[71] See e.g. J. Snell, 'The notion of market access: a concept or a slogan?' (2010) 47 *CMLRev.* 437; C. Barnard and S. Deakin, 'Market access and regulatory competition', in C. Barnard and J. Scott (eds.), *The Legal Foundations of the Single Market: Unpacking the Premises* (Oxford, Hart Publishing, 2002); G. Davies, 'Understanding market access: exploring the economic rationality of different conceptions of free movement law' (2010) 10 *German Law Journal* 673, E. Spaventa, 'From *Gebhard* to *Carpenter*: towards a (non-)economic European Constitution' (2004) 41 *CMLRev.* 743, 757–8.

[72] Case C–255/04 *Commission* v. *France (performing artists)* [2006] ECR I-5251, para. 38.

The Court said that the French system was 'likely both to discourage the artists in question from providing their services in France and discourage French organisers of events from engaging such artists'.[73] The rules were therefore presumptively unlawful unless they could be justified and were proportionate (which was not the case on the facts). Likewise in *Commission* v. *Germany (Volkswagen)*[74] the German law which privatized Volkswagen in the 1960s gave the German state and the *Land* considerable influence over the affairs of Volkswagen on the basis of a lower level of investment than would be required under general law. This, the Court found, was liable to deter direct investors from other Member States and so in principle breached Article 63 TFEU on free movement of capital. The justifications offered by the German government were also rejected: Germany failed to explain why, in order to meet the objective of protecting workers, it was appropriate and necessary for the Federal and State authorities to maintain a strengthened and irremovable position in the capital of Volkswagen. It also failed to explain why the provisions of the Volkswagen Law were appropriate and necessary to preserve the jobs generated by Volkswagen's activity.

These cases suggest that a full scale application of the market access test could jeopardize the entire edifice of national labour law. This was more than amply demonstrated by the *Viking* litigation.

2. FREEDOM OF ESTABLISHMENT AND LABOUR LAW: *VIKING*

2.1. Introduction

Viking concerned a Finnish company wanting to reflag its vessel, the Rosella, under the Estonian flag so that it could man the ship with an Estonian crew, who would be paid considerably less than the existing Finnish crew. The International Transport Workers' Federation (ITF) told its affiliates to boycott the Rosella and to take other solidarity industrial action. Viking therefore sought an injunction in the English High Court, restraining the ITF and the Finnish Seaman's Union (FSU), now threatening strike action, from breaching Article 49 TFEU (ex Article 43 EC) on freedom of establishment. In essence, the judgments in both *Viking* and *Laval* (see later in this chapter) raised four issues:[75]

---

[73] Para. 38.

[74] Case C-112/05 *Commission* v. *Germany* [2007] ECR I-8995.

[75] This section draws on the discussion in C. Barnard, 'Viking and Laval: a Single Market Perspective' in K. Ewing and J. Hendy (eds.), *The New Spectre Haunting Europe: The ECJ, Trade Union Rights and the British Government, Institute of Employment Rights* (The Institute of Employment Rights, 2009) 19. There is now a huge volume of literature on these cases. See e.g. (2007–08) 10 *CYELS* chs. 17–22; N. Reich, 'Free Movementt v. Social Rights in an Enlarged Union' (2008) 9 *German Law Journal*; P. Syrpis and T. Novitz, 'Economic and Social Rights in Conflict: Political and Judicial Approaches to their Reconciliation' (2008) 33 *ELRev*. 411; J. Malmberg and T. Sigeman, 'Industrial Actions and EU Economic Freedoms: The Autonomous Collective Bargaining Model Curtailed by the European Court of Justice' (2008) 45 *CMLRev*. 1115; C. Kilpatrick, 'Laval's Regulatory Conundrum: Collective Standard-setting and the Court's New Approach to Posted Workers' (2009) 34 *ELRev*. 844; C. Joerges and F. Rödl, 'Informal politics, formalized law and the "Social deficit" of European integration: Reflections after the

- Does EU (economic) law apply to the exercise of fundamental social rights, in particular the right to take industrial action?
- If it does, does EU law apply to trade unions?
- If so, does the collective action constitute a restriction on free movement?
- If it does, can it be justified and are the steps taken proportionate?

We shall consider these issues in turn.

2.2. Does EU law apply?

In respect of the first question, the trade unions and certain governments argued that Union law should not apply to national social policy because the application of Union economic freedoms to national social policy would undermine the integrity of national law. They relied, in particular, on Article 153(5) TFEU which, as we saw in Chapter 2, excludes Union competence in respect of, *inter alia*, the right to strike. These arguments resonated with the original settlement agreed at the time of the Treaty of Rome but were rejected by both the Advocates General and the Court. For example, the Court in *Viking* said that collective action fell in principle 'within the scope of Article [49 TFEU]'.[76] In respect of Article 153(5) TFEU, the Court said that just because Article 153(5) TFEU excluded Union competence in respect of, *inter alia*, the right to strike, this did not mean that strike action, as a whole, fell outside the scope of Union law.[77] This is not a surprising conclusion: in a number of areas of law (e.g. social security, healthcare, taxation) the Court has held that, even though Member States have the powers to organize their national systems, their action must nevertheless comply with Union law when exercising those powers.[78]

Somewhat more surprisingly, the Court also refused to extend to the context of free movement[79] the principle it had recognized in *Albany*[80] (considered above), thereby suggesting that while it is prepared to protect collective bargaining—and the resulting collective agreements[81]—from the scope of Union law, it will not protect collective action in the same way. Many trade unionists would argue that this misses the point: collective bargaining cannot exist without at least the threat of collective action.[82]

---

judgments of the ECJ in *Viking* and *Laval*' (2009) 15 *ELJ* 1; L. Azoulaï, 'The Court of Justice and the Social Market Economy: the emergence of an ideal and the conditions for its realisation' (2008) 45 *CMLRev.* 1335; S. Prechal and S. de Vries, 'Seamless web of judicial protecton in the internal market' (2009) *ELRev.* 5. A fuller list of all published work on this topic can be found at <http://www.etui.org/Topics/Social-dialogue-collective-bargaining/Social-legislation/The-interpretation-by-the-European-Court-of-Justice/Reaction-to-the-judgements/Articles-in-academic-literature-on-the-judgements> (last accessed 29 March 2012).

[76] *Viking*, para. 37.
[77] *Viking*, ibid., paras. 39–41; *Laval* para. 88.
[78] See e.g. Case C–158/96 *Kohll* v. *Union des caisses de maladie* [1998] ECR I–1931, paras. 17–19.
[79] *Viking*, para. 51.
[80] Case C–67/96 *Albany* [1999] ECR I–5751.
[81] *Viking*, para. 65.
[82] A point that the Court appears to acknowledge, ibid., para. 36.

Finally, the Court also rejected the argument that fundamental rights, including the right to strike, fell outside Union law. For labour lawyers, the significance of this section of the judgment lies in the (probably long overdue) recognition of 'the right to strike' as a 'fundamental right which forms an integral part of the general principles of Union law the observance of which the Court ensures'.[83] However, this observation comes with a sting in its tail: the right to take industrial action is not absolute; its 'exercise' may be subject to 'certain restrictions'. The Court then spelt out those restrictions: 'As is reaffirmed by Article 28 of the Charter of Fundamental Rights of the European Union', those rights are to be protected in accordance with national law and practices (such as rules on balloting and notice requirements) *and* Union law (in particular the rules on free movement).[84] The importance of the latter limitation becomes apparent only later in the judgment.[85]

2.3. Does EU law apply to trade unions?

Having ruled that Union law in principle applied, the Court then said that Article 49 TFEU could be 'relied on by a private undertaking against a trade union or an association of trade unions'.[86] While it is not surprising that the Court said that the Treaties applied to the trade unions,[87] the Court's ruling generates a particular problem for trade unions which have now been placed in the same position as states, with the same responsibilities. Yet, unlike states, trade unions do not need to balance the interests of those losing their jobs with the interests of the citizen body as a whole in receiving cheaper services; the principal objective of trade unions is to protect the interests of their members.[88] The invidious position that trade unions now find themselves in is exacerbated by the fact that while trade unions are subject to the same obligations as states it will be hard for them ever to be able to invoke any of the defences in Article 52 TFEU (ex Article 46 EC), such as public policy, which were drafted with states in mind. This point has particular resonance on the facts of *Laval*: as we shall see later, trade unions 'not being bodies governed by public law' could not rely on the public policy derogation in Article 3(10) PWD.[89]

---

[83] Although cf. Davies' description of 'the Court's "defensive" recognition of the right to strike' which colours the way in which the right can be used: A.C.L. Davies, 'One Step Forward, Two Steps Back? The *Viking* and *Laval* cases in the ECJ' (2008) 37 *ILJ* 126, 139.

[84] *Viking*, para. 44.

[85] See further G. Orlandini, 'Trade Union Rights and Market Freedoms: the European Court of Justice sets out the rules' (2008) 29 *Comp. Labor Law and Pol'y Journal* 573.

[86] *Viking*, para. 61.

[87] Case 36/74 *Walrave and Koch* [1974] ECR 1405. See D. Wyatt, 'The Horizontal Effect of Articles 43 and 49' (2008) 4 *Croatian Ybk of Intl L* 1.

[88] A point the Court expressly noted in Case C-319/07 *3F* v. *Commission* [2009] ECR I-5963, para. 52: 'the appellant as an organisation representing workers is by definition established to promote the collective interests of its members'.

[89] *Laval*, para. 84.

2.4. Does strike action constitute a restriction on free movement?

Having established that EU law in principle applied to the case and could be invoked by the employers against trade unions, it was a relatively easy step for the Court to find that European Union law was breached. Relying on the 'market access' reasoning, the Advocates General and the Court concluded that the collective action constituted a restriction on free movement. So, in *Viking* the Court found a breach of Article 49 both by FSU[90] and by the ITF.[91] Nevertheless, for Continental labour lawyers the Court's approach came as a shock. It changes the presumption that striking is lawful into a presumption that striking, at least in the context of transnational disputes, is unlawful.

2.5. Can the strike action be justified?

Having established a breach of the Treaty, the next question was whether the collective action could be justified and the steps taken were proportionate. Rejecting the nuanced approach proposed by Advocate General Poiares Maduro in *Viking*, the Court adopted a robust stance to the question of justification. It began by recognizing the need to reconcile and balance[92] the competing objectives of the Union: on the one hand, the completion of the internal market and, on the other, 'a policy in the social sphere'.[93] The significance of this observation lies in the fact that the Court has now confirmed just how far the Union has come from its purely economic origins in 1957 as the European *Economic* Community. Social policy is, apparently, no longer residual; it is as important as the economic policies of the Union.[94] Yet, in fact, the reference to balance is largely rhetorical and had no substantive influence on the outcome of the decisions in *Viking* and *Laval*.

In *Viking*, the Court then noted that 'the right to take collective action for the protection of workers is a legitimate interest which, in principle, justifies a restriction of one of the fundamental freedoms guaranteed by the [Treaties]' and that 'the protection of workers is one of the overriding reasons of public interest recognised by the Court'.[95] It is striking, as Novitz notes,[96] that the Court is not prepared to protect the right to strike *per se*, as it did with freedom of expression in *Schmidberger*, but will only protect industrial action which achieves a wider 'approved' purpose, namely worker protection. By implication, industrial action taken to achieve other goals (e.g. political strikes) may not be lawful. This highlights the limited significance of the Court's recognition of the right to strike in the earlier—and less significant—part of the judgment.

The Court of Justice gave the national court a strong steer as to whether the collective action did actually concern the protection of workers.[97] In respect of the collective action taken by the FSU, it said:

---

[90] *Viking*, para. 72.   [91] Ibid., para. 73.   [92] *Viking*, para. 79; *Laval*, para. 105.

[93] *Viking*, para. 78; *Laval*, para. 104.

[94] See further the earlier decision in Joined Cases C–270/97 and C–271/97 *Deutsche Post AG* v. *Elisabeth Sievers and Brunhilde Schrage* [2000] ECR I–929.

[95] *Viking*, para. 77.

[96] T. Novitz, 'The Right to Strike as a Human Right' (2007–08) 10 *CYELS* 357.

[97] *Viking*, para. 80.

[E]ven if that action—aimed at protecting the *jobs and conditions of employment* of the members of that union *liable to be adversely affected* by the reflagging of the *Rosella*—could reasonably be considered to fall, at first sight, within the objective of protecting workers, such a view would no longer be tenable if it were established that the jobs or conditions of employment at issue were not jeopardised or under serious threat.[98]

This is a reference to the fact that Viking, presumably on good advice, had given an undertaking that neither it nor companies in the same group would 'by reason of the reflagging terminate the employment of any person employed by them'.[99] However, since the exact legal scope of the undertaking was not clear from the order for reference, 'it is for the national court to determine whether the jobs or conditions of employment of that trade union's members who are liable to be affected by the reflagging of the *Rosella* were jeopardised or under serious threat'.[100]

2.6. Was the strike action proportionate?

Even though the Court of Justice clearly thought that the FSU had not made out the justification, it did nevertheless give guidance on the question of proportionality, i.e. whether the collective action initiated by FSU was (1) suitable for ensuring the achievement of the objective pursued and (2) did not go beyond what was necessary to attain that objective.[101] On question (1), suitability, the Court said that 'collective action, like collective negotiations and collective agreements, may, in the particular circumstances of a case, be one of the main ways in which trade unions protect the interests of their members'.[102] This reasoning coincides with a labour lawyer's understanding of the right to strike. However, this is undermined by the Court's approach to question (2), necessity, where the Court said it is for the national court to examine whether the 'FSU did not have other means at its disposal which were less restrictive of freedom of establishment' to bring to a successful conclusion the collective negotiations entered into with Viking, and, 'whether that trade union had exhausted those means before initiating such action'.[103]

Thus, the Court of Justice suggests that industrial action should be the last resort; and national courts will have to verify whether the union has exhausted all other avenues under Finnish law before the industrial action is found proportionate. This test poses significant problems for trade unions in the future. Unfortunately no further guidance

---

[98] *Viking*, para. 81.

[99] Viking's cost savings would presumably have come from its decision not to renew short-term employment contracts and redeploying employees on equivalent terms and conditions: see question 10 referred by the national court.

[100] *Viking*, para. 83.

[101] Ibid., para. 84.

[102] Citing two ECtHR decisions in support: *Syndicat national de la police belge* v. *Belgium* Series Application 4464/70 (1975) and *Wilson, National Union of Journalists and Others* v. *United Kingdom* Applications 30668/96, 30671/96 and 30678/96 EHHR 2002-V, 44.

[103] *Viking*, para. 87.

will be offered by the Court of Appeal, the referring court, because the case was set-tled.[104] It is, however, known that the *Rosella* is now registered in Sweden.

2.7. Assessment

Given the classic 'market access' structure adopted in *Viking* (and *Laval*), it was inevi-table that the Court would find the collective action a restriction on freedom of estab-lishment.[105] This put the 'social' arguments on the back foot: collective action was presumptively unlawful unless the trade unions could justify it and show the action taken was proportionate.[106] Despite the talk of 'balance' between the economic and the social, most regarded the result as a victory for the economic freedoms.[107]

Further, the Court applied a strict approach to the question of justification and pro-portionality. As we have seen, the Court that said the right to take collective action under Union law is justified only where jobs or conditions of employment are jeopard-ized or under serious threat (note, it seems that collective action is not possible to *improve* jobs and conditions, the traditional role of collective action), and collective action is the last resort. These are the *Union* limits on the right to strike which are imposed in addition to any national law limits. And this will apply equally to Article 28 of the Charter which contains reference to the same limitations.

It is also remarkable that in an area of such sensitivity—national social policy and collective action in particular—the Court still insisted on applying a strict proportion-ality test to the trade unions, with no reference to any margin of appreciation, which appears to be confined to Member States.[108] This leads to a further paradox, noted by Davies, on the application of the proportionality test to industrial action: the more the strike restricts the employer's free movement rights—and thus the more effective it is from the union's perspective—the harder it will be to justify.[109]

If the decisions in *Viking* and *Laval* essentially ensure free movement, subject to a narrow possibility of taking industrial action, then this is clearly good news for the accession states[110] and for their workers. They will continue to take advantage of their

---

[104] <http://www.itfglobal.org/news-online/index.cfm/newsdetail/1842> (last accessed 12 March 2012).

[105] Cf. R. O'Donoghue and B. Carr, 'Dealing with *Viking* and *Laval*: from Theory to Practice' (2008–09) 11 *CYELS* 123.

[106] Cf. V. Skouris, 'Das Verhältnis der Grundfreiheiten zu den Gemeinschaftsgrundrechten' [2009] *Recht der Arbeit-Beil*, 25.

[107] Cf. D. Kukovec 'Myths of Social Europe: The *Laval* judgment and the prosperity gap', talk delivered to the Harvard Law School, 16 April 2010 available on SSRN. Kukovec argues '...like Wittgenstein's duck-rabbit picture, what appears as economic is social and what social is economic, depending on the angle from which we see the dilemma. The debate could just as well be framed in terms of social rights of [Estonian] workers against the [Finnish] interpretation of the freedom of movement provisions which ignores their realisation'.

[108] For contemporary examples of the Court applying the margin of appreciation to states, see e.g. Case C–250/06 *United Pan-Europe Communications Belgium SA* v. *Etat Belge* [2007] ECR I–11135; Case C–244/06 *Dynamic Medien* [2008] ECR I–505. J. Sweeney, 'A "Margin of Appreciation" in the Internal Market: Lessons from the European Court of Human Rights' (2007) 34 *LIEI* 27.

[109] Davies, above, n 83.

[110] For a full discussion of the views of the new Member States, see B. Bercusson, 'The Trade Union Movement and the European Union: Judgment Day' (2007) 13 *ELJ* 279.

cheaper labour for so long as their wage costs remain significantly lower than in the West. They are the winners; the trade union movement in the West the losers, a point made by John Monks, General Secretary of the ETUC, to the European Parliament in 2008:

> So we are told that the right to strike is a fundamental right but not so fundamental as the EU's free movement provisions. This is a licence for social dumping and for unions being prevented from taking action to improve matters. Any company in a transnational dispute has the opportunity to use this judgment against union actions, alleging disproportionality.[111]

The ETUC has therefore called for the adoption of a social progress clause which would say that '[n]othing in the Treaty, and in particular neither fundamental freedoms nor competition rules shall have priority over fundamental social rights and social progress'. It adds: 'In case of conflict, fundamental social rights shall take precedence'.[112]

This line may find some support following the judgment of the European Court of Human Rights in *Demir and Baykara*[113] which ruled that both a right to collective bargaining and a right to take collective action can be inferred from Article 11, the freedom of association provision of the European Convention on Human Rights. In reaching this conclusion the Court of Human Rights made wide-ranging reference to a number of international sources including the EU's Charter of Fundamental Rights and the ILO Conventions. This latter reference is of particular significance because, following a complaint by BALPA (the British Airline Pilot's Association) to the ILO's Committee of Experts on the Application of Conventions and Recommendations, that the effect of the judgments in *Viking* and *Laval* was to expose the unions to crippling damages[114] if they went on strike without complying with the (unclear) terms of the judgments, the Committee observed:

> with *serious concern* the practical limitations on the effective exercise of the right to strike of the BALPA workers in this case. The Committee takes the view that the omnipresent threat of an action for damages that could bankrupt the union, possibly now in the light of the *Viking* and *Laval* judgments, creates a situation where the rights under the Convention cannot be exercised.... The Committee thus considers that the doctrine that is being articulated in these ECJ judgments is likely to have a significant restrictive effect on the exercise of the right to strike in practice in a manner contrary to the Convention.

---

[111] See additionally J. Monks, 'European Court of Justice and Social Europe: A divorce based on irreconcilable differences?' [2008] *Social Europe Journal* 22.

[112] ETUC's Resolution adopted on 4 March 2008: <http://www.etuc.org/IMG/pdf_ETUC_Viking_Laval_-_resolution_070308.pdf> (last accessed 12 March 2012). Cf. Report on joint work of the European social partners on the ECJ rulings in the Viking, Laval, Rüffert and Luxembourg cases, 19 March 2010: <http://www.etuc.org/IMG/pdf_Joint_report_ECJ_rulings_FINAL_logos_19.03.10.pdf> (last accessed 12 March 2012).

[113] *Demir and Baykara* v. *Turkey*, Application No 34503/97, 12 November 2008. See further *Enerji Yapi-Yol* (Application no. 68959/01) which confirms that right to strike is part of Art. 11 (see further Ch. 16).

[114] K. Apps, 'Damages Claims Against Trade Unions after Viking and Laval' (2009) 34 *ELRev.* 141.

2.8. The Monti II proposal

However, when the Commission published its Monti II proposal[115] it did not go so far as expressly to prioritize the social interests over the economic. Article 2 says:

> The exercise of the freedom of establishment and the freedom to provide services enshrined in the Treaty shall respect the fundamental right to take collective action, including the right or freedom to strike, and conversely, the exercise of the fundamental right to take collective action, including the right or freedom to strike, shall respect these economic freedoms.

At first glance this appears to make matters worse for trade unions by prioritizing, in the first part of the clause, the economic right over the social. Yet, in fact had the Article opened with the second part of the sentence coming first ('the exercise of the fundamental right to take collective action … shall respect these economic freedoms') this would have sent a strong message as to the priority of the economic freedoms.[116] Further, Article 2 must be read in the light of the Preamble and the Explanatory memorandum. The latter is particularly supportive of the right to strike (which should not be 'a mere slogan or metaphor'[117]) and makes extensive reference to obligations under international law, including ILO Conventions 87 and 98,[118] to the case law of the Court of Human Rights in cases such as *Demir* and *Enerji Yapi-Yol*,[119] as well as to the EU's own Charter of Fundamental Rights. These documents (and others) are all mentioned in the first recital to the proposed regulation which also contains the important statement that '[t]he right to take collective action … is the corollary of the right to collective bargaining', a point which the Court appeared to overlook in *Viking* and *Laval*.

Further, the reference to the Charter means that Article 52 is engaged. Article 52(1) requires that any limitation on the exercise of the rights and freedoms recognized by the Charter must be provided for by law and 'respect the essence of those rights and freedoms', a point expressly noted in the Explanatory Memorandum[120] and in the 12th Recital. This might mean that if, under the *Viking* formula, strike action is considered disproportionate because of the costs entailed—as in *Balpa* where British Airways claimed that it would lose £50 million if its pilots went on strike—and so an injunction restraining strike action is granted, the effect of that injunction might be to undermine the essence of the right to strike. In the light of this reasoning, an injunction cannot be granted. Further, Article 52(3) says that in so far as the Charter contains rights which correspond to rights guaranteed by the Convention, 'the meaning and scope of those rights shall be the same as those laid down' by the Convention. Given the links between

---

[115] COM(2012) 130.

[116] The widely leaked draft of 2011 did start with that order: 'The exercise of the fundamental right to take collective action, including the right to freedom to strike, should *fully* respect the economic freedoms enshrined in the Treaty…'. It also added 'No primacy exists between the two'. This last sentence was dropped, as was the word 'fully'.

[117] At p. 10.

[118] ILO Convention 98 is mentioned in the first Recital of the proposal.

[119] At pp. 3–4.   [120] At p. 13.

Article 11 of the Convention and Article 28 of the Charter, there is an argument that the Regulation must be interpreted in the light of the *Demir* case law, which includes the right to strike as its starting point.

Article 1(2) of the proposed Regulation, along with Article 1(2) of the proposed enforcement Directive (see further in Section 4), contains a so-called Monti clause, combining the text of Article 2 of the Monti I Regulation 2679/98 and Article 1(7) of the Services Directive:

> This Regulation shall not affect in any way the exercise of fundamental rights as recognised in the Member States, including the right or freedom to strike or to take other action covered by the specific industrial relations systems in Member States in accordance with national law and practices. Nor does it affect the right to negotiate, conclude and enforce collective agreements and to take collective action in accordance with national law and practices.

However, there is a significant omission: unlike Article 1(7) of the Services Directive (cited in Section B above) no reference is made to the limitations laid down by 'Union law'. It could thus be argued that there is an attempt to make clear that matters affecting strike action are very much a matter for national law, a point reinforced by Article 3(4) which emphasizes that national courts have a role (in addition to, or in the alternative to, ADR where it exists in the Member States to which cross-border cases must enjoy equal access[121]), 'in particular to assess the facts and interpret the national legislation, and, as far as the scope of this Regulation is concerned, to determine whether and to what extent collective action, *under the national legislation and collective agreement law* applicable to that action, does not go beyond what is necessary to attain the objective(s) pursued, without prejudice to the role and competences of the Court of Justice' (emphasis added).

The reference to the content of the proportionality principle in Article 3(4) (albeit that the word 'proportionality' has now gone from the Article itself although it is still present in the Preamble (Recitals 11 and 12)) has caused particular concern for trade unions in states such as the UK where a substantive proportionality review of strike action is not undertaken by the courts. National courts merely check to see whether strike action complies with the complex terms of the national legislation. They do not do an additional substantive proportionality review check. In other countries, such as Germany, there is a possibility of carrying out a substantive proportionality review of the strike action, but since the review is undertaken in the framework of a constitutional right to strike, the German (specialist labour) courts are reluctant to find strike action disproportionate.[122]

But there are a number of ways of using the proportionality principle——which does not have to entail strict two-limbed approach to proportionality review envisaged by

---

[121] Arts. 3(1)–(3).
[122] Cf. T. Novitz, 'The Impact of *Viking* and *Laval*. Contesting the social function and the legal regulation of the right to strike' in E. Ales and T. Novitz (eds.) *Collective Action and Fundamental Freedoms in Europe* (Intersentia, Antwerp, 2010).

the Court in *Viking*. The new fundamental rights context provided by the Regulation might suggest time has come for a reconsideration of how proportionality should be applied in cases such as this. Should a more procedural rather than a substantive approach to proportionality be taken into account?[123] Does the reference to the three-limbed test of proportionality in the Preamble ('appropriate, necessary and reasonable') pave the way for incorporating a test to see whether the essence of the right has been infringed?

The 2011 leaked draft of the Regulation contained another clause, Article 2(3), which also created controversy:

> When cross border elements are lacking or hypothetical, any collective or industrial action shall be assumed prima facie not to constitute a violation of the freedom of establishment or the freedom to provide services and therefore in principle be legitimate and lawful under Union law.
>
> This presumption is rebuttable and without prejudice to the conformity of the collective action with national law and practices.

At first sight, this provision looks peculiar: why does it take a Regulation to make a well-known point of EU law that if there is no cross-border element then EU law does not apply? The provision was in fact introduced to help address a particular problem created by EU law itself: it is enough for there to be a potential impact on inter-state movement for EU law to be engaged.[124] This rule, together with *Viking*, has had a chilling effect on strike action in some states. If, for example, there is a strike at a local postal sorting office over, say, the dismissal of a colleague, would that strike action have to comply with both domestic law *and* EU law (the *Viking* conditions which are unlikely to be satisfied on these facts), given that there is a potential inter-state element (some of the post currently being delayed is destined for other EU Member States), or, should only domestic law apply (as common sense might dictate). The trade union risks getting this decision wrong and being challenged by the employer, which could lead to bankruptcy for the union. Article 3(2) was therefore intended to assist trade unions in this situation. Although Article 3(2) has now gone from the final version of the proposed Regulation, echoes of its presence still remain, in particular in the 12th recital of the Preamble and in the Explanatory Memorandum.[125]

The only substantive provision in the Regulation is the alert mechanism in Article 4, modelled on the alert mechanism in the Monti I Regulation 2679/98. This provides:

> 1. Whenever serious acts or circumstances affecting the effective exercise of the freedom of establishment or the freedom to provide services which could cause grave disruption to the proper functioning of the internal market and/or which may cause serious damage to its industrial relations system or create serious social unrest in its territory or in the territory of other Member States, arise, the Member State concerned shall immediately inform and

---

[123] See further C. Barnard, 'A Proportionate Response to Proportionality: the case of collective action' (2012) 37 *ELRev.* 117.

[124] See e.g. Case C–321/94 *Pistre* [1997] ECR I–2343; Case C–60/00 *Carpenter* [2002] ECR I–6279.

[125] At p.12.

notify the Member State of establishment or origin of the service provider and/or other relevant Member States concerned as well as the Commission.

2. The Member State(s) concerned shall respond as soon as possible to requests for information from the Commission and from other Member States concerning the nature of the obstacle or threat. Any information exchange between Member States shall also be transmitted to the Commission.

So since the Monti II Regulation is intended to respond to the judgments in *Viking* and *Laval* in the same way that Monti I responded to *Commission v. France (Spanish strawberries)*,[126] then presumably strike action on the scale envisaged in those two cases would need to be subject to an alert. Some would argue that this renders Article 4 unlawful since it imposes an additional restriction on strike action. However, it is an obligation on the states, not the trade unions, to make the alert, and Article 4 makes no reference to any sanctions for non-compliance by a state (although presumably an Article 258 TFEU enforcement action could be brought against a defaulting state). Further, Article 4 is a weaker provision than its Monti I forebears since it does not require Member States to take any 'remedial' action other than to respond to requests for information.

The fate of the Monti II proposal is uncertain. The trade unions have already come out against it,[127] as has BusinessEurope[128] which argues that the proposal 'disrespects the exclusion of the right to strike from the competences in the Treaty'. The proposed Regulation is based on Article 352 TFEU, the residual legal basis. Article 153 TFEU, the more obvious choice, was ruled out because of the exclusion of competence in respect of the right to strike under Article 153(5) TFEU.[129] The argument is that if the Court declares strike action to be a 'restriction' on free movement and thus in principle unlawful, the EU must have the power to re-regulate at EU level. Article 352 TFEU provides just such powers—but subject to some major limitations, not least unanimous voting in Council (the French have already indicated that they are opposed given the weakness of the measure[130]), and only consent from the European Parliament. Further, Article 352(2) TFEU expressly requires the Commission to draw the proposal to the attention of the national parliaments, in accordance with the Subsidiarity Protocol, and the Member States' parliaments have issued a yellow card for the first time.

However, even if Monti II is not adopted, following the Lisbon Treaty there is evidence of striving for a better balance between the economic and social, on the part of the Advocates General, at least. This is mandated by Article 3(3) TEU which talks of attaining a 'social market economy'.[131] Perhaps the fullest expression of this desire can

---

[126] Case C–265/95 *Commission v. France* [1995] ECR I–6959.

[127] 'ETUC says no to a regulation that undermines the right to strike': <http://www.etuc.org/a/9823> (last accessed 2 April 2012).

[128] <http://www.businesseurope.eu/content/default.asp?PageID=568&DocID=30033> (last accessed 2 April 2012).

[129] This is discussed further in Ch. 2.

[130] <http://www.euractiv.com/socialeurope/new-rights-posted-workers-problematic-business-news-511672> (last accessed 2 April 2012).

[131] A view given some support by e.g. AG Cruz Villalon in Case C–515/08 *Santos Palhota* [2010] ECR I–000, paras. 51–53.

be seen in Advocate General Trstenjak's Opinion in *Commission* v. *Germany (occupational pensions)*.[132] Having noted that fundamental rights and fundamental freedoms are of equal rank,[133] she was critical of the approach adopted in *Viking* that suggested the existence of a 'hierarchical relationship between fundamental freedoms and fundamental rights in which fundamental rights are subordinated to fundamental freedoms and, consequently, may restrict fundamental freedoms only with the assistance of a written or unwritten ground of justification'.[134] She offered a different perspective:

> 188.... [I]t must be presumed that the realisation of a fundamental freedom constitutes a legitimate objective which may limit a fundamental right. Conversely, however, the realisation of a fundamental right must be recognised also as a legitimate objective which may restrict a fundamental freedom.

> 189. For the purposes of drawing an exact boundary between fundamental freedoms and fundamental rights, the principle of proportionality is of particular importance....

> 190. A fair balance between fundamental rights and fundamental freedoms is ensured in the case of a conflict only when the restriction by a fundamental right on a fundamental freedom is not permitted to go beyond what is appropriate, necessary and reasonable to realise that fundamental right. Conversely, however, nor may the restriction on a fundamental right by a fundamental freedom go beyond what is appropriate, necessary and reasonable to realise the fundamental freedom.

In other words, Advocate General Trstenjak is proposing a 'symmetrical' approach, checking that the economic right is limited to the least extent possible and that the social right is also limited to the least extent possible.[135] However, even she found it difficult to release this in practice and her opinion came down in favour of the economic freedom.

3. FREE MOVEMENT OF SERVICES, POSTED WORKERS, AND NATIONAL LABOUR LAW: AN INTRODUCTION

So far, we have concentrated on freedom of establishment. We turn now to free movement of services. The comparative advantage in terms of labour costs enjoyed by the EU-10 states means that they are in a strong position to win contracts put out to tender by contracting authorities in EU-15 host states. They can fulfil the contract using their own staff—who can be EU nationals or third country nationals[136]—'posted' to the host state but employed under their home country's terms and conditions of employment.[137]

---

[132] Case C–271/08 [2010] ECR I–7087.   [133] Para. 183.   [134] Para. 184.

[135] Her views did, however, influence the drafting of the Monti II proposal: Recital 12 (COM(2012) 130).

[136] Case C–113/89 *Rush Portuguesa* v. *Office nationale d'immigration* [1990] ECR I–1417. If the workforce comes from a third country, the staff must return to the home state after completing the assignment: Case C–43/93 *Vander Elst* v. *Office des Migrations Internationales* [1994] ECR I–3803. Both cases confirmed that the host state cannot require these staff to have work permits but the host state can insist on TCNs having a short-stay visa permitting them to remain in the host state for as long as necessary to carry out the work, a so-called '*Vander Elst* visa' which was subsequently adopted by Germany. The Court suggested that the prior checks connected with the visa procedure were unlawful in Case C–244/04 *Commission* v. *Germany* [2006] ECR I–885, para. 18.

[137] Posted workers represent about 0.4 per cent of the EU's working-age population.

This is compatible with the Rome I Regulation (see later in this chapter). Nevertheless, it undercuts the terms and conditions of employment of the host state which, in accordance with the principles of equal treatment, the posted workers might expect to enjoy on the same terms as nationals. Some host states, such as the UK, do apply the principle of equal treatment as a result of the territorial application of labour law, according to which host states apply all of their terms and conditions of employment to all those working in their territory. Is this compatible with Article 56 TFEU? In *Rush Portuguesa*[138] the Court (obiter) said yes:[139]

> [Union] law does not preclude Member States from extending their legislation, or collective labour agreements entered into by both sides of industry, to any person who is employed, even temporarily, within their territory, no matter in which country the employer is established; nor does [Union] law prohibit Member States from enforcing those rules by appropriate means.[140]

Thus, in one (unreasoned) paragraph the Court allowed the host state to extend all of its labour laws and conditions to the staff employed by service providers working in its country. By requiring equal treatment of the in-state and out-of state-workers, the Court either, depending on your perspective, put a stop to the threat of social dumping, or undermined the out-of-state company's comparative advantage.

While *Rush Portuguesa* came as a relief to a number of countries, in particular Germany, that receive a large number of posted workers, and paved the way for the adoption of the PWD (see later in this chapter), its compatibility with Article 56 TFEU was soon questioned. In its subsequent case law the Court retreated somewhat from its bold but unreasoned approach in *Rush Portuguesa*, and brought its case law more into line with its *Säger*[141] jurisprudence. Therefore, in its subsequent decisions, the Court has looked to see:

(1) whether the requirements imposed by the host state on the service provider restrict or impede the freedom to provide services (the answer is usually yes);

(2) whether the measure can be justified on the non-economic[142] grounds of, for example, worker protection,[143] especially the interests of the posted workers[144] (again the answer is usually yes);[145]

---

[138] Case C–113/89 *Rush Portuguesa* [1990] ECR I–1417.

[139] Para. 12, emphasis added.

[140] Para. 18.

[141] Case C–76/90 [1991] ECR I–4221.

[142] Emphasized in Case E-2/11 *STX Norway Offshore*, judgment of EFTA Court of 23 January 2012, para. 83.

[143] Joined Cases C–49, 50, 52, 54, 68, and 71/98 *Finalarte Sociedade de Construção Civil Lda* [2001] ECR I–7831, paras. 41–9, for a careful scrutiny of the worker protection justification and that the national measures did actually confer a genuine benefit on the posted worker. See additionally Case C–164/99 *Portugaia Construções Lda* [2002] ECR I–787, paras. 28–9.

[144] Joined Cases C–49, 50, 52, 54, 68 and 71/98 *Finalarte* [2001] ECR I–7831, para. 41.

[145] If the rules are directly discriminatory they can be saved only by reference to one of the express derogations found in the Treaties i.e. public policy, public security or public health (Arts. 52 and 62 TFEU):

(3) whether the same interest is already protected in the state of establishment (this is usually left to the national court to decide);[146] and

(4) whether the steps taken are proportionate.[147] While the proportionality question should be considered by the national court, sometimes the Court of Justice provides the answer itself.

Stage three is particularly important in the context of the provision of services: the presumption is that the rules of the country of origin (*home* state) apply. This distinguishes the rules on the provision of services from those on free movement of workers and freedom of establishment where *host* state rules apply. As we saw in Chapter 4, under Article 45 TFEU migrant workers enjoy equal treatment with *host* state workers. Likewise, staff employed by companies with branches or agencies established in the host state under Article 49 TFEU enjoy equal treatment with host state staff. This distinction between home and host state control in respect of temporary and permanent migrants is also reflected in the Rome I Regulation[148] which is discussed further below.

A number of the post *Rush Portuguesa* cases focused on the procedural safeguards that host states can apply in posting situations. Some rules concerned procedural protection that host states could apply to posted workers themselves. So, for example, in *Wolff*[149] the Court said the host state was justified in extending to service providers measures intended to 'reinforce the procedural arrangements enabling a posted worker usefully to assert his right to a minimum rate of pay'. Other cases concerned procedural rules which host states could apply to companies doing the posting, often to check that immigration and other host state rules had been complied with, safeguards which the proposed enforcement Directive has confirmed.[150] In *Commission* v. *Germany*[151] the Court said that the host state could insist that the service provider furnished a 'simple prior

Case C–490/04 *Commission* v. *Germany* [2007] ECR I–6095, para. 86; Case C–546/07 *Commission* v. *Germany* [2010] ECR I-439. This was also at issue in respect of the so-called *Lex Britannia* in Case C–341/05 *Laval* [2007] ECR I–11767. National rules failed to take into account, irrespective of their content, collective agreements to which undertakings that post workers to Sweden were already bound in the Member State in which they are established. This gave rise to discrimination against these undertakings, in so far as under those national rules they were treated in the same way as national undertakings which had not concluded a collective agreement. The Court said that the application of those rules to foreign undertakings which are bound by collective agreements to which Swedish law does not directly apply is intended, first, to allow trade unions to take action to ensure that all employers active on the Swedish labour market pay wages and apply other terms and conditions of employment in line with those usual in Sweden, and, secondly, to create a climate of fair competition, on an equal basis, between Swedish employers and entrepreneurs from other Member States. Since none of these considerations constitute grounds of public policy, public security, or public health within the meaning of Arts. 52 and 62 TFEU the discrimination could not be justified (paras. 118–119).

[146] See e.g. Case C–458/08 *Commission* v. *Portugal* [2010] ECR I–000.
[147] See e.g. Joined Cases C–369 and 376/96 *Criminal Proceedings against Jean-Claude Arblade and Arblade & Fils SARL and against Bernard Leloup and others* [1999] ECR I–8453.
[148] Regulation 593/2008 (OJ [2008] L177/6).
[149] Case C–60/03 *Wolff & Müller* v. *Pereira Félix* [2004] ECR I–9553, paras. 36 and 41.
[150] COM(2012) 131.
[151] Case C–244/04 *Commission* v. *Germany* [2006] ECR I-885, confirmed in Case C–219/08 *Commission* v. *Belgium* [2009] ECR I-9213.

declaration certifying that the situation of the workers concerned is lawful', particularly in the light of the requirements of residence, work visas and social security cover in the Member States where the provider employs them.[152] In *Commission* v. *Luxembourg*[153] the Court also said that the host state could require the service provider to report beforehand to the local authorities on the presence of one or more posted workers, the anticipated duration of their presence and the provision or provisions of services justifying the deployment.[154] In *Arblade*[155] the Court said that the host Member State could insist that the service provider keep social and labour documents available on site or in an accessible and clearly-identified place in the host state, where such a measure was necessary to enable it effectively to monitor compliance with the host state's legislation[156] and, in *Commission* v. *Germany (language)*,[157] that the host state could require a (reasonable) number of those documents to be translated into German.[158] Finally, in *Finalarte*[159] the Court added that businesses established outside the Member State could be required to provide more information than businesses established in the host state to the extent that this difference in treatment could be attributed to objective differences between those businesses and businesses established in the host state.[160]

The Court has not, however, allowed the host state to impose all of its procedural rules on posting companies. So, for example, it has said that host state laws requiring the posted worker to have been employed by the service provider for at least six months in the case of Luxembourg[161] (a year in the case of Germany[162]) were not lawful. A requirement for the posted workers to have individual work permits which were only granted where the labour market situation so allowed was also not compatible with the EU law.[163] The Court has also said that a requirement for the service provider to provide, for the purposes of obtaining a work permit, a bank guarantee to cover costs in the event of repatriation of the worker at the end of his deployment was not permitted,[164] nor was a

---

[152] However, the host state cannot require the declaration to be sent in advance so that a registration number can be issued without which the planned posting cannot take place: Case C–515/08 *Santos Palhota* [2010] ECR I–000.

[153] Case C–445/03 [2004] ECR I–10191.

[154] Para. 31. These rules are confirmed in Art. 9(1)(a) of the proposed enforcement Dir. (COM(2012) 131).

[155] Joined Cases C–369/96 and C–376/96 [1999] ECR I–8453. See Case C–515/08 *Santos Palhota* [2010] ECR I–000.

[156] See Art. 9(1)(b) of the proposed enforcement Dir. (COM(2012) 131).

[157] Case C–490/04 *Commission* v. *Germany* [2007] ECR I- 6095, para. 76.

[158] See Art. 9(1)(c) of the proposed enforcement Dir. (COM(2012) 131).

[159] Joined Cases C–49/98, C–50/98, C–52/98 to C–54/98 and C–68/98 to C–71/98 [2001] ECR I–7831.

[160] This might mean, as Art. 9(1)(d) of the proposed enforcement Dir. (COM(2012) 131) says, an obligation to designate a contact person to negotiate, if necessary, on behalf of the employer with the relevant social partners in the Member State to which the posting takes place, in accordance with national legislation and practice, during the period in which the services are provided.

[161] Case C–445/03 *Commission* v. *Luxembourg* [2004] ECR I–10191, paras. 32–3.

[162] Case C–244/04 *Commission* v. *Germany* [2006] ECR I–885.

[163] Case C–445/03 *Commission* v. *Luxembourg* [2004] ECR I–10191, paras. 42–3. See further Case C–43/93 *Vander Elst* [1994] ECR I–3803 considered above.

[164] Ibid., para. 47.

requirement that the work be licensed,[165] nor was a rule that in order for an EU posting confirmation to be issued, the posted worker must have been employed by the sending company for at least a year prior to the posting and to have an indefinite contract with that company.[166] In the explanatory memorandum accompanying the proposed enforcement Directive, there is a list of other measures a host state may not impose, based on the case law of the Court:

- an obligation for the provider to have an establishment in their territory;
- an obligation for the provider to obtain an authorization from or to be registered with their competent authorities, including entry in a register or registration with a professional body or association in their territory, or to satisfy any other equivalent requirement, except where provided for in other instruments of EU law;
- an obligation to designate a representative or ad hoc agent established, domiciled or residing in the host Member State;
- a ban on the provider setting up a certain form or type of infrastructure in their territory, including an office or chambers, which the provider needs in order to be able to provide the services in question;
- an obligation to keep certain social documents on its territory, without any exception and/or time limitation, when the information can be obtained via the employer or the authorities in the Member State of establishment within a reasonable period of time;
- an obligation to draw up relevant social documents in accordance with the rules of the host country.[167]

While the cases on the procedural rules are likely to remain good law since they fall outside the scope of the Posted Workers Directive,[168] and, as we have seen, are likely to be endorsed by the proposed enforcement Directive, a number of other decisions on the application of substantive employment law by the host state (e.g. *Finalarte*[169] which says that the host state can require the service provider to give the posted workers 30 days worked, or 36 working days, of paid leave per year) now need to be reconsidered in the light of the Directive, which had not come into force at the time when those decisions were handed down. We turn now to consider the PWD.

---

[165] Ibid., para. 30.

[166] Case C–168/04 *Commission v. Austria* [2006] ECR I–9041.

[167] This list broadly replicates Art. 24(1) of the ill-fated 'Bolkestein' draft of the Services Directive (COM(2004) 2). When that Directive failed, the Commission published Guidance (COM(2006) 159) which broadly replicated the content of Article 24. This was followed up by COM(2007) 304.

[168] Case C–515/08 *Santos Palhota* [2010] ECR I–000, paras. 26–7.

[169] Joined Cases C–49/98, C–50/98, C–52/98 to C–54/98 and C–68/98 to C–71/98 *Finalarte Sociedade de Construção Civil Lda* (C–49/98) [2001] ECR I–7831, para. 58.

4. THE POSTED WORKERS DIRECTIVE 96/71/EC

4.1. Introduction

Directive 96/71 on the posting of workers in the framework of the provision of services,[170] based on Articles 53(1) and 62 TFEU on the provision of services and not on the social policy legal bases in the Treaties, is intended to promote the transnational provision of services in a 'climate of fair competition' while 'guaranteeing respect for the rights of workers'.[171] As Vladimir Špidla, the then EU Employment, Social Affairs and Equal Opportunities Commissioner bluntly put it, 'This Directive is a key instrument both to ensure freedom to provide services and to prevent social dumping'.[172] It aims to co-ordinate the legislation in the Member States and to lay down and give detail of the hard core of mandatory EU rules which *must* be respected by undertakings assigning their employees to work in another Member State. In this way, the Directive goes further than *Rush Portuguesa* which merely permitted (as opposed to requiring) host Member States to extend some or all of their rules to employees posted to their territory.

4.2. The scope of the Directive

The Directive applies to undertakings established in a Member State[173] which, in the framework of the transnational provision of services, post workers to the territory of another Member State (the host state).[174] According to Article 1(3), the posting of workers can take one of three forms:[175]

(a) posting under a contract concluded between the undertaking making the posting and the party for whom the services are intended;

(b) posting to an establishment or an undertaking owned by the group (this category, referred to as intra-firm or intra-group mobility,[176] has been included to prevent an undertaking from opening a subsidiary in another Member State purely to place some of its workers there to carry out temporary assignments, and thereby to avoid the scope of the Directive);

(c) posting by a temporary employment or placement agency (temp agency) to a user undertaking established or operating in the territory of another Member State, provided there is an employment relationship between the temp agency and the worker during the period of posting.

---

[170] OJ [1996] L18/1. See additionally COM(93) 225 final—SYN 346.

[171] Preambular, para. 5 cited in, e.g. Case E-2/11 *STX Norway Offshore AS* v. *Norway*, judgment of the EFTA Court 23 Jan. 2012, para. 23.

[172] IP/06/423.

[173] Art. 1(1). Art. 1(4) provides that undertakings established in non-Member States must not be given more favourable treatment than undertakings established in a Member State.

[174] Art. 1(1).   [175] Art. 1(3).   [176] Arts. 1 and 2.

In all three cases the key feature is that an employment relationship exists between the posted worker and the service provider which is established in a Member State other than that where the service is provided. This point was emphasized by the Court in *Vicoplus*[177] in the context of Article 1(3)(c) of Directive 96/71. It said that the hiring-out of workers is a service provided for remuneration in respect of which the worker who has been hired out remains in the employ of the undertaking providing the service, no contract of employment being entered into with the user undertaking. Unlike the situation under Article 1(3)(a) where the posting of workers is ancillary to the provision of services, Article 1(3)(c) is characterized by the fact that the movement of the worker to the host Member State constitutes the very purpose of the provision of services effected by the undertaking providing the services and that that worker carries out his tasks under the control and direction of the user undertaking.

The third situation, posting by a temp agency,[178] potentially raises an issue with the Temporary Agency Work Directive (TAWD) 2008/104[179] which requires in Article 5(1) equal treatment between agency workers and workers of the user undertaking.[180] However, Article 5(4) TAWD allows Member States, in agreement with the social partners, to establish arrangements concerning the basic working and employment conditions which derogate from the principle of equal treatment. It continues: 'Such arrangements may include a qualifying period for equal treatment'. The UK has taken advantage of this, not extending the principle of equal treatment to agency workers working in the user undertaking for less than three months. With an average posting lasting 44 days, many posted workers will therefore fall within the scope of any Article 5(4) derogation. However, if Member States do choose to apply the principle of equal treatment to posted agency workers, Article 3(9) permits them to do so. It provides that Member States 'may provide' that undertakings 'must guarantee workers referred to in Article 1(3)(c) the terms and conditions which apply to temporary workers in the Member States in which the work is carried out'. If a Member State extends all employment rights to domestic agency workers and that Member State also takes advantage of Article 3(9) then posted agency workers will enjoy all the rules of the host Member State. They will thus find themselves in a better position than, say, workers posted under Article 1(3)(a) who will enjoy only the rights laid down in Article 3(1).

A posted worker means a worker, as defined by the law of the host state, who for a limited period, carries out his work in the territory of a Member State other than the state in which he normally works.[181] The proposed enforcement

---

[177] Joined Cases C–307/09 and C–309/09 *Vicoplus* v. *Minister van Sociale Zaken en Werkgelegenheid* [2011] ECR I-000, paras. 45–47.

[178] In practice, a lot of the large temp agencies are actually established in the host state so the PWD will not apply. The agency will therefore be bound by Dir. 2008/104 only.

[179] OJ [2008] L327/9.

[180] It is thus a stronger obligation than that found in Art. 3(9) PWD which, although using a different comparator, provides that Member States *may* provide temp agencies must guarantee to the workers they employ the terms and conditions which apply to temporary workers in the Member State where the work is carried out.

[181] Art. 2(1) and (2).

Directive,[182] published at the same time as the proposed Monti II Regulation, aims to provide some clarity as to whether posted workers temporarily carry out their work in another Member State. Article 3(2) contains a non-exhaustive qualitative (not quantitative) list of elements which can be included:

(a) the work is carried out for a limited period of time in another Member State;

(b) the posting takes place to a Member State other than the one in or from which the posted worker habitually carries out his or her work according to Regulation (EC) No 593/2008 and/or the Rome Convention;

(c) the posted worker returns to or is expected to resume working in the Member State from which he/she is posted after completion of the work or the provision of services for which he or she was posted;

(d) travel, board and lodging/accommodation is provided or reimbursed by the employer who posts the worker, and if so, how this is done; as well as

(e) any repeated previous periods during which the post was filled by the same or another (posted) worker.

This list is complemented by a further list in Article 3(1) as to the criteria relating to what genuinely constitutes an establishment in another Member State (e.g. the place where the undertaking has its registered office and administration, uses office space, pays taxes, has a professional licence or is registered with the chambers of commerce or professional bodies; the place where posted workers are recruited; the law applicable to the contracts concluded by the undertaking with its workers, on the one hand, and with its clients, on the other hand; the place where the undertaking performs its substantial business activity and where it employs administrative staff; the abnormally limited number of contracts performed and/or size of turnover realized in the Member State of establishment). These factors are intended to help competent authorities decide whether the undertaking genuinely performs substantial activities, other than purely internal management and/or administrative activities, in the state.

According to Article 3(1) PWD, whatever the law applicable to the employment relationship, the undertakings identified above *must* guarantee posted workers the host state's terms and conditions of employment in respect of:

(a) maximum work periods and minimum rest periods;[183]

(b) minimum paid holidays;

---

[182] COM(2012) 131.

[183] This may include several maximum levels contained in different legal provisions: Case E–2/11 *STX Norway Offshore AS*, judgment of the EFTA Court 23 Jan. 2012, para. 56.

(c) minimum rates of pay,[184] as defined by the host state's law and/or practice, including overtime.[185] This does not apply to supplementary occupational retirement pension schemes; case law indicates it also does not cover sick pay;[186]

(d) the conditions of hiring out of workers, in particular the supply of workers by temp agencies;

(e) health, safety, and hygiene at work;

(f) protective measures with regard to the terms and conditions of employment of pregnant women or women who have recently given birth, children, and young people;

(g) equality of treatment between men and women and other provisions on non-discrimination.

Social security is not covered: Regulation 883/2004,[187] applies instead.[188] Furthermore, the rules listed in Article 3 of Directive 96/71 must be laid down by law, regulation or administrative provision.[189] In the case of the building industry[190] these rules can also be laid down by collective agreement provided strict conditions, laid down in Article 3(8) (outlined later in this chapter), are satisfied. In other industries Member States can, under Article 3(10) second indent, require the application of 'terms and conditions of employment laid down in collective agreements or arbitration awards within the meaning of paragraph [3(8)]'.

This Directive is thus different to other more traditional social policy measures in that it is not a harmonization measure but a coordination Directive.[191] This means that where host States have rules in the areas listed in Article 3(1) these must be applied to posted workers, but where no such rules exist the Member States do not need to create them. Since some of the areas listed in Article 3(1) are covered by EU harmonization legislation (e.g. working time, equal treatment), Member States will (or at least should) have such legislation.

---

[184] Allowances specific to the posting shall be considered to be part of the minimum wage, unless they are paid in reimbursement of expenditure actually incurred on account of the posting, such as expenditure on travel, board and lodging (Art. 3(7), para. 2).

[185] The overtime rates must also be minima: Case E-2/11 *STX Norway Offshore AS* v. *Norway*, judgment of the EFTA Court 23 Jan. 2012, para. 57.

[186] Case E-12/10 *EFTA Surveillance Authority* v. *Iceland*, judgment of the EFTA Court, 28 June 2011, para. 47.

[187] OJ [2004] L166/1.

[188] This is confirmed in Case E-12/10 *EFTA Surveillance Authority* v. *Iceland*, judgment of the EFTA Court, 28 June 2011, para. 50 For details see text attached to n. 193.

[189] Art. 3(1).

[190] That is all work relating to the construction, repair, upkeep, alteration, or demolition of buildings, including excavation, earth-moving, actual building work, assembly and dismantling of prefabricated elements, fitting out or installation, alterations, renovation, repairs, dismantling, demolition, maintenance, upkeep, painting and cleaning work, and improvements (Annex).

[191] *Laval*, paras. 60 and 108; Case E-2/11 *STX Norway Offshore*, judgment of the EFTA Court 23 Jan. 2012, para. 31.

However, Directive 96/71 was unclear as to whether the areas identified in Article 3(1) were an exhaustive list in which the host state must apply its laws or merely minimum standards upon which host states could improve. Take, for example, the case of dismissal law or redundancy (dismissal for economic reasons) which is not listed in Article 3(1). Can the host state decide to apply its rules on dismissal law to posted workers? It can do so only if the Directive provides for minimum standards. The arguments in favour of a minimum standards reading are primarily legal: (1) that Article 3(7) of the Directive appears to provide a minimum standards clause; (2) that *Rush Portuguesa* which concerned a reading of the (hierarchically superior) norm (Article 56 TFEU) appeared to allow host states to apply all of their rules to posted workers; and (3) a minimum standards reading would coincide with the territorial application of labour law which a number of Member States apply. This means that all labour laws apply to those in the host state, irrespective of their nationality or the duration of their stay. The territorial application of labour law coincides with the principle of equal treatment.

The arguments against a reading of Article 3 as a minimum standards provision are both legal and economic. The economic argument is that if out-of-state service providers are obliged to comply with all of the host state's employment laws in respect of their posted workers, the service providers would lose their competitive advantage. The legal argument is that allowing host states to apply all of their employment laws to posted workers would be inconsistent with Article 56 TFEU which applies a principle of home, not host, state control. This view is reinforced by Art. 8(2) of the Rome I Regulation which, in the case of posted workers, says that home state laws apply:

> To the extent that the law applicable to the individual employment contract has not been chosen by the parties, the contract shall be governed by the law of the country in which or, failing that, *from which* the employee habitually carries out his work in performance of the contract. *The country where the work is habitually carried out **shall** not be deemed to have changed if he is temporarily employed in another country.* [Emphasis added to show the major changes from the language of the original Article 6(2)(a) of the Rome Convention.]

This reading is reinforced by Article 12(1) of Regulation 883/2004 which says:

> A person who pursues an activity as an employed person in a Member State on behalf of an employer which normally carries out its activities there and who is posted by that employer to another Member State to perform work on that employer's behalf shall continue to be subject to the legislation of the first Member State, provided that the anticipated duration of such work does not exceed twenty-four months[192] and that he is not sent to replace another person.[193]

---

[192] This gives a useful rule of thumb as to a possible distinction between when the services provisions apply (less than 24 months) and when the establishment rules apply (over 24 months) although in Case C–458/08 *Commission* v. *Poland* [2010] ECR I–000, para. 85 the Court emphasized that service provision can last several years.

[193] See additionally Case C–202/97 *Fitzwilliam Executive Search Ltd* v. *Bestuur van het Landelijk Instituut Sociale Verzekeringen* [2000] ECR I–883.

Broadly speaking, the minimum standards reading was advocated by labour lawyers, the exhaustive reading (which sees the list of areas on Article 3(1) as a ceiling not a floor) was supported by single market lawyers. Eventually, it fell to the Court to decide between the two readings in three momentous decisions: *Laval*, *Rüffert*,[194] and *Luxembourg*.[195]

4.3. *Laval* and *Rüffert*

(a) *The decision*

Laval concerned a Latvian company which won a contract to refurbish a school in Sweden using its own Latvian workers who earned about 40 per cent less than comparable Swedish workers. The Swedish construction union wanted Laval to apply the Swedish collective agreement but Laval refused, in part because the collective agreement was unclear as to how much Laval would have to pay its workers, and in part because it imposed various supplementary obligations on Laval such as paying a 'special building supplement' to an insurance company to finance group life insurance contracts. There followed a union picket at the school site, a blockade by construction workers, and sympathy industrial action by the electricians' unions. Although this industrial action was permissible under Swedish law, Laval (funded by the Swedish employers association) brought proceedings in the Swedish labour court, claiming that this action was contrary to Article 56 TFEU and the PWD.[196]

As with *Viking*, the Court found that EU law did apply to this case[197] and that Article 56 applied to trade unions.[198] This enabled it then to use its standard *Säger* formulation. It found that the collective action was a restriction on free movement[199] and so presumptively unlawful unless it could be justified and was proportionate.[200] Intriguingly and without explanation, the Court said that the right to take collective action for the protection of workers in the host state against 'possible social dumping may constitute an overriding reason of the public interest'.[201] However, the Court then seems to suggest that the justification can only be made out where the terms of the PWD are complied with to the letter.

The problem facing the Swedish trade unions was that Article 3(1) did not cover matters such as the 'special building supplement' and the other insurance premiums employers were required to pay in Sweden under the relevant collective agreement.[202] The unions therefore argued that they could insist on requiring service providers to

---

[194] Case C–346/06 *Dirk Rüffert* v. *Land Niedersachsen* [2008] ECR I–1989.

[195] Case C–319/06 *Commission* v. *Luxembourg* [2008] ECR I–4323.

[196] For a full description of the dispute, see C. Woolfson and J. Sommers, 'Labour Mobility in Construction: European Implications of the Laval un Partneri Dispute with Swedish Labour' (2006) 12 *EJIR* 49.

[197] Para. 95.

[198] Para. 98.

[199] Para. 99.

[200] Para. 101.

[201] Para. 103.

[202] The fact that supplements for insurance constitute a rule of national tort law or insurance law is irrelevant. Because insurance concerns terms and conditions of employment the PWD applies: Case E–12/10 *EFTA Surveillance Authority* v. *Iceland*, judgment of the EFTA Court, 28 June 2011, para. 52.

apply these provisions under Article 3(10) of the Directive. This allows Member States to apply terms and conditions of employment on matters other than those referred to in Article 3(1) in the case of so-called 'public policy provisions'. But, Member States must positively opt to rely on Article 3(10) which Sweden had not done. And, since trade unions were not a public body, they could not rely on Article 3(10) either, so the trade union could not apply the various insurance premiums to Laval under the Directive.[203] This highlights the predicament that trade unions now find themselves in: they are treated as states for the purposes of liability but not when it comes to defences.

The trade unions also relied on the minimum standards clause in Article 3(7), which provides: 'Paragraphs 1 to 6 shall not prevent application of terms and conditions of employment which are more favourable to workers'. As we have seen, many labour lawyers had thought that Article 3(7) meant that while the Directive provided the floor, the state—always assumed to be the host state—could go further and impose higher standards, subject to the ceiling of Article 56 TFEU. This was certainly the view of Advocate General Bot in *Rüffert*.[204] However, this was not the Court's understanding of Article 3(7). It said in *Laval*—and repeated in *Rüffert*[205]—that Article 3(7) applied to the situation of out-of-state service providers *voluntarily* signing a collective agreement in the host state which offered superior terms and conditions to their employees. It also covered the situation where the *home* state laws or collective agreements were more favourable and these could be applied to the posted workers.[206] In other words, a German service provider could continue to apply German labour law rules to its workers posted to Poland—the situation originally envisaged by the Directive. However, the Court made clear that Article 3(7) did not allow the *host* state to impose terms and conditions employment which went 'beyond the mandatory rules [in Article 3(1)] for minimum protection'.[207] The Court thus came close to making Article 3(1) not a floor but a ceiling. And, in reaching this conclusion, the Court prevented the Swedish trade unions from relying on Article 3(7) to impose higher standards on the Latvian employer.

The Court also limited the utility of the PWD to posted workers by insisting on a strict reading of Article 3(1) and 3(8). Here the issue becomes complex. Matters listed in Article 3(1) must be laid down by:

(1) law, regulation, or administrative provision; and/or

(2) in respect of activities referred to in the Annex (primarily building work[208]), collective agreements or arbitration awards which have been declared universally applicable within the meaning of Article 3(8).

---

[203] Ibid., paras. 83–4. See further Case C–319/06 *Commission* v. *Luxembourg* [2008] ECR I–4323.
[204] Case C–346/06 *Rüffert* v. *Land Niedersachsen* [2008] ECR I–1989, paras. 82–3.
[205] *Rüffert*, para. 33.
[206] *Laval*, para. 81.
[207] Ibid., para. 80. See further *Rüffert*, para. 33.
[208] Member States can choose to extend collective agreements or arbitration awards within the meaning of Art. 3(8) to activities other than those listed in the Annex: Art. 3(10) second para.

If they are not laid down in one of these ways, then they cannot be applied to the posted workers. Since there is no *law* on the minimum wage in Sweden (or Germany)[209] (i.e. limb (1) does not apply), both cases focused on Article 3(8) dealing with collective agreements (i.e. limb (2)).

Article 3(8) also has two paragraphs. The first deals with those systems which do have a doctrine of extension (also known as the *erga omnes* effect) of collective agreements. It explains that collective agreements, or arbitration awards which have been declared universally applicable,[210] are those which must be observed by all undertakings in the geographical area and in the profession or industry concerned. This paragraph was at issue in *Rüffert*. Germany has a system for declaring collective agreements universally applicable. However, in the particular situation at issue, the collective agreement setting pay in the building industry had not been declared universally applicable,[211] and so the collectively agreed rules on pay rates could not be applied to the posted workers,[212] no matter that the German state law on the award of public contracts required contractors and their subcontractors to pay posted workers at least the remuneration prescribed by the collective agreement in force at the place where those services were performed.

The second paragraph of Article 3(8) deals with those systems which do not have a procedure for extending collective agreements to all workers (systems such as those in the UK and Sweden). In these situations:

Member States may, *if they so decide*, base themselves on:
- collective agreements or arbitration awards which are generally applicable to all similar undertakings in the geographical area and in the profession or industry concerned,[213] and/or
- collective agreements which have been concluded by the most representative employers' and labour organizations at national level and which are applied throughout national territory…

Once again, as with Article 3(10), the Court required Member States positively to opt for either of these possibilities.[214] Because Sweden had not taken advantage of the

---

[209] *Laval*, para. 8; *Rüffert*, para. 24. All other terms and conditions laid down by Art. 3(1) of the Posted Workers Directive have been implemented by Swedish law: *Laval*, para. 63.

[210] The proportion of employees covered by the relevant collective agreement prior to it being declared universally applicable is irrelevant: Case E–2/11 *Norway Offshore*, judgment of the EFTA Court of 23 January 2012, para. 105.

[211] Ibid., para. 26.

[212] Ibid., para. 31.

[213] (Emphasis added.) It is for the national court to verify whether these conditions are fulfilled: Case E–2/11 *STX Norway Offshore AS v. Norway*, judgment of the EFTA Court 23 Jan. 2012, para. 53. If they are fulfilled, they allow limits on, say working time, to be adapted to specific professions or industries (paras. 54–5).

[214] Cf. AG Mengozzi in *Laval*, especially paras. 179–181*ff*. He concluded at para. 187: 'It is therefore beyond doubt, in my view, that the right to take collective action granted by Swedish law to trade unions to enable then to impose the wage conditions laid down or governed by Swedish collective agreements provides a suitable means of attaining the aim of protecting posted workers laid down in Article 3 of Directive 96/71'.

second paragraph of Article 3(8),[215] it could not impose enterprise-level collective bargaining on Laval.[216] More generally, the Court objected to a number of aspects of the Swedish system of industrial relations, in particular its lack of transparency in respect of pay,[217] the fact that Laval was 'required' to negotiate with trade unions 'in order to ascertain the wages to be paid to workers and to sign the collective agreement for the building sector',[218] and that these negotiations might be of 'unspecified duration'.[219]

Because the terms of the PWD had not been complied with, the collective action could not be justified. And because the collective action could not be justified, the question of proportionality was not relevant. The result of the decision is that the perspective of single market lawyers seems to have prevailed over that of labour lawyers. When the case returned to the Swedish court, exemplary damages were awarded to Laval of about 60,000 euros and the trade union had to pay Laval's costs of about 230,000 euros.[220]

(b) Assessment

Four observations can be made about the Court's approach to the PWD in *Laval* and *Rüffert*. The first, and perhaps most obvious, is that the Court takes a restrictive view of Article 3(1). It contains an 'exhaustive list' of the matters in respect of which the host state laws will prevail.[221] In this respect, its position stands in sharp contrast to that of its Advocate Generals, Advocate General Bot in particular, but coincide with the arguments advanced by the Commission. A clue to understanding the Court's approach can perhaps be gained from Advocate General Mengozzi's Opinion: he says Article 3(1) is a 'derogation'[222] from the principle of home state control laid down in Article 8(2) of the Rome I Regulation. According to traditional jurisprudence, derogations must be narrowly construed.[223]

The second observation concerns the use of the PWD to interpret Article 56 TFEU: if the detailed terms of the PWD are not complied with to the letter, there will be a

---

[215] *Laval*, para. 67.

[216] Ibid., para. 71. By implication, therefore, the fact that the Directive did not apply meant that the Preambular paragraph in Dir. 96/71, to the effect that 'this Directive is without prejudice to the law of the Member States concerning collective action to defend the interests of trades and professions', becomes irrelevant.

[217] *Laval*, paras. 36 and 110. Cf. Art. 5(4) of the Temporary Agency Directive 2008/104 which explicitly says that where a collective agreement derogates from the principle of equal treatment, the arrangements 'shall be sufficiently precise and accessible to allow the sectors and firms concerned to identify and comply with their obligations'. See additionally Case E–2/11 *Norway Offshore*, judgment of the EFTA Court of 23 January 2012, where the need for transparency in pay arrangements for posted workers was repeatedly stressed (e.g. paras. 72 and 73).

[218] Ibid., para. 63. See further para. 71. It also did not like the rigidity of the Swedish system: e.g. the collective agreement was for an hourly not a monthly rate (para. 25).

[219] Ibid., para. 100.

[220] U. Bernitz and N. Reich (2011) 48 *CMLRev.* 603.

[221] Case E–12/10 *EFTA Surveillance Authority v. Iceland,* judgment of the EFTA Court, 28 June 2011, para. 40.

[222] *Laval*, Opinion, para. 132, cited with approval in Case E–2/11 *STX Norway Offshore AS v. Norway*, judgment of the EFTA Court 23 Jan. 2012, para. 28.

[223] If this reasoning is correct, then Arts. 3(7) and (10), as derogations to derogations, must be particularly narrowly construed.

breach of Article 56 TFEU.[224] The interdependency between the PWD and Article 56 TFEU is confirmed in paragraph 36 of *Rüffert*, where the Court said that its interpretation of Directive 96/71 is 'confirmed by reading it in the light of Article [56 TFEU], since that Directive seeks in particular to bring about the freedom to provide services, which is one of the fundamental freedoms guaranteed by the Treaty'. The EFTA Court reached a similar conclusion in *STX Norway Offshore*[225] where it said that, in determining the meaning of minimum rates of pay and whether it includes an entitlement to remuneration requiring an overnight stay away from home—a matter for national law—the EEA states must also respect the Treaty provison on services. As Deakin points out, the Directive and Article 56 TFEU are mutually reinforcing: the restrictive interpretation of the Directive is derived from Article 56 TFEU and the substance of Article 56 TFEU is derived from the Directive.[226]

The third observation concerns the deterritorialization of labour law. Laval was essentially arguing to be allowed to keep the competitive advantage of less protective (and hence less costly) Latvian labour laws and collective agreements while, through its subsidiary, it operated on Swedish territory.[227] In *Rüffert* the issue was whether Polish subcontractors working in Germany should 'lose the competitive advantage which they enjoy by reason of their lower wage costs'.[228] In deciding in favour of the service providers in these cases, the Court appeared to treat corporate location in a low-cost jurisdiction as a matter of competitive advantage, which it was the role of the free movement principle to protect.[229] The claim that differences in labour standards across the Member States gave rise, in and of themselves, to a restriction on free movement, opened a Pandora's Box.[230]

This was precisely the argument rejected by the authors of the Spaak report in 1956. They had foreseen the need to consider whether, 'leaving aside cases of overt discrimination and interventions aimed at favouring certain firms or modes of production, legislative and regulatory provisions may have such an impact on costs and prices' that the results would be to 'distort conditions of competition among the national economies as a whole or in particular branches of economic activity'.[231] The Spaak report concluded, however, that simple differences in regulatory regimes

---

[224] See additionally AG Mengozzi's Opinion in *Laval*, para. 149.

[225] Case E–2/11, judgment of 23 January 2012, para. 74.

[226] See, by analogy, the Court's interpretation of the (then) Equal Pay Dir. 75/117 (now Sex Equality Dir. 2006/54) and its relationship with Article 157 TFEU. In Case 96/80 *Jenkins* v. *Kingsgate* [1981] ECR 911 the Court said that Art. 1 of the Dir. 'is principally designed to facilitate the practical application of the principle of equal pay outlined in Article [157] of the [Treaties] [and] in no way alters the content or scope of that principle as defined in the [Treaties]'. See further Ch. 6.

[227] See the Opinion of Mengozzi AG in *Laval* at para. 133.

[228] This was the way the issue was put by the referring court. See *Rüffert*, Opinion of Bot AG, at para. 41.

[229] What follows comes from C. Barnard and S. Deakin, 'European Labour Law after *Laval*' in M. Moreau (ed.), *Before and After the Economic Crisis: What Implications for the 'European Social Model'?* (Edward Elgar, Cheltenham, 2011).

[230] R. Eklund, 'A Swedish Perspective on *Laval*' (2008) 29 *Comparative Labor Law and Policy Journal* 551, at p. 572.

[231] See further Ch. 1.

could not amount to a distortion of competition, insisting that to think otherwise was to 'misunderstand' the way international trade worked. This was because 'competition does not necessarily require a complete harmonization of the different elements in costs'; rather, 'it is only on the basis of certain differences—such as wage differences due to productivity—that an equilibrium can be established and trade develop'. The Spaak report took this line in order to forestall arguments for (among other things) a comprehensive labour code at European level, but precisely the same argument applies, *mutatis mutandis*, to attempts to bring about the 'negative harmonisation' or levelling down of labour laws through free movement jurisprudence. Other federal systems can and do perfectly well combine an internal market based on free movement for economic resources, with the retention of jurisdiction over labour law and other matters of social policy at state or local level. Differences in labour law regulation across US states do not give rise to a prima facie breach of the Commerce Clause requiring justification by reference to a proportionality test.[232] In principle, diversity of regulatory regimes is desirable as it makes it possible for labour law rules to be matched to local conditions, reflecting political priorities and social compromises at state level. Such diversity also facilitates learning across systems, an important aspect, more generally, of open coordination methods within the EU's emergent federal regime.[233]

The fourth observation is that it is a mistake to think of the PWD as a worker protection measure as such. Its legal basis (Articles 53(1) and 62 TFEU) is in the chapter on freedom to provide services not social policy.[234] And yet the Court in *Laval* and *Rüffert* did manage to preserve a social dimension to the Directive: posted workers will enjoy the rights listed in Article 3(1), and they will enjoy better terms and conditions of employment in the host state provided that the host state has complied with the letter of the Directive. And in reaching this conclusion, the Court has actually saved the Directive from allegations made by some single market lawyers that the Directive is *ultra vires* the Treaties because the application of any host state employment laws constitute a restriction on the freedom to provide services. And in so doing the Court also managed to respect the general principle of interpretation that a Union measure must be interpreted, as far as possible, in such a way as not to affect its validity and in conformity with primary law as a whole.[235] Thus, it could be said that the Court reached a careful compromise—recognizing that, in the context of the provision of services, generally home state laws apply, but in those areas listed in Article 3 of the Directive, the host state laws will apply. How, then, does this fit with the Rome I Regulation?

---

[232] S. Deakin, 'Regulatory Competition after *Laval*' (2007–8) 10 *CYELS* 581, 608. See further, D. Nicol, 'Europe's *Lochner* Moment' [2011] PL 308.

[233] See S. Deakin, 'Reflexive Harmonisation and European Company Law' (2009) 15 *ELJ* 224.

[234] See additionally *Laval*, para. 74.

[235] Case C–149/10 *Chatzi* v. *Ipourgos Ikonomikon* [2010] ECR I–000, para. 43.

4.4. The relationship between Directive 96/71 and the Rome I Regulation

The Rome Convention of 19 June 1980[236] and now the Rome I Regulation on the law applicable to contractual obligations lay down choice-of-law rules for application in contractual disputes.[237] The Rome I Regulation envisages two situations: (1) where the parties have chosen the applicable law, and (2) where they have not. Where the parties have *not* chosen the applicable law, in the field of employment Article 8(2) applies.[238] It will be recalled that this says:

> To the extent that the law applicable to the individual employment contract has not been chosen by the parties, the contract shall be governed by the law of the country in which or, failing that, *from which* the employee habitually carries out his work in performance of the contract.[239] *The country where the work is habitually carried out shall not be deemed to have changed if he is temporarily employed in another country.*[240]

So, in the case of a Polish worker who has come to the UK as a *migrant* worker under Article 45 TFEU but without a choice of law clause in his contract, Article 8(2) says that English law will be the objectively applicable law. However, in the case of a Polish worker *temporarily* posted to the UK by a Polish company under Article 56 TFEU, the objectively applicable law will be Polish. According to the 36th Recital of the Rome I Regulation, work is regarded as temporary 'if the employee is expected to resume working in the country of origin after carrying out his tasks abroad'. In an attempt to deal with evasion techniques, it continues 'The conclusion of a new contract of employment with the original employer or an employer belonging to the same group of companies as the original employer should not preclude the employee from being regarded as carrying out his work in another country temporarily'.

Where, on the other hand, the parties have chosen the applicable law (which they are permitted to do under Article 3 of the Rome I Regulation[241]), Article 8(1) of the Rome I Regulation says 'An individual employment contract shall be governed by the law chosen by the parties in accordance with Article 3.' However, Article 8(1) continues: 'Such a choice of law may not, however, have the result of depriving the employee of the protection afforded to him by provisions that cannot be derogated from by agreement under the law that, in the absence of choice, would have been applicable pursuant to [Article 8(2)]...'. So if the parties have chosen English law to govern the employment contract and the English workers are posted temporarily to Poland then English law is

---

[236] OJ [1980] L266/1. See further the Report by Giuliano and Lagarde (OJ [1980] C282/1).
[237] The following is taken from C. Barnard, 'The UK and Posted Workers: The Effect of *Commission v Luxembourg* on the Territorial Application of British Labour Law' (2009) 38 *ILJ* 122.
[238] For a full discussion of these issues, see L. Merrett, *Employment Contracts in Private International Law* (OUP, Oxford, 2011); L. Merrett, 'The Extra-territorial reach of Employment Legislation' (2010) 39 *ILJ* 355.
[239] In Case C–29/10 *Koelzsch* v. *Luxembourg* [2011] ECR I–000 the Court said that 'the country in which the employee habitually carries out his work in performance of the contract, within the meaning of that provision, is that in which or from which, in the light of all the factors which characterise that activity, the employee performs the greater part of his obligations towards his employer'.
[240] Emphasis added.
[241] This provides: 'A contract shall be governed by the law chosen by the parties'.

likely to be the objectively applicable law under Article 8(2) as well as the chosen law. Furthermore, even if, in this situation, the parties have chosen Polish law to apply this will be subject to the provisions of Article 8(1) which say that the choice of law cannot deprive the employee of the protection afforded to him by the '*provisions* that cannot be derogated from by agreement under the law that, in the absence of choice, would have been applicable pursuant to [Article 8(2)], namely mandatory provisions of English law'. So generally English law would remain the objectively applicable law, provided that English law is more favourable to the employee and it is suitable to apply English law under the principles laid down in *Lawson* v. *Serco*.[242] Similarly, where the Polish employer, posting Polish workers to the UK, has chosen Polish law to govern the contract, the chosen law will be, and the objectively applicable law is likely to be, Polish.

This analysis shows that when considering the position of the Polish worker temporarily posted to the UK, with or without Polish law being the choice of law, Polish law may well apply to the contract. Even if the parties have chosen a different law, such as English law, the contract will remain subject to mandatory provisions of Polish law which cannot be derogated from. English courts will be able to apply English law only if: (1) English law applies as an overriding mandatory rule of the forum under Article 7(2) of the Rome Convention, now Article 9(2) of the Rome I Regulation; or (2) on the basis of the foreign law being contrary to UK public policy under Article 21 of the Rome Regulation. For the purposes of this chapter the position under Article 9(2) is the most relevant and we shall focus on that.

The original Article 7(2) provided: 'Nothing in this Convention shall restrict the application of the rules of the law of the forum in a situation where they are *mandatory* irrespective of the law otherwise applicable to the contract'. The new Article 9(2) appears to be more restrictive. It provides: 'Nothing in this Regulation shall restrict the application of the *overriding mandatory provisions* of the law of the forum'. 'Overriding mandatory provisions' are defined in Article 9(1) as 'provisions the respect for which is regarded as *crucial* by a country for safeguarding its public interests, such as its political, social or economic organisation, to such an extent that they are applicable to any situation falling within their scope, irrespective of the law otherwise applicable to the contract under this Regulation' (emphasis added). As the Commission's explanatory memorandum says,[243] this test explicitly draws on the Court of Justice's decision in *Arblade*.[244] It is hard to argue that, for example, laws on unfair dismissal, however central to a system of employment protection, are 'crucial' to safeguard a country's social organization. It will therefore be harder to argue in future that Polish workers temporarily posted to the UK will be subject to key aspects of UK employment protection legislation which the UK might argue should apply as an overriding mandatory provision of the forum.

---

[242] [2006] UKHL 3, [2006] IRLR 289, Dicey, Morris & Collins, *The Conflicts of Law* (Sweet & Maxwell, London, 2006).

[243] COM(2005) 650, 7.

[244] Cases C–369/96 and C–374/96 *Arblade* [1999] ECR I–8453, para. 31.

The limited scope offered by Article 7(2)/Article 9(2) to host Member States wanting to apply their employment laws has now been emphasized by the decision in *Commission* v. *Luxembourg*. In that case the Commission argued that by declaring that most of its labour law provisions and collective agreements to be mandatory rules under Article 7(2) of the Rome Convention and applying them to posted workers, Luxembourg breached Article 3(1) PWD and Article 56 TFEU. In its defence, Luxembourg argued that it could extend its legislation to posted workers because the rules all related to mandatory provisions falling under national public policy under Article 3(10) PWD. In other words, Luxembourg said that Article 7(2) of the Rome Convention (now Article 9(2) of the Rome I Regulation) and Article 3(10) PWD were co-extensive. The Court effectively agreed with Luxembourg's analysis that the provisions were co-extensive but reached the opposite conclusion as to result.

The Court began by recalling its observations in *Arblade*[245] that 'the classification of national provisions by a Member State as public order legislation applies to national provisions compliance with which has been deemed to be so crucial for the protection of the political, social or economic order in the Member State concerned as to require compliance therewith by all persons present on the national territory of that Member State and all legal relationships within that State'.[246] As we have already seen, this is the same test used to define overriding mandatory provisions in Article 9(2) of the Rome I Regulation, thus supporting the view that Article 3(10) PWD and Article 9(2) of Rome I are co-extensive.

Having laid down this narrow reading of public policy the Court then said that the public policy exception, as a derogation from the fundamental principle of freedom to provide services, had to be interpreted strictly.[247] In support, it cited Declaration No 10 on Article 3(10) PWD recorded in the Council minutes which provides that the expression 'public policy provisions' should be construed as covering 'those *mandatory* rules from which there can be no derogation and which, by their nature and objective, meet the imperative requirements of the public interest. These may include, in particular, the prohibition of forced labour or the involvement of public authorities in monitoring compliance with legislation on working conditions'.[248]

These observations further emphasize the idea that Article 7(2) of the Rome Convention, now Article 9(2) of the Rome I Regulation, and Article 3(10) PWD are co-extensive. Both suggest that only exceptionally can the host state insist on applying its law to temporary/posted workers. This conclusion sits rather uncomfortably with the observations made by the Commission in its Green Paper on the Conversion of the Rome Convention that Article 3(1) 'determines a "focal point" of mandatory rules to be complied with throughout the period of assignment to the host Member State ... The Directive must therefore be regarded as an implementation of Article 7 of the Rome

---

[245] Cases C–369/96 and C–374/96 *Arblade* [1999] ECR I–8453, para. 31.
[246] *Luxembourg*, para. 29.
[247] Ibid., paras. 30 and 31. This view was confirmed in Case E–12/10 *EFTA Surveillance Authority* v. *Iceland*, judgment of the EFTA Court, 28 June 2011, para. 56.
[248] Ibid., para. 33, emphasis added.

Convention, concerning overriding mandatory rules,'[249] a view which appears to be repeated in the 34th Recital of the Rome I Regulation: 'The rule on individual employment contracts should not prejudice the application of the overriding mandatory provisions of the country to which a worker is posted in accordance with Directive 96/71/EC...concerning the posting of workers in the framework of the provision of services'. It is hard to argue that maximum work periods, minimum rest periods, and minimum paid holidays, satisfy the *Arblade* test of being 'crucial for a country for safeguarding its public interests'. Yet they are listed in Articles 3(1)(a) and (b) as part of the PWD's nucleus of 'mandatory rules' which the host state must apply.

How can this circle be squared? Perhaps the only way is through reliance on the doctrine of pre-emption. The Union legislature has selected those matters listed in Article 3(1)(a)–(g) PWD to be the mandatory rules under Article 7(2) of the Rome Convention/Article 9(2) of the Rome I Regulation. Therefore, Member States cannot unilaterally rely on Article 7(2)/Article 9(2) and Article 3(10) to impose additional requirements on posted workers over and above those laid down by Article 3(1) PWD, except in truly exceptional circumstances (which may, in fact, never arise).

The exceptional nature of Article 3(10) was emphasized later in the *Commission* v. *Luxembourg* when, in paragraph 50, the Court tightened up the criteria for public policy still further:

> ...while the Member States are still, in principle, free to determine the requirements of public policy in the light of national needs, the notion of public policy in the [Union] context,... may be relied on only if there is a genuine and sufficiently serious threat to a fundamental interest of society.

For good measure, the Court added that the Member State invoking the derogation must produce 'appropriate evidence or by an analysis of the expediency and proportionality of the restrictive measure adopted by that State, and precise evidence enabling its arguments to be substantiated'.[250]

The test set out in paragraph 50 of *Commission* v. *Luxembourg* replicates the well-known test for public policy used by the Court in the context of free movement of persons[251] to consider whether a Member State is justified in *deporting* a migrant. It is surprising that the Court has transplanted this test to the very different context of labour law, although it may have been influenced by the Commission's own view of public policy set out in its Communication on the implementation of the Directive.[252] With the exception of laws against slavery (referred to in Declaration No.10), it is difficult to see how states can argue that any labour laws, however fundamental to the system of employment protection, satisfy this extraordinarily high standard, as we saw from the working time example. The group of experts advising the Commission thought that public policy provisions would cover fundamental rights and freedoms such as free-

---

[249] COM(2002) 654, 36.   [250] Ibid., para. 51.
[251] Case 30/77 *Bouchereau* [1977] ECR 1999, now enshrined in Art. 27 CRD.
[252] COM(2003) 458, 13.

dom of association and collective bargaining, prohibition of forced labour, the principle of non-discrimination and elimination of exploitative forms of child labour, data protection, and the right to privacy but there is no evidence that the Commission agreed with this.[253] The effect of *Commission* v. *Luxembourg* is to interpret Article 3(10) PWD and Article 7(2)/Article 9(2) of the Rome Convention/Regulation almost out of existence.[254]

With the *Bouchereau* test as its yardstick, it is not at all surprising that the Court then found that specific aspects of Luxembourg labour law that were applied to posted workers could not be justified under Article 3(10). For example, Luxembourg law required a written contract or document established pursuant to Directive 91/533 on the written statement, a matter not covered by Article 3(1) PWD. The Court pointed out that since employers were required by the law of the home state to provide a written statement, the Luxembourg law was likely to dissuade undertakings established in another Member State from exercising their freedom to provide services. The Court therefore concluded that the Luxembourg rule did not 'comply with the first indent of Article 3(10) of Directive 96/71, in so far as it is not applied in compliance with the Treaty'.[255] Likewise, the Court rejected Luxembourg's attempt to apply a 'living wage' to posted workers (i.e. all wages indexed to the cost of living) in order to ensure 'good labour relations in Luxembourg' and to protect 'workers from the effects of inflation'.[256] Such general assertions, made in the absence of 'appropriate evidence', meant that Luxembourg had failed to make out the public policy derogation.[257]

Luxembourg also applied its own laws implementing the Part-time Work Directive 97/81 and the Fixed-term Work Directive 99/70 to posted workers. Once again, the Court noted that the requirement 'concerns a matter which is not mentioned in the list in the first subparagraph of Article 3(1)'.[258] This is a surprising observation since Article 3(1)(g) talks of 'equality of treatment between men and women *and other provisions on non-discrimination*'. Both Directives 97/81 and 99/70 have the principle of non-discrimination at their core. Nevertheless, the Court continued that such rules were likely to hinder the exercise of freedom to provide services by undertakings wishing to post workers to Luxembourg,[259] and that since the home law already ensures the protection of these rights, Luxembourg again could not rely on the public policy exception.[260] Finally, the Court said that collective agreements could not constitute a public policy exception under the first indent of Article 3(10)[261] nor did the second indent of Article 3(10) apply to them since that related exclusively to the terms and conditions

---

[253] COM(2003) 458, 14.
[254] Cf. Case E–2/11 *Norway Offshore*, judgment of the EFTA Court of 23 January 2012, para. 100 which adopts a much more lenient view.
[255] *Luxembourg*, para. 44.
[256] Ibid., para. 48.
[257] Ibid., paras. 54–5.
[258] Ibid., para. 57.
[259] Ibid., para. 58.
[260] Ibid., para. 60.   [261] Ibid., paras. 64–5.

of employment laid down in collective agreement which have been declared universally applicable.[262]

4.5. Exceptions and derogations to the Directive

The provisions of the Directive do not apply to merchant navy undertakings as regards seagoing personnel.[263] In addition to this total exclusion, Article 3 lists four potential derogations. First, Article 3(1) provides that the rules relating to minimum rates of pay and paid holidays do not apply to skilled or specialist workers employed by an undertaking involved in a contract for supplying goods, where the workers are engaged in the initial assembly or installation of goods which is an integral part of the contract and the period of posting does not exceed eight days.[264] Secondly, Article 3(3) provides that Member States may, after consulting employers and labour, in accordance with the traditions and practices of each Member State, decide not to apply the provision relating to pay in the case of all posted workers, with the exception of those employed by a temp agency, where the posting does not exceed one month. Thirdly, Article 3(4) provides that Member States may, in accordance with national laws or practices, provide that exemptions may be made from the provisions relating to pay in the case of all posted workers with the exception of those employed by a temp agency, and from a decision of a Member State within the meaning of Article 3(3), by means of a collective agreement,[265] where the posting does not exceed one month.[266] Fourthly, Article 3(5) provides that Member States may provide for exemptions to be granted from the provisions relating to pay and holidays in the case of all posted workers, with the exception of those employed by a temp agency, on the grounds that the amount of work to be done is not significant.[267]

In fact, these derogations are more apparent than real since, following the social dumping thesis, it is usually not in the host state's interest to exempt service providers from the domestic rules. This is the position taken by the UK, which has not taken advantage of any derogations.

4.6. Other provisions in the Posted Workers Directive

(a) Access to Information and Administrative Co-operation

While much attention has been given to key rights in the Directive, from a practical point of view the Directive also contains some key provisions. One such provision is the

---

[262] Ibid., para. 67.   [263] Art. 1(2).

[264] Art. 3(6) provides that the length of the posting shall be calculated on the basis of a reference period of one year from the beginning of the posting. In calculating the one-year period, account shall be taken of any previous periods for which the post has been filled by a posted worker. This provision does not apply to the building activities described above, see Art. 3(2).

[265] As defined in Art. 3(8).

[266] Art. 3(4).

[267] Art. 3(5). Member States must lay down the criteria to determine whether the work is considered non-significant.

'one-stop shop' or single point of contact approach for service providers to find out about the requirements laid down by national law and/or collective agreement. So, in order to implement this Directive, Member States must, in accordance with national legislation or practice, designate one or more liaison offices or one or more competent national bodies.[268] It is striking that one of the reasons why the Court so objected to the Swedish position in *Laval* was that the designated liaison office set up under the PWD could not help;[269] nor would the police step in to assist Laval since the blockade was lawful under Swedish law.[270] Article 5 of the proposed enforcement Directive aims to address this problem by prescribing a number of detailed measures to help ensure easily accessible and generally available information (e.g. on the web) on the terms and conditions to be respected in the host state, including where these are laid down in collective agreements.

The Directive also requires that Member States must make provision for co-operation between the public authorities which, in accordance with national legislation, are responsible for monitoring the terms and conditions of employment. This co-operation must, in particular, consist of replying (free of charge) to reasoned requests about information on transnational supply of workers, including manifest abuses[271] or possible cases of unlawful transnational activities.[272] The Commission and the public authorities must co-operate, especially in respect of any difficulties which might arise in the application of Article 3(10).[273] A high level Committee must, inter alia, examine any difficulties arising under Article 3(10).

These provisions were emphasized by the Commission in its Communication on the posting or workers adopted following the failure of the Bolkestein draft of the Services Directive.[274] It provides that the national authorities of the countries of origin have to cooperate loyally with the authorities in the host Member States and provide them all the required information, in order to enable these authorities to perform their controlling duties and fight illegal practices. Liaison offices and the monitoring authorities have to be sufficiently equipped and resourced in order to be able to reply correctly and swiftly to any kind of demand.[275]

(b) Remedies

Article 5(1) of Directive 96/71 requires the Member States to 'take appropriate measures in the event of failure to comply with this Directive'. They must ensure that 'ade-

---

[268] Art. 4(1). Member States must notify the other Member States and the Commission of the liaison offices and/or competent bodies.

[269] Ibid., para. 35.

[270] Ibid., para. 34.

[271] It can also be inferred from Case 113/89 *Rush Portuguesa* [1990] ECR I–1417 that the provisions on the freedom to provide services must not be abused to achieve some other purpose (para. 17).

[272] Art. 4(2). On the importance of this cooperation, see Joined Cases C–369 and 376/96 *Arblade* [1999] ECR I–8453.

[273] Art. 4(2) of Commission Recommendation 2008/C 85/01 on enhanced administrative cooperation in the context of posting of workers in the framework of the provision of services (OJ [2008] C85/1).

[274] COM(2007) 304.

[275] See additionally Commission Recommendation 2008/C 85/01.

quate procedures are available to workers and/or their representatives for the enforcement of the obligations under this Directive'.[276] According to *Wolff*,[277] the Member States have a wide margin of appreciation in determining the form and detailed rules governing these adequate procedures. Article 6 provides that in order to enforce the right to the terms and conditions guaranteed by Article 3, judicial proceedings may be instituted in the Member State in whose territory the worker is or was posted, without prejudice, where applicable, to the right, under existing international conventions on jurisdiction, to institute proceedings in another Member State.[278] This provision adds to the rules laid down in the Brussels I Regulation.[279] Under the Regulation, the general principle is that persons domiciled in a contracting state must, whatever their nationality, be sued in the courts of that state.[280] However, in respect of employment contracts, Articles 18–21 of the Regulation lay down special rules. They provide that if the employer is domiciled in a Member State, the employee may sue the employer either:

1. In the Member State of the employer's domicile;[281] or
2. In the courts of the place where the employee *habitually* carries out his work[282] (or the place where he last did so).[283] If the employee does not carry out his or her work in any one country then jurisdiction is conferred on the courts of the place where the business which engaged the employee is situated.[284]

---

[276] Art. 5(2).
[277] Case C–60/03 *Wolff & Müller* v. *Pereira Félix* [2004] ECR I–9553, para. 30.
[278] Art. 6.
[279] Council Reg. 44/2001 (OJ [2001] L12/1). In the proposal for a recast version of the Brussels I Reg., a new 'Monti' clause has been introduced into Art. 85 (COM(2010) 748), along the lines of Art. 1(7) of the Services Directive 2006/123 (see previously).
[280] Art. 2(1).
[281] Art. 19(1).
[282] See Case C–383/95 *Rutten* v. *Cross Medical Ltd* [1997] ECR I–57. See additionally Case C–125/92 *Geels* [1993] ECR I–4075 where the Court had to consider the application of the principles laid down by the Brussels Convention before its amendment. Geels, a Dutch national domiciled in France, sued his employer Mulox, a limited company established under English law in London, in the French, courts for terminating his contract of employment. Geels had set up his office in France but marketed Mulox products in Germany, Belgium, the Netherlands, and Scandinavia. The Court pointed out that employment contracts differed from other contracts by virtue of the 'lasting bond which brings the worker to some extent within the organisational framework of the business' and consequently the link between the place where the activities are pursued which determines the application of mandatory rules and collective agreements. The Court therefore recognized that, given the peculiarities of contracts of employment, it was the courts of the place where the work was carried out which were best suited to resolving disputes in which one or more obligations under the contract of employment gave rise. The Court also added that the provisions of the Convention should be interpreted so as to take account of the need to ensure adequate protection for the socially weaker contracting party, namely the employee. Such adequate protection was better assured if the cases relating to contracts of employment fell within the jurisdiction of the courts in the place where the employee discharged his obligations to the employer to carry out the work agreed. The Court said that it was in this place that the employee could, at less cost, apply to the tribunals or defend himself before them. Consequently, the place of performance of the relevant obligation was the place where the employee carried out the activities agreed with the employer.
[283] Art. 19(2)(a).   [284] Art. 19(2)(b).

Article 6 of Directive 96/71 therefore adds to the Brussels Regulation by allowing the posted worker to bring proceedings in the courts of the host state even though the worker is employed there only *temporarily*.[285]

4.7. Proposed enforcement Directive

Most agree that these provisions, while important, have not been effective in practice and Member States and employers have had difficulty in implementing, applying, and enforcing the Directive. Does this really matter given the relatively small number of posted workers? In fact, the number of posted workers are not really known. The Commission estimates that around one million workers are posted each year by their employers from one Member State to another, a small share of the active population (0.4 per cent of the active population of EU-15 sending countries and 0.7 per cent of the active population of EU-12 sending countries). However, in terms of labour mobility within the EU, the number of postings represented 18.5 per cent of non-national EU-27 citizens in the labour force in 2007.[286] There was little appetite in the Commission to reopen the substance of the PWD but the Commission obtained political agreement on legislation aimed at improving and reinforcing the transposition, implementation and enforcement in practice of the Posting of Workers Directive, which will include measures to prevent and sanction any abuse and circumvention of the applicable rules.[287] The proposed Directive therefore contains the following:

- *provisions aiming at preventing abuses, circumvention, or disrespect of law* such as in the case of 'letterbox' companies;[288]

- *specific provisions improving the access to information* for posting companies so that they know what host state terms and conditions of employment are applicable;[289]

- *enhancing administrative cooperation and mutual assistance.* General principles, rules and procedures necessary for effective administrative cooperation and assistance are laid down in Article 6, whereas the role of the Member State from which the posting takes place is covered by Article 7. In addition, the Directive provides an appropriate legal basis for the development of an electronic information exchange system to facilitate administrative cooperation between the Member States;

- *monitoring compliance.* Closely allied with administrative cooperation are national control measures such as inspections. As the Commission notes,[290] for certain aspects of the notion of posting, such as the genuine link of the employer with the sending Member State, the Member State from which the posting takes place plays the key role, whereas matters such as compliance with the terms and conditions of employment to be respected in the country where the services are

---

[285] This is a provision governing a specific matter as permitted by Art. 67 of Reg. 44/2001.
[286] COM(2012) 131, 5.
[287] COM(2011) 206.
[288] Arts. 2 and 3 discussed previously.
[289] Arts. 4 and 5.   [290] COM(2012) 131, 16.

provided can only be controlled in the host Member State. Close collaboration by both countries is also necessary on other matters, such as the indicative qualitative criteria to be used in the context of the notion of posting. Therefore, both countries are an essential part of an effectively functioning system of cooperation and exchange of information, even if the actual scope of their activities in this context may differ. If the system works well, there may no longer be any need for further compliance measures, so a review clause has been included;[291]

- *ways to increase the effectiveness of controls and sanctions and posted workers' possibilities to better defend their rights.* In essence there are two limbs to this. First, Article 11 requires Member States to ensure that there are effective mechanisms for posted workers to lodge complaints against their employers directly, as well as the right to institute judicial or administrative proceedings, also in the Member State in whose territory the workers are or were posted, where such workers consider they have sustained loss or damage as a result of a failure to apply the applicable rules, even after the relationship in which the failure is alleged to have occurred has ended. It also makes provision for posted workers to receive any outstanding remuneration as well as a refund of excessive costs charge for accommodation provided to the employer.[292] Secondly, the Directive makes provision for joint and several liability in subcontracting sub-chains,[293] albeit limited to the construction sector. These measures raise issues about the cross border enforcement of administrative fines and penalties based on the system established for the recovery of social security claims by Regulation 987/2009[294] and for tax claims by Directive 2010/24/EU[295] were used as a source of inspiration.

The fate of this measure, like Monti II, remains uncertain but seems to command greater support.

5. CONCLUSION

In his 2010 report on the single market, Mario Monti[296] recognized that the Court rulings in *Viking* and *Laval* reveal 'the fault lines that run between the single market and the social dimension at national level', showing 'an old split that had never been healed: the divide between advocates of greater market integration and those who feel that the call for economic freedoms and breaking up regulatory barriers is code for dismantling social rights protected at national level'. But in fact the apocalypse that some predicted has not, in fact occurred. Why is this? First, there is evidence of the continuing will and capacity of Member States to pursue social policy goals at national level and to take steps to limit the impact of the *Viking* and *Laval* judgments. This is clearest in the case

---

[291] Art. 9(3).   [292] Art. 11.
[293] Art. 12. See further Case C–60/03 *Wolff & Müller* [2004] ECR I–9553.
[294] OJ [2009] L284/1.
[295] OJ [2010 L18/15.
[296] <http://ec.europa.eu/bepa/pdf/monti_report_final_10_05_2010_en.pdf> (last accessed 15 April 2012).

of the immediate reaction of the Nordic systems to *Laval* and in the regional German response to *Rüffert*. The Nordic reaction has essentially involved reaffirmation of the role of the social partners in setting market-wide labour standards through collective bargaining, a core feature of those systems which complements their widely praised active labour market policies.[297] The Swedish legislation which came into force in April 2010, although promoted by a Conservative-led government, was premised on the goal of allowing 'as far as possible the application of the Swedish labour market model to workers posted to Sweden from another country'.[298] It permits industrial action to support the application to posted workers of a sector-level collective agreement that is applied throughout national territory to workers of the relevant description, under the terms of Article 3(8) PWD. Although only minimum conditions of employment as set out in Article 3(1) may be enforced this way, the law can be seen as a limited accommodation of *Laval*. In Denmark reforms have been undertaken to confirm the legality of strike action in support of multi-employer collective agreements even in cases of minimum wages above subsistence level, and in Norway the courts have so far regarded powers to extend the effects of sector-level collective agreements by legal decree as compatible with *Laval*, a view also adopted by the EFTA Surveillance Authority.[299] Meanwhile, in reaction to *Rüffert*, the Land of Lower Saxony has enacted a law which requires compliance with *erga omnes* collective agreements, again under Article 3(8) of the Directive, and generally leaves the law on the application of market-wide labour standards stronger than it was before.[300]

A second reason to be more optimistic is the role which sectoral social dialogue can play in responding to the Court's interventions. In 2009 a Council Directive was adopted giving effect to a framework agreement made by the European-level federations of employers' associations and trade unions in the maritime sector, governing terms and conditions of employment of workers affected by the use of flags of convenience. The Directive is intended to come into force alongside an ILO Convention which was adopted in 2006.[301] While by no means reversing *Viking*, these developments indicate the scope for norms based on transnational collective bargaining to fill the void left by court-led deregulatory initiatives.[302]

---

[297] The Commission Green Paper, *Modernising Labour Law to Meet the Challenges of the Twenty-First Century*, COM(2006) 708, highlighted flexible employment law and active labour market policy as important elements of the Nordic model, but market-wide labour standards play a critical role in complementing these mechanisms: see C. McLaughlin, 'On the productivity enhancing impacts of the minimum wage: evidence from Denmark and New Zealand' (2008) 47 *British Journal of Industrial Relations* 327.

[298] M. Rönnmar, '*Laval* returns to Sweden: the final judgment of the Swedish labour court and Swedish legislative reforms' (2010) 39 *ILJ* 280, 285.

[299] T. Skjeie, 'European economic integration: a threat to the Scandinavian labour law systems?' LL.M. Dissertation, University of Cambridge (2010).

[300] S. Sciarra, 'Notions of solidarity in times of economic uncertainty' (2010) 39 *ILJ* 223, 240.

[301] See Council Directive 2009/13 implementing the agreement concluded by the European Community Ship Owners' Associations and the European Transport Workers' Federation, OJ [2009] L 124/30; ILO Convention No. 186 on Maritime Labour, adopted 23 February 2006; S. Sciarra, 'Notions of solidarity', above, n. 300, 232–3.

[302] Barnard and Deakin, previously, at n. 229.

D. ATTEMPTS AT RECONCILING THE INTERNAL MARKET WITH LABOUR LAW AND POLICY: THE CASE OF PUBLIC PROCUREMENT

1. INTRODUCTION

One of the reasons why *Laval* and particularly *Rüffert* were so criticized was that the Court failed to take into account the public procurement context in which they were decided.[303] It must be said that public procurement and labour law have had an awkward co-existence. Purists would argue that public procurement is about achieving value for money; social considerations should not be taken into account. Others would argue that public procurement involves the expenditure of large sums of public money and that money should be used to achieve social as well as economic objectives. The social objectives might include an obligation on the successful contractor to hire a certain number of the local unemployed or to ensure that those workers fulfilling the contract enjoy certain minimum terms and conditions.

The ambivalence towards the purpose of the procurement regime can be detected largely in the legislation. By contrast, with the exception of *Rüffert*, the Court has generally been pushing for a more socially sensitive reading of the legislation. What follows is a brief consideration of the General Procurement Directive (GPD) 2004/18/EC[304] and its interpretation by the Court. The position has been complicated by the fact that, following the decisions in *Laval* and *Rüffert*, the labour law regime which applies depends on whether the successful bidder is merely providing services under Article 56 or is established in the state where the services are to be provided.

2. THE PROCUREMENT REGIME

2.1. Introduction

Where the value of a tender exceeds a prescribed minimum, it must be publicly advertised in accordance with the GPD. Where the thresholds laid down in the Directive are not satisfied, the procurement regime must nevertheless still respect the Treaty principles of equal treatment, mutual recognition and proportionality.[305]

---

[303] See further S. Arrowsmith and P. Kunzlik, *Social and Environmental Policies in EC Procurement Law: New Directives and New Directions* (CUP, Cambridge, 2009).

[304] Directive 2004/18 on the award of public works contracts, public supply contracts, and public service contracts [2004] OJ L134/114.

[305] See, e.g., Case C–264/03 *Commission* v. *France* [2005] ECR I–8831, para. 33; Case C–6/05 *Medipac-Kazantzidis AE* v. *Venizelio-Pananio (PE.S.Y KRITIS)* [2007] ECR I–4557, paras. 32–3.

There are five main stages in a procurement regime under the Directive:

(1) pre-procurement: where the contracting authorities identify whether and what to purchase, and which procedure to apply;

(2) specification: where the contracting authorities set out technical specifications in the contract documentation;[306]

(3) identification of suitable potential suppliers;

(4) contract award; and

(5) performance stage.

Stages (3)–(5) are the most relevant for employment law issues and we shall focus on these.

2.2. Supplier selection stage

Directive 2004/18 prescribes a list of criteria for the selection of contractors permitted to submit a tender.[307] These are:

1. the personal situation of the candidate or tenderer;[308]

2. their suitability to pursue a professional activity (for example, their membership of a professional organization);[309]

3. their economic and financial standing (for example, are they financially sound based on their annual accounts?);[310]

4. their technical capacity (for example, are they adequately equipped to do the job and do they have a good track record?).[311]

On their face, it does not seem as though these provisions provide much scope for social matters to be taken into account. However, one of the discretionary grounds on which a tenderer can be excluded, under the first heading 'personal situation', is that the tenderer has been found 'guilty of grave professional misconduct'. According to the Recitals,[312] this includes non-compliance with the obligations under the PWD, the Equality Framework Directive 2000/78,[313] and the Equal Treatment Directive 76/207[314] (now Directive 2006/54[315]).[316]

2.3. The contract award stage

(a) MEAT and social clauses

The next stage in the procurement process is the award of the contract. According to Article 53, contracts can be awarded on one of two bases: (1) the lowest price; or (2) the most economically advantageous tender (MEAT). The former offers no room for

---

[306] Art. 23.
[307] Case C–94/99 *ARGE* [2000] ECR I–11037, para. 27. This list is exhaustive: Case C–368/10 *Commission* v. *Netherlands (eco-labels)* [2012] ECR I-000, para. 105.
[308] Art. 45.   [309] Art. 46.   [310] Art. 47.   [311] Arts. 46–48.   [312] Recitals 34 and 43.
[313] OJ [2000] L303/16.   [314] OJ [1976] L39/40.   [315] OJ [2006] L204/23.
[316] Art. 7(1)(b) of Dir. 2009/52 on sanctions against employers employing illegally staying TCNs expressly provides that Member States can exclude such employers from participation in a public contract for up to five years.

contracting authorities to take into account additional factors and so is rarely used in more complex procurements procurement. The latter basis, MEAT, might offer space for social factors to be taken into account but the precise scope is unclear.

According to the 1993 version of the public procurement Directive:

> the most economically advantageous tender, [involves] various criteria depending on the contract in question, such as: delivery or completion date, running costs, cost-effectiveness, quality, aesthetic and functional characteristics, technical merit, after-sales service and technical assistance, commitments with regard to spare parts, security of supplies and price.[317]

While the purists had argued that this provision provided no scope for non-economic matters to be taken into account by contract-awarding bodies, in *Nord-Pas-de-Calais*[318] the Court disagreed: 'that provision does not preclude all possibility for the contracting authorities to use as a criterion a condition linked to the campaign against unemployment provided that that condition is consistent with all the fundamental principles of [Union] law, in particular the principle of non-discrimination...'.[319] However, the Court added that such an award criterion had to be expressly mentioned in the contract notice 'so that contractors may become aware of its existence'.[320]

In *Concordia Bus Finland*[321] the Court added a further limitation on the use of social clauses. It said: 'Since a tender necessarily relates to the subject matter of the contract, it follows that the award criteria which may be applied in accordance with that provision must themselves also be linked to the subject-matter of the contract'.[322] This conclusion indirectly made it harder for contracting authorities to include social criteria in their tenders because the link between social criteria and the specific nature of the product/service can be tenuous.[323] This problem is exacerbated by the revisions made in the 2004 public procurement Directives (key revisions in italics). Article 53(1)(a) now provides:

> when the award is made to the tender most economically advantageous *from the point of view of the contracting authority*, various criteria *linked to the subject-matter of the public contract* in question, for example, quality, price, technical merit, aesthetic and functional characteristics, *environmental characteristics*, running costs, cost-effectiveness, after-sales service and technical assistance, delivery date and delivery period or period of completion [can be taken into account].

As can be seen, not only must the criteria now be linked to the subject matter of the contract but the tender must be the most economically advantageous from the point of

---

[317] This is taken from Art. 34 of the Utilities Dir. 93/38 (OJ [1993] L199/84).

[318] Case C–225/98 *Commission* v. *France* [2000] ECR I–7445.

[319] Para. 50.

[320] Para. 51.

[321] Case C–513/99 [2002] ECR I–7213.

[322] Para. 59. See further Case C–448/01 *EVN* v. *Republik Osterreich* [2003] ECR I–14527, para. 33; Case C–331/04 *ATI EAC Srl e Viaggi di Maio Snc* v. *ACTV Venzia SpA* [2005] ECR I–10109, para. 21.

[323] P. Charro, (2003) 40 *CML Rev.* 179, 187.

view of the contracting authority, the point the Commission had lost in *Concordia* but had already included as an accurate statement of the law in its 2001 Interpretative Communication.[324] It is hard to argue that a condition relating to the specification of improved terms and conditions of employment is economically advantageous from the point of view of the contracting authority, apart from in the most general terms that improving labour standards ultimately improves productivity. Moreover, the failure to refer to social matters is exacerbated by the fact that environmental characteristics are listed for the first time in Article 53.[325]

Why did the 2004 version of the Directive not reflect the case law more closely?[326] Although the European Parliament pushed for greater recognition of social matters, the Commission (DG Internal Market) and the Council were opposed. The compromise was to move a number of the social clauses from the body of the Directive to the Preamble. Contrast, for example, Article 53(1)(a) of the Directive (set out above) with Recital 46 which does offer some space for social matters to be taken into account in determining the MEAT:

> ...a contracting authority may use criteria aiming to meet social requirements, in response in particular to the needs—defined in the specifications of the contract—of particularly disadvantaged groups of people to which those receiving/using the works, supplies or services which are the object of the contract belong.[327]

This is still a long way removed from requiring tenderers to take into account improved terms and conditions of employment. *Commission* v. *Germany (occupational pensions)* considered below might provide further openings, especially if read in the light of the Commission's 2001 Interpretative Communication which says that working conditions 'more favourable to workers may, however, also be applied (and must then also be complied with), provided they are compatible with [Union] law'.[328]

(b) Abnormally low tenders

There is one other area, in the context of the award, where social matters can be taken into account: where the bid appears abnormally low, the contracting authority must request the details of the constituent elements of the tender including 'compliance with the provisions relating to employment protection and working conditions in force at the place where the work, service or supply is to be performed'. This might indicate that

---

[324] Commission, *Interpretative Communication on the Community law applicable to public procurement and the possibilities for integrating social considerations into public procurement*, COM(2001) 566, 13.

[325] Although cf. the first Recital which says that the 2004 Directive is 'based on the Court of Justice case law, in particular the case law on award criteria, which clarifies the possibilities for the contracting authorities to meet the needs of the public concerned, including in the environmental and/or social area'.

[326] See further, C. Kilpatrick, 'Internal market architecture and the accommodation of labour rights: posting of workers, public procurement and the Court of Justice', on file with the author.

[327] Recent case law shows the extent to which the Court is now prepared to refer to Preambles: see, e.g., Case C–307/05 *Del Cerro Alonso* v. *Osakidetza-Servicio Vasco de Salud* [2007] ECR I–7109, para. 36. Case C–368/10 *Commission* v. *Netherlands (eco-labels)* [2012] ECR I-000, para. 85. However, recitals have only interpretative value and cannot be used to contradict express provisions in a Directive: Case C–267/06 *Maruko* v. *Versorgungsanstalt der deutschen Bühnen* [2008] ECR I–1757, para. 60.

[328] Commission, above n. 324, 20.

only minimum terms and conditions can be requested but the vagueness of the phrase 'place where the work … is to be performed' might be broad enough to include improved terms and conditions in that particular workplace.

2.4. The performance stage

From the public authority's point of view, including social clauses is best considered as a condition at the performance stage of the contract. Here the Directive appears to offer greater flexibility to the contracting authority since, as with the pre-procurement stage, it is the area least regulated by the Directive. Article 26 of the Directive merely says:

> Contracting authorities may lay down special conditions relating to the performance of a contract, provided that these are compatible with [Union] law and are indicated in the contract notice or in the specifications. The conditions governing the performance of a contract may, in particular, concern *social and environmental considerations*. (Emphasis added.)

Most of the situations envisaged by the Preamble to the Directive concern local hiring.[329] However, the Preamble adds that 'mention may be made, amongst other things of the requirements—applicable during performance of the contract—…to comply in substance with the provisions of the basic International Labour Organization (ILO) Conventions,[330] assuming that such provisions have not been implemented in national laws'. This view is now reinforced by the Commission's 2010 Staff Working Document, *Buying Social: A guide to taking account of social criteria in public procurement*,[331] which says that 'Sustainability criteria (including social criteria) may also be incorporated in the contract performance condition, provided they are linked to performance of the contract in question (e.g. minimum salary and decent labour conditions for the workers involved in the performance of the contract)'.

This suggests that it would be possible at least at performance stage to include requirements for tenderers to take into account minimum terms and conditions of employment and possibly improved terms and conditions, a view now given further support by *Commission* v. *Germany (occupational pensions)*, provided those social conditions are 'not directly or indirectly discriminatory and are indicated in the contract notice or in the contract documents'.[332]

2.5. *Commission* v. *Germany (occupational pensions)*

In *Commission* v. *Germany* a number of local authorities entered into a collective agreement with the trade unions concerning the conversion of earnings into pension savings. The collective agreement identified a limited list of pension providers entrusted with implementing the salary conversion measure. Given the existence of this collective agreement, the local authorities did not issue a call for tenders, as required by Directive

---

[329] Recital 33. See additionally the Commission's Interpretative Communication, above n. 324, 17.
[330] See e.g. Convention 94 Labour Clauses (Public Contracts Convention) 1949.
[331] SEC(2010) 1258 final, 34 and 51.   [332] First sentence of Recital 33.

2004/18, with the result that other pension providers were denied the chance to offer their services.

As with *Viking* and *Laval* the case therefore pitted the fundamental social right to engage in collective bargaining against the fundamental economic freedoms, freedom of establishment, and free movement of services, as enshrined in the Public Procurement Directive. The Court noted the need for balance between the competing interests[333] but found that this balance had not been struck on the facts because the effect of the collective agreement was 'to disapply the public procurement rules completely, and for an indefinite period, in the field of local authority employees' pension saving'.[334] It rejected the German government's argument that the public procurement Directives should not be applied because (1) they did not provide room for worker participation; and (2) the collective agreement was a manifestation of the principle of solidarity (with good risks offsetting the bad). However, it did say at paragraph 56 that the 'application of the procurement procedures [do not] preclude the call for tenders from imposing upon interested tenderers conditions reflecting the interests of the workers concerned'. It also said that the Directives do not prevent 'a local authority employer from specifying, in the terms of the call for tenders, the conditions to be complied with by tenderers in order to prevent, or place limits on, workers interested in salary conversion being selected on the basis of medical grounds'.[335] It added that the preservation of 'elements of solidarity is not inherently irreconcilable with the application of a procurement procedure'.[336]

From a single market perspective the outcome of this case is not surprising: earlier case law had already rejected attempts to ring-fence sensitive matters from the scope of the procurement Directives.[337] However, from a practical perspective the implications of subjecting pensions arrangements negotiated collectively to the full rigours of the public procurement Directives[338] are serious and have caused consternation in some states, particularly in Scandinavia. The procurement rules are bureaucratic and burdensome for local authorities without necessarily resulting in actually attracting tenders from other Member States. This is particularly so in respect of pension provision in Germany, a highly specialized and localized field.[339]

---

[333] Case C-271/08 *Commission v. Germany* [2000] ECR I-000, paras. 44 and 52. The Court has extended this to the field of state aid: Case C-319/07 *3F v. Commission* [2009] ECR I-5963, para. 58.

[334] Para. 53.

[335] Para. 58.

[336] Ibid.

[337] E.g. Case C-160/08 *Commission v. Germany (ambulance)* [2010] ECR I-000, paras. 125-31. More recently, see Case C-45/09 *Rosenbladt* [2010] ECR I-000, para. 52 (collective agreements not exempt from review under the equality legislation).

[338] These are Annex IIA services to which the full procedure applies, not Annex IIB. This distinction is to be dropped in the reforms to the public procurement rules: COM(2011) 896, 8.

[339] Cf. Case C-507/03 *Commission v. Ireland (An Post)* [2007] ECR I-9777, para. 34 where, in a case that involved a tender which was not subject to the full rules of the Directive, the Court found that the contract lacked cross-border interest and so EU law did not apply.

A more positive note, from the perspective of labour law, is the fact that in paragraph 56 of *Commission* v. *Germany* the Court appears to countenance significantly more space for social matters in the tendering process. Further, unlike its previous decisions on social clauses in procurement, the Court is not prescriptive at which stage the social factors can be included (albeit, unlike its earlier case law on social clauses, the complaint concerned a total failure to tender, rather than a criticism of the terms included in the tender document or controls on the actual performance of the contract). In this way, the Court gives some backbone to Article 27 of Directive 2004/18 (considered above) and possibly paves the way for the inclusion of improved labour standards as a requirement in the contract documentation.

Change is in the air. The Commission's 2010 'Buying Social' Guide indicated greater enthusiasm for taking social considerations into account. The Single Market Act 2011 also identified public procurement as one of the 12 projects to be delivered. The Commission commits itself to modernizing 'this legislative framework in order to arrive at a balanced policy sustaining the demand for environmentally friendly, socially responsible and innovative goods and services, provide contracting authorities with simpler and more flexible procedures'. In the Commission's proposal,[340] social matters do feature more prominently[341] but not to the extent of opening up the procurement regime to enable contracting authorities to require the hiring of a certain number of, for example, young local unemployed. One feature is, however, noteworthy for this chapter. Various of the Articles make reference to Annex XI which lists international social and environmental law provisions. These include ILO Conventions 87 on freedom of association and Convention 98 on the right to organize. So, for example, Article 55(3) provides that a contracting authority may exclude from participation in a public contract an economic operator who has violated obligations established by Union legislation in the field of social or labour law or international provisions listed in Annex XI.

2.6. Public procurement, posted workers, and labour law

So far, we have concentrated on the public procurement regime to see what scope it provides for mandating both minimum and improved labour standards. It has been argued that, particularly following *Commission* v. *Germany*, it may be possible for contracting authorities to require more of contractors by way of specified terms and conditions of employment. However, in *Laval* and, more importantly for our purposes, *Rüffert*, the space for contracting authorities to impose even minimum labour standards on a successful tenderer from another Member State has been reduced when the work is being performed by posted workers. This is because, as we have seen, under Article 3(1) PWD, as interpreted in *Laval*,[342] only those host state rules listed in Article 3(1) (e.g. rules on working time, health and safety, equality, and minimum rates of pay. but not other key aspects of labour law such as protection against unfair dismissal and

---

[340] COM(2011) 896.   [341] See e.g. Arts. 17, 41, 54(2), 55(2)m 55(3)(c), 63(5), 69(3)–(4) and 70.
[342] *Laval*, para. 70.

redundancy) can be applied by the host state to posted workers. All other matters are governed by the law of the home state. So Latvian posted workers working on a contract in the UK will enjoy the benefit of UK rules in respect of the matters listed in Article 3(1) but Latvian law in respect of all other matters. The potential 'get out' clauses for host States (the so-called minimum standards clause in Article 3(7) and the Article 3(10) public policy provision) have effectively been neutered by the Court in *Laval*, *Rüffert* and *Luxembourg*, thereby curtailing the possibility for host states (the UK) to require contractors to respect its terms and conditions in areas outside those listed in Article 3(1). The PWD therefore seems to apply—and possibly take precedence over—matters covered by the Public Procurement Directives. This can be seen in *Rüffert*.

The case concerned the Law of Lower Saxony on the award of public contracts, introduced to counteract 'distortions of competition which arise in the field of construction'. This law provided that public (but not private) contracting authorities could award contracts for building works but only to undertakings and subcontractors which paid the wage laid down in the collective agreements at the place where the service was provided. Following a public invitation to tender, Lower Saxony awarded Objekt und Bauregie (O&B) a contract for the structural work in the building of a prison. The contract contained a declaration regarding compliance with certain collective agreements and, more specifically, with the collective agreement regarding payment to employees employed on the building site of at least the minimum wage in force at the place where those services were to be performed. However, when it was discovered that O&B's Polish sub-contractor employed workers on the site at a wage well below that provided for in the collective agreement, the Land terminated the contract with O&B.

By requiring respect for the German collective agreement by both domestic and foreign tenderers, Lower Saxony was complying with the key principle of equal treatment, expressly articulated in Article 2 of Directive 2004/18. This point was noted by the Advocate General[343] who added that while the aim of public procurement was to meet an identified administrative need for works, services or supplies, 'the award of public contracts also authorises the attainment of other public interest requirements, such as environmental policy or, as in the present case, social objectives'.

However, the Court adopted a different approach. It found that the German law contravened the PWD because the German authorities had failed to comply with the detailed provisions of Article 3(8). In particular, they had failed to declare the collectively agreed pay in the building industry to be universally applicable[344] with the result that the collectively agreed rules on pay rates could not be applied to the posted workers.[345] The Court added that by requiring undertakings performing public works contracts and, indirectly their subcontractors to apply the minimum wage laid down by the collective agreement, the German law could impose on undertakings established in another Member State where minimum rates of pay are lower 'an additional economic

---

[343] Para. 131.   [344] Ibid., para. 26.   [345] Ibid., para. 31.

burden' that is 'capable of constituting a restriction within the meaning of Article [56 TFEU]'.[346] In other words, the application of social provisions constituted a restriction on market access and was presumptively unlawful. Even more striking in this regard was the Court's reference to the procurement context but its failure to mention the public procurement Directives.

The divergence between the Court and its Advocate General highlights the fundamental problem at the core of the decision: should the Land insist on an equal treatment approach (as the Advocate General would suggest) or a single market perspective (as the Court would suggest). The effect of the Advocate General's approach would be to allow contracting authorities to impose on contractors all labour standards justified in the name of equal treatment. The effect of the Court's approach is that the imposition of the host state's labour standards on the staff of temporary service providers—with the exception of those areas listed in Article 3(1) PWD—is an impediment to market access. The Court's stance therefore significantly restricts the extent to which even minimum terms and conditions can be imposed on posted workers through any procurement regime.

Yet, in reaching this conclusion the Court created its own (reverse) discrimination: domestic service providers and established service providers exercising their rights under Article 56 TFEU will be subject to all the employment conditions of the procuring state (e.g. the UK), to the extent this is compatible with the public procurement regime. By contrast, out-of-state (e.g. Latvian) service providers will not be subject to host state (UK) laws except in the areas listed in Article 3(1) PWD. Could the domestic/ established service providers claim that they have been subject to unequal treatment contrary to Article 2 of Directive 2004/18? If they can, does this mean that the domestic/established service providers can demand a 'levelling down' (at least from a labour law perspective) of requirements,[347] resulting in them being subject to UK laws only in those areas listed in Article 3(1). If this argument was accepted it would have three unexpected consequences.

First, it would mean that the effect of applying EU law would be to reduce the level of terms and conditions for the employees of domestic/established service providers, contrary to Article 151(1) TFEU which identifies 'improved living and working conditions' as one of the objectives of the Union. Second, in areas outside those listed in Article 3(1) PWD the employees of domestic/established service providers no longer enjoy the protection of national laws, contrary to Article 8(2) of the Rome I Regulation. Third, the Latvian service provider would now itself be subject to discrimination: its employees will be subject to two sets of rules (UK law in respect of matters listed in Article 3(1) PWD and Latvian law in respect of all other employment-related issues), whereas domestic/

---

[346] Ibid., para. 37.

[347] A 'levelling up' (i.e. service providers being treated in the same way as domestic providers) would not be permissible because, according to well-established case law, by making the provision of services in a state's territory subject to compliance with all the conditions required for freedom of establishment would undermine the Treaty provision on services: Case 33/74 *Van Binsbergen* [1974] ECR 1299, para. 11; Case 205/84 *Commission v. Germany (the insurance cases)* [1986] ECR 3755, para. 26.

established service providers would have to respect one set of rules only (the UK's) and a reduced set of rules at that. This could be resolved only by applying Latvian law to the employees of domestic/established service providers. This would mean the extra-territorial application of Latvian labour law not just to Latvian workers (which is envisaged by Article 8(2) of the Rome I Regulation when they carry their home state laws to the place where they are temporarily working) but to UK workers (which is not).

The only apparent way out of this conundrum is to say that, in respect of working conditions at least, the situation of domestic/established service providers is not comparable with that of (Latvian) service providers and so the principle of equal treatment in Article 2 GPD is not engaged. Nevertheless, the practical effect of this is that the Treaty provisions on free movement of services trump the principle of equal treatment found in the Directive.[348]

E. CONCLUSIONS

While the rights of free movement of persons have been the cornerstone of the Treaties since its inception, in fact remarkably few people actually took advantage of these provisions; and the derogations and justifications gave the Member States an important tool to exclude those they did not wish to see admitted and to apply their own rules if they were justified. However, the world now is a very different place and while workers still might not want to relocate permanently to another Member State, they are much more willing to go for short periods when posted by their employers. The Treaty provisions on services have enjoyed a renaissance over the last 20 years or so. When terms and conditions of employment did not differ substantially between the original 12 Member States, the free market did not pose a significant threat to the integrity of national social orders. But as the EU began to expand, first to the south (Portugal, Spain, and Greece) and, more importantly to the east, the tensions between the free market and the preservation of national social models began to resurface. It has been the Court which has been in the frontline dealing with the fall-out from the structural imbalance embedded in the Treaty since its inception.

* * *

---

[348] This point seems to have been recognized in the proposed Directive on the award of concession contracts COM (2011) 897 where the 29th Recital does recognize a greater role for social considerations: 'In order to better integrate social considerations in the award of concessions, procurers may also be allowed to include, in the award criteria, characteristics related to the working conditions. However, where the contracting authorities or contracting entities use the most economically advantageous tender, such criteria may only relate to the working conditions of the persons directly participating in the process of production or provision in question. Those characteristics may only concern the protection of health of the staff involved in the production process or the favouring of social integration of disadvantaged persons or members of vulnerable groups amongst the persons assigned to performing the contract, including accessibility for persons with disabilities'. However, it adds: 'In this case, any award criteria which include those characteristics should in any event remain limited to characteristics that have immediate consequences on staff members in their working environment. They should be applied in accordance with Directive 96/71/EC…'.

According to the PWD, one of the areas in which the out-of-state service provider must respect the host state's terms and conditions of employment concerns 'equality of treatment between men and women and other provisions on non-discrimination'. This is one area of law where the Union has now developed a substantial body of acquis. It is to this subject that we now turn.

PART III

EQUALITY LAW

6

EQUALITY LAW: DEVELOPMENT AND PRINCIPLES

A. INTRODUCTION

The quest for equality—and in particular sex equality—has been the central and most highly developed pillar of the European Union's social policy. It lies at the core of the European social model and it has served as a catalyst for change in the Member States.[1] The pursuit of *sex* equality has been in the Union's sight since the signing of the Treaty of Rome in 1957. The pursuit of equality on other grounds—in particular race, ethnic origin, sexual orientation, religion, belief, age, and disability—is of much more recent vintage. Indeed, it took concrete form only in the Treaty of Amsterdam in 1997, four decades after the Treaty of Rome, when Article 19 TFEU (ex 13 EC) was included as a legal basis for legislation to prohibit discrimination on these grounds.

It is not entirely clear why sex equality[2] has maintained such a unique hold on the attentions of EU legislators and litigators for so long.[3] It is true that women represent more than a third of the workforce, are more likely to occupy 'atypical' jobs, especially part-time jobs, and are particularly affected by long-term unemployment. Perhaps, as Ellis suggests, the attainment of sex equality served political and economic goals: on an economic level, it was important to prevent competitive distortions in a now quite highly integrated market; and on a political level, sex equality provided a relatively innocuous, even high-sounding platform, by which the Union could demonstrate its commitment to social progress.[4] Less cynically, it could be argued that the drive to achieve sex equality has provided the EU with a readily accessible human face.[5]

---

[1] White Paper on Social Policy COM(94) 333, 41.

[2] For a comprehensive discussion of this subject, see E. Ellis, *EU Anti-discrimination Law* (OUP, Oxford, 2005) and M. Bell, *Anti-discrimination Law and the European Union* (OUP, Oxford, 2002). For a general, positive review, see S. Prechal, 'Equality of Treatment, Non-discrimination and Social Policy: Achievements in Three Themes' (2004) 41 *CMLRev.* 533.

[3] See C. Kilpatrick, 'Gender Equality: A Fundamental Dialogue' in S. Sciarra (ed.), *Labour Law in the Courts: National Judges and the ECJ* (Hart Publishing, Oxford, 2001).

[4] Ellis, above n. 2, 22.

[5] C. Kilpatrick, 'Emancipation through law or the Emasculation of Law? The Nation State, the EU, and Gender Equality at Work' in J. Conaghan *et al. Labour Law in an Era of Globalization* (OUP, Oxford, 2002).

The aim of this chapter is to outline the development of equality law in the EU as well as placing these developments in context. We begin by considering the evolution of the Union's approach to the realization of equal treatment. An understanding of this evolution is necessary to appreciate the twists and turns in the case law. We then examine the meaning of equality, both theoretically and in practice, in the EU's legal order. Inevitably, because Union law on sex equality has been around for almost 50 years, many of the key concepts have been developed in respect of this strand and this is reflected in the discussion in this chapter.

The following chapters then consider in detail the interpretation of the law: Chapter 7 considers equal pay for men and women; Chapter 8 looks at equal treatment across the strands; Chapter 9 examines various aspects of so-called 'family friendly' policies; while Chapter 10 considers the thorny question of equality in respect of social security and, in particular, pensions.

B. THE DEVELOPMENT OF EU LAW AND POLICY ON EQUALITY

1. SEX EQUALITY

1.1. Introduction

Article 157 TFEU (ex 141 EC) established the principle that men and women should receive equal pay for equal work. Article 157 TFEU was introduced into the Treaty of Rome largely to serve the economic purpose of 'correcting or eliminating the effect of specific distortions which advantage or disadvantage certain branches of activity'.[6] France insisted on the inclusion of Article 157 TFEU because it feared that, in the absence of Union regulation, its worker protection legislation, including its laws on equal pay, would put it at a competitive disadvantage in a common market due to the additional costs borne by French industry.[7] Thus, the original rationale for including a provision on sex equality in the EEC Treaty was a negative one: to stop social dumping.[8]

---

[6] The Spaak Report, 61 (author's translation). Comité Intergouvernemental Crée par la Conférence de Messine, Rapport des Chefs de Délégations aux Ministères des Affaires Etrangères of 21 April 1956. The Committee, comprising of the heads of delegations, was established at the Messina conference in June 1955 under the chairmanship of M Paul Henri Spaak, then Belgian foreign minister. See generally C. Barnard, 'EC Sex Equality Law: A Balance Sheet', in P. Alston (ed.), *The EU and Human Rights* (OUP, Oxford, 1999) on which this section draws.

[7] See O. Kahn-Freund, 'Labour Law and Social Security', in E. Stein and T. Nicholson (eds.), *American Enterprise in the European Common Market: A Legal Profile* (University of Michigan Press, Ann Arbor, Mich., 1960) 300, discussed in C. Barnard, 'The Economic Objectives of Article 119', in T. Hervey and D. O'Keeffe (eds.), *Sex Equality Law in the European Union* (Wiley, Chichester, 1996); G. More, 'The Principle of Equal Treatment: From Market Unifier to Fundamental Right', in P. Craig and G. De Búrca (eds.), *The Evolution of EU Law* (OUP, Oxford, 1999). See further the influence of ILO Convention 100: C. Hoskyns, *Integrating Gender* (Verso, London, 1996) Ch. 4.

[8] See further Ch. 1.

The social and moral justification for sex equality was largely overlooked. Yet, within 20 years the Union had adopted three Directives on equality, and the Court had started to recognize the principle of equality as a fundamental right which served a social, as well as an economic, function. This was first identified in the landmark judgment in *Defrenne (No. 2)*,[9] a case brought against the backcloth of serious industrial unrest by women in Belgium about the absence of equal pay.[10] The Court famously observed:

> Article [157] pursues a double aim. *First*,... the aim of Article [157] is to avoid a situation in which undertakings established in states which have actually implemented the principle of equal pay suffer a competitive disadvantage in intra-[Union] competition as compared with undertakings established in states which have not yet eliminated discrimination against women workers as regards pay. *Second*, this provision forms part of the social objectives of the [Union], which is not merely an economic union, but is at the same time intended, by common action to ensure social progress and seek the constant improvement of living and working conditions of their peoples...This double aim, which is at once economic and social, shows that the principle of equal pay forms part of the foundations of the [Union].

In *Defrenne (No. 3)*[11] the Court took the social dimension of equality one stage further and elevated the principle to the status of a fundamental right. It said that 'respect for fundamental personal human rights is one of the general principles of [Union] law... there can be no doubt that the elimination of discrimination based on sex forms part of those fundamental rights'. As we shall see, despite such statements, the yoke of the economic justification for Union sex equality legislation has far from been cast off. While the EU has never followed the neo-liberal route which opposes all anti-discrimination legislation on the grounds that the market will achieve the optimal outcome without there being any need for the legislature to interfere with freedom of contract,[12] the EU viewed equal opportunities as acceptable in the early 1970s so long as they did not interfere significantly with the operation of the Single Market. Then, the late 1990s saw a shift in approach with the European employment strategy where the European Union viewed discrimination laws as promoting efficiency by inducing potential productivity, and by reducing the inefficiencies associated with statistical discrimination.[13] In other words, equality—together with other social rights—came to be seen as inputs into growth.[14]

The view that equality was socially and economically important was reinforced by the prominent position of equality both in the Charter of Fundamental Rights adopted

[9] Case 43/75 *Defrenne (No. 2)* v. *SABENA* [1976] ECR 455.
[10] C. Hoskyns, *Integrating Gender* (Verso, London, 1996), 65–75.
[11] Case 149/77 *Defrenne (No. 3)* v. *SABENA* [1978] ECR 1365, 1378.
[12] See, e.g., G. Becker, *The Economics of Discrimination*, 2nd edn (Univ. of Chicago Press, Chicago, 1971). Cf. B. Hepple, 'The Principle of Equal Treatment in Article 119 EC and the Possibilities for Reform', in A. Dashwood and S. O'Leary (eds.), *The Principle of Equal Treatment in EC Law* (Sweet & Maxwell, London, 1997) 141.
[13] J. Donohue, 'Prohibiting Sex Discrimination in the Workplace: An Economic Perspective' (1989) 56 *U. Chicago L.Rev.* 1337.
[14] This was recognized at a relatively early stage by the European Commission in its White Paper on Social Policy where it said that the 'adaptability and creativity of women is a strength which should be harnessed to

at Nice in December 2000 and the Lisbon Treaty. Title III of the Charter opens with the classic assertion that, 'Everyone is equal before the law'.[15] Article 23(1) of the Charter requires equality between men and women in 'all areas, including employment, work and pay'. Article 23(2) of the Charter contains the positive action provision. It specifies that the principle of equality 'shall not prevent the maintenance or adoption of measures providing for specific advantages in favour of the under-represented sex'.[16]

This changing perspective fed into rulings of the Court of Justice. In *Deutsche Post*[17] the Court said that in view of the case law recognizing that equality was a fundamental right, the priority between the economic and social aims of Article 157 was reversed:

> ...it must be concluded that the economic aim pursued by Article [157 TFEU], namely the elimination of distortions of competition between undertakings established in different Member States, is *secondary* to the social aim pursued by the same provision, which constitutes the expression of a fundamental human right.[18]

1.2. The development of EU law and policy on sex equality

(a) Hard law

Following the inclusion of the original Article 119 EEC into the Treaty of 1957, little happened in the field of sex equality until the Social Action Programme 1974 which followed the Paris Communiqué in 1972. This said that the Union aspired to create a 'situation in which equality between men and women obtains in the labour market throughout the [Union], through the improvement of economic and psychological conditions, and of the social and educational infrastructure'.[19] Three important Directives were adopted as a result:

- Directive 75/117/EEC[20] on equal pay for male and female workers, enshrining the principle of 'equal pay for equal work' laid down in Article 157 TFEU and introducing the concept of 'equal pay for work of equal value'. This has been supplemented by two codes of practice intended to give practical advice on measures to ensure the effective implementation of equal pay.[21]

- Directive 76/207/EEC[22] on equal treatment with regard to access to employment, vocational training, promotion and working conditions, aimed at eliminating all discrimination, both direct and indirect, in the world of work and providing an opportunity for positive measures. This Directive was amended by Directive

---

the drive for growth and competitiveness in the EU' (COM(94) 333, 41).

[15] Art. 20 of the Charter. This was relied on in Case C-2-8/09 *Sayn-Wittgenstein* v. *Landeshauptmann von Wien* [2010] ECR I-000, para. 89.

[16] For a full discussion, see C. Costello, 'Gender Equalities and the Charter of Fundamental Rights of the European Union' in T. Hervey and J. Kenner (eds.), *Economic and Social Rights under the EU Charter of Fundamental Rights* (Hart Publishing, Oxford, 2003).

[17] Joined Cases C–270/97 and C–271/97 *Deutsche Post* v. *Sievers and Schrage* [2000] ECR I–929, para. 57.

[18] Emphasis added. See additionally Joined Cases C–234/96 and C–235/96 *Deutsche Telekom AG* v. *Vick and Conze* [2000] ECR I–799, para. 57.

[19] See Council Resolution of 21 January 1974 concerning a Social Action Programme OJ [1974] L14/10.

[20] OJ [1975] L45/19.   [21] COM(94) 6; COM(96)336 final.

[22] OJ [1976] L39/40. The Directive was based on Art. 352 TFEU (ex Art. 308 EC).

2002/73[23] to bring the sex equality strand into line with the principles expressed in the 'Article 19' Directives (see later in this chapter).

- Directive 79/7/EEC[24] on the progressive implementation of equal treatment with regard to statutory social security schemes.

There followed five Action Programmes aimed specifically at equal opportunities for men and women.[25]

In the 1980s, at a time of stagnation in Union social policy more generally, two specific Directives were adopted on sex equality:

- Directive 86/378/EEC[26] on the implementation of equal treatment in occupational schemes of social security. The Directive was amended by Directive 96/97/EC[27] in the light of the *Barber*[28] judgment.

- Directive 86/613/EEC[29] on equal treatment for men and women carrying out a self-employed activity, including agriculture (now repealed and replaced by Directive 2010/41/EU).[30]

The Directives considered so far were all adopted under Articles 115 and/or 352 TFEU (ex Articles 94 and 308 EC) requiring unanimous voting.[31] The 1989 Social Action Programme,[32] implementing the Community Social Charter 1989, led to the enactment of one measure in the field of equality, Directive 92/85/EC[33] improving the health and safety of workers who are pregnant or have recently given birth. This Directive was based on Article 153 TFEU (ex Article 137 EC) which required qualified majority voting.

Two further Directives were adopted under the Social Policy Agreement (SPA) annexed to the Treaty on European Union from which the UK initially secured an opt-out:

- Directive 96/34/EC on reconciling family and working life (parental leave),[34] the first Directive adopted as a result of an agreement concluded by the Social Partners (now replaced by Directive 2010/18/EU[35]).

- Directive 97/80/EC[36] on the burden of proof in cases of discrimination based on sex.

---

[23] OJ [2002] L269/15.
[24] OJ [1979] L6/24. This is considered in detail in Ch. 10.
[25] Action Programme 1982–5 OJ [1982] C186/3, EC Bull. 5–1982, point 2.1.48 and EC Bull. 7/8–1982, point 2.1.67; Equal Opportunities for Women Medium-term Community Programme 1986–1990, EC Bull. Supp. 3/86 and EC Bull. 6–1986, point 2.1.116; Third Medium-term Action Programme COM(90) 449 final; Fourth Medium Term Action Programme (1996–2000) Council Decision 95/593/EC (OJ [1995] L335/37); Fifth Action Programme (2001–2006) Council Decision, 2001/95 (OJ [2001] L17/22).
[26] OJ [1986] L225/40.   [27] OJ [1997] L46/20.
[28] Case 262/88 *Barber* v. *Guardian Royal Exchange* [1990] ECR I–1889. This is considered in detail in Ch. 10.
[29] OJ [1997] L359/56.
[30] OJ [2010] L180/1. This Dir. was adopted under Art. 157(3) TFEU.
[31] E.g., Dir. 75/117 was adopted under Art. 115 TFEU, Dir. 76/207 under Art. 352 TFEU, and Dir. 86/378 under both Arts. 115 TFEU and 352 TFEU.
[32] COM(89) 568.   [33] OJ [1992] L245/23.
[34] OJ [1996] L145/4, amended by Dir. 97/75/EC (OJ [1998] L10/24), consolidated OJ [1998] L10/11.
[35] OJ [2010] L68/13.
[36] OJ [1998] L14/6, amended by Directive 98/52/EC (OJ [1998] L205/66).

When the UK signed up to the Social Chapter in 1997 these two measures were readopted under Article 115 TFEU and applied to the UK.[37] In addition, two other Directives adopted in this period, also using the collective route to legislation, the Part-time Work Directive 97/81[38] and the Fixed-term Work Directive 99/70,[39] although not specifically part of the equality agenda, modelled themselves on the equality Directives, and inevitably helped women, who dominate the part-time and (to a lesser extent) the fixed-term workforce.

Seven of the equality Directives (the Equal Pay Directive 75/117, the Equal Treatment Directive 76/207 as amended by Directive 2002/73, the Burden of Proof Directive 97/80 as amended by Directive 98/52, and Directive 86/378/EEC on equal treatment in occupational schemes of social security as amended by Directive 96/97/EC) were recast into a single consolidated Directive 2006/54/EC, repealing the earlier Directives from 15 August 2009.[40]

The common feature of all of the hard law Directives outlined above is that they are based on the 'human rights' model.[41] Fredman explains this model in the following terms: the function of human rights is to protect the individual against interference by the state, the rights are vested in the individual who must bring a claim before the courts (which are seen as the primary means of enforcing rights) and remedies are available only if the individual victim can prove the right has been breached. Remedies are retrospective, individual, and based on proof of breach, or 'fault'. She adds, 'Corresponding to this paradigm is also a particular view of equality as a negative duty, restraining the state or private individuals from discriminating against individuals'.

While this model offers a number of benefits—the language of fundamental rights has symbolic value, it provides litigants with an avenue of recourse, and it helps shape employer behaviour and establish a culture of compliance—the disadvantages are also well known. Litigation is stressful for those involved, particularly if the employment relationship is ongoing, it is expensive and it depends on the courts understanding, and being responsive to, the issues involved. It also overlooks the fact that, particularly with gender, breaches of rights operate in a 'collective and institutional way'.[42] As Fredman points out, the human rights approach fails to see that gender inequality is often not individualized; it 'affects individuals as a result of their group membership and inequality is frequently a consequence of institutional arrangements for which no single actor is "to blame"'. When viewed through this lens, it is clear that the courts do not have the competence to intervene to seek to resolve wider social issues; and that the responsibility more often lies with the state. Yet, as Fredman argues, the human rights model assumes that the state is a potential threat to liberty, rather than a potential force for enhancing freedom through the provision of social goods. She therefore advocates a 'proactive

---

[37] The Social Partners were also consulted with regard to combating sexual harassment at work: COM(96) 373 (first round consultation) and SEC(97) 373 (second round consultation). UNICE (now BusinessEurope) pulled out of their negotiations in September 1997.

[38] OJ [1998] L14/9, as amended by Dir. 97/81/EC (OJ [1998] L131/10).

[39] OJ [1999] L175/43.   [40] OJ [2006] L204/23.

[41] 'Changing the Norm: Positive Duties in Equal Treatment Legislation' (2005) 12 *MJ* 369, 370.

[42] Ibid., 371.

model' where the initiative lies with policy makers, implementers and employers to identify and address the institutional and structural causes for inequality.[43] It is in this context that some of the other Union developments are worth examining.

(b) Soft law and the Open Method of Co-ordination (OMC)

From the mid-1980s the Union started adopting a variety of soft law measures on, for example, equal opportunities,[44] the integration of equal opportunities into the Structural Funds,[45] balanced participation by men and women in decision making[46] and in family and working life,[47] women in vocational training in general[48] and science in particular,[49] and equal participation by women in an employment-intensive growth strategy in the EU.[50] Although these texts are not legally binding, they form part of the 'softening up process', paving the way for the Commission's preferred course of action should a 'policy window' open up.[51] More importantly, they steer the Union institutions and the Member States to take positive steps to address inequality through policy, and not just legal, means. They also provide an opportunity for decision makers to see a problem in the round rather than through the prism of legal categorization. Thus, policy may be more responsive to the problems experienced by those facing multiple levels of discrimination such as being an ethnic minority, single mother.[52] Funding for some of these policy initiatives was made available through the European Social Fund, especially its EQUAL programme,[53] and now through PROGRESS,[54] the EU's employment and social solidarity programme.

The Commission has now brought some of these soft-law initiatives under the broader umbrella of 'mainstreaming'.[55] As the Commission explains:

> Gender mainstreaming is the integration of the gender perspective into every stage of policy processes—design, implementation, monitoring and evaluation—with a view to promoting

---

[43] Ibid., 373.

[44] See e.g. Council Resolution on the promotion of equal opportunities for women OJ [1986] L203/2.

[45] 94/C 231/01 OJ [1994] C231/1. See additionally Council Res. of 2 December 1996 on mainstreaming equal opportunities for men and women into the structural funds (OJ [1996] C386/1).

[46] Council Res. of 27 March 1995 (OJ [1995] L168/3) and Council Rec. 96/694/EC (OJ [1996] L319/11).

[47] OJ [2000] C218/5.

[48] Commission Rec. of 24 November 1987 on vocational training for women (OJ [1987] L342/35). See additionally e.g., Council Res. on social and human capital building in the knowledge society: learning, work, social cohesion and gender (OJ [2003] C175/3) and Council Res. on equal access to and participation of women and men in the knowledge society for growth and innovation (OJ [2003] C317/6).

[49] Council Resolution of 20 May 1999 (OJ [1999] C201/1).   [50] 94/C 368/02.

[51] L. Cram, Policy Making in the EU: Conceptual Lenses and the Integration Process (Routledge, London, 1997).

[52] D. Schiek, 'Broadening the Scope and the Norms of EU Gender Equality law: Towards a Multi-Dimensional Conception of Equality Law' (2005) 12 MJ 427. Although the Commission is considering other ways of dealing with such 'multiple' discrimination: COM(2010) 491, 11. See further Ch. 8.

[53] <http://ec.europa.eu/employment_social/equal/about/index_en.cfm> (last accessed 12 January 2012).

[54] <http://ec.europa.eu/social/main.jsp?langId=en&catId=987> (last accessed 12 January 2012). EP and Council Dec. 1672/2006/EC establishing a programme for Employment and Social Solidarity (OJ [2006] L315/1), as amended.

[55] <http://ec.europa.eu/comm/employment_social/gender_equality/gender_mainstreaming/general_overview_en.html> (this website has now been removed). See The Equal Guide on Gender Mainstreaming:

equality between women and men. It means assessing how policies impact on the life and position of both women and men—and taking responsibility to re-address them if necessary.

The mainstreaming agenda spans issues as diverse as gender balance in decision making,[56] women and science,[57] development co-operation,[58] and gender-based violence and trafficking in women.[59]

The importance of mainstreaming was emphasized in the Commission's Framework Strategy on Gender Equality (2001–2005)[60] and Article 29 of the Sex Equality Directive 2006/54. As the Commission explained, this integrated approach marks an important change from previous Union action, mainly based on compartmental activities and pro-grammes funded under different specific budget headings. The Framework Strategy aims at 'coordinating all the different initiatives and programmes under a single umbrella built around clear assessment criteria, monitoring tools, the setting of benchmarks, gender proofing, and evaluation'.[61] Thus, OMC techniques—together with the hallmark proliferation of declaratory documents—are now being applied to gender equality.[62] The Framework Strategy was followed by the European Pact for Gender Equality of 2006[63] which in turn was supported by the Roadmap for Equality (2006–2010) between women and men.[64] The Roadmap identified six priority areas for action:

- Achieving equal economic independence for women and men.

- Enhancing reconciliation of work, private, and family life.

- Promoting equal participation of men and women in decision making.

<http://ec.europa.eu/employment_social/equal/data/document/gendermain_en.pdf> (last accessed 12 January 2012); DG Empl's *Manual on Gender Mainstreaming* (2008) and for more detailed discussion, see F. Beveridge and S. Velluti (eds.), *Gender and the Open Method of Coordination: Perspectives on Law, Governance and Equality in the EU* (Ashgate, Aldershot, 2008).

[56] According to the Commission, just one in four MPs and government ministers is a woman. In business, women represent only one in ten board members of the largest publicly listed companies and 3 per cent of presidents of boards: COM(2010) 491, 7, and *Women in Economic Decision making in the EU* (OPEC, Luxembourg, 2012). See, e.g., Commission Dec. relating to Gender Balance within the Committees and Expert Groups (OJ [2000] L154/34).

[57] Council Res. of 27 November 2003 on equal access to and participation of women and men in the knowledge society for growth and innovation (OJ [2003] C317/6).

[58] See, in particular, Co. Reg. (EC) No. 2836/98 on integrating gender issues in development cooperation (OJ [1998] L354/5) and EP and Co. Reg. 806/2004 on promoting gender equality in development co-operation (OJ [2004] L143/40) together with the Commission's Communication (COM(2001) 295).

[59] See, e.g., Council Res. on initiatives to combat trafficking in human beings, in particular women (OJ [2003] C260/4) and Council Framework Dec. 2002/629/JHA (OJ [2002] L203/1) on combating trafficking in human beings. See further <http://ec.europa.eu/justice/gender-equality/document/index_en.htm#h2-6> (last accessed 12 January 2011).

[60] COM(2000) 335 implemented by Council Dec. 2001/51 (OJ [2001] L17/22). The Council Decision envisages intervention in five areas: economic life, equal participation and representation, social rights, civil life, and gender roles and stereotypes.

[61] COM(2000) 335, para. 2.1.

[62] See e.g., the annual reports from the Commission on equality between women and men such as COM(2006) 71. OMC is considered in detail in Ch. 3.

[63] European Council Conclusions March 2006, 7775/1/06 REV 1.

[64] COM(2006) 92.

- Eradicating gender-based violence and trafficking.
- Eliminating gender stereotypes in society.
- Promoting gender equality outside the EU.

This was subject to a mid-term review which concluded that although there had been significant progress, that progress was uneven, with particular difficulty encountered in implementing equality policy.[65] There followed a 'Women's Charter' adopted in commemoration of the 15th anniversary of the adoption of a Declaration and Platform for Action at the Beijing UN World Conference on women and on the 30th anniversary of the CEDAW Convention. This identified five principles of equality which were to underpin the Commission's term of office, principles which built on the priority areas for action identified in the 2006–10 Roadmap: equal economic independence (which considers question of childcare); equal pay for work of equal value; equality in decision making (while in 2005 the EU set the goal of having 25 per cent of leading positions in the public research sector filled by women, the target has now been generalized to having 25 per cent of women in top decision making positions); dignity, integrity, and an end to gender-based violence; and gender equality beyond the Union.[66] These principles were fleshed out by the Strategy for Equality between Men and Women (2010–2015) and were reinforced by the renewed European Pact for Gender Equality (2011–2020).[67]

These strategies and pacts are intended to feed into the EU2020 agenda.[68] In order to achieve the objectives of EU2020, 'the potential and the talent pool of women need to be used more extensively and more effectively'.[69] So under the heading 'equal economic independence' priority is given to employment (the female employment rate currently stands at 62.5 per cent and should be raised to 75 per cent by 2020[70]), education, closing gender gaps, and combating gender discrimination.

In this respect, the gender equality strategy dovetails with the European Employment Strategy (EES). The promotion of equal opportunities formed one of the four key pillars of the EES initiated in Luxembourg in November 1997.[71] Initially, the Guidelines under the equal opportunities pillar focused on specific measures to strengthen gender equality such as the need to tackle gender gaps, especially in respect of unemployment rates and, according to the 1999 Guidelines, pay inequalities. Other measures included helping to reconcile work and family life, particularly through policies on career breaks, parental leave, and part time work and adequate provision of good quality childcare, and facilitating return to work after a period of absence.[72] Subsequently, the 2001 Guidelines[73] placed

---

[65] COM(2008) 760 final.   [66] COM(2010) 78.

[67] <http://www.consilium.europa.eu/uedocs/cms_data/docs/pressdata/en/lsa/119628.pdf> (last accessed 11 January 2011).

[68] See further Ch. 3.   [69] COM(2010) 491, 3.   [70] COM(2010) 491, 4.

[71] See further Ch. 1.

[72] See, e.g., the original (1998) Employment Guidelines OJ [1998] C30/1. See further Ch. 9.

[73] Council Dec. 2001/63 (OJ [2001] L22/18). Gender mainstreaming had in fact been a feature of the Employment Guidelines since 1999 (OJ [1999] C69/2).

emphasis on a gender mainstreaming approach in implementing the Guidelines across all four pillars by developing and reinforcing consultative systems with gender equality bodies, applying procedures for gender impact assessment under each Guideline, and developing indicators to measure progress in gender equality in relation to each guideline. These ideas still resonate in the 2010 Employment Guidelines[74] (maintained for 2011[75]). Guideline 7, 'Increasing labour market participation and reducing structural unemployment', requires Member States to integrate flexicurity principles into their labour market policies with a view to increasing labour market participation, combating segmentation and gender inequality. The Guideline continues:

> [Member States] should promote active ageing, gender equality including equal pay, and the integration in the labour market of young people, people with disabilities, legal migrants and other vulnerable groups. Work-life balance policies with the provision of affordable care and innovation in the manner in which work is organised should be geared to raising employment rates, particularly among young people, older workers and women. Member States should also remove barriers to labour market entry for newcomers, promote self-employment [now supported by Directive 2010/41/EU on equal treatment for the self-employed], entrepreneurship and job creation in all areas including green employment and care and promote social innovation.

Guideline 10, 'Promoting social inclusion and combating poverty', emphasizes the need for extending employment opportunities 'with special attention to women', and requires Member States to put in place 'effective anti-discrimination measures'. This is what Fagan *et al.* criticize as the 'narrow and instrumental focus on gender equality in the EES which focuses on using anti-discrimination to raise the employment rate rather than seeing anti-discrimination legislation and its capacity to deliver equal opportunity'.[76]

Mainstreaming gender equality now enjoys Treaty support. Not only does Article 3(3), second paragraph TEU provide that the Union shall combat social exclusion and discrimination and promote social justice and protection of equality between men and women, but Article 8 TFEU also says that in all its activities, the EU shall aim to eliminate inequalities and to promote equality between men and women. These provisions were referred to in *Test Achats*[77] to buttress the conclusion that the principle of equality is a fundamental right, that action taken by the EU legislature has to contribute in a 'coherent manner to the achievement of the intended objective'[78] and so any derogation from the principle of equality has to be time limited.

While the pro-active model has much to commend it, it is of course dependent on the Union institutions and the Member States actually being pro-active rather than merely talking about being pro-active. As Pollack and Hafner-Burton show,[79] the success of

---

[74] Decision 2010/707/EU (OJ [2010] L138/57).

[75] Decision 2011/308/EU (OJ [2011] L138/56).

[76] 'The subordination of the gender equality objective: the National Reform Programme and "making work pay" policies' (2006) 37 *IRJ* 571.

[77] Case C–236/09 *Association Belge des Consommateurs Test-Achats ASBL and Others* v. *Conseil des ministres* [2011] ECR I–000, paras. 19–20 considered in detail later in this chapter.

[78] Para. 21.   [79] 'Mainstreaming Gender in the European Union' (2000) 7 *JEPP* 432.

gender mainstreaming in the EU has depended very much on the commitment of the various actors to its aims. Beveridge has shown that in fact there is little evidence that the shift towards mainstreaming is much reflected in the day-to-day routines of the DGs and services.[80] Sanctions are therefore necessary to ensure that, in the absence of voluntary compliance, remedies are available in default. So in practice, a combination of hard law and soft law is necessary, as Hervey advocates: '[W]here we seek to resolve complex social problems, such as inequality of women and men, a notion of "mixity" or "hybridity" of old governance [hard law equality Directives] and new governance [soft law resolutions and OMC techniques such as indicators and benchmarking] probably holds the key to the realization of our goals'.[81]

As lawyers, our task is to analyse the 'old governance' measures (principally Directives), but against a backcloth of an appreciation of the new governance agenda, and it is a consideration of these Directives that will predominantly form the subject-matter of the next five chapters.

(c) The Treaty of Amsterdam

The Treaty of Amsterdam explicitly introduced equality between men and women as one of the tasks of the Union (Article 3 TEU (ex 2 EC)) and one of its activities (Article 3 EC (now repealed)). The Lisbon Treaty identified 'equality' as one of the five values of the EU (Article 2 TEU). It also expanded the objectives of the EU in this field (Article 3(3) TEU, second paragraph considered above). In addition, the Amsterdam Treaty introduced a new article, Article 19 TFEU (ex 13 EC), allowing the Council to take action on various grounds including sex. The Amsterdam Treaty also amended the equal pay provision, Article 157 TFEU, for the first time since 1957. Article 157(1) TFEU extended the principle of equal pay for equal work to include 'work of equal value', thereby bringing the Treaty into line with the Court's case law.[82]

Further, the Treaty of Amsterdam introduced two new provisions into Article 157. First, Article 157(3) TFEU finally provided an express legal basis for the Council to adopt measures, in accordance with the ordinary legislative procedure, 'to ensure the application of the principle of equal opportunities and equal treatment of men and women in matters of employment and occupation, including the principle of equal pay for equal work or work of equal value'. Second, Article 157(4) TFEU allows Member States to adopt or maintain positive action measures for the under-represented sex in respect of professional careers.

The first measure adopted under Article 157(3) TFEU was the Equal Treatment Directive 2002/73[83] amending the Equal Treatment Directive 76/207.[84] This Directive

---

[80] F. Beveridge, 'Building against the Past: the Impact of Mainstreaming on EU Gender Law and Policy' (2007) 32 *ELRev.* 193, 211.

[81] 'Thirty Years of EU Sex Equality Law: Looking Backwards, Looking Forwards' (2005) 12 *MJ* 307, 322.

[82] Art. 1 of Dir. 75/117/EEC already made provision for this. In Case 96/80 *Jenkins* v. *Kingsgate* [1981] ECR 911 the Court said that Art. 1 'is principally designed to facilitate the practical application of the principle of equal pay outlined in [what was then] Article 119 of the [EEC] Treaty [and] in no way alters the content or scope of that principle as defined in the Treaty'.

[83] OJ [2002] L269/15.

[84] The Sex Equality Directive 2006/54 was also adopted under this legal basis.

was introduced to ensure coherence of key principles in the field of sex discrimination with the Article 19 Directives (see later in this chapter) and to incorporate some of the decisions of the Court. Most significantly, in its proposal for the 2002 Directive, the Commission noted that the 'provision for equal opportunities in the framework of the Treaty has been greatly enhanced since the entry into force of the Treaty of Amsterdam'.[85] The Commission continued:

> Originally regarded as a means of preventing distortion of competition, equal treatment between men and women is now an explicit objective of the [Union] enshrined in Article [3(3) TEU]…These Treaty developments constitute an explicit embodiment of the Court's statement that the elimination of discrimination based on sex forms part of fundamental rights.

In 2004 the Council adopted, under Article 19 TFEU, Directive 2004/113 which, following the pattern of the Race Directive 2000/43, extended the principle of equal treatment between men and women to access to and supply of goods and services.[86] A Directive is currently proposed to do the same for religion, belief, disability, age, and sexual orientation.[87]

(d) Institutional support

Institutional support for the realization of sex equality has also been provided: for example, there are special committees concerned with women's issues in the European Parliament, including: the Committee on Women's Rights and Gender Equality; an 'Equality between men and women' Unit within DGEmpl of the European Commission but under the responsibility of the Commissioner for Justice, Fundamental Rights and Citizenship; and an Advisory Committee on Equal Opportunities for men and women which assists the Commission in formulating and implementing the EU activities aimed at promoting equality between men and women.[88]

In addition, the Inter-Service Group on Gender Equality brings together representatives of all Commission services to develop gender mainstreaming activities. There is also a high level group on gender mainstreaming which is an informal group of representatives responsible for gender mainstreaming at national level in the Member States. This meets to exchange information on best practices and experience 'to support and improve the synergy among national policies on gender equality and strategies for mainstreaming at national level'.[89] At its instigation, the Commission adopted a communication on incorporating equal opportunities for women and men into all Union policies and activities.[90] However, perhaps the most

---

[85] Para. 7.   [86] OJ [2004] L373/37.   [87] COM(2008) 426.

[88] Established by Commission Decision 82/43/EEC (OJ [1982] L20/35), as amended by Decision 95/420/EEC (OJ [1995] 249/43). See <http://ec.europa.eu/justice/gender-equality/other-institutions/advisory-comittee/index_en.htm> (last accessed 11 January 2012).

[89] <http://ec.europa.eu/justice/gender-equality/other-institutions/gender-mainstreaming/index_en.htm> (last accessed 11 January 2011).

[90] COM(96) 67 and the Commission's Progress Report COM(98) 122. The Commission has also begun to put its own house in order: Commission Decision 2000/407/EC (OJ [2000] L154/34) relating to gender balance within the committees and expert groups established by it.

visible demonstration of institutional commitment to achieving sex equality is the establishment in Vilnius of a European Institute for Gender Equality whose task is to review all existing EU gender equality law, increase awareness of gender inequality, facilitate an exchange of good practice, and ensure that gender equality is considered in all policies.[91]

2. EQUALITY IN OTHER FIELDS

2.1. The Race and the Horizontal Directives

The EU institutions had long been concerned about discrimination on grounds other than sex, especially racism and xenophobia, but doubted the Union's competence to act. The position changed with the inclusion of Article 19 TFEU by the Treaty of Amsterdam which provides:

> Without prejudice to the other provisions of the Treaties and within the limits of the powers conferred by them upon the Union, the Council, acting unanimously in accordance with a special legislative procedure and after obtaining the consent of the European Parliament, may take appropriate action to combat discrimination based on sex, racial or ethnic origin, religion or belief, disability, age or sexual orientation.

Article 19 TFEU can be compared with Article 21(1) of the Charter which contains a specific, but non-exhaustive, list of the grounds of discrimination which are prohibited including 'sex, race, colour, ethnic or social origin, genetic features, language, religion or belief, political or any other opinion, membership of a national minority, property, birth, disability, age or sexual orientation'. However, while Article 19 TFEU provides the legal power for the Union to act, Article 21(1) of the Charter has a different function: it addresses discrimination by the institutions and bodies of the Union themselves, and by Member States when they are implementing Union law.

Until Article 19 TFEU was included in the Treaty, the EU institutions had limited their activities to issuing non legally binding declarations and resolutions.[92] In addition, the European Union Monitoring Centre on Racism and Xenophobia (EUMC) was set up, now replaced by the Fundamental Rights Agency.[93] Thus, unlike gender equality where hard law preceded soft, in the context of race much soft law work had been done, preparing the ground prior to the adoption of the (hard law) Directive

[91] EP and Council Reg. 1922/2006 on establishing a European Institute for Gender Equality (OJ [2006] L403/9).
[92] For a full list see Annex II of the Commission's Communication on certain Community measures to combat discrimination (COM(99) 564). See further C. Gearty, 'The Internal and External "Other" in the Union Legal Order: Racism, Religious Intolerance and Xenophobia in Europe' in Alston (ed.), *The EU and Human Rights* (OUP, Oxford, 1999). Some anti-racism provisions have been included in other legally binding instruments. For example, Art. 9(1)(c)(ii) of Dir. 2010/13/EU (OJ [2010] L95/1) provides that audiovisual commercial communications must not include any discrimination on grounds of race, sex, or nationality nor offend any religious or political beliefs, and Art. 6 provides that Member States shall ensure that audiovisual media services do not contain any incitement to hatred based on race, sex, religion, or nationality.
[93] Council Reg. 168/2007 (OJ [2007] L53/1). See n. 116.

2000/43[94] under Article 19 TFEU.[95] As the Commission noted in its explanatory memorandum:[96]

> It is widely acknowledged that legal measures are of paramount importance for combating racism and intolerance. The law not only protects victims and gives them a remedy, but also demonstrates society's firm opposition to racism and the genuine commitment of the authorities to curb discrimination. The enforcement of anti-racist laws can have a significant effect on the shaping of attitudes.

The Directive lays down 'broad objectives to ensure that discrimination is prohibited and that the victims of discrimination enjoy a basic minimum entitlement to redress'. In so doing the Directive aims to reinforce the 'fundamental values on which the Union in founded—liberty, democracy, the respect for human rights and fundamental freedoms and the rule of law—and contribute to the development of the Union as an area of freedom, security and justice. And it will help to strengthen economic and social cohesion'.[97]

Close on the heels of the Race Directive, the Union adopted the 'horizontal' or 'framework' labour market Directive 2000/78[98] prohibiting discrimination on all the other grounds listed in Article 19 TFEU except sex; and a Communication on certain Union measures to combat discrimination.[99] As part of the launch for a 'Renewed Social Agenda' in 2008 the Commission adopted another Communication, *Non-discrimination and equal opportunities: A renewed commitment*.[100] The striking feature of this document was its recognition that there are differences between the protected strands, which make a tailored response necessary.[101] In this regard age and disability are singled out. This has led to a proposal for a European Accessibility Act[102] as part of the European Disability Strategy 2010–2020,[103] containing measures to improve the accessibility of goods and services in the European market. In addition, the needs of the Roma have now also been identified as requiring serious attention following the high profile criticism

---

[94] OJ [2000] L180/22. The Tampere European Council (October 1999) urged the Commission to bring forward proposals for a Race Directive under Art. 19 TFEU, in part due to concern about the rise of the far right in countries such as Austria (S. Douglas-Scott, *Constitutional Law of the European Union* (Longman, Harlow, 2002) 435) and in part because of concerns about levels of discrimination in some of the Accession states, especially in respect of the Roma.

[95] Art. 19(1) TFEU provides for the special legislative procedure. A new paragraph was added at Nice to allow for incentive measures to be adopted under the ordinary legislative procedure but excluding any harmonization of the Member States' legislation.

[96] COM(99) 566, 2.   [97] COM(99) 566, 4.

[98] Council Dir. 2000/78/EC (OJ [2000] L303/16).

[99] COM(99) 564. In the same package there was also an Action Plan to combat discrimination 2001–2006 (which became Decision 2000/750 (OJ [2000] L303/23)). There followed a framework strategy against discrimination in 2005.

[100] COM(2008) 420.   [101] Ibid., 6.

[102] <http://ec.europa.eu/justice/newsroom/discrimination/opinion/111207_en.htm> (last accessed 12 January 2012). See additionally L. Waddington, 'A Disabled Market: Free Movement of Goods and Services in the EU and Disability Accessibility' (2009) 15 *ELJ* 575.

[103] COM(2010) 636.

of France for its policy towards deporting the Roma.[104] This has led to an EU framework for national Roma integration strategies by 2020.[105]

2.2. The scope of the Directives

The Framework Directive prohibited discrimination on wide grounds (sexual orientation, religion or belief, disability, and age) but in narrow circumstances (matters relating to employment and vocational training). By contrast the Race Directive prohibited discrimination on narrow grounds (race and ethnic origin but not colour or nationality) but in broad circumstances (employment, vocational training as well as social protection, including social security and healthcare, social advantages, education, access to and supply of goods and services which are available to the public, including housing). However, both Directives share, with the sex equality Directives, a symmetrical approach to equality. Thus homosexuals must be treated in the same way as heterosexuals and vice versa. This means that more favourable treatment of the disadvantaged group will always breach the principle of equality. The exception to the rule of symmetry is disability: disabled persons can demand equal treatment with non-disabled but not vice versa and, in this way, the non-disabled cannot complain of more favourable treatment enjoyed by the disabled. As Ellis puts it,[106] this formulation can be seen 'to reflect a different underlying philosophy for the disability provisions from the rest of anti-discrimination legislation; they are more clearly directed to relieving the disadvantage experienced by the disabled section of society than to protecting a fundamental human right possessed by everyone'.

2.3. A common approach: Social inclusion

The two Article 19 Directives, like the sex equality Directives, broadly adopt the classic, human rights model to combating discrimination: individual and rights based.[107] However, as with sex discrimination, the legislative approach is complemented by an action plan[108] which envisages action under three strands: analysis and evaluation, capacity building, and awareness raising.[109] In addition, the weight of the EES has also been deployed to combat discrimination.[110] Thus, those who are socially excluded, especially the disabled, older workers, and ethnic minorities, can become included through employment because 'employment is the best guarantee against social exclusion',[111] and

---

[104] M. Dawson and E. Muir, 'Individual, Institutional and Collective Vigilance in Protecting Fundamental Rights in the EU: Lessons from the Roma' (2011) 48 *CMLRev*. 751. See further Commission, *The social and economic integration of the Roma in Europe*, COM(2010) 133.

[105] COM(2011) 173.   [106] At n. 2, 91.

[107] This is recognized by the Commission, 'Equality and non-discrimination in an enlarged European Union' (COM(2004) 379, 6).

[108] Co. Dec. 2000/750 (OJ [2000] L303/23). See G. de Búrca, 'EU Race Discrimination Law: a Hybrid Model' in G. de Búrca and J. Scott (eds.), *Law and New Governance in the EU and US* (Hart Publishing, Oxford, 2006).

[109] On the future of this approach, see Commission Green Paper, *Equality and Non-discrimination in an enlarged European Union*, COM(2004) 379.

[110] M. Bell, 'Combating Racial Discrimination through the Employment Strategy' (2003–4) 6 *CYELS* 55.

[111] Barcelona European Council, Presidency Conclusions, Bull. EU 3/2001, para. 22. See additionally Case C–54/07 *Centrum voor gelijkheid van kansen en voor racismebestrijding* v. *Firma Feryn NV* [2008] ECR I–5187, paras. 23–4.

the Article 19 Directives provide those excluded with a vehicle to challenge that exclusion. The link between social exclusion and employment policy was expressly noted in the Preambles to the Article 19 Directives. The Race Directive refers to the 2000 Employment Guidelines which 'stress the need to foster conditions for a socially inclusive labour market by formulating a coherent set of policies aimed at combating discrimination against groups such as ethnic minorities'[112] while the Framework Directive adds: 'Employment and occupation are key elements in guaranteeing equal opportunities for all and contribute strongly to the full participation of citizens in economic, cultural and social life and to realising their potential.'[113]

2.4. Institutional support

Institutional support for the elimination of discrimination is provided at a number of levels. For example, the Race Directive, like the Sex Directive 2002/73 (but not the horizontal Directive), requires Member States to designate a body or bodies for the promotion of equal treatment.[114] At Union level there is an anti-discrimination unit in DGEmpl but under the responsibility of DG Justice which has regular contact with civil society and the NGOs.[115] In particular, under the PROGRESS Programme, the Commission itself funds five European umbrella NGO networks representing and defending the rights of people exposed to discrimination—one per ground of discrimination: AGE (The European Older People's Platform); ILGA Europe (International Lesbian and Gay Association—Europe); ENAR (European Network Against Racism); EDF (European Disability Forum); and ERIO (European Roma Information Office). The European Parliament has a committee on civil liberties, justice and home affairs which deals with all issues of discrimination on grounds other than sex.

The Union's work is supported by the establishment of an EU Agency for Fundamental Rights,[116] albeit that its powers are limited to collecting evidence about the situation of fundamental rights across the EU and providing advice. It does not have a campaigning role, and, unlike some of its counterparts in the Member States such as the British Equality and Human Rights Commission (EHRC), it cannot fund legal cases. There are also four European networks active in the field of anti-discrimination: the government expert group which examines the impact of national and EU level non-discrimination measures and validates good practice through peer learning; the network of socio-economic experts which supports the sharing of good practice between members of the government expert group; the network of legal experts providing independent information and advice mainly on national law developments; and a network of equality bodies, Equinet.[117]

---

[112] 8th Preambular para. of Dir. 2000/43. See further the 8th Preambular para. of Dir. 2000/78.
[113] 9th Preambular para.   [114] Art. 13.
[115] <http://ec.europa.eu/social/main.jsp?catId=330&langId=en> (last accessed 11 January 2011).
[116] <http://fra.europa.eu/fraWebsite/home/home_en.htm> (last accessed 12 January 2012).
[117] <http://ec.europa.eu/justice/discrimination/experts/index_en.htm> (last accessed 11 January 2012).

C. THE CONSTITUTIONAL USE OF THE EQUALITY PRINCIPLE IN EU LAW

1. INTRODUCTION

It is clear that the attainment of the principle of equality has a central role to play in the EU. But what is actually meant by 'equality'?[118] This question has been debated for millennia. Aristotle famously explained, albeit in the context of a very different, highly stratified society, that '[e]quality in morals' meant 'things that are alike should be treated alike',[119] an understanding often described as formal equality. But who is alike? The very nature of human beings is that they are all unique—and different. It is a moral judgment as to who is alike. This leads Westen to conclude that the concept of equality is tautological. He says equality 'tells us to treat like people alike; but when we ask who "like people" are, we are told they are "people who should be treated alike"'. He therefore argues that equality is an empty vessel with no substantive moral content of its own. Without moral standards, equality remains meaningless, 'a formula that has nothing to say about how we should act'.[120]

Since equality provides no internal guidance as to the relevance of particular characteristics of individuals or groups, the principle of non-discrimination helps to fill this vacuum. At Union level this can be seen in Article 157 TFEU which provides for 'Equal pay without discrimination on the grounds of sex'.[121] The original Article 2(1) of Directive 76/207 said that the 'principle of equal treatment' means 'there shall be no discrimination whatsoever on grounds of sex either directly or indirectly'. Thus, it is the legislature which has defined the principle of non-discrimination, prohibiting, as Article 2(1) and now Article 14(1) of the Sex Equality Directive 2006/14 make clear, both direct and indirect discrimination. Further, it is the legislature, and not the court, which has taken the policy decision and identified which people should be treated alike. In Section D below we shall examine the meaning of the terms direct and indirect discrimination as well as considering the values underpinning the Union's approach to equality. This is the programmatic use of the equality principle as manifested through the principle of non-discrimination. There is however an additional—and increasingly important use of equality—as a general principle of law. In this 'Constitutional' context, the Court takes the view that equality requires consistent treatment ('equality as consistency')—or in the Aristotelian formulation 'like must be

---

[118] This section draws on C. Barnard, 'The Principle of Equality in the Community Context. *P, Grant, Kalanke* and *Marschall*: Four Uneasy Bedfellows?' (1998) 57 *CLJ* 352.

[119] Aristotle, *Ethica Nicomachea* V.3.1131a–1131b (Ross, trans., 1925), cited in P. Westen, 'The Empty Idea of Equality' (1982) 95 *Harvard Law Review* 537, 543.

[120] Westen, above, n. 119, 547. Cf. A. Somek, 'A Constitution for Anti-discrimination: Exploring the Vanguard Moment of Community Law' (1999) 5 *ELJ* 243 and A. Somek, *Engineering Equality: An Essay on European Anti-discrimination Law* (Oxford, OUP, 2011).

[121] Art. 1 of Dir. 75/117 explains that the principle of equal pay outlined in Art. 157 TFEU means 'the elimination of all discrimination on grounds of sex'.

treated with like'.[122] Equality in this context is shorn of the detailed elaboration of the principles of direct and indirect discrimination which seem to apply only to the programmatic field.

2. EQUALITY AS A GENERAL PRINCIPLE OF LAW

As we have already seen, since *Defrenne (No. 3)* the Court has recognized equality as a general principle of law.[123] In developing general principles of law the Court has often drawn inspiration from the European Convention on Human Rights. Article 14 ECHR contains a non-exhaustive list of grounds on which discrimination is prohibited. It provides:

> The enjoyment of the rights and freedoms set forth in this Convention shall be secured without discrimination on any ground such as sex, race, colour, language, religion, political or other opinion, national or social origin, association with a national minority, property, birth or other status.

However, in fact, the case law of the ECHR has had less impact in the field of EU equality law than in respect of other areas of fundamental rights, partly because in the past, Article 14 has not been directly enforceable in its own right[124] (it needs to be read in conjunction with another Article in the Convention or its protocols);[125] partly because it can be invoked only in respect of state action; and partly because the EU's rules are consciously stricter than those applied by the European Court of Human Rights.[126]

The 'Constitutional' use of the general principle of equality (or non-discrimination) can be seen in four contexts: (1) as a ground for challenging the validity of Union acts of a general legislative nature as well as specific acts in respect of the EU's own staff; (2) as a value against which other Union measures are interpreted; (3) as a ground to challenge rules of the Member States when acting in the sphere of Union Law; and (4) as a freestanding principle to challenge national acts. We shall consider these situations in turn.

---

[122] See further C. McCrudden, 'Equality and Non-Discrimination' in D. Feldman, *English Public Law* (OUP, Oxford, 2004).

[123] See e.g. Case 152/84 *Marshall* v. *Southampton and South West Hampshire Area Health Authority (Teaching) (No. 1)* [1986] ECR 723, para. 36; Case 151/84 *Roberts* v. *Tate & Lyle Industries Ltd* [1986] ECR 703, para. 35, and Case C–132/92 *Birds Eye Walls Ltd* v. *Roberts* [1993] ECR I–5579, para. 17; Joined Cases C–270/97 and C–271/97 *Deutsche Post* [2000] ECR I–929, para. 57; Case C–25/01 *Rinke* v. *Ärztekammer Hamburg* [2003] ECR I–8349, para. 25. On the principle of equality more generally, see *Land Oberösterreich* v. *ČEZ as* [2009] ECR I–10265, paras. 88–90. See additionally C. Docksey, 'The Principle of Equality between Women and Men as a Fundamental Right Under Community Law' (1991) 20 *ILJ* 258 and T. Tridimas, *The General Principles of EU Law* (OUP, Oxford, 2006).

[124] *National Union of Belgian Police* v. *Belgium* [1979] 1 EHRR 578.

[125] Cf. Protocol 12, agreed and opened for signature by Member States of the Council of Europe in November 2000 which, once signed by 10 states (this occurred in April 2005), establishes a free-standing right to equality on the same grounds as those set out in Art. 14. However, a number of large states, including the UK, have not signed or ratified the Protocol.

[126] See S. Fredman, 'Equality Issues' in B.S. Markesinis (ed.), *The Impact of the Human Rights Bill on English Law* (OUP, Oxford, 1998) 111–32, 115–18.

3. THE USE OF THE PRINCIPLE OF EQUALITY
TO CHALLENGE THE VALIDITY OF UNION ACTS

General principles of law can be invoked to challenge the validity of Union legislative acts on the ground that they breach the principle of equality. In this context, the principle of equal treatment requires that comparable situations must not be treated differently and that different situations must not be treated in the same way unless such treatment is objectively justified.[127] Usually, the Court finds that the two situations are not comparable, or that the differences can be objectively justified. Therefore, in the *Alliance* case[128] the Court found that the distinction drawn by the challenged Directive between (1) those substances which had already been approved when the Directive was adopted which were automatically added to the positive list, and (2) those which had not already been approved which had to go through an onerous approval process, did not breach the principle of equality because the two situations were not comparable.

This use of the equality principle to challenge the validity of Union acts has now been reinforced by the coming into force of the Charter, as *Test-Achats*[129] demonstrates. The case concerned Directive 2004/113 on equal treatment between men and women in the access to and supply of goods and services. While Article 5(1) laid down the principle of equal treatment, Article 5(2) allowed Member States to derogate from that principle to allow sex based actuarial factors to be used to calculate insurance premiums. This derogation was challenged as being contrary to Articles 21 and 23 of the Charter. The Court agreed and said that because Article 5(2) enabled the Member States 'to maintain without temporal limitation an exemption from the rule of unisex premiums and benefits, this works against the achievement of the objective of equal treatment'.[130] The Court therefore ruled that the derogation was invalid from 21 December 2012, the date when the Member States had to review the use of the derogation.

Test–Achats was only the second case in which the Court struck down EU legislation as contrary to the Charter. It was met by a chorus of disapproval in those states, such as the UK, which have taken advantage of the derogation.[131] Yet the logic of the ruling is clear: sex-based actuarial factors are based on stereotypical assumptions which are incompatible with the case-by-case merit-based approach that should be taken to decision making.

Test–Achats also demonstrates how the general principle of equal treatment can mean non-discrimination on a prohibited ground. More commonly this use of the equality principle arises in the case of employees of the Union institutions challenging

---

[127] Joined Cases C–184/02 and C–223/02 *Spain and Finland* v. *Parliament and Council* [2004] ECR I–7789, para. 64.

[128] Joined Cases C–154/04 and C–155/04 *R* v. *Secretary of State for Health, ex parte Alliance for Natural Health* [2005] ECR I–6451, para. 116; Case C–221/09 *AJD Tuna Ltd* v. *Direttur tal-Agrikoltura u s-Sajd* [2011] ECR I–000.

[129] Case C–236/09 *Test-Achats* [2011] ECR I–000.   [130] Para. 32.

[131] See Commission Communication, *Guidelines on the application of Council Directive 2004/113/EC to insurance in the light of the judgment of the Court of Justice of the European Union in Case C-236/09* Test-Achats, C(2011) 9497.

EU rules and practices. Such claims have enjoyed mixed success. On the one hand, in *Razzouk and Beydoun*[132] the Court said the Union's staff regulations which distinguished between the treatment of widows and widowers for the purpose of a survivor's pension breached the principle of equal treatment on the grounds of sex.[133] On the other hand, in *Rinke*[134] the discrimination claim failed. At issue was the validity of two Directives on training for doctors which were challenged on the grounds that the provision requiring part-time training in general medicine to include a certain number of full-time training periods was indirectly discriminatory against women. The Court said that 'compliance with the prohibition of indirect discrimination on grounds of sex is a condition governing the legality of all measures adopted by the [Union] institutions'.[135] However, on the facts the Court found that the training requirements could be objectively justified and so were lawful.

In *Prais*,[136] another staff case, the Court appeared to recognize the right to freedom of religion under Article 9 ECHR but said that it was not absolute. This meant that while the Union institutions should avoid having recruitment tests on dates which might be unsuitable for religious reasons and seek to avoid fixing such dates for tests, fundamental rights did not impose on the Union institutions a duty to avoid a conflict with a religious requirement of which they had not previously been informed.[137] The Court adopted a similarly cautious approach in *D* v. *Council*,[138] a case concerning the EU's refusal to pay a household allowance, which would have been payable to a married employee, to a homosexual employee who was in a stable partnership registered under Swedish law. While the Court appeared to recognize that the principle of non-discrimination extended to sexual orientation,[139] it found that the principle had not been breached on the facts of the case. The Court said that the principle of equal treatment could apply only to persons in comparable situations, and so it was necessary to consider whether the situation of an official who had registered a partnership between persons of the same sex was comparable to that of a married official.[140] The Court then noted that because there was a wide range of laws in the Member States on recognition of partnerships between persons of the same sex or of the opposite sex and because of the absence of any general assimilation of marriage and other forms of statutory union,[141] the situation of an official who had registered a partnership in Sweden was not comparable, for the purposes of applying the Staff Regulations, to that of a married official.[142]

---

[132] Joined Cases 75 and 117/82 *Razzouk and Beydoun* v. *Commission* [1984] ECR 1509.

[133] Paras. 17–18. See further Case 212/74 *Airola* v. *Commission* [1975] ECR 221. For a successful challenge to an indirectly discriminatory measure, see Case 20/71 *Sabbatini* v. *European Parliament* [1972] ECR 345.

[134] Case C–25/01 *Rinke* v. *Ärztekammer Hamburg* [2003] ECR I–8349.

[135] Para. 28.   [136] Case 30/75 *Prais* v. *Council* [1976] ECR 1589.

[137] Para. 18.   [138] Case C–125/99P [2001] ECR I–4319.

[139] At para. 47 the Court said 'as regards infringement of the principle of equal treatment of officials irrespective of their sexual orientation, it is clear that it is not the sex of the partner which determines whether the household allowance is granted, but the legal nature of the ties between the official and the partner'.

[140] Para. 48.   [141] Para. 50.   [142] Para. 51.

These cases demonstrate that the Court of Justice's approach to the principle of equality is evolving and rather ad hoc. By contrast, the US Supreme Court has developed a sophisticated framework for analysing such cases, with strict scrutiny requiring a compelling state interest to be shown for measures which discriminate on the grounds of race, alien status (citizenship), national origin, and religion and political opinion; heightened scrutiny for discrimination on the grounds of sex and illegitimacy; and only rational basis review[143] for ordinary grounds of discrimination such as the distinction between the permitted activities of opthalmologists and opticians.[144]

4. EQUALITY AS A VEHICLE FOR INTERPRETATION

The second 'Constitutional' use of the equality principle is to interpret potentially ambiguous provisions of Union law. The significance of this can be seen in *P* v. *S.*[145] The case concerned the dismissal of a male to female transsexual on the grounds of her gender reassignment. The question referred to the Court of Justice was whether the word 'sex' in the phrase there should be 'no discrimination whatsoever on the grounds of sex' in the Equal Treatment Directive 76/207 was broad enough to include 'change of sex'. Drawing on the general principle of equality, the Court said that the Equal Treatment Directive was 'simply the expression, in the relevant field, of the principle of equality, which is one of the fundamental principles of [Union] law'.[146] This enabled the Court to conclude that the scope of the Directive could not be confined simply to discrimination based on the fact that a person is of one or other sex and so would also apply to discrimination based on gender reassignment.[147]

This was a quite remarkable decision.[148] It seems that a strong opinion on the part of the Advocate General was highly influential. He declared:

> I am well aware that I am asking the Court to make a 'courageous' decision. I am asking it to do so, however, in the profound conviction that what is at stake is a universal fundamental value, indelibly etched in modern legal traditions and in the constitutions of the more advanced countries: the irrelevance of a person's sex with regard to the rules regulating relations in society.... I consider that it would be a great pity to miss this opportunity of

---

[143] See *City of Cleburne, Texas* v. *Cleburne Living Center, Inc.* 473 US 432, 440: 'The general rule is that legislation is presumed to be valid, and will be sustained if the classification drawn by the statute is *rationally related to a legitimate state interest....* When social or economic legislation is at issue, the Equal Protection Clause allows the States wide latitude'.

[144] *Wiliamson* v. *Lee Optical of Oklahoma Inc* 348 US 483 (1955). The European Court of Human Rights has also adopted an approach which distinguishes between sensitive grounds such as sex, race, religion, nationality, and sexual orientation where differences in treatment by the state must be for 'very weighty reasons' and ordinary grounds which are easier to justify: Ellis, above n. 2, 321. See further the House of Lords' Decision in *R* v. *Secretary of State for Work and Pensions, ex parte Carson* [2005] UKHL 37.

[145] Case C–13/94 [1996] ECR I–2143. See further Case C-149/10 *Chatzi* v. *Ipourgos Ikonomikon* [2010] ECR I-000, paras. 63–75.   [146] Para. 17.   [147] Para. 20.

[148] See, in a similar vein, Case–C 391/09 *Wardyn* v. *Vilniaus miesto savivaldybės administracija* [2011] ECR I–000, para. 43 where the Court said that the fact that Dir. 200/43 is one of the general principles of EU law, as recognized in Art. 21 of the Charter, meant that the scope of that Directive cannot be defined restrictively.

leaving a mark of undeniable civil substance, by taking a decision which is bold but fair and legally correct, inasmuch as it is undeniably based on and consonant with the great value of equality.[149]

The guiding hand of the principle of equality—and another impassioned opinion by the Advocate General, this time Ruiz-Jarabo Colomer—seems also to have helped a transsexual couple in *KB*.[150] The case concerned a decision by the NHS Pensions Agency not to award a widower's pension to KB's transsexual partner on the grounds that they were not married. KB was a woman who lived with R. R had been born a woman but, following gender reassignment, had become a man. Under English law, a birth certificate could not be amended to reflect this change in gender. This meant that the couple could not marry under English law because the Matrimonial Causes Act 1973 required marriage to take place between a man and a woman; according to their birth certificates KB and R were both female. As a result, R was not entitled to a survivor's pension, should KB predecease R, because under the NHS pension scheme a survivor's pension could be paid only to a spouse and R was not—and could never be—a spouse.

The Court began by finding that there was no discrimination on the grounds of sex because, for the purposes of awarding the survivor's pension, it was irrelevant whether the claimant was a man or a woman.[151] However, the Court then changed tack.[152] It noted that there was inequality in treatment, not in respect of the right to the pension itself, but in respect of one of the conditions for the grant of that right: the capacity to marry.[153] As the Court explained, while a heterosexual couple always had the option of getting married (and thus benefiting from the survivor's pension), a couple such as KB and R, where one of the partners had undergone gender reassignment, could never marry. The Court of Justice then noted that the European Court of Human Rights had already condemned the UK for not allowing transsexuals to marry a person of the sex to which they once belonged.[154] This enabled the Court of Justice to conclude that British legislation which, in breach of the ECHR, prevented a couple such as KB and R from being able to marry and thus to benefit from part of KB's pay, had to be 'regarded as being, in principle, incompatible with the requirements of Article [157 TFEU]'.[155] However, the Court then added that since it was for the Member States to determine the conditions under which legal recognition was given to the change of gender of a person in R's situation, it was for the national court to decide whether a person in KB's situation could rely on Article 157 TFEU to gain recognition of her right to nominate her partner as a beneficiary of a survivor's pension.

---

[149] Para. 24.

[150] Case C-117/01 *KB* v. *National Health Service Pensions Agency* [2004] ECR I-541, AG's Opinion esp. paras. 79-80. See additionally Case C-423/04 *Richards* v. *Secretary of State for Work and Pensions* [2006] ECR I-3585.

[151] Para. 29.   [152] Para. 30.

[153] Ibid. Cf. Joined Cases C-122/99P and C-125/99P *D* v. *Council* [2001] ECR I-4319, para. 47, considered above, where the Court said '... as regards infringement of the principle of equal treatment of officials irrespective of their sexual orientation, it is clear that it is not the sex of the partner which determines whether the household allowance is granted, but the legal nature of ties between the official and the partner'.

[154] *Goodwin* v. *UK* (2002) 13 BHRC 120 and *I* v. *UK* [2002] 2 FCR 613.

[155] Para. 34.

5. THE USE OF THE PRINCIPLE OF EQUALITY
TO CHALLENGE THE ACTS OF THE MEMBER STATES
WHEN ACTING IN THE SPHERE OF UNION LAW

So far we have concentrated on the Court of Justice's approach to reviewing the validity of *Union* acts and interpreting of Union acts in the light of the principle of equality. However, the Court of Justice has not limited itself to using general principles in this way. It has also said that when *Member States* are acting within the sphere of Union law (i.e. when they are implementing Union law[156] and when they are derogating from Union law[157]), their actions must also be compatible with fundamental rights, including the principle of equality. That said, to date there has been no case where a Member State has been found to breach the equality principle in these circumstances. However, this possibility paved the way for the Court's decision in *Mangold* where the Court used the equality principle, or at least one aspect of it, to set aside national acts.

6. THE EU PRINCIPLE OF EQUALITY AS A FREE STANDING
GROUND OF CHALLENGE TO NATIONAL ACTS

Mangold[158] concerned the German law implementing the Fixed Term Work Directive 99/70.[159] According to this law, a fixed-term employment contract could be concluded only where there were objective grounds for so doing. However, until December 2006 (when the age discrimination provisions of the Horizontal Directive 2000/78 came into force) the need for objective justification did not apply to fixed term contracts for workers aged over 52. The Court of Justice upheld Mangold's challenge to this rule that it was discriminatory on the grounds of age. Even though the age discrimination provisions of the Directive had not yet come into force, the Court said the source of the principle of non-discrimination found in the Horizontal Directive was various international instruments and the constitutional traditions common in the Member States.[160] It continued: 'The principle of non-discrimination on grounds of age must thus be regarded as a general principle of [Union] law'[161] and the observance of this general principle could not be made conditional on the expiry of the transposition date of the Framework Directive.

Most striking of all, the Court indicated that this general principle of law could be invoked in the national courts. The Court said that:

> In those circumstances it is the responsibility of the national court, hearing a dispute involving the principle of non-discrimination in respect of age, to provide, in a case within its jurisdiction, the legal protection which individuals derive from the rules of [Union] law and to ensure that those rules are fully effective, setting aside any provision of national law which may conflict with that law.[162]

---

[156] Case 5/88 *Wachauf* [1989] ECR 2609, para. 19 and Case C–2/92 *Bostock* [1994] ECR I–995, para. 16.
[157] Case C–260/89 *ERT* [1991] ECR 2925.
[158] Case C–144/04 *Mangold* v. *Helm* [2005] ECR I–9981. Cf. Case C–212/04 *Adeneler* v. *ELOG* [2006] ECR I–6057.
[159] OJ [1999] L175/43.   [160] Para. 74.   [161] Para. 75.   [162] Para. 77.

Thus, national courts had to provide a genuine and effective remedy to enforce a general principle of Union law which applied in a horizontal situation.[163]

It would be fair to say that this ruling was greeted with consternation in many quarters[164] and was criticized by a number of Advocates General themselves.[165] In *Bartsch*[166] the Grand Chamber, on advice from the Advocate General, appeared to narrow the scope of *Mangold*. It said that in *Mangold* the age-discriminatory national rules were introduced when implementing another Directive (the Fixed Term Work Directive 1999/70/EC). As a result, those national rules fell within the scope of EU law and were thus subject to the application of general principles of Union law, including the prohibition of age discrimination. Thus, because there was an underlying Union measure, the *Mangold* principle applied. *A contrario*, and on the facts of *Bartsch*, in the absence of an underlying Union measure *Mangold* would not apply.

Thus, *Bartsch* was a useful attempt at reconciling *Mangold* with the orthodoxy but it was not to last. In the seminal decision of *Kücükdeveci* the Court reiterated *Mangold*. The case concerned German legislation under which periods of employment completed before the age of 25 were not taken into account for calculating the notice period. The claimant, who was 28, therefore could claim notice based on three years employment with her (private sector) employer but not the full 10 years she had actually been working. She argued that this was directly discriminatory on the grounds of age. The Court agreed. The problem was that the case arose in a horizontal situation, and unimplemented or incorrectly implemented Directives cannot have horizontal direct effect (the deadline for the implementation of the Directives had now expired), a point the Court confirmed in *Kücükdeveci*,[167] nor could the *Marleasing*[168] interpretation approach (sometimes referred to as indirect effect) be used on the facts of the case. The Court therefore said that:

> 50. It must be recalled here that ... Directive 2000/78 merely gives expression to, but does not lay down, the principle of equal treatment in employment and occupation, and that the principle of non-discrimination on grounds of age is a general principle of European Union law in that it constitutes a specific application of the general principle of equal treatment.
>
> 51. In those circumstances, it for the national court, hearing a dispute involving the principle of non-discrimination on grounds of age as given expression in Directive 2000/78, to provide, within the limits of its jurisdiction, the legal protection which individuals derive from European Union law and to ensure the full effectiveness of that law, disapplying if need be any provision of national legislation contrary to that principle.

---

[163] See additionally AG Tizzano's opinion, para. 99ff.

[164] See e.g. A. Dashwood, 'From *Van Duyn* to *Mangold* via *Marshall*: Reducing Direct Effect to Absurdity' (2006/07) 9 *CYELS* 81.

[165] E.g. Advocate General Geelhoed in Case C–13/05 *Chacón Navas* v. *Eurest Colectividades SA* [2006] ECR I–6467 and Advocate General Mazak in Case C–411/05 *Félix Palacios de la Villa* v. *Cortefiel Servicios SA* [2007] ECR I–8531.

[166] Case C–427/06 *Bartsch* v. *Bosch und Siemens Hausgeräte (BSH) Altersfürsorge GmbH* [2008] ECR I–7245.

[167] Paras. 45–6.   [168] Case C–106/89 [1990] ECR I–4135.

In other words, where a Directive embodies a general principle of law that general principle can be used to 'disapply' any conflicting provisions of national law. The broad reading of this is that general principles have horizontal direct effect even though provisions of unimplemented or incorrectly implemented Directives do not. This would lead to the paradoxical result that for reasons of legal certainty, unimplemented or incorrectly implemented Directives do not have horizontal direct effect, yet general principles of law (concepts which are themselves inherently uncertain) may have horizontal direct effect in the name of effectiveness. The narrower reading is that general principles are not being used as a sword (as in the case of direct effect) but as a shield (a view supported by paragraph 51 where the Court uses the language of 'disapplying' national law[169]); Whichever reading is adopted, the consequences (other than the damage to legal certainty) are perhaps less severe than might first have been thought. In *Kücükdeveci* the Court appeared to draw on the substance of the Directive to flesh out the meaning of the general principle; and so far the Court has applied its ruling only to two cases both involving the general principle of non-discrimination on the grounds of age.

D. NON-DISCRIMINATION ON PROHIBITED GROUNDS

1. INTRODUCTION

So far, we have focused on the 'Constitutional' use of equality as a general principle of law. In essence, it requires like situations to be treated with like unless there are objectively justified reasons why not. We turn now to consider the programmatic use of equality: how the law, specifically Directives, have fleshed out the equality principle in order to address specific long-standing entrenched inequalities between groups of persons (e.g. men/women, black/white, able-bodied/disabled). In this context, the law distinguishes between direct discrimination and indirect discrimination. These key terms will now be considered.

2. DIRECT DISCRIMINATION

Direct or 'overt' discrimination involves one prohibited group being treated less favourably than another. So for example in *Macarthys*[170] the woman received less pay than the man doing the same job. As Directive 2006/54 puts it, direct discrimination is where 'one person is treated less favourably on the grounds of sex than another is, has been or would be treated in a comparable situation'.[171] Equivalent rules apply in respect of the other strands. Thus, in order to claim direct discrimination the applicant needs to

---

[169] This, is reminiscent of the contested substitution/exclusion distinction which had been floated by some of the Advocates General in the early 2000s (see e.g. Advocate General Léger in Case C–287/98 *Linster* [2000] ECR I–6917, paras. 24–90.

[170] Case 129/79 *Macarthys* v. *Smith* [1980] ECR 1275.   [171] Art. 2(1)(a).

identify a comparator —actual or hypothetical—who has been treated more favourably. The issue of the choice of comparator is considered in more detail in Chapters 7 and 8.

The motive or intention to discriminate is not a necessary element of direct discrimination:[172] it is enough that that the adverse treatment is grounded upon, or caused by, a prohibited classification.[173] In English law this causation-based approach is reflected in the so-called 'but for' test recognized by the House of Lords in *James v. Eastleigh Borough Council*.[174] According to this test, 'but for' the person's sex/race, etc. they would have enjoyed the more favourable treatment experienced by the comparator. Directly discriminatory measures are unlawful unless they can be saved by an express derogation. No such derogations can be found in respect of Article 157 TFEU but express derogations are found in the Equal Treatment Directives (see Figure 6.1).

3. INDIRECT DISCRIMINATION

3.1. The definition of indirect discrimination

The notion of indirect discrimination is designed to target those measures which are discriminatory in *effect*. Talking in the context of sex discrimination, indirect discrimination arises when the application of a gender-neutral criterion or practice[175] in fact disadvantages a much higher percentage of women than men, unless that difference can be justified by objective factors unrelated to any discrimination on the grounds of sex.[176]

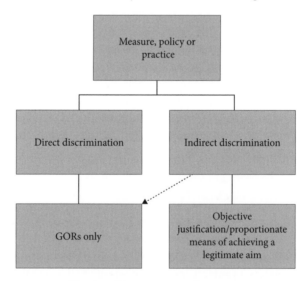

Fig. 6.1. Discrimination: Overview.

---

[172] Case 69/80 *Worringham* v. *Lloyds Bank* [1981] ECR 767. See further AG Lenz in Case C–127/92 *Enderby* [1993] ECR I–5535, 5558.

[173] Ellis, at n. 2, 103.   [174] [1990] 3 WLR 55.

[175] Case 170/84 *Bilka-Kaufhaus* [1986] ECR 1607; Case C–127/92 *Enderby* [1993] ECR I–5535.

[176] Case 171/88 *Rinner-Kühn* v. *FWW Spezial-Gebäudereinignung* [1989] ECR 2743.

The Court's approach to indirect discrimination is neatly summed up in *Kachelmann*[177] where it said:

> ...it is well settled that where national rules, although worded in neutral terms, work to the disadvantage of a much higher percentage of women than men, they discriminate indirectly against women, unless that difference in treatment is justified by objective factors unrelated to any discrimination on grounds of sex.

Thus, for a measure to be indirectly discriminatory *the Court* has required that (1) the apparently neutral rule or practice[178] (2) actually disadvantages (3) a considerably[179] higher percentage of women than men and (4) cannot be objectively justified by factors other than sex. The Court's approach has been used, but adapted, by the legislature. The first legislative definition was found in the Burden of Proof Directive 97/80[180] which provided that:

> ...indirect discrimination shall exist where an apparently neutral provision, criterion or practice *disadvantages a substantially higher proportion* of the members of one sex, unless that provision, criterion or practice is appropriate and necessary and can be justified by objective factors unrelated to sex.[181]

The reference to '*disadvantages a substantially higher proportion*' emphasized the need for some statistical analysis. By contrast, Article 2(1)(b) of the Sex Equality Directive 2006/54 and the 'Article 19' Directives offer a somewhat different formulation. They provide that in the case of indirect discrimination:

> ...an apparently neutral provision, criterion or practice *would put* persons of one sex at a *particular disadvantage* compared with persons of the other sex, unless that provision, criterion or practice is objectively justified by a legitimate aim, and the means of achieving that aim are appropriate and necessary.

There are three important points of difference in this definition. First, there is a shift from showing actual disparate impact (as required by the CJEU and the Burden of Proof Directive) to potential disparate impact ('would put'). Second, the emphasis on statistical analysis (as strongly required by the CJEU, less strongly by the Burden of Proof Directive) is reduced, if not removed altogether. Thirdly, the language of justification is differently formulated. For the purposes of this chapter, we shall work with the definition contained in the 'Article 19' Directives and Sex Equality Directive 2006/54 but with reference to the other definitions where appropriate.

3.2. 'Provision, criterion or practice'

The first requirement—that there be a provision, criterion or practice—is derived from *Enderby*[182] where the Court talked freely of 'measure' and 'practice' without distinguishing

---

[177] Cf. Case C–322/98 *Kachelmann* v. *Bankhaus Hermann Lampe KG* [2000] ECR I–7505, para. 23.
[178] Case C–127/92 *Enderby* v. *Frenchay Health Authority* [1993] ECR I–5535.
[179] Case C–236/98 *Jämställdhetsombudsmannen* v. *Örebro läns landsting* [2000] ECR I–2189, para. 50.
[180] OJ [1998] L14/6, amended by Directive 98/52/EC (OJ [1998] L205/66).
[181] Art. 2(2), emphasis added.   [182] Case C–127/92 [1993] ECR I–5535.

between the terms. The phrase is deliberately broad and catches both legal and non-legal requirements. Cases do not usually fail at this hurdle.[183]

3.3. '... would put persons of one sex at a particular disadvantage'

(a) Introduction

It will be recalled that the Sex Equality Directive 2006/54 and the Article 19 Directives define indirect discrimination in terms of the potential *disadvantage* experienced by the protected group, language which is derived from the test of indirect discrimination in the field of free movement of workers laid down in *O'Flynn*.[184] This compares with the requirement of 'substantially higher proportion' in the Burden of Proof Directive and 'considerably larger' or 'considerably smaller' used by the Court—both tests apparently requiring actual disparate impact. To what extent does this change of words make a difference?

First, the shift from actual to potential disparate impact recognizes that in some areas common sense would dictate that there may well be disparate impact but it is difficult to obtain statistical proof (particularly in those countries which prohibit the collection of data on sensitive issues such as race). Secondly—and related to the first point—the absence of references to 'significantly larger' or 'smaller' seems to rule out the mandatory use of statistics to show disparate impact. As the Commission says in its explanatory memorandum, the new test for indirect discrimination may be proven on the basis of statistical evidence or by any other means that demonstrate that a provision would be intrinsically disadvantageous for the person or persons concerned. This point is confirmed in the preamble to the Sex Directive 2002/73: '[National] rules may provide in particular for indirect discrimination to be established by *any means including* on the basis of statistical evidence'.[185] However, the new test does not altogether do away with the need to identify advantaged and disadvantaged groups and thus a need to construct a pool from which these groups are drawn. For this reason we shall now examine some of the older case law examining these requirements, but always bearing in mind that the new approach is intended to encourage national courts and the CJEU to take a more flexible approach.

(b) Selecting the pool

It is important to identify the group or groups of workers that are to be used for the purposes of comparing the treatment of men and women. Indirect discrimination is detected by showing that the impact of a practice on women—as a group—is greater

---

[183] See, e.g. in the UK context *British Airways* v. *Starmer* [2005] IRLR 863: an ad hoc decision of an employer constituted a provision, criterion or practice.

[184] Case C–237/94 *O'Flynn* v. *Adjudication Officer* [1996] ECR I–2617, para. 18, considered in Ch. 4, to which COM(99) 565 refers.

[185] Para. 10, emphasis added. This view is shared by the British government which says that 'Employment Tribunals will still need to consider whether a provision, criterion or practice causes disadvantage to a particular group of people. Statistics could be helpful in establishing evidence of particular disadvantage, although the new test makes clear that such evidence could also come from experts or other witnesses'. (*Equality and Diversity: Updating the Sex Discrimination Act*, para. 23). See additionally *Homer* v. *Chief Constable of West Yorkshire Police* [2012] UKSC 15, para. 14.

than the effect on men. It is often critical to identify which groups of workers are to be used for that comparison. Generally, in the case of discrimination alleged against an *employer*, the pool is drawn from the undertaking where workers perform or performed comparable work.[186] However, when discriminatory *legislation* is at issue, then the pool is generally the workforce as a whole[187] or at least workers throughout the country satisfying the requirements of the particular rule. Thus, in *Allonby*[188] the Court was asked to consider whether the requirement of being an 'employee' (which as we saw in Chapter 4 is a narrower concept in English law than 'worker' as defined by Union law) engaged as a teacher in a specified category of educational institution (which included Allonby's college) in order to be a member of the Teachers' Superannuation Scheme (TSS) (a condition deriving from state rules) was indirectly discriminatory against women. The Court took as the pool teachers across the country who were workers within the meaning of Article 157(1) TFEU and who fulfilled all the conditions of membership of the pension scheme except that of being employed under a contract of employment.[189]

The choice of the pool is usually a matter for the national court or tribunal but it is an issue that has bedevilled indirect discrimination case law. The British case of *Rutherford*[190] provides a very good example of just how difficult it is to determine the correct pool. Rutherford, aged 67, was dismissed but he was prevented from bringing a claim for unfair dismissal/redundancy because the then British statute precluded claims brought by those over 65. This, he argued, was indirectly discriminatory against men (the case pre-dated age discrimination legislation which would have been the more natural claim). The Industrial Tribunal agreed and said that 8 per cent of men over 65 were economically active (in employment or available to work) which was considerably higher than the 3 per cent of women. However, the Employment Appeal Tribunal allowed the appeal on the basis that a 5 per cent difference was not considerably higher and remitted the case to the tribunal. The Employment Tribunal took the new pool of those aged between 55 and 74 (i.e. those for whom retirement had real meaning) and concluded that the relevant measures disadvantaged a substantially higher proportion of men than women. However, the EAT again allowed the Secretary of State's appeal and said that the appropriate pool was those aged between 16 and 79 with one year's continuous service (the then requirement to bring a claim for unfair dismissal). In applying these statistics 98.88 per cent of men could comply as compared with 99.01 per cent of women. Therefore, there was no disparate impact. This approach was upheld by Court of Appeal. The House of Lords was also divided on this issue[191] and gave five different speeches from which it is not easy to extract 'a single easily stated principle'.[192] They did, however, all agree that there was no indirect discrimination, either because there was no discrimination at all or because the disparate impact was too small.

[186] See, e.g., Case C–256/01 *Allonby* v. *Accrington & Rosendale College* [2004] ECR I–873, para. 74.
[187] Case C–300/06 *Voß* v. *Land Berlin* [2007] ECR I-10573, para. 41.
[188] Case C–256/01 *Allonby* [2004] ECR I–873.   [189] Para. 75.
[190] *Secretary of State for Trade and Industry* v. *Rutherford (No. 2)* [2004] IRLR 892.
[191] [2006] UKHL 19.   [192] Lord Walker, para. 70.

This case demonstrates that, in widening the pool, Rutherford's claim was undermined because, while there were more men than women in the category of older workers, the proportions of the sexes in the workforce as a whole was almost identical. At the other end of the spectrum, if the pool is too small then this might also undermine the individual's claim. This can be seen in the controversial decision of the British Court of Appeal in *Coker* v. *Lord Chancellor*.[193] The Lord Chancellor appointed his friend, Gary Hart, a partner in a City law firm, to be his special adviser. The post was never advertised and it was accepted that the Lord Chancellor did not look outside his personal acquaintances for the appointment. Jane Coker, a solicitor, unsuccessfully complained of indirect discrimination. The Court of Appeal said that if a requirement excluded almost the entirety of the pool (on the facts, the members of the pool were reduced to a single man—Hart) it could not constitute indirect discrimination; it could only have a discriminatory effect if a significant proportion of the pool were able to satisfy the requirement. However, as Pannick points out, the principle of disparate impact is not intended to make individuals' rights dependent on the arbitrary factors of where they work, and the number of men and women who do particular jobs there.[194]

(c) Determining disparate impact

Once the pool has been established the Court then needs to determine whether the rule has a disparate impact on (i.e. puts at a particular disadvantage) the protected group. How can this be shown? Taking as our starting point *Seymour-Smith*[195] where, in a case concerning the issue of whether a two-year service requirement[196] prior to bringing a claim for unfair dismissal in the UK was indirectly discriminatory against women contrary to Article 157 TFEU, the parties presented the Court with four ways of considering the question of disparate impact[197] (the case arose before the new approach was adopted by the EU legislature in Article 2(1)(b) of the Sex Equality Directive 2006/54). The first was a rule-of-thumb of the kind adopted in the US Equal Employment Opportunity Commission (EEOC) Uniform Guidelines on Employee Selection Procedures.[198] These state that a selection rate for any race, sex, or ethnic group which is less than four-fifths (80 per cent) of the group with the highest rate will generally be regarded as evidence of adverse impact. Smaller differences in selection rates may nevertheless constitute adverse impact where they are 'significant' in both statistical and practical terms or where a user's actions have discouraged applicants disproportionately. This rule has the advantage of being relatively easy to apply.

---

[193] [2002] IRLR 80.   [194] *Sex Discrimination Law* (OUP, Oxford, 1985) 47.

[195] Case C–167/97 [1999] ECR I–623.

[196] The two-year service requirement was reduced to one year by SI 1999/1436, Unfair Dismissal and Statement of Reasons for Dismissal (Variation of Qualifying Period) Order 1999, and it was raised to two years again in April 2012.

[197] This is taken from C. Barnard and B. Hepple, 'Indirect discrimination: interpreting *Seymour-Smith*' (1999) 58 *CLJ* 399.

[198] *Federal Register*, Vol. 43, No. 166, 25 August 1978.

The second option was an impressionistic or 'eyeball' approach which asks, as the original British Sex Discrimination Act 1975 did, whether the difference in impact is 'considerable'. In *Seymour-Smith* the UK government argued for this approach, attaching to the word 'considerable' the meaning of a 'large disparity'. The advantage of this approach is that it does not rely solely on numbers, which may be an unreliable guide since they depend upon the size and male/female composition of the employer's workforce or (in the case of a legislative measure) the national labour force.

A third approach, for which the applicants argued in *Seymour-Smith*, is to ask whether there is an inherent risk that a measure adopted by a Member State will have a disparate impact as between men and women.[199] This approach has the advantage of allowing the tribunal to use its general knowledge and to look outside the pool for comparison to take account of social facts, such as the fact that 10 times as many women as men are likely to be single parents and responsible for a child. The language used in *O'Flynn* and in the Article 19 Directives, as well as Article 2(1)(b) of the Sex Equality Directive 2006/54, would support this approach.[200]

The fourth approach, for which the European Commission argued in *Seymour-Smith*, was to adopt a 'statistically significant' test, whereby a provision is indirectly discriminatory when it affects a significantly different number of members of one sex.[201] This test was said to enable the national court to determine whether a difference in impact is due to a mere chance or whether it reflects a social fact or structural phenomenon.

The Court did not consider the first of these options (the four-fifths rule), and failed to give any clear guidelines as to whether the second, third, or fourth options was to be preferred. Instead, the Court suggested that there were two ways of judging disparate impact. The first, found at paragraph 60, was to consider whether a 'considerably smaller proportion of women than men' was able to satisfy the two-year requirement (i.e. the second or third option).[202] It then went on to adopt a test of statistical significance (the fourth option).[203] It said that in 1985, the year in which the requirement of two years' employment was introduced, 77.4 per cent of men and 68.9 per cent of women fulfilled that condition.[204] According to the Court, such statistics did not appear, on the face of it, to show that a considerably smaller percentage of women than men was able to fulfil the requirement imposed by the disputed rule.[205] The Court seems to be equating

---

[199] [1999] IRLR 253, 258. This accords with the important decision of the Court of Appeal in *London Underground Ltd* v. *Edwards* [1998] IRLR 364 upholding a tribunal finding that a rostering system requiring an early morning start had an adverse impact on women with family responsibilities, even though only one of 21 women train drivers positively complained about the arrangements.

[200] See further Case C–25/01 *Rinke* v. *Ärztekammer Hamburg* [2003] ECR I–8349, para. 35 where, after considering the statistics produced, the Advocate General said: 'That fact [the percentage of women working part-time is much higher than that of men working on a part-time basis], which can be explained in particular by the unequal division of domestic tasks between women and men, shows that a much higher percentage of women than men wishing to train in general medicine have difficulties in working full-time during part of their training'.

[201] Para. 57.   [202] Para. 60.   [203] Para. 62.   [204] Para. 63.

[205] Para. 64. Cf. Case C–123/10 *Brachner* v. *Pensionsversicherungsanstalt* [2011] ECR I–000, para. 62 where a difference between 75 per cent of men entitled to a benefit as compared to 43 per cent of women represented a large enough disparity to constitute a significant indication capable of justifying the conclusion that the rule placed at a disadvantage a significantly higher percentage of men than women.

statistical significance with a 'considerable' difference, since, where the sample is relatively small, a difference of less than 10 per cent is insufficient to prove indirect sex discrimination.[206]

At paragraph 61 it then proposed a second, alternative test for disparate impact. It said that there would be evidence of apparent sex discrimination 'if the statistical evidence revealed a lesser but persistent and relatively constant disparity over a long period between men and women who satisfy the requirement of two years' employment'. So, where it is not possible to establish indirect discrimination when a snapshot is used (para. 60), it is possible to establish indirect discrimination using a longer time frame (para. 61). The Court did not have the evidence to propose an answer to the paragraph 61 test.[207]

What is clear from this decision is that the Court attached considerable weight to the need to produce statistics to show indirect discrimination. However, these statistics must be valid: i.e. they must cover enough individuals, they must not illustrate purely fortuitous or short-term phenomena, and must appear to be significant.[208] In *Jørgensen* the statistics failed to satisfy these requirements. The case concerned a reorganization of medical practices based on turnover which, Jørgensen argued, was indirectly discriminatory against women. The Court noted that the application affected only 22 specialized medical practitioners, of whom 14 were women, out of a total of 1,680, of whom 302 were women. The Court concluded that '[i]t seems doubtful that such data could be treated as significant'.[209]

Assuming the statistics are significant, what can they show? They can show how many people (the qualifiers) *can* comply with the requirement (the so-called 'success rates' approach) or how many people (the non-qualifiers) *cannot* comply with the requirement (the so-called 'failure rates' approach). The first focuses on the proportion of men and women who are able to benefit. The second considers the proportion of men and women within the group who cannot obtain the benefit to determine whether the proportion of women in the disadvantaged group is greater than the proportion of men and, in particular, whether the proportion of women in the disadvantaged group is higher than the proportion of women in the workforce generally, which might indicate that the practice does adversely affect women more than men.

The difference between these approaches was highlighted by Lord Nicholls in the House of Lords in *Barry* v. *Midland Bank*.[210] He took the example of an employer whose workforce of 1,000 employees comprised an equal number of men and women. In his example, 10 per cent of the staff (100 people) worked part time and of these 90 per cent were women. If the employer offered a pension or redundancy scheme that favoured full-time workers

---

[206] For criticisms of this approach see Barnard and Hepple, previously, at n. 197.

[207] When the case returned to the House of Lords the majority considered that the para. 61 test, but not the para. 60 test, had been satisfied. Therefore, there was evidence of indirect discrimination but that it was not unlawful because it could be objectively justified.

[208] Case C–226/98 *Jørgensen* v. *Foreningen af Speciallæger and Sygesikringens Forhandlingsudvalg* [2000] ECR I–2447, para. 33.

[209] Para. 33.   [210] [1999] IRLR 581.

would this be indirectly discriminatory? If the success rates question was asked (how many men and women can comply with the requirement to work full time?) the answer would be 98 per cent of men (490/500) and 82 per cent of women (410/500) could comply with the requirement. A difference of 16 per cent would probably satisfy the paragraph 60 test of whether a 'considerably smaller proportion of women than men' could satisfy the two-year requirement (although not the EEOC rule of thumb guidelines).

However, if the failure rates question was asked (how many men and women cannot satisfy the requirement of working full time?) the figures are much more stark: 2 per cent of men (10/500) compared with 18 per cent of women (90/500) would be disadvantaged, a ratio of 1:9. Putting it another way, of those who were non-qualifiers 10 per cent were men and 90 per cent were women. Some have argued that the language of 'disadvantage' used in the Burden of Proof Directive, the Sex Equality Directive 2006/54 and the Article 19 Directives favours the failure rates approach. However, such arguments have not found favour, with the British courts at least.[211]

In *Seymour-Smith* the Court seemed to accept an amalgam of the 'can' and 'cannot' comply tests (the success and the failure rates test). It said that the best approach to comparing statistics was to consider:

[o]n the one hand, the respective proportions of men in the workforce *able* to satisfy the requirement of two years' employment under the disputed rule and of those *unable* to do so, and on the other, to compare those proportions as regards women in the workforce.[212]

However, the later part of the judgment focused, especially in paragraph 60, on the success rates 'can' comply test.[213] More recently, the British House of Lords in *Rutherford* has also preferred the success rates test.

Seymour-Smith also considered the question of when the discrimination should be judged. The statistics in this case showed that over the period 1985 to 1993 the proportion of men and women who had two years' or more service with their current employer ranged for men, from a minimum of 72.5 per cent to a maximum of 78.4 per cent, and for women from a minimum of 63.8 per cent to a maximum of 74.1 per cent. Throughout the period 1985 to 1991 the ratio of the proportion of men qualified to the proportion of women qualified was about 10:9 reducing to about 20:19 in 1993. Therefore, the disparate impact appears to have diminished over time. This makes it crucial to determine the moment in time at which the disparate impact test is to be applied, not least because the objective justification which existed at one time may not exist at another. The Court failed to give an unequivocal answer to this question, preferring to throw it back to the national court, stating that 'the point in time at which the legality of a rule of the kind at issue in this case is to be assessed by the national court may depend on various circumstances, both factual and legal'.[214] It was suggested that if the legislator

---

[211] *Secretary of State for Trade and Industry* v. *Rutherford (No. 2)* [2003] IRLR 858 and [2004] IRLR 892; although cf. Lord Nicholls in the House of Lords [2006] UKHL 19.

[212] Para. 59 (emphasis added).

[213] See further Case C–236/98 *Örebro läns landsting* [2000] ECR I–2189, paras. 50–1.

[214] Para. 46.

was alleged to have acted *ultra vires* (as in these judicial review proceedings), then this was in principle the time when the rule was adopted[215] but in cases of application of the rule to an individual, it was the time of application which is relevant.

(d) Intention

In its earliest case law, the Court required discriminatory intention by the employer before the indirect discrimination was declared unlawful. For example, in *Jenkins*,[216] a case where part-time workers received a lower hourly rate than full time workers, the Court required national courts to look at the employer's intention[217] to see whether discrimination had occurred. Confining indirect discrimination to intentional acts only would have significantly limited its effectiveness. However, in *Bilka-Kaufhaus*[218] the Court recognized that the prohibition on discrimination also included *unintentional* indirect discrimination, that is, it covers those situations where the employer does not intend to discriminate but the effects of any policy are discriminatory.[219]

3.4. '…unless that provision, criterion or practice is justified by a legitimate aim, and the means of achieving that aim are appropriate and necessary'

(a) Indirect discrimination

As we saw in *Jämo*,[220] the Court of Justice has long recognized that indirect discrimination can be objectively justified on grounds other than sex. Thus, once it is established that the measure is indirectly discriminatory the burden shifts to the defendant to show that the measure is justified by objective factors unrelated to sex, and the steps taken are proportionate. If the measure can be objectively justified it avoids being classified as discriminatory.[221] The Court's approach was replicated in the Burden of Proof Directive which provided that indirectly discriminatory practices could be 'justified by objective factors unrelated to sex', provided that the practices were 'appropriate and necessary'.[222] The approach found in the Article 19 Directives and the Sex Equality Directive 2006/54, which requires the practice to be 'justified by a legitimate aim, and the means of achieving that aim are appropriate and necessary', follows the classic formulation in *Bilka-Kaufhaus*:[223] that the measures chosen must 'correspond to a real need on the part of the undertaking, are appropriate with a view to achieving the objectives pursued and

---

[215] Para. 47 and implicit in para. 63.   [216] Case 96/80 [1981] ECR 911.

[217] Para. 14. The employer, who had previously paid men and women at different rates, changed his system so that he paid part-time workers, the majority of whom were women, less than full-time workers. There was a concern that the employer had replaced a directly discriminatory system by an intentionally indirectly discriminatory system.

[218] Case 170/84 [1986] ECR 1607; Case 171/88 *Rinner-Kühn* [1989] ECR 2743.

[219] The culpability of the employer should be reflected in the remedy.

[220] Case C–236/98 *Jämställdhetsombudsmannen* v. *Örebro läns landsting* [2000] ECR I–2189, para. 50.

[221] Case C–356/09 *Pensionsversicherungsanstalt* v. *Kleist* [2010] ECR I–000, para. 41.

[222] Case 96/80 *Jenkins* [1981] ECR 911, para. 114. See T. Hervey, 'Justification of Indirect Sex Discrimination in Employment: European Community Law and United Kingdom Law Compared' (1991) 40 *ICLQ* 807 and *Justifications for Sex Discrimination in Employment* (Butterworths, London, 1993) Ch. 8.

[223] Case 170/84 [1986] ECR 1607, para. 36.

are necessary to that end'. The new approach drops the requirement that the justification must be 'on grounds other than sex', prompting some to suggest that a legitimate aim could be sex, race etc. related. Others argue that the strong trend in the case law that the justification must not be connected to the protected ground rules out any such suggestion.

Given the importance of objective justification, especially in the context of equal pay, it will be considered in more detail in the next chapter. However, there is one further issue that needs to be considered here: can *direct* discrimination be objectively justified?

(b) Can direct discrimination be justified?

As mentioned, the open–ended 'objective justification' applies only to *indirect* discrimination.[224] Can it ever apply to direct discrimination? The orthodox answer—found in the Sex Equality Directive 2006/54 and in the Race and Horizontal Directives in respect of all strands, except age—is no.[225] Direct discrimination can be saved only by reference to the derogations expressly provided for by the legislation.

However, as we shall see in Chapter 7, the absence of any such derogations in Article 157 TFEU has generated particular difficulties. For example, in *Roberts*[226] the employer paid a former male employee a bridging pension between the ages of 60 and 65 but did not pay the same to a former female employee who received the equivalent from the state, as she had a lower state pension age. The woman therefore received less pay from her employer than a man. Ostensibly she suffered direct discrimination but there were no derogations available for the employer. This prompted the Commission in *Roberts*[227] to follow the Continental view that direct discrimination could be objectively justified 'since the very concept of discrimination, whether direct or indirect, involves a difference in treatment which is unjustified'. The Advocate General, while noting that direct and indirect discrimination could not always be distinguished with clarity,[228] said that the Court had not ruled that direct discrimination could never be justified by objective factors,[229] making it arbitrary to permit the possibility of justifying a clear inequality of treatment dependent on whether that inequality was direct or indirect. On the other hand, in *Grant*[230] Advocate General Elmer reasserted the orthodox position: 'direct discrimination cannot be justified by reference to objective circumstances'.

---

[224] The detail of objective justification is considered below. Cf. Section C of Ch. 5.

[225] Case C–262/88 *Barber* [1990] ECR I–1889, para. 32, and Case C–177/88 *Dekker* v. *Stichting Vormingscentrum voor Junge Volwassen Plus* [1990] ECR I–3941, para. 12; Case C–356/09 *Kleist* [2010] ECR I–000, paras. 41–3.

[226] Case C–132/92 [1993] ECR I–5579. See further Ch. 10.

[227] Ibid.

[228] E.g. while *Roberts* looked like a case of direct discrimination, if emphasis were laid on the fact that the employer calculated the bridging pension in the same way but the result of such calculation was that for five years women receive a lower bridging pension, this constitutes indirect discrimination.

[229] See e.g. Case C–217/91 *Spain* v. *Commission* [1993] ECR I–3923, para. 37: 'The principle of equal treatment viewed as a general principle of [Union] law requires that similar situations shall not be treated differently and that different situations shall not be treated in the same manner unless such differentiation is objectively justified'.

[230] Case C–249/96 *Grant* v. *South West Trains* [1998] ECR I–621, para. 38.

Although the Court did not expressly rule on this point in *Roberts*, in *Smith*[231] it did contemplate taking objective justification into account in the context of not applying the equality principle to pension benefits payable immediately post the *Barber* judgment.[232] Similarly, in *Webb*[233] the Court ruled in the context of the Sex Equality Directive that the termination of a contract for an indefinite period on grounds of the woman's pregnancy, which constitutes direct discrimination '*cannot be justified* by the fact that she is prevented, on a purely temporary basis, from performing the work for which she has been engaged' (emphasis added). The implication of this statement is that termination of a fixed term contract on the grounds of pregnancy could be justified.[234]

Although subsequent case law has removed this possibility in respect of pregnancy,[235] it does mark a further stage in the erosion of the clear distinction between direct and indirect discrimination. Does this matter? For most commentators, the answer is yes because, as Deakin and Morris put it, the application of the equality principle would become highly contingent, being dependent, in effect, on the courts' assessment of the justification defence in individual cases.[236]

Ellis has argued that those advocating that direct discrimination can be objectively justified misunderstand the structural elements of discrimination. Since discrimination means detrimental treatment which is grounded on sex, it consists of two elements—harm (adverse treatment) and causation (the grounding of that treatment in a prohibited classification).[237] The concept of justification is used in relation to indirect discrimination, where the root cause of the detrimental treatment is not clear and the defendant is seeking to show that its cause is unrelated to sex. The Court recognized this point in *Jørgensen*:[238]

> Thus, once it is established that a measure adversely affects a much higher percentage of women than men, or vice versa, that measure will be presumed to constitute indirect discrimination on grounds of sex and it will be for the employer or the person who drafted the measure to prove the contrary.

Thus, if the adverse consequence to one group can be shown to be 'attributable to an acceptable and discrimination-neutral factor, then there is no discrimination'.[239] By contrast, in *direct* discrimination cases, where it is proved that the detrimental treatment is grounded upon the plaintiff's sex, cause has been established and there is no room to argue about justification.

---

[231] Case C–408/92 [1994] ECR I–4435.   [232] Paras. 30 and 31.

[233] Case C–32/93 *Webb* v. *EMO Air Cargo* [1994] ECR I–3567.

[234] The justification will not include the financial loss which an employer who appointed a pregnant woman would suffer during her maternity leave (Case C–207/98 *Mahlburg* [2000] ECR I–549, para. 29).

[235] Case C–109/00 *Tele Danmark A/S* v. *Kontorfunktionaerernes Forbund I Danmark* [2001] ECR I–6993.

[236] S. Deakin and G. Morris, *Labour Law* (Hart Publishing, Oxford, 2009) para. 6.30. See additionally J. Bowers and E. Moran, 'Justification in Direct Sex Discrimination Law: Breaking the Taboo' (2002) 31 *ILJ* 307 and the responses (2003) 32 *ILJ* 115 and (2003) 32 *ILJ* 185.

[237] Previously, at n. 2, 112.

[238] Case C–226/98 *Jørgensen* v. *Foreningen af Speciallæger and Sygesikringens Forhandlingsudvalg* [2000] ECR I–2447, para. 30.

[239] Ellis, previously, at n. 2, 112.

Ellis also makes the practical point that the introduction of a concept of justification into direct discrimination would have the effect of extending the range of defences available to the employer in an open-ended manner, contrary to the intention of the drafters of the legislation,[240] and would seriously undermine discrimination law as it now stands.

3.5. Conclusions

In the 1970s sex equality Directives, the principles of direct and indirect discrimination were the main pillars of protection for individuals. In the 'younger' Directives, the legislature deemed other conduct to be discriminatory including harassment and instructions to discriminate. The inclusion of these concepts, which are discussed in detail in the next two chapters, together with the prohibition of victimization and the duty of reasonable accommodation in respect of disability, is a reminder that equality law is not simply about formal equality but also about protecting a person's dignity at work. We shall now turn to consider the values underpinning Union equality law.

E. FORMAL AND SUBSTANTIVE EQUALITY

1. THE FORMAL EQUALITY MODEL

At one level, equality is about protecting the dignity and autonomy of the *individual*. This is perhaps the most prevalent view of equality: people should be treated according to their own merits and characteristics; irrelevant factors such as gender or race should not be taken into account. So decisions taken on the basis of stereotypes undermine a person's dignity and autonomy and thus the principle of equality.[241] This perspective most closely maps on to what is described as the formal equality model which requires, for example, women to be treated like men and those who belong to an ethnic minority to be treated in the same way as those who are white. In law, this perspective is embodied in the concept of direct discrimination. The strength of this approach is that it assumes that all people are equal and so should be paid the same and treated in the same way, irrespective of any dissimilarities they possess. As Ellis puts it, this is frequently referred to as the 'merit' principle: individuals ought to be rewarded according to their merit and not according to stereotypical assumptions made about them on account of the group to which they belong.[242]

This approach also exemplifies what Deakin and Morris describe as 'equality within the market order'. According to this concept, the principal aim is to do what is necessary to ensure free and equal competition in the labour market, while regulating outcomes in

---

[240] See E. Ellis, 'The Definition of Discrimination in European Community Sex Equality Law' (1994) 19 *ELRev*. 563.
[241] Values such as these did influence the Court of Justice in Case C–13/94 *P* v. *S* [1996] ECR I–2143, para. 22 where it said that to tolerate discrimination on the grounds of gender reassignment would be 'tantamount, as regards such a person, to a failure to respect the dignity and freedom to which he or she is entitled, and which the Court has a duty to safeguard'.
[242] Ellis, previously, at n. 2, 5.

terms of the distribution of economic and social resources as little as possible.[243] This approach is particularly resonant in the EU, with its origins in the creation of a common, now single, market.

There are three main criticisms of the formal equality approach. First, hidden behind the apparent neutrality is a reality which is white, straight, and male. For women, it disregards the context in which many find themselves, balancing work with domestic and caring responsibilities.[244] This results in decisions such as *Hofman*[245] where the Court made clear that the then Equal Treatment Directive 76/207 was not 'designed to settle questions concerning the organisation of the family or to alter the division of responsibility between parents'.[246] Similarly, in *Helmig*[247] the Court ruled that there was no discrimination when part-timers, who were predominantly women, did not receive overtime rates for hours worked over their normal contractual hours but less than the full-time hours, even though the social consequences for part-timers to work one hour's overtime was likely to be more disruptive than for full-timers.[248] These decisions serve to highlight the fact that while the Court will require non-discrimination in the world of work, it has been reluctant to look at the effects of its decisions in the domestic sphere. The creation of an artificial distinction between the world of work and the family further prejudices the many women who are not 'well-assimilated' to the male norm and denies them *de facto* equality.[249]

Second, the concept of formal equality embodies a notion of procedural justice which does not guarantee any particular outcome. So there is no violation of the principle if an employer treats white and black workers equally badly. A claim to equal treatment can be satisfied by depriving both the persons compared of a particular benefit (levelling down) as well as by conferring the benefit on them both (levelling up).[250]

[243] *Labour Law* (Hart Publishing, Oxford, 2009), 524–5.

[244] See further C. Mackinnon, *Feminism Unmodified—Discourses on Life and Law* (Harvard University Press, Cambridge, Mass., 1987) 32–45; C. Mackinnon, 'Reflections on Sex Equality under Law' (1991) 100 *Yale Law Journal* 1281. See generally G. Mancini and S. O'Leary, 'The New Frontiers of Sex Equality Law in the European Union' (1999) 24 *ELRev.* 331.

[245] Case 184/83 *Hofman* v. *Barmer Ersatzkasse* [1984] ECR 3047. See T. Hervey and J. Shaw, 'Women, Work and Care: Women's Dual Role and Double Burden in EC Sex Equality Law' (1998) 8 *Journal of European Social Policy Law* 43.

[246] See further Case 170/84 *Bilka-Kaufhaus* v. *Weber von Hartz* [1986] ECR 1607 where the Court stopped short of imposing a positive requirement on companies to organize their occupational pension schemes in such a way as to accommodate the needs of their employees, and Case C–297/93 *Grau-Hupka* v. *Stadtgemeinde Bremen* [1994] ECR I–5535 where the Court said that since Union law on equal treatment did not oblige Member States to take into account in calculating the statutory pension years spent bringing up children, the national rules also did not breach Art. 157 TFEU.

[247] Case C–399/92 *Stadt Lengerich* v. *Helmig* [1994] ECR I–5727. On the serious consequences of this decision, see the House of Lords' decision in *Barry* v. *Midland Bank* [1999] IRLR 581. However cf. Case C–285/02 *Elsner-Lakeberg* v. *Land Nordrhein-Westfalen* [2004] ECR I–5861.

[248] See M. Rubinstein [1995] IRLR 183. These cases are considered further in Ch. 9.

[249] See H. Cullen, 'The Subsidiary Woman' (1994) 16 *JSWL* 407, 408.

[250] E.g., Case C–408/92 *Smith* v. *Avdel* [1994] ECR I–4435 (raising of pension age for women to the same as that for men satisfies principle of equal treatment).

Third, the formal equality model is also dependent on a comparator: it is impossible for a woman to achieve equal pay for work of equal value if there is no male comparator in her establishment or an establishment of the same employer with common terms and conditions of employment.[251] Further, the choice of comparators can be determinative of the claim. So where a travel concession was denied to the lesbian partner of a female employee, in *Grant*, the CJEU made the comparison with the way in which the male partner of a gay employee would have been treated. Since the gay man would have been treated in the same way, there was no discrimination.[252] Had the comparator been a male employee with a female partner, she would have received the travel concession and this would have revealed a breach of the principle of equal treatment.[253]

The need for a comparator is particularly unrealistic when a male comparator has to be sought in claims of unequal treatment on grounds of pregnancy or childbirth.[254] Consequently the limited, formal notion of equality adopted by the law can assist only the minority who are able to conform to the male stereotype but cannot reach or correct underlying structural impediments.[255] Thus, as Fredman puts it, the formal equality model reinforces the liberal ideas of 'the primacy of the neutrality of law, the rights of the individual as individual, and the freedom of the market'.[256] Further, she argues, equal treatment of individuals who are not socially equal perpetuates inequalities.[257] This prompts some to advocate the need for steps to remedy *group* disadvantage.

2. THE SUBSTANTIVE EQUALITY MODEL

Women, ethnic minorities, homosexuals, and persons with disabilities have suffered from a history of *group* disadvantage which requires more radical, group-based action to remedy. Thus, unlike the individualist perspective where a person's sex/race, etc. is considered an *irrelevant* factor, the group-based disadvantage perspective considers these factors to be *relevant* and requires decisions to be taken based on the real situation of the protected group.[258] Some commentators describe this as 'substantive equality', one aimed at achieving equality of outcome or results.[259] Writing in the context of sex

---

[251] Equality Act 2010, s. 79. EU law appears to be slightly wider allowing a comparison with those in the same (public) service: *Scullard* v. *Knowles* [1996] IRLR 344, EAT; cf. *Lawrence* v. *Regent Office Care Ltd* [1999] IRLR 148, EAT.

[252] Case C–249/96 *Grant* v. *South West Trains* [1998] IRLR 165.

[253] See C. Barnard, 'The Principle of Equality in the Community Context: *P, Grant, Kalanke* and *Marschall*: Four Uneasy Bedfellows?' (1998) 57 *CLJ* 352–73 at 364–6.

[254] See S. Fredman, *Women and the Law* (Clarendon Press, Oxford, 1997) 179–224.

[255] S. Fredman, 'European Community Discrimination Law' (1992) 21 *ILJ* 119, 121.

[256] S. Fredman, *Women and the Law* (Clarendon Press, Oxford, 1997) 383.

[257] S. Fredman, 'Reversing Discrimination' (1997) 113 *LQR* 575.

[258] H. Fenwick and T. Hervey, 'Sex Equality in the Single Market: New Directions for the European Court of Justice' (1995) 32 *CMLRev.* 443, 445.

[259] In Case C–136/95 *Caisse Nationale d'Assurance Vieillesse des Travailleurs Salariés (CNAVTS)* v. *Évelyne Thibault* [1998] ECR I–2011 the Court claimed that the result pursued by the Directive was substantive, not formal, equality (para. 26).

discrimination, Fredman[260] explains that equality of results can itself be used in three different senses. The first focuses on the impact of apparently equal treatment on the individual. The second is concerned with the results on a group (e.g. women, ethnic minorities, etc.), and the third demands an outcome which is equal, for example equal pay for women doing work of equal value with that of men or equal representation of women and men in the same grade.

The concept of indirect discrimination is results-oriented in the first sense, in that the treatment must be detrimental to an individual, but it also involves equality of results in the second sense (i.e. that an apparently neutral practice has an unjustifiable adverse disparate impact upon the group to which the individual belongs). However, the concept of indirect discrimination is not redistributive in the third sense. If there is no exclusionary practice or criterion, or if no significant disparate impact can be shown, or if there is an objective business or administrative justification for the practice, then there is no breach.

An approach which is more results-oriented in a redistributive sense is to define equality in terms of 'fair' (sometimes referred to as 'full') participation of groups in the workforce. This aims to overcome under-representation of disadvantaged groups in the workplace and to ensure their fair share in the distribution of benefits. This may involve special measures to overcome disadvantage. Thus in Northern Ireland, 'affirmative action' designed 'to secure fair participation in employment by members of the Protestant, or members of the Roman Catholic, community in Northern Ireland'[261] has been a cornerstone of the legislation against religious discrimination since the Fair Employment Act 1989. A similar redistributive approach is taken by the Canadian Employment Equity Act 1995, which utilizes the concept of 'employment equity' to indicate that equality 'means more than treating persons in the same way but requires special measures and the accommodation of differences'.[262] In the EU, Article 157(4) TFEU talks of 'full equality in practice' yet the precise scope of this is far from clear.[263]

Positive action—and more radically positive discrimination—provide perhaps the best example of measures intended to achieve substantive equality, often at the price of formal equality. The original Article 2(4) of Directive 76/207 permitted positive action and it was relied on by the Court in *Marschall*[264] to uphold the state's law which gave

[260] S. Fredman, 'A Critical Review of the Concept of Equality in U.K. Anti-Discrimination Law', Independent Review of the Enforcement of U.K. Anti-Discrimination Legislation, Working Paper No. 3 (Cambridge Centre for Public Law and Judge Institute of Management Studies, November 1999), paras. 3.7–3.19. This Section is taken from C. Barnard and B. Hepple, 'Substantive Equality' (2000) 59 *CLJ* 562.

[261] Fair Employment and Treatment (Northern Ireland) Order 1998, Art. 4(1). The FETO does not define 'fair participation'. The Fair Employment Commission (now merged in the Equality Commission for Northern Ireland), which administered the legislation, adopted an interpretation which involves redressing imbalances and under-representation between the two communities in Northern Ireland. The aims are to secure greater fairness in the distribution of jobs and opportunities and to reduce the relative segregation of the two communities at work.

[262] Employment Equity Act 1995 [Can.], s. 2.   [263] Considered further in Ch. 8.

[264] Case C-409/95 *Marschall* v. *Land Nordrhein-Westfalen* [1997] ECR I-6363. Cf. Case C-450/93 *Kalanke* v. *Stadt Bremen* [1995] ECR I-3051. These cases are considered in detail in Ch. 8.

preference to a woman in a tie-break situation, subject to a saving clause operating in favour of the man. The Court said that this national rule was compatible with (the original) Article 2(4) because:

> even where male and female candidates are equally qualified, male candidates tend to be promoted in preference to female candidates particularly because of prejudices and stereotypes concerning the role and capacities of women in working life and the fear, for example, that women will interrupt their careers more frequently, that owing to household and family duties they will be less flexible in their working hours, or that they will be absent from work more frequently because of pregnancy, childbirth and breastfeeding.[265] For these reasons, the mere fact that a male candidate and a female candidate are equally qualified does not mean that they have the same chances.[266]

This case is not an isolated example. On a number of occasions the Court has said, as in *Thibault*,[267] that 'the result pursued by the Directive [2006/54] is substantive, not formal, equality'. This change in approach from *Hofman* and *Helmig* to *Marschall* and *Thibault* may in turn reflect something of a change in the European Union's self-perception from being a European *Economic* Community to a Union based on solidarity[268] and social inclusion[269] where attempts need to be made to accommodate those—particularly women with caring responsibilities—who have often been excluded from the labour market.

3. THE EU MODEL OF EQUALITY: EQUAL OPPORTUNITIES

Falling somewhere between formal and substantive equality lies the notion of equality of opportunity. Fredman points out that 'using the graphic metaphor of competitors in a race, [this approach] asserts that true equality cannot be achieved if individuals begin the race from different starting points. An equal opportunities approach therefore aims to equalise

---

[265] See further the views of the Federal Labour Court when the *Kalanke* case returned to it (No. 226), Urteil of 5 March 1996–1 AZR 590/92 (A). It said that it was impossible to distinguish between opportunity and result, especially in the case of engagement and promotion because the selection itself was influenced by circumstances, expectations, and prejudices that typically diminish the chances of women.

[266] Paras. 29 and 30.

[267] Case C–136/94 [1998] ECRI–2011, repeated in Case C–207/98 *Mahlburg* [2000] ECR I–549, para. 26; Case C–284/02 *Land Brandenburg* v. *Sass* [2004] ECR I–11143, para. 34. See additionally Case 109/88 *Handels-og Kontorfunktionærernes Forbund i Danmark* v. *Dansk Arbejdsgiverforening, acting on behalf of Danfoss (Danfoss)* [1989] ECR 3199 where the Court ruled that a criterion rewarding employees' mobility—their adaptability to variable hours and places of work—may work to the disadvantage of female employees who, because of household and family duties, are not as able as men to organize their working time with such flexibility. Similarly, the criterion of training may work to the disadvantage of women in so far as they have had less opportunity than men for training or have taken less advantage of that opportunity. In both cases the employer may only justify the remuneration of such adaptability or training by showing it is of importance for the performance of specific tasks entrusted to the employee.

[268] C. Barnard, 'The Future of Equality Law: Equality and Beyond?' in C. Barnard *et al.*, *The Future of Labour Law* (Hart Publishing, Oxford, 2004). See additionally Arts. 2 and 3 TEU and the Commission's Social Agenda documents 'Opportunities, access and solidarity': COM(2007) 726; COM(2008) 412.

[269] H. Collins, 'Human Rights; Employment Discrimination, Equality and Social Inclusion' (2003) 66 *MLR* 16; see additionally B. Hepple, 'Race and Law in Fortress Europe' (2004) 67 *MLR* 1.

the starting point....[270] The EU has expressly endorsed the equal opportunities approach.[271] But what does it mean? The *procedural* view of equal opportunities involves the removal of obstacles or barriers, such as word-of-mouth recruitment or non-job-related selection criteria. This opens up more opportunities but does 'not guarantee that more women or minorities will in fact be in a position to take advantage of those opportunities' because their capacities have been limited by the effects of social disadvantage.[272]

A more substantive approach to equality of opportunity would require a range of other special measures to compensate for disadvantages. These measures might include positive action (see previously) and positive duties being imposed on employers to 'promote equality of opportunity'. Elements of this positive duty can be found in Article 29 of the Sex Equality Directive 2006/54 which provides that 'Member States shall actively take into account the objective of equality between men and women when formulating and implementing laws, regulations, administrative provisions, policies and activities'. Measures which tackle inequality in the labour market, such as specific rights for part-time workers and workers on fixed-term contracts (predominantly women) may also be substantive in nature, but as we shall see in Chapter 9 they have been framed in EU Directives and UK law in terms of a principle of formal equality.

F. CONCLUSIONS

The Commission's 2010 Equality Strategy says in its opening paragraphs that:

> Inequalities between women and men violate fundamental rights. They also impose a heavy toll on the economy and result in under utilisation of talent. On the other hand, economic and business benefits can be gained from enhancing gender equality.

This statement reflects some of the tensions that have bedevilled EU equality law since its inception. Is it about protecting fundamental rights per se or is it, in fact, about the use of fundamental rights to achieve economic objectives? Often the two are interlinked, and there is a positive narrative about using discrimination law to remove artificial barriers preventing the most marginalized from working and thus securing independence though that work. That narrative appears particularly strongly in the 2010 Equality Strategy. However, this depends on individuals being prepared to enforce their rights which many choose not to do. From that point of view, other policy choices become more important and more effective (e.g. mainstreaming).

---

[270] Fredman, Working Paper (n. 260 previously), para. 3.12.

[271] See Art. 2(4) of Dir. 76/207 and now Art. 1 of the Sex Equality Dir. 2006/54 and Case C–450/93 *Kalanke* v. *Freie und Hansestadt Bremen* [1995] ECR I–3051, para. 23.

[272] FETO, Art. 5 provides that a person of any religious belief has equality of employment opportunity with a person of any other religious belief if he or she 'has the same opportunity...as that other person has or would have...due allowance being made for any material difference in their suitability'. Art. 5(4) sets out the kinds of opportunity encompassed by the duty. Section 75 of the Northern Ireland Act 1998 requires public authorities in carrying out their functions relating to Northern Ireland to 'have due regard to promote equality of opportunity' between a wide range of groups.

But there is a time when the fundamental rights argument and the economic imperative collide and there is a risk that, in straitened economic times, the economic needs will prevail. Sometimes the Court has resisted, but not always. Equal pay (Chapter 7) and occupational pension age (Chapter 9) provide some good examples of this collision. It is to equal pay that we now turn.

7

EQUAL PAY

A. INTRODUCTION

Article 157 TFEU (ex 141 EC) on equal pay is the cornerstone of the employment law provisions of the EU Treaties. The basic principle is laid down in Article 157(1) TFEU:

> Each Member State shall ensure that the principle of equal pay for male and female workers for equal work or work of equal value[1] is applied.

The significance of Article 157 TFEU first became apparent in the case of *Defrenne (No. 2)*.[2] Ms Defrenne was an air hostess employed by Sabena Airlines. Although she did identical work to a male cabin steward she was paid less than him contrary, she claimed, to Article 157 TFEU. The Court, recognizing that the principle of equal pay forms part of the 'foundations of the [Union]', decided, despite strong objections from the Member States, that Article 157 TFEU was both horizontally and vertically directly effective, and could thus give rise to 'individual rights which the courts may protect'.[3] However, realizing the number of potential claims arising from this decision which might seriously affect the solvency of many companies, the Court ruled that, in the interests of legal certainty, the direct effect of Article 157 TFEU could not be relied on to support the claims in respect of periods of employment prior to the date of the judgment (8 April 1976), except in the case of workers who had already brought legal proceedings.

This case captures the Court's dynamic approach towards Article 157 TFEU. On the one hand, the Court sees Article 157 TFEU as a key pillar of Union social policy and so fights to make it meaningful to victims of discrimination; on the other, it recognizes that changes in legal understanding can have profound consequences for individuals, particularly employers, who had no reason to believe that they were acting unlawfully. This has become a major issue in respect of addressing discrimination arising in the field of occupational pensions. This issue is considered separately in Chapter 10. In this chapter we focus on the meaning of equal pay primarily in the context of an ongoing employment relationship.

---

[1] Reference to 'work of equal value' was added by the Treaty of Amsterdam.
[2] Case 43/75 *Defrenne v. Sabena (No. 2)* [1976] ECR 455. For the background to this case, see C. Hoskyns, *Integrating Gender* (Verso, London, 1996) 65–75.
[3] Para. 24. See additionally Case C–28/93 *Van den Akker v. Stichting Shell Pensioenfonds* [1994] ECR I–4527, para. 21.

B. THE PERSONAL SCOPE OF ARTICLE 157 TFEU

The criterion on which Article 157(1) TFEU is based is the comparability of the work done by 'workers' of each sex.[4] Yet unlike the field of free movement of workers where there is a voluminous case law on the meaning of the 'worker',[5] it was not until the 2004 decision of *Allonby*[6] that the Court grappled with the meaning of 'worker' in the context of equal pay. It began by noting that there was no single definition of 'worker', in Union law: the definition varied according to the area in which the definition was applied.[7] However, as with the definition of 'worker' under Article 45 TFEU (ex 39 EC), the Court began by noting that 'worker' used in Article 157(1) TFEU had a broad, Union meaning.[8] Drawing on its Article 45 TFEU case law,[9] the Court said:

> For the purposes of that provision [Article 157(1) TFEU], there must be considered as a worker a person who, for a certain period of time, performs services for and under the direction of another person in return for which he receives remuneration.

Then, referring to the definition of pay found in Article 157(2) TFEU (see later in this chapter), the Court added:[10]

> It is clear from that definition that the authors of the Treaty did not intend that the term 'worker', within the meaning of Article [157(1) TFEU], should include independent providers of services who are not in a relationship of subordination with the person who receives the services.

However, the Court added the caveat that formal classification of a self-employed person under national law did not exclude the possibility that a person had to be classified as a worker within the meaning of Article 157(1) TFEU if that person's independence was 'merely notional, thereby disguising an employment relationship within the meaning of that Article'.[11]

Allonby concerned teachers who used to be employed directly by a further education (FE) college on fixed-term contracts. Once their contracts expired they were engaged on a self-employed basis by an agency, ELS. Allonby worked on specific assignments agreed by her with ELS at the FE college. The college agreed with ELS the fee it would pay for each lecturer. ELS then agreed with Allonby the fee she was to receive for each assignment and set the conditions under which its lecturers were to work. The effect of these changes was to reduce Allonby's pay. The question for the Court was whether the lecturers

---

[4] Case 149/77 *Defrenne (No. 3)* [1978] ECR 1365, para. 22.

[5] See further Ch. 4.

[6] Case C–256/01 *Allonby* v. *Accrington & Rosendale College* [2004] ECR I–873.

[7] Case C–85/96 *Martínez Sala* [1998] ECR I–2691, para. 31.

[8] Para. 66.

[9] Case 66/85 *Lawrie-Blum* [1986] ECR 2121, para. 17, and Case C–85/96 *Martínez Sala* [1998] ECR I–2691, para. 32.

[10] Para. 68. See additionally, in the context of free movement of workers, Case C–337/97 *Meeusen* [1999] ECR I–3289, para. 15.

[11] See additionally Case C–276/07 *Delay* v. *Università degli studi di Firenze* [2008] ECR I–3635, para. 29 where similar sentiments were expressed albeit in a different context: 'only an analysis concentrating on substance rather than the form, of statutory schemes will make it possible to establish' the true situation.

were genuinely self-employed. It said that it was necessary 'in particular to consider the extent of any limitation on their freedom to choose their timetable, and the place and content of their work'. It continued: 'The fact that no obligation is imposed on them to accept an assignment is of no consequence in that context'.[12] The result of this decision is to broaden the scope of the definition of worker, send a strong signal that it is the substance and not the form of the legal relationship which is relevant and, in the context of the UK, to reduce the long-established requirement that there must be mutuality of obligation (namely the obligation on the employer obligation to offer work and on the individual to accept that work) prior to employee or worker status being established.

C. THE MEANING OF 'PAY'

1. WHAT REMUNERATION CONSTITUTES 'PAY'?

Article 157(2) TFEU defines 'pay' broadly. It refers to the 'ordinary basic minimum wage or salary', which would include pay received as piece rates[13] or time rates, 'and any other consideration, whether in cash or in kind, which the worker receives directly or indirectly in respect of his employment from his employer'.[14] The Court has added that pay can be 'immediate or future' provided that the worker receives it, albeit indirectly,[15] in respect of his employment from his employer.[16] Thus, in *Garland*[17] the Court found that concessionary travel facilities granted voluntarily to ex-employees fell within the scope of Article 157 TFEU. The Court has also said that the legal nature of the facilities is not important: they can be granted under a contract of employment, a collective agreement,[18] as a result of legislative provisions,[19] or made *ex gratia*[20] by the employer,[21] provided always that they are granted to the worker by reason of the employment relationship between the worker and the employer in respect of employment.[22] This is the decisive criterion.[23]

---

[12] Citing Case C–357/89 *Raulin* [1992] ECR I–1027, paras. 9 and 10.

[13] See additionally Case C–400/93 *Specialarbejderforbundet i Danmark v. Dansk Industri* [1995] ECR I–1275.

[14] This definition is repeated in Art. 2(1)(e) of Dir. 2006/54.

[15] Since Art. 157 TFEU also applies to money received indirectly from an employer, it would cover occupational pensions paid out of a trust fund, administered by trustees who are technically independent of the employer: see Case C–262/88 *Barber v. Guardian Royal Exchange* [1990] ECR I–1889. Joined Cases C–270 and C–271/97 *Deutsche Post AG v. Sievers and Schrage* [2000] ECR I–929; Joined Cases C–234 and C–235/96 *Deutsche Telekom AG v. Vick and Conze* [2000] ECR I–799; and Case C–50/96 *Deutsche Telekom AG v. Schröder* [2000] ECR I–743.

[16] Case 80/70 *Defrenne (No. 1) v. Belgian State* [1971] ECR 445.

[17] Case 12/81 *Garland v. British Railways Board* [1982] ECR 359.

[18] Case C–281/97 *Krüger v. Kreiskrankenhaus Ebersberg* [1999] ECR I–5127, para. 17.

[19] See Cases 43/75 *Defrenne (No. 2)* [1976] ECR 455, para. 40, and C–262/88 *Barber* [1990] ECR I–1889.

[20] *Ex gratia* payments are 'advantages which an employer grants to workers although he is not required to do so by contract' (Case C–262/88 *Barber* [1990] ECR I–1889, para. 19, and Case 12/81 *Garland* [1982] ECR 359).

[21] Case C–360/90 *Arbeiterwohlfahrt der Stadt Berlin e.V v. Bötel* [1992] ECR I–3589.

[22] Cf. the position with additional voluntary contributions which are not granted in respect of employment: see Case C–200/91 *Coloroll v. Russell* [1994] ECR I–4389.

[23] Case C–366/99 *Griesmar v. Ministre de l'Économie, des Finances et de l'Industrie* [2001] ECR I–9383, para. 28.

Therefore, the Court has ruled that all employer-based payments constitute pay. Thus sick pay,[24] redundancy payments resulting from voluntary or compulsory redundancy,[25] unfair dismissal compensation,[26] occupational pensions,[27] survivors' benefits,[28] bridging pensions,[29] additional statutory redundancy payments,[30] maternity benefits paid under legislation or collective agreements,[31] special bonus payments made by the employer[32] (including an end-of-year bonus[33] and an 'inconvenient hours' supplement[34]), payment for extra hours,[35] concessionary train fares,[36] family and marriage allowances granted by collective agreement,[37] and a severance grant payable on the termination of an employment relationship,[38] all constitute pay. Similarly, compensation in the form of paid leave or overtime pay for participation in training courses given by an employer to Staff Committee members[39] and rules governing the automatic reclassification to a higher salary grade can constitute pay.[40]

---

[24] Case 171/88 *Rinner-Kühn* v. *FWW Spezial-Gebäudereinigung GmbH & Co. KG* [1989] ECR 2743.

[25] Case C-262/88 *Barber* [1990] ECR I-1889 concerned *compulsory* redundancy. Case 19/81 *Burton* v. *British Rail* [1982] ECR 555 concerned *voluntary* redundancy where the Court suggested that the (then) Equal Treatment Dir. 76/207 did not apply to discriminatory age conditions. The Court seems *sotto voce* to have overruled this decision (see D. Curtin, 'Scalping the Community Legislator: Occupational Pensions after *Barber*' (1990) 27 *CMLRev.* 475, 482) and it seems likely that Art. 157 TFEU would apply to both.

[26] Case C-167/97 *Seymour-Smith* [1999] ECR I-623. In Case C-249/97 *Gruber* v. *Silhouette International Schmied GmbH & Co. KG* [1999] ECR I-5295, the Court said that 'termination payments' constitute pay.

[27] Case 170/84 *Bilka-Kaufhaus* v. *Weber von Hartz* [1986] ECR 1607 and Case C-50/99 *Podesta* v. *CRICA* [2000] ECR I-4039 (supplementary pensions); Case C-262/88 *Barber* [1990] ECR I-1889 (contracted-out pensions).

[28] Case C-109/91 *Ten Oever* [1993] ECR I-4879; Case C-147/95 *DEI* v. *Efthimios Evrenopoulos* [1997] ECR I-2057.

[29] Case C-132/92 *Roberts* v. *Birds Eye Walls* [1993] ECR I-5579. See additionally Case C-19/02 *Hlozek* v. *Roche Austria Gesellschaft mbH* [2004] ECR I-11491, para. 51.

[30] Case C-173/91 *Commission* v. *Belgium* [1993] ECR I-673.

[31] C-342/93 *Gillespie* v. *Northern Health and Social Services Boards* [1996] ECR I-475. The Court did, however, rule that neither Art. 157 TFEU nor Art. 1 of the then Dir. 75/117 required that women should continue to receive full pay during maternity leave, nor did those provisions lay down any specific criteria for determining the amount of benefit to be paid to them during that period. See additionally Case C-218/98 *Abdoulaye* v. *Régie nationale des usines Renault SA* [1999] ECR I-5723, para. 14.

[32] Case 58/81 *Commission* v. *Luxembourg* [1982] ECR 2175 where a special 'head of house hold' allowance was deemed to be pay. Individual supplements to basic pay (Case 109/88 *Handels- og Kontorfunktionærernes Forbund I Danmark* v. *Dansk Arbejdsgiverforening, acting on behalf of Danfoss (Danfoss)* [1989] ECR 3199) and increments based on seniority (Case 184/89 *Nimz* v. *Freie und Hansestadt Hamburg* [1991] ECR 297) are considered to be pay. So, presumably, would shift premia, overtime, and all forms of merit and performance pay constitute 'pay' within Art. 157 TFEU (COM(94) 6 final).

[33] Case C-281/97 *Krüger* v. *Kreiskrankenhaus Ebersberg* [1999] ECR I-5127; Case C-333/97 *Lewen* v. *Lothar Denda* [2000] ECR I-7243 (a Christmas bonus paid on a voluntary basis as an incentive for future work or loyalty to the undertaking constituted pay (para. 22)).

[34] Case C-236/98 *Örebo läns landsting* [2000] ECR I-2189, para. 42.

[35] Case C-285/02 *Elsner-Lakeberg* v. *Land Nordrhein-Westfalen* [2004] ECR I-58561, para. 16.

[36] Case C-249/96 *Grant* v. *South West Trains* [1998] ECR I-621.

[37] Case C-187/98 *Commission* v. *Greece* [1999] ECR I-7713.

[38] Case C-33/89 *Kowalska* v. *Freie und Hansestadt Hamburg* [1990] ECR I-2591. Such payments are deemed to be deferred pay.

[39] Case C-360/90 *Bötel* [1992] ECR I-3589.

[40] Case C-184/89 *Nimz* [1991] ECR I-297.

2. REMUNERATION CONSIDERED TO BE SOCIAL SECURITY PAYMENTS

Payments do not constitute pay where they are considered to be social security payments[41] and so fall under Directive 79/7. In *Beune*[42] the Court provided some guidance as to how to identify whether a payment formed part of a state social security scheme (to which Directive 79/7 would apply) or part of the employment relationship (to which Article 157 TFEU would apply). The case concerned a pension scheme governed directly by statute. The Court said that Article 157 TFEU did not cover social security schemes or benefits, such as retirement pensions, directly governed by statute which were obligatorily applicable to general categories of employees, where no element of negotiation within the undertaking or occupational sector was involved.[43] It said that although these schemes were funded by the contributions of workers, employers, and possibly the public authorities, the funding was determined not so much by the employment relationship between the employer and the worker as by considerations of social policy. Since Article 157 TFEU did not apply to these payments, they fell within the scope of Directive 79/7 on equal treatment.

In subsequent cases the Court has identified three conditions necessary for retirement pensions to fall within the scope of Article 157 TFEU. These were summarized in *Schönheit*[44] where the Court said that a scheme, although established by law, fell within Article 157 TFEU if: (1) it concerned only a particular category of workers;[45] (2) it was directly related to the period of service completed; and (3) its amount was calculated by reference to the individual's final salary.[46] Where these conditions are satisfied a pension paid by a public sector employer is comparable to a pension paid by a private employer to his former employees; in other words it is equivalent to an occupational pension.[47] This definition has now been broadly incorporated into Article 7(2) of Directive 2006/54.

---

[41] Case 80/70 *Defrenne (No. 1)* [1971] ECR 445. This is considered further in Ch. 10.

[42] Case C-7/93 *Bestuur van het Algemeen Burgerlijk Pensioenfonds* v. *Beune* [1994] ECR I-4471.

[43] This language is actually taken from Case C-366/99 *Griesmar* v. *Ministre de l'Économie, des Finances et de l'Industrie* [2001] ECR I-9383, para. 27.

[44] Joined Cases C-4/02 and C-5/02 *Schönheit* v. *Stadt Frankfurt am Main* [2003] ECR I-12575. For a careful analysis of whether a particular scheme satisfies these requirements, see Case C-50/99 *Podesta* v. *CRICA* [2000] ECR I-4039.

[45] The particular category of workers is 'distinguished from employees grouped within an undertaking or group of undertakings in a particular sector of the economy, or in a trade or inter-trade sector, only by reason of the specific features governing their employment relationship with the state or with other public employers or bodies'. This is wide enough to cover a group comprising all public servants: Case C-366/99 *Griesmar* [2001] ECR I-9383, para. 31.

[46] Para. 58. See additionally Case C-366/99 *Griesmar* [2001] ECR I-9383, paras. 28-34; Case C-351/00 *Niemi* [2002] ECR I-7007, paras. 47-52.

[47] Joined Cases C-4/02 and C-5/02 *Schönheit* [2003] ECR I-12575, para. 65.

3. THE RELATIONSHIP BETWEEN 'PAY' AND 'EQUAL TREATMENT'

As the definition of pay becomes broader it might be thought that the role for the provisions on equal treatment in respect of conditions of employment which were once covered by the Equal Treatment Directive 76/207 would diminish, especially since Article 157 TFEU has both vertical and horizontal direct effect. It might also be thought that the advent of the Sex Equality Directive 2006/54 would have further eroded the distinction between pay and other conditions of employment since both are now brought under one and the same prohibition on discrimination. However, in *Gillespie*,[48] a case decided before Directive 2006/54, the Court emphasized that there was still a clear distinction between equal pay matters governed by Article 157 TFEU and equal treatment in respect of working conditions covered by Directive 76/207. The Court also emphasized this distinction in *Wippel*,[49] a case concerning a casual worker employed on a 'work on demand' contract. The Court said that where a contract affects the pursuit of an occupational activity by scheduling working time according to need, the contract laid down rules concerning working conditions and so fell within the Equal Treatment Directive 76/207 (and also the Part-time Work Directive 97/81) but not Article 157 TFEU.[50] The Court added that the fact that the contract had financial consequences for the worker concerned was 'not sufficient to bring such conditions within the scope of Article [157 TFEU] or of [what was then] Directive 75/117, those provisions being based on the close connection which exists between the nature of the work done and the amount of the worker's pay.'[51] These cases therefore suggest that close attention needs to be paid to the material scope of the equal pay on the one hand and equal treatment in respect of working conditions on the other even though both now fall under the umbrella of Directive 2006/54.

D. THE SCOPE OF THE COMPARISON

1. INTRODUCTION

Article 157 TFEU talks about equal pay for male and female workers for equal work or work of equal value. Thus, the model originally envisaged by Article 157 TFEU is (usually) a woman claiming equal pay against her *employer* using a man engaged in like work or work of equal value as a comparator. Therefore, in order to determine whether

---

[48] Case C–342/93 [1996] ECR I–475, para. 24. See further Case C–281/97 *Krüger* [1999] ECR I–5127, para. 14.

[49] Case C–313/02 *Wippel* [2004] ECR I–9483.

[50] Para. 32.

[51] Para. 33. See additionally Case C–476/99 *Lommers* v. *Minister van Landbouw* [2002] ECR I–2891, para. 27: provision of workplace nurseries is a working condition under what was Dir. 76/207 and does not constitute 'pay' under Art. 157 TFEU; the measure does not constitute pay just because the cost of the nursery places is partly borne by the employer.

the woman is entitled to equal pay, there must be (1) a comparator of the opposite sex who is, or has been, (2) engaged in equal work or work of equal value. In its case law the Court has added an additional requirement: (3) that the comparator has to be employed in the same establishment or service. In this section we shall focus on the application of Article 157 TFEU to cases where an employer is the defendant. It will be suggested below that the Court adopts a rather different approach when the defendant is the state and discriminatory legislation is at issue.

2. DISCRIMINATORY PRACTICES BY EMPLOYERS

2.1. Identifying the comparator

(a) Real comparator similarly situated

To bring an equal pay claim under Article 157 TFEU, the applicant needs to point to a comparator of the opposite sex, who is paid better for doing equal work or work of equal value. The Court has said that the comparator does not need to be employed at the same time as the applicant[52] but the comparator must be a real, identifiable person and not a 'hypothetical worker'.[53] This requirement prevents a woman from arguing that she was the victim of discrimination because, had she been a man, she would have received a higher salary. In *Macarthys* the Court explained that such claims should be excluded on the grounds that it would necessitate comparative studies of entire branches of industry which would require further Union legislation.

While hypothetical comparators do present considerable problems of proof, the requirement for an actual comparator limits the effectiveness of the equality legislation in sectors—such as cleaning and catering—dominated by women. However, with Directive 2006/54 bringing pay and treatment under the same 'roof', it has been argued that key principles relating to equal treatment, in particular the possibility of using a hypothetical comparator, should now apply to equal pay claims as well. The UK government has contested this, pointing to the 16th Recital of Directive 2002/73,[54] to suggest that the two regimes remain distinct.[55] Some support for the UK's view can be found in Directive 2006/54 which, in Article 4, also suggests that the equal pay provisions are separate.

---

[52] Case 129/79 *Macarthys* [1980] ECR 1275.

[53] Ibid. This argument was based on the distinction the Court had drawn between direct and indirect discrimination. If the comparator were to be a hypothetical male this would be classed as indirect, disguised discrimination which would require comparative studies of entire industries. At that stage Art. 157 TFEU was only directly effective in respect of direct discrimination. Since the law has now changed this approach may require reassessment. See additionally Case C–200/91 *Coloroll Pension Trustees Ltd* v. *Russell* [1994] ECR I–4389.

[54] This says: 'The principle of equal pay for men and women is already firmly established by Article [157] of the Treaty and Council Directive 75/117/EEC of 10 February 1975 on the approximation of the laws of the Member States relating to the application of the principle of equal pay for men and women and is consistently upheld by the case-law of the Court of Justice; the principle constitutes an essential and indispensable part of the acquis communautaire concerning sex discrimination'. This paragraph has been removed from Dir. 2006/54.

[55] The Government response to the amended Equal Treatment Directive, paras. 18.2–18.4 <http://webarchive.nationalarchives.gov.uk/20080910135031/http://equalities.gov.uk/legislation/archive.htm>.

Not only must the comparator be real, he must also be in an 'identical' situation with the woman.[56] In *Roberts*[57] the employer paid the man a bridging pension between the ages of 60 and 65 but paid Mrs Roberts only a reduced bridging pension on the grounds that she received a state pension at the age of 60 but her male comparator did not. The Court ruled that no discrimination occurred since the 'difference as regards the objective premise, which necessarily entails that the amount of the bridging pension is not the same for men and women, cannot be considered discriminatory'. Similarly, in *Abdoulaye*[58] the Court said that it was not contrary to Article 157 TFEU for women but not men to receive a maternity bonus intended to offset the occupational disadvantages inherent in maternity leave, since the two situations were not comparable.[59]

There have been some concerns in the past that, in selecting a comparator group, particularly in the context of equal value claims, the applicant 'cherry-picks'—carves a group of women and a group of men out of larger groups—to facilitate an equal pay claim. In *Dansk Industri*[60] the Court sought to put a stop to this. It said that the two groups had to encompass all the workers who could be considered to be in a comparable situation, taking into account factors such as the nature of the work, training requirements, and working conditions. The group also had to comprise a relatively large number of workers and that any differences could not be due to purely fortuitous or short-term factors or to differences in the individual output of the workers concerned.

(b) Hard cases

In most cases the selection of the comparator is straightforward. However, as *Grant* demonstrates,[61] this is not always the case. Lisa Grant, a lesbian, was denied benefits (concessionary train fares) for her female partner. One of her claims was that she was (directly) discriminated against on the grounds of sex contrary to Article 157 TFEU since her (heterosexual) male colleague had received those benefits for his female partner. The Court, however, chose a homosexual male as the comparator. Grant lost her case since both (homosexual) men and women would have been treated equally (albeit equally badly).[62] Had the Court chosen a heterosexual male comparator, as Grant had

---

[56] Case C-132/92 *Roberts* [1993] ECR I-5579. See additionally Case C-342/93 *Gillespie and Others* v. *Northern Health and Social Services Board and Others* [1996] ECR I-475; Case C-249/97 *Gruber* [1999] ECR I-5295; Case C-309/97 *Wiener Gebietskrankenkasse* [1999] ECR I-2865; and Case C-333/97 *Lewen* v. *Lothar Denda* [2000] ECR I-7243, para. 38. Such differences in circumstances (such as the hours worked) may, however, constitute an objective justification: Case C-236/98 *Jämo* [2000] ECR I-2189, para. 61.

[57] Case C-132/92 *Roberts* [1993] ECR I-5579. In a similar vein, see further Case C-19/02 *Hlozek* [2004] ECR I-11491.

[58] Case C-218/98 *Abdoulaye* v. *Régre Nationale des Usines Renault SA* [1999] ECR I-5723.

[59] Cf. Case C-366/99 *Griesmar* [2001] ECR I-9383, considered in Ch. 9.

[60] Case C-400/93 [1995] ECR I-1275.

[61] Case C-249/86 *Grant* [1998] ECR I-621.

[62] This is sometimes referred to as 'equal misery': C. Denys, 'Homosexuality: a non-issue in Community law' (1999) 24 *ELRev.* 419, 422. See additionally Joined Cases C-122/99P and C-125/99P *D and Kingdom of Sweden* v. *Council* [2001] ECR I-4319.

argued, there would have been discrimination on the grounds of sex.[63] In *P* v. *S*,[64] by contrast, a case decided under the then Equal Treatment Directive 76/207, a male to female transsexual was dismissed on the grounds of her sex change. The comparator selected by the Court was a person of the sex to which P was deemed to have belonged prior to the gender reassignment (i.e. a male). Discrimination was found. As the Advocate General recognized, had the Court selected a female to male transsexual as a comparator, (which the UK government had argued for), the result might have been different.

2.2. Type of work undertaken by the comparator

The chosen comparator must be engaged in (a) 'equal work' or (b) work rated as equivalent/'work of equal value' with the claimant. We shall look at these situations in turn.

(a) Equal work

'Equal work' embraces the concept of equal pay for the same[65] or similar work (also known as 'like work'). Various factors need to be taken into account, such as:

- the nature of the work actually entrusted to the individual employees;
- the training requirements for carrying out those tasks;
- the working conditions in which the activities are actually carried out.[66]

The importance of weighing up a number of factors in determining 'like work' was highlighted in *Wiener Gebietskrankenkasse*.[67] There the Court ruled that where the same activities were performed over a considerable length of time by persons the bases of whose qualification to exercise their profession were different, this did not constitute 'same work'. Therefore, graduate psychologists, most of whom were women, could not claim equal pay with medical doctors who were paid 50 per cent more, even though both groups worked as psychotherapists and the patients were charged the same irrespective of whether they were treated by a psychologist or a doctor.

An individual can bring a 'like work' claim even if the work of the applicant and her comparator is not performed contemporaneously. Thus, in *Macarthys*,[68] the complainant successfully claimed that she had been discriminated against on the grounds of her sex. She worked as a warehouse manageress earning £50 a week. Her predecessor, a man, had earned £10 more. According to the Court, an assessment of whether the work

---

[63] Cf. *Baehr* v. *Lewin* 852 P.2d 44 (Hawaii 1993). See further C. Barnard, 'Some are More Equal than Others: the Case of *Grant* v. *South-West Trains*' (1999) 1, 147; M. Bell, 'Shifting Conceptions of Sexual Discrimination at the Court of Justice': from *P* v. *S* to *Grant* v. *SWT*' (1999) 5 *ELJ* 63.

[64] Case C–13/94 [1996] ECR I–2143.

[65] Art. 1 of Dir. 75/117 and Art. 4. of the Sex Equality Dir.

[66] Case C–381/99 *Brunnhofer* v. *Bank der Österreichischen Postsparkasse AG* [2001] ECR I–4961, para. 48.

[67] Case C–309/97 *Angestelltenbetriebsrat der Wiener Gebietskrankenkasse* v. *Wiener Gebietskrankenkasse* [1999] ECR I–2865.

[68] Case 129/79 [1980] ECR 1275.

was equal was 'entirely qualitative in character in that it is exclusively concerned with the nature of the services in question'. The Court said that the scope of Article 157 TFEU could not be restricted by the introduction of a 'requirement of contemporaneity'.

(b) Equal pay for work of equal value

The principle of equal pay for work of equal value, originally found in Article 1 of Directive 75/117 and now in the amended Article 157(1) TFEU, is intended to redress the undervaluing of jobs undertaken primarily by women (such as cleaning) where they are found to be as demanding as different jobs more usually undertaken by men (such as maintenance work or gardening).

A job classification or job evaluation scheme,[69] while not obligatory,[70] offers one method of determining whether a man and woman's work is of equal value. This is recognized by Article 4(2) of Directive 2006/54 which provides:

> ..., where a job classification system is used for determining pay, it shall be based on the same criteria for both men and women and so drawn up so as to exclude any discrimination on grounds of sex.

However, job classification systems themselves can embody discrimination. This was considered in *Rummler*.[71] A German printing firm adopted a grading scheme which classified jobs according to the previous knowledge required, concentration, effort, exertion, and responsibility. Grade II jobs involved slight to medium muscular effort; Grade III jobs medium to high muscular effort, and Grade IV jobs involved on occasion high levels of muscular exertion. Mrs Rummler's job was classified as Grade III. She argued that it should have been classified as Grade IV because it involved lifting packages of 20kg which, *for her*, was heavy physical work. She therefore asked that account be taken of her own (subjective) characteristics.

The Court said that the nature of the work had to be considered objectively. It recognized that a criterion which took account of an objectively measurable level of physical strength needed to do the job was compatible with Article 1(2) provided that the work, by its very nature, did actually require physical exertion. However, the Court said that when calculating the amount of physical exertion needed, a criterion based solely on the values of one sex, for example, the average strength of a woman, brought with it the threat of discrimination since it might result in work requiring use of greater physical strength being paid in the same way as work requiring less physical strength.

The Court did, however, accept that even though a strength criterion might generally favour male employees, the classification system was not discriminatory on this ground

---

[69] Job classification is a non-analytical process used to categorize jobs. Job evaluation, used in the UK and Ireland, is a more analytical approach to assess the relative demands of a job. The analytical approach involves breaking the jobs down into their component elements for the process of comparison whereas the non-analytical approach considers the relative worth of the job based on a whole job comparison. While analytical schemes are more objective the whole process is still subject to judgments made by evaluators which reflect their own background, experience, and attitudes (COM(94) 6 final).

[70] Case 61/81 *Commission v. UK* [1982] ECR 2601.

[71] Case 237/85 *Rummler v. Dato-Druck* [1986] ECR 2101.

alone. Instead, the Court said that the scheme had to be considered overall and, in order for it to accord with the principles of the Directive, it had to be designed to include, if the nature of the work permitted, work in which other criteria were taken into account for which female employees might show 'particular aptitude'. Thus, as the United Kingdom government suggested, a system based on the criterion of muscular effort was only discriminatory if it excluded from consideration the activation of small groups of muscles which typifies manual dexterity, where women tend to score highly. The Court concluded that it was the task of national courts to decide in individual cases whether the job classification scheme in its entirety permitted fair account to be taken of all the criteria on the basis of which pay was determined.

A job classification system initiated by the employer is not the only method for determining whether work is of equal value. In *Commission* v. *United Kingdom*[72] the Court said that the individual should have the right to initiate an equal value claim in the national court, notwithstanding objections from her employer, since Article 6 of Directive 75/117 (now essentially Article 17 of Directive 2006/54) required Member States to endow an authority with the requisite jurisdiction to decide whether different jobs were of equal value, even though national courts might have difficulty in applying such an abstract concept.

(c) Equal pay for work of greater value

Does Article 157(1) TFEU cover the (unusual) situation where the woman is doing work of greater value than the man, is being paid less than the man, and wishes to be paid the same as the man. In *Murphy*[73] the Court said yes. The case concerned female factory workers who dismantled, oiled, and reassembled telephones. They wished to be paid the same rate as a male worker employed in the same factory as a labourer who also cleaned, collected, and delivered equipment. The equality officer considered the women's work, taken as a whole, was of a higher value than the man's. The Court said that since the principle of equal pay forbade women engaged in work of equal value to men from being paid less than men on the grounds of sex, *a fortiori* it prohibited a difference in pay where the woman is engaged in work of higher value.[74] To adopt a contrary interpretation, said the Court, would be 'tantamount to rendering the principle of equal pay ineffective and nugatory' since an employer could circumvent the principle by assigning additional duties to women who could then be paid a lower wage.[75]

2.3. Same establishment or service

Under English law, the ability of the British statute, originally the Equal Pay Act 1970 and now the Equality Act 2010, to combat low pay in occupationally segregated sectors, such as

---

[72] Case 61/81 [1982] ECR 2601. The Member States have adopted different mechanisms for resolving whether, in the light of the nature and demands of the different jobs, the work is of equal value. In Belgium, France, Italy, and Luxembourg, disputes may be resolved by labour inspectorates, while under Irish legislation any dispute on the subject of equal pay can be referred to one of three equality officers (COM(94) 6 final).

[73] Case 157/86 *Murphy* v. *Bord Telecomm Eireann* [1988] ECR 673.

[74] Para. 9.   [75] Para. 10.

cleaning and catering, has been curtailed by the requirement that the comparator be employed in the same employment as the woman. This means that the woman and the man have to employed (1) by the same employer or an associated employer,[76] and (2) at the same establishment or at different establishments where common terms and conditions of employment are observed.[77] This requirement prevents a woman from making comparisons with colleagues in other establishments belonging to the same employer but with different terms and conditions or with comparators working for different employers in the same industry. It also prevents female workers, in a sector predominated by women, from making cross-industry comparisons.

However, no 'same employment' requirement is expressly mentioned in Article 157 TFEU or in the original Equal Pay Directive 75/117. Nevertheless, the Court alluded to some similar restriction in *Defrenne (No. 2)*[78] where it said:

> 21 Among the forms of direct discrimination which may be identified solely by reference to the criteria laid down by Article [157 TFEU] must be included in particular those which have their origin in legislative provisions or in collective labour agreements and which may be detected on the basis of a purely legal analysis of the situation.
>
> 22 This applies even more in cases where men and women receive unequal pay for equal work carried out in the same establishment or service, whether public or private.

These paragraphs appeared to suggest that while envisaging some limits to the selection of comparator, these limits were not as tightly drawn as those prescribed by English law.[79] Thus, it would seem that under EU law, the comparator is not confined to those working in the 'same establishment' but also covers those working in the same 'service' (para. 22). Paragraph 21 suggests that it is sufficient for the comparator to be covered by the same legislative provisions or collective agreements.

Although the language in *Defrenne (No. 2)* is not especially clear, it was relied on by the Scottish Court of Session in *South Ayrshire Council* v. *Morton*[80] to allow primary school head teachers (75 per cent of whom were women) to bring an equal pay claim using as a comparator secondary school head teachers (75 per cent of whom were men) employed by a different local education authority but whose salary scale was set by the same negotiating body under the aegis of the Secretary of State. The court allowed comparison across authorities because, under paragraph 21 of *Defrenne (No. 2)*, a comparison could be made where the discrimination arises from common legislation or collective bargaining.

However, it was not until *Lawrence*[81] in 2002 that the Court of Justice had the chance to (re)consider the significance of its earlier remarks in *Defrenne (No. 2)*. *Lawrence*

---

[76] Two employers are treated as associated if one is a company of which the other (directly or indirectly) has control or if both are companies of which a third person (directly or indirectly) has control: s. 79(9) Equality Act 2010.

[77] S. 79 Equality Act 2010.

[78] Case 43/75 [1976] ECR 455.

[79] In Case 143/83 *Commission* v. *Denmark* [1985] ECR 427 the Advocate General also expressed doubts about the validity of the single workplace rule which might defeat the purpose of the principle of equal pay.

[80] [2001] IRLR 28.

[81] Case C–320/00 *Lawrence* v. *Regent Office Care Ltd* [2002] ECR I–7325.

arose out of a long dispute concerning the pay rates of 'female catering assistants' (dinner ladies). Following the introduction of equal pay for work of equal value into UK law in 1983,[82] a job evaluation scheme was carried out by the employer, North Yorkshire County Council, in 1987 which rated the work of dinner ladies and cleaners as being of equal value to that of men performing jobs such as gardening, refuse collection, and sewage treatment. As a result of this exercise, the pay for the women's work was increased.

The following year, the Local Government Act (LGA) 1988 required 'defined activities', including school catering and cleaning, to be subject to compulsory competitive tendering (CCT). However, when selecting a contractor, local authorities could not consider 'non-commercial matters' such as wages and conditions or gender equality. In order to compete with external contractors, who were tendering on the basis of significantly lower contract costs, North Yorkshire County Council (NYCC) therefore cut the dinner ladies' pay. In *Ratcliffe v. North Yorkshire County Council*[83] the dinner ladies successfully argued that they were entitled to be paid the same as male NYCC employees whose work had been rated as equivalent to theirs under the 1987 job evaluation scheme (i.e. road sweepers and dustbin men).[84]

However, while *Ratcliffe* was ongoing, NYCC had to engage in a further round of CCT. The catering and cleaning contracts were won by three external contractors which employed (some of) the dinner ladies but on inferior terms and conditions. The dinner ladies then brought equal pay claims against the contractors, using as comparators the road sweepers and dustbin men still employed by NYCC, whose work had been rated as equivalent to theirs under the 1987 job evaluation scheme. However, as we saw above, under the British Equal Pay Act, the fact that the women and their comparators were employed by different employers (the dinner ladies were now employed by private companies while their comparators worked for NYCC) was fatal to their claim. Would Article 157 TFEU help the dinner ladies or did it contain equivalent limitations? This was the issue in *Lawrence*.[85]

The Court of Justice said that there was nothing in the wording of Article 157(1) TFEU to suggest that it could be applied only to situations in which men and women work for the same employer.[86] However, it continued:

> where ... the differences identified in the pay conditions of workers performing equal work or work of equal value *cannot be attributed to a single source*, there is no body which is responsible for the inequality and which could restore equal treatment. Such a situation does not come within the scope of Article [157(1) TFEU]. The work and the pay of those workers cannot therefore be compared on the basis of that provision. [Emphasis added.]

---

[82] As a result of successful infringement proceedings before the ECJ: Case 61/81 *Commission v. UK* [1982] ECR 2601.

[83] [1995] IRLR 439. For full details of the background, see C. Barnard, S. Deakin, and C. Kilpatrick, 'Equality, Non-discrimination and the Labour Market in the UK' (2002) 18 *IJCLLIR* 129.

[84] The House of Lords said that NYCC's need to cut wages to compete effectively with external contractors, though the genuine reason for the pay cuts, was not a 'material factor which is not the difference of sex' as required by the Equal Pay Act 1970, s. 1(3).

[85] Case C–320/00 *Lawrence* [2002] ECR I–7325.   [86] Para. 17.

Thus, the Court said that there could only be a cross-employer comparison where the differences in pay could be attributed to a single source. That was not the case in *Lawrence* as there was no one body responsible for the inequality which could restore equal treatment.

So what is meant by single source? The paradigm case would be where the applicant and her comparator work for the same legal person or group of persons or for public authorities operating under joint control[87] or where their pay is covered by the same collective agreement or legislative provisions,[88] i.e. common terms and conditions (paragraph 21 of *Defrenne*). This is particularly important in the public sector where, as in *Morton*, comparators are drawn from different public authorities who operate under the same government department.

However, in the absence of such a single source, the equal pay claim will fail. This was confirmed in *Allonby*.[89] Ms Allonby was employed by an FE college on a series of part-time, one-year contracts. Because of its worries about the effects of the Part-time Work Directive,[90] the college decided not to renew the existing contracts of part-time lecturers and instead use the services of an agency, ELS, which provided the same lecturers to the college, including Allonby. ELS engaged the lecturers under self-employed contracts. The effect of these changes was to reduce Allonby's overall pay. She brought an equal pay claim against the college, using a male full-time lecturer who had a permanent, full-time contract with the college as her comparator.

The Court of Justice said that Article 157 TFEU would not permit such a claim. It explained that while Article 157(1) TFEU could be invoked 'in particular in cases of discrimination arising directly from legislative provisions or collective labour agreements, as well as in cases in which work is carried out in the same establishment or service, whether private or public', where the differences in pay could not be attributed to a single source, there was 'no body which is responsible for the inequality and which could restore equal treatment' and so the situation did not come within the scope of Article 157(1) TFEU. The Court concluded that even though the level of pay received by Ms Allonby was influenced by the amount which the college paid ELS, this was not a sufficient basis for concluding that the college and ELS constituted a single source to which the differences identified in Ms Allonby's conditions of pay and those of the male worker paid by the college could be attributed.

As Fredman points out,[91] the fault-oriented model of equal pay introduced in *Lawrence* and applied with such damaging effect in *Allonby*, overlooks the widely recognized fact that inequality of pay is frequently a consequence of institutional arrangements for which no single actor is 'to blame'. Because the Court could not find fault on the part of either the college or ELS—even though the Advocate General

---

[87] Cf. *Robertson* v. *DEFRA* [2005] IRLR 363.
[88] AG Geelhoed's Opinion in *Lawrence*, para. 54.
[89] Case C–256/01 *Allonby* v. *Accrington & Rosendale College* [2004] ECR I–873.
[90] See further Ch. 9.
[91] S. Fredman, 'Marginalising Equal Pay Laws' (2004) 33 *ILJ* 281, 281.

acknowledged that the institutional arrangements had been deliberately manipulated to secure savings for the college and to avoid the consequences of the Part-time Work Directive—the loss fell on those who were least at fault—the part-time lecturers, the majority of whom were women.[92] Thus, the triangulation of the managerial function (with the college having control over the worker but ELS having control over their remuneration) successfully drew the teeth of the (fundamental) principle of equal pay and this was condoned by a Court unable 'to see beyond the formal boundaries of the employing enterprise'.[93] The effect of *Allonby* is that workers working alongside each other in the same establishment but with contracts of employment with different legal entities do not enjoy equal pay.[94]

Deakin and Morris point out that the *Lawrence* and *Allonby* reference to 'single source' represents an unjustified gloss on the wording of Article 157 TFEU, which makes no reference to the employment unit as the sole basis for comparison.[95] Although there may be practical difficulties in allowing comparisons across employment boundaries, such difficulties did not arise in these two cases: *Lawrence* was a case of a unified job evaluation scheme, and *Allonby* involved work in a single establishment where there was a contract between the college and the agency. In both cases comparisons were made with former co-workers.[96]

E. THE PROHIBITION OF DISCRIMINATION ON THE GROUNDS OF SEX

1. INTRODUCTION

In the description above of the three criteria necessary to bring an equal pay claim (comparator, engaged in equal work/work of equal value, in the same establishment or service) there is no reference to the principle of discrimination. Yet, Article 157 TFEU does envisage a role for the discrimination principle. Talking in the specific context of piece and time rates, it says:

> Equal pay *without discrimination based on sex* means:
>
> (a) that pay for the same work at piece rates shall be calculated on the basis of the same unit of measurement;
>
> (b) that pay for work at time rates shall be the same for the same job.[97]

Similarly, in the original Equal Pay Directive 75/117 and in Directive 2006/54, the principle of non-discrimination is central. Article 4 of Directive 2006/54 provides:

---

[92] Ibid.   [93] Ibid.

[94] S. Deakin and G. Morris, *Labour Law* (Hart Publishing, Oxford, 2009) para. 6.83.

[95] Ibid.

[96] Ibid.

[97] Emphasis added. The wording of Art. 157 TFEU is based on Art. 2(1) of ILO Convention 100, 1951 (UNTS, Vol. 165, 303).

For the same work or for work to which equal value is attributed, *direct and indirect discrimination on grounds of sex* with regard to all aspects and conditions of remuneration shall be eliminated.[98]

In this Section we consider the meaning of the term non-discrimination on the grounds of sex before considering the problems associated with applying the principle in the specific context of equal pay.

2. NON-DISCRIMINATION

2.1. The principle of non-discrimination

In cases where discrimination is raised, the Court draws the conventional distinction between *direct* and *indirect* discrimination which was considered in detail in Chapter 6. In essence, direct discrimination involves one sex being treated less favourably than the other. In the case of *Macarthys*[99] this meant that the woman received less pay than the man doing the same job. In *Moufflin*[100] French law provided that female civil servants with husbands suffering from a disability or an incurable illness were entitled to a retirement pension with immediate effect; male civil servants in an equivalent situation were not. In both cases the Court found the rule to be directly discriminatory contrary to Article 157 TFEU.

Indirect discrimination means, according to Article 2(1)(b) of Directive 2006/54, that:

Where an apparently neutral provision, criterion or practice *would put* persons of one sex at a *particular disadvantage* compared with persons of the other sex, unless that provision, criterion or practice is objectively justified by a legitimate aim and the means of achieving that aim are appropriate and necessary.

As we saw in Chapter 6, the Court's approach to proving indirect discrimination has generally been more strict than the test laid down by Article 2(1)(b). Nevertheless, both the legislative and judicial routes allow the defendant to justify the differential treatment for objective reasons unrelated to sex.

2.2. On the grounds of sex

The discrimination (either direct or indirect) must be 'on the grounds of sex'. This raises the question as to what constitutes 'sex': does it mean merely gender or is the term broader than that? Although this question is considered in more detail in the next chapter, for the purpose of equal pay we can observe the following. At first, it seemed that the Court would construe the concept of 'sex' broadly. For example, in *Liefting*[101] it recognized that 'gender-plus' (e.g. gender and marriage) discrimination was caught by

---

[98] Emphasis added.   [99] Case 129/79 *Macarthys* v. *Smith* [1980] ECR 1275.
[100] Case C–206/00 *Mouflin* v. *Recteur de l'académie de Reims* [2001] ECR I–10201.
[101] Case 23/83 *Liefting* v. *Academisch Ziekenhuis bij de Universiteit van Amsterdam* [1984] ECR 3225.

Article 157 TFEU. In that case employer contributions to a pension scheme discriminated against female civil servants married to (male) civil servants. Although there was
no allegation that women were being discriminated against generally, the Court found
that discrimination against this particular category of female civil servants was nevertheless caught by Article 157 TFEU.[102] However, as we have already seen, in *Grant*[103] the
Court was not prepared to allow the definition of sex in Article 157 TFEU to include
sexual orientation.[104]

Discrimination for reasons other than sex is compatible with Union law. Sometimes
this notion is dealt with through the defence of 'objective justification *on grounds other
than sex*' (see later in this chapter). In other cases this question forms an integral part of
the assessment of whether the threshold criteria for liability have been made out. For
example, in *Danfoss*[105] the Court said that a criterion for awarding a pay increase based
on the quality of work done by the employee is 'undoubtedly wholly neutral from the
point of view of sex'.[106]

The Court reiterated the point in the complex case of *Dansk Industri*[107] where it had
to consider a collective agreement in a Danish ceramics factory under which the majority of workers opted to be paid largely on a piecework basis. Their pay consisted of a
fixed element, paid as a basic hourly wage, and a variable element, paid by reference to
the number of items produced. In April 1990 a comparison was made between the average hourly wage of three sub-groups of workers.[108] The workers' union argued that the
difference in pay between the predominantly female blue-pattern painters and the male
automatic machine operators breached the requirement under Article 157 TFEU of
equal pay for work of equal value.

The Court said that while the principle of equal pay applied to piecework pay systems
the mere finding that there was a difference in the average pay of two groups of workers,
calculated on the basis of the total individual pay of all the workers belonging to the
group, did not suffice to establish discrimination, since that difference might have been
due to differences in the individual output of the workers constituting the two groups,

---

[102] See additionally Case C–7/93 *Beune* [1994] ECR I–4471 (discrimination against married men) and Case
C–128/93 *Fisscher* v. *Voorhuis Hengelo and Stichting Bedrijfspensioenfonds voor de Detailhandel* [1994] ECR
I–4583 (discrimination against married women). In *Beune* the Court ruled that married men placed at a
disadvantage by discrimination must be treated in the same way and have the same rules applied to them as
married women.

[103] Case C–249/96 [1998] ECR I–621.

[104] Cf. the decision of the European Court of Human Rights concerning Art. 8 of the European Convention
in *Smith and Grady* v. *United Kingdom* [1999] IRLR 734.

[105] Case 109/88 [1989] ECR I–3199.

[106] Although it did say that if the application of such a wholly neutral criterion systematically works to the
disadvantage of women, then the only explanation is that the employer has misapplied the criterion and so
cannot objectively justify its application.

[107] Case C–400/93 [1995] ECR I–1275.

[108] This found that the average hourly pay of the automatic machine operators (an all-male group of 26 turners)
was Danish Krone (DKR) 103.93, including a fixed element of DKR 71.69, the pay of the blue-pattern painters
(155 women and 1 man) was DKR 91, including a fixed element of DKR 57, and the pay of the ornamental plate
painters (an all-female group of 51) was DKR 116.20, including a fixed element of DKR 35.85.

rather than to a difference between the units of measurement applicable to the two groups. Further, the Court said that it was for the national court to decide whether a pay differential relied on by a worker belonging to a group consisting predominantly of women as evidence of sex discrimination against that worker compared with a worker belonging to a group consisting predominantly of men was due to a difference between the units of measurement, which would contravene Article 157 TFEU, or to a difference in output, which would not.

3. THE PROBLEM WITH APPLYING THE PRINCIPLE OF NON-DISCRIMINATION IN EQUAL PAY CASES

Even though the principle of non-discrimination is well established in the case law on Article 157 TFEU, it is not always easy to see how non-discrimination principles actually fit with those of equal pay, particularly where work of equal value is at stake. This is because the equal pay model is intended to eliminate pay practices which have, over time, worked to depress the pay of certain jobs typically carried out by women. This is not simply about removing direct or indirect discrimination on the grounds of sex but addressing structural failings in the system. Thus, it could be argued that the equal pay legislation can and should go beyond the non-discrimination model. However, the Court has not always appreciated this and this helps to explain the tensions in the case law.

One line of case law suggests the claimant needs to show the three equal pay criteria we have considered (comparator, engaged in equal work/work of equal value, in the same establishment or service) *and* an element of discrimination (we shall refer to this as the discrimination model). This was the approach adopted by the Court in *Jämo*.[109] Two midwives claimed equal pay, arguing that they were engaged in work of equal value with a (male) clinical technician. The Court said that if the national court found that they were engaged on work of equal value, it (the CJEU) found that midwives were paid less. It continued:[110]

> It follows that, in order to establish whether it is contrary to Article [157] of the Treaty and to Directive [2006/54] for the midwives to be paid less, the national court must verify whether the statistics available indicate that a considerably higher percentage of women than men work as midwives. If so, there is indirect sex discrimination, unless the measure in point is justified by objective factors unrelated to any discrimination based on sex.[111]

The other line of case law suggests that once the three criteria outlined above have been shown, it is sufficient to raise the presumption that the difference in pay is due to

---

[109] Case C–236/98 *Örebro läns landsting* [2000] ECR I–2189.

[110] Para. 50.

[111] Case C–196/02 *Nikoloudi* v. *Organismos Tilepikinonion Ellados AE* [2005] ECR I–1789, where the Court said: 'It must be considered first of all whether equal work, or work of equal value exists' (para. 26). It then said: 'If that is the case . . . the alleged difference in treatment must then be considered in order to determine whether it is directly based on sex' (para. 30).

discrimination on the grounds of sex.[112] In other words, all the claimant needs to show is that a man and a woman are factually doing the same work but paid differently: this alone is sufficient to trigger the application of Article 157 TFEU. This is the approach adopted by the original British Equal Pay Act 1970 (now Equality Act 2010) which made no reference to the concept of discrimination.[113] Under the Equal Pay Act model all the complainants have to establish are the three conditions outlined above and then the burden shifts to the employer to show objective reasons for the pay differential unrelated to sex (the so-called material factor defence). Thus, all pay differentials between men and women can be objectively justified (and no account is taken of whether those differentials are directly or indirectly discriminatory). We shall refer to this as the 'equal pay' model.

This 'equal pay' model appears to have influenced the Court in *Enderby*.[114] The case concerned a female speech therapist, doing a job predominantly carried out by women, who claimed equal pay with pharmacists and clinical psychologists, jobs predominantly carried out by men.[115] Instead of raising questions of direct and indirect discrimination, the Court merely said:[116]

> … if the pay of speech therapists is significantly lower than that of pharmacists and if the former are almost exclusively women while the latter are predominantly men, there is a prima facie case of sex discrimination, at least where the two jobs in question are of equal value and the statistics describing that situation are valid.

In this case the burden shifted to the employer to show that the difference was based on objectively justified factors unrelated to any discrimination on the grounds of sex.[117] This approach has the advantage of allowing the employer to justify any pay differential without undermining the fundamental distinction (considered in the previous chapter) between direct discrimination (which can only be saved by express derogations which do not exist in Article 157 TFEU) and indirect discrimination (which can be objectively justified).

Two other cases appear to follow the *Enderby* approach: *Elsner-Lakeberg*[118] and *Brunnhofer*.[119] In *Elsner-Lakeberg* the Court said:[120]

---

[112] Lord Nicholls in the British House of Lords decision in *Glasgow* v. *Marshall* [2000] IRLR 272 said the scheme of the British Equal Pay Act was that a rebuttable presumption arose once a gender-based comparison shows that a woman doing like work/work rated as equivalent/work of equal value to that of a man was being treated less favourably than a man. The variation between his and her contract was presumed to be due to sex. In order to discharge the burden, the employer had to satisfy the tribunal of several matters: (1) the preferred reason is not a sham or pretence; (2) the less favourable treatment is due to this reason (the factor relied on is the cause of the disparity); (3) the reason is not the 'difference of sex' whether due to direct or indirect discrimination; and (4) the factor is a 'material one' between the woman and the man's case.

[113] Cf. Lord Browne-Wilkinson's approach in *Strathclyde* v. *Wallace* [1998] IRLR 146 which is now reflected in s. 69(2) Equality Act 2010.

[114] Case C–127/92 [1993] ECR I–5535.

[115] Para. 3.

[116] Para. 16.

[117] Para. 18.

[118] Case C–285/02 *Elsner-Lakeberg* v. *Land Nordrhein-Westfalen* [2004] ECR I–5861.

[119] Case C–381/99 *Brunnhofer* v. *Bank der österreichischen Postsparkasse AG* [2001] ECR I–4961.

[120] Para. 12, emphasis added.

Article [157] and Article [4 of Directive 2006/54], mean that, for the same work or for work to which equal value is attributed, *all discrimination* on grounds of sex with regard to the aspects and conditions of remuneration is prohibited unless that different treatment is *justified by an objective* unrelated to sex.

Although the case concerned a measure which discriminated against part-time workers and so was indirectly discriminatory, the Court nevertheless suggested that *all* discrimination could be objectively justified.

A stark example of this 'equal pay' model can be seen in *Brunnhofer*. Ms Brunnhofer was paid less than a male colleague recruited after her, even though they were both employed in the same salary group. Assuming that the difference in pay was on the ground of sex (the facts were disputed on this point), the discrimination at issue here was direct and so, according to a conventional analysis, could not be objectively justified. However, the Court, making no reference to the principle of discrimination, merely said:[121]

> ...the fundamental principle laid down in Article [157] of the Treaty...precludes unequal pay as between men and women for the same job or work of equal value, whatever the mechanism which produces such inequality..., unless the difference in pay is justified by objective factors unrelated to any discrimination linked to the difference in sex.

One possible way of squaring this circle would be to say that most equal value claims concern indirect discrimination. *Enderby*[122] could be explained on this basis: the Court assumed that speech therapists were predominantly women and pharmacists predominantly men so that rules paying speech therapists less were indirectly discriminatory unless they could be objectively justified.

The dichotomy between the discrimination model and the equal pay model is less acute when the defendant in an equal pay case is not an employer but the *state* and the challenge is to *legislation*. In these cases the Court places much less emphasis on establishing the three equal pay criteria and focuses instead on the need to prove discrimination. *Allonby*[123] shows this clearly. In her first claim (considered previously), Allonby, a teacher employed by an agency, tried to bring an equal pay claim against her day-to-day *employer* (the FE college), using one of her former male colleagues as a comparator. Although this claim was ultimately unsuccessful (because there was no single source to address the inequality), the case shows how the Court set about the task of determining whether an equal pay claim had been established. It focused on the three equal pay criteria[124] and not on the question of any discrimination. In other words, it adopted the equal pay model. However, in respect of Allonby's second claim, this time brought against the state (the Department for Education), that her exclusion from the Teachers' Superannuation Scheme (an exclusion based on *legislation*) was contrary to Article 157 TFEU—she was more successful. The Court did not apply the traditional, three equal pay criteria. Instead it concentrated on the question of discrimination.[125]

---

[121] Para. 30.   [122] Case C–127/92 [1993] ECR I–5535.
[123] Case C–256/01 *Allonby* v. *Accrington & Rosendale College* [2004] ECR I–873.
[124] Para. 42.   [125] Para. 81.

We shall now examine the application of the principle of non-discrimination to legislative rules.

4. DISCRIMINATORY LEGISLATIVE RULES

Article 23(a) of Directive 2006/54 confirms that Member States are required to abolish all discrimination arising from laws, regulations, or administrative provisions which are contrary to the principle of equal pay. Once again, both direct and indirect discrimination are prohibited. *Commission v. Greece*[126] was a case of direct discrimination: regulations provided for the grant of family and marriage allowances exclusively to married men workers. The Court said this contravened Article 157 TFEU.

Rinner-Kühn[127] concerned indirect discrimination. There the Court found that a German law obliging an employer to pay sick pay only to those employees who worked more than 10 hours a week or 45 hours a month discriminated against female workers and contravened Article 157 TFEU unless it could be objectively justified.[128] Similarly, in *Seymour-Smith*,[129] considered in detail in the previous chapter, the Court suggested that a rule requiring employees to work for two years before they acquired the right to claim unfair dismissal, might discriminate indirectly against women, where the statistics revealed a 'persistent and relatively constant disparity over a long period between men and women'[130] who were able to satisfy the requirement of two years' employment.

F. JUSTIFICATIONS

1. INTRODUCTION

The possibility for the employer or the state to justify unequal pay for objective factors unrelated to sex is of great importance. This possibility is certainly available where indirect discrimination is alleged; increasingly, the Court is referring to the possibility of objective justification where the discrimination is direct[131] and more generally when, in cases such as *Enderby*, the Court applies the 'equal pay' model without considering issues of discrimination.

In *Bilka-Kaufhaus*[132] the Court first recognized the possibility of the defendant being able to objectively justify pay differentials if the measures chosen 'correspond to a real need on the part of the undertaking, are appropriate with a view to achieving the objectives pursued and are necessary to that end'. The strictness of this test would suggest that concrete evidence is required: generalizations about certain categories of workers—

---

[126] Case C-187/98 *Commission v. Greece* [1999] ECR I-7713.   [127] Case 171/88 [1989] ECR 2743.
[128] See later, text attached to nn. 139–201.   [129] Case C-167/97 [1999] ECR I-623.
[130] Para. 61.   [131] Case C-381/99 *Brunnhofer* [2001] ECR I-4961.
[132] Case 170/84 [1986] ECR 1607, para. 36.

such as the belief that part-time workers are not as integrated in, or as dependent upon, the undertaking employing them as full-time workers—do not constitute objectively justified grounds.[133] The Court made this point clearly in *Hill* where the Court rejected the Irish government's argument that its reward system maintained staff motivation, commitment, and morale because it was 'no more than a general assertion unsupported by objective criteria'. Similarly, in *Kutz-Bauer*[134] the Court said that mere generalizations about the capacity of a specific measure to encourage recruitment were not enough to show that the aim of the disputed provisions was unrelated to any discrimination on the grounds of sex or to provide evidence on the basis of which it could be reasonably considered that the means chosen were or could be suitable for achieving that aim.

We begin by considering the factors that can be put forward to justify unequal pay (personal factors, market forces, and collective bargaining) before looking at the different approaches the Court adopts to those factors depending on the nature of the rule (and the defendant) being challenged. We conclude with an examination of proportionality.

2. THE FACTORS

2.1. Personal factors

(a) Examples of personal factors

Common personal factors invoked by employers to justify paying one person more than another include seniority, training, productivity, the quality of the work done, the difference between permanently established workers and secondees, and so-called 'red circling'.[135] Personal factors might also include the nature of the work done and the conditions in which it is carried out, including differences in the hours worked.[136]

The Court will check that the personal factor put forward is relevant. Thus in *Brunnhofer*[137] the Court said that if a male and female employee engaged on like work or work of equal value were appointed on different rates of pay, with the woman being paid less, the employer could not *later* justify that difference on the ground that the man's work was superior or that the woman's work had steadily deteriorated after her appointment.[138]

(b) Mobility and training

The Court has also been willing to scrutinize the justifications put forward to check that they do not themselves contain some form of unjustified discrimination. Its approach to personal factors, such as mobility and training, provides a good example. In *Danfoss*[139] it

---

[133] Case 171/88 *Rinner-Kühn* [1989] ECR 2743.
[134] Case C–187/00 *Kutz-Bauer v. Freie und Hansestadt Hamburg* [2003] ECR I–000, para. 58.
[135] *Snoxell v. Vauxhall Motors Ltd* [1977] IRLR 123, 125 (Philips J): red circling occurs where 'it is necessary to protect the wages of an employee, or a group of employees, moved from a better paid type of work to a worse paid type of work, perhaps because the first type is no longer undertaken'.
[136] Case C–236/98 *JämO* [2000] ECR I–2189.   [137] Case C–381/99 [2001] ECR I–4961.
[138] Para. 79.   [139] Case 109/88 [1989] ECR I–3199.

recognized that a criterion for awarding a pay increase to reward employees' adaptability to variable hours and places of work could work to the disadvantage of female employees who, because of household and family duties, were not as able as men to organize their working time with such flexibility.[140] Similarly, the criterion of training may work to the disadvantage of women in so far as they have had less opportunity than men for training or have taken less advantage of that opportunity.[141] In both cases the employer may only justify the remuneration of such adaptability or training by showing it is of importance for the performance of specific tasks entrusted to the employee.[142]

(c) Seniority

The Court's approach to seniority has been less consistent. Pay based on length of service indirectly discriminates against women since they generally have more interrupted careers and so less continuous service. This would suggest that such pay scales should be subject to the full rigours of the *Bilka-Kaufhaus* test. On the other hand, seniority based pay scales are deeply entrenched in pay structures in the Member States. This might suggest a lower standard of scrutiny, or even none at all. It is this last approach which the Court adopted in *Danfoss*[143] where it said that a criterion which rewarded length of service, while operating to the prejudice of women in so far as women have entered the labour market more recently than men or more frequently take a career break, did not require special justification.[144] It reasoned that since length of service went hand-in-hand with experience, and since experience generally enabled employees to perform their duties better, the employer was free to reward length of service without having to establish the importance service had in the performance of specific tasks entrusted to the employee.

However, *Nimz*[145] suggests that the Court was prepared to offer a more nuanced view, at least in the context of part-time work. Once again it recognized that experience went hand in hand with length of service but this time it added that 'the objectivity of such a criterion depends on all the circumstances in a particular case, and in particular on the relationship between the nature of the work performed and the experience gained from the performance of the work upon completion of a certain number of working hours'.[146] This was a matter for the national court to determine.[147]

Gerster[148] and *Kording*[149] also concerned the application of length of service rules for the purposes of promotion and accreditation. In *Gerster* part-time workers had their service counted at either zero (for part-time work at less than half time), two-thirds (for part-time work at one-half to two-thirds time), or full-time (for part-time work over two-thirds time). As the Advocate General pointed out, such a system totally lacked the internal coherence necessitated by the requirement of objective justification. While not going as far as its Advocate General, the Court pointed out, as it had previously held in *Nimz*, that:[150]

---

[140] Para. 21.   [141] Para. 23.

[142] Paras. 22–3. Cf. Case C–309/97 *Wiener Gebietskrankenkasse* [1999] ECR I–2865, para. 19.

[143] Case 109/88 [1989] ECR I–3199.   [144] Para. 24.   [145] Case C–184/89 [1991] ECR I–297.

[146] Para. 14.   [147] Ibid.   [148] Case C–1/95 [1997] ECR I–5253.

[149] Case C–100/95 [1997] ECR I–5289.   [150] Para. 39.

it is impossible to identify objective criteria... on the basis of an alleged special link between length of service and acquisition of a certain level of knowledge and experience, since such a claim amounts to no more than a generalisation concerning certain categories of worker.

Rather, it said, an individual assessment had to be made by the national court, on the basis of all the circumstances of the individual case, and the nature of the work and the experience acquired through time by the particular employee.

The Court was forced to address the issue of seniority, outside the context of part-time work, in *Cadman*.[151] Mrs Cadman earned about £35,000 pa while her male comparators earned between £39,000 and £44,000 pa. These differences derived from their greater length of service since the pay scale was broadly service related and she argued that this was indirectly discriminatory against women. Advocate General Poiares Maduro neatly encapsulated the dilemma facing the Court. He said that if it is admitted that length of service is a valid proxy for rewarding experience and efficiency, then it will be impossible for an employee to challenge a pay system that relies on length of service even if such a system in fact works to the disadvantage of women. Conversely, if it is found that an employer must justify any difference in treatment which arises out of the use of length of service as a criterion in the pay system, it may prove difficult for the employer to give precise and detailed evidence of the extent to which efficiency and productivity increase with seniority.[152]

The Court appeared to recognize the force of the second argument over the first. It said that since, as a general rule, recourse to the criterion of length of service is appropriate to attain the legitimate objective of rewarding experience acquired which enables the worker to perform his/her duties better, the employer does not have to establish specifically that recourse to that criterion is appropriate to attain that objective as regards a particular job. Thus, in the ordinary case there is a presumption that the service criterion is lawful.[153] However, in a nod to the Advocate General's first point, the Court provided a window for an individual to challenge seniority criteria because it added 'unless the worker provides evidence capable of raising serious doubts' as to the appropriateness of using service as a criteria for awarding experience.[154] While an apparently neat solution, the practicalities thrown up by the decision are numerous: how will individuals know they are a normal case or an exceptional case? How much evidence will they need to produce to show that longer service does not lead to better performance? And how will they obtain that evidence given that the judgment suggests that only in exceptional cases are they entitled to ask. Further, the Court's added remarks—that 'where a job classification system based on an evaluation of the work to be carried out is used in determining pay, there is no need to show that an individual worker has acquired experience during the relevant period which has enabled him to

[151] Case C–17/05 *Cadman v. Health and Safety Executive* [2006] ECR I-9583.   [152] Para. 1.

[153] See additionally Joined Cases C–297/10 and C–298/10 *Hennigs v. Eisenbahn-Bundesamt* [2011] ECR I–000, para. 74.

[154] Para. 40.

perform his duties better'—seem to negate the earlier premise on which the judgment was based, namely that length of service equates to greater efficiency.[155]

2.2. Market forces/labour market factors

The Court has also allowed objective justifications to take account of economic factors relating to the needs and objectives of the undertaking[156] and of the state.[157] Thus, when the *state* is defending its indirectly discriminatory legislation, the Court has recognized that the encouragement of recruitment constitutes a legitimate aim of social policy.[158] When *employers* are seeking to justify their practices, the Court has permitted them to justify paying full-time workers more than part-time workers in order to encourage full-time work,[159] and paying certain jobs more in order to attract candidates when the market indicates that such workers are in short supply.[160] However, the Court does not permit employers to pay part-time workers less simply because they are part-time,[161] or job-sharers less solely on the grounds that avoidance of such discrimination would involve increased costs.[162] In a similar vein, it also impermissible for a state to argue that public utilities should not bear excessive costs.[163]

While the Court will not usually accept economic justifications put forward by *employers* that it costs too much to secure equal pay,[164] it tends to be more deferential to a state's arguments based on budgets when the state is defending its own legislative

---

[155] For more general criticism, see G. Beck, 'The State of EC anti-discrimination law and the judgment in *Cadman*, or how the legal can become the political' (2007) 33 *ELRev.* 549.

[156] Case 96/80 *Jenkins* [1981] ECR 911.

[157] Case C–189/91 *Kirsammer-Hack* v. *Sidal* [1993] ECR I–6185, paras. 33–4: measures which excluded part-time workers from the calculation of the threshold of five employees (if the employer employed less than five employees the rules on unfair dismissal did not apply) could be objectively justified by reference to the need 'to alleviate the constraints burdening small businesses which play an essential role in economic development and the creation of employment in the [Union]'.

[158] Case C–167/97 *Seymour-Smith and Perez* [1999] ECR I–623, para. 71.

[159] See e.g. Case C–170/84 *Bilka-Kaufhaus* [1984] ECR 1607 where Bilka-Kaufhaus argued that the employment of full-time workers entailed lower ancillary costs and permitted the use of staff throughout opening hours. In general part-time workers refused to work in the late afternoons and on Saturdays. However, see now the Part-time Work Dir. 97/81 (OJ [1998] L14/9), considered in Ch. 9.

[160] Case C–127/92 *Enderby* [1993] ECR I–5535. If the national court can determine precisely what proportion of the increase in pay is attributable to market forces, it must necessarily accept that the pay differential is objectively justified to the extent of that proportion.

[161] Case C–196/02 *Nikoloudi* [2005] ECR I–1789, para. 51. See further Joined Cases C–4/02 and C–5/02 *Schönheit* [2003] ECR I–12575, para. 97 where the Court ruled that part-timers could not be paid less to stop them being placed at an advantage compared to full-timers. See now the Part-time Work Dir. 97/81 (OJ [1998] L14/9).

[162] Case C–243/95 *Hill* [1998] ECR I–3739, para. 40. In Case C–226/98 *Jørgensen* [2000] ECR I–2447, para. 42, the Court said that budgetary considerations could not in themselves justify discrimination on grounds of sex. However, measures intended to ensure sound management of public expenditure on specialized medical care and to guarantee people's access to such care could be justified if they met a legitimate objective of social policy, were appropriate and necessary. This is a 'costs plus' argument.

[163] Case C–196/02 *Nikoloudi* [2005] ECR I–1789, paras. 51–2.

[164] Case C–226/98 *Jørgensen* [2000] ECR I–2447, para. 39; Case C–243/95 *Hill and Stapleton* [1998] ECR I–3739, para. 40.

choices, provided the state's argument is carefully tailored. Thus in *Jørgensen*[165] the Court said that although budgetary considerations might underlie a Member State's choice of social policy and influence the nature or scope of the social protection measures which it wishes to adopt, they did not in themselves constitute an aim pursued by that policy and could not therefore justify discrimination against one of the sexes.[166] As the Court explained in *Kutz-Bauer*,[167] if budgetary considerations could justify a difference in treatment, the scope of the fundamental principle of equality could vary in time and place according to the state of the public finances of Member States. However, in *Jørgensen*[168] the Court went on to recognize that reasons relating to the need to ensure sound management of public expenditure on specialized medical care and to guarantee people's access to such care were legitimate and could justify measures of social policy.

2.3. Collective bargaining

The Court has also examined the validity of the justification that the discrimination was the result of separate structures of collective bargaining. In *Enderby*[169] the Court ruled that the fact that collective bargaining had led to the rates of pay of two jobs of equal value (speech therapy carried out almost exclusively by women and pharmacy performed predominantly by men) was not sufficient objective justification for the difference in pay between the two jobs. The Court reached this conclusion despite the fact that the collective bargaining was carried out by the same parties, and, taken separately, had in itself no discriminatory effect.

However, in *Dansk Industri*[170] the Court seems to have relaxed its view. It said that the national court could take into account the fact that the elements of pay were determined by separate collective bargaining in its assessment as to whether the differences between the two groups of workers were due to objective factors unrelated to sex.

3. DIFFERENT LEVELS OF SCRUTINY

3.1. Introduction

The (strict) *Bilka* test for objective justification was developed in the context of indirectly discriminatory conduct by *employers*. That test was broadly reflected in the Burden of Proof Directive[171] and now Directive 2006/54. It provides that an indirectly discriminatory measure is unlawful unless the measure is 'objectively justified by a legitimate aim, and the means of achieving that aim are appropriate and necessary'.[172] However, despite the fact that these two Directives lay down only the one test for objective justification, the Court of Justice seems to apply at least three tests for objective justification depending on the circumstances: the strict *Bilka* test for indirectly

---

[165] Case C-226/98 *Jørgensen* [2000] ECR I-2447, para. 30.
[166] Case C-343/92 *De Weerd and Others* [1994] ECR I-571, para. 35.
[167] Case C-187/00 [2003] ECR I-2741, para. 60.
[168] Case C-226/98 *Jørgensen* [2000] ECR I-2447, para. 30.   [169] Case C-127/92 [1993] ECR I-5535.
[170] Case C-400/93 *Dansk Industri* [1995] ECR I-1275.   [171] Dir. 97/80 ([1998] OJ L14/6).
[172] Art. 2(1)(b).

discriminatory conduct by *employers*,[173] the weaker *Seymour-Smith*[174] test for indirectly discriminatory *employment legislation*, and the very dilute test for *social security legislation* in *Nolte/Megner*.[175]

3.2. The sliding scale of objective justification

In the context of indirectly discriminatory *legislation*, the Court initially formulated a test similar to that in *Bilka*. In *Rinner-Kühn*,[176] a case concerning indirectly discriminatory employment legislation, the Court ruled that the Member State could justify such legislation provided that it could show that the means chosen met a necessary aim of its social policy and that the legislation was suitable for attaining that aim. In *De Weerd*[177] the Court applied *Rinner-Kühn* in the context of social security.

Subsequently, however, the Court has shown signs of diluting this test, at least in the context of social security cases. *Nolte*[178] and *Megner*[179] concerned German social security law under which individuals working less than 15 hours per week and whose income did not exceed one seventh of the monthly reference wage[180] were termed 'minor' or 'marginal' part-time workers. Since these workers were not subject to the statutory old-age insurance scheme covering invalidity and sickness benefit, they did not have to pay contributions. They were also exempt from paying contributions for unemployment benefit. Although the legislation affected considerably more women than men, the German government argued that the exclusion of people in minor employment corresponded to a structural principle of the German social security scheme, that there was a social demand for minor employment and that if it subjected marginal workers to compulsory insurance there would be an increase in unlawful employment and an increase in avoidance techniques (for instance false self-employment).

The Court began by citing *De Weerd*[181] and repeated the standard *Rinner-Kühn* test for objective justification. It said that social policy was a matter for the Member States which had a broad margin of discretion and could choose the measures capable of achieving the aim of their social and employment policy. It then said:

> It should be noted that the social and employment policy aim relied on by the German government is objectively unrelated to any discrimination on the grounds of sex and that,

---

[173] Case C–243/95 *Hill* [1998] ECR I–3739 (job sharers returning to full-time work).

[174] Case C–167/97 [1999] ECR I–623.

[175] Case C–317/93 *Nolte* [1996] ECR I–4625. Cf. Case C-123/10 *Brachner* [2011] ECR I-000, para. 62 where, in the social security context, the Court thought it was applying the most relaxed test but cited only *Seymour-Smith* (see e.g. paras. 73–4). For a full discussion, see S. O'Leary, *Employment Law at the European Court of Justice: Judicial Structures, Policies and Processes* (Hart Publishing, Oxford, 2002), Ch. 4.

[176] Case 171/88 [1989] ECR 2743.

[177] Case C–343/92 [1994] ECR I–571.

[178] Case C–317/93 *Nolte* [1996] ECR I–4625.

[179] Case C–444/93 *Megner*[1995] ECR I–4741.

[180] The average monthly salary of persons insured under the statutory old-age insurance scheme during the previous calendar year.

[181] Case C–343/92 [1994] ECR I–571.

in exercising its competence, the national legislature was *reasonably entitled* to consider that the legislation in question was necessary in order to achieve that aim.[182]

The Court reached similar conclusions in *Laperre*[183] and *Van Damme*.[184] The test of 'reasonableness' applied here is weaker than the more rigorous test envisaged by *Rinner-Kühn* and the subsequent cases. It is also striking that the Court itself decided in *Megner* that 'the legislation in question was necessary to achieve a social policy aim unrelated to any discrimination on the grounds of sex',[185] even though in *Lewark* the Court said that drawing such conclusions was a task for the national court. The Court reached this conclusion in *Megner* without citing any evidence, nor considering whether the social policy aim in question could be achieved by other means.[186] The Court also accepted that, with the exception of mere budgetary considerations,[187] almost any other social policy reason (provided it met the proportionality test) would justify indirect discrimination in state social security schemes.[188]

In *Seymour-Smith*[189] the Court was asked to choose between the *Rinner-Kühn* and *Nolte/Megner* tests when the state sought to justify indirectly discriminatory *employment* legislation. The answer was inconclusive. The Court's initial observations favoured the *Rinner-Kühn* test. It said:

It must also be ascertained, in the light of all the relevant factors and taking into account the possibility of achieving the social policy aim [encouragement of recruitment][190] in question by other means, whether such an aim appears to be unrelated to any discrimination based on sex and whether the disputed rule, as a means to its achievement, is capable of advancing that aim.[191]

The UK government, introducing the language of reasonableness, maintained that a Member State should merely have to show that it was reasonably entitled to consider that the measure would advance a social policy aim. The Court recalled that in *Nolte/Megner* it had observed that, in choosing the measures capable of achieving the aims of their social and employment policy, the Member States have a broad margin of discretion. It added:

75. However, although social policy is essentially a matter for the Member States under [Union] law as it stands, the fact remains that the broad margin of discretion available to

---

[182] Para. 30, emphasis added.   [183] Case C–8/94 *Laperre* [1996] ECR I–273.

[184] Case C–280/94 *Posthuma-van Damme* [1996] ECR I–179.

[185] It decided similarly in Case C–317/93 *Nolte* [1996] ECR I–4625 and Case C–8/84 *Laperre* [1996] ECR I–273.

[186] Cf. the British House of Lords' ruling in *R v. Secretary of State for Employment, ex parte EOC* [1994] IRLR 176 that the Secretary of State had failed to show that discriminatory service thresholds could be objectively justified.

[187] Case C–343/92 *De Weerd* [1994] ECR I–571.

[188] Case C–280/94 *Posthuma-van Damme* [1996] ECR I–179 and Case C–8/94 *Laperre* [1996] ECR I–273. See additionally Case C–25/01 *Rinke* [2003] ECR I–8349, para. 39 where the Court applied the relaxed test of justification when faced by a challenge to the validity of Union legislation.

[189] Case C–167/97 [1999] ECR I–623.

[190] The Court accepted that this was a legitimate aim of social policy (para. 71).

[191] Para. 72.

the Member States in that connection cannot have the effect of frustrating the implementation of a fundamental principle of [Union] law such as that of equal pay for men and women.

76. Mere generalisations concerning the capacity of a specific measure to encourage recruitment are not enough to show that the aim of the disputed rule is unrelated to any discrimination based on sex nor to provide evidence on the basis of which it could reasonably be considered that the means chosen were suitable for achieving that aim.

The Court then reformulated the test for justification in its answer to the national court in terms of the *Nolte/Megner* test:

77. Accordingly, the answer to the fifth question must be that if a considerably smaller percentage of women than men is capable of fulfilling the requirement of two years' employment imposed by the disputed rule, it is for the Member State, as the author of the allegedly discriminatory rule, to show that the said rule reflects a legitimate aim of its social policy, that that aim is unrelated to any discrimination based on sex, and that it could reasonably consider that the means chosen were suitable for attaining that aim.

It is still not clear which test is being applied: judges favouring a more rigorous approach to equality got their way in paragraphs 75 and 76; those favouring a more market-oriented concept, winning through in paragraph 77.[192]

So far we have been concentrating on indirectly discriminatory *state* legislation. However, in *Rinke*[193] the Court extended the same flexible approach to indirectly discriminatory *Union* legislation. At issue was a provision in the then Directive 86/457[194] requiring doctors to undertake certain periods of full-time training during part-time training in general medical practice. Although 'such a requirement does in fact place women at a particular disadvantage as compared with men',[195] the Court considered that:

It was reasonable for the legislature to take the view that that requirement enables doctors to acquire the experience necessary, by following patients' pathological conditions as they may evolve over time, and to obtain sufficient experience in the various situations likely to arise more particularly in general medical practice.

The existence of a sliding scale of tests is supported by the Court's decision in *Krüger*.[196] The case concerned the exclusion of those employed in 'minor' employment, as defined in *Nolte/Megner*, from an end of year bonus paid by the *employer* under a collective agreement. The Court, noting that the case concerned a situation 'which is different from ... *Nolte* and *Megner*',[197] said:

In this case, it is not a question of either a measure adopted by the national legislature in the context of its discretionary power or a basic principle of the German social security system, but of the exclusion of persons in minor employment from the benefit of a collective

---

[192] For a further example of a relaxed approach to indirectly discriminatory state legislation, see Case C–322/98 *Kachelmann* v. *Bankhaus Hermann Lampe KG* [2000] ECR I–7505, para. 34.
[193] Case C–25/02 *Rinke* [2003] ECR I–8349.   [194] OJ [1986] L267/26.   [195] Para. 35.
[196] Case C–281/97 *Krüger* v. *Kreiskrankenhaus Ebersberg* [1999] ECR I–5127.   [197] Para. 29.

agreement which provides for the grant of a special annual bonus, the result of this being that, in respect of pay, those persons are treated differently from those governed by that collective agreement.

This confirms that employers cannot rely on the more lenient test of justification available to the state. The Court itself then went on to find that the exclusion was indirectly discriminatory and, by implication, could not be objectively justified.[198]

4. PROPORTIONALITY

While proportionality has always been an integral part of the test for objective justification, in the more recent cases the Court has sought to re-emphasize its importance. We have already seen the Court's reference in *Kutz-Bauer* and *Seymour-Smith* to the fact that mere generalizations are not sufficient to show either that the discrimination was not based on sex or that the steps taken were proportionate. In *Steinicke*[199] the Court underlined this point. In order to benefit from a law permitting public servants approaching retirement to work part time, an individual employee was required to have worked full time for three of the five years immediately preceding the period of part-time work. Ms Steinicke, a part-time worker who could not satisfy these conditions, argued that the scheme was indirectly discriminatory contrary to Article 14 of Directive 2006/54. The Court agreed[200] and also found that the national law was not a proportionate means of achieving the objective. It noted that the national rules excluded from access to part-time working scheme the very group of people (public servants working part-time) who made a considerable contribution to the unblocking of the employment market.[201] It continued:

> As a result, a provision of national law which poses the risk that workers may be discouraged from accepting part-time work for older employees cannot *a priori* be considered to be an apt or suitable means of attaining the objective of unblocking the employment market.

G. ENFORCEMENT OF EQUALITY RIGHTS

1. DIRECT EFFECT

In *Defrenne (No. 2)*[202] the Court ruled that Article 157 TFEU was directly effective and could thus give rise to individual rights which the courts had to protect.[203] This means that the prohibition of discrimination applies 'not only to the actions of public authorities, but also extends to all agreements which are intended to regulate paid

---

[198] Para. 30.   [199] Case C–77/02 *Steinicke* v. *Bundesanstalt für Arbeit* [2003] ECR I–9027.
[200] Para. 57.   [201] Para. 65.   [202] Case 43/75 [1976] ECR 455.
[203] On the background to the direct effect of Article 157 TFEU, see AG Lamothe's opinion in Case 80/60 *Defrenne (No. 1)* [1971] ECR 445, 456.

labour collectively,[204] as well as contracts between individuals'.[205] Thus, Article 157 TFEU has both vertical *and* horizontal direct effect. At first the Court suggested that Article 157 TFEU was not directly effective in the context of 'indirect or disguised discrimination' which requires the 'elaboration by the [Union] and national legislative bodies of criteria of assessment',[206] but in *Bilka-Kaufhaus*[207] the Court said that individuals could rely on Article 157 TFEU to secure the elimination of indirect discrimination. It now seems that although the Court continues to pay lipservice to this potential limit on the direct effect of Article 157 TFEU,[208] the limitation is, in reality, redundant for the Court has found Article 157 TFEU to be directly effective in areas of great complexity, including occupational pensions and survivors' benefits.[209]

Since Article 1 of Directive 75/117 was essentially designed 'to facilitate the practical application of the principle of equal pay laid down in Article [157]' and in no way altered the scope or content of that principle,[210] exceptionally it had both vertical and horizontal direct effect. It is likely that the same approach will apply to Article 4 of the Sex Equality Directive 2006/54.

2. BURDEN OF PROOF

The Court has ruled that in principle the burden of proving the existence of sex discrimination lies with the complainant.[211] It has, however, recognized that adjustments to national rules on the burden of proof may be necessary to ensure the effective implementation of the principle of equality. This can be seen in *Danfoss*.[212] In that case the employer's pay structure provided the same basic wage to all employees but paid additional individual supplements on the basis of mobility, training, and seniority. This resulted in the average wage paid to men being 6.86 per cent higher than that paid to women. This system was so lacking in transparency that female employees could only establish differences between their pay and that received by their male colleagues by reference to average pay. Consequently, the Court concluded that the applicants would be deprived of any effective means of enforcing the principle of equal pay before the

---

[204] Article 23(b) of the Sex Equality Dir. 2006/54 obliges Member States to take the necessary measures to ensure that provisions appearing in collective agreements, wage scales, wage agreements, or individual contracts of employment, which are contrary to the principle of equal pay, are declared null and void or can be amended. In Case C–33/89 *Kowalska* [1990] ECR I–2591 the Court confirmed that Art. 157 TFEU applied to collective agreements.

[205] See additionally Case C–28/93 *Van den Akker* [1994] ECR I–4527, para. 21; Case C–320/00 *Lawrence* [2002] ECR I–7325, para. 13.

[206] Case 43/75 *Defrenne (No. 2)* [1996] ECR 455, para. 19, and Case 129/79 *Macarthys* [1980] ECR 1275, para. 15.

[207] Case 170/84 [1986] ECR 1607.

[208] See e.g. Case C–262/88 *Barber* [1990] ECR I–1889, para. 37.

[209] Case C–262/88 *Barber* [1990] ECR I–1889 and Case 109/91 *Ten Oever* [1993] ECR I–5535, respectively.

[210] Case 96/80 *Jenkins v. Kingsgate* 1981] ECR 911; Case C–381/99 *Brunnhofer* [2001] ECR I–4961, para. 29.

[211] Case C–127/92 *Enderby* [1993] ECR I–5535.

[212] Case 109/88 [1989] ECR I–3199. See further Case 318/86 *Commission v. France* [1988] ECR 3559; Case 248/83 *Commission v. Germany* [1985] ECR 1459; Case C–127/92 *Enderby* [1993] ECR I–5535.

national courts if the effect of producing such evidence was not to impose upon employers the burden of proving that their pay practices were not in fact discriminatory.

Similarly, in *Enderby* the Court concluded that if the pay of speech therapists was significantly lower than that of pharmacists, and the speech therapists were almost exclusively women while the pharmacists were predominantly men, there was a prima facie case of discrimination, at least where the two jobs were of equal value and the statistics describing the situation were valid. As a result it was for the employers to show that there were objective reasons for the difference in pay and for the national court to assess whether it could take those statistics into account and to assess whether they covered a large enough number of individuals, whether they illustrated purely fortuitous or short-term phenomena, and whether in general they appeared to be significant.[213]

However, in *Dansk Industri*[214] the Court sounded a note of caution. It said that in a piecework pay scheme a prima facie case of discrimination did not arise solely because significant statistics disclose appreciable differences between the average pay of two groups of workers, since those statistics might be due to differences in individual output of the workers in the two groups. However, where the individual pay consisted of both a fixed and a variable element, and it was not possible to identify the factors which determined the rates or units of measurement used to calculate the variable element in the pay, the employer might have to bear the burden of proving that the differences found were not due to sex discrimination. Again, it was for the national court to decide whether the conditions for shifting the burden of proof were satisfied.

This case law, allowing a reversal of the burden of proof,[215] helped to unblock a Directive on the Burden of Proof proposed under Articles 115 and 352 TFEU (ex 94 and 308 EC),[216] but which had not made progress in Council. Eventually the Commission initiated the procedure under Article 154 TFEU,[217] which led to the adoption (via the legislative route)[218] of Directive 97/80 on the burden of proof.[219] The Directive, now incorporated into Directive 2006/54, is a minimum standards measure[220] which applies to the situations covered by the Directive, together with Article 157 TFEU, and, in so far as discrimination based on sex is concerned, the Directives on Pregnant Workers and Parental Leave.[221] It also applies to any civil or adminis-

---

[213] See additionally Case C–400/93 *Dansk Industri* [1995] ECR I–1275; Case C–236/98 *Örebro läns landsting* [2000] ECR I–2189, para. 53.

[214] Case C–400/93 [1995] ECR I–1275.

[215] According to E. Ellis, *EU Anti-discrimination Law* (OUP, Oxford, 2005) 99 the Court meant the legal, as distinct from the evidential, burden of proof.

[216] The Commission's original proposal can be found at OJ [1988] C176/5.

[217] The first round of consultations was launched on 5 July 1995. The Social Partners' opinions differed. Some did not consider any action in the area to be justified, since a series of national legal instruments and the Court's case law had already achieved the desired aim. Others thought that action should be taken at European level while respecting the principle of subsidiarity. As far as the proper level and nature of the action to be taken, some organizations preferred a binding Union measure and others a less rigid approach, such as a recommendation.

[218] See further Ch. 2.   [219] OJ [1998] L14/16, amended by Council Dir. 98/52 (OJ [1998] L205/66).

[220] Art. 19(2).   [221] Art. 20(4)(a).

trative procedure concerning the public or private sector which provides for means of redress under national law pursuant to Article 157 TFEU and the Equality Directives.[222] Article 19(1) provides that Member States shall take such measures as are necessary, in accordance with their national judicial systems, to ensure that:

> when persons who consider themselves wronged because the principle of equal treatment has not been applied to them establish, before a court or other competent authority, facts from which it may be presumed that there has been direct or indirect discrimination, it shall be for the respondent to prove that there has been no breach of the principle of equal treatment.[223]

Although the reversal of the burden of proof is unpopular with employers, it is now firmly entrenched in the Union acquis, including in the Article 19 Directives.

3. JUDICIAL REMEDIES

3.1. Effectiveness of the remedy

It is a long-established principle of Union law that under the duty of co-operation laid down in Article 4(3) TEU (ex 10 EC), the Member States must ensure the legal protection which individuals derive from the direct effect of Union law.[224] In the absence of Union rules governing a matter, it is for the domestic legal system of each Member State to designate the courts having jurisdiction and to lay down detailed procedural rules governing actions for safeguarding rights for individuals (the principle of procedural autonomy). However, such rules must not be less favourable than those governing similar domestic actions (the principle of equivalence) nor render virtually impossible or excessively difficult the exercise of rights conferred by Union law (the principle of effective judicial protection).[225]

The question of the adequacy of national remedies has been of central importance to the procedural protection conferred by the Equality Directives. Originally, Article 6 of the Equal Pay Directive 75/117/EEC required Member States to ensure that the principle

---

[222] Art. 20(4)(b). It does not apply to out-of-court procedures of a voluntary nature or provided for in national law.

[223] Art. 19(1). Art. 19(2) says that para. 1 does not prevent Member States from introducing rules of evidence which are more favourable to claimants; Art. 19(3) says that Member States do not need to apply para. 1 to proceedings in which it is for the court or competent body to investigate the facts of the case; and Art. 19(5) says that the rules on the reversal of the burden of proof will not apply to criminal procedures unless otherwise provided by the Member States.

[224] According to Case C–187/98 *Commission* v. *Greece* [1999] ECR I–7713, para. 45, a Member State cannot plead practical, administrative or financial difficulties to justify non-compliance with the obligations and time limits laid down by the Directive.

[225] See e.g. Case 33/76 *Rewe-Zentralfinanz eG* v. *Landwirtschaftskammer für das Saarland* [1976] ECR 1989, para. 5. See generally M. Dougan, 'The Vicissitudes of Life at the Coalface: remedies and procedures for enforcing Union law before the national courts', in P. Craig and G. De Búrca (eds.), *The Evolution of EU Law* (OUP, Oxford, 2011).

of equal pay was applied,[226] and that effective means were available to ensure that the principle is observed. This provision has been repealed by Directive 2006/54. In addition, Article 2 of Directive 75/117 required Member States to allow those who consider themselves wronged by the failure to apply the principle of equal pay to pursue their claims by judicial process. This has now been replaced by Article 17 of Directive 2006/54, which requires Member States to ensure that, after possible recourse to other competent authorities including conciliation procedures:

> judicial and/or administrative procedures
> for the enforcement of obligations under this Directive are available to all persons who consider themselves wronged by failure to apply the principle of equal treatment to them, even after the relationship in which the discrimination is alleged to have occurred has ended.

In addition, Article 18 of Directive 2006/54 requires Member States to introduce into their legal systems such measures as are necessary:

> to ensure real and effective compensation or reparation as the Member States so determine for the loss and damage sustained by a person injured as a result of discrimination on grounds of sex, in a way which is dissuasive and proportionate to the damage suffered.

Since these provisions are largely based on the case law decided under the original Equal Treatment Directive 76/207 they will be discussed in more detail in the next chapter. In this chapter we shall focus on the issues specific to equal pay.

The Court has required that the amount of *each* individual benefit paid be non-discriminatory[227] and that access to the benefits (such as membership of an occupational pension scheme) be non-discriminatory.[228] The pensions case law has thrown up two other major remedies issues:[229] (1) claims for arrears of pay where national law only allows arrears to be recovered for a limited period; and (2) time limits for bringing a claim (e.g. six months from the end of employment). The first issue is considered in this chapter, the second in Chapter 10.

In respect of the first issue, an individual may wish to claim for arrears in respect of periods which predate the period for which recovery is permitted under national law.[230] In this context, the Court has had to strike a balance between, on the one hand, legal certainty (and the cost to an individual pension scheme, government, or employer) and, on the other, the principle of effective judicial protection. In two social security

---

[226] According to the Court, Member States may leave the implementation of the principle of equal pay to representatives of management and labour but this does not discharge Member States from the obligation of ensuring that all workers are afforded the full protection of the Directive, especially where the workers are not union members, where the sector is not covered by a collective agreement, or where the agreement does not fully guarantee the principle of equal pay: Case 143/83 *Commission* v. *Denmark* [1985] ECR 427.

[227] Case C–262/88 *Barber* [1990] ECR I–1889 The same principle of transparency was applied to the original Dirs 76/207 and 86/613 in Case C–226/98 *Jørgensen* [2000] ECR I–2447, paras. 27 and 36.

[228] Case 170/84 *Bilka-Kaufhaus* [1986] ECR 1607. See further Ch. 10.

[229] See further Ch. 10.

[230] These issues will be examined further in respect of social security claims under Dir. 79/7, considered in Ch. 10.

cases, *Johnson*[231] and *Steenhorst Neerings*,[232] the Court held that a restriction on back-dating was valid under Union law. However, in the context of equal pay this might have the effect of denying the individual the benefit of the entitlement. The interplay of these two issues can be seen in the cases of *Magorrian*[233] and *Levez*.[234]

In *Magorrian* the applicants began employment as full-time workers and then became part-time workers when they had children. When they retired they were not entitled to the more favourable pension benefits available to full-time workers and so they brought a claim under Article 157 TFEU. In response, it was argued that, under the relevant statute, no award for arrears of pay could be made relating to a period earlier than two years before the date on which the proceedings had been instituted. However, the Court said the fact that the right to be admitted to a scheme might have effect from a date no earlier than two years before the institution of proceedings would deprive the applicants of the additional benefits under the scheme to which they were entitled to be affiliated, since those benefits could be calculated only by reference to periods of service completed by them two years prior to the commencement of proceedings. The Court then distinguished *Magorrian* from *Johnson*. It said that in *Magorrian* the claim was not for the retroactive award of certain additional benefits but for recognition of entitlement to full membership of an occupational scheme (which would lead to payment in the future of benefits based on that membership). The rules at issue in *Johnson* merely limited the period, prior to the commencement of proceedings, in respect of which backdated benefits could be obtained. In *Magorrian* the rule at issue prevented the entire record of service completed by those concerned after 8 April 1976 (the date of the judgment in *Defrenne (No. 2)*) until 1990 (two years prior to the start of proceedings) from being taken into account for the purposes of calculating the additional benefits which would be payable even after the date of the claim. Consequently, the Court said that the two-year rule rendered any action by individuals relying on Union law impossible in practice.

The Court also emphasized the principle of effectiveness in *Levez*.[235] In February 1991 Mrs Levez was appointed manager of a betting shop owned by Jennings at a salary of £10,800 per annum. The employer falsely declared to her that this had been her male predecessor's salary. In fact, Mrs Levez's salary did not reach that of the predecessor (£11,400 per annum) until April 1992. Mrs Levez did not find this out until September 1993, whereupon she brought a claim for equal pay. The UK Industrial Tribunal said that Mrs Levez was entitled to a salary of £11,400 from the date on which she had taken up the job, and ordered Jennings to pay her arrears. Jennings appealed this decision, arguing that, in view of the national law concerning damages for failure to

[231] Case C–410/92 *Johnson* v. *Chief Adjudication Officer* [1994] ECR I–5483.
[232] Case C–338/91 *Steenhorst-Neerings* v. *Bestuur van de Bedrijfsvereniging* [1993] ECR I–5475.
[233] Case C–246/96 *Magorrian and Cunningham* v. *Eastern Health and Social Services Board and Department of Health and Social Services* [1997] ECR I–7153. See additionally Case C–78/98 *Preston* v. *Wolverhampton Health Care NHS Trust* [2000] ECR I–3201 which is considered in detail in Ch. 10.
[234] Case C–326/96 *Levez* v. *TH Jennings (Harlow Pools) Ltd* [1998] ECR I–7835.
[235] Case C–326/96 [1998] ECR I–7835.

comply with the equal pay principle, the Industrial Tribunal had no power to award arrears of remuneration in respect of a time earlier than two years before the date on which the proceedings were instituted before the tribunal.[236] Thus, as Mrs Levez's application to the Industrial Tribunal was dated 17 September 1993, arrears could not be awarded in respect of the period before 17 September 1991.

The Court, having reviewed its jurisprudence on effective judicial protection, concluded that in principle it was compatible with Union law for national rules to prescribe reasonable limitation periods for bringing proceedings, in the interests of legal certainty. Therefore, a national procedural rule, such as that at issue in *Levez*, would not in itself be incompatible with Union law.[237] However, the Court went on to consider the circumstances of Mrs Levez's case, and in particular the fact that the employer had concealed from Mrs Levez the pay of her predecessor. The Court pointed out that in such circumstances, an employee would have no means of determining whether she was being discriminated against. Thus the employer would effectively be able to deprive the employee of the entitlement to enforce the principle of equal pay before the courts.[238] To allow an employer, in such a situation, to rely on a procedural rule of national law, would make it virtually impossible or excessively difficult for the employee to obtain arrears of remuneration in respect of sex discrimination in pay. In these circumstances, the Court said, there existed no justification for the application of the national rules in terms of legal certainty or the proper conduct of proceedings.[239]

Levez also raised the issue as to what the principle of equivalence actually meant in practice. It was argued by the employer and the United Kingdom government that Mrs Levez did have an adequate remedy in national law, in that she could bring proceedings not before the Industrial Tribunal, but before the county court on the basis of breach of contract pursuant to the (then) UK Equal Pay Act 1970 and the tort of deceit committed by the employer. The national court asked the Court what would constitute a 'similar domestic action', in the context of the principle of equivalence, where national law made different provision for equal pay than that made for other employment rights. The Court essentially said that it was for the national court to determine this issue. Where the alternative remedy in the county court was likely to entail procedural rules or other conditions which were less favourable than those appertaining before an Industrial Tribunal, then the principle of equivalence would be breached. In making this determination, the national court would need to take into account matters such as the relative costs and delays involved in each proceedings.[240]

---

[236] UK Equal Pay Act 1970, s. 2(5).   [237] Para. 20.

[238] Cf. the Court's approach in respect of transparency and the burden of proof in Case 109/88 *Danfoss* [1989] ECR 3199.

[239] Paras. 31–4. In *Levez (No. 2)* [1999] IRLR 764 the British EAT ruled that the two-year limitation on arrears of remuneration in EPA 1970, s. 2(5) breached Union law in that it was less favourable than those governing similar claims, such as for unlawful deduction from wages and unlawful discrimination on the grounds of race. It ruled that the six-year limit in the Limitation Act 1980 would apply.

[240] See further on this issue T. Hervey and P. Rostant, 'After *Francovich*: State Liability and British Employment Law' (1996) 25 *ILJ* 259. See further Case C–78/98 *Preston* v. *Wolverhampton Health Care NHS Trust* [2000] ECR I–3201, considered further in Ch. 10.

The Court in *Levez* showed some sensitivity to the practicalities of bringing an equal pay claim.[241] The reality of such claims is often that the employer is in a much stronger position than the employee, in terms of holding relevant information on comparative pay of men and women employees. In the absence of any duties of transparency, the remedial effect of equal pay law would be significantly reduced if an employer, particularly a deliberately deceitful employer, could hide behind technical procedural rules to escape an equal pay claim. What seems certain is that the Court is not going anywhere near so far as to impose on employers a duty to disclose sufficient information to allow women employees to ensure that they are paid equally with male comparators. Although to do so would no doubt improve the position of those seeking to bring an equal pay claim, it would also go a long way beyond the requirements of Article 157 TFEU and, in the absence of legislation requiring such disclosure, would constitute too great an infringement of national procedural autonomy.

3.2. Levelling up or down?

It might be expected that the realization of equality necessarily equates with a levelling up of entitlement. In *Defrenne (No. 2)*[242] the Court accepted this. It said that in view of the connection between Article 157 TFEU and the harmonization of working conditions while the improvement is being maintained,[243] it was not possible to comply with Article 157 TFEU in other ways than by raising the lowest salaries.[244] This point was reinforced by *Kutz-Bauer*[245] where the Court said that national courts were required to set aside discrimination, using all the means at their disposal, and 'in particular by applying those provisions for the benefit of the class placed at a disadvantage, and are not required to await the setting aside of the provisions by the legislature, by collective negotiation or otherwise.'[246]

Thus Union law envisages levelling up by national courts once a finding of discrimination has been made. However, if an employer subsequently decides to level down, this is compatible with Union law. This is because, under Union law there is no background requirement of distributive justice (since formal equality is satisfied whether the two parties are treated equally well or equally badly). This can be seen in *Smith*[247] where the Court said that where the employer had decided to achieve equality by levelling down of entitlement (so that women received their pension at 65, the age at which the men had received it, rather than men receiving their pension at 60, as women had previously), this was compatible with Union law.

---

[241] See further C. Barnard and T. Hervey, 'European Union Employment and Social Policy Survey 1998' (1998) 18 *Yearbook of European Law* 613, 638–40.

[242] Case 43/75 [1976] ECR 455. See further Case C–102/88 *Ruzius Wilbrink* [1989] ECR 4311.

[243] See Art. 117 EEC (new Art. 151 TFEU) and Case 126/86 *Zaera* [1987] ECR 3697.

[244] See further Case C–102/88 *Ruzius Wilbrink* [1989] ECR I–4311 where the Court said that part-timers are entitled to have the same system applied to them as other workers in proportion to their working hours. The principle of this case was applied to collective agreements in Case 33/89 *Kowalska* [1990] ECR I–2591.

[245] Case C–187/00 [2003] ECR I–2741, para. 75.

[246] Case C–184/89 *Nimz* [1991] ECR I–297, para. 21.

[247] Case C–408/92 [1994] ECR I–4435.

Transitional arrangements, whereby, for example, a collective agreement, which replaces a system of pay leading to discrimination by a system of pay based on objective criteria while maintaining, for a transitional period limited in time, some of the discriminatory effects of the earlier system, in order to ensure that arrangements made to allow employees in post to be transferred to the new system without suffering a loss of income are compatible with EU law.[248]

3.3. Proportionate value?

The Court has not yet decided the question of how equal in value the men and women's work must be to receive equal pay. Since the Court has insisted that 'equal work be remunerated with equal pay'[249] this suggests that only work of exactly equal value should receive equal pay. The Court has also not yet considered the question of whether Article 157 TFEU should secure a woman proportionate pay, that is, a proportionate increase in pay when her work is valued. For example, if her work is valued at 60 per cent of the man's, yet she receives only 40 per cent of his pay, can she rely on Union law to receive the additional 20 per cent?[250] There are straws in the wind to suggest that the Court might consider such a claim. For example, in *Rummler*[251] the Court said that it followed from the principle that equal work must be remunerated with equal pay that work performed must be remunerated according to its nature. This case, when read in conjunction with Article 151 TFEU (ex 136 EC) and the Directive on Part-time Work,[252] might suggest that part-time workers should receive a proportionate share of full-time earnings.[253]

Enderby[254] lends some support to this view. When considering the market forces justification for paying one group of (predominantly male) workers more than another (predominantly female) group, the Court said that if the national court has been able to determine precisely what proportion of the increase in pay is attributable to market forces, 'it must necessarily accept that the pay differential is objectively justified to the extent of that proportion'.[255] The Court then added that 'When national authorities have to apply [Union] law, they must apply the principle of proportionality'.[256] This sentence has prompted some commentators to suggest that Union law might provide a basis for a proportionate pay claim.

---

[248] Joined Cases C-297/10 and C-298/10 *Hennigs* [2011] ECR I-000, para. 99. The case was decided in the context of age discrimination.

[249] Case 237/85 *Rummler* [1986] ECR 2101.

[250] See perhaps Case C-127/92 *Enderby* [1993] ECR I-5535. See further M. Rubinstein, 'The Equal Treatment Directive and UK Law', in C. McCrudden (ed.), *Women, Employment and European Equality Law* (Eclipse, London, 1987).

[251] Case 237/85 [1986] ECR 2101.

[252] Dir. 97/81/EC (OJ [1997] L14/9), as amended by Council Dir. 98/23/EC (OJ [1998] L131/10) and consolidated OJ [1998] L131/13.

[253] See further Case C-102/88 *Ruzius Wilbrink* [1989] ECR 4311.

[254] Case C-127/92 [1993] ECR I-5535.   [255] Para. 21.   [256] Ibid.

H. CONCLUSIONS

Although the principle of equal pay has been enshrined in the Treaties since 1957, women are still paid less than men for the same work or for work of equal value. The gender pay gap remains at 17.8 per cent for the EU as a whole (with Estonia at 30.9 per cent at one of end of the scale and Belgium at 9 per cent at the other). The pay gap is due to a variety of factors.[257] First, women are segregated both in terms of occupation and establishment. Predominantly female occupations attract consistently lower rates of pay than do male occupations. This is particularly the case where women work part-time, as the facts of *Enderby* highlight. In that case the majority of the speech therapists were women working part time while the majority of pharmacists were men working full time. Speech therapists earned up to 60 per cent less than pharmacists.

The second explanation for the difference in pay is that even where men and women do the same kind of work in the same organizations, women tend to attract lower pay because they are concentrated in lower paying specialisms, they occupy lower status jobs, and the method of remuneration impacts differently on men and women (by, for example, rewarding seniority or flexibility). Further, women's skills are often undervalued. This is exacerbated by the fact that, while much of the unfavourable stereotyping of women and their abilities has been swept away, many girls and young women are still following traditional routes in education and training, and being paid less than men as a result.[258]

Once again, this highlights the limits of the law, especially a complex law such as the one on equal pay, in achieving full equality. The law, dependent as it is on individual enforcement, cannot really address the heart of structural inequalities. Further, decisions such as *Lawrence* and *Allonby* serve only to underline the limits of the law. On the other hand, law can trigger social change and the inclusion, in the second paragraph of Article 21(4) of Directive 2006/54, of the possible obligation on employers to provide information to employees and their representatives about pay and pay differentials is a small but important step. Such transparency may reveal that there is a problem of a gender pay gap. The Directive also suggests that employers must put forward possible measures of how to improve it. The Commission also wants to experiment with new governance tools in an attempt to crack this persistent problem which the law has failed to address fully. So the Commission talks about supporting equal pay initiatives at the workplace such as equality labels, 'charters', and awards, as well as the development of tools for employers to correct unjustified gender pay gaps. In addition, it has instituted an annual European Equal Pay Day to be held each year to increase awareness on how much longer women need to work than men to earn the same.[259]

---

[257] See further Commission Communication, *Tackling the pay gap between men and women*, COM(2007) 424.
[258] Women and Work Commission, *Shaping a Fairer Future*, February 2006, vii.
[259] COM(2010) 491, 7.

8

EQUAL TREATMENT

A. INTRODUCTION

As we have already seen, the European Union has enjoyed a long history of prohibiting discrimination on the grounds of sex in the context of employment. The inclusion of Article 19 TFEU into the Treaty at Amsterdam gave the Union the power to prohibit discrimination on other grounds, notably race and ethnic origin, sexual orientation, religion and belief, age, and disability. Two Directives were subsequently adopted, Directive 2000/43 on race and ethnic origin and the so-called 'horizontal' or 'framework' Directive 2000/78, covering the remaining grounds. These built on the experience gained in the field of sex equality. This process of learning was, in turn, extended back into the sex equality field when Directive 2002/73 was adopted (under Article 157(3) TFEU (ex 141(3) EC)) amending the Equal Treatment Directive 76/207, to bring it into line with the employment aspects of the Article 19 Directives, and to reflect developments in the case law. The content of the Equal Treatment Directive 76/207 is now found in Directive 2006/54. The aim of this chapter is to consider the principle of equal treatment in these disparate areas.

B. THE PROHIBITED GROUNDS OF DISCRIMINATION

1. INTRODUCTION

The list of grounds on which discrimination is prohibited by the Union Directives—sex, sex change, marital status, race, ethnic origin, religion or belief, sexual orientation, age, and disability—largely mirrors those found in major international instruments[1] and other domestic Charters such as section 15(1) of the Canadian Charter of Fundamental Rights. The conventional argument for the prohibition of discrimination on grounds of

---

[1] E.g. Art. 2 Universal Declaration of Human Rights; Art. 2(2) International Covenant of Economic, Social and Cultural Rights; Art. 2(1) International Covenant of Civil and Political Rights.

sex, race, and ethnic origin is that these characteristics are immutable, clearly identifiable to employers, and are (usually) irrelevant to an individual's ability to do a job. By
taking these characteristics into account when making employment decisions, employers narrow any pool of applicants, often based on stereotypical assumptions associated
with the particular ground, with the result that the employer is not selecting the best
candidate on merit and suitability alone.

In respect of the other prohibited grounds of discrimination—sexual orientation,
religion or belief, age, and disability—they do not share all the characteristics associated with sex and race. For example, sexual orientation and disability may not be
clearly identifiable to an employer, and religion or belief is not necessarily immutable.
Age and disability may actually impact on an individual's ability to do a job. However,
what these groups do have in common is the risk that the individuals are excluded
from the possibility of participating fully in working life based on stereotypical
assumptions rather than because of an assessment of the individual's personal characteristics.[2] Thus, in the name of social inclusion, anti-discrimination legislation is
necessary to prevent such stereotyping from occurring. This line of argument has
influenced the European Employment Strategy. For example guideline 10 of the 2010
Council Decision[3] says:

> The extension of employment opportunities is an essential aspect of Member States' inte-
> grated strategies to prevent and reduce poverty and to promote full participation in soci-
> ety and economy.... Member States should put in place effective anti-discrimination
> measures. Empowering people and promoting labour market participation for those
> furthest away from the labour market while preventing in-work poverty will help fight
> social exclusion.

Thus, while the rationale for selecting these grounds as prohibited categories varies, in
fact the law generally deems them to be equivalent and has applied similar rules to each
strand. So, for example, direct and indirect discrimination are prohibited across all
strands, as are harassment and instructions to discriminate. The differences between
the strands are then reflected in adaptations to the basic non-discrimination model. In
the sections that follow we shall look at the prohibited grounds in more detail before
moving on to examine the legal rules which apply in each case.

2. SEX, GENDER REASSIGNMENT, MARITAL, AND FAMILY STATUS

The prohibition of discrimination on the grounds of sex is the longest standing prohibited ground. The term 'sex' is not defined in the Directive. However, its meaning is
neither obvious nor uncontentious. In general the courts have taken the view that 'sex'
refers to the biological or birth sex of the individual. The term 'sex' is *not* therefore
understood legally as 'gender', that is to say, as a socially constructed category. However,

---

[2] H. Collins, 'Discrimination, Equality and Social Inclusion' (2003) 66 *MLR* 16.
[3] Council Dec. 2010/707/EU (OJ [2010] L308/46).

in *P* v. *S*,[4] Advocate General Tesauro did recognize that the biological understanding of sex may well include a sociological understanding. He said:[5]

> Sex is important as a convention, a social parameter. The discrimination of which women are frequently the victims is not of course due to their physical characteristics, but rather to their role, to the image which society has of women. Hence the rationale for less favourable treatment is the social role which women are supposed to play and certainly not their physical characteristics.

For these very reasons—both biological and sociological—the differences between the sexes might apparently justify different treatment. However, the law requires men and women to be treated in the same way, as the strong language of the original Article 2(1) of the original Equal Treatment Directive 76/207 makes clear: 'there shall be no discrimination *whatsoever* on grounds of sex either directly or indirectly by reference in particular to marital or family status'.[6] The biological differences between the sexes are accommodated in the various, narrowly tailored derogations, relating in particular to pregnancy and maternity. The historical and social differences between the sexes (notably the woman's caring function) are addressed—to a limited extent at least—by the prohibition against indirect discrimination and the provision for positive action.

Most famously, in *P* v. *S*[7] the Court ruled that 'sex' included change of sex or gender reassignment: a characteristic which is also irrelevant to the individual's ability to do a job. This point was recognized by Advocate General Tesauro in *P* v. *S*:[8] 'the unfavourable treatment suffered by transsexuals is most often linked to a negative image, a moral judgment which has nothing to do with their abilities in the sphere of employment'. Therefore, a male to female transsexual dismissed on the grounds of her sex change had a remedy in EU law. The Court reasoned that since the right not to be discriminated against on grounds of sex was one of the fundamental human rights whose observance the Court had a duty to ensure, the scope of the Directive could not be confined simply to discrimination based on the fact that a person was of one sex or another.[9] It then said that in view of the purpose and the nature of the rights which it sought to safeguard, the scope of the Directive applied to discrimination arising from the gender reassignment of the person concerned, since 'such discrimination is based, essentially if not exclusively, on the sex of the person concerned'.[10]

In *Grant*,[11] however, the Court drew the line at extending the concept of 'sex' to include sexual orientation. The Court explained its reluctance by referring to the fact

---

[4] Case C–13/94 [1996] ECR I–2143.   [5] Para. 20.

[6] Emphasis added. Art. 14(1) of the Sex Equality Dir. is less explicit.

[7] Case C–13/94 [1996] ECR I–2143.

[8] Para. 20.

[9] Paras. 18–19. The Court reached this conclusion even though AG Tesauro pointed out that it was indisputable that the *wording* of the principle of equal treatment laid down by the Directive referred to the traditional man/woman dichotomy.

[10] Paras. 20–21. See now the 3rd preambular para. of Dir. 2006/54. R. Wintemute, 'Sexual Orientation Discrimination', in C. McCrudden and G. Chambers (eds.), *Individual Rights and the Law in Britain* (Clarendon, Oxford, 1995).

[11] Case C–249/96 [1998] ECR I–621. Cf. the decision of the European Court of Human Rights concerning Art. 8 of the European Convention in *Smith and Grady* v. *United Kingdom* [1999] IRLR 734.

that the Amsterdam Treaty gave the Council the power under Article 19 TFEU 'to take appropriate action to eliminate various forms of discrimination, including discrimination based on sexual orientation',[12] and so deferred to the legislature to act, which it has now done. The Framework Directive does prohibit discrimination on the grounds of sexual orientation and, according to Article 3(1)(c) the principle of non-discrimination applies to 'employment and working conditions, including dismissals and pay'.[13]

Article 2(1) of the original Equal Treatment Directive 76/207 also prohibited discrimination on the grounds of marital and family status. This precludes discrimination against those who are married and presumably, those who are unmarried, as well as those who do or do not have children, irrespective of their marital status.[14] Again, these grounds are irrelevant to an individual's ability to do a job but not immutable. This provision has not been included in Directive 2006/54.

3. RACE AND ETHNIC ORIGIN

Directive 2000/43 itself does not define the key terms racial and ethnic origin.[15] The *Shorter Oxford English Dictionary*[16] defines race as a 'group or set, especially of people having a common feature or features'. The Preamble adds that the 'European Union rejects theories which attempt to determine the existence of separate human races. The use of the term "racial origin" in this Directive does not imply an acceptance of such theories.'

The British House of Lords has considered the meaning of the phrase 'ethnic origin' in *Mandla* v. *Lee*[17] in the context of a question whether Sikhs formed an ethnic group. Lord Fraser said an 'ethnic group' must regard itself, and be regarded by others, as a distinct community by virtue of certain characteristics. He then said that some of these characteristics are essential; others are not essential but one or more of them will commonly be found and will help to distinguish the group from the surrounding community. The essential conditions are: (1) a long shared history, of which the group is conscious as distinguishing it from other groups, and the memory of which it keeps alive; (2) a cultural tradition of its own, including family and social customs and manners, often but not necessarily associated with religious observance. He then listed those characteristics which are relevant: (3) either a common geographical origin, or descent from a small number of common ancestors; (4) a common language, not necessarily peculiar to the group; (5) a common literature peculiar to the group; (6) a common

---

[12] Para. 48.

[13] In Case C-267/06 *Maruko* [2008] ECR I–1757, para. 41 the Court said that the term 'pay' should be defined in the same way as for Art. 157 TFEU (see Ch. 7). Therefore a survivor's benefit granted under an occupational scheme constitutes 'pay'; in Case C–147/08 *Römer* v. *Freie und Hansestadt Hamburg* [2011] ECR I–000, para. 36 the Court said that supplementary retirement pensions were also covered.

[14] The phrase 'family status' may also embrace those with other caring responsibilities including looking after elderly relatives. Presumably, 'marital status' could also apply to those who are no longer married, either because of death or divorce, or those who are unmarried.

[15] The Directive does not expressly cover caste discrimination although it might be included if the term 'ethnic origin' is broadly construed.

[16] OUP, Oxford, 2002, 5th edn.   [17] [1983] IRLR 209.

religion different from that of neighbouring groups or from the general community surrounding it; (7) being a minority or being an oppressed or a dominant group within a larger community, for example a conquered people (say, the inhabitants of England shortly after the Norman conquest) and their conquerors might both be ethnic groups. He concluded that Sikhs did form part of an ethnic group because they are a distinctive and self-conscious community, with a history dating back to the fifteenth century, with a written language, a common religion, and a common origin: they were at one time politically supreme in the Punjab.

The British courts have subsequently applied this test to find that members of the 'traveller' community (formerly known as gypsies) were an ethnic group because of their shared history and common geographic origin, common customs, and a shared language and culture of folktales and music.[18] The courts have also found that Jewish people formed an ethnic group.[19] However, Rastafarians did not form part of an ethnic group (60 years did not amount to a long shared history)[20] nor did Muslims because of the many different nationalities and languages spoken by them[21] (although these groups would be protected by the prohibition of discrimination on the grounds of religion).

Finally, unlike the British statute, the Directive says nothing about colour. This is surprising because the principal trigger for racially discriminatory behaviour is frequently colour: discriminators will seldom know their victims' ethnic or national origins and sometimes not their racial group, but 'colour' is a visibly different characteristic.[22]

4. RELIGION OR BELIEF

Once again, the Directive does not define the grounds 'religion or belief'. In the UK the implementing Act says: 'Religion means any religion and a reference to religion includes a reference to a lack of religion'.[23] It continues: 'Belief means any religious or philosophical belief and reference to belief includes a reference to a lack of belief'.[24] The guidance issued by the government gives further explanation:[25] the reference to 'religion' is a broad one, and is in line with the freedom of religion guaranteed by Article 9 ECHR. It includes those religions widely recognized, such as Christianity, Islam, Hinduism, Judaism, Buddhism, Sikhism, Rastafarianism, Baha'is, Zoroastrians, and Jains. Equally, branches or sects within a religion can be considered as a religion or religious belief,

---

[18] *CRE v. Dutton* [1989] QB 783.

[19] *Seide v. Gillette Industries Ltd* [1980] IRLR 427.

[20] *Crown Suppliers v. Dawkins* [1993] ICR 517.

[21] *J H Walkers Ltd v. Hussain* [1996] IRLR 11.

[22] Commission for Racial Equality quoted by Rubinstein, 'New Discrimination Regulations: An EOR Guide' (2003) 119 *EOR* 20, 21.

[23] S. 10(1) Equality Act 2010.

[24] S. 10(2) Eq. A. 2010. The ACAS guide provides a useful list of the religions that are likely to be covered: <http://www.acas.org.uk/publications/pdf/religion.pdf> (last accessed 5 February 2012).

[25] <http://webarchive.nationalarchives.gov.uk/+/http://www.dti.gov.uk/er/equality/eeregs.htm> (last accessed 31 March 2012).

such as Catholics or Protestants within the Christian church.[26] The European Court of Human Rights has recognized other collective religions including Druidism, the Church of Scientology, and the Divine Light Zentrum. The guidance adds that the main limitation on what constitutes a 'religion' for the purposes of Article 9 ECHR, is that it must have a clear structure and belief system.[27]

As far as religious belief is concerned,[28] the guidance points out that it may go further than simply a belief about adherence to a religion or its central articles of faith to include other beliefs founded in a religion, if they 'attain a certain level of cogency, seriousness, cohesion and importance, provided the beliefs are worthy of respect in a democratic society and are not incompatible with human dignity'.[29] Finally, the guidance explains that the reference to 'similar philosophical belief' does not include any philosophical or political belief unless it is similar to a religious belief. Thus, the belief in question should be 'a profound belief affecting a person's way of life, or perception of the world'. It suggests that atheism and humanism satisfy this test; support for a political party and support for a football team do not.[30] It also says that non-belief is protected.

The guidance draws a distinction between holding a religion or belief and its manifestation. The notes explain that, following the distinction drawn in Article 9 ECHR, the definition of 'religion or belief' does not include the 'manifestation' of, or conduct based on or expressing a religion or belief. This may well create problems. Take the case of a Muslim teacher who wears the full veil being refused a post in a secular state school on the grounds that she refuses to remove her veil. Is she being discriminated against on the grounds of her religion or its manifestation?[31]

As with the other grounds of discrimination, religion and belief may be immutable and are generally irrelevant to an individual's ability to do a particular task. Where an individual's religion is relevant to his or her ability to do a task (e.g. refusal by a Muslim shelf stacker to handle alcohol), this may be dealt with through a narrowly tailored exception a so-called 'genuine occupational requirement' (considered later in this chapter) or, if indirectly discriminatory, by objective justification. Unlike other grounds of discrimination, an individual's religion or belief may not be visible (except those religions which do require particular clothing or conduct).

5. SEXUAL ORIENTATION

The decision in *Grant* v. *South West Trains*,[32] where the Court ruled that the word 'sex' in Article 157 TFEU could not be construed to include sexual orientation, together with

---

[26] Para. 11.

[27] *X* v. *UK* (1977) 11 DR 55. See futher, L. Vickers, *Religious Freedom, Religious Discrimination and the Workplace* (Hart Publishing, Oxford, 2008).

[28] Para. 12.

[29] Citing the judgment of the European Court of Human Rights in *Campbell and Cosans* v. *UK* (1982) 4 EHRR 293 at 304.

[30] Para. 13.

[31] See *Azmi* v. *Kirklees BC* [2007] IRLR 484. See further, G. Pitt, 'Keeping the faith: Trends and Tensions in Religion or Belief Discrimination' (2011) 40 *ILJ* 384.

[32] Case C–249/86 *Grant* v. *South West Trains* [1998] ECR I–621.

rulings by the European Court of Human Rights recognizing that discrimination on the grounds of sexual orientation infringed an individual's right to family life,[33] put pressure on the Union legislature to prohibit discrimination on the grounds of sexual orientation. The horizontal Directive adopted under Article 19 TFEU did just that.

Once again, sexual orientation is not defined by EU law. By contrast, in the UK, sexual orientation is defined to mean orientation towards persons of the same sex (lesbians and gays), the opposite sex (hetero-sexuals), and the same and opposite sex (bisexuals). The Commission's explanatory memorandum accompanying the proposed Directive makes clear that a 'dividing line should be drawn between sexual orientation which is covered by this proposal, and sexual behaviour, which is not'.[34] The memo continues that the proposal does not affect marital status and therefore does not impinge upon entitlements to benefits for married couples, a point emphasized in Recital 22. However, in *Maruko*[35] the Court cast doubt on this proposition. Maruko was a gay man in a 'life partnership' with another man who had contributed to an occupational pension scheme. When his partner died, Maruko was denied a survivors' benefit on the ground that he was not a spouse. The Court said that if the national court found that the position of surviving spouses and surviving life partners was comparable, the national legislation was directly discriminatory on the grounds of sexual orientation contrary to the Directive.[36]

At first glance, sexual orientation shares certain common features with the other prohibited grounds: it is immutable and irrelevant to an individual's ability to do a particular task. However, it differs from other grounds in that sexual orientation is usually not visible to a third party and may be intensely personal.[37] To that extent it shares certain common features with religion and belief. Many gay and lesbian employees do not come 'out' in the workplace, often for fear of discrimination.

6. AGE

The need to address the problems of an ageing population have become a central feature of the European Employment Strategy. A policy based on 'active ageing' was first highlighted in the 1999 Guidelines.[38] By the time of the 2005 revisions,[39] a 'new intergenerational approach' had become an overriding objective of Member State employment policies. Specifically, Guideline 18 headed 'Promote a lifecycle approach to work', says that there is a need to provide 'support for active ageing, including appropriate working conditions, improved (occupational) health status and adequate incentives to work and

---

[33] See, e.g. *Smith and Grady* v. *United Kingdom* [1999] IRLR 734.

[34] COM(99)565.

[35] Case C–267/06 *Maruko* [2008] ECR I–1757.

[36] Para. 72. See additionally Case C–147/08 *Römer* v. *Freie und Hansestadt Hamburg* [2011] ECR I–000.

[37] H. Oliver, 'Sexual Orientation Discrimination: Perceptions, Definitions and Genuine Occupational Requirements' (2004) 33 *ILJ* 1.

[38] Co. Res. of 22 February 1999 (OJ [1999] C69/2), para. 4.

[39] Council Dec. 2005/600 (OJ [2005] L205/21). See further Art. 25 of the Charter which talks of the rights of the elderly.

discouragement of early retirement'. Early soft law measures[40] hardened with the inclusion of age as a prohibited ground in the Directive. Once again, age is not defined in the Directive. This generates its own problems. The early soft law measures focus on the age discrimination experienced by older people, yet young people also experience age discrimination: the Directive does not distinguish between the two situations and the interests of the two groups may well conflict especially over issues such as retirement (considered below).

Further, while age, like sex and race, is visible and immutable, age differs from the other grounds of discrimination in that age is a process not a fixed status.[40A] Thus, while most people will never experience life as a person of the opposite sex, everyone will have experience of being both young and (hopefully) old. This raises the question of whether older people should be able to demand all the opportunities now enjoyed by younger people, given that they themselves were once young and could have taken advantage of those opportunities (the 'good innings' argument). The converse is also true. This difference between age and the other grounds is reflected in the broader, but opaque, derogations available in the framework Directive, together with the possibility that direct discrimination can be objectively justified.

7. DISABILITY

Early measures aimed at helping those with disabilities adopted a welfare approach,[41] aimed at promoting the employment and vocational training of disabled people, including policies relating to sheltered employment, vocational rehabilitation and training, and providing incentives to employers to assist with the special costs incurred when employing a disabled worker.[42] The Directive, by contrast, embodies a human rights-based approach which focuses on prevention and removal of barriers that denied equality of access to people with disabilities to, *inter alia*, the labour market.[43] Once again, disability is not defined in the Directive although there are extensive international and national definitions which would help provide meaning to the term.[44] The British statute, the Equality Act 2010, adopts a 'medical' approach to the definition of disability. Section 6(1) defines disability as 'a physical or mental impairment' which has a 'substantial and long-term adverse effect on [the person's] ability to carry out normal day-to-day activities'. This definition of disability can be contrasted with a more social constructed view of disability. As Wells explains, while 'the medical model sees disability as a functional impair-

---

[40] These are detailed in the third edition of this book (*EC Employment Law*).

[40A] 'Age is not a "binary" in nature…but a continuum which changes over time' per Lady Hale, *Seldon v. Clarkson Wright and Jakes* [2012] UKSC 16, para. 4.

[41] See e.g. Council Recommendation 86/379/EEC of 24 July 1986 (OJ [1986] L225/43). This measure also envisaged setting targets for the employment of people with disabilities.

[42] Considerable help has been given from the European Social Fund.

[43] COM(99)565, 4. See further COM(99) 565, para. 2.

[44] The EU's commitment to removing discrimination on the grounds of disability has been significantly reinforced by its accession to the Convention on the Rights of Persons with Disabilities (CRPD). See G. de Búrca, 'The European Union in the negotiation of the UN Disability Convention' (2010) 35 *ELRev.* 174. See

ment, the social model sees disability as a particular relationship between the impaired individual and society'.[45] In *Chacón Navas*[46] the Grand Chamber favoured the medical definition of disability. It ruled that 'disability', a term which had to be given a Union meaning, referred to a limitation that resulted in particular from 'physical, mental or psychological impairments' which hindered the person's participation in professional life, and would probably 'last for a long time'. It also made clear that sickness and disability were different and that a person dismissed for sickness was not protected by the disability provisions of the Framework Directive.

Disability differs from the other grounds of discrimination for a number of reasons. First, it may or may not be immutable (in the case of some disabilities, an individual is born with them or a condition develops later in life and the disabilities will never improve; in respect of others the individual may recover). Second, the disability may be visible (e.g. a wheelchair user) or it may not (e.g. a person suffering from a mental disability). Third, the disability may prevent an individual from being able to do a job (e.g. those with some types of learning disability would not be able to do a job requiring high skills), or it may not (e.g. a wheelchair user could perform a variety of jobs), or it may affect an individual's ability to do a job but a certain amount of assistance would overcome that difficulty (e.g. a person with arthritis may be able to undertake an office-based job with the help of an adapted keyboard). The key issue with disability is that there are all kinds of disabilities and one rule does not fit all situations.[47]

8. EXTENSION OF THE STRANDS

The language of 'on grounds of sex [race etc]' used in the Directives is broader than the wording sometimes used in discrimination legislation of 'on the grounds of her sex [race etc]'. While the latter wording prohibits discrimination against a person because of his or her sex, race, etc., the former wording is wide enough to cover not only less favourable treatment on the grounds of the victim's sex (race, etc.) but also because of the victim's association with a person of a particular race or false assumptions about the claimant's race, sexual orientation, disability etc. The protection based on false assumptions is of particular importance in the field of sexual orientation. As Oliver points out, sexual orientation discrimination and harassment are often based on stereotypical assumptions about a person's sexuality drawn from the way in which that person is perceived as projecting him/herself, whether through clothing, speech, or other characteristics (men seen as acting 'gay' and women 'butch'), irrespective of their actual orientation.

also O. M. Arnardóttir and G. Quinn (eds.), 'The UN Convention on the Rights of Persons with Disabilities' (Martinus Nijhoff, Leiden, 2009).

[45] 'The Impact of the Framework Employment Directive on UK Disability Discrimination Law' (2003) 32 *ILJ* 253.

[46] Case C–13/05 *Chacón Navas* v. *Eurest Colectividades SA* [2006] ECR I–6467, paras. 43 and 45.

[47] For a full discussion of the Directive's provisions relating to disability, see S. Whittle, 'The Framework Directive for equal treatment in employment and occupation: an analysis from a disability rights perspective' (2002) 27 *ELRev.* 303.

The Court has now confirmed that the equal treatment Directives can apply to associative discrimination. In *Coleman* v. *Attridge Law*[48] a mother was dismissed by her employers due to the amount of time she took off from work to look after her disabled son. She claimed that she had been discriminated against on the grounds of being associated with a person with a disability. The Court agreed:[49]

> Directive 2000/78 . . . must be interpreted as meaning that the prohibition of direct discrimination laid down by those provisions is not limited only to people who are themselves disabled. Where an employer treats an employee who is not himself disabled less favourably than another employee is, has been or would be treated in a comparable situation, and it is established that the less favourable treatment of that employee is based on the disability of his child, whose care is provided primarily by that employee, such treatment is contrary to the prohibition of direct discrimination laid down by Article 2(2)(a).

C. THE PERSONAL SCOPE

1. INTRODUCTION

The personal scope of employment rights—that is, who benefits from employment rights—has long been a vexed issue, as we saw in Chapter 4. Neo-liberals would argue for employment rights to be given to as few people as possible because, they argue, employment rights distort the way in which the market operates. By contrast, human rights lawyers would favour giving employment rights to as wide a group as possible since employment rights form a key pillar of human rights and human rights are universal. Somewhere in between are new institutionalists who would argue that rights can be justified but only where they are seen as an input into growth. Both neo-liberals and new institutionalists would, however, agree that in order to enjoy employment rights there must be some sort of dependence by the individual on the employer. They would certainly argue that the genuinely self-employed—that is those who are *in*dependent of any particular employer—should not enjoy employment rights.

These different strands of thinking can be detected in various Commission documents[50] as a well as in the personal scope of the social policy Directives. For example, the Transfer of Undertakings Directive 2001/23 applies to 'employees', as defined by national law,[51] thereby perhaps reflecting the neo-liberal approach. The Working Time Directive 2003/88 appears to have a broader scope in that it applies to 'workers', reflect-

---

[48] Case C–303/06 [2008] ECR I–5603.

[49] Para. 56.

[50] See e.g. Communication from the Commission: Towards Common Principles of Flexicurity: More and better jobs through flexibility and security, COM(2007) 359 final.

[51] Art. 2(d), although Art. 2(2) says 'This Directive shall be without prejudice to national law as regards the definition of contract of employment *or employment relationship*' (emphasis added) which suggests a broader personal scope.

ing perhaps the new institutionalist reading of the role of law. And the two Article 19 Directives on non-discrimination have the widest personal scope because they apply to 'all persons', reflecting a human rights approach. A broad reading of personal scope is supported by, for example, the reference to fundamental human rights in the fifth and sixth recital of the preamble to Directive 2000/78 and the third and fourth recital of Directive 2000/43. However, since Directives 2000/78 and 2006/54 are Directives on 'employment', there must be outer limits to the personal scope. If so, what are they?

2. THE OUTER LIMITS

Article 3(1) of the two Article 19 Directives 2000/43 and 2000/78, together with Article 14 of the Sex Equality Directive 2006/54/EC, say that the Directives apply to:

> all persons, as regards both the public and private sectors, including public bodies, in rela-
> tion to—
>
> (a) conditions for access to employment, to self-employment or to occupation, including
>   selection criteria and recruitment conditions, whatever the branch of activity and at all
>   levels of the professional hierarchy, including promotion...[52]

Articles 3(1)(b)–(d) add that the Directives also apply to access to vocational training, to employment and working conditions, and membership of, and involvement in, workers' organizations (see later in this chapter). Article 3(1)(a) thus makes it clear that the Directives are intended to apply not only to employees and workers but to the self-employed and the liberal professions. This broad reading is supported by *Danosa*[53] which suggests that if the individual (a pregnant member of a capital company's board of directors) was not considered a pregnant worker for the purposes of the Pregnant Workers Directive 92/85, she would still fall within the scope of the Sex Equality Directive 2006/54. However, the fact that the scope of the Directives is explicitly linked to 'employment and occupation' (Article 1 of all three Directives) indicates that there are outer limits to the reach of the Directives.[54] This might indicate that there must be some notion of economic, if not personal, subordination and thus the Directive should be confined in its application to employees, workers and the dependent self-employed (see Figure 4.1). In other words, these Directives should not apply to the genuinely self-employed.

This view receives some support by reference to the rest of Directive 2006/54 which, in Article 1, makes no reference to self-employment, merely to 'access to employment, including promotion, and to vocational training'. Further, the detailed reference to the self-employed in Chapter 2 of Title II of Directive 2006/54 on equal treatment in

---

[52] The quote is taken from Directive 2000/78.
[53] Case C–232/09 *Danosa* [2010] ECR I–000, para. 74. See additionally Case C–393/10 *O'Brien* [2012] ECR I-000 considered in Ch. 9.
[54] See further N. Countouris, *The Changing Law of the Employment Relationship* (Aldershot, Ashgate, 2007), esp. Ch. 5.

occupational social security schemes might indicate that the self-employed do not benefit from the rest of the Directive.[55]

However, others would argue that the reference to 'self-employed' covers even the independent self-employed (entrepreneurs), at least in respect of conditions for access to self-employment, and that the self-employed will also benefit from access to supply of goods and services under Article 3(1)(h) of Directive 2000/43 and Directive 2004/113 on equal treatment of men and women in access to and supply of goods and services. Article 3 of Directive 2004/113 provides:

> This Directive shall apply to all persons who provide goods and services, which are available to the public irrespective of the person concerned as regards both the public and private sectors, including public bodies, and which are offered outside the area of private and family life and the transactions carried out in this context.

The Member States' approach to this question has varied significantly. Perhaps most interesting in terms of implementation is the position of the UK, Ireland, and Malta, which largely follow a common pattern. Looking at the position under UK law, s. 39(1) of the Equality Act 2010 says: an employer (A) must not discriminate against a person (B) in the arrangements A makes for deciding to whom to offer employment, as to the terms on which A offers B employment and by not offering B employment. Section 83(2) then provides that:

> 'Employment' means—
>
> (a) employment under a contract of employment, a contract of apprenticeship or a contract personally to do work ...

Therefore it covers applicants, employees, apprentices, workers, and those who are self-employed with a contract for personal services.[56] For our purposes, it is the last two categories which are of importance. The concept of worker covers the dependent self-employed but, as we saw in Chapter 4, generally excludes the provision of services to a client or customer in the course of practising a profession or running a business. However, there is no such limitation in the Equality Act 2010, which applies to 'employment under...a contract personally to do work' which may include the genuinely self-employed who are in business on their own account.[57]

---

[55] Likewise, the express reference to the self-employed in Directive 2010/41/EU on the application of the principle of equal treatment between men and women engaged in an activity in a self-employed capacity (considered in Section I below) and the definition of self-employed workers in Article 2(a) (namely 'all persons pursuing a gainful activity for their own account, under the conditions laid down by national law') suggests, by implication, that the other equality Directives do not cover entrepreneurs.

[56] The UK legislation also extends the rights of equal treatment to, for example, partners in law firms, barristers, and office holders.

[57] Cf. the important Supreme Court decision in the UK, *Jivraj* v. *Hashwani* [2011] UKSC 40, where an arbitrator was found not to fall in the scope of the Equality Act because the role of an arbitrator is 'not naturally described as an employment under a contract personally to do work. That is because his role is not naturally described as one of employment at all'. For a full discussion compare C. McCrudden (2012) 41 *ILJ* 30 and N. Kountouras and M. Freedland (2012) 41 *ILJ* 56.

However, it must be a contract which places the provider of services under some obligation to provide services personally, and where the 'dominant purpose' is the execution of personal work or labour. If the dominant purpose is the provision of services rather than the execution of personal work, the individual will not be considered as being in 'employment'.[58] This introduces yet a further nuance in the definition of self-employed.

D. THE MATERIAL SCOPE

1. SEX

1.1. Field of application

Article 13 of Directive 2006/54 provides that 'there shall be no direct or indirect discrimination on the grounds of sex in the public or private sectors, including public bodies',[59] in relation to:

(a) conditions for access to employment, to self-employment, or to occupation, including selection criteria and recruitment conditions, whatever the branch of activity and at all levels of the professional hierarchy, including promotion;

(b) access to all types and to all levels of vocational guidance, vocational training, advanced vocational training, and retraining, including practical work experience;

(c) employment and working conditions, including dismissals, as well as pay;[60]

(d) membership of, and involvement in, an organization of workers or employers, or any organization whose members carry on a particular profession, including the benefits provided for by such organizations.

For our purposes, paragraph (c) is of most interest. The reference to 'pay', albeit mirroring the equivalent provision in the Race and Framework Directives, has raised the question as to the extent to which the equal treatment and the equal pay regimes have become merged, despite the Court's careful attempts to distinguish their different fields of application.[61] If so, this opens up the possibility that principles which have hitherto been applied only to equal treatment cases now apply equally to pay cases.[62] Most notable among those is the possibility that directly discriminatory pay policies can be saved by

---

[58] *Mirror Group Newspapers Limited v. Gunning* [1986] IRLR 27. On the question on whether this also applies to volunteers: *X v. Mid Sussex Citizens Advice Bureau and others* [2011] EWCA Civ 28.

[59] This confirms Case 248/83 *Commission v. Germany* [1985] ECR 1459.

[60] Originally, the Directive 2002/73 version of this provision contained the addition 'as provided for in Directive 75/117/EEC'. The Equality Directive refers to Article 157 TFEU.

[61] This is discussed further in Ch. 7.

[62] The Commission takes the view that the exclusion of pay by Art. 153(5) TEFU (ex 137(5) EC) refers only to Directives adopted under Art. 153 TFEU and so does not apply to Directives adopted under other legal bases: COM(99) 565.

reference to the express derogations found in the equal treatment Directive and the possibility that pay claims can be brought using a hypothetical comparator. However, there
is no indication in either the Preamble or the travaux préparatoires that this was the
intention behind either the amendment Directive or the Equality Directive.

The reference to 'working conditions' has already been the subject of litigation. In
Meyers[63] the Court refused to confine 'working conditions' to those conditions set out
in a contract of employment or applied by the employer in respect of a worker's employment. It therefore said that a benefit such as family credit constituted a working condition within the meaning of the original Article 5 of Directive 76/207 (Article 14(1)(c) of
the Equality Directive). This is consistent with its earlier case law. In *Burton*[64] the Court
said that the phrase 'working conditions, including the conditions governing dismissal'
had to be 'widely construed so as to include termination of the employment relationship between a worker and his employer, even as part of a voluntary redundancy scheme'.
This idea was developed in *Marshall (No. 1)*[65] where the Court made it clear that compulsory retirement fell within the scope of the original Article 5.[66] It was therefore
unlawful for any employer to have different retirement ages for men and women.

1.2. Social security

Social security remains largely excluded from the scope of the equal treatment principle. Article 1(2) of Directive 76/207 (but not the Equality Directive) provided that 'with
a view to ensuring the progressive implementation of the principle of equal treatment
in matters of social security, the Council… will adopt provisions defining its substance,
its scope and the arrangements of its application' (now Directive 79/7 considered in
Chapter 10). The Court has consistently held that Article 1(2), as a derogation from a
fundamental principle, must be narrowly construed.[67] Therefore, in *Jackson*[68] the Court
said that a benefit could not be excluded from the scope of the Directive simply because
it was formally part of the social security system; it might fall within the scope of the
Directive if its subject-matter was access to employment, including vocational training
and working conditions.[69] In *Meyers*[70] the Court considered that family credit, a social

[63] Case C–116/94 [1995] ECR I–2131. Working conditions also covers the provision of workplace nurseries:
Case C–476/99 *Lommers v. Mininster van Landbouw* [2002] ECR I–2891, para. 26.

[64] Case 19/81 [1982] ECR 555.

[65] Case 152/84 [1986] ECR 723.

[66] See additionally Case C–13/94 *P v. S* [1996] ECR I–2143. The conditions determining whether an
employee was entitled, where they are unfairly dismissed, to obtain reinstatement or re-engagement are also
covered by the Equal Treatment Directive (and not Art. 157 TFEU): Case C–167/97 *Seymour-Smith* [1999]
ECR I–623. See further Case C–236/98 *Örebro läns landsting* [2000] ECR I–2189, para. 60, where the Court
ruled that the reduction in working time related to working conditions (and not pay under Art. 157 TFEU).

[67] Case 151/84 *Roberts* [1986] ECR 703 and Case 152/84 *Marshall (No. 1)* [1986] ECR 723.

[68] Case C–63–4/91 *Jackson v. Chief Adjudication Officer* [1992] ECR I–4737.

[69] The fact that the Court in Case C–78/91 *Hughes v. Chief Adjudication Officer* [1992] ECR I–4839 found
that family credit fell within Reg. 1408/71 (now 883/2004) and also did not prevent the benefit from falling
within the scope of Dir. 76/207.

[70] Case C–116/94 *Meyers v. Adjudication Officer* [1995] ECR I–2131.

security benefit 'designed to encourage workers who are poorly paid to continue work-ing and to meet family expenses'[71] did fall within the scope of Directive 76/207. It said that family credit, which was necessarily linked to an employment relationship, was concerned with access to employment under Article 3 of Directive 76/207 (Article 14(1)(a) of the Equality Directive), since the prospect of receiving family credit might encourage an unemployed worker to accept work.

2. RACE AND ETHNIC ORIGIN

The Race Directive is the most ambitious equal treatment measure going well beyond the sphere of employment. It applies the principles of non-discrimination to 'all persons, as regards both the public and private sectors, including public bodies', in relation not only to[72] the four areas outlined above ((a)–(d)) for sex but also, more controversially,[73] to:

(e) social protection including social security and healthcare;

(f) social advantages;[74]

(g) education;

(h) access to and supply of goods and services which are available to the public, including housing.

The Goods and Services Directive 2004/113 has extended the material scope of the Sex Directive[75] to cover:

all persons who provide goods and services, which are available to the public irrespective of the person concerned as regards both the public and private sectors, including public bodies, and which are offered outside the area of private and family life and the transactions carried out in this context.

The Commission justified the broad material scope of the Race Directive in order 'to make a serious contribution to curbing racism and xenophobia in Europe'.[76] It said that 'social protection systems play a fundamental role in ensuring social cohesion, and in

---

[71] See the judgment in Case C–78/91 *Hughes* [1992] ECR I–4839.

[72] Art. 3(1). Art. 11(2) requires Member States to encourage the two sides of the industry to conclude at the appropriate level, including at undertaking level, agreements laying down antidiscrimination rules in these fields which fall within the scope of collective bargaining. These agreements must respect the minimum requirements laid down by this Directive and the relevant national implementing measures.

[73] For a discussion on the scope of the Art. 19 TFEU legal basis, see Whittle, 'Disability Discrimination and the Amsterdam Treaty' (1998) 23 *ELRev.* 50, 53.

[74] See further Ch. 4.

[75] Art. 3(1). The Directive expressly does not apply to the content of media and advertising nor to education (Art. 3(3)). Special provision is made in Art. 5 concerning actuarial factors.

[76] COM(99) 566, 5. The Directive does not apply to difference of treatment based on nationality and is without prejudice to provisions and conditions relating to entry and residence of third country nationals and to any treatment which arises from the legal status of third country nationals and stateless persons.

maintaining political stability and economic progress across the Union'.[77] It also recognized that 'discrimination in access to benefits and other forms of support from the social protection system [and social advantages] contributes to and compounds the marginalization of individuals from ethnic minority and immigrant backgrounds';[78] and that high quality education was a prerequisite for successful integration into society.

Article 3(2) says that the Directive does not cover difference of treatment based on nationality. Nationality discrimination, at least against those holding the nationality of one of the Member States, is covered by Article 45 TFEU (ex 39 EC). In addition, the Directive is 'without prejudice to provisions and conditions relating to the entry into and residence of third country nationals and stateless persons on the territory of Member States, and to any treatment which arises from the legal status of the third country nationals and stateless persons'.

3. FRAMEWORK DIRECTIVE

The material scope of the Directive is narrower than that of the Race Directive. According to Article 3, the principle of equal treatment applies only to employment issues (i.e. the four areas outlined above ((a)–(d)) for sex). The Directive then envisages three exclusions from its scope, two mandatory, one permissive: first, as with the Race Directive, the Framework Directive does not cover differences of treatment based on nationality, and is without prejudice to provisions and conditions relating to the entry into and residence of TCNs and stateless persons in the territory of Member States, and to any treatment which arises from the legal status of TCNs and stateless persons.[79] Second, the Directive does not apply to payments of any kind made by state schemes or similar, including state social security or social protection schemes.[80] And third, Member States *may* provide that the Directive does not apply to the armed forces, but only in so far as it relates to discrimination on the grounds of disability and age.[81]

E. PROHIBITION OF DISCRIMINATION

The Directives prohibit four types of discrimination:

- Direct discrimination
- Indirect discrimination
- Harassment
- Instruction to discriminate

We shall consider each in turn.

---

[77] Ibid.   [78] Ibid.   [79] Art. 3(2).   [80] Art. 3(3).   [81] Art. 3(4).

1. DIRECT DISCRIMINATION

1.1. The basic rule

Article 2(2)(a) of the Race Directive provides that direct discrimination 'shall be taken to occur where one person is treated less favourably than another is, has been or would be treated in a comparable situation on grounds of racial or ethnic origin'. The other Directives contain an equivalent provision. The Directives therefore envisage a symmetrical approach to equality: the complainant needs to point to a comparator in a comparable situation[82] who is better treated. The comparator can be either actual or potential. *Firma Feryn*[83] considered an unexpected dimension to a direct discrimination claim: what happens when a potential employer publicly announces that when looking to recruit new employees (fitters for the sale and installation of up-and-over and sectional doors) it could not employ 'immigrants' because its customers were reluctant to give them access to their private residences for the period of the works. The Court said the fact that an employer declares publicly that it would not recruit employees of a certain ethnic or racial origin, something which is clearly likely to strongly dissuade certain candidates from submitting their candidature and, accordingly, to hinder their access to the labour market, constituted direct discrimination in respect of recruitment within the meaning of Directive 2000/43. It added that the existence of such direct discrimination was not dependent on the identification of a complainant who claims to have been the victim.[84]

1.2. Sex discrimination

The principal drawback with the requirement of a comparator in the context of sex equality is that, as we saw in Chapter 6, it takes the male as the norm and assumes that a woman is like a man and should be placed in the same position as a man. In some contexts, notably pregnancy, this makes no sense. Comparisons adopted by some courts between a pregnant woman and a sick man are artificial, inaccurate, and misleading. This point was recognized in both *Dekker*[85] and *Webb*.[86] In *Dekker* a woman was refused a job on the grounds that she was pregnant; another woman was appointed and there were no male candidates. Nevertheless, the Court found that discrimination had occurred. It reasoned that since employment can only be refused because of pregnancy to a woman, such a refusal constituted discrimination on the grounds of sex. In *Webb* the Court confirmed that 'there can be no question of comparing the situation of a [pregnant] woman ... with that of a man similarly incapable for medical or other reason'.

[82] Case C–147/08 *Römer v. Freie und Hansestadt Hamburg* [2011] ECR I–000, para. 42: 'first, it is required not that the situations be identical, but only that they be comparable and, second, the assessment of that comparability must be carried out not in a global and abstract manner, but in a specific and concrete manner in the light of the benefit concerned'.

[83] Case C–54/07 *Centrum voor gelijkheid van kansen en voor racismebestrijding v. Firma Feryn NV* [2008] ECR I–5187. See additionally Case C–81/12 Asociaţia ACCEPT, pending.

[84] Para. 25.   [85] Case C–177/88 [1990] ECR I–3941. This issue is considered in detail in Ch. 9.

[86] Case C–32/93 [1994] ECR I–3567, para. 24.

Thus, the Court has recognized that discrimination on the grounds of pregnancy is *per se* unlawful: a male comparator is not needed when a woman has clearly been disadvantaged by the use of a sex-specific criterion, such as pregnancy (the asymmetrical approach). This approach was confirmed by Article 2(7) of Directive 76/207, now Article 2(2)(c) of the Equality Directive:

> Less favourable treatment of a woman related to pregnancy or maternity leave within the meaning of Directive 92/85/EEC shall constitute discrimination within the meaning of this Directive.

Outside of the field of pregnancy, the Court has taken a narrow and literal view of the concept of direct discrimination: it appears that the discrimination must be overt and explicit to engage the prohibition.[87] This can be seen in *Schnorbus*.[88] Julia Schnorbus applied to the Hessian Ministry of Justice for her practical legal training. Her application was rejected because, due to the number of applicants, preference was given to those applicants who had completed compulsory military or civilian service. Since only men could do military or civilian service, it might be thought that, following *Dekker*, more favourable treatment on the grounds of having done military or civilian service would constitute direct discrimination. Yet, the Court did not go down this route, arguing that the priority given to those having done military or civilian service could not be regarded as directly based on the sex of the persons concerned.[89] Nevertheless, the Court did recognize that the rule was indirectly discriminatory but could be justified.

2. INDIRECT DISCRIMINATION

2.1. Sex, race and ethnic origin, religion or belief, age, sexual orientation

As we saw in Chapter 6, the case law has long given guidance on the principle of indirect discrimination on the grounds of sex. For example, in *Rinke*[90] the Court defined indirect discrimination as a provision which, although worded in neutral terms, 'works to the disadvantage of a much higher percentage of women than men, unless that difference in treatment is justified by objective factors unrelated to any discrimination on grounds of sex'.[91]

The amended Equal Treatment Directive and the Sex Equality Directive both provide that 'the apparently neutral provision, criterion or practice *would put* persons of one sex at a *particular disadvantage* compared *with persons of the other sex*, unless that provision, criterion or practice is objectively justified by a legitimate aim, and the means of achieving that aim are appropriate and necessary'. Equivalent definitions can be found in the

---

[87] See additionally Case C–207/04 *Vergani* v. *Agenzia delle Entrate* [2005] ECR I–7453, para. 35 (national law granted to workers over 50 (for women) and 55 (for men) a favourable taxation rate as an incentive for them to take voluntary redundancy. This provision was directly discriminatory on the grounds of sex.

[88] Case C–79/99 *Schnorbus* v. *Land Hessen* [2000] ECR I–10997.

[89] Para. 32.

[90] Case C–25/01 *Rinke* v. *Ärztekammer Hamburg* [2003] ECR I–8349, para. 33.

[91] Case C–226/98 *Jørgensen* [2000] ECR I–2447, para. 29.

Article 19 Directives, albeit with slight differences. For example, Article 2(2)(b) of the Race Directive says indirect discrimination shall be taken to occur 'where an apparently neutral provision, criterion or practice would put persons of a racial or ethnic origin at a particular disadvantage compared *with other persons*, unless that provision, criterion or practice is objectively justified by a legitimate aim and the means of achieving that aim are appropriate and necessary'.[92] Thus, in respect of the Article 19 Directives (but not the Sex Equality Directive 2006/54) a comparison needs to be made between persons of a particular group (e.g. racial group) with 'other persons' (i.e. with any other person), and a particular disadvantage can be established if any detriment is proven.

2.2. Disability and the duty of reasonable accommodation

Special rules apply to indirect discrimination on the grounds of disability. Article 1(2)(b) defines indirect discrimination in the same terms as for the other grounds (an apparently neutral provision, criterion, or practice which would put persons having a particular disability at a particular disadvantage compared with other persons). It continues that such a measure is unlawful unless *either* (i) that provision, criterion, or practice is objectively justified by a legitimate aim and the means of achieving that aim are appropriate and necessary, *or* (ii) 'the employer or any person or organisation to whom this Directive applies, is obliged, under national legislation, to take appropriate measures in line with the principles contained in Article 5 in order to eliminate disadvantages entailed by such provision, criterion or practice'. Article 5 refers to the duty of 'reasonable accommodation'.[93] This means that:

> ...employers shall take appropriate measures,[94] where needed in a particular case, to enable a person with a disability to have access to, participate in, or advance in employment, or to undergo training, unless such measures would impose a disproportionate burden on the employer. This burden shall not be disproportionate[95] when it is sufficiently remedied by measures existing within the framework of the disability policy of the Member State concerned.

Thus, the obligation of reasonable accommodation is limited in two respects. First, it only pertains to what is reasonable. Secondly, it is limited if it would give rise to undue hardship.

---

[92] Art. 2(2)(b), drawing on Case C–237/94 *O'Flynn* v. *Adjudication Officer* [1996] ECR I–2617, para. 18.

[93] This provision supplements the employer's obligation to adapt the workplace to disabled workers, as provided by the framework Directive on health and safety 89/391/EEC (OJ [1989] L 183/1), considered in Ch. 11.

[94] See Recital 20 which explains that 'appropriate measures' mean effective and practical measures to adapt the workplace to the disability, e.g. adapting premises and equipment, patterns of working time, the distribution of tasks or the provision of training or the integration of resources.

[95] See Recital 21: to determine whether the measures give rise to a disproportionate burden, account should be taken in particular of the financial and other costs entailed, the scale and the financial resources of the organization or undertaking and the possibility of obtaining public funding or other assistance.

The duty of reasonable accommodation is a core element of the new human rights-based approach to the elimination of discrimination against people with a disability, and a key feature of recent national legislation. The concept stems from the realization that the achievement of equal treatment can only become a reality where some reasonable allowance is made for disability in order to enable the abilities of the individual concerned to be put to work. However, as the Commission makes clear,[96] the duty of reasonable accommodation does not create any obligations with respect to individuals who, even with reasonable accommodation, cannot perform the essential functions of any given job.

Whittle provides a helpful example as to how the limitations in Article 1(2)(b) (i) and (ii) interrelate.[97] If an employer says that it is an advantage that the employee be able to drive, such a rule would place blind people at a particular disadvantage when compared to other persons and so would constitute an indirectly discriminatory rule. However, it may be possible for the employer to objectively justify this requirement. The second 'unless' clause (clause (ii)) provides the employer another opportunity to retain the driving requirement. If the employer is obliged to provide the blind person with 'reasonable accommodation' (e.g. swapping some of the blind person's tasks with a sighted colleague or providing a taxi on the necessary occasions) then, by virtue of the second 'unless' clause, the job requirement for an ability to drive will be allowed to remain.

2.3. Justification/proportionate means of achieving a legitimate aim

It has long been established in the Court's case law on sex discrimination that a measure which is prima facie indirectly discriminatory is unlawful unless it is objectively justified on grounds other than sex and the steps taken are proportionate. *Schnorbus*[98] provides an example of how objective justification operates. It will be recalled that Julia Schnorbus unsuccessfully applied to the Hessian Ministry of Justice for her practical legal training but, due to the high level of applications, preference was given to those (men) who had completed compulsory military or civilian service. Although the Court found the rule indirectly discriminatory, it said that it could be justified: the national rule took into account the fact that doing military or civilian service delayed male applicants' education. The national rule was therefore objective in nature and prompted solely by the desire to counterbalance to some extent the effects of that delay.[99]

While the Article 19 Directives and the Sex Equality Directive 2006/54 permit indirectly discriminatory measures to be justified, the language through which this is achieved is slightly different from the case law. Each Directive refers to the measure being 'objectively justified by a legitimate aim and the means of achieving that aim are appropriate and necessary'. Unlike the Burden of Proof Directive which expressly prohibits the objective aim being sex based, the new Directives do not contain an equivalent prohibition, thereby opening up the possibility that the justification could relate to the prohibited ground.

---

[96] COM(99) 565.
[97] S. Whittle, 'The Framework Directive for equal treatment in employment and occupation: an analysis from a disability rights perspective' (2002) 27 *ELRev.* 303, 310.
[98] Case C–79/99 *Schnorbus* [2000] ECR I–10997.   [99] Para. 44.

3. INSTRUCTION TO DISCRIMINATE

According to Article 2(4) of revised Directive 76/207, 'An instruction to discriminate against persons on grounds of sex shall be deemed to be discrimination within the meaning of this Directive'. Equivalent provisions can be found in the Article 19 Directives[100] and Article 2(2)(b) of the Sex Equality Directive 2006/54.

4. HARASSMENT

4.1. Sex

(a) Recommendation and Code

Despite the considerable weight of evidence concerning the serious consequences of sexual harassment, a Commission report found that in most countries there was no effective legal remedy against sexual harassment.[101] It therefore proposed that a specific Directive be passed with the aim of protecting workers from the risk of sexual harassment[102] but this suggestion was initially not followed. Instead, the Council passed a non-legally binding Resolution on the protection of the dignity of women and men at work.[103] This was followed by a Commission Recommendation and a Code of Conduct[104] which was approved by a Council Declaration.[105]

The Council Resolution contained a detailed definition of sexual harassment: it is 'conduct of a sexual nature, or other conduct based on sex affecting the dignity of women and men at work, including conduct of superiors and colleagues'. This conduct is deemed to constitute an 'intolerable violation of the dignity of workers or trainees' and is unacceptable if:

---

[100] Art. 2(4) of Dirs 2000/43 and 2000/78.

[101] M. Rubinstein, *The Dignity of Women at Work: a Report on the Problem of Sexual Harassment in the Member States of the European Communities* (OPEC, Luxembourg, October 1987).

[102] The Social Partners started to negotiate an agreement on the prevention of sexual harassment at work with a view to concluding a Directive. UNICE pulled out of the negotiations: COM(96) 373 and SEC(97) 568. However, the social partners did successfully negotiate a framework agreement on harassment and violence at work (signed on 26 April 2007; the ETUC's interpretation guide also contains its provisions: <http://www.etuc. org/a/4758>). The agreement aims at increasing the awareness and understanding of employers, workers and their representatives of workplace harassment and violence and to provide employers, workers, and their representatives at all levels with an action-oriented framework to identify, prevent and manage problems of harassment and violence at work.

[103] Resolution of 29 May 1990 (OJ [1990] C157/3).

[104] Commission Recommendation 92/131/EEC of 27 November 1991 on the protection and dignity of men and women at work (OJ [1992] L49/1). See Case 322/88 *Grimaldi v. Fonds des Maladies Professionnelles* [1989] ECR 4407 where the Court said in the context of a Recommendation on compensation for persons with occupational diseases, that national courts are bound to take Recommendations into account in order to decide disputes before them, in particular where they clarify the interpretation of national rules adopted in order to implement them or when they are designed to supplement binding Union measures, such as the Equal Treatment Directive.

[105] Council Declaration of 19 December 1991 on the Implementation of the Commission Recommendation on the Protection of the Dignity of Women and Men at Work including the Code of Practice to Combat Sexual Harassment (92/C 27/01).

(a) such conduct is unwanted, unreasonable, and offensive to the recipient;

(b) a person's rejection of or submission to such conduct on the part of employers or workers (including superiors or colleagues) is used explicitly or implicitly as a basis for a decision which affects that person's access to vocational training, access to employment, promotion, salary, or any other employment decisions; and/or

(c) such conduct creates an intimidating, hostile, or humiliating work environment for the recipient.[106]

Thus, the definition of what constitutes sexual harassment is subjective not objective: account is taken of the effect of the conduct upon the particular individual concerned rather than examining the effect of equivalent conduct on a 'reasonable person'. The motive of the perpetrator is largely irrelevant.

The Code suggests that conduct constituting sexual harassment may take the form of physical conduct of a sexual nature, ranging from unnecessary touching to assault, verbal conduct of a sexual nature, including unwelcome sexual advances, suggestive remarks and innuendoes, non-verbal conduct of a sexual nature, including the display of pornographic or sexually explicit pictures, leering, whistling or making sexually suggestive gestures, and sex-based conduct, such as sex-based comments about appearance or dress. The essence of the definition is that the conduct is unwanted by the recipient. In the words of the Code, 'sexual attention becomes sexual harassment *if it is persisted in once it has been made clear that it is regarded by the recipient as offensive*, although one incident of harassment may constitute sexual harassment if sufficiently serious' (emphasis added).[107] The definition of sexual harassment also distinguishes between conduct which damages the employee's working environment creating a 'hostile work environment'[108] (Article 1(c)), and conduct which is used as a basis for employment decisions affecting the victim (Article 1(b)).

(b) The Directive

These soft law measures 'softened up' the legislature to introduce a hard law, freestanding wrong of harassment in the amendments to the Equal Treatment Directive which deem harassment to constitute discrimination, now incorporated into Article 2(2)(a) of the Equality Directive. The Directive recognizes two forms of harassment: harassment and sexual harassment. Article 2(1)(c) of the Equality Directive defines *harassment* as the situation 'where unwanted conduct *related to the sex* of a person occurs with the purpose or effect of violating the dignity of a person, and of creating an

---

[106] Art. 1 of the Council's Resolution on the Dignity of Women and Men at Work (OJ [1990] C157/3). For further definitions see the American EEOC's Guidelines on Sexual Harassment, 980, 29 CFR, s. 1604. 11(f) and the discussion in E. Ellis, *EU Anti-discrimination Law* (OUP, Oxford, 2005), 215ff.

[107] See, in the British context, *Bracebridge Engineering* v. *Darby* [1990] IRLR 3 where the EAT accepted that a single serious sexual assault constituted unlawful sexual discrimination.

[108] In *Meritor Savings Bank* v. *Vinson* 477 US 57, 65 the US Supreme Court distinguished between hostile work environment and *quid pro quo* claims. Both are cognizable under Title VII though a hostile environment claim requires harassment that is severe or perverse. In *Burlington Industries* v. *Ellerth*, 524 U.S. 742 (1998) the Supreme Court doubted the utility of these terms and it is not proposed to adopt this distinction here.

intimidating, hostile, degrading, humiliating or offensive environment'. The language of 'related to the sex' (as opposed to the more traditional 'on the grounds of sex') catches a wider range of conduct, argues for a lower threshold of proof,[109] and can be satisfied without reference to how someone of the opposite sex was or would have been treated. By contrast, whether there has been unwanted conduct towards a woman 'on the ground of her sex' can be determined only by reference to the treatment of a man.[110]

Article 2(1)(d) of the Equality Directive defines *sexual harassment* as the situation 'where any form of unwanted verbal, non-verbal or physical conduct of a sexual nature occurs, with the purpose or effect of violating the dignity of a person, in particular when creating an intimidating, hostile, degrading, humiliating or offensive environment'. Thus, sexual harassment is a distinct concept covering situations where the behaviour is sexual in nature, rather than on the grounds of a person's sex. The Code of Conduct would help provide examples of the type of conduct prohibited by the Directive. Article 2(2)(a) then defines discrimination to include '[h]arassment and sexual harassment, as well as any less favourable treatment based on a person's rejection of or submission to such conduct'.

Article 26 of the Equality Directive requires Member States to encourage employers and those responsible for access to vocational training 'to take measures to prevent all forms of discrimination on grounds of sex, in particular harassment and sexual harassment at the workplace'. Here the Code may serve a useful function as guidance for employers as to good practice. For example, the Code recommends that employers, both in the public and private sectors should issue a policy statement, preferably linked to a broader policy promoting equal opportunities, which expressly states that all employees have a right to be treated with dignity, that sexual harassment will not be permitted, and that all employees have a right to complain about any sexual harassment. Furthermore, the policy should state that employees' complaints will be taken seriously, will be dealt with expeditiously, and that they will not suffer victimization or retaliation as a result of making the complaint. The Code also recommends that the policy statement should leave no doubt as to what is considered inappropriate behaviour and it should also specify that appropriate disciplinary measures will be taken against employees found guilty of sexual harassment. This statement must be communicated to all concerned to ensure maximum awareness.

The Code also expects that provision be made for both informal and formal means of resolving disputes. Employers should designate a specially trained officer to provide advice and assistance to employees subjected to sexual harassment and identify to whom a victim can make a complaint. Developing this idea, the European Parliament adopted a resolution calling for Member States to adopt legislation obliging employers to appoint an in-house confidential counsellor to deal with cases of sexual harassment.[111] Normally, formal proceedings should be commenced only after an unsuccessful informal approach to the alleged harasser has been made. This informal approach should

---

[109] M. Rubinstein, 'Amending the Sex Discrimination Act' (2005) 140 *EOR* 20.
[110] Ibid., 21.   [111] B3–1735/91 OJ [1994] C61/246.

make clear that particular behaviour is not welcome. Any investigations must be independent, objective, and handled with sensitivity, with due respect for the rights of both the complainant and the alleged harasser. Employers should monitor and review these procedures to ensure they are working effectively. Finally, the Code emphasizes that both trade unions and employees have a key role to play: trade unions by encouraging employers to develop policies on sexual harassment and advising their members of their rights not to be sexually harassed and supporting them when complaints arise; employees by discouraging any form of reprehensible behaviour and making it clear that it is unacceptable.

4.2. The Article 19 Directives

The Article 19 Directives also introduce the innovation that '[h]arassment shall be deemed to be discrimination' when, in the case of Article 2(3) of the Race Directive, 'unwanted conduct related to racial or ethnic origin takes place with the purpose *or* effect of violating the dignity of a person *and* of creating an intimidating, hostile, degrading, humiliating or offensive environment'.[112] While the definition of harassment is broadly drawn so as to include conduct which has the purpose or effect of violating the victim's dignity, its scope is reduced by the fact that not only must the individual's dignity be violated but also the conduct must create a hostile environment. Therefore, as Rubinstein points out, a one-off incident of racial abuse might be said to violate the recipient's dignity without its creating a hostile working environment. This phrase implies something of greater breadth and duration than a one-off incident.[113] The Directives permit the concept of harassment to be defined in accordance with national laws or practice of the Member States.[114]

F. DEROGATIONS

1. SEX

1.1. Introduction

So far we have focused on the rights to equal treatment. We turn now to look at the derogations from that right. The original version of the Equal Treatment Directive 76/207 contained three express exceptions to the principle of equal treatment: first, where the sex of the worker constituted a determining factor (Article 2(2)); secondly, where women needed to be protected, particularly as regards pregnancy and maternity (Article 2(3)); and, thirdly, where the state has implemented 'positive action' programmes (Article 2(4)). These exceptions, being derogations from an individual right

---

[112] Emphasis added. Cf. Case F-61/06 *Sapara* v. *Eurojust*, judgment of the EU Civil Service Tribunal, 10 July 2008.

[113] 'New Discrimination Regulations: An EOR Guide' (2003) 118 *EOR* 17.

[114] Art. 2(3) of both Directives.

laid down in the Directive, had to be interpreted strictly,[115] had to be regularly reviewed,[116] and were subject to the principle of proportionality.[117] Although the Member States retained a reasonable margin of discretion as to the detailed arrangements for the implementation of these exceptions,[118] the list of exceptions was exhaustive. The Court made this clear in *Johnston*[119] where it said that the principle of equal treatment could not be subject to, for example, any general reservation as regards measures taken on the grounds of public safety.

A different approach has been adopted by the Sex Equality Directive 2006/54, bringing sex discrimination into line with the Article 19 Directives. The first derogation has been replaced by an apparently more open-ended derogation. Article 14(2) provides:

> Member States may provide, as regards access to employment including the training leading thereto, that a difference of treatment which is based on a characteristic related to sex shall not constitute discrimination where, by reason of the nature of the particular occupational activities concerned or of the context in which they are carried out, such a characteristic constitutes a *genuine and determining* occupational requirement, provided that its objective is legitimate and the requirement is proportionate.

This provision allows sex-based criteria to be used provided that reliance on sex (1) constitutes a genuine and determining occupational requirement (so-called 'GOR'); (2) that the objective is legitimate; and (3) the requirement is proportionate. This is narrower than the objective justification defence because the requirement must be connected with the doing of the occupation itself. On the other hand, the open-ended nature of the GOR defence erodes the once clear dichotomy between direct and indirect discrimination.

The second derogation in Directive 76/207 has been expanded. The Sex Equality Directive 2006/54 now provides that the Directive is without prejudice to:

- provisions concerning the protection of women, particularly as regards pregnancy and maternity (Article 28(1) of Directive 2006/54);
- provisions of the Parental Leave Directive 2010/18 and the Pregnant Workers Directive 92/85 (Article 28(2) of Directive 2006/54);
- national provisions giving distinct rights to paternity or adoption leave (Article 16 of Directive 2006/54).

The third derogation has been recast. Article 3 of the Sex Equality Directive 2006/54 now provides that '*Member States* may maintain or adopt measures within the meaning of Article [157(4)] of the Treaty with a view to ensuring full equality in practice between men and women'. The wording suggests that this is no longer a derogation

---

[115] See e.g. Case C–450/93 *Kalanke* v. *Freie und Hansestadt Bremen* [1995] ECR I–3051.
[116] See additionally Arts. 3(2)(c), 5(2)(c), 9(1)–(2). See further Case 222/84 *Johnston* v. *Chief Constable of the RUC* [1986] ECR 1651.
[117] Ibid., para. 36.
[118] See e.g. Case 184/83 *Hofmann* [1984] ECR 3047, para. 27.
[119] Case 222/84 [1986] ECR 1651.

but an important way of realizing equality, provided that the Member States take advantage of the provision. If this is the case, a position which is considered below, the rules outlined above which apply to derogations, no longer apply to Article 3.

In the section that follows we shall consider the first two derogations as originally drafted. The case law decided under these original derogations is likely to offer guidance as to the scope of the new provisions. Positive action—since it is now no longer a true derogation—will be considered separately.

1.2. Sex of the worker constitutes a determining factor/GOR

According to the original Article 2(2) of Directive 76/207, Member States had the option not to apply the principle of equal treatment to 'those occupational activities and, where appropriate, the training leading thereto, for which, by reason of their nature or the context in which they are carried out, the sex of the worker constitutes the determining factor'. Article 2(2) did not oblige Member States to exclude certain occupational activities from the scope of the Directive, nor did it require Member States to exercise the power of derogation in a particular manner.[120]

Certain clearly defined occupations such as singing, acting, dancing, and artistic or fashion modelling fell under Article 2(2).[121] The Court also accepted that certain kinds of employment in private households might fall within Article 2(2)[122] but ruled that a general exclusion of the application of the principle of equal treatment to employment in a private household or in undertakings with no more than five employees went beyond the objective which could be lawfully pursued under Article 2(2).[123] On the other hand, the Court found that it was lawful to limit access by men to the post of midwife in view of the 'personal sensitivities' which may play 'an important role in relations between midwife and patient'.[124] Similar reasoning can explain the Court's acceptance that it was lawful to reserve posts primarily for men in male prisons and for women in female prisons.[125]

More surprisingly, however, the Court accepted in *Johnston*[126] that certain policing activities in Northern Ireland might be such that the sex of the police officers constituted a determining factor. In that case the Chief Constable of the RUC decided not to renew the contract of Mrs Johnston and other women, and not to give them training in the handling of firearms. The Court unquestioningly accepted that the justification for this policy was that 'in a situation characterised by serious internal disturbances the carrying of firearms by policewomen might create additional risks of their being assassinated and

---

[120] Case 248/83 *Commission v. Germany* [1985] ECR 1459.
[121] Commission survey on the implementation of Art. 2(2) of Directive 76/207 cited in Case 248/83 *Commission v. Germany* [1985] ECR 1459.
[122] Case 165/82 *Commission v. UK* [1983] ECR 3431.
[123] Ibid. See further Case E-1/02 *EFTA Surveillance Authority v. The Kingdom of Norway*, judgment of the Court 24 January 2003, para. 46.
[124] Ibid.
[125] Case 318/86 *Commission v. France* [1988] ECR 3559.
[126] Case 222/84 [1986] ECR 1651.

might therefore be contrary to the requirements of public safety'.[127] The Court did, however, insist that Member States had to assess the activities periodically in order to decide whether, in the light of social developments, the derogation from the general scheme of the Directive should be maintained.[128] The Court also recognized that it was for the national court to ensure that the principle of proportionality be maintained.

The Court re-emphasized the limited nature of the Article 2(2) derogation in *Commission* v. *France (prison warders)*.[129] It said that the exceptions provided for in Article 2(2) could relate only to specific activities and that they had to be sufficiently transparent to permit effective supervision by the Commission. Therefore a system of separate recruitment according to sex fell outside Article 2(2).

Despite the caveats in *Johnston* and *Commission* v. *France*, the Court again adopted a respectful approach to state policy in *Sirdar*.[130] Mrs Sirdar had been in the British army since 1983 and had served as a chef in a commando regiment since 1990. When she was made redundant she was invited to apply for a job as a chef in the Royal Marines provided that she satisfied a selection board and a commando training course. The invitation was subsequently withdrawn when the authorities realized that she was a woman, because women were excluded from this regiment. The existence of this policy was justified by the state on the grounds that the presence of women was incompatible with the requirement of 'interoperability'—the need for every Marine, irrespective of his specialization, to be capable of fighting in a commando unit.

Having ruled that Union law in principle applies to the case, since there was no general exception from Union law covering all measures taken for reasons of public security,[131] the Court considered the application of the Article 2(2) derogation to see whether the measures had 'the purpose of guaranteeing public security and whether they are appropriate and necessary to achieve that aim'.[132] The Court said that it was clear that 'the organisation of the Royal Marines differs fundamentally from that of other units in the British armed forces, of which they are the "point of the arrow head"'.[133] They were a small force and were intended to be the first line of attack. The Court noted that it had also been established that, within this corps, chefs were required to serve as front-line commandos, that all members of the corps were engaged and trained for that purpose, and that there were no exceptions to this rule at the time of recruitment.[134] The Advocate General added that the evidence given by the Royal Marines showed the 'negative effects' which the presence of any female element might have on the operational cohesion of a commando unit, 'resulting from the foreseeable preoccupation of infanteers to protect women, quite apart from the latter's (as yet untested) physical suitability for difficult offensive operations involving hand-to-hand combat for which the marines are trained'.[135] Therefore the Court concluded:[136]

---

[127] Para. 36.
[128] See further Art. 9(2) and the requirement to notify the Commission of the results of the assessment and see Case 248/83 *Commission* v. *Germany* [1985] ECR 1459, para. 37.
[129] Case 318/86 [1988] ECR 3559.
[130] Case C–273/97 *Sirdar* v. *Secretary of State for Defence* [1999] ECR I–7403.
[131] Para. 19.   [132] Para. 28.   [133] Para. 30.   [134] Ibid.   [135] Para. 33.   [136] Para. 31.

In such circumstances, the competent authorities were entitled, in the exercise of their
discretion as to whether to maintain the exclusion in question in the light of social developments, and without abusing the principle of proportionality, to come to the view that the
specific conditions for deployment of the assault units of which the Royal Marines are
composed, and in particular the rule of interoperability to which they are subject, justified
their composition remaining exclusively male.

In the light of *Johnston,* the outcome of *Sirdar* is unsurprising. It does, however, reveal how
easy it is for a Member State (condoned by the Court) to use the derogations as a shield for
gender stereotyping and untested assumptions about male soldiers' attitudes to women.
However, the limited nature of the exclusion of women in *Sirdar* was emphasized by the
Court in *Kreil.*[137] It reiterated the point already made in *Johnston* and *Sirdar* that the principle of proportionality had to be observed in determining the scope of any derogation.
Proportionality requires that 'derogations remain within the limits of what is appropriate
and necessary in order to achieve the aim in view'.[138] The Court then ruled that the German
law which excluded women from *all* military posts involving the use of arms and which
allowed women access only to medical services and military music services could not be
regarded as a derogating measure justified by the specific nature of the posts in question or
by the particular context in which the activities in question were carried out.[139]

However, the Court's deference to Member State policy was again repeated in
Dory,[140] this time outside the context of the professional army. Dory objected to being
called up for compulsory military service, arguing, in the light of *Kreil*, that the German law on military service was contrary to Union law, in particular because women
were not required to do military service. The Court accepted the German argument
without criticism that compulsory military service was 'the expression of such a
choice of military organisation to which [Union] law is consequently not applicable'.[141] The fact that, unlike women, the careers of men called up for military service
were delayed was not enough to bring the matter within the scope of Union law. The
Court added that:

> The existence of adverse consequences for access to employment cannot, without encroach-
> ing on the competences of the Member States, have the effect of compelling the Member
> State in question either to extend the obligation of military service to women, thus impos-
> ing on them the same disadvantages with regard to access to employment, or to abolish
> compulsory military service.

As Anagnostaras points out,[142] *Sidar, Kreil,* and *Dory* show that the Court draws a distinction between, on the one hand, the army as a profession and, on the other, military
service as a civilian obligation aimed at protecting external security. It is only in the

---

[137] Case C–285/98 *Kreil v. Bundesrepublik Deutschland* [2000] ECR I–69.
[138] Para. 23.
[139] Para. 27.
[140] Case C–186/01 *Dory v. Federal Republic of Germany* [2003] ECR I–2479.
[141] Para. 39. See M. Trybus (2003) 40 *CMLRev.* 1269.
[142] 'Sex Equality and Compulsory Military Service: the Limits of National Sovereignty over Matters of Army
Organisation' (2003) 28 *ELRev.* 713, 718.

context of the former that Union sex equality law applies. Outside the professional army, it is for each country to decide on the necessity of military service and to determine which people will be affected by it.

The Commission summarized the Court's case law under Article 2(2) in the following terms:[143]

> The main conclusion which can be drawn from this jurisprudence is that the 'certain degree of discretion' enjoyed by Member States to exclude some occupational activities from the scope of the Directive is subject to strict scrutiny. First, the exclusion can only concern specific posts. Secondly, Member States are under the obligation to reassess periodically the legitimacy of the exclusion, so that it may be authorised at a certain date, but become illegal subsequently.[144]

The Commission clearly had this case law in mind when drafting Article 14(2) of the Sex Equality Directive 2006/54 whose scope is unlikely to differ significantly from the original Article 2(2), a point the Commission expressly made when it said: 'In accordance with the above case law, where a difference of treatment, which relates to a genuine occupational qualification exists, it is not to be considered as discrimination'.[145] Emphasizing the exceptional nature of the derogation, the Commission said that 'the term "genuine occupational [requirement]" should be construed narrowly to cover only those occupational requirements where a particular sex is necessary for the performance of the activities concerned'.[146]

1.3. Protection of women, particularly as regards pregnancy and maternity

Article 2(3) of Directive 76/207 and now Article 28(1) of the Sex Equality Directive 2006/54 permits a derogation from the principle of equal treatment to protect women 'particularly as regards pregnancy and maternity'. In *Johnston*[147] the Court made clear that this provision was intended 'to protect a woman's biological condition and the special relationship which exists between a woman and her child'. The significance of this observation can be seen in *Hofmann*.[148] The case concerned a father who took unpaid paternity leave to look after his new-born child while the mother, having completed the initial obligatory period of maternity leave, returned to work. When the father's claim for the state maternity allowance, which was payable to mothers, was refused, he claimed direct discrimination. The Court accepted that Article 2(3)/Article 28(1) permitted Member States to introduce provisions which were designed to protect both 'a woman's

---

[143] COM(2000) 334, para. 24.

[144] The example the Commission gives is that of the situation of midwives. In 1983, the Court ruled that 'at the present time personal sensitivities may play an important role in relations between midwife and patient' so that the United Kingdom had not exceeded the limits of the power granted to the Member States by the Directive in excluding men from that profession and the training leading thereto. However, even at that time, the United Kingdom stated that it intended to progressively fully open up the profession of midwives to men. More than 15 years later, that profession is fully open to men in all the Member States.

[145] COM(2000) 334, para. 27. See additionally Case C-447/09 *Prigge* v. *Deutsche Lufthansa* [2011] ECR I-000, para. 72.

[146] Ibid.

[147] Case 222/84 [1986] ECR 1651.

[148] Case 184/83 [1984] ECR 3047. This case is considered further in Ch. 9.

biological condition during pregnancy and thereafter until such time as her physiological and mental functions have returned to normal after childbirth' and 'to protect the special relationship between a woman and her child over the period which follows between pregnancy and childbirth,[149] by preventing that relationship from being disturbed by the multiple burdens which would result from the simultaneous pursuit of employment'.[150] Thus, the Court ruled that the Directive did not require Member States to grant leave to fathers, even where the parents had decided differently.

While the derogation can be used to justify the special protection of women where their condition requires it, it cannot be used to justify a total exclusion of women from a post of indefinite duration just because they are pregnant at the start of the employment[151] or to exclude women from an occupation, such as the police force, because public opinion demands that women be given greater protection than men, even though the risks are not specific to women.[152] It also cannot be used to exclude women from certain types of employment solely because they are on average smaller and less strong than average men, while men with similar features are accepted for that employment.[153] Women also cannot be excluded from certain types of employment, such as night work[154] or mining and diving,[155] where, with the exception of pregnancy and its aftermath,[156] the risks are common to men and women.

2. RACE AND ETHNIC ORIGIN

As with sex, direct discrimination on the grounds of race or ethnic origin can be saved only by reference to an express defence, the 'genuine and determining occupational

---

[149] See additionally Case C–394/96 Brown v. Rentokil [1998] ECR I–4185.

[150] Both requirements need not be present: in Case 163/82 Commission v. Italy [1983] ECR 3273 the Court found that an Italian law which gave a woman but not her husband the entitlement to the equivalent of maternity leave when they adopted a child under six years old was justified 'by the legitimate concern to assimilate as far as possible the conditions of entry of the child into the adoptive family to those of the arrival of a new born child in the family during the very delicate initial period'. Although Art. 2(3) was not cited, the thinking is very similar to the requirement of safeguarding the 'special relationship' between mother and child.

[151] Case C–207/98 Mahlburg v. Land Mecklenburg-Vorpommern [2000] ECR I–549, para. 25.

[152] Case 222/84 Johnston [1986] ECR 1651 and Case C–285/98 Kreil [2000] ECR I–69, para. 30. The Commission discussed the implications of the Johnston decision in its Communication on Protective Legislation for Women (COM(87) 105 final); Council Conclusions of 26 May 1987 on Protective Legislation for Women in the Member States of the European Community (OJ [1987] C178/04). It examined all national protective provisions, especially in the light of the Arts. 3(2)(c) and 5(2)(c) of the original Equal Treatment Directive 76/207 which require Member States to revise all protective legislation which is no longer justified. It found that 'a mosaic of extremely varied and highly specific regulations exist, the reasons for which are not clearly defined' and concluded that protective legislation which does not relate to pregnancy or maternity should be made to apply equally to both sexes or be repealed.

[153] Case C–203/03 Commission v. Austria [2005] ECR I–935, para. 46.

[154] Case C–345/89 Stoeckel [1991] ECR I–4047. See further Case C–13/93 Office national de l'emploi v. Minne [1994] ECR I–371 where discriminatory derogations from the prohibition of nightwork contravened the Directive.

[155] Case C–203/03 Commission v. Austria [2005] ECR I–935, para. 47.

[156] Case C–421/92 Habermann-Beltermann v. Arbeiterwohlfahrt [1994] ECR I–1657, para. 18; and Art. 7 of Dir. 92/85 (OJ [1992] L348/1) on pregnant workers.

requirement' (GOR).[157] In its explanatory memorandum, the Commission gave examples of such GORs: where a person of a particular racial or ethnic origin is required for reasons of authenticity in a dramatic performance or where the holder of a particular job provides persons of a particular ethnic group with personal services promoting their welfare and those services can most effectively be provided by a person of that ethnic group. The Commission does, however, note that these GORs will be highly exceptional.

3. THE FRAMEWORK DIRECTIVE

3.1. Introduction

The Framework Directive contains a general exclusion, a GOR, and then some specific provisions for the affected grounds. The general exclusion is found in Article 2(5). This provides:

> This Directive shall be without prejudice to measures laid down by national law which, in a democratic society, are necessary for public security, for the maintenance of public order and the prevention of criminal offences, for the protection of health and for the protection of the rights and freedoms of others.

This provision was included in the Directive at the last minute and is intended to prevent members of harmful cults, paedophiles, and people with dangerous physical or mental illnesses from gaining the protection of the Directive.[158] In fact, as we shall see in the context of age discrimination, it has been used more widely than that.

The GOR is found in Article 4(1):

> Notwithstanding Article 2(1) and (2), Member States may provide that a difference of treatment which is based on a characteristic related to any of the grounds referred to in Article 1 shall not constitute discrimination where, by reason of the nature of the particular occupational activities concerned or of the context in which they are carried out, such a characteristic constitutes a *genuine and determining occupational requirement*, provided that the objective is legitimate and the requirement is proportionate.[159]

However, due to the different issues affecting the various strands, the derogations are more tailored for the framework Directive than in respect of sex and race and ethnic origin. We shall therefore now consider the unique issues arising in respect of the different strands.

3.2. Religion or belief

(a) Ethos-based organizations

In addition to the general GOR in Article 4(1) which would be available to all employers wishing to employ someone of a particular religion (e.g. a non-denominational hospital wishing to employ a Christian chaplain), Article 4(2) makes special provision for 'entreprises de tendences', that is organizations which promote certain religious values where the jobs need to be performed by employees who share the relevant religious belief. According to Article 4(2), Member States may provide that, 'in the case of occupational

---

[157] Art. 4.   [158] Ellis, previously, at n. 107, 291.   [159] Emphasis added.

activities within churches and other public or private organisations the ethos of which is based on religion or belief, a difference of treatment based on a person's religion or belief shall not constitute discrimination where, by reason of the nature of these activities or of the context in which they are carried out, a person's religion or belief constitute a *genuine, legitimate and justified occupational requirement*, having regard to an organisation's ethos'.[160] Thus a faith school would be allowed to insist under Article 4(2) that its teachers are a member of that particular faith provided that a person's religion or belief constitutes 'a genuine, legitimate and justified occupational requirement' (the requirement of 'determining' does not apply under Article 4(2)). However, the same school might not be able to insist that a member of its ground or works' staff also be an adherent to that particular faith since such individuals do not have the same contact with children and are not responsible for the children's spiritual life.

(b) Special provisions relating to Northern Ireland

The political difficulties in Northern Ireland are well known and the peace process remains fragile. In order not to undermine the careful negotiations which have already taken place, Article 15 of the Framework Directive makes two special provisions, one concerning the police and the other concerning teachers. In respect of preserving the Patten reforms to the police service which require an equal number of Catholic and Protestant recruits, Article 15(1) provides that in order to tackle the under-representation of 'one of the major religious communities' in the police service in Northern Ireland, differences in treatment regarding recruitment into that service, including its support staff 'shall not constitute discrimination in so far as those differences in treatment are expressly authorised by national legislation'. In respect of teachers, Article 15(2) provides that '[i]n order to maintain a balance of opportunity in employment for teachers in Northern Ireland while furthering the reconciliation of historical divisions between the major religious communities there' the religion and belief provisions of the Directive do not apply to the recruitment of teachers in schools insofar as this is expressly authorized by national legislation.

3.3. Age

(a) Introduction

The derogations in the field of age have attracted the most attention from litigators and there is now a large body of case law interpreting the relevant provisions. In addition to the general derogation in Article 2(5) and the general GOR in Article 4(1), Article 6(1) contains a further, unique, derogation in respect of age, permitting Member States to discriminate on the grounds of age for labour market reasons. Since all three provisions are derogations from the fundamental principle of equal treatment they have to be narrowly construed.[161]

---

[160] Emphasis added.
[161] Case C–447/09 *Prigge* [2011] ECR I–000, para. 56 (Art. 2(5)), para. 71 (Art. 4(1)) quoting Recital 23 that in 'very limited circumstances can a difference of treatment be justified where a characteristic related to, inter alia, age constitute a GOR'.

(b) Article 2(5)

The first of the derogations, Article 2(5), was considered in *Petersen*[162] which concerned the upper age limit of 68 for practising as a panel dentist in the German statutory health insurance scheme. The Court recognized that while directly discriminatory, the rules could in principle be justified in the basis of public health under Article 2(5). The public health argument had two strands. The first concerned the protection of public health of patients. The Court recognized as a fact that the performance of dentists declined with age—without asking for any supporting evidence.[163] However, the Court found that the retirement age was not proportionate because it applied only to panel dentists covered by statutory health insurance scheme; outside the scheme there was no age limit. This lack of consistency meant that the age limit imposed on panel dentists was not necessary for the protection of public health.[164] The Court did, however, accept the second strand of the public health argument put forward: the financial balance of the healthcare system. The argument was that the departure of the oldest dentists reduced expenditure and so averted serious harm to the balance of social security system.[165] The Court also considered that setting the age at 68 was sufficiently high to serve as an endpoint to practise as a dentist. The fact that the private sector did otherwise was irrelevant for the purposes of this argument.[166]

In *Prigge*[167] public security, as opposed to public health, was at stake and the Court confirmed in a case concerning the compulsory retirement of pilots at age 60 that as regards air traffic safety, measures aimed at avoiding aeronautical accidents by monitoring pilots' aptitude and physical capabilities with the aim of ensuring that human failure did not cause accidents were 'undeniably measures of a nature to ensure public security within the meaning of Article 2(5) of the Directive'.[168] However, there was a glitch: the retirement age had been laid down by collective agreement and Article 2(5) expressly refers to measures being laid down by 'national law'. The collective agreement was therefore insufficient.[169] However, the Court did say that Member States could authorize the social partners to adopt rules by collective agreement provided that any such rules were 'sufficiently precise'.[170] Yet even with Member State authorization the requirements had to be proportionate. They were not in this case since national and international rules fixed the age at 65. The measure was therefore not necessary for public security and the protection of health.[171]

(c) Article 4(1)

Given the breadth of the justification available in Article 6(1), it was thought that Article 4(1) would not be much used in age discrimination cases. The opposite has, in fact,

---

[162] Case C–341/08 *Petersen v. Berufungsausschuss für Zahnärzte für den Bezirk Westfalen-Lippe* [2010] ECR I–000.

[163] Cf. Joined Cases C–250/09 and C–268/09 *Georgiev v. Tehnicheski universitet—Sofia, filial Plovdiv* [2010] ECR I–000 considered below.

[164] Para. 62.   [165] Para. 52.   [166] Para. 63.

[167] Case C–447/09 *Prigge v. Deutsche Lufthansa* [2011] ECR I–000.

[168] Para. 58.   [169] Para. 60.   [170] Para. 61.   [171] Para. 64.

turned out to be true. The issue first arose in *Wolf*[172] which concerned a German rule setting the upper age limit of 30 for entering employment as active fire fighter. Mr Wolf was 31 so his application to join the fire service was not considered. The German government justified its rule by reference to Recital 18:

> This Directive does not require, in particular, the armed forces and the police, prison or emergency services to recruit or maintain in employment persons who do not have the required capacity to carry out the range of functions that they may be called upon to perform with regard to the legitimate objective of preserving the operational capacity of those services.

The Court accepted that the concern to ensure the operational capacity and proper functioning of the professional fire service constituted a legitimate objective within the meaning of Article 4(1) of the Directive.[173] The Court then said that unlike those in the higher management grades, those in the intermediate career of the fire service perform tasks of professional firefighters on the ground: 'fighting fires, rescuing persons, environment protection tasks, helping animals and dealing with dangerous animals, as well as supporting tasks such as the maintenance and control of protective equipment and vehicles'. The Court therefore concluded that 'the possession of especially high physical capacities may be regarded as a genuine and determining occupational requirement within the meaning of Article 4(1) of the Directive for carrying on the occupation of a person in the intermediate career of the fire service'.[174] This GOR was, according to the Court, related to age. The Court accepted the German government's evidence that respiratory capacity, musculature and endurance diminish with age and that 'very few officials over 45 years of age have sufficient physical capacity to perform the fire-fighting part of their activities'.[175] The Court also found the German rules to be proportionate. It noted that an official recruited before the age of 30, who would have to follow a training programme lasting two years, could be assigned to those duties for a minimum of 15 to 20 years. By contrast, if he was recruited at the age of 40, that period would be a maximum of 5 to 10 years only. Recruitment at an older age would mean too many employees could not be assigned to the most physically demanding duties or could be so assigned but not for a sufficiently long period.[176]

This judgment was met with disappointment in many quarters. While all commentators would accept that active fire fighters need to be physically fit, they objected to the fact that the German government produced, and the Court relied on, generalized data. Surely an individual assessment of a young applicant would have been more proportionate than having a blanket cut-off age? The avalanche of criticism heaped on the Court may help to explain why in *Prigge* it reached the opposite conclusion. As we saw above, the case concerned the mandatory retirement age for pilots of 60. Lufthansa

---

[172] Case C–229/08 *Wolf v. Stadt Frankfurt am Main* [2010] ECR I–1.
[173] Para. 39.   [174] Para. 40.   [175] Para. 41.   [176] Para. 43.

argued this was compatible with Article 4(1). The Court made clear that, following *Wolf*, there were four stages to the analysis:

(i) the difference in treatment had to be based on a characteristic related to one of the grounds referred to in Article 1;

(ii) the characteristic had to constitute a genuine and determining occupational requirement;

(iii) the requirement pursued a legitimate objective; and

(iv) the requirement was proportionate.

Following *Wolf* the Court found that (i) possessing particular physical capabilities, capabilities which 'undeniably' diminish with age (ii) constituted a genuine and determining occupational requirement. The requirement (iii) pursued a legitimate aim (of guaranteeing air traffic safety). However, the Court found the rule disproportionate because of the difference in treatment of airline pilots by national and international legislation which allowed those pilots aged between 60 and 65 to continue carrying out their activities, albeit under certain restrictions, while the collective agreement at issue in *Prigge* contained an outright prohibition of continued employment.

(d) Article 6(1)

The principal derogation invoked in the context of age discrimination is Article 6(1). This says that Member States may provide that differences of treatment on grounds of age shall not constitute discrimination—either direct *or* indirect—if, within the context of national law, 'they are objectively and reasonably justified by a legitimate aim, including legitimate employment policy, labour market and vocational training objectives, and if the means of achieving that aim are appropriate and necessary'.[177] The provision then goes on to provide (a non-exhaustive) list of measures of what might constitute differences of treatment:

• the setting of special conditions on access to employment and vocational training, employment and occupation, including dismissal and remuneration conditions, for young people, older workers, and persons with caring responsibilities in order to promote their vocational integration or ensure their protection;

• the fixing of minimum conditions of age, professional experience, or seniority in service for access to employment or to certain advantages linked to employment;

---

[177] This is not the same test as for objective justification under Art. 2(2)(b). As the Court explained in Case C–388/07 *R (on the application of The Incorporated Trustees of the National Council on Ageing (Age Concern England))* v. *Secretary of State for Business, Enterprise and regulatory Reform* [2009] ECR I–1569, paras. 59–60, Art. 2 draws a distinction, in para. 2, between, on the one hand, discrimination directly on those grounds and, on the other, 'indirect' discrimination. Only provisions, criteria or practices liable to constitute indirect discrimination may, by virtue of Art. 2(2)(b) of Dir. 2000/78, escape classification as discrimination if objectively justified. For differences in treatment constituting direct discrimination, Art. 2(1) does not provide for any derogation. However, Art. 6 establishes a scheme of derogation specific to differences of treatment on grounds of age, on account of the recognized specificity of age among the grounds of discrimination prohibited by the Directive.

- the fixing of a maximum age for recruitment which is based on the training requirements of the post in question or the need for a reasonable period of employment before retirement.

Thus, Article 6(1) gives Member States the option of allowing employers to objectively justify not only indirect discrimination on the grounds of age but also direct discrimination. This constitutes an important departure from the basic model (see Figure 6.1 in Chapter 6) but has been introduced to reflect the fact that age may genuinely be a relevant factor for certain aspects of employment and vocational training. Article 6(1) therefore means that employers can in principle lay down a retirement age, length of service criteria and, for jobs such as those in medicine involving a lengthy period of training, a maximum age for recruitment, provided always that the employer can show, on a case-by-case basis and on the production of evidence and not general assertions,[178] that the age criteria are objectively justifiable and the means of achieving the aim are appropriate and necessary. In addition, Article 6(2) of the Framework Directive permits Member States to provide that the fixing for occupational social security schemes of ages for admission or entitlement to retirement or invalidity benefits and the use, in the context of such schemes, of age criteria in actuarial calculations, does not constitute discrimination on the grounds of age, provided this does not result in discrimination on the grounds of sex.

The practical significance of Article 6(1) is enormous since nearly all Member States have some form of retirement age. In the absence of Article 6(1) such retirement ages would constitute unlawful direct discrimination unless justified under Article 4(1) or 2(5). However, the Court has not given the Member States a totally free hand. It has insisted that the criteria in Article 6(1) be strictly complied with.[179] These criteria are:

(1) *Member States* may provide that differences of treatment on grounds of age shall not constitute discrimination, if,

(2) within the context of national law,

(3) they are objectively and reasonably justified by a legitimate aim, including legitimate employment policy, labour market and vocational training objectives, and

(4) if the means of achieving that aim are appropriate and necessary.

Palacios de la Villa[180] provides a good example of how the Court applies these criteria. In that case national legislation enabled the social partners to negotiate collective agreements providing for compulsory retirement, set at 65 by national legislation, on condition that the workers have fulfilled the social security conditions entitling them to draw a contributory retirement pension. Criteria (1) and (2) had both been satis-

---

[178] Ibid., para. 4.1.14.

[179] C–388/07 *Age Concern* [2009] ECR I–1569, para. 62: Art. 6, as an 'exception to the principle prohibiting discrimination, is however strictly limited by the conditions laid down in Article 6(1) itself'.

[180] Case C–411/05 *Palacios de la Villa* [2007] ECR I–8531.

fied. In respect of criteria (3) the Court recognized that promoting employment,[181] or 'intergenerational employment' as Advocate General Mazak[182] put it, was a good justification.

On the question of proportionality, the Court said that the Member States and social partners enjoyed a broad discretion in their choice of the aim of social policy measures and the definition of measures able to achieve it.[183] The Advocate General set the bar even higher: 'only a manifestly disproportionate national measure should be censured' at EU level.[184] The Court said that it did not appear unreasonable for the Spanish authorities to take the view that their measure could be appropriate and necessary in order to achieve a legitimate aim in the context of national employment policy, consisting in the promotion of full employment by facilitating access to the labour market.[185] Furthermore, the Spanish system combined retirement with an entitlement to a pension[186] and it also incorporated a degree of flexibility because the collective agreements took into account the specific features of jobs in question.

In *Palacios* the Court was dealing with the standard situation anticipated when the Directive was drafted: national law makes provision for a retirement age. What happens when, as in the UK, the government abolishes the statutory framework for retirement? Can employers nevertheless rely on Article 6(1)?[187] And, if they can, what sort of objective reasons can they rely on? The case law so far has not answered questions (1) and (2). As for the third, the Court has recognized a range of justifications which a *state* can produce. It has left open the question as to whether they can be invoked by an employer. The justifications recognized so far include:

(1) Striking a balance between political, social, economic, demographic and/or budgetary considerations (*Rosenbladt*[188]).

(2) Workforce planning—to enable employers and employees to plan work, retirement and succession planning *(Georgiev*[189]*)*.

(3) Prevention of 'job blocking' by older workers, thereby providing opportunities for the retention of younger workers (*Palacios*). This is also referred to as facilitating access to employment/promotion for younger employees (*Palacios, Petersen, Rosenbladt, Fuchs*[190]).

(4) Promoting exchange of experiences and innovation through mixing the generation of employees (*Fuchs*).

[181] Paras. 63–4.   [182] Para. 71.   [183] Para. 68.   [184] Para. 74.   [185] Para. 72.   [186] Para. 73.
[187] Possibly: Case C–88/08 *Hütter* v. *Technische Universität Graz* [2009] ECR I–5325, albeit that the employer was the state; Case C–555/07 *Kücükdeveci* v. *Swedex* [2010] ECR I–365, albeit that the case was decided under the general principle of non-discrimination on the grounds of age (see Ch. 6). See additionally *Seldon* [2012] UKSC 16, para. 55. Cf. Case C–388/07 *Age Concern* [2009] ECR I–1569, para. 61: 'Article 6(1) of Directive 2000/78 authorises *Member States* to provide, notwithstanding Article 2(2) thereof, that certain differences of treatment on grounds of age do not constitute discrimination if, "within the context of national law, they are objectively and reasonably justified by a legitimate aim, [etc …]"' (emphasis added). See further, M. Sargeant, 'The Default Retirement Age: Legitimate Aims and Disproportionate Means' (2010) 39 *ILJ* 244.
[188] Case C–45/09 *Rosenbladt* v. *Oellerking Gebäudereinigungsges. mbH* [2010] ECR I–000.
[189] Joined Cases C–250/09 and C–268/09 *Georgiev* [2010] ECR I–000.
[190] Joined Cases C–159/10 and C–160/10 *Fuchs* v. *Land Hessen* [2011] ECR I–000.

(5) Protection of dignity at work, avoiding the need to performance manage long serving employees, avoiding disputes over fitness to work (*Fuchs*).

(6) Ensuring high quality of service and continued competence (*Petersen, Fuchs*).

While in some cases the Court has waived the justifications through with little or no scrutiny,[191] in other cases the Court has insisted that 'mere assertion' is not sufficient and that evidence needs to be adduced.[192] Therefore, in *Georgiev*, the Court insisted that the university had to show that there were younger academics waiting to take up posts vacated by the retiring older professors.

The Court has also given attention to the question of proportionality.[193] *Rosenbladt* provides a good example. The Court accepted that the automatic termination of employment contracts of employees meeting certain age conditions could be justified. The Court also thought that the scheme at issue was proportionate: the national legislation was based on (a relatively high) age and entitlement to pension.[194] In addition, and importantly, the national scheme also offered flexibility:[195]

> That allows not only employees and employers, by means of individual agreements, but also the social partners, by means of collective agreements,—and therefore with considerable flexibility—to opt for application of that mechanism so that due account may be taken not only of the overall situation in the labour market concerned, but also of the specific features of the jobs in question.

How relevant, then, is consistency?[196] This is an important question in the labour law context. Good industrial relations would seem to require all employees to be treated equally (i.e. the same retirement age) but a proportionality review might suggest there should be exceptions to the rule (i.e. different retirement ages), provided that the exceptions do not undermine the rule.[197] *Rosenbladt* suggests that each case should, indeed, be judged on its own merits, a point reiterated in *Fuchs*.[198] Land Hessen had a retirement age of 65 for civil servants. However, the retirement could be postponed on request 'if it is in the interests of the service' (e.g. to finalize a pending case) for one year at a time up to the age of 68. Fuchs, a state prosecutor, had his request declined. The Court accepted that there were good justifications for the retirement age. On the question of

---

[191] See e.g. Case C–45/09 *Rosenbladt* [2010] ECR I–000, para. 47, where the Court came close to a presumption of legality of such clauses: 'The authorisation of clauses on automatic termination of employment contracts on the ground that an employee has reached retirement age cannot, generally, be regarded as unduly prejudicing the legitimate interests of the workers concerned'.

[192] Case C–388/07 *Age Concern* [2009] ECR I–1569, para. 51 where the Court also said that Art. 6(1) imposes on Member States the burden of establishing to a 'high standard of proof' the legitimacy of the aim relied on as a justification (para. 67).

[193] For full discussion, see C. Kilpatrick, 'The Court of Justice and labour law in 2010: A New EU Discrimination Law Architecture' (2011) 40 *ILJ* 280.

[194] Para. 48.

[195] Para. 49. See additionally Case C–499/08 *Andersen* v. *Region Syddanmark* [2010] ECR I–000 where the failure to take individual circumstances into account led to the downfall of the scheme.

[196] See Case C–88/08 *Hütter* [2009] ECR I–5325 more generally on the question of consistency.

[197] Joined Cases C–159/10 and C–160/10 *Fuchs* [2011] ECR I–000, para. 86

[198] Joined Cases C–159/10 and C–160/10 [2011] ECR I–000.

coherence, the Court said that coherence is important but narrowly tailored exceptions introduced to achieve flexibility could be justified.[199] For good measure, the Court added that the fact that the federal government and other regions had different retirement ages did not undermine the coherence of the rule because the pace of change inevitably varies from region to region.[200]

4. CONFLICTS BETWEEN THE GROUNDS

With the extension of the scope of the non-discrimination principle, there will inevitably come a time when the different grounds of protection come into conflict. The derogations provide some guidance as to hierarchy. Thus Article 4(2) of Directive 2000/78 allows ethos-based organizations to discriminate against those who do not share their ethos. It also seems to permit such organizations to discriminate against those who once shared their ethos but through their conduct no longer adhere to it: ethos-based organizations can require 'individuals working for them to act in good faith and with loyalty to the organisation's ethos'. Therefore, the dismissal of a Catholic teacher employed in a Catholic school who gets divorced may be compatible with the Directive. However, this example demonstrates the potential conflict which arises between the different strands of protection: the dismissal of such a teacher might also contravene Directive 76/207's prohibition against discrimination on the grounds of marital status (not replicated in Directive 2006/54). Thus, the question is raised whether ethos-based organizations can discriminate against people who are protected on other grounds, such as women and homosexuals. Article 4(2) suggests that the answer is no: it provides that '[t]his difference of treatment... should not justify discrimination on another ground'. However, the same restriction does not apply in the case of non-ethos-based employers considered in Article 4(1). Furthermore, Article 2(5) expressly refers to the fact that the Directive is without prejudice to the 'rights and freedoms of others'.

G. POSITIVE ACTION

1. SEX

1.1. Introduction

Article 2(4) of the original version of the Equal Treatment Directive 76/207 provided that the Directive was 'without prejudice to measures which promote equal opportunity for men and women, in particular by removing existing inequalities which affect women's opportunities'. The importance of positive action as a way of securing women more senior positions in the labour market was recognized relatively early by a Commission

---

[199] Paras. 86–7.   [200] Paras. 96–7.

report on occupational segregation.[201] The report concluded, first, that despite rising
female participation in the workforce, occupational segregation remains a central characteristic of all European labour markets; and, secondly, that although women have
made entry into high level jobs, they have also increased their shares of lower level
service and clerical work. The authors argued that positive action programmes, particularly those implemented in a favourable labour market context, have a role to play in
reducing this segregation.

Positive *action* is a management approach intended to identify and remedy situations
which lead to or perpetuate inequalities in the workplace. It is intended to put women
in the position to be able to compete equally with men but does not interfere with the
selection process. Thus, positive action aims to complement legislation on equal treatment and includes any measure contributing to the elimination of inequalities in practice. It focuses on balancing family and professional responsibilities, in particular
looking at the development of childcare structures, the arrangement of working hours,
and the reintegration of women who have taken career breaks into the workplace.[202]
Positive *discrimination*, by contrast, consists of setting recruitment targets or quotas
and discriminating in favour of women at the point of selection in order to meet these
targets. Although ostensibly contravening the principle of formal equality,[203] such discrimination can be justified in that it compensates for past discrimination, providing an
immediate remedy to a long-standing problem.[204]

The Union has traditionally favoured positive action over positive discrimination.
The Council's Recommendation on the Promotion of Positive Action for Women[205]
recommends that Member States adopt a positive action policy 'designed to eliminate
existing inequalities affecting women in working life and to promote a better balance
between the sexes in employment'. The policy is intended, first, to eliminate the prejudicial effects on women which arise from existing attitudes, behaviour, and structures
based on the idea of a traditional division of roles in society for men and women; and,
secondly, to encourage the participation of women in sectors where they are currently
under-represented and at higher levels of responsibility in order to achieve better use of
human resources.[206] Article 4 contains a list of the steps that Member States might take,
including encouraging women to participate in vocational and continuous training,[207]

---

[201] J. Rubery and C. Fagan, *Occupational Segregation of Women and Men in the European Community*,
Commission of the European Communities, V/5409/93-EN, 1993.

[202] See additionally Advocate General Tesauro's Opinion in Case C–450/93 *Kalanke* [1995] ECR I–3051 and
COM(96) 88.

[203] See S. Fredman, *Women and the Law* (Clarendon, Oxford, 1997), 380–3.

[204] But see B. Parekh, 'A Case for Positive Discrimination' in B. Hepple and E. Szyszczak (eds.), *Discrimination:
The Limits of the Law* (Mansell, London, 1992). See further chaps 16–21 from the same book. For some lively
discussion on the positive discrimination debate, see the essays by R. Kennedy and R. Delgado in J. D. Donohue
(ed.), *Foundations of Employment Discrimination Law* (OUP, New York, 1997).

[205] Recommendation 84/635/EEC (OJ [1984] L331/34).

[206] Art. 1.

[207] See further the Commission Recommendation 87/567/EEC of 24 November 1987 on Vocational
Training for Women (OJ [1987] C342/5); the Council Resolution of 16 December on the Reintegration and
Late Integration of Women into Working Life (OJ [1988] C333/01).

encouraging women candidates in making applications, adapting working conditions, and adjusting working time. Article 8 emphasizes that the public sector should promote equal opportunities to serve as an example.[208]

The Commission published an extensive guide to positive action,[209] listing the organizational advantages of a positive action programme and the means by which to put it into place. Nevertheless, a report produced for the Commission found that 'despite almost a decade of the active promotion of positive action for women progress is slow... Many organisations do not appear to have a policy for equality of opportunity. Even [fewer] appear to have a programme of practical actions.'[210]

1.2. The role of the Court of Justice

(a) The early days

Given the sensitivities surrounding positive action it was inevitable that the Court would eventually become drawn into the debate, not least because some of the German *Länder* have quite extensive positive action programmes in the public sector. In some of its earlier case law the Court took a very narrow view of what was permissible. For example, in *Commission* v. *France*[211] it said that the Article 2(4) of Directive 76/207 exception was specifically and exclusively designed to allow measures which, although discriminatory in appearance, were in fact intended to eliminate or reduce actual instances of inequalities which might exist in the reality of social life. It ruled out, however, 'a generalised preservation of special rights for women in collective agreements'. This led one commentator to suggest that special measures—perhaps even positively discriminatory ones—would be excused by Article 2(4) to the extent that they compensated for specific instances of pre-existing inequality, albeit that Article 2(4) would not justify positive discrimination in favour of women in employment generally.[212]

(b) Kalanke *and* Marschall

The decision in *Kalanke*[213] cast doubt on any such broad reading of Article 2(4) of Directive 76/207. The case concerned the Bremen law on positive discrimination which, in the case of a tie-break situation, gave priority to an equally qualified woman over a man if women were under-represented in the workforce.[214] Relying on this provision, the State of Bremen promoted Ms Glißman to the post of section manager in the parks department in preference to Mr Kalanke. He argued that he had been discriminated

---

[208] The Commission itself introduced a positive action programme on 8 March 1988.

[209] *Positive Action. Equal Opportunities for Women in Employment. A Guide*, Commission of the European Communities (1988) CB–48–87–525–EN–C.

[210] *An Evaluation Study of Positive Action in Favour of Women*, ER Consultants (1990), Commission V/587/91-EN, 39. For the Commission's own assessment, see its report to Council COM(88) 370 final.

[211] Case 318/86 [1988] ECR I–6315. See additionally Case 111/86 *Delauche* v. *Commission* [1987] ECR 5345.

[212] Ellis, previously, at n. 107, 246.

[213] Case C–450/93 [1995] ECR I–3051.

[214] Under-representation exists where women 'do not make up at least half the staff in the individual pay, remuneration and salary brackets in the relevant personnel group within a department'.

against on the grounds of sex, contrary to Article 2(1) of the Directive 76/207 (now Article 14 of the Equality Directive); Bremen relied on the Article 2(4) derogation.

The Court explained that Article 2(4) did permit national measures relating to access to employment, including promotion, which gave a specific advantage to women, with a view to improving their ability to compete on the labour market and to pursue their career on an equal footing with men.[215] However, it said that measures which, at the decision stage, departed from the principle of individual merit contravened Article 2(4). It continued that national rules which guaranteed women 'absolute and unconditional priority for appointment or promotion' went beyond promoting equal opportunities and overstepped the limits of the exception in Article 2(4) of the Directive.[216] Consequently, the Bremen system 'substitutes for equality of opportunity as envisaged in Article 2(4) the result which is only to be arrived at by providing such equality of opportunity'.[217]

Advocate General Tesauro's Opinion was equally narrow. He said: '[G]iving equal opportunities can only mean putting people in a position to attain equal results and hence restoring conditions of equality between members of the two sexes as regards starting points'.[218] This means removing existing barriers to achieve such a result. He then reasoned that since the man and woman in *Kalanke* had equivalent qualifications they must have had, and continued to have, equal opportunities: 'they are therefore on an equal footing at the starting block'.[219] Consequently, by favouring the woman, he said this created a position of equality of results which exceeded the scope of Article 2(4). He said:[220]

> In the final analysis, must each individual's right not to be discriminated against on grounds of sex—which the Court itself has held is a fundamental right the observance of which it ensures—yield to the rights of the disadvantaged group, in this case women, in order to compensate for the discrimination suffered by that group in the past?

Put this way the answer was, inevitably, no. He said that positive discrimination brought about a quantitative increase in female employment but it also most affected the principle of equality as between individuals. He concluded:

> I am convinced that women do not merit the attainment of numerical—and hence only formal—equality—moreover at the cost of an incontestable violation of a fundamental value of every civil society: equal rights, equal treatment for all. Formal numerical equality is an objective which may salve some consciences, but it will remain illusory and devoid of all substance unless it goes together with measures which are genuinely destined to achieve equality... [W]hat is necessary above all is a substantial change in the economic, social and cultural model which is at the root of the inequalities.[221]

---

[215] Para. 19, referring to the Preamble of the Recommendation on Positive Action (84/635/EEC OJ [1984] L331/34).

[216] Para. 22. See additionally Case C–407/98 *Abrahamsson v. Fogelqvist* [2000] ECR I–5539 where the Court ruled that a national rule which gave automatic priority to a person of the under-represented sex who had adequate qualifications but qualifications which were inferior to those of the person who would otherwise have been appointed, albeit that the difference in qualifications was not important, breached Art. 2(4) of Directive 76/207 and Art. 157(4) TFEU. This outcome was not affected by the limited number of posts to which the rule applied or the level of the appointment.

[217] Para. 23.   [218] Para. 13.   [219] Ibid.   [220] Para. 7.   [221] Para. 28.

The judgment (and the opinion) were much criticized for their excessive reliance on the formal non-discrimination model, their focus on the individual, their failure both to show any sensitivity towards the position of women,[222] and to respect the principle of subsidiarity, and the absence of any attempt to weigh up any policy arguments. They also cast doubt on the legality of a variety of different forms of positive action. As a result, the Commission issued a Communication on *Kalanke*.[223] It took the view that the Court only condemned the special feature of the Bremen law which *automatically* gave women the absolute and unconditional right to appointment or promotion over men. Therefore, it considered that only those quota systems which were completely rigid and did not leave any possibility to take account of individual circumstances were unlawful. It therefore proposed an amendment to Article 2(4) of Directive 76/207/EEC to the effect that:

> This Directive shall be without prejudice to measures to promote equal opportunity for men and women in particular by removing existing inequalities which affect the opportunities of the underrepresented sex in the areas referred to in Article 1(1). Possible measures shall include the giving of preference, as regards access to employment or promotion, to a member of the underrepresented sex, provided that such measures do not preclude the assessment of the particular circumstances of the individual case.

The Commission's approach was reflected in the Court's decision in the subsequent case of *Marschall*.[224] Mr Marschall, a teacher, applied for promotion. The District Authority informed him that it intended to appoint a female candidate on the basis of the state law which provided for priority to an equally qualified woman where women were underrepresented. However, unlike *Kalanke*,[225] the state law contained a saving clause (*Öffnungsklausel*): priority was given to the woman 'unless reasons specific to an individual [male] candidate tilt the balance in his favour'. Advocate General Jacobs thought that the saving clause did not alter the discriminatory nature of the rule in general. He agreed with Advocate General Tesauro in *Kalanke* that the measures permitted by Article 2(4) were those designed to remove the obstacles preventing women from pursuing the same results on equal terms. He said Article 2(4) did not permit measures designed 'to confer the results on them [women] directly, or, in any event, to grant them priority in attaining those results simply because they are women'. He said that the reasoning in *Kalanke* suggested that the rule in *Marschall* was also unlawful: if an absolute rule giving preference to women on the grounds of sex was unlawful, then a conditional rule which gave preference to men on the basis of admittedly discriminatory criteria *a fortiori* had to be unlawful.[226]

---

[222] See e.g. D. Schiek 'Positive Action in Community Law' (1996) 25 *ILJ*. 239; S. Prechal (1996) 33 *CMLRev.* 1245; A. Peters, 'The Many Meanings of Equality and Positive Action in Favour of Women under European Community Law—A Conceptual Analysis' (1996) 2 *ELJ* 177.

[223] COM(96) 88.

[224] Case C-409/95 [1997] ECR I-6363.

[225] The Bremen law at issue in *Kalanke* did not contain a saving clause. The Federal Labour Court, however, read exceptions into the Bremen law in accordance with the *Grundgesetz*. While this was mentioned to the Court (see para. 9), the questions referred made no reference to these exceptions. It therefore seems that the Court answered the question in *Kalanke* on the basis of the absence of such a clause.

[226] Para. 36.

The Court disagreed. While recognizing that a rule which automatically gave priority to women when they were equally qualified to men involved discrimination on grounds of sex, it distinguished *Marschall* from *Kalanke* on the basis of the saving clause. Having noted the 'prejudices and stereotypes concerning the role and capacities of women in working life',[227] it said that:[228]

> It follows that a national rule in terms of which, subject to the application of the saving clause, female candidates for promotion who are equally as qualified as the male candidates are to be treated preferentially in sectors where they are under-represented may fall within the scope of Article 2(4) if such a rule may counteract the prejudicial effects on female candidates of the attitudes and behaviour described above and thus reduce actual instances of inequality which may exist in the real world.

The Court then added a proviso. The state rule did not breach Article 2(4) provided that the national rule contained a saving clause. This means that:

> ...in each individual case the rule provides for male candidates who are equally as qualified as the female candidates a guarantee that the candidatures will be the subject of an objective assessment which will take account of all criteria specific to the individual candidates and will override the priority accorded to female candidates where one or more of those criteria tilts the balance in favour of the male candidate. In this respect it should be remembered that those criteria must not be such as to discriminate against the female candidates.[229]

It that said that it was for the national court to determine whether those conditions were fulfilled.

Marschall therefore suggests that so-called soft quotas (quotas with a saving clause) fell within Article 2(4) of Directive 76/207, as an exception to the equal treatment principle, provided that the state law contains a proviso.[230] The ruling in *Marschall* therefore confines *Kalanke* to the (unusual) situation of an unqualified ('hard') quota rule. However, the qualification introduced by the Court to the types of saving clause permitted, and the limitations on the criteria which may be applied to tilt the balance (back) in favour of the man, in effect restricts the operation of such saving clauses. The criteria applied must be based on the individual concerned and 'not such as to discriminate against *female candidates*',[231] that is, they must be non-discriminatory in a general sense. Therefore, the criteria applied to bring the saving clause into operation may not be based on generalizations about men, such as, for instance, their need to bring home a 'household wage' (an indirectly discriminatory requirement), or the fact that the man is a sole breadwinner[232] (again an indirectly discriminatory assumption), or reasons of

---

[227] Paras. 29 and 30.   [228] Para. 31.   [229] Para. 33.

[230] On the different types of quota, see D. Schiek, 'Sex Equality Law after *Kalanke* and *Marschall*' (1998) 4 *ELJ* 148.

[231] Para. 33, emphasis added.

[232] It was suggested by the national court that this might be precisely one such criterion applied in the assessment. Mr Kalanke had argued that he should have been promoted on social grounds since he had to maintain three dependants (wife and two children) whereas Ms Glißman had no such obligation.

seniority (also potentially indirectly discriminatory).[233] This was Advocate General Jacobs' concern about the use of such a proviso. He said that such a saving clause would have 'the result that the post will be offered to the male candidate on the basis of criteria which are accepted as discriminatory'.[234]

The Commission summarized the *Kalanke* and *Marschall* line of case law in the following terms:[235]

- the possibility to adopt positive action measures is to be regarded as an exception to the principle of equal treatment;

- the exception is specifically and exclusively designed to allow for measures which, although discriminatory in appearance, are in fact intended to eliminate or reduce actual instances of inequality which may exist in the reality of social life;

- automatic priority to women, as regards access to employment or promotion, in sectors where they are under-represented cannot be justified;

- conversely, such a priority is justified if it is not automatic and if the national measure in question guarantees equally qualified male candidates that their situation will be the subject of an objective assessment which takes into account all criteria specific to the candidates, whatever their gender.

(c) The effect of Article 157(4) TFEU

Marschall is a delicate balance by the Court, echoing a compromise adopted by the US Supreme Court in *Johnson* v. *Santa Clara*[236] 10 years earlier. In *Johnson* the US Supreme Court upheld an affirmative plan under Title VII of the Civil Rights Act 1964 which 'sought to take a moderate, gradual approach to eliminating the imbalance in its workforce, one which establishes realistic guidance for employment decisions, and which visits minimal intrusion on the legitimate expectations of other employees'. The Court of Justice also shows an understanding of the real situation of women—that the private sphere cannot be divorced from the public—and that concepts such as equality of opportunity and equality of results are not mutually exclusive. There is much to suggest that the Court was adopting a more substantive approach to equality in *Marschall*[237] and the introduction of what is now Article 157(4) TFEU, by the Amsterdam Treaty, may have offered some guidance. Article 157(4) TFEU provides:

> With a view to ensuring *full equality in practice between men and women* in working life, the principle of equal treatment shall not prevent any Member State from maintaining or adopting measures providing for specific advantage, in order to make it easier for the

---

[233] On the question of seniority, see Ch. 7. For an analysis of the proviso, see L. Charpentier, 'The European Court of Justice and the Rhetoric of Affirmative Action' (1998) 4 *ELJ* 167.

[234] C. Barnard and T. Hervey, 'Softening the Approach to Quotas: Positive Action after *Marschall*' (1998) 20 *JSWL*. 333.

[235] COM(2000) 334, para. 29.   [236] 107 S.Ct 1442, 480 US 616 (1987).

[237] P. Cabral, 'A Step Closer to Substantive Equality' (1998) 23 *ELRev*. 481, 486. See additionally Case C–407/98 *Abrahamsson* v. *Fogelqvist* [2000] ECR I–5539, para. 48.

underrepresented sex to pursue a vocational activity or to prevent or compensate for disadvantages in their professional careers.[238]

This appears to go further than Article 2(4) of Directive 76/207 by permitting a wider range of measures—possibly even positively discriminatory measures.[239] The Article 157(4) TFEU approach has now replaced Article 2(4) in the revised Equal Treatment Directive. Article 3 of the Sex Equality Directive 2006/54 provides:

> Member States may maintain or adopt measures within the meaning of Article [157(4)] of the Treaty with a view to ensuring full equality in practice between men and women.

This provision 'makes obsolete' the Commission's former proposal to amend Directive 76/207 in the light of *Kalanke*.[240] The question remains whether Article 157(4) TFEU and Article 3 of the Sex Equality Directive 2006/54 continue to be viewed as 'exceptions' to the principle of equality (as the Commission seems to think—see later), in which case the usual rules apply (exceptions are narrowly construed, are subject to the principle of proportionality and need to be reviewed over time), or whether these provisions are free standing and form an integral step to achieving equality of opportunity (as the prominent position of Article 3 in the Equality Directive indicates) in which case the usual rules do not apply. Certainly, the Norwegian government, in its submissions in the *EFTA* case,[241] favoured the broad approach, advocating an interpretation of the original Article 2(4) (Article 157(4) TFEU does not form part of EFTA law) that views affirmative action measures aimed at gender equality in practice, 'not as constituting discrimination but rather as an intrinsic dimension of the very prohibition thereof'. The EFTA Court, apparently rather reluctantly, referred to the 'homogeneity objective underlying the EEA Agreement' which meant that it could not 'accept the invitation to redefine the concept of discrimination on grounds of gender in the way the defendant has suggested'.[242]

The Court of Justice's case law does not provide a clear answer as to whether Article 157(4) TFEU goes further than and thus differs from Article 2(4) of Directive 76/207. In *Griesmar*[243] the Court merely noted that national measures covered by Article 157(4) TFEU (in its original form as Article 6(3) of the SPA) had to 'contribute to helping women conduct their professional life on an equal footing with men'. On the facts the Court suggested that the measure at issue—a service credit provided to female (but not male) civil servants in respect of each of their children for the purposes of calculating a pension—did not offset the disadvantages to which the careers of female civil servants were exposed by helping those women in their professional life.[244] It continued that the measure was limited to granting female civil servants who were mothers a service credit at the date of their retirement, without providing a remedy for the problems which they might encounter in the course of their professional career.[245]

[238] Emphasis added.   [239] See Ellis, previously, at n. 107, 259.   [240] COM(2000) 334, para. 12.
[241] Case E–1/02 *EFTA Surveillance Authority* v. *Kingdom of Norway* [2003] IRLR 318.
[242] Para. 45. See C. Tobler (2004) 41 *CMLRev.* 245.
[243] Case C–366/99 *Griesmar* v. *Ministre de l'Économie, des Finances et de l'Industrie* [2001] ECR I–9383, para. 46.
[244] Para. 64.   [245] Para. 65.

In *Briheche*[246] the Court considered the arguments under Article 2(4) of Directive 76/207 and Article 157(4) TFEU separately. It first examined whether a national rule—which applied to widows who had not remarried, but not to widowers—could be saved by Article 2(4). This rule removed the maximum age at which individuals could take public exams if they wanted to work in the public sector. Because the rule gave automatic and unconditional priority to women, the Court found that it 'could not be allowed under Article 2(4)'.[247] However, the Court then went on to consider whether the national provision was 'nevertheless allowed under Article [157(4)]'.[248] On the facts, it found the national rule to be unjustified because it was disproportionate.[249] However, the interesting point in this case is that the Court's approach suggested that the two Articles are not co-extensive.[250]

(d) Beyond Kalanke *and* Marschall

In other cases the Court does not engage directly with the detail of Article 157(4) TFEU but does refer to it to support its findings. In reality, the case law seems to ebb and flow, depending on the circumstances.[251] The broader approach to positive action can be seen in the multi-faceted case of *Badeck*.[252] The Court ruled that Articles 2(1) and 2(4) of Directive 76/207/EEC did not preclude:

- national rules which allocated at least half of all training places in the public service to women, where women were under-represented, unless despite appropriate measures for drawing the attention of women to the training places available, there were not enough applications from women;

- national rules where male and female candidates have equal qualifications, but guarantees that qualified women who satisfy all the conditions required or laid down were called to interview, in sectors in which they were underrepresented;

- national rules relating to the composition of employees' representative bodies and administrative and supervisory bodies, that recommended that the legislative provisions adopted for their implementation take into account the objective that at least half the members of those bodies had to be women.

These aspects of the ruling are unsurprising. Two important issues did, however, arise in the case.

---

[246] Case C–319/03 *Briheche v. Ministre de l'Interieur, Ministre de l'Education nationale and Ministre de la Justice* [2004] ECR I–8807.
[247] Para. 28.
[248] See additionally Case C–407/98 *Abrahamsson v. Folgequist* [2000] ECR I–5539, para. 54.
[249] Para. 31.
[250] Ibid. See additionally Case C–407/98 *Abrahamsson* [2000] ECR I–5539, para. 40.
[251] C. Tobler (2004) 41 *CMLRev*. 245, 255 citing para. 41 of Case E–1/02 *EFTA Surveillance Authority v. Kingdom of Norway* [2003] IRLR 318.
[252] Case C–158/97 *Badeck v. Hessicher Ministerpräsident und Landesanwalt beim Staatsgerichtshof des Landes Hessen* [2000] ECR I–1875.

The first concerned the legality of the so-called 'flexible result quota' ('*flexible Ergebnisquote*'). According to this rule, in sectors of the public service where women are under-represented, priority is given to female candidates, where male and female candidates for selection have equal qualifications, where this proves necessary for complying with the binding targets in the women's advancement plan, if no reasons of 'greater legal weight' are put forward.[253] The Court said that this priority rule was not 'absolute and unconditional' in the *Kalanke* sense and so was compatible with Directive 76/207. Following *Marschall* this outcome is not surprising.

Of more interest is the Court's (cursory) discussion of the criteria by which the initial selection of candidates occurred, before the flexible quota was applied.[254] For example, capabilities and experience acquired by carrying out work in the home were to be taken into account in so far as they were of importance for the suitability, performance, and capability of candidates. By contrast seniority, age, and the date of last promotion were to be taken into account only in so far as they were of importance to the job. The family status or income of the partner was immaterial. Further, part-time work, leave, and delays in completing training as a result of looking after children or other dependants could not have a negative effect on the selection process. As the Court simply noted:

> Such criteria, although formulated in terms which are neutral as regards sex and thus capable of benefiting men too, in general favour women. They are manifestly intended to lead to an equality which is substantive rather than formal, by reducing the inequalities which may occur in practice in social life. Their legitimacy is not challenged in the main proceedings.

Thus, the Court seems to allow some (indirect) discrimination against men in the application of the selection criteria. Only if a female candidate and a male candidate could not be distinguished on the basis of their qualifications could the woman be chosen according to the flexible quota. However, as the Court emphasized in *Abrahamsson*,[255] the application of such criteria had to be transparent and amenable to review in order to 'obviate any arbitrary assessment of the qualifications of the candidates'.

The second interesting aspect of *Badeck* concerned the rule which prescribed binding targets for women for *temporary* posts in the academic service and for academic assistants where women were equally qualified to the men. These targets required that the minimum percentage of women be at least equal to the percentage of women among graduates, holders of higher degrees, and students in each discipline. The *Land* Attorney noted that this minimum quota system came very close to equality as to results which had been rejected in *Kalanke*. Nevertheless, the Court said that this rule was compatible with Union law. It pointed out that this system did not fix an absolute ceiling

---

[253] These reasons of 'greater legal weight' concern five rules of law, described as 'social aspects' which make no reference to sex, whereby preferential treatment is given, first, to former employees in the public service who have left the service because of family commitments; secondly, to individuals who worked on a part-time basis for family reasons and now wish to resume full-time employment; thirdly, to former temporary soldiers; fourthly, to seriously disabled people; and fifthly, to the long-term unemployed.

[254] Paras. 31–2.

[255] Case C–407/98 *Abrahamsson* [2000] ECR I–5539, para. 49.

but only a ceiling by reference to the number of persons who had received appropriate training. It said that this amounted to using an actual fact as a quantitative criterion for giving preference to women.

This aspect of *Badeck* can be contrasted with *Abrahamsson* which concerned a Swedish rule which applied in the public sector, allowing the appointment of women in preference to men where they were under-represented, provided that the difference between the respective merits of the two candidates was not so great as to give rise to a breach of the requirement of objectivity in making public appointments. Folgequist, a woman, was appointed to a chair in hydrospheric sciences even though Abrahamsson, a man, was superior 'from the scientific point of view'. As the Court noted, unlike the rules at issue in *Kalanke*, *Marschall*, and *Badeck*, the Swedish measure allowed preference to be given to those who were 'sufficiently qualified' but not equally qualified.[256] For this reason, it said that the Swedish measure giving automatic preference to a person of the under-represented sex with merely sufficient qualifications failed to satisfy the requirements of Article 2(4) of Directive 76/207 and Article 157(4) TFEU.

Concern that posts would be awarded to female applicants with inadequate qualifications if there was an insufficient number of qualified women candidates also underpinned the *EFTA* case.[257] Norwegian law allowed for academic posts to be advertised as being open only to members of the under-represented sex. Based on this law, 10 post-doctoral posts and 12 permanent posts were earmarked for women only by the University of Oslo. This decision was challenged by the EFTA Surveillance Authority (the equivalent to the Commission). The Norwegian government argued that its legislation fell under Article 2(4) of the Equal Treatment Directive 76/207. However, the EFTA Court considered that the Norwegian legislation went further than the Swedish rule in *Abrahamsson* (where a selection procedure, involving an assessment of all candidates was foreseen, at least in principle). Since the CJEU found that the Swedish rule breached the equal treatment principle, *a fortiori* the Norwegian rule also fell foul of that principle:[258] the national rule, as applied by the University of Oslo, gave absolute and unconditional priority to women. There was no provision for flexibility and the outcome was determined automatically in favour of a female candidate.

Abrahamsson and the *EFTA* case can, in turn, be contrasted with *Lommers*[259] which adopted a more generous approach to positive action in a similar vein to *Marschall*. A male employee challenged the policy of the Dutch Ministry of Agriculture to provide subsidized nursery places 'only to female employees... save in the case of an emergency'. The Court of Justice ruled that this was compatible with Union law. Because women were significantly under-represented in the Ministry of Agriculture, both in

---

[256] Para. 45.
[257] Case E–1/02 *EFTA Surveillance Authority v. Kingdom of Norway* [2003] IRLR 318, para. 45.
[258] Para. 51.
[259] Case C–476/99 *Lommers* [2002] ECR I–2891. For a full discussion of this and other cases, see C. Costello and G. Davies, 'The Case Law of the Court of Justice in the Field of Sex Equality Since 2000' (2006) 43 *CMLRev.* 1567, esp. at 1595–1602.

terms of their number and their occupation of higher grades, the Court said that a measure which formed part of:[260]

> ...the restricted concept of equality of opportunity in so far as it is not places of employment which are reserved for women but enjoyment of certain working conditions designed to facilitate their pursuit of, and progression in, their career, falls in principle into the category of measures designed to eliminate the causes of women's reduced opportunities for access to employment and careers and are intended to improve their ability to compete on the labour market and to pursue a career on an equal footing with men.

Having recognized that Article 2(4) was potentially satisfied, the Court then considered the question of proportionality.[261] It recognized that the number of nursery places was limited, that not all women got the places they wanted and that places were open to single fathers who had responsibility for children.[262] The Court therefore concluded that the Dutch measure was proportionate.[263]

The striking feature about *Lommers* is the shift in emphasis away from viewing Article 2(4) of Directive 76/207 as a derogation to the principle of equal treatment which must be narrowly construed, to subjecting measures taken under Article 2(4) to a (relatively relaxed) proportionality analysis. This was also emphasized by the Court in the *EFTA* case[264] and, given the redrafting, is likely to apply with more justification to Article 3 of the Sex Equality Directive 2006/54.

2. THE ARTICLE 19 DIRECTIVES

The Article 19 Directives contain an equivalent positive action provision to Article 3 of the Sex Equality Directive 2006/54, albeit that the reference to the workplace has been dropped. For example, Article 5 of the Race Directive provides:

> With a view to ensuring full equality in practice, the principle of equal treatment shall not prevent any Member State from maintaining or adopting specific measures to prevent or compensate for disadvantages linked to racial or ethnic origin.

In its explanatory memorandum, the Commission notes that the need for positive action has already been addressed by the Court of Justice in *Kalanke* and *Marschall*. It then says that the wording is based on Article 157(4) TFEU and that as positive action measures are a derogation from the principle of equality 'they should be interpreted strictly, in the light of the current case law on sex discrimination'.

However, in respect of two strands, age and disability, positive action raises particular issues. First, in respect of age, since direct age discrimination can be objectively justified, the need for a specific provision concerning positive action is significantly reduced. Second, in respect of disability, since the prohibition of discrimination is

---

[260] Para. 38. Similar sentiments underpinned AG Alber's reasoning in Case C–218/98 *Abdoulaye v. Régre Nationale des Usines Renault SA* [1999] ECR I–5723, paras. 57–8.

[261] Paras. 42–3.   [262] Para. 46.   [263] Para. 48.

[264] Case E–1/02 *EFTA Surveillance Authority v. Kingdom of Norway* [2003] IRLR 318, para. 43.

asymmetrical, positively discriminatory measures could be taken in favour of the disabled and the able-bodied would not have legal grounds for complaint. Furthermore, Article 7(2) contains the following provision:

> With regard to disabled persons, the principle of equal treatment shall be without prejudice to the right of Member States to maintain or adopt provisions on the protection of health and safety at work or to measures aimed at creating or maintaining provisions or facilities for safeguarding or promoting their integration into the working environment.

The first part of Article 7(2) suggests the opposite of positive action: apparently allowing Member States to restrict opportunities for disabled people on the grounds of health and safety. On the other hand, the second limb of Article 7(2) is seemingly broader than the general positive action provision in that it does not require the measures taken to 'compensate for previous disadvantages'.

H. POSITIVE DUTY TO PROMOTE EQUALITY

The standard non-discrimination model contained in the various Directives plays a valuable role in sending out a signal about conduct which is considered unacceptable and in providing individuals with a means of redress. But, by its very nature, such an approach is dependent on individuals taking action which may lead to ad hoc, *ad personam* solutions rather than more general structural change. In this respect the Revised Equal Treatment Directive contained an important innovation: it imposed a duty on Member States 'actively [to] take into account the objective of equality between men and women when formulating and implementing laws, regulations, administrative provisions, policies and activities' (Article 29 of the Sex Equality Directive 2006/54). In addition, Member States must take the necessary measures to ensure that they abolish any laws, regulations, or administrative provisions contrary to the principle of equal treatment and to ensure that any discriminatory provisions contained in collective agreements,[265] individual contracts of employment, staff handbooks, and other internal rules of undertakings, or in rules governing the independent occupations or professions and workers' and employers' organizations are or shall be declared null and void or are amended.[266]

Thus the Directive imposes positive duties on the state to be pro-active in the elimination of discrimination and promoting equality. As Fredman points out, such duties go beyond compensating identified victims and aim at restructuring institutions. The duty bearer is not the person at fault for creating the problem but is, nevertheless,

---

[265] The Directive covers all collective agreements, irrespective of whether they have legal effects or not because they have important *de facto* consequences for employment relationships: see Case 165/82 *Commission v. UK* [1982] ECR 3431.

[266] Art. 23(a) and (b) of the Sex Equality Directive 2006/54.

responsible for identifying the problem and for participating in its eradication.[267] So far, the Union legislature has not introduced equivalent duties in respect of the other strands.

This 'mainstreaming' of equality is another important feature of Union policy which requires the institutions to be pro-active in their drive to achieve equality. As we saw in Chapter 6, the Union institutions have already applied it to their own policies in respect of sex,[268] as mandated by Article 8 TFEU, and now require Member States to consider gender equality in respect of their employment policies. Gender mainstreaming has been a key aspect of the Employment Guidelines since 2001.[269] For example, in the chapeau to the 2005 Guidelines, the Council says that 'Equal opportunities and combating discrimination are essential for progress. Gender mainstreaming and the promotion of gender equality should be ensured in all action taken'.[270] But by 2010 the language of gender mainstreaming has gone and, with it some of its influence, albeit the sentiment remains: 'Member States should promote active ageing, gender equality including equal pay, and the integration in the labour market of young people, people with disabilities, legal migrants and other vulnerable groups'.[271]

I. DIRECTIVE 2010/41 ON EQUAL TREATMENT OF THE SELF-EMPLOYED

We turn now to consider the position of the self-employed and the Cinderella Directive 86/613. Directive 86/613,[272] and now Directive 2010/41,[273] applies the principle of equal treatment to (1) self-employed workers who are defined as 'all persons pursuing a gainful activity for their own account, under the conditions laid down by national law',[274] and (2) to their spouses, or, when and in so far as recognized by national law, the

---

[267] 'The Age of Equality' in S. Fredman and S. Spencer (eds.), *Age as an Equality Issue. Legal and Policy Perspectives* (Hart Publishing, Oxford, 2003) 62. See additionally S. Fredman, 'Breaking the Mold: Equality as a Proactive Duty' (2012) 60 Am. J. Comp. L. 265.

[268] Commission, *Incorporating Equal Opportunities for Men and Women into all Community Policies and Activities*, COM(96) 67. This is considered further in Ch. 6.

[269] Co. Dec. 2001/63/EC (OJ [2001] L22/18, para. 16: 'Therefore, the Member States will adopt a gender-mainstreaming approach in implementing the Guidelines across all four pillars:

—developing and reinforcing consultative systems with gender equality bodies;
—applying procedures for gender impact assessment under each guideline;
—developing indicators to measure progress in gender equality in relation to each guideline.'

[270] Council Dec. 2005/600 (OJ [2005] L205/21).

[271] Council Dec. 2010/707/EU (OJ [2010] L308/46).

[272] Council Dir. 86/613/EEC, based on Arts. 115 and 352 TFEU on the application of the principle of equal treatment between men and women engaged in an activity, including agriculture, in a self-employed capacity, and on the protection of self-employed women during pregnancy and motherhood (OJ [1986] L359/56).

[273] Dir. 2010/41 on the application of the principle of equal treatment between men and women engaged in an activity in a self-employed capacity (OJ [2010] L180/1) was based on Art. 157(3) TFEU.

[274] Art. 2(a). The phrase 'including farmers and members of the liberal professions' has been dropped from the original version, showing that the orientation of the measure has broadened significantly beyond its initial narrow focus.

life partners of self-employed workers,[275] not being employees or partners, who habitually participate in the activities of the self-employed worker and perform the same
tasks or ancillary tasks.[276]

The 2010 Directive significantly overhauled the rather eclectic and weak provisions
of its 1986 predecessor; it now more resembles a standard equality Directive. So it
begins, in Article 4, with the non-discrimination principle as formulated in the original Directive 76/207, that 'there shall be no discrimination whatsoever on grounds of
sex in the public or private sectors, either directly or indirectly' (the definitions, set
out in Article 3(a) and (b), follow the standard pattern of the Sex Equality Directive
2006/54) 'for instance in relation to the establishment, equipment or extension of a
business or the launching or extension of any other form of self-employed activity'.[277]
It then deems harassment and sexual harassment, as defined in the Sex Equality
Directive 2006/54, to be discrimination,[278] as is an instruction to discriminate.[279] It
also permits positive action measures aimed at, for instance promoting entrepreneurship initiatives among women.[280] In this way the Directive responds directly to the
Equality Strategy 2010–15 which identifies promoting female entrepreneurship and
self-employment as a key action for the Commission.[281]

There then follows a more eclectic mix of provisions speaking to a range of issues.
First, the Directive deals with the establishment of a company. It requires that the conditions imposed on spouses, or between life partners, when forming a company be no
more restrictive than the conditions for the establishment of a company between other
persons.[282]

Second, the Directive addresses, in a rather light-touch way, the sensitive question of
social protection for the families of self-employed workers. Thus, Article 7 says that if
the Member State provides for social protection for the self-employed, a spouse or life
partner must be able to benefit in accordance with national law. However, it is up to the
Member States to decide whether the social protection is implemented on a mandatory
or voluntary basis. This provision closely reflects its predecessor, suggesting just how
little progress has been made in the intervening quarter century.

Thirdly, Article 8 concerns maternity benefits. Here, under pressure from the
European Parliament, the situation has improved somewhat. The Member States must
take the necessary measures to ensure that female self-employed workers and female
spouses and life partners 'may, in accordance with national law, be granted a sufficient
maternity allowance[283] enabling interruptions in their occupational activity owing to
pregnancy or motherhood for at least 14 weeks'. For good measure Article 8(2) adds:
'The Member States may decide whether the maternity allowance referred to in paragraph 1 is granted on a mandatory or voluntary basis'.

---

[275] This was added by the 2010 Directive.
[276] Art. 2(b).   [277] Art. 4(1).   [278] Art. 4(2).   [279] Art. 4(3).   [280] Art. 5.
[281] COM(2010) 491, 5.   [282] Art. 6.
[283] Art. 8(3) then gives guidance as to the adequacy of the allowance.

Finally, Article 9 obliges Member States to allow those who consider that they have been discriminated against to pursue their claims by judicial process; Article 10 that they should have an effective remedy; and Article 11 that the competence of the Equality Body designated in accordance with Article 20 of Directive 2006/54 should be extended to this Directive. We turn now to examine the remedies provision of all of the Equality Directives in more detail.

J. REMEDIES

1. INTRODUCTION

The remedies provision of the original Equal Treatment Directive 76/207 inspired much litigation, raising issues which not only profoundly affected national social policy but also raised points of fundamental constitutional importance. Some of the issues addressed by the Court's case law on sex equality have been incorporated into the Article 19 Directives and have now been included in the Sex Equality Directive 2006/54. In the section that follows we shall therefore focus on the Court's case law in the field of sex discrimination.

2. SEX

2.1. Direct effect and beyond

It is well established that provisions of a Directive which are unconditional and sufficiently precise and which have not been implemented correctly or at all, can have vertical direct effect.[284] This means that an individual may, after the expiry of the period prescribed for implementation, rely on such provisions directly against the Member State in default.[285] This prevents Member States from taking advantage of their own failure to comply with Union law to deny rights to individuals.[286] The same argument does not apply to private individuals, as the Court explained in *Marshall (No. 1)*.[287] Consequently, clear and unambiguous provisions of an unimplemented or incorrectly implemented Directive cannot have horizontal direct effect. On the facts of the case, Helen Marshall was able to rely on the principle of equal treatment laid down in Article 14(1) of the Sex Equality Directive 2006/54, as applied to conditions governing dismissal

---

[284] Case 152/84 *Marshall (No. 1)* [1986] ECR 723.
[285] Case 148/78 *Pubblico Ministero* v. *Ratti* [1979] ECR 1629 and Case 8/81 *Becker* v. *Finanzamt Munster-Innenstadt* [1982] ECR 53.
[286] Case 152/84 *Marshall (No. 1)* v. *Southampton Area Health Authority* [1986] ECR 723, para. 47. Cf. Case C-144/04 *Mangold* v. *Helm* [2005] ECR I-9981 considered in Ch. 6.
[287] Case 152/84 *Marshall (No. 1)* [1986] ECR 723, para. 48.

referred to in Article 14(1)(c), which were directly effective, to complain against her state employer of a discriminatory dismissal.

Early cases suggested that the terms of Article 17 of the Sex Equality Directive 2006/54 on remedies were not, however, sufficiently unconditional or precise to be directly effective.[288] There was merely an obligation to interpret national law in the light of the wording and purpose of the Directive.[289] In *Marshall (No. 2)*,[290] however, the Court said that Articles 14 and 17 conferred rights on a victim of a discriminatory dismissal which that person had to be able to rely upon before the national courts as against the state and authorities which were an emanation of the state.

The Court has taken three steps to address the hardship caused by the distinction between horizontal and vertical direct effect. First, it has given a broad definition to the term 'state'. In *Marshall (No. 1)*[291] the Court said a person can rely on a Directive against the state regardless of the capacity in which the state is acting, whether as an employer or as a public authority, such as Southampton and South West Hampshire Area Health Authority. Subsequently, in *Foster*[292] the Court defined 'state' as 'organisations or bodies which were subject to the authority and control of the state or had special powers beyond those which result from the normal rules applicable to relations between individuals'. Therefore, Mrs Foster could rely on Article 14 of the Sex Equality Directive 2006/54 against British Gas, at that time a nationalized company, to claim compensation for a discriminatory dismissal.[293] The directly effective provisions of the Sex Equality Directive have also been relied on against constitutionally independent authorities responsible for maintaining law and order,[294] public authorities providing public health services,[295] and a nationalized industry responsible for providing energy.[296] The case of *Dekker*,[297] however, concerned a private employer who was nevertheless held bound to comply with the provisions of the Directive which had not been fully implemented by the Dutch government.[298]

---

[288] Case 14/83 *Von Colson and Kamann v. Land Nordrhein Westfalen* [1984] ECR 1891, para. 27; Case 79/83 *Harz v. Deutsche Tradax* [1984] ECR 1921, para. 27.

[289] Case 14/83 *Von Colson* [1984] ECR 1891, para. 26.

[290] Case C–271/91 *Marshall v. Southampton and South West Hampshire Area Health Authority (Teaching) (No. 2)* [1993] ECR I–4367.

[291] Case 152/84 [1986] ECR 723, para. 49.

[292] Case C–188/89 *Foster v. British Gas* [1990] ECR I–3313, para. 18.

[293] *Foster v. British Gas* [1991] IRLR 268 (House of Lords).

[294] Case 222/84 *Johnston* [1986] ECR 1651.

[295] Case 152/84 *Marshall (No. 1)* [1986] ECR 723.

[296] Case C–188/89 *Foster* [1990] ECR I–3313.

[297] Case C–177/88 [1990] ECR I–3941.

[298] It has been argued that this case is in reality an application of the *Marleasing/Von Colson* 'interpretation' mechanism: K. Banks, 'Equal Pay and Equal Treatment for Men and Women in Community Law', *Social Europe* 3/91, Ch. 2. A similar point was raised in Case C–421/92 *Habermann-Beltermann* [1994] ECR I–1657. See additionally Case C–180/95 *Nils Draehmpaehl v. Urania Immobilienservice ohG* [1997] ECR I–2195, and A. Ward, 'New Frontiers in Private Enforcement of EC Directives' (1998) 23 *ELRev.* 65.

Secondly, in *Von Colson, Marleasing*,[299] and *Pfeiffer*[300] the Court imposed a broad obligation on all state institutions, especially the national courts, arising from both the Directive and Article 4(3) TEU, to interpret national law, as far as possible, in conformity with the requirements of Union law, subject to the general principles of law, especially the principles of legal certainty and non-retroactivity.[301] Therefore, in *Von Colson* the national court was obliged to interpret the national rules on compensation in the light of Directive 76/207. The *Von Colson* approach may well explain the Court's decision in *Dekker*.[302]

The third step taken by the Court was to introduce the principle of state liability in *Francovich*,[303] saying that Union law requires the Member States to make good damage caused to individuals through failure to transpose a Directive. Subsequently, in *Brasserie du Pêcheur and Factortame (No. 3)*[304] and *British Telecommunications*[305] (cases concerning breaches of Treaty provisions involving wide discretion and an incorrectly implemented Directive respectively) the Court made clear that the principle of state liability was inherent in the system of the Treaty. It did not merely apply in a situation where the provisions of Union law were directly effective: direct effect was only a 'minimum guarantee' and could not ensure in every case that individuals enjoyed their Union law rights. The Court then established a threefold test for liability: first, the rule of law infringed must be intended to confer rights on individuals; secondly, the breach must be sufficiently serious; and, thirdly, there must be a direct causal link between the breach of the obligation resting on the state and the damage suffered by the injured parties. If the state totally failed to transpose a Directive the Court ruled in *Dillenkofer*[306] that the breach was *per se* sufficiently serious.

Following *Mangold*[307] and *Kücükdeveci*,[308] a fourth route might be emerging: that if the unimplemented or incorrectly implemented Directive encapsulates a general principle of law that general principle can be used to disapply conflicting national rules, even in a horizontal situation.[309] So far the case law has, however, been confined to breach of the general principle of non-discrimination on the grounds of age.

[299] The is also known as the doctrine of indirect effects: see Cases 14/83 *Von Colson and Kamann* [1984] ECR 1891 and C–106/89 *Marleasing SA* v. *La Comercial Internacional de Alimentacion* [1990] ECR I–4135; and confirmed in Case C–185/97 *Coote* v. *Granada Hospitality Ltd* [1998] ECR I–5199. In Case C–54/96 *Dorsch Consult* [1997] ECR I–4961 the Court said that this minimum guarantee could not justify a Member State absolving itself from taking, in due time, implementing measures sufficient to meet the purpose of each Directive.
[300] Joined Cases C–397/01 to C–403/01 *Pfeiffer* v. *Deutsches Rotes Kreuz, Kreisverband Waldshut eV* [2004] ECR I–8835 considered in detail in Ch. 12.
[301] Case 14/86 *Pretore di Salò* v. *X* [1987] ECR 2545; Case C–168/95 *Criminal Proceedings against Arcaro* [1996] ECR I–4705.
[302] Case C–177/88 [1990] ECR I–3941, considered previously, at n. 298.
[303] Joined Cases C–6 and C–9/90 *Francovich and Bonifaci* v. *Italian State* [1991] ECR I–5357.
[304] Joined Cases C–46/93 *Brasserie du Pêcheur* v. *Bundesrepublik Deutschland* and C–48/95 *R* v. *Secretary of State for Transport, ex parte Factortame (No. 3)* [1996] ECR I–1029.
[305] Case C–392/93 *R* v. *HM Treasury, ex part British Telecommunications* [1996] ECR I–1631.
[306] Joined Cases C–178, C–179, C–188, C–189 and C–190/94 *Dillenkofer and Others* v. *Bundesrepublik Deutschland* [1996] ECR I–4845.
[307] Case C–144/04 *Mangold* v. *Helm* [2005] ECR I–9981.
[308] Case C–555/07 *Kücükdeveci* v. *Swedex* [2010] ECR I–365.
[309] See further Ch. 6. See additionally AG Trstenjak's Opinion in Case C–282/10 *Dominguez* [2012] ECR I–000.

2.2. Effectiveness of the remedy

It is a long established principle of Union law that under the duty of co-operation laid down in Article 4(3) TEU the Member States must ensure the legal protection which individuals derive from the direct effect of Union law. In the absence of Union rules governing a matter, it is for the domestic legal system of each Member State to designate the courts having jurisdiction and to lay down detailed procedural rules governing actions for safeguarding rights for individuals (the principle of procedural autonomy).[310] However, such rules must not be less favourable than those governing similar domestic actions (the principle of non-discrimination or equivalence) or render virtually impossible or excessively difficult the exercise of rights conferred by Union law (the principle of effective judicial protection or 'effectiveness').[311]

The question of the adequacy of national remedies has been of central importance to the procedural protection conferred by the Equality Directives. Article 17(1) of the Sex Equality Directive 2006/54 provides that Member States must ensure that 'after possible recourse to other competent authorities including, where they deem it appropriate, conciliation procedures, judicial procedures for the enforcement of obligations under this Directive are available to all persons who consider themselves wronged by failure to apply the principle of equal treatment to them'.[312]

The Court has, however, circumscribed the Member States' discretion as to the remedies available for sex discrimination. First, as the Court ruled in *Johnston*,[313] Member States cannot exclude judicial control altogether. In *Johnston* the Secretary of State issued a certificate declaring that the decisions taken by the Chief Constable of the Royal Ulster Constabulary were made for the purpose of safeguarding national security and protecting public safety and public order. Under the national law at the time, such a declaration constituted conclusive evidence that the conditions for derogating from the principle of equal treatment had been fulfilled and therefore excluded the exercise of any power of review by the courts. The Court held that such a provision deprived an individual of the possibility of asserting the rights conferred by the Sex Equality Directive by judicial process and so was contrary to the Directive. The Court added that Article 17 'reflects a general principle of law which underlies the constitutional traditions common to the Member States, including Articles 6 and 13 of the European Convention on Human Rights'.[314]

---

[310] See Case C–246/09 *Bulicke* v. *Deutsche Büro Service GmbH* [2010] ECR I–000.

[311] See e.g. Case 33/76 *Rewe-Zentralfinanz eG* v. *Landwirtschaftskammer für das Saarland* [1976] ECR 1989, para. 5. For a more recent restatement in the equal treatment context, see Case C–63/08 *Pontin* v. *T-Comalux SA* [2009] ECR I–10467.

[312] For an example of a system which 'undeniably satisfies the requirement of adequate and effective judicial protection' see the Austrian law at issue in Case C–380/01 *Schneider* v. *Bundesminister für Justiz* [2004] ECR I–1389, paras. 27–8.

[313] Case 222/84 [1986] ECR 1651.

[314] See additionally Case C–185/97 *Coote* [1998] ECR I–5199 where the Court said the requirement laid down by Art. 17 that recourse be available to the courts reflects a general principle of law which underlies the constitutional traditions common to the Member States and which is also enshrined in Art. 6 of the European Convention for the Protection of Human Rights and Fundamental Freedoms of 4 November 1950. It added that by virtue of Art. 17 of the Directive, interpreted in the light of the general principle, all persons have the right to obtain an effective remedy in a competent court against measures which they consider to interfere with the equal treatment for men and women laid down in the Directive.

The second area in which the Court has limited Member States' discretion concerns the actual remedy itself. The Court has insisted that any sanction provided for by the national system must be such as to 'guarantee real and effective judicial protection... it must also have a real deterrent effect on the employer.'[315] This case law has now been incorporated into Article 18 of the Sex Equality Directive 2006/54. Therefore, if the Member State chooses to penalize the discrimination by the award of compensation that compensation must be adequate in relation to the damage sustained.[316] In both *Von Colson* and *Harz*[317] the compensation was limited to a purely nominal amount: the reimbursement of the travelling expenses incurred. The Court considered that this would not satisfy the requirements of Article 18.[318] Similarly, the Court held in *Marshall (No. 2)*[319] that the imposition of an upper limit on the amount of compensation received and the exclusion of an award of interest did not constitute proper implementation of Article 18, a point now incorporated into Article 18 itself. The Court reasoned that such limits restricted the amount of compensation 'a priori to a level which is not necessarily consistent with the requirement of ensuring real equality of opportunity through adequate reparation for the loss and damage sustained as a result of discriminatory dismissal'. In addition, the Court said that excluding an award of interest to compensate for the loss sustained by the recipient of the compensation, as a result of the effluxion of time, until the capital sum awarded is actually paid, breached Article 18.

The Court adopted a similarly broad, purposive interpretation of Article 18 in *Draehmpaehl*,[320] a case concerning the measure of damages for an individual involved in a discriminatory recruitment process. Having noted that the Directive precluded provisions of domestic law making reparation of damage suffered as a result of discrimination on the grounds of sex subject to the requirement of fault,[321] the Court then considered the question of the adequacy of compensation. It drew a distinction between, on the one hand, less qualified applicants who would not have got the job, even if there had been no discrimination in the recruitment process, and on the other, those applicants who would have got the job but for the discrimination.

As far as the latter group was concerned, the Court, basing its ruling on the principle of non-discrimination, said that the Directive precluded provisions of domestic law which, unlike other provisions of domestic civil and labour law, prescribed an upper limit of three months' salary for the amount of compensation which could be claimed. As far as the former category was concerned, the Court said that although reparation

---

[315] Case 14/83 *Von Colson* [1984] ECR 1891, para. 23.

[316] Ibid., Case C–271/91 *Marshall (No. 2)* v. *Southampton and South West Hampshire Area Health Authority (Teaching) (No. 2)* [1993] ECR I–4367, para. 26; C. McCrudden, 'The Effectiveness of European Equality Law: National Mechanisms for Enforcing Gender Equality Law in the Light of European Requirements' (1993) 13 *OJLS* 320.

[317] Case 79/83 [1984] ECR 1921.

[318] See further D. Curtin, 'Effective Sanctions and the Equal Treatment Directive: the *Von Colson* and *Harz* Cases' (1985) 22 *CMLRev.* 505.

[319] Case C–271/91 [1993] ECR I–4367. See Art. 18, second sentence.

[320] Case C–180/95 [1997] ECR I–2195. Cf. the Court's robust approach to remedies with its attitude in Case C–66/95 *R* v. *Secretary of State for Social Security, ex parte Sutton* [1997] ECR I–2163, considered in Ch. 10.

[321] See additionally Case C–177/88 *Dekker* [1990] ECR I–3941, para. 22.

had to be adequate in relation to the damage sustained, the reparation could take into account the fact that even if there had been no discrimination in the process some applicants would not have obtained the position because the applicant appointed had superior qualifications. It said, therefore, that given that the only damage suffered by less qualified applicants was that resulting from the failure, because of the sex discrimination, to take their applications into consideration, it was not unreasonable for a Member State to lay down a statutory presumption that the damage suffered could not exceed a ceiling of three months' salary.[322] However, the burden of proof rested with the employer, who had all the applications submitted, to show that the applicant would not have obtained the vacant position even if there had been no discrimination.

2.3. Victimization

While most cases on effective remedies concern compensation, *Coote*[323] is authority for the fact that the obligation to provide an effective remedy includes protection against victimization. In that case the Court said that the principle of effective judicial control would be deprived of an essential part of its effectiveness if the protection which it provided did not cover measures which an employer might take as a reaction to legal proceedings brought by an employee to enforce compliance with the principle of equal treatment. Therefore, it ruled Member States had to introduce into their national legal systems measures necessary to ensure judicial protection for workers whose employer refused to provide them with a reference as a result of victimization. Article 24 of the Sex Equality Directive 2006/54 now provides:

> Member States shall introduce into their national legal systems such measures as are necessary to protect employees, including those who are employees' representatives provided for by national laws and/or practices, against dismissal or other adverse treatment by the employer as a reaction to a complaint within the undertaking or to any legal proceedings aimed at enforcing compliance with the principle of equal treatment.

3. BURDEN OF PROOF

Normally, the burden of proof rests on the complainant. However, in a number of equal pay cases discussed in Chapter 7 the Court indicated that the burden of proof should be reversed, and this led to the adoption of Directive 97/80 on the burden of proof[324] which did just that. The Directive laid down minimum standards[325] which applied to situations covered by Article 157 TEFU, the Directives on Equal Pay and Equal Treatment and, in so far as discrimination based on sex is concerned, the Directives on Pregnant Workers' and Parental Leave. It has now been incorporated into the Sex Equality Directive

---

[322] This is now confirmed in Article 18, second sentence of Dir. 2006/54.
[323] Case C–185/97 [1998] ECR I–5199. See M. Dougan, 'The Equal Treatment Directive: Retaliation, Remedies and Direct Effect' (1999) 24 *ELRev.* 664.
[324] OJ [1998] L14/16, amended by Council Directive 98/52 (OJ [1998] L205/66).
[325] Art. 4(2).

2006/54. Article 19 provides that Member States must take such measures as are necessary, in accordance with their national judicial systems, to ensure that:

> ...when persons who consider themselves wronged because the principle of equal treatment has not been applied to them establish, before a court or other competent authority, facts from which it may be presumed that there has been direct or indirect discrimination, it shall be for the respondent to prove that there has been no breach of the principle of equal treatment.

While this is a significant provision intended to help individual applicants, its effectiveness in practice has been doubted. There is considerable uncertainty in the minds of claimants and the courts as to just how much evidence needs to be adduced before the burden of proof is reversed. Some of these difficulties were aired in *Kelly*.[326] An unsuccessful applicant for vocational training believed that his application was rejected because of an infringement of the principle of equal treatment. The Court said he was not entitled to information held by the course provider on the qualifications of the other applicants for the course in order that he may establish 'facts from which it may be presumed that there has been direct or indirect discrimination' in accordance with the provision on burden of proof. However, the Court added that it cannot be ruled out that a refusal of disclosure by the defendant, in the context of establishing such facts, could risk compromising the achievement of the objective pursued by that Directive and thus depriving, in particular, the provision on the burden of proof of its effectiveness. Rather weakly, the Court said that it was for the national court to ascertain whether that was the case in the main proceedings.

4. REPRESENTATIVE ORGANIZATIONS

Some of the Court's most important decisions on equality have arisen in the context of cases referred by the British courts. In the early days, a disproportionate number of cases testing the limits of Article 157 TFEU on equal pay and the other equality Directives came from the United Kingdom. This was largely due to the fact that the British legislation gave powers to the (then) Equal Opportunities Commission (EOC) to fund individual cases which included support for Article 267 TFEU (ex 234 EC) references to the Court of Justice. Strategically selecting cases to fund to the Court of Justice eventually became part of the EOC's litigation strategy.[327]

Inspired by this model, and tempering somewhat the problems faced by individual litigants bringing claims, Article 17(2) of the Sex Equality Directive 2006/54 requires other Member States to make similar provision:

> Member States shall ensure that associations, organisations or other legal entities which have, in accordance with the criteria laid down by their national law, a legitimate interest in ensuring that the provisions of this Directive are complied with, may engage, either on

---

[326] Case C-104/10 *Kelly* v. *National University of Ireland (UCD)* [2011] ECR I-000. See further Case C-415/10 *Moister* [2012] ECR I-000 where the unsuccessful candidate was not entitled to have access to information as to whether the employer engaged another applicant.

[327] C. Barnard, 'A European Litigation Strategy: the Case of the Equal Opportunities Commission', in J. Shaw and G. More (eds.), *Dynamics of European Integration* (Clarendon, Oxford, 1996).

behalf or in support of the complainant, with his/her approval, in any judicial and/or administrative procedure provided for the enforcement of obligations under this Directive.

In addition, Article 20 of the Sex Equality Directive 2006/54 requires Member States to designate a body or bodies for the promotion, analysis, monitoring and support of equal treatment of all persons without discrimination on the grounds of sex. These bodies may form part of any agency with responsibility at national level for the protection of human rights or the safeguard of individuals' rights. These bodies should be able to:

- provide independent assistance to victims of discrimination in pursuing their complaints about discrimination (without prejudice to the bodies laid down in Article 17(2), namely organizations with a legitimate interest in ensuring that the provisions of the Directive are complied with);
- conduct independent surveys concerning discrimination;
- publish independent reports and make recommendations on any issue relating to such discrimination;
- exchange information with corresponding European bodies including the European Institute for Gender Equality.

Furthermore, Article 22 requires Member States to encourage dialogue with appropriate non-governmental organizations with a legitimate interest in contributing to the fight against discrimination on grounds of sex.

In addition, the Directive envisages a significant role for the Social Partners. Article Article 21(1) provides that Member States must take adequate measures to promote social dialogue between the Social Partners with a view to fostering equal treatment, including through the monitoring of workplace practices, collective agreements, codes of conduct, research, or exchange of experiences and good practices. Article 21(2) provides that Member States should also encourage the Social Partners, without prejudice to their autonomy, to promote equality between women and men and, according to the Equality Directive, flexible working arrangements, and to conclude, at the appropriate level, agreements laying down anti-discrimination rules in the fields coming within the material scope of the Directive which fall within the scope of collective bargaining.

Individual employers also have a role: Article 21(3) says that Member States must encourage employers to promote equal treatment for men and women in the workplace in a 'planned and systematic' way in access to employment, training, and promotion. Employers must also be encouraged, according to Article 21(4), to provide employees and/or their representatives with appropriate information on equal treatment for men and women in the undertaking at appropriate regular intervals. Such information may include:

- statistics on proportions of men and women at different levels of the organization;
- their pay and pay differentials; and

- possible measures to improve the situation in co-operation with employees'
  representatives.

These provisions, introduced by the Equal Treatment Directive 2002/73, are intended
to introduce a 'new governance' approach into what is broadly an 'old governance'
measure. Thus, it encourages a wider range of actors to become involved in the process
of securing equality, largely through mainstreaming and 'gender proofing' workplace
practices and collective agreements.

5. RACE DIRECTIVE 2000/43

The remedies provisions in the Sex Equality Directive 2006/54 drew extensively on the
remedies provisions found in the Race Directive 2000/43. The Race Directive envisages
two rights: the right of victims to a personal remedy against the discriminator (Article 7),
as well as the duty on each Member State to lay down rules on penalties for breach of the
Directive (Article 15). As far as the first right is concerned, Member States must ensure
that 'judicial and/or administrative procedures, including where they deem it appropriate conciliation procedures, for the enforcement of obligations under this Directive are
available to all persons who consider themselves wronged by failure to apply the principle of equal treatment to them, even after the relationship in which the discrimination
is alleged to have occurred has ended' (Article 7(1)). As with Article 17(2) of the Sex
Equality Directive 2006/54, Member States must ensure that relevant interest groups
can bring a claim on the individual's behalf or support the individual in his or her
claim.[328] National time limits will apply (Article 7(3)). Protection against victimization
is found in Article 9; the burden of proof is reversed in Article 8.

As far as Article 15 is concerned, the sanctions must be 'effective, proportionate and
dissuasive' but leaves Member States free to choose between the different solutions suitable for achieving its objective.[329] This was at issue in *Firma Feryn*. In a case such as this
where there is no direct victim of discrimination but a body empowered to do so by law
seeks a finding of discrimination and the imposition of a penalty, the Court of Justice
said that the sanctions could, where necessary, include a finding of discrimination by
the court or the competent administrative authority in conjunction with an adequate
level of publicity, the cost of which was to be borne by the defendant. They could also
take the form of a prohibitory injunction, in accordance with the rules of national law,
ordering the employer to cease the discriminatory practice, and, where appropriate, a
fine. They could, moreover, take the form of the award of damages to the body bringing
the proceedings.[330]

Member States are under an obligation to ensure the elimination of discrimination
from any legal or administrative provisions, as well as from collective agreements or
individual contracts of employment, rules of profit making and non-profit making

---

[328] Provision is also made for Member States to encourage dialogue with appropriate NGOs (Art. 12).
[329] Case C–54/07 *Firma-Feryn* [2008] ECR I–5187, para. 37.
[330] Paras. 38–9.

associations, and workers' and employers' associations (Article 14). States must also disseminate information about the content of the Directive (Article 10). They must also take 'adequate measures to promote the social dialogue between the two sides of industry with a view to fostering equal treatment, including through the monitoring of workplace practices, collective agreements, codes of conduct, research or exchange of experiences and good practices' (Article 11). The European Social Partners have already concluded a Joint Declaration on Racism and Xenophobia in the Workplace adopted in Florence in 1995 and, at national level in certain states, have adopted framework agreements and codes of conduct on combating racial and ethnic discrimination in companies. States must also promote dialogue with NGOs (Article 12).

Perhaps the most striking feature of the Race Directive (not found in the Framework Directive) is the obligation for Member States to 'designate a body or bodies for the promotion of equal treatment of all persons without discrimination on the grounds of racial or ethnic origin' (Article 13). These bodies may form part of agencies charged at national level with the defence of human rights or the safeguard of individuals' rights. Not only must an agency be set up but, following the model of the original UK Commission for Racial Equality (now the Equality and Human Rights Commission (EHRC)), these bodies must have the following among their functions: providing independent assistance to victims of discrimination in pursuing complaints about discrimination on grounds of racial or ethnic origin; conducting independent surveys concerning discrimination based on racial or ethnic origin; and publishing independent reports and making recommendations on issues relating to discrimination based on racial or ethnic origin.

6. FRAMEWORK DIRECTIVE 2000/78

The remedies provisions in the Framework Directive mirror those in the Race Directive: individuals or associations acting for them should have access to the judicial process (Article 9); the burden of proof is reversed (Article 10); there is protection against victimization (Article 11); states are under an obligation to disseminate information (Article 12); and states are to encourage social dialogue to foster equal treatment (Article 13) and dialogue with NGOs. States are, however, under no obligation to set up an independent agency to promote and enforce these rights.

K. CONCLUSIONS

Equality is a multi-layered, multi-faceted concept, and nowhere is this more clearly identified than in the field of equal treatment. The law in this area, through a combination of legislative and judicial intervention, has produced a sophisticated framework of rights for individuals which they can enforce in their national courts. The dialogue between the courts and the legislature has been productive, and the learning that has been gained in the field of sex equality has been extended to the other strands; and developments in respect of the other strands have spilled back into the field of sex discrimination. To date, the intervention has, however, been broadly confined to achieving the negative objective of prohibiting discrimination, and not the more positive approach of realizing equality. Some of the means of achieving equality, particularly in the field of gender, require policy intervention rather than just legal rights. Such intervention may take the form of encouraging the provision of childcare and care for elderly relatives. This is one strand of what are now referred to as 'family friendly' policies, which form the subject of the next chapter.

9

FAMILY FRIENDLY POLICIES

A. INTRODUCTION

With women historically taking primary responsibility for child and elder care in most western societies, their flexibility to participate fully in paid employment has often been limited. Since the first equality action programme, the Commission has recognized that full equality of opportunity can be achieved only by taking measures which will 'enable men and women to reconcile their occupational and family obligations'.[1] The Union's approach to what is now generally referred to as 'family friendly' policies or 'work-life balance' has three strands. The first relates to pregnancy, birth, and maternity. Directive 76/207 and now the Sex Equality Directive 2006/54, as expansively interpreted by the Court, together with Directive 92/85 on Pregnant Workers,[2] are the principal instruments. It is this aspect of the work-life balance which is emphasized in Article 33(2) of the EU Charter of Fundamental Rights:

> To reconcile family and professional life, everyone shall have the right to protection for dismissal for a reason connected with maternity and the right to paid maternity leave and to parental leave following the birth or adoption of a child.

The second strand of the EU's family friendly policies concerns attempts at reconciling work and family life: on the one hand, Directive 96/34 on Parental Leave,[3] repealed and replaced by Directive 2010/18/EU,[4] gives rights to working parents to take time off for domestic reasons while, on the other, Directive 97/81 on Part-time Work, Directive 99/70 on Fixed-term Work, and Directive 2008/104 on agency work,[5] together with the Social Partners' agreement on telework,[6] give some protection to atypical workers,

---

[1] Third para. of point 16 of the Social Charter of 1989. The 'family' in this context tends to be viewed as the 'traditional' family, cf. E. Caracciolo di Torella and E. Reid, 'The Changing Shape of the "European Family" and Fundamental Rights' (2002) 27 *ELRev.* 80.

[2] Council Dir. 92/85/EEC (OJ [1992] L348/1).

[3] OJ [1996] L145/4.

[4] OJ [2010] L68/13.

[5] OJ [1998] L14/9, as amended by Council Dir. 98/23/EC (OJ [1998] L131/10) (consolidated OJ [1998] L131/13), OJ [1999] L175/43 and OJ [2008] L327/9 respectively.

[6] <http://resourcecentre.etuc.org/Agreements-57.html> (last accessed 31 March 2012). See further the Social Partners' agreement on an inclusive labour market, 25 March 2010 (<http://resourcecentre.etuc.org/Agreements-57.html>), especially para. 4.5, where work-life balance issues are identified as an obstacle to an inclusive labour market, albeit that addressing this obstacle is not highlighted as one of the actions of the social partners.

the majority of whom are women seeking to balance work and caring commitments. To a limited extent, Directive 2003/88 on Working Time[7] should also be considered as part of this strategy in that part of its aim of limiting working hours is to enable workers to have sufficient time to spend with their families. However, since the Working Time Directive's principal aim is health and safety, it is considered in detail in Part IV of this book (health, safety, and working conditions).

The third, and least developed, strand of the EU's family friendly policy concerns provision for childcare and, to a limited extent, care for other dependants. The adoption of a Council Recommendation on childcare represents one step in this direction.[8] The European Pact for Gender Equality, launched by the Spring European Council in March 2006,[9] is also significant for it recognizes clearly that in order to promote a better 'work-life balance for all' not only must there be provision of childcare facilities but also the 'provision of care facilities for other dependants' has to be improved, a point reiterated in the 2011 European Pact for Gender Equality.[10]

The importance of these three policy strands was recognized in the original equal opportunities pillar of the Luxembourg Employment Guidelines.[11] Under the heading 'Reconciling work and family life', the Council agreed:

> Policies on career breaks, parental leave and part-time work, as well as flexible working arrangements which serve the interests of both employers and employees, are of particular importance to women and men. Implementation of the various Directives and social partner agreements in this area should be accelerated and monitored regularly. There must be an adequate provision of good quality care for children and other dependants in order to support women's and men's entry and continued participation in the labour market. An equal sharing of family responsibilities is crucial in this respect.

In order to strengthen equal opportunities the Member States and the Social Partners were to 'design, implement and promote family-friendly policies, including affordable, accessible and high quality care services for children and other dependants, as well as parental and other leave schemes'. By the 2010 Employment Guidelines, the Council was still saying that '[w]ork-life balance policies with the provision of affordable care and innovation in the manner in which work is organised should be geared to raising employment rates, particularly among young people, older workers and women'.[12]

We begin by examining the rights given to women in respect of pregnancy and maternity before moving on to look at the question of parental leave and childcare. We conclude with an examination of atypical work.

---

[7] This is considered further in Ch. 12.

[8] 92/241/EEC OJ [1992] L123/16.

[9] Presidency Conclusions, Brussels European Council, 23–24 March 2006, Annex II. See further Ch. 6.

[10] Council Conclusions on the European Pact for Gender Equality for the Period 2011–2020, 7 March 2011.

[11] Council Resolution of 15 December 1997 on the 1998 Employment Guidelines (OJ [1998] C30/1), as amended by Council Resolution of 22 February 1999 on the 1999 Employment Guidelines (OJ [1999] C69/2).

[12] Council Dec. 2010/707/EU (OJ [2010] L 308/46).

B. PREGNANCY, MATERNITY, AND BEYOND

1. INTRODUCTION

The original version of the Equal Treatment Directive 76/207 made no specific provision for rights for pregnant workers. It merely allowed employers, derogating from the principle of equal treatment, to take *special* provisions to protect pregnant workers and women on maternity leave, such as preventing them from working at night (Article 2(3) of Directive 76/207, now Article 28(1) of the Sex Equality Directive 2006/54). In *Johnston*[13] the Court made clear that this provision was intended 'to protect a woman's biological condition and the special relationship which exists between a woman and her child'.

Nevertheless, cases started coming before the Court where pregnant women argued that they wanted to be treated in the *same way* as their (non-pregnant) colleagues. It is in this context that the discrimination model shows its limitations: since pregnancy is unique to women, trying to find a similarly-situated male comparator 'suffering from an equivalent problem' for the purposes of arguing less favourable treatment has always been an artificial exercise.[14] In fact, the Court of Justice has shown some sense in addressing the issue, making pregnancy discrimination per se unlawful, thereby obviating the need to find a comparator.[15] Nevertheless, to shoehorn pregnancy and maternity into an anti-discrimination model has always proved difficult. The adoption of the Pregnant Workers Directive 92/85, with its specific provisions dealing with pregnant workers not dependent on the anti-discrimination model, was a positive step. Nevertheless, the Pregnant Workers Directive does not exhaustively regulate the whole area of the treatment of pregnant women and women on maternity leave. There is therefore still a role for the Equal Treatment Directive/Sex Equality Directive 2006/54. For this reason, we begin by considering the position under the Sex Equality Directive 2006/54, and Article 157 TFEU (ex 141 EC) on equal pay before considering the position under the Pregnant Workers Directive.

2. THE APPROACH UNDER THE SEX EQUALITY DIRECTIVE 2006/54

2.1. The (equal) treatment of pregnant women

(a) Appointment and dismissal

The leading judgment in which the Court first addressed the rights of pregnant workers is *Dekker*.[16] In that case, the employer decided not to appoint the applicant who was

---

[13] Case 222/84 [1986] ECR 1651.
[14] See e.g. the approach of the Court of Appeal in the English case of *Webb* v. *EMO Air Cargo* [1992] 1 CMLR 793. The Court in Case C–32/93 *Webb* [1994] ECR I–3567 said 'pregnancy is not in any way comparable with a pathological condition'.
[15] Cf. R. Wintemute, 'When is Pregnancy Discrimination Indirect Discrimination' (1998) 27 *ILJ* 23.
[16] Case C–177/88 [1990] ECR I–3941.

pregnant, even though she was considered the best person for the job, on the grounds
that the employer's insurers refused to cover the costs of her maternity leave. Despite
the fact that all the other candidates for the job were women, the Court ruled that since
employment could only be refused because of pregnancy to a woman, refusal to appoint
a woman on the grounds of her pregnancy constituted direct discrimination on the
grounds of sex, contrary to Article 14 of the Sex Equality Directive.[17] The Court also
dismissed concerns about the cost implications of its decision: it said that a refusal to
employ a woman on account of her pregnancy could not be justified on the grounds of
the financial loss which an employer who appointed a pregnant woman would suffer for
the duration of her maternity leave.[18]

The Court extended the same rationale to a woman undergoing IVF treatment in
Mayr:[19] because IVF treatment directly affects only women then unfavourable treatment because of it (*in casu* dismissal) constitutes direct discrimination on the grounds
of sex. *Mayr* was therefore a mix of the rationale of *Dekker* and the fact pattern of *Hertz*[20]
where the Court had ruled that the *dismissal* of a female worker on account of pregnancy constituted direct discrimination on the grounds of sex contrary to the Sex
Equality Directive 2006/54.[21]

The rationale underpinning these cases was tested in *Webb*.[22] Ms Webb was appointed
by EMO Air Cargo Ltd, initially to replace another employee, Ms Stewart, who was
about to go on maternity leave, but then to continue working on Ms Stewart's return.
Shortly after starting work, Ms Webb announced that she too was pregnant. The employers dismissed her not, they said, because of her pregnancy but because of her unavaila-
bility, at least at first, to work during the period for which she was needed.

The Court rejected this argument and ruled that her dismissal was on the grounds of
pregnancy and so contravened the Directive. Emphasizing the fact that Ms Webb was
not employed on a fixed-term contract, the Court ruled that 'dismissal of a pregnant
woman recruited for an indefinite period *cannot be justified* on grounds relating to her
inability to fulfil a fundamental condition of her employment contract'. This suggestion
that direct discrimination due to pregnancy could in some circumstances be justified
(e.g. the dismissal of a pregnant woman employed under a fixed-term contract), in situations beyond those listed in Article 28(1) of the Directive, set alarm bells ringing.[23]
However, in *Tele-Denmark*[24] the Court appeared to reject that possibility. It said that the

---

[17] See additionally Case C–207/98 *Mahlburg* v. *Land Mecklenburg-Vorpommern* [2000] ECR I–549, para. 27.
[18] Para. 12. The same conclusion must be drawn as regards the financial loss caused by the fact that the
woman appointed cannot be employed in the post for the duration of her pregnancy: Case C–207/98 *Mahlburg*
[2000] ECR I–549, para. 29.
[19] Case C–505/06 *Mayr* v. *Bäckerei und Konditorei Gerhard Flöckner OHG* [2008] ECR I–1017, para. 50.
[20] Case C–179/88 *Handels- og Kontorfunktionaerernes Forbund i Danmark (Hertz)* v. *Dansk
Arbejdsgiverforening* [1990] ECR I–3979.
[21] This view was confirmed in Case C–421/92 *Habermann-Beltermann* [1994] ECR I–1657. See further Art.
10 of Dir. 92/85/EC [1992] OJ L348/1 considered below.
[22] Case C–32/93 [1994] ECR I–3567.
[23] See further Ch. 6.
[24] Case C–109/00 *Tele Danmark A/S* v. *Kontorfunktionarernes Forbund I Danmark* [2001] ECR I–6993.

ruling in *Webb* could not be 'altered by the fact that the contract of employment was concluded for a fixed-term'.[25] Therefore a woman who took a fixed-term job, knowing she was pregnant and so would not be able to do the job for some of the period of employment, but did not tell the employer of this fact, could claim discrimination on the grounds of sex if she was dismissed.

The approach to pregnancy discrimination first laid down by the Court in *Dekker* has now been confirmed by Article 2(2)(c) of the Sex Equality Directive (2006/54):

> For the purposes of this Directive, discrimination includes…any less favourable treatment of a woman related to pregnancy or maternity leave within the meaning of Directive 92/85/EEC.

The advantage of this approach—deeming less favourable treatment on the grounds of pregnancy to be discrimination—is that it avoids doing damage to the concept of direct discrimination since direct discrimination presupposes the existence of a comparator of the opposite sex. However, the concept 'less favourable' does presuppose that there is someone being treated more favourably. It seems that that person can be either a male or female worker who is not pregnant.

(b) Terms and conditions of employment

The Court has extended the approach adopted in *Dekker* to discrimination against pregnant workers in respect of terms and conditions of employment. Thus, in *Thibault*[26] the Court ruled that a woman who continued to be bound to her employer by her contract of employment during maternity leave could not be deprived of the benefit of working conditions which applied to both men and women and were the result of that employment relationship. Therefore, the Court said, to deny a female employee the right to have her performance assessed annually would discriminate against her in her capacity as a worker because, had she not been pregnant and not taken the maternity leave, she would have been assessed for the year in question and could therefore have qualified for promotion. Such conduct constituted discrimination on grounds of sex within the meaning of the Directive.[27]

Similar issues arose in *Sarkatzis Herrero*,[28] this time in the context of a new appointment. Ms Sarkatzis Herrero was appointed to a permanent post in the Spanish health service, having previously been employed on a temporary post. She asked to defer taking up that post until the end of her maternity leave, a request which was granted, but her request meant that her seniority dated from the time of the appointment and not the time when she took up the post. The Court found that she had been discriminated against contrary to the Sex Equality Directive. The Directive, it said, precluded a national law which did not afford a woman who was on maternity leave the same rights as other successful applicants from the same recruitment competition by deferring the start of

---

[25] Para. 30.   [26] Case C–136/95 *Thibault* [1998] ECR I–2011.

[27] See additionally Case C–333/97 *Lewen* [1999] ECR I–7243, para. 48, discussed below, where the Court ruled that Art. 157 TFEU precludes an employer taking periods of maternity leave into account when granting a Christmas bonus so as to reduce the benefit *pro rata*.

[28] Case C–294/04 *Sarkatzis Herrero* v. *Imsalud* [2006] ECR I–1513.

her career to the end of that leave, without taking account of the duration of the leave, for the purpose of calculating her seniority of service.[29]

In *Busch*[30] the Court pushed the principle of non-discrimination to its outermost limits. After the birth of her first child in June 2000, Ms Busch, a nurse, took parental leave which was supposed to be for three years. In October 2000, she became pregnant again. In January 2001, she successfully requested permission to terminate her parental leave early and returned to full-time work as a nurse in April 2001. The day after she returned to work, she informed her employer that she was seven months' pregnant. Given that German law prohibited pregnant women from working in certain circumstances, the clinic which employed Ms Busch said that she was not able to carry out her duties effectively. It therefore rescinded its consent to her returning to work on grounds of fraudulent misrepresentation and mistake.

The Court disagreed. It said that where an employer took an employee's pregnancy into consideration when refusing to allow her to return to work before the end of her parental leave, that constituted direct discrimination on grounds of sex;[31] and since the employer could not take the employee's pregnancy into account in deciding whether she could return to work early, she was not obliged to inform the employer that she was pregnant.[32] The Court also said that the discrimination could not be justified by the fact that she was temporarily prevented, by a legislative prohibition imposed because of pregnancy, from performing all of her duties; and that discrimination on the grounds of sex could not be justified on grounds relating to the financial loss for an employer.[33] For good measure, the Court added that the fact that, in asking to return to work, Ms Busch intended to receive a maternity allowance higher than the parental leave allowance, as well as the supplementary allowance paid by the employer, did not legally justify sex discrimination over working conditions.

However, pregnant and breastfeeding women do not get it all their own way. In Spain a law dating back to 1900 allowed women who are breastfeeding an hour off from work a day to feed their babies. However, the law has long since lost its original purpose and now men and women can enjoy the right but, in the case of men, only when their wives are employees. Since this condition did not apply to women (i.e. their husbands did not have to be employees), the Court found in *Roca Álvarez*[34] that this was a directly discriminatory condition against men.

(c) Sick leave

Despite the long line of case law beginning with *Dekker* which finds that less favourable treatment on the grounds of pregnancy is directly discriminatory, the Court has not provided women suffering from physical or mental problems connected with pregnancy or childbirth with absolute protection. This was shown by the case of *Hertz*.[35] Hertz suffered a

[29] Para. 47.
[30] Case C–320/01 *Busch* v. *Klinikum Neustadt GmbH & Co. Betriebs-KG* [2003] ECR I–2041.
[31] Para. 39. [32] Para. 40. [33] Para. 44.
[34] Case C–104/09 *Roca Álvarez* v. *Sesa Start España ETT SA* [2010] ECR I–000.
[35] Case C–179/88 [1990] ECR I–3979.

complicated pregnancy, causing her to take a lot of sick leave. When the maternity leave came to an end she returned to work but, shortly afterwards, had to take a further 100 days' sick leave due to an illness resulting from her pregnancy. As a result, she was dismissed.

The Court distinguished between two situations: first, the period of maternity leave, and, secondly, the period after the maternity leave. During the first period the Court said that a woman was protected from being dismissed due to her absence from work (the *per se* discriminatory approach). However, during the second period the Court said it saw no reason to distinguish an illness attributable to pregnancy or confinement from any other illness. It therefore applied a comparative test. It reasoned that although certain disorders were specific to one or other sex, the only question was whether a woman was dismissed on account of absence due to illness in the same circumstances as a man. If this was so, then there was no direct or indirect discrimination on the grounds of sex.

While this decision can be justified by reference to practicality and economic necessity,[36] it cannot be defended in terms of logic: if the dismissal of a female worker on account of pregnancy constitutes direct discrimination, the dismissal of a woman on account of a pregnancy-related illness which arises after the end of her maternity leave should also constitute direct discrimination. Nevertheless, the Court reaffirmed this ruling in *Larsson*[37] and took it one stage further. It said that the Directive did not preclude dismissals which were the result of absences due to an illness attributable to pregnancy or confinement even where that illness arose during pregnancy and continued during and after maternity leave. This decision was much criticized and the Court reconsidered it in *Brown*.[38]

In *Brown* the employer had a policy of dismissing any employee who took more than 26 weeks' sick leave. Ms Brown, who suffered from a pregnancy-related disorder, was dismissed after 26 weeks' absence in line with the policy. The Court said that although pregnancy was not in any way comparable to a pathological condition, pregnancy was a period during which disorders and complications might arise compelling a woman to undergo strict medical supervision and, in some cases, to rest absolutely for all or part of her pregnancy. The Court then said that the principle of non-discrimination required protection against dismissal 'throughout the period of pregnancy'[39] so that, reversing *Larsson*, periods of sick leave during pregnancy could not be taken into account for calculating the 26 weeks of sick leave. The clock would, however, start ticking in respect of periods of sick leave taken after the end of her maternity leave on the same terms as a man. Thus, looking to see how a sick man would be treated applies only in respect of the post maternity leave period.

---

[36] See esp. Advocate General Darmon's discussion in his Joined Opinion in Cases C–177/88 *Dekker* ECR I–3941 and C–179/88 *Hertz* [1990] ECR I–3979, para. 43.

[37] Case C–400/95 *Larsson* v. *Føtex Supermarked* [1997] ECR I–2757.

[38] Case C–394/96 [1998] ECR I–4185. See C. Boch, 'Official: During Pregnancy, Females are Pregnant' (1998) 23 *ELRev.* 488.

[39] For criticism of this approach, see E. Ellis (1999) 36 *CMLRev.* 625.

However, sometimes the requirement to find a comparator does spill over to the pre-maternity leave phase, despite the Court's professed attempts to keep the pre-maternity leave period free of such a requirement. This can be seen in *Høj Pedersen*.⁴⁰ The Court said that Article 157 TFEU required a woman taking sick leave due to a pathological condition connected with her pregnancy,⁴¹ in a period prior to the start of her maternity leave, to receive full pay from her employer (and not, as in this case, part pay with additional benefits being paid by the local authority). The Court then added the comparator element. It said that a pregnant woman taking sick leave should receive full pay when, in the event of incapacity for work on grounds of illness, a worker is in principle entitled to receive full pay from his or her employer.⁴² Similarly, in *McKenna*⁴³ the Court ruled that Article 157 TFEU permits a rule of a sick leave scheme which provides, in regard to female workers absent prior to maternity leave by reason of an illness related to their pregnancy, for a reduction in pay in the case where the absence exceeds a certain duration, provided that the female worker is treated in the same way as a male worker who is absent on grounds of illness, and provided that the amount of payment made is not so low as to undermine the objective of protecting pregnant workers.

2.2. Maternity leave

Once a woman goes on maternity leave her situation changes. This was made clear by the Court in *Gillespie*,⁴⁴ where it said that since the case concerned women taking maternity leave provided for by the national legislation they were in a special position requiring them to be afforded special protection.⁴⁵ This situation was not comparable either with that of a man or woman actually at work.⁴⁶ In respect of the payment during maternity leave, the Court said that, although maternity benefit constituted pay within the meaning of Article 157 TFEU, neither Article 157 TFEU nor Article 4 of the Sex Equality Directive 2006/54 required that women should continue to receive full pay during maternity leave,⁴⁷ nor did those provisions lay down

⁴⁰ Case C–66/96 *Høj Pedersen* v. *Kvickly Skive* [1998] ECR I–7327. See additionally Case C–284/02 *Land Brandenburg* v. *Sass* [2004] ECR I–11143, para. 37 cf. Case C–294/04 *Sarkatzis Herrero* [2006] ECR I–1513, para. 47.

⁴¹ The position is different in respect of a woman's absence due to 'routine pregnancy-related minor complaints when there is no incapacity for work or of a medical recommendation intended to protect the unborn child but not based on any actual pathological condition or any special risks for the unborn child': para. 50.

⁴² Para. 41. The only exception to this rule was where the sums received by employees by way of state benefits were equal to the amount of their pay. It would then be for the national court to ascertain whether the circumstance that the benefits were paid by a local authority was such as to bring about discrimination in breach of Art. 157 TFEU.

⁴³ Case C–191/03 [2005] ECR I–7631.

⁴⁴ Case C–342/93 [1996] ECR I–475. See J. Conaghan, 'Pregnancy, Equality and the European Court of Justice: Interrogating *Gillespie*' (1998) 3 *IJLD* 115.

⁴⁵ Para. 17. It said that 'discrimination involves the application of different rules to comparable situations or the application of the same rule to different situations'.

⁴⁶ See additionally Case C–218/98 *Abdoulaye* [1999] ECR I–5723 (women could be paid a maternity bonus not payable to new fathers).

⁴⁷ Para. 20.

any specific criteria for determining the amount of benefit to be paid to them during that period.

The Court did, however, add that the amount payable could not be so low as to undermine the purpose of the maternity leave, namely the protection of women before and after giving birth. In order to assess the adequacy of the amount payable, the national court had to take into account not only the length of the maternity leave but also the other forms of social protection afforded by the national law in the case of justified absence from work. On the facts of the case there was nothing to suggest that the amount of benefit granted was such as to undermine the objective of protecting maternity leave.

The Court also said in *Gillespie* that a woman on maternity leave should receive a pay rise awarded before or during that period. It said that the benefit paid during maternity leave was equivalent to a weekly payment calculated on the basis of the average pay received by the worker at the time when she was actually working and which was paid to her week by week, just like any other worker. The principle of non-discrimination therefore required that a woman who was still linked to her employer by a contract of employment or by an employment relationship during maternity leave had to benefit from any pay rise, even if backdated.[48] To deny her such an increase would discriminate against her purely in her capacity as a worker since, had she not been pregnant, she would have received the pay rise.

In *Gillespie*, the maternity pay was calculated on the basis of a woman's average earnings over an eight-week reference period which was taken between the fourth and sixth month of pregnancy when the woman was most likely to be well. The pay increase she benefited from occurred after the reference period but was backdated to the reference period. In *Alabaster*[49] the woman also benefited from a pay rise prior to her maternity leave but after the reference period, but this time the pay rise was not backdated. The Court extended its ruling in *Gillespie* to this situation so that 'any pay rise awarded after the beginning of the period covered by her reference pay must be included in the elements of pay used to determine the amount of pay owed to the worker during her maternity leave'.[50]

Directive 2002/73 amended Directive 76/207 by expressly giving a woman the right to return to her job after her maternity leave and to enjoy any improved terms and conditions of employment. Article 15 of the Sex Equality Directive 2006/54 now provides:

> A woman on maternity leave shall be entitled, after the end of her period of maternity leave, to return to her job or to an equivalent post on terms and conditions which are no less favourable to her and to benefit from any improvement in working conditions to which she would have been entitled during her absence.

---

[48] Para. 22.
[49] Case C–147/02 *Alabaster* v. *Woolwich plc, Secretary of State for Social Security* [2004] ECR I–3101.
[50] Para. 49.

2.3. Express derogation from the principle of equal treatment

As we saw in the last chapter, different treatment on the grounds of pregnancy may be lawful if the employer's actions are caught within the derogation contained in Article 28(1) of the Sex Equality Directive 2006/54 (protection of women, particularly on the grounds of pregnancy and maternity).[51] In *Habermann-Beltermann*[52] the Court held that the prohibition on night-time work by pregnant women was 'unquestionably compatible with Article [28(1)]'. However, since the prohibition on night-time work by pregnant women takes effect only for a limited period in relation to the total length of an indefinite contract 'the termination of a contract without a fixed term on account of the woman's pregnancy...cannot be justified on the ground that a statutory prohibition, imposed because of pregnancy, temporarily prevents the employee from performing night-work'.[53]

3. DIRECTIVE 92/85 ON PREGNANT WORKERS

3.1. Introduction

The significance of the decisions of the Court under the Sex Equality Directive in respect of dismissals[54] (but not in respect to other discriminatory treatment) have been reduced in the light of Directive 92/85/EC[55] which is designed to protect pregnant workers,[56] including those already on childcare leave with a previous child,[57] and workers who have recently given birth or who are breastfeeding.[58] The Directive is intended to provide minimum requirements for encouraging improvements,[59] especially in the

---

[51] Cf. Art. 5(3) of the Goods and Services Dir. 2004/113/EC (OJ [2004] L373/37): when considering actuarial factors, the Directive says that 'costs related to pregnancy and maternity shall not result in differences in individuals' premiums'.

[52] Case C–421/92 [1994] ECR I–1657.

[53] See additionally Art. 7 of Dir. 92/85 [1992] OJ L348/1 and Case C–320/01 *Busch* [2003] ECR I–2041 considered previously.

[54] However, if the woman falls outside the personal scope of the Pregnant Workers Directive she may still be covered by the Sex Equality Dir. 2006/54: Case C–232/09 *Danosa* [2010] ECR I–000, para. 74.

[55] Council Dir. 92/85/EEC (OJ [1992] L348/1) (tenth individual Directive adopted within the meaning of Art. 16(1) of Dir. 89/391, considered further in Ch. 11) on the introduction of measures to encourage improvements in the safety and health at work of pregnant workers who have recently given birth or are breastfeeding. The Directive was based on Art. 153 TFEU (ex 137 EC). See further V. Cromack, 'The EC Pregnancy Directive: Principle or Pragmatism?' (1993) 6 *JSWL* 261.

[56] The term worker is defined in the same way as for Article 45 TFEU discussed in Ch. 4: Case C–116/06 *Kiiski* v. *Tampereen kaupunki* [2007] ECR I–7643, para. 25.

[57] Case C–116/06 *Kiiski* [2007] ECR I–7643, para. 33.

[58] These three terms are defined by reference to national law and practice and are dependent on the worker informing her employer of her condition (Art. 2). The term 'pregnant worker' will be used to apply to the three situations unless otherwise stated. The term does not, however, apply to a female worker who is at an advanced stage of *in vitro* fertilization treatment, that is, between the follicular puncture and the immediate transfer of the *in vitro* fertilized ova into her uterus, inasmuch as it is established that the dismissal is essentially based on the fact that the woman has undergone such treatment: Case C–505/06 *Mayr* [2008] ECR I–1017, para. 53. See additionally the reference in Case C-167/12 CD as to whether 'with mothers' and 'surrogate mothers' are covered by the Dir.

[59] Art. 1(3) provides that the Directive may not have the effect of reducing the level of protection afforded to pregnant workers.

working environment, to protect the health and safety of pregnant workers.[60] The Directive applies to 'workers', as defined by EU law. The definition draws on the Court's case law on Article 45 TFEU on free movement of workers and Article 157 TFEU on equal pay.[61] The key issue is subordination in fact.[62] In *Danosa*[63] the Court said that a member of the board of directors of a capital company who regularly and in return for remuneration performed the duties assigned to her under the company's statutes and rules of procedure of the board of directors, could have the status of worker for the purposes of the Pregnant Workers Directive.

3.2. 'Employment' rights

The Directive provides three specific forms of 'employment' protection[64] to pregnant workers and workers on maternity leave, which, with one exception relating to payment during maternity leave, exist from the first day of employment. Firstly, they are entitled to time off, without loss of pay, in order to attend ante-natal examinations, if such examinations have to take place within working hours.[65]

Secondly, they are entitled to a continuous period of at least 14 weeks' maternity leave, of which at least two weeks must be allocated before and/or after confinement.[66] The purpose of maternity leave is 'to protect a woman's biological condition and the special relationship between a woman and her child over the period which follows pregnancy and childbirth, by preventing that relationship from being disturbed by the multiple burdens which would result from the simultaneous pursuit of employment'.[67] In *Kiiski*[68] the Court referred, *inter alia*, to the European Social Charter 1961 and 1996 to support its conclusion that 'the right to maternity leave granted to pregnant workers must be regarded as a particularly important mechanism of protection under employment law'. Therefore the Court has interpreted the requirements of the Directive in a way which most protects pregnant women. So in *Boyle*[69] the Court said that the Pregnant Workers Directive did not preclude a clause in an employment contract from requiring an employee who had expressed her intention to commence her maternity leave during the six weeks preceding the expected week of childbirth, but who was on sick leave with a pregnancy-related illness immediately before that date and gave birth during the period of sick leave, to bring forward the date on which her paid maternity leave commenced either to the beginning of the sixth week preceding the expected week of childbirth or to the beginning of the period of sick leave, whichever was the later.

---

[60] See further Ch. 11.   [61] See further Chs. 4 and 7 respectively.
[62] Case C–232/09 *Danosa* [2010] ECR I–000, para. 46.
[63] Ibid., para. 47.
[64] The Directive was adopted under Art. 153 TFEU on health and safety.
[65] Art. 9, which applies only to pregnant workers.
[66] Art. 8(1) and (2).
[67] Case C–519/03 *Commission* v. *Luxembourg* [2005] ECR I–3067, para. 32.
[68] Case C–116/06 *Kiiski* [2007] ECR I–7643, para. 49.
[69] Case C–411/96 *Boyle* v. *EOC* [1998] ECR I–6401.

Taking maternity leave cannot affect the right to take any other period of leave guaranteed by Union law, such as annual leave under the Working Time Directive.[70] However, in *Boyle*[71] the Court said that the contract of employment could limit the period during which annual leave accrued to the minimum period of 14 weeks' maternity leave. Thus, annual leave would not accrue in respect of any period of supplementary maternity leave granted by the employer.

During her (minimum 14-week) maternity leave, a woman's rights connected with the contract of employment must be maintained.[72] To date, the Court has answered some very specific questions on this point. For example, in *Boyle*,[73] the Court said that a clause in an employment contract which prohibited a woman from taking sick leave during the minimum period of 14 weeks' maternity leave to which a female worker was entitled pursuant to Article 8(1) of Directive 92/85, unless she elected to return to work and thus terminated her maternity leave, was not compatible with Directive 92/85. By contrast, a clause in an employment contract which prohibited a woman from taking sick leave during a period of supplementary maternity leave granted to her by the employer, unless she elected to return to work and thus terminated her maternity leave, was compatible with the Sex Equality Directive and the Pregnant Workers Directive 92/85. The Court also said that Directive 92/85 precluded a clause in an employment contract from limiting, in the context of an occupational scheme wholly financed by the employer, the accrual of pension rights during the period of maternity leave referred to by Article 8 to the period during which the woman received the pay provided for by that contract or national legislation.

The (major) exception to the rule that a woman's rights connected with the contract of employment must be maintained relates to pay. All the Directive requires is the maintenance of pay or the payment of an (unspecified) 'adequate' allowance,[74] but Member States may make entitlement to pay conditional upon the worker fulfilling the conditions of eligibility for such benefits laid down by national legislation. These conditions may not, however, provide for periods of previous employment in excess of 12 months immediately prior to the presumed date of confinement.[75] As far as the level of

---

[70] Dir. 2003/88: Case C-342/01 *Merino Gómez* [2004] ECR I-2605, para. 41 considered further in Ch. 12.

[71] Case C-411/96 *Boyle* v. *EOC* [1998] ECR I-6401.

[72] Art. 11(2)(a). See Case C-342/93 *Gillespie* [1996] ECR I-475; Case C-284/02 *Land Brandenburg* v. *Sass* [2004] ECR I-11143, para. 44.

[73] Case C-411/96 *Boyle* v. *EOC* [1998] ECR I-6401.

[74] Art. 11(2)(b). An allowance is adequate (Art. 11(3)) if it guarantees income at least equivalent to that which the worker concerned would receive in the event of a break in her activities on grounds connected with her state of health, subject to any ceiling laid down by national legislation (in other words, sick pay). However, a statement of the Council and the Commission added to the Directive (OJ [1992] L348/8) states that the reference to the state of health is not 'intended in any way to imply that pregnancy and childbirth be equated with sickness'. The link with such allowance is intended to serve as a concrete fixed reference in all Member States for the determination of the minimum amount of maternity allowance. In Case C-66/96 *Høj Pedersen* [1998] ECR I-7327 the Court said that Art. 11(3) applied only to pay or benefits received in the context of *maternity* leave and did not apply to allowances which a woman could claim when pregnant.

[75] Arts. 11(2)(b) and (4).

maternity pay is concerned, the Court ruled in *Gillespie*[76] that the allowance must not be paid at such a derisory level as to undermine the purpose of the maternity leave. However, if the employer pays maternity pay higher than the statutory payments in respect of maternity leave, the Court ruled in *Boyle*[77] that Union law permitted the employer making those payments conditional on the worker undertaking to return to work after the birth of the child for at least one month, failing which she would be required to repay the difference between the statutory and the higher rate of pay.

The third employment right can be found in Article 10(1), which provides that pregnant workers cannot be dismissed[78] during the period from the beginning of their pregnancy to the end of their maternity leave, save in exceptional cases not connected with their condition which are permitted under national law or practice.[79] Employers must provide pregnant workers who are dismissed within this period with duly substantiated written grounds for dismissal[80] and Member States must provide a remedy for pregnant workers who are dismissed.[81]

In *Jiménez Melgar*[82] the Court confirmed that Article 10 was directly effective.[83] It also made clear that the prohibition of dismissal laid down in Article 10 applied both to fixed-term contracts of employment and to those concluded for an indefinite duration.[84] In reaching this conclusion, the Court helped to lay to rest the suggestion made in *Webb*[85] (above), a case decided under the Equal Treatment Directive 76/207, that the dismissal of a worker employed on a fixed-term contract (as opposed to a contract of indefinite duration) could be justified if she was unable to do the job because she was pregnant. Thus, where an employer unilaterally terminates a contract—whether for a fixed-term or an indefinite duration—this contravenes Article 10. As the Court made clear in *Jiménez Melgar*, and in *Tele Danmark*[86] which was decided the same day, had the Union legislature wished to exclude fixed-term contracts, which represent a substantial proportion of employment relationships, it would have done so expressly.[87]

Where, however, a fixed-term contract has expired because it has come to the end of its stipulated term, and it is not subsequently renewed, the Court said in *Jiménez Melgar*

---

[76] Case C–342/93 [1996] ECR I–475.

[77] Case C–411/96 *Boyle* v. *EOC* [1998] ECR I–6401.

[78] The prohibition of dismissal extends not just to the notification of a decision to dismiss on the grounds of pregnancy and/or of the birth of a child but also the taking of preparatory steps for such a decision before the end of that period: Case C–460/06 *Paquay* [2007] ECR I–8511.

[79] Member States do not have to specify the particular grounds on which workers may be dismissed: Case C–438/99 *Jiménez Melgar* v. *Ayuntamiento de Los Barrios* [2001] ECR I–6915, para. 38. Member States are also not obliged to have a national authority in place which is required to give consent prior to the employer's dismissal of a pregnant worker (para. 52).

[80] Art. 10(2).

[81] Art. 10(3). In addition, Art. 12 provides more generally that Member States must allow those who consider themselves wronged by the failure to comply with the obligations of the Directive to pursue their claims by judicial process.

[82] Case C–438/99 *Jiménez Melgar* [2001] ECR I–6915.

[83] Ibid., para. 34.

[84] Ibid., para. 44.

[85] Case C–32/93 [1994] ECR I–3567.

[86] Case C–109/00 *Tele Danmark A/S* v. *Kontorfunktionaerernes Forbund I Danmark* [2001] ECR I–6993.

[87] See now the Fixed-term Work Dir. 99/70 considered later at, nn. 250–295.

that this could not be regarded as a dismissal;[88] and so its non-renewal did not contravene Article 10 of Directive 92/85.[89] However, the Court added that since the non-renewal of a fixed-term contract could be viewed as a refusal of employment then the Court's case law (*Dekker* and *Mahlburg*) on the Sex Equality Directive 2006/54 would apply. Thus, if the non-renewal of a fixed-term contract was motivated by the worker's pregnancy this would constitute direct discrimination contrary to Article 14 of the Sex Equality Directive 2006/54.[90]

Jiménez Melgar makes clear that Article 10 of Directive 92/85 has largely replaced the Court's case law on pregnancy-related dismissals under the Equal Treatment Directive 76/207/EEC and the Sex Equality Directive 2006/54 (which in turn was developed against the backcloth of Article 10 of the Pregnant Workers Directive[91]). However, given the limited scope of Directive 92/85, the Court's case law under Directive 76/207 continues to be important in respect of other forms of discrimination occurring during pregnancy (such as refusal to appoint or discriminatory terms and conditions).

Finally, Article 12 requires Member States to provide pregnant women with the possibility of bringing a claim by judicial or other process to protect their rights under the Pregnant Workers Directive. Since Article 12 is a 'specific expression... of the principle of effective judicial protection of an individual's rights under Union law',[92] the principles developed in the field of remedies apply equally here. So, the remedy chosen by the Member State must have a genuine dissuasive effect on the employer and must be commensurate with the injury suffered.[93] Further, the detailed procedural rules governing actions for safeguarding individual's rights are subject to the principles of equivalence and effectiveness.[94]

3.3. Health and safety protection

Directive 92/85 also provides more specific rights to protect the health and safety of the pregnant worker.[95] The Directive makes a distinction between the risks contained in Annex I (certain physical, biological, and chemical agents, certain industrial processes,

---

[88] Cf. the position under British law, s. 95(1)(b) Employment Rights Act 1996, which provides that an employee is dismissed if... 'he is employed under a limited-term contract and that contract terminates by virtue of the limiting event without being renewed under the same contract'.

[89] Para. 45.   [90] Para. 46.

[91] As the Court said in Case C–394/96 *Brown* [1998] ECR I–2757, it was 'precisely in view of the harmful effects which the risk of dismissal may have on the physical and mental state of women who are pregnant, women who have recently given birth or women who are breastfeeding, including the particularly serious risk that pregnant women may be prompted voluntarily to terminate their pregnancy, that the [Union] legislature, pursuant to Article 10 of Council Directive 92/85/EEC ....provided for special protection to be given to women, by prohibiting dismissal during the period from the beginning of their pregnancy to the end of their maternity leave'. Therefore the Court took this 'general context' into account in construing the relevant provisions in *Brown*.

[92] Case C–63/08 *Pontin* v. *T-Comalux SA* [2009] ECR I–10467, para. 41.

[93] Ibid., para. 42.   [94] Ibid., para. 43.

[95] Commission Communication on the guidelines on the assessment of the chemical, physical, and biological agents and industrial processes considered hazardous for the safety or health of pregnant workers and workers who have recently given birth or are breast feeding: COM(2000) 466.

and underground mining) and those contained in Annex II (a more limited list of physical, biological, and chemical agents, and underground mining). In the case of the
Annex I risks, the employer is obliged to examine the nature, degree and duration of
exposure of the pregnant worker to these risks.[96] The pregnant worker and/or the worker's representatives are to be informed of any risks and of the measures to be taken.
These measures may include a temporary adjustment to the working conditions or
working hours of the pregnant worker. If this is not technically or objectively feasible,
or cannot reasonably be required on duly substantiated grounds, the employer must
take the necessary measures to move the worker to another job.[97] The pay does not need
to be the same as her previous job provided: (1) the pay she receives does not undermine the Directive's objective of protecting the health and safety of pregnant workers;
(2) the pay received does not ignore the fact that the woman is continuing to work;
(3) the transferred employee must not be paid less than employees performing the job to
which she is temporarily assigned; and (4) she should not lose any pay components or
supplementary allowances that relate to her professional status, such as seniority, length
of service or professional qualifications.[98]

If it is not possible to transfer the worker concerned, she must be granted leave in
accordance with the national legislation for the whole of the period necessary to protect
her health and safety.[99] These rules apply equally to Annex II risks. In addition, Article
6 provides that neither pregnant workers nor workers who are breastfeeding may be
obliged to perform duties for which the assessment has revealed a risk of exposure to
the agents and working conditions listed in Annex II, section A, in the case of pregnant
workers, and Annex II, section B in the case of workers who are breastfeeding.[100]

In *Høj Pedersen*[101] the Court has insisted that these provisions be strictly applied. The
case concerned a Danish law allowing employers to send home a pregnant woman,
although not unfit to work, without paying her salary in full, when they considered that
they could not provide work for her. The Court said that this law did not comply with
the requirements laid down in Directive 92/85 on the grounds that giving leave to the
employee was based on the interests of the employer and that decision could be taken
by the employer without first examining the possibility of adjusting the employee's
working conditions and/or hours or even the possibility of moving her to another job.

Article 7 recognizes that pregnant workers have the right not to have to work at night
during their pregnancy and for a period to be determined by the national authorities

---

[96] Art. 4(1). Technical adjustments to Annex I can be made according to the provisions in Art. 12. Art. 3
obliges the Commission to draw up guidelines in conjunction with the Advisory Committee on Safety and
Health at work, on the assessment of the chemical, physical, and biological agents and industrial processes
considered hazardous for the health and safety of pregnant workers.

[97] Art. 5(2).

[98] Art. 11(1) read in conjunction with Case C–471/08 *Parviainen* v. *Finnair Oyj* [2010] ECR I–000. See
additionally Case C–194/08 *Gassmayr* v. *Bundesminister für Wissenschaft und Forschung* [2010] ECR I–000
which makes clear that Art. 11(1) is directly effective.

[99] Art. 5(3).

[100] Art. 6. Annex II may only be amended in accordance with the Art. 153 TFEU procedure.

[101] Case C–66/96 *Høj Pedersen* v. *Kvickly Skive* [1998] ECR I–7327.

following childbirth. These rights are dependent on the production of a medical certificate stating that these arrangements are necessary for the safety or health of the
worker. If this is the case then the pregnant worker must be transferred to day work or
be granted leave from work or an extension of maternity leave where such a transfer is
not possible.

3.4. Revisions to the Directive

In 2009, the Commission proposed some significant amendments to the Pregnant
Workers Directive.[102] These included extending paid maternity leave to 18 weeks (with
remuneration at the level of full pay subject to a statutory cap), providing still longer
leave for mothers with premature babies, babies sick at birth, and multiple births,
increasing the flexibility for women to decide when to take their leave before or after
giving birth, improving protection in respect of sickness absence and in respect of dismissal, including protection against victimization, and reversing the burden of proof.
The European Parliament went even further and demanded, *inter alia*, 20 weeks maternity leave. These proposals were, however, rejected by the Council and the matter has
returned to the Commission.

C. DIVISION OF RESPONSIBILITIES IN THE FAMILY: THE BALANCE BETWEEN WORK AND CARING

1. INTRODUCTION

In the previous section we considered how European Union law regulated the position
of women workers from the start of their pregnancy to the end of their maternity leave.
We now turn to the question of how the law has responded to the challenge confronted
by parents seeking to combine raising a family with employment. Traditionally, once a
child was born the woman gave up work as a matter of choice or social expectation or
because the law required it. Women have therefore always been associated with the role
of principal childcarer and/or carer for elderly dependent relatives. However, for many
families this is no longer an option, because of the economic need for two salaries, particularly where the family unit has broken down, and/or because the woman wants to
work. Yet, children (and increasingly, with an ageing society, elderly relatives) need to
be cared for, school days are short and holidays long. The question for women, and
increasingly men, is how to balance work and family life. For some families it has meant
that one partner, often the woman, opts for working part time, doing a job share, being
employed under fixed-term contracts or doing agency work which fits around school

---

[102] COM(2008) 600.

terms, or, perhaps, becoming self-employed. For others it has meant working full time and paying others to help care for children or elderly relatives.

The Court has been at the frontline of fielding questions raising the issue of how the law balances the rights of those with families with the interests of employers. As we shall see in the next section, in the last 20 years the Court has moved quite a long way from supporting the traditional male breadwinner/female carer model towards recognizing a 'dual breadwinner/dual carer' model. In searching for a resolution to the work-life balance dilemma, the Court has sought to reconcile its desire not to deprive women of hard-won benefits that reward the childcare function[103] and its wish not to stereotype the woman as carer.[104]

The work-life balance issue has also become a central concern for many western governments—for economic as well as moral reasons. Addressing work-life balance issues is seen as a way of attracting and retaining more people in employment, increasing the labour supply, and modernizing social protection systems,[105] in other words to make 'full and effective use of the productive capacities of all sections of the population.'[106] The European Employment Strategy recognized the need to reconcile 'work and family life' in its first set of Guidelines in 1997.[107] In 2000 the Council issued a Resolution on the Balanced Participation of women and men in family and working life[108] which recognized the new 'social contract' on gender in which the principle of equality between men and women in relation to employment and labour 'implies equal sharing between working fathers and mothers, in particular of time off work to look after children or other dependants',[109] that the balanced participation of women and of men in both the labour market and in family life is 'an advantage to both men and women' and is an essential aspect of the development of society; and that maternity, paternity, and the rights of children are 'eminent social values to be protected by society, the Member States and the European [Union]'.[110] The Preamble concludes with the radical statement that:

> The beginning of the twenty-first century is a symbolic moment to give shape to the new social contract on gender, in which the de facto equality of men and women in the public and private domains will be socially accepted as a condition for democracy, a prerequisite for citizenship and a guarantee of individual autonomy and freedom, and will be reflected in all European Union policies.

---

[103] Case C–218/98 *Abdoulaye* [1999] ECR I–5723.

[104] Case C–476/99 *Lommers* v. *Mininster van Landbouw* [2002] ECR I–2891.

[105] This is the chapeau to Guidelines 18 ('Promote a lifecycle approach to work' which includes 'better reconciliation of work and private life and the provision of accessible and affordable childcare facilities and care for other dependants'), 19 ('Ensure inclusive labour markets'), and 20 ('Improve Matching of Labour Market needs'): Co. Dec. 2005/600 (OJ [2005] L205/21).

[106] Commission's own summary of the four pillars cited in D. Ashiagbor, 'European–Employment Strategy and Regulation' in S. Sciarra, P. Davies, and M. Freedland (eds), *Employment Policy and the Regulation of Part-time Work in the European Union: A Comparative Analysis* (CUP, Cambridge, 2004) 53.

[107] Para. 16 of the Community Social Charter 1989 had already recognized that 'measures should also be developed enabling men and women to reconcile their occupational and family obligations'.

[108] OJ [2000] C218/5.

[109] 3rd Preambular paragraph.

[110] 4th Preambular paragraph.

In the Employment Guidelines adopted the following year, the EES policy towards work/life balance issues had become more fully articulated. Under the heading of 'Reconciling work and family life', the Guidelines provide:[111]

> Policies on career breaks, parental leave and part-time work, as well as flexible working arrangements which serve the interests of both employers and employees, are of particular importance to women and men. Implementation of the various Directives and social-partner agreements in this area should be accelerated and monitored regularly. There must be an adequate provision of good quality care for children and other dependants in order to support the entry of women and men into, and their continued participation in, the labour market. An equal sharing of family responsibilities is crucial in this respect. Those returning to the labour market after an absence may also have outmoded skills, and experience difficulty in gaining access to training. Reintegration of women and men into the labour market after an absence must be facilitated.

The 'various Directives and social partner agreements' referred to include the Parental Leave Directive and the Part-time and Fixed-term Work Directives which we shall examine below. However, first, we shall look at the Court's approach to balancing a work and family life.

2. EQUAL TREATMENT AND THE CHANGING APPROACH OF THE COURT OF JUSTICE

As we have seen, the Court has been forced to address the issue of work-life balance through Article 267 TFEU (ex 234 EC) references made in the context of the Sex Equality Directive 2006/54. Initially its response was to reinforce the traditional gender division of roles: women as childcarers, men as breadwinners. For example, *Commission* v. *Italy*[112] concerned an Italian law granting a mother, but not a father, who adopted a child under six, compulsory maternity leave and the corresponding financial allowance. The Court said that the difference in treatment could not be regarded as discrimination within the meaning of the Directive.[113] Similarly, in *Hofmann*[114] the Court's response to a complaint by a father that he was not allowed a maternity leave payment was that (then) Directive 76/207 was not 'designed to settle questions concerning the organisation of the family or to alter the division of responsibility between parents'.[115]

---

[111] Co. Dec. 2001/63/EC (OJ [2001] L22/18).

[112] Case 163/82 [1983] ECR 3273.

[113] Para. 17. Once again, in this case the Court appears to suggest that direct discrimination can be justified. The Court said that the difference in treatment between the mother and the father was 'justified…by the legitimate concern to assimilate as far as possible the conditions of entry of the child into the adoptive family to those of the arrival of a newborn child in the family during the very delicate initial period' (para. 16).

[114] Case 184/83 *Hofmann* v. *Barmer Ersatzkasse* [1984] ECR 3047. See T. Hervey and J. Shaw, 'Women, Work and Care: Women's Dual Role and Double Burden in EC Sex Equality Law' (1998) 8 *Journal of European Social Policy Law* 43.

[115] See additionally Case 170/84 *Bilka-Kaufhaus* v. *Weber von Hartz* [1986] ECR 1607 where the Court stopped short of imposing a positive requirement on companies to organize their occupational pension schemes in such a way as to accommodate the needs of their employees, and Case C–297/93 *Grau-Hupka* v. *Stadtgemeinde Bremen* [1994] ECR I–5535 where the Court said that since Union law on equal treatment did not oblige Member States to take into account, in calculating the statutory pension, years spent bringing up children, the national rules also did not breach Art. 157 TFEU.

Fifteen years later, in *Abdoulaye*[116] the Court upheld a benefit paid by Renault to women on maternity leave. This benefit was intended to offset the 'occupational disadvantages experienced by women on maternity leave'.[117] Certain male employees argued that, since this benefit was payable only to women, it contravened Article 157 TFEU. The Court disagreed. It said that in respect of benefits intended to offset occupational disadvantages, male and female workers were 'in different situations, which excludes any breach of the principle of equal pay laid down in Article [157 TFEU]'.[118]

Concern was expressed at the time that the ruling in *Abdoulaye* served only to reinforce the position of women as principal childcarers.[119] *Lommers*,[120] the positive action case considered in Chapter 8, can also be criticized in this regard, where the Court upheld the female employees' preferential entitlement to nursery places. Yet the Court did itself note the paradox—that a measure whose purported aim was to abolish a *de facto* inequality, might nevertheless also help 'to perpetuate a traditional division of roles between men and women'.[121]

The Court showed itself increasingly sensitive to these issues in *Griesmar*[122] where it distinguished between benefits which were directly related to the maternity and post-maternity period from those which apply to child rearing more generally. The Court said that where a benefit was designed to offset the occupational disadvantages which 'arise for female workers as a result of being absent from work *during the period following childbirth*' the situation of a male worker was not comparable to that of a female worker and so Article 157 TFEU did not apply. By contrast, where a benefit was designed essentially to offset the occupational disadvantages which arise for female workers as a result of having brought up children, it was necessary to examine the question of whether the situations of a male civil servant and a female civil servant were comparable. This was the situation in *Griesmar* itself which concerned a service credit applied to the calculation of pensions for female but not male civil servants in respect of each of their children. The Court said that the national law infringed Article 157 TFEU inasmuch as it excluded male civil servants who could prove that they assumed the task of bringing up their children from entitlement to the credit.

The new 'social contract' referred to in the Council's Resolution on balanced participation between men and women (considered above) had already been anticipated by the Court in *Hill*[123] where it noted that most of the women who choose to job share use

---

[116] Case C–218/98 *Abdoulaye* [1999] ECR I–5723.

[117] Renault listed these disadvantages as first, that a woman on maternity leave might not be proposed for promotion; second, that on her return, her period of service would be reduced by the length of her absence; third, that a pregnant woman could not claim performance-related salary increases; fourth, a female worker could not take part in training; lastly, since new technology was constantly changing the nature of jobs, the adaptation of a female worker returning from maternity leave became complicated (para. 19).

[118] Para. 20.

[119] C. McGlynn, 'Pregnancy, Parenthood and the Court of Justice in *Abdoulaye*' (2000) 6 *ELJ* 39.

[120] Case C–476/99 *Lommers* v. *Mininster van Landbouw* [2002] ECR I–2891.

[121] Para. 41.

[122] Case C–366/99 *Griesmar* v. *Ministre de l'Économie, des Finances et de l'Industrie* [2001] ECR I–9383, para. 46.

[123] Case C–243/95 *Kathleen Hill and Ann Stapleton* v. *Revenue Commissioners* [1998] ECR I–3739, paras. 41–2.

that option 'in order to be able to combine work and family responsibilities which invariably involve caring for children'. The Court then added:

> [Union] policy in this area is to encourage and, if possible, adapt working conditions to family responsibilities. Protection of women within family life and in the course of their professional activities is, in the same way as for men, a principle which is widely regarded in the legal systems of the Member States as being the natural corollary of the equality between men and women, and which is recognised by [Union] law.

However, there are limits to what the Court can achieve when interpreting the Equality Directives. In *Grau-Hupka*[124] the woman complained that her state pension was reduced because it had been calculated without taking into account the five years she had spent looking after her child (and this had consequences for other payments she received). Under German law, as it then stood, a woman could claim only one year spent looking after her child to count towards her state pension. Because the case concerned the *state* pension, Article 157 TFEU did not apply;[125] and the Social Security Directive 79/7 did not help her either because it did not require Member States to grant advantages in respect of old-age pension schemes to people who had brought up children, nor did it require states to provide benefit entitlements where employment had been interrupted to bring up children.[126]

3. PARENTAL LEAVE DIRECTIVE

The question of taking time off to care for young children was addressed for the first time by the legislature in the Parental Leave Directive 96/34/EC.[127] It gave effect to the first collective agreement concluded by the Social Partners under the collective route to legislation contained in the (then) Social Policy Agreement.[128] The agreement lays down minimum requirements designed to facilitate the reconciliation of parental and professional responsibilities for working parents.[129] It applies to all workers, both men and women who have an employment contract or an employment relationship.[130] It was

---

[124] Case C–297/93 *Grau-Hupka* v. *Stadtgemeinde Bremen* [1994] ECR I–5535.

[125] See further Ch. 10.

[126] Para. 27. In a rather similar vein, see Case C–160/01 *Mau* v. *Bundesanstalt für Arbeit* [2003] ECR I–4791, paras. 52–3 concerning the Insolvency Dir. 2008/94 considered further in Ch. 14.

[127] OJ [1996] L145/4, amended by Council Dir. 97/75/EC (OJ [1998] L10/24), consolidated 16 January 1998. A question was referred to the CJEU as to whether the right to parental leave should apply to all parents after 15 December 1999 or only to those whose children were born or adopted after 15 December 1999: *R* v. *Secretary of State, ex parte TUC*, 23 May 2000 but was subsequently withdrawn (OJ [2003] C184/28) because the UK amended its law: SI 2001/4010 the Maternity and Parental Leave (Amendment) Regulations 2001 to ensure that both groups of parents, with the necessary qualifying service benefit from the right.

[128] The draft agreement was concluded on 6 November 1995 by ETUC, CEEP and UNICE and formally agreed on 14 December 1995. The process for adopting this agreement and the subsequent litigation are considered in Ch. 2.

[129] Clause 1(1), a point reiterated by the Court in Case C–116/08 *Meerts* v. *Proost* [2009] ECR I–10063, para. 35.

[130] Clause 1(2). Clause 1(3) adds that Member States and/or social partners must not exclude from the scope and application of this agreement 'workers, contracts of employment or employment relationships solely because they relate to part-time workers, fixed-term contract workers or persons with a contract of employment or employment relationship with a temporary agency'.

revised in 2010 by a further agreement between the social partners and extended to all workers by Directive 2010/18.

The Parental Leave Directive envisages two main rights. First, it entitles men and women workers to parental leave on the birth or adoption of a child to enable them to take care of that child, for at least three (now extended to four) months, until a given age up to eight years, to be defined by the Member States or the Social Partners.[131] Clause 2(2) adds:

> …to promote equal opportunities and equal treatment between men and women, [the leave] should, in principle, be provided on a non-transferable basis. To encourage a more equal take-up of leave by both parents, at least one of the four months shall be provided on a non-transferable basis. The modalities of application of the non-transferable period shall be set down at national level through legislation and/or collective agreements taking into account existing leave arrangements in the Member States.

No requirement is imposed that the leave be paid. As the Court made clear in *Commission* v. *Luxembourg*,[132] parental leave and maternity leave are different: parental leave enables either parent to look after their child; maternity leave applies to mothers only, immediately after childbirth. Therefore, each parent is entitled to parental leave of at least four months and that period cannot be reduced when it is interrupted by another period of leave such as maternity leave (which is paid). In *Chatzi*[133] the Court said that if there are multiple births, the periods of parental leave are not multiplied by the number of children born. However, the Court added that Clause 2.1 of the framework agreement, read in the light of the principle of equal treatment, obliges the national legislature to establish a parental leave regime which, according to the situation obtaining in the Member State concerned, ensures that the parents of twins receive treatment that takes due account of their particular needs. The Court said that it is incumbent upon national courts to determine whether the national rules meet that requirement and, if necessary, to interpret those national rules, so far as possible, in conformity with European Union law.

The Parental Leave Directive leaves a large number of issues to be resolved by the Member State and/or Social Partners.[134] For example, the Member States and/or the Social Partners may decide whether parental leave is granted on a full-time or part-time basis, in a fragmented way or in the form of a time credit system; whether entitlement to parental leave be subject to a period of work qualification and/or length of service qualification (which cannot exceed one year); and any requirement as to notice periods that are to be given by the worker to the employer specifying the beginning and the end of the parental leave.[135] In addition, the Member States, in consultation with the Social

---

[131] Clause 2(1) and Clause 2(2). Clause 2(1) does not confer an individual right to parental leave on the child: Case C–149/10 *Chatzi* [2010] ECR I–000, para. 40.

[132] Case C–519/03 *Commission* v. *Luxembourg* [2005] ECR I–3067, para. 32.

[133] Case C–149/10 *Chatzi* [2010] ECR I–000.

[134] Clause 2(3).

[135] Clause 2(3)(a)–(d).

Partners, can define the circumstances in which the employer is allowed to postpone the granting of parental leave for justifiable reasons relating to the operation of the undertaking[136] and can authorize that special arrangements be made for small undertakings.[137] Special provision is made for parents with disabled children or children with a long-term illness,[138] and adoption.[139] In addition, Member States and/or the Social Partners must define the status of the employment contract or employment relationship for the period of the parental leave.[140] All matters relating to social security in relation to the agreement are left to be determined by the Member States according to national law.[141]

In order to ensure that workers can exercise their right to parental leave, they must be protected against dismissal or other discrimination on the grounds of applying for, or taking parental leave, in accordance with national legislation, collective agreements or practice.[142] At the end of the parental leave, workers have the right to return to the same job, or, if that is not possible, to an equivalent or similar job consistent with their employment contract or employment relationship.[143] In addition, rights acquired by the worker or in the process of being acquired on the date on which parental leave starts must be maintained as they stand until the end of the parental leave.[144] This means, for example, that a national rule under which workers exercising their right to parental leave, lose their right, following that leave, to paid annual leave under the Working Time Directive 2003/88 accumulated during the year preceding the birth of their child, is contrary to the Parental Leave Directive.[145] These rights, including any changes arising from national law, agreements or practice, will apply to the worker at the end of the parental leave.[146]

---

[136] Clause 3(1)(c). E.g. where the work is of a seasonal nature, where a replacement cannot be found within the notice period, where a significant proportion of the workforce applies for parental leave at the same time, and where a specific function is of strategic importance.

[137] Clause 3(1)(d). The Court has been sensitive to the realities of such leave for business: Case C–116/06 *Kiiski* [2007] ECR I–7643, para. 37: 'Since the grant of such leave affects the organisation of the business or of the service for which the worker enjoying that leave is employed and may in particular necessitate recruitment of a replacement, it is reasonable that national law should attach strict conditions to the grant of any alterations of the period of such leave'.

[138] Clause 3(3).

[139] Clause 4.

[140] Clause 5(3).

[141] Clause 5(5). This provision is not directly effective, nor does it require states to ensure that during parental leave employees continue to receive social security benefits: Case C–537/07 *Sánchez-Camacho* [2009] ECR I–6525, para. 51.

[142] Clause 5(4).

[143] Clause 5(2).

[144] This provision is directly effective: Case C–537/07 *Sánchez-Camacho v. INSS* [2009] ECR I–6525, para. 37. It is also a 'particularly important' provision which cannot be interpreted restrictively so that where an employer unilaterally terminates a worker's full-time employment contract of indefinite duration, while the parent is on part-time parental leave, the compensation to be paid must not be determined on the basis of the reduced salary being received when the dismissal takes place (Case C–116/08 *Meerts v. Proost NV* [2009] ECR I–10063).

[145] Case C–486/08 *Land Tirol* [2010] ECR I–000, para. 56.

[146] Clause 5(2).

The new agreement introduced a provision on the return to work. Clause 6(1) provides:

> In order to promote better reconciliation, Member States and/or social partners shall take the necessary measures to ensure that workers, when returning from parental leave, may request changes to their working hours and/or patterns for a set period of time. Employers shall consider and respond to such requests, taking into account both employers' and workers' needs.

The modalities of this paragraph must be determined in accordance with national law, collective agreements, and/or practice. This reflects the right to request flexible working which has been adopted in the UK since 2002. It is not a right to change terms, merely a right to request. But many employers in fact agree to the change and the right has been judged remarkably successful. Clause 6(2) adds that in order to facilitate the return to work following parental leave, workers and employers are encouraged to maintain contact during the period of leave and may make arrangements for any appropriate reintegration measures.

The second right given to workers by the agreement is to time off on the grounds of *force majeure* for urgent family reasons in cases of sickness or accident, making the immediate presence of the worker indispensable.[147] Member States and/or Social Partners may specify the conditions of access and the detailed rules for applying this rule and can limit the entitlement to a certain amount of time per year and/or per case.[148]

As we have seen, the rights provided here are minima and Member States can maintain or introduce more favourable provisions.[149] Further, the implementation of the provisions of the collective agreement must not constitute grounds for reducing the general level of protection afforded to workers in the field of this agreement.[150] However, 'this does not prejudice the right of the Member States and/or Social Partners to develop different legislative, regulatory or contractual provisions, in the light of changing circumstances (including the introduction of non-transferability), as long as the minimum requirements provided for in this agreement are complied with'.[151]

While there have not yet been any comprehensive studies on the use made by parents to their right to leave under the Directive,[152] experience from the Nordic countries, where parental leave already exists, indicates that it is usually the woman who takes the parental leave.[153] This fact was recognized by the Court in *Lewen*[154] where it said that failure to pay a Christmas bonus to employees on parental leave was *prima facie* indirectly discriminatory against women. Such discrimination contravened Article 157 TFEU if the bonus was awarded retroactively for work performed in the course of the year and the woman did not receive an amount proportionate to the time worked. If, on

---

[147] Clause 7(1).   [148] Clause 7(2).   [149] Clause 8(1).
[150] Clause 8(2): the standard non-regression clause.
[151] Clause 4(2), second sentence.
[152] A legal assessment on the implementation of the Directive can be found in COM(2003) 358.
[153] Bruning and Plontenga, 'Parental Leave and Equal Opportunities' (1999) 9 *JESP* 195.
[154] Case C–333/97 *Lewen v. Lothar Denda* [1999] ECR I–7243, para. 35.

the other hand, the bonus was paid as a way of encouraging those in active employment to work hard and to reward *future* loyalty to an employer, then failure to pay such a bonus was not discriminatory since a woman on parental leave was in a 'special situation' which could not be 'assimilated to that of a man or woman at work since such leave involves suspension of the contract of employment and, therefore, of the respective obligations of the employer and the worker'. Thus, if the payment is made *prospectively* the Court treats those on parental leave, just like those on maternity leave,[155] as being in a 'special situation' and so Article 157 TFEU offers no protection. It also offers no protection against employers taking into account periods of parental leave (but not maternity leave) to reduce the benefit *pro rata*.[156]

4. THE RELATIONSHIP BETWEEN THE PARENTAL LEAVE DIRECTIVE AND OTHER MEASURES

The Parental Leave Directive is about just that: leave for parents (mothers *and* fathers[157]). It is not to be confused with paternity leave (granted to fathers on the birth of their child) for which Union law makes no provision. That said, Article 28(2) of the Sex Equality Directive 2006/54 makes clear that not only are the Equal Treatment Directives without prejudice to the provisions of Parental Leave Directive, but they are also without prejudice to the right of Member States to recognize distinct rights to paternity and/or adoption leave (Article 16 of the Sex Equality Directive 2006/54). Those Member States which recognize such rights must take the necessary measures to protect working men and women against dismissal due to exercising those rights and ensure that, at the end of such leave, they are entitled to return to their jobs or to equivalent posts on terms and conditions which are no less favourable to them, and to benefit from any improvement in working conditions to which they would have been entitled during their absence.

D. CHILDCARE

Parental leave enables workers to take some time off to look after young children but for the rest of the time they are dependent on childcare. The Union is conscious of this issue (but less so of care for elderly relatives). To date, it has issued a Recommendation 92/241 on Childcare Services[158] and the Barcelona European Council agreed that by 2010 Member States should provide childcare for at least 90 per cent of children between three years old and the mandatory school age and for at least 33 per cent of children

---

[155] See previously, at nn. 44–50.

[156] Case C–333/97 *Lewen* [1999] ECR I–7243, paras. 48–9.

[157] Cf. *Markin* v. *Russia* [2010] ECHR 1435 where the Court of Human Rights ruled that the exclusion of servicemen from parental leave but not servicewomen constituted unlawful discrimination contrary to Article 8 and Article 14 ECHR.

[158] Council Recommendation 92/241/EEC of 31 March 1992 on childcare (OJ [1992] L123/16).

under three years of age. These targets became an integral part of the EES and the Lisbon Strategy. Yet, unsurprisingly, the Commission found that Member States were not meeting the targets, especially for children under three. Where childcare facilities do exist, they were found to be costly and not compatible with full time work or jobs with atypical hours, and the quality of the facilities (the qualifications of the staff and the staff/child ratio) deter parents from using them.[159] However, as the Commission notes, while better support for the reconciliation of work and family enable men and women to exercise greater choice in balancing the work and private sides of their life, and will also contribute to achieving major policy objectives of the EU, notably growth and jobs, the primary responsibility for developing and promoting reconciliation belongs to the Member States.[160] All the Commission can do is exhort, and this has not proved very successful to date.

According to the Commission, the rationale for a (non-binding) Recommendation on Childcare is both economic and social. Despite increasing numbers of women entering the labour force there has not been a correlative decrease in women's share of family responsibilities. According to the Commission, women will only be able to take advantage of the new jobs due to be created by the advent of the Single European Market if affordable support measures—including childcare—are available, enabling them time to train or retrain in order to be able to meet the demands of a restructured labour market.

Article 1 recommends that Member States, possibly in co-operation with national, regional or local authorities, management and labour, and other relevant organizations and private individuals, take and encourage initiatives in four areas:

- the provision of childcare services[161] while parents are working, following a course of education or training in order to obtain employment, or are seeking a job or a course of education or training in order to obtain employment;

- special leave for employed parents with responsibility for the care and upbringing of children;[162]

- adapting the environment, structure and organization of work to make them responsive to the needs of workers with children;[163]

---

[159] Commission, *A better work-life balance: stronger support for reconciling professional, private and family life* (COM(2008) 635).

[160] Ibid., 9.

[161] Childcare services, defined as any type of childcare whether public or private, individual or collective, should be affordable, flexible and diverse. They should combine reliable care, from the point of view of health and safety, with a general upbringing and a pedagogical approach. They should be available in all areas and regions of the Member States, and be accessible to parents and children, including children with special needs (Art. 3).

[162] These special leave initiatives apply to both men and women. They are intended to combine some flexibility as to how leave may be taken (Art. 4).

[163] This includes action, esp. within the framework of a collective agreement to create an environment which takes into account the needs of all working parents with childcare responsibilities, ensures that due recognition is given to persons engaged in childcare services and the social value of their work; and promotes action, especially in the public sector, which can serve as an example in developing initiatives in this area (Art. 5).

- sharing of occupational, family, and upbringing responsibilities arising from the care of children between women and men. This includes, according to Article 6, encouraging increased participation by men in order to achieve a more equal sharing of parental responsibilities.

Because this measure is a recommendation, it lacks the legal force of a Directive.[164] Furthermore, the broad strategic nature of the policy—and the complexities created by the recognition of subsidiarity in the provision of the services—means that it will be very difficult for an individual to raise provisions of the Recommendation before a national court. Nevertheless, the Recommendation has a symbolic value in demonstrating the EU's commitment to childcare and Member States are obliged to inform the Commission of the measures taken to give effect to the Recommendation;[165] and in this respect, the Recommendation sits comfortably with the OMC techniques envisaged by the European Employment and Lisbon strategies.

E. ATYPICAL WORKERS: PART-TIME, FIXED-TERM, AND AGENCY WORK

1. INTRODUCTION

One way of balancing work and family life is to work part-time, or under a short fixed-term contract, or as an agency worker (temp). While these arrangements offer flexibility, they can be the most precarious types of contract. As far back as 1989, the Community Social Charter identified the need for action to ensure the improvement in living and working conditions as regards 'forms of employment other than open-ended contracts, such as fixed-term contracts, part-time working, temporary work and seasonal work'. The Action Programme noted that atypical workers constitute an 'important component in the organisation of the labour market', and said that the growth of atypical work, 'often in a quite anarchical manner' raised a 'danger of seeing the development of terms of employment such as to cause problems of social dumping, or even distortion of competition, at [Union] level' unless safeguards were introduced.

Although Directive 91/533/EEC on proof of the employment contract[166] provided some transparency in contracts of employment, the Commission proposed three specific Directives concerning atypical workers, intended to improve the operation of the internal market and introduce greater transparency into the labour market, to improve living and working conditions of workers, and to protect the health and safety of work-

---

[164] The Court has not been prepared to extend Art. 157 TFEU to reinforce this Recommendation: Case C–249/97 *Gruber* [1999] ECR I–5295.

[165] The Commission intends to follow up the Childcare Recommendation by assessing the implementation of the Recommendation and establishing baseline data on childcare infrastructure and services in the Member States (COM(94) 333, 43).

[166] OJ [1991] L288/32. See Ch. 12.

ers at the workplace. The three Directives were proposed on three different legal bases. The first, and least radical Directive, Directive 91/383/EEC, proposed on the basis of Article 153 TFEU, concerned health and safety and was the only measure successfully adopted. This is considered below. The second Directive, proposed on the basis of Article 115 TFEU (ex 94 EC),[167] applied the principle of non-discrimination to atypical workers,[168] in a limited set of circumstances, subject to objective justification. This eventually formed the intellectual basis of Directive 97/81 on Part-time Work and Directive 99/70 on Fixed-term Work considered below.

The third Directive, proposed on the basis of Article 114 TFEU (ex 95 EC), contained the more ambitious aim of creating a level playing field of indirect costs for employing atypical workers. As the Commission explained,[169] variations in wage costs relating to atypical employment are often due to factors unrelated to productivity—principally to national laws and collectively agreed regulations. Cost differences 'not justified by the workers' performance over time unit' are mainly related to costs arising from social protection and indirect costs associated with the duration of the contract, such as seniority. For example, costs to employers in some Member States arising from statutory social protection schemes, such as sickness, unemployment, insurance, and pensions, vary according to whether the worker concerned is employed full-time or part-time. As a result, some states can produce with lower labour costs than others for reasons unrelated to productivity, thus placing them at a competitive advantage.[170]

This draft Directive therefore proposed imposing three obligations on the Member States. First, Member States had to ensure that atypical employees were afforded, vis-à-vis full-time employees, social protection under statutory and occupational social security schemes underpinned by the same groundwork and the same criteria, taking

---

[167] COM(90) 228 final (OJ [1990] C224/90).

[168] Atypical work was defined in both the Arts. 115 and 114 TFEU Directives as including:

(i) part-time employment involving shorter working hours than statutory, collectively agreed or usual working hours;

(ii) temporary employment relationships in the form of: (a) fixed-term contracts, including seasonal work, concluded directly between the employer and the employee, where the end of the contract is established by objective conditions such as reaching a specific date, completing a specific task or the occurrence of a specific event; and (b) temporary employment covers any relationship between the temporary employment business (a temp agency), which is the employer, and its employees (the temps), where the employees have no contract with the user undertaking where they perform their activities. In other words, the employees have a contract with the temp agency which sends them to work as a temp for a company needing additional staff.

[169] Proposal for a Council Directive on the Approximation of Laws of the Member States Relating to Certain Employment Relationships with Regard to Distortions of Competition COM(90) 228 final (OJ [1990] C224/90); amended proposal in COM(90) 533 final (OJ [1990] C305/90).

[170] In Denmark e.g. complementary pensions scheme contributions amounting to about 2.5 per cent of the gross wages of the employees concerned are not paid by employers in respect of employment of less than 10 hours per week. In Ireland, social security contributions amounting to 15.95 per cent of gross wages are not paid in respect of employment for less than 18 hours a week. (1990) 200 EIRR 13 (September 1990).

into account the duration of work and/or pay.[171] Therefore, those employees working more than eight hours a week would be entitled to maternity protection, protection against unfair dismissal, redundancy payments, occupational pensions, sickness benefits, and survivor's benefits. Secondly, Member States had to ensure that part-time workers (but not the other classes of atypical worker) received the same entitlements to annual holidays, dismissal allowances, and seniority allowances as full-time employees, in proportion to the total hours worked.[172] Thirdly, Member States had to ensure that national laws provided a limit on the renewal of temporary employment relationships of 12 months or less, so that the total period of employment did not exceed 36 months.[173] In addition, an equitable allowance had to be paid in the event of an unjustified break in the employment relationship before the end of the fixed term.[174] Neither this Directive, nor the Article 115 TFEU Directive, were adopted. It took two agreements by the Social Partners to apply the principle of non-discrimination (similar to the Article 115 TFEU Directive) to part-time and fixed-term workers.[175] Elements of the Article 114 TFEU Directive were also included in the Fixed-term Work Directive.

In none of these proposals, nor the Directives themselves, is any attempt made to challenge the need for these 'new' forms of employment. The Commission recognizes that the marked increase in the more flexible forms of work contract is 'not only because management wants to increase flexibility but also because the workers involved quite often prefer alternative work patterns'. Nevertheless, the Commission also recognizes that if these flexible forms of work are to be generally accepted there is a need to ensure that such workers are given broadly equivalent working conditions in comparison to standard workers.[176]

2. DIRECTIVE 91/383/EEC ON HEALTH AND SAFETY OF ATYPICAL WORKERS

Council Directive 91/383/EEC[177] encourages improvement in the health and safety of atypical workers who are defined as those on fixed-term contracts and those in temporary employment relationships.[178] By applying the principle of equal treatment, the Directive requires atypical workers to be given the same level of health and safety protection as other workers in the user undertaking.[179] The Directive warns that the existence of an atypical employment relationship does not justify different treatment in respect of health and safety, especially as regards access to personal protective equipment.[180] Consequently, as a bare minimum,[181] the Framework Directive 89/391/

---

[171] Art. 2.   [172] Art. 3.   [173] Art. 4(a).   [174] Art. 4(b).

[175] See now Dir. 97/81/EC (OJ [1998] L14/9) on part-time work and Dir. 99/70/EC (OJ [1999] L175/43).

[176] COM(94) 333, 30.

[177] OJ [1991] L206/19. See further COM(90) 228 final.

[178] Art. 1. No reference is made to part-time workers.

[179] Art. 2(1).

[180] Art. 2(2).

[181] Art. 9 provides that the Directive is without prejudice to existing or future national or Union legislation which is more favourable to the health and safety protection of atypical workers.

EEC[182] on health and safety and all the individual daughter Directives apply equally to atypical workers.[183]

In addition, all atypical workers must be informed of the risks they face before taking up a particular activity, including any special occupational qualifications or skills they need or any special medical surveillance that is required.[184] In the case of temporary employment relationships (temps), the user undertaking must also specify to the temp agency, possibly in a contract of assignment, the occupational qualifications required, and the specific features of the job to be filled, and these details must be conveyed by the temp agency to the workers concerned.[185] It is, however, the user undertaking which is responsible for the conditions in which the temp's work is performed. This is without prejudice to any responsibility imposed on the temp agency by national law.[186] This is perhaps the most controversial feature of the Directive. Although it is useful to identify one individual as being responsible for the temp, at times it may be preferable for the employer, usually the temp agency, to take responsibility, because usually it is the agency who has the ongoing relationship with the temp, and it is the agency which can monitor the individual's long-term exposure to, for example, radiation, over a variety of temporary jobs.

Atypical workers must also receive sufficient training appropriate to the job, taking into account the qualifications and experience[187] of the worker, who must be provided with special medical surveillance where the nature of the work demands it.[188] Member States have the option to extend that medical surveillance beyond the end of the employment relationship or to exclude atypical workers from work which is particularly dangerous to their health and safety.[189]

3. PART-TIME WORK

3.1. The equal treatment approach

In the days before the Part-time Work Directive,[190] indirect discrimination was a useful tool to address less favourable treatment of part-time workers on the grounds that considerably fewer men than women work part time.[191] Unless the differential treatment could be objectively justified, the part-time workers were entitled to have the same

---

[182] OJ [1989] L183/1. See further Ch. 11.

[183] Art. 2(3).   [184] Art. 3.   [185] Art. 7.   [186] Art. 8.   [187] Art. 4.

[188] Art. 5. The existence of atypical workers at an undertaking must be notified to workers designated to protect and prevent occupational risks in accordance with Art. 7 of Dir. 89/391 (Art. 6).

[189] Art. 5.

[190] Dir. 97/81 (OJ [1998] L14/9).

[191] See additionally Case 96/80 *Jenkins* [1981] ECR 911; Case 170/84 *Bilka-Kaufhaus* [1986] ECR 1607; Case 171/88 *Rinner-Kühn* [1989] ECR 2743; Case 33/89 *Kowalska v. Freie und Hansestadt Hamburg* [1990] ECR I–2591; Case C–360/90 *Arbeiterwohlfahrt der Stadt Berlin eV v. Bötel* [1992] ECR I–3589; Case C–184/89 *Nimz* [1991] ECR I–297; Case C–1/95 *Gerster* [1997] ECR I–5253; and Case C–100/95 *Kording v. Senator für Finanz* [1997] ECR I–5289. These cases are discussed by E. Traversa, 'Protection of Part-time Workers in the Case Law of the Court of Justice of the European Communities' (2003) 19 *IJCLLIR* 219.

scheme applied to them as applied to other workers, on a basis proportional to their working time.[192]

The German works council cases provide a good example of how the principle of indirect discrimination has been used to assist part-time workers. German law provided that both full- and part-time workers attending training courses connected with their functions as staff representatives could be compensated up to the limit of their respective normal working hours. In *Bötel*[193] the Court found that this legislation discriminated against part-time workers, and thus against women, because, while both part-time and full-time employees participated in the same number of hours of training, part-timers received less compensation due to the lower number of hours worked. The Court said that this method of compensation acted as a disincentive to part-time workers from attending such training courses and acquiring further skills and knowledge.

This decision led to considerable concern in Germany since it interfered with the special status of works and staff councils in the organization of German employment policy and labour relations. In particular, it interfered with the principle that members of staff councils carry out their duties without loss of earnings and without any financial incentives to take on such a responsibility. As a result, in *Lewark*[194] the Court was asked to reconsider its decision in *Bötel*.[195] Once again the Court recognized that the application of the legislation discriminated against women contrary to Article 157 TFEU unless it could be objectively justified, which was a matter for the national court. However, the Court did note that such legislation was likely to deter part-time workers from performing staff council functions or from acquiring the knowledge necessary for performing them, which made it more difficult for part-time workers to be represented by qualified staff council members.[196]

In some cases, however, the Court has been unable to see the issue affecting part-time workers at all. For example, in *Helmig*[197] the Court ruled that there was no discrimination when part-timers, who were predominantly women, did not receive overtime rates for hours worked over their normal contractual hours but less than the full-time hours, even though the social consequences for part-timers to work one hour's overtime were likely to be more disruptive than for full-timers.[198] However, 10 years later,

---

[192] Case C–102/88 *Ruzius Wilbrink v. Bestuur van de Bedrijfsvereniging voor Overheidsdiensten* [1989] ECR 4311.

[193] Case C–360/90 [1992] ECR I–3589. Cf. Case C–399/92 *Helmig* [1994] ECR I–5727, a case where part-timers did not receive the higher rate of overtime pay until they worked in excess of the normal working hours for full-timers.

[194] Case C–457/93 [1996] ECR I–243.

[195] Case C–360/90 [1992] ECR I–3589.

[196] See additionally Case C–278/93 *Freers and Speckmann v. Deutsche Bundespost* [1996] ECR I–1165 and see J. Shaw, 'Works Councils in German Enterprises and Article 119 EC' (1997) 22 *ELRev*. 256.

[197] Case C–399/92 *Stadt Lengerich v. Helmig* [1994] ECR I–5727. On the serious consequences of this decision, see the House of Lords' decision in *Barry v. Midland Bank* [1999] IRLR 581.

[198] See Rubinstein [1995] IRLR 183.

in *Elsner-Lakeberg*[199] the Court had a change of heart, albeit without making any reference to *Helmig*. Ms Elsner-Lakeberg worked part-time as a secondary school teacher. Full-time teachers worked for 24.5 hours per week (98 hours per month) whereas Ms Elsner-Lakeberg taught for 15 hours per week (60 hours per month). In one month she was required to teach 2.5 additional hours. Her request for remuneration of those hours was refused on the basis that the legislation provided that excess hours worked by a teacher would be remunerated only when the additional work exceeded three hours in a month. She therefore received no pay at all for the additional hours worked.

The Court said that although the pay appeared to be equal, inasmuch as the entitlement to remuneration for additional hours was triggered only after three additional hours had been worked by part-time and full-time teachers, three additional hours was in fact a greater burden for part-time teachers than for full-time teachers: a full-time teacher had to work an additional three hours over his or her regular monthly schedule of 98 hours (approximately 3 per cent extra) in order to be paid for the additional hours, while a part-time teacher had to work three hours more than his or her monthly 60 hours (5 per cent extra). Since the number of additional teaching hours giving entitlement to pay was not reduced for part-time teachers in a manner proportionate to their working hours, they received different treatment compared with full-time teachers as regards pay for additional teaching hours.[200] Having reached this conclusion, the Court said that it was for the national court to determine whether the different treatment affected considerably more women than men and, if so, whether the rule could be objectively justified.

The drawback with the indirect discrimination approach to dealing with less favourable treatment of part-time workers is that it is dependent on the part-timers showing that the rule actually[201] disadvantaged a considerably higher percentage of women than men.[202] Thus, female part-time workers have to show disparate impact; male part-time workers cannot make the claim at all. In this respect the Part-time Work Directive 97/81 represented an important step forward in terms of protection for all part-time workers, both male and female. Nevertheless, the equal treatment model still has a residual role to play in respect of matters which fall outside the scope of the Directive including, for example, a woman returning from maternity leave wanting to challenge a decision by her employer not to allow her to change from full-time to part-time work.

---

[199] Case C–285/02 *Elsner-Lakeberg* v. *Nordrhein-Westfalen* [2004] ECR I–5861. More recently, see Case C–300/06 *Voß* v. *Land Berlin* [2007] ECR I–10573.

[200] Para. 17.

[201] Cf. the statutory language of the amended Equal Treatment Directive (Article 2(1)(b) the Sex Equality Dir. 2006/54) considered in Ch. 6.

[202] Case C–236/98 *Örebro läns landsting* [2000] ECR I–2189, para. 50.

3.2. The Part-time Work Directive 97/81

(a) Introduction

Given that the two proposals for the Directives based on Articles 115 and 114 TFEU had been blocked in Council, the Commission decided to initiate the procedure under Article 154 TFEU. In June 1996, the Social Partners (UNICE (now BusinessEurope), ETUC, and CEEP) announced their intention to begin negotiations.[203] On 6 June 1997, they agreed the 'European Framework Agreement on Part-time Work' which, following the procedure under Article 155 TFEU, was subsequently implemented by Council Directive 97/81/EC[204] and extended to the UK by Council Directive 98/23/EC.[205] The drafting of the Agreement was much influenced by the 1994 ILO Convention No. 175 establishing minimum standards on part-time work and the supplementary Recommendation 182.[206]

The purpose of the framework agreement is, first and foremost, 'to provide for the removal of discrimination against part-time workers and to improve the quality of part-time work'.[207] However, as the Preamble makes clear, the Directive applies the principle of non-discrimination to employment conditions and not to social security. Thus, an important aspect of the Article 114 TFEU proposal has disappeared.

The Directive has two other objectives:[208] 'to facilitate the development of part-time work on a voluntary basis *and* to contribute to the flexible organisation of working time in a manner which takes into account the needs of employers and workers'.[209] Thus, the Part-time Work Directive forms part of the EU's flexibility agenda aimed at encouraging adaptability of business and, in particular, modernizing work organization.[210] But what sort of flexibility—supply-side (where part-time work is encouraged to enable those with family commitments to combine work with family life) or demand-side (where flexible working arrangements such as part-time, fixed-term, or temporary work is used by management to adapt their staffing needs to market conditions)?[211]

---

[203] For a fuller description of the background, see S. Sciarra, 'New discourses in labour law: part-time work and the paradigm of flexibility' in S. Sciarra *et al.*, previously, at n. 107, 21–6.

[204] OJ [1998] L14/9.

[205] OJ [1998] L131/10. Consolidated legislation OJ [1998] L131/13. On the background to the legislation, see M. Jeffery, 'Not Really Going to Work? Of the Directive on Part-time Work, "Atypical Work" and Attempts to Regulate It' (1998) 3 *ILJ* 193.

[206] See J. Murray 'Social Justice for Women? The ILO's Convention on Part-time Work' (1999) 15 *IJCLLIR* 3.

[207] Clause 1(a).   [208] Clause 1(b), emphasis added.

[209] This, the Court notes in Joined Cases C–395/08 and C–396/08 *INPS* v. *Bruno* [2010] ECR I–000, para. 24, is the first objective of the Directive.

[210] See, e.g., Guideline 13 of the 2001 Employment Guidelines (OJ [2002] L22/18) which encourages the Social Partners to 'negotiate and implement at all appropriate levels agreements to modernise the organisation of work, including flexible working arrangements, with the aim of making undertakings productive and competitive, achieving the required balance between flexibility and security, and increasing the quality of jobs. Subjects to be covered may, for example, include the introduction of new technologies, new forms of work and working time issues such as…the development of part-time working, access to career breaks, and associated job security issues'.

[211] See generally, S. Deakin and H. Reed, 'Between Social Policy and EMU: the New Employment Title of the EC Treaty' in J. Shaw (ed.), *Social Law and Policy in an Evolving European Union*, (Hart Publishing, Oxford, 2000).

If the latter,[212] then, as Ashiagbor notes, the first objective of the Directive risks being undermined by the second and third objectives: the reason why atypical work has been promoted is to provide a way of circumventing the high levels of employment protection associated with typical work.[213]

Given the dualism of the Directive, this chapter focuses on its role as part of the Union's agenda on family friendly policies. However, comments made in this respect must be considered against the broader backcloth of the Directive's role in 'increasing the employment-intensiveness of growth, in particular by a more flexible organization of work in a way which fulfils both the wishes of the employees and the requirements of competition'.[214]

(b) Personal scope

The Directive applies to part-time workers who have an employment contract or employment relationship as defined by the law, collective agreement, or practice in force in each Member State. [215] Once again, personal style has proved to be a vexed question. In the UK the Directive has been implemented to cover a person who works under a contract of employment or under any other contract for the personal performance of work or services. However, services provided for a client or customer on a professional basis or by a business undertaking are not covered. Thus, the employees and the dependent self-employed are covered but not the genuine self-employed (entrepreneurs) and professionals.

In *O'Brien*[216] the Court provided some detailed criteria as to who falls within the personal scope of the Part-time Work Directive. The case arose in the context of the exclusion under UK law of judges generally, and part-time judges remunerated on a daily fee-paid basis in particular, from employment law, including the Part-time Work Regulations, because they do not have a contract of employment. The Court said first, that the sole fact that judges are treated as judicial office holders was insufficient in itself to exclude them from enjoying the rights provided for by the Part-time Work Directive.[217] Second, stressing 'the need to safeguard the effectiveness of the principle of equal treatment enshrined in that framework agreement', the Court said that an exclusion is permitted 'only if the nature of the employment relationship concerned is substantially different from the relationship between employers and their employees which fall within the category of "workers" under national law',[218] bearing in mind 'the differentiation between that category and self-employed persons'.[219] The Court then noted the following points:

- judges are expected to work during defined times and periods, even though this can be managed by the judges themselves with a greater degree of flexibility than members of other professions.

- judges are entitled to sick pay, maternity or paternity pay and other similar benefits.[220]

---

[212] A perspective supported by Guideline 13.
[213] 'European Employment Strategy and Regulation' in S. Sciarra *et al.*, previously, at n. 107, 54–5.
[214] Fifth Preambular paragraph.
[215] Clause 2(1).   [216] Case C–393/10 *O'Brien* v. *Ministry of Justice* [2012] ECR I–000.
[217] Para. 41.   [218] Para. 42.   [219] Para. 44.   [220] Paras. 45–6.

It added: 'the fact that judges are subject to terms of service and that they might be regarded as workers within the meaning of Clause 2.1 of the Framework Agreement on part-time work in no way undermines the principle of the independence of the judiciary'.[221] The Court therefore provided a strong steer that these judges were in fact covered by the Directive and in so doing moved the debate away from merely looking at the question of control and subordination, the traditional indicia of 'employee/worker' status, and focused more on the question of integration.[222]

The term *'part-time* worker'[223] refers to 'an employee whose normal hours of work, calculated on a weekly basis or on average over a period of employment of up to one year, are less than the normal hours of work of a comparable full-time worker'.[224] Clause 3(2) explains that the term 'comparable full-time worker' means 'a full-time worker in the same establishment having the same type of employment contract or relationship, who is engaged in the same or a similar work/occupation, due regard being given to other considerations which may include seniority, qualification/skills'. Where there is no comparable full-time worker in the same establishment, the comparison must be made by reference to the applicable collective agreement or, where there is no applicable collective agreement, in accordance with national law, collective agreements, or practice.

The scope of the comparator may well prove to be the Achilles heel of the Directive.[225] First, it seems likely that the comparator must be actual, not hypothetical.[226] Second, the requirement of the same type of contract means that, for example, part-time workers providing services on a self-employed basis cannot compare themselves with full-time employees with a contract of employment even if they are doing similar work. Some of these problems can be seen in *Wippel*.[227] The applicant was a casual worker employed on a 'work on demand' contract (zero hours contract). She brought an action claiming the same treatment as a regular full-time worker. Her contract did not stipulate either weekly working hours or the manner in which her working time was to be organized, leaving it up to her whether to accept or reject the work offered by the employer. Her comparator, a full-time worker, worked under a contract with a fixed working week of 38.5 hours. The full-time worker had to work for the employer for the whole working week without being able to refuse to work if the worker could not or did not wish to do it. Because of these differences between the full-timers' and part-timers'

---

[221] Para. 47.

[222] See further Section B in Ch. 4.

[223] In Case C–313/02 *Nicole Wippel* v. *Peek & Cloppenburg GmbH & Co. KG* [2004] ECR I–9483, para. 40 the Court said that a part-time worker employed under a 'framework contract' (like a zero hours contract), working as and when the employer required it, was a worker for the purposes of the Directive provided that she satisfied the requirement of national law for the existence of an employment contract or relationship, and did not fall under any derogation by the Member States under Clause 2(2).

[224] Clause 3(1). Cf. Case C–322/98 *Kachelmann* v. *Bankhaus Hermann Lampe KG* [2000] ECR I–7505, paras. 26 and 28 which suggests that part-time and full-time work are not comparable.

[225] For a discussion of the position under British law, see A. McColgan, 'Missing the Point? The Part-time Workers (Prevention of Less Favourable Treatment) Regulations 2000 (SI 2000/1551)' (2000) 29 *ILJ* 260.

[226] *Carl* v. *University of Sheffield* UKEAT/0261/08.

[227] See Case C–313/02 *Wippel* [2004] ECR I–9483.

contracts, the Court found that there was no full-time worker comparable to Ms Wippel.[228]

Third, the part-time and full-time worker must be engaged in the same or a similar work/occupation, due regard being given to other considerations which may include seniority, qualification/skills. So far there has been no guidance on this point from the Court of Justice. However, the British House of Lords said in *Matthews v. Kent and Medway Towns Fire Authority*[229] that retained firefighters who work on a part-time basis and are called on to respond to emergencies did similar work to full-time fire fighters, since the core work of both involved putting out fires, even though full-time fire fighters had additional educative, administrative and preventative functions. The House of Lords said the focus should be on the similarity of the jobs rather than the differences. Baroness Hale said:[230]

> ...the extent to which the work that they do is *exactly the same* must be of great importance. If a large component of their work is exactly the same, the question is whether any differences are of such importance as to prevent their work being regarded overall as 'the same or broadly similar'. It is easy to imagine workplaces where both full and part-timers do the same work, but the full-timers have extra activities with which to fill their time. This should not prevent their work being regarded as the same or broadly similar overall....In other words, in answering that question particular weight should be given to the extent to which their work is in fact the same and to the importance of that work to the enterprise as a whole. Otherwise one runs the risk of giving too much weight to differences which are the almost inevitable result of one worker working full-time and another working less than full-time.

On remission from the House of Lords, the tribunal in *Matthews* found that the part-time firefighters were carrying out the same or broadly similar work to the full-time firefighters. There was a substantial body of work comprising the fire-fighter's 'central duties' that were the same for both roles, and the full-timers' additional skills and experience, while relevant, did not contribute 'something different to the work'.

(c) The principle of non-discrimination

The essence of the Directive can be found in Clause 4. This provides that:

1. In respect of *employment conditions*, part-time workers shall not be treated in a less favourable manner than comparable full-time workers *solely* because they work part-time unless different treatment is justified on objective grounds.

2. Where appropriate, the principle of *pro rata temporis* shall apply. (Emphasis added.)

Clause 4(3) concludes: 'The arrangements for the application of this clause shall be defined by the Member States and/or Social Partners, having regard to European legislation, national law, collective agreements and practice'.

---

[228] Para. 62.   [229] [2006] UKHL 8.   [230] Para. 44.

Thus, Clause 4(1) prohibits discrimination against part-timers vis-à-vis full-timers in respect of 'employment conditions'. According to *Bruno*,[231] Clause 4 articulates a principle of EU social law which cannot be 'interpreted restrictively'. This enabled the Court to conclude that the phrase 'employment conditions' is broad enough to include not only pay but also (occupational) pensions,[232] but not pensions forming part of the social security scheme. In the light of the case law on equal pay, it is likely that the Court will ensure equal treatment on a term-for-term basis,[233] rather than looking at the over-all package enjoyed by the part-time and the full-time worker. However, only where the difference in treatment is *solely* (as opposed to mainly or even one of the reasons[234]) based on the grounds of the part-time worker's status is the different treatment unlaw-ful. This is the first limitation on the use of Clause 4(1). The second limitation is that any difference in treatment can be justified on (unspecified) objective grounds.[235] In addi-tion, Clause 4(4) provides:

> When justified by objective reasons, Member States, after consultation of the Social Part-ners in accordance with national law or practice and/or Social Partners may, where appro-priate, make access to particular conditions of employment subject to a period of service, time worked or earnings qualification. Qualifications relating to access by part-time work-ers to particular conditions of employment should be reviewed periodically having regard to the principle of non-discrimination as expressed in clause 4.1.

Thus, the significant feature of Directive 97/81 is that part-time workers no longer have to rely on the difficult concepts of indirect discrimination to make their case to ensure that they are not treated less favourably than full-time workers in respect of working conditions.[236] The Part-time Work Directive will remove the need for two stages of the indirect discrimination analysis. First, the Directive removes the obligation to show that a full-time work requirement has an adverse impact on women in a particular pool: merely discriminating against the part-timer will be unlawful *per se* unless it can be justified. Secondly, it would seem that a worker will not have to show that he or she can-not comply with a full-time work requirement to seek to challenge it: treating full-time and part-time staff differently requires justification of itself. However, these advances come at a price: *direct* discrimination on the grounds of being a part-time worker can be objectively justified.

---

[231] Joined Cases C-395/08 and C-396/08 *INPS* v. *Bruno* [2010] ECR I-000, para. 32.

[232] Joined Cases C-395/08 and C-396/08 *Bruno* [2010] ECR I-000, paras. 24 and 64. See further the case law under Art. 157 as discussed in Ch. 10.

[233] See by analogy Case C-236/98 *Örebro läns landsting* [2000] ECR I-2189.

[234] The English courts have favoured this more relaxed test to bring protection against discrimination against part-time work into line with discrimination on other grounds: *Sharma* v. *Manchester City Council* [2008] IRLR 336 although the Scottish courts adopt a stricter line (*McMenemy* v. *Capita Business Services Ltd* [2007] IRLR 400).

[235] Case 170/84 *Bilka Kaufhaus* v. *Weber von Hartz* [1986] ECR 1607. See further Ch. 4.

[236] Case C-313/02 *Wippel* [2004] ECR I-9483, paras. 30-3 suggests that the phrase 'working conditions' has the same meaning as in Art. 14(1)(c) of Dir. 2006/54. It continues: 'The fact that that type of contract has financial consequences for the worker concerned is not, however, sufficient to bring such conditions within the scope of Art. [157 TFEU]…'.

If, however, the discrimination cannot be justified, the part-timer worker will enjoy equal treatment with the full-time worker subject, *where appropriate*, to the principle of *pro rata temporis*. So, if a full-timer working five days a week enjoys 30 days leave a year, a part-time worker working three days a week will enjoy 3/5ths of that, namely 18 days leave.[237] But where benefits are not easily subject to division, e.g. the use of the company car, then the employer might use the 'where appropriate' clause and not subject them to the pro rata principle or adopt a more imaginative solution (e.g. providing the part-time workers with a less valuable car).

It is, however, remarkable that, despite the existence of the Part-time Work Directive, the Court continues to decide cases based on the existing Equal Treatment Directives. *Steinicke*[238] is one such case. Although the case largely predated the Directive, the Court was not prepared to consider Directive 97/81 at all because the scheme fell within the scope of Article 14 of the Sex Equality Directive 2006/54.

(d) Encouragement of part-time work

Much of the remainder of Directive 97/81 has the feel of an exhortatory resolution rather than a hard law measure.[239] Clause 5(1) charges the Member States and, within their spheres of responsibility, the Social Partners, with responsibility for identifying and, where possible, removing obstacles (in legislation, administrative practice, and collective agreements) to part-time work. This particular provision could be read as inviting the removal of protective legislation which, according to neo-liberal thinking, might hinder opportunities for part-time work. Although it is too broadly phrased to amount to an instruction to deregulate, it could be prayed in aid by a Member State to justify the exclusion of part-time workers from protective measures. However, the obligation to remove such obstacles is subject to the principle of non-discrimination and to the non-regression provision found in Clause 6(2). In fact, the only case where this provision has been considered is *Michaeler*,[240] where the Court used Clause 5(1) to remove an obligation on all employers to notify part-time contracts to the relevant authorities because it discouraged employers from making use of part-time work.[241]

The Directive also considers the question of the movement of workers from full-time to part-time work, and vice versa. A worker's refusal to transfer from the one form of work to the other is not to constitute, of itself, a valid ground for dismissal;[242] conversely, the employer must give consideration to requests by workers to transfer between full-time and part-time work[243] and must provide information about opportunities for transfers.[244] However, it is not required to accede to workers' requests. Finally, the least

---

[237] Case C–486/08 *Zentralbetriebsrat der Landeskrankenhäuser Tirols* v. *Land Tirol* [2010] ECR I–000, para. 33. That principle cannot, however, be retrospectively applied to leave entitlement accrued during periods of full-time work.

[238] Case C–77/02 *Steinicke* v. *Bundesanstalt für Arbeit* [2003] ECR I–9027, para. 52.

[239] C. Barnard and B. Hepple, 'Substantive Equality' (2000) 59 *CLJ* 562, 582 cf. C. Kilpatrick and M. Freedland, 'The United Kingdom: How is EU Governance Transformative?' in S. Sciarra *et al.*, previously, at n. 107, 329.

[240] Joined Cases C–55/07 and C–56/07 *Michaeler* v. *Amt für sozialen Arbeitsschutz* [2008] ECR I–3135.

[241] Para. 28.   [242] Clause 5(2).   [243] Clause 5(3)(a) and (b).   [244] Clause 5(3)(c) and (e).

strong provision in clause 5 provides that employers should give consideration to measures to facilitate access to part-time work at all levels in the enterprise, including skilled
and managerial positions, and, where appropriate, to facilitate access by part-time
workers to vocational training to enhance career opportunities and occupational
mobility.[245]

The Court has already considered the situation of a part-time worker—a job sharer—
wishing to return to full-time work under Article 157 TFEU. In *Hill*[246] two women who
had shared a job found themselves at a disadvantage when they converted to full-time
employment when compared with those who had worked on a full-time basis for the
same number of years. When converting, a job-sharing worker was placed on the full-
time pay scale at a level below that which she had previously occupied on the pay scale
applicable to job-sharing staff and, consequently, at a level lower than that of a full-time
worker employed for the same period of time. The court noted that 99.2 per cent of
clerical assistants who job-shared were women, as were 98 per cent of all civil servants
employed under job-sharing contracts and so a provision which adversely affected the
legal position of those workers had discriminatory effects based on sex.[247] Because the
rule was indirectly discriminatory, the defendants had to establish before the national
court that the rule could be objectively justified.[248]

4. FIXED-TERM WORK

4.1. Introduction

In the Preamble to the Part-time Work Agreement the Social Partners announced their
intention to consider the need for similar agreements relating to other forms of flexible
work. On 23 March 1998, the European Social Partners said they would start negotiations on fixed-term work. They concluded a framework agreement on 18 March 1999
which the Council put into effect by Directive 99/70 on 28 June 1999.[249]

The purpose of the 1999 agreement is to 'improve the quality of fixed-term work by
ensuring the application of the principle of non-discrimination; and to establish a
framework to prevent abuse arising from the use of successive fixed term employment contracts or relationships'.[250] Thus, unlike the Part-time Work Directive the dual
purpose of the Fixed-term Work Directive is not so stark. The Fixed-term Work
Directive is more obviously about worker protection, a point recognized by the Court
in *Adeneler*: 'the benefit of stable employment is viewed as a major element in the
protection of workers …, whereas it is only in certain circumstances that fixed term
employment contracts are liable to respond to the needs of both employers and workers'.[251] In *Kumpan*[252] the Court went further: the use of fixed-term contracts as opposed
to contracts of indefinite duration is therefore 'exceptional'. That said, the Preamble to

---

[245] Clause 5(3)(d).   [246] Case C–243/95 *Kathleen Hill and Ann Stapleton* [1998] ECR I–3739, para. 42.
[247] Para. 25.   [248] Para. 43.   [249] OJ [1999] L175/143.   [250] Clause 1.
[251] Case C–212/04 *Adeneler* [2006] ECR I–6057, para. 62.
[252] Case C–109/09 *Deutsche Lufthansa AG* v. *Kumpan* [2011] ECR I–000, para. 30.

both the Directive and the Framework Agreement refer to the EES and, in particular to the need to achieve a better balance between 'flexibility in working time and security for workers'.

4.2. Personal scope

The Directive applies to 'fixed-term *workers* who have an employment contract or employment relationship as defined in law, collective agreements or practice in each Member State'.[253] It covers workers in both the public and private sector.[254] Controversially, the UK has limited its application to 'employees' only.[255] Clause 3 provides that '*fixed-term* worker' means 'a person having an employment contract or relationship entered into directly between an employer and a worker where the end of the employment contract or relationship is determined by objective conditions such as reaching a specific date, completing a specific task, or the occurrence of a specific event'. The Preamble to the agreement makes clear that the 'agreement applies to fixed term workers with the exception of those placed by a temporary work agency at the disposition of a user enterprise', since the Social Partners intend to 'consider the need' for a similar agreement relating to temporary agency work (see later).

In addition, Member States, after consultation with the Social Partners, and/or the Social Partners themselves, may provide that the Directive does not apply to:[256]

(a) initial vocational training relationships and apprenticeship schemes;

(b) employment contracts and relationships which have been concluded within the framework of a specific public or publicly supported training, integration and vocational retraining programme.

4.3. Equal treatment

The Directive contains three main rights for fixed-term workers. First, as with the Part-time Work Directive, the principle of non-discrimination applies. Clause 4(1) provides that in respect of employment conditions, fixed-term workers are not to be treated in a less favourable manner than comparable permanent workers solely because they have a fixed-term contract or relationship unless justified on objective grounds.[257] Where appropriate, the principle of *pro rata temporis* applies.[258] The Court said in *Impact* that Clause 4 must be 'interpreted as articulating a principle of [Union] social law which cannot be interpreted restrictively'.[259]

The term 'comparable permanent worker' means a worker (1) with an employment contract or relationship of indefinite duration, (2) in the same establishment, (3) engaged

---

[253] Clause 2.   [254] Case C–212/04 *Adeneler* [2006] ECR I–6057, para. 55.   [255] See further Ch. 4.

[256] Clause 2(2).

[257] The arrangements for the application of Clause 4(1) are to be defined by the Member States after consultation with the Social Partners, and/or the Social Partners, having regard to Union law, national law, collective agreements and practice. According to Case C–268/06 *Impact* v. *Minster for Agriculture* [2008] ECR I–2483, para. 80. Clause 4(1) is directly effective.

[258] Clause 4(2).   [259] Case C–268/06 *Impact* [2008] ECR I–2483.

in the same or similar work/occupation, due regard being given to qualifications/skills.[260] These terms are likely to be interpreted in a similar way to their equivalents in the Part-time Work Directive. Where there is no comparable permanent worker in the same establishment, the comparison is to be made by reference to the applicable collective agreement, or where there is no applicable collective agreement, in accordance with national law, collective agreements or practice.[261] This would suggest that where there is no permanent comparator in the same establishment, the fixed-term worker can look to employees in the employer's other establishments but not to former employees or hypothetical comparators.

Clause 4(1) applies to 'employment conditions'. These include pay and occupational pensions,[262] and length of service allowance.[263] The case law contains a wide range of examples of less favourable treatment such as exclusion from a pension scheme, a redundancy policy, eligibility for service-related pay.[264] The prohibition against discrimination is also likely to cover other disadvantages for fixed-term employees such as being denied promotion opportunities. However, the expiry of the fixed-term contract, in and of itself, is unlikely to constitute discrimination since this is the essence of a fixed-term contract.

The less favourable treatment must be 'solely' because the individual has a fixed-term contract. As with the Part-time Work Directive this raises issues as to causation and whether a lower threshold (e.g. mainly connected with, or even one of the causes) would suffice which is the test elsewhere in discrimination law. The pro rata principle also applies[265] so that a fixed-term worker on a six month contract cannot complain of discrimination if he receives only 50 per cent of the bonus of a full-time worker.

Again, as with the Part-time Work Directive, the principle of non-discrimination is subject to objective justification. The test for this is likely to be similar to that laid down in *Bilka-Kaufhaus*:[266] (1) the different treatment must serve a legitimate aim; (2) must be necessary to achieve that aim; and must be appropriate to achieve that aim. One example might be where a fixed-term worker on a three-month contract is not given his own company car, while his permanent comparator does receive one, where the business need for the fixed-term worker to travel can be met in some other way (e.g. use of a pool car).

The Court of Justice is, only now, beginning to provide some guidance on the meaning of the phrase objective justification. For example, in *Del Cerro Alonso*,[267] the Court relying on the case law interpreting Clause 5(1)(a) (see later), said that the concept objective reasons must be understood as referring to 'precise and concrete circum-

---

[260] Clause 3(2).   [261] Clause 3(2), second paragraph.
[262] Case C–307/05 *Del Cerro Alonso v. Osakidetza-Servicio Vasco de salud* [2007] ECR I–7109; Case C–268/06 *Impact v. Minster for Agriculture* [2008] ECR I–2483.
[263] Case C–307/05 *Del Cerro Alonso* [2007] ECR I–7109.
[264] Joined Cases C–444/09 and C–456/09 *Gavieiro Gavieiro and Iglesias Torres* [2010] ECR I–000; Case C–177/10 *Rosado Santana* [2011] ECR I–000.
[265] Clause 4(2).   [266] Case 170/84[2004] ECR I–9483.
[267] Case C–307/05 *Del Cerro Alonso* [2007] ECR I–7109, para. 53.

stances characterising a given activity, which are therefore capable, in that particular context' of justifying a difference in treatment. So it is not possible to objectively justify a difference in treatment between fixed term and permanent employees simply because the collective agreement or statute says so[268] or because the contract is temporary.[269] Nor, according to the Court in *Land Tirol*,[270] are arguments based on budgetary considerations, such as 'rigorous personnel management', acceptable justifications. On the other hand, the Court said in *Rosado Santana*[271] the differences in treatment based on the qualifications required and the nature of the duties undertaken could justify a difference in treatment.

Finally, clause 4(4) provides that period of service qualifications relating to particular conditions of employment are to be the same for fixed-term workers as for permanent workers except where different length of service qualifications are justified on objective grounds.

4.4. Use of successive fixed-term contracts

The second pillar of protection found in the Directive concerns the prevention of abuse of fixed-term contracts. In countries such as the UK there were, prior to the Directive, no limits on the number of occasions on which fixed-term contracts could be renewed and in some sectors (notably the media and higher education) repeated use of fixed-term contracts was widespread. As a result, Clause 5(1) provides that:

> …Member States, after consultation with social partners in accordance with national law, collective agreements or practice, and/or the social partners, shall, where there are no equivalent legal measures to prevent abuse,[272] introduce in a manner which takes account of the needs of specific sectors and/or categories of workers, one or more of the following measures:
>
> a) objective reasons justifying the renewal of such contracts or relationships;[273]
>
> b) the maximum total duration of successive fixed-term employment contracts or relationships;[274]
>
> c) the number of renewals of such contracts or relationships.

---

[268] Para. 59.

[269] Joined Cases C–444/09 and C–456/09 *Gavieiro Gavieiro and Iglesias Torres* [2010] ECR I–000.

[270] Case C–486/08 [2010] ECR I–000, para. 46.

[271] Case C–177/10 *Rosado Santana* [2011] ECR I–000.

[272] This principle is discussed in Joined Case C–378/07 to C–380/07 *Angelidaki* v. *Organismos Nomarkhiaki Aftodiikisi Rethimnis* [2009] ECR I–3071.

[273] Joined Case C–378/07 to C–380/07 *Angelidaki* [2009] ECR I–3071: this provision does not apply to the first or single use of a fixed-term contract.

[274] Member States after consultation with the Social Partners, and/or the Social Partners, shall, where appropriate, determine under what conditions fixed-term employment contracts or relationships: (a) shall be regarded as 'successive'; (b) shall be deemed to be contracts or relationships of an indefinite duration (Clause 5(2)).

Thus Member States have a significant margin of appreciation as to how to implement this provision,[275] discretion which must be exercised in compliance with EU law and in particular the general principles and other provision of the framework agreement.[276] The UK has implemented this provision by saying that a renewal of a fixed-term contract after four years will become a permanent contract[277] unless there are objectively justifiable reasons why not. Therefore, an employee with a two-year fixed-term contract that is renewed and followed by a three-year fixed-term contract will become permanent after four years' service (i.e. 2/3 of the way through the second contract) unless there are objectively justified reason as to why it should not. Likewise, employees with a five-year fixed-term contract which is extended by a further two-year fixed-term contract will discover that their contract has become permanent[278] at the moment of renewal unless there are objective reasons why not. The key issue is the fact of renewal: an employee on one five-year fixed-term contract will never enjoy permanent status under the UK's implementing rules. Unlike some Continental systems, such as Germany, the (initial) use of a fixed-term contract in the UK does not need justification.

So what then constitutes objective justification? In *Adeneler*[279] the Court, when interpreting Clause 5(1)(a), said that the concept of 'objective reasons' referred to 'precise and concrete circumstances characterising a given activity, which are capable in that particular context of justifying the use of successive fixed term contracts'. In other words, the employer must point to the presence of 'specific factors relating in particular to the activity in question and the conditions under which it is carried out'.[280] The mere fact that the use of fixed-term contracts was provided for in national law 'in a general and abstract manner' could not be an objective reason[281] In *Kücük*[282] the Court said that the temporary replacement of another employee in order to satisfy, in essence, the employer's temporary staffing requirements could, in principle, constitute an objective reason under clause 5(1)(a), especially when the cover is being provided for other staff taking other types of EU leave such as maternity or parental leave. However, on the facts, Ms *Kücük* had had 13 fixed-term contracts over 11 years. The Commission said that this amounted to abuse. The Court was less categoric: 'It is for all the authorities of the Member State concerned to ensure, for matters within their respective spheres of competence, that clause 5(1)(a) of the FTW Framework Agreement is complied with by

---

[275] Case C–212/04 *Adeneler* [2006] ECR I–6057, para. 68.

[276] Case C–109/09 *Kumpan* [2011] ECR I–000, para. 37.

[277] Case C–251/11 *Huet v. Université de Bretagne Occidentale* [2012] ECR I–000 says that when a fixed-term contract is converted to a permanent contract, the principal terms of the fixed term and the permanent contract do not need to be identical but there must not be material amendments that are overall unfavourable to the employee.

[278] This does not have to be the sanction if other Member States exercise their discretion to choose another remedy, provided the remedy is effective and punishes the abuse of successive fixed-term contracts: Case C–53/04 *Marrosu v. Azienda Ospedaliera Ospedale San Martino di Genova e Cliniche Universitarie Convenzionate* [2006] ECR I–7213.

[279] Case C–212/04 *Adeneler* [2006] ECR I–6057, para. 69.

[280] Ibid., para. 75.   [281] Para. 71.

[282] Case C–586/10 *Kücük v. Land Nordrhein-Westfalen* [2012] ECR I–000, para. 30.

ascertaining that the renewal of successive fixed-term employment contracts or relationships is actually intended to cover temporary needs' and that the possibility of hiring one employee temporarily to replace another is 'not, in fact, being used to meet fixed and permanent needs'.[283] Factors that the authorities should take into account include the number of successive contracts concluded with the same person or for the purposes of performing the same work[284] and the circumstances surrounding the renewal of those employment contracts or relationships.[285] The Court has also stamped on other avoidance techniques. For example, in *Adeneler* it said that a national rule, under which fixed-term contracts that were separated from one another by a period of more than 20 working days could not be regarded as successive, was not compatible with the Fixed-Term Work Directive.[286]

So how might the rules on objective justification apply in practice? Take a rather familiar example of a researcher working in a university being awarded a grant for five years. The researcher is given a five-year fixed-term contract. In the UK, at least, this initial decision does not need to be objectively justified. At the end of that five-year period some more money is found to give the researcher another two years of employment to finish the research. In principle, the renewal would trigger the provision on abuse and so that second contract would become permanent unless an objectively justified case could be made as to why not. Here the justification would relate to the limited pot of money and the completion of the research. The second contract would therefore probably continue to be fixed term.

4.5. The right to information

The third right given by the Directive to fixed-term workers relates to information. Clause 6(1) requires employers to inform fixed-term workers about vacancies (all vacancies and not just suitable vacancies) which become available in the undertaking or establishment by, for example, displaying a general announcement at a suitable place in the undertaking, to ensure that fixed-term workers have the same opportunity to secure permanent positions as other workers. Clause 6(2) adds that, as far as possible, employers should facilitate access by fixed-term workers to appropriate training opportunities to enhance their skills, career development, and occupational mobility. Clause 7(1) requires that fixed-term workers be taken into consideration in calculating the threshold above which workers' representative bodies provided for in national and Community law may be constituted in the undertaking as required by national provisions.[287] In addition, Clause 7(2) requires employers, as far as possible, to give consideration to the provision of appropriate information to existing workers' representative bodies about fixed-term work in the undertaking.

---

[283] Para. 39.   [284] Para. 40.   [285] Para. 43.

[286] Case C–212/04 *Adeneler* [2006] ECR I–6057, para. 89.

[287] The arrangements for the application of Clause 7.1 are to be defined by Member States after consultation with the Social Partners and/or the Social Partners in accordance with national law, collective agreements or practice and having regard to Clause 4.1.

4.6. Implementation

Directive 99/70 is a minimum standards Directive: Member States and/or the social partners can maintain or introduce provisions more favourable to workers.[288] The Directive also contains a non-regression clause: Clause 8(3) provides that the implementation of the agreement shall not constitute valid grounds for reducing the general level of protection afforded to workers. In *Sorge*[289] the Court said that in the light of its objectives Clause 8(3) of the framework agreement cannot be interpreted restrictively and that the existence of a 'reduction' for the purposes of Clause 8(3) of the framework agreement must be considered in relation to the whole of a Member State's domestic law relating to the protection of workers in the context of fixed-term employment contracts. This implies that only a reduction on a scale likely to have an effect *overall* on national legislation relating to fixed-term employment contracts is capable of being covered by Clause 8(3) of the framework agreement.[290] Thus a reduction in protection affecting only a limited category of workers is not sufficient to trigger Clause 8(3).[291] Alternatively, where the reduction in protection is offset by other safeguards or protective measures, Clause 8(3) is also not breached.[292] The Court in *Sorge* also said that because Clause 8(3) of the framework agreement has no direct effect, it is for the national court, if it should be led to conclude that the national legislation at issue in the main proceedings is incompatible with European Union law, not to disapply it but, so far as possible, to give it an interpretation in conformity with Directive 99/70 and with the objective pursued by the framework agreement.[293]

Clause 8(4) allows the social partners 'to conclude at the appropriate level...agreements adapting and/or complementing the provision of this agreement in a manner which will take note of the specific needs of the social partners concerned'. The UK has taken advantage of this provision to allow collective agreements or, where there is no recognized trade union, workforce agreements, to be used to vary the rules on successive fixed-term contracts by, for example, increasing or decreasing the four-year limit.[294]

4.7. Remedies

Clause 8(5) says that the prevention and settlement of disputes and grievances arising from the application of the agreement shall be dealt with in accordance with national law, collective agreements and practice. The Court applied its standard case law on effective remedies to this provision. So in *Impact*[295] it said that the principle of effectiveness, requires that where, as in that case, a specialized court was called upon to

---

[288] Clause 8(1).   [289] Case C–98/09 *Sorge* v. *Poste Italiane* [2010] ECR I–5837, para. 34.
[290] Para. 42.
[291] See additionally Joined Case C–378/07 to C–380/07 *Angelidaki* v. *Organismos Nomarkhiaki Aftodiikisi Rethimnis* [2009] ECR I–3071.
[292] Para. 47.   [293] Para. 55.
[294] For discussion about the limited use made of this provision, see A. Koukiadaki, 'Case Law Developments in the Area of Fixed-Term Work' (2009) 38 *ILJ* 89.
[295] Case C–268/06 *Impact* [2008] ECR I–2483, para. 55.

hear and determine a claim based on an infringement of the legislation implementing Directive 99/70, it also had to have jurisdiction to hear and determine an applicant's claims arising directly from the Directive itself. This applied in respect of the period between the deadline for transposing the Directive and the date on which the transposing legislation entered into force if it was established that the obligation on that applicant to bring, at the same time, a separate claim based directly on the Directive before an ordinary court would involve procedural disadvantages liable to render excessively difficult the exercise of the rights conferred on him by Union law. It is for the national court to undertake the necessary checks in that regard.

5. AGENCY WORK

5.1. Introduction

Addressing the problems experienced by agency workers was always going to prove the most problematic for the Union legislature, due to the triangulation of the relationships involved. Agency workers (temps) are usually employed by an agency (a temping agency) which then offers their services to a user undertaking which normally controls the individual's day to day activities (see Fig. 9.1). Where the engagement with the user is for a short term, then it is likely that the agency remains the temp's employer. But where the engagement is for a longer term, the position is much less clear.

Although negotiations between the *intersectoral* social partners on this subject started in May 2000, they proved difficult and eventually broke down a year later over

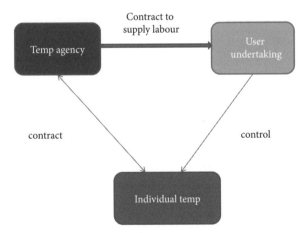

Fig. 9.1. The triangulation of employment relationships in temping situations.

the issue of the definition of a comparable worker for the purposes of equal treatment (the ETUC had insisted on a comparator being a worker in the user undertaking, UNICE (now BusinessEurope) rejected this). In October 2001 the *sectoral* Social Partners Euro-CIETT (the European Committee of the International Confederation of Temporary Work Businesses) and Uni-Europa (the European regional organization of Union Network International) issued a joint declaration on temporary agency work which, they hoped, would form the basis for a future European Directive. Indeed, in March 2002 the Commission put forward a proposal for a Directive on agency work[296] which built on the sectoral partners' joint declaration and on those areas where the intersectoral Social Partners had been able to agree.

Directive 2008/104, a minimum standards measure,[297] was eventually adopted in November 2008. It is more limited in its objectives than the sectoral partners' declaration (e.g. it contains no Article prohibiting temp agencies from making workers available to user undertakings in order to replace striking workers[298]) but it retains the basic dual aim: on the one hand to improve the quality of temporary work by ensuring that the principle of non-discrimination is applied to temporary workers (reference is made in the first preambular paragraph to Article 31 of the Charter) and, on the other, to establish a suitable framework for the use of temporary work to contribute to the creation of jobs and the development of flexible forms of working,[299] as well as enabling employees to reconcile their working and private lives.[300] The overriding message from the Directive is that temp work is good and should be encouraged.[301] This is a far cry from the position in a number of Member States up until the 1980s, where agency work was actually prohibited or very strictly controlled.[302]

---

[296] COM(2002)149 final.

[297] Art. 9. A non-regression clause can be found in Art. 9(2). The remedies clause is in Article 10. For a discussion of the implementation of the Directive in the UK, France, the Netherlands, Spain, and Sweden, see (2010) 1 *European Labour Law Journal*.

[298] Although cf. the 20th Recital which says that the provisions of the Dir. are without prejudice to national legislation or practices that prohibit workers on strike being replaced by temporary agency workers. As N. Countouris and R. Horton point out ('The Temporary Agency Work Directive: Another Broken Promise' (2009) 38 *ILJ* 329, 336), the Directive should have introduced a positive duty not to make agency workers available to a user undertaking to replace workers exercising their right to strike, as required by para. 6 of ILO Private Employment Agencies Recommendation C–188 of 1997.

[299] Art. 2.   [300] 11th Recital.

[301] Art. 4 of the Dir. Requires the Member States and the social partners to review their legislation and collective agreements for restrictions or prohibitions on the use of agency work unless those restrictions can be justified on the grounds of 'general interest relating in particular to the protection of temporary agency workers, the requirements of health and safety at work or the need to ensure that the labour market functions properly and abuses are prevented'.

[302] See e.g. Case C–279/00 *Commission v. Italy* [2009] ECR I–1425. This point was recognized in the 10th recital of the Dir.

5.2. Scope

The Directive applies to workers with a contract of employment or employment relationship with a temporary work agency[303] who are assigned[304] to user undertakings[305] to
work temporarily under their supervision and direction. It applies to public and private
undertakings which are temporary-work agencies or user undertakings engaged in
economic activities whether or not they are operating for gain,[306] although Member
States may, after consulting the social partners, provide that the Directive does not
apply to employment contracts or relationships concluded under a specific public or
publicly-supported vocational training, integration or retraining programme.[307]

Once again, the language of 'workers' is used; and once again reference is made to the
national systems. Article 3(1)(a) says that ' "worker" means any person who, in the
Member State concerned, is protected as a worker under national employment law'. For
good measure, Article 3(2) adds that the Directive is without prejudice to national law
as regards the definition of 'contract of employment, employment relationship or
worker', although the Directive does provide that Member States must not exclude from
the scope of the Directive 'workers, contracts of employment or employment relationships solely because they relate to part-time workers, fixed-term contract workers or
persons with a contract of employment or employment relationship with a temporary
work agency.'

The question of who is a worker is significant because, as we saw in *Allonby*, agencies,
in order to circumvent obligations as employers, describe staff employed by them as
'self-employed' and so outside the scope of employment legislation. In some cases the
legislation may apply the rules to such staff anyway regardless of their professed status.[308] The UK rules implementing the Directive seem particularly narrow: they apply
to employees (an individual who has a contract of employment with the agency) as well
as the (very small) group of individuals who have 'any other contract to perform work
and services personally for the agency'.[309] The UK implementing regulations are also
interesting because they apply not only to agency workers who find temporary work
through a temporary work agency but also agency workers contracted via an 'umbrella
company' or other intermediary.[310] However, the Regulations do not apply to the genuinely self-employed, or those who are employed on a managed service contract or in-
house staffing banks.

---

[303] Art. 3(1)(b) 'temporary-work agency' means any natural or legal person who, in compliance with national
law, concludes contracts of employment or employment relationships with temporary agency workers in order
to assign them to user undertakings to work there temporarily under their supervision and direction.

[304] Art. 3(1)(e) 'assignment' means the period during which the temporary agency worker is placed at the
user undertaking to work temporarily under its supervision and direction.

[305] Art. 3(1)(d) 'user undertaking' means any natural or legal person for whom and under the supervision
and direction of whom a temporary agency worker works temporarily.

[306] Art. 1(2).   [307] Art. 1(3).

[308] See e.g. Reg. 36 of SI 1998/1833 The Working Time Regulations 1998.

[309] Reg. 3(1) of SI 2010/93 The Agency Workers Regulations 2010.

[310] Regs 3(3)–(5).

5.3. Equal treatment

On the crucial issue of equal treatment, Article 5(1) provides that temporary workers shall, during their assignment with the user, enjoy at least the *basic* working and employment conditions (a qualification not found in the other Directives), laid down by legislation, regulations, administrative provisions, collective agreements, and/or other binding general provisions in force in the *user* undertaking[311] (relating to the duration of working time, overtime, breaks, rest periods, night work, holidays, public holidays, pay,[312] as well as the rules on maternity protection, protection of children and young workers, and rules on non-discrimination on the grounds of sex and those areas covered in the Article 19 Directives[313]), as those that 'would apply if they had been recruited directly by that undertaking to occupy the same job'.

The rather unusual language in Article 5(1) contains an implicit reference a comparator but no substantive guidance about that comparator. Presumably the comparator would be a person engaged in the same or broadly similar work involving a similar level of qualifications and skills working at the same establishment as the agency worker or at different establishments with common terms and conditions. The Directive leaves open the question whether the comparator needs to be actual or whether hypothetical suffices. The language of 'would' suggests that a hypothetical comparator should be acceptable. The Directive also leaves open the question as to whether the comparator should be a person on a permanent contract with the user or someone on a short fixed-term contract. In the latter case, the fixed-term worker might have inferior terms and conditions vis-à-vis permanent workers for objectively justified reasons.

The Directive then contains a number of important limitations to the general principle of equality. Member States can decide not to apply the principle of equal treatment in respect of pay to temporary agency workers who have a permanent contract of employment with the temp agency and who continue to be paid between postings, the so-called 'Swedish' derogation.[314] Member States can also allow the Social Partners to conclude collective agreements which derogate from the principle of equal treatment in Article 5(1), provided an adequate overall level of protection is given to temporary workers.[315] Most significantly, the Directive provides for a derogation from the principle of equal treatment in a system, such as the UK's, where there is no possibility for declaring collective agreements universally applicable. The Member State, while ensuring an adequate level of protection for the temporary agency workers, and after consulting the social partners and on the basis of an agreement concluded by them, must establish arrangements concerning the basic working and employment conditions. This includes the possibility of introducing a service period[316] (in the UK's case, 12 weeks which, according to the government's own evidence, has the effect of depriving of protection the 55 per cent of agency work-

---

[311] Art. 3(1)(f).

[312] Pay is to be defined in accordance with national law: Art. 3(2). It is likely to cover basic play plus other contractual entitlements that are directly undertaken by the agency worker while on assignment. However, Art. 5(4), second para. requires Member States to specify whether occupational social security schemes, including pension, sick pay or financial participation schemes are incuded in the definition of pay.

[313] Art. 5(1) second para.   [314] Art. 5(2).   [315] Art. 5(3).   [316] Art. 5(4).

ers with contracts of less than 12 weeks). More generally, Member States must introduce measures to prevent avoidance of these rules and, in particular, prevent successive assignments designed to circumvent provision of the Directive.[317]

These derogations, combined with the limitation that the agency worker enjoys only the basic employment conditions in the user undertaking, mean that there is no possibility for objectively justifying any general less favourable treatment[318] (unlike the position under the Part-time Work and Fixed-term Work Directives). In effect the derogations and the limitations determine ex ante the sorts of matters that might otherwise be raised as objective justification.

5.4. Access to employment and facilities

The Directive also lays down a range of rights to give the temp every chance of being employed on a permanent basis by the user, '[e]mployment contracts of an indefinite duration [being] the general form of employment relationship'.[319] So, from the *start* of their assignment, an agency worker has the right to be told of any relevant vacancies in the hirer during the assignment,[320] and any national rule prohibiting the temp and the user from concluding a contract of employment or an employment relationship is null and void (although the agency can still receive a reasonable fee for the assignment, recruitment and training of the temp).[321] Temp agencies cannot charge any fees for arranging for the temp to be recruited by a user undertaking or for concluding a contract of employment with the user after carrying out an assignment.[322]

Article 6(4) expands the basis for equal treatment. It provides that without prejudice to Article 5(1), temporary agency workers must be given 'access to the amenities or collective facilities in the user undertaking, in particular any canteen, child-care facilities and transport services, under the same conditions as workers employed directly by the undertaking'. This time, unlike under Article 5(1), a difference in treatment can be objectively justified.

5.5. Collective matters

The Directive makes provision for dialogue with the social partners to improve temporary agency workers' access to training and to child-care facilities in the temporary-work agencies, even in the periods between their assignments, in order to enhance their career development and employability and to improve temporary agency workers' access to training for user undertakings' workers.[323] In order to ensure the representation of temps, Member States can choose whether to make temps count for the purpose of calculating the threshold for forming worker representative bodies either at the agency or at the user undertaking.[324] In addition, the user undertaking must provide suitable information on the use of temporary agency workers when providing information on the employment situation in that undertaking to bodies representing workers set up in accordance with national and EU legislation, in particular the Information and Consultation Directive 2002/14.[325]

---

[317] Art. 5(5).   [318] Cf. Art. 6(4).   [319] 15th Recital.   [320] Art. 6(1).   [321] Art. 6(2).
[322] Art. 6(3).   [323] Art. 6(5).   [324] Art. 7.   [325] Art. 8.

6. TELEWORK

Although the EU social partners did not manage to agree a measure on agency work, they did manage to conclude an intersectoral agreement on telework.[326] and two sectoral agreements in commerce and telecommunications. The intersectoral agreement, one of the first 'autonomous agreements' to be implemented at national level by collective agreement rather than through legally binding measures derived from a Directive,[327] is intended to facilitate telework 'both as a way for companies and public service organisations to modernise work organisation, and as a way for workers to reconcile work and social life and giving them greater autonomy in the accomplishment of their tasks'. Thus, the telework agreement falls squarely within the Lisbon priorities. As the Social Partners put it, 'If Europe wants to make the most out of the information society, it must encourage this new form of work organisation in such a way, that flexibility and security go together and the quality of jobs is enhanced, and that the chances of disabled people on the labour market are increased'.

The agreement defines telework as 'a form of organising and/or performing work, using information technology, in the context of an employment contract/relationship, where work, which could also be performed at the employer's premises, is carried out away from those premises on a regular basis'. It also emphasizes that telework is voluntary for the worker and the employer and that a worker's refusal to opt for telework is not, as such, a reason for terminating the employment relationship or changing the terms and conditions of employment of that worker. Further, if telework is not part of the original job description the decision to move to telework is reversible by individual and/or collective agreement.

The agreement then details a number of substantive rights for teleworkers and obligations for employers. These include the requirement that:

- the employer is to provide teleworkers with the relevant written information as required by Directive 91/533[328] but supplemented by information connected with telework (e.g. the department to which the teleworkers is attached, his/her immediate superior);[329]

- teleworkers benefit from the same rights, guaranteed by applicable legislation and collective agreements, as comparable workers at the employers' premises, although specific collective agreements may be needed to take into account the particularities of telework.[330] They also enjoy the same collective rights as workers at the employer's premises;[331]

- the employer is responsible for ensuring the protection of the data used and processed by the teleworkers and for respecting the teleworker's privacy;[332]

---

[326] <http://resourcecentre.etuc.org/Agreements-57.html> (last accessed 31 March 2012).
[327] See further Ch. 2.   [328] OJ [1991] L288/32 considered further in Ch. 12.   [329] Clause 3.
[330] Clause 4.   [331] Clause 11.   [332] Clauses 5 and 6.

- generally the employer is responsible for providing, installing and maintaining the equipment necessary for regular telework unless the teleworker uses his/her own equipment. If telework is performed on a regular basis the employer compensates or covers the costs directly caused by the work, in particular those relating to communication;[333]

- the employer is responsible for the protection of the teleworker's health and safety in accordance with the Framework Directive on health and safety 89/391 and its daughters,[334] together with the teleworker's training.[335] Teleworkers can manage their own time but the workload and performance standards must be equivalent to those of comparable workers at the employer's premises.[336] The employer is also responsible for ensuring that the teleworker is not isolated from the rest of the working community in the company.[337]

This Directive is innovative in terms of its method of implementation, relying as it does solely on the Social Partners rather than the Member States for its implementation. However, the absence of a Directive, and thus the lack of an obligation for the Member States to guarantee the outcome, has meant that this agreement lacks the visibility of its predecessors.

7. ASSESSMENT

During the 1980s, the Commission attempted to *limit* the use of temporary work.[338] In a proposed Directive of 1982[339] it listed limited grounds in which fixed-term and temporary work provided by employment agencies could be used. In the intervening 15 or so years there was a sea change in attitude and now the focus is on *encouraging* atypical work as part of the agenda of modernizing 'the organisation of work, including flexible working arrangements, with the aim of making undertakings productive and competitive and achieving the required balance between flexibility and security'.[340] The two Directives on Part-time and Fixed-term Work do attempt to reconcile, on the one hand, demand-side needs for numerical flexibility, allowing the firm to modulate the numbers employed, and supply-side needs for family friendly policies. In respect of those working part time in the EU there may be a degree of coalescence of interests: from the employer's point of view part-time work provides the flexibility necessary to meet changing consumer demands. From the worker's point of view it provides the flexibility

---

[333] Clause 7.   [334] Clause 8, considered further in Ch. 11.   [335] Clause 10.   [336] Clause 9.
[337] Ibid. See further Commission Recommendation 98/370/EC on the ratification of ILO Convention No. 177 on homework of 20 June 1996 (notified under Doc. No. C(1998)764) (OJ [1998] L165/32).
[338] See J. Murray, 'Normalising Temporary Work' (1999) 28 *ILJ* 269.
[339] OJ [1982] C128/2.
[340] Council Resolution of 15 December 1997 on the 1998 Employment Guidelines (OJ [1998] C30/1). See additionally the Supiot report, *Transformation of Labour Law in Europe* (June 1998), para. 755, and D. Ashiagbor, 'Promoting Precariousness? The Response of the EU Employment Policies to Precarious Work' in J. Fudge (ed.), *Precarious Work, Women and the New Economy* (Hart Publishing, Oxford, 2006).

to make it easier to combine work with other family responsibilities.[341] Through the principle of non-discrimination the Directives provide a degree of protection for these workers in respect of employment conditions but not in respect of job security. This leads Bell to conclude that the text of the Directives suggest that their rationale is strongly linked to the pursuit of flexicurity, 'albeit with a stronger accent on flexibility than security'. This is particularly clear in the case of the Agency Work Directive, the first hard law social measure adopted by the EU after the launch of the flexicurity agenda in 2006–7.[342] The Directive is fully signed up to the new discourse when it talks of flexicurity striking 'a balance between flexibility and security in the labour market and help both workers and employers to seize the opportunities offered by globalisation'.[343] Countouris and Horton argue that what in fact emerges is a 'regulatory instrument that seeks to remove any remaining stigma, restriction or prohibition, associated with temporary agency work without providing for a sufficiently protective, equitable and fair regulatory regime'.[344] Worse still is the fact that all three directives are precluded on the idea that it is legitimate that workers—not employers—bear the [...] of flexibility.

However, Bell notes that the Court of Justice has rejected the labour market orientation of the Directives, and so has refused to interpret the principle of equal treatment in a highly flexible manner.[345] Rather, he says, the Court favours the more traditional social rights based approach. But, he makes one major caveat to this observation. He suggests that the Court's use of the comparator test acts as a filtering mechanism:[346] only those non-standard workers whose employment relationship is relatively proximate to the standard worker are able to access the benefits of the principle of equal treatment.[347]

Both the Part-time Work and Fixed-term Work Directives are drafted in a similar manner. However, they employ the same tool to address different problems. While part-time work may well represent a positive 'choice' for many workers, those engaged under fixed-term contracts would usually choose, given the choice, contracts of indefinite duration,[348] since fixed-term contracts, by their very nature are insecure and precarious. To a limited extent this is recognized in the two Directives: the Fixed-term Work Directive does not contain a clause requiring Member States and the Social Partners to remove obstacles to fixed-term work. Further, the Preamble to the Directive expressly states that 'contracts of an indefinite duration are, and will continue to be, the general form of employment relationship'. Given the differences between the nature of fixed-term and part-time work, Murray argues[349] the protection that temporary workers

---

[341] Green Paper, *Partnership for a New Organisation of Work*, COM(97) 127 final, para. 52.

[342] See further Ch. 3.   [343] 9th Recital.   [344] Previously, at n. 298, 338.

[345] M. Bell, 'Between Flexicurity and Fundamental Social Rights: The EU Directives on Atypical Work' (2012) 37 *ELRev.* 31, 38–9. See additionally M. Rönnmar, 'Flexicurity, Labour Law and the Notion of Equal Treatment' in M. Rönnmar, *Labour Law, Fundamental Rights and Social Europe* (Hart Publishing, Oxford, 2011); L. Rodgers, 'Labour Law and Employment Policy in the EU: Conflict or Consensus' (2011) 27 *IJCLLIR* 387.

[346] Citing Case C–313/02 *Wippel* [2004] ECR I–9483, considered previously, at n. 223, and Case F–65/07 *Aayhan* v. *European Parliament* [2007] OJ C269/70.

[347] Ibid., 41.

[348] See L. Delsen, 'Atypical Employment Relations and Government Policy in Europe' (1991) 5 *Labour* 123.

[349] J. Murray, 'Normalising Temporary Work' (1999) 28 *ILJ* 269.

need is actually a fully-fledged scheme of portability of entitlements which recognizes all relevant working experience, even if undertaken with different employers and with breaks in between, to qualify for employment rights. This, rather than the principle of non-discrimination, would provide security for fixed-term workers which would counter-balance the flexibility offered by fixed-term contracts to employers.

F. CONCLUSIONS

The European Union's approach to work-life balance issues has undergone a rapid evolution. There is now recognition at the highest level that work/life balance is a Union concern and steps need to be taken to address it. Yet, the rhetoric in the Council's radical resolution on the balanced participation of women and men in family life was undermined by the limited and carefully tailored language of Article 33(2) of the Charter. The original drafting of this provision, which referred to the 'right to reconciliation', was dropped before the Charter was finally adopted.[350] McGlynn says, 'rhetoric and reality could not be further apart'[351] but, as we have already seen, the law can only go so far and in this key *policy* domain, it is employers, the Social Partners, and workers themselves who need to make this work. This is now recognized in Article 21(2) of the Sex Equality Directive 2006/54, which requires the Member States to encourage the social partners to promote 'equality between men and women, and flexible working arrangements, with the aim of facilitating the reconciliation of work and private life'. In this respect there is a clear role for softer policy coordination, perhaps underpinned by law, including the Charter rights. Until these various policy actors manage to work together, women will continue to suffer from the gender segregation of labour, 'wage disparities and extra workload (the "double working day")'.[352]

---

[350] C. McGlynn, 'Reclaiming a Feminist Vision: The Reconciliation of Paid Work and Family Life in European Union Law and Policy' (2001) 7 *Columbia Jo. E.L.* 241, 262.

[351] Ibid., 263.

[352] The Supiot report, *Beyond Employment: Changes in Work and the Future of Labour Law in Europe* (OUP, Oxford, 2001) 229.

10

EQUAL TREATMENT IN RESPECT OF SOCIAL SECURITY AND PENSIONS

A. INTRODUCTION

While the previous chapter looked mainly at the position of those at an earlier stage of their careers seeking to juggle work and family life, this final chapter on equality considers how the non-discrimination principle applies to those coming out of the workforce either involuntarily—through sickness, invalidity, or unemployment—or through the effluxion of time, on retirement. This chapter focuses in particular on two issues. First, it examines Directive 79/7[1] on equal treatment in *state* social security systems which was intended to complement the two original sex equality Directives: Directive 75/117 on equal pay,[2] and Directive 76/207 on equal treatment.[3] In particular, it considers the derogation from the equality principle in respect of benefits based on a discriminatory state pension age. This aspect of the chapter provides the relevant legislative background to the second issue considered here: the controversial question of the discriminatory retirement age and the discriminatory age at which occupational pensions are payable. 'Retirement age' relates to the age at which a worker retires—the upper age at which the worker stops working. Pension age is the age at which a worker is entitled to receive a pension, from the state (state pension) or the employer (occupational pension). Originally, Directive 86/378/EEC[4] was adopted to ensure equal treatment in respect of *occu-*

---

[1] Council Dir. 79/7 of 19 December 1978 on the progressive implementation of the principle of equal treatment for men and women in matters of social security (OJ [1979] L6/1). The original draft of Dir. 79/7 referred to both statutory and occupational social security schemes. During negotiations the occupational dimension was postponed to a further Directive: Dir. 86/378/EEC (OJ [1986] L225/40) as amended by Council Dir. 96/97 (OJ [1997] L46/20). Dir. 79/7 came into force on 23 December 1984. Member States therefore had six years to implement the Directive, the longest period ever set for a Directive (see C. Hoskyns, *Integrating Gender* (Verso, London, 1996), 111). Art. 5 requires Member States to take the measures necessary to abolish any laws, regulations and administrative provisions contrary to the principle of equal treatment. See L. Luckhaus, 'Changing Rules Enduring Structures' (1990) 53 *MLR* 655.

[2] OJ [1975] L45/19.

[3] OJ [1976] L39/40. In addition, Dir. 92/85/EEC (OJ [1992] L348/1) makes specific provision for entitlement to maternity leave and maternity benefits. These three Directives are considered in Chs. 6–9.

[4] OJ [1986] L225/40 as amended by Council Dir. 96/97 (OJ [1997] L46/20).

pational social security benefits. However, the contents of this Directive were largely superseded by the Court's case law on sex equality in respect of occupational pensions and survivors' benefits under Article 157 TFEU (ex 141 EC). The Court's complex case law has now been incorporated into the Sex Equality Directive 2006/54. However, we begin by examining Directive 79/7 on Equal Treatment in Social Security.

B. DIRECTIVE 79/7: EQUAL TREATMENT IN SOCIAL SECURITY

1. THE MATERIAL AND PERSONAL SCOPE OF THE DIRECTIVE

1.1. Material scope

According to Article 1, the purpose of Directive 79/7 is the *progressive implementation*[5] of the principle of equal treatment in matters of social security and other areas of social protection provided for in Article 3(1). These areas are:

(a) statutory schemes which provide protection against:
- sickness;
- invalidity;
- old age;
- accidents at work and occupational diseases;
- unemployment;[6] and

(b) social assistance, in so far as it is intended to supplement or replace schemes referred to in (a).

Thus the principle of equal treatment, as defined in Article 4 (see later) will apply only if the benefit is intended to protect against one of the risks listed in Article 3(1).

At first the Court adopted a generous approach to the material scope of the Directive. In *Drake*[7] the Court expanded the scope of Article 3(1) to include benefits which constitute 'the whole *or part*' of a statutory scheme providing protection against one of the specified risks, including, on the facts of the case, invalidity.

However, *Drake* now appears to be a somewhat exceptional case and the Court has since shown signs of retrenchment.[8] In *ex parte Smithson*,[9] a case concerning housing benefit which was paid to people on a low income, the Court said that, since Article 3(1)(a) did not refer to statutory schemes relating to housing costs, the British legislation fell outside the scope of the Directive because the benefit was not 'directly and effectively linked to the protection provided against one of the risks specified in

---

[5] The significance of this point was reiterated by the Court in Case 150/85 *Drake* v. *Chief Adjudication Officer* [1986] ECR 1995.

[6] Cf. the eight risks covered by Art. 4(1) of Reg. 1408/71.

[7] Case 150/85 [1986] ECR 1995. This case is considered further below.

[8] M. Cousins, 'Equal Treatment and Social Security' (1994) 19 *ELRev.* 123.

[9] Case 243/90 *R* v. *Secretary of State for Social Security, ex parte Smithson* [1992] ECR I–467.

Article 3(1)',[10] even though the recipient of the benefit was in one of the circumstances listed in Article 3(1). Similarly, in *Jackson and Cresswell*[11] the Court said that benefits designed to supplement the income of claimants (supplementary allowance and income support) were excluded from the scope of Directive 79/7. The Court pointed out that because the national scheme exempted claimants from being available for work this showed that the benefits in question could not be regarded as being directly and effectively linked to protection against the risk of unemployment.[12]

Thus, for the benefit to fall within the material scope of the Directive it must provide direct and effective protection against one of the risks specified in Article 3(1), rather than merely 'incidental' protection against such a risk.[13] *Atkins*[14] is an example of a case which fell on the 'incidental' protection side of the line. It concerned a concessionary travel scheme which allowed men over the age of 65 and women aged over 60 reduced fares on public transport. The Court said that this benefit was not directly and effectively linked to the protection provided against one of the risks specified in Article 3(1). The purpose of concessionary travel was to facilitate access to public transport for certain classes of persons who, for various reasons, were recognized as having a particular need for public transport and who were, for the same reasons, less well-off financially and materially. It said that although old age and invalidity were among the categories covered by Directive 79/7 they were only two of the criteria which might be applied to define the classes of beneficiaries of such a scheme of concessionary fares. The fact that the recipient of the benefit happened to fall within one of the categories envisaged by Article 3(1) was not sufficient to bring the benefit within the scope of EU law. A similar argument can be made to explain why benefits designed to supplement the income of claimants (*Jackson and Cresswell*) and a child-raising allowance (*Hoever and Zachow*)[15] fell outside the scope of the Directive.[16] By contrast, in *ex parte Richardson*[17] the Court ruled that exemption from prescription charges fell within the scope of Article 3(1) because it provided direct and effective protection against sickness; and in *ex parte Taylor*[18] the Court ruled that a winter fuel payment directly and effectively protected against the risk of old age.

1.2. Personal scope

The potential beneficiaries of the Directive are widely drawn by Article 2. The Directive applies to the 'working population' which covers 'self-employed persons, workers and

---

[10] Para. 12.
[11] Joined Cases C–63/91 and 64/91 [1992] ECR I–4737. This case concerned a challenge to the national legislation which prevented child-minding expenses from being taken into account in assessing entitlement to various means-tested payments on the grounds that it indirectly discriminated against women.
[12] Para. 21.
[13] R. White, *EC Social Security Law* (Longman, Harlow, 1999) 121.
[14] Case C–228/94 *Atkins v. Wrekin DC and Department of Transport* [1996] ECR I–3633.
[15] Joined Cases C–245/94 and C–312/94 *Hoever and Zachow* [1996] ECR I–4895.
[16] Cf. Case C–139/95 *Livia Balestra v. Istituto Nazionale della Presidenza Sociale* [1997] ECR I–549 where early retirement benefits fell within Art. 3(1) because they provide protection against the 'risk' of old age.
[17] Case C–137/94 [1995] ECR I–3633.
[18] Case C–382/98 *R v. Secretary of State for Social Security, ex parte Taylor* [1999] ECR I–8955, para. 23.

self-employed persons whose activity is interrupted by illness, accident or involuntary unemployment and persons seeking employment—and to retired or invalided workers and self-employed persons'. A person is still a member of the working population even if one of the risks mentioned in Article 3 happens not to the worker herself but to a relative of the worker, forcing the worker to interrupt her occupational activity. This was the situation in *Drake*.[19] Mrs Drake, who had given up work to care for her invalid mother, was regarded as being a member of the working population, because her employment had been interrupted, albeit by the invalidity of another. The Court justified this conclusion by reference to the objectives of the Treaty and the Directive. It emphasized that 'there is a *clear economic link* between the benefit and the disabled person, since the disabled person derives an advantage from the fact that an allowance is paid to the person caring for him...the fact that a benefit...is paid to a third party and not directly to the disabled person does not place it outside the scope of Directive 79/7'.[20]

A person is also a member of the working population where the risk materializes while the person concerned is seeking employment immediately after a period without occupational activity,[21] or where the employment in question is regarded as minor since it consists of less than 15 hours' work a week and attracts remuneration of less than one-seventh of the average monthly salary[22] or where, as in *Verholen*,[23] the individual who is not within the Article 'bears the effect' of the discriminatory treatment directed at another who does fall within the scope of Article 2.

On the other hand, the Court said, the Directive does not apply to people who are not working and are not seeking work or to people whose occupation or efforts to find work were not interrupted by one of the risks referred to in Article 3 of the Directive.[24] Therefore, in *Achterberg-te Riele* the Court held that a person who has given up his or her occupational activity to bring up children did not fall within the scope of the Directive.[25] This point was confirmed in *Züchner*[26] where the Court ruled that Article 2 of Directive

[19] Case 150/85 [1986] ECR 1995.
[20] Case 150/85 *Drake* [1986] ECR 1995. This case was the subject of a well orchestrated campaign: L. Luckhaus, 'Payment for Caring: A European Solution' [1986] *PL*. 526, who suggests that the Court was motivated by its desire to condemn such unabashed discrimination and so engaged in 'some well meaning subterfuge' in order to extend the reach of Union law into the realm of domestic unpaid work. See further. Case C–343/92 *De Weerd, née Roks and Others* v. *Bestuur van de Bedrijfsverenigning voor de Gezondheid* [1994] ECR I–571.
[21] Case C–31/90 *Johnson (No. 1)* v. *Chief Adjudication Officer* [1991] ECR I–3723. The onus of proof is on applicants to show that they were seeking work in these circumstances. This is a matter for the national court to decide, taking into account such factors as whether they were registered with an employment organization, whether they had sent out job applications, and whether they could produce certificates to show that they had attended interviews.
[22] Case C–317/93 *Nolte* v. *Landversicherungsanstalt Hannover* [1995] ECR I–4625 and Case C–444/93 *Megner and Scheffel* v. *Innungskrankenkasse Vorderpfalz* [1995] ECR I–4741. See additionally Case C–280/94 *Posthuma-van Damme* v. *Bestuur van de Bedrijfsvereniging voor Detailhandel* [1996] ECR I–179.
[23] Joined Cases C–87/90, 88/90 and 89/90 *Verholen* v. *Verzekeringsbank Amsterdam* [1991] ECR I–3757. Cf. Case C–77/95 *Bruna-Alessandra Züchner* v. *Handelskrankenkasse (Ersatzkasse) Bremen* [1996] ECR I–5689, and Waddington (1997) 22 *ELRev*. 587.
[24] Case 48/88 *Achterberg-te Riele and Others* v. *Sociale Verzekeringsbank* [1989] ECR 1963.
[25] Case C–31/90 *Johnson (No. 1)* [1991] ECR I–3723.
[26] Case C–77/95 [1996] ECR I–5689.

79/7/EEC did not cover a woman who was not 'economically active' (neither in paid employment, nor seeking work, nor whose employment was interrupted by one of the risks listed in Article 3 of the Directive) who undertook the unpaid care of her invalid husband, even though she had to undertake special training to care for him properly.

In the light of *Verholen, Züchner* seems particularly harsh. It also takes no account of the social circumstances in which women's relationship with the paid employment market and social security systems is constituted.[27] If Mrs Züchner's husband had had no relative to care for him, the caring work would have been remunerated, either privately or by the state through its social security provision. Yet it seems that the caring work carried out by women on a private basis is not characterized by EU law as 'work' and therefore falls outside the scope of EU sex equality provisions. In reaching its conclusion in *Züchner* the Court seems to have been concerned with limiting the scope of Directive 79/7. To have extended the application of the Directive to women such as Mrs Züchner would, as the Court put it, 'have the effect of infinitely extending the scope of the directive'.[28] Such an extension might severely disrupt national social security systems, whose conceptual (and financial) basis is the protection of economically active persons, whose employment is interrupted by a risk against which the social security system provides protection.

2. THE PRINCIPLE OF EQUAL TREATMENT

2.1. Direct and indirect discrimination

Article 4(1) gives concrete expression to the principle of equal treatment set out in Article 1 of the Directive.[29] It provides that:

> ... there shall be no discrimination whatsoever on the ground of sex either directly, or indirectly, by reference in particular to marital or family status,[30] in particular, as concerns:
> — the scope of the schemes and the conditions of access thereto;
> — the obligation to contribute and the calculation of the contributions;
> — the calculations of benefits including increases[31] due in respect of a spouse[32] and for dependants[33] and the conditions governing the duration and retention of entitlements to benefits.[34]

---

[27] J. Sohrab, *Sexing the Benefit: Women, Social Security and Financial Independence in EC Sex Equality Law* (Dartmouth, Aldershot, 1996).

[28] Para. 15.   [29] Case 150/85 *Drake* [1986] ECR 1995.

[30] This definition closely mirrors that found in the Equal Treatment Directive 76/207. The reference to 'marital status' is particularly important because the national social security systems of the Member States are in general based on the model of the family unit, consisting of one breadwinner (male), one adult dependant (female) and dependent children. This model is prone to discrimination against the female sex.

[31] Member States are entitled to stipulate whatever increases they wish for entitlement to increases in social security benefits, provided they comply fully with the principle of equal treatment laid down in Art. 4(1): Case C–377/89 *Cotter and Others* v. *Minister for Social Welfare* [1991] ECR I–1155.

[32] Spouses do not need to be dependent (Case C–377/89 *Cotter and Others* [1991] ECR I–1155).

[33] No proof of their dependency is actually required under the Directive as a prior condition of the application of the principle of equal treatment (Case C–377/89 *Cotter and Others* [1991] ECR I–1155).

[34] Art. 4(1). Art. 4(2) contains an exclusion for provisions relating to the protection of women on the grounds of maternity.

The 'fundamental' principle of equal treatment was recognized in *Drake*.[35] Under British law an Invalid Care Allowance (ICA) was not payable to a married woman who lived with her husband although it was payable in corresponding circumstances to a man. The Court found that this legislation was directly discriminatory and contravened Articles 1 and 4(1).[36] In *FNV*[37] the Court said that Article 4(1) was sufficiently precise and unconditional to be directly effective.[38] Together, these decisions paved the way to challenge a wide variety of national legislation which discriminated either directly or indirectly, usually against women.

For example, in *Borrie Clarke*[39] the Court held that Article 4(1) did not permit Member States to make conditional or to limit the application of the principle of equal treatment, nor did it allow Member States to maintain beyond 22 December 1984 (the deadline for implementing the Directive) any inequalities of treatment which had their origin in the fact that conditions of entitlement to the benefit were those which applied before that date. *Borrie Clarke* concerned Severe Disablement Allowance (SDA), introduced to replace the discriminatory Non-Contributory Invalidity Pension (NCIP). In order to receive NCIP the household duties test was applied to women but not men. This test asked whether the woman was capable of performing 'normal household duties'. Under the transitional provisions, automatic entitlement to the SDA was subject to the same discriminatory criteria as for NCIP (i.e. the household duties test). The Court found that women were entitled to be treated in the same manner and to have the same rules applied to them as men.[40] Therefore, since a man was automatically entitled to the new SDA, a woman should also receive the new benefit automatically.

Relying on the decision in *Borrie Clarke*, Mrs Johnson also claimed SDA.[41] She gave up work to look after her daughter in 1970. By 1980 she wished to return to work but, since she was unable to do so due to a back condition, she received NCIP. However, this payment was stopped when Mrs Johnson began to cohabit because she was considered capable of performing normal household duties. Mrs Johnson applied for SDA on the

---

[35] Case 150/85 [1986] ECR 1995.

[36] E.g. Case C–337/91 *A. M. van Gemert-Derks* v. *Bestuur van de Nieuwe Industriele Bedrijfsvereniging* [1993] ECR I–5435.

[37] Case 71/85 *Netherlands* v. *Federatie Nederlandse Vakbeweging* [1986] ECR 3855.

[38] The derogations contained in Arts. 5 and 7 of the Directive do not confer on the Member States the power to make conditional or limit the application of the principle of equal treatment and thus do not prevent Art.4(1) from having direct effect. See Arnull (1987) 12 *ELRev*. 276. The fact that Art. 4(1) is directly effective (and has been since 23 December 1984) has been endorsed by the Court in numerous cases including Case 150/85 *Drake* [1986] ECR 1995, Case 286/85 *McDermott and Cotter* v. *Minister for Social Welfare and Attorney General* [1987] ECR 1453, and Case 384/85 *J. B. Clarke* v. *Chief Adjudication Officer* [1987] ECR 2865. Member States can belatedly introduce legislation and make it retroactive to the date when implementation was required, see Case 80/87 *Dik and Mencutos-Demirci* v. *College van Burgermeester en Wethouders Arnhem and Winterswijk* [1988] ECR 1601.

[39] Case C–384/85 [1987] ECR 2865.

[40] The Court applied *Borrie Clark* in another case concerning discriminatory transitional provisions, Case 80/87 *Dik and Mencutos-Demirci* [1988] ECR 1601, which in turn was applied in Case C–377/89 *Cotter and Others* [1991] ECR I–1155. See further Case 286/85 *McDermott and Cotter* [1987] ECR 1453 and Case C–154/92 *Van Cant* v. *Rijksdienst voor Pensionenen* [1993] ECR I–3811.

[41] Case C–31/90 *Johnson (No. 1)* [1991] ECR I–3723, noted by Laske (1992) *CMLRev*. 101.

basis that she would have been entitled to the NCIP immediately prior to the abolition of the benefit, had the discriminatory household duties test not been applied to her in 1980. The Court supported her arguments, concluding that national legislation making entitlement to a benefit, such as the SDA, subject to an earlier claim for a benefit which incorporated a discriminatory requirement was incompatible with Article 4(1) of Directive 79/7. The national legislation therefore had to be set aside. Similarly, in *Cotter and Others*[42] the Court ruled that if married men have automatically received increases in social security benefits in respect of a spouse and children deemed to be dependants without having to prove actual dependency, married women without actual dependants were also entitled to those increases, even if in some circumstances that would result in double payment of the increases.

While many of the cases concern discrimination against women, *Integrity*[43] is an example of a case of discrimination against men. Belgian law provided a possibility for married women and widows to be exempted from having to make social security contributions without granting the same possibility to married men or widowers who otherwise satisfied the same conditions. The Court said this rule contravened Article 4(1).[44] *Richards*,[45] on the other hand, is a case about discrimination on the grounds of gender reassignment. Richards, born a man, underwent gender reassignment. In the UK, women receive their state pension at 60, men at 65. When Ms Richards applied for a pension at 60 she was turned down on the grounds that the law, at that time, considered her still to be a man and so she was not entitled to receive a pension until she was 65. The Court ruled that this unequal treatment arose from her gender reassignment and so was regarded as discrimination contrary to Article 4(1).[46]

The cases considered so far concern legislation which was directly discriminatory. *Teuling*[47] confirms that Article 4(1) also outlaws indirectly discriminatory measures, that is, measures which although formulated in neutral terms, work to the disadvantage of far more women than men,[48] unless they can be objectively justified. *Teuling* concerned a system of benefits where supplements were provided which, although not

[42] Case C–377/89 [1991] ECR I–1155. See further Case C–338/91 *Steenhorst-Neerings* v. *Bestuur van de Bedrijfsvereniging* [1993] ECR I–5475 where a national law deprived women of benefits which men continued to receive, even though the national court applied the law in a non-discriminatory manner; see additionally Case C–187/98 *Commission* v. *Greece* [1999] ECR I–7713; Case C–577/08 *Rijksdient voor Pensioenen* v. *Brouwer* [2010] ECR I–000.

[43] Case C–373/89 *Caisse d'assurances sociales pour travailleurs independents 'Integrity'* v. *Rouvroy* [1990] ECR I–4243.

[44] Para. 15.

[45] Case C–423/04 *Richards* v. *Secretary of State for Work and Pensions* [2006] ECR I–000. See further *Grant* v. *UK* (Application no. 32570/03), judgment of 23 May 2006 where the European Court of Human Rights ruled that denying the state pension at age 60 from a male to female transsexual was a breach of the right to respect for private life contrary to Art. 8 ECHR.

[46] Para. 30.

[47] Case 30/85 *Teuling* v. *Bedrijfsvereniging voor de Chemische Industrie* [1987] ECR 2497.

[48] Case C–343/92 *De Weerd* [1994] ECR I–571, para. 33, Case C–229/89 *Commission* v. *Belgium* [1991] ECR I–2205, para. 13; Case C–123/10 *Brachner* v. *Pensionsversicherungsanstalt* [2011] ECR I–000, para. 62. See generally J. Steiner, 'The Principle of Equal Treatment for Men and Women in Social Security' in T. Hervey and D. O'Keeffe (eds.), *Sex Equality Law in the European Union* (Wiley, London, 1996).

directly based on the sex of the beneficiaries, took account of their marital status or family situation. It became apparent that a considerably smaller number of women than men were entitled to such supplements and that the scheme was therefore indirectly discriminatory and contrary to Article 4(1), unless the system could be justified on grounds other than sex. The Court, however, accepted the justification that the system sought to ensure an adequate minimum subsistence income for beneficiaries who had a dependent spouse or dependent children, by means of a supplement to the social security benefit which compensated for the greater burdens they had to bear in comparison with single people.

This approach was confirmed in *Ruzius Wilbrink*.[49] This case concerned Dutch legislation providing disability allowances to workers which were lower for part-time workers than for full-time workers. The Court found, first, that such a provision was indirectly discriminatory against female workers, and secondly, that the discrimination could not be objectively justified. The Court therefore concluded that since in the case of direct discrimination women were entitled to be treated in the same manner as men, so part-time workers had to be treated in the same way as full-timers in the case of indirect discrimination (a levelling up of benefit), because such rules relating to full-timers remained the only valid point of reference so long as the Directive had not been implemented correctly.[50]

2.2. Objective justification

The question of objective justification was considered further in *De Weerd*.[51] The case concerned national legislation making receipt of a benefit for incapacity for work subject to the requirement of having received a certain income from or in connection with work in the year preceding the commencement of the incapacity. That requirement was indirectly discriminatory because it affected more women than men and therefore breached Article 4(1), 'unless that measure is based on objectively justified factors unrelated to any discrimination on grounds of sex' (para. 33).[52] The Court continued: 'That is the case where the measures chosen reflect a legitimate social policy aim of the Member State whose legislation is at issue, are appropriate to achieve that aim and are necessary in order to do so' (para. 34).[53] Budgetary considerations did not, however, justify a difference in treatment. As the Court said, '[A]lthough budgetary considerations may influence a Member State's choice of social policy and affect the nature or scope of the social protection measures it wishes to adopt, they cannot themselves constitute the aim pursued by that policy and cannot therefore justify discrimination against one of

---

[49] Case C–102/88 *Ruzius-Wilbrink* v. *Bedrijfsvereniging voor Overheidsdiensten* [1989] ECR 4311.
[50] Para. 16.   [51] Case C–343/92 [1994] ECR I–571.
[52] Para. 33, citing Case C–229/89 *Commission* v. *Belgium* [1991] ECR I–2205.
[53] This follows Case 171/88 *Rinner-Kühn* v. *FWW Spezial-Gebäudereinigung GmbH* [1989] ECR 2743, para. 14, concerning legislation which was prima facie indirectly discriminatory contrary to Art. 157 TFEU. In Case C–226/91 *Molenbroeck* v. *Sociale Verzekeringsbank* [1992] ECR I–5943 the Court emphasized 'the reasonable margin of discretion' allowed to Member States as to the nature of the social protection measures and the detailed arrangements for their implementation.

the sexes'. However, the Court did say that Union law did not prevent budgetary constraints being taken into account when making the continuance of entitlement to social
security benefit dependent on certain conditions, the effect of which was to withdraw
benefits from certain categories of people, provided that when they did so they did not
infringe the rule of equal treatment laid down in Article 4(1).[54]

In *Nolte*[55] and *Megner and Scheffel*[56] the Court relaxed the rigorous test for objective
justification laid down in *De Weerd*. These cases concerned a German social security
law under which individuals working fewer than 15 hours per week and whose income
did not exceed one-seventh of the monthly reference wage[57] ('minor' or 'marginal' part-
time workers) were not subject to the statutory old-age insurance scheme and were also
exempt from paying contributions for unemployment benefit. Although the legislation
affected considerably more women than men, the German government argued that the
exclusion of persons in minor employment corresponded to a structural principle of
the German social security scheme. Having cited the test contained in paragraphs 33
and 34 of the judgment in *De Weerd* (see previously), the Court then said that in the
current state of Union law, social policy was a matter for the Member States.[58] Consequently, it was for the Member States to choose the measures capable of achieving the
aim of their social and employment policy. In exercising that competence Member
States had a broad margin of discretion. It then said:

> It should be noted that the social and employment policy aim relied on by the German
> government is objectively unrelated to any discrimination on the grounds of sex and that,
> in exercising its competence, the national legislature was *reasonably entitled* to consider
> that the legislation in question was necessary in order to achieve that aim. [Emphasis
> added]

It therefore said that the legislation could not be described as indirectly discriminatory within the meaning of Article 4(1).[59] Thus, in the context of social security at
least, a weaker test of objective justification applies than is applied in respect of
employment.[60]

---

[54] Para. 29.

[55] Case C–317/93 [1995] ECR I–4625. See generally T. Hervey, 'Sex Equality in Social Protection: New
Institutional Perspectives on Allocation of Competence' (1998) 4 *ELJ* 196.

[56] Case C–444/93 [1995] ECR I–4741.

[57] The average monthly salary of persons insured under the statutory old-age insurance scheme during the
previous calendar year.

[58] This point was made clearly by the Court in Case C–343/92 *De Weerd* [1994] ECR I–571, para. 28:
'Directive 79/7 leaves intact, however, the powers reserved by Articles [151 and 156 TFEU] to the Member
States to define their social policy within the framework of close co-operation organised by the Commission,
and consequently the nature and extent of the measures of social protection, including those relating to
social security and the way in which they are implemented', citing Case C–229/89 *Commission v. Belgium*
[1991] ECR I–2205. The point was again repeated in Case C–280/94 *Posthuma-van Damme* [1996] ECR
I–179, para. 26.

[59] Case C–317/93 *Nolte* [1995] ECR I–4625, paras. 34 and 35; Case C–444/93 *Megner and Scheffel* [1995]
ECR I–571, paras. 30 and 31.

[60] See further the discussion of this subject in Ch. 7.

The weaker test of justification was applied again in *Laperre*.[61] The case concerned the conditions of access (previous employment, age, and incapacity) to a non-means-tested social security benefit, the IOAW, which Mrs Laperre argued gave rise to indirect sex discrimination. Another scheme, the RWW, also provided a minimum income but was subject to a means test. The Netherlands government said that while the RWW aimed to bring the unemployed back to work by providing income for those of 'modest assets', the IOAW was not means-tested because the legislature sought to protect potential beneficiaries from having to break into their life savings given that they had little chance of rebuilding their assets by resuming gainful employment. The Court said that the aim relied on by the Dutch government was a matter of social policy, that it was objectively unrelated to any discrimination on the grounds of sex and that, in exercising their competence, the national legislature was reasonably entitled to consider that the legislation in question was necessary in order to achieve that aim.[62]

The Court showed the same deference to the national system in *Posthuma van Damme*.[63] In that case the Court was asked to consider whether its judgment in *De Weerd* meant that the national law could not be justified at all or only that it could not be justified on budgetary grounds. The Court confirmed the latter interpretation. It also accepted the Dutch government's arguments that guaranteeing a minimum income to people who had given up work on the grounds of incapacity satisfied a legitimate aim of social policy. It also agreed that imposing conditions on access to the benefit constituted a measure appropriate to achieve the objective which the national legislature, in the exercise of its competence, was reasonably entitled to consider necessary. The fact that the scheme replaced a scheme of pure national insurance and that the number of people who actually benefited was further reduced did not affect the finding. This case, more than any other, sounded the death knell to the rigorous approach adopted in *De Weerd*.

3. EXCEPTIONS AND DEROGATIONS

Directive 79/7 contains (1) permanent exceptions, and (2) temporary, 'permissive' derogations. Into the first category fall survivors' benefits, family benefits,[64] occupational pension schemes,[65] and provisions relating to the protection of women on the grounds of maternity.[66] Into the second category fall the derogations found in Article 7. Member

---

[61] Case C–8/94 *Laperre v. Bestuurcommissie beroepszaken in de provincie Zuid-Holland* [1996] ECR I–273.

[62] Although the Court was not provided with a detailed explanation of the employment conditions at issue, Advocate General Lenz was prepared to assume that the condition relating to employment operated to the disadvantage of women whose employment histories often had long gaps because of their need to fulfil their family obligations. Nevertheless, he accepted that the provisions were not contrary to Union law because Dutch law was entitled to offer specific protection to those who had maintained themselves from earned income over a long period.

[63] Case C–280/94 [1996] ECR I–179.   [64] Art. 3(2).

[65] Art. 3(3). See now Dir. 86/378 (OJ [1986] L225/40) on equal treatment in occupational social security as amended by Council Dir. 96/97/EC (OJ [1997] L46/20).

[66] Art. 4(2).

States have the right to exclude from the scope of the Directive a long list of benefits,[67] the most significant of which is Article 7(1)(a), the determination of pensionable age for the purposes of granting old-age and retirement benefits, and the possible consequences for other benefits.[68] In respect of all derogations, the basic rule applies: that derogations are narrowly construed.[69]

3.1. Article 7(1)(a) on the determination of pensionable age for granting old-age and retirement benefits

According to Article 7(1)(a), the Directive is without prejudice to the right of Member States to exclude from its scope the determination of pensionable age for the purposes of (1) granting old-age and retirement pensions, and (2) the possible consequences for other benefits which, the Court has added, are 'necessarily and objectively linked to the difference in pensionable age'. However, in view of the fundamental importance of the principle of equal treatment, the exception to the prohibition of discrimination on the grounds of sex has to be interpreted strictly.[70]

(a) Discrimination for the Purposes of granting old-age and retirement benefits

The first part of Article 7(1)(a) was at issue in *ex parte EOC*[71] where it was argued that the British state pension scheme, which allowed women to receive their state pension at 60, while men had to wait until 65, unlawfully discriminated against men in two ways. First, it required men to pay contributions for 44 years to qualify for the same basic retirement pension as women who had contributed for only 39 years. The corollary of this was that a man who had made contributions for 39 years received a lower basic pension than a woman who had contributed for 39 years. Secondly, men working between the ages of 60 and 64 had to pay contributions but women in the same situation did not.

---

[67] The other exclusions relate to entitlements granted to those who have brought up children, derived entitlements of a wife, and the exercise of a right of option not to acquire rights or incur obligations under a statutory scheme. See further S. Atkins, 'The EEC Directive on Equal Treatment in Social Security Benefits' (1978–79) 1 *JSWL* 244.

[68] Art. 7(1), discussed further below. Member States must periodically examine matters excluded under Art. 7(1) in order to ascertain whether there is justification for maintaining the particular exclusion (Art. 7(2)). Art. 8(2) obliges the Member State to notify the Commission of the reasons for maintaining the derogation under Art. 7(2). A Directive on the Implementation of the Principle of Equal Treatment for Men and Women in Statutory and Occupational Social Security Schemes was proposed (OJ [1988] C95/4), designed to fill the gaps left by Directives 79/7 and 86/378, although its purpose may have been overtaken in part by decisions of the Court. It extends the principle of equal treatment to the areas previously excluded by the earlier Directives, esp. pensionable age in both statutory and occupational schemes. Art. 9 proposes two alternatives for achieving this objective: the first involves selecting a uniform age for men and women but with safeguards for those who have already reached a certain age close to retirement; the second envisages flexible retirement, allowing workers to choose their retirement age during a specified period, provided that the conditions, esp. with regard to the number of contribution years, are identical for both sexes.

[69] See e.g., Case C–423/04 *Richards* v. *Secretary of State for Work and Pensions* [2006] ECR I–3585, para. 36.

[70] Case C–328/91 *Secretary of State for Social Security* v. *Thomas and Others* [1993] ECR I–1247.

[71] Case C–9/91 *R* v. *Secretary of State for Social Security, ex parte Equal Opportunities Commission* [1992] ECR I–4297.

According to the Court, the purpose of the Directive was to achieve *progressive* implementation of the principle of equal treatment in social security. The progressive nature of the implementation was reflected in the number of derogations. The purpose of the derogations, allowing Member States to maintain temporarily advantageous treatment of women in the field of state pensions, was to enable Member States 'progressively to adapt their pension systems [towards equality] without disrupting the complex financial equilibrium of those systems'. Therefore, the Court said that any derogation under Article 7(1)(a) would be rendered nugatory if it did not apply to contribution periods, such as those in *ex parte EOC*, as well as at the moment at which they become entitled to a pension. If the derogation did not apply, Member States would be obliged to alter the existing financial equilibrium substantially.

(b) Discrimination in respect of other benefits objectively linked to old-age and retirement benefits

The second part of Article 7(1)(a) provides that sex discrimination is still permitted in respect of other benefits which, the Court has added, are 'necessarily and objectively linked to the difference in pensionable age'. That will be the case where the discrimination is necessary (a) to avoid disturbing the financial equilibrium of the social-security system or (b) to ensure coherence between the retirement pension scheme and other benefit schemes.[72]

Graham[73] illustrates how the Court will approach the question of whether the benefit is 'necessarily and objectively linked to the difference in pensionable age'. The case concerned two benefits, an invalidity pension and an invalidity allowance. The first part of Graham's claim related to the *invalidity pension*. Graham had to stop working before reaching pensionable age due to ill health. Initially she received sickness benefit and then invalidity pension at the full retirement pension rate. When she reached pensionable age (65 for men, 60 for women) she opted to continue receiving the invalidity pension, which was not taxable, rather than a retirement pension which was taxable. As she had not fulfilled the contribution conditions for the grant of a full retirement pension, the amount of her invalidity pension was reduced to the rate of the retirement pension which would have been paid to her. Had Graham been a man, she would have continued to receive the invalidity pension at the full retirement pension rate until she was 65 and only then would a reduction have been made to reflect the number of years that she had paid contributions.

Graham also complained about the discriminatory effect of the *invalidity allowance* which was paid in addition to the invalidity pension to a person who was more than five years below pensionable age on the first day of incapacity for work. Mrs Graham, who was aged over 55 when she became incapacitated for work, was refused invalidity allowance. Had she been a man she would have received the payment.

---

[72] Case C–92/94 *Secretary of State for Social Security and Chief Adjudication Officer* v. *Graham and Others* [1995] ECR I–2521, para. 11, and Case C–139/95 *Balestra* v. *INPS* [1997] ECR I–549, para. 33.

[73] Case C–92/94 *Secretary of State for Social Security* v. *Graham* [1995] ECR I–2521.

The Court found that the forms of discrimination at issue were objectively linked to the setting of different pensionable ages for men and women. It said that since invalidity benefit was designed to replace income from an occupational activity there was nothing to prevent a Member State from providing for its cessation and replacement by a retirement pension at the time when the recipients would have stopped work because they had reached pensionable age.[74] The Court continued that to prohibit a Member State which has set different pensionable ages from limiting, in the case of individuals becoming incapacitated for work before reaching pensionable age, the rate of invalidity benefit payable to them from that age to the actual rate of the retirement pension to which they were entitled under the retirement pension scheme would mean restricting the very right enjoyed by the UK under Article 7(1)(a) of Directive 79/7 to set different pensionable ages.

The Court added that such a prohibition would also undermine the coherence between the retirement pension scheme and the invalidity benefit scheme in two ways. First, the UK would be prevented from granting to men who became incapacitated for work before reaching pensionable age invalidity benefits greater than the retirement pensions which would actually have been payable to them if they had continued to work until reaching pensionable age, unless it granted to women over pensionable age retirement pensions greater than those actually payable to them. Secondly, if women did not have their invalidity pension reduced to the level of their retirement pension until they reached the age of 65, as in the case of men, women aged between 60 and 65, thus over pensionable age, would receive an invalidity pension at the rate of a full retirement pension if their incapacity for work commenced before they reached pensionable age and a retirement pension corresponding to the rate actually payable if it did not. Consequently, the Court ruled that the derogation in Article 7(1)(a) applied to the differences between the rates of invalidity pension payable to men and women from the time when they reached pensionable age. The Court added that, due to the link between invalidity pension and invalidity allowance, the same conclusion applied with regard to the difference between the qualifying dates for the grant of invalidity allowance.

The Court will check to see if the defendant state can make out the necessary link. For example, in *Buchner*[75] the Court said that the Austrian government had failed to make out the case that the link between, in that case, the early old-age pension on account of incapacity for work and the old-age pension was necessary to preserve coherence between the two. The Court pointed out that there was no precise relationship between the minimum qualifying age for the early old-age pension on account of incapacity for work and the statutory retirement age (55 for women, five years before the statutory retirement age, and 57 for men, eight years before the statutory retirement age) and that this difference in the age condition was introduced essentially for budgetary reasons. Therefore the discrimination was not covered by Article 7(1)(a) of Directive 79/7.

---

[74] Para. 14.
[75] Case C–104/98 *Buchner v. Soxialversicherungsanstalt der Bauern* [2000] ECR I–3625.

Cases involving non-contributory benefits are unlikely to satisfy the requirement of the need to avoid disturbing the financial equilibrium of the social security system. For example, *Thomas*[76] concerned the refusal under British law to grant severe disablement allowance and invalid care allowance to those who had reached state pensionable age. The Court suggested that discrimination between men and women under such *non-contributory* schemes was unnecessary to preserve the financial equilibrium of the entire social security system and therefore Article 7(1)(a) could not be invoked. Similarly, in *ex parte Richardson*[77] a retired man of 64 claimed that he was discriminated against on the grounds of his sex by national legislation which exempted women, but not men, aged between 60 and 64 from paying prescription charges. The Court agreed. It said that Article 7(1)(a) did not apply to the rules on prescription charges since the removal of the discrimination would not affect the financial equilibrium of the pension scheme and that the discrimination was not objectively necessary to ensure coherence between the retirement pension system and regulations concerning prescription charges.[78] And again, in *ex parte Taylor*,[79] the Court said that arguments concerning financial equilibrium did not apply to other non-contributory benefits, such as a winter fuel payment. Consequently eliminating discrimination had no impact on the financial equilibrium of the social security scheme as a whole and so was not covered by the Article 7(1)(a) derogation.

In cases which do not involve non-contributory schemes, the Court will scrutinize any claim about the serious effect on the financial equilibrium of the scheme with care. Thus, in *Haackert*,[80] a case with rather similar facts to *Graham*, the Court said that the percentage of early old-age pensions on account of unemployment paid in relation to the total of old-age pensions represented barely 1.2 per cent. The Court therefore concluded that the removal of such discrimination could not have any serious effect on the financial equilibrium of social security system.[81] However, on the facts, the Court found that the discrimination could be justified on the grounds of preserving coherence between early old-age pensions on account of unemployment and the old-age pension.[82]

---

[76] Case C–328/91 *Secretary of State for Social Security* v. *Thomas and Others* [1993] ECR I–1247.

[77] Case C–137/94 [1995] ECR I–3633.

[78] In Case C–228/94 *Atkins* [1996] ECR I–3633 (reduced fares on public transport) the Advocate General urged the Court to follow *ex parte Richardson* rather than *Graham*. He said that the scheme fell within the material scope of the Directive, and that the derogation contained in Art. 7(1)(a) did not apply since the travel concessions had no connection with the extent of entitlement to an old-age pension or with the overall financing of the pensions system. To remove the discrimination would not, he said, affect the financial equilibrium of the pensions scheme. However, as we saw above, the Court decided that the case fell outside the material scope of the Directive.

[79] Case C–382/98 [1999] ECR I–8955, paras. 30–1.

[80] See further Case C–303/02 *Haackert* v. *Pensionsversicherungsanstalt der Angestellten* [2004] ECR I–2195 concerning the discriminatory ages at which a Belgian early old-age pension on account of unemployment was paid which was 'objectively necessary in order to ensure coherence between early old-age pension on account of unemployment and the old-age pension' (para. 37).

[81] See additionally Case C–104/98 *Buchner* v. *Sozialversicherungsanstalt der Bauern* [2000] ECR I–3625, para. 30.

[82] See additionally Case C–196/98 *Hepple* v. *Adjudication Officer* [2000] ECR I–3701.

(c) Transitional arrangements

Can Member States continue to rely on Article 7(1)(a) when they are in the process of removing discrimination in state pension ages? This was the issue in *Van Cant*.[83] From 1991 Belgian law allowed both men and women to receive their state pension from age 60, but it maintained a different method of calculating the pension for each sex. The Court ruled that this was discriminatory contrary to Article 4(1) of the Directive and could not be justified under Article 7(1)(a). It said that once the national system took the step of abolishing the difference in state pensionable ages Article 7(1)(a) could no longer be relied on to justify maintaining a difference in the method of calculating the retirement pension which was linked to the difference in retirement ages.

This decision in *Van Cant* seemed to allow no scope for (necessary) transitional arrangements which may incorporate the discriminatory features of the earlier scheme. Paradoxically, had the Belgian government maintained different state pension ages it could have continued to rely on Article 7(1)(a) in respect of the method of calculating the pension.[84] There was some dispute in *Van Cant* as to whether the national law had in fact maintained different pensionable ages. The Court ruled that this was a matter for the national court to decide, but because different Belgian courts had reached different conclusions on this question, an interpretative law was passed which indicated that the different pensionable ages had not been removed.[85]

The consequences of these developments were at issue in *De Vriendt*[86] and *Wolfs*.[87] The references in these cases concerned the new Belgian law establishing a flexible retirement age for men and women, which allowed all workers to retire 'early' at age 60 during a transitional period. The amount of pension paid was accrued on an annual basis and calculated based on a proportion of the worker's remuneration for that year. For men the highest number of years taken into account to determine the pension was 45, but only 40 for women. If a worker worked longer than this, the most advantageous 45 or 40 years were used as the basis for the calculation of the pension. Even under the new system, for men the relevant proportion of salary was one-forty-fifth, but for women it was one-fortieth of salary. A number of Belgian men applied for their pensions to be calculated on the basis of fortieths of salary, rather than forty-fifths. Subsequent amendments to, and implementations of, Belgian law were to the effect that for men, pensionable age was to be 65 and pension calculated in forty-fifths; for women, pensionable age was to be progressively raised to 65 over a transitional period of 13 years, and the rate of pension was to be progressively raised over that period. The flexible retirement age was to be maintained, allowing both men and women to take their pension 'early' at 60, if they met an employment-record entitlement. The employment-record entitlement was to be 20 years in 1997, and to be progressively raised to 35 years in 2005. The question arose as to whether these provisions were compatible with Union law.

---

[83] Case C–154/92 [1993] ECR I–3811.   [84] Rubinstein [1994] IRLR 1.

[85] White, previously, at n. 13, 125.

[86] Joined Cases C–377–384/96 *De Vriendt and Others* v. *Rijksdienst voor Pensioen* [1998] ECR I–2105.

[87] Case C–154/96 *Wolfs* v. *Office national des pensions* [1998] ECR I–6173.

Once again, the Court repeated its test whether the rules in question were 'necessarily and objectively linked' to the difference in state pensionable age. The national court was to determine, as an issue of fact, whether the national legislation maintained a different pensionable age for men and women. If there was a difference, then 'the specification of the age for the award of a retirement pension effectively determines the length of the period during which persons can contribute to the pension scheme'.[88] In such a case, the method of calculating pensions would be necessarily and objectively linked to the pensionable age difference. Thus, if national legislation had maintained a different pensionable age for male and female workers, the Member State could calculate the amount of pension differently depending on the worker's sex. Differences in state pensionable ages could lawfully be maintained under Article 7(1)(a) to 'enable [Member States] progressively to adapt their pension systems in this respect without disrupting the complex financial equilibrium of those systems'.[89] Thus the principle established in *Van Cant* did not apply to transitional arrangements. The effect of these rulings was to leave it to the national court to decide whether the net effect of the Belgian legislation was to equalize state pensionable age. If it was not, then the different mechanisms for calculation were lawful, within Article 7(1)(a).

(d) Levelling up or down?

This litigation raises a variation on the long-standing debate about whether Union sex equality law requires 'levelling up' of benefits, or pay, or treatment, to the level of the better treated sex, or whether it is permissible to achieve formal equality between men and women by 'levelling down' benefits to those enjoyed by the worse treated sex.[90] The Court's case law makes it clear that nothing in Directive 79/7 requires equalization of state pensionable ages by levelling up. This of course leaves maximum discretion for Member States in this sensitive area of national social policy. The Court's rulings also make clear that Union law implies no specific duty on Member States to undertake the equalization process in any particular way. This conclusion is problematic, as the economics of the situation mean that any equalization is bound to take time. Provision must be made for an interim or transitional period, often of several years or even decades. On the Court's interpretation in *De Vriendt* and *Wolfs*, Directive 79/7 seems to leave Member States with full discretion even during that period. This is, at the least, a rather minimalist approach to the duties imposed by Directive 79/7.

3.2. Other derogations

Article 7(1) provides other grounds for derogating from the Directive. For example, Article 7(1)(c) allows Member States to exclude from the scope of the Directive the granting of entitlement to old-age benefits by virtue of the derived entitlement of a spouse. Therefore, in *Van Munster*[91] the Court said Directive 79/7 permitted a Member

---

[88] Joined Cases C–377–384/96 *De Vriendt* [1998] ECR I–2105, para. 29.
[89] Case C–154/96 *Wolfs* [1998] ECR I–6173, para. 25.   [90] See later in this chapter, at, n. 210–14.
[91] Case C–165/91 *Van Munster* v. *Rijksdienst voor Pensioenen* [1994] ECR I–4661.

State not to apply to a retired person's pension the 'household rate', which took account of the position of both the retired person and his dependent spouse, where the spouse was entitled to a retirement pension in his or her own right.[92]

Article 7(1)(d) allows Member States to exclude from the scope of the Directive the granting of increases of long-term invalidity benefits, old-age benefits, accidents at work, and occupational disease benefits for a dependent wife. This exception was successfully relied on by the UK in *Bramhill*.[93] The UK had abolished discrimination in respect of the rules relating to increases in long-term old-age benefits but only for certain categories of women. The Court said that the retention of the discriminatory rules in respect of the women not benefiting from the changed rules fell within the scope of Article 7(1)(d).

4. REMEDIES

4.1. Adequacy of compensation

Article 6 of Directive 79/7 repeats almost verbatim the requirement laid down in the original Article 6 of the Equal Treatment Directive 76/207 (now Article 17 of the Sex Equality Directive 2006/54) for complainants to have the right to pursue their claims by judicial process.[94] The parallels between the two Directives, and especially in the content of the remedies provisions, led many to think that the Court would interpret Article 6 similarly in both cases. Therefore, the decision in *ex parte Sutton*,[95] a Directive 79/7 case, delivered on the same day as *Draehmpaehl*,[96] a Directive 76/207 case, came as a surprise, and marked a departure from the emphasis on effective protection laid down in *Von Colson*[97] and *Marshall (No. 2)*.[98] In *Sutton*, a question was raised concerning the payment of interest on arrears of a social security benefit, invalid care allowance (ICA), when the delay in payment of the benefit was the result of discrimination prohibited by Directive 79/7 which had been declared unlawful by the Court in *Thomas*.[99] In the light of the Court's ruling in *Marshall (No. 2)* that interest was payable for an award under Directive 76/207, Mrs Sutton and the Commission argued that interest should also be paid under Directive 79/7. They pointed out, first, that the wording of Article 6 of Directive 79/7 was practically identical to that of Article 6 of Directive 76/207; secondly, that both Directives pursued the same objective, namely real equality of treatment for men and women; and thirdly, that Directive 79/7 gave effect to the legislative programme initiated by the adoption of Directive 76/207, which provided that subsequent instruments would be adopted with a view to ensuring the progressive implementation of the principle of equal treatment in matters of social security.

---

[92] Para. 17.   [93] Case C–420/92 *Bramhill* v. *Chief Adjudication Officer* [1994] ECR I–3191.

[94] The Burden of Proof Directive also applies to Dir. 79/7. See further Ch. 7.

[95] Case C–66/95 *The Queen* v. *Secretary of State for Social Security, ex parte Sutton* [1997] ECR I–2163.

[96] Case C–180/95 *Draehmpaehl* [1997] ECR I–2195, considered in Ch. 8.

[97] Case 14/83 *Von Colson* [1984] ECR 1891.

[98] Case C–271/91 *Marshall (No. 2)* [1993] ECR I–4367.   [99] Case C–328/91 [1993] ECR I–1247.

The Court, however, rejected these submissions. It said that the judgment in *Marshall (No. 2)* concerned the award of interest on amounts payable by way of reparation for loss and damage sustained as a result of discriminatory dismissal, where full compensation for the loss and damage sustained could not leave out of account factors such as the effluxion of time, which might have reduced its value. Therefore, in accordance with the applicable national rules, the award of interest had to be regarded as an essential component of compensation for the purposes of restoring real equality of treatment. By contrast, *Sutton* concerned the right to receive interest on amounts payable by way of social security benefits. Those benefits were paid to the person concerned by the competent bodies which had to examine whether the conditions laid down in the relevant legislation were fulfilled. Consequently, the Court said, the amounts paid by way of social security benefit were not compensatory in nature and in no way constituted reparation for loss or damage sustained. Therefore, it said its reasoning in *Marshall (No. 2)* could not be applied; and that Article 6 of Directive 79/7 merely required that the Member States adopt the measures necessary to enable all persons who consider themselves to have been wronged by discrimination prohibited under the Directive to establish the unlawfulness of such discrimination and to obtain the benefits to which they would have been entitled in the absence of discrimination. The payment of interest on arrears of benefits could not be regarded as an essential component of the right.

These arguments are not convincing: the purpose of any remedy by way of arrears of payment is to place complainants in the position they would have been in but for the discrimination. That must include interest on the money they would have otherwise received.[100] The Court did not, however, leave Mrs Sutton entirely without a remedy. It said (without having received a question on the point) that the state might be liable, following the cases of *Francovich No. 1*[101] and *ex parte Factortame (No. 3)*,[102] for loss and damage caused to individuals as a result of breaches of Union law for which the State could be held responsible. It said that a Member State's obligation to make reparation for the loss and damage was, however, subject to three conditions: the rule of law infringed had to be intended to confer rights on individuals; the breach had to be sufficiently serious; and there had to be a direct causal link between the breach of the obligation resting on the state and the damage sustained by the injured parties. It then added that, while the right to reparation was founded directly on Union law where the three conditions were fulfilled, the national law on liability provided the framework within which the state had to make reparation for the consequences of the loss and damage caused (the principle of national procedural autonomy).[103] It therefore said that it was for the national court to assess, in the light of this principle, whether Mrs Sutton was entitled to reparation for the loss which she claimed to have suffered as a result of

---

[100] Rubinstein [1997] IRLR 487.

[101] Joined Cases C–6/90 and C–9/90 *Francovich* [1990] ECR I–5357.

[102] Joined Cases C–46/93 *Brasserie du Pecheur* and C–48/95 *R v. Secretary of State for Transport, ex parte Factortame (No. 3)* [1996] ECR I–1029.

[103] Case 199/82 *Amministrazione delle finanze dello Stato v. San Giorgio* [1983] ECR 3595.

the breach of Union law by the UK, and, if appropriate, to determine the amount of such reparation.

The other perennial problem facing the Court has been the discrimination in the air hostess pension scheme for those working at Belgian Sabena airlines. This was at dispute in the *Defrenne* litigation[104] and the problems continue today in unravelling the discriminatory effect of the pension scheme, as *Jonkman*[105] shows. The first question concerned whether it was possible for a Member State, when adopting rules intended to allow those women who had been discriminated against to become eligible for the pension scheme only on condition that they make a payment, in a single sum and together with interest at the annual rate of 10 per cent, of adjustment contributions consisting of the difference between what the women had paid and what the men had paid. The Court said that Directive 79/7 does allow Member States to demand adjustment contributions plus interest but only interest to compensate for inflation. The Court also said that the Member State could not demand payment as a single sum, where that condition makes the adjustment concerned impossible or excessively difficult in practice. That is the case in particular where the sum to be paid exceeds the annual pension of the interested party.[106]

4.2. Time limits

The principle of national procedural autonomy outlined in *Sutton* has been a long-established rule of Union law. In essence it means that national procedural rules apply provided that they satisfy the requirements of equivalence (i.e. the same rules apply for breaches of Union law as for breaches of domestic law) and effectiveness (i.e. the national rules must not make it virtually impossible to bring a claim). Generally, reasonable national rules about time limits for bringing a claim do satisfy these tests.

However, in one of the earliest Directive 79/7 cases on this issue, *Emmott*,[107] the Court appeared to interfere with the principle of national procedural autonomy by saying that a Member State was precluded from relying on national procedural rules relating to time limits for bringing proceedings so long as the state had not properly transposed the Directive into its domestic legal system. The facts of *Emmott* were striking. The applicant had relied on the Court's judgment in *McDermott and Cotter*[108] to claim entitlement to invalidity benefit under Article 4(1) of Directive 79/7. The administrative authorities declined to adjudicate on her claim since Directive 79/7 was the subject of proceedings before the national court. Once these proceedings were completed, Emmott's claim was out of time, even though Directive 79/7 had still not been correctly transposed into national law. The Court ruled that:[109]

> ... until such time as a Directive has been properly transposed, a defaulting Member State may not rely on an individual's delay in initiating proceedings against it in order to protect rights

---

[104] See further Ch. 7 and later in this chapter.
[105] Joined Cases C–231/06 to C–233/06 *National Pensions Office* v. *Jonkman* [2007] ECR I–5149.
[106] Para. 35.   [107] Case C–208/90 *Emmott* v. *Minister for Social Welfare* [1991] ECR I–4269.
[108] Case 286/85 [1987] ECR 1453.   [109] Para. 23.

conferred upon him by the provisions of the directive and that a period laid down by national law within which proceedings must be initiated cannot begin to run before that time.

Given the potential implications of the ruling in *Emmott* it is not surprising that the Court began to backtrack. In *Steenhorst-Neerings*,[110] for example, the Court said that *Emmott* did not establish an automatic entitlement to *damages* backdated to the date on which an EU Directive should have been implemented into domestic law. This case concerned a national procedural rule limiting to one year the retroactive effect of claims made for the purpose of obtaining a particular benefit. The Court distinguished *Steenhorst-Neerings* from *Emmott* on the ground that while *Emmott* concerned a domestic rule fixing time limits for bringing actions, which had the effect of denying the right to rely on the Directive in order to claim, the rule in *Steenhorst* concerned only the amount of benefit. The limit in *Steenhorst* also served 'to ensure sound administration, most importantly so that it may be ascertained whether the claimant satisfied the conditions for eligibility, and so that the degree of incapacity which may vary over time, can be fixed'. The case also reflected 'the need to preserve financial balance in a scheme'.[111]

Similarly, in *Johnson (No. 2)*,[112] Mrs Johnson, who had been discriminated against in respect of her claim for NCIP and SDA,[113] was given SDA for a period of 12 months prior to her claim but was refused payments in respect of any period prior to that date. The Court said that the decision in *Emmott* was justified by the particular circumstance of the case. The national rule in *Johnson (No. 2)*, on the other hand, was similar to that in *Steenhorst-Neerings* where 'Neither rule constitutes a bar to proceedings; they merely limit the period prior to the bringing of the claim in respect of which arrears of benefit are payable'.[114]

In *Fantask*[115] the Court confirmed the limits to the rulings in *Emmott*. Having reasserted the principle of national procedural autonomy the Court pointed out that, in the interests of legal certainty, the setting of reasonable limitation periods for bringing proceedings was compatible with Union law. It said that such periods could not be regarded as rendering virtually impossible or excessively difficult the exercise of rights conferred by Union law, even if expiry of those periods necessarily entailed the dismissal, in whole or in part, of the action brought. The Court therefore ruled that the five-year limitation period at issue in *Fantask* had to be considered reasonable, especially since the period applied without distinction to actions based on Union law and those based on national law. The Court then referred to its decisions in *Johnson (No. 2)* and *Steenhorst-Neerings* and said that the solution adopted in *Emmott* was justified by the particular circumstances of the case, in which the time bar had the result of depriving the applicant of any opportunity whatever to rely on her right to equal treatment under a Union Directive. Where the time bar did not have that effect, as in *Fantask* itself, Member States could rely on national time limits, provided that they were not less favourable for

---

[110] Case C–338/91 [1993] ECR I–5475.   [111] Para. 23.
[112] Case C–410/92 *Johnson (No. 2)* v. *Chief Adjudication Officer* [1994] ECR I–5483.
[113] Case C–31/90 *Johnson (No. 1)* [1991] ECR I–3723.   [114] Para. 30.
[115] Case C–188/95 *Fantask and Others* v. *Industriministeriet* [1997] ECR I–6783.

actions based on Union law than for actions based on national law, and did not render virtually impossible or excessively difficult the exercise of rights conferred by Union law (as was the case in *Emmott*),[116] even where a Member State had not properly transposed the Directive.

C. EQUALITY, RETIREMENT, AND PENSIONS

1. INTRODUCTION

The application of the principle of equality to the highly controversial field of retirement and pension ages demonstrates both the interface between Article 157 TFEU and the equality Directives, and the potential cost to employers and the state of granting equality to men and women. Some Member States have directly discriminated between men and women in respect of state pension age, allowing men to receive their *state pension* at 65, but women at 60. As we saw above, Article 7(1)(a) of Directive 79/7 allows Member States to derogate from the principle of equality when determining pensionable age for the granting of (state) old-age and retirement benefits. And because the state pension age has (lawfully) discriminated against men and women, employers and trustees of occupational pensions schemes followed suit and set their retirement ages and the consequential entitlement to occupational pension ages in line with the state pension age, with the result that, for decades these ages have also discriminated (against men). As we shall see, this was in fact not a wise decision. In the following sections we shall consider the law in relation to retirement age and occupational pensions.

2. RETIREMENT AGE

Although the Court has now decided, in *Marshall (No. 1)*,[117] that men and women must not suffer discrimination in respect of retirement age, it had some difficulty reaching this conclusion. In the earliest case on this point, *Defrenne (No. 3)*,[118] the Court held that Article 157 TFEU did not apply to discriminatory retirement ages. In that case air hostesses, but not cabin stewards, had to retire when they reached the age of 40. The Court said that since retirement age related to working conditions, Article 157 TFEU did not apply.

The next decision, *Burton*,[119] arose after the enactment of the Equal Treatment Directive 76/207. This case concerned a voluntary redundancy scheme under which male

---

[116] J. Coppel 'Domestic Law Limitations on Recovery for Breach of EC Law' (1998) 27 *ILJ* 259, 260.

[117] Case 152/84 *Marshall (No. 1) v. Southampton and South West Hampshire Area Health Authority* [1986] ECR 723.

[118] Case 149/77 *Defrenne (No. 3) v. SABENA* [1978] ECR 1365.

[119] Case 19/81 *Burton v. British Railways Board* [1982] ECR 555. For criticism of this decision, see A. Lester, 'The Uncertain Trumpet, References to the Court of Justice from the United Kingdom: Equal Pay and Equal Treatment without Sex Discrimination' in H. Schermers, C. Timmermans, J. Kellermann, and A. Watson (eds.), *Article 177 EEC: Experiences and Problems* (The Asser Institute, The Hague, 1987).

employees could take voluntary redundancy at 60, women at 55 (in each case five years earlier than the British state pension age). Burton, a man of 58 who was refused redundancy on the grounds that he was too young, claimed that he was a victim of discrimination: had he been a woman he could have taken voluntary redundancy at 58. The Court argued that the case concerned not the benefit itself—the same amount was paid to men and women—but *the conditions of access to the benefit*.[120] The matter therefore fell to be considered under the Equal Treatment Directive 76/207 and not under Article 157 TFEU.[121] It then decided that although the term 'dismissal' in Article 5(1) of Directive 76/207 (now Article 14(1)(c) of the Sex Equality Directive) had to be broadly construed to include the termination of an employment relationship even as part of a voluntary redundancy scheme,[122] British Rail's redundancy scheme was not discriminatory because the only difference in treatment stemmed from the fact that the *state pension age* was not the same for both sexes. This difference in ages did not amount to discrimination prohibited by Union law because Article 7(1)(a) of *Directive 79/7* expressly excluded the determination of pensionable age from the application of the equality principle.[123] Thus, to much criticism, the Court decided that discriminatory retirement ages under Directive 76/207 could be saved by a derogation from another Directive (i.e. Directive 79/7).[124]

The issue was finally resolved in *Marshall (No. 1)*.[125] Helen Marshall worked for an area health authority whose policy was that women should retire at 60 but men could carry on working until 65, ages which once again coincided with the state pension age. Miss Marshall wanted to work until she was 65 but was forced to retire at 62. She claimed that she had been discriminated against, again contrary to Article 5(1) of the Directive 76/207 (now Article 14(1)(c) of the Sex Equality Directive). Her case was referred to the Court at the same time as *Roberts v. Tate & Lyle*.[126] Tate & Lyle's occupational pension scheme provided for compulsory retirement with a pension at 65 for men and 60 for women. When Tate & Lyle closed down one of its depots employees up to five years away from normal retirement age (60 for men and 55 for women) were entitled to receive an early pension. When the men complained that this was discriminatory, the company agreed that both men and women would receive the pension at 55. Miss Roberts, who was 53, then argued that the revised plan was also discriminatory since a male employee

---

[120] It is widely thought that *Burton* has been *sotto voce* overruled on this point. The distinction between access to payment as opposed to the amount of benefit was not maintained in Case 170/84 *Bilka-Kaufhaus* v. *Weber von Hartz* [1986] ECR 1607 where the Court recognized that access to benefits for part-timers fell within Art. 157 TFEU, see D. Curtin (1990) 27 *CMLRev.* 475, 482.

[121] For a more recent reaffirmation of this point, see Case C–207/04 *Vergani* v. *Agenzia delle Entrate* [2005] ECR I–7453, para. 26.

[122] Again this was confirmed in Case C–207/04 *Vergani* [2005] ECR I–7453, para. 27.

[123] It now seems that the exceptions to Directive 79/7 are confined exclusively to the field of social security benefits, see Case 152/84 *Marshall (No. 1)* [1986] ECR 723, 746.

[124] Without reference to *Burton* on this point, the Court reversed itself in Case C–207/04 *Vergani* [2005] ECR I–7453, para. 33: 'That exception [Art. 7(1)(a) of Dir. 79/7] to the prohibition of discrimination on grounds of sex is therefore not applicable in the case of a tax concession such as that at issue [to which Dir. 76/207 applies]…, which is not a social security benefit'.

[125] Case 152/84 [1986] ECR 723.   [126] Case 151/84 *Roberts* v. *Tate & Lyle* [1986] ECR 703.

was entitled to receive a pension 10 years before the normal retirement age whereas women could receive the pension only five years before the normal retirement age.

Marshall (No. 1), Roberts and a third case, *Beets Proper,*[127] the facts of which were very similar to those in *Marshall (No. 1),* presented the Court with a menu of options, forcing the Court to examine whether to require equality in respect of retirement ages and, if so, how. In the event, the Court opted for the formal equality model offered by *Marshall (No. 1).*[128] However, in order to achieve this, the Court had to address the problems caused by *Burton.* Its solution was to sever the link between retirement age and state pension age. It argued that *Marshall (No. 1)* was not about the conditions for paying an old-age pension; it actually concerned the fixing of an age limit in connection with the termination of employment pursuant to a general policy concerning dismissal. This situation was covered by Article 5(1) of Directive 76/207 (now Article 14(1)(c) of Directive 2006/54). Consequently, Article 7(1)(a) of the Social Security Directive 79/7 did not apply since it covered only the determination of *pensionable* age for the purpose of granting old-age and retirement pensions. Therefore, since Article 5 was directly effective it could be invoked by Miss Marshall against her state employer to insist on equal treatment.[129] Similarly, in *Roberts* the Court concluded that the case concerned dismissal as a result of mass redundancy and not the granting of old-age or retirement pensions and so Article 5(1) of Directive 76/207 again applied. It then ruled that it was compatible with Article 5 to lay down a single age for the dismissal of men and women and the grant of an early retirement pension.

As a consequence of these decisions the Court has ensured formal equality in respect of retirement age but in so doing it has created an artificial distinction between retirement age and pension age. This presents a particular problem for men: while it may now be possible for men to (be obliged to) retire at 60[130] with their female colleagues, the right to retire is of limited value if the men are dependent on a state pension which is not payable until they are 65. These inconsistencies are due to the maintenance of discriminatory state pension ages which, as we have seen, are compatible with Union law.

3. STATE PENSION AGE

In *Defrenne (No. 1)*[131] the Court made it clear that differences in the state pension age would not fall within the ambit of Article 157 TFEU. In the words of the Court:

---

[127] Case 262/84 *Beets Proper v. F. van Landschot Bankers NV* [1986] ECR 773. See further T. Millett, 'European Community Law: Sex Equality and Retirement Age' (1987) 36 *ICLQ.* 616.

[128] For a more recent example, see Case C–356/09 *Pensionsversicherungsanstalt v. Kleist* [2010] ECR I–000. See further K. Koldinska, 'Case law of the European Court of Justice on Sex Discrimination 2006–11' (2011) 48 *CMLRev.* 1599.

[129] In Case 262/84 *Beets Proper* [1986] ECR 773 the Court reiterated the principle laid down in *Marshall* but this time applied it to discriminatory retirement ages contained in a contract of employment based on a collective agreement. No reference to direct effect was made in that case.

[130] Subject now to the Age Discrimination provisions of the Framework Directive 2000/78 considered in detail in Ch. 8.

[131] Case 80/70 *Defrenne (No. 1) v. Belgian State* [1971] ECR 445.

Although payment in the nature of social security benefits is not excluded in principle from the concept of pay it is not possible to include in this concept as defined in Article [157] TFEU social security schemes and benefits especially retirement pensions which are directly settled by law without any reference to any element of consultation within the undertaking or industry concerned and which cover without exception all workers in general.[132]

The case concerned a pension scheme which applied to flight personnel of civil airlines with the exception of air hostesses. Miss Defrenne, an air hostess, argued that the scheme was discriminatory, contrary to Article 157 TFEU. The Court disagreed, arguing first, that the scheme was determined less by the employment relationship between the employer and the worker than by considerations of social policy; and second, that the worker would receive the benefits not by reason of the employer's contributions but solely because the worker fulfilled the legal conditions for the grant of the benefits. Therefore, the Court said that the retirement pension did not constitute consideration which the workers received indirectly from their employer within the meaning of Article 157 TFEU.

Since Article 157 TFEU cannot be used to eliminate a discriminatory state pension age then it is compatible with Union law to maintain this discrimination. As we saw in section B above and in *Burton*,[133] this is confirmed by Article 7(1)(a) of the Social Security Directive 79/7, and accepted by the Court in *ex parte EOC*.[134] Furthermore, measures taken by an employer to mitigate the consequences of a discriminatory pension age are also compatible with Union law. In *Roberts*[135] the employer reduced a woman's bridging pension by the amount of the state pension from the age of 60 but made no such reduction in respect of a man until the age of 65. While acknowledging that bridging pensions are 'pay' within the meaning of Article 157 TFEU, the Court ruled that the difference in the 'objective premise'—that women receive a state pension at 60 but men do not—leading to differences in the amount of the bridging pension paid to men and women 'cannot be considered discriminatory'. This view can be contrasted with the approach adopted by the British House of Lords in *James*[136] which ruled that gender-based criteria are discriminatory, *per se*, regardless of their purpose or justification. However, the Court's decision in *Roberts* is now confirmed by Article 8(2) of the Sex Equality Directive 2006/54.

4. OCCUPATIONAL PENSIONS

4.1. Introduction

Occupational pensions are offered by employers to their employees in connection with their employment. In defined contribution or money purchase schemes the employer

---

[132] Para. 7.   [133] Case 19/87 [1982] ECR 555.

[134] Case C–9/91 [1992] 3 ECR I–4297. In the UK from 2018 men and women will both receive their state pension at 65, which represents a levelling down of benefit for women. From 2020 the age will increase to 66 for both.

[135] Case C–132/92 *Birds Eye Walls* v. *Roberts* [1993] ECR I–5579. See additionally Case C–19/02 *Hlozek* [2004] ECR I–11491.

[136] *James* v. *Eastleigh Borough Council* [1990] 3 WLR 55.

and employee agree to a level of contributions, usually a fixed percentage of salary, and the resulting lump sum saved is used to purchase a pension at the time of retirement. In defined benefit or final salary schemes there is usually a fixed employee contribution (although in some schemes the employer funds the total cost) but the employer undertakes to provide a level of benefits according to a formula. Consequently the employer's contribution to the scheme will vary from year to year.[137] These occupational pensions can be a substitute for a state pension (such as a pension contracted-out from the state scheme) or a supplement to a state pension. Following the model of state schemes, the occupational pension age for many schemes was also discriminatory. For this reason Directive 86/378,[138] introduced to implement the principle of equal treatment in occupational social security schemes, allowed for derogations in respect of, *inter alia*, occupational pension age. This Directive has now been repealed and replaced by the Sex Equality Directive 2006/54.

4.2. Directive 86/378 on Equal Treatment in Occupational Social Security (Articles 5–13 of the Sex Equality Directive 2006/54)

Directive 86/378 (and now Directive 2006/54) was intended to complement Directive 79/7,[139] and the beneficiaries of the principle of equal treatment[140] were almost identical in both. Occupational social security schemes are defined as those schemes not governed by Directive 79/7 whose purpose is to provide workers, whether employees or self-employed, in an 'undertaking or group of undertakings, area of economic activity, occupational sector or group of sectors with benefits intended to supplement the benefits provided by the statutory social schemes or to replace them, whether membership of such schemes is compulsory or optional'.[141] It applies to occupational social security schemes which provide protection against sickness, invalidity, old age, including early retirement, industrial accidents, occupational diseases, and unemployment. It also applies to occupational schemes which provide for other social benefits, in cash or in kind, and in particular survivors' benefits and family allowances, if such benefits constitute a consideration paid by the employer to the worker by reason of the worker's employment.[142]

Article 5 (of both Directive 86/378 and the Sex Equality Directive 2006/54) spells out the scope of the principle of equal treatment: without prejudice to the principle of equal pay, there is to be no direct or indirect discrimination on the grounds of sex in occupational social security schemes, in particular as regards:

- the scope of such schemes and the conditions of access to them;
- the obligation to contribute and the calculation of contributions;

---

[137] R. Nobles, *Pensions, Employment and the Law* (Clarendon Press, Oxford, 1993) 8.
[138] OJ [1986] L225/40.
[139] Art. 3(3) of Dir. 79/7 said that the Council will adopt provisions defining the principle of equal treatment in occupational pension schemes.   [140] Art. 3.
[141] Art. 2(1)(f) of the Sex Equality Dir. 2006/54.   [142] Art. 7 of the Sex Equality Dir. 2006/54.

- the calculation of benefits, including supplementary benefits due in respect of a spouse or dependants, and the conditions governing the duration and retention of entitlement to benefits.

Article 9 of the Sex Equality Directive 2006/54 gives examples of provisions which contravene the principle of equal treatment. The list includes determining people who can participate in occupational schemes, fixing the compulsory or optional nature of participation in an occupational scheme; laying down different rules as regards the age of entry into the scheme or minimum periods of employment or membership of the scheme required to obtain the benefits of the scheme; laying down different rules for the reimbursement of contributions when a worker leaves a scheme without having fulfilled the conditions guaranteeing a deferred right to long-term benefits; setting different conditions for granting of benefits or restricting the benefits to workers of one or other of the sexes; fixing different retirement ages; suspending the retention or acquisition of rights during periods of maternity leave or leave for family reasons which are granted by law or agreement and paid by the employer; setting different levels of benefit;[143] setting different levels of worker contribution[144] and employer's contribution;[145] and laying down different standards applicable to workers of only one sex.[146]

Article 9 of the original Directive 86/378 did, however, contain an extensive list of derogations. In particular, Member States could defer compulsory application of the principle of equal treatment with regard to:

(a) the determination of pensionable age for the purposes of granting old-age and retirement pensions, and the possible implications for other benefits, either until the date on which such equality is achieved in statutory schemes, or at the latest until such equality is required by a Directive;

(b) survivors' pensions until a Directive requires the application of the principle of equal treatment, and

(c) setting the levels of worker contributions to take account of the different actuarial calculations factors, at least until the expiry of a 13-year period as from 30 July 1986.

As we shall see, considerable doubt was cast on the legality of these derogations, with the exception of the derogation relating to actuarial factors, by *Barber*[147] (occupational pensions age) which 'automatically invalidates certain provisions of Directive 86/378',[148] and *Ten Oever*[149] (survivors' benefits). In each case the benefit concerned was

---

[143] Special provision is made in respect of actuarial factors which is considered further in this chapter..

[144] See additionally case C–152/91 *Neath* v. *Steeper* [1993] ECR I–6935 and Case C–200/91 *Coloroll* [1994] ECR I–4389 and 10th Preambular paragraph.

[145] Certain exceptions are provided here in the case of defined contribution and defined benefit schemes.

[146] Again certain exceptions are provided here too.

[147] Case C–262/88 *Barber* v. *Guardian Royal Exchange Assurance Group* [1990] ECR I–1889.

[148] Preamble to Council Dir. 96/97/EC (OJ [1997] L46/20).

[149] Case C–109/91 *Ten Oever* v. *Stichting Bedrijfspensionenfonds voor het Glazenwassers—en Schoomaakbedrijf* [1993] ECR I–4879.

deemed to fall within the definition of 'pay' in Article 157 TFEU, a *Treaty* provision which took precedence over the Directive. As the Court said in *Moroni*,[150] the 'effects of the Directive do not matter, for its provisions cannot in any way restrict the scope of Article [157]'. This led to the adoption of a new Directive 96/97/EC,[151] amending Directive 86/378 to 'adapt the provisions affected by the *Barber* case law',[152] the content of which is now found in the Sex Equality Directive 2006/54. The derogations from the Directive now apply largely to the self-employed.[153]

4.3. Occupational pensions, 'pay', and Article 157 TFEU

(a) The early case law

So, how then did Article 157 TFEU apply? There had been hints in the early case law that occupational pensions could fall within the definition of pay in Article 157 TFEU. For example, in *Garland*[154] the Court said that the concept of pay embraced both 'immediate and *future* benefits',[155] which in that case included free travel after retirement. Consequently, occupational pensions, although received after employment, could be construed as a type of remuneration received directly or indirectly from the employer. Advocate General Dutheillet de Lamothe in *Defrenne (No. 1)*[156] had also taken this view. He considered that pensions payable directly by the employer came within the scope of Article 157 TFEU since they could be regarded as a form of deferred pay. He also regarded *supplementary* pensions as falling within the scope of Article 157 TFEU if they could be regarded as being independent of the state scheme. On the facts of *Defrenne (No. 1)* the Court found that this was not the case.

Advocate General Dutheillet de Lamothe's approach in *Defrenne (No. 1)* was endorsed by the Court in *Bilka-Kaufhaus*.[157] The case concerned an occupational pension scheme which, although adopted in accordance with German legislation, was voluntary in origin and arose from an agreement between the employer and the works council.[158] It *supplemented* the social security legislation with benefits financed entirely by the employer. In the words of the Court, the scheme was contractual rather than statutory and formed an integral part of the contracts of employment. The scheme therefore offered the necessary link between pay and the employment relationship which was absent from the scheme in *Defrenne (No. 1)*.[159]

---

[150] Case C–110/91 *Moroni* v. *Collo* [1993] ECR I–6591, para. 24.   [151] OJ [1996] L46/20.

[152] Preamble to Dir. 96/97.

[153] E.g. Arts. 8(1)(a) and (b) and Art. 11 of the Sex Equality Dir. 2006/54. Art. 10 of the Sex Equality Dir. 2006/54 requires Member States to take the necessary steps to ensure that the provisions of occupational schemes for self-employed workers contrary to the principle of equal treatment are revised with effect from 1 January 1993.

[154] Case 12/81 *Garland* v. *British Rail Engineering* [1982] ECR 359.   [155] Para. 5.

[156] Case 80/70 [1971] ECR 445.   [157] Case 170/84 [1986] ECR 1607.

[158] The emphasis on agreement is important. It takes precedence over the criterion of statutory origin. However, the negotiations between the employer's and the employees' representatives must result in a formal agreement and not just consultation (Case C–7/93 *Beune* [1994] ECR I–4471, para. 32).

[159] Case 80/70 [1971] ECR 445.

However, Advocate General Warner in *Worringham*[160] did not feel the distinctions made by Advocate General Dutheillet de Lamothe in *Defrenne (No. 1)* were so easy to apply in the context of the British system of contracted-out schemes which were a *substitute for* the state scheme and not a *supplement to* the state scheme. Because he was worried that an unbalanced result would arise if equalization was required in the context of occupational schemes and not in the case of the state scheme, he argued that such contracted-out occupational schemes had to fall outside Article 157 TFEU. *Worringham* concerned a pension scheme under which men were required to contribute to the bank's pension scheme from the date on which they started work but women could start making contributions only when they reached the age of 25. The contributions amounted to 5 per cent of an employee's salary. In order to make up for this difference in pay, men under 25 received a 5 per cent addition to their gross pay. If a man left the bank before he was 25 he was entitled to a refund on his contributions but women leaving before the age of 25 received nothing. Women also suffered other disadvantages: any redundancy pay, unemployment benefit, and credit facilities were calculated by reference to gross earnings which would be less for women than for men.

The bank argued that the case concerned a contracted-out scheme and so Article 157 TFEU did not apply; the women argued that the scheme was a supplementary scheme to which Article 157 TFEU did apply. The Court, by examining the discriminatory effects of the scheme rather than its legal nature, focused on the way in which the contributions affected the calculation of gross pay. It concluded that contributions to a retirement benefits scheme, which were paid by the employer in the name of the employees by means of an addition to the gross salary, were 'pay' within the meaning of Article 157 TFEU[161] and therefore no discrimination was permitted.

By contrast, in *Newstead*,[162] the Court found that because the deduction in question resulted in a reduction in *net* pay, due to a contribution paid to a social security scheme, and in no way affected gross pay, Article 157 TFEU did not apply. Newstead was a civil servant employed by the Department of Transport. He was required to contribute to an occupational pension scheme which made provision for a widow's pension fund. All male civil servants were obliged to contribute to this scheme at a rate of 1.5 per cent of their gross salary, irrespective of their marital status; female civil servants had the choice whether to contribute to the scheme. Civil servants who remained unmarried throughout the period during which they were covered by the scheme were entitled to a refund of their contributions plus interest at 4 per cent when they left the service. Newstead, a confirmed bachelor in his fifties, objected to making this payment, albeit temporarily, and claimed that he was the victim of unlawful discrimination. The Court decided that the pension scheme was a substitute for a social security scheme and consequently any contribution to such a scheme was 'considered to fall within the scope of Article [156] TFEU and not Article [157]'. This decision was the subject of much criticism and

---

[160] Case 69/80 *Worringham* v. *Lloyds Bank* [1981] ECR 767.
[161] Cf. Case 23/83 *Liefting* v. *Academisch Zieckenhuis bij de Universiteit van Amsterdam* [1984] ECR 3225.
[162] Case 192/85 *Newstead* v. *Department of Transport* [1987] ECR 4753.

it is difficult to reconcile it with the earlier cases.[163] It took the momentous decision by the Court in *Barber* to cut through this muddle and state authoritatively that occupational pensions, including contracted-out pension schemes,[164] constituted 'pay' within the meaning of Article 157 TFEU.[165]

(b) The decision in Barber

Mr Barber belonged to a non-contributory pension scheme (a scheme wholly financed by the employer). Since the scheme was contracted-out from the state pension scheme it was a substitute for the state scheme. Under the terms of the scheme the normal pensionable age was fixed at 62 for men and 57 for women—three years prior to the state pension age. In the event of redundancy, members of the pension fund were entitled to an immediate pension at 55 for men and 50 for women, seven years before the scheme's normal pensionable age. Staff who did not fulfil these conditions but who had been made redundant received cash benefits calculated on the basis of their years of service and a deferred pension payable at the normal pensionable age. Barber found himself in this position. Made redundant at 52, he received the cash benefits, statutory redundancy pay and an *ex gratia* payment but he was not entitled to his occupational pension until he was 62. A woman of 52 would have received the pension immediately, as well as the statutory redundancy payment, and the total value of those benefits would have been greater than the amount paid to him. Barber claimed that he had been discriminated against on the grounds of his sex.[166]

The Court began by distinguishing contracted-out private *occupational* schemes from the state *social security* scheme at issue in *Defrenne (No. 1)*.[167] First, it noted that contracted-out schemes resulted from either an agreement between workers and employers or a unilateral decision by the employer. The schemes were funded by the employer or by the employer and the workers, with no contribution from the public authorities. The Court therefore concluded that such occupational pension schemes formed part of the consideration offered to the workers by the employer. Secondly, the Court said that such schemes were not compulsorily applicable to general categories of workers: they applied only to workers employed in certain undertakings, with the result that affiliation to those schemes derived from the employment relationship with a given employer. In addition, such schemes were governed by their own rules, even if they were established in conformity with national legislation. Thirdly, the Court reasoned that even if such occupational schemes were substitutes for the general statutory scheme these schemes might

---

[163] See e.g. Arnull (1988) 13 *ELRev.* 136.

[164] In Case C–7/93 *Beune* [1994] ECR I–4471, para. 37, the Court said that benefits awarded under an occupational scheme which *partly or entirely* take the place of the benefits paid by a statutory social security scheme may also fall within the scope of Art. 157 TFEU.

[165] Case C–262/88 *Barber* [1990] ECR I–1887. On the effect of *Barber* on the pensions industry see G. Moffat and L. Luckhaus, 'Occupational Pension Schemes, Equality and Europe: a Decade of Change' (1998) 20 *JSWL* 1.

[166] A comparator is necessary. In Case C–200/91 *Coloroll Pension Trustees* v. *Russell* [1994] ECR I–4389 the Court ruled that Art. 157 TFEU did not apply to schemes whose members were all of one sex (para. 104).

[167] Case 80/70 [1971] ECR 445.

grant their members benefits greater than those paid under the statutory scheme, with the result that their economic function was similar to that of supplementary schemes, which, as the Court had held in *Bilka-Kaufhaus*,[168] fell within the concept of pay within the meaning of Article 157 TFEU. Therefore, a pension paid under a contracted-out scheme constituted consideration paid by an employer in respect of his employment and consequently fell within the scope of Article 157 TFEU.[169]

4.4. The application of the equality principle to occupational pension schemes

It is clear that the principle of non-discrimination laid down by Article 157 TFEU relates to the *quantum* of benefit[170] so that men and women receive the same amount. In *Barber*[171] the Court established that *each* benefit received under an occupational pension scheme was to be paid on a non-discriminatory basis:[172] it was not sufficient to make a comprehensive assessment of the total consideration paid to workers. The Court's justification for reaching this conclusion was pragmatic: it referred to the fundamental principle of transparency which would enable national courts to review schemes with a view to eliminating discrimination based on sex. The Court argued that such judicial review would be difficult and the effectiveness of Article 157 TFEU would be diminished if the national courts were required to make a comparative assessment of the package of consideration granted.

However, Article 157 TFEU does not only apply to the quantum of benefits. As Article 9 of the Sex Equality Directive 2006/54 indicated, it also applies to *access and conditions of access* to the scheme.[173] The question of *access* was first raised in *Bilka-Kaufhaus*[174] where the Court ruled that Article 157 TFEU covered not only entitlement to benefits paid by an occupational pensions scheme but also the right to be a member of such a scheme. In *Bilka-Kaufhaus* the employers refused to pay Mrs Weber, a part-time worker, an occupational pension since she had not worked full time for the minimum period of 15 years. She alleged that the exclusion of part-time workers from the occupational pension scheme constituted indirect discrimination, contrary to Article 157 TFEU. As the Court had explained in *Jenkins*,[175] if a pay policy setting a lower hourly rate for part-

---

[168] Case 170/84 [1986] ECR 1607.   [169] See additionally Case C–46/07 *Commission* v. *Italy* [2008] ECR I–151*.

[170] Curtin suggests that *Barber* does not require that the total amount of a particular benefit be mathematically equal since neither the costs nor the value of the total pension benefits will ever be known in advance. She argues that *Barber* requires that the *rate* at which the benefit is enjoyed be equal ((1990) 27 *CMLRev*. 475, 484–5). See further Case E-2/07 *EFTA Surveillance Authority* v. *Norway*, judgment of the EFTA Court 2007.

[171] Case C–262/88 [1990] ECR I–1889.

[172] This is also the approach which had been adopted by the House of Lords in *Haywards* v. *Cammell Laird* [1988] 2 WLR 1134 concerning the interpretation of the equal pay provisions of the Equality Act 2010.

[173] See further Art. 5(9) and Art. 9(1)(a) of the Sex Equality Directive 2006/54.

[174] Case 170/84 [1986] ECR 1607. However, in Case C–256/01 *Allonby* v. *Accrington & Rosendale College* [2004] ECR I–873, para. 57 the Court said that a teacher employed by an agency could not rely on the principle of equal pay in order to secure entitlement to membership of an occupational pension scheme for teachers set up by state legislation of which only teachers with a contract of employment could become members, using as a basis for comparison the remuneration, including such a right of membership, received for equal work or work of the same value by a man employed by the woman's previous employer.

[175] Case 96/80 *Jenkins* v. *Kingsgate* [1981] ECR 911.

time work than for full-time work entailed discrimination between men and women, then the same applied where part-time workers were refused access to a company pension. Since a pension fell within the definition of pay, it followed that hour for hour the total remuneration paid by the employer to full-time workers was higher than that paid to part-time workers.

The Court followed this approach in *Vroege*.[176] It said that an occupational pension scheme which excluded part-time workers from membership contravened Article 157 TFEU if the exclusion affected a much greater number of women than men, and which the employer could not explain by objectively justified factors unrelated to any discrimination on grounds of sex. In *Vroege* the Court also recognized that the exclusion of married women from membership of an occupational pension scheme did entail discrimination directly based on sex and was contrary to Article 157 TFEU.[177]

As far as *conditions of access* are concerned, the principle of equality in Article 157 TFEU also applies. As the Court ruled in *Barber*,[178] Article 157 TFEU prohibited any discrimination with regard to pay as between men and women, *whatever the system which gives rise to such inequality*. Thus, the Court said it was contrary to Article 157 TFEU to impose an age condition which differed according to sex in respect of pensions paid under a contracted-out scheme, even if the difference between the pensionable age for men and women was based on the age laid down by the national statutory scheme.[179] The Court extended this ruling to supplementary (non-contracted-out) occupational pension schemes in *Moroni*[180] and *Coloroll*.[181]

Earlier cases, such as *Burton*,[182] *Marshall (No. 1)*,[183] and *Roberts*,[184] had, however, suggested that the fixing of pensionable ages related to the *conditions of access* to the pension and consequently was governed by the Equal Treatment Directives, despite the consequences that such discrimination might have for the worker's pay.[185] On the other hand, Article 1 of the (original) Equal Pay Directive 75/117, which was designed to facilitate the application of Article 157 TFEU,[186] made clear that 'the principle of equal pay...means the elimination of all discrimination on the grounds of sex with regard to all aspects and *conditions of remuneration*' (emphasis added) and so in this respect the *Barber* judgment only serves to confirm the position under Directive 75/117.[187] Nevertheless, the distinction between the Equal Treatment Directive and Article 157 TFEU is no longer as clear as it once was.[188]

[176] Case C–57/93 *Vroege v. NCIV* [1994] ECR I–4541.
[177] See additionally Case C–128/93 *Fisscher v. Voorhuis Hengelo BV* [1994] ECR I–4583.
[178] Case C–262/88 [1990] ECR I–1889. See additionally Art. 9(1)(e) of the Sex Equality Dir. 2006/54.
[179] See additionally Case C–351/00 *Niemi* [2002] ECR I–7007, para. 53.
[180] Case C–110/91 [1993] ECR I–6591.   [181] Case C–200/91 [1994] ECR I–4389.
[182] Case 19/81 [1982] ECR 555.   [183] Case 152/84 [1986] ECR 723.
[184] Case 151/84 [1986] ECR 703.   [185] Art. 5 of Dir. 76/207 and Art. 6(f) of Dir. 86/378.
[186] Case 96/80 *Jenkins* [1981] ECR 911.
[187] See additionally Arts. 5(a) and 9(1)(e) of the Sex Equality Dir. 2006/54.
[188] AG Van Gerven in *Barber* [1990] ECR I–1889 did suggest that the two are not mutually exclusive, a point now reinforced by the Sex Equality Dir. 2006/54. See further Ch. 7.

4.5. The non-retrospective effect of the *Barber* judgment: the temporal limitation

The Court, aware of the potential financial consequences of any decision on equalization of benefits under an occupational pension scheme, decided to limit the retrospective effect of its judgment. It had already restricted the retrospective effect of its judgment
in *Defrenne (No. 2)*[189] 'by way of exception, taking account of the serious difficulties
which its judgment may create as regards events in the past'. Thus, the direct effect of
Article 157 TFEU which was established in that case for the first time could not be
invoked in respect of periods of service prior to 8 April 1976, the date of the judgment
in *Defrenne (No. 2)*. In *Barber* the Court considered that, in the light of the exclusion of
pensionable age from the scope of Directive 79/7 and the formal extension of this derogation by Article 9(a) of Directive 86/378/EEC to occupational pension schemes, Member States were reasonably entitled to consider that Article 157 TFEU did not apply to
pensions paid under contracted-out schemes. Therefore, in the interests of legal certainty and out of a wish to avoid upsetting the financial balance of many contracted-out
pension schemes, the Court concluded that:

> ...the direct effect of Article [157 TFEU] may not be relied upon in order to claim entitle-
> ment to a pension with effect from a date prior to that of this judgment (17 May 1990),
> except in the case of workers or those claiming under them who have before that date initi-
> ated proceedings or raised an equivalent claim under the applicable national law.

The Court then added that 'no restriction on the effects of the aforesaid interpretation
can be permitted as regards the acquisition of entitlement to a pension as from the date
of this judgment'.

Such statements caused considerable uncertainty as to the precise meaning of the
scope of the non-retrospectivity ruling. Advocate General Van Gerven discussed four
possible interpretations:[190]

> A *first interpretation* would be to apply the principle of equal treatment only to workers
> who became members of, and began to pay contributions to, an occupational pension
> scheme as from 17 May 1990. This view would deprive the *Barber* judgment of almost all
> retroactive effect. In practical terms, it would mean that the full effect of the judgment
> would be felt only after a period of about 40 years.
>
> A *second interpretation* is that the principle of equal treatment should only be applied
> to benefits payable in respect of periods of service after 17 May 1990. Periods of service
> prior to that date would not be affected by the direct effect of Article [157].
>
> According to a *third interpretation*, the principle of equal treatment must be applied
> to all pensions which are payable or paid for the first time after 17 May 1990, irrespec-
> tive of the fact that all or some of the pension accrued during, and on the basis of, peri-
> ods of service completed or contributions paid prior to that date. In other words, it is

---

[189] Case 43/75 [1976] ECR 455.
[190] Cases C–109/91, C–110/91, C–152/91, and C–200/91 *Ten Oever, Moroni, Neath*, and *Coloroll* [1993]
ECR I–4879. See further S. Honeyball and J. Shaw, 'Sex and the Retiring Man' (1991) 16 *ELRev*. 56 and D.
Curtin (1990) 27 *CMLRev*. 475, 487.

not the periods of service (before or after the judgment in *Barber*) which are decisive, but the date on which the pension falls to be paid.

A *fourth interpretation* would be to apply equal treatment to all pension payments made after 17 May 1990, including benefits or pensions which had already fallen due and, here again, as in the previous interpretation, irrespective of the date of the periods of service during which the pension accrued. This interpretation undoubtedly has the most far-reaching effect.

At the Intergovernmental Conference at Maastricht the heads of state added Protocol No. 2 (now called the Protocol concerning Article 157 TFEU (Protocol No. 33)) to 'clarify' the temporal limitation of *Barber*. This provides:

> For the purposes of Article [157] of the [Treaty on the Functioning of the European Union], benefits under occupational social security schemes shall not be considered as remuneration if and insofar as they are attributable to periods of employment prior to 17 May 1990, except in the case of workers or those claiming under them who have before that date initiated legal proceedings or introduced an equivalent claim under the applicable national law.

The Protocol favours the second approach identified by Advocate General Van Gerven that benefits need to be equal only in respect of periods of employment after 17 May 1990. The approach contained in the Protocol was followed by the Court in *Ten Oever*[191] (thereby avoiding a constitutional conflict with the European Council). The Court said that account had to be taken of the fact that in the case of pensions 'there is a time lag between the accrual of entitlement to the pension, which occurred gradually throughout the employee's working life and its actual payment, which is deferred until a particular age'.[192] It noted the way in which occupational pension funds are financed and the accounting links existing in each individual case between the periodic contributions and the future amounts paid. It continued that 'equality of treatment in the matter of occupational pensions may be claimed only in relation to benefits payable in respect of periods of employment subsequent to 17 May 1990, the date of the *Barber* judgment, subject to the exception prescribed therein for workers or those claiming under them who have, before that date, initiated legal proceedings or raised an equivalent claim under the applicable national law'.[193]

The Protocol concerning Article 157 TFEU made no distinction between contracted-out and supplementary occupational schemes, talking only in general terms of 'benefits under occupational social security schemes'. This suggested that the *Barber* time limit also applied to supplementary schemes. This was confirmed by *Moroni*[194]

---

[191] Case C–109/91 [1993] ECR I–4879 and applied in Case C–152/91 *Neath* v. *Steeper* [1993] ECR I–6935 and Case C–200/91 *Coloroll* [1994] ECR I–4389.

[192] See further Advocate General Van Gerven in Case C–109/91 *Ten Oever* [1993] ECR I–4879. The same justification was given by the Court apply the *Barber* limitation to transfer benefits and lump-sum options in Case C–152/91 *Neath* [1993] ECR I–6953.

[193] The Court has refused to permit any further exception to the rule: Joined Cases C–4/02 and C–5/02 *Schönheit* v. *Stadt Frankfurt am Main* [2003] ECR I–12575, para. 103.

[194] Case C–110/91 [1993] ECR I–6591, para. 33.

and *Coloroll*,[195] despite the fact that in the earlier case of *Bilka-Kaufhaus*,[196] which also concerned supplementary occupational schemes, no temporal limitation was imposed. This position is now confirmed in Article 12(1) of the Sex Equality Directive 2006/54 which provides that any measure implementing the Chapter (on occupational social security) as regards workers must cover 'all benefits under occupational social security schemes derived from periods of employment subsequent to 17 May 1990[197] and shall apply retroactively to that date, without prejudice to workers or those claiming under them who have, before that date, initiated legal proceedings or raised an equivalent claim under national law'. In respect of this latter group the implementation measures apply retroactively to 8 April 1976 (the date of the judgment in *Defrenne (No. 2)*).[198]

It is now quite clear that Article 157 TFEU does not apply to any benefit or part of any benefit relating to service before 17 May 1990 (except for legal claims started before that date)[199] and true equality of pension *benefits* will not be achieved under Union law until all those employed prior to 17 May 1990 have retired. However, *Barber* does require all occupational schemes to allow men and women to receive their occupational pensions at the same age, as from 17 May 1990, albeit that the payments which relate to service prior to 17 May 1990 are of different amounts.

A simple example may serve to illustrate the application of the *Barber* principles.[200] In May 1984 ABC Ltd employs Mrs X and Mr Y, both aged 50. ABC Ltd runs an occupational pension scheme with a normal pension age of 60 for women and 65 for men. An actuarial reduction of 4 per cent per annum is made for each year by which retirement precedes the normal pension age. Mrs X and Mr Y both retire in May 1994 aged 60. Mr Y's pension is subject to a 20 per cent actuarial reduction (4 per cent × 5 years). Therefore, if Mrs X receives an occupational pension of £1,000 per month, Mr Y will receive only £800 due to the 20 per cent actuarial reduction. As a result of the decision in *Barber* he is now able to claim an additional £80 per month calculated as follows:

May 1984–May 1990
(period of service between date of commencement of
employment and date of *Barber* judgment)
6/10 of service   £600
Minus 20% actuarial reduction   (£120)   ——
                                                                        £480

[195] Case C–200/91 [1994] ECR I–4389, para. 71.   [196] Case 170/84 [1986] ECR 1607.

[197] Art. 12(4) of the Sex Equality Dir. 2006/54 adds that for states that acceded to the EU after 17 May 1990, the date of 17 May 1990 is replaced by the date on which Art. 157 TFEU became applicable in their territory. Art. 12(3) provides that for states that were not members of the EU on 17 May 1990 but were members of the EEA on 1 January 1994, the date of 17 May 1990 is replaced by 1 January 1994. See, e.g., Case C–351/00 *Niemi* [2002] ECR I–7007, para. 54.

[198] For states that acceded to the EU after 8 April 1976, that date is replaced by the date on which Art. 157 TFEU became applicable on their territory.

[199] This was confirmed by Advocate General Ruiz-Jarabo Colomer in Case C–166/99 *Defreyne* v. *SABENA* [2000] ECR I–6155.

[200] I am grateful for Lorraine Fletcher for help with this illustration.

May 1990–May 1994
(period of service between date of *Barber* judgment and
date of retirement when no deduction can be made)
4/10 of service   £400

                                                                                            £400
                                                                                        _____
Total   £880

The temporal limitation in *Barber* also applies to survivors' benefits[201] and to benefits not linked to actual service, such as a lump sum payment in the event of an employee's death, where the operative event (the death) occurred before 17 May 1990.[202] However, according to the Court in *Vroege*[203] and *Fisscher*,[204] the temporal limitation does not apply to conditions of membership of occupational schemes which are governed by the judgment in *Bilka-Kaufhaus*[205] where no temporal limitation was prescribed. This serves to emphasize the Court's ambivalence towards financial costs. While accepting that retrospective rights to equality in *benefits* might upset the financial balance of pension schemes, it did not seem aware of the costs of granting retrospective *access* to those benefits. Consequently, the direct effect of Article 157 TFEU can be relied on in order to claim equal treatment retroactively in relation to the right to join an occupational pension scheme and this may apply from 8 April 1976,[206] the date of the judgment in *Defrenne (No. 2)*.[207] This may mean that both the employer and the employee have to make contributions from 8 April 1976, although national time limits may preclude such extensive retrospective claims.[208] In the case of part-timers claiming access to a pension scheme, the employers may attempt to show that any indirect discrimination that occurred from 1976 could at any given moment be objectively justified and so no discrimination occurred, hence no contribution would be needed to be paid for that period. If national law allows retrospective claims before 8 April 1976, this is compatible

---

[201] Case C–109/91 *Ten Oever* [1993] ECR I–4879, considered below.

[202] Case C–200/91 *Coloroll* [1994] ECR I–4389.

[203] Case C–57/93 [1994] ECR I–4541, para. 32. In *Vroege* the Court pointed out that a limitation of the effects in time of an interpretative preliminary ruling can only be in the actual judgment ruling upon the interpretation sought. Consequently, if the Court had considered it necessary to impose a limit in time, it would have done so in *Bilka-Kaufhaus*. See further Case C–7/93 *Beune* [1994] ECR I–4471, paras. 61–2, and Case C–128/93 *Fisscher* [1994] ECR I–4583, para. 28.

[204] Case C–128/93 [1994] ECR I–4583.

[205] Case 170/84 [1986] ECR 1607. The Court has repeated this in Joined Cases C–270/97 and C–271/97 *Deutsche Post AG* [2000] ECR I–929, paras. 34 and 35; Joined Cases C–234/96 and C–235/96 *Deutsche Telekom AG* v. *Vick and Conze* [2000] ECR I–799, para. 40; and Case C–50/96 *Deutsche Telekom* v. *Schröder* [2000] ECR I–743, para. 38.

[206] Case C–57/93 *Vroege* [1994] ECR I–4541.   [207] Case 43/75 [1976] ECR 455.

[208] Case C–128/93 *Fisscher* [1994] ECR I–4583, but cf. Case C–246/96 *Mary Teresa Magorrian and Irene Patricia Cunningham* v. *Eastern Health and Social Services Board and Department of Health and Social Services* [1997] ECR I–7153. See further Case C–78/98 *Preston* v. *Wolverhampton Health Care NHS Trust* [2000] ECR I–3201. The requirement to bring a claim within six months from the end of the contract of employment struck out quite a lot of the 60,000 plus pension claims in those cases.

with Union law, despite the risk of competition being distorted between economic operators in the different Member States.[209]

4.6. Levelling up or down?

The *Barber* judgment did not, however, make clear whether the equalization demanded by Article 157 TFEU required levelling the man's terms up to the more favourable terms enjoyed by the women or whether it permitted levelling the woman's terms down to the inferior terms 'enjoyed' by the man. A question was referred to the Court on this point in *Smith* v. *Avdel Systems*.[210] In that case the employer, in order to give effect to the *Barber* judgment in its own occupational pension scheme, decided that as from 1 July 1991 both men and women would receive their occupational pensions at 65 (levelling down of the women's conditions) rather than providing that the men would receive their occupational pensions at 60 at the same age as the women (levelling up). The Court was faced with a difficult choice: levelling down was more affordable for the pension schemes, particularly in the light of an ageing population, but levelling up was more consistent with the Treaty's aspiration of an improvement in working conditions and its earlier jurisprudence. In *Defrenne (No. 2)*[211] the Court said that in view of the connection between Article 157 TFEU and the harmonization of working conditions while the improvement is being maintained,[212] compliance with Article 157 TFEU could not be achieved in ways other than by raising the lowest salaries.[213] Similarly, in *Nimz*[214] the Court ruled that the national court was obliged to apply to the members who had been victims of discrimination 'the same arrangements as are applied to other employees, arrangements which, failing the correct application of Article [157 TFEU] in national law, remain the only valid system of reference'—in other words, levelling up.

In *Smith* v. *Avdel Systems* the Court reached a compromise solution. It identified three separate points of time: first, the period before 17 May 1990, the date of the *Barber* judgment; second, after 17 May 1990 but before any remedial action had been taken by the employer; and third, once remedial action had been taken. In respect of the first

---

[209] Case C–50/96 *Schröder* [2000] ECR I–743, paras. 50 and 59; Joined Cases C–234/96 and C–235/96 *Vick and Conze* [2000] ECR I–799, para. 50; and Joined Cases C–270/97 and C–271/97 *Sievers and Schrage* [2000] ECR I–929, para. 59.

[210] Case C–408/92 *Smith* [1994] ECR I–4435. The Court reached similar conclusions in Case C–28/93 *Van den Akker* v. *Stichting Shell Pensioenfonds* [1994] ECR I–4527 and Case C–200/91 *Coloroll* [1994] ECR I–4389, para. 36.

[211] Case 43/75 [1976] ECR 455.

[212] See Art. 151 (ex 136 EC) and Case 126/86 *Zaera* v. *Instituto Nacional de la Seguridad Social* [1987] ECR 3697.

[213] Case 43/75 [1976] ECR 455. See further Case C–102/88 *Ruzius Wilbrink* [1989] ECR 4311 where the Court stated that part-timers are entitled to have the same system applied to them as other workers in proportion to their working hours, and the application of this in the case of collective agreements (Case 33/89 *Kowalska* v. *Freie und Hansestadt Hamburg* [1990] ECR I–2591).

[214] Case C–184/89 [1991] ECR I–297. See further Joined Cases C–231/06 to C–233/06 *Jonkman* [2007] ECR I–5149, para. 41.

period (service prior to 17 May 1990), the *Barber* judgment excluded the application of Article 157 TFEU to pension benefits payable in respect of those periods so that employers and trustees were not required to ensure equal treatment as far as those benefits were concerned. However, in respect of the second period (periods after 17 May 1990), when the Court found that discrimination in relation to pay existed, and so long as measures bringing about equal treatment had not been adopted by the scheme, the Court ruled that the only proper way of complying with Article 157 TFEU was to grant those in the disadvantaged class, the men, the same advantages as those enjoyed by the people in the favoured class, the women (levelling up).

As regards the third period (periods of service completed after the entry into force of rules designed to eliminate discrimination (1 July 1991)), the Court said that Article 157 TFEU did not preclude measures which achieve equal treatment by reducing the advantages of persons previously favoured (levelling down) since Article 157 TFEU merely required that men and women should receive the same pay for the same work without imposing any specific level of pay. The Court added that since equal treatment was a fundamental principle of Union law its application by employers had to be 'immediate and full'. As a result, 'the achievement of equality cannot be made progressive on a basis that still maintains discrimination, even if only temporarily'. Therefore, it was not possible to phase in the process of levelling down.

If the principles laid down in *Smith* v. *Avdel* are applied to the example outlined above, with the modification that the employer equalized the occupational pension age to 65 for both men and women in May 1991, Mrs X will receive £940 a month, and Mr Y £820. This is calculated as follows:

Mrs X's position

1984–1990	6/10 of service	£600	
			£600
1990–1991	1/10 of service	£100	
			£100
1991–1994	(period of service for which levelling down is permitted)		
	3/10 of service	£300	
	Minus 20% of actuarial reduction for early retirement	(£60)	
			£240
	Total		£940

Mr Y's position

1984–1990	(no equality required)		
	6/10 of service	£600	
	Minus 20% of actuarial reduction for early retirement	(£120)	
			£480

1990–1991	(period of service between date of *Barber* judgment and date on which pension scheme adopts measures to achieve equality: levelling up required and no actuarial reduction can be made)	
	1/10 of service	£100
		£100
1991–1994	(period of service for which levelling down is permitted)	
	3/10 of service	£300
	Minus 20% of actuarial reduction for early retirement	(£60)
		£240
	Total	£820

4.7. *Barber* and beyond

In the light of the decision in *Barber* a series of other pension practices have been examined for unlawful discrimination.

(a) *Survivors' benefits*

In *Ten Oever*[215] the Court established that the concept of pay in Article 157 TFEU included survivors' benefits. Mr Ten Oever's wife belonged to an occupational pension scheme which provided for a survivor's pension for widows only. It was not until 1 January 1989 that this entitlement was extended to widowers. Mrs Ten Oever died on 13 October 1988 and Mr Ten Oever unsuccessfully claimed entitlement to a survivor's pension. The Court ruled that since this scheme was a result of an agreement between both sides of industry and was funded wholly by the employees and the employers without any financial contribution from the public purse,[216] this survivors' pension fell within the scope of Article 157 TFEU. The Court added that it was not relevant that a survivors' pension was paid, by definition, not to the employee but to the employee's survivor.[217] Entitlement to such a benefit was consideration deriving from the survivor's spouse's membership of the scheme, the pension being vested in the survivor by reason of the employment relationship that had existed between the employer and the survivor's spouse and being paid to him or her by reason of the spouse's employment.[218] In *Coloroll*[219] the Court confirmed that the survivor could

---

[215] Case C–109/91 [1993] ECR I–4879.   [216] Cf. Case 80/70 *Defrenne (No. 1)* [1971] ECR 445.

[217] This is now recognized in Art. 6 of the Sex Equality Dir. 2006/54.

[218] Since survivors' pensions now fall in principle within Art. 157 TFEU the exclusion of survivors' pensions from the application of the principle of equal treatment in Art. 9(b) of Dir. 86/378 was *ultra vires*.

[219] Case C–200/91 [1994] ECR I–4389.

rely on Article 157 TFEU to assert his or her rights since the right to payment of a survivors' pension arose at the time of the death of an employee affiliated to the scheme and the survivor was the only person in a position to assert the right. The Court also confirmed in *Coloroll* that the temporal limitation laid down in *Barber* applied to survivors' pensions.[220]

(b) Actuarial factors

In *Neath*[221] the Court drew the line at expanding the definition of 'pay' in Article 157 TFEU to include the use of actuarial factors differing according to sex in funded and defined-benefit schemes. Mr Neath belonged to a contributory defined-benefit/final salary scheme where male and female employees' contributions were identical[222] but the employer's contributions varied over time to ensure that the pension scheme was properly funded to cover the cost of pensions promised. The employer's contributions were higher for female than for male employees, due to a variety of actuarial factors in the mechanism for funding the scheme, including the fact that women live, on average, longer than men. This meant that when part of the pension was converted into capital, the male employees received lower sums than the female employees.

While recognizing that the commitment by the employer to pay a periodic pension to the employees fell within the definition of pay in Article 157 TFEU, the Court ruled that that 'commitment does not necessarily have to do with the funding arrangements (including the selection of actuarial factors) chosen to secure the periodic payment of the pension' which remained outside the scope of Article 157 TFEU. Consequently, since the use of sex-based actuarial factors in funded defined-benefit schemes did not fall within Article 157 TFEU, inequalities in the amounts of capital benefits 'whose value can only be determined on the basis of the arrangements chosen for funding the scheme are likewise not struck at by Article [157 TFEU]'.[223]

However, sex-based actuarial factors run directly contrary to the essence of anti-discrimination laws which require that workers be regarded on the basis of their individual characteristics and not on the basis of gender stereotypes.[224] As Advocate-General

---

[220] See further Case C–50/99 *Podesta* v. *CRICA* [2000] ECR I–4039, para. 46.

[221] Case C–152/91 [1993] ECR I–6935 affirmed in Case C–200/91 *Coloroll* [1994] ECR I–4389, para. 85.

[222] The employees' contributions are an element of pay since they are deducted directly from an employee's salary which, according to the Court in Case 69/80 *Worringham* [1981] ECR 767, is pay. In Case C–200/91 *Coloroll* [1994] ECR I–4389 the Court added that whether contributions are payable by the employer or the employees has no bearing on the concept of pay (para. 88).

[223] Case C–152/91 *Neath* [1993] ECR I–6935, para. 33, and Case C–200/91 *Coloroll* [1994] ECR I–4389, para. 85.

[224] Cf. Art. 5(1) of the Goods and Services Dir. 2004/113/EC (OJ [2004] L373/37). However, Art. 5(2) does permit proportionate differences in individuals' premiums and benefits where the use of sex is a determining factor in the assessment of risk based on relevant and accurate actuarial and statistical data. Yet, in Case C–236/09 *Test-Achats* [2011] ECR I–000 the Court said that since Art. 5(2) did not contain a sunset clause it was incompatible with the Charter (see further Ch. 6).

Van Gerven recognized, health, race, occupation, and social class provide better indicators of life expectancy, and other Union countries manage their occupation pension
schemes without reference to sex-based actuarial factors. However, in the UK sex-based
actuarial assumptions are used not only by employers but also by pension providers to
whom it would be difficult to extend the application of Article 157 TFEU.[225]

The rationale behind the decision in *Neath* focuses on the fact that the case concerns
a defined benefit scheme where the employer knows the extent of the commitment. The
same considerations may not apply to money purchase schemes. The Court has yet to
rule on this point.

In the amendments to Directive 86/378, now found in Article 9(1)(h) of the Sex
Equality Directive 2006/54, the Directive provides that setting different levels of benefit
is unlawful 'except in so far as may be necessary to take account of actuarial calculation
factors which differ according to sex in the case of defined-contribution schemes; in the
case of funded defined-benefit schemes, certain elements may be unequal where the
inequality of the amounts results from the effects of the use of actuarial factors differing
according to sex at the time when the scheme's funding is implemented'.[226]

(c) Additional Voluntary Contributions

The Court also took a strict line in respect of Additional Voluntary Contributions
(AVCs) paid by employees to secure additional benefits such as an additional tax-free
lump sum.[227] Since the AVCs are paid into a separate fund merely administered by the
occupational scheme, and since they secure benefits additional to those connected with
their employment, the Court said in *Coloroll*[228] that AVCs were not pay within the
meaning of Article 157 TFEU and this has now been confirmed by Article 8(1)(e) of the
Sex Equality Directive 2006/54.

4.8. Remedies

The obligation to secure equality applies not only to employers but also to the trustees
of a pension scheme. The Court made this clear in *Barber*.[229] The Court recognized that
Article 157 TFEU applied to an occupational pension scheme set up in the form of a
trust and administered by trustees who were technically independent of the employer
because Article 157 TFEU applied to 'consideration received indirectly from the

---

[225] Rubinstein, Editorial [1994] IRLR 51.

[226] The Directive also provides that setting different levels for employers' contributions contravenes the
principle of equal treatment except:

- in the case of defined-contribution schemes if the aim is to equalize the amount of the final benefits to
  make them more nearly equal for both sexes;
- in the case of funded defined-benefit schemes where the employer's contributions are intended to ensure
  the adequacy of the funds necessary to cover the cost of the benefits defined.

[227] Case C–200/91 *Coloroll* [1994] ECR I–4389.

[228] Case C–200/91 [1994] ECR I–4389.

[229] Case C–262/88 [1990] ECR I–1889, paras. 28 and 29. See further Art. 9(2) of the Sex Equality Dir. 2006/54.

employer'.[230] In *Coloroll*[231] the Court added that the trustees were bound to do everything within the scope of their powers to ensure compliance with the principle of equal treatment, especially when a worker changes job, transferring pension rights from one occupational scheme to another. When the worker reaches retirement age, the *second* scheme is obliged to increase the benefits it undertook to pay him when accepting the transfer so as to eliminate the effects, contrary to Article 157 TFEU, suffered by the worker due to the inadequacy of the capital transferred because of discrimination suffered under the first scheme.[232]

If securing the principle of equality is beyond the powers of trustees, employers and trustees are bound to use all means available under domestic law, such as having recourse to the national courts, especially where the involvement of the courts is necessary to amend the provisions of the pension scheme or trust deed.[233] The courts are bound to provide the legal protection which individuals derive from the direct effect of provisions of the Treaties,[234] and where necessary they must disapply any incompatible domestic provisions.

Given the long-term investment involved in accumulating a pension, the question of national time limits has become a major issue which has arisen in the context of remedies, particularly in respect of access to occupational pensions as a result of the decisions in *Vroege*[235] and *Fisscher*.[236] It will be recalled that the temporal limitation laid down in *Barber*[237] did not apply to the right of access to occupational pension schemes. Consequently, the direct effect of Article 157 TFEU could be relied on in order retroactively to claim equal treatment in relation to the right to join an occupational pension scheme and this could be done as from 8 April 1976. However, the Court said that in those cases national time limits might preclude such extensive retrospective claims.[238]

Doubt has been cast on that rule by *Magorrian*.[239] In that case the applicants began employment as full-time workers and then became part-time workers when they had children. When they retired they were not entitled to the more favourable pension benefits available to full-time workers. In response to their claim under Article 157 TFEU, the UK government argued that under the relevant statute no award of arrears of pay

---

[230] The Court has also said that Art. 157 TFEU applies to administrators of a pension scheme (Case C–128/93 *Fisscher* [1994] ECR I–4583, para. 32).

[231] Case C–200/91 [1994] ECR I–4389.

[232] This only applies to benefits payable in periods of service subsequent to 17 May 1990.

[233] Case C–200/91 *Coloroll* [1994] ECR I–4389, para. 39. The same applies to the administrators of an occupational pension scheme: Case C–128/93 *Fisscher v. Voorhuis Hengelo BV* [1994] ECR I–4583, para. 31; and insuring bodies responsible for administering occupational pension schemes in Germany: Case C–379/99 *Pensionskasse für die Angestellten der Barmer Ersatzkasse VVaG v. Hans Menauer* [2001] ECR I–7275, para. 24. If the funds held by the pension scheme are insufficient to meet the principle of equal pay, this is a matter for national law to resolve: Case C–200/91 *Coloroll* [1994] ECR I–4389, paras. 42 and 43.

[234] Case C–213/89 *R v. Secretary of State for Transport, ex parte Factortame* [1990] ECR I–2433, para. 19.

[235] Case C–57/93 [1994] ECR I–4541.

[236] Case C–128/93 [1994] ECR I–4583.

[237] Case 262/88 [1990] ECR I–1889.

[238] See 5th Preambular paragraph of Dir. 96/97. See additionally Art. 12(2) of the Sex Equality Dir. 2006/54.

[239] Case C–246/96 [1997] ECR I–7153.

could be made relating to a period earlier than two years before the date on which the proceedings were instituted. The Court, reaffirming its decisions in *Vroege* and *Fisscher*, said that the direct effect of Article 157 TFEU could be relied on, as from 8 April 1976, in order retroactively to claim equal treatment in relation to the *right to join* (access to) an occupational pension scheme. The UK, however, argued that this case concerned the amount of *benefits* payable under the scheme (to which the *Barber* temporal limitation would apply) and not the right to belong to the scheme.

The Court said that membership of a scheme would be of no interest to employees if it did not confer entitlement to the benefits provided by the scheme in question.[240] Therefore, entitlement to a retirement pension under an occupational scheme was indissolubly linked to the right to join such a scheme. It continued that the same was true in *Magorrian* where the discrimination suffered by part-time workers stemmed from discrimination concerning access to a special scheme which conferred entitlement to additional benefits. While helpful to the applicants in *Magorrian*, this observation creates a problematic distinction because benefit claims can usually be defined in terms of claims for full access to that benefit and access claims can usually be described in terms of a claim for benefit which flows from the access.[241]

As far as the backdating was concerned, the Court said the fact that the right to be admitted to a scheme could take place no earlier than two years before the institution of proceedings deprived the applicants of the additional benefits under the scheme to which they were entitled to be affiliated. However, the UK argued that following *Johnson (No. 1)*[242] and *Steenhorst Neerings*[243] a restriction on backdating was valid under Union law. The Court disagreed. It said that in *Magorrian* the claim was not for the retroactive award of certain additional benefits but for recognition of entitlement to full membership of an occupational scheme. Whereas the rules at issue in *Johnson* merely limited the period, prior to commencement of proceedings, in respect of which backdated benefits could be obtained, the rule at issue in *Magorrian* prevented the entire record of service completed by those concerned after 8 April 1976 until 1990 from being taken into account for the purposes of calculating the additional benefits which would be payable even after the date of the claim. Consequently, the Court said that the UK rule rendered any action by individuals relying on Union law impossible in practice and limited the direct effect of Article 157 TFEU in cases in which no such limitation had been laid down either in the Court's case law or in Protocol No. 33.

The scope of this aspect of the ruling is not clear and sits uncomfortably with the earlier decisions in *Fisscher* and *Fantask*.[244] It seems that in the ordinary case of a limitation on the retroactive effect of such claims, the claim is limited in terms of periods

---

[240] Case C–435/93 *Dietz v. Stichting Thuiszorg Rotterdam* [1996] ECR I–5223.

[241] Rubinstein [1998] IRLR 55.

[242] Case C–31/90 [1991] ECR I–3723.

[243] Case C–338/91 [1993] ECR I–5475.   [244] Case C–188/95 [1997] ECR I–6783.

which are prior to the date of institution of proceedings but claimants are able to vindicate their rights for the future. The Court's view of the effect of the rule in *Magorrian*
was that it prevented the applicants from claiming access to the scheme for the future as
well: if each woman could count only two years of past part-time service towards the
20-year requirement, the applicants would have had to come out of retirement and seek
to work for some considerable time into the future to vindicate their rights of access
under Article 157 TFEU.[245]

Nevertheless, in *Preston*[246] the Court repeated its approach in *Magorrian*. It thus continued to draw a distinction between arrears of benefits (time limited by *Barber*) and
access to retroactive membership of the scheme (time limited back to April 1976[247]),
thereby enabling the part-time workers, who formed part of 22 test cases co-ordinated
by the TUC, to claim retrospective membership of occupational pension schemes in
respect of periods of employment since April 1976, despite the fact that English law
limited retrospective membership to two years, although these women would, if necessary, have to pay employee contributions relating to the period of membership.[248]

The other issue raised in *Preston* concerned time limits for bringing a claim. Under
English law claimants had six months from the end of the contract of employment to
lodge a claim. The Court said this was compatible with Union law provided that it did
not contravene the principle of equivalence.[249] When the case returned to the House of
Lords,[250] the Lords found that the six-month time limit did not breach the principle of
equivalence because it was not less favourable than the six-year limitation period for
bringing a claim for breach of contract, given the difference in the procedural rules
governing the two claims. This meant that some of the 60,000 test cases failed because
the part-timers had not brought their claims in time, even though they could not reasonably have known of their right to bring claims. However, for those still in the same
employment, the clock had yet to start ticking and they could claim back to the start of
the employment relationship.

But what about those applicants who were employed on a series of fixed-term contracts but with intervals in between those contracts? Should they have brought their
claim at the end of each individual contract or at the end of the employment relationship as a whole? The Court of Justice, opting for the latter approach, said that the former
approach made it excessively difficult to bring a claim.[251] The House of Lords followed
this and said that fixed-term employees did not have to bring their claim within six
months of the end of each contract so long as there was a 'stable employment relationship'. However, where there were intermittent contracts of service without a stable
employment relationship, the period of six months ran from the end of each contract of
service.

---

[245] J. Coppel (1998) 27 *ILJ* 259, 261.
[246] Case C–78/98 *Preston* v. *Wolverhampton Healthcare NHS Trust* [2000] ECR I–3201.
[247] Para. 37.
[248] Para. 39.
[249] Para. 35.   [250] [2001] IRLR 237.   [251] Para. 72.

D. CONCLUSIONS

The Court's case law on pensions shows just how radical the application of the equality principle can be. It also demonstrates that the Court is prepared to disregard the views of the legislature to give full effect to the 'fundamental' principle of equality. While in some respects, women, especially women who work part time, have benefited from the Court's case law, in others their position may have deteriorated as a result of the employer's need to secure equality for men in occupational pension schemes.

The pensions issue will not go away. Far from it, with an ageing population and shortfalls in the funding of pensions,[252] the pension age will continue to rise, there may well be moves towards flexible retirement and, in some countries, such as the UK, the abolition of a retirement age all together. This in turn may create difficulties for younger people seeking employment. The EU2020 strategy recognizes these problems:

> Demographic ageing is accelerating. As the baby-boom generation retires, the EU's active population will start to shrink as from 2013/2014. The number of people aged over 60 is now increasing twice as fast as it did before 2007—by about two million every year compared to one million previously. The combination of a smaller working population and a higher share of retired people will place additional strains on our welfare systems.[253]

At a legal level some of these issues will be played out through the interrelationship between pension provision and the age discrimination provisions in the Framework Directive. The other issue for the future will be portability of pensions. At present the legislation that does exist concerns portability of pensions in a cross-border situation.[254] For an EU committed to 'flexicurity', employment security and a life cycle approach to work, the transferability of pension entitlement is an important issue. So far this has proved too politically controversial.

---

[252] See the Commission's Green Paper, *Towards adequate, sustainable and safe European pensions systems* COM(2010) 365.

[253] <http://ec.europa.eu/europe2020/documents/related-document-type/index_en.htm> (last accessed 4 April 2012).

[254] Dir. 98/49 (OJ [2009] L209/46).

PART IV

HEALTH AND SAFETY AND WORKING CONDITIONS

11

HEALTH AND SAFETY

A. INTRODUCTION

The Union has been concerned about health and safety issues since its inception. Article 151 TFEU (ex 136 EC) calls for the improvement in working conditions and standards of living of workers while Article 156 TFEU (ex 140 EC) empowers the Commission to promote close co-operation between Member States in the field of occupational hygiene. There is a two-fold justification for addressing health and safety. The first is personal, the second economic. Industrial accidents and work-related ill health represent not only a cost in terms of human suffering but also a financial cost estimated at between 1.5 and 4 per cent of GDP.[1] Four sectors (fishing, agriculture, construction, and health and social services) have an accident rate 30 per cent above average; four others (the extractive industries, manufacturing, hotels and restaurants, and transport) have an accident rate 15 per cent above average.[2] The Commission therefore argues that higher health and safety standards, while initially imposing increased costs, should guarantee in the long term a reduction in the number of accidents and occupational diseases, thereby reducing costs to business and increasing competitiveness without reducing the number of jobs. This feeds into the EU's 'quality' agenda identified as part of its Lisbon strategy of creating more and better jobs. Health and safety are essential elements in terms of the quality of work, and feature among the indicators adopted in the wake of the Commission's communication *Investing in quality*.[3]

The other main economic justification for EU action in the field of health and safety is to create a level playing field. Union rules deprive those countries with low health and safety standards of a perceived competitive advantage over those countries with higher standards and thus greater costs. This argument has particular resonance within the UK, which has always guaranteed relatively high levels of health and safety protection for its workforce, for which British industry has incurred a heavier financial burden.

This chapter looks at the Union measures traditionally regarded—certainly from a common law perspective—as health and safety matters: the Framework Directive 89/391 on health and safety and, in outline, its daughters. Chapter 12 then examines those measures which fall within a rather broader—and more Scandinavian—definition

---

[1] COM(2002) 118, 6.
[2] COM(88) 74, Commission's Memorandum to the Framework Dir. 89/391/EEC.
[3] COM(2001) 313.

of health and safety, which encompasses references to the working environment. In particular, it examines the Working Time Directive 2003/88 and the Young Workers Directive 94/33 as well as considering two measures which are traditionally considered labour law matters: proof of the contract of employment, and pay.

B. THE DEVELOPMENT OF A UNION POLICY IN RESPECT OF HEALTH AND SAFETY

1. INTRODUCTION

All Member States have traditionally regulated the health and safety of workers, through constitutional provisions (Greece, Portugal, Italy, and Luxembourg), codes or statutes (France, Netherlands, Germany, Spain, and the UK) and/or through implied terms in the contract of employment (for example, UK and Ireland).[4] Moreover, in all states employers are under a general duty to provide safe and healthy working conditions. This is variously described as: the duty to ensure 'with the diligence of a good father' that work takes place in suitable conditions for health and safety and to observe the requirements of the law (Belgium); 'to take measures necessary in relation to the type of work and the state of technology to protect the physical and mental welfare for employees' and to observe the requirements of the law (Italy); and to ensure so far as reasonably practicable the health, safety, and welfare of all employees (UK).

Individual Member States have also evolved a common pattern to the legislative control of occupational health and safety. This involves a basic framework of primary legislation establishing general principles and some specific requirements.[5] This framework may provide the basis for more detailed and specific secondary legislation which then sets out detailed requirements based on general principles established in the primary legislation. Finally, codes of practice and technical guidance may provide a third tier of control. While breaches of codes and guidelines are not generally offences, evidence of compliance or non-compliance may be used in legal proceedings. This national approach has influenced the Commission's strategy to legislation. It has adopted framework Directives prescribing general duties and more specific daughter Directives.

2. HISTORICAL PERSPECTIVE

2.1. The early days

Under the ECSC Treaty[6] various health and safety research programmes were carried out and attempts were made to reduce the number of explosions and fires in coal mines.

---

[4] See generally *The Regulation of Working Conditions in the Member States of the European Community*, Vol. I, *Social Europe* 4/92, 108–11.

[5] See e.g. Denmark—Working Environment Act 1975; Greece—Health and Safety of Workers Act 1985; Ireland—Safety, Health and Welfare at Work Act 1989; Netherlands—Working Environment Act 1980; UK—Health and Safety at Work Act 1974.

[6] Art. 55(2) ECSC.

Similarly, in the early stages of the evolution of a Union policy on health and safety under the Treaty of Rome the emphasis was on 'mapping' the area and identifying the problems.[7] The 1974 Social Action Programme[8] talked of establishing a programme for workers 'aimed at the humanisation of their living and working conditions... with particular reference to:... improvement in safety and health conditions at work'. This led to the creation of the Advisory Committee for Safety, Hygiene and Health Protection at Work[9] (now replaced by the tripartite Advisory Committee on safety and health at work (ACSH)),[10] designed to assist the Commission in preparing and implementing activities in the fields of health, safety, and hygiene, and the adoption of the first two health and safety Directives, concerning signs at the workplace and protection against vinyl chloride monomers (VCMs). The safety signs Directive 77/576[11] was introduced at a time of increasing freedom of movement of persons[12] to reduce both the risk of accidents at work and occupational diseases due to language problems. The Directive provided a comprehensive set of colour co-ordinated signs to draw workers' attention to specific hazards.[13] This Directive was superseded by Directive 92/58.[14]

The VCM Directive 78/610/EEC[15] provided the model which was to be applied in subsequent Directives. Employers were required:

(1) to take technical preventive measures (reducing the concentration of VCM to which workers are exposed;[16] setting limits on the atmospheric concentration of VCM in the working area;[17] making provisions for monitoring the atmospheric

---

[7] For a detailed discussion of the development of a Union policy on health and safety, see A. Neal and F. Wright (eds.), *The European Communities' Health and Safety Legislation* (Chapman & Hall, London, 1992) Preface.

[8] Council Resolution 74/C 13/1 of 21 January 1974.

[9] Council Decision 74/325/EEC (OJ [1975] C185/15). A year later the European Foundation for the Improvement of Living and Working Conditions (the Dublin Foundation) was established (Reg. 1365/75) (OJ [1975] C139/1), a body engaged in applied research in areas of social policy, including the improvement and protection of the environment. As a result of the Community Social Charter 1989 there is now a European Agency for Safety and Health at Work (in Bilbao) Council Reg. (EC) No. 2062/94 (OJ [1994] L216/1) amended by Council Reg. (EC) No. 1643/95 (OJ [1995] L156/1) COM(90) 564 final (OJ [1991] C27/3) which is intended to provide support for the implementation of programmes relating to the workplace, including technical and scientific assistance and co-ordination as well as assistance in the field of training. The Agency works closely with European Foundation.

[10] Council Decision 2003/C 218/01 (OJ [2003] C218/1). [11] OJ [1977] L229/12.

[12] Considered further in Chs. 4 and 5.

[13] Art. 1(1): red means stop or prohibition and is also used to identify fire-fighting equipment; yellow means caution or possible danger and can be used to identify particular dangers, such as fire, radiation, and chemical hazards, as well as to identify steps and dangerous obstacles; green means no danger or first aid and can be used to identify emergency routes and exits, first aid stations, and rescue points; and blue indicates a mandatory sign or conveys information and is used to demonstrate the obligation to wear individual safety equipment and the location of a telephone.

[14] Council Dir. 92/58/EEC of 24 June 1992 on the minimum requirements for the provision of safety and/ or health signs at work (OJ [1992] L245/23) (ninth individual Directive within the meaning of Art. 16(1) of Dir. 89/391). The principles relating to Dir. 89/391 (see later in the chapter), including information and consultation of workers, apply equally to this Directive.

[15] Council Dir. 78/610/EEC on the approximation of laws, regulations and administrative provisions of the Member States on the protection of the health of workers exposed to VCM (OJ [1978] L197/12). This Directive was repealed by Council Dir. 1999/38/EC on the protection of workers from the risks related to exposure to carcinogens at work and extending it to mutagens (OJ [1999] L138/66) which in turn was repealed and replaced by Dir. 2004/37/EC (OJ [2004] L 158/50) considered below.

[16] Art. 3(1). [17] Arts. 2(b) and 4 and Annex I.

concentration of VCM;[18] and, where necessary, making provision for personal protection measures[19]);

(2) to provide adequate information to the workers on the risks to which they are exposed and the precautions to be taken;[20] to keep a register of workers with particulars of the type and duration of their work and the exposure to which they have been subjected;[21] and

(3) to provide medical surveillance, ensuring that workers are examined by a competent doctor, both on recruitment or prior to taking up the activities and subsequently.

This period (1978–1982) also saw the adoption of the first action programme on safety and health at work,[22] focusing on the causes of occupational accidents and disease, the protection against dangerous substances, prevention of hazards caused by machinery, and the improvement of human behaviour. The second action programme 1982–1986, added measures on training, information, statistics and research. The 1978–1982 action programme resulted in the enactment of the first Framework Directive on hazardous agents (Directive 80/1107/EEC),[23] which was intended to protect workers against risks to their health and safety, including the prevention of such risks arising from exposure to harmful chemical, physical and biological agents.[24] The Directive said that exposure of workers to agents had to be avoided or kept at as low a level *as is reasonably practicable*.[25] This provided a margin of discretion in the application of the Directive, particularly for small companies, a discretion which has largely been removed in the Directives adopted under the subsequent Framework Directive (Directive 89/391/EEC),[26] despite strong arguments made to the contrary by the UK and the Commission.[27]

The 1980 Directive was followed by Directives designed to protect workers from lead[28] and asbestos,[29] and noise.[30] The Directives laid down limit values on the exposure to the

---

[18] Arts. 5 and 6.   [19] Art. 7.   [20] Art. 8.   [21] Art. 9.

[22] Council Resolution of 29 June 1978 (OJ [1978] C165/1), supplemented and revised by the second action programme—Council Resolution of 27 February 1984 (OJ [1984] C67/02).

[23] Council Dir. 80/1107/EEC of 27 November 1980 on the protection of workers from the risks related to exposure to chemical, physical and biological agents at work (OJ [1980] L327/8). This Directive was repealed by the Chemical Agents Dir. 98/24/EC (OJ [1998] L131/8) which in turn has been partially repealed by Directive 2009/148/EC on the protection of workers from the risks related to exposure to asbestos at work (OJ [2009] L330/28).

[24] Art. 1(1).   [25] Art. 3(1).

[26] Although, as we shall see, certain Articles of the Directive make specific provisions for SMEs.

[27] See additionally Case C–5/00 *Commission* v. *Germany* [2002] ECR I–1305 where Germany was condemned for exempting businesses employing fewer than 10 workers from being in possession of an assessment in documentary form of the health and safety risks at work under Dir. 89/391.

[28] Council Dir. 82/605/EEC on the protection of workers from the risks related to the exposure to metallic lead and its ionic compounds at work (OJ [1982] L247/12). See now Dir. 98/24 (OJ [1998] L131/11).

[29] Council Dir. 83/477/EEC of 19 September 1983 on the protection of workers from the risks relating to exposure to asbestos at work (OJ [1983] L263/25), amended by Council Dir. 91/382/EEC (OJ [1991] L 206/16); Council Dir. 98/24/EC (OJ [1998] L131/8) and Dir. 2003/18/EC (OJ [2003] L097/48); and EP and Council Dir. 2009/148/EC on the protection of workers from the risks related to exposure to asbestos at work (OJ [2009] L330/28). Despite the adoption of the Carcinogens Dir. 2004/37 (see in this chapter), Dir. 83/477 continues to apply whenever its provisions are more favourable.

[30] Council Dir. 86/188/EEC on the protection of workers from the risks relating to exposure to noise at work (OJ [1983] L137/28). This Directive was repealed by the Physical Agents Dir. 2003/10 (OJ [2003] L42/38).

agents and require risk assessment, risk reduction, medical surveillance, and the provision of workers with information, following the pattern of the parent Directive. The fourth daughter Directive 88/364 banned the use of certain specified substances altogether[31] because precautions were not sufficient to ensure a satisfactory level of worker protection. The parent Directive, as amended, and Directive 82/605/EEC on lead and Directive 88/364/EEC on banned substances have been reviewed and are now included in Directive 98/24/EC on chemical agents.[32]

2.2. The Single European Act 1986 and beyond

The Single European Act, passed to facilitate the completion of the internal market in goods, persons, services and capital by 31 December 1992, also contained some recognition of the role of a social dimension to the internal market programme by means of the addition of Article 118a EEC (now Article 153 TFEU). Article 118a(1) EEC contained the commitment that:

> Member States shall pay particular attention to encouraging improvements, especially in the working environment, as regards the health and safety of workers, and shall set as their objective the harmonisation of conditions in this area, while maintaining the improvements made.

In order to achieve this objective a new legal basis was introduced. Article 118a(2) EEC provided that:

> the Council, acting by a qualified majority on a proposal from the Commission, in co-operation with the European Parliament,[33]... shall adopt, by means of directives, minimum requirements[34] for gradual implementation, having regard to the conditions and technical rules obtaining in each of the Member States.

The introduction of qualified majority voting marked a significant departure from the unanimous vote required by Article 115 TFEU (ex 94 EC) for measures directly affecting the establishment or functioning of the Common Market. For the Commission this represented an ideal opportunity to push through social measures on the basis that they were health and safety matters, thereby circumventing any veto that the UK might wish to exercise. The only constraint imposed upon the Commission was that the Directives had

---

[31] Council Dir. 88/364/EEC on the protection of workers by the banning of certain specified agents and/or certain work activities (OJ [1988] L179/44). See now Dir. 98/24/EC (OJ [1998] L131/11), partially repealed by Directive 2009/148/EC on the protection of workers from the risks related to exposure to asbestos at work (OJ [2009] L330/28).

[32] OJ [1998] L131/11. This has been partially repealed by Directive 2009/148/EC on the protection of workers from the risks related to exposure to asbestos at work (OJ [2009] L330/28).

[33] These procedures have been replaced by the ordinary legislative procedure following the Lisbon Treaty.

[34] The reference to minimum standards does not imply lowest common denominator standards. Instead it refers to the power granted by Art. 118a(3) EEC, introduced at the behest of the Danes in an attempt to avoid downward harmonization, enabling Member States to maintain or introduce more stringent conditions. This view was confirmed in Case C–84/96 UK v. Council [1996] ECR I–5755, para. 17, and again in Case C–2/97 IP v. Borsana [1998] ECR I–8597, para. 35.

to avoid imposing 'administrative, financial and legal constraints in a way which would hold back the creation and development of small and medium-sized undertakings'.[35]

In addition to the new legal basis on health and safety, the Single European Act introduced Article 100a(2) EEC (new Article 114(2) TFEU) which provided that measures relating to 'the rights and interests of employed persons' could not be adopted by qualified majority voting, as provided by Article 100a(1) EEC (new Article 114(1) TFEU). This meant that the unanimous voting rules laid down by Article 115 TFEU applied. As the UK government discovered in *Working Time*,[36] there was no clear line distinguishing Article 100a(2) EEC from Article 118a EEC. However, in that case the Court ruled that measures which had as their 'principal aim' the protection of health and safety, albeit with ancillary objectives such as employment rights, could be adopted under Article 118a EEC.

The Treaty of Amsterdam revised the wording of Article 118a. What is now Article 153(1) TFEU (ex 137 EC) provides that 'the Union shall support and complement the activities of the Member States' in the fields of, *inter alia*, 'improvement in particular of the working environment to protect workers' health and safety' and 'working conditions'. The inclusion of working conditions is significant for it recognizes that there is a blurring of the distinction between health and safety matters, which required qualified majority voting, and other issues affecting working conditions which, prior to Amsterdam, might have required unanimous voting under Article 115 TFEU and Article 114(2) TFEU. The Treaty of Amsterdam also applied the co-decision procedure (Article 294 TFEU (ex 251 EC)) for the adoption of measures listed in Article 153(1) TFEU, replacing the co-operation procedure.

Equipped with Article 118a EEC, the Commission drew up a third action programme (1988–1992).[37] The action programme took a broad approach to the meaning of health and safety, determined that workers should have adequate protection from accidents at work and occupational diseases and insisted that the competitive pressures of the single market did not jeopardize the safety and health protection of workers. This programme was therefore focused on legislation. This was emphasized by the 1989 Social Charter[38] and its related action programme.[39] Paragraph 19(1) of the Social Charter provides that:

> Every worker must enjoy satisfactory health and safety conditions in his working environment. Appropriate measures must be taken in order to achieve further harmonisation of conditions in this area while maintaining the improvements made.

Article 19(3) adds that 'the provisions regarding implementation of the internal market shall help to ensure such protection'. Thus, the Social Charter Action Programme identified a two-pronged approach: first, the adoption of 'product' or 'trading' Directives

---

[35] Art. 153 TFEU, para 2(b).
[36] Case C–84/94 *UK* v. *Council* [1996] ECR I–5755. See further Ch. 2.
[37] COM(87) 520 final and Council Resolution on Safety, Hygiene and Health at Work of 21 December 1987 (OJ [1987] C28/88).
[38] COM(89) 471 final.   [39] COM(89) 568 final.

based on Article 114(1) TFEU to ensure that equipment being used by workers was safe, and secondly, provisions concerning protection in the working environment based on Article 153 TFEU, including a new Framework Directive 89/391/EEC[40] and its daughter Directives laying down minimum health and safety requirements for the workplace, the use of work equipment, personal protective equipment, and chemical, physical, and biological agents. The Commission emphasized that priority would be given to new initiatives in areas where safety caused significant problems, such as the building industry, and fisheries. It also urged Member States to put forward ideas for a schedule of industrial diseases. This led to a Commission Recommendation,[41] suggesting that Member States introduce into their national laws provisions concerning scientifically recognized occupational diseases liable to compensation and subject to preventive measures. Although this Recommendation is only soft law, in *Grimaldi* v. *Fonds des Maladies Professionnelles*[42] the Court ruled that recommendations had to be taken into account by national courts when deciding disputes before them, in particular when Recommendations clarify the interpretation of national rules adopted in order to implement them or when they are designed to supplement binding Union measures.

The fourth Union action programme (1996–2000)[43] was designed to support the implementation and the application of the existing legislation. It too put increased emphasis on non-legislative measures, especially providing information. In particular, the Commission focused on making legislation more effective, preparing for enlargement, strengthening the link with (what was to become) the employability pillar of the Employment Guidelines, especially after the Amsterdam and Luxembourg Summits, and examining the new health and safety risks faced by the changing structure of the working population and employment patterns (an ageing workforce; a steady increase in the proportion of female workers; an increase in casual and part-time work and, in economic sectors other than agriculture, self-employment, with a continuing increase in jobs in the service sector). Social dialogue was also emphasized as central to successful action on health and safety.

2.3. The European Employment Strategy and the Commission's Strategy on Health and Safety at Work

At first, health and safety did not feature in the European Employment Strategy. It was not until the 2001 Employment Guidelines,[44] under the heading 'Modernisation of Work', that the Guidelines provided that Member States would, where appropriate in partnership with the Social Partners or drawing upon agreements negotiated by the Social Partners:[45]

> Endeavour to ensure a better application at workplace level of existing health and safety legislation by stepping up and strengthening enforcement, by providing guidance to help enterprises, especially SMEs, to comply with existing legislation, by improving training on

---

[40] OJ [1989] L183/1.

[41] Commission Recommendation 90/326/EEC of 22 May 1990 to the Member States concerning the adoption of a European Schedule of Occupational Diseases (OJ [1990] L160/90). See additionally the Commission's earlier Recommendations 2188/62 of 23 July 1962 and 66/462/CEE of 20 July 1966.

[42] Case C–222/88 [1989] ECR 4407.   [43] COM(95) 282 final (OJ [1995] C262/18).

[44] Co. Dec. 2001/53 (OJ [2001] L22/18).   [45] Para. 14.

occupational health and safety, and by promoting measures for the reduction of occupational accidents and diseases in traditional high risk sectors.

In its Social Policy Agenda of 2000, the Commission had emphasized the importance of promoting health and safety at work as part of the quality agenda. Thus, it committed itself to codifying and simplifying health and safety legislation and adapting and improving existing legislation, taking into account Union case law and the changing world of work.[46] The Nice European Council's Social Agenda was more prescriptive.[47] It emphasized not only consolidation and simplification of the existing acquis but also required the Union to respond to new risks, such as work-related stress, by initiatives on standards and exchanges of good practice; to promote the application of legislation in SMEs, taking into account the special constraints to which they are exposed, to apply them by means of a specific programme, and to develop exchanges of good practice and collaboration between labour inspection institutions in order to satisfy the common essential requirements more effectively. This concern with health and safety also fed into the Charter of Fundamental Rights 2000. Under the heading 'Fair and Just Working Conditions', Article 31(1) of the Charter provides: 'Every worker has the right to working conditions which respect his or her health, safety and dignity'.

Health and safety also formed one of the indicators of quality at work in the Commission's communication on quality.[48] Thus, it said that the key policy objective is to ensure that working conditions are safe, healthy, and supportive—in both physical and psychological terms. Indicators to be adopted include accidents at work (fatal and serious), rates of occupational disease including new risks (e.g. repetitive strain), stress levels (so-called psychosocial issues[49]), and other difficulties concerning working arrangements. This was followed up by the Commission's Strategy on Health and Safety at Work 2002–6[50] which had three 'novel' features.[51]

First, it adopted a 'global approach' to 'well being at work', taking account of:

- changes in the world of work (a changing profile of the workforce—an increasingly feminized society with a particular susceptibility to allergies, infectious diseases, neurological and skin complaints, and an increasingly diverse active population, where older workers have an above average fatality rate and younger workers tend to suffer from more accidents at work; and changes in the forms of employment with strong growth in atypical employment relationships, where there is a higher risk of accidents at work especially in the construction industry and in health and social services);

---

[46] COM(2000) 379, 18.

[47] Annexes to the Presidency Conclusions Nice European Council Meeting 7, 8 and 9 December 2000, II.

[48] COM(2001) 313.

[49] <http://ec.europa.eu/social/main.jsp?catId=716&langId=en&intPageId=227> (last accessed on 27 January 2012).

[50] COM(2002) 118.

[51] Ibid., 3.

- the emergence of new 'social' risks, especially stress,[52] depression, anxiety, violence at work,[53] harassment and intimidation, and risks related to dependence on alcohol, drugs and medicines; and

- increasing flexibilization of work, with more work being done by SMEs,[54] very small businesses, the self-employed, and at home. The global approach has eight objectives including a continuing reduction in occupational accidents and illnesses at work, mainstreaming the gender dimension, prevention of social risks, enhanced prevention of occupational illnesses (especially illnesses due to asbestos exposure, hearing loss, and musculo-skeletal problems), and analysis of new or emerging risks with special reference to risks associated with the interaction between chemical, physical, and biological agents and those associated with the general working environment (ergonomic, psychological, and social risks).[55]

The second aspect of the Commission's strategy is based on consolidating the culture of risk prevention. This, like the Lisbon strategy itself, is to be achieved through a variety of political instruments: legislation (adapting and update existing Directives, addressing new risks and consolidating existing Directives); the social dialogue (especially at the sectoral level where codes of conduct already exists and best practice has already been identified); progressive measures (benchmarking and identifying best practices); CSR (corporate social responsibility—health at work has been used as a criterion in the choice of subcontractors, and it has been included in voluntary certification and labelling initiatives);[56] and economic incentives (such as through reduced insurance premiums for those with a low accident record). The Council, in endorsing the strategy, emphasized the importance of preparing non-binding instruments (technical handbooks, codes of good practice) to make it easier to implement legal provisions in businesses.[57] The Commission also called upon a variety of actors to be involved. For example, a 'fundamental role' is given to the Senior Labour Inspectors Committee (SLIC) to encourage exchanges of information and experience and organizing mutual co-operation and assistance;[58] and the Social Partners are given an important role, especially at sectoral level, together with public authorities, companies, and public and private insurers. The Commission also wants to 'mainstream' health and safety at work:

---

[52] The Commission has issued Guidance on work-related stress: <http://osha.europa.eu/en/topics/stress/index_html> (last accessed 26 January 2012).

[53] The Commission has issued Guidance on the prevention of violence at work: <http://osha.europa.eu/en/topics/stress/index_html/violence> (last accessed 26 January 2012).

[54] In the construction industry the mean accident rate is 41 per cent above the average. It jumps to 124 per cent for firms with between 1 and 9 workers and 130 per cent for firms with between 10 and 49 workers.

[55] The European Agency for Health and Safety at Work (<http://osha.europa.eu/en>) (last accessed 26 January 2012) is responsible for acting as the driving force in matters concerning awareness building and risk anticipation.

[56] See additionally the CSR Green Paper where health at work was identified as one of the ideal areas for 'voluntary good practices' on the part of firms that want to go beyond existing rules and standards: COM(2001) 366.

[57] Res. 2002/C 161/01 (OJ [2002] L161/1), para. 3.

[58] <http://ec.europa.eu/social/main.jsp?catId=153&langId=en&intPageId=685> (last accessed 26 January 2012).

at the micro-level, in individual firms, and at the macro-level. In particular, it should be more prominent in the EES and there should be an improved linkage between health and safety and the Union rules on the manufacture and marketing of work equipment and chemical products and Union policies in the fields of public health, disability, transport, the environment, and fisheries.[59]

The third feature of the Union's strategy, again dovetailing with the Social Policy Agenda 2000, is that 'an ambitious social policy is a factor in the competitiveness equation and that, on the other side of the coin, having a non-policy engenders costs which weigh heavily on economies and societies'.[60]

The Commission's 2002 Strategy—and its enthusiastic endorsement by the Council of Ministers[61]—fed into the 2003 Employment Guidelines.[62] Health and safety formed part of the second of the three 'overarching and interrelated objectives', quality and productivity at work,[63] and formed part of the third specific Guideline (address change and promote adaptability and mobility in the labour market) which urged Member States to improve working conditions, including health and safety. Specifically, policies are to achieve 'a substantial reduction in the incidence rate of accidents at work and occupational disease' but, contrary to the Commission's hope,[64] no national quantified targets are set. Yet, by the time of the Lisbon relaunch and the 2005 Guidelines,[65] the prominence of health and safety was reduced to a brief reference in Guideline 21.

However, the Commission's 2005 Communication on the Social Agenda[66] proposed a new strategy for 2007–12 based on the idea that prevention pays off: fewer work-related accidents and less disease push up productivity, contain costs, strengthen quality in work and hence improve the value of Europe's human capital. The 2007–12 strategy also focuses on new and emerging risks and safeguarding minimum levels of protection in workplace situations and to workers not adequately covered. Specific attention is to be given to the quality of prevention services, a policy emphasized in the 2010 Employment Guidelines,[67] health and safety training, as well as other tools to ensure a better application of health and safety standards. Since the quality of implementation is of vital importance, the Commission is also committed to pursuing its efforts to monitor the transposition and implementation of legislation. Moreover, in order to ensure effective implementation, all the players concerned must have the capacity to take on their responsibilities, including the Social Partners who proved their worth in concluding an agreement on work-related stress.

---

[59] This was also emphasized by the Council in its Res. 2002/C 161/01 (OJ [2002] L161/1), paras. 2(e)(a) and 5.

[60] COM(2002) 118, 3.

[61] Co. Res. 2002/C 161/01 on a new Union strategy on health and safety at work (2002–6) (OJ [2002] L161/1).

[62] Co. Dec. 2003/578/EC (OJ [2003] L197/13).

[63] For a full discussion of this approach, see Ch. 3.   [64] COM(2002) 118, 15.

[65] Co. Dec. 2005/600/EC (OJ [2005] L205/21).   [66] COM(2005) 33, 7.

[67] Dec. 2010/707/EU (OJ [2010] L308/46): Guideline 7 *Increasing labour market participation of women and men, reducing structural unemployment and promoting job quality* says: 'The quality of jobs and employment conditions should be addressed. Member States should combat in-work poverty and promote occupational health and safety'.

2.4. The Social Partners' agreement on work-related stress

In recognition of the 'new and emerging risks', and their own responsibilities, the Social Partners produced an agreement on work-related stress in October 2004.[68] Stress is defined as 'a state, which is accompanied by physical, psychological or social complaints or dysfunction and which results from individuals feeling unable to bridge a gap with the requirements or expectations placed on them'. It continues that '[s]tress is not a disease but prolonged exposure to it may reduce effectiveness at work and may cause ill health'. The agreement then outlines various anti-stress measures:

- management and communication measures such as clarifying the company's objectives and the role of individual workers, ensuring adequate management support for individuals and teams, matching responsibility and control over work, improving work organization and processes, working conditions and environment;

- training managers and workers to raise awareness and understanding of stress, its possible causes and how to deal with it, and/or to adapt to change;

- provision of information to, and consultation with, workers and/or their representatives in accordance with EU and national legislation, collective agreements, and practices.

The Social Partners agreed to implement the agreement in accordance with the procedures and practices specific to management and labour in the Member States and in the EEA.[69]

The Stress Agreement makes express reference to the employer's legal obligation to protect the occupational safety and health of workers including from the problems of work-related stress. This obligation comes from the cornerstone of Union health and safety law, Framework Directive 89/391.

C. FRAMEWORK DIRECTIVE 89/391 ON HEALTH AND SAFETY

1. INTRODUCTION

The most important legislative measure adopted under the Social Action Programme 1989 was the Framework Directive, Directive 89/391/EEC,[70] which marked the advent of a new approach to health and safety. While building on the principles laid down in the parent Directive 80/1107, Directive 89/391/EEC and its more specific daughter Directives[71] lack the detailed technical requirements found in the earlier Directives and

---

[68] <http://www.etuc.org/a/529> (last accessed 2 April 2012). See additionally the Framework Agreement on harassment and violence at work: <http://www.etuc.org/a/8574> considered in Ch. 2.

[69] This is an autonomous agreement: see further Ch. 2.   [70] OJ [1989] L183/1.

[71] The enactment of these daughter Directives is provided for under Art. 16(1) of Dir. 89/391. See further Communication from the Commission on the practical implementation of the provisions of the Health and Safety at Work Dirs 89/391 (Framework), 89/654 (Workplaces), 89/655 (Work Equipment), 89/656 (Personal Protective Equipment), 90/269 (Manual Handling of Loads), and 90/270 (Display Screen Equipment): COM (2004) 62.

rely instead on broad general principles of prevention.[72] Article 1(1) makes clear that the object of Directive 89/391 is to introduce measures to encourage improvements in the health and safety of workers at work. To that end, it contains 'general principles concerning the prevention of occupational risks, the protection of safety and health, the elimination of risk and accident factors, the informing, consultation [and] balanced participation of workers and their representatives'.[73] Thus, as the Court put it in *Commission* v. *Netherlands*,[74] the aim of the Directive is not only to improve the protection of workers against accidents at work and the prevention of occupational risks but also to introduce specific measures to organize that protection and prevention. This approach, based on principles rather than detailed technical requirements, obviated the need for lengthy technical debates.[75] The specification of any relevant technical standards has been left to be resolved through a Technical Adaptation Procedure.[76]

Directive 89/391 lays down minimum standards but it does not justify any reduction in the levels of protection already achieved in Member States, since the states are committed to encouraging improvements in working conditions and harmonizing conditions while maintaining the improvements made.[77] This is specifically recognized in Article 1(3) which provides that the Directive is without prejudice to 'existing or future national and [Union] provisions which are more favourable to protection of safety and health of workers at work'. Article 4 makes clear that the responsibility for ensuring that employers, workers, and workers' representatives are subject to the legal provisions necessary for the implementation of the Directive lies with the Member States.

2. THE PERSONAL SCOPE OF THE DIRECTIVE

The Directive applies to all sectors of activity, both public and private. This includes, in a non-exhaustive list, industrial activity, agricultural, commercial, administrative, service, educational and cultural activities, and leisure.[78] There are limited derogations in the case of 'certain specific *public sector* activities' (emphasis added), such as the armed forces or police, and 'certain specific activities in the civil protection services'.[79] The Directive recognizes that these occupations inevitably conflict with the principle of health and safety. Nevertheless, even in these situations, the health and safety of workers must be 'ensured as far as possible in the light of the objectives of the Directive'.[80] The Directive applies to 'workers', defined as meaning any person employed by an employer, including trainees

---

[72] Art. 3(d) defines 'prevention' as 'all steps or measures taken or planned at all stages of work in the undertaking to prevent or reduce occupational risks'.

[73] Art. 1(2).

[74] Case C–441/01 *Commission* v. *Netherlands* [2003] ECR I–5463, para. 38.

[75] See P. James, *The European Community: A Positive Force in UK Health and Safety Law* (1993) *IER* 6.

[76] See e.g. Art. 17 of Dir. 89/391/EEC replaced by Reg. 1137/2008 (OJ [2008] L311/1) adapting a number of instruments with regard to the regulatory procedure with scrutiny.

[77] Para. 5 of the Preamble.   [78] Art. 2(1).   [79] Art. 2(2).   [80] Art. 2(2).

and apprentices but excluding domestic servants.[81] Thus, by implication, the self-employed are excluded from the benefit of the Directives unless otherwise provided.[82] 'Employers' means natural or legal persons having an employment relationship with the worker and having responsibility for the undertaking and/or the establishment.[83]

3. EMPLOYERS' OBLIGATIONS

3.1. The basic requirements

(a) Article 5(1)

Article 5(1) contains the demanding obligation that the employer has the duty 'to ensure the health and safety of workers in *every aspect* related to the work'.[84] This duty extends to taking responsibility for services provided by third parties[85] and is not diminished by the workers' own obligations for their health and safety.[86] Such a definitive statement, when read in conjunction with Article 1(1), clearly sets the tenor of the Directive: worker protection. Member States may, however:

> provide for the exclusion or the limitation of employers' responsibility where occurrences are due to unusual *and* unforeseeable circumstances, beyond the employers' control, or to *exceptional* events, the consequence of which could not have been avoided despite the exercise of *all due care*.[87]

This derogation, being an exception to the basic principle of the Directive, will be narrowly construed[88] and is unlikely to permit broad defences based on financial considerations or arguments related to lack of time or effort to deal with the risk. The emphasis on the exceptional nature of the events also suggests that, on its face, a defence that the employer took all reasonably practicable steps to avoid the risk would not be acceptable. On the other hand, since the general principle of proportionality applies to the Directive as a whole, it may well be that a more general defence based on proportionality applies to all the provisions in the Directive.

The scope of Article 5(1) was considered in *Commission v. UK*.[89] The UK restricted the duty on employers to ensure the safety and health of workers in all aspects related to work to only 'so far as is reasonably practicable'. The Commission argued that an employer's liability extended 'to the consequences of any event detrimental to workers' health and safety, regardless of whether that event or those consequences can be attributed to any form of negligence on the part of the employer in adopting preventive measures'; i.e. a 'no-fault liability, whether civil or criminal'. The Court disagreed with the Commission.

---

[81] Art. 3(a). See additionally Ch. 4.
[82] Cf. Council Rec. 2003/134/EC (OJ [2003] L53/45) which recognizes the precarious position of the self-employed and encourages Member States to promote health and safety for self-employed workers.
[83] Art. 3(b).   [84] Emphasis added.   [85] Arts. 5(2), 7(3).
[86] Art. 5(3).   [87] Art. 5(4). Emphasis added.
[88] See, by analogy, Case 41/74 *Van Duyn* v. *Home Office* [1974] ECR 1337, para. 18.
[89] Case C-127/05 [2007] ECR I-4619.

It said Article 5(1) 'simply embodies the general duty of safety to which the employer is subject, without specifying any form of liability'. It referred to the legislative history of Directive 89/391, and in particular, to the joint statement by the Council and the Commission recorded in the minutes of the Council meeting of 12 June 1989, that the insertion of such a clause was suggested in order to resolve the problems that formulating the employer's duty to ensure safety in absolute terms would have raised in the common-law systems, bearing in mind the obligation on the courts concerned to interpret written law literally. The Court said the refusal to insert a clause comparable to the disputed clause in Article 5(1) of Directive 89/391 could not suffice to justify an interpretation of that provision to the effect that the employer is subject to a form of no-fault liability in the event of accident. It also said that such an interpretation could not be based on the scheme of Article 5 of Directive 89/391 either.

So what then is the extent of the duty on employers to ensure the safety and health of workers? Although the Commission submitted that the duty on the employer was absolute, it expressly acknowledged that that duty did not imply that the employer was required to ensure a zero-risk working environment. The Commission also recognized that, as a result of carrying out a risk assessment, the employer could conclude that the risks were so small that no preventive measures were necessary. In those circumstances, the key point, according to the Commission, was that the employer would remain responsible if an accident were to occur. The Court did not express a view on this issue, finding that the Commission had not established in what way the disputed clause infringed Article 5(1).

(b) Article 6

Article 6 fleshes out the wide-ranging general obligations on employers: not only must they take the measures *necessary* for safety and health protection of workers, but they must also prevent the occurrence of occupational risks, provide information and training and establish the necessary organization and means.[90] These measures must be further adjusted to take account of changing circumstances.[91]

Article 6(2) then details the following general principles of prevention[92] designed to guide the employer:

(a) avoiding risks;

(b) evaluating the risks which cannot be avoided;

(c) combating the risks at source;

(d) adapting the work to the individual, especially as regards the design of work places, the choice of work equipment and the choice of working and production methods, with a view, in particular, to alleviating monotonous work and work

---

[90] Art. 6(1).   [91] Ibid.
[92] Defined in Art. 3(d) to mean all steps or measures taken or planned at all stages of work in the undertaking to prevent or reduce occupational risks.

at a predetermined work rate, thus reducing the effects on health. This provision probably goes further than legislation in all Member States. It is a key requirement which addresses the well-being of workers in a comprehensive way rather than focusing on specific hazards;[93]

(e) adapting to technical progress;

(f) replacing the dangerous by the non-dangerous or the less dangerous (the principle of substitution);

(g) developing a coherent prevention policy which covers technology, organization of work, working conditions, social relationships, and the influence of factors related to the working environment;

(h) giving collective protective measures priority over individual protective measures; and

(i) giving appropriate instructions to the workers.

Article 6(3) then provides more specifics. Taking into account the nature of the activities of the enterprise and/or establishment, the employers must:

(a) evaluate the risks to the safety and health of workers, *inter alia*[94] in the choice of work equipment, the chemical substances or preparations used, and the fitting-out of work places. Subsequent to this evaluation and as necessary, the preventive measures and the working and production methods implemented by the employer must:
— assure an improvement in the level of protection afforded to workers with regard to safety and health,
— be integrated into all the activities of the undertaking and/or establishment and at all hierarchical levels;

(b) take into consideration the worker's capabilities as regards health and safety;

(c) ensure that the planning and introduction of new technologies are the subject of consultation with the workers and/or their representatives, as regards the consequences of the choice of equipment, the working conditions and the working environment for the safety and health of workers;

(d) take appropriate steps to ensure that only workers who have received adequate instructions may have access to areas where there is serious and specific danger.

The Directive also contains more specific employers' duties which can be subdivided into the following five categories:[95] duty of awareness and evaluation; duty to plan and

[93] For a similar idea see the principle of the humanization of work contained in Art. 13 of the Working Time Dir. 2003/88/EC (OJ [2003] L299/9).
[94] This is a non-exhaustive list: Case C–49/00 *Commission v. Italy* [2001] ECR I–8575, para. 12.
[95] See further Neal and Wright, previously, at n. 7, 18, and A. Neal, 'The European Framework Directive on the Health and Safety of Workers: Challenges for the UK' (1990) 6 *IJCLLIR* 80, 82.

take action; duty to train and direct the workforce; duty to inform and consult workers and their representatives; and duty to report. These will be considered in turn.

3.2. Duty of awareness and evaluation

Article 9(1)(a) requires the employer to have conducted an assessment of health and safety risks and be aware of the situation of groups of workers who are exposed to particular risks. Respecting the principle of subsidiarity, the Directive prescribes the objectives but allows Member States to decide how these are to be achieved. There is thus no guidance as to how this risk assessment is to be carried out or any indication of the minimum enquiry necessary.

Employers must then evaluate both the risks to the safety and health of workers, *inter alia*, in the choice of work equipment, the chemical substances or preparations used, and the fitting out of the workplace,[96] and decide on the protective measures and equipment needed.[97] The employer, when entrusting tasks to a worker, must take account of the capabilities of the individual workers as regards health and safety.[98] This is particularly relevant in the case of pregnant women or women who have recently given birth or who are breastfeeding.[99] Further, Article 14 requires that workers receive health surveillance appropriate to the risks they incur at work. These checks may be provided as part of the national health system. According to the Preamble, employers must also keep themselves informed of the latest advances in technology and scientific findings concerning workplace design.[100] This suggests that the review of health and safety measures should be a continuous process, requiring constant reassessment and evaluation.

3.3. Duty to plan and take action

Having completed the assessment, the employer must, where necessary, introduce preventive measures and changes to working and production to improve the health and safety of workers. Any steps taken must form part of a coherent prevention policy[101] and be integrated into all the activities of the undertaking and at all hierarchical levels.[102] In addition, particularly sensitive risk groups must be protected against the dangers which specifically affect them.[103]

The Framework Directive, when read in conjunction with the various daughter Directives, envisages a hierarchy of control measures as follows:[104]

- Elimination of risk from the workplace. While this is clearly advantageous from a health and safety perspective it may not be feasible in practice. Consequently, employers must consider means by which those risks can be reduced.

- The principle of substitution. This may involve replacing one chemical with another one which is less dangerous but is still capable of working as effectively. It

---

[96] Art. 6(3)(a).   [97] Art. 9(1)(b).   [98] Art. 6(3)(b).
[99] See further Dir. 92/85/EEC (OJ [1992] L348/1) which is considered in Ch. 9.
[100] See further Art. 6(2)(e).   [101] Art. 6(2)(g).   [102] Art. 6(3)(a), para. 2.
[103] Art. 15.   [104] *HSIB* 200, 5.

may also involve the substitution of another form of the same substance which is likely to be less hazardous, for example, by replacing powdered ingredients with a less dusty form.[105]

- Engineering control. This may involve introducing ventilation, enclosing dangerous processes,[106] using mechanical handling aids,[107] or automation.

- Personal protective equipment (PPE).[108] From a health and safety perspective this is the least advantageous because much PPE is not 100 per cent effective (e.g. the effectiveness of respiratory protective equipment can be reduced if the user wears glasses or has a beard) and its success is largely dependent on the correct selection of the most appropriate type of PPE. Further, PPE protects only the individual rather than the workforce as a whole. The disadvantages of this approach are reflected in Article 6(2)(h) of the Framework Directive which requires employers to give collective (as against individual) protective measures priority.

Where several undertakings share a workplace it is possible that the different employers may co-operate in implementing the health and safety provisions and co-ordinate their action in protecting and preventing occupational risks.[109] Nevertheless, whatever action is taken 'may in no circumstances involve the worker in financial cost'.[110] This refrain also appears in various daughter Directives.[111]

In order to carry out activities related to the protection and prevention of occupational risks, including the risks faced by young workers,[112] the employer must designate one or more workers to fulfil these tasks.[113] Where—and only where[114]—no appropriate workers exist then the employer can enlist 'competent external services or persons' who must be fully informed by the employer of the factors which may affect the health and safety of workers.[115] Delegating the tasks does not mean, however, that the employer is able to delegate responsibility.[116] Both the internal and external health and safety staff must have the necessary skills and be sufficient in number to deal with the organization of the health and safety measures, taking into account the size of the undertaking, the hazards to which the workers are exposed, and their distribution throughout the entire undertaking or establishment.[117] This provision does allow a certain degree of flexibility, particularly for SMEs,

---

[105] See further *HSIB* 200, 5.

[106] See e.g. Art. 5 of Dir. 90/394/EEC (OJ [1990] L196/1). This Directive was repealed and replaced by Dir. 2004/37/EC (OJ [2004] L158/50).

[107] See Art. 3(1) of Dir. 90/269/EEC (OJ [1990] L156/9).

[108] See Dir. 89/656/EEC (OJ [1989] L393/181).

[109] Art. 6(4).   [110] Art. 6(5).

[111] E.g. Dir. 90/270 on VDUs and Dir. 89/656 on PPE discussed below.

[112] Arts. 6(4) and 7(3) of Dir. 94/33/EEC (OJ [1994] L216/12).

[113] Art. 7(1).

[114] Case C–441/01 *Commission* v. *Netherlands* [2003] ECR I–5463, paras. 20–1; Case C–428/04 *Commission* v. *Austria* [2006] ECR I–3325, para. 54.

[115] Art. 7(3) and (4).   [116] Art. 5(2).

[117] Art. 7(5). Member States may specify the appropriate numbers, see Art. 7(8). Member States must lay down sufficiently clear and detailed rules relating to the capabilities required of the persons concerned with the organization of protective and preventive measures: Case C–49/00 *Commission* v. *Italy* [2001] ECR I–8575.

as to the appointment of health and safety personnel. Finally, Article 7(2) provides that those workers to whom responsibility for health and safety has been designated must be given adequate time for the task[118] and must not be placed at a disadvantage in respect of their careers because of their health and safety role.[119]

In the specific context of first-aid, fire-fighting, and the evacuation of workers, Article 8(1) allows the employer to take the necessary measures, *adapted to the nature of the activities and the size of the undertaking*, while Article 8(2) provides that the employer can designate workers who are required to implement such measures.[120] However, the most significant feature of Article 8 is the right to stop work. Article 8(3) provides that the employer must also give instructions to enable workers in the event of serious, imminent, and unavoidable danger to stop work and/or immediately leave the workplace and proceed to a place of safety. If, in these circumstances workers do leave their workplace under instruction from the employer, or at their own initiative when an immediate supervisor cannot be contacted, they must not be placed at 'any disadvantage because of their action and must be protected against any harmful and unjustified conduct'.[121] Therefore, they should be protected from dismissal or any lesser disciplinary measure. Furthermore, where workers have acted on their own initiative because a superior cannot be contacted and have taken appropriate steps in the face of serious and imminent danger, a subjective test is applied and account is taken of their knowledge and the technical means at their disposal. They are only liable to censure if they acted carelessly or negligently.[122]

The employer must also refrain from asking for workers to resume work where a serious and imminent danger still exists, save in exceptional cases for reasons duly substantiated.[123] This provision is principally designed to apply to safety and repair workers.

3.4. Duty to train and direct the workforce

Article 12 provides that all workers must receive adequate health and safety training, particularly relating to the operation of their work stations. This training must be given on recruitment, if and when workers change jobs, if the work equipment is changed, or if new technology is introduced. The training must be adapted to take account of new or changed risks and repeated periodically where necessary.[124] Special training must be provided for workers' representatives with a specific role in the health and safety protection of workers.[125] In either case, training must not be at the workers' or workers' representatives' expense and must take place during working hours.[126]

In addition, the Directive recognizes the role of the responsible exercise of managerial prerogative. Article 6(2)(i) talks of an employer giving 'appropriate instructions to

---

[118] There is no provision for time off without loss of pay in the case of designated workers. Cf. Art. 11(5) which does, expressly, provide for this. This might be explained by the fact that responsibility for health and safety may be part of a designated worker's job and therefore they will be paid for it.

[119] Art. 7(2).

[120] Art. 8(2), unlike Art. 8(1), is not subject to a caveat for SMEs: Case C–428/04 *Commission v. Austria* [2006] ECR I–3325, para. 66.

[121] Art. 8(4) and (5).   [122] Art. 8(5).   [123] Art. 8(3)(c).   [124] Art. 12(1).

[125] Art. 12(3).   [126] Art. 12(4).

the workers' and where there are specific danger areas the employer must ensure that only workers who have received adequate instructions may have access to them.[127]

3.5. Duty to inform workers and workers' representatives, to consult, and to encourage the participation of the workforce

The EU has long had ambitions of incorporating contributions of both management and labour in decisions and initiatives in this field.[128] This was given further impetus by Article 154 TFEU (ex 138 EC) providing for a social dialogue, and the Community Social Charter 1989 which required that health and safety measures to take account of the need for 'the training, information, consultation and balanced participation of workers as regards the risks incurred and the steps taken to eliminate or reduce them'.[129]

It is possible to identify three distinct approaches to workplace organization on health and safety.[130] In the first system, found in Germany, Luxembourg, Italy, and the Netherlands, works councils elected by employees occupy a central position, and safety delegates or committees play only a secondary role. Works councils have the right to approve or reject measures proposed by the employer, assist in planning, monitor compliance with the legislation, be informed of relevant information, and accompany inspectors on visits and consult with them. The second system sees joint safety committees as the main channel of participation. In Belgium a special committee must be established to act as a forum for consultation between the employer and employee in all undertakings with more than 50 employees. Similarly, health and safety committees must be set up in all establishments which employ over 50 people in France and Portugal. In Spain committees are compulsory for certain companies, depending on the number of employees and the nature of the risk. The third system, found in Denmark and the UK, involves the workers electing safety representatives who become members of safety committees and are entitled to be informed of all relevant information and to consult the relevant inspectorates.

Directive 89/391/EEC does impose onerous requirements on employers in respect of the provision of information to the workers themselves and/or to their representatives. The term 'workers' representatives with specific responsibility for the safety and health of workers' is defined by Article 3(c) as any person elected, chosen *or designated* in accordance with national laws and/or practices to represent workers where problems arise relating to safety and health protection of workers at work. In *Commission* v. *Portugal*[131] the Court confirmed that the Directive does not oblige Member States to provide for an election procedure for workers' representatives but envisages other possibilities for

---

[127] Art. 6(3)(d). This provision may be read in conjunction with Art. 8(3)(c).

[128] See the Preambles to the 1978 and 1984 Action Programmes and the 1988 Action Programme which envisaged that the Advisory Committee on Safety, Health and Hygiene as a 'highly appropriate forum for consultation between two sides of industry'. See Neal and Wright, above, n. 7, 19–20.

[129] COM(89) 471 final, para. 19(2).

[130] See previously, at n. 5, 114, and COM(88) 73 final. See additionally J. Korostoff, L. Zimmermann, and C. Ryan, 'Rethinking the OSHA Approach to Workplace Safety: A Look at Worker Participation in the Enforcement of Safety Regulations in Sweden, France and Great Britain' (1991) 13 *Comparative Labour Law Journal* 45.

[131] Case C–425/01 [2003] ECR I–6025.

choosing or designating such representatives.[132] If the Member State does decide to hold an election, the Directive does not require the national legislation to state all the detailed rules applying to the procedure,[133] although the workers' representatives must be elected by workers in accordance with national law or practice.

The duty to inform extends to temporary and hired workers currently working in the enterprise or establishment[134] and workers from any outside undertakings working in the employer's establishment.[135] Depending on the size of the undertaking, and in accordance with national laws and/or practices, the employer must, according to Article 10, provide all necessary information concerning:

(a) the safety and health risks and protective and preventive measures and activities in respect of both of the undertakings and/or establishments in general, and each type of work station and job; and

(b) the measures taken to deal with first-aid, fire-fighting, and evacuation.[136]

In order to help workers or workers' representatives, they must be provided with the results of the risk assessment conducted by the employer and details of the necessary protective measures to be taken, as well as details about occupational accidents and illnesses and any health and safety reports made to national authorities.[137]

Article 11(1) provides that employers must also consult workers and/or their representatives and allow them to take part in discussions on all questions including working conditions and the working environment, the planning and introduction of new technology,[138] and the consequences of the choice of equipment on the safety and health of workers.[139] The Article presupposes:[140]

• the consultation of workers;

• the right of workers and/or their representatives to make proposals, including making proposals which mitigate hazards for workers and/or remove sources of danger;[141]

• balanced participation in accordance with national laws and/or practices.[142]

The phrase 'balanced participation' is not defined.[143] It has been suggested that the qualification 'in accordance with national laws and practices' has caused particular problems of interpretation,[144] allowing a diversity of potentially inadequate implementation.

---

[132] Para. 20.   [133] Para. 21.

[134] Art. 10(2). See further Arts. 3 and 7 of Dir. 91/383/EEC (OJ [1991] L206/19) on Atypical Workers considered in Ch. 9.

[135] Ibid.   [136] Art. 10(1).   [137] Art. 10(3).

[138] A study found that only 60 per cent of firms in Europe satisfied this requirement, see N. Krieger, 'Employee Participation in Health and Safety Protection' (1990) 6 *IJCLLIR* 217.

[139] Art. 6(3)(c).   [140] Art. 11(1).   [141] Art. 11(3).   [142] Art. 11(1).

[143] This issue is considered further in Ch. 15.

[144] D. Walters and R. Freeman, 'Employee Representation in Health and Safety in the Workplace: a Comparative Study in Five European Countries', OPEC, cited in *HSIB* 201, 6. See additionally D. Walters, *Worker Participation in Health and Safety: A European Comparison* (IER, London, 1990).

Workers or workers' representatives must be consulted in advance *and in good time*[145] with regard to any measure which may substantially affect health and safety, the appointment of designated workers, risk assessment and the provision of information, the enlistment of services or personnel, and the planning and organization of training.[146] If they consider that the measures taken and the means employed by the employer are inadequate they are entitled to appeal to the national authority responsible for health and safety protection.[147] They must also be given the opportunity to submit their observations during official inspection visits.[148]

As with designated workers, workers and their representatives entitled to be consulted about health and safety matters must be given adequate time off work without loss of pay to fulfil their duties. They must also be provided with the necessary means to enable them to exercise their rights and functions[149] and must not be placed at a disadvantage because of their activities.[150] In other words, they cannot be dismissed or suffer any other detriment. The full requirements of the information and consultation provisions have been incorporated into the daughter Directives.

Research conducted for the Commission has revealed a picture of only partial implementation in the Member States of the provisions relating to worker representation, particularly in the case of small workplaces and those in the tertiary sector. The same report criticized the Directive's provisions on worker involvement and consultation in that they allow Member States to continue to exempt small workplaces from participative arrangements, they do little to stimulate the development of more general institutions of workforce representation, and they fail to encourage state enforcement agencies to adopt a more interventionist role where such institutions are absent.[151]

3.6. Duty to report

The employer must draw up a list of accidents which resulted in the worker being unfit for work for more than three working days[152] and provide these reports to the responsible national authorities.[153] The detail and scope of the reports may be determined by the Member States, taking into account the size of the undertaking and the nature of its activities.[154]

4. WORKERS' RESPONSIBILITIES

Complementing the duties imposed on the employer, the Directive also places significant and detailed obligations on workers. We have already seen, in Article 7, that employers must designate one or more workers to carry out activities related to the protection and prevention of occupational risks. This, according to the Court,[155] is an

---

[145] Cf. Council Dir. 98/59/EC on Collective Redundancies (OJ [1998] L225/16), discussed in Ch. 14.
[146] Art. 11(2).   [147] Art. 11(6).   [148] Ibid.   [149] Art. 11(5).
[150] Art. 11(4).   [151] Walters and Freeman, previously, at n. 144.   [152] Art. 9(1)(b).
[153] Art. 9(1)(d).   [154] Art. 9(2).
[155] Case C–441/01 *Commission v. Netherlands* [2003] ECR I–5463, para. 40.

'organisational measure consistent with the aim of participation of workers in their own safety'. In addition, Article 13(1) lays down the general principle that:

> It shall be the responsibility of each worker to take care as far as possible of his own safety and health and that of other persons affected by his acts or commissions at work in accordance with his training and the instructions given by his employer.

This is part of the Union's preventive policy bringing in all players, including the workers themselves, with a view to developing a genuine culture of risk prevention.[156]

Article 13(2) fleshes out the workers' general obligation, with examples of three specific duties. The first requires the worker to make correct use of personal protective equipment,[157] machinery, apparatus, tools, dangerous substances, transport equipment, and other means of production.[158] This includes refraining from disconnecting, changing, or arbitrarily removing safety devices fitted to the machinery and equipment.[159]

The second obligation is for the worker to inform immediately the employer or workers with responsibility for health and safety whenever they have reasonable grounds for fearing a serious and immediate danger or highlight any shortcomings in the protection arrangements.[160] Thirdly, workers must co-operate with the implementation of health and safety measures[161] and ensure that the working environment and working conditions are safe.[162] Nevertheless, the final responsibility rests with the employer.[163]

5. REMEDIES

Article 4 of the Directive provides that Member States must take the necessary steps 'to ensure that the employers, workers and workers' representatives are subject to the legal provisions necessary for the implementation of [the] Directive' but the final responsibility rests with the Member States who must ensure 'adequate controls and supervision'. Although the Directive does not expressly state that Member States must provide workers with recourse to the judicial process if they are denied the rights conferred by the Directive, as a general principle of Union law[164] some remedy must be provided to secure full implementation of the Directive. In *Commission* v. *Greece*[165] the Court made clear that an infringement of Union law must be 'penalised under conditions, both procedural and substantive, which are analogous to those applicable to infringements of national law of similar nature and importance' and that the penalty must be 'effective, proportionate and dissuasive'.

---

[156] COM(2002) 118, 9.   [157] Art. 13(2)(b).   [158] Art. 13(2)(a).
[159] Art. 13(2)(c).   [160] Art. 13(2)(d).   [161] Art. 13(2)(e).
[162] Art. 13(2)(f).   [163] Art. 5(3).
[164] See e.g. Case C–326/88 *Hansen* [1990] ECR I–2911.
[165] Case 68/88 *Commission* v. *Greece* [1989] ECR I–2965.

D. THE DAUGHTER DIRECTIVES

1. INTRODUCTION

The Framework Directive provides that a series of individual Directives will be passed to cover specific risks.[166] The general principles contained in the parent Directive apply to the daughter Directives, without prejudice to the more specific provisions of the daughter Directives.[167] These daughter Directives can loosely be divided into three categories: those affecting the workplace, those laying down requirements relating to work equipment, and those relating to chemical, physical, and biological agents. They will be considered in outline under these headings.

2. THE WORKPLACE DIRECTIVES

Union legislation on the workplace has adopted a twin-track approach: a general Directive covering most industries running parallel with a number of complementary measures targeting specific sectors.

2.1. Directive 89/654/EEC on the Minimum Safety and Health Requirements for the Workplace

The principal aim of this Directive[168] is to protect the health and safety of workers through the proper layout of the workplace. A workplace is defined as 'the place intended to house workstations on the premises of undertakings and/or establishments and any other place within the area of the undertaking to which the worker has access in the course of his employment'.[169] Article 6 imposes general requirements on the employer to safeguard the health and safety of workers by ensuring that:

- traffic routes to emergency exits and the exits themselves are kept clear at all times;
- technical maintenance of the workplace and of the equipment and devices is carried out, and that any faults are rectified as quickly as possible;
- the workplace, the equipment and any devices are regularly cleaned to an adequate level of hygiene;
- safety equipment and devices intended to prevent or eliminate hazards are regularly maintained and checked.

Workers must be informed and consulted about any measures to be taken concerning health and safety at the workplace.[170] More detailed obligations imposed on employers

---

[166] Art. 16(1). [167] See e.g. Art. 1(3) of Dir. 89/654.
[168] Council Dir. 89/654/EEC on the minimum health and safety requirements for the workplace (first individual Directive within the meaning of Art. 16(1) of Dir. 89/391/EEC) (OJ [1989] L393/1). See additionally COM(88) 74 final.
[169] Art. 2. [170] Arts. 7 and 8.

in connection with their workplaces are found in the Annexes to the Directive. The nature of the obligations depends on whether the workplace was used for the first time after 31 December 1992 or was already in use. The obligations do not, however, apply to specific risk sectors, where there is a particularly high incidence of accidents[171] which are covered by specific Directives.

2.2. Specific risk sectors

Developing and expanding the principles in Directive 89/654; specific Directives are intended to address the special problems relating to industries identified as creating a particular risk. Directive 92/57 concerns temporary or mobile construction sites.[172] It acknowledges that the work site[173] brings together the self-employed and a number of different undertakings working at the site simultaneously or in succession, and that the self-employed, as well as employed workers, must be bound by certain obligations to avoid exposing other workers to various risks.[174] The Directive aims at a 'global approach to accident prevention': by establishing a chain of responsibility linking all the parties concerned—the clients, the project supervisors, the employers, the co-ordinators, and the self-employed—and by integrating health and safety requirements at all stages of the project, in particular by strengthening co-ordination between the parties.[175]

Two Directives concern the mineral extracting industry: Directive 92/91/EEC concerns the safety and health protection of workers in the mineral extracting industries through drilling,[176] which takes into account the findings of the Cullen inquiry into the Piper Alpha oil platform disaster,[177] and Directive 92/104/EEC[178] concerns the health and safety protection of workers in surface and underground mineral extracting industries. Both Directives follow a common format, obliging employers to ensure that:[179]

- workplaces are designed, constructed, equipped, commissioned, operated, and maintained in such a way that workers can perform the work assigned to them without endangering their safety and/or health and/or those of other workers;

- the operation of workplaces when workers are present takes place under the supervision of a person in charge;

- work involving special risk is entrusted only to competent staff and carried out in accordance with instructions given;

---

[171] Art. 1(2).

[172] Council Dir. 92/57/EEC on the implementation of minimum health and safety requirements at temporary or mobile construction sites (eighth individual Directive) (OJ [1992] L245/6).

[173] Defined to include any construction site at which building or civil engineering works are carried out (Art. 2(a)). A non-exhaustive list of building and civil engineering works is contained in Annex I.

[174] COM(90) 275 final.

[175] See esp. Art. 3 considered in Case C-224/09 *Nussbaumer* [2010] ECR I-000.

[176] Council Dir. 92/91/EEC on the minimum requirements for improving the safety and health protection of workers in the mineral-extracting industries through drilling (eleventh individual Directive) (OJ [1992] L348/9).

[177] *HSIB* 196, 12, and *HSIB* 181, 2.

[178] Council Dir. 92/104/EEC on the minimum requirements for improving the safety and health protection of workers in surface and underground mineral-extracting industries (twelfth individual Directive) (OJ [1992] L404/10). See additionally COM(92) 14 final/2.   [179] Art. 3.

- safety instructions are comprehensible to all the workers concerned;
- appropriate first-aid facilities are provided;
- any relevant safety drills are performed at regular intervals.

Directive 93/103/EC[180] concerns the minimum health and safety requirements on board fishing vessels. The Directive imposes general duties relating to all vessels and specific obligations on vessels depending on their age and size. Owners must ensure that their boats are used without endangering the health and safety of workers, in particular in foreseeable meteorological conditions, without prejudice to the responsibility of the skipper.[181] Owners also have responsibility in respect of equipment and maintenance: they must ensure that the vessels and their fittings and equipment are technically maintained, that any defects are rectified as quickly as possible, and that the equipment is hygienic.[182] Moreover the vessel must be supplied with an adequate quantity of suitable emergency and survival equipment.[183]

Finally, Directive 99/92/EC on explosive atmospheres[184] requires the establishment of a coherent strategy for the prevention of explosions.[185]

3. EQUIPMENT USED AT WORK

The Directives examined so far address the health and safety problems arising from the layout of the workplace. The next group of Directives concerns the rules relating to the equipment used by workers. The principal Directive, Directive 89/655/EEC,[186] now repealed and replaced by Directive 2009/104/EC,[187] concerning the minimum health and safety requirements for the use of work equipment by workers, obliges employers to ensure that the work equipment made available to workers is suitable for the work to be carried out, or properly adapted for that purpose, and may be used by workers without impairment to their health and safety.[188] Work equipment, defined

---

[180] Council Dir. 93/103/EEC of 23 November 1993 (thirteenth individual Directive) (OJ [1993] L307/1). See additionally Council Dir. 92/29/EEC (OJ [1992] L113/19) on minimum health and safety requirements for improved medical treatment on board vessels.

[181] Art. 3(1)(a). The skipper is the person commanding the vessel or having responsibility for it (Art. 2(g)).

[182] Art. 7.   [183] Ibid.

[184] European Parliament and Council Dir. 99/92/EC on minimum requirements for improving safety and health protection of workers potentially at risk from explosive atmospheres (15th individual Directive) (OJ [2000] L23/57). See additionally European Parliament and Council Dir. 94/9/EC (OJ [1994] L100/1) on equipment and protective systems in potentially explosive atmospheres.

[185] Non-binding guide to good practice for implementing the European Parliament and Council Directive 1999/92/EC on minimum requirements for improving the safety and health protection of workers potentially at risk from explosive atmospheres: COM(2003)515.

[186] Council Dir. 89/655/EEC (second individual Directive) (OJ [1989] L393/13).

[187] Directive 2009/104/EC of the European Parliament and of the Council of 16 September 2009 concerning the minimum safety and health requirements for the use of work equipment by workers at work (second individual Directive within the meaning of Article 16(1) of Directive 89/391/EEC) (OJ [2009] L260/5).

[188] Art. 3.

to include any machine, apparatus, tool or installation used at work,[189] must be selected to take account of the specific working conditions and hazards existing in the workplace.[190] The equipment provided must satisfy the minimum requirements laid down in the Annex.[191]

Three Directives supplement Directive 89/655 providing individual, as opposed to collective,[192] protection. First, Directive 89/656/EEC concerns the use of personal protective equipment (PPE) in the workplace.[193] PPE can be used only when the risks cannot be avoided or sufficiently limited by technical means of collective protection or by measures, methods of procedures or work organization. PPE means all equipment designed to be worn or held by workers to protect them against one or more hazards likely to endanger their health and safety.[194] PPE must comply with the relevant Union provisions in the design and manufacture of the equipment,[195] and must:[196]

- be appropriate for the risks involved, without itself leading to any increased risk;
- correspond to existing conditions in the workplace;
- take account of ergonomic requirements and the worker's state of health;
- fit the wearer correctly after any necessary adjustment.

Any PPE which is chosen must be provided free of charge by the employer,[197] who must ensure that it is in good working order and in a satisfactory and hygienic condition. The employer must also inform workers of the purpose of the PPE and arrange appropriate training and demonstrations.[198]

---

[189] Art. 2(a). This is much broader than the original draft which envisaged minimum requirements for machinery only.

[190] Art. 3(1).

[191] Art. 4(1)(a)(ii). The equipment must satisfy these requirements by 31 December 1992 in the case of equipment provided for the first time after that date or within four years in the case of existing equipment. This delay in implementation is designed to lessen the immediate financial burden, particularly on small businesses. Member States can set a shorter time limit provided that the time limit is not so short that it does not enable employers to make the changes or it entails a cost that is excessive compared with what they would have had to meet if the time limit had been longer, see Case C–2/97 *Borsana* [1998] ECR–8597, para. 53.

[192] Collective protection is considered more favourable: Art. 6(2)(b) of Dir. 89/391/EEC (OJ [1989] L183/1). See additionally Art. 4 of the original Dir. 80/1107 (OJ [1980] L327/7).

[193] Dir. 89/656/EEC on the minimum health and safety requirements for the use by workers of personal protective equipment at the workplace (third individual Directive) (OJ [1989] L393/18) due to be implemented by 31 December 1992. See additionally the Commission Communication of 30 December 1989 (89/C 328/02) on the implementation of Council Dir. 89/656/EEC.

[194] Art. 2(1).

[195] Both Dir. 89/655/EEC on work equipment, now Directive 2009/104/EC, and Dir. 89/656/EEC on PPE provide a social supplement to two specific, technical 'product' Directives setting minimum safety standards in respect of machinery, Council Dir. 89/392/EEC (OJ [1989] L183/9), now Dir 2006/42 (OJ [2006] L 157/24) on machinery, and PPE, Council Dir. 89/686/EEC on the approximation of the laws of the Member States relating to PPE (OJ [1989] L399/19) as amended. See additionally Commission Communication 2000/C76/03 (OJ [2000] C76/3); OJ [2000] C 159/03; OJ [2000] C 185/04; OJ [2000] C 40/07; OJ [2000] C 40/08; OJ [2000] C 40/09; OJ C315/24.

[196] Art. 4(1).

[197] Art. 4(b). The worker can be asked to make a contribution towards the cost of the PPE where its use is not exclusive to the workplace.

[198] Art. 4(7)–(8).

The second Directive, Directive 90/269/EEC, addresses the health and safety requirements involved in the manual handling of heavy loads.[199] Manual handling is defined to mean 'any transporting or supporting of a load, by one or more workers, including lifting, putting down, pushing, pulling, carrying or moving of a load, which by reason of its characteristics or of unfavourable ergonomic conditions involves a risk particularly of back injury to workers'.[200] The Directive envisages a hierarchy of measures which employers must consider. Primarily, they are obliged to take appropriate organizational measures, in particular by providing for the use of mechanical equipment, to avoid the need for manual handling of loads by workers.[201] Other steps might include redesigning the job to eliminate manual handling altogether or automating the process. If this is not possible, employers must strive to reduce the risk involved.[202]

The third Directive, Directive 90/270/EEC, lays down minimum health and safety requirements for work with display screen equipment (VDUs).[203] Article 2(a) defines display screen equipment as 'an alphanumeric or graphic display screen, regardless of the display process employed'. In *Dietrich*[204] the Court ruled that the phrase 'graphic display screen' included screens that displayed film recordings in analogue or digital form. Therefore, the applicant, a film cutter, could rely on the Directive against her employers, a German public broadcasting company.[205]

The Directive applies to any worker, as defined in Article 3(a) of Directive 89/391/EEC, 'who habitually uses display screen equipment as a significant part of his normal work'.[206] Neither the term 'habitual' nor 'significant' is defined. In *X*[207] the Court ruled that Article 3(a) could not be defined in the abstract and that it was for the Member States who, given the vagueness of the phrase, had a broad discretion to specify its meaning when adopting national implementing measures.

The specific obligations imposed on employers are fivefold. First, they must analyse the workstations[208] to evaluate the health and safety conditions affecting their workers, particularly as regards possible risks to eyesight, physical problems, and mental stress, and to take measures to remedy the risks found.[209] Secondly, they must ensure that workstations comply with the minimum requirements set out in the Annex.[210]

---

[199] Council Dir. 90/269/EEC on the minimum health and safety requirements for the manual handling of loads where there is a risk particularly of back injury to workers (fourth individual Directive) (OJ [1990] L156/9).

[200] Art. 2.   [201] Art. 3(1).   [202] Art. 3(2).

[203] Council Dir. 90/270/EEC (fifth individual Directive) (OJ [1990] L156/14), COM(88) 77.

[204] Case C–11/99 *Dietrich* v. *Westdeutscher Rundfunk* [2000] ECR I–5589.

[205] The case is also authority for the proposition that the exclusions form the Directive, found in Art. 1(3) should be narrowly construed (para. 50).

[206] Art. 2(c).

[207] Joined Cases C–74/95 and C–129/95 *Criminal Proceedings* v. *X* [1996] ECR I–6609, para. 30.

[208] Workstation is defined to mean an assembly comprising display screen equipment, which may be provided with a keyboard or input device and/or software determining the operator/machine interface, optional accessories, peripherals including the diskette drive, telephone, modem, printer, document holder, work chair, and work desk or work surface, and the immediate work environment (Art. 2(b)).

[209] Art. 3.

[210] Arts. 4 and 5 respectively. These requirements apply to all workstations and not just those used by 'habitual users' (Case C–74/95 *X* [1996] ECR I–6609, para. 41).

Thirdly, the employee must receive training on the use of the workstation before commencing work and further training whenever the organization of the workstation is substantially modified.[211] Fourthly, employers are obliged to keep themselves informed of the latest advances in technology and scientific findings concerning workstation design so that they can make any changes necessary to guarantee better levels of health and safety protection.[212] Fifthly, the employer must plan the worker's activities in such a way that daily work on a display screen is periodically interrupted by breaks or changes of activity reducing the workload at the display screen.[213] In addition, workers are entitled[214] to an appropriate eye and eyesight test carried out by a person with the necessary skills before commencing display screen work, at regular intervals thereafter, and whenever they experience visual difficulties which may be due to display screen work.[215] If, as a result of this examination, workers need further assistance they are entitled to an ophthalmological examination[216] and, if need be, they must be provided with 'special corrective appliances appropriate for the work concerned' if normal appliances cannot be used.[217] Protection of workers' eyes and eyesight may be provided as part of the national health system[218] but in any case, measures taken pursuant to this Article may 'in no circumstances involve workers in additional financial cost'.[219]

4. CARCINOGENS, CHEMICAL, PHYSICAL, AND BIOLOGICAL AGENTS

As we have already seen, the four daughters under the original parent Directive 80/1107/EEC concerned specific agents (for example asbestos and lead). The new approach, adopted under the Framework Directive 89/391, is to address the problems of classes of agents—biological, physical and chemical agents, and carcinogens. The first of these new Directives, Directive 90/394/EEC,[220] originally one of the daughter Directives under Directive 80/1107/EEC, introduced general and specific measures for a list of occupational carcinogens[221] and

---

[211] Art. 6(2).   [212] Preamble to the Directive.   [213] Art. 7.

[214] Art. 9. Earlier drafts talked of workers being obliged to have an appropriate eyesight test but this was considered an invasion of workers' privacy.

[215] Art. 9(1). According to Case C–74/95 X [1996] ECR I–6609, para. 36, regular eye tests are carried out on all workers to whom the Directive applies and not just to certain categories of workers.

[216] Art. 9(2). The X case makes clear that this applies only to those for whom an Art. 9(1) test reveals that they need further assistance.

[217] Art. 9(3). See further Case C–455/00 Commission v. Italy [2002] ECR I–9231.

[218] Art. 9(5).   [219] Art. 9(4).

[220] Dir. 90/394/EEC on the protection of workers from the risks relating to exposure to carcinogens at work (sixth individual Directive) (OJ [1990] L196/1). Its adoption was also inspired by the 'Europe Against Cancer' campaign, see Decisions 88/351/EEC and 90/238/Euratom, EEC and ECSC.

[221] Defined as a process which may cause cancer and with reference to Dir. 67/548/EEC (OJ [1967] L196/1), Dir. 88/379/EEC (OJ [1988] L187/14) and Annex I of this Directive. An IARC (International Agreement for Research on Cancer) survey found that of 107 chemical substances examined, 38 were carcinogens and 68 were probably carcinogens COM(87) 641 final.

reputedly carcinogenic processes.[222] This Directive was modified a number of times and has now been codified by Directive 2004/37/EC.[223] The Directive aims to protect workers against risks arising or likely to arise from exposure to carcinogens and mutagens at work. The Directive provides that where workers are, or are likely to be, exposed to carcinogens, employers must determine the nature, degree, and duration of workers' exposure in order to assess the risk posed to their health and safety.[224] Article 4 applies the principle of substitution, requiring employers to use non-carcinogenic substitutes which are not dangerous or are less dangerous to a worker's health and safety.[225] Where that is technically unfeasible, employers must ensure that production is carried out in a closed system. Where a closed system is not technically possible, the employer must ensure that the level of exposure of workers is reduced to as low as is technically possible.[226] Exposure cannot exceed the limit values set out in the Annex.[227] Whenever a carcinogen or mutagen is used the employer must protect workers[228] by, for example, limiting the quantities of carcinogen in the workplace,[229] reducing the number of workers likely to be exposed,[230] designing work processes and engineering control measures to avoid or minimize the release of carcinogens and mutagens,[231] providing collective protection measures and/or individual protective equipment[232] and appropriate hygiene measures,[233] laying emergency plans,[234] providing for safe storage and disposal of the waste,[235] organizing continuous ad hoc training,[236] providing information to workers[237] and/or their representatives,[238] and, on request, to the appropriate competent authority, and arranging medical surveillance.[239] Whatever the cost of these measures, it must not be imposed on the workers.[240] Finally, the list of the persons exposed within the firm must always be accessible to the workers themselves and to their medical representatives.[241]

The scope of this Directive is potentially very broad, for Article 11 expressly recognizes that employers must inform workers of 'the potential risks to health, including the additional risk due to tobacco consumption'. Since there is a recognized link between cigarettes and cancer, the obligations imposed by this Directive on all employers are

---

[222] The Directive does not apply to workers exposed to radiation (Art. 1(2)). This is covered by the Euratom Treaty and Directives adopted under that Treaty, in particular Dir. 80/836/Euratom (OJ [1980] L246/1) repealed by Dir. 96/29/Euratom (OJ [1996] L159/1) laying down the fundamental principles governing operational protection of exposed workers and Dir. 90/641/Euratom (OJ [1990] L349/21) on the operational protection of outside workers exposed to the risk of ionizing radiation during their activities in a controlled area. Council Dir. 96/29/Euratom laying down basic safety standards for the protection of the health of workers and the general public against the dangers arising from ionizing radiation (OJ [1996] L159/1).

[223] OJ [2004] L 158/50.

[224] Art. 3.

[225] This is not contingent on the outcome of the assessment of risks under Art. 3: Case C–2/97 *Borsana* [1998] ECR I–8597.

[226] Art. 5(3).   [227] Art. 5(4).

[228] Art. 5(5). This is contingent on the outcome of the assessment of risks under Art. 3: Case C–2/97 *Borsana* [1998] ECR I–8597, para. 41.

[229] Art. 5(5)(a).   [230] Art. 5(5)(b).   [231] Art. 5(5)(c).   [232] Art. 5(5)(g).

[233] Art. 5(5)(h).   [234] Art. 5(5)(k).   [235] Art. 5(5)(m).   [236] Art. 11.

[237] Arts. 5(5)(i) and 12.

[238] Art. 12. There must also be consultation and participation of workers under Art. 13.

[239] Art. 14.   [240] Art. 10(2).   [241] Art. 12(d) and (e).

far-reaching. The Commission recognizes that this Directive will impose a financial burden particularly on industries such as those producing chemicals, fibre, sterilizing agents, crystal glass, and wood preservatives. It argues, however, that enterprises will benefit in the long term through reduced sickness absence and rehabilitation costs, and fewer retirements due to ill health.

The structure and approach adopted in what is now Directive 2004/37 on carcinogens is mirrored in what was Directive 90/679/EEC on biological agents[242] which has now been codified by Directive 2000/54/EC.[243] This Directive relates to those who work in laboratories, hospitals and veterinary clinics and those who are employed in the manufacturing industries, particularly those manufacturing vaccines, and those dealing with sewage and breweries.[244] The Directive classes biological agents, defined as micro-organisms, including those which have been genetically modified,[245] cell cultures and human endo-parasites, which may be able to provoke any infection, allergy or toxicity,[246] into four categories according to their intrinsic danger,[247] and defines appropriate confinement measures. Once again the Directive requires the employer to assess the risks posed by the exposure to the biological agent,[248] replace the harmful agent where possible,[249] and, if not, reduce the risks connected with the exposure to the agents.[250] Detailed requirements as to worker training, information and consultation,[251] and medical surveillance,[252] also apply.

Directive 98/24/EC on chemical agents,[253] replaces in a single Directive the first parent Directive 80/1107/EEC, as amended, the lead Directive 82/605/EEC and Directive 88/364/EEC banning specific agents at work. It is thus an example of 'simplified and rationalised legislation'. Chemical agents are defined as any chemical element or compound, on its own or admixed, as it occurs in the natural state or as produced by any work activity, whether produced intentionally and whether or not placed on the market. The Directive follows the pattern of its sister Directives: it requires a risk assessment to

---

[242] Council Dir. 90/679/EEC of 26 November 1990 on the protection of workers from the risks related to exposure to biological agents at work (seventh individual Directive) (OJ [1990] L374/1).

[243] OJ [2000] L262/21.   [244] Arts. 15 and 16.

[245] Two further Directives have been passed concerning genetically modified organisms (GMOs). The first, Dir. 90/219/EEC of 23 April 1990 (OJ [1990] L117/1), now Dir. 2009/41/EC (OJ [2009] L125/75) concerns the contained use of GMOs which refers to any work in conditions which are intended to prevent the escape of GMOs into the environment with a view to protecting human health and the environment. The Directive requires risk assessment, minimizing the level of risk, and drawing up emergency plans. The second, Dir. 90/220/EEC (OJ [1990] L117/15), now Dir. 2001/18/EC (OJ [2001] L 106/01) concerns the deliberate release of GMOs into the environment for research purposes and the marketing of products involving GMOs. Those enterprises proposing to undertake either of these activities must notify the competent authorities, assess and provide information on the risks, and may make specified information available to the public.

[246] Art. 2(a).   [247] Art. 2(d).   [248] Arts. 3 and 4.

[249] Art. 5.   [250] Art. 6.   [251] Arts. 7, 9, 10, and 12.   [252] Art. 14.

[253] Council Dir. 98/24/EC of 7 April 1998 on the protection of the health and safety of workers from the risks related to chemical agents at work (fourteenth individual Directive within the meaning of Art. 16(1) of Dir. 89/391/EEC) (OJ [1998] L131/11), partially repealed by Dir. 2009/148. The Scientific Committee on Occupational Exposure Limits advises the Commission on occupational exposure limits both in respect of this Directive and Dir. 2004/37.

be made, it lays down occupational exposure levels, and it provides for worker consultation, information, and medical surveillance.

The Directives on physical agents also follow this pattern. They aim to harmonize the minimum health and safety requirements regarding exposure of workers to the risks arising from physical agents. The physical agents covered to date are noise,[254] vibration,[255] electromagnetic fields,[256] and artificial optical radiation.[257] The Directives establish threshold action and ceiling levels for exposure to the agents. In addition, employers are required to: conduct exposure risk assessments; avoid risks where possible, failing which reduce any risks; provide personal protective equipment; conduct health surveillance depending on levels of exposure; and engage in worker information, consultation, participation, and training.

The Noise Directive was at issue in *Barcenilla Fernández*[258] where the Court recognized the hierarchy between the obligations of the employer. It noted that first, the employer is obliged, under Article 5(2) of that Directive, to implement a programme intended to reduce the noise exposure where the workers are exposed to a noise level exceeding 85 dB(A), measured without taking into account the effect of the individual hearing protectors. It is only in the event that that programme does not allow such noise exposure to be reduced that Article 6 of Directive 2003/10 sets out, secondly, the additional obligation to make individual hearing protectors available to workers. Thirdly and finally, Article 7 of that Directive provides specific obligations for the case where use of individual hearing protectors does not prevent exposure limit values being exceeded. The Court concluded that:

> It therefore follows from the clear wording and arrangement of these provisions that an employer cannot fulfil its obligations under Article 5(2) of Directive 2003/10 by simply providing the workers with individual hearing protectors, but that it must implement a programme intended to reduce exposure to noise where workers are exposed to a noise level exceeding 85 dB(A), measured without taking into account the effect of the use of individual hearing protectors.[259]

[254] Dir. 2003/10/EC of the European Parliament and of the Council on the minimum health and safety requirements regarding the exposure of workers to the risks arising from physical agents (noise) (seventeenth individual Directive within the meaning of Article 16(1) of Dir. 89/391/EEC) (OJ [2003] L 042/38).

[255] Dir. 2002/44/EC of the European Parliament and of the Council on the minimum health and safety requirements regarding the exposure of workers to the risks arising from physical agents (vibration) (sixteenth individual Directive within the meaning of Article 16(1) of Dir. 89/391/EEC) (OJ [2002] L 177/13).

[256] Dir. 2004/40/EC of the European Parliament and of the Council on the minimum health and safety requirements regarding the exposure of workers to the risks arising from physical agents (electromagnetic fields) (eighteenth individual Directive within the meaning of Art. 16(1) of Dir. 89/391/EEC) (OJ [2004] L 159/01), as amended by Dir. 2012/11/EU (OJ [2012] L110/1).

[257] Dir. 2006/25/EC of the European Parliament and of the Council on the minimum health and safety requirements regarding the exposure of workers to the risks arising from physical agents (artificial optical radiation) (nineteenth individual Directive within the meaning of Art. 16(1) of Dir. 89/391/EEC) OJ [2006] L 114/38.

[258] Joined Cases C-256/10 and C-261/10 *Barcenilla Fernández* v. *Gerardo García SL* [2011] ECR I-000.

[259] Para. 32.

E. CONCLUSIONS

The volume of legislation in this field supports the Commission's claim that '[h]ealth and safety at work represents today one of the most important [and] most advanced fields of the social policy of the Union'.[260] Less clear is the Commission's claim that the solid corpus of legislation covers 'the maximum number of risks with the minimum number of regulations'. That said, the EU's approach, based on prevention, is clearly the sensible one, albeit an approach which has yet to bear full fruit, especially in the EU-10.[261]

Despite its undoubted importance, health and safety has always been the Cinderella area of Union employment law, even though there is more regulation in this area than any other area of EU social law. Yet when the delicate issue of working time is thrown into the equation, the whole issue assumes a rather different complexion. It is to this subject that we now turn.

---

[260] <http://ec.europa.eu/social/main.jsp?catId=148&langId=en> (last accessed 2 April 2012).
[261] COM(2002) 118, 4.

12

WORKING CONDITIONS

A. INTRODUCTION

In the last chapter we concentrated on those measures traditionally considered to concern health and safety in the narrow, common law sense. Since the introduction of Article 118a into the (E)EC Treaty by the Single European Act 1986,[1] all such measures have been adopted under this legal basis and its successor, Article 153 TFEU (ex 137 EC). More controversially, Article 118a EEC was also used to adopt other measures which, some considered, were less intimately connected with (an Anglo-Saxon conception of) health and safety, notably the Working Time Directive 93/104,[2] now Directive 2003/88.[3] This chapter will begin by examining this controversial measure, together with the Young Workers' Directive 94/33,[4] before moving on to look at measures which are more clearly linked to employment conditions, notably pay, as well as examining the Proof of Employment Contract Directive which aims at introducing transparency in respect of the terms and conditions of an employment relationship.

B. WORKING TIME

1. INTRODUCTION

The Working Time Directive is situated in the grey area between traditional health and safety measures and the rights of employed persons. The Working Time Directive 93/104/EEC and the Young Workers' Directive 94/33/EC were both adopted under Article 118a EEC (new Article 153 TFEU) and formed key pillars of the EU's Social Charter Action Programme 1989. Previously there existed only certain sectoral legislation[5] and some soft law measures on working time, such as a Council Recommendation

---

[1] See further Ch. 2.   [2] OJ [1993] L307/18.
[3] OJ [2003] L299/9. A report on its implementation can be found at COM(2010) 802.
[4] OJ [1994] L216/12.
[5] See Reg. 561/2006 on the harmonization of certain social legislation relating to road transport (OJ [2006] L102/1) repealing Reg. (EEC) No. 3820/85 (OJ [1985] L370/1) on the harmonization of certain social legislation relating to road transport; Reg. (EEC) No. 3821/85 (OJ [1985] L207/1) on recording equipment in road transport was amended by Reg. 561/2006. There are proposals to amend these measures: COM(2011) 451. See additionally Dir. 88/599/EEC (OJ [1988] L325/1) on standard checking procedures on recording equipment in road transport, repealed by Dir. 2006/22 (OJ [2006] L102/35).

of 1975 on the principle of the 40-hour week and four weeks' annual paid holiday,[6] and a Resolution of 1979 on the adaptation of working time.[7] Both the recommendation and the Resolution focused on the reduction in working time for the purposes of *job creation*.[8] The Community Social Charter 1989 marked a change in emphasis. Articles 7 and 8 advocated action on the duration and organization of working time so that the completion of the internal market would lead to an improvement in the living and working conditions of workers in the EU. This enabled the Commission to conceive a Directive on working time, not as a job creation measure, but a health and safety matter, enabling it to select Article 118a EEC as the appropriate legal basis. To support its choice the Commission cited a variety of studies which variously showed that weekly working time of more than 50 hours could, in the long run, be harmful to health and safety, that working weeks of more than six days showed some correlation with health problems including fatigue and disturbed sleep, and that longer working hours substantially increased the probability of accidents at work.[9] This evidence was, however, disputed[10] and the UK challenged the choice of legal basis,[11] a challenge which, as we saw in Chapter 2, was ultimately unsuccessful.

The health and safety legal basis of the Directive has subsequently proved influential in the interpretation of the Directive's provisions.[12] For example, in *Wippel*[13] the Court said:[14]

> [I]t is clear both from Article 118a [EEC]...and from the first, fourth, seventh and eighth recitals in the preamble as well as the wording of Article 1(1) of [Directive 2003/88] itself, that the purpose of the directive is to lay down minimum requirements intended to improve the living and working conditions of workers through approximation of national provisions concerning, in particular, the duration of working time.

The Court continued that such harmonization at Union level in relation to the organization of working time is intended 'to guarantee better protection of the safety and health of workers' by ensuring that they are entitled to minimum rest periods and adequate breaks and by providing for a ceiling on the duration of the working week.[15] It concluded: 'That protection constitutes a social right conferred on each worker as an essential minimum requirement in order to ensure the protection of his security and health'.[16] In a similar vein, the Court said in the earlier case of *BECTU*[17] that the

---

[6] Recommendation 75/457/EEC (OJ [1975] L199/32).   [7] OJ [1982] L357/27.

[8] See additionally Council Recommendation 82/857/EEC on the principles of a Community policy with regard to retirement age (OJ [1982] L357/27) which also has the objective of lower activity levels.

[9] COM(90) 317.

[10] See B. Bercusson, 'Working Time in Britain: Towards a European Model, Part I' (1993) *IER* 4.

[11] Case C–84/94 *UK* v. *Council* [1996] ECR I–5755, considered further in Ch. 2.

[12] As the Court emphasized in Case C–84/94 *UK* v. *Council* [1996] ECR I–5755 and again in Case C–151/02 *Landeshauptstadt Kiel* v. *Jaeger* [2003] ECR I–8389, para. 93, health and safety is interpreted widely, embracing all factors, physical or otherwise, capable of affecting the health and safety of workers in his working environment. The other factor that has shaped the interpretation of the Directive is the reference in the 6th recital to the ILO: Joined Cases C–350/06 and C–520/06 *Schultz-Hoff* [2009] ECR I–179, para. 37.

[13] Case C–313/02 *Wippel* [2004] ECR I–9483.   [14] Para. 46.   [15] Para. 47.   [16] Ibid.

[17] Case C–173/99 *R* v. *Secretary of State for Trade and Industry, ex parte Broadcasting, Entertainment, Cinematographic and Theatre Union (BECTU)* [2001] ECR I–4881.

objective of improving workers' health and safety could not be subjected to 'purely economic considerations'.[18] Therefore, increases in administrative costs in providing the rights laid down by the Directive (in this case annual leave to staff on short contracts) which would weigh more on small and medium-sized undertakings, could not be taken into account.

The Advocate General in *BECTU* went further, suggesting that the right to annual paid leave was a fundamental social right.[19] Citing various international instruments on human rights, including Article 8 of the Community Social Charter of 1989,[20] he noted that the Directive 'specifically upheld the right to paid leave as a manifestation of the right to fair and equitable working conditions'. He continued, 'Even more significant, it seems to me, is the fact that that right is now solemnly upheld in the Charter of Fundamental Rights [2000]'. Article 31(2) of the Charter declares: 'Every worker has the right to limitation of maximum working hours, to daily and weekly rest periods and to an annual period of paid leave'. That statement, which is inspired by Article 2 of the European Social Charter 1961 and by Article 8 of the Community Social Charter 1989, also took account of the existence of the Working Time Directive.[21] Even prior to the Charter having legal effect, Advocate General Tizzano said that the Charter included statements which appeared, in large measure, to reaffirm rights which were enshrined in other instruments.[22] He therefore concluded that 'in proceedings concerned with the nature and scope of a fundamental right, the relevant statement of the Charter cannot be ignored'.[23]

As the Court's remarks in *Wippel* emphasize, the Working Time Directive does not affect the right of Member States or the two sides of industry to conclude agreements which are more favourable to the health and safety protection of workers.[24] The Court recognized this possibility in *Dellas*[25] where it acknowledged that France had made use of this option by laying down a maximum weekly working time of 44 hours over 12 consecutive weeks, while the Directive imposes a limit of 48 hours over four consecutive months.[26] However, the Court was at pains to point out that it will verify compliance with the rules laid down by the Directive by reference solely to the limits fixed by the Directive, to the exclusion of the national provisions that provide greater protection.[27] As we shall see later, in this respect the French rules were found wanting.

The original Working Time Directive contained a number of important sectors to which the Directive did not apply, including doctors in training and the transport sector. Both mobile and non-mobile (office) transport staff[28] were excluded.[29] This led to

---

[18] Para. 59. See additionally Case C–151/02 *Jaeger* [2003] ECR I–8389, paras. 66–7.
[19] See additionally his views in Case C–133/00 *BECTU* [2001] ECR I–7031, para. 31.
[20] This was expressly referred to by the Court in Case C–151/02 *Jaeger* [2003] ECR I–8389.
[21] Para. 26. [22] Para. 27. [23] Para. 28. [24] Art. 15.
[25] Case C–14/04 *Dellas and Others* v. *Premier ministre and Others* [2005] ECR I–10253, para. 51.
[26] Para. 52. [27] Ibid.
[28] Art. 1(3) of Dir. 93/104. See further Case C–133/00 *Bowden* v. *Tuffnells Parcels Express Ltd* [2001] ECR I–7031, para. 44.
[29] These exclusions were interpreted strictly: Case C–303/98 *Sindicato de Médicos de Asistencia Pública (Simap)* v. *Conselleria de Sanidad y Consumo de la Generalidad Valenciana* [2000] ECR I–7963, para. 35.

various sectoral agreements being negotiated by the transport sector Social Partners which were given legal effect by Directive,[30] notably:

- Directive 99/63 on the organization of working time of seafarers;[31]
- Directive 2000/79 on the organization of mobile staff in civil aviation;[32]
- Directive 2005/47 on certain aspects of the working conditions of mobile workers engaged in interoperable cross-border services in the railway sector.[33]

A further sectoral Directive, Directive 2002/15,[34] this time concluded via the conventional legislative route, made provision for the working time of persons performing mobile road transport activities (commercial drivers and crew).[35]

The main Working Time Directive 93/104 was amended by Directive 2000/34[36] to include the sectors previously excluded from the scope of the Directive that were not covered by the sectoral Directives. Both Directives 93/104 and 2000/34 have now been consolidated and repealed and replaced by Directive 2003/88/EC.[37]

2. PERSONAL AND MATERIAL SCOPE OF DIRECTIVE 2003/88

Directive 2003/88 concerns all sectors of activity,[38] both public and private, as defined by Article 2 of the Framework Directive 89/391 on health and safety (industrial, agricultural, commercial, administrative, service, educational, cultural, leisure, etc.).[39] As we have seen, in the original Directive the transport sector (both mobile and

---

[30] See further Ch. 2.

[31] OJ [1999] L167/33. Dir. 99/63 implements the sectoral agreement on the organization of working time of seafarers concluded by the European Community Ship Owners Association (ECSA) and the Federation of Transport Workers in the European Union (FST). This agreement reflects the provision of the ILO Convention 180 on seafarers' hours of work. It provides for either a maximum number of working hours (14 hours in any 24-hour period and 72 hours in any seven-day period) or a minimum rest period regime (10 hours in any 24-hour period and 77 hours in any seven-day period). A second Directive (Dir. 99/95/EC (OJ [2000] L14/29)) concerns enforcement of seafarers' hours of work on board ships using Union ports. In addition, a Recommendation (Commission Recommendation 99/130/EC on ratification of ILO Convention 180) concerning seafarers' hours of work and the manning of ships, and ratification of the 1996 Protocol to the 1976 Merchant Shipping (minimum standards) Convention (OJ [1999] L43/9) were also adopted. ILO Convention 180 was consolidated by the ILO's Maritime Labour Convention (MLC), adopted in 2006. This led to Council Directive 2009/13/EC of 16 February 2009 implementing the Agreement concluded by the European Community Shipowners' Associations (ECSA) and the European Transport Workers' Federation (ETF) on the Maritime Labour Convention 2006, and amending Dir. 1999/63/EC (OJ [2009] L124/30). See additionally the proposed enforcement Directive: COM(2012) 134. An enforcement has now also been concluded on working time for inland waterways (5 Feb. 2012).

[32] OJ [2000] L302/57.   [33] OJ [2005] L195/15.   [34] OJ [2002] L80/35.

[35] This Directive applies to mobile workers employed by enterprises carrying out transport work on their own account. Self-employed drivers, when driving a bus, coach, or heavy goods vehicle, are also included from 2009. This Directive supplements the provisions of Reg. (EEC) 3820/85 now Reg. 561/2006 (OJ [2006] L102/1) on driving rest periods. The Directive is without prejudice to this Regulation, which remains applicable in its entirety as does the European agreement on international road transport (AETR). On whether to apply the Regulation and the Agreement, see Case C–439/01 *Cipra* v. *Bezirkshauptmannschaft Mistelbach* [2003] ECR I–745.

[36] OJ [2000] L195/41.   [37] OJ [2003] L299/9.

[38] Art. 1(3). Given the health and safety objective of the Directive, the scope is interpreted broadly: Case C–303/98 *Simap* [2000] ECR I–7963, para. 34.

[39] OJ [1989] L183/1. Considered in detail in Ch. 11.

non-mobile) was excluded, as were the activities of doctors in training. This exclusion has now been removed; the only express exception relates to seafarers, as defined in Directive 99/63.[40] In addition, the Directive does not apply to certain specific activities such as the armed forces or the police, or to certain specific activities in the civil protection services, but only where the characteristics of those activities inevitably conflict with the requirements of the Framework Directive 89/391.[41]

The Directive applies to 'workers' which are defined in Article 3 of Directive 89/391[42] as 'any person employed by an employer, including trainees and apprentices but excluding domestic servants'.[43] It does not apply to those normally regarded as self-employed[44] but does cover those on fixed-term contracts as much as those on indefinite contracts.[45] The Court has drawn on its case law on Article 45 TFEU[46] to give a *Union* meaning to the term 'worker', with no reference being made to national law.[47] This can be seen in *Union syndicale Solidaires Isère* where the question was raised whether people employed under 'educational commitment contracts' carrying out 'casual and seasonal activities in holiday and leisure centres' (ie kids' camps), and completing a maximum of 80 working days per annum, could fall within the personal scope of the Directive. The Court said:[48]

> The concept must be defined in accordance with objective criteria which distinguish the employment relationship by reference to the rights and duties of the persons concerned. The essential feature of an employment relationship, however, is that for a certain period of time a person performs services for and under the direction of another person in return for which he receives remuneration.

The Court continued that the *sui generis* legal nature of the employment relationship under national law did not have any consequence as to whether the person was a worker for the purposes of EU law.[49] The Court therefore concluded that these education commitment contracts fell within the scope of the Directive.

3. 'ENTITLEMENTS' AND 'LIMITS'

3.1. Introduction

The English language version of the Directive makes a distinction between limits and entitlements. The provisions concerning working time and night work are *limits*. This

---

[40] Art. 1(3), para. 2. Similarly, the provisions of the Working Time Directive do not apply where other Union instruments exist relating to specific occupations: Art. 14.

[41] Art. 2(2) of Dir. 89/391. This exclusion is included due to the reference in Art. 1(3) of Dir. 89/391. See Ch. 11.

[42] Art. 1(3) and (4).

[43] The provisions of Framework Dir. 89/391 on health and safety are fully applicable to the Working Time Directive, without prejudice to the more stringent and/or specific provisions contained in the Working Time Directive: Art. 1(4).

[44] Although cf. Dir. 2002/15 (OJ [2002] L80/35) considered above.

[45] Case C–428/09 *Union syndicale Solidaires Isère* v. *Premier ministre and Others* [2010] ECR I–000, para. 31.

[46] See further Ch. 4.   [47] Case C–428/09 *Union syndicale Solidaires Isère* [2010] ECR I–000.

[48] Para. 28.   [49] Para. 30. See additionally Case C-337/10 *Neidel* [2012] ECR I-000, paras. 23–25.

means employers must not allow workers to exceed those limits, subject to derogations and, where appropriate, the individual opt-out. By contrast, the rest provisions (in-work rest breaks and daily, weekly, and annual rest) all concern worker *entitlements*: the employer cannot lawfully require the worker to work during any such period. On the other hand, if workers choose to work in a way which means forgoing a rest period to which they are entitled this is not unlawful and workers are free to do so. At least, this is the British perspective on the Directive. As the DTI (now BIS) put it in its original guidance accompanying the implementing Regulations, 'Employers must make sure that workers *can* take their rest, but are not required to make sure that they do take their rest' (discussed further below). In the UK, the distinction between limits and entitlements is also reflected in the way in which the provisions are enforced: limits are enforced through criminal sanctions against the employer, entitlements through civil action in an Employment Tribunal.

However, in *Commission* v. *UK*[50] Advocate General Kokott cast doubt on the validity of the distinction between limits and entitlements.[51] She argued that 'no qualitative distinction can be derived from the respective choice of wording between the requirements of Articles 6 and 8 [maximum working time and night work] of the Directive, on the one hand, and Articles 3 and 5 [daily and weekly rest periods] at issue here, on the other'. She continued that the eighth recital in the Preamble to the Directive in particular militated against such a distinction, because it referred to minimum rest periods and maximum working time in one breath and against the background of the same defined objective—both serve to ensure the safety and health of workers.[52] The Court agreed with the Advocate General. On the general point the Court said that neither the various language versions of the Directive nor the Court's case-law relating to the Directive, its objective, and the nature of the rights to rest which it lays down, support the distinction between entitlements and limits.[53]

On the facts of the case, the Commission criticized the DTI's Guidelines on entitlements which 'clearly endorse and encourage a practice of non-compliance with the requirements of the Directive'.[54] The Advocate General agreed. She said that in order to secure effective

---

[50] Case C–484/04 *Commission* v. *UK* [2006] ECR I–7471.

[51] At para. 62 she examines the wording of the different provisions of the Directive which, she admits, is highly inconsistent. She says: 'Admittedly, for example, in its English version in Articles 3, 4, 5, and 7 the term "entitled to" is used throughout, which could be interpreted as meaning a mere entitlement. However, in the French, Italian and Portuguese language versions of those articles the terms "bénéficie" (French), "benefici" (Italian) and "beneficiem" (Portuguese) are used, which may be translated into German as "genießen" ("enjoy") or "zugute kommen" ("benefit") and therefore could also be interpreted as meaning an obligation of result. In other language versions again, the use of terminology is not even consistent within the various provisions on rest periods (Articles 3, 4, 5, and 7). Thus for example the German version of Articles 3, 4 and 5 contains the expression "gewährt wird", whereas Article 7 uses "erhält". Articles 3 and 5 of the Spanish version use the term "disfruten", whilst Article 4 reads "tengan derecho a disfrutar" and Article 7 simply "dispongan". In a similarly inconsistent manner the Dutch version uses the word "genieten" in Articles 3 and 5 but the word "hebben" in Article 4, and the expression "wordt toegekend" in Article 7'.

[52] Para. 64.   [53] Para. 45.

[54] The guidelines said that employers must make sure that workers can take their rest 'but are not required to make sure they do take their rest'.

protection of the safety and health of workers, it was necessary that workers are *actually granted* the minimum periods of rest provided for, and that presupposes that they are put in a position by their employer to take the rest periods which are due to them and are not, for example, deterred from doing so by what she describes as 'factual constraints',[55] such as the risk of becoming unpopular within the business.[56] However, she did concede that it would normally be excessive, if not even impossible, to demand that employers *force* their workers to claim the rest periods due to them; the employer's responsibility concerning observance of rest periods cannot be without limits.[57] But she added that an employer could not withdraw into a purely passive role and grant rest periods only to those workers who expressly request them and if necessary enforce them at law.[58] The Court agreed: by restricting the obligations on employers as regards the workers' right to actually benefit from the minimum rest periods provided for in Articles 3 and 5 of Directive 93/104 and letting it be understood that, while they cannot prevent those rest periods from being taken by the workers, they are under no obligation to ensure that the workers are actually able to exercise such a right, the British guidelines were 'clearly liable to render the rights enshrined in Articles 3 and 5 of that directive meaningless and are incompatible with the objective of that directive, in which minimum rest periods are considered to be essential for the protection of workers' health and safety'.

The limits and entitlements must also be read subject to the general organizing principle of the Directive, found in Article 13, of 'humanisation of work'.[59] This provides that an employer intending to organize work according to a certain pattern must take account of the:

> general principle of adapting work to the worker, with a view, in particular, to alleviating monotonous work and work at a pre-determined work rate, depending on the type of activity, *and* of health and safety requirements, especially as regards breaks during working time. [Emphasis added]

This provision envisages not only implementing health and safety measures but also respecting the general principle of adapting the work to the worker, an idea which is not directly related to narrowly construed health and safety requirements. This principle is entirely consistent with the broader duty imposed on employers by some Continental systems. In Italy, for example, Article 1087 of the Civil Code provides that, in the organization of the enterprise, the employer must adopt all measures which, according to the nature of the work, experience, and technical possibilities, are required to protect the physical integrity and moral personality of the employees. From the common law perspective, this breaks down the distinction between, on the one hand, the duty of mutual trust and confidence and, on the other, health and safety, and may help to explain the debate about the choice of legal basis.

---

[55] Para. 66.   [56] Para. 68.   [57] Para. 67.   [58] Para. 68.

[59] See B. Bercusson, previously, at n. 10. Although Art. 13 is located at the end of Section III on night work there is no evidence that it is confined to this section, particularly since the Article makes express reference to breaks during working time which is found in Section II. Indeed, it would appear from the breadth of Art. 13 that all provisions must be interpreted in the light of the principle of humanization of work.

3.2. 'Entitlements' to rest

(a) Daily rest and in-work rest breaks (Articles 3 and 4)

Every worker is entitled to a minimum daily rest period of 11 *consecutive* hours per 24-hour period.[60] Although this implies a 13-hour working day, the principle of the 'humanisation of work' would prevent an employer from requiring an employee to work such long hours regularly.

If the working day is longer than six hours every worker is entitled to an in-work rest break, the details of which, including the duration of the break and the terms on which it is taken must, by preference, be laid down by collective agreement between the two sides of industry or, failing that, by national legislation.[61] In the British decision of *Gallagher* v. *Alpha Catering Services*[62] the Court of Appeal gave a purposive reading to the rest provisions. The claimants were responsible for delivering food to aircraft. Between loading assignments they were on downtime—they were not physically working but were required to remain in radio contact with their employers and at their disposal. The employers said that these periods of downtime constituted the workers' rest breaks. The Court of Appeal disagreed. Peter Gibson LJ said that a period of downtime could not retrospectively become a rest break only because it could be seen, after it was over, that it had been an uninterrupted period of at least 20 minutes. He said that the worker had to know, at the start of a rest break, that it was a rest break which he could use as he pleased.

(b) Weekly rest (Article 5)

In addition to the daily rest period, workers are also entitled to weekly rest. Article 5 provides for a minimum uninterrupted rest period of 24 hours for each 7-day period worked plus the 11 hours' daily rest. Therefore, workers are entitled to 35 consecutive hours of rest (11 hours' daily rest plus 24 hours' weekly rest) at least once a week averaged over 14 days.[63] However, if objective, technical, or work organization conditions justify it, a minimum rest period of 24 hours (instead of 35 hours) may be applied.[64]

Article 5(2) originally provided that the minimum weekly rest period 'shall in principle include Sunday'. Although this provision was consistent with the Court's jurisprudence on Sunday trading,[65] the UK government successfully challenged its validity in the *Working Time*[66] case. The Court said that the 'Council has failed to explain why Sunday as a weekly rest day, is more closely connected with health and safety of workers than any other day of the week'. As a result, the provision 'which is severable from the other provisions of the Directive', had to be annulled.

[60] Art. 3.   [61] Art. 4.
[62] [2005] IRLR 102. See additionally *MacCartney* v. *Overley House Management*, UKEAT/0500/05/MAA.
[63] Art. 16(1).   [64] Art. 5(3).
[65] See e.g. Case C–169/91 *Stoke on Trent* v. *B & Q* [1992] ECR I–6457.
[66] Case C–84/94 *UK* v. *Council* [1996] ECR I–5755.

(c) Annual leave (Article 7)

The basic rules

According to the Directive, every worker is entitled to *paid* annual leave of at least four weeks,[67] in accordance with conditions for entitlement to, and granting of, such leave laid down by national legislation and/or practice.[68] This provision, says the Court, is a 'particularly important principle of [Union] social law' and is intended to enable the worker 'actually to take the leave to which he is entitled'.[69] The minimum period of paid annual leave cannot be replaced by an allowance in lieu, except where the employment relationship is terminated.[70] This point was emphasized in *Federatie Nederlandse Vakbeweging*[71] where the Court said that the employer could not buy out leave which was not taken in one year by paying an allowance in lieu in the following year.

Pay is the 'normal remuneration received by the worker' so that he enjoys, during the period of 'rest and relaxation, economic conditions which are comparable to those relating to the exercise of his employment'.[72] Therefore pay includes basic salary, all the components intrinsically linked to the performance of the tasks he is required to carry out under the contract of employment and all the elements relating to his personal and professional status (e.g. allowances for seniority, length of service and professional qualification) but not e.g. amounts intended to cover expenses for being away from home.[73]

Article 7 is the only substantive provision in the Directive from which there are no derogations.[74] It would therefore appear that the right to four weeks' paid annual leave applies to all workers falling within the scope of the Directive, including part-timers and those on other atypical contracts for whom, presumably, the entitlement will be provided on a pro-rata basis (although this is not expressly provided for in the Directive).[75] As the Court made clear in *BECTU*,[76] such workers often find themselves in a

---

[67] Member States did, however, have the option under Article 18(1)(b)(ii) (now Article 22(2)) of 'making use' of a transitional period of not more than three years from 23 November 1996 (i.e. until 22 November 1999), during which every worker could receive *three* weeks' paid annual leave. Prior to the UK's implementation of the Directive, the EAT found in *Gibson* v. *East Riding of Yorkshire Council* [1999] IRLR 358 that, notwithstanding the derogations, Art. 7 was sufficiently clear and precise to have direct effect so that during the period from 23 November 1996 to 1 October 1998 an employee of an emanation of the state (such as Ms Gibson, a swimming instructor at a leisure centre) could take advantage of four weeks' paid leave and not three, since the UK had not enacted legislation to take advantage of the period of delayed implementation. The tribunal left the question open as to whether an individual in private sector employment would have an action for *Francovich* damages. This decision now receives implicit support from the CJEU in Case C-227/09 *Accardo* v. *Comune di Torino* [2010] ECR I-000, para. 51.

[68] Art. 7(1). Thus, pre-existing national rules permitting workers to qualify for the minimum entitlement to annual leave after, say, 12 months' service would continue to apply. The introduction of a service requirement where none existed previously might breach the non-regression clause found in Art. 18(3).

[69] Joined Cases C-131/04 and C-257/04 *Robinson-Steele* [2006] ECR I-2531.

[70] Art. 7(2), including on retirement: Case C-337/10 *Niedel* [2012] ECR I-000, para. 2.

[71] Case C-124/05 *Federatie Nederlandse Vakbeweging* v. *Staat der Nederlanden* [2006] ECR I-3423.

[72] Case C-155/10 *Williams* v. *British Airways* [2011] ECR I-000, paras. 21–23.

[73] Ibid., paras. 24–5 and 30.

[74] According to Case C-173/99 *BECTU* [2001] ECR I-4881, para. 43, the absence of any derogations emphasizes Art. 7's importance as a principle of Union social law.

[75] Case C-313/02 *Wippel* [2004] ECR I-9483, para. 48.

[76] Case C-173/99 *BECTU* [2001] ECR I-4881.

more precarious situation than those employed under longer term contracts, so that 'it is all the more important to ensure that their health and safety are protected in a manner consonant with the purpose of Directive [2003/88]'.[77] For this reason the UK could not provide that a worker did not begin to accrue rights to paid annual leave until he had completed a minimum period of 13 weeks' uninterrupted employment with the same employer.[78]

The annual leave provisions have been more litigated than most. Two issues, in particular, have proved particularly problematic: rolled up holiday pay, and the relationship between sick leave/maternity leave and annual leave. It is these matters that we shall now consider.

Rolled up holiday pay

As we have seen, the Directive requires four weeks' annual leave which cannot be contracted out from, save on termination. But how do casual workers enjoy paid leave? In the past, employers have argued that an element of the hourly pay includes holiday pay ('a rolled up rate'). While some tribunals accepted this, provided that the situation was clear to the worker,[79] others were less sure,[80] expressing concern whether rolled up holiday pay was compatible with the health and safety basis of the Directive. In the light of this confused case law, the EAT tried to offer some guidance in *Marshalls Clay Products* v. *Caulfield*.[81] It identified five types of 'rolling-up' provisions, namely:

(1) contracts which are silent as to holiday pay;

(2) contracts which purport to exclude liability for holiday pay;

(3) contracts where rates are said to include an amount for holiday pay, but there is no indication or specification of an amount;

(4) contracts providing for a basic wage or rate topped up by a specific sum or percentage in respect of holiday pay;

(5) contracts where holiday pay is allocated to and paid during (or immediately before or after) specific periods of holiday.

The EAT said that (1), (2), and (3) offended the Working Time Directive but that categories (4) and (5) were permissible. Subsequently, in *Smith* v. *Morrisroe*[82] the EAT provided further general guidance as to the circumstances where a rolled up rate would be legitimate. It said that there had to be *mutual agreement* for genuine payment for holidays, representing a *true addition* to the contractual rate of pay for time

---

[77] Para. 63.

[78] Para. 64. See additionally Case C–282/10 *Dominguez* v. *Centre Informatique du Centre Ouest Atlantique* [2012] ECR I–000.

[79] *College of North East London* v. *Leather*, EAT/0528/00 and *Blackburn* v. *Gridquest Ltd* [2002] IRLR 604.

[80] *MPB Structure Ltd* v. *Munro* [2002] IRLR 601 (EAT); Court of Session [2003] IRLR 350.

[81] [2003] IRLR 552.

[82] [2005] IRLR 72.

worked.[83] In *Robinson-Steele* v. *RF Retail Services Ltd*[84] an employment tribunal decided that it did not want to follow the EAT's decision in *Marshalls Clay*. In *Robinson-Steele* the employer provided in the applicant's contract that:

> Entitlement to payment for leave accrues in proportion to the amount of time worked continuously by the temporary worker on assignment during the leave year. The temporary worker agrees that payment in respect of the entitlement to paid leave shall be made together with and in addition to the temporary worker's hourly rate at 8.33% of his hourly rate.

This sum reflected one week's pay after the worker had worked continuously for three months. The ET thought that only situation (5) of the EAT's catalogue in *Marshall's Clay* of the five types of rolled up holiday pay situations was compatible with the Directive and so the employer's rolled up holiday pay practice contravened the Directive.

Marshalls Clay and *Robinson-Steele* were joined by the Court of Justice which ruled out the possibility of rolled up holiday pay altogether. It noted that the term 'paid annual leave' meant that, for the duration of annual leave, remuneration had to be maintained. In other words, 'workers must receive their normal remuneration for that period of rest'.[85] The Court continued that 'an agreement under which the amount payable to the worker, as both remuneration for work done and part payment for minimum annual leave, would be identical to the amount payable, prior to the entry into force of that agreement, as remuneration solely for work done, effectively negates, by means of a reduction in the amount of that remuneration, the worker's entitlement to paid annual leave under Article 7 of the directive'.[86] Thus, the Court of Justice ruled out the situation which arose in *Smith* v. *Morrisroe*. Smith was employed as a sub-contractor earning £150 per day; holiday pay was not paid. From the end of 2002, Smith was informed by his site manager that he would be receiving £138 per day, while the employer would retain £12 from the £150 and then pay it to Smith as and when he took holiday. He protested: 'I was not paying for my own holiday pay out of my wages and for them to give it back to us as holiday pay'. Even prior to *Robinson-Steele* the EAT had accepted that such an arrangement was not compatible with the Directive: there was no mutual agreement for genuine payment for holidays representing a true addition to the contractual rate of pay for time worked and the Court of Justice agreed.

The Court of Justice also ruled out the possibility, practised by many employers, of rolling up holiday pay in weekly or monthly pay cheques. It said that Article 7 of the Directive precluded the payment for minimum annual leave from being made in the form of part payments, staggered over the corresponding annual period of work and paid together with the remuneration for work done, rather than in the form of a pay-

---

[83] The best way of evidencing this was for: (a) the provision for rolled up holiday pay to be clearly incorporated into the contract of employment; (b) the percentage or amount allocated to holiday pay (or particulars sufficient to enable it to be calculated) to be identified in the contract, and preferably also in the payslip; (c) records to be kept of holidays taken (or of absences from work when holidays can be taken) and for reasonably practicable steps to be taken to ensure that workers take their holidays before the end of the relevant holiday year.

[84] Case No. 1800174/2004.   [85] Para. 50.   [86] Para. 51.

ment in respect of a specific period during which the worker actually takes leave.[87] As the Court said, a regime of rolled up holiday pay could lead to situations in which 'the minimum period of paid annual leave is, in effect, replaced by an allowance in lieu'.[88] Advocate General Stix-Hackl in *Robinson-Steele* expressed a different concern. She said that if rolled up holiday pay were allowed, low paid workers, in particular, could use most, if not all of their pay for subsistence, with the risk that holiday pay would be used up and so they would forgo leave in favour of carrying on working; the possibility of earning money was a substantial encouragement for forgoing leave.

Thus, it seems that employers must pay holiday pay during the specific period during which the worker takes leave; it is unlawful to stagger payment over the year. However, given the implications of its rulings for many thousands of employers employing casual staff, the Court endorsed what is, in essence, a transitional regime. It allowed employers to set off part payments staggered over the corresponding annual period of work and paid together with the remuneration for work done (i.e. rolled up holiday pay) against the payment for specific leave which was actually taken by the worker,[89] provided that the sums paid were *additional* to remuneration which has been paid and that the sums were *transparent* and comprehensible.[90] In other words, provided that the rolled up holiday pay arrangements satisfied these conditions (essentially those of the EAT in *Marshall's Clay* and *Smith*), with the burden of proof on the employer,[91] they were lawful. However, Member States were under an obligation to rectify this illegality, ensuring that 'practices incompatible with Article 7 of the Directive are not continued'.[92] This the DTI /BIS did in its revised guidance which says:[93]

> Following an [CJEU] Judgement on 16 March 2006, Rolled Up Holiday Pay (RHP) is considered unlawful and employers should renegotiate contracts involving RHP for existing employees/workers *as soon as possible* so that payment for statutory annual leave is made at the time when the leave is taken. Where an employer has already given RHP in relation to work undertaken, and the payments have been made in a transparent and comprehensible manner, they can be set off against any future leave payments made at the proper time.

The effect of sick leave and maternity leave

The other question that frequently arises is whether the four weeks' paid leave will be added to any period of maternity leave or long-term sick leave. In *Merino Gómez*[94] the Court of Justice considered the issue in respect of maternity leave. Factory workers could take leave only during certain periods over the summer. Gomez was on maternity leave during those periods and was denied the right to take the annual leave after her maternity leave. The Court distinguished maternity leave from annual leave. Maternity leave, it noted, was intended to protect a woman's biological condition during and after

---

[87] Para. 63.   [88] Para. 61.   [89] Para. 69.
[90] Para. 66.   [91] Para. 68.   [92] Para. 67.
[93] <http://webarchive.nationalarchives.gov.uk/+/http://www.dti.gov.uk/employment/employment-legislation/employment-guidance/page14382.html> (last accessed 12 March 2012).
[94] Case C–342/01 *Gómez* v. *Continental Industrias del Caucho SA* [2004] ECR I–2605.

the calculation.[115] In *Pfeiffer* the Court said that the 48-hour upper limit on working time constitutes a rule of Union social law of particular importance from which every worker must benefit.[116] The Court also ruled that Article 6 was sufficiently clear and precise to be directly effective.[117] The problem for the Court was that the case concerned two individuals (emergency workers working for the German Red Cross who argued that they were being required to work in excess of the 48-hour working week). The Court did not reverse its long-standing rule that unimplemented Directives have only vertical direct effect. Instead, it imposed on the German courts a very broad interpretative obligation. It said:

> [W]hen hearing a case between individuals, a national court is required, when applying the provisions of domestic law adopted for the purpose of transposing obligations laid down by a directive, to consider the whole body of rules of national law and to interpret them, so far as possible, in the light of the wording and purpose of the directive in order to achieve an outcome consistent with the objective pursued by the directive. In the main proceedings, the national court must thus do whatever lies within its jurisdiction to ensure that the maximum period of weekly working time, which is set at 48 hours by Article 6(2) of Directive [2003/88], is not exceeded.[118]

The definition of working time

The key issue, then, is, what constitutes working time? Article 2(1) defines 'working time' as having three elements: (1) any period during which the worker is working, (2) at the employer's disposal, and (3) carrying out his activities or duties, in accordance with national laws and/or practices. The question is whether these three elements are cumulative or disjunctive, an issue of particular significance to 'on-call workers'. If read disjunctively then, for on-call workers waiting at home, this time constitutes working time. If read cumulatively, then this time may not represent working time since the worker is not 'working'. The Court of Justice, insisting on a Union definition of working time (and rest periods),[119] has supported the cumulative reading,[120] but with the lightest touch in respect of the third criteria.[121] This can be seen in various cases concerning the emergency services: *Simap* (doctors in primary care teams),[122] *CIG* (nursing staff in the emergency services),[123] and *Jaeger* (doctor in the surgical department of a hospital).[124] In these cases, the Court ruled that the time spent by these medical and emergency

---

[115] Art. 16(b). By virtue of Art. 17 it is possible to derogate from this provision but any derogations must not result in the establishment of a reference period exceeding six months. However, Member States have the option, subject to compliance with the general principles relating to the protection of health and safety of workers, and allowing for objective or technical reasons or reasons concerning the organization of work, to allow collective agreements to set reference periods which do not exceed 12 months (Art. 19, para. 2).

[116] Joined Cases C–397/01 to C–403/01 *Pfeiffer* v. *Deutsches Rotes Kreuz* [2004] ECR I–8835, para. 69.

[117] Para. 73.   [118] Para. 88. See additionally Case C-282/10 *Dominguez* [2012] ECR I-000.

[119] Case C–151/02 *Jaeger* [2003] ECR I–8389, para. 58.

[120] See e.g., Case C–303/98 *Simap* [2000] ECR I–7963, para. 48.

[121] For a full discussion, see J. Kenner, 'Re-evaluating the concept of working time: an analysis of recent case law' (2004) 32 *IRJ* 588, 594.

[122] Case C–303/98 *Simap* [2000] ECR I–7963.   [123] Case C–241/99 *CIG* v. *Sergas* [2001] ECR I–5139.

[124] Case C–151/02 *Jaeger* [2003] ECR I–8389.

workers at their workplace on-call *and* on the premises of the employer (even where they could sleep in a bed provided by the employer[125]) constituted working time. As the Court explained in *Jaeger*,[126] an on-call doctor who is required to keep himself available to the employer at a place designated by the employer is subject to appreciably greater constraints than a doctor on standby (i.e. a doctor required to be permanently accessible but not present at the health centre) since he has 'to remain apart from his family and social environment and has less freedom to manage the time during which his professional services are not required'.

Furthermore, the time spent asleep or otherwise inactive on the employer's premises does not count towards the rest periods because the worker must be able 'to remove himself from the working environment . . . to enable him to relax and dispel the fatigue caused by the performance of his duties'.[127] As the Court put it in *Simap*, in the scheme of the Directive, working time is placed 'in opposition to rest periods, the two being mutually exclusive'.[128]

In *Dellas*[129] the Court confirmed that on-call duty was classified as working time (on the facts, time spent by a teacher on night duty in an establishment for handicapped persons) and had to be taken into account in its entirety for the purposes of calculating the 48-hour week. The case concerned a French law which provided a weighting mechanism to reflect periods of inactivity during on-call duty, when calculating pay and overtime. The decree established a 3 to 1 ratio for the first nine hours followed by a 2 to 1 ratio for subsequent hours between the hours of presence and the working hours actually counted. The Court said that while the Directive did not apply to the remuneration of workers, it did apply to working hours; and because the weighting mechanism took into account only in part the number of hours a worker was actually present, the total working time of a worker could amount to at least 60 hours a week contrary to the Directive. The Court noted that the Directive did not provide for any intermediate category between working time and rest periods.[130] It also noted that the definition of working time did not include any reference to 'the intensity of work done by the employee and his output'.[131] It therefore said: 'The fact that on-call duty includes some period of inactivity is thus completely irrelevant in this connection'.[132]

The consequences of a broad definition of working time

The decisions of the CJEU defining working time so broadly as to encompass time spent on the employer's premises, even when asleep, have caused many problems for employers, especially in the health care sector. This has led to far greater attention being given to the derogations from the Directive. As we shall see, a complex set of derogations apply to Article 6. In the case of those with 'unmeasured working time', Member States can derogate both from Article 6 (48-hour week) *and* Article 16(b) (the reference

---

[125] Case C–151/02 *Jaeger* [2003] ECR I–8389, paras. 60–4.
[126] Case C–151/02 *Jaeger* [2003] ECR I–8389, para. 65.   [127] Para. 95.
[128] Para. 47.   [129] Case C–14/04 *Dellas* [2005] ECR I–10253.
[130] Cf. the various proposals for reform considered below.
[131] Para. 43.   [132] Para. 47.

period) provided due regard is paid to the general principles of the protection of the safety and health of workers. In the case of other workers (i.e. those considered to be special cases and those covered by a collective agreement) Member States can derogate, but only from Article 16(b) (reference period). Furthermore, according to Article 19(1), the option to derogate may not result in the establishment of a reference period exceeding six months. However, Member States have the option, subject to compliance with general health and safety principles, of allowing for objective or technical reasons concerning the organization of work, collective agreements, or agreements concluded between the two sides of industry to set longer reference periods but in no event exceeding 12 months.[133] But, perhaps more important than all the derogations is the highly controversial 'opt-out'.

The opt-out

Article 22(1) (formerly Article 18(1)(b)(i)) provides that Member States need not apply Article 6 on the maximum 48-hour week provided certain conditions are satisfied. Member States must ensure that:

- the general principles of the protection of health and safety of workers are respected;
- no employer requires a worker to work more than 48 hours over a seven-day period calculated as an average for the reference period referred to in Article 16(b) unless the workers' consent has been obtained previously;
- any worker refusing to give this consent must not be subjected to any detriment by the employer as a result;
- the employer must keep up-to-date records of all workers who work more than 48 hours a week;
- records must be placed at the disposal of the competent authorities, which may, for reasons connected with the health and safety of workers, prohibit or restrict the possibility of exceeding the maximum weekly working hours;
- the employer provides the competent authorities at their request with information on cases in which agreement has been given by workers to perform work exceeding 48 hours over a period of seven days (calculated as an average for any reference period set down under the option available in Article 16(b)).

The Court considered the use of the opt-out in *Pfeiffer*:[134]

Any derogation from those minimum requirements must therefore be accompanied by all the safeguards necessary to ensure that, if the worker concerned is encouraged to relinquish a social right which has been directly conferred on him by the directive, he must do so freely and with full knowledge of all the facts. Those requirements are all the more important given that the worker must be regarded as the weaker party to the employment

---

[133] Art. 19(2).   [134] Joined Cases C–397/01 to C–403/01 [2004] ECR I–8835.

contract and it is therefore necessary to prevent the employer being in a position to disregard the intentions of the other party to the contract or to impose on that party a restriction of his rights without him having expressly given his consent in that regard.

The Court added that, for a derogation to Article 6 to be valid, 'the worker's consent must be given not only individually but expressly and freely'.[135] Consent given by trade union representatives in the context of a collective or other agreement was not equivalent to that given by the worker himself.[136] Therefore, in *Pfeiffer*, individual contracts of employment incorporating a collective agreement allowing working hours to be extended breached the Directive.

Originally, the UK (and Ireland) were the only countries to take advantage of the opt-out. Ireland abandoned the opt-out but the UK has hung on to it tenaciously. The use of the opt-out by the UK was subject to review in 2003,[137] and the Commission then issued a Communication[138] which criticized the UK's implementation, noting that[139] legislation and practice do not appear to offer all the guarantees laid down by the Directive. In particular, the Commission was critical of the practice of employers giving new recruits the opt-out to sign at the same time as signing the contract of employment, thereby compromising the workers' freedom of choice. The Commission noted that this practice undermined Article 22(1)(b), which aims to guarantee the worker's free consent by ensuring that no worker may suffer harm due to the fact that he is not prepared to give his agreement. The Communication concludes with a general criticism of the UK's approach:

> The only experience that is applicable here (in the United Kingdom …) has shown the existing difficulties in ensuring that the spirit and terms of the Directive are respected and that real guarantees are provided for workers. It also brings out an unexpected effect in that it is difficult to ensure (or at least check) that the other provisions in the Directive have been complied with, concerning whether workers have signed the opt-out agreement.

Despite the Commission's desire to remove the opt-out from a (health and safety) Directive, it discovered that, following the *Simap* line of case law, the use of the opt-out was becoming more widespread across other Member States (it is now used by 16 Member States,[140] particularly in the healthcare sector).[141] The UK Presidency of the Council in the second half of 2005 came close to securing a deal on revisions to the Working Time Directive according to which the opt-out would have been preserved but with its conditions tightened. However, the deal failed over another matter entirely: whether the 48-hour week (and all other limits) applied per worker (as in the UK, Germany,

---

[135] Para. 84.   [136] Para. 81. See additionally Case C–303/98 *Simap* [2000] ECR I–7963, para. 74.

[137] C. Barnard, S. Deakin. and R. Hobbs, 'Opting Out of the 48 Hour Week: Employer Necessity or Individual Choice?' (2003) 32 *ILJ* 223. See further the Deloitte report (2010): <ec.europa.eu/social/BlobServlet?docId=64 21&langId=en> (last accessed 22 January 2012).

[138] COM(2003) 843.   [139] Para. 2.2.1.2.

[140] <http://www.eurofound.europa.eu/eiro/2011/01/articles/eu1101021i.htm> (last accessed 12 March 2012).

[141] See C. Barnard, 'The EU Agenda for Regulating Labour Markets: Lessons from the UK in the Field of Working Time' in G. Bermann and K. Pistor (eds), *Law and Governance in an Enlarged Europe* (Hart Publishing, Oxford, 2004).

Italy, Ireland, and the Netherlands) or per contract (in a number of other Member States such as France, Portugal, and the Scandinavian countries). The Austrian Presidency had another go in June 2006, hoping to bridge the divide between those Member States wanting to see the opt-out phased out and those determined to keep it, by proposing that the opt-out be retained but with increased safeguards for workers. These included a 'cooling-off period' of one month within which new recruits could change their mind about the opt-out and a requirement that opt-outs be renewed annually, with a statement by the employer as to the reason why long hours are needed. These attempts also failed.[142] Further attempts were also unsuccessful in 2009.[143] So what was intended as a temporary derogation to be reviewed before 23 November 2003 has become semipermanent. The interesting question is whether, following *Test-Achats*,[144] the absence of a sunset clause on the opt-out might be challenged as contrary to Article 31(2) of the Charter.

Remedy

The question of what remedies are available to employees who have suffered a breach of Article 6 was at issue in *Fuß II*.[145] The Court ruled that EU law precluded national legislation which makes a public sector worker's right to reparation for loss or damage conditional on a concept of fault going beyond that of a sufficiently serious breach of European Union law and conditional on a prior application having been made to his or her employer in order to secure compliance with that provision. The Court also said that the reparation for the loss or damage caused to individuals as a result of breaches of European Union law had to be commensurate with the loss or damage sustained. Where the loss concerned overtime it was for national law to determine whether the compensation should take the form of additional time off in lieu or financial compensation for the worker as well as the rules concerning the method of calculation of that reparation.

(b) Night work (Article 8)

The other 'limit' concerns night work. Night time is any period of not less than seven hours, *as defined by national law*, which must include, in any case, the period between midnight and 5 a.m.[146] This gives the national systems a possible range of the hours between 10 p.m. and 7 a.m. to designate as night time.

Night workers are defined in two ways by the Directive. First, 'night workers' are those who, during night time, work at least three hours of their daily working time as a normal course.[147] Secondly, the Directive defines night workers as those who are likely to work a certain proportion of their working time during night time, as defined by national legislation *or* collective agreements concluded by the two sides of industry at national or regional

---

[142] 2733rd Council Meeting, Employment, Social Policy, Health and Consumer Affairs, EU Council press release, 1–2 June 2006.

[143] <http://www.eurofound.europa.eu/eiro/2009/06/articles/eu0906039i.htm> (last accessed 12 March 2012).

[144] Case C–236/09 [2011] ECR I–000, considered in Ch. 6.

[145] Case C–429/09 *Fuß v. Stadt Halle* [2010] ECR I–000.   [146] Art. 2(3).   [147] Art. 2(4)(a).

level.[148] The definition of night worker was considered by the High Court in Northern Ireland in *ex parte Burns*.[149] The applicant had a rotating shift pattern during which she worked one week in three from 9 p.m. to 7 a.m. The government argued that she was not a night worker since night workers were those who worked night shifts exclusively or pre-dominantly. Kerr J rejected this, arguing that it was sufficient that night working be a 'regular feature' of the employment. In *Simap*[150] Advocate General Saggio said that doctors working at night or who were contactable at night constituted night workers.

Normal working hours for night work must not exceed an average of eight hours in any 24-hour period.[151] The reference period is to be determined after consulting the two sides of industry or by collective agreements or agreements concluded between the two sides of industry at national or regional level.[152] Night workers whose work involves special hazards or mental strain—to be defined by national legislation or collective agreements or agreements concluded between the two sides of industry—must not work more than eight hours in any period of 24 hours during which they work at night.[153] Thus, no reference period exists in the case of such workers.

In addition, night workers are entitled to a free and confidential health assessment, possibly conducted within the national health system, before their assignment and then at regular intervals thereafter.[154] If night workers are found to suffer from health problems related to night work they must be transferred wherever possible to suitable day work.[155] In addition, Member States can make the work of 'certain categories of night workers subject to certain guarantees, under the conditions laid down by national law and practice, in the case of workers who incur risks to their safety or health linked to night time working'.[156] However, any guarantees made must be careful not to offend the principle of equal treatment of men and women.[157] Employers who *regularly* use night workers must inform the competent authorities on request.[158] Finally, Article 12 provides that both night workers and shift workers must both enjoy health and safety protection appropriate to the nature of their work, and that such protection is equivalent to that applicable to other workers and is available at all times.

4. DEROGATIONS

The Directive contains a complex series of derogations which Member States can choose to apply.[159] However, they can take advantage of the derogations only if they have

---

[148] Art. 2(4)(b).   [149] [1999] IRLR 315.   [150] Case C–303/98 [2000] ECR I–7963.

[151] Art. 8(a).   [152] Art. 16(c).   [153] Art. 8(b).

[154] Arts. 9(1)(a), (2) and (3).   [155] Art. 9(1)(b).   [156] Art. 10.

[157] See Case 312/86 *Commission v. France* [1988] ECR 3559, Case 345/89 *Criminal Proceedings Against Stoeckel* [1991] ECR I–4047, and Case C–158/91 *Ministère public and Direction du travail et de l'emploi v. Levy* [1993] ECR I–4287.

[158] Art. 11.

[159] Case C–227/09 *Accardo* [2010] ECR I–000, para. 51: 'Since the derogations available under the derogating provisions in question are optional, European Union law does not require Member States to implement them in domestic law. In order to exercise the option provided for by those provisions to derogate, in certain circumstances, from the requirements laid down, inter alia, in Article 5 of the Working Time Directives, the Member States are required to make a choice to rely on it'.

implemented them.[160] As always, with derogations, they have to be interpreted in such a way that their scope is limited to what is strictly necessary in order to safeguard the interests which those derogations enable to be protected'.[161] In summary, the derogations fall into six categories, discussed below.

4.1. Unmeasured working time (Article 17(1))

With due regard for the general principles of the protection of the safety and health of workers, Member States may derogate from Articles 3, 4, 5, 6, 8, and 16 of the Directive (i.e. all limits and entitlements except annual leave) when 'on account of the specific characteristics of the activity concerned, the duration of the working time is not measured and/or predetermined or can be determined by the workers themselves', particularly in the case of managing executives, family workers, and 'religious' workers.[162] As the guidance notes accompanying the British implementation of the Directive explain,[163] this derogation essentially applies to workers who have complete control over the hours they work and whose time is not monitored or determined by their employer. Such a situation may occur if a worker can decide when the work is to be done, or may adjust the time worked as they see fit. An indicator may be if the worker has discretion over whether to work on a given day without needing to consult the employer.[164] A number of universities consider that academics fall into this category.

4.2. Other special cases (Article 17(3))

In the case of security and surveillance activities requiring a permanent presence in order to protect property and persons, particularly security guards and caretakers or security firms,[165] and, following *Union syndicale Solidaires Isère*,[166] instructors and leaders working at summer camps for children, or in the case of industries requiring 'continuity of service or production' (for example prisons, hospitals,[167] the utilities, the press[168]), again including leaders at kids' camps,[169] or industries where there is a foreseeable surge of activity (for example, tourism, agriculture, postal industry),[170] or where the worker's home and work are distant,[171] or for people working in railway transport,[172]

---

[160] Case C–303/98 *Simap* [2000] ECR I–7963.

[161] Case C–151/02 *Jaeger* [2003] ECR I–8389, para. 89.   [162] Art. 17(1).

[163] Para. 2.2.2. of DTI, Regulatory Guidance on the Working Time Regulations 28 August 1998.

[164] SI 1999/3372 added a new clause in Reg. 20(2) which was intended to deal with workers whose working time was partly measured, predetermined or determined by the worker and partly not. The 48-hour limit applied to the work which was predetermined or measured. In respect of the part of the job which was not predetermined, the 48-hour limit did not apply. The trade union Amicus complained about this Regulation, which was repealed two days before the hearing in Case C–484/04 *Commission* v. *UK*: SI 2006/99 The Working Time (Amendment) Regulations 2006.   [165] Art. 17(3)(b).

[166] Case C–428/09 *Union syndicale Solidaires Isère* [2010] ECR I–000, para. 46.

[167] See Case C–151/02 *Jaeger* [2003] ECR I–8389, para. 87: the organization of teams of on-call services in hospitals and similar establishments falls within this derogation.   [168] Art. 17(3) (c).

[169] Case C–428/09 *Union syndicale Solidaires Isère* [2010] ECR I–000, para. 47.

[170] Art. 17(3)(d).   [171] Art. 17(3)(a).

[172] Art. 17(3)(e) (i.e. where the activities are intermittent, where the people spend their time working on board trains or whose activities are linked to transport timetables and to ensuring the continuity and regulation of traffic).

or where there is a dangerous situation,[173] derogations can be adopted from Articles 3, 4, 5, 8, and 16 of the Directive (i.e. from the entitlements, night work, and the reference period but not from the working time limit itself) by laws, regulations, administrative provisions, collective agreements, or agreements between the two sides of industry.[174] These derogations are subject to the requirement that the workers concerned are afforded equivalent periods of compensatory rest. This rest must, according to *Jaeger*,[175] follow on immediately from the working time in order to prevent the worker from experiencing a state of fatigue or overload owing to the accumulation of consecutive periods of work. In exceptional cases in which it is not possible for objective reasons to grant such rest, the workers concerned must be afforded appropriate protection.[176]

As far as the option to derogate from Article 16(b) is concerned (reference period of four months for calculating average weekly working time), the reference period may not exceed six months, or 12 months where there are objective, technical or work organization reasons and a collective agreement or agreement between the two sides of industry has been concluded.[177]

4.3. Shift work (Article 17(4))

Shift work is defined as any method of organizing work in shifts, whereby workers succeed each other, at the same work stations, according to a *certain pattern*, including a rotating pattern, which may be continuous or discontinuous, entailing the need for workers to work at different times over a given period of days or weeks.[178] This period is not defined by the Directive. In *Simap*[179] the Court said that working time spent both on call where doctors in primary care teams are required to be present at health centres and on the actual provision of primary care services when doctors are on call by having merely to be contactable at all times, fulfilled all the requirements of the definition of shift work. It added that the work of doctors in primary care teams is organized in such a way that workers are assigned successively to the same work posts on a rotational basis, which makes it necessary for them to perform work at different hours over a given period of days or weeks.[180]

Articles 3 and 5 (daily rest and weekly rest) do not apply in relation to shift workers when they change shift and cannot take a daily and/or weekly rest period between the end of one shift and the start of the next one or in the case of activities involving periods of work split up over the day, as may be the case for cleaning staff.[181] As with 'Other Special Cases' (Article 17(3)) considered above, the derogation can be laid down by laws, regulations, administrative provisions, collective agreements, or agreements between the two sides of industry.[182] These derogations are subject to the requirement

---

[173] Defined as circumstances described in Art. 5(4) of Dir. 89/391 and in cases of accident or imminent risk of accident (Art. 17(3)(f) and (g)).   [174] Art. 17(3) and Art. 17(2).

[175] C–151/02 *Landeshauptstadt Kiel* v. *Jaeger* [2003] ECR I–8389, paras. 94 and 97.

[176] Art. 17(2). In Case C–428/09 *Union syndicale Solidaires Isère* [2010] ECR I–000, para. 55 emphasized the 'absolutely exceptional' nature of this exception.   [177] Art. 19.

[178] Art. 2(5).   [179] Case C–303/98 *Simap* [2000] ECR I–7963, para. 61.

[180] Para. 62.   [181] Art. 17(4).   [182] Art. 17(2).

that the workers concerned are afforded equivalent periods of compensatory rest or appropriate protection.[183]

4.4. Collective agreements or agreements between the two sides of industry (Article 18)

Derogations may be made from Articles 3, 4, 5, 8, and 16[184] (entitlements, night work limit, and reference period) by means of collective agreements or agreements between the two sides of industry at national or regional level.[185] These derogations are allowed on condition that equivalent compensating rest periods are granted to the workers concerned or, in exceptional cases where it is not possible for objective reasons to grant such periods, the workers concerned are afforded appropriate protection.[186] Once again, as with 'other special cases'—Article 17(3) considered above—the option to derogate from the reference period in Article 16(b) (of four months for calculating average weekly working time) the reference period may not exceed six months, or 12 months where there are objective, technical, or work organization reasons and a collective agreement or agreement between the two sides of industry has been concluded.[187] Therefore, collective agreements are permitted to lower the standard of protection provided by the legislation, subject to the provision on compensatory rest.

In the UK, one of the states envisaged by Article 18, second paragraph, in which there is no statutory system for ensuring the conclusion of collective agreements, the collective dimension of the Directive has posed considerable problems for a traditionally single channel system where worker representation has been performed by recognized trade unions.[188] With the decline in trade union membership and recognition, the approach adopted by the British Working Time Regulations 1998 is to give a role to elected worker representatives where there is no recognized trade union. While trade unions can enter collective agreements, worker representatives can enter workforce agreements. To be valid a 'workforce agreement' it must:

- be in writing;
- have effect for a specified period not exceeding five years;
- apply either to all of the relevant members of the workforce (other than those covered by collective agreement—thus employers cannot by-pass a recognized trade union), or to all of the relevant members of the workforce who belong to a particular group;

---

[183] Ibid.

[184] As far as derogations from Art. 16(b) are concerned, the same periods apply as for other special cases (Art. 19).

[185] Art. 18, para. 1. Where it is in conformity with the rules laid down by such agreements, derogations can be made by means of collective agreements or agreements between the two sides of industry at a lower level (Art. 18, para. 1). Member States where there is no statutory system for ensuring the conclusion of collective agreements or agreements between the two sides of industry, or Member States where there is a specific legislative framework, may allow derogations by collective agreement or agreement between the two sides of industry at the appropriate collective level (Art. 18, para. 2).

[186] Art. 18, para. 3.   [187] Art. 19.   [188] See further Ch. 15.

- be signed by the representatives of the workforce[189] or the representatives of the group where appropriate (excluding in either case any representative not a relevant member of the workforce on the date on which the agreement was first made available for signature). If the employer employs 20 or fewer workers on the date on which the agreement was first made available for signature, it must be signed either by the appropriate representatives *or* by the majority of workers. Thus, in a small workforce the British regulations envisage a form of direct representation to achieve a collective goal.

Thus, collective or workforce agreements can be used to secure so-called 'statutory bargained adjustments'[190] to the rules on working time.

4.5. Doctors in training (Article 17(5))

The Directive applies to doctors in training from 2 August 2004 but it also makes provision for transitional arrangements in respect of the maximum working week and the reference period over which it is calculated.[191] In essence, derogations from the maximum working week are permitted for five years (or seven years in those states having difficulties in meeting the working time provision or eight years in those states having particular difficulties).[192] However, Member States must ensure that in no case will the number of weekly working hours exceed an average of 52 hours for any remaining period which can be averaged over a maximum of six months.[193] The employer must consult the representatives of employees in good time with a view to reaching agreement on the arrangements applying to the transitional period.[194]

Thus, unlike the other derogations, this derogation is temporary. Once the transitional periods have expired, doctors in training are treated like all other workers with a maximum 48-hour working week. Member States will then have to rely on the other derogations outlined in the Directive (e.g. the opt-out in Article 22) if they want to allow doctors in training to work more than 48 hours a week.

---

[189] Para. 2 of Sch. 1 provides that 'representatives of the workforce' are workers duly elected to represent the relevant members of the workforce; 'representatives of the group' are workers duly elected to represent the members of a particular group, and representatives are 'duly elected' if their election satisfies the requirements of para. 3 of the Schedule. The Working Time Regulations provide some details of the method of carrying out elections (Sch. 1, para. 3). The Working Time Regulations are, however, far less prescriptive than those rules contained in TULR(C)A 1992 for the election of trade union officials and, as the TUC has pointed out, employers have too much power in deciding how the representatives are to be elected and there are no controls on ballot-rigging (Research Paper 98/82, 25). This has prompted concern as to whether the elected worker representatives will pass the test of representativity laid down by the Court in Case T–135/96 *UEAPME* v. *Council of the European Union* [1998] ECR II–2335, considered in Ch. 2.

[190] P. Davies and C. Kilpatrick, 'UK Worker Representation after Single Channel' (2004) 33 *ILJ* 121, 137.

[191] Art. 17(2) also applies to this provision.   [192] Art. 17(5), paras. 2–4.

[193] Art. 17(5), para. 5. This was phased in as follows: 58 hours for the first three years which could be averaged over 12 months (i.e. until 31 July 2007); 56 hours for the following two years which could be averaged over a maximum of six months (i.e. until 31 July 2009); 52 hours until the end of the transitional period (31 July 2011 or 31 July 2012 for states with special difficulties).

[194] Art. 17(5), para. 6.

4.6. Transport workers (Articles 20 and 21)

The provisions on daily rest, in work rest breaks, weekly rest, and night work do not apply to mobile workers,[195] defined to mean any worker employed as a member of travelling or flying personnel by an undertaking which operates transport services for passengers or goods by road or air.[196] Member States must, however, take the necessary measures to ensure that such workers are entitled to adequate rest except in a dangerous situation or cases of accident or imminent risk of accident.[197] Member States can derogate from the reference period laid down in Article 16(b) in respect of offshore workers provided that there is compliance with the general principles of health and safety and provided that there is consultation of representatives of the employer and employees.[198]

The provisions on daily rest, in-work rest breaks, weekly rest, the 48-hour working week, and night work do not apply to any worker on board a sea-going fishing vessel flying the flag of a Member State[199] but states are required to take the necessary measures to ensure that any such worker is entitled to adequate rest and that they do not have to work more than 48 hours a week referenced over 12 months. Within these confines, the Directive then lays down details of maximum hours of work and minimum hours of rest.

5. CONCLUSIONS

The adaptability pillar of the Luxembourg Employment Guidelines saw the reform of working time as a key component of realizing demand-side flexibility. According to the 1998 Employment Guidelines,[200] the Social Partners were invited to negotiate, at the appropriate levels, agreements to 'modernise the organisation of work, including flexible working arrangements, with the aim of making undertakings productive and competitive and achieving the required balance between flexibility and security'. The 1999 Guidelines offered some further suggestions: the Social Partners might negotiate agreements on the expression of working time as an annual figure, the reduction of working hours, the reduction of overtime, the development of part-time working, lifelong training, and career breaks—issues which far exceed the scope of the Working Time Directive.[201] However, in subsequent Guidelines, working time has featured less prominently. For example, the 2005 Guidelines[202] contained only two brief references to working time, the first under Guideline 21 (promoting flexibility); the second under Guideline 24 (adapt education and training systems). By 2010, reference to working time as such

---

[195] Art. 20.   [196] Art. 2(7).   [197] Art. 20(1), para. 2.

[198] 'Offshore work' means work that is performed 'mainly on or from offshore installations (including drilling rigs) directly or indirectly in connection with the exploration, extraction or exploitation of mineral resources, including hydrocarbons, and diving in connection with such activities, whether performed from an offshore installation or vessel' (Art. 2(8)).

[199] Art. 21.   [200] Council Res. 98/C 30/01.   [201] Council Res. 99/C 69/02, para. 16.

[202] Council Dec. 2005/600/EC (OJ [2005] L205/21).

had disappeared altogether, replaced instead by concerns about work-life balance more generally.[203]

Nevertheless, working time remains a key issue on the Union's flexibility agenda. The sectoral specific Directives, negotiated by the Social Partners, represent a step in this direction. However, many businesses viewed the Working Time Directive as a significant constraint on their ability to introduce flexible working arrangements, not least because its provisions are so prescriptive (especially when compared with the Framework Directives on, for example, Parental Leave (Directive 2010/18/EU[204])), and the content of the derogations unclear. This helps to explain why so many employers, in the UK at least, have taken advantage of the opt-out. In many cases they do not actually need it, but it provides them with a security blanket in case of breach. However, the negative effect of the use of the opt-out is that it has insulated employers from the need to consider whether organizational changes are necessary to reduce the length of the working week and improve productivity.[205]

Amendments to the Working Time Directive have proved elusive. In December 2010, the European Commission launched the second stage of consultations with EU-level social partners[206] on possible amendments to the Working Time Directive, suggesting either a 'focused' review, limited to the issues of on-call time and compensatory rest, or a wider-ranging 'comprehensive' review covering issues as varied as the individual opt-out from the Directive's 48-hour maximum working week; greater flexibility in working patterns; work-life balance; autonomous workers; workers with multiple contracts; specific sectoral problems; and paid annual leave.[207] The European social partners wrote to the European Commission in November 2011 confirming their intention to open formal negotiations on revising the legislation.[208]

Yet, the debate has moved on. The economic crisis has forced firms to experiment with a variety of 'flexible' working arrangements in order retain skilled staff at a time of reduced need.[209] Thus, firms have tried offering their staff unpaid or reduced-pay sabbaticals, short-time working, and extended holiday leave. None of this is envisaged by the Working Time Directive or the proposed reforms. Much has been worked out between employers and trade unions in the traditional way. Recent years have also witnessed an increased use of unpaid 'internships' where firms have offered work experience, usually to those who are young and unemployed—often over a number of months and doing work normally undertaken by paid employees—but with no pay. Many see this as exploitation.[210] Once again, neither the Working Time Directive nor the Young

---

[203] Council Dec. 2010/707/EU (OJ [2010] L308/46).

[204] OJ [2010] L68/13 considered further in Ch. 9.

[205] Barnard, Deakin, and Hobbs, previously, at n. 137.   [206] COM(2010) 801.

[207] <http://www.eurofound.europa.eu/eiro/2011/01/articles/eu1101021i.htm> (last accessed 12 March 2012).

[208] <http://ec.europa.eu/social/main.jsp?langId=en&catId=329&newsId=1116&furtherNews=yes> (last accessed 12 March 2012).

[209] Cf. J. Plantenga and C. Remery, 'Flexible working time arrangements and gender equality—A comparative review of 30 European countries' 2010, <http://europa.eu/rapid/pressReleasesAction.do?reference=IP/10/1377&format=HTML&a> (last accessed 22 January 2012). See additionally, Commission, *Restructuring and anticipation of change: What lessons from recent experience?* COM(2012) 7, 8–11.

[210] <http://www.tuc.org.uk/union/tuc-17759-f0.cfm> (last accessed 22 January 2012).

Workers Directive (see later in this chapter) touch this issue. It is not even clear whether such 'volunteers' fall within the personal scope of these measures.

C. YOUNG WORKERS

1. INTRODUCTION

The Court's decision in *UK* v. *Council* to uphold the choice of Article 153 TFEU as the legal basis for the Working Time Directive saved three other Directives designed to protect specific groups of workers adopted in the same period as the original Working Time Directive—pregnant workers,[211] young workers,[212] and atypical workers[213]—all adopted under Article 153 TFEU but combining a mixture of health and safety with working conditions and employment rights.[214] This section will consider the Young Workers' Directive, where the same dilemmas as with the Working Time Directive emerge.

The Young Workers' Directive[215] is intended to prevent abuse of young people's labour while allowing sufficient flexibility in schemes providing both work experience and training. The Directive requires Member States to ensure that employers guarantee that young people (any person under 18 'having an employment contract or employment relationship')[216] have working conditions which suit their age, and are protected against 'economic exploitation and against any work likely to harm their safety, health or physical, mental, moral or social development or to jeopardise their education'.[217] Since this is the purpose of the Directive, any subsequent provisions must be interpreted in the light of this objective. These points are now reinforced by Article 32 of the Charter of Fundamental Rights of the European Union which provides:

> The employment of children is prohibited. The minimum age of admission to employment may not be lower than the minimum school-leaving age, without prejudice to such rules as may be more favourable to young people and except for limited derogations.

---

[211] Council Dir. 92/85/EEC (OJ [1992] L348/1). See further Ch. 9.

[212] Council Dir. 94/33/EC (OJ [1994] L216/12).

[213] Council Dir. 91/383/EC (OJ [1991] L206/19). See further Ch. 9.

[214] Art. 31(1) of the Charter of Fundamental Rights of the European Union recognizes this bridge between health and safety and working conditions. It provides that '[e]very worker has the right to working conditions which respect his or her health safety and dignity'.

[215] Council Dir. 94/33/EC (OJ [1994] L216/12). SEC (2010) 1339 contains a report on the application of the Dir. See additionally Commission Recommendation 67/125/EEC (OJ [1967] 25/405). Inspiration for the Directive came, in particular, from various ILO Conventions, the European Social Charter 1961 Art. 7, and Art. 32 of the UN Convention on the Rights of the Child: COM(91) 543 final. Member States were required either to implement the Directive by 22 June 1996 or to ensure that the two sides of industry introduced the requisite provisions by means of collective agreements (Art. 17(1)(a)). The UK, however, did not need to implement certain provisions (Art. 8(1)(b) limiting the working time of children to two hours a day on a school day and 12 hours a week; Art. 8(2), limiting the working time of adolescents to eight hours a day and 40 hours a week; and Art. 9(1)(b) and (2), relating to the night work of adolescents) of the Directive until 2000 (Art. 17(1)(b)). This was the first time in the social field that a named Member State had secured at least a significant delay in implementing a Directive.

[216] Arts. 3(a) and 2(1).   [217] Art. 1(3).

Young people admitted to work must have working conditions appropriate to their age and be protected against economic exploitation and any work likely to harm their safety, health or physical, mental, moral or social development or to interfere with their education.

2. THE PERSONAL SCOPE OF THE DIRECTIVE AND DEROGATIONS

The Young Workers' Directive envisages two categories of young workers: (1) children, defined as any young person less than 15 years old or who is still subject to compulsory full-time schooling under national law,[218] and (2) adolescents, defined as any young person who is at least 15 years old but younger than 18, who is no longer subject to compulsory full-time schooling.[219] The basic premise of the Directive is that while work by adolescents must be strictly regulated under the conditions laid down by the Directive, work by children is prohibited.[220]

In the case of children, Member States do, however, have the option to derogate from this basic prohibition in three circumstances. First, children can perform cultural, artistic, sports, or advertising work, subject to prior authorization by a competent authority,[221] provided that the activities are not harmful either to the safety, health, and development of children or to their attendance at school or their participation in vocational training programmes.[222] The Member States must also prescribe the working conditions for children taking advantage of this exception. Secondly, children over 14 can work under a combined work/training scheme or an 'in-plant work experience scheme'.[223] Thirdly, children over 14 can perform light work, defined to mean all work, taking into account the inherent nature of the tasks involved and the particular conditions under which they are to be performed, which is not likely to harm the health and safety or development of young people nor harm their attendance at school, their participation in vocational guidance and training or their capacity to benefit from the instruction received.[224] This exception would appear to allow children over 14 to continue to do newspaper rounds and baby-sitting, provided in both cases the time taken does not jeopardize their health, safety, and schooling. Member States can also permit 13-year-olds to perform designated types of light work provided that the Member States specify the conditions in which the work is to be performed.[225]

In addition, Member States have the option not to apply the Directive to occasional work or short-term work involving either domestic service in a private household or to work in family undertakings provided the work is not regarded as being harmful,

---

[218] Art. 3(b).

[219] Art. 3(c). Member States must ensure that the minimum working or employment age is not lower than the minimum age at which compulsory full-time schooling, as imposed by national law, ends or 15 years in any event.

[220] Arts. 1(1) and 4(1).

[221] However, in the case of children over 13, Member States can authorize the employment of children in cultural, artistic, sports, or advertising agencies (Art. 5(3)). Member States with a specific authorization system for modelling agencies can retain that system (Art. 5(4)).

[222] Art. 5(2)(ii).   [223] Art. 4(2)(b).   [224] Art. 3(d).   [225] Art. 4(3).

damaging, or dangerous to young people.[226] The accompanying memorandum explains that the Directive is not intended to apply to occasional or limited work in the family context, for example, work in the household or in the family business, whether agriculture (for example, grape picking or crop harvesting) or in a distributive or craft trade (for example, shelf-filling or other light shop work).[227]

3. HEALTH AND SAFETY

As with the Framework Directive 89/391 on health and safety, the Young Workers' Directive imposes general obligations on employers to take the necessary measures to protect the safety and health of all young workers permitted to work by the Directive.[228] This requires the employer to conduct a risk assessment before young people begin work and when there is any major change in their working conditions.[229] In particular, employers must have regard to the fitting-out and layout of the workplace, the nature, degree and duration of exposure to physical, biological, and chemical agents, the form, range and use of work equipment, the arrangement of the work process and the level of training and instruction given to young workers.[230] If this assessment reveals a risk to the physical or mental health, safety, or development of young people 'an appropriate *free* assessment and monitoring of their health must be provided',[231] possibly as part of the national health system, and involving the protective and preventive services referred to in Article 7 of Directive 89/391/EEC.[232] In addition, employers must inform both the young workers and their legal representatives of possible risks and measures adopted to protect their health and safety.[233]

Given the 'vulnerability of young people', due to their 'absence of awareness of existing or potential risks' or because 'young people have not yet fully matured', Member States must ensure that young people are protected from any specific risks[234] to their health, safety, and development. Young workers are also prohibited from being employed in the following categories of work:

- work which is beyond their physical or psychological capacity;
- work involving harmful radiation or exposure to agents which are toxic, carcinogenic, cause heritable genetic damage or chronically affect human health in any other way
- work which puts them at risk of accidents; or
- work where their health may suffer from extreme cold, heat, noise, vibration, or from handling heavy loads.

---

[226] Art. 2(2).   [227] COM(91) 543, 10.   [228] Art. 6(1).   [229] Art. 6(2).
[230] Art. 6(1) and (2).   [231] Art. 6(2).   [232] OJ [1989] L183/1. See Ch. 11.   [233] Art. 6(3).
[234] Art. 7(2). This includes work involving harmful exposure to the physical, biological and chemical agents referred to in point I of the Annex to the Young Workers' Directive and to the processes and work referred to in point II of the Annex. Changes to the Annex can be made in accordance with the procedure in Art. 17 of Dir. 89/391/EEC.

Exceptionally, derogations from these provisions can be made in the case of adolescents where it is indispensable for their vocational training, provided that their work is performed under the supervision of a 'designated worker'.[235]

4. WORKING TIME LIMITS

In the case of children permitted to perform light work or engage in a training scheme, the Directive limits their working time to:[236]

- eight hours a day and 40 hours a week for work performed under a combined work/training scheme or work experience scheme;[237]
- two hours on a school day and 12 hours a week for work performed outside the hours fixed for school attendance if this is permitted by national law; daily working time must not exceed seven hours, or eight hours in the case of children over the age of 15;
- seven hours a day and 35 hours a week for work performed during the school holiday period; eight hours a day and 40 hours a week in the case of the over 15s;
- seven hours a day and 35 hours a week for light work performed by children no longer subject to compulsory full-time schooling.

Adolescents can work up to eight hours a day and 40 hours a week.[238] Where daily working time is more than four-and-a-half hours, young people are entitled to a break of at least 30 minutes.[239]

Children cannot work between 8.00 p.m. and 6.00 a.m.[240] and adolescents between 10.00 p.m. and 6.00 a.m. or between 11.00 p.m. and 7.00 a.m.,[241] although adolescents may work at night under the supervision of an adult if Member States so provide, but not between midnight and 4.00 a.m.[242] However, Member States may authorize adolescents to work between midnight and 4.00 a.m. in the shipping or fisheries sectors, the armed forces, and the police, hospitals, and similar establishments, in cultural, artistic, sports, or advertising activities, where there are objective grounds for doing so and provided that adolescents are allowed suitable compensatory rest.[243]

---

[235] See Art. 7 of Dir. 89/391/EEC.   [236] Art. 8(1).
[237] Art. 8(1)(a). Time spent training counts as working time (Art. 8(3)). Member States can derogate from Art. 8(1)(a) but must determine the conditions for such derogation (Art. 8(5)).
[238] Art. 8(2). Member States can derogate from this provision either by way of exception or where there are objective grounds for so doing provided the Member State determines the conditions, limits and procedure for implementing such derogations (Art. 8(5)).
[239] Art. 12.   [240] Art. 9(1)(a).   [241] Art. 9(1)(b).   [242] Art. 9(2).
[243] Art. 9(2). Adolescents are also entitled to a free health assessment prior to any assignment to night work and at regular intervals thereafter, unless their work is of 'an exceptional nature' (Art. 9(3)).

5. REST PERIODS

For each 24-hour period, children are entitled to a minimum rest period of 14 consecutive hours and adolescents to 12 consecutive hours.[244] Although it appears that children can therefore work 10 hours a day and adolescents 14 hours a day, such an interpretation directly contradicts the requirements of Article 8 on working time. Further, for each seven-day period worked, both children and adolescents are entitled to a minimum rest period of two days, consecutive if possible, including in principle a Sunday.[245] Where justified by technical or organizational reasons, the minimum rest period may be reduced, but may in no circumstance be less than 36 consecutive hours.[246] However, extensive derogations are permitted to this rule, in the case of the shipping and fisheries sector, the armed forces or the police, work performed in hospitals or similar establishments, agriculture, tourism, hotels and catering, and activities involving periods of work split up over the day.[247]

It is also possible, in the case of adolescents, to derogate from the provisions on working time, night work, and rest periods in the case of *force majeure*, provided that the work is temporary, must be performed immediately, that adult workers are not available and that the adolescents are allowed equivalent compensatory rest time in the following three weeks.[248] Finally, children are permitted to work on a combined work/training scheme and must have a period free from work including, as far as possible, in the school holidays.[249] No minimum period of leave is specified nor is the situation of adolescents addressed. It had been thought that the Working Time Directive 2003/88[250] would fill the gap but a decision of the British Employment Appeal Tribunal[251] suggested that while the Working Time Directive applied to adult workers and young workers it did not apply to children.[252] Therefore a 15-year-old paper-boy who had delivered papers six days a week from the age of 13 was not entitled to four weeks' paid holiday.

6. CONCLUSIONS

The parallels between the Young Workers' Directive and Directive 2003/88 on Working Time are obvious, and concerns about its lack of flexibility and the burdens on small business apply to both. The Directive applies to all types of business regardless of size, in both the public and private sector.[253] Certain sectors of the economy are particularly affected, including the distributive trades, hotels and catering, services and events for the young. On the other hand, the ILO has criticized the Directive for not being compatible with the international conventions (a point strongly denied by the Commission).[254]

---

[244] Art. 10(1).

[245] Art. 10(2). The equivalent provision in the original Working Time Dir. 93/104 was annulled.

[246] Ibid.

[247] Art. 10(4). There must be objective grounds for derogation, workers must be granted compensatory rest time and the objectives set out in Art. 1 of the Directive must not be called into question.

[248] Art. 13.   [249] Art. 11.   [250] OJ [1993] L307/18.   [251] *Ashby* v. *Addison* [2003] IRLR 211.

[252] Under English law, children were covered by the Children and Young Persons Act 1933 which made no specific reference to annual leave entitlement but provided that a child was entitled to at least two consecutive weeks without employment during the school holidays.

[253] COM(91) 543 final—SYN 383, 51.   [254] WE/2/94, 20 January 1994.

Yet the Directive does not go as far as the Community Social Charter 1989 intended: Article 21 requires that young people who are in gainful employment must receive equitable remuneration in accordance with national practice, and Article 23 provides that following the end of compulsory education, young people must be entitled to receive initial vocational training of a sufficient duration to enable them to adapt to the requirements of their future working life. The choice of Article 153 TFEU as the appropriate legal basis has prevented the development of a more ambitious programme for young workers. This has been left to the European Employment Strategy (EES) which places much emphasis on the need to improve employment prospects for young people, especially those who leave school without relevant skills. Since its inception, tackling youth unemployment has been a priority for the EES and it is one of the areas in which substantive targets are laid down. Thus, under the 'employability' pillar the 1998 Guidelines required that every unemployed young person be offered a new start before reaching six months of unemployment (e.g. training, retraining) within five years, that Member States improve the quality of school to reduce 'substantially' the number of young people who drop out from school early, to ensure that they equip young people with greater ability to adapt to technological and economic changes.[255] In 2001 the Council added that Member States should develop measures aimed at halving by 2010 the number of 18 to 24-year-olds with only lower secondary level education who are not in further education and training.[256] This is now reinforced by the European Youth Pact, adopted at the same time as the Lisbon relaunch in March 2005, which aims to improve the education, training, mobility, vocational integration, and social inclusion of 'young Europeans' while facilitating the reconciliation of work and family life. The 2010 Employment Guidelines identifies similar aims.[257] For example, under Guideline 8, 'Developing a skilled workforce responding to labour market needs and promoting lifelong learning', the following is required:

> To support young people and in particular those not in employment, education or training, Member States, in cooperation with the social partners, should enact schemes to help those people find initial employment, job experience, or further education and training opportunities, including apprenticeships, and should intervene rapidly when young people become unemployed.

But all of this rings rather hollow when youth unemployment has reached nearly 20% in some peripheral euro-zone states.

D. WORKING CONDITIONS

Finally, this chapter considers two further measures adopted under the Social Charter Action Programme 1989 concerning working conditions: a Directive on the Proof of the Employment Contract 91/533/EEC[258] which is intended to harmonize the diverse

---

[255] Co. Res. 98/C 30/01.   [256] Council Dec. 2001/63 (OJ [2001] L22/18).
[257] Council Dec. 2010/707/EU (OJ [2010] L308/46).
[258] Council Dir. 91/533/EEC (OJ [1991] L288/32) on an employer's obligation to inform employees of the conditions applicable to the contract or employment relationship. See additionally COM(90) 563 final. Although the UK and Ireland were the only countries with pre-existing rules providing that most workers are entitled to a written statement of their terms and conditions, the UK abstained in the final vote.

national laws concerning the provision of information about working conditions, and an Opinion on an equitable wage.

1. PROOF OF EMPLOYMENT CONTRACT

1.1. Introduction

The Social Charter Action Programme 1989 recognized that the great diversity of terms of recruitment and multiplicity of types of employment contract might hinder the mobility of workers. It concluded that Union workers, particularly those covered by atypical contracts, must have their working conditions set out in writing, to ensure greater transparency in the respective rights and obligations of employers and employees throughout the Union market. The final text of Directive 91/533/EEC, inspired by British law, was rapidly adopted and is richer, more precise, and more demanding than the Commission's original proposal. In essence, the Directive obliges employers to provide all employees with a document containing information about the essential elements of their contract or employment relationship.

1.2. Material and personal scope of the Directive

The Directive applies to every paid employee having a contract *or* an employment relationship defined by the law in force in a Member State and/or governed by the law in force in a Member State.[259] These terms reflect a Continental distinction. For example, under German law the contract of employment (*Arbeitsvertrag*) is a contract of service by which the employee undertakes to perform work in accordance with instructions.[260] The contract of employment establishes an employment relationship (*Arbeitsverhältnis*). While the contract of employment consists only of the specific arrangements relating to work that are agreed between employer and employee, the employment relationship encompasses the entire legal relationship between the contracting parties. The rights and obligations concerned may be laid down either by the individual contract or by collective agreement or by law. If the contract of employment is invalid but the employee has already entered into employment, there still exists a valid employment relationship with retrospective effect, including all the rights and obligations between employer and employee in the form of a *de facto* employment relationship.[261] In a similar way, Italian law also recognizes a distinction between employment contract and employment relationship. An employment relationship (*rapporto di lavoro*) is the legal relationship in which the worker is obliged to work and the employer to remunerate this work. The employment relationship is brought about by the conclusion of a contract of employment (*contratto di lavoro*) between the worker and the employer.[262]

---

[259] Art. 1(1). It would appear that this definition does not apply to the self-employed.

[260] Civil Code 611.

[261] M. Weiss, *European Employment and Industrial Relations Glossary, Germany* (Sweet & Maxwell, London, 1992) paras. 82 and 85.

[262] T. Treu, *European Employment and Industrial Relations Glossary* (Sweet & Maxwell, London, 1991) paras. 188 and 561.

In considering the term 'employment relationship' the Commission, in its memo accompanying the draft Directive, envisaged both new forms of employment as well as variations on traditional forms, including distance work,[263] training schemes, work/training contracts, work outside the traditional workplace, job-sharing and on-call work. However, in order to 'maintain a certain degree of flexibility in employment relationships',[264] Member States can exclude two categories of employees from the Directive's scope. The first are those who have a contract or employment relationship not exceeding one month and/or with a working week not exceeding eight hours. It has been suggested[265] that such an exclusion may be indirectly discriminatory against women since a higher proportion of woman than men work part time. However, if the Court's reasoning in *Kirsammer*[266] is accepted, such discrimination may be objectively justified in order to secure flexibility.

The second category who may be excluded from the scope of the Directive are those employees of a casual and/or specific nature, provided that the non-application of the Directive is justified by objective considerations.[267] This derogation might apply to casual workers or seasonal workers such as fruit pickers, cleaners, hotel staff and others on very short-term contracts for occasional days or for a fixed purpose. The burden of proof would rest on the employer to justify the failure to provide the employee with the relevant information.

1.3. The employer's obligations to notify

Under Article 2(1) the employer must notify the employees of the *essential aspects* of the contract or employment relationship.[268] This must include—in a non-exhaustive list:[269]

(a) the identity of the parties;

(b) the place of work or, if there is no fixed or main place of work, a statement to that effect and details of the registered place of business or, where appropriate, the domicile of the employer;

(c) the title, grade, nature or category of work, and a brief description of the work;

(d) the date of commencement of the contract and,

(e) in the case of a temporary contract, its duration;

(f) the amount of paid leave;[270]

---

[263] See now the Telework Agreement concluded between the European intersectoral social partners (<http://www.etuc.org/a/579>, last accessed on 2 April 2012) considered further in Ch. 9.

[264] Preamble to Dir. 91/533/EEC.

[265] See J. Clark and M. Hall, 'The Cinderella Directive? Employee Rights to Information about Conditions Applicable to their Contract or Employment Relationship' (1992) 21 *ILJ* 106, 111.

[266] Case C–189/91 *Petra Kirsammer-Hack* v. *Sidal* [1993] ECR I–6185.   [267] Art. 1(2).

[268] Art. 2(1). 'Contract' will be used to refer to both contracts and employment relationships.

[269] Art. 2(2). The Court ruled in Case C–253/96 *Kampelmann and Others* v. *Landschaftsverband Westfalen-Lippe and Others* [1997] ECR I–6907 that Art. 2(2)(c) is sufficiently precise and unconditional to have direct effect.

[270] This information, together with the information in (g), (h), and (i) may be given by reference to the laws, regulations, administrative or statutory provisions or collective agreements governing those particular points: Art. 2(3). In Case C–350/99 *Lange* [2001] ECR I–1061, para. 24, the Court said that, by analogy, information about overtime could also be provided in this way.

(g) the length of the notice periods;

(h) the initial basic amount, the other component elements, and the frequency of payment of the employee's remuneration;

(i) the length of the employee's normal working day or working week;[271]

(j) where necessary the collective agreements governing the employee's conditions of work.

In *Lange*[272] the Court said that since Article 2(1) lays down the basic rule, Article 2(2) cannot reduce the scope of the general requirement.[273] Therefore, the Court ruled that, in addition to the elements listed in Article 2(2), any element which, in view of its importance, must be considered an essential element of the contract of employment of which it forms part must be notified to the employee.[274] On the facts of the case, the Court said that this applies in particular to a term under which an employee is obliged to work overtime whenever requested to do so by his employer.

Some Continental commentators suggest that the obligation to inform the employee of the essential aspects of the contract indicates that all these aspects must have been agreed for the relationship to have been formed correctly. However, the position under English law is different. As Parker LJ said in *Eagland*,[275] where no terms exist relating to, for example, holiday pay and sick pay, the requirement to have a written statement does not empower or require the tribunal to impose on the parties terms which had not been agreed.

Article 3(1) provides that this information must be given to the employee 'not later than two months[276] after the commencement of employment' in the form of a written contract of employment and/or a letter of engagement and/or one or more other written documents, where one of these documents contains at least all the information required by (a)–(d), (h), and (i). Alternatively, the employer can provide the employee with a written declaration signed by the employer containing the information listed in (a)–(j). The written declaration can either take the place of the written documents or can supplement these documents. Employees going to work abroad for more than a month must be provided with additional information, including details of the duration of the period abroad, the currency to be used for the payment of remuneration, benefits in cash or kind, and details of their repatriation.[277]

Article 5 provides that if the terms and conditions of employment are changed in the course of the contract, the employee must be notified in writing at the earliest opportunity, and not later than one month after the date of entry into force of the change. This rule does not apply if the contractual terms are altered as a result of a change in the laws, regulations, and administrative or statutory provisions or collective agreements.

---

[271] But not including overtime: Case C–350/99 *Lange* [2001] ECR I–1061, paras. 16–19.

[272] Case C–350/99 *Lange* [2001] ECR I–1061.   [273] Paras. 21–2.

[274] Para. 23.   [275] *Eagland* v. *British Telecommunications* [1992] IRLR 323.

[276] If the work comes to an end before the two months expires the information must be provided by the end of the contract at the latest.

[277] Art. 4.

1.4. The probative value of the written statement

According to Article 6, the rules laid down by the Directive do not prejudice national rules and practice concerning the form of the contract, proof of the existence and the content of the contract, and any relevant procedural rules. In the UK the written statement of terms is merely evidence of the terms of the contract; it does not constitute the contract itself. However, as Browne-Wilkinson J said in *Systems Floors* v. *Daniel*,[278] the written particulars represent 'strong prima facie evidence' of the contract terms. The written terms do however, place a 'heavy burden on the employer to show that the actual terms of the contract are different from those which he has set out in the statutory statement'. This 'heavy burden' does not apply to the employee who wishes to show that the contract terms are different to those in the statement.[279]

The probative value of the written statement of terms was considered by the Court of Justice in *Kampelmann*.[280] It said that although under Article 6 of the Directive national rules concerning the burden of proof are not to be affected by the Directive, the employer's obligation to notify an employee of the essential aspects of the contract or employment relationship had to be given some meaning. Therefore, employees had to be able to use the information contained in the notification referred to in Article 2(1) as evidence before the national courts, particularly in disputes concerning essential aspects of the contract or employment relationship. The Court therefore ruled that national courts had to apply and interpret their national rules on the burden of proof in the light of the purpose of the Directive. Thus, they had to give the notification referred to in Article 2(1) such evidential weight as to allow it to serve as factual proof of the essential aspects of the contract of employment or employment relationship. The notification also had to enjoy the same presumption as to its correctness as would attach, in domestic law, to any similar document drawn up by the employer and communicated to the employee.[281]

The Court added that since the Directive did not itself lay down any rules of evidence, proof of the essential aspects of the contract or employment relationship could not depend solely on the employer's notification under Article 2(1). The employer therefore had to be allowed to bring any evidence to the contrary, by showing that the information in the notification was either inherently incorrect or had been shown to be so in fact.[282] Thus, the judgment in *Kampelmann* is compatible with the approach adopted by the British courts outlined above. Nevertheless, as Kenner concludes,[283] while the central thrust of *Kampelmann* has fortified Directive 91/533 as a means of transmitting contractual information in a transparent form, it has also helped to reveal its most serious limitation. Article 6 ensures that the employer retains a large measure of control over the contractual bargain; the Directive is merely concerned with how that information is conveyed. Where the framework of regulation at national level is stripped

---

[278] [1982] ICR 54, 58.   [279] *Robertson* v. *British Gas Corporation* [1983] ICR 351.
[280] Case C–253/96 *Kampelmann* [1997] ECR I–6907.   [281] Para. 33.   [282] Para. 34.
[283] J. Kenner, 'Statement or Contract—Some Reflections on the EC Employee Information (Contract or Employment Relationship) Directive after *Kampelmann*' (1999) 28 *ILJ* 205.

away and no longer offers a minimum level of protection in the enumerated areas there is no compulsion on the employer to include them in the contractual terms and the Directive offers no protection.

1.5. Implementation and remedies

Member States may introduce rules which are more favourable to employees.[284] They must also ensure that employees who consider themselves wronged by failure to comply with the obligations arising from the Directive can pursue their claims by judicial process.[285] Thus, as usual, remedies are a matter for the Member States. The most effective remedy in the circumstances would be an order that the employer produce a written statement compatible with the provisions of the Directive. The Directive does not require this but clearly envisages it as a possibility: Article 15(2) provides that, with the exception of expatriate employees, workers on temporary contracts and employees not covered by collective agreements, prior to seeking a judicial remedy the employee must notify the employer who has 15 days to reply. In *Lange*[286] the Court made clear that no provision of the Directive requires an essential element of the contract of employment that has not been mentioned in a written document or has not been mentioned with sufficient precision to be regarded as inapplicable.[287]

2. PAY

2.1. Introduction

Article 5 of the Community Social Charter 1989 provides that 'all employment shall be fairly remunerated'. To this end, and in accordance with arrangements applying in each country, 'workers shall be assured of an equitable wage, i.e. a wage sufficient to enable them to have a decent standard of living'. The term 'equitable' wage is carefully selected. No reference is made to a 'minimum' wage. Respecting the principle of subsidiarity, the Commission said in its Action Programme that wage setting is a matter for the Member States and the two sides of industry alone. It recognizes that the majority of the Member States, either through their constitution, legislation or by means of international agreements to which they are party, guarantee the right of workers to sufficient remuneration to provide them and their families with a decent standard of living. As a result, it recognizes that it is not the Union's task to set a decent reference wage. It argued that low pay gives a competitive advantage: minimum wage provision means that richer countries would deprive poorer countries of their competitive advantage.[288] Although the link between low pay and competitiveness has been disputed,[289] and the evidence suggesting that the introduction of a minimum wage would cause large-scale unemployment is not conclusive, the Commission has nevertheless exercised extreme caution in this area, being prepared only to 'outline certain basic

---

[284] Art. 7.   [285] Art. 8(1).   [286] Case C–350/99 *Lange* [2001] ECR I–1061, para. 29.
[287] Para. 29.   [288] House of Lords Evidence 1989, 16.
[289] S. Deakin and F. Wilkinson, *The Economics of Employment Rights* (IER, London, 1991), esp. at 32–3.

principles on equitable wages' in a non-legally-binding Opinion.[290] Otherwise its activities have concentrated on the reform of national systems of social protection to ensure that individuals are not discouraged by the operation of national social security systems from going back to work and therefore earning enough money to support themselves. We consider this issue in outline in the final part of this chapter; first we shall look at the Opinion on an equitable wage.

2.2. The Opinion on an equitable wage

Article 1 of the Opinion defines an equitable wage as meaning 'that all workers should receive a reward for work done which in the context of the society in which they live and work is fair and sufficient to enable them to have a decent standard of living'. Four principles underpin the Commission's approach: the first involves the recognition of the role of investment and training in order to achieve high productivity and high quality employment; the second restates the proposition that the pursuit of equitable wages is to be seen as part of the Union's basic objectives of greater economic and social cohesion and more harmonious development; the third recognizes that discriminatory wage practices should be eliminated; and the fourth recommends that attitudes to traditionally low-paid groups should be reassessed. In the context of discrimination, the commitment to pay an equitable wage to all workers, 'irrespective of gender, disability, race, religion, ethnic origin or nationality', was, at the time, an important step forward because it went further than the commitment contained elsewhere in Union law merely to equal pay without discrimination on the grounds of sex or nationality.

The Commission envisaged a three-pronged plan of action. First, there needs to be improved transparency of the labour market by better collection and dissemination of comparable statistical information about wage structures in the Union. Secondly, the right to an equitable wage must be respected, in particular by prohibiting discrimination, ensuring fair treatment for workers in all age groups and for home workers, and establishing the mechanisms for negotiated minima and the strengthening of collective bargaining arrangements. In addition, Member States must check that wages agreed under the contract of employment are paid in full and that employees are 'correctly paid in respect of periods of leave and sickness'. In addition, Member States must ensure that 'the measures taken do not force low-paid workers into the informal economy and do not encourage unlawful employment practices'. However, by 2006, undeclared work had become 'a particularly worrying and enduring feature of today's labour markets, often associated with cross-border labour movements. Being the main contributing factor to social dumping, it is responsible not only for the exploitation of workers but also for distortions to competition'.[291]

Thirdly, the Opinion says that action should be taken to improve the long-term productivity and earnings potential of the workforce. Again this has become a matter of major interest for the EU. For example, in the 2010 Employment Guidelines, a key

---

[290] COM(93) 388 final.   [291] 'The Modernisation of Labour Law' Green Paper: COM(2006) 708.

aspect of Guideline 7 (Increasing labour market participation of women and men, reducing structural unemployment and promoting job quality), says:

> Policies to make work pay remain important. In order to increase competitiveness and raise participation levels, particularly for the low-skilled, and in line with economic policy guideline 2, Member States should encourage the right framework conditions for wage bargaining and labour cost development consistent with price stability and productivity trends. Member States should review tax and benefit systems, and public services capacity to provide the support needed, in order to increase labour force participation and stimulate labour demand.

Finally, the Social Partners are invited to address all the issues raised in the Opinion, in particular to examine what contribution they can make to ensuring the right of every worker to an equitable wage. Indeed, the Social Partners have already considered questions relating to the adaptation of remuneration systems as part of the social dialogue.[292] However, little further action can be expected at Union level on matters relating to pay. Article 153(5) TFEU provides that the provisions of Article 153 do not apply to pay, and so the Union's competence is at best circumscribed. Nevertheless, countries in receipt of a bailout have cut wages as part of their labour market reform programmes. Yet the Commission maintained that 'setting minimum wages at appropriate levels can help prevent growing in-work poverty'.[292A]

2.3. Supporting measures

(a) Recommendation 92/441

Accompanying the Commission's Opinion on an equitable wage is the Council Recommendation 92/441/EEC on common criteria concerning sufficient resources and social assistance in the social protection systems.[293] While the former concentrates on fair remuneration for work performed with particular attention paid to the more vulnerable members of the labour force, the latter concerns guaranteed minimum income from all sources, and contains a more resounding commitment to respect for human rights. Article 1 requires Member States to:

> recognise the basic right of a person to sufficient resources and social assistance to live in a manner compatible with human dignity as part of a comprehensive and consistent drive to combat social exclusion, and to adapt their social protection systems.

It then lays down principles according to which this right must be assured. In particular, the resources should be provided on an individual basis,[294] should not be time-limited,[295] and should be fixed at a level considered 'sufficient to cover essential needs with regard to respect for human dignity, taking account of living standards and price levels in the Member State concerned, for different types and sizes of household'.[296] Thus, the Recommendation guidance is carefully circumscribed by respect for the principle of subsidiarity and the divergence of national systems.[297]

---

[292] Commission, *Adaptation of Remuneration Systems*, Luxembourg, 1993.   [292A] COM(2012) 173, 9.

[293] COM(91) 161 final (OJ [1992] L245/46). See additionally Art. 10 of the Community Social Charter 1989 and Art. 34 of the Charter of Fundamental Rights of the European Union 2000.

[294] Para. I.B.2.   [295] Para. I.B.4.   [296] Para. I.C.1(a).

[297] See further the emphasis on subsidiarity in COM(97) 102.

(b) Recommendation 92/442

Recommendation 92/442,[298] by contrast, provides guidance on the co-ordination of national policies. Although still hemmed in by the principle of subsidiarity and respect for the autonomy of the national systems, it is more ambitious. It begins with four basic principles for social protection policies. First, it recommends that Member States give any person legally resident in its territory, regardless of resources, access to the state's health service.[299] It also recommends that states provide employed workers who retire or interrupt their careers with replacement income to maintain their standard of living.[300] Second, social benefits must be provided on a non-discriminatory basis without regard to 'nationality, race, sex, religion, customs or political opinion'[301] and must be granted according to the principles of fairness,[302] so that beneficiaries of social benefits receive their share from the improvements in the standard of living of the population as a whole. Third, it recommends that social policies should adapt to the development of behaviour and of family structures responsive to changes in the labour market; and fourth, that social protection should be administered with maximum efficiency. The Recommendation then makes specific suggestions in respect of six policy areas including sickness, maternity, and unemployment.[303]

(c) Reform of the National Systems of Social Protection

Reform of the social protection systems has now become a major concern of the European Union. In its 1993 the White Paper on Growth, Competitiveness and Employment[304] the Commission argued that, due to inappropriate social protection schemes and employment services, there was insufficient motivation to work. It also expressed concerns about the funding of these schemes by high non-wage costs, particularly in the form of statutory levies and charges, through which an equivalent of 40 per cent of the Union's GDP was channelled. These concerns were picked up in the Commission's 1997 Communication *Modernising and Improving Social Protection in the European Union*.[305] While recognizing that publicly funded social protection systems (social security and social assistance) established decades ago have played a 'fundamental role in ensuring income redistribution and cohesion, and in maintaining political stability and economic progress over the life of the Union', the systems were in need of modernization to ensure their continued effectiveness. Although it said that social protection could be a productive factor, it expressed concerns about the level of non-wage costs and the need for policies designed to improve flexibility and to provide security. This was reflected in the Entrepreneurship pillar of the Employment Guidelines which envisaged setting a target for gradually reducing the overall tax burden and, where appropriate, a target for gradually reducing the fiscal pressure on labour and non-wage

---

[298] OJ [1992] L245/46.   [299] Para. I.A.1(b).   [300] Para. I.A.1(d).

[301] Para. I.A.2(a).   [302] Para. I.A.2(b).

[303] See additionally Council Resolution on the role of social protection systems in the fight against unemployment (OJ [1996] C386/3).

[304] Bull. Supp. 6/93, 124, 136ff.   [305] COM(97) 102.

labour costs, in particular on relatively unskilled and low-paid labour.[306] This theme was carried through into the Integrated Guidelines of the Lisbon relaunch.[307] The tenor of these statements suggests that the results of future co-ordination of social protection may lead to the reduction in the level of benefits rather than their improvement, especially for those Member States participating in EMU which have agreed to limit public deficit to 3 per cent and have a maximum of 60 per cent of GDP in public debt.[308] This has certainly come to pass in those countries, such as Portugal at the heart of the Eurozone storm, where the troika has insisted on significant cuts to benefits.

The Commission followed up its 1997 Communication with a Concerted strategy on Modernization of Social Protection[309] which argued for an agenda of deepened co-operation based on four key objectives within the overall challenge of modernization: (1) to make work pay and to provide secure income; (2) to make pensions safe and pension systems sustainable; (3) to promote social inclusion; and (4) to ensure high quality and sustainable health care.[310] This strategy was to be supported by 'enhanced mechanisms for exchanging information and monitoring policy developments in order to give the process more visibility and political profile'—in essence OMC-style techniques facilitated by the establishment of a Social Protection Committee.[311] This approach was endorsed by the Lisbon European Council,[312] which noted that developed social protection systems were a key pillar of the European Social model, and confirmed by the Commission.[313] Member States now present National Action Plans for Inclusion and National Strategy reports on pensions, on the basis of which the Commission and Council agree a Joint Inclusion Report and a Joint Pensions report. The OMC processes have now been strengthened and streamlined with the Integrated Guidelines.[314]

E. CONCLUSIONS

With the discussion of social protection, we have come a long way from the health and safety Directives with which we started this chapter. The discussion does, however, emphasize that it is not possible easily to compartmentalize those areas of law in which the European Union has intervened. In its Green Paper on Social Policy 1993[315] the

---

[306] Council Res. 98/128 on the 1998 Employment Guidelines (OJ [1998] 30/1).

[307] See, e.g., Council Dec. 2005/600 (OJ [2005] L205/21): Guideline No. 22.

[308] See E. Guild, 'How Can Social Protection Survive EMU? A United Kingdom Perspective' (1999) 24 ELRev. 22.

[309] COM(99) 347, 4.

[310] This was endorsed by the Council in its conclusions of 17 December 1999 on the strengthening of cooperation for modernizing and improving social protection (OJ [2000] C8/7).

[311] Initially established by Council Dec. 2000/436/EC (OJ [2000] L172/26) which was repealed and replaced by Council Dec. 2004/689/EC (OJ [2004] L314/8) based on Art. 160 TFEU (ex 144 EC).

[312] Lisbon European Council, Presidency Conclusions, 23–24 March 2000, para. 31.

[313] Communication, Strengthening the social dimension of the Lisbon strategy: streamlining open coordination in the field of social protection (COM(2003) 261).

[314] COM(2005) 706.   [315] COM(93) 551.

Commission advocated extending legislative action at Union level still further to include protection against: individual dismissal; the prohibition of discrimination against workers who wish to enforce their rights or who refuse to perform unlawful tasks; the right to payment of wages on public holidays and during illness; and the right of the worker to be heard in internal company matters which concern him or her personally. With the exception of worker information and consultation, none of these plans for a 'European labour law' have come to fruition. Worse still, from a labour law point of view, is the challenge to national law rules (in these key areas where there is no EU legislation) by the troika's conditions attached to those states in receipt of bail-out funds. Pay has been cut, pensions frozen and dismissal law deregulated. For those states, EU law no longer equates with raising the standard of living, but a deterioration. Challenges to these reforms based on the Charter[316] are unlikely to succeed, although challenges based on the European Social Charter 1961 may be more successful.[317] The Lisbon strategy has diverted the Union's attention away from enacting an ever wider range of employment rights and focused more on different forms of regulation, especially OMC, aimed at co-ordinating national policies in a range of areas, including social protection. Where there has been legislation, it has concentrated on the EU's areas of specialism: equality, health and safety, information and consultation, and employees' rights on the restructuring of a business. It is to this latter subject that we now turn.

[316]   See C. Barnard, 'Equality, Solidarity and the Charter in Crisis: the case of dismissal' in N. Countouris and M. Freedland (eds), Resocialising Europe and the Mutualisation of Risks to Workers, forthcoming.
[317]   See e.g. the various complaints against Greece registered in Jan. and Feb. 2011 and Jan. 2012.

PART V

EMPLOYEE RIGHTS ON RESTRUCTURING ENTERPRISES

13

TRANSFERS OF
UNDERTAKINGS

A. INTRODUCTION

In the early 1970s there was much concern about the absence of a 'social face' to the then Common Market. In particular there was a fear that, in the inevitable process of restructuring brought about by increased competition as barriers to trade were removed, individual employees would suffer. For example, they might see their part of the business transferred to another owner who would either want to dismiss extraneous employees or at least change their terms and conditions of employment. Alternatively, they might face redundancy when their employer decided to downsize and so make a large number of workers redundant, or they might find that their employer could not compete and became insolvent, leaving the employees with arrears of salary outstanding.

As a result, three important Directives were adopted as part of the 1974–1976 Social Action Programme aimed at addressing the social consequences of economic change: Directive 77/187 on employees' rights on the transfer of undertakings,[1] Directive 75/129 on collective redundancies[2] and Directive 80/987 on insolvency.[3] Since these Directives were drafted to facilitate the restructuring of enterprises with a view to making them more competitive and efficient, they did not question the managerial prerogative either to undertake the restructuring or to dismiss employees. Instead, the Directives aimed to address the social consequences of these managerial decisions and mitigate their effects. In this respect the Directives were intended both to encourage a greater degree of industrial democracy and to provide an element of social protection.[4]

The three Directives, as originally conceived, focused on restructuring at *national* level. With the advent of the internal market programme in 1986 the focus shifted towards the social consequences of *transnational* corporate restructuring, caused by the need of a market economy to establish, on the most appropriate sites, 'businesses capable of implementing the large-scale economic operations which a large market is likely to require'.[5] As a result, the Collective Redundancies Directive was revised by Directive

---

[1] Council Dir. 77/187/EEC (OJ [1977] L61/126).   [2] OJ [1975] L48/29.   [3] OJ [1980] L283/23.
[4] R. Blainpain, recalling the discussions held in a group of labour law experts from different Member States, *Labour Law and Industrial Relations of the European Community* (Kluwer, Deventer, 1991), 153.
[5] COM(94) 300, 3.

92/56[6] to give it a transnational dimension. It was subsequently consolidated in Directive 98/59.[7] Directive 77/187 on Transfers of Undertakings was also revised by Directive 98/50,[8] in the light of the Court's now extensive jurisprudence, and was subsequently consolidated in Directive 2001/23.[9] The Insolvency Directive was amended by Directive 87/164,[10] substantially revised by Directive 2002/74,[11] and finally replaced by Directive 2008/94.[12]

We shall now examine these Directives in turn. In this chapter we consider the most litigated Directive, Directive 2001/23 on Transfers of Undertakings, sometimes referred to as the Acquired Rights Directive; in the next chapter we examine the Directives on Collective Redundancies and Insolvency.

B. TRANSFERS OF UNDERTAKINGS: OVERVIEW

Since 1928 French law has required that, if there is a change in the juridical situation of an employer, for example as a result of succession, sale, or fusion, all contracts of employment existing on the date of the transfer will continue between the new employer and the employees of the enterprise. This provision was introduced at the behest of employers to ensure that, on the date of the transfer, not only were the assets of the business transferred but so was the workforce, thereby ensuring that the new employer had the necessary skilled workers to operate the equipment. The French position can, however, be contrasted with the approach adopted by other states. For example, in the UK the employment contract was considered to be a personal contract which could not be transferred to another employer. The new employer could therefore not expect to receive a trained workforce in the event of a transfer, but neither could employees be guaranteed any job security.

Directive 77/187 (now Directive 2001/23) on transfers of undertakings favoured the French position in preference to the common law rule.[13] The Preamble to the Directive recognized that 'economic trends are bringing in their wake, at both national and [Union] level, changes in the structure of undertakings, through transfers of undertakings'. The Preamble continued that it was 'necessary to provide for the protection of employees in the event of a change of employer, in particular, to ensure that their rights are safeguarded'. The Court has been particularly influenced by this wording,[14] and has,

---

[6] Council Dir. 92/56/EEC (OJ [1992] L245/3).   [7] OJ [1998] L225/16.   [8] OJ [1998] L201/88.
[9] OJ [2001] L82/16.   [10] OJ [1987] L66/11.   [11] OJ [2002] L270/10.   [12] OJ [2008] L283/36.
[13] The original (1977) Directive was significantly watered down from earlier drafts: P. Elias, 'The Transfer of Undertakings: A Reluctantly Acquired Right' (1982) 3 *Company Lawyer* 147, 156, described the 'protections afforded to employees are now but a pale shadow of what might once have been anticipated'.
[14] See e.g. Case 135/83 *Abels* v. *Bedrijfsvereniging voor de Metaalindustrie en de Electrotechnische Industrie* [1985] ECR 469, para. 6; Case 19/83 *Wendelboe* v. *L J Music* [1985] ECR 457, para. 8; Case 105/84 *Foreningen af Arbejdsledere i Danmark* v. *Danmols Inventar* [1985] ECR 2639, para. 15; Case 24/85 *Spijkers* v. *Benedik* [1986] ECR 1119, para. 6; Case C–29/91 *Sophie Redmond Stichting* v. *Bartol* [1992] ECR I–3189; Case C–392/92 *Schmidt* v. *Spar und Leihkasse* [1994] ECR I–1311, para. 15; Case C–399/96 *Europièces* v. *Wilfried Sanders and Automotive Industries Holding Company SA* [1998] ECR I–6965, para. 37.

at times, been prepared to give a purposive interpretation to the Directive to 'ensure as far as possible that the contract of employment or employment relationship continues unchanged with the transferee, in order to prevent the workers concerned from being placed in a less favourable position solely as a result of the transfer'.[15]

The Directive establishes three pillars of protection for employees. First, it provides for the automatic transfer of the employment relationship with all of its rights and obligations from the transferor A, the natural or legal person who, by reason of the transfer, ceases to be the employer in the undertaking[16] to the transferee B, the natural or legal person who becomes the employer[17] in the event of a transfer (see Figure 13.1).[18] Secondly, it protects workers against dismissal[19] by the transferor or transferee. This is, however, subject to the employer's right to dismiss employees for 'economic, technical or organisational reasons entailing changes in the workforce'.[20] Thirdly, the Directive requires the transferor and the transferee to inform and consult the representatives of the employees affected by the transfer.[21] These three pillars of protection are minimum requirements:[22] Member States are free either to apply laws, regulations or administrative provisions which are more favourable to employees or to promote or permit more favourable collective agreements or agreements between the Social Partners[23] which are more favourable to employees.

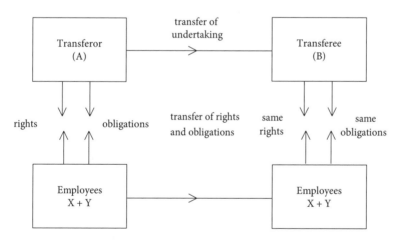

FIG. 13.1. Consequences of a transfer of an undertaking.

---

[15] Case 287/86 *Landsorganisationen i Danmark for Tjenerforbundet i Danmark* v. *Ny Mølle Kro*, [1987] ECR 5465, para. 25; Case C–478/03 *Celtec Ltd* v. *Astley* [2005] ECR I–4389, para. 26.

[16] Art. 2(1)(a). In Case C–242/09 *Albron Catering* v. *FNV Bondgenoten* [2010] ECR I–000 the Court ruled that the transferor could be the non-contractual employer to which the employees were assigned on a permanent basis.

[17] Arts. 2(1)(b).   [18] Art. 3(1).   [19] Art. 4(1).   [20] Art. 4(1), second sentence.
[21] Art. 7.   [22] Art. 8.   [23] Ibid.

The Directive is intended as a means of 'partial harmonisation'.[24] This means that it is not intended to 'establish a uniform level of protection throughout the [Union] on the basis of common criteria'.[25] Therefore national law still has a significant role to play, particularly in defining key terms such as 'employee'.[26] National law also prescribes the consequences of a refusal to be transferred[27] and the sanction in the case of the failure to inform and consult worker representatives and the dismissal of a worker in the event of a transfer.[28] The inevitable consequence of partial harmonization is a certain divergence in the level of employee protection across the European Union.

The Directive is not without its critics, who argue that it interferes with free enterprise. They say that it severely restricts contractors in their ability to restructure their workforces, or to devise new, performance-related arrangements or to introduce innovative ways of doing the work, thus interfering with any anticipated increase in efficiency. They also say that it dissuades a potential transferee from acquiring the undertaking.[29] Not surprisingly, the Commission makes a different assessment. It says:

> Generally speaking, as far as legislation is concerned, the effectiveness in social terms of the protection afforded by the Directive is beyond dispute. The Directive has proved to be an invaluable instrument for the protection of workers in the event of the reorganisation of an undertaking, by ensuring peaceful and consensual economic and technological restructuring and providing minimum standards for promoting fair competition in the context of such changes.[30]

The rights outlined above are dependent on there being a transfer of an undertaking. Determining the meaning of this crucial gateway criterion is therefore the starting point of the discussion that follows.

---

[24] Case 105/84 *Foreningen af Arbejdsledere i Danmark* v. *Danmols Inventar* [1985] ECR 2639, para. 26. See A. Garde, 'Partial harmonisation and European Social Policy: A Case Study on the Acquired Rights Directive' (2002–3) 5 *CYELS*. 173.

[25] Case 105/84 [1985] ECR 2639, para. 26.

[26] Case 105/84 *Danmols Inventar* [1985] ECR 2639, para. 16, and now Art. 2(1)(d) of Dir. 2001/23 considered below.

[27] Joined Cases C–132, 138 and 139/91 *Katsikas* v. *Konstantinidis* and *Skreb and Schroll* v. *PCO Stavereibetrieb Paetz & Co. Nachfolger GmbH* [1992] ECR I–6577.

[28] Art. 9.

[29] Earl Howe, Hansard, HL, Vol. 533, col. 148, discussed in B. Napier, 'CCT, Marketing Testing and Employment Rights: The Effects of TUPE and the Acquired Rights Directive' (1993) *Institute of Employment Rights*, 12. See additionally the arguments of the Italian government in Case C–362/89 *d'Urso* [1991] ECR I–4105.

[30] Commission memorandum on Acquired Rights of Workers in Cases of Transfers of Undertakings (<http://europa.eu/rapid/pressReleasesAction.do?reference=IP/97/199&format=HTML&aged=1&language=EN&guiLanguage=en> (last accessed 2 April 2012)). This memo provides guidelines on the application of Directive 2001/23 based on the Court's case law. See generally J. Hunt, 'The Court of Justice as a Policy Actor: the Acquired Rights Directive' (1998) 18 *Legal Studies* 336.

C. WHEN IS THERE A TRANSFER OF AN UNDERTAKING?

1. INTRODUCTION

According to Article 1(1)(a), the Directive applies to 'any transfer of an undertaking, business or part of an undertaking or business to another employer as a result of a legal transfer or merger'.[31] This provision has been the subject of considerable litigation, particularly regarding the meaning of the two key terms 'transfer of an undertaking' and 'legal transfer'. At first it seemed that the transfer of an undertaking had to occur as a direct consequence of a legal transfer or merger.[32] However, depending on the nature of the questions referred,[33] subsequent cases indicate that the two concepts are distinct and require the answer to two separate questions:[34]

- is the transfer a legal transfer within the meaning of the Directive (e.g. sale, contracting-out, leasing)? If so,

- is there a transfer of an undertaking on the facts, applying the criteria laid down by the Court in *Spijkers*[35] (considered below). This decision is usually a matter for the national courts.

Some of the uncertainty generated by the subsequent case law was supposed to have been removed by the amendment to the 1977 Directive, now found in Article 1(b) of Directive 2001/23. This provides that 'there is a transfer, within the meaning of this Directive, where there is a transfer of an economic entity which retains its identity'. There are now three elements that need to be shown: (1) there is an economic entity; (2) which has been transferred; and (3) that entity retains its identity following the transfer. We shall look at these in turn.

2. ECONOMIC ENTITY

Article 1(b) provides that the economic entity (the undertaking) is an 'organised grouping of resources which has the objective of pursuing an economic activity, whether or not that activity is central or ancillary'. An organized grouping of resources can be a single employee.[36]

---

[31] The Directive does not apply to sea-going vessels (Art. 1(3)). The Commission proposed that the rights conferred by the Directive, with the exception of rights relating to information and consultation, should also apply to sea-going vessels (Art. 1(4) of 94/C274/08) but this was not adopted in the final draft.

[32] Case 135/83 *Abels* [1985] ECR 469.

[33] C. De Groot, 'The Council Directive on the Safeguarding of Employees Rights in the Event of Transfers of Undertakings: An Overview of the Case Law' (1993) 30 *CMLRev.* 331.

[34] Case C–29/91 *Dr Sophie Redmond v Bartol* [1992] ECR I–3189, para. 9. See additionally Case C–392/92 *Schmidt* v. *Spar und Leihkasse* [1994] ECR I–1311.

[35] Case 24/85 *Spijkers* v. *Benedik* [1986] ECR 1119.

[36] Case C–392/92 *Schmidt* [1994] ECR I–1311.

Scattolon[37] provides more detail as to what constitutes an undertaking. The Court (Grand Chamber) said:[38]

> The term 'undertaking'... covers any economic entity organised on a stable basis, whatever its legal status and method of financing. Any grouping of persons and assets enabling the exercise of an economic activity pursuing a specific objective and which is sufficiently structured and independent will therefore constitute such an entity...

The Court continued that the term 'economic activity' covers 'any activity consisting in offering goods or services on a given market', adding that 'services which, without falling within the exercise of public powers, are carried out in the public interest and without a profit motive and are in competition with those offered by operators pursuing a profit motive have been classified as economic activities'. It therefore found on the facts that the activities carried out by the transferred workers (cleaning and maintenance of the premises and administrative tasks) were of an economic nature.

However, the Court added in *Scattolon* that activities falling within the exercise of public powers do not constitute an economic activity, citing inter alia *Henke*.[39] Henke was employed as secretary to the mayor's office of the municipality of Schierke. When the municipality of Schierke and other municipalities formed an 'administrative collectivity', to which they transferred administrative functions, Henke was dismissed. The Court ruled that the reorganization of structures of the public administration or the transfer of administrative functions between public administrative authorities did not constitute a 'transfer of an undertaking' within the meaning of the Directive.[40] In a terse judgment in which no cases were cited, the Court said that the purpose of a number of municipalities grouping together was to improve the performance of those municipalities' administrative tasks.[41] The transfer carried out between the municipality and the administrative collectivity related only to activities involving 'the exercise of public authority'.[42] The Court said that even if it was assumed that those activities had aspects of an economic nature, they could only be ancillary.[43]

Therefore, in *Henke* the Court focused on the fact that the authority was not a business exercising an economic activity but was involved with public administration exercising public law powers. The Court, however, made no reference to its earlier decision in *Sophie Redmond*[44] where it had considered that the term 'legal transfer' covered the situation where a public authority decided to terminate the subsidy paid to one legal person, as a result of which the activities of that person were fully and definitively terminated, and to transfer it to another legal person with a similar aim. It also did not refer to *Commission* v. *UK*[45] where the Court found that the 'non-commercial venture' exclusion from the then British Regulations implementing the Directive breached the Directive.

Nevertheless, the legislature has followed the Court's approach in *Henke*. Article 1(1)(c), introduced by Directive 98/50, provides: 'An administrative reorganisation of public

---

[37] Case C–101/10 *Scattolon* v. *Ministero dell'Istruzione, dell'Universita et della ricerca* [2011] ECR I–000.
[38] Para. 42.   [39] Case C–298/94 *Henke* [1996] ECR I–4989, para. 17.
[40] Para. 14.   [41] Para. 16.   [42] Para. 17.   [43] Ibid.
[44] Case C–29/91 [1992] ECR I–1311.   [45] Case C–382/92 [1994] ECR I–2435.

administrative authorities, or the transfer of administrative functions between public administrative authorities, is not a transfer within the meaning of this Directive'. However, in subsequent cases, the Court appears to have given a restrictive reading to its decision in *Henke*.[46] For example, in *Sánchez Hidalgo*,[47] the Court said that where a public body, such as a municipality, contracted out a service (the provision of home help for disadvantaged people), this did not involve the exercise of public authority, and so the Directive still applied.[48] In *Collino*,[49] a case concerning the reorganization of the Italian telephone services and the transfer of the employees from a state body to a state owned company, the Court endorsed *Sánchez Hidalgo*, upheld *Sophie Redmond*, and concluded that the Italian reorganization fell within the scope of the Directive.[50]

The Court reached similar conclusions in *Mayeur*.[51] It found that the transfer to the city of Metz of activities previously carried out by APIM, a non-profit making association set up as an independent entity by the city of Metz, funded by the city to promote the attractions of Metz, did constitute a transfer of an undertaking. By referring to the broad definition of undertaking,[52] to the fact that APIM was a distinct legal entity from the city of Metz,[53] and to the fact that APIM carried out an economic activity (publicity and information services on behalf of the city of Metz) the Court concluded that there was a transfer of an undertaking. It said that 'activity of this kind, consisting in the provision of services, is economic in nature and cannot be regarded as deriving from the exercise of public authority'.

Thus, the key feature distinguishing public sector reorganization cases to which the Directive does not apply (*Henke*) from those cases to which the Directive does apply (*Collino*, *Mayeur*) is the 'exercise of public authority'.[54] While the meaning of this phrase is not entirely clear, it is likely that the exclusion will apply only in cases with facts similar to those in *Henke* (i.e. those involving the reorganization of structures of the public administration or the transfer of administrative functions between public administrative authorities).[55] The Directive will, however, apply where the activity is non-profit making or carried out in the public interest. This is confirmed by Article 1(1)(c) of Directive 2001/23 which provides that the Directive applies to *public* or private undertakings engaged in economic activities, whether or not they are operating for gain.[56]

---

[46] See e.g. Case 108/10 *Scattolon* [2011] ECR I–000, para. 58.

[47] Joined Cases C–173/96 and 247/96 [1998] ECR I–8237, para. 24.

[48] Para. 24, distinguishing *Henke*.

[49] Case C–343/98 *Collino* v. *Telecom Italia SpA* [2000] ECR I–6659.

[50] Paras. 35 and 41. See additionally E–3/01 *Alda Viggósdóttir* v. *Iceland Post Ltd*, judgment of the EFTA Court, 22 March 2002, para. 23.

[51] Case C–175/99 *Mayeur* v. *Association Promotion de l'Information Meesine* [2000] ECR I–7755. See further Case C–425/02 *Delahaye* v. *Ministre de la Fonction publique et de la Réforme administrative* [2004] ECR I–10823 where the Court noted that the transfer of an economic activity from a legal person governed by private law to a legal person governed by public law was in principle within the scope of Directive.

[52] '[A]ny stable economic entity, that is to say, an organised grouping of persons and assets facilitating the exercise of an economic entity which pursues a specific objective.... Such a concept is independent of the legal status of that entity and the manner in which it is financed' (para. 32).

[53] Paras. 36–7.   [54] Para. 39.

[55] A view confirmed by Case C–425/02 *Delahaye* [2004] ECR I–10823, para. 30.

[56] Emphasis added.

3. A TRANSFER OF AN UNDERTAKING AS A RESULT OF A LEGAL TRANSFER OR MERGER

3.1. Legal transfer

(a) Introduction

Having established that the body is a stable economic entity, the next question is whether it has been transferred. Article 1(1)(a) provides that the Directive applies to the transfer of an undertaking as a result of a legal transfer or merger.[57] We begin by considering the meaning of the term 'legal transfer'; 'merger' is considered below.

The notion of 'legal' transfer relates to the method of the transfer. At first the cases concerned contractual relations—the sale of a business being the paradigm example.[58] Subsequently, the Court had to consider more complex transactions, including leasing arrangements and contracting out of services where there was no direct contractual link between the transferor and transferee (see Figures 13.2 and 13.3 below). This raised the problem whether the Directive covered only transfers arising directly from a contract, as the Dutch, German, French, Greek, Italian, Spanish, and Portuguese language versions suggested,[59] or whether the scope of the Directive was wide enough to cover other types of transfer which did not necessarily result from a contract, as the English phrase ('legal transfer') and the Danish version (*overdragelse*)[60] suggested.

The Court adopted a broad purposive interpretation of the notion of a legal transfer[61] and it is now clear that the Directive can apply to all transfers, including those involving a (unilateral) administrative or legislative act,[62] a court decision,[63] and those where there is no contract at all.[64] Thus, as the Court said in *Allen*,[65] the Directive covers 'any legal change in the person of the employer'. Therefore, it could apply to a transfer between two subsidiary companies in the same group, which were distinct legal persons, each with specific employment relationships with their employees,[66] albeit that

---

[57] The Directive does not apply to sea-going vessels (Art. 1(3)). The Commission proposed that the rights conferred by the Directive, with the exception of rights relating to and consultation, should also apply to sea-going vessels (Art. 1(4) of 94/C274/08) but this was not adopted in the final draft.

[58] See Case 287/86 *Ny Mølle Kro* [1987] ECR 5465, para. 12, discussed below.

[59] *Overdracht krachtens overeen kommst, vertragliche Ubertragung, cession conventionnelle, sumbatkij exphoorijsij, cessione contrattuale, cesion contractual, cesio contractual.*

[60] The Danish version includes transfers by way of gift as well as by contract, but not by court order or inheritance.

[61] Case 135/83 *Abels* [1985] ECR 469.

[62] See e.g., Case C–29/91 *Bartol* [1992] ECR I–3189; Case C–478/03 *Celtec* [2005] ECR I–4389; E–3/01 *Alda Viggósdóttir* v. *Iceland Post Ltd*, judgment of the EFTA Court, 22 March 2002, para. 23.

[63] See e.g. Case 135/83 *Abels* [1985] ECR 469 (surséance van betaling proceedings); Case C–362/89 *d'Urso* [1991] ECR I–4105 (special administration for large companies in critical difficulties); Case C–319/94 *Déthier Equipement* v. *Dassy* [1998] ECR I–1061 (winding up by the Court where the undertaking continues to trade); and Case C–399/96 *Europièces* [1998] ECR I–6965 (voluntary liquidation of a company).

[64] See e.g., Joined Cases C–171/94 and C–172/94 *Merckx* v. *Ford Motor Company and Neuhuys* [1996] ECR I–1253.

[65] Case C–234/98 *Allen* v. *Amalgamated Construction Co. Ltd* [1999] ECR I–8643, para. 17.

[66] The Court expressly did not apply its case law on competition (Art. 101 TFEU (ex 81 EC)), esp. Case C–73/95P *Viho* v. *Commission* [1996] ECR I–5457.

the companies had the same ownership, management, and premises and were engaged in the same work.[67] In a similar vein, the Court said in *Temco*[68] that the Directive could apply in respect of a transfer between a contractor and its subcontractor which was a subsidiary of the contractor.

We turn now to consider some examples of the more complex arrangements which are covered by the Directive.

(b) Leasing arrangements

Several cases have concerned leasing arrangements and the rescission of leases (see Figure 13.2). *Ny Mølle Kro*[69] provides a good example. A leased a restaurant to B. When B failed to comply with the terms of the agreement, A rescinded the lease and ran the restaurant herself. The Court reasoned that 'employees of an undertaking whose employer changes without any change in ownership are in a situation *comparable to that of employees of an undertaking which is sold* and require equivalent protection'.[70] Consequently, it said that the Directive would apply to this type of situation. Similarly, in *Daddy's Dance Hall*[71] A leased a restaurant to B. A subsequently terminated the lease with B and agreed that C should take on the lease. Once again the Court found that this could constitute a legal transfer and so the Directive in principle applied. It added that the fact that the transfer was effected in two stages, in that the undertaking was first retransferred from the original lessee (B) to the owner (A) which then transferred it to the new lessee (C), did not prevent the Directive from applying, provided that the economic unit retained its identity.[72]

The are two common features of these cases: first, there is a change in the legal or natural person who is responsible for carrying out the business, regardless of whether or not ownership of the undertaking is transferred;[73] and second, that while there is a contract between the lessor and the lessee there is no contract between the successive lessees. As the Court made clear in *Merckx*,[74] a case concerning the termination of a motor vehicle dealership with one undertaking and its award to another undertaking pursuing the same activities, for the Directive to apply, it was not necessary for there to be a direct contractual relationship between the transferor and the transferee.[75]

---

[67] Case C–234/98 *Allen* [1999] ECR I–8643, para. 17.

[68] Case C–51/00 *Temco* [2002] ECR I–969. See further the emphasis placed by AG Geelhoed on the need for a contractual link and more generally his criticism of the Court's case law in this field.

[69] Case 287/86 [1987] ECR 5465. See additionally Joined Cases 144 and 145/87 *Berg* [1988] ECR 2559 where the Court found that the transfer of a bar-discotheque by means of a lease-purchase agreement and the restoration of the undertaking to its owner as a result of a judicial decision constituted a legal transfer.

[70] Para. 12, emphasis added.

[71] Case 324/86 [1988] ECR 739.

[72] Para. 10. See further Case 101/87 *Bork* [1988] ECR 3057; Case C–340/01 *Abler v. Sodexho MM Catering Gesellschaft mbH* [2003] ECR I–14023, para. 39.

[73] Case C–478/03 *Celtec* [2005] ECR I–4389, para. 33.

[74] Joined Cases C–171/94 and C–172/94 [1996] ECR I–1253.

[75] Para. 30.

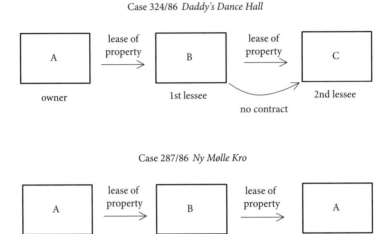

FIG. 13.2. Leasing arrangements.

(c) Contracting out

The absence of the need for a direct contractual relationship between the transferor and the transferee paved the way for the Directive to apply to contracting out. Contracting out is the process by which services previously provided in-house, and often ancillary to the main activity of the company (e.g. cleaning and catering), are offered out to tender to be performed by contractors which usually specialize in providing those specific services. This specialization should mean that the contractor can perform the work at lower costs,[76] in part due to economies of scale and in part through paying lower wages. If the Transfer of Undertakings Directive applied to contracting out then the contractor would be obliged to take on all of the staff previously employed by the company *and* on the same terms and conditions, including pay, therefore losing an important dimension of the cost saving. The question of whether contracting out constituted a legal transfer within the meaning of the Directive was therefore one of fundamental economic importance.[77]

Following the leasing cases discussed above, it was not surprising when the Court ruled in *Rask*[78] that contracting out fell in principle within the scope of the Directive. *Rask* concerned an agreement between Philips and ISS that ISS would assume full responsibility for the running of Philips' canteens, in particular, for menu planning, purchasing, and preparation of the food and for the recruitment and training of staff. In return, Philips agreed to pay ISS a fixed monthly sum and allowed ISS to use, free of charge, Philips' premises, including the canteens, equipment and utilities. The Court

---

[76] See G. More, 'The Acquired Rights Directive: Frustrating or Facilitating Labour Market Flexibility' in J. Shaw and G. More (eds.), *New Legal Dynamics of European Union* (Clarendon, Oxford, 1995).

[77] It was also of considerable political importance because in countries such as the UK with successive governments committed to cost-saving in the public sector, there was a statutory obligation on local authorities to put certain services out to tender.

[78] Case C–209/91 *Rask and Christensen* v. *ISS Kantineservice A/S* [1992] ECR I–5755.

ruled that the Directive could apply to a situation in which the owner of an undertaking by contract assigns to the owner of another undertaking the responsibility for running a facility for staff, previously operated directly, in return for a fee and various other benefits the terms of which were determined by the agreement made between them.[79]

Rask concerned the contracting out of services in the private sector; *Sánchez Hidalgo*[80] confirmed that the principle also applied to contracting out in the public sector. The Court said in *Rask* that it was irrelevant both that the activity transferred was only an ancillary activity[81] of the transferor undertaking,[82] not necessarily related to its main activities, and that the agreement between the transferor and the transferee related to the provision of services exclusively for the benefit of the transferor.[83] The Court repeated this conclusion in *Schmidt*[84] where it held that the fact that the activity concerned (cleaning) was performed, prior to the transfer, by only a single employee was not sufficient to preclude the application of the Directive.

The cases considered so far concern 'first round' contracting out (i.e. the first time the user undertaking contracts out part of its business to the contractor) where there was a contract between transferor and transferee (see Figure 13.3). The leasing cases, such as *Ny Mølle Kro*[85] and *Bork*,[86] suggested that the Directive would also apply, at least in principle, to second (and subsequent) round contracting out (i.e. after the expiry of the contract with the first contractor (B), the user undertaking (A) puts the work out to tender again and then enters into a contract with a second contractor (C)), as well as to contracting back in (i.e. after the expiry of the contract with the first contractor (B), the user undertaking (A) brings the work back in-house), where there is a contract between the user undertaking and the contractors but no contract between the different contractors B and C (see Figure 13.3). *Süzen*[87] and *Hernández Vidal*[88] confirmed that the Directive applied to second round contracting out, while *Sánchez Hidalgo*[89] said the Directive applied to contracting back in. The Court also confirmed in these cases that there was no need for any direct contractual relationship between the transferor (B) and transferee (C);[90] and that the transfer could take place in two stages (first-round contractor (B) to user undertaking (A) to second-round contractor (C)).[91]

(d) Transfer as a result of a legislative or administrative decision

Bartol[92] said that the approach adopted in the leasing and contracting out cases applied equally[93] to the situation where a municipal authority terminated the subsidy

---

[79] Para. 21.
[80] Joined Cases C–173/96 and C–247/96 *Sánchez Hidalgo and Others* [1998] ECR I–8237.
[81] This is confirmed by Art. 1(b) of Dir. 2001/23 introduced by Dir. 98/50.
[82] Para. 17.   [83] Ibid.
[84] Case C–392/92 [1994] ECR I–1311, para. 15.   [85] Case 287/86 [1987] ECR 5456.
[86] Case 101/87 [1988] ECR 3057.   [87] Case C–13/95 *Süzen* [1997] ECR I–1259.
[88] Joined Cases C–127/96, C–229/96 and C–74/97 *Hernández Vidal and Others* [1998] ECR I–8179.
[89] Joined Cases C–173/96 and C–247/96 [1998] ECR I–8237.
[90] Case C–13/95 *Süzen* [1997] ECR I–1259, para. 12.
[91] Joined Cases C–173/96 and C–247/96 *Sánchez Hidalgo* [1998] ECR I–8237, para. 23.
[92] Case C–29/91 [1992] ECR I–3189.   [93] See, e.g., Case C–51/00 *Temco* [2002] ECR I–969, para. 31.

First Round Contracting Out: *Rask, Schmidt*

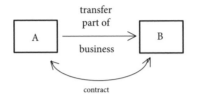

Second Round Contracting Out

1) Contracting out to Third Parties: *Süzen, Sanchez Hidalgo*

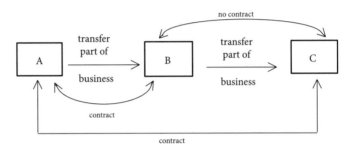

2) Contracting back in: *Hernández Vidal*

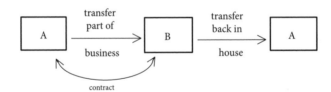

FIG. 13.3. First and second round contracting out and contracting in.

payable to one association which then closed and awarded the subsidy to another association with a similar aim. The Dr Sophie Redmond foundation provided assistance to drug addicts in the Netherlands, with funding provided by grants from the local authority. When the local authority decided to terminate the grant to the foundation the staff were dismissed and the foundation was closed. The local authority then switched the grant to another organization concerned with drug dependency, Sigma, which decided not to take on all of the former Redmond staff. The Court ruled that such a situation was capable of constituting a legal transfer and so the Directive could apply; it was irrelevant that the decision was taken unilaterally by the local authority rather than by agreement.[94]

[94] Paras. 15–17.

In a similar vein, the Court has ruled that the Directive will also apply to privatization situations, as in *Beckmann*[95] concerning the transfer of a quantity surveyor from the (public) National Health Service (NHS) to a private company, or the transfer of nursing lecturers from a college which was part of the NHS to South Bank University in *Martin*,[96] and the transfer of training from the Department of Employment to private Training and Enterprise Councils (TECs) in *Celtec*.[97]

(e) Conclusion

The Court's case law suggests that its interpretation of the phrase 'legal transfer' is now so broad that it is no longer a serious impediment to the application of the Directive. It has accepted that nearly all dispositions are covered by the phrase:[98] the Directive applies to contracting out (*Rask, Schmidt, Sánchez, Hidalgo*), subcontracting (*Allen, Temco*), privatization (*Beckmann, Martin, Celtec*), and some types of corporate reorganization (*Allen, Temco*) as well as to the more usual transfer situations involving a contract. That said, the Court is not consistent and does, from time to time, resurrect the need for some form of contractual link, albeit of the broadest kind, before the Directive can apply. For example, in *Temco* the Court appeared to talk of the need for the transfer 'to be part of the web of contractual relations even if they are indirect'.[99] In order to clarify the situation the Commission proposed that all language versions of the Directive be revised to make clear that it covered any transfer effected by contract or by some other disposition or operation of law, judicial decision or administrative measure.[100] This proposal was not adopted in the final version of the Directive but does indicate how broadly the requirement of 'legal transfer' is now drawn.

3.2. Merger

According to Article 1(1)(a), the Directive applies to any transfer of an undertaking as a result not only of a legal transfer but also of a merger. The concept of a merger is not defined in Directive 2001/23, although it has always been assumed that the term refers to a merger within the meaning of Articles 3 and 4 of Directive 2011/35/EU replacing

---

[95] Case C-164/00 *Beckmann v. Dynamco Whicheloe Macfarlane Ltd* [2002] ECR I-4893. In this case the applicability of the Directive was assumed. Cf. AG Alber's Opinion, para. 48. See additionally Case C-343/98 *Collino* [2000] ECR I-6659.

[96] Case C-4/01 *Martin v. South Bank University* [2003] ECR I-12859.

[97] Case C-478/03 *Celtec* [2005] ECR I-4389.

[98] See AG Poiares Maduro's approach in Case C-478/03 *Celtec* [2005] ECR I-4389. The Directive is therefore likely to apply, at least in principle, to other dispositions, such as gifts and transfers of ownership on the basis of succession.

[99] Para. 32. See further Joined Case C-232/04 and C-233/04 *Güney-Gorres v. Securicor Aviation* [2005] ECR I-11237, para. 37 'whenever, in the context of contractual relations, there is a change in the legal or natural person who is responsible for carrying on the undertaking'; and Advocate General Van Gerven's Opinion in Case C-29/91 *Bartol* [1992] ECR I-3189 that a contract was an essential prerequisite to any transfer but he insisted that 'contract' be given an extremely broad interpretation, including any situation where there was an element of consensus between the parties. Such an interpretation is so broad that it significantly undermines the concept of a contract.

[100] Art. 1(1), para. 1, 94/C274/08.

Directive 78/855/EEC.[101] Article 12 of this Directive makes express reference to the fact that employees' rights are to be protected in accordance with Directive 2001/23 in the event of a merger. Article 11 of Council Directive 82/891/EEC[102] contains similar wording in the context of a division[103] of a public limited company. However, although the 45th recital of Council Regulation 139/2004 on the control of concentrations between undertakings[104] (the EU Merger Regulation) expressly states that it does not detract from 'the collective rights of employees as recognised in the undertakings concerned', it provides no machinery for ensuring these rights.

The crucial point is that the merger for the purposes of Directive 2001/23 must involve a change of identity of the employer. Consequently, the operation of the Directive is said to be confined to 'assets-mergers', for example by the sale of an undertaking by private contract, provided that the original employer is not retained in some nominal capacity, in which case the Directive does not apply. 'Share sales' or takeovers by the acquisition of share capital—where one company acquires the control of another without any change in the identity of the employer—are excluded from the scope of the Directive[105] because the rules relating to transfers are intended to deal with legal problems arising when the identity of the *employer* is changed. When a change of share ownership occurs, legal theory considers that there is only a change in the identity of the proprietor of the share capital and not a change in the legal identity of the employer, albeit that, *in reality*, this change may be just as important to an employee as the change in identity of the employer following the transfer of the undertaking as recognized by the Directive. The majority shareholder may have plans for a major restructuring of the enterprise with a significant impact on the employees who are denied protection under the Directive. Earlier drafts of the original Directive (77/187) did extend its provisions to takeovers by acquisition of share capital but this was omitted from the final draft. This omission may be attributed to the difficult interface between labour law and

---

[101] (OJ [2011] L110/1). For an additional discussion of the definition of mergers in the context of taxation, see Art. 2 of Council Dir. 2009/133/EC (OJ [2009] L310/34).

[102] OJ [1982] L378/47.

[103] A division, or rather, using the language of the Directive, a 'division by acquisition', is defined in Art. 2(1) to mean the operation whereby, after being wound up without going into liquidation, a company transfers to more than one company all its assets and liabilities in exchange for the allocation to the shareholders of the company being divided of shares in the companies receiving contributions as a result of the division (hereinafter referred to as 'recipient companies') and possibly a cash payment not exceeding 10 per cent of the nominal value of the shares allocated or, where they have no nominal value, of their accounting par value.

[104] OJ [2004] L24/1. This is considered further in Ch. 15.

[105] B. Hepple, 'The Transfer of Undertakings (Protection of Employment) Regulations' (1982) 11 *ILJ* 29. However, doubt has been cast on this view by Advocate General Van Gerven in Case C–29/91 *Sophie Redmond* [1992] ECR I–3189. He argued that since the term merger had not been defined it should be given the usual commercial definition. In other words, it referred to a case where two or more undertakings which were formerly independent of each other unite or amalgamate giving rise to a merger in the broader sense of the term. He therefore invoked Art. 3(1) of what is now Council Reg. 139/2004, the EU Merger Regulation, which provides that a merger occurs where: '(a) two or more previously independent undertakings merge, or (b) one or more persons already controlling at least one undertaking, or one or more undertakings acquire, *whether by purchase of securities or assets*, by contract or other means direct or indirect control of the whole or parts of one or more other undertakings' (emphasis added). The Court has yet to rule on this point.

company law and the corresponding overlap between the responsibilities of the different Directorates General of the Commission. Nevertheless, it is a serious omission for many employees because in states such as the UK transfer by the sale of share capital is the most common form of transfer.[106]

4. THE ENTITY RETAINS ITS IDENTITY

4.1. Introduction

Having established that there is (1) a stable economic entity, and (2) that it has been transferred as a result of a legal transfer or merger, the final question is (3) whether the entity retains its identity following the transfer. *Spijkers*[107] listed a series of factors to be taken into account in deciding whether the entity has retained its identity. Subsequently the Court prioritized the similarity of the activity before and after transfer. If the activities were similar then the entity retained its identity. However, subsequent cases, starting with *Süzen*,[108] rejected the similarity test: the mere fact that the activity carried out by the transferor and that carried out by the transferee are 'similar, even identical, does not lead to the conclusion that an economic entity has retained its identity'. As the Court put it in *CLECE*:[109] 'An entity cannot be reduced to the activity entrusted to it. Its identity emerges from several indissociable factors, such as its workforce, its management staff, the way in which its work is organized, its operating methods or indeed, where appropriate, the operational resources to it'.[110] We shall now examine the evolution of the Court's approach to the question of whether an entity retains its identity.

4.2. The *Spijkers* criteria

Spijkers[111] provides the national courts with guidance on how to answer the question whether an entity retains its identity. Spijkers was employed by Colaris as an assistant manager of a slaughterhouse. By December 1982, when the business activities of Colaris had ceased and no goodwill remained, Benedik Abbatoir purchased the entire slaughterhouse, various rooms and offices, the land, and certain specified goods. From February 1983 Benedik Abbatoir operated the slaughterhouse, having taken on all of Colaris' employees except Spijkers and one other. Spijkers contended that there had been a transfer of an undertaking within the meaning of the Directive.

The Court ruled that the decisive criterion for establishing the existence of a transfer of an undertaking for the purposes of the Directive was whether:

> the business in question *retains its identity inasmuch as it is transferred as a going concern*, which may be indicated in particular by the fact that its operation is actually continued or resumed by the new employer with the same or similar activities.[112]

---

[106] Although cf *Millam v. The Print Factory (London) 1991* [2007] EWCA Civ 322.
[107] Case 24/85 [1986] ECR 1119.
[108] Case C–13/95 *Süzen v. Zehnacker Gebäudereinigung GmbH Krankenhausservice* [1997] ECR I–1259.
[109] Case C–463/09 *CLECE v. Ayuntamiento de Cobisa* [2011] ECR I–000.
[110] Para. 41.   [111] Case 24/85 [1986] ECR 1119.
[112] Wording actually taken from para. 18 of Case 287/86 *Ny Mølle Kro* [1987] ECR 5465 approving Case 24/85 *Spijkers* [1986] ECR 1119 and Case 29/91 *Bartol* [1992] ECR I–3189, para. 23.

In order to decide whether the business is transferred as a going concern the Court ruled that 'it is necessary to consider all the facts characterising the transaction', including:

- the type of undertaking or business:
- whether the business' tangible assets,[113] such as buildings and moveable property, and intangible assets,[114] were transferred;[115]
- the value of intangible assets at the time of transfer;
- whether the majority of the business' employees are taken over by the new employer;
- whether its customers are transferred;
- the degree of similarity between the activities carried on before and after the transfer;
- the period, if any, for which those activities were suspended.[116]

The Court said that no single factor was decisive;[117] national courts had to make an assessment of the overall position.

The advantage of the *Spijkers* ruling was that its breadth provided plenty of scope for national courts with long experience of working with the concept of transfer of undertaking to continue applying their own case law. The disadvantage was that the absence of any weighting of the *Spijkers* criteria caused a number of problems for national courts. This eventually led the Court to focus—and vacillate between—two elements of the *Spijkers* formula: 'activity' and 'economic entity'. These two elements are based on two contrasting conceptualizations of the undertaking which lie at the heart of the French debate over the scope of the transfer rule: that of the *entreprise-activité*, the labour law approach,

---

[113] It is clear that a transfer does *not* occur merely because the assets of a business are disposed of, see Case 24/85 *Spijkers* [1986] ECR 1119, para. 12. However, as Advocate General Slynn pointed out, the courts will identify any sham agreements for the disposal of assets designed to avoid the provisions of the Directive.

[114] Added by Case 101/87 *Bork* [1988] ECR 305. See additionally Case C–29/91 *Bartol* [1992] ECR I–3189.

[115] In Case 24/85 *Spijkers* [1986] ECR 1119 Advocate General Slynn suggested that the fact that at the date of transfer trading has ceased or has been substantially reduced does not prevent there from being a transfer of business if the wherewithal to carry on the business, such as plant, is available to be transferred. He also suggested that just because goodwill or existing contracts were not transferred was not conclusive against there being a transfer because the transferee might want to take over the activities of the business to supply existing customers.

[116] In Case 24/85 *Spijkers* [1986] ECR 1119 AG Slynn suggested that the transferee might want to spend time reorganizing or renovating the premises before reopening. If the employees were kept on and trading was resumed a national court was entitled to find that there was a transfer. In Case 287/86 *Ny Mølle Kro* [1987] ECR 5465 the undertaking, a restaurant, was regularly closed for part of the year. The transfer occurred when the undertaking was temporarily closed and the staff were absent. The Court decided that while this was a relevant factor it did not preclude the application of the Directive. The seasonal closure of a business did not mean that the undertaking has ceased to be a going concern. It was, however, for the national court to make the relevant factual appraisal. See additionally Case 101/87 *Bork* [1988] ECR 3057 where the closure coincided with the Christmas and New Year holiday.

[117] Case C–392/92 *Schmidt* [1994] ECR I–1311, para. 16; Case C–13/95 *Süzen* [1997] ECR I–1259, para. 14.

and that of the *entreprise-organisation*, the commercial law approach.[118] Pre-*Süzen*[119] the Court tended to look at the labour law test focusing on 'activity': has the new employer taken over the running of the same or similar business activities as its predecessor? Post-*Süzen*, the Court emphasized the application of the more commercial test, focusing on whether the business had been transferred as an 'economic entity', dependent on the transfer of tangible or intangible assets. The labour law test was more likely to produce the result that there had been a transfer of an undertaking, which is consistent with the employment protection objectives of the Directive; but the commercial law approach had been preferred by the Italian and German courts and was increasingly being favoured by the French courts.[120] We shall examine the two approaches in turn.

(a) The labour law approach: Similarity of activity

In the early cases, the Court focused on the question of whether one employer stepped into the shoes of another. This was a practical, rather than a legal, enquiry and certainly one which did not focus on questions of ownership.[121] As the Court said in *Ny Mølle Kro*:[122]

> The Directive is therefore applicable where, following a legal transfer or a merger, there is a change in the legal or natural person who is responsible for carrying on the business and who by virtue of that fact incurs the obligations of an employer *vis-à-vis* employees of the undertaking, regardless of whether or not the ownership of the undertaking is transferred.[123]

In subsequent cases the Court focused less on the employer and more on the similarity between the activity performed by the new employer compared with those carried out by its predecessor.[124] This approach reached its zenith in the controversial case of *Schmidt*[125] which concerned the contracting out of cleaning services where the work was performed by a single employee. The Court emphasized that the decisive criterion for establishing whether there was a transfer of an undertaking was whether the business in question retained its identity which was indicated by actual continuation or resumption by the new employer of the same or similar activities (namely, cleaning work performed by the same employee). The Court therefore rejected the arguments

---

[118] P. Davies, 'Transfers of Undertakings' in S. Sciarra (ed.), *Labour Law in the Courts: National Judges and the European Court of Justice* (Hart Publishing, Oxford, 2001) 136.

[119] Case C–13/95 [1997] ECR I–1259.

[120] For detailed consideration of the national rules, see A. Jeammaud and M. Le Friant, *La Directive 77/187 CEE, la Cour de Justice et le Droit Français*, EUI Working Paper 97/3; M. Körner, *The Impact of Community Law on German Labour Law—The Example of Transfer of Undertakings*, EUI Working Paper 96/8; V. Leccese, 'Italian Courts, the ECJ and Transfers of Undertakings: A Multi-Speed Dialogue?' (1999) 5 *EZW* 311.

[121] See additionally Case 101/87 *Bork* [1988] ECR 3057 and Joined Cases 144 and 145/87 *Berg* [1988] ECR 2559.

[122] Case 287/86 [1987] ECR 5465.

[123] Para. 12. For similar wording see Case 101/87 *Bork* [1988] ECR 3057, para. 13 approving the decision in Joined Cases 144 and 145/87 *Berg* [1988] ECR 2559.

[124] The fact that the business was carried on in a different way is not conclusive against there being a transfer— new methods, new types of machinery, and new customers are relevant factors but they do not prevent there being *in reality* a transfer. The activities before and after the transfer do not need to be the same for this would undermine the broad scope of the Directive (per AG Van Gerven in Case C–29/91 *Bartol* [1992] ECR I–3189).

[125] Case C–392/92 [1994] ECR I–1311, para. 16.

made by the German and UK governments that the absence of any transfer of tangible assets precluded the existence of a transfer.[126]

This decision attracted a considerable amount of adverse comment. In its prescription of the *entreprise-activité* approach, the Court, contrary to the advice of its Advocate General, had abandoned the flexibility offered by the broad *Spijkers* formulation and offended the national courts (especially the German and Italian courts) which favoured the *entreprise-organisation* approach. *Schmidt* also produced the surprising result, noted famously by Rubinstein, that the *reductio ad absurdum* of the decision was that the Directive and its national implementing legislation would apply 'when I changed the contractor who cut my lawn. Absurd or not, there is nothing in *Schmidt* which provides a basis for concluding that that is not the law'.[127]

The Court was sensitive to this criticism and the decision in *Rygaard*[128] suggested that it was considering a change of approach. Rygaard was employed by Pedersen, a firm of carpenters, building SAS's canteen. Pedersen told SAS that it wanted part of the work to be carried out by Strø Mølle. Strø Mølle and SAS agreed that Strø Mølle would perform the contract, that some of Pedersen's workers would continue working for Strø Mølle, and that Strø Mølle would take over materials on the building site to complete the contracted work. Pedersen then wrote to Rygaard informing him that he would be dismissed, explaining that the firm was to be wound up and that the work would be taken over by Strø Mølle. The letter added that Rygaard would be transferred to Strø Mølle.

Following *Schmidt*, Rygaard argued that a transfer of an undertaking had occurred because the works taken over by Strø Mølle were the same as those entrusted to Pedersen, and that the duration of the works could not be decisive in determining whether a transfer of an undertaking had taken place. The Court rejected his arguments and said that the similarity between the activities of Pedersen and Strø Mølle was not sufficient. It said that the case law presupposed that 'the transfer relates to a *stable economic entity* whose activity is not limited to performing one specific works contract'.[129] On the facts of this case, the transfer did not relate to a stable economic entity because all that was transferred was one particular building project.[130] The Court continued that such a transfer could come within the terms of the Directive only if it included the transfer of a body of assets enabling the activities or certain activities of the transferor undertaking to be carried on in a stable way.[131] That was not so where the transferor undertaking merely makes available to the new contractor certain workers and material.[132]

Rygaard therefore served to remind national courts of the relevance of the existence of a body of assets (even though this was not of paramount importance); and the requirement of a stable economic entity confirmed that there was a distinction between

---

[126] Para. 16.   [127] Rubinstein [1994] ECR I–257.

[128] Case C–48/94 *Ledernes Hovedorganisation, acting for Rygaard v. Dansk Arbejdsgiverforening, acting for Strø Mølle Akustik* [1995] ECR I–2745.

[129] Para. 20. Emphasis added.   [130] Para. 23.   [131] Para. 21.

[132] Cf. Case C–234/98 *Allen* [1999] ECR I–8643, para. 37 where the Court distinguished Case C–48/84 *Rygaard* [1995] ECR I–2745 on its facts, because in *Allen* a complete works project was transferred, probably along with some assets.

a one-off project of limited duration and contracting out of a continuing function.[133] And in concentrating on the need for a stable economic entity the Court's focus appeared to be shifting towards the conception of an *entreprise-organisation*.

However, *Rygaard* did not entirely bury the *Schmidt* 'same activity' approach which could still be detected in *Merckx*.[134] M and N were employed as salesmen by Anfo Motors, a Ford dealership in which Ford was the major shareholder. When Anfo Motors ceased its activities, the dealership was transferred to Novorabel which employed 14 of the 64 Anfo Motors employees on the same terms and conditions. Anfo Motors informed its customers of the situation and recommended the services of the new dealer. The Court, having cited the *Spijkers* criteria, considered that the transfer of the dealership was a transfer of an undertaking.[135] It reached this conclusion even though, as in *Schmidt*, there was no transfer of tangible assets, the business was carried on under a different name, from different premises with different facilities, and was situated in a different area of the same conurbation. For the Court it was sufficient that the contract territory remained the same.[136] Furthermore, the fact that a majority of the staff had been dismissed when the transfer occurred did not preclude the application of the Directive. The Court said that the dismissals might have taken place for economic, technical, or organizational reasons, in compliance with Article 4(1) (considered below), but failure to comply with Article 4(1) did not preclude the application of the Directive. The Court concluded that 'where a motor vehicle dealership concluded with one undertaking is terminated and a new dealership is awarded to another undertaking *pursuing the same activities*, the transfer of the undertaking is the result of a legal transfer'.[137]

(b) The commercial approach: Economic entity

Despite *Merckx*, *Rygaard* essentially paved the way for the Court's new, tougher approach found in the seminal decision of *Süzen*.[138] The case concerned second round contracting out: A, having entrusted the cleaning of its premises to B, terminated this contract and, for the performance of similar work, entered into a new contract with C without any concomitant transfer of tangible or intangible business assets from one undertaking to the other. Did this constitute a transfer of an undertaking? The Court began in an orthodox manner, referring to the aim of the Directive (to ensure continuity of employment relationships within an economic entity, irrespective of any change of ownership[139]) and to the *Spijkers* test.[140] However, following *Rygaard*, the Court said that, for the Directive to be applicable, the transfer had to relate to a stable economic entity. It continued that the term 'entity' referred to an 'organised grouping of persons and assets facilitating the exercise of an economic activity which pursues a specific objective'.[141] Having emphasized the importance of the 'economic entity' test,

---

[133] Rubinstein [1996] IRLR 1.
[134] Joined Cases C–171/94 and C–172/94 [1996] ECR I–1253, esp. paras. 18, 23, and 30.
[135] Para. 19.   [136] Para. 21.   [137] Para. 30. Emphasis added.
[138] Case C–13/95 [1997] ECR I–1259 (noted P. Davies (1997) 26 *ILJ* 193).
[139] Para. 10.   [140] Ibid.   [141] Para. 13.

the Court then appeared to reject—or at least reduce the importance of—the labour law 'activity' test accepted in *Schmidt*.[142] It said that:

> the mere fact that the service provided by the old and the new awardees of a contract is similar does not therefore support the conclusion that an economic entity has been transferred. An entity cannot be reduced to the activity entrusted to it. Its identity also emerged from other factors, such as its workforce, its management staff, the way in which its work is organised, its operating methods or indeed, where appropriate, the operational resources available to it.[143]

The Court continued that the mere loss of a service contract to a competitor could not, therefore, by itself indicate the existence of a transfer within the meaning of the Directive. In those circumstances, the service undertaking previously entrusted with the contract (B) did not, on losing a customer, thereby cease fully to exist, and a business or part of a business belonging to it could not be considered to have been transferred to the new awardee of the contract (C).

So how does a national court know whether an 'economic entity' has been transferred? The Court distinguished between two types of business: those which were assets-based and those which were not.[144] In the case of an *assets-based* business, the Court said that there was a transfer of an undertaking only where there was a transfer of 'significant tangible or intangible assets'.[145] On the other hand, in the case of a *non-assets based* business (i.e. a business based essentially on manpower such as cleaning[146] or security[147]), the Court said that 'the maintenance of its identity following the transaction affecting it [could] not, logically, depend on the transfer of such assets'.[148] Therefore, the Court said in certain labour-intensive sectors (such as services) a group of workers engaged in a joint activity on a permanent basis could themselves constitute an economic entity.[149] The Court said it had to be recognized that such an entity was capable of maintaining its identity after it had been transferred where the new employer (C) did not merely pursue the activity in question but also took over a major part, in terms of their numbers and skills, of the employees specially assigned by its predecessor (B) to that task.[150] In those circumstances, the new employer took over a body of assets enabling him to carry on the activities or certain activities of the transferor undertaking on a regular basis.[151]

Thus, in the case of a *non-assets* business, there is only a transfer of an undertaking where the transferee takes over a majority of the transferor's staff, in terms of their

---

[142] Cf. para. 20.   [143] Para. 15.

[144] The EFTA Court said that if neither assets nor personnel are transferred then there is no transfer: see further Case E–3/96 *Tor Angeir Ask and Others v. ABD Offshore Technology AS and Aker Offshore Partner AS*, Advisory Opinion of the Court 14 March 1997 (OJ [1997] C136/7).

[145] Para. 23.

[146] Joined C–229/96 and C–74/97 *Hernández Vidal and Others* [1998] ECR I–8179.

[147] C–247/96 *Sánchez Hidalgo and Others* [1998] ECR I–8237, para. 26.

[148] Para. 18.   [149] Para. 21.   [150] Ibid.

[151] This was for the national court to establish: para. 21.

numbers and skills.[152] As Davies points out, this test has a peculiar 'boot strap' quality to it. Since an adviser may need to know whether the Directive applies in order to determine whether the transferee ought to take the employees of the transferor into its employ, it is unhelpful to try to answer that question by application of the test whether the transferee has in fact done that very thing.[153] In *Hernández Vidal* Advocate General Cosmas made a similar point: the result achieved by the Directive (continuation of employment contracts by the transferee) 'becomes a condition determining whether [the Directive] is to apply'.[154] This test enables transferees to avoid their obligations under the Directive: if few assets are transferred the transferee can avoid the Directive by refusing to employ the 'major part' of the workforce. This test renders the Directive in many cases a 'voluntary obligation', contrary to the spirit of a Directive designed to give employment protection.

A similar problem also arises in the case of an *assets-based* business. This can be seen in *Oy Liikenne*,[155] a case concerning second round contracting out of bus services in Helsinki. When the first contractor (B) lost the contract, it dismissed its 45 drivers. The second contractor (C) then took on 33 of those drivers (all those who applied) but none of B's buses since C had ordered new buses for use on the routes. The Court considered that bus transport could not be 'regarded as an activity based essentially on manpower, as it requires substantial plant and equipment'.[156] It continued that where the tangible assets contribute significantly to the performance of the activity, the absence of the transfer of such assets from the old to the new contractor meant that the entity did not retain its identity[157] and so the Directive did not apply.[158]

Thus, the classification of whether a transfer is assets or non-assets based is crucial. If it is non-assets based the transferee can circumvent the provisions of the Directive by refusing to take on the majority of the staff; if it is assets-based the transferee can circumvent the provisions of the Directive by refusing to take on the majority of the assets. But transferees get this wrong at their peril, as *Abler*[159] shows. This was a contracting out case concerning a transfer of the catering operation for a hospital. The transferee refused to take on the outgoing transferor's staff but did take on the equipment used by the transferor because it belonged to the hospital for whom the transferor, and now the transferee, was preparing meals. Somewhat surprisingly, the Court said: 'Catering cannot be regarded as an activity based essentially on manpower since it requires a significant

---

[152] Para. 21. See additionally Case C–51/00 *Temco* [2002] ECR I–969, para. 27 which makes clear that this rule applies even where a sectoral collective agreement obliges the transferee to take on, as far as possible, the transferor's staff. See additionally E–2/04 *Rasmussen* v. *Total E&P Norge AS*, judgment of the EFTA Court 10 December 2004, para. 43.

[153] Davies, above, n. 118, 196.

[154] Joined Cases C–229/96 and C–74/97 *Hernández Vidal and Others* [1998] ECR I–8179, para. 80. The Court itself appeared to recognize the force of this criticism in Case C–463/09 *CLECE* [2011] ECR I–000, para. 38 but still applied the *Süzen* line of case law.

[155] Case C–172/99 *Oy Liikenne Ab* v. *Liskojärvi* [2001] ECR I–745. See additionally Case C–234/98 *Allen* [1999] ECR I–8643, para. 30.

[156] Para. 39.   [157] Para. 42.   [158] Para. 43.

[159] Case C–340/01 *Abler* [2003] ECR I–14023.

amount of equipment.[160] As this was therefore an assets transfer case and (use of)[161] the tangible assets needed—the premises, water and energy, the appliances, and the dish-washers—had been taken over by the transferee,[162] even though the tangible assets belonged to the contracting authority (the hospital) and not the transferor,[163] the Court found that there was a transfer of an economic entity. And because this case concerned an assets-based business, the transferee's failure to take over, in terms of numbers and skills, an essential part of the staff employed by its predecessor was not sufficient to preclude the existence of a transfer of an undertaking.[164]

To avoid this uncertainty, the UK, in its 2006 version of the implementing legislation, took the policy decision to apply the Regulations—and thus the Directive—not only to 'standard' transfer situations as identified in Articles 1(1)(a) and (b) of the Directive but also to 'service provision changes' (SPCs). Regulation 3 provides:

3.—(1) These Regulations apply to—

(a) a transfer of an undertaking, business or part of an undertaking or business situated immediately before the transfer in the United Kingdom to another person where there is a transfer of an economic entity which retains its identity;

(b) a service provision change, that is a situation in which—

  (i) activities cease to be carried out by a person ('a client') on his own behalf and are carried out instead by another person on the client's behalf ('a contractor');
  (ii) activities cease to be carried out by a contractor on a client's behalf (whether or not those activities had previously been carried out by the client on his own behalf) and are carried out instead by another person ('a subsequent contractor') on the client's behalf; or
  (iii) activities cease to be carried out by a contractor or a subsequent contractor on a cli-ent's behalf (whether or not those activities had previously been carried out by the client on his own behalf) and are carried out instead by the client on his own behalf, …[165]

Thus Regulation 3(1)(a) applies to standard transfers (to which the *Spijkers* formula will apply) while Regulation 3(1)(b) applies to service provision changes (to which the

---

[160] Para. 36.
[161] As opposed to ownership of the assets: G. Barrett, 'Light Acquired on Acquired Rights: Examining Developments in Employment Rights on Transfers of Undertakings' (2005) 42 *CMLRev.* 1053, 1063.
[162] Para. 36.
[163] Para. 42. See additionally Joined Cases C–232/04 and C–233/04 *Güney-Görres* [2005] ECR I–11237, para. 42.
[164] Para. 37.
[165] This is read subject to Reg 3(3) which provides: 'The conditions referred to in paragraph (1)(b) are that—

(a) immediately before the service provision change—
  (i) there is an organised grouping of employees situated in Great Britain which has as its principal purpose the carrying out of the activities concerned on behalf of the client;
  (ii) the client intends that the activities will, following the service provision change, be carried out by the transferee other than in connection with a single specific event or task of short-term duration; and
(b) the activities concerned do not consist wholly or mainly of the supply of goods for the client's use.'

Spijkers formula will not apply since SPCs are deemed to fall within the scope of the regulations). The SPCs cover first generation contracting out, subsequent transfers, and the return of work in-house. While the Coalition government considers that this Labour innovation might represent gold-plating of the implementation of the EU Directive, many contractors are in favour since it provides certainty and creates a level playing field from which contractors can bid.

The decision in *CLECE*[166] highlights the difference between the EU and the UK approach. The case concerned contracting back in, a classic example of an SPC under UK law to which the protection under the transfer rules would apply. However, the Court found that 'the identity of an economic entity, [such as one performing cleaning], which is essentially based on manpower, cannot be retained if the majority of its employees are not taken on by the alleged transferee'.[167] Therefore, the Directive did not apply.

The *Süzen* 'economic entity' test is now the principal authority in determining whether there has been a transfer of an undertaking.[168] It has been applied with more or less strictness in subsequent cases.[169] And, in a move described as 'reverse codification',[170] the Court has *de facto* implemented the Commission's 1997 proposed definition of 'transfer of an undertaking' which had been successfully blocked by the European Parliament. The Commission had defined a transfer of an undertaking as a 'transfer of an activity which is accompanied by the transfer of an economic entity which retains its identity'. The proposal added that the 'transfer only of an activity of an undertaking...does not in itself constitute a transfer of an undertaking'.[171] The dialogue between the Court and the Commission has continued: the emphasis on 'economic entity' which has retained its identity has now been picked up in what is now the Article 1(1)(b) definition of 'transfer' introduced by Directive 98/50. It defines transfer as 'the transfer of an economic entity which retains its identity, meaning an organised grouping of resources which has the objective of pursuing an economic activity whether or not that activity is central or ancillary'.[172] So what then is an 'organized grouping of resources'?

---

[166] Case C–463/09 *CLECE v. Ayuntamiento de Cobisa* [2011] ECR I–000.

[167] Para. 41.

[168] Initially, there was some suggestion that *Süzen* might be confined to second-round contracting out (*Süzen*, paras. 8 and 9) but its extensive citation subsequently suggests that this is not the case: see e.g., Case C–172/99 *Oy Liikenne Ab* v. *Liskojärvi* [2001] ECR I–745; Case C–51/00 *Temco Service Industries SA* [2002] ECR I–969.

[169] Some commentators detected a slight relaxation of approach in, for example, Joined Cases C–173/96 and C–247/96 *Sánchez Hidalgo and Others* [1998] ECR I–8237 and Joined Cases C–127/96, Joined Cases C–229/96 and C–74/97 *Hernández Vidal and Others* [1998] ECR I–8179 but recognize that *Süzen* was applied with full rigour in Case C–172/99 *Oy Liikenne Ab* [2001] ECR I–745. There is also some evidence of greater flexibility shown by the EFTA Court which, in E–2/04 *Rasmussen* v. *Total E&P Norge AS*, judgment of the EFTA Court 10 December 2004, [2004] EFTA Court Reports 57, paras. 28 and 38, emphasized the need to take account of 'various factors'.

[170] J. Kenner, *EU Employment Law: From Rome to Amsterdam and Beyond* (Hart Publishing, Oxford, 2003), 347.

[171] COM(97) 60 final.

[172] Art. 1(b) of Dir. 2001/23.

4.3. Organized grouping of resources

The cases considered so far focus on the traditional situation where one part of a business is transferred in its entirety to another business. But what happens where the unit transferred is reorganized or dispersed? Consider a situation where care services were previously provided in a care setting (e.g. a publicly funded residential care home) but those cared for were then put into independent accommodation and the care was provided at the individual's own home by a private provider. Has there been a transfer of an economic entity which has retained its identity? This issue has troubled the German courts which took the view that if the transferred parts of a business lost their autonomy and were fully integrated into a transferee's business then there was no transfer of an undertaking. This approach would have significantly limited the effectiveness of the Directive. However, the Court in *Klarenberg*[173] rejected this view. It said that a mere alteration in the organizational structure of the entity transferred did not prevent the application of the Directive.[174] In respect of a more radical reorganization the Court said that the phrase 'organised grouping of resources' covers not only the organizational element of the entity transferred but also the element of pursuing an economic activity.[175] It continued that the Directive did apply to a transfer of an undertaking not retaining its organizational autonomy, provided that the 'functional link between the various elements of production transferred is preserved, and that that link enables the transferee to use those elements to pursue an identical or analogous economic activity'.[176] This seems to mean that even if the transferred business is integrated into the transferee's structure provided the organized grouping of resources such as labour and material, which formed the economic entity prior to the transfer, continue to be linked together then the grouping retains its identity. Therefore, following *Klarenberg*, in the care home example described above, given the absence of a functional link between the carers and the way the care is provided (even though those needing care still receive care), it will not be a transfer situation, and this is the view taken by the UK Courts. The Employment Appeal Tribunal (EAT) said that the situation was not covered by the Directive either under the standard transfer test or the SPC test because of the fundamental difference in ethos between the old and new care providers with the result that the transferor was liable for successful claims brought by any staff.[177]

5. TERRITORIAL SCOPE

Article 1(2) provides that the Directive applies 'where and in so far as the undertaking, business or part of the undertaking or business to be transferred is situated in the territorial scope of the Treaty'.[178] It is the physical location of the business and not the location of the ownership that is the determinative feature. This may lead to a significant

---

[173] Case C–466/07 *Klarenberg* [2011] ECR I–000.   [174] Para. 44.
[175] Para. 45.   [176] Para. 53.
[177] *Nottinghamshire Healthcare NHS Trust* v. *Hamshaw* UKEAT/0037/11.
[178] This includes a Member State of the EEA (Norway, Iceland, and Liechtenstein).

gap in the protection of workers within the Union since, if the business transferred from outside the EU is transferred to a Union undertaking, workers in the acquiring Union enterprise may be adversely affected by the transfer but not covered by the Directive. The Directive also does not apply to transfers of businesses located outside the Union but which belong to a company whose head office is in the territory of a Member State. However, in a case decided by the British Courts *Holis Metal Industries* v. *GMB*,[179] a transfer of a UK business to an Israeli company operating in Israel did in principle fall in the scope of the UK rules implementing Directive 2001/23.

D. SAFEGUARDING INDIVIDUAL EMPLOYEES' RIGHTS

1. INTRODUCTION

If the transfer is a transfer of an undertaking within the meaning of Directive 2001/23, then according to the Court in *Wendelboe*:[180]

> ... the scheme and purposes of the Directive, ... is intended to ensure, as far as possible, that the employment relationship continues unchanged with the transferee and by protecting workers against dismissals motivated solely by the fact of the transfer...[181]

In other words, the Directive is intended to protect those employees who are performing the same job but under the orders of a different employer. The protection conferred has two pillars: first, the transfer of rights and obligations arising from the contract of employment or employment relationship[182] and collective agreements (Article 3) and, secondly, the protection against dismissal (Article 4). We shall consider these situations in turn below. First, we consider who is the beneficiary of these rights.

2. 'EMPLOYEES'

2.1. Employee v. worker

The rights laid down by the Directive are conferred, in the English language version, on 'employees'[183] who are defined by Directive 2001/23 as 'any person who, in the Member

---

[179] [2008] IRLR 187. It is likely that a transfer to Israel would constitute a substantial change to working conditions which would fall in the rules on constructive dismissal under Art. 4(2).

[180] Case 19/83 [1985] ECR 457.

[181] Para. 15. Similar sentiments are expressed in Joined Cases C–132, 138 and 139/91 *Katsikas* [1992] ECR I–6577, para. 21, and Cases C–362/89 *d'Urso* [1991] ECR I–4105, para. 9.

[182] For ease of reference 'contract of employment' will be used and should be interpreted as including 'employment relationship'.

[183] Although the English version of the Directive uses the term 'employee', other language versions use 'worker' and the Court uses the terms interchangeably. See e.g. para. 15 in Case 19/83 *Wendelboe* [1985] ECR 457. See translator's note in Case 105/84 *Danmols Inventar* [1985] ECR 2639.

State concerned, is protected as an employee under national employment law'.[184] Article 2(2) of Directive 2001/23 adds that the Directive shall be 'without prejudice to national law as regards the definition of the contract of employment or employment relationship'.[185] However, Article 2(2) continues that Member States must not exclude contracts of employment or employment relationships from the Directive solely because:

- of the number of working hours performed or to be performed;
- they are employment relationships governed by a fixed-term contract as defined by Article 1(1) of Directive 91/383;[186]
- they are temporary employment relationships within the meaning of Article 1(2) of Directive 91/383 and the undertaking transferred is or is part of the temp agency which is the employer.

This definition of employees, which refers back to *national* law, confirms the Court's earlier jurisprudence[187] but stands in sharp contrast to the case law on Article 45 TFEU (ex 39 EC) on free movement of workers[188] where the Court has insisted on a *Union* definition of the term 'worker'.[189]

As we have seen elsewhere, in English law, an 'employee' means an individual who has entered into or works under a 'contract of employment' and a contract of employment is defined as 'a contract of service or apprenticeship, whether express or implied, and (if it is express) whether oral or in writing'.[190] This traditional definition excludes the broader category of workers. However, while the language in the UK statute refers to 'employees' in fact the definition covers those under a contract of service, apprenticeship or 'otherwise' and thus does, in fact, include workers.

2.2. Part of the business

The Directive confers rights only on those employees[191] who, during their working hours, are *wholly* engaged in the part[192] of the business transferred. Advocate General Slynn in *Botzen*[193] suggested that in order to determine whether an employee was 'wholly engaged'

---

[184] Art. 2(1)(d). Public service employees are not covered by the Directive insofar as they are not subject to the labour law in force in the Member States: Case C–343/98 *Collino* v. *Telecom Italia SpA* [2000] ECR I–6659, paras. 39–40. See AG Poiares Maduro's criticisim of this in Case C–425/02 *Delahaye* [2004] ECR I–108273, para. 17.

[185] The reference to the 'contract of employment or employment relationship' may embrace the German *Arbeitsvertrag* and *Arbeitsverhältnis* and the Italian *contratto di lavoro* and *rapporto di lavoro* where the employment relationship arises out of the contract of employment.

[186] OJ [1991] L206/19; see further Ch. 9.

[187] Case 19/83 *Wendelboe* [1985] ECR 457, para. 16; Case 105/84 *Danmols Inventar* [1985] ECR 2639, para. 16.

[188] Case 105/84 *Danmols Inventar* [1985] ECR 2639. In the same case Advocate General Slynn agreed (p. 2644) that the Directive did not envisage a Union definition of the term 'worker'.

[189] See e.g. Case 53/81 *Levin* [1982] ECR 1035. This is considered further in Ch. 4.

[190] S. 230(1)–(2) ERA 1996.

[191] This will cover full-time and part-time workers: Advocate General Slynn in Case 186/83 *Botzen* [1985] ECR 519.

[192] The Court has also refused to define comprehensively what is meant by 'part of' a business. In Case 186/83 *Botzen* [1985] ECR 519, 521 Advocate General Slynn suggested that this was a question of fact but that 'it will usually involve the transfer of a department or a factory or facet of the business' or the sale of 'a fraction or a single unit of business'.

[193] Case 186/83 [1985] ECR 519, 521.

in the part of the organization transferred it was necessary to consider whether the employee would have been employed by the owners of that part or by the owners of the remaining part, if that part of the business had been separately owned before the transfer. The only exception made by Advocate General Slynn to the requirement of being 'wholly engaged' was where an employee was required to perform other duties to an extent which could be described as *de minimis*. If, however, an employee was in fact engaged in the activities of the whole business or in several parts then he could not be regarded as an employee of the part of the business transferred for the purpose of the Directive. Thus, a person who works for several parts of a company, including the part transferred—for example, a sales representative or a personnel officer—cannot claim to be transferred to the new employer, for their jobs may be different in scope, a position which is not envisaged by the Directive.

This view was taken by the Court in *Botzen*. In that case the transferee took over the general engineering departments of the transferor and the relevant staff but not the departments containing the support staff. The Court ruled that an employment relationship was essentially characterized by the link existing between the employee and the part of the undertaking or business to which he was assigned to carry out his duties.[194] As the Commission put it, a transfer takes place of the departments to which the employee was assigned and which formed the organizational framework within which their employment relationship took effect.[195] Therefore, the Directive would not apply to those employees who, although not employees in the transferred part of the undertaking, performed certain duties which involved the use of assets assigned to the part transferred or who, while being employed in an administration department of the undertaking which was not transferred, carried out certain duties for the benefit of the part transferred.[196]

2.3. Employed at the date of transfer

As the Court made clear in *Wendelboe*,[197] the employees must be employed by the transferor undertaking on the date of transfer. The transferee is therefore not liable for holiday pay and compensation in respect of those employees who were not employed in the undertaking on the date of transfer.[198] Subsequent employees also cannot enjoy the benefits of the Directive;[199] nor can employees who have decided *of their own volition*[200] that they do not wish to continue the employment relationship with the new employer after transfer.[201]

---

[194] Case 186/83 *Botzen* [1985] ECR 519 and Case C–392/92 *Schmidt* [1994] ECR I–1311.
[195] Para. 14.   [196] Para. 16.
[197] Case 19/83 *Wendleboe* [1985] ECR 457. The Court reached this conclusion after examining the various language versions of the Directive. In the Dutch, French, German, Greek, and Italian versions the phrase 'existing on the date of the transfer' relates unequivocally to the expression 'contract of employment... or employment relationship' and that the English and Danish versions were capable of bearing the same interpretation. Furthermore, Art. 3(4) distinguishes between 'employees' and 'persons no longer employed'. Art. 3(1) does not make that distinction.
[198] This is considered further below.   [199] Case 287/86 *Ny Mølle Kro* [1987] ECR 5465, para. 26.
[200] Advocate General Slynn in Case 105/84 *Danmols Inventar* [1985] ECR 2639, however, stressed that it was crucial for the national courts to ensure that any such agreement is 'genuine and not tainted by duress on the part of the transferor or the transferee'.
[201] Case 105/84 *Danmols Inventar* [1985] ECR 2639, para. 26.

So when is the 'date of transfer'? According to *Celtec*,[202] it is the 'date on which responsibility as employer for carrying on the business of the unit in question moves from the transferor to the transferee'. Furthermore, according to the Court in *Rotsart*[203] the transfer of the contracts of employment 'necessarily takes place on the date of the transfer of the undertaking and cannot be postponed to another date at the will of the transferor or the transferee'.[204] If it were otherwise and the transferor or transferee could choose the date from which the contract of employment was transferred, this would amount to allowing employers to derogate, at least temporarily, from the provisions of the Directive which was not possible 'since the provisions are mandatory'.[205]

The importance of this ruling can be seen on the facts of *Celtec*. The British Department of Employment transferred responsibilities for vocational training to Training and Enterprise Councils (TECs) run by private sector employers. Civil servants who had been responsible for running the vocational training were initially seconded to the TECs for three years. At this point they resigned from the civil service and were employed by the TEC. Although the Advocate General suggested that the Directive did not require there to be a particular point in time at which all the aspects of the undertaking were transferred, thereby allowing the contracts of employment to be transferred after the transfer of assets, the Court of Justice adopted the simple approach it had applied in *Rotsart*. It ruled that the date of transfer was the date on which responsibility as employer for carrying on the business moves from the transferor (the government) to the transferee (Celtec). Thus, the contracts of employment existing on the date of transfer were deemed to be handed over on that date from the transferor to the transferee 'regardless of what has been agreed between the parties in that respect'.[206]

3. PROTECTION OF RIGHTS ARISING FROM THE CONTRACT OF EMPLOYMENT

3.1. Transfer of rights and obligations

(a) The basic rule: Transfer of responsibility to the transferee

Article 3(1) paragraph 1, as amended, requires the transferee to respect the transferor's rights and obligations towards the employees, thereby limiting the managerial autonomy of the transferee. It provides:

> The transferor's rights and obligations arising from a contract of employment or from an employment relationship existing on the date of a transfer shall, by reason of such transfer, be transferred to the transferee.

---

[202] Case C–478/03 *Celtec* [2005] ECR I–4389, para. 36.

[203] Case C–305/94 *Claude Rotsart de Hertaing* v. *J. Benoidt SA, in liquidation and Others* [1996] ECR I–5927.

[204] Para. 26.   [205] Paras. 17 and 25.   [206] Para. 44.

Therefore, the transferor's rights and obligations, a phrase which is broadly construed,[207] arising from a contract of employment—or from non-contractual employment relationships[208]—which exist at the time of transfer, the details of which are determined by national law, are *automatically* transferred to the transferee.[209]

The Court applies Article 3(1) strictly. For example, in *Rask*[210] the transferee changed the date of payment of the employee's salary from the last Thursday in the month to the last day in the month. The transferee also changed the composition of the payment: the claimants no longer received allowances for laundry or for shoes, although the total amount of their pay remained unchanged. Nevertheless, the Court ruled that Article 3(1) required that the terms of the contract of employment could not be varied on the transfer.[211] In *Collino*[212] the Court said that the transferee had to take into account the entire length of service of the employees transferred in calculating rights of a financial nature such as a termination payment or salary increases.[213] While the transferred employees' length of service with the transferor did not, as such, constitute a right which they could assert against their new employer, where length of service was used to determine financial rights, those rights would have to be maintained by the transferee in the same way as by the transferor.[214]

New Article 3(2), added at the last minute by Directive 98/50, provides, in the interests of transparency, that Member States *may* adopt appropriate measures to ensure that the transferor notifies the transferee of all the rights and obligations which will be transferred to the transferee under Article 3, in so far as the transferor knew or ought to have known of the existence of those rights and obligations. However, a failure to notify will not affect the transfer of any of the rights or obligations nor will it affect the rights of any employees against the transferee and/or transferor in respect of that right or obligation.

(b) The effect of the transfer on the transferor

Berg[215] makes clear that the effect of Article 3(1) is to discharge the transferor from all its obligations arising under the contract of employment[216] from the date of transfer.

---

[207] See e.g. Case C–4/01 *Martin* [2003] ECR I–12859, para. 30 where the Court found that rights contingent on dismissal or the grant of early retirement by agreement with the employer were included within the definition.

[208] Case C–242/09 *Albron* [2011] ECR I-000.

[209] See e.g. Joined Cases 144 and 145/87 *Berg* [1988] ECR 2559, para. 13. In technical terms this means subrogating the rights and obligations of the transferor to the transferee.

[210] Case C–209/91 [1992] ECR I–5755.

[211] Case C–392/92 *Schmidt* [1994] ECR I–1311, para. 19. On the facts, although the transferee offered to employ the transferred employee for a higher wage than she had received previously, she was not prepared to work on those terms because she thought that her hourly wage would, in fact, be lower due to the increase in the surface area to be cleaned.

[212] Case C–343/98 *Collino* v. *Telecom Italia SpA* [2000] ECR I–6659. See further Case C–108/10 *Scattolon* [2011] ECR I-000.

[213] Para. 51.   [214] Para. 50.

[215] Joined Cases 144 and 145/87 [1988] ECR 2559.

[216] The British EAT ruled in *Kerry Foods Ltd* v. *Kreber* [2000] IRLR 10 that the duty to consult was a right which arose from the individual contracts between each employee and the employer and therefore fell within Art. 3(1).

In that case some employees objected to the transfer of certain contractual obligations which the transferor had, prior to the transfer contracted with them to observe, although they did not object to the transfer of their contract of employment. Nevertheless, the Court said that the transferor was released from his obligations as an employer solely by reason of the transfer and irrespective of the consent of the employees concerned.[217]

That said, Member States can provide for joint liability for both the transferor and transferee after the date of the transfer in respect of obligations which arose before the transfer from a contract of employment existing on the date of transfer.[218] Various Member States (for example, Spain, France, Greece, Italy, the Netherlands, Portugal, and Germany) have adopted some form of co-liability rule so that the transferor continues to be liable for pre-transfer debts with the transferee. The period during which the transferor remains liable varies from six months (Portugal) to three years (Spain), while no time limit is fixed in France and Greece. Other Member States have not adopted a co-liability rule, so only the transferee is liable.[219]

(c) Contractual variation

A question which has long troubled employers is whether the transferee (or even the transferor) can vary the contractual terms of the transferred employees to bring the transferred employees' terms and conditions into line with those of the staff already employed by the transferee. For the transferee this is important in terms of administrative convenience, good industrial relations, and, probably, cost saving. However, as we saw in *Rask*, the Court appears to prohibit any changes to the terms and conditions of employment even where the changes are small and the employees consent to their variation. This point was made clearly in *Daddy's Dance Hall*,[220] where the Court said that since the protection conferred by the Directive was a 'matter of public policy, and therefore independent of the will of the parties to the contract of employment', the rules of the Directive had to be considered 'mandatory, so that it is not possible to derogate from them in a manner unfavourable to employees.'[221] The Court continued:[222]

> It follows that employees are not entitled to waive the rights conferred on them by the Directive and that those rights cannot be restricted even with their consent. This interpretation is not affected by the fact that, as in this case, the employee obtains new benefits in compensation for the disadvantages resulting from an amendment to his contract of employment so that, taking the matter as a whole, he is not placed in a worse position than before.

---

[217] Case C–305/94 *Rotsart* [1996] ECR I–5927.   [218] Art. 3(1), para. 2.
[219] COM(94) 300.   [220] Case 324/86 [1988] ECR 739.
[221] Para. 14. See additionally Case 362/89 *d'Urso* [1991] ECR I–4105 where the Court said that the implementation of rights laid down by the Directive could not be made dependent on the agreement of the transferor, transferee, employees' representative, or employees themselves. For the problems experienced by the UK House of Lords in addressing the issue, see *Wilson* v. *St Helens B.C., British Fuels* v. *Meade* [1999] IRLR 706. The Commission proposed that the Directive should contain a declaratory provision that, with the exception of insolvency situations, the transferee and the employees cannot by consent restrict any of the rights contained in the Directive, and that no provision should be made for waiver by collective agreements. This was not adopted in the final version.
[222] Para. 15.

Thus, it seems that a transferee cannot vary the terms and conditions of employment because of the transfer itself. *Martin*[223] adds that contractual variation also cannot occur for a reason connected to the transfer.[224] The case concerned the transfer of a nursing college from the NHS to South Bank University (SBU). The college lecturers had enjoyed the benefits of the NHS Whitley Council terms and conditions, including those relating to early retirement. SBU sought to change those terms to bring them into line with those offered to its other employees. The Court said the alteration of the employment relationship had to be regarded as 'connected to the transfer'.[225] Thus the transferee had to offer the transferred employees early retirement on the same terms as had been offered by the transferor, including to those employees who had already accepted early retirement on the inferior terms.[226]

Martin gave no clue as to whether it is necessary to wait for a certain period of time to elapse before the transfer of an undertaking is not 'the reason' for the variation?[227] It also did not answer the causation question referred: did the transfer have to be the sole or main reason for the change in terms, or was it sufficient that the transfer was only one of a number of reasons to explain the change in terms (the Court in *Martin* assumed that the change in terms was caused by the transfer)? If the former, then the transferee might enjoy some latitude to change terms; if the latter then it becomes very difficult for the transferee to change the employees' terms and conditions.

The corollary of the judgments in *Daddy's Dance Hall* and *Martin* is that the terms and conditions of employment can be amended, even in a manner unfavourable to employees,[228] provided that national law allows such an amendment, on condition that the sole or principal reason for the change is not the transfer of an undertaking itself or for a reason connected to the transfer.[229] The reasoning behind this is that because the Directive is a Directive of partial harmonization, it is only intended to prevent employees affected by a transfer of an undertaking from being placed in a less favourable position than had the transfer not occurred;[230] the Directive was not intended to establish a uniform level of protection throughout the Union on the basis of common criteria.[231]

[223] Case C–4/01 [2003] ECR I–12859.
[224] In *Smith and others v Trustees of Brooklands College* UKEAT/0128/11 the rates had been changed consensually following a transfer because the transferee believed that the existing rates were a mistake in that they did not reflect standard practice. This was not a reason connected with a transfer.
[225] Para. 44.   [226] Para. 54.
[227] See, by analogy, with the one-year period for collective agreements contained in Art. 3(3) considered later, at n. 239.
[228] Case C–392/92 *Schmidt* [1994] ECR I–1311, para. 19. See additionally Case C–343/98 *Collino* v. *Telecom Italia SpA* [2000] ECR I–6659, para. 52.
[229] Reg 4(4) of the TUPE 2006 in the UK allows contractual variation for a reason connected with the transfer which is for an ETOR (see later in this chapter). This is not expressly permitted by the Directive but the UK argues that if a dismissal for a reason connected with the transfer can be justified for ETOR then the lesser step of contractual variation should also be permitted for ETOR.
[230] Case 324/86 *Daddy's Dance Hall* [1988] ECR 739, para. 16; AG Léger's Opinion in Case C–425/02 *Boor, neé Delahaye* v. *Ministre de la Fonction publique et de la Réforme administrative* [2004] ECR I–10823, para. 33.
[231] Case 324/86 *Daddy's Dance Hall* [1988] ECR 739, para. 17; Case C–343/98 *Collino* [2000] ECR I–6659, para. 52.

However, two more recent cases suggest that the Court is beginning to relax its approach. The first is *Delahaye*[232] where the Court suggested that even changes of contract *connected with* the transfer are permissible provided that they are not substantial.[233] The case concerned the transfer of training services in Luxembourg from the private sector to the public sector. Mrs Boor was duly transferred but her pay was cut by 37 per cent due to the fact that her years of service with the transferor had not been taken into account. In another terse judgment, the Court said the Directive had to be interpreted as 'not precluding in principle', in the event of a transfer, the new employer, 'from reducing the amount of the remuneration of the employees concerned for the purpose of complying with the national rules'.[234] However, the Court went on to say that the competent authorities responsible for applying and interpreting those rules were obliged to do so as far as possible in the light of the purpose of the Directive (namely to provide for protection of employees in the event of a change of employer). It continued that if the reduction in pay was substantial, such a reduction constituted a substantial change in working conditions to the detriment of the employees concerned by the transfer and this gave grounds for a claim of constructive dismissal against the transferee under Article 4(2) (considered further below). This point was reiterated by the Grand Chamber in *Scattolon*[235] where it also suggested that variations in terms and conditions by a collective agreement are permissible where 'overall' (not term-by-term) the terms and conditions are no less favourable than those prevailing before the transfer.[236]

3.2. Rights arising from a collective agreement

Article 3(3) provides that, following the transfer, the transferee is obliged to observe the terms and conditions of any collective agreement on the same terms as the transferor.[237] In many Member States this is merely a corollary of contractual subrogation, since in most systems the conditions of employment established by collective agreements are automatically incorporated in individual contracts.[238] This may well mean that different collective agreements regulate the employment conditions of different sections of the transferee's workforce which may interfere with the 'unité du personnel'. Consequently, in some states, such as Spain, the law provides that if the terms of the collective agreements enjoyed by the transferee's workers are superior to those of the transferor's workers, the transferor's workers enjoy the better terms.

However, the obligation on the transferee to respect the terms of pre-existing collective agreements is not indefinite: it lasts until the date of termination or expiry of the

---

[232] Case C–425/02 *Delahaye* [2004] ECR I–10823.

[233] See additionally AG Léger's opinion, paras. 54–6 which seems to have influenced the Court's judgment.

[234] Para. 35.   [235] Case C-108/10 [2011] ECR I-000, para. 83.   [236] Para. 76.

[237] The requirement that the transferee must respect 'customary industrial practice', which would include rules and practices governing the working environment which are not contractually binding, was removed from the final draft of the Directive (Hepple, previously, at n. 105).

[238] Commission report to Council on progress with regard to the implementation of Dir. 77/187/EEC, SEC (92) 857 final, 2 June 1992, 29.

collective agreement or the entry into force or application of another collective agreement. Member States may also limit the period for observing the terms and conditions laid down in the agreement to one year.[239] This would be another way for the transferee to change the terms and conditions of employment, provided that they are contained in a collective agreement. As the Court explained in *Martin*,[240] if, at the time the transferred employees accepted early retirement on terms other than those laid down in the Whitley Council agreement, and the collective agreement giving rise to that provision had, as a matter of law, ceased to apply to them, the employees would lose their rights under the Whitley Council agreement.

The Court in *Werhof*[241] confirmed these points. It considered whether a transferee was bound by a collective agreement subsequent to the one in force at the time of the transfer of the business, when the transferee was not party to the collective agreement. The Court favoured a 'static' interpretation of the Directive, so that a transferee who was not party to a collective agreement, was not bound by future changes to that agreement.[242] The Court said that this interpretation safeguarded the transferee's right not to join an association and thus not to be bound by a collective agreement subsequent to the agreement in force at the time of the transfer.[243]

Scattolon[244] raised a different problem. If the transferor and the transferee both have collective agreements, can the transferee apply its own collective agreement straightaway? Yes, said the Court provided that the conditions which the transferred workers enjoy under the new collective agreement do not have 'the aim or effect of imposing on those workers conditions which are, *overall*, less favourable than those applicable before the transfer.'[245] This remarkable statement suggests that the rule which appeared absolute before (no contractual variation) is less absolute than might first appear.

3.3. Pension rights, invalidity, and survivors' benefits

The final draft of Directive 77/187 excluded employees' rights to 'old age, invalidity or survivor's benefits under supplementary company or inter-company schemes outside the statutory social security schemes' from the scope of the Directive,[246] unless Member States provide otherwise.[247] This provision is now found in Article 3(4)(a) of Directive 2001/23. In *Eidesund*[248] the EFTA Court confirmed that the new contractor was not obliged under Article 3(4)(a) to maintain contributions to the employee's occupational

---

[239] Art. 3(3), para. 2.

[240] Case C–4/01 *Martin* [2003] ECR I–12859, para. 48.

[241] Case C–499/04 *Werhof* v. *Freeway Traffic System GmbH & Co. KG* [2006] ECR I–000. See additionally the reference in *Parkwood Leisure* v. *Alemo-Herron & Ors* [2011] UKSC 26.

[242] Para. 35.   [243] Para. 36.   [244] Case C-108/10 [2011] ECR I-000.

[245] Para. 76.

[246] The British Employment Appeal Tribunal confirmed in *Walden Engineering* v. *Warrener* [1993] IRLR 420 that contracted out occupational pension schemes fell within the definition of 'supplementary schemes' and consequently were excluded from the Directive.

[247] Added by Dir. 98/50. See further B. Hepple and K. Mumgaard, 'Pension Rights in Business Transfers' (1998) 27 *ILJ* 309.

[248] Case E–2/95 [1996] IRLR 684. See additionally the British Court of Appeal's ruling to the same effect in *Adams* v. *Lancashire County Council* [1997] IRLR 436.

pension scheme. From an employee's perspective, this is a grave omission from the protective scheme of the Directive. Since an occupational pension scheme may constitute an integral part of any remuneration package, its loss would make any transfer considerably less attractive. The transferor, who may be insolvent, remains responsible under the terms of the scheme for any liabilities but neither the transferred employee nor the transferor would continue to make contributions.

The severity of this rule is, however, mitigated in two ways. First, Article 3(4)(b) provides that if the Directive does not apply to these benefits, the Member States must adopt the measures necessary to protect the interests of employees and persons no longer employed in the transferor's business at the time of transfer in respect of rights conferring on them immediate or prospective entitlement to old age benefits, including survivors' benefits, under supplementary schemes. Thus, the obligation falls on the Member State[249] and not the transferee, and it extends to persons no longer employed, as well as to employees.

Secondly, the Court of Justice ruled in *Beckmann*[250] that, since Article 3(4)(a) is an exception to the general rule found in Articles 3(1) and (3), it has to be interpreted strictly[251] so that the exception applies 'only to the benefits listed exhaustively in that provision and they must be construed in a narrow sense'. The case concerned an employee, a quantity surveyor, who was transferred from the NHS to a private sector employer, Dynamco Whicheloe Macfarlane Ltd (DWM). Under the terms of the NHS Whitley Council agreement, which was implemented by statutory instrument, employees over 50 and with more than five years' service in the NHS Superannuation Scheme were entitled to immediate payment of their retirement pension and compensation when they were dismissed for redundancy. Beckmann satisfied these conditions but still did not receive the benefits.

The (Full) Court ruled that DWM could not rely on the Article 3(4)(a) exception, declaring that 'it is only benefits paid from the time when an employee reaches the end of his normal working life as laid down by the general structure of the pension scheme in question, and not benefits paid in circumstances such as...[dismissal for redundancy] that can be classified as old-age benefits, even if they are calculated by reference to the rules for calculating normal pension benefits'.[252] Because these rights did not fall within the Article 3(4) exception, they were transferred under Article 3. It did not matter that the rights derived from a statutory instrument or were implemented by such instruments.[253] The effect of this judgment is that early retirement benefits payable on redundancy and all aspects of early retirement schemes are automatically transferred under Article 3; the exclusion applies only to pension benefits paid on or after normal retirement age.[254] In *Martin*[255] the Court extended the ruling in *Beckmann* to benefits applied for on early retirement agreed between the employer and the employee.

---

[249] Failure to implement may result in enforcement proceedings. See Case 235/84 *Commission v. Italy* [1986] ECR 2291 but the provision is unlikely to be directly effective, see e.g. the views of the British EAT in *Warrener* [1993] IRLR 420.
[250] Case C–164/00 *Beckmann v. Dynamco Whicheloe Macfarlane Ltd* [2002] ECR I–4893.
[251] Para. 29.   [252] Para. 32.   [253] Para. 38.
[254] Rubinstein [2002] IRLR 509.   [255] Case C–4/01 *Martin* [2003] ECR I–000, para. 35.

3.4. Consent to transfer

The protection provided by the Directive is a matter of public policy and, as we have seen, operates independently of the will of the parties.[256] This approach contradicts the deep seated, particularly common law, notion that contract is based on a voluntary agreement between the parties. Thus, it is a principle of English law that contracts can be transferred only by novation, which requires the consent of both parties to the contract and of the substituting party. Nevertheless, the Court expressly rejected the common law approach in *Berg*, maintaining that the Directive overrode these principles[257] and did not permit derogations unfavourable to employees. Therefore, as we have seen in *Daddy's Dance Hall*,[258] the Court has said that employees could not waive the rights conferred on them by the Directive nor could these rights be restricted even with their consent.

Following *Daddy's Dance Hall* it was also thought that employees' consent was not relevant as to whether their contract as a whole could be transferred,[259] since it had always been assumed that continued employment by the transferee would be the more attractive proposition for the employee. In fact, this might not always be the case. If the transferor is a public sector undertaking and the transferee a small private company of uncertain financial stability, with a doubtful commercial strategy or less favourable employment policies (including, perhaps, the policy relating to preservation and payment of pensions),[260] the employee may be well advised not to transfer. The Court opened up this possibility in *Katsikas* and *Skreb*,[261] where it made clear that employees could refuse to be transferred. In the first case, Katsikas, an employee in a restaurant run by Konstantinidis, refused to work for Mitossis to whom Konstantinidis had sub-let the restaurant. As a result, Konstantinidis dismissed Katsikas. In the second case, two employees were dismissed by their employers when they refused to accept the transfer of their employment relationship to another company to whom their employers had transferred their section of the business.

The Court reasoned that although the Directive permitted an employee to remain in employment with the new employer on the same terms and conditions as those agreed with the transferor, the Directive did not impose an *obligation* on the employee to continue the employment relationship with the transferee. Such an obligation would undermine the fundamental rights of employees who had to be free to choose their employer and could not be obliged to work for an employer whom they had not freely

---

[256] Case 324/86 *Daddy's Dance Hall* [1988] ECR 739.

[257] Joined Cases 144 and 145/87 *Berg* [1988] ECR 2559, para. 13.

[258] Case 324/86 *Daddy's Dance Hall* [1988] ECR 739.

[259] See para. 11 of Joined Cases 144 and 145/87 *Berg* [1988] ECR 2559, Case C–362/89 *d'Urso* [1991] ECR I–4105, para. 12, and Case 101/87 *Bork* [1988] ECR 3057, para. 17.

[260] See further Advocate General Van Gerven's Opinion in Joined Cases C–132, 138 and 139/91 *Katsikas* [1992] ECR I–6577.

[261] Joined Cases C–132/91, C–138/91 and C–139/91 [1992] ECR I–6577. See additionally Case C–51/00 *Temco Service Industries SA* [2002] ECR I–969, para. 36.

chosen.[262] This means that although employees can neither agree to waive their rights under the Directive nor contract for different terms since the provisions of the Directive are mandatory, they can decide not to be transferred.[263]

However, the judgment came with a sting in its tail: if the employee did voluntarily decide not to transfer, then it was for the Member States to determine the fate of the contract of employment. The Court made clear that the Directive did not oblige Member States to provide that the contract of employment or employment relationship be continued with the transferor. This is the approach adopted by the UK where the contract of employment is considered as terminated with no protection from the law of dismissal. This is a significant practical limitation to the fundamental rights recognized in the judgment.

4. RIGHTS RELATING TO DISMISSAL

4.1. The basic rules

The second pillar of employment protection offered by the Directive relates to rights on dismissal. The first sentence of Article 4(1) provides that the transfer of the undertaking shall not *in itself* constitute grounds for dismissal by the transferor or the transferee. Therefore any dismissal is automatically unfair or unlawful, unless it is for an ETOR (considered below).

Article 4(2) concerns quasi constructive dismissal. It provides that if the contract of employment is terminated because the transfer involves a substantial change in *working conditions*[264] (and not just contractual terms (e.g. major relocation of workplace)) to the detriment of the employee, the employer shall be regarded as having been responsible for termination of the contract. In *Merckx*[265] the Court ruled that a change in the level of remuneration awarded to an employee by the transferee constituted a substantial change in working conditions, even where the remuneration depended on the turnover achieved.[266] Similarly, in *Delahaye*[267] the Court ruled that a substantial reduction in the level of remuneration awarded to an employee (in this case a reduction of 37 per cent due to the fact that on the transfer the transferee took no account of the employee's length of service with the transferor) constituted a substantial change in working conditions.[268] In the UK such dismissals are automatically unfair[269] and the transferee is responsible.[270]

---

[262] The decision accords with the English common law position, stated by Lord Atkin in *Noakes* v. *Doncaster Amalgamated Collieries* [1940] AC 1014, 1026: 'I had fancied that ingrained in the personal status of a citizen under our laws was the right to choose for himself whom he would serve and that this right of choice constituted the main difference between a servant and a serf'. See further Art. 4(2) of the European Convention on Human Rights concerning the prohibition of forced or compulsory labour and in the UK, s. 236 TULR(C)A 1992.

[263] The Court confirmed this ruling in Joined Cases C–171/94 and 172/94 *Merckx* [1996] ECR I–1253, Case C–399/96 *Europièces* [1998] ECR I–6965, para. 38.

[264] This is a matter for the national court to decide, see Case C–399/96 *Europièces* [1998] ECR I–6965, para. 43.

[265] Joined Cases C–171/94 and 172/94 [1996] ECR I–1253.

[266] Para. 38.   [267] Case C–425/02 *Delahaye* [2004] ECR I–10823.   [268] Para. 33.

[269] Unlike other categories of unfair dismissal, the employee is required to satisfy the normal qualifying period to claim for unfair dismissal (two years), see TUPE Reg. 8(5)(b) inserted by SI 1995/2587 reversing *Milligan* v. *Securicor* [1995] IRLR 288. Such dismissals are, however, legally effective, according to the House of Lords in *Wilson* [1998] IRLR 706, and not a legal nullity, as the Court of Appeal had thought [1997] IRLR 505.

[270] As confirmed by AG Léger's Opinion in Case C–425/02 *Delahaye* [2004] ECR I–10823, para. 37.

In *Juuri*[271] the Court had to consider the implications of a breach by the employer of Article 4(2). Emphasizing the partial harmonization envisaged by the Directive, the Court said that the Directive did not impose an obligation on the states to ensure employees benefit from a particular compensation scheme.[272] However, in order to ensure an effective remedy, the national court must ensure that the transferee employer 'bears the consequences that the applicable national law attaches to termination by an employer of the contract of employment or the employment relationship, such as the payment of the salary and other benefits relating, under that law, to the notice period with which an employer must comply'.[273]

4.2. The relationship between Articles 3 and 4

The Court has refused to allow a wedge to be driven between the two pillars of employment protection contained in Articles 3 and 4. As has already been seen, the employment protection provision applies only to those workers who have a contract of employment at the date of transfer,[274] which must be decided on the basis of national law.[275] Thus, in order to avoid the effect of Article 3, a transferor (possibly at the behest of the transferee) might dismiss the workforce shortly before the transfer and then the transferee would re-engage the workforce after the transfer with inferior terms and conditions. In *Bork*[276] the Court tried to eliminate such practices. It said that it was for the national court to decide whether the reason for dismissal was the transfer itself. In reaching its decision the national court had to take account of the objective circumstances in which the dismissal occurred, noting, in particular, the fact that the dismissal took place on a date close to that of the transfer and that the workers concerned were re-engaged by the transferee.[277] If the national court decided that the dismissal occurred because of the transfer then those employees 'dismissed' in breach of Article 4(1), had to be considered as still employed by the undertaking on the date of the transfer with the result that the transferor's obligations towards the employees were automatically transferred to the transferee.[278]

Does this mean that employees, dismissed by the transferor for a transfer-related reason before the transfer or by the transferee after the transfer, can enforce the primary obligation to continued employment or is their remedy confined to compensation enforceable against the transferee for loss of employment? The cases suggest that there is no right to continued employment. In *Dethier*[279] the Court said that the contract of employment of a person unlawfully dismissed shortly before the transfer had to be

---

[271] Case C-396/07 *Juuri* v. *Fazer Amica Oy* [2008] ECR I-8883.
[272] Para. 22.   [273] Para. 30.   [274] Case 19/83 *Wendleboe* [1985] ECR 457, para. 13.
[275] Case 101/87 *Bork* [1988] ECR 3057, para. 17.
[276] Case 101/87 [1988] ECR 3057. See additionally the decision of the British House of Lords in *Litster* v. *Forth Dry Dock & Engineering Co. Ltd* [1990] 1 AC 546 where it said that the Directive applied both to those who were employed immediately before the transfer and those who would have been so employed had they not been unfairly dismissed.
[277] Case 101/87 *Bork* [1988] ECR 3057, paras. 18 and 19.
[278] See additionally Case C-51/00 *Temco* [2002] ECR I-969, para. 28.
[279] Case C-319/94 [1998] ECR I-1061.

regarded as still extant as against the transferee even if the dismissed employee was not taken on by him after the undertaking was transferred.[280] This employee can claim that his dismissal was unlawful against the transferee. This suggests that the transferee is liable for all secondary contractual obligations, such as the right to claim unfair dismissal, but not the primary obligation to continued employment. This approach was adopted by the British House of Lords in *British Fuels and Wilson*[281] where Lord Slynn said the transferee had to meet all of the transferor's contractual and statutory obligations unless either the employee objected to being employed by the transferee or the reason or principal reason for dismissal was for an economic, technical, or organizational reason (ETOR). This is considered in the next section.

4.3. The limits to the protection contained in Article 4(1)

The general rule contained in Article 4(1) that the transfer shall not constitute grounds for dismissal is subject to two limitations. First, Member States may exclude certain specific categories of employees who are not covered by the dismissal laws or practice of the Member States from the protection conferred by the first sentence of Article 4(1).[282] However, in *Commission* v. *Belgium*[283] the Court ruled that Member States cannot use this exception as a means of depriving rights from workers in the event of a transfer who already enjoy some protection, albeit limited, against dismissal under national law.

Second, Article 4(1), second sentence, contains the ETOR defence. It provides that:

> This provision shall not stand in the way of dismissals that may take place for economic, technical or organisational reasons [ETOR] entailing changes in the workforce.

The Court has offered surprisingly little guidance on the meaning of ETOR, often only paying lip service to the existence of the provision.[284] The only case where there has been some discussion of ETOR is *Vigano*[285] where a transferor in the course of insolvency proceedings decided to award some of its stores to the transferee which took on the transferor's staff. However, the assignment of the leases to the transferee was done in breach of the original lease, and since the lessor and the new lessee (the transferee) could not reach an agreement the store had to be closed leading to the dismissal of the staff. The Court said:

> the possible termination of the contracts of employment would not be due solely to the transfer of the undertaking. It would be caused by additional circumstances such as the failure of the transferee and the landlords to agree a new lease, the impossibility of finding other commercial premises or the impossibility of transferring the staff to other stores. Those circumstances can be described as economic, technical or organisational reasons for the purposes of Article 4(1).[286]

---

[280] Para. 41.
[281] *British Fuels Ltd* v. *Baxendale; Wilson* v. *St Helens Borough Council* [1998] 4 All ER 609.
[282] Art. 4(1), third sentence.   [283] Case 237/84 [1986] ECR 1247.
[284] See, e.g., Case C–171/94 *Merckx* [1996] ECR I–1253.
[285] Case C–313/07 *Vigano* v. *Red Elite* [2008] ECR I–7907.   [286] Para. 46.

The English courts have considered the ETOR defence in more detail. They have found that an 'economic' reason has to relate to the conduct of the business. Therefore, dismissals for reasons of redundancy fall within the ETOR[287] exception and so the transferee must make a redundancy payment. On the other hand, broader economic reasons, such as the desire on the part of the transferor to achieve a higher sale price or achieve a sale at all, do not constitute an economic reason.[288] Flexibility and cost-cutting measures also do not constitute an ETOR because the 'reason itself does not involve any change either in the number or the functions of the workforce'.[289]

The employer must be motivated by a genuine economic, technical, or organizational reason and that reason must result in the dismissals. Therefore, any attempt by a transferee to rely on this provision to dismiss employees who are later re-engaged by the same transferee, usually on inferior terms, is regarded with suspicion. This view receives some support from Advocate General Van Gerven in *d'Urso*.[290] He refused to countenance the argument that the Directive permits *any* dismissal for economic, technical, or organizational reasons. In fact, he says, the Directive expressly prohibits such dismissals when they occur as a result of the transfer of the undertaking. Only dismissals which would have been made in any case, for instance if the decision had been taken before there was any question of transferring the undertaking, fall within the exclusion. He therefore said that Article 4 could not be relied on as justification for dismissing some employees because the undertaking has been transferred.

E. COLLECTIVE RIGHTS

1. INTRODUCTION

The Directive envisages an important role for employee representatives in respect of information and consultation. They are defined in Article 2(1)(c) as the representatives of the employees provided for by the laws or practice of the Member States. These representatives may be trade unionists and/or works councillors. The Continental European tradition has typically provided for this 'dual channel' approach. However, in the UK the information and consultation procedures laid down by the original national rules implementing the Directive applied only to recognized trade unions (with the decision to recognize being entirely a matter for the employer). This was in line with the British 'single channel' approach through which all worker representation was traditionally directed.

In *Commission* v. *UK*[291] the Court ruled that, by confining the information and consultation obligations to recognized trade unions only, the UK had failed to transpose the

---

[287] It was confirmed in Case C–319/94 *Dethier* [1998] ECR I–1061 that the ETOR exception applies to both the transferor and the transferee.
[288] *Wheeler* v. *Patel* [1987] IRLR 631.   [289] *Berriman* v. *Delabole Slate* [1990] ICR 85.
[290] Case C–362/89 *d'Urso* [1991] ECR I–4105.
[291] Case C–382/92 *Commission* v. *UK* [1994] ECR I–2435.

Directive fully because British law did not provide a mechanism for the designation of workers' representatives where an employer refused to recognize a trade union. The UK government argued that, as a Directive of partial harmonization,[292] the term employees' representatives referred to those representatives provided for by the laws and practices of the Member States which, in the UK, meant recognized trade unions only. The Court rejected this argument, saying that the Directive was not simply a *renvoi* to the rules in force in the Member States.[293] Focusing on the effective application of Union law rather than the concept of partial harmonization, the Court said that the duty to inform and consult would be deprived of its full effect if Member States allowed only recognized employee representatives to be informed and consulted,[294] leaving employees in a workplace without a recognized trade union without information and consultation rights.[295]

The UK gave effect to the ruling by expanding the scope of those who could be consulted.[296] Where a recognized trade union exists, it still needs to be consulted. In the absence of a recognized trade union, consultation takes place with elected representatives.[297] The creation of elected 'employee representatives' marked the first substantial inroad into the single channel in the UK. However, the Labour government's amendments ensured that consultation with employee representatives is considered very much a secondary channel, prompting Davies to describe the current British rules as 'a modified single channel'.[298]

2. INFORMATION AND CONSULTATION

As far as information is concerned, Article 7(1) requires that the representatives of the employees must be informed and consulted. As far as information is concerned, Article 7(1) requires the transferor *and* the transferee to inform the representatives of their respective employees affected by a transfer of the following:

- the date or proposed date of the transfer;
- the reasons for the transfer;
- the legal, economic, and social implications of the transfer for the employees;
- any measures envisaged in relation to the employees.

---

[292] Para. 27.

[293] Para. 18. The Court cited Case 61/81 *Commission* v. *UK* [1982] ECR 2601 which held that national legislation making it possible to impede protection unconditionally granted to employees by a Directive is contrary to Union law.

[294] Para. 19.   [295] Para. 29.

[296] The initial implementation can be found in SI 1995/2587 The Collective Redundancies and Transfer of Undertakings (Protection of Employment) (Amendment) Regulations 1995, amending SI 1981/1794 Transfer of Undertakings (Protection of Employment) Regulations 1981, Reg. 10.

[297] Unsuccessful judicial review proceedings were brought in R v. *Secretary of State for Trade and Industry, ex parte Unison* [1996] IRLR 438, challenging the implementation. The relevant Regulations are now found in SI 1999/1925 The Collective Redundancies and Transfer of Undertakings Regulations (Protection of Employment) (Amendment) Regulations 1999. These Regulations also make some provision for the election of worker representatives.

[298] P. Davies, 'A Challenge to Single Channel' (1994) 23 *ILJ* 272, 279. This issue is considered further in Ch. 15.

Both the transferor and the transferee are obliged to give the information to the employees' representatives in 'good time'. In the case of the transferor, the information must be given before the transfer is carried out but no specific time limit is set.[299] In the case of the transferee, it is under an obligation to provide its own employees' representatives with information before its employees are directly affected by the transfer as regards their conditions of work and employment.[300]

Employees' representatives have direct input only in respect of 'measures' envisaged by the transferor or transferee in relation to the employees (such as a reduction in the workforce, or the introduction of new working methods):[301] under Article 7(2) the transferor or the transferee must *consult* the employees' representatives,[302] again in good time, with a *view to seeking their agreement*. Thus, the Directive does provide for an element of employee participation, at least through their representatives, in commercial decisions but neither the employees nor their representatives have the right to veto any such decisions.

German law provides that the works council and the head of the undertaking may agree on a social plan intended to compensate for or mitigate the detrimental economic consequences which the worker might suffer as a result of the envisaged change. In the event of disagreement about the social plan, either of the two sides may bring the matter before the conciliation committee, an arbitration body comprising an equal number of members appointed by the head of the firm and the works council, with a Chair acceptable to both sides, whose decision is binding.[303] This can continue: Article 7(3) provides that if the national system permits employees' representatives to have recourse to an arbitration board to obtain a decision on the 'measures to be taken in relation to employees', the duties of information and consultation may be limited to cases where the transfer is likely to entail 'serious disadvantages for a considerable number of employees'. Nevertheless, the information and consultations must concern the measures envisaged in relation to employees and must take place in good time before the transfer is effected.[304]

Article 7(4), introduced by Directive 98/50, addresses the situation of transnational companies where decisions may be taken by the parent in one state which affects a subsidiary in another state. In line with the amendments to the Directive on Collective Redundancies,[305] Article 7(4) provides that it is no 'excuse' for an employer subsidiary which is in breach of the information and consultation provisions to argue that the

---

[299] Art. 7(1), para. 2.   [300] Art. 7(1), para. 3.

[301] European Works Councils may also have to be informed and consulted in respect of the progress of the business and its prospects and to be informed of decisions affecting the employees' interests to a considerable extent: see paras. 2 and 3 of the Annex to Dir. 2009/38/EC (OJ [2009] L122/28). Cf. Art. 9 of The Information and Consultation Dir. 2002/14 (OJ [2002] L80/29) which gives precedence to the specific information and consultation procedures set out in the Collective Redundancies and Transfer of Undertakings Directives.

[302] The first draft envisaged negotiations by the employees' representatives with the transferor or transferee with a view to seeking agreement and in default the matter could be referred to arbitration.

[303] Commission Report to the Council, SEC (92) 857 final, 93.

[304] Art. 7(3), paras. 2 and 3.

[305] Council Directive 92/56/EEC (OJ [1992] L245/3).

information was not provided by the controlling parent undertaking which took the decision. Article 7 applies irrespective of whether the decision resulting in the transfer is taken by the employer or an undertaking controlling the employer.[306]

Finally, Member States have the option of limiting the information and consultation rights to those businesses which in terms of the number of employees meet 'the conditions for the election or nomination of a collegiate body representing the employees'.[307] This provision addresses a situation such as that in the Netherlands where the statutory requirement of information and consultation of representatives of workers applies only to works councils,[308] and consequently to undertakings employing at least 100 people, or at least 35 people for more than one-third of the normal working hours, where the election of a works council is mandatory.[309] In the case of smaller undertakings where there are no employee representatives, Article 7(6) provides that the employees themselves must be given the same information 'in advance' (not 'in good time') as would have been given to the employee representatives.

Given the importance of the information and consultation provisions to the Directive, Article 6 aims to safeguard and preserve the status and function of the 'representatives' or of the representation of the employees affected by the transfer, as laid down by the laws, regulations or administrative provisions of the Member States, on the same terms and subject to the same conditions as existed before the transfer. This protection is subject to two conditions. First, the business must preserve its autonomy.[310] The term 'autonomy' is not equivalent to 'identity' in Article 1(1)(b). Rather, as the Court explained in *UGT-FSP*,[311] it describes the right to self-government, namely:[312]

> the powers, granted to those in charge of that entity, to organise, relatively freely and independently, the work within that entity in the pursuit of its specific economic activity and, more particularly, the powers to give orders and instructions, to allocate tasks to employees of the entity concerned and to determine the use of assets available to the entity, all without direct intervention from other organisational structures of the employer ('the organisational powers').

The Court continued that autonomy is, as a general rule preserved, if, after the transfer, the organizational powers of those in charge of the entity transferred remain, within the organizational structures of the transferee, essentially unchanged as compared with the situation pertaining before the transfer. Where the part of the business transferred does

---

[306] Art. 7(4), para. 1.   [307] Art. 7(5).

[308] Art. 25 of the Law on Works Councils.

[309] The proposed Directive (94/C274/08) provided that the Member States could limit the information and consultation requirements to undertakings or businesses which normally employ 50 or more employees. This was not included in the final version but reflects the Commission's thinking in the more general information and consultation proposal discussed in Ch. 8.

[310] Art. 6(1). If the business does not preserve its autonomy, the Member States must take the necessary measures to ensure that the employees transferred, who were represented before the transfer, continue to be properly represented during the period prior to the reconstitution or reappointment of the representatives of the employees (Art. 6(1), para. 4).

[311] Case C–151/09 *UGT-FSP v. Ayuntamiento de la Línea de la Concepción* [2010] ECR I–000, para. 42.

[312] Para. 43.

not retain its autonomy the Member States must take the necessary measures to ensure that the employees transferred who were represented before the transfer continue to be properly represented during the period necessary for the reconstitution or reappointment of the representation of employees in accordance with national law and practice.[313]

The second limit on preserving the status of existing employee representatives is that if 'the conditions necessary for the re-appointment of the representatives of the employees or for the reconstitution of the representation of the employees are fulfilled', the status and function of the original representatives will not be preserved.[314] This may occur where the transfer results in an increase in the workforce necessitating a change in the number of representatives or in the structure of the representation.[315] Nevertheless, workers representatives whose term of office expires as a result of the transfer continue to enjoy the protection afforded by legislation in the Member States against action taken by employers which may be detrimental to workers' representatives.[316]

Finally, Article 6(1) makes special provision for a transferor which is the subject of bankruptcy proceedings or any analogous insolvency proceedings. Article 6(1), paragraph 3 provides that Member States *may* take the necessary measures to ensure that the employees transferred who were represented before the transfer continue to be properly represented during the period necessary for the reconstitution or reappointment of the representation of employees in accordance with national law or practice.

F. INSOLVENCY AND MEASURES FALLING SHORT OF A DECLARATION OF INSOLVENCY

1. THE BASIC RULES

Transfers on insolvency raise particular issues. Although the original Directive 77/187/EEC did not expressly exclude transfers on insolvency from its scope, in *Abels*[317] the Court achieved that result. It said that the Directive did not apply to transfers of undertakings 'taking place in the context of insolvency proceedings instituted with a view to the liquidation of assets of the transferor under the supervision of the competent judicial authority'.[318] The explanation of the Court's ruling lies in the special nature of the laws on insolvency[319] which are designed to weigh up the various interests involved, in

---

[313] Art. 6(1), para. 4.   [314] Art. 6(1), para. 2.

[315] See Art. 6(1), para. 2, Commission Report to the Council, SEC (92) 857 final, Brussels 2 June 1992.

[316] Art. 6(2).

[317] The Court repeated its decision in Case 135/83 [1985] ECR 469 in three cases decided on the same day as *Abels*: Case 186/83 *Botzen* [1985] ECR 519, Case 19/83 *Wendelboe* [1985] ECR 457 and Case 179/83 *Industrie Bond FNV* [1985] ECR 511.

[318] Para. 23. This was deemed important by Advocate General Van Gerven in Case C–362/89 *d'Urso* [1991] ECR I–4105. He said it was insufficient that the preconditions to insolvency have been fulfilled.

[319] Para. 16. In the Union context, see Council Dir. 80/987/EEC (OJ [1980] L283/23) (now Dir. 2008/94 (OJ [2008] L283/36)). The Council did not take the opportunity of the enactment of Dir. 80/987 to apply the original Dir. 77/187/EEC to an insolvency situation.

particular, those of the creditors.[320] Consequently, insolvency rules derogate, at least in part, from the provisions of social law, both at national and Union level.[321] Therefore, the Court concluded, rather unusually, that an express provision in the Directive would have been *required* before it applied to an insolvency situation.[322]

In *Abels* the claimant was employed by Thole when, by successive decisions of the District Court, Thole was granted *surséance van betaling* (judicial leave to suspend payment of debts) in 1981 and then went into liquidation in 1982. During the liquidation proceedings Thole's business was transferred to TPP which continued to operate the undertaking and took over most of the workforce, including the claimant. The claimant, however, complained that he had not received his wages or various other payments as required by the Directive.

It was argued by the Danish government that the transfer rules should apply to employees whose employer had become insolvent because this was the time when the workers were in most need of protection.[323] By contrast, the Dutch government and the Commission argued that if the Directive applied this might dissuade a potential transferee from acquiring an undertaking on conditions acceptable to the creditors, who might then prefer instead to sell the assets of the undertaking separately, thereby avoiding the scope of the Directive.[324] This, they argued, would entail the loss of all the jobs in the enterprise, which would detract from the utility of the Directive.[325] As the Commission has subsequently recognized, the underlying problem here is the conflict between the acquired rights of employees and those of other creditors upon insolvency. If the employees of the insolvent transferor undertaking and all their rights and entitlements are transferred to the new solvent transferee, the effect is to treat those employees more favourably than other creditors of the insolvent undertaking. The creditors will assert that the transferee will pay less for the transferred undertaking, as a result of having to take over all liabilities to the new employees, and hence the pool of assets against which the creditors of the insolvent undertaking can claim will be reduced.[326]

The Court, while acknowledging that 'considerable uncertainty exists regarding the impact on the labour market of transfer of undertakings in the case of the employer's insolvency',[327] seemed to accept the Dutch government's view. It therefore decided that the interests of employees would be better served if the Directive did *not* apply 'otherwise a serious risk of general deterioration in living and working conditions of workers, contrary to the social objectives of the Treaty',[328] could not be ruled out.

The Court has, however, refused to extend the scope of its ruling in *Abels*. In *Sophie Redmond*,[329] for example, the Court rejected arguments that the Directive did not

---

[320] Para. 15.
[321] Para. 16. In the Union context, see Art. 1(2)(d) of the original Dir. 75/129/EEC (OJ L48/29) on collective redundancies which expressly excluded from its scope workers affected by termination of an establishment's activities 'where that is a result of a judicial decision' (now removed by Dir. 98/59/EC (OJ [1998] L225/16)).
[322] Para. 17.   [323] Para. 20.
[324] Assets only sales fall outside the scope of the Directive, see Case 24/85 *Spijkers* [1986] ECR 1119.
[325] Para. 21.   [326] Explanatory memorandum, COM(94) 300, para. 23.   [327] Para. 22.
[328] Para. 23.   [329] Case C–29/91 [1992] ECR I–3189.

apply to situations comparable with insolvency, such as the closure of a foundation due to the withdrawal of its subsidy by the local authority. In *Merckx*,[330] the Court ruled that the application of the Directive could not be excluded merely because the transferor discontinued its activities when the transfer was made and was then put into liquidation. It added that if the business of that undertaking was carried on by another undertaking this tended to confirm that there had been a transfer for the purposes of the Directive.

Even in *Abels*[331] the Court imposed two limits to its own ruling. First, it said that Member States could, if they wished, apply the provisions of the Directive to a transfer arising in the event of insolvency.[332] Secondly, it said that the Directive did apply to situations where an undertaking was transferred to another employer in the course of a pre-insolvency procedure, such as the Dutch *surséance van betaling*.[333] This procedure allows a company, with the leave of the court, to suspend payment of its debts with a view to reaching a settlement. Such a settlement is intended to ensure that the undertaking is able to continue operating in the future.

The distinction drawn by the Court between insolvency and pre-insolvency proceedings may be based on a false premise. Although it acknowledged that the two types of proceedings share many common characteristics,[334] the Court failed to recognize that the reason why many companies go into pre-insolvent procedures is that there is a greater chance of selling off at least part of the company's business as a going concern, thereby securing some of the workers' jobs. This is precisely the situation which justified excluding insolvent companies from the operation of the Directive.[335] Nevertheless, the distinction between liquidation of insolvent companies and other ways of dealing with them was incorporated into the Directive by Directive 98/50/EEC.[336] Article 5(1) of what is now Directive 2001/23 provides that unless Member States provide otherwise, Articles 3 and 4 of the Directive (concerning transfer of the contract of employment and dismissals) do not apply to a transfer where the transferor is 'the subject of bankruptcy proceedings or any analogous insolvency proceedings which have been instituted with a view to the liquidation of the assets of the transferor and are under the supervision of a competent public authority'.[337]

If Member States do decide that Articles 3 and 4 are to apply to a transfer during insolvency proceedings which have been opened in relation to a transferor (whether or

---

[330] Joined Cases C–171/94 and C–172/94 [1996] ECR I–1253.
[331] Case 135/83 [1985] ECR 469.   [332] Para. 24.
[333] This point was confirmed in three cases decided on the same day: Case 135/83 *Abels* [1985] ECR 469, Case 186/83 *Botzen* [1985] ECR 519, Case 19/83 *Wendleboe* [1985] ECR 457, Case 179/83 *Industrie Bond FNV* [1985] ECR 511, and Case 105/84 *Danmols Inventar* [1985] ECR 2639.
[334] *Abels*, para. 28. See additionally Case C–362/89 *d'Urso* [1991] ECR I–4105, para. 24.
[335] P. Davies, 'Acquired Rights, Creditors' Rights, Freedom of Contract, and Industrial Democracy' (1989) 9 *YEL* 21, 47.
[336] OJ [1998] L201/88.
[337] The supervision of a competent public authority may be an insolvency practitioner authorized by a competent public authority.

not those proceedings have been instituted with a view to the liquidation of the assets of the transferor), the Directive says that a Member State may provide that:[338]

(a) the transferor's debts arising from any contracts of employment or employment relationships and payable before the transfer or before the opening of the insolvency proceedings are not transferred to the transferee, provided that the proceedings give rise to protection at least equivalent to that provided for by Directive 2008/94 on the protection of employees in the event of the insolvency of their employer; and/or

(b) the transferee or transferor on the one hand, and the representatives of the employees on the other hand, may agree alterations, in so far as current law and practice permits,[339] to the employees' terms and conditions of employment designed to safeguard employment opportunities by ensuring the survival of the economic entity being transferred.[340] Further, a Member State may apply this provision to *any* transfers where the transferor is in a situation of 'serious economic crisis'[341] and open to judicial supervision, on condition that such provisions already existed in national law by 17 July 1998.[342]

Therefore in situation (b) worker representatives can agree collectively to the modification of terms and conditions of employment. Thus, the Directive, like the Working Time Directive 2003/88,[343] permits derogations from the legislative minima *in pejus*. In addition, as we saw above, new Article 6(1), paragraph 3 provides that where the transferor is the subject of bankruptcy proceedings or analogous proceedings, as described in Article 5(1), Member States 'may take the necessary measures to ensure that the transferred employees are properly represented until the new election or designation of representatives of the employees'. These new provisions are striking for their 'pick-and-mix' quality. Member States are given a great deal of discretion which provisions to apply.

Finally, Article 5(4) requires Member States to take appropriate measures with a view to preventing misuse of insolvency proceedings in such a way as to deprive employees of their rights in the event of a transfer.

2. DISTINGUISHING BETWEEN INSOLVENCY AND PRE-INSOLVENCY PROCEEDINGS

Given that the Directive now distinguishes between insolvency proceedings, to which the Directive will (usually) not apply, and pre-insolvency proceedings such as *surséance*

---

[338] Art. 5(2).

[339] Thus, the representatives cannot agree anything which the individual employee could not negotiate him or herself.

[340] Cf. Case C–362/89 *d'Urso* [1991] ECR I–4105.

[341] Art. 5(3). A situation of 'serious economic crisis' is to be defined by public law and declared by a competent public authority. In Italy an enterprise in crisis can go into *amministrazione controllata*, a procedure similar to the Dutch *surséance van betaling*, which allows the trade unions, as a derogation from Art. 2112 of the Civil Code, to agree to the reduction in protection for those workers transferred to the solvent transferee.

[342] Art. 5(3).   [343] OJ [2003] L299/9 considered in detail in Ch. 12.

proceedings, to which the Directive will apply, how are these different types of procedure to be identified? Advocate General Van Gerven in *d'Urso*[344] offered some guidance. First, he distinguished between the two proceedings by reference to their purpose. He suggested that an inherent characteristic of *surséance* proceedings was that they were intended to resolve temporary cash-flow problems and not to liquidate the assets of the debtor—in other words, to *prevent* insolvency.[345] By contrast, he said, insolvency proceedings, were fundamentally different: their purpose was the liquidation of property by selling the assets with a view to offsetting the liabilities.

Secondly, Advocate General Van Gerven distinguished between the two proceedings, by reference to judicial control. In the case of *surséance* proceedings he noted that the supervision of the Court over the commencement and the course of the proceedings was much more limited than in the case of insolvency.[346] The judge's control extended only to ensuring that the debtor respected the obligations he had entered into. On the other hand, in insolvency the judge had more extensive control. This might be accompanied by the creation of an administration or a trust with special powers to determine the value of the undertaking, to sell off the assets and to meet the liabilities, which in turn is accompanied by the creation of a compulsory trust over the affairs of the debtor, who is deprived of any power to manage or to dispose of the assets. In *surséance* proceedings, there will be one or more designated receivers or administrators who will exercise control over the debtor, to whom they must give assistance or authorization before the debtor may carry out certain acts, but without ever depriving the debtor of the rights to manage or dispose of this property. In subsequent cases, the Court has placed less emphasis on the importance of judicial supervision than on the objective of the procedure at issue[347] as the distinguishing criteria.

The Court has been asked by various national courts to decide on which side of the line the national rules fall. For example, in *d'Urso* the Court said that the Directive did not apply to transfers of undertakings made as part of a creditor's settlement of the kind provided for in Italian legislation on 'compulsory administrative liquidation' whose effects were comparable to bankruptcy proceedings; while in *Spano*[348] the Court held that the Directive did apply to a transfer of an undertaking declared to be in critical difficulties pursuant to Italian Law No. 675 of 12 August 1977. It pointed out that the purpose of such a declaration was to enable the undertaking to retrieve its economic and financial situation and above all to preserve jobs, that the procedure in question was designed to promote the continuation of its business with a view to its subsequent recovery, and that, by contrast with insolvency proceedings, it did not involve any judicial supervision or any measure whereby the assets of the undertaking were put under administration and did not provide for any suspension of payments.[349]

---

[344] Case C–362/89 [1991] ECR I–4105.   [345] See additionally the Court of Justice in *Abels*, para. 28.
[346] Ibid.   [347] Case C–362/89 *d'Urso* [1991] ECR I–4105.
[348] Case C–472/93 *Spano and Others* v. *Fiat Geotech and Fiat Hitachi* [1995] ECR I–4321.
[349] Paras. 26, 28, and 29.

In *Dethier*[350] the Court was obliged to give more detailed guidance about the nature of the distinction between the two types of proceedings in the context of Belgian law on liquidation. In May 1991 the Tribunal de Commerce made an order putting Sovam into liquidation and appointing a liquidator. Three weeks later the liquidator dismissed Dassy and shortly afterwards transferred the assets of Sovam to Dethier under an agreement approved by the Tribunal de Commerce. In deciding whether the Directive applied to this Belgian winding-up procedure, the Court said that the determining factor to be taken into consideration was the *purpose* of the procedure in question, but that account also had to be taken of the *form* of the procedure in question, in particular, in so far as it meant that the undertaking continues or ceases trading, and also of the Directive's objectives.[351] On the facts of the case, the Court said that it was apparent that although the objective of the Belgian procedure could sometimes be similar to those of insolvency proceedings, this was not necessarily the case, since liquidation proceedings could be used whenever it was wished to bring a company's activities to an end and whatever the reasons for that decision.[352]

Since the criterion relating to the *purpose* of the procedure for winding up was not conclusive, the Court examined the procedure in detail.[353] It pointed out that the liquidator, although appointed by the court, was an organ of the company who sells the assets under the supervision of the general meeting; that there was no special procedure for establishing liabilities under the supervision of the court; and that a creditor could enforce his debt against the company and obtain judgment against it. By contrast, in the case of an insolvency, the administrator was a third party vis-à-vis the company and realized the assets under the supervision of the court; that the liabilities of the company were established in accordance with a special procedure and individual enforcement actions were prohibited.[354] Therefore, the Court concluded that there was no insolvency situation where an undertaking continued to trade while it was being wound up by the court and so the Directive applied.[355]

In *Europièces*[356] the Court applied its ruling in *Dethier* to the case of voluntary liquidation which, it noted, is 'essentially similar to winding up by the court, save for the fact that it falls to the shareholders in general meeting, and not to the court, to take the decision to wind up the company, appoint the liquidators and determine their powers'.[357] Since, at least in some procedural respects, voluntary liquidation had even less in common with insolvency than winding up by the court,[358] the Court said the Directive applied.

---

[350] Case C–319/94 [1998] ECR I–1061.   [351] Para. 25.   [352] Para. 27.   [353] Para. 28.
[354] Para. 29.   [355] Para. 32.   [356] Case C–399/96 [1998] ECR I–6965.
[357] Para. 33. Only where a majority of the shareholders cannot be assembled must the company apply to the court for a declaration putting it into liquidation. The court then designates the liquidators in accordance with the company's articles of association or pursuant to the decision of the shareholders in general meeting, unless it is clear that disagreement between the shareholders will prevent them from taking a decision in general meeting, in which case the court itself appoints a liquidator.
[358] Para. 34.

G. IMPLEMENTATION AND REMEDIES

1. IMPLEMENTATION

Directive 2001/23 is a minimum standards Directive: states are free to enact provisions more favourable to employees or to promote or permit collective agreements more favourable to employees.[359] Even if Member States do not take advantage of improving upon the minimum protection laid down by the Directive, they do have to implement the Directive's minima either through laws, regulations, or administrative provisions[360] or through collective agreements. This second possibility was introduced by Article 2(1) of Directive 98/50 which permitted employers and the employees' representatives to introduce the required provisions 'by means of agreement',[361] albeit that the Member States retained responsibility for ensuring that all workers were afforded the full protection provided by the Directive.[362] In the words of the Court, 'the state guarantee must cover all cases where effective protection is not ensured by other means'.[363] Thus, in *Commission* v. *Italy*,[364] the Court accepted that collective agreements could be used as a means of laying down procedures for informing and consulting employees' representatives affected by a transfer.[365] However, since these agreements covered only specific economic sectors, the Italian government was obliged to enact appropriate laws, regulations or administrative measures to ensure full compliance with the Directive.

2. REMEDIES

While the original Directive 77/187 provided rights for employees and their representatives it made no provision for remedies in the event of the failure by a transferor or transferee to recognize those rights. However, in *Commission* v. *UK*[366] the Court said that where a Union Directive did not specifically provide any penalty for an infringement, or refers to national laws, regulations, and administrative provisions, Article 4(3) TEU (ex 10 EC) required the Member States to take all measures necessary to guarantee the application and effectiveness of Union law. While the choice of penalties remained within their discretion (the principle of national procedural autonomy), Member States had to ensure, in particular, that infringements of Union law were penalized under conditions, both procedural and substantive, which were analogous to those applicable to infringements of national law of a similar nature and importance and which, in any

---

[359] Art. 8.   [360] Art. 8 of the original Dir. 77/187.

[361] As approved by the Court: Case 143/83 *Commission* v. *Denmark* [1985] ECR 427, and confirmed by Case 235/84 *Commission* v. *Italy* [1986] ECR 2291.

[362] Art. 2(1) of Dir. 98/50/EC. There is no equivalent provision in Dir. 2001/23 although Art. 12 refers to Annex I Part B which retains the deadline for implementation.

[363] Case 235/84 *Commission* v. *Italy* [1986] ECR 2291, para. 20.   [364] Ibid.

[365] Cf. Advocate General Slynn, in Case 235/84 *Commission* v. *Italy* [1986] ECR 2291 who doubted whether collective agreements could be used as a means of implementing a Directive.

[366] Case C–382/92 [1994] ECR I–2435.

event, made the penalty effective, proportionate, and dissuasive.[367] Under UK law, an employer who failed to consult employee representatives at the time of the transfer could be ordered to pay a penalty of up to a maximum of four weeks' pay to employees affected by the transfer. However, any protective award made against the employer for failing to consult employees' representatives in the event of collective redundancies could be set off against any penalty payment received by the employee which, when combined with the financial ceiling on the penalty, significantly weakened the initial financial penalty. In the eyes of the Court such a penalty was not a true deterrent and consequently the UK legislation did not comply with Article 4, para 3 TEU.

The Directive has now been amended to introduce a standard remedies clause. Article 9 requires those employees and employee representatives who consider themselves wronged by failure to comply with the obligations arising from the Directive to pursue their claims by judicial process after possible recourse to other competent authorities.

H. CONCLUSIONS

Despite the overt recognition that the Directive on transfers of undertakings has a welfarist or market-correcting purpose (the protection of labour standards), it has become increasingly clear that the Court is also motivated by the desire to ensure a level playing field of costs so that the financial burden of restructuring an enterprise is the same in all Member States (the market-making rationale).[368] Express acknowledgement of this can be found in *Commission* v. *UK*[369] where the Court said:

> By harmonising the rules applicable to collective redundancies,[370] the [Union] legislature intended both to ensure comparable protection of workers' rights in the different Member States and *to harmonise the costs which such protective rules entail for [Union] undertakings.*[371]

However, the effectiveness of this level playing field of costs is significantly reduced by the degree to which key matters are dictated by national legislation or practice. As we have seen in *Katsikas*,[372] while the Court recognized the worker's right to refuse to be transferred it allowed national law to prescribe the consequences for the worker of his or her refusal. As a result some Member States have said that the worker's contract of employment is treated as terminated while in others the contract with the transferor

---

[367] With regard to Union regulations see the judgments in Case 68/88 *Commission* v. *Greece* [1989] ECR 2965, paras. 23 and 24, and in Case C–7/90 *Criminal Proceedings against Vandevenne and Others* [1991] ECR I–4371, para. 11.

[368] As a result, Art. 115 TFEU (ex 94 EC), concerning the approximation of measures which directly affect the establishment and functioning of the Common Market, was chosen as the legal base for all three Directives.

[369] Case C–383/92 [1994] ECR I–2479.

[370] The Court used the same words in the context of the Directive on safeguarding employees' rights in the event of transfers of undertakings in Case C–382/92 *Commission* v. *UK* [1994] ECR I–2435.

[371] Emphasis added. See additionally Case C–55/02 *Commission* v. *Portugal* [2004] ECR I–9387, para. 48, citing the third, fourth and seventh recitals of the preamble to Dir. 98/59.

[372] Joined Case C–132, C–138 and 139/91 [1992] ECR I–6577.

will usually continue. If the Court was genuinely committed to worker protection it could have provided that workers must not be prejudiced as a result of their decision not to be transferred.

It is perhaps concern about high levels of unemployment that has prompted the Court to re-orientate its case law, particularly in the context of transfers after *Süzen*,[373] in favour of the economic imperative to pursue the most cost-efficient forms of organizing a business such as contracting out, thereby at least preserving some jobs. Concerns about unemployment are also reflected in the amendments to the Directives on Collective Redundancies and Transfers and show a shift towards an increasing flexibility and adaptability which, as we have seen,[374] form a key pillar of the Union's employment policy. Yet, the lack of clarity and consistency in the Court's rulings carry their own cost and it is in this context that the criticism of the Court is most deserved. The next chapter considers how the Court has addressed the parallel issues raised by the Directives on collective redundancies and insolvency.

[373] Case C–13/95 [1997] ECR I–1259.
[374] See further Ch. 1.

14

COLLECTIVE REDUNDANCIES AND EMPLOYEES' RIGHTS ON THE EMPLOYER'S INSOLVENCY

A. INTRODUCTION

In the last chapter we focused on the important and much-discussed Directive on Transfers of Undertakings 2001/23. Now we consider the two other Directives adopted at around the same time as the original Transfers Directive: Directive 75/129 on Collective Redundancies,[1] revised by Directive 92/56[2] to give it a transnational dimension and subsequently consolidated in Directive 98/59,[3] and Directive 80/987 on insolvency,[4] also amended to take account of the transnational dimension of corporate activities by Directive 2002/74[5] and finally replaced by Directive 2008/94.[6] As with the Directive on Transfers, neither Directive 98/59 nor 2008/94 interferes with the employer's decision to restructure; both focus instead on the consequences of restructuring.

B. THE COLLECTIVE REDUNDANCIES DIRECTIVE

1. INTRODUCTION

Council Directive 75/129/EEC[7] was agreed by the Council of Ministers as part of the 1974–6 Social Action Programme. According to Blanpain,[8] the Directive had its origins in the conduct of AKZO, a Dutch–German multinational enterprise which wanted to make 5,000 workers redundant as part of a programme of restructuring. AKZO compared the costs of dismissing workers in the various states where it had subsidiaries and chose to dismiss workers in the country where costs were lowest. This led to calls for

---

[1] OJ [1975] L48/29.   [2] Council Directive 92/56/EEC (OJ [1992] L245/3).
[3] OJ [1998] L225/16.   [4] OJ [1980] L283/23, as amended by Dir. 87/164 (OJ [1987] L66/11).
[5] OJ [2002] L270/10.   [6] OJ [2008] L283/36.   [7] OJ [1975] L48/29.
[8] See further, R. Blanpain, *Labour Law and Industrial Relations of the European Community* (Kluwer, Deventer, 1991) 153.

action at European level to prevent this from happening again: Directive 75/129 was the Union's response. The purpose of the Directive was two-fold:[9] first, that 'greater protection be afforded to workers in the event of collective redundancies,[10] while taking into account the need for balanced economic and social development within the [Union]';[11] and secondly, to promote 'approximation...while the improvement (in living and working conditions) is being maintained within the meaning of Article [151 TFEU].[12]

The Directive set minimum standards[13] to ensure both that major redundancies were subjected to proper consultation with worker representatives and that the competent public authority was notified prior to dismissal.[14] The Directive was not, however, designed to harmonize national practices and procedures for actually making *individuals* redundant;[15] nor was it designed to interfere with the employer's freedom to effect, or refrain from effecting, collective dismissals.[16] This was confirmed in *Rockfon*[17] where the Court said that companies retained autonomy to manage their internal affairs, adding 'it is sufficient to state that the sole purpose of the Directive is the partial harmonization of *collective* redundancy procedures and that its aim is not to restrict the freedom of undertakings to organize their activities and arrange their personnel departments in the way which they think best suits their needs'.

Directive 75/129 was amended by Directive 92/56/EEC[18] which was drafted against the backcloth of increasing transnationalization of companies, with decisions affecting employees in a subsidiary in State A being taken by controlling parent companies in State B. Directive 75/129 and Directive 92/56 were consolidated and repealed by Council Directive 98/59/EC[19] to which all subsequent references relate.

2. THE MATERIAL AND PERSONAL SCOPE OF THE DIRECTIVE

2.1. The meaning of collective redundancies

Article 1(1)(a) defines collective redundancies as 'dismissals effected by an employer for one or more reasons *not related to the individual* workers concerned'. In *Commission*

---

[9] Case 215/83 *Commission* v. *Belgium* [1985] ECR 103.

[10] Second recital in the Preamble, cited in Case C–449/93 *Rockfon A/S* v. *Specialarbejderforbundet i Danmark, acting for Nielsen* [1995] ECR I–4291, para. 29; Case C–250/97 *Lauge* v. *Lønmodtagernes Garantifond* [1998] ECR I–8737, para. 19. See further the weight given to this recital by AG Tizzano in Case C–55/02 *Commission* v. *Portugal* [2004] ECR I–9387, para. 31 in influencing the interpretation given to the meaning of terms in the Directive.   [11] Second recital in the Preamble.

[12] Case 215/83 *Commission* v. *Belgium* [1985] ECR I–1039, para. 2.

[13] National laws, regulations, and administrative provisions can lay down laws more favourable to workers and, since Dir. 92/56, Member States can promote or allow the application of collective agreements more favourable to workers (Art. 5).

[14] Case 284/83 *Dansk Metalarbeiderforbund and special arbeiderforbundet i Danmark* v. *Nielsen & Son Maskin-fabrik A/S in liquidation* [1985] ECR 553, para. 10.

[15] Case 284/83 *Nielsen* [1985] ECR 553 and Case C–383/92 *Commission* v. *UK* [1994] ECR I–2435.

[16] Case 284/83 *Nielsen* [1985] ECR 553, para. 10.

[17] Case C–449/93 *Rockfon A/S* v. *Specialarbejderforbundet i Danmark, acting for Nielsen* [1995] ECR I–4291, para. 21, emphasis added.

[18] OJ [1992] L245/3.   [19] OJ [1998] L225/16.

v. *Portugal*[20] the Court insisted that the concept 'redundancy' be given a Union mean-ing,[21] namely 'any termination of [a] contract of employment not sought by[22] the worker, and therefore without his consent'.[23]

For the redundancies to be *collective*, the Directive adds a quantitative and temporal hurdle: it says that the number of redundancies must be:

(i) either, over a period of 30 days:

— at least 10 redundancies[24] in establishments normally employing more than 20 and less than 100 workers;

— at least 10 per cent of the number of workers in establishments normally employing at least 100 but less than 300 workers;

— at least 30 in establishments normally employing 300 workers or more;

(ii) or, over a period of 90 days, at least 20 redundancies, irrespective of the number of workers normally employed in the establishments in question.

The choice between these alternatives is left to the Member State. Directive 92/56 added that for the purpose of calculating the number of redundancies 'terminations of an employment contract which occur on the employer's initiative for one or more reasons not related to the individual workers concerned' (so-called 'redundancies by assimila-tion')[25] are to be treated as redundancies, provided at least five redundancies occur.[26] Thus, other forms of termination, such as voluntary early retirement, or where the employment relationship is terminated on the employer's initiative but with the agree-ment of the worker, where the worker is encouraged to give his agreement (for example in exchange for financial advantages),[27] or solely on the employer's volition,[28] are included within the scope of the Directive, but these must be, like the redundancies themselves, for a reason not related to the individual worker.[29]

From this we can see that the definition of collective redundancies contains both an *objective* element, concerning the scale of the redundancies (number or percentage of workers to be made redundant over a given period), and a *subjective* element concern-ing the reasons for the redundancies.[30] As far as the *objective* element is concerned, the Court gave some guidance in *Rockfon*[31] as to the definition of an establishment for the

---

[20] Case C–55/02 [2004] ECR I–9387.   [21] Para. 49.

[22] Also translated as 'against the will of the worker' (para. 62).   [23] Para. 50.

[24] Case C–385/05 CFDT v. *Premier* Ministre [2007] ECR I–611. 'Article 1(1)(a) of Council Directive 98/59/EC must be interpreted as precluding national legislation which excludes, even temporarily, a specific category of workers from the calculation of staff numbers set out in that provision.'

[25] AG Tizzano in Case C–55/02 *Commission* v. *Portugal* [2004] ECR I–9387, para. 42.

[26] Art. 1(1), final para.

[27] AG Tizzano in Case C–55/02 *Commission* v. *Portugal* [2004] ECR I–9387, para. 46.

[28] Case C–270/05 *Panagiotidis* [2007] ECR I–1499, para. 37.

[29] C. Bourn, 'Amending the Collective Dismissals Directive: a Case of Rearranging the Deckchairs' (1993) 9 *Int. Jo. Comp. LLIR.* 227, 234.

[30] See Commission Report to Council, SEC(91) 1639 final, Brussels 13 September 1991, 11.

[31] Case C–449/93 [1995] ECR I–4291.

purposes of calculating the scale of redundancies. Rockfon, part of a multinational group, shared a joint personnel department responsible for recruitment and dismissals with three other companies in the group.[32] Internal rules required that any dismissal decision had to be taken in consultation with the personnel department. In less than a month, Rockfon dismissed 25 employees from its workforce of 162. Rockfon, considering itself to be part of the multinational group and not an independent establishment, did not consult the employees nor did it inform the relevant public authority. The question for the Court was whether Rockfon by itself constituted an establishment. If it did, then the dismissals were carried out in breach of the consultation requirements of the Directive since Danish law had chosen the first option provided by Article 1(1)(a) (over a period of 30 days, at least 10 dismissals in establishments normally employing between 20 and 100 workers, 10 per cent of the number of workers in establishments normally employing between 100 and 300 workers) to implement the Directive.

Although 'establishment' is not defined in the Directive, the Court said that the term had to be given a Union meaning.[33] The different language versions of the Directive use different terms:[34] 'establishment', 'undertaking', 'work centre', 'local unit', and 'place of work'.[35] The Court said that a broad interpretation of the term 'establishment' would allow companies belonging to the same group to try to make it more difficult for the Directive to apply to them by conferring on a separate decision-making body the power to take decisions concerning redundancies. They would thus be able to escape the obligation to follow the procedures provided by the Directive.[36] It therefore said that the term 'establishment' had to be interpreted as the unit to which the workers made redundant were assigned to carry out their duties.[37] It was not essential for the unit in question to be endowed with a management which could independently effect collective redundancies.[38] In *Panagiotidis*[39] the definition was more elaborate: 'establishment', in the context of an undertaking, may consist of a distinct entity, having a certain degree of permanence and stability, which is assigned to perform one or more given tasks and which has a workforce, technical means, and a certain organizational structure allowing for the accomplishment of those tasks. The entity does not, however, have to have any legal autonomy, nor need it have economic, financial, administrative, or technological autonomy.

Since Danish law had chosen the first option provided for by Article 1(1)(a) the purposive construction set out in *Rockfon* defining 'establishment' *narrowly* was of benefit to Danish workers. The Court expressly said that the purpose of the Directive was to afford workers greater protection in the event of collective redundancies.[40] However, for countries such as the UK, which have chosen the second option provided for by Article 1(1)(a)

---

[32] Para. 17.   [33] Paras. 23 and 25.

[34] Danish *virksomhed*, Dutch *plaatselijke eenheid*, English 'establishment', Finnish *yritys*, German *Betrieb*, Italian *stabilemento*, Portugese *estabelecimento*, Spanish *centro de trabajo*, Swedish *arbetsplats*.

[35] Para. 27.   [36] Para. 30.

[37] Para. 31, citing Case 186/83 *Botzen* [1985] ECR 519, discussed in Ch. 13.

[38] Para. 32. This approach is supported by the fact that the Commission's initial proposal for the Directive used the term 'undertaking' and that term was defined as 'local employment unit'.

[39] Case C–270/05 *Athinaiki Chartopoiia AE v Panagiotidis* [2007] ECR I–1499.   [40] Para. 29.

(20 employees at one establishment within a period of 90 days), the decision in *Rockfon* threatens to undermine the position of those employees,[41] since for them the more *broadly* defined the establishment, the more likely the threshold of 20 employees will be met.

As far as the *subjective* element is concerned, the reasons for the redundancies must not be 'related to the individual workers concerned'. Therefore, dismissals for reasons relating to a worker's behaviour (e.g. disciplinary dismissals) are excluded from the scope of the Directive. Otherwise the scope of the Directive is broad,[42] as the Court made clear in two enforcement actions. First, in *Commission v. UK*[43] the Court found that the British definition of redundancy (used for the purposes of receiving a redundancy payment, namely the cessation of a business or cessation or diminution in the requirements of a business to carry out work of a particular kind) was too narrow since it did not cover cases where workers were dismissed as a result of new working arrangements which were unconnected with the volume of business.[44] Secondly, in *Commission v. Portugal*[45] the Court found that the Portuguese definition of redundancy which confined the concept of collective redundancies to redundancies for structural, technological or cyclical reasons (i.e. redundancies as a result of a 'willed' or 'voluntary' act of the employer) and excluded redundancies resulting from compulsory and other types of liquidation, compulsory purchase, fire, other *force majeure*, or death of the trader (i.e. redundancies not resulting from a voluntary act of the employer) also failed to implement the Directive correctly. The Court said that it was not necessary that the underlying reasons for the redundancies should 'reflect the will of the employer'.[46]

The Directive applies only when the *employer* dismisses the employees. The phrase employer is broadly construed, consistent with the worker protection aims of the Directive, and therefore applies to all employers.[47] Under Italian law, employers engaged in non-profit-making activities, such as trade unions, political parties, and NGOs, were excluded from the scope of the national rules implementing the Directive. In *Commission v. Italy*[48] the Court found that this exclusion contravened the Directive. In support of its arguments, the Commission referred to Article 1(1)(c) of Directive 2001/23 on transfer of undertakings[49] which provides that the Directive applies to 'public and private undertakings engaged in economic activities whether or not they are operating for gain'. While the Court did not refer to Directive 2001/23 in its findings, its long reference to the Directive when summarizing the Commission's arguments, may suggest that the Court is prepared to see parallel developments in the two fields.[50]

---

[41] Rubinstein [1996] IRLR 113.   [42] Case C–55/02 [2004] ECR I–9387, para. 58.
[43] Case C–383/92 [1994] ECR I–2435.
[44] S. 195 TULR(C)A 1992 was amended by s. 34 TURERA 1993 to bring British law in line with the Directive. This now provides that 'references to dismissal as redundant are references to dismissal for a reason not related to the individual concerned or for a number of reasons all of which are not so related'.
[45] Case C–55/02 [2004] ECR I–9387.   [46] Ibid.
[47] Case C–32/02 *Commission v. Italy* [2003] ECR I–12063, para. 26.
[48] Case C–32/02 [2003] ECR I–12063.   [49] See Ch. 13.
[50] For further examples of cross-fertilization, this time with European Works' Councils Dir. 2009/38 (OJ [2009] L 122/28) see AG Tizzano's Opinion in Case C–440/00 *Gesamtbetriebsrat der Kühne & Nagel AG & Co. KG v. Kühne & Nagel AG & Co. KG* [2004] ECR I–787, para. 32 in Ch. 15.

The Directive does not apply to termination of employment by the employees them-selves[51] since such resignations might be contrary to the employer's wishes. If the Direc-tive did apply to voluntary resignations, the effect of an employee resigning would be to prevent the employer from discharging the obligations laid down by the Directive. This, according to the Court in *Nielsen*,[52] would lead to a result contrary to that sought by the Directive, namely to avoid or reduce collective redundancies.[53] The position may, how-ever, be different if the employer is actively seeking to close the business and has forced the workers to give notice in order to escape the obligations imposed by the Directive.[54]

2.2. Where the Directive does not apply

The Directive does not apply to:[55]

- collective redundancies resulting from the expiry of fixed-term contracts or the completion of a particular task in the case of a contract to perform a particular task;[56]
- workers employed by public administrative bodies or by establishments governed by public law (or, in Member States where this concept is unknown, by equivalent bodies);[57]
- the crews of sea-going vessels.[58]

Since these instances are exceptions to the general rule they must be construed narrowly. Article 1(2)(d) of Directive 75/129 also excluded workers affected by the ter-mination of an establishment's activities where that is the result of a judicial decision (e.g. an insolvency situation). Directive 92/56 removed this exception.[59] As the Court said in *Claes*:[60] 'That amendment was emphasised by the European Union legislator in the third recital in the preamble to Directive 92/56, which states that Directive 75/129 also applies in principle to collective redundancies arising where the establishment's activities are terminated as a result of a judicial decision'. The Court has held that since the amendment of Directive 75/129, in all cases of collective redundancy following the termination of an establishment's activities, even where their termination was the result of a judicial decision, employers (either the management team if still in place or the liquidators) are obliged to inform and consult workers.[61]

---

[51] AG Tizzano's Opinion in Case C–188/03 *Junk* [2005] ECR I–885, para. 49.
[52] Case 284/83 [1985] ECR 553.   [53] Para. 10.
[54] Advocate General Lenz, Case 284/83 *Nielsen* [1985] ECR 553.
[55] Art. 1(2). The Belgian government was condemned for failing to implement these provisions correctly in Case 215/83 *Commission* v. *Belgium* [1985] ECR 1039.
[56] Art. 1(2)(a). The Directive does, however, apply to redundancies which take place prior to the date of expiry of fixed term contracts or to the completion of the specific task.
[57] Art. 1(2)(b).   [58] Art. 1(2)(c).
[59] Ninth recital to the Dir. and Case C–55/02 *Commission* v. *Portugal* [2004] ECR I–9387, para. 54.
[60] Joined Cases C–235/10 to 239/10 *Claes* v. *Landsbanki Luxembourg* [2011] ECR I–000.
[61] Cases C–187/05 to C–190/05 *Agorastoudis and Others* [2006] ECR I–7775, para. 33. This is confirmed in Joined Cases C–235/10 to 239/10 *Claes* [2011] ECR I–000.

To compensate for this amendment, Directive 92/56 introduced two new provisions on the termination of an establishment's activities as a result of judicial decision. Article 3(1), paragraph 2 says that Member States have the discretion whether to require dismissals arising in such circumstances to be notified to the competent public authority and Article 4(4) provides that Member States need not apply Article 4 (notification of collective redundancies to competent public authorities) to collective redundancies arising in these circumstances. These provision are not, however, derogations.

The most notable omission from this list of exceptions concerns cases of emergency or *force majeure*. The Court considered such a situation in *Nielsen*.[62] In February 1980 the employer, Nielsen, informed workers' representatives of its financial difficulties. On 14 March 1980 it informed the bankruptcy court that it was suspending payment of its debts, and, when it failed to provide a bank guarantee for the future payment of wages, the trade unions advised their members to stop work. On 25 March 1980 the employer was declared insolvent and the following day the workers were given notice of dismissal. The trade union argued that as soon as the employer experienced financial difficulties it ought to have contemplated collective redundancies and thus the application of the Directive. The Court disagreed. It argued that this interpretation would cause employers to incur penalties for failing to have foreseen the collective redundancies and consequently failing to implement the procedure required by the Directive. This would run counter to the wording of Article 1(2)(d) which excluded from the scope of the Directive collective redundancies caused by 'the termination of an establishment's activities where that is the result of a judicial decision'.[63] The logic of these arguments is undermined now that Article 1(2)(d) has been deleted from the Directive 92/56/EEC,[64] so the position in respect of *force majeure* is unclear.

3. THE EMPLOYER'S OBLIGATIONS

An employer who is contemplating collective redundancies has two obligations: first, to inform and consult with worker representatives under Article 2, and second, to notify the relevant public authority under Articles 3 and 4.

3.1. Consultation of workers' representatives

Article 2(1) provides that 'where an employer is contemplating collective redundancies, he shall begin consultations with the workers' representatives in good time with a view to reaching an agreement'. There has been much writing and litigation over the meaning of each aspect of Article 2(1). We shall examine each limb in turn.

(a) 'Contemplating' collective redundancies

This entire consultation procedure is only triggered when the employer who must be living, not dead,[65] is *contemplating* redundancies and has drawn up a 'project' to that

[62] Case 284/83 [1985] ECR 553. [63] Para. 16.

[64] Although the Court still refers to it: Case C–55/02 *Commission v. Portugal* [2004] ECR I–9387, para. 55.

[65] Case C–323/08 *Ovidio Rodriguez Mayor and others v. Herencia yacente de Rafael de las Heras Dávila and Others* [2009] ECR I–11621.

end.[66] At what moment in time does 'contemplation' occur? Is it earlier in time than when the employer is 'proposing' to make people redundant (the language used in the British implementing legislation)? This issue has now been considered three times by the Court. First, in *Junk*[67] the Court made clear that the obligations to consult and to notify the competent public authority 'arise prior to any decision by the employer to terminate contracts of employment'.[68] The case concerned an employee who worked as a care assistant until her employer went into liquidation. The liquidator gave notice to her and a number of other staff at the end of June that her contract would be terminated at the end of September 2002. At the end of August the liquidator notified the labour office of the collective redundancies. This went well beyond 'contemplating'. As the Court said, the case in which the employer 'is contemplating' collective redundancies corresponds to a situation in which 'no decision has yet been taken'[69] or, using Advocate General Tizzano's language, when the redundancies are still at the 'projection stage'.[70] By contrast, the notification to a worker that his or her contract of employment has been terminated (i.e. giving notice) is the expression of a decision to sever the employment relationship, and the actual cessation of that relationship on the expiry of the period of notice (i.e. the date when the dismissal takes effect) is no more than the effect of that decision.[71] As the Court explained,[72] given that the purpose of the Directive is to avoid terminations of contracts of employment or at least to reduce their number, the achievement of that purpose would be jeopardized if the consultation of worker representatives were to be subsequent to the employer's decision.

The Court therefore concluded that 'the event constituting redundancy consists in the declaration by an employer of his intention to terminate the contract of employment'[73] (i.e. giving notice of dismissal or *Kündigung* in German)[74] with the result that an employer cannot terminate contracts of employment before the employer has engaged in the consultation and notification process.[75] The effect of this decision is that the consultation process must take place before employees are given notice of dismissal, rather than after individual notices have been given but before they have taken effect. However, as Rubinstein points out,[76] the Court does not require that the full period for consultation provided under national law must elapse before the employees can be given notice of dismissal. The focus is on the substance of consultation.[77]

In the second case, *Fujitsu Siemens*,[78] the Court suggested that consultations might begin somewhat later in the day than had been first thought. Drawing on the Advocate General's Opinion, the Court said that it was clear from comparison of various language

---

[66] Case C–188/03 *Junk* v. *Kühnel* [2005] ECR I–885, para. 36.   [67] Ibid.

[68] Para. 37.   [69] Para. 36.   [70] Para. 47.   [71] Ibid.   [72] Para. 38.   [73] Para. 39.

[74] And not *Entlassung*, the word used in the German version of the Directive, which means the time when the redundancy becomes effective, i.e. when the employment relationship is actually at an end.

[75] Para. 41.   [76] [2005] IRLR 225.   [77] Para. 45.

[78] Case C–44/08 *Akavan Erityisalojen Keskusliitto and others* v. *Fujitsu Siemens Computers Oy* [2009] ECR I–8163.

versions of that provision that the Union legislature 'envisaged that the obligation at issue to hold consultations would arise in connection with the existence of an intention on the part of the employer to make collective redundancies'.[79] The Court added that 'the consultation procedure must be started by the employer once a strategic or commercial decision compelling him to contemplate or to plan for collective redundancies has been taken'.[80] This seems to come closer to the idea of 'proposing' found in the UK statute. Nevertheless, employers must still respect the obligation in the Directive that the consultations must be in good time.[81]

Thirdly, when redundancies occur which have not been 'contemplated' it seems that the consultation requirements under the Directive do not apply since, as the Court recognized in *Nielsen*,[82] there is no implied obligation under the Directive to foresee collective redundancies. The Court said that the Directive did not stipulate the circumstances in which employers must contemplate collective redundancies and in no way affected their freedom to decide whether and when they must formulate plans for collective dismissals. This ruling favours the disorganized employer who would not have contemplated redundancies, to whom the Directive may not apply.

(b) Consultations with the workers' representatives

These consultations are with 'workers' representatives', defined as those representatives provided for by the laws or practices of the Member States.[83] This enables consultation to continue within established frameworks of the German and Dutch works councils, the French *comité d'entreprise*, and collective bargaining in Britain, Ireland, and Denmark.[84] The UK's implementation of this provision (along with the equivalent term in Directive 2001/23 on transfers of undertakings) was found by the Court to be defective since only recognized trade unions could be consulted.[85] The fact that the consultations are with workers representatives, a term which is defined in the Directive, and not with 'workers', a term which is not defined, enabled the Court to conclude in *Mono Car Styling*[86] that the rights in particular in Article 2 are 'intended to benefit workers as a collective group and is therefore collective in nature'.

(c) The subject-matter of consultation

The substance of these consultations must cover, as a minimum, two matters: first, ways and means of avoiding collective redundancies or reducing the number of employees affected; and secondly, ways of mitigating the consequences of the redundancies by recourse to 'social measures aimed, *inter alia*, at aid for redeploying or retraining

---

[79] Para. 39. [80] Para. 48. See additionally the reference in Case C-583/10 *USA v. Nolan*.

[81] See the *obiter dicta* of Glidewell LJ in *R v. British Coal Corporation and Secretary of State for Trade and Industry, ex parte Vardy* [1993] IRLR 104 which envisages consultation at an early stage when the employer is first envisaging the possibility that he may have to make employees redundant.

[82] Case 284/83 [1985] ECR 553. [83] Art. 1(1)(b).

[84] B. Hepple, 'Community Measures for the Protection of Workers on Dismissal' (1977) 14 *CMLRev.* 489.

[85] Case C–383/92 *Commission v. UK* [1994] ECR I–2479. This is considered in detail in Ch. 13.

[86] Case C–12/08 *Mono Car Styling v. Dervis Odemis* [2009] ECR I–6653, para. 42.

workers made redundant'.[87] This is a pale reflection of the 'social plan' recognized by German law—a special form of redundancy programme drawn up by management and the works council in a legally binding agreement designed to 'compensate or reduce economic disadvantages for employees in the event of a substantial alteration to the establishment'.[88] The fact that ways of avoiding collective redundancies appear as the first item on the list suggests that the drafters of the Directive did not presume that redundancies would occur[89] and considered that the avoidance of redundancies was at least as important as giving rights to those who will be made redundant.

This raises the practical question: in considering ways of avoiding dismissals does that require the employer to consult on the reasons for the proposed redundancies. The British courts had been divided on the issue[90] but *UK Coal Mining*[91] said definitively that an employer must consult on the business reasons for avoiding redundancies. A reference has been made to the Court of Justice in *USA* v. *Nolan*[92] on this point.

Since the emphasis is on consultation and not just information the Directive also makes provision to ensure that the consultations are effective. To enable the workers' representatives to make constructive proposals the employer is obliged to supply the workers' representatives[93] in good time during the course of the consultations with all relevant information[94] *and* the employer must 'in any event' give in writing:[95]

- the reasons for the projected redundancies;
- the number of categories of workers to be made redundant[96] (Directive 75/129/EEC talked of the number of workers to be made redundant);
- the number of workers normally employed;
- the period over which the redundancies are to be effected.

Directive 92/56 added two further items to this list:

- the criteria proposed for the selection of workers to be made redundant in so far as national legislation and/or practice confers this power on the employer; and

---

[87] Art. 2(2). This is reinforced by Joined Cases C–235/10 to 239/10 *Claes* v. *Landsbanki Luxembourg* [2011] ECR I–000, para. 56. Furthermore, according to para. 2, Member States can provide that the workers' representatives can call upon the services of experts in accordance with national law or practice. Thus, there will still be a contrast between the position in France where employees may call upon the services of an accountant (*expert comptable*) and in Denmark and the UK where no such obligation exists (Bourn, previously, at n. 29, 236).

[88] M. Weiss, *European Employment and Industrial Relations Glossary: Germany* (Sweet & Maxwell, London, 1992), para. 657.

[89] On the importance of this, see Case C–188/03 *Junk* [2005] ECR I–885, para. 38.

[90] See e.g. *R* v. *British Coal Corporation, ex parte Vardy* [1993] IRLR 104.

[91] *UK Coalmining Ltd v National Union of Mineworkers* EAT/0397/06.

[92] Case C–583/10 [2010] EWCA 1223, [2011] IRLR 40.

[93] The European Works Council will also need to be informed, see para. 3 of Annex to Directive 2009/38/EC (OJ [2009] L122/28).

[94] Art. 2(3)(a).   [95] Art. 2(3)(b).

[96] The language of this provision suggests that redundancies will occur. This appears to contradict the tenor of Art. 2(1) and (2).

- the method for calculating any redundancy payments other than those arising out of national legislation and/or practice.

This information does not need to be given all at once at the start of the consultation process. The Court made this clear in *Fujitsu Siemens*:[97]

> the information can be provided during consultations, and not necessarily at the time when they start. The logic of the provision is that the employer is to supply to the workers' representatives the relevant information throughout the course of the consultations. Flexibility is essential, given, firstly, that the information may become available only at various stages in the consultation process, which implies that the employer both can and must add to the information supplied in the course of that process. Secondly, the purpose of the employer being under that obligation is to enable the workers' representatives to participate in the consultation process as fully and effectively as possible, and therefore any new relevant information must be supplied up to the end of the process.

The most important addition made by Directive 92/56 is that the obligation to consult workers' representatives applies 'irrespective of whether the decision regarding collective redundancies is being taken by the employer *or by an undertaking controlling the employer*'.[98] It is no defence for an employer to argue that the parent or controlling undertaking had not provided the employer with the necessary information.[99] This provision was introduced in the light of the increasing 'transnationalization' of commercial ventures. As the Commission said, the dismantling of national barriers has led to major corporate reorganization, involving a significant increase in takeovers, mergers, and joint ventures.[100] As a result, decisions affecting the workforce might be taken by a controlling undertaking which might not be situated in one of the Member States, or possibly not even in the Union. The obligation to acquire the information is, however, placed on the controlled undertaking to avoid the problem of extraterritoriality. The approach adopted by the Collective Redundancies Directive to complex corporate structures contrasts favourably with that adopted under the European Works Council Directive 2009/38/EC[101] where rights are given against central management at a time when there is an increasing tendency towards decentralizing decision making in corporate groups.

(d) With a view to reaching an agreement

The reference to 'consultation' with a view to reaching an 'agreement'[102] blurs the distinction between consultation and collective bargaining. The Court confirms this in

---

[97] Case C–44/08 *Akavan Erityisalojen Keskusliitto AEK ry and others* v. *Fujitsu Siemens Computers Oy* [2009] ECR I–8163, para. 53.

[98] Art. 2(4), para. 1.   [99] Art. 2(4), para. 2.

[100] According to the Commission's figures, the number of mergers and acquisitions carried out by the top 1,000 European industrial enterprises doubled every three years during the 1980s, increasing from 208 in 1984–85 to 492 in 1988–89: Commission, XXth Report on Competition Policy, cited in COM(94) 300, 2.

[101] OJ [2009] L122/28. Dir. 2009/38/95 is considered further in Ch. 15.

[102] A concept initially absent from the UK legislation, see Case C–383/92 *Commission* v. *UK* [1994] ECR I–2479. Implemented by s. 34(2)(c) TURERA 1993 and included in s. 188 TULR(C)A 1992.

Junk,[103] where it said with stark simplicity: 'It thus appears that Article 2 of the Directive imposes an obligation to negotiate'.[104] The Court continued that the effectiveness of the obligation to negotiate would be compromised if an employer was entitled to terminate contracts of employment during the course of the procedure or even at the beginning of the procedure. It added that it would be significantly more difficult for workers' representatives to achieve the withdrawal of a decision that has been taken than to secure the abandonment of a decision that is being contemplated.[105] The Court therefore concluded that a contract of employment could be terminated only after the conclusion of the consultation procedure laid down by Article 2.[106]

3.2. Notification of the 'competent public authority'

In France and the Netherlands the competent authorities have long-established powers to authorize or prohibit redundancies. In the Netherlands the procedure involves a system whereby the Dutch labour office issues a number of permits to dismiss.[107] Due to resistance from the UK, this principle was not included in the Directive.[108] Instead, Article 3(1) imposes an administrative obligation on employers to notify 'the competent public authority' in writing of 'any projected collective redundancies'.[109] The notification must contain all information relevant to the projected redundancies, the consultations with the workers' representatives provided for in Article 2,[110] and particularly the reasons for the redundancies, the number of workers to be made redundant, the number of workers normally employed, and the period over which the redundancies are to be effected.[111] In the case of planned collective redundancies arising from termination of the establishment's activities as a result of a judicial decision, the Member States can provide that the employer is obliged to notify the competent public authority on the request of the authority.[112] The employer must also send a copy of the Article 3(1) notification to the workers' representatives, who may send any comments they have to the competent authority.[113]

---

[103] Case C–188/03 *Junk* [2005] ECR I–885.

[104] Para. 44. See further AG Tizzano's Opinion in Case C–188/03 *Junk* [2005] ECR I–885, para. 59: '*At the least*, Article 2 therefore imposes an obligation to negotiate' (emphasis added).

[105] Para. 45.   [106] Para. 45.

[107] In the Netherlands the employer wishing to terminate employment contracts unilaterally must apply to the District Labour Office for a permit. In 1980 98,387 permits were requested by employers of which 16 per cent concerned 20 employees or more. In 1993 107,998 permits were requested of which 15 per cent concerned 20 employees or more, based on figures for the Dutch Ministry for Social Affairs and Employment.

[108] M. Freedland, 'Employment Protection: Redundancy Procedures and the EEC' (1976) 5–6 *ILJ* 24, 27.

[109] AG Lenz argues that the employer must give notice to the competent authorities if he actually plans to make collective redundancies, whereas representatives of workers must be consulted at an earlier stage (Case 284/83 *Nielsen* [1985] ECR 553, 557).

[110] Art. 2(3), para. 2, obliges the employer to forward to the competent authority all written communications referred to in Art. 2(3)(b) except the method for calculating any redundancy payments.

[111] Art. 3(1), para. 2.   [112] Added by Dir. 92/56 as second sentence of para. 1 of Art. 3(1).

[113] Art. 3(2).

In principle, the proposed redundancies cannot take place until at least 30 days after the Article 3(1) notification, 'without prejudice to any provisions governing individual rights with regard to notice of dismissal'.[114] The reference to national provisions with regard to 'notice of dismissal' safeguards the application of notice periods which are longer than the 30 days provided by the Directive.[115] The purpose of this delay is, according to Article 4(2), to enable the competent authority to seek solutions to 'the problems raised by the projected redundancies'. It is not clear whether this means that the authority should intervene in an attempt to stave off the redundancies or rather that it should make provision for coping with those employees facing unemployment. Advocate General Tizzano's Opinion in *Junk*[116] suggests the latter. He saw the Article 2 consultation stage and the Article 3 notification stage as separate, consecutive stages,[117] serving different purposes: 'the notification stage, which, unlike the stage of consultation with workers' representatives, does not relate to the principle of redundancy but rather to its consequences, or "the *problems* raised by the . . . collective redundancies"'.[118] Thus, the consultation stage concerns 'managing' the effects of the redundancy[119] and for that reason, as the Court said in *Junk*,[120] it was possible for the contracts of employment to be terminated in the course of the notification procedure provided that such termination occurred after the projected collective redundancies have been notified to the competent public authority.[121]

The Member State can grant the competent authority the power to reduce or extend the 30-day period.[122] If, however, the initial period of delay is for less than 60 days Member States can grant the competent authority the power to extend the initial period to 60 days or longer[123] following notification, where the problems raised by the projected collective redundancies are not likely to be solved within the initial period.[124] The employer (but not the workers' representatives) must be informed of the extension and the reason why such an extension has been granted before the expiry of the initial 30-day period.[125]

4. IMPLEMENTATION AND REMEDIES

4.1. Implementation

As with the Transfer of Undertakings Directive 2001/23, the Collective Redundancies Directive is a minimum standards Directive.[126] So Member States could implement the Directive or promote collective agreements more favourable to employees. In any event, the Member States were obliged to implement both Directives 75/129 and 92/56 within two years of their notification.[127] The Court is strict about ensuring correct implementation, as the Belgian government found to its cost:

---

[114] Art. 4(1).   [115] AG Tizzano's Opinion in Case C–188/03 *Junk* [2005] ECR I–885, para. 66.
[116] Case C–188/03 *Junk* [2005] ECR I–885.   [117] Para. 61.   [118] Para. 67.
[119] Ibid.   [120] Case C–188/03 *Junk* [2005] ECR I–885.   [121] Para. 53.
[122] Art. 4(1), para. 2.   [123] Art. 4(3), para. 2.   [124] Art. 4(3), para. 1.
[125] Art. 4(3), para. 3.   [126] Art. 5.   [127] Art. 6, 19 February 1977 and 24 June 1994, respectively.

Member States must fulfil their obligations under [Union] Directives in every respect and may not plead provisions, practices or circumstances existing in their internal legal system in order to justify a failure to comply with those obligations.[128]

The Court said that the Belgian government could not plead that in practice very few workers were excluded from the benefits of the Directive, nor that the government's failure to comply fully with the Directive was justified by the fact that Belgian law provides the workers in question with other forms of security. The Italian government was equally unsuccessful in the arguments it raised in enforcement proceedings brought against it. Although it claimed that the Italian system as a whole created conditions and established procedures making it possible to attain the objectives of the Directive, it did concede that in certain sectors the legislation was not as comprehensive as the Directive required.[129] It was therefore found to be in breach of its obligations under the Directive.

4.2. Remedies

Directive 75/129/EEC, like Directive 77/187, made no express provision for remedies in the event of employers' failure to comply with their obligations. However, in the case of the *Commission* v. *UK*[130] the Court insisted that Member States had to ensure that infringements of Union law were penalized under conditions, both procedural and substantive, which were analogous to those applicable to infringements of national law and which made the penalty effective, proportionate, and dissuasive. Consequently the Court ruled that a British law which allowed that a protective award, payable by an employer who had failed to consult workers' representatives to dismissed employees, could be set off in full or in part against any other amounts owed by the employer to the employees, deprived the sanction of its practical effect and deterrent value.

In several Member States collective redundancies carried out in contravention of the Directive are null and void.[131] Originally this was also included in the new draft Directive but, faced with opposition from ECOSOC, the UK government, and employers, it was deleted from the final version. Instead, Article 6, introduced by Directive 92/56, requires Member States to ensure 'that judicial and/or administrative procedures for the enforcement of obligations under this Directive are available to the workers' representatives or to the workers'. However, in *Mono Car Styling*[132] the Court emphasized the collective nature of the rights in the Directive and thus the collective nature of the remedy. It therefore considered a Belgian law which provided unrestricted rights of challenge to worker representatives but only limited grounds of challenge to individual claimants and imposed on them additional requirements (that their right of action is subject to the conditions that workers' representatives should first have raised objections and that the worker concerned has informed the employer in advance of his intention to challenge compliance with the information and consultation procedure) to be compatible with Article 6.[133]

---

[128] Case 215/83 *Commission* v. *Belgium* [1985] ECR 1039.
[129] Case 91/81 *Commission* v. *Italy* [1982] ECR 2133. Further enforcement proceedings were later brought for failing to implement the judgment in Case 91/81, see Case 131/84 *Commission* v. *Italy* [1985] ECR 3531.
[130] Case C–383/92 [1994] ECR I–2479.   [131] Bourn, previously, at n. 29.
[132] Case C–12/08 *Mono Car Styling* v. *Dervis Odemis* [2009] ECR I–6653, para. 42.   [133] Para. 44.

C. THE INSOLVENCY DIRECTIVE 2008/94/EC

1. INTRODUCTION

The Insolvency Directive[134] was the third in the trilogy of measures designed to confer some protection on employees faced with their employers' insolvency due to increased competition caused by the advent of the Common Market and, subsequently, Single Market. Also based on Article 115 TFEU (ex 94 EC), the Directive has dual objectives: to promote the approximation of laws and to improve the living and working conditions by protecting employees in the event of the insolvency of their employer.[135] As with the Directives on Transfers of Undertakings and Collective Redundancies, the Insolvency Directive does not interfere with any decision about the employer's insolvency; instead it provides employees with a minimum degree of protection under Union law in the event of their employer becoming insolvent, in particular by requiring Member States to put in place an institution guaranteeing employees the payment of their outstanding claims to remuneration for a specific period. This is an important right. Between 2006–9 almost 147,000 claims were made against the German guarantee institution, over 90,000 in France, and almost 55,000 in Spain, and nearly 18 billion euros have been paid out by the Guarantee institutions in the EU as a whole.[136]

The Directive has been the subject of much litigation and it was amended by Directive 2002/74.[137] This Directive retained the basic structure of Directive 80/987, whose results are 'beyond dispute,'[138] but was adapted to reflect changes in insolvency law in the Member States. In the interests of 'clarity and rationality' the Directive was codified in 2008.[139]

2. THE MATERIAL AND PERSONAL SCOPE OF THE DIRECTIVE

According to Article 1(1), the Directive applies to employees' claims arising from contracts of employment or employment relationships[140] and existing against employers who are in a state of insolvency. This raises two questions: what is meant by insolvency and who are employees?

2.1. The definition of insolvency

According to Article 2(1), an employer is considered to be in a state of insolvency:

> where a request has been made for the opening of collective proceedings based on insolvency of the employer, as provided for under the laws, regulations and administrative

---

[134] Council Dir. 80/987/EEC (OJ [1980] L283/23) on the approximation of the laws of the Member States relating to the protection of employees in the event of insolvency of their employer, as amended by Dir. 87/164 (OJ [1987] L66/11). See COM(96) 696 on the implementation of the Directive.

[135] Third Preambular paras. See additionally Case 22/87 *Commission v. Italy* [1989] ECR 143.

[136] COM(2011) 84, 9.   [137] OJ [2002] L270/10.

[138] COM(2000) 832, 2.   [139] OJ [2008] L283/37.

[140] The term 'contract of employment' will be now be used to describe both the contract of employment and the employment relationship unless otherwise stated.

provisions of a Member State, and involving the partial or total divestment of the employer's assets and the appointment of a liquidator or a person performing a similar task, and
the authority which is competent pursuant to national provisions has:

(a)   either decided to open the proceedings, or
(b)   established that the employer's undertaking or business has been definitively closed
      down and that the available assets are insufficient to warrant the opening of the
      proceedings.

This new—and broader[141]—definition of insolvency was introduced by Directive
2002/74 and is based on the definition found in Article 1(1) of Regulation 1346/2000 on
insolvency proceedings.[142] It covers bankruptcy (liquidation) proceedings as well as
other collective insolvency proceedings. Article 2(4) adds that the Directive allows
Member States to extend workers' protection to other situations of insolvency (for
example, where payments have been *de facto* stopped on a permanent basis) established
by proceedings different from those laid down in Article 2(1).

2.2. Employees

'Insolvency' is the only term defined by the Directive; other terms used—employee,
employer, pay, and rights conferring immediate or prospective entitlement—are defined
by reference to national law.[143] This measure is thus a further example of a partial harmonization Directive.

As far as 'employees' are concerned, the Court made clear in *Wagner-Miret*[144] that the
Directive was intended to apply to all categories of employee defined as employees
under national law. Therefore, the Spanish exclusion of higher management staff from
the scope of the Directive was incompatible with Union law.

The Commission did, however, become increasingly concerned that the reference to
national law for determining the definition of concepts such as 'employee' could limit the
scope of the protection provided by the Directive.[145] Therefore, although Directive 2002/74
did not define 'employee', the Directive followed the model used in the Transfers Directive
2001/23 and prohibited Member States from excluding part-time workers, within the meaning of Directive 97/81, workers with fixed term contracts within the meaning of Directive
99/70, and workers with a temporary employment relationship within the meaning of
Directive 91/383/EEC.[146] Directive 2002/74 also provides that Member States may not set a
minimum service requirement for workers to qualify for claims under the Directive.[147]

However, under Articles 1(2) and (3), Member States may exclude two categories of
employees from the scope of the Directive. First, 'certain categories of employee' can be
excluded where other forms of guarantee offer the employee protection equivalent to

---

[141] The original definition contained in the 1980 Directive was restricted to liquidation proceedings
(collective settlement of creditors' claims). This definition was given a narrow interpretation by the Court in
Case C–479/93 *Francovich (No. 2)* v. *Italy* [1995] ECR I–3843.
[142] OJ [2000] L160/1.   [143] Art. 2(2).
[144] Case C–334/92 *Wagner-Miret* v. *Fondo de Garant'a Salarial* [1993] ECR I–6911.
[145] COM(2000) 832, 5.   [146] Art. 2(2).   [147] Art. 2(3).

that conferred by the Directive.[148] In the original Directive an Annex provided further details[149] but the Annex was considered unnecessary and was removed by Directive 2002/74. Yet the principle identified by the Court in *Commission v. Greece*[150] remains valid: since the purpose of the Directive is to ensure a minimum degree of protection for all employees, these exclusions are possible only by way of exception and must be interpreted strictly.[151]

Secondly, the Directive allows Member States to 'continue to exclude' from the scope of the Directive (1) domestic servants employed by a natural person; and (2) share fisherman, where 'such provision already applies in their national legislation'.[152] The exclusion will apply only to those categories of workers which are expressly listed.[153]

2.3. The application of the provisions

The interrelationship between Articles 1 and 2 was considered in *Francovich (No. 1)* and *(No. 2)*. In *Francovich (No. 1)*[154] the applicants' employer went into liquidation leaving them with arrears of salary outstanding at a time when the Italian government had failed to implement the Directive. The Court ruled that in order to determine whether a person should be regarded as intended to benefit under the Directive a national court must verify, (1) whether the person concerned was an employed person under national law and whether he was excluded from the scope of the Directive, and then ascertain (2) whether a state of insolvency exists, as provided for in Article 2 of the Directive.

After the Court's decision in *Francovich (No. 1)* the Italian government adopted Decree-Law No. 80 (13 February 1992) transposing the Directive into national law. However, under this law, several categories of employer were excluded from proceedings to satisfy the claims of creditors collectively. In *Francovich (No. 2)*[155] the national court asked whether this was compatible with Article 2 of the Directive. Since the case concerned the definition of insolvency prior to the 2002 amendments the Court ruled that the Directive could not be relied on by employees whose contract of employment was with an employer who could not, under national law, be subject to proceedings to satisfy collectively the claims of creditors. The position is now different under the amendments.

---

[148] Art. 1(2).

[149] E.g. the crews of sea-going vessels in Greece, Italy, and the UK, and permanent and pensionable employees of local or other public authorities and certain groups of teachers in Ireland.

[150] Case C–53/88 *Commission v. Greece* [1990] ECR I–3931.

[151] Case C–441/99 *Riksskatteverket v. Gharehveran* [2001] ECR I–7687, para. 26.

[152] Art. 1(3). Originally the excluded groups included, e.g. domestic servants in Spain and the Netherlands, outworkers, employees who are relatives of the employer, seasonal, casual or part-time workers in Ireland, and crews of fishing vessels in Greece and the UK. The rump of this list is now found in Art. 1(3) as a result of the amendments introduced by Dir. 2002/74.

[153] Case C–334/92 *Wagner-Miret v. Fondo de Garantía Salarial* [1993] ECR I–6911.

[154] Joined Cases C–6 and 9/90 [1991] ECR I–5357.

[155] Case C–479/93 *Francovich (No. 2) v. Italy* [1995] ECR I–3843.

3. THE PROTECTION CONFERRED BY THE DIRECTIVE

The Directive provides three forms of protection for the worker: first, the payment of outstanding claims against the employer, including arrears of wages, by a specially established guarantee institution; secondly, the guarantee by the Member States that the insolvent employer's non-payment of state social security contributions does not adversely affect employees' benefit entitlement; and thirdly, in the case of former employees, the protection of their entitlement to old-age benefits under supplementary company or inter-company pension schemes. We shall examine these different types of protection in turn.

3.1. Payment by guarantee institutions of employees' claims

(a) The content of the right

The Directive obliges Member States to set up guarantee institutions to 'guarantee' the payment of employees' outstanding claims resulting from contracts of employment or employment relationships,[156] including, where provided for by national law, severance pay on termination of employment relationships.[157] The onus is on the Member State to lay down the detailed rules for the organization, financing (including by way of employer's contributions) and operation of the guarantee institution (Article 5).[158] By way of derogation,[159] Article 4 allows Member States to limit the liability of the guarantee institutions[160] subject to a minimum that the guarantee institution must cover the remuneration of the last three months of the employment relationship.[161] The original version of the Directive offered Member States a choice of three dates marking the beginning of the reference period within which the minimum period of guaranteed remuneration had to fall,[162] but this was considered too complicated. Directive 2002/74 simplified the rules by allowing the Member States to fix a date and reference period.[163] So, Article 4(2) provides that Member States may include the minimum period of three months in a reference period with a duration of not less than six months.[164] Member States having a reference period of not less than 18 months may limit the period for which outstanding claims are met by the guarantee institution to eight weeks. In this case, those periods which are most favourable to the employee are used for the calculation of the minimum period.[165]

---

[156] These terms are given Union meanings: Case C–160/01 *Mau v. Bundesanstalt für Arbeit* [2003] ECR I–4791, para. 41 where the Court ruled that periods during which the employment relationship is suspended on account of child raising are excluded from the period of three months in Article 4(2) because no remuneration is due in those periods.

[157] Art. 3, para. 1. Words which apply to the actual determination of the minimum guarantee must be given a uniform interpretation: Case C–160/01 *Mau* [2003] ECR I–4791, para. 41.

[158] The Member States must, however, take three principles into account: the assets of the guarantee institution must be independent of the employers' operating capital and be inaccessible to proceedings for insolvency; employers must contribute to the financing of the institution unless the costs are fully covered by the public authorities; and the guarantee institution's liabilities must not depend on whether obligations to contribute to the financing have been fulfilled.

[159] Case C–125/97 *Regeling v. Bestuur van de Bedrijfsvereniiging voor de Metaalnijverheid* [1998] ECR I–4493, para. 20.

[160] Art. 4(1).   [161] Art. 4(2), para. 1.   [162] Original Art. 3(2).

[163] Art. 3, para. 2.   [164] Art. 4(2), para. 1.   [165] Art. 4(2), para. 2.

Finally, in recognition that the Directive does not have solely welfarist objectives, Article 4(3) permits the Member States to set a ceiling for payment, so that the sums paid do not exceed 'the social objective of the Directive'. The Commission must be notified of the means of calculating this ceiling.[166] Even if the Commission has not been informed, Member States are still free to set a ceiling.[167] In *Barsotti*[168] the Court said while Member States are entitled to set a ceiling, they are bound to ensure, within the limit of that ceiling, the payment of all outstanding claims in question.[169] Any part payments received on account by employees had to be deducted from the total owed to employees[170] but they could not be deducted from the ceiling because this would undermine the social purpose of the Directive.[171]

The question of what constitutes payments that can be claimed was addressed in *Rodríguez Caballero*[172] which concerned unpaid unfair dismissal compensation (*salarios de tramitación*). The Court ruled that the Directive covers only employees' claims arising from contracts of employment or employment relationships where those claims relate to pay[173] and that pay is defined by national law.[174] This would suggest that unfair dismissal compensation could not be claimed. However, under Spanish law the guarantee institutions could meet claims relating to unfair dismissal compensation but only when the compensation had been awarded by judicial decision. In this case the compensation had been awarded as a result of conciliation, albeit supervized by a judicial body,[175] and so the individual could not recover the money owed. This, the Court ruled, constituted unlawful discrimination contrary to the fundamental principle of equality which could not be objectively justified.[176]

The Spanish courts sought further clarification of this ruling in *Olaso Valero*.[177] Once again, the Court reiterated that the definition of pay was a matter for national law. However, it pointed out that Directive 2002/74 now expressly referred, in Article 3, to compensation for the termination of the employment relationship as pay.

(b) Enforcement of the rights

In *Francovich (No. 1)*[178] the Court considered Articles 3 and 4 (relating to the determination of the beneficiaries of the guarantee as well as those relating to the content of the guarantee) to be sufficiently precise and unconditional to be directly effective. The fact that the Member States had a choice as to the date from which payment of the claims were to be guaranteed (in what was old Article 3(2)) presented no obstacle.[179] However,

---

[166] Art. 4(3), para. 2.

[167] Case C–235/95 *AGS Assedic Pas-de-Calais* v. *Dumon and Froment* [1998] ECR I–4531.

[168] Joined Cases C–19/01, C–50/01 and C–84/01 *INPS* v. *Barsotti* [2004] ECR I–2005.

[169] Para. 36.   [170] Para. 37.   [171] Para. 38.

[172] Case C–442/00 *Rodríguez Caballero* v. *Fondo de Garantia Salarial* [2002] ECR I–11915.

[173] Para. 26.   [174] Art. 2(2) and para. 27.

[175] Cf Case C–498/06 *Robledillo Núñez* v. *Fogasa* [2008] ECR I–921 (extra-judicial conciliation).

[176] Para. 40.

[177] Case C–520/03 *José Vicente Olaso Valero* v. *Fondo de garantia salarial* [2004] ECR I–2065, para. 32.

[178] Joined Cases C–6 and C–9/90 [1991] ECR I–5357.

[179] Case 71/85 *Netherlands* v. *FNV* [1986] ECR 3855 and Case 286/85 *McDermott and Cotter* v. *Minister for Social Welfare and Attorney-General* [1987] ECR 1453.

the wide discretion conferred on the Member States by Article 5 in establishing the guarantee institution meant that Article 5 was not sufficiently precise to enable individuals to rely on it before the national court.[180] Nevertheless, in what became a seminal decision with ramifications extending far beyond the Insolvency Directive, the Court went on to say that the state would nevertheless be liable for failing to implement the Directive.[181]

Similarly in *Wagner-Miret*,[182] the Court said that the discretion given to the Member States by Article 5 of the Directive with regard to the organization, operation, and financing of the guarantee institutions meant that higher management staff could not rely on the Directive to request payment of amounts owing by way of salary from the guarantee institution established for the other categories of employee. The Court then added that even when interpreted in the light of the Directive, in accordance with the principles laid down in *Marleasing*,[183] national law did not enable higher management staff to obtain the benefits provided by the guarantee institutions. However, such staff were entitled, as in *Francovich (No. 1)* itself, to request the state concerned to make good the loss and damage sustained as a result of the failure to implement the Directive.

The Directive does not lay down any time limit in which to lodge an application for insolvency compensation. Nevertheless, the Court said in *Pflücke*[184] that Member States were free to lay down such a time limit provided it was no less favourable than that governing similar domestic applications and was not framed in such as way as to render impossible in practice the exercise of rights conferred by Union law.[185]

3.2. Provisions concerning social security benefits

Article 6 says that Member States have the option to provide that the guarantee institution is not responsible for the contributions owed by the insolvent employer either to the national statutory social security scheme or to supplementary company or intercompany pension schemes.[186] Nevertheless, Article 7 provides that Member States *must* ensure that the non-payment by the insolvent employer of compulsory contributions to their insurance institutions under the state social security scheme does not adversely affect employees' benefit entitlement inasmuch as the employees' contributions are deducted at source from the remuneration paid.[187] In other words, as the Court explained in *Commission* v. *Italy*,[188] Member States had to choose another system for guaranteeing employees' entitlement to social security benefits.

---

[180] Joined Cases C–6 and 9/90 *Francovich (No. 1)* [1991] ECR I–5357.　　[181] See later, at nn. 213–217.

[182] Case C–334/92 [1993] ECR I–6911. Cf. Case C–441/99 *Gharehveran* [2001] ECR I–7687, para. 46 where the Member State has designated itself as liable to meet the claims under the Directive, an individual may rely on the direct effect of the provision against the states.

[183] Case 109/89 [1990] ECR I–4135.

[184] Case C–125/01 *Pflücke* v. *Bundesanstalt für Arbeit* [2003] ECR I–9375.　　[185] Para. 46.

[186] Art. 6. This view was confirmed by Case 22/87 *Commission* v. *Italy* [1989] ECR 143, para. 32.

[187] Art. 7. This does not explain the fate of an insolvent employer's unpaid contributions to an occupational scheme.

[188] Case 22/87 [1989] ECR 143.

3.3. Provisions concerning old-age benefits

Not only does the Directive provide some protection to workers employed at the time of employer's insolvency but it also requires, in Article 8, that Member States protect 'the interests of employees and of persons having already left the employer's undertaking or business at the date of the onset of the employer's insolvency' in respect of rights conferring on them immediate or prospective entitlement to old-age benefits, including survivors' benefits, under occupational or supplementary schemes which fall outside the national statutory social security system.[189] In *Robins*[190] the Court said that this provision gives the Member States, for the purposes of determining the level of protection, considerable latitude which excludes an obligation to guarantee in full. Therefore, where the employer is insolvent and the assets of the supplementary company or inter-company pension schemes are insufficient, accrued pension rights need not necessarily be funded by the Member States themselves or be funded in full. However, the Court did say that where the provisions of domestic law lead to a guarantee of benefits limited to 20 or 49 per cent of the benefits to which an employee was entitled, i.e. less than half of that entitlement, this could not be considered to fall within the definition of the word 'protect' used in Article 8 of the Directive.[191] Given the lack of clarity of the drafting of Article 8, the Court gave a strong indication that the UK's incorrect transposition of the Directive did not constitute a sufficiently serious breach for the purposes of a claim for state liability.[192]

This is not the only limitation on Article 8. Article 8 also provides that the protective provisions do not prevent Member States from either taking measures to avoid abuses or refusing or reducing the liability of the guarantee institution if it appears that 'fulfilment of the obligation is unjustifiable because of the existence of special links between the employee and the employer and of common interests resulting in collusion between them'.[193]

4. PROVISIONS CONCERNING TRANSNATIONAL SITUATIONS

The original version of the Directive did not address the problems which inevitably arose in transnational companies where the parent in State A becomes insolvent and the guarantee institution in State B where the employee works refuses to make payments to the employees. The Court of Justice considered this situation in two cases. First, *Mosbæk*[194] concerned a Danish woman working as an agent for a British company in Denmark. She was paid directly and no tax or social security contributions were deducted under Danish law. The British company was not established or registered in Denmark. The Court considered that the opening of proceedings was most often requested in the state in which the employer is established[195] and in which the employer contributed to the financing of the guarantee institution.[196] In *Mosbæk* the UK satisfied both criteria and so it was the UK's guarantee institution which had to pay.

---

[189] Art. 8.
[190] Case C–278/05 *Robins v. Secretary of State for Work and Pensions* [2007] ECR I–1053, paras. 45–6.
[191] Para. 57.   [192] Paras. 79–81.   [193] Art. 12.
[194] Case C–117/96 *Mosbæk v. Lønmodtagernes Garantifond* [1997] ECR I–5017.
[195] Para. 23.   [196] Para. 24.

Thus, despite the apparent transnational dimension, in fact the case really concerned a single state. This can be contrasted with *Everson*[197] where there was a true transnational dimension. An Irish company was established and registered in the UK and paid its workers through its branch there, collecting the taxes and social security contributions under UK law. In this case the guarantee institution of the state of employment (the UK) was liable for payment of outstanding claims to the employees employed on that territory when the employer was placed in liquidation.

In the interests of clarity, Directive 2002/74 introduced new rules to deal with these transnational situations. Article 9(1) of (what is now) Directive 2008/94 provides that when an undertaking with activities in the territories of at least two countries is in a state of insolvency 'the institution responsible for meeting employees' outstanding claims shall be that in the Member State in whose territory they work or habitually work'.[198] Article 9(3) adds that Member States must take the measures necessary to ensure that decisions taken in the context of insolvency proceedings which have been requested in another Member State, are taken into account when determining the employer's state of insolvency. Article 10 makes provision for information sharing between the competent institutions of the Member States.

So what then constitutes 'habitual work'? This question arose in *Holmquist*[199] concerning a lorry driver, who was employed by a Swedish company which was declared insolvent, who drove between Sweden and Italy in order to deliver goods. The unloading was done by the Italian customers. The Swedish institution argued that it was not liable for the guarantee payment. The Court disagreed. It said that in order for an undertaking established in a Member State to be regarded as having activities in the territory of another Member State, that undertaking does not need to have a branch or fixed establishment in that other State. The undertaking must, however, have a stable economic presence in the latter State, featuring human resources which enable it to perform activities there. In the case of a transport undertaking established in a Member State, the mere fact that a worker employed by it in that State delivers goods between that State and another Member State cannot demonstrate that the undertaking has a stable economic presence in another Member State.[200]

5. ABUSE

Article 12 of Directive 2008/94 deals with the misuse of the Directive. As a derogation to the minimum guarantee laid down by the Directive, this provision is narrowly construed.[201] Article 12(a) provides that Member States can take measures necessary

---

[197] Case C–198/98 *Everson and Barrass v. Secretary of State for Trade and Industry* [1999] ECR I–8903, para. 19.

[198] Art. 9(2) adds: 'The extent of employees' rights shall be determined by the law governing the competent guarantee institution'. Cf. Case C–477/09 *Defossez v. Wiart* [2011] ECR I–000 for the position under the 1980 Directive.

[199] Case C–310/07 *Svenska Staten v. Anders Holmqvist* [2008] ECR I–7871.   [200] Para. 36.

[201] Case C–201/01 *Walcher v. Bundesamt für Soziales und Behinderten wesen Steiermark* [2003] ECR I–8827, para. 38.

to avoid abuses.[202] According to *Walcher*,[203] the abuses referred to in Article 12(a) are 'abusive practices that adversely affect the guarantee institutions by artificially giving rise to a claim for salary, thereby illegally triggering a payment obligation on the part of those institutions'. The case concerned a husband and wife team running a company. She was an employee and a shareholder of the company. The company ran into difficulties in spring 1998. The following year the business was placed in judicial liquidation. Although Mrs Walcher had not been paid since September 1998 she was nevertheless refused a compensation payment. The Court said that while it was not abusive to try to enforce a claim against the employer who did not appear able to pay,[204] it might be abusive (although not in all cases)[205] to carry on in an employment relationship beyond the date on which an employee who was not a shareholder would have resigned (since such conduct sets up the preconditions for payment by the guarantee institution).[206]

Article 12 also provides that Member States can refuse or reduce the liability under Article 3 or the guarantee obligation under Article 7 if it appears that fulfilment of the obligation is either unjustifiable because of the existence of special links between the employee and the employer and of common interests resulting in collusion between them[207] or where the employee, on his or her own or together with his or her close relatives, is the owner of an essential part of the employer's undertaking or business and had a considerable influence on its activities.[208]

6. IMPLEMENTATION AND REMEDIES

6.1. Implementation

The rules laid down are the minimum: Member States have the option of introducing laws, regulations, or administrative provisions which are more favourable to employees.[209] Furthermore, the implementation of the amendments to Directive 80/987 cannot be used as an excuse to lower the levels of protection already provided in the Member States.[210]

6.2. Remedies

Directive 2008/94 differs from the Directives on Transfers and Collective Redundancies in that it envisages a particular role for the state which cannot be fulfilled by any other body. Consequently, as the Court recognized in *Francovich (No. 1)*,[211] while Articles 1 and 2 were sufficiently precise and unconditional to be directly effective, the key provision of the Directive—Article 5 on the establishment of a guarantee institution—

---

[202] Note the careful scrutiny adopted by the Court to this (eventually unsuccessful) claim in Case C–442/00 *Rodríguez Caballero* v. *Fondo de Garantía Salarial* [2002] ECR I–11915, para. 36.

[203] Case C–201/01 [2003] ECR I–8827, para. 39.   [204] Para. 44.

[205] Para. 49.   [206] Paras. 47–8.   [207] Art. 12(b).

[208] Art. 12(c). See further Case C–30/10 *Lotta Andersson* [2011] ECR I–000.

[209] Art. 11.   [210] Art. 11, para. 2.

[211] Joined Cases C–6/90 and C–9/90 *Francovich (No. 1)* v. *Italy* [1991] ECR I–5357.

did not satisfy the requirements to be directly effective[212] and so could not be relied on by the applicants in the national court to claim arrears of salary. Instead, the Court ruled that Francovich and Bonifaci were obliged to sue the state for damages for the loss suffered due to the Italian government's failure to implement the Directive. Famously, the Court said that Member States were required to make good loss or damage caused to individuals by their failure to transpose a Directive since the principle of state liability was inherent in the system of the Treaty.[213] In *Francovich (No. 1)* the Court laid down three conditions for state liability, which it subsequently refined,[214] namely, that the rule of law infringed was intended to confer rights on individuals; the breach had to be sufficiently serious (always satisfied in the case of total failure to implement a Directive);[215] and there had to be a direct causal link between the breach of the obligation resting on the state and the damage sustained by the injured parties.[216] In *ex parte Factortame*,[217] the Court established that the reparation had to be commensurate with the loss or damage sustained, so as to ensure effective protection for the rights of the individuals harmed. Subject to this, it was on the basis of the rules of national law on liability that the state had to make reparation for the consequences of the loss or damage caused. However, the conditions for reparation of loss or damage laid down by national law could not be less favourable than those relating to similar domestic claims and could not be framed as to make it virtually impossible or excessively difficult to obtain reparation.

Finally, in *Maso*[218] and *Bonifaci*[219] the Court considered the extent of the reparation for the loss or damage arising from such failure. The Court said that in making good the loss or damage sustained by employees as a result of the belated transposition of the Directive, a Member State was entitled to apply retroactively the belated implementing measures to such employees, including rules against aggregation or other limitations on the liability of the guarantee institution, provided that the Directive had been properly transposed. However, it was for the national court to ensure that reparation of the loss or damage sustained by the beneficiaries was adequate. Retroactive and proper application in full of the measures implementing the Directive would suffice, unless the

---

[212] In Joined Cases C–140/91, C–141/91, C–278/91 and C–279/91 *Suffritti* v. *INPS* [1992] ECR I–6337 the Court, however, held that the claimants could not rely on the provisions of the Directive since both the declarations of insolvency and the termination of the employment relationships took place before the expiry of the time limit for the implementation of the Directive. The Court reminded the parties that it is only where a Member State has not correctly implemented a Directive within the period of implementation laid down that individuals can rely on rights which derive directly from provisions of the Directive before their national courts.

[213] Joined Cases C–6 and C–9/90 *Francovich (No. 1)* [1991] ECR I–5357.

[214] Joined Cases C–6 and C–9/90 [1991] ECR I–5357, para. 35; Joined Cases C–46/93 and C–48/93 *Brasserie du pêcheur and ex parte Factortame and Others* [1996] ECR I–1029, para. 31; Case C–392/93 *R* v. *Secretary of State for Trade and Industry, ex parte British Telecommunications* [1996] ECR I–1631, para. 38.

[215] Joined Cases C–178/94, C–179/94, C–188/94, C–189/94 and C–190/94 *Dillenkofer and Others* v. *Bundesrepublik Deutschland* [1996] ECR I–4845, para. 20.

[216] Joined Cases C–46/93 and C–48/93 *ex parte Factortame* [1996] ECR I–1029, para. 51.

[217] Para. 82.   [218] Case C–373/95 [1997] ECR I–4051.

[219] Joined Cases C–94/95 and C–95/95 *Bonifaci* v. *INPS* [1997] ECR I–3969.

beneficiaries established the existence of complementary loss sustained on account of the fact that they were unable to benefit at the appropriate time from the financial advantages guaranteed by the Directive. If so, such loss also had to be made good.

Finally, in *Palmisani*[220] the Court ruled that Union law allowed Member States to require any action for reparation of the loss or damage sustained as a result of the belated transposition of Directive 2008/94 to be brought within a limitation period of one year from the date of its transposition into national law, provided that the limitation period was no less favourable than procedural requirements in respect of similar actions of a domestic nature.

D. CONCLUSIONS

Restructuring is currently the name of the game for the European Union. As the Commission put it in its Communication, *Restructuring and Employment*,[221] drafted in connection with the relaunched Lisbon strategy, restructuring must be well-managed to meet a two-fold economic and social requirement. *Enterprises* have to adapt to change and must do so rapidly to preserve and enhance their competitiveness; and *workers* have to be adaptable to be able to move from one job to another 'of equivalent quality'. This is, of course, not new, and the 1970s Directives on Employee Rights on Restructuring Enterprises, broadly aimed to achieve very similar objectives. What is new is that the Social Partners are now being used to achieve these objectives. The emphasis on a legal approach found in the 1970s is being replaced by softer methods, in particular OMC. For example, the Commission encourages the Social Partners to reach agreement on the requisite ways and means for implementing mechanisms for applying and monitoring existing Guidelines on restructuring. It also encourages the adoption of best practices through guidelines on restructuring. An interactive website, 'anticipedia',[222] has been launched by the Commission as a discussion forum on restructuring. More substantively, various EU funds, such as the European Social Fund[223] and the European Globalisation Adjustment Fund (now specifically adapted to respond to the economic crisis)[224] have been used to invest in retraining workers who have lost their jobs. The role of the Social Partners—and other forms of worker representatives—in managing change is considered further in the next two chapters.

---

[220] Case C–261/95 *Palmisani v. INPS* [1997] ECR I–4025.

[221] Communication, *Restructuring and employment. Anticipating and accompanying restructuring in order to develop employment: the role of the European Union* COM(2005) 120.

[222] <https://ec.europa.eu/employment_social/anticipedia/> (last accessed 25 January 2012).

[223] <http://ec.europa.eu/esf/main.jsp?catId=381&langId=en> (last accessed 25 January 2012).

[224] <http://ec.europa.eu/social/main.jsp?catId=326&langId=en> (last accessed 25 January 2012).

PART VI

COLLECTIVE LABOUR LAW

15

WORKER INVOLVEMENT
IN DECISION-MAKING:
INFORMATION,
CONSULTATION, AND
WORKER PARTICIPATION

A. INTRODUCTION

This chapter and the next concern the collective dimension of EU labour law. Collective labour law traditionally embraces the body of rules regulating the relationship between the collectivity of employees and employers/groups of employers. The diversity of collective labour law is reflected in the Community Social Charter 1989 and the EU Charter of Fundamental Rights 2000. Both documents envisage a range of collective rights: rights of information, consultation, and participation for workers,[1] freedom of association for employers and workers,[2] the right to negotiate and conclude collective agreements,[3] and the right to resort to collective action, including strikes.[4] With the exception of the right to join or not to join a trade union, reference is made in all cases to national legislation and practice to clarify the substance and exercise of these rights. The reference to national law is explained in part by the absence of clear Union competence in the broad field of collective labour law. In particular, Article 153(5) TFEU (ex 137(5) EC) excludes 'pay, the right of association, the right to strike or the right to impose lock-outs' from the Union's competence, or at least from its competence under Article 153 TFEU.[5] Because of this uncertainty about competence, only the rights to

---

[1] Arts. 17–18 of the Social Charter 1989 and Arts. 27–28 of the Charter of Fundamental Rights of the EU.
[2] Art. 11 of the Social Charter 1989 and Art. 12 of the Charter of Fundament Rights of the EU.
[3] Art. 12 of the Social Charter 1989 and Art. 28 of the Charter of Fundamental Rights of the EU.
[4] Art. 13 of the Social Charter 1989 and Art. 28 of the Charter of Fundamental Rights of the EU. The internal orders of the Member States are free to determine the conditions and the extent of the application of the rights laid down in Arts. 11–13 of the Social Charter 1989 to the armed forces, police, and civil service.
[5] Cf. the proposal for the Monti II Reg. which has Art. 352 TFEU as its legal basis. This is discussed further in Ch. 5.

information, consultation, and participation of workers' representatives, and collective bargaining have assumed any concrete form in the Union legal order.

In this chapter we shall consider the various steps taken by the Union to require employees—or more usually their representatives (union or non-union)—to be informed, consulted, and even to participate in the employer's decision-making. In the next chapter we consider the (limited) action taken by the Union in the field of collective rights as they affect trade unions and their members. In particular, we focus on the extent to which the Union has encouraged the development of collective bargaining at EU, national, and sub-national levels.

B. INFORMATION, CONSULTATION, AND PARTICIPATION: SETTING THE SCENE

1. INTRODUCTION

In recent years, the Union has focused particular attention on encouraging dialogue between workers/their representatives and their employers. This is because the Union sees a clear link between dialogue and greater productivity:[6]

> Regular, transparent, comprehensive dialogue creates trust...The systematic development of social dialogue within companies, nationally and at European level is fundamental to managing change and preventing negative social consequences and deterioration of the social fabric...Social dialogue ensures a balance is maintained between corporate flexibility and workers' [security].[7]

The argument runs that workers who participate in decisions which affect them enjoy a greater degree of job satisfaction and should be more productive than those who simply accept orders.[8] Social dialogue, replacing the more traditional hierarchical management arrangements, is therefore seen as the cornerstone of corporate governance designed to create a high skill, high effort, high trust European labour market which now lies at the core of the European Employment Strategy (EES).[9]

Some have doubted the validity of these claims. Cheffins,[10] for example, argues that employees are often cynical about worker participation measures and so employers have little to gain by keeping in place whatever participative measures they have introduced; that, over time, employees in high-effort work places have an incentive to free-ride off the efforts of fellow members; that the *quid pro quo* for flexibility, job security, creates a cozy environment where there is little likelihood of being fired, which might hurt production levels, and a low turnover of staff gives little chance for promotion. This, in turn,

---

[6] See COM(98) 592 discussed further in this chapter.

[7] Final Report of the High Level Group on economic and social implications of industrial change, November 1998, 9.

[8] B. Cheffins, *Company Law: Theory, Structure and Operation* (OUP, Oxford, 1997).

[9] See further Ch. 3.   [10] Cheffins, previously, at n. 8, 583–5, 588.

may have a negative impact on flexibility, as would any formalized, bureaucratic deci-sion-making process[11] which might cause a company to postpone facing economic reali-ties and defer changes which are required to foster the company's long-term growth and development.

Nevertheless, the EU documents continue to emphasize the value of social dialogue. For example, the Final Report of the High Level Group on the economic and social implications of industrial change,[12] published late in 1998, concluded that 'top-performing companies have a good social dialogue with their employees because moti-vated people are the vital component for commercial success'. The Group considered necessary 'the initiatives taken by the European Union, corporations, the social part-ners and governments to create a broader, high quality system of information and consultation'.[13]

Some of the inspiration for the Union's emphasis on the benefits of social dialogue comes from an examination of the success in the past of the German economy, which has been attributed in part to the well-established system of co-determination (*Mit-bestimmung*). Under this system workers are involved in decision-making not only at plant level through works councils,[14] but also at company level through the mem-bership of workers' representatives on the supervisory board controlling the company.[15]

However, while a positive case can be made for social dialogue, the development of EU rules also serves a defensive function. A co-determination system is expensive and has inevitably raised fears about social dumping[16]—that in the absence of Union regulation companies will incorporate in countries which take a low-cost approach to employment relations.[17] Until relatively recently this was not a real problem in the EU since most countries operate the *siège réel* doctrine whereby a company's 'real seat' is

---

[11] Citing C. Lane, *Management and Labour in Europe: The Industrial Enterprise in Germany, Britain and France* (E. Elgar Ltd, Aldershot, 1989) 232 and 236, and K. Hopt, 'Labor Representation on Corporate Boards: Impacts and Problems for Corporate Governance and Integration in Europe' (1994) 14 *Int. Rev. of Law and Econ.*, 203, 207–8, 210–11, 214.

[12] Commission, *Managing Change*, Gyllenhamer Report, November 1998, 5 and now Commission, Restructuring and employment: the contribution of the European Union, COM(2008) 419.

[13] Ibid. See additionally the Davignon Report, 'European System of Worker Involvement, with regard to the European Company Statute and Other Pending Proposals', and the Gyllenhammer Report, 'Interim Report of the High Level Expert Group on the Economic and Social Impact of Industrial Change'.

[14] Co-determination means employee representatives sharing responsibility with management for making decisions in areas such as organization of working time, methods of remuneration, leave arrangements, health and safety, and bonus arrangements.

[15] See R. J. Adams, 'The Right to Participate' (1992) 5 *Employee Resp. and Rts J.*, 91, 94 and 97, and K. Thelan, *Union of Parts: Labor Politics in Postwar Germany* (Cornell University Press, Ithaca, NY, 1991) 1–5, 25–32, cited and discussed in Cheffins, above, n. 8, 582. Cf. K. Kraft, 'Empirical Studies on Codetermination: A Selective Survey and Research Design' in H. Nutzinger and J. Backhaus (eds.), *Co-determination: A Discussion of Different Approaches* (Springer-Verlag, Berlin, 1989).

[16] These arguments are considered further in Ch. 1.

[17] See, e.g., G. Wiesmann, 'German Companies flee to the UK', *Financial Times*, 24 May 2006 which reports that Air Berlin, the low-cost airline, opted to become Germany's first UK plc, in part due to its desire to avoid the German system of co-determination.

the country where its central administration or principal place of business is located. Therefore, a company incorporated in the UK, but with its plant and operations in Germany, will be considered under German law to have its real seat in Germany. The decision of the Court in *Centros*[18] has, however, cast doubt on the compatibility of the real seat doctrine with Union law. This, in turn, may create further pressure for the enactment of Union legislation on worker representation to protect existing worker participation structures.

2. DIFFERENT FORMS OF WORKER INVOLVEMENT

What forms, then, can worker involvement take? *Participation* can be regarded as a generic term[19] embracing all types of industrial democracy,[20] ranging from information, consultation, and collective bargaining to more extensive involvement in the employer's decision-making process. The provision of *information*, the least intense form of worker involvement, is unilateral: the information is provided by management to workers or their representatives (trade unions or elected worker representatives). *Consultation*, on the other hand, is bilateral, giving workers' representatives the opportunity to make their views known. However, the final decision usually remains with the employers and that decision may or may not reflect the workers' views. This is the weak form of consultation.[21] A stronger approach to consultation brings consultation closer to collective bargaining because, as with Article 2 of Directive 98/59/EC on collective redundancies,[22] employers must consult with the workers' representatives 'with a view to reaching agreement'.[23]

At the other end of the spectrum, the most intense forms of worker involvement are, on the one hand participation on the company's board, a distinguishing feature of the German and Dutch systems, which is now a possibility provided for by the European Company Statute,[24] and, on the other, collective bargaining. Traditionally, collective bargaining is a function carried out by trade unions and is usually linked to the right to strike:[25] strike action is a union's principal sanction if the employer does not co-operate in the negotiations. This issue is considered further in Chapter 16.

---

[18] Case C–212/97 *Centros v. Erhvervs-og Selskabsstyrelsen* [1999] ECR I–1459. S. Deakin, 'Two Types of Regulatory Competition: Competitive Federalism Versus Reflexive Harmonisation. A Law and Economics Perspective on *Centros*' (1999) 2 *CYELS* 231; M. Siems (2002) 27 *ELRev.* 47.

[19] As we shall see later, in the context of certain Directives, 'participation' has a specific legal meaning.

[20] See generally O. Kahn-Freund, 'Industrial Democracy' (1977) 6 *ILJ* 65; P. Davies and B. Wedderburn, 'The Land of Industrial Democracy' (1977) 6 *ILJ* 197.

[21] See, e.g., Art. 2(g) of ECS Dir. 2003/72 (OJ [2003] L207/25); '"consultation" means the establishment of dialogue and exchange of views between the body representative of the employees and/or the employees' representatives and the competent organ of the SCE, at a time, in a manner and with a content which allows the employees' representatives, on the basis of information provided, to express an opinion on measures envisaged by the competent organ which may be taken into account in the decision-making process within the SCE'.

[22] OJ [1999] L225/16.

[23] See additionally Case C–188/03 *Junk* [2005] ECR I–885, para. 44: 'It thus appears that Article 2 of the Directive imposes an obligation to negotiate'. See further Ch. 14.

[24] See e.g. Art. 7(2) of Dir. 2003/72 (OJ [2003] L207/25).

[25] This point is recognised in the first Recital to the proposed Monti II Regulation (COM(2012) 130).

Participation (used in its generic sense) can be direct or indirect.[26] *Direct participation* permits *individual* employees to take part directly in decision-making or other company processes by, for example, participating in company finances through profit-related pay or equity sharing. It can also include involvement in decision-making, particularly at workplace level. Such participation is designed primarily to promote motivation in order to achieve company goals such as increased productivity, better quality control and a greater sense of loyalty. However, it is also considered the least legitimate form of worker participation since workers, unlike trade unions, are not independent from their employers.

Indirect or 'representative' participation, by contrast, involves procedures through which workers are *collectively* represented in the company's decision-making processes. The purpose of such participation is primarily the representation of interests. This participation can loosely be divided into three categories: first, collective bargaining; second, employee representatives sitting on the company's board (where their involvement is limited to structural matters at company level);[27] and thirdly, the establishment of works councils (or equivalent bodies) whose rights comprise the disclosure of information, consultation, and co-determination over areas of concern at plant, company, or group level. These types of indirect participation are designed to improve worker representation in the decision-making process. This, it is believed, will improve operational efficiency because problems are identified and resolved at an earlier stage, employers can put into practice employee's ideas to improve production processes, and workers feel a greater commitment to decisions in which they are involved or represented.[28] Further, it is thought that giving workers a voice discourages them from 'quitting', thereby reducing labour costs.

3. DEVELOPMENTS AT UNION LEVEL

At Union level, the communiqué issued by the heads of state at the Paris summit in 1972 made reference to the importance of increasing the involvement of the Social Partners in the economic and social decisions of the Union,[29] a view endorsed by the 1974 Action Programme.[30]

At first the Union concentrated its efforts on the provision of information and the requirement to consult in specific fields, most notably health and safety,[31] collective

---

[26] M. Gold and M. Hall, 'Legal Regulation and the Practice of Employee Participation in the European Community, European Foundation for the Improvement of Living and Working Conditions', EF/WP/90/41/EN, 26.

[27] Ibid.

[28] See, e.g. the British Labour Government's *Fairness at Work* White Paper, Cm. 3968 HMSO, London, 1998, 12.

[29] Final declaration, EC Bull. 10/1972, 15–24.

[30] OJ [1974] C13/1, EC Bull. 2/1974. The Commission has also taken the view that the structure and activities of Union enterprises, esp. transnational enterprises, must be sufficiently transparent for the benefit of shareholders, creditors, employees, and the public interest in general. See Commission's Communication on *Multinational Undertakings and the Community*, EC Bull. Supp. 15/1973.

[31] The Framework Dir. 89/391/EEC on health and safety (OJ [1989] L183/1), discussed in Ch. 11.

redundancies,[32] and transfer of undertakings.[33] However, there was continued resistance to the introduction of a more general, systematic, and institutionalized right to employee participation in corporate decision-making for fear that it would cut across established national systems of worker involvement. The long and tortuous legislative history of various proposals over the last four decades bears testimony to this.[34] In particular, proposals for a European Company Statute date back to 1970 while proposals for national level information and consultation go back to 1980 with the 'Vredling' proposal. The difficulties created by radically different perceptions of worker representation in the Member States made it difficult to agree on a single approach. However, the Social Charter of 1989 and subsequently the EU Charter of Fundamental Rights 2000 recognized workers' rights to information and consultation as fundamental social rights. For example, Article 27 of the Charter of Fundamental Rights provides:

> Workers or their representatives must, at the appropriate levels, be guaranteed information and consultation in good time in the cases and under the conditions provided for by Union law and national laws and practices.

Article 21 of the revised European Social Charter 1996 of the Council of Europe is more prescriptive, encouraging workers or their representatives, again in accordance with national legislation and practice, to be informed regularly about the economic and financial situation of the undertaking employing them, and to be consulted in good time on proposed decisions which could substantially affect the interests of workers, particularly in respect of those decisions which could have an important impact on the employment situation of the undertaking. Article 21 is supplemented by Article 28 which requires states to support worker representatives by protecting them against detrimental treatment, including dismissal, and providing them with facilities to carry out their tasks.

As Davies points out, some rights theorists are sceptical about the value of the right to be informed and consulted, arguing that it is the 'second best' option to collective bargaining which offers a more effective form of participation because the presence of a trade union helps to equalize the bargaining power of workers and management. On the other hand, others argue that the right to be consulted sits closely alongside other procedural rights such as a right to a hearing, and, on this basis, the right to consultation is an important aspect of the more general right to a fair hearing at work.[35] This argument, together with the more general view that worker participation is good for productivity, has influenced the EU's approach to the need for legislation in this field. But how was the Union to push through the

---

[32] Council Dir. 75/129/EEC (OJ [1975] L48/29) as amended by Council Dir. 92/56/EC (OJ [1992] L245/3) and consolidated in Council Dir. 98/59/EC (OJ [1998] L225/16) considered in Ch. 14.

[33] See Council Dir. 77/187/EEC (OJ [1977] L61/126) as amended by Council Dir. 98/50/EC (OJ [1998] L201/88) and consolidated in Dir. 2001/23 (OJ [2001] L82/16) considered in Ch. 13.

[34] See generally, W. Kolvenbach, 'EEC Company Law Harmonisation and Worker Participation' (1990) 11 *University of Pennsylvania Journal of International Business Law* 709.

[35] A. C. L. Davies, *Perspectives on Labour Law* (CUP, Cambridge, 2008), 180–181.

long-standing proposals on worker consultation provision? The answer lay in a new approach: a shift away from requiring consultation on specific issues (collective redundancies, health and safety, etc.) and instead requiring employers to set up a mechanism, when asked to do so by their staff, in which to consult workers or their representatives on a regular basis. The adoption of the European Works Council Directive 94/45 (now Directive 2009/38), based on encouraging workers and their employers to reach an agreement on what form worker participation should take in their workplace, with the sanction that the stricter subsidiary requirements found in the Annex would apply if they did not, paved the way for the adoption of a number of other Directives, notably Directive 2002/14 on national-level informa-tion and consultation[36] and Directive 2003/72 on worker participation in the European Company.[37]

C. EUROPEAN WORKS COUNCILS

1. BACKGROUND TO THE ADOPTION OF THE DIRECTIVE

While the focus on developing Union rules on information and consultation at *national* level risked stepping on the toes of existing national structures, the Union realized that there might be a role for Union legislation dealing with the *transnational* provision of information. While the Directives on Collective Redundancies[38] and Transfer of Undertakings[39] did address the problem in part, their limited scope proved to be inadequate. A number of multinationals, mostly French and German (BSN, Bull, Elf-Aquitaine, Pechiney, Rhône-Poulenc, Saint Gobain, Thomson, Nestlé, Allianz, Volkswagen, and Mercedes-Benz), were already ahead of the game. They had established various types of jointly agreed European-level information and consulta-tion arrangements.[40] These were influenced by the French basic model: a joint man-agement/employee forum meeting annually, at the employer's expense, to discuss information provided by management about group-level matters relating to corpo-rate strategy, finances, and employment.[41]

---

[36] OJ [2002] L80/29.   [37] OJ [2003] L207/25.

[38] Council Dir. 75/129/EEC (OJ [1975] L48/29). This Directive was amended by Council Dir. 92/56/EEC (OJ [1992] L245/13) to reflect the increasing transnationalization of companies and consolidated by Council Dir. 98/59/EC (OJ [1998] L225/16). See further Ch. 14.

[39] Council Dir. 77/187/EEC (OJ [1977] L61/26). This Directive was revised by Dir. 98/50 (OJ [1998] L201/88) and was subsequently consolidated in Dir. 2001/23 (OJ [2001] L82/16). See further Ch. 13.

[40] P. Marginson, 'European Integration and Trans-national Management—Union Relations in the Enterprise' (1992) BJIR. 529, 540. The operation of these bodies is considered in M. Gold and M. Hall, *European Level Information and Consultation in Multi-National Companies: An Evaluation of Practice*, European Foundation for the Improvement of Living and Working Conditions (OPEC, Luxembourg, 1992).

[41] M. Hall, *Legislating for Employee Participation: A Case Study of the European Works Council Directive*, 1992, Warwick Papers in Industrial Relations, 4. An expanded version of this can be found in M. Hall, 'Behind the European Works Councils Directive: The European Commission's Legislative Strategy' (1992) 30 BJIR 547.

These precedents showed the Commission the way forward:[42] Union legislation could focus on the transnational dimension of employee information and consultation,[43] accommodating, but not cutting across, national practice in respect of employee representation,[44] in order to bridge the gap between increasingly transnational corporate decision-making and workers' nationally defined and nationally confined information and consultation rights.[45]

However, the UK remained implacably opposed to the principle of the proposed Directive,[46] arguing that such a Directive would undermine existing successful arrangements for consultation, particularly at local levels; that it would impose new statutory restrictions on a company's freedom to implement decisions and consequently would cause costly delays; and that the Directive would deter inward investment, rendering firms more prone to settle in only one Member State[47] or discourage them from expanding above the employee threshold set by the Directive. Since the proposal was based on Article 115 TFEU (ex 94 EC), the UK was able to block its adoption.

In October 1993 the Commission abandoned its attempt to secure unanimous agreement on the Directive and proposed reintroducing the measure under the Social Policy Agreement (SPA) instead, but this time providing for a choice between a European Works Council (EWC) and an Information and Consultation Procedure (ICP). The Social Partners were consulted, as required by Article 154(2) TFEU (ex 138(2) EC),[48] and then the Commission produced a revised draft where the term 'European Works Council' was dropped and replaced by 'information and consultation structure', albeit that the structure remained very similar to the EWC of earlier drafts.[49] This draft formed the basis for unsuccessful negotiations between the Social Partners. UNICE (now BusinessEurope), the employers' association, considered that employee participation measures should not be regulated or harmonized by the Union but should be allowed to evolve naturally, to reflect local circumstances. It also considered that too much emphasis was placed by the Commission on regulated collective relationships between employers and trade unions or workers' representatives and not enough on direct employee contact and involvement with management.[50] Meanwhile, ETUC, the trade union body, strongly favoured the introduction of measures encouraging employee participation and called for a basic European legal framework to guarantee the information, consultation and participation rights of workers' representatives at all levels of decision-making within undertakings.

[42] COM(90) 581, para. 17.
[43] See further the Opinion of the Economic and Social Committee on the social consequences of cross-frontier mergers (OJ [1989] C329/10).
[44] Commission Social Charter Action Programme, *Social Europe* (Special Edn) 1/90, 66.
[45] M. Gold and M. Hall, 'Statutory European Works Councils: the Final Countdown?' (1994) 25 *IRJ* 177, 178.
[46] See COM(90) 581.
[47] Cf. J. Visser, 'Works Councils and Trade Unions in the Netherlands: Rivals or Allies?' (1993) 29 *The Netherlands' Journal of Social Sciences* 64, esp. 86–7.
[48] EIRR 241, 28.   [49] See further EIRR 242, 13.
[50] UNICE Press Release, 24 October 1989, cited in M. Gold and M. Hall, *Legal Regulation and the Practice of Employee Participation in the European Community*, European Foundation for the Improvement of Living and Working Conditions, Working Paper No. EF/WP/90/41/EN.

With the breakdown of talks between the Social Partners, the Commission issued a further proposal aimed at establishing either a 'European Committee',[51] *or* a procedure for informing and consulting employees,[52] the more flexible alternative emphasized by the Belgian Presidency in 1993.[53] However, the term 'European Works Council' was reinstated in the final version of the Directive 94/45/EC[54] adopted in September 1994. Since the Directive was adopted under the SPA, the UK was initially excluded, but when the Labour government signed up to the Social Chapter in 1997, the Directive was extended to the UK.[55]

Directive 94/45 was repealed and replaced in 2009 by the recast Directive 2009/38.[56] While much of Directive 2009/38 replicated Directive 94/45/EC, Directive 2009/38 emphasized that information and consultation had to be conducted at the most appropriate level but that the role of the EWC was confined to transnational issues, defined in Article 1(4), as concerning the Union-scale undertaking or Union-scale group of undertakings as a whole, or at least two undertakings or establishments of the undertaking or group situated in two different Member States.[57]

2. THE THRESHOLDS LAID DOWN BY THE DIRECTIVE

The requirement to establish an EWC or a procedure for informing and consulting (ICP) employees applies only to Union-scale undertakings and Union-scale groups of undertakings[58] with more than 1,000 employees across the 30 Member States[59] and with at least two establishments[60] in different Member States each employing at least 150 people.[61] In *Bofrost*[62] the Court said that the employees' right to information in Article 11 existed even before it was ascertained whether there existed within the group a controlling undertaking.[63] This right to information enabled workers' representatives to

---

[51] This term reflects the terminology used in voluntary information and consultation arrangements.

[52] COM(94) 134 final (OJ [1994] C199/10).

[53] Art. 1(2).   [54] OJ [1994] L254/64.

[55] Council Directive 97/74/EC (OJ [1997] L10/20).   [56] OJ [2009] L122/28.

[57] For a discussion of the changes introduced, see S. Sciarra, 'Notions of Solidarity in Times of Economic Uncertainty' (2010) 39 *ILJ* 280.

[58] Arts. 1(1) and (2). A group of undertakings means a controlling undertaking, defined to mean an undertaking which can exercise a dominant influence over another undertaking by virtue of ownership, financial participation or the rules which govern it (Art. 3(1) and (2)) and its controlled undertakings (Art. 2(1)(b)). These definitions are based on EP and Council Dir. 2004/18 (OJ [2004] L134/114), on the co-ordination of procedures for the award of public works contracts, public supply contracts, and public service contracts.

[59] Art. 2(1)(a). The prescribed thresholds for the size of the workforce are to be based on the average number of employees, including part-time employees, employed during the previous two years calculated according to national legislation and/or practice (Art. 2(2)).

[60] In the case of Community scale groups of undertakings, read 'groups of undertakings' in the place of 'establishments' (Art. 2(1)(c)).

[61] Art. 2(1)(a) and (c). Member States may provide that this Directive does not apply to merchant navy crews (Art. 1(7)).

[62] Case C–62/99 *Betriebsrat de Bofrost v. Bofrost Josef H. Boquoi Deutschland West GmbH & Co. KG* [2001] ECR I–2579. See generally, B. Waas, 'The European Court of Justice and Directive 94/45/EC on the Establishment of European Works Councils' [2005] *European Company Law* 138.

[63] Para. 34. Controlling undertaking is defined in Art. 3.

obtain information about, for example, the structure or organization of a group of undertakings,[64] and the average total number of employees and their distribution across the Member States,[65] in order to establish whether the thresholds laid down by the Directive had been met to support a demand that negotiations for the establishment of an EWC/ICP be opened.[66]

The Directive also applies where Union-scale undertakings or groups of undertakings have their headquarters outside the territory of the Member States but meet the threshold requirements in the 30 Member States.[67] In this 'extra-territorial' situation, the Directive deems legal responsibility for carrying out the Directive's requirements: responsibility falls on either a representative agent of the undertaking or group of undertakings or the undertaking with the highest number of employees in the territory of the Member States.[68]

The importance of the deeming provisions have been highlighted by *Kühne* v. *Nagel*[69] and *Anker*.[70] In *Kühne* v. *Nagel* the Court said that the other undertakings belonging to the group and located in the Member States were under an obligation to assist the deemed central management in creating the conditions necessary for the establishment of an EWC or ICP, in particular by supplying it with the necessary information. *Anker* concerned the reverse situation: the obligation by the central management or deemed central management to supply information to workers' representatives. The Court said that not only must the information be supplied but also the Directive required that the information be supplied to employees' representatives through their undertaking in the group to which those representatives submitted a request in the first place.[71] The representatives were not required to submit requests for information directly to central management or deemed central management since this might discourage employees from exercising their rights.[72]

3. THE NEGOTIATING PROCEDURE

The Directive envisages a two-stage approach to the establishment of an EWC or ICP. The first stage involves voluntary negotiations. If there is no agreement or the parties so decide, then the mandatory ('subsidiary') provisions laid down in the annex of the Directive are triggered at the second stage.

---

[64] Para. 39.

[65] Case C–349/01 *Betriebsrat der Firma ADS Anker GmbH* v. *ADS Anker GmbH* [2004] ECR I–6803, para. 65. The Advocate General suggested that the provision of information on corporate structure and documentation should be subject to confidentiality requirements but the Court of Justice did not add this requirement.

[66] Para. 32. See additionally Case C–440/00 *Kühne* v. *Nagel* [2004] ECR I–787, para. 46.

[67] Art. 4(2).   [68] Art. 4(2), para. 2.

[69] Case C–440/00 *Kühne* v. *Nagel* [2004] ECR I–787.

[70] Case C–349/01 *Betriebsrat der Firma ADS Anker GmbH* v. *ADS Anker GmbH* [2004] ECR I–6803, para. 49.

[71] Para. 56.   [72] Para. 59.

3.1. Starting the negotiations

The procedure for the first stage is activated at the initiative of central management of the undertaking or the controlling undertaking in a group of undertakings[73] or at the written request of at least 100 employees or their representatives[74] in at least two undertakings in at least two Member States.[75] This prevents an EWC from being imposed from the outside: the parties must actually want it. However, the onus is on central management to create the conditions and means necessary for the establishment of an EWC or ICP.[76]

3.2. The outcome of the negotiations

When a request has been received, a 'special negotiating body' (SNB)—essentially an employee representation body[77]—must be set up. Individual Member States must determine the method to be used for the election or appointment of the members of the SNB.[78] Central management must then convene a meeting with the SNB.[79] Both central management and the SNB must negotiate 'in the spirit of cooperation with a view to reaching an agreement'.[80]

There are three possible outcomes of the meetings between the SNB and central management. First, they are able to conclude, possibly with the assistance of experts,[81] a written agreement on the scope, composition, functions and term of office of the EWC(s) or the arrangements for implementing an ICP.[82] If they succeed in reaching an agreement to establish an EWC, the agreement should include: details of the undertakings covered by the agreement; the composition of the EWC; the number of members; the allocation of seats and the term of office; the function and procedure for informing and consulting the EWC; the venue, frequency, and duration of meetings of the EWC; the financial and material resources to be allocated to the EWC; the duration of the agreement; and the procedure for its renegotiation.[83]

If central management and the SNB decide to establish an ICP instead, the agreement must specify the methods by which the employees' representatives have the right to meet to discuss the information conveyed to them.[84] The information supplied must relate, in particular, to transnational questions which significantly affect workers' interests.[85]

---

[73] Art. 2(1)(e).

[74] Employees' representatives means the employees' representatives provided for by national law or practice (Art. 2(1)(d)), a definition drawn from Council Dirs. 98/59 on collective redundancies and 2001/23 on transfers of undertakings.

[75] Art. 5(1).   [76] Art. 4(1).

[77] Case C–349/01 *Betriebsrat der Firma ADS Anker GmbH* v. *ADS Anker GmbH* [2004] ECR I–6803, para. 49.

[78] Art. 5(2)(a). The right to elect or appoint members of the SNB must apply equally to employees in those undertakings 'in which there are no employees' representatives through no fault of their own'. Special rules apply to ensure an even representation of employees (Art. 5(2)(b)). Central management and local management must be informed of the composition of the SNB (Art. 5(2)(c)).

[79] Art. 5(4). Expenses relating to the negotiations must be borne by the central management (Art. 5(6)).

[80] Art. 6(1).

[81] Art. 5(4), para. 3. Member States may limit funding to one expert only (Art. 5(6), para. 2). Experts can be present at the negotiation.

[82] Art. 5(3).   [83] Art. 6(2).   [84] Art. 6(3), paras. 1 and 2.   [85] Art. 6(3), para. 3.

Whether an EWC or ICP is established, the minimum requirements laid down in the Annex do not need to be incorporated into the agreement.[86]

The second possible outcome is that the SNB decides, by at least two-thirds of the votes, not to open negotiations or to terminate the negotiations already opened. In this case the provisions in the Annex again do not apply and a new request to convene the SNB cannot be made for at least two years, unless the parties lay down a shorter period.[87]

The third possible outcome is that, after three years of negotiations, the parties cannot reach an agreement on the nature, function, or powers of the EWC, or if management fails to initiate negotiations within six months of the request being made, or if the two parties prefer, then the requirements laid down by the legislation of the Member State in which the central management is situated will apply, which must include the 'subsidiary' requirements set out in the annex.[88] Thus negotiators are fully aware that failure to reach an agreement will result in a mandatory procedure being imposed, or as Bercusson describes it, they bargain in the shadow of the law.[89] Putting it another way, law 'steers' negotiation: through the use of a 'penalty default' rule (the application of the subsidiary requirements), the more powerfully placed and better-informed party (the employer) is induced to enter into a bargaining process when it would otherwise lack an incentive to do so.[90]

4. THE SUBSIDIARY REQUIREMENTS

So what do the subsidiary requirements provide? In fact, Annex I lays down fairly modest requirements regarding the composition[91] and operating methods of the EWC, requiring a minimum of one information and consultation meeting per year on the basis of a report drawn up by central management.[92] Information must be provided covering such issues as:

- the structure, economic and financial situation of the business;
- the probable development of the business and of production and sales;
- the employment situation and future trends;
- investments and substantial changes concerning the organization of the business;
- the introduction of new working methods or production processes;

---

[86] Art. 6(4).   [87] Art. 5(5).

[88] Art. 7(1) and (2). Four years after the EWC has been established to which the subsidiary requirements apply, the EWC must consider whether it wants to open negotiations for an Article 6 agreement (Annex I, para. 1(f)).

[89] B. Bercusson, 'Maastricht: A Fundamental Change in European Labour Law' (1992) 23 *IRJ* 177.

[90] I. Ayres and R. Gertner, 'Filling Gaps in Incomplete Contracts: a Theory of Default Rules' (1989) 99 *YLJ* 87.

[91] The EWC shall be composed of employees of the Union scale undertaking or group of undertakings or appointed from their number by the employees' representatives or in their absence the entire body of employees. The EWC will have between 3 and 30 members.

[92] Annex I, para. 2

- transfers of production;
- mergers and cut-backs or closures of undertakings or collective redundancies.[93]

Information is defined as the:

> transmission of data by the employer to the employees' representatives in order to enable them to acquaint themselves with the subject matter and to examine it; information shall be given at such time, in such fashion and with such content as are appropriate to enable employees' representatives to undertake an in-depth assessment of the possible impact and, where appropriate, prepare for consultations with the competent organ of the [Union]-scale undertaking or [Union]-scale group of undertakings.[94]

In respect of consultation, it must be conducted in such a way that the employees' representatives can meet with the central management and obtain a response, and the reasons for that response, to any opinion they might express.[95] Consultation is defined as the:

> establishment of dialogue and exchange of views between employees' representatives and central management or any more appropriate level of management, at such time, in such fashion and with such content as enables employees' representatives to express an opinion on the basis of the information provided about the proposed measures to which the consultation is related, without prejudice to the responsibilities of the management, and within a reasonable time, which may be taken into account within the Union-scale undertaking or Union-scale group of undertakings.[96]

In addition to the annual information and consultation meeting of the EWC, Annex I requires that a 'select' committee, a type of executive committee of the EWC, be set up, comprising of no more than five members,[97] which can be informed of important decisions on matters such as relocation, closures, and collective redundancies.[98] At its request, the select committee will have the right to meet central management or any other more appropriate level of management so as to be informed and consulted on measures significantly affecting employees' interests.[99]

The meeting with the select committee must take place as soon as possible. There must be a report drawn up by central management on which the select committee can give its opinion, either at a meeting or within a reasonable time. However, Annex I provides that this meeting will not affect the prerogatives of the central management.[100] This is a compromise between the employers, who were concerned about the disruptive effects of having too many consultation meetings every time an important decision was to be taken, and the Commission, which felt that the consultation of workers was an essential element in achieving the objectives of the Directive.

---

[93] Annex I, para. 1(a). Art.12 gives details as to how to address potential overlaps between this Directive and the other Directives providing for information and consultation.

[94] Art. 2(1)(f).   [95] Annex I, para. 1(a).   [96] Art. 2(1)(g).   [97] Annex I, Article 1(d).

[98] Annex I, para. 3. If there is no select committee the EWC must be informed.

[99] The members of the EWC who have been elected or appointed by undertakings which are directly affected have a right to participate in the meeting organized with the select committee.

[100] Annex, para. 3, 4th subpara.

Finally, the Annex provides that the operating expenses of the EWC must be borne by the Union-scale undertaking or group of undertakings, thereby reflecting the current practice of undertakings which have already set up information and consultation groups of this kind. According to the Commission,[101] given the substantial advantages that such EWCs can bring for the two parties, in particular by contributing to a better mutual flow of information and a constructive dialogue, it seems reasonable to suppose that these subsidiary requirements will not impose a significant additional burden on central management.

5. RELATED PROVISIONS

The Directive contains three provisions designed to ensure that the EWCs/ICPs function smoothly. The first deals with confidentiality of the information received. While in principle the members of the EWC or ICP can inform the employees' representatives, or, in their absence, the employees themselves, of the content and outcome of the process, Member States can provide that members of the SNBs, or of the EWCs, or employee representatives in the ICPs, and any experts who assist them, are not authorized to reveal any information which has been expressly given to them in confidence,[102] even after the expiry of their terms of office.[103] In addition, Member States must provide that management can withhold any information which, according to objective criteria, would seriously harm the functioning of the undertakings concerned or would be prejudicial to them.[104] In response to a fear that these provisions could be abused by management, the Commission has said that the EWCs should be run by respecting the principles of transparency and mutual respect, particularly as prescribed by Article 9 (see later in this chapter). The Directive also provides a practical solution to these concerns: Article 11(3) requires that complainants should have access to administrative or judicial appeal procedures where central management requires confidentiality or does not give information.

---

[101] COM(94) 134.

[102] Cf. Case C–384/02 *Grøngard* [2005] ECR I–9939 concerning the prohibition under the Insider Dealing Dir. 89/592 (OJ [1989] L334/30), now Dir. 2003/6 (OJ [2003] L96/16) of disclosing information to third parties. The Court ruled that Dir. 89/592 precludes a person who receives inside information in his or her capacity as an employees' representative on a company's board of directors or in his or her capacity as a member of the liaison committee of a group of undertakings, from disclosing such information to the general secretary of the professional organization which organizes those employees and which appointed that person as a member of the liaison committee, unless (1) there is a close link between the disclosure and the exercise of his or her employment, profession, or duties, and (2) that disclosure is strictly necessary for the exercise of that employment, profession, or duties. The Court added that, as part of its examination, the national court must, in the light of the applicable national rules, take particular account of: (1) the fact that that exception to the prohibition of disclosure of inside information must be interpreted strictly; (2) the fact that each additional disclosure is liable to increase the risk of that information being exploited for a purpose contrary to Dir. 89/592; and (3) the sensitivity of the inside information. The same rules also apply to a general secretary wishing to disclose information to colleagues.

[103] Art. 8(1). Special provisions apply to 'entreprises de tendences' in Art. 8(3), i.e. undertakings which pursue 'directly and essentially the aim of ideological guidance with respect to information and the expression of opinions'.

[104] Art. 8(2). Member States can make such dispensation subject to prior administrative or judicial authorization.

The second provision designed to ensure the smooth functioning of the EWC/ICP is Article 9 itself, which requires that '[t]he central management and the European Works Council shall work in a spirit of cooperation with due regard to their reciprocal rights and obligations'.[105] The same applies to cooperation between the central management and employees' representatives in the framework of an information and consultation procedure.[106] Such statements are designed to set the tenor of the Directive and it seems likely that the Directive will be interpreted in light of Article 9.

The third is Article 10 which provides that employees involved in the SNB, EWC, or ICP should enjoy the same protection and guarantees provided for employees' representatives under national law and or practice, including the payment of wages. Directive 2009/38 adds that members of the SNB and the EWC can be trained without loss of wages where it is necessary for the exercise of their duties.[107]

6. ASSESSMENT

6.1. Flexibility

Despite the complex legislative history of this Directive its substance has remained remarkably intact from the earliest proposals. Its provisions draw heavily on the structure of the French and German works councils but lack the sophisticated co-determination principles found in the German system. Perhaps the most striking feature of the Directive, when contrasted with the earlier Vredling proposal, is its flexibility: the Directive now allows the Member States to determine practical matters, such as election methods, and encourages the Social Partners to negotiate the details of the operation of the agreement in order to accommodate local requirements. The result is what Streeck describes as convergence rather than harmonization[108] and what, for Weiss, amounts to a 'change of paradigm from substantial regulation to a merely procedural solution'.[109] In other words, the Directive takes effect not by imposing a uniform solution but by encouraging *both* Member States, through their laws, *and* companies themselves, through negotiations with employee representatives, to develop local-level solutions. There are now about a thousand EWCs.[110]

The greatest flexibility was provided by the so-called Article 13 voluntary agreements (now Article 14). Article 13 said that where an agreement was already in existence on 22 September 1996,[111] and covered the entire workforce, the obligations contained in

---

[105] This draws on the joint opinion adopted by the two sides of industry in March 1987.

[106] Art. 9, second para. See additionally Art. 6(1).

[107] Art. 10(4).

[108] W. Streeck, 'Citizenship under Regime Competition: The Case of European Works Councils', *MPIfG Working Paper* 97/3.

[109] 'The Future of Worker's Participation in the EU' in C. Barnard *et al.* (eds.), *The Future of Labour Law: Liber Amicorum Sir Bob Hepple QC* (Hart Publishing, Oxford, 2004) 234.

[110] <http://www.worker-participation.eu/European-Works-Councils/Facts-Figures> (last accessed 29 January 2012).

[111] 15 December 1999 for the UK or earlier if the date of transposition in the UK is before then: Art. 3(1) of Dir. 97/74/EC (OJ [1998] L10/22).

the Directive did not apply; and when these agreements expire the parties can decide jointly to renew them, failing which the provision of the Directive will apply. By the September 1996 deadline 386 such agreements had been signed,[112] including 58 signed by British companies, even though the UK was not initially bound by the Directive.

6.2. The EWC's success as a model?

Commentators are divided as to whether the EWC Directive has been a successful experiment. For Ramsay, EWCs have a symbolic significance for industrial democracy:[113] the assertion of the right of labour to information and consultation provides some fetter on rights of ownership and management. Schulten, on the other hand, argues that the establishment of a new transnational micro-corporatism will not be free from tensions and contradictions because the Euro-company will also continue regime shopping to take advantage of the different national and local social standards, thereby playing off its national personnel against each other.[114] He also suggests that the EWCs might exacerbate the trend towards decentralized, company-specific regulation by detaching an multi-national company's national subsidiaries from their national or sectoral systems.

Others express concerns that the lack of co-determination leads to the danger that EWCs will become a vehicle for 'Europeanised human resource management strategy';[115] and that they will subside into hearing management reports and offering some 'desultory discussion on the information offered but remaining insignificant to an employee relations still driven through local and national negotiations'.[116] In particular, Ramsay is concerned that MNCs, if they choose to take the initiative, may be able to increase management control by selling their own message convincingly, and by increasing enterprise consciousness by squeezing out external union representation.

The unions are generally more positive. Aided by generous EU funding for preparatory EWC meetings,[117] they swiftly grasped the benefits of EWCs.[118] They are especially keen on sharing information and strategy and on exchanging ideas. They also think that EWCs help in countering perceived management attempts to misinform national

---

[112] See P. Marginson et al., Negotiating European Works Councils: an Analysis of Agreements under Article 13, European Foundation of Living and Working Conditions, EF9839. A particularly high incidence of such agreements can be found in Norway, see H. Knudsen and N. Bruun, 'European Works Councils in the Nordic Countries: An Opportunity and a Challenge for Trade Unionism' (1998) 4 EJIR 131.

[113] H. Ramsay, 'Fool's Gold? European Works Councils and Workplace Democracy' (1997) 28 IRJ 314, 320.

[114] T. Schulten, 'European Works Councils: Prospects for a New System of European Industrial Relations' (1996) 2 EJIR 303.

[115] W. Lecher and S. Rüb, 'The Constitution of European Works Councils: from Information Forum to Social Actor' (1999) 5 EJIR 7, 8.

[116] Ramsay, previously, at n. 113.

[117] The budget was intended 'to finance transnational meetings of employees' representatives from undertakings operating on a transfrontier basis in the [Union]'. The budget was for 17 million ECU in 1993 and 1994, comprising about 30 per cent of the Commission's entire 'social dialogue and employment budget'. This prompted criticism from the employers who argued that their organizations did not receive similar financial assistance, contrary to the requirements of what is now Art.154(1) TFEU which obliged the Commission to provide 'balanced support' to management and labour at Union level.

[118] EIRR 246, 16, and Gold and Hall, previously, at n. 26, 49.

workforces or 'play them off' against one another. Longer term, they think EWCs might lead to a more coordinated approach to collective bargaining among national unions—albeit restricted in the first instance to issues such as health and safety—although research by Gold and Hall found that management was implacably opposed to the development of European-level collective bargaining.[119]

However, TUC research has reported some problems in tailoring meetings of representatives to the complex business structures of multinationals where decision-making may well occur, not centrally, but at product division level or lower. This view was supported by a study conducted by the Multinational Business Forum[120] which argued that meaningful ICPs must follow company decision-making machinery: a statutory obligation to inform and consult at a level at which business decisions are not routinely taken is 'at best a waste of resources, and at worst necessitates the creation of a parallel and irrelevant organisation'.[121] Some of the amendments introduced by the 2009 Directive were intended to address this, especially Article 1(3) considered above.

Marginson considers that the success of European industrial relations is dependent upon the structure of the multi-national enterprise. He argues that common management approaches across borders are less likely in companies which have expanded their access to markets in different European countries through licensing or franchise arrangements with local producers or joint ventures with enterprises based in other Member States. On the other hand, he suggests that in those transnationals that are organized to face the market on a European-wide basis, and where the primary axis of internal organization is around international product divisions, management is more likely to have an interest in developing common, cross-border approaches to the management of its workforce.

D. EUROPEAN COMPANY STATUTE

1. INTRODUCTION

The successful adoption of the EWC Directive has led to its basic model being adapted and applied to the worker participation provisions in other areas, notably the European company (Societas Europaea (SE)), which has been established by Regulation 2157/2001 and the accompanying Directive 2001/86.[122] The conclusion of these two measures was the final chapter in 40 years of negotiations[123] about the creation of an SE—a free-standing, cross-frontier European Company which could be estab-

---

[119] Gold and Hall, previously, at n. 26, 65.

[120] 'Thriving on Diversity: Informing and Consulting Employees in Multinational Enterprises' (September 1993) *EIRR* 238.

[121] See additionally P. Marginson *et al.*, 'The Emergence of the Euro-company: Towards a European Industrial Relations' (1993) 24 *IRJ* 182.

[122] OJ [2001] L294/1, as amended, and OJ [2001] L294/22 respectively.

[123] OJ [1970] C124/2, EC Bull. 8/1970 amended by COM(75) 150 final.

lished independently from existing national laws. The Commission had long argued that the SE was the only way that European industry and services could take full advantage of the internal market, and pool their resources to be able to compete with Japan and the US.

The stumbling block in the creation of an SE has always been worker participation. This is because existing national systems vary so radically in this respect. For example, some Member States, notably the UK and Ireland, adopt a unitary or one-tiered system where the company is managed by a single administrative board which does not contain worker representation. Other Member States, notably Germany and the Netherlands, adopt a two-tier system under which the company is managed by a management board under the supervision of a supervisory board. Under German law, elected employees or trade unionists are members of the supervisory organ (*Aufsichsrat*) of the company.[124] While they constitute one-third of the members in companies employing between 500 and 2,000 employees, in companies employing 2,000 employees or more a system of quasi-parity operates where there are as many members representing the employees as representing the shareholders. However, the chair is always a representative of the shareholders and has a casting vote in the case of deadlock.

The Dutch system approaches the issue of worker participation from a different perspective. It views the supervisory board as a genuinely non-executive body, reflecting as far as possible the views of the outside world and divorced from the internal power politics of the company. Its role is to guide and supervise management on behalf of the shareholders and the employees. Consequently, it considers that there is no place on the supervisory board for either trade union representatives or employees. Whenever a vacancy on the board arises, the remaining members of the board co-opt a person from a list of candidates nominated separately by the shareholders, management and the works council. The new member must be independent and so cannot be an employee or a trade unionist. If one of the groups objects to the appointment it can pronounce a veto, in which case the matter is decided by the Enterprise Chamber Court.

How have these differences been accommodated by the EU? The original Commission proposal was for a regulation,[125] comprising 284 articles, which included provisions for an *obligatory* two-tier board with German style worker participation. This combined one-third to one-half employee representation on the supervisory board, charged with overseeing and appointing the management board, and the mandatory establishment of a works council. The amended proposal strengthened the original version by proposing that the supervisory board be made up of one-third employee representatives and one-third shareholder representatives, with the remainder being co-opted by these two

---

[124] See generally M. Weiss and M. Schmidt, *Labour Law and Industrial Relations in Germany* (Kluwer, The Hague, 2008).

[125] OJ [1970] C124/1, EC Bull. Supp. 8/1970. For a full discussion of the birth of the European Company Statute (ECS), see J. Kenner, 'Worker Involvement on the *Societas Europaea*: Integrating Company and Labour Law in the European Union' (2005) 24 *YEL* 223.

groups.[126] The main area for disagreement in Council related to worker participation, particularly following the accession to the (then) EEC of the 'unitary' Member States (UK and Ireland). Negotiations ceased in 1982.

Over the next decade other proposals were put forward[127] offering various approaches to the seemingly intractable problem of worker participation in the European Company.[128] However, it took the determination of a number of presidencies in the late 1990s (including the British presidency in 1998) to push the matter forward. The final piece of the jigsaw was secured by the French presidency at Nice: Spain, which had been holding out against the proposal on board-level participation, agreed to the European Company Statute (ECS) when a quasi-exemption was granted authorizing the Member States not to implement the Directive on workers' participation in the case of European companies created by merger (the so-called Nice compromise). The Regulation establishing a European company (70 Articles) and the Directive (17 Articles) on employee involvement were finally adopted in October 2001 by the Belgian presidency, the 63rd presidency to deal with the statute.[129]

Adoption of the ECS was soon followed by the adoption of a Regulation establishing a European Co-operative Society (SCE)[130] and its Directive, Directive 2003/72,[131] concerning the involvement of employees in the SCE. The SCE is intended to provide co-operatives with the same opportunities for European level operation as the ECS provides for private limited companies. In addition, Directive 2005/56 on cross-border mergers of limited liability companies[132] takes the employee involvement provisions in the ECS Directive as its basis. Given the importance of the ECS model, it is this that we shall focus on. However, in order to understand the worker participation provisions of the Directive, it is first necessary to appreciate the key elements of the Regulation establishing a European Company (SE).

2. THE KEY FEATURES OF THE REGULATION ESTABLISHING A EUROPEAN COMPANY (SE)

According to the Regulation, an SE can be created in one of four ways. The first is by the merger of two or more *public* limited companies[133] formed under the laws of the

---

[126] Bull. Supp. 4/75. See additionally EIRR 223, 25.

[127] OJ [1989] C263/41; COM(89) final—SYN 218 and 219, 1. Later (p. 3) the Directive is described as an 'indispensable complement to the regulation'. Modified proposal COM(91) 174 Final—SYN 219.

[128] For more detailed discussion see the second edition of this book (*EC Employment Law*).

[129] V. Edwards, 'The European Company—Essential Tool or Eviscerated Dream?' (2003) 40 *CMLRev.* 443, 450. See further C. Villiers, 'The Directive on Employee Involvement in the European Company' (2006) 22 *IJCLLIR* 183.

[130] The SCE itself was set up by Reg. 1435/2003 (OJ [2003] L207/25). The choice of legal basis of this Reg (Art. 352 TFEU) was unsuccessfully challenged in Case C–436/03 *Parliament v. Council* [2006] ECR I–3733. See further I. Snaith, 'Employee Involvement in the European Cooperative Society' (2006) 22 *IJCLLIR* 213.

[131] OJ [2003] L207/25. [132] OJ [2005] L310/1.

[133] Groups involving subsidiaries incorporated as private companies will have to preface any consolidation as an SE by the conversion of such subsidiaries to public companies. This will make the process even more cumbersome: Edwards, previously, at n. 129, 463.

Member States, provided at least two of the companies are governed by the laws of different Member States (the merger route).[134] The second and third options concern two or more public or private companies, formed under the law of a Member State. They can set up either (a) a holding *or* (b) a subsidiary SE, provided that at least two of the companies are governed by the law of different Member States or have, for at least two years, had a subsidiary governed by the law of another Member State or a branch situated in another Member State. (These two options will be referred to as (a) 'creating a holding company' or (b) 'forming a subsidiary'.)[135] The fourth option involves the conversion of a public company, formed under the law of a Member State and with its registered office and head office within the Union, if, for at least two years, it has had a subsidiary company governed by the law of another Member State (the transformation route).[136] As we shall see, these different procedures for creating an SE affect the application of the employee involvement provisions.

To accommodate the different national approaches to the management body of the SE, the Regulation provides that an SE will comprise a general meeting of shareholders and *either* a supervisory organ and management organ (two-tier system) *or* an administrative organ (one-tier) depending on its statutes.

3. THE CONTENT OF THE EMPLOYEE INVOLVEMENT PROVISIONS

3.1. Introduction

Central to the SE concept is the involvement of employee representatives. They can be involved in one, or possibly two, ways. At a minimum, employees must be informed and consulted through a representative body (RB). The rules on information and consultation are mandatory,[137] although they can be customized by the Social Partners.[138] In addition, the Directive envisages a role for employees in electing or appointing or otherwise influencing the selection of the members of the SE's (one-tier or two-tier) board.[139] This is the more controversial aspect of the Directive.

Article 12(2) of the Regulation makes clear that an SE may not be registered unless an agreement on arrangements for employee involvement has been concluded (which may include an explicit decision not to have special involvement provisions for the SE). And the employee involvement provisions draw heavily on the EWC model. As Keller notes, both the EWC and the ECS Directives give priority to voluntary negotiations

---

[134] Art. 2(1). However, as Edwards notes, previously, at n. 129, 463 the adoption of the Cross-Border Mergers Dir. 2005/56 (OJ [2005] L310/1) means that mergers will be achievable without resorting to an SE. Using an SE for a cross-border merger gives no right to more favourable merger control review at either EU or national level.

[135] Arts. 2(2) and 2(3).   [136] Art. 2(4).

[137] 6th Preambular recital to the Directive.

[138] P. Davies, 'Workers on the Board of the European Company?' (2003) 32 *ILJ* 75, 81.

[139] Ibid.

between the Social Partners instead of binding legislation, both require the establishment of an SNB procedure to negotiate and agree with management, both specify the subject and scope of the employee involvement, and both introduce binding fall-back provisions if the negotiations fail. However, there are notable differences between the two models and the ECS provisions are considerably more complex and detailed. The reason for this, as Davies explains,[140] is that the Union legislator was unwilling to give the employee representatives freedom to decide or agree that the system to operate in the SE would be less advanced than that applying under national law in one of the founding companies and, where more than one system operated in the founding companies, the Directive also had to provide rules to determine which system was in fact the most advanced.

While much is made of the centrality of the employee involvement provisions to the Directive, in fact the so-called 'avant-après' or 'before and after' system identified in the Preamble[141] means that the Directive actually only requires employee participation where employee participation already existed in the companies involved in setting up the SE.[142] In other words, the Directive aims only to preserve existing rights unless the parties decide otherwise;[143] the aim of the Directive is not to promote board-level participation in all SEs. The Directive's approach is therefore negative rather than positive, a policy aimed at ensuring that the possibility of forming[144] an SE is not used to circumvent national-level provisions on board-level participation.[145] Edwards summarizes the position in the following terms:

- there will be no participation in the management of the SE where there was none in the founding companies;

- where an SE is formed by the conversion of a public company, any existing participation must be continued in the SE;

- where an SE is formed by merger or the creation of a holding or subsidiary company and participation covered at least 25 per cent (in the case of formation by merger) or 50 per cent (in the case of SEs established by creating a holding company or a subsidiary) of the total employees involved, participation rights may be reduced only with the approval of two-thirds of the total employees.

We turn now to consider how the employee involvement provisions are negotiated.

---

[140] Davies, previously, at n. 138, 80.
[141] Particularly in the 3rd, 7th and 18th recitals.
[142] Cf. Worker participation provisions do not exist in Reg. 2137/85 (OJ [1995] L199/1) on European Economic Interest Groupings (EEIGs). The Preamble, however, states that national and EU law apply to matters not covered by the Regulation, including social and labour law. The Regulation provides that an EEIG must not employ more than 500 workers (Art. 3(2)(c)), a threshold inserted to avoid circumvention of the German employee participation provisions by German companies forming or joining an EEIG registered in another Member State with more lax worker participation rules.
[143] Edwards, previously, at n. 129, 459.
[144] Edwards, previously, at n. 129.   [145] Davies, previously, at n. 138, 84.

3.2. Negotiating procedure

According to Article 3(1), it is the management or administrative organs of the participating companies (not the employees or their representatives) which trigger the Directive's procedure for negotiating the arrangements for the involvement of the employees
in the SE. When the management draws up a plan for the establishment of an SE it must,
as soon as possible after publishing the draft terms of the mechanism for creating an SE
(by any one of the four routes outlined above), take the necessary steps to start negotiations with the representatives of the companies' employees. This includes providing the
employees' representatives with information about the identity of the participating
companies/subsidiaries/establishments and the number of their employees affected.

To this end, an SNB must be set up, either by election or appointment. It must be
representative of the employees of the companies, subsidiaries, and establishments
involved, based on geographic and proportional criteria. In particular, the Directive
provides for one seat per portion of employees employed in that Member State which
equals 10 per cent, or a fraction thereof, of the number of employees employed by the
participating companies and concerned subsidiaries or establishments in all the Member States taken together.[146] The Directive expressly states that these representatives can
include representatives of trade unions.[147] The SNBs can be assisted by experts who[148]
can actually be present at negotiation meetings in an advisory capacity. These experts
can also include representatives of appropriate Union level trade unions.[149] Any expenses
relating to the functioning of the SNB and to the negotiations more generally are to be
borne by the participating companies.[150] The legislation applicable to the negotiation
procedure is that of the Member State in which the registered office of the SE is to be
situated.[151]

As with the EWC Directive, the SNB's role, together with that of the competent organs
of the participating companies is to determine, by written agreement, arrangements for
the involvement of employees within the SE.[152] The SNB and management must start
negotiations as soon as the SNB is established[153] and must negotiate in a spirit of co-
operation with a view to reaching an agreement.[154] Normally, the SNB is to take decisions by absolute majority of members representing an absolute majority of employees.
However, where the negotiations lead to a reduction of existing participation rights
then a two-thirds majority is required representing at least two-thirds of the employees
including the votes of members representing employees employed in at least two Member States (the so-called 'enhanced majority').[155]

3.3. The possible outcomes of the negotiations

As with the EWC Directive, there are three possible outcomes to the negotiations. The
first possibility is that a voluntary agreement[156] is reached within six months (or a year

---

[146] Art. 3(2)(a)(i).   [147] Art. 3(2)(b), para. 2.
[148] Member States can choose to limit the experts to one: Art. 3(7), para. 2.
[149] Art. 3(5).   [150] Art. 3(7), para. 1.   [151] Art. 6.   [152] Art. 3(5).
[153] Art. 5(1).   [154] Art. 4(1).   [155] Art. 3(4).   [156] Art. 4(1).

if the parties agree to extend the period) to set up a representative body (RB). The RB is similar to an EWC or ICP. The agreement setting up the RB must cover:[157]

- the composition, number of members and allocation of seats on the representative body, which will be the discussion partner of the competent organ of the SE in connection with arrangements for informing[158] and consulting[159] the employees of the SE and its subsidiaries and establishments. This would also apply if the parties decide to establish an information and consultation procedure instead;
- the functions and the procedure for the information and consultation of the representative body;
- the frequency of meetings of the representative body;
- the financial and material resources to be allocated to the representative body;
- the date of the entry into force of the agreement, its duration, and any procedure for renegotiation.

For the purposes of the Directive, information means informing the body representative of the employees and/or employees' representatives by the competent organ of the SE on questions which concern the SE itself and any of its subsidiaries or establishments situated in another Member State or which exceed the powers of the decision-making organs in a single Member State at a time, in a manner and with a content which allows the employees' representatives to undertake an in-depth assessment of the possible impact and, where appropriate, prepare consultations with the competent organ of the SE.[160] The Directive envisages the soft form of 'consultation'. Article 2(j) defines 'consultation' as the establishment of dialogue and exchange of views between the body representative of the employees and/or the employees' representatives and the competent organ of the SE, at a time, in a manner and with a content which allows the employees' representatives, on the basis of information provided, to express an opinion on the measures envisaged by the competent organ. This opinion 'may be taken into account in the decision-making process within the SE'.

In addition, Article 4(2) permits the parties to agree details of arrangements for participation, if they so choose (although this is compulsory in some cases (considered above)). Participation means the influence of the body representative of the employees and/or employees representatives in the affairs of the company by way of either the right to elect or appoint some of the members of the company's supervisory or administrative organ or the right to recommend and/or oppose the appointment of some or all of the members of the company's supervisory or administrative organ.[161] The agreement must

---

[157] Art. 4(2).   [158] Defined in Art. 2(i).

[159] Defined in Art. 2(j). The definition of consultation is the weaker form: it means the establishment of a dialogue and exchange of views between the body representative of the employees or the employees' representatives and the competent organ of the SE in a manner which allows the employees' representatives to express an opinion on measures envisaged by the competent organ which may be taken into account in the decision-making process of the SE.

[160] Art. 2(i).   [161] Art. 2(k).

specify which, if any, of these options it wishes to take advantage of and whether the employees will be entitled to elect, appoint, recommend or oppose, and the procedures for putting this into effect.

Finally, Article 4(4) makes specific provision for an SE established by means of transformation: any voluntary agreement must provide for at least the same level of all elements of employee involvement as the ones already existing within the company to be transformed to an SE.

The second possible outcome (which is not available to SEs established by transformation)[162] is an agreement, by enhanced majority,[163] not to open negotiations or to terminate negotiations already opened and to rely on the rules on information and consultation of employees in force in the Member States where the SE has employees,[164] which will mean, as a minimum, complying with the information and consultation obligations under Directive 2002/14 (see later in this chapter) and, more importantly given the transnational context of the ECS, the European Works Council Directive (otherwise excluded from the Directive).[165]

In neither the first nor the second possible outcome of the negotiations do the provisions of the standard rules found in the Annex apply.[166] By contrast, the standard rules (functionally equivalent to the 'subsidiary requirements' in the EWC Directive) will apply to the third situation. This is where no voluntary agreement is reached within six months (or a year if the parties agree to extend the period). The standard rules will also apply if the parties so choose[167] and if the SNB has not reached agreement under Article 3(6) in the case of an SE established by transformation. They will also apply, according to Article 7(2), if:

- in an SE established by transformation, the rules of a Member State relating to employee participation in the administrative or supervisory body applied to a company transformed into an SE;[168]

- in the case of an SE established by merger, one or more forms of participation applied in one or more of the companies covering at least 25 per cent of the total number of employees in all the participating companies or less than 25 per cent and the SNB decides to apply the participation rules;[169]

- in the case of an SE established as a holding or subsidiary company, if before registration of the SE, one or more forms of participation applied in one or more of the participating companies covering at least 50 per cent of the total number of employees in all the participating companies or less than 50 per cent and the SNB so decided.[170]

Therefore, the standard rules apply where all or most workers were covered by mandatory participation and here the 'highest level' principle (considered later in this chapter)

---

[162] Art. 3(6), para. 2.   [163] Art. 3(6), para. 2.
[164] Art. 3(6), para. 1. This decision can be revisited two years after the decision or earlier if the parties so agree: Art. 3(6), para. 4.
[165] Art. 13(1), para. 2.   [166] Art. 4(3) and Art. 3(6) respectively.   [167] Art. 7(1).   [168] Art. 7(2)(a).
[169] Art. 7(2)(b).   [170] Art. 7(2)(c).

operates freely. By contrast, where large numbers of employees were not covered by mandatory participation (e.g. in an SE formed by merger 75 per cent of employees were not covered by participation rules, and in the case of a formation of a joint holding or subsidiary company 50 per cent of the employees are not covered by mandatory participation rules) then the standard rules do not automatically apply.[171]

The results of the Nice compromise can be found in Article 7(3) which says that Member States may provide that the standard participation provisions will not apply in the case of an SE established by merger. However, an SE established by merger of companies one or more of which was governed by participation rules, may be registered in a Member State which has made use of the Article 7(3) option only where an agreement pursuant to Article 4 of the Directive has been concluded.[172]

3.4. The standard rules

So what do the standard rules say? Inevitably, like the rest of the Directive, they are complex. They are also more detailed than those found in the EWC Directive and cover a broader range of situations. In essence they provide for a standard RB, similar to the statutory EWC laid down in the EWC Directive's subsidiary requirements, and board-level participation where this existed in the participating companies.

The standard rules are contained in three parts. The first part relates to the composition of the RB. It provides that the RB must be composed of employees of the SE and its subsidiaries and establishments elected or appointed (in accordance with national legislation and/or practice) from their number by the employees' representatives or, in the absence thereof, by the entire body of employees. The members of the representative body are elected or appointed in proportion to the number of employees employed in each Member State by the participating companies and concerned subsidiaries or establishments, by allocating one seat per portion of employees employed in that Member State which equals 10 per cent, or a fraction thereof, of the number of employees employed by the participating companies and concerned subsidiaries or establishments in all the Member States taken together. In other words, the membership of the RB reflects that of the SNB set up under Article 3. The competent organ of the SE must be informed of the composition of the RB. The RB must lay down its own rules of procedure. In addition, where its size so warrants, the RB must elect a select committee from among its members, comprising at the most three members. Four years after the RB is established, it must examine whether to open negotiations for the conclusion of an agreement referred to in Articles 4 and 7 or to continue to apply the standard rules adopted in accordance with the Annex.

The second part concerns the standard rules for information and consultation. These broadly map the subsidiary requirements in the EWC Directive. In essence, the RB has the right to be informed and consulted and, for that purpose, to meet with the competent organ of the SE at least once a year. On the basis of regular reports drawn up by the competent organ, the RB has the right to be informed and consulted on the progress of

---

[171] Davies, previously, at n. 138, 88.   [172] Art. 12(3) of the Regulation.

the business of the SE and its prospects. In addition, the competent organ of the SE must provide the RB with the agenda for meetings of the administrative, or, where appropriate, the management and supervisory organ, and with copies of all documents submitted to the general meeting of its shareholders. The meeting itself must relate to:

- the structure, economic and financial situation of the business;

- the probable development of the business and of production and sales;

- the situation and probable trend of employment, investments, and substantial changes concerning organization, introduction of new working methods or production processes, transfers of production, mergers, cutbacks or closures of undertakings, establishments or important parts thereof, and collective redundancies.

Where there are exceptional circumstances affecting the employees' interests to a considerable extent, particularly in the event of relocations, transfers, the closure of establishments or undertakings or collective redundancies, the RB has the right to be *informed*. The RB or, where it so decides, in particular for reasons of urgency, the select committee,[173] has the right to meet the competent organ of the SE or any more appropriate level of management within the SE, so as to be *informed and consulted* on measures significantly affecting employees' interests. However, unlike the EWC Directive, the ECS Directive provides that where the competent organ decides not to act in accordance with the opinion expressed by the representative body, the RB has the right to a further meeting with the competent organ of the SE *with a view to seeking agreement*. However, the standard rules then add: 'The meetings referred to above shall not affect the prerogatives of the competent organ.' Finally, the standard rules expressly permit the members of the RB to inform the representatives of the employees of the SE and of its subsidiaries and establishments of the content and outcome of the information and consultation procedures.

As with the EWC Directive, the standard rules also contain provisions to ensure the smooth operation of the RB: the RB or the select committee can be assisted by experts of its choice, the members of the RB are entitled to time off for training without loss of wages (but no reference is made to paid time off for actual attendance at the meetings themselves), and the costs of the RB are to be borne by the SE, which must provide the body's members with the financial and material resources needed to enable them to perform their duties in an appropriate manner.

The third part of the standard rules concern participation. In essence these rules are premised on the 'no escape' principle: that forming an SE cannot be used as a means to escape from employee participation rules. The rules distinguish between SEs established by transformation and those formed in one of the three other ways outline above

---

[173] In the case of a meeting organized with the select committee, those members of the representative body who represent employees who are directly concerned by the measures in question shall also have the right to participate.

(merger, creating a holding company, or forming a subsidiary). In respect of SEs established by transformation, if the rules of a Member State relating to employee participation in the administrative or supervisory body applied before registration, all aspects of employee participation will continue to apply to the SE. In the other three cases establishing an SE, the employees of the SE, its subsidiaries, and establishments and/or their representative body have the right to elect, appoint, recommend, or oppose the appointment of a number of members of the administrative or supervisory body of the SE equal to the *highest proportion* in force in the participating companies concerned before registration of the SE. Thus, the form of participation in principle to be adopted by the SE is the most advanced of the systems required by national laws applying to the founding companies.[174] The most advanced system is the one with the 'highest' proportion of members of the board subject to employee influence, irrespective of the form that influence might take. As Davies points out, there is no qualitative judgment among the various forms in which employee influence over board membership might express itself.[175] Once the highest level is determined, the most 'advanced' system will then be exported to the employees previously subject to less advanced systems. However, if none of the participating companies was governed by participation rules before registration of the SE (i.e. companies subject to the law of, for example, Belgium, France, Ireland, Italy, Portugal, Spain, and the UK)[176], the SE is not required to establish provisions for employee participation.

The RB must decide on the allocation of seats within the administrative or supervisory body among the members representing the employees from the various Member States or on the way in which the SE's employees may recommend or oppose the appointment of the members of these bodies according to the proportion of the SE's employees in each Member State. If the employees of one or more Member States are not covered by this proportional criterion, the representative body must appoint a member from one of those Member States, in particular the Member State of the SE's registered office, where that is appropriate. Each Member State may determine the allocation of the seats it is given within the administrative or supervisory body. The rules also provide that every member of the administrative body or, where appropriate, the supervisory body of the SE, who has been elected, appointed or recommended by the representative body or, depending on the circumstances, by the employees, is a full member, with the same rights and obligations as the members representing the shareholders, including the right to vote.

3.5. Supporting provisions

In keeping with the Directive's aim of preventing the avoidance of national employee involvement rules, Article 11 of the Directive obliges Member States to take appropriate measures to prevent the misuse of an SE for the purpose of depriving employees of rights to employee involvement or withholding such rights.[177] More generally, Article 9

---

[174] Davies, previously, at n. 138, 84. For a fuller discussion of the 'highest-level' rules, see Davies, previously, at n. 138, 85.

[175] Ibid.   [176] Edwards, previously, at n. 129, 462.   [177] Art. 11.

provides that the competent organ of the SE and the RB must work together in 'a spirit of cooperation with due regard for the reciprocal rights and obligations'.

As with the EWC Directive, the ECS Directive also lays down rules on issues such as confidentiality of information given to members of the SNB and RB or to experts which assist them,[178] on protection of employee representatives,[179] its relationship with other provisions (in essence the ECS Directive 2001/86 takes precedence over the EWC Directive unless the SNB decides not to open negotiations or terminate negotiations already opened), and compliance (each Member State must ensure that the management of establishments of an SE, and the supervisory or administrative organs of subsidiaries and of participating companies which are situated within its territory and the employees' representatives or the employees themselves abide by the obligations laid down by the Directive, regardless of whether the SE has its registered office in its territory).[180] Member States must also provide for appropriate remedies.[181]

3.6. Assessment

It is not clear how much use will actually be made of the possibility of setting up an SE. While some view the possibility of creating an SE as beneficial in terms of administrative costs savings, others are concerned about the weaknesses of the ECS Regulation and Directive. In particular, they are critical of the absence of a genuine Union legal instrument, given that essentially 25 different statutes have been created, the absence of an agreed tax regime, the complexity of the rules on employee involvement, and the existence of too many options and references to national law. Davies describes the SE Regulation as 'but a shadow of its former self', with the disappearance of the goal of a non-national corporate law regime.[182]

That said, the German Insurance group Allianz merged with its Italian subsidiary RAS to create an SE. Allianz, and its subsidiary Dresdner Bank, have operations in Germany, France, the UK, Italy, Austria, Hungary, Slovakia, Spain, and Ireland. The legal seat of the company is Germany. In terms of employee representation, the German legislation implementing the European Company Statute's employee involvement Directive was applied, because the seat of the new company is Germany. So the new company has a dual board structure, comprising a management board (*Vorstand*) and a supervisory board (*Aufsichtsrat*). Employee representation on the supervisory board is 50 per cent, which is in line with current practice at Allianz.[183]

---

[178] Art. 8.   [179] Art. 10.   [180] Art. 12(1).   [181] Art. 12(2).

[182] Davies, previously, at n. 138, 77–8.

[183] <https://www.allianz.com/en/press/news_dossiers/allianz_se/index.html (last accessed 2 April 2012)>. Other examples of SEs are BASF SE, Strabag SE, Gfk SE, and MAN SE. For more details, see <http://ecdb. worker-participation.eu/index.php> (last accessed 12 March 2012).

E. NATIONAL-LEVEL INFORMATION
AND CONSULTATION PROVISIONS

1. INTRODUCTION

The adoption of Directive 2002/14 on national level information and consultation (I&C)[184] is of greater practical significance than the ECS. This Directive also had a long gestation and, once again, was finalized in the light of the EWC Directive, which provided a model to help unblock long-standing proposals, in particular the ill-fated and highly controversial 'Vredling' Directive of 1980[185] and the substantially amended 'Richard' proposal in 1983.[186] These proposals were considered sisters to the Directives on collective redundancies (now 98/59), transfers of undertakings (now 2001/23), and the proposed Fifth Company Law Directive.[187] The 'Vredling' proposal contained two key rights: the right to periodic information and the right to be consulted in advance of important decisions in the life of the undertaking. Nevertheless, the various proposals prompted heated opposition and were accused, first, of being complicated and unfamiliar, and secondly, of interfering with information and consultation practices already in existence at national level (because the proposal covered large undertakings or groups of undertakings in a single state), and thirdly, of disrupting voluntarist systems of industrial relations.[188] Allegations that the Commission was trying to harmonize diverse national industrial relations systems were not new,[189] but became an increasingly sensitive issue as the doctrine of subsidiarity gained in importance.

Various attempts were subsequently made to resurrect the proposals[190] but these attempts assumed new importance with the launch of the EES where worker participation was seen as the key to achieving flexibility in the workplace. As the Green Paper on Partnership explained,[191] flexibility within organizations is to be encouraged by reinforcing mechanisms for employee participation at the level of the plant or enterprise; 'the role of workers in decision-making and the need to review and strengthen the existing arrangements for workers' involvement in their companies will…become essential issues.'[192]

---

[184] OJ [2002] L80/29.
[185] OJ [1980] C297/3, Bull. Supp. 3/80, discussed by F. Vandamme, 'L'Information et la Consultation des Travailleurs dans la proposition de directive sur les entreprises a structure complexe, en particulier transnationale' [1982] *Revue du Marché Commun* 368 and R. Blanpain *et al.*, *The Vredling Proposal. Information and Consultation of Employees in Multinational Enterprises* (Kluwer, Deventer, 1983).
[186] OJ [1983] C217/3, Bull. Supp. 2/83, 3.
[187] J. Pipkorn, 'The Draft Directive on Procedures for Informing and Consulting Employees' (1983) 20 *CMLRev.* 725, 726–7.
[188] Ibid., 281.
[189] See the Commission's concern expressed in its Green Paper on Employee Participation and Company Structures, EC Bull. Supp. 8/75.
[190] COM(95) 547.
[191] Green Paper on Partnership, COM(97) 127 final, Executive Summary.
[192] Ibid., para. 44.

The Commission hoped that the Social Partners would be able to negotiate a Euro-pean-level collective agreement on national-level information and consultation, but, as with the EWC Directive, while the ETUC and CEEP were willing, UNICE/Business-Europe was not, largely due to resistance from the British CBI. UNICE argued that any such agreement would not conform with the principle of subsidiarity; that there were adequate legal frameworks at national level; that there was no link between employee information and consultation and job security; and that labour management should be the exclusive preserve of the company's internal organization. Indeed there was real concern that any EU initiative would cut across the very varied, culturally specific sys-tems of worker involvement in the Member States. This was a particular issue for the UK where worker representation has traditionally been channelled through recognized unions.[193] This is known as the single-channel approach. The concept of works councils or their equivalents has been largely unfamiliar, albeit that larger firms often have joint consultative committees which comprise both union and non-union representatives.

The British 'single channel' can be contrasted with the 'dual channel' found in, for example, Germany[194] where unions and employers' associations are responsible for col-lective bargaining, traditionally at a *sectoral or regional* level, concerning quantitative matters (especially wages and hours). By contrast, works councils and management are responsible for relations in respect of essentially qualitative issues within a *company* (such as personnel planning and changes in work processes, the working environment, new technology, and job content). Works councils in Germany have wide powers rang-ing from information and consultation rights to co-determination rights, which include the right of veto over individual cases of hiring, grading, transfer, and dismissal.[195]

The German model thus has a clear 'space' in which works councils can operate, i.e. at firm level. This is not the case in the UK, where collective bargaining is conducted largely at the enterprise/company or even plant/establishment level. Furthermore, while competition between unions is regulated by the so-called Bridlington principles, no such rules apply to 'competition' between trade unions and works councils/elected worker representatives. Therefore, in the UK any second channel might be perceived as a threat to established trade unions and might risk undermining collective bargaining, hence the concerns.

Regretting 'this lack of willingness to negotiate',[196] the Commission nevertheless decided to present a proposal,[197] even though it was faced with objections from the UK

---

[193] Traditionally, recognition has been entirely a matter for employers. This position has been changed in part by s. 1 and Sch. AI of the Employment Relations Act 1999, amending TULR(C)A 1992, introducing a statutory recognition procedure. See B. Wedderburn, 'Collective Bargaining or Legal Enactment: the 1999 Act and Union Recognition' (2000) 29 *ILJ* 1; G. Gaal, 'The First Five Years of Britain's Third Statutory Recognition Procedure' (2005) 34 *ILJ* 345.

[194] The following draws on Jacobi *et al.*, 'Germany: Facing New Challenges' in A. Ferner and R. Hyman (eds), *Changing Industrial Relations in Europe* (Blackwell, Oxford, 1998).

[195] S. 87 BetrVG. If the parties cannot reach an agreement, either side may appeal to the conciliation board which would then rule on the matter.

[196] COM(98) 612, 2.   [197] OJ [1999] C2/3.

government.[198] The Renault affair gave new impetus to these proposals. In 1997 the French car manufacturer, Renault, closed its plant at Vilvoorde in Belgium without prior information and consultation of the workforce. As the Commission explained, 'Several events, which have given rise to enormous political and media attention, have illustrated the weakness of national and Union law. In fact, it has become clear that, even where information and consultation provisions existed, they were not effective as they were either only ritual in nature or effective only *a posteriori*'.[199]

The UK, with the initial support of Germany (and Denmark and Ireland), managed to block the proposal for a while but, once its blocking majority collapsed, the UK abandoned its hostility to the measure and focused instead on making the measure more UK-friendly.[200] The result, Directive 2002/14, is a measure which provides the minimum framework in which information and consultation (I&C) can take place: all the detail is left to be worked out by the Member States or the national or subnational Social Partners. The UK (under the Labour government) then became an enthusiastic supporter of the measure, seeing it as an important step in its partnership agenda.

2. THE DIRECTIVE

2.1. The scope of the Directive

Article 1 says that the Directive's objective is to establish a general framework for informing and consulting employees in the EU. It refers to a 'right' to information and consultation.[201] Unlike the Collective Redundancies Directive where consultation is mandatory, employers do not have to inform and consult an unwilling workforce; employees need to request the right to be informed and consulted.

Information is defined in Article 2(e) as transmission by the employer to the employees' representatives of data in order to enable them to acquaint themselves with the subject-matter and to examine it. 'Employees' representatives' means 'the employees' representatives provided for by national laws and/or practices'.[202] This formulation allows Member States to use not only collegiate forms of employee representation, but also individual representatives (workforce delegates, trade union delegates, and others).[203] 'Consultation' means the exchange of views and establishment of dialogue between the

---

[198] *Fairness at Work* White Paper, previously, at n. 28, para. 4.5.

[199] See generally 'Employee Representatives in Europe and their Economic Prerogatives', Supp. *Social Europe* 3/96.

[200] M. Hall, 'Assessing the Information and Consultation of Employees Regulations' (2005) 34 *ILJ* 103, 108.

[201] Art. 1(1).

[202] Art. 2(e). For the difficulty this definition creates see Case C–382/92 *Commission* v. *UK* [1994] ECR I–2435 considered in Ch. 13. See additionally the Joint declaration of the European Parliament, the Council and the Commission on employee representation: 'With regard to employee representation, the European Parliament, the Council and the Commission recall the judgements of the European Court of Justice of 8 June 1994 in Cases C–382/92 (Safeguarding of employees rights in the event of transfers of undertakings) and C–383/92 (Collective redundancies)'.

[203] For the problems associated with this formula see Ch. 13.

employees' representatives and the employer. Finally, Article 2(d) defines 'employee' by reference to national law. It provides that 'employee' means any person who, in the Member State concerned, is protected as an employee under national employment law and in accordance with national practice.

The Member States have the choice to apply the Directive to:

(a) undertakings employing at least 50 employees[204] in any one Member State,[205] or

(b) establishments employing at least 20 employees in any one Member State.

Article 2(a) defines 'undertaking' as a public or private undertaking carrying out an economic activity, whether or not operating for gain, which is located within the territory of the Member States. This definition draws on the revisions to the Transfer of Undertakings Directive 2001/23.[206] Article 2(b) defines 'establishment' as a unit of business defined in accordance with national law and practice, and located within the territory of a Member State, where an economic activity is carried out on an ongoing basis with human and material resources.

Member States are to determine the method for calculating the thresholds of employees employed. This is consistent with the overall aim of the Directive to ensure that it sits comfortably within the national industrial relations systems. This ethos is confirmed by Article 1(2) which provides: 'The practical arrangements for information and consultation shall be defined and implemented in accordance with national law and industrial relations practices in individual Member States in such a way as to ensure their effectiveness'. In much the same vein, the Directive permits Member States to lay down special rules applicable to so-called *entreprises de tendences*, i.e. undertakings or establishments which pursue 'directly and essentially political, professional organisational, religious, charitable, educational, scientific or artistic aims, as well as aims involving information and the expression of opinions', on condition that, at the date of entry into force of the Directive, provisions of that nature already exist in national legislation.[207]

2.2. Information and consultation agreements

Unlike the EWC and ECS Directives, Directive 2002/14 makes no provision for a special negotiating body to be set up to negotiate the content of the agreement. Instead, the Directive identifies three possible outcomes. These are referred to in the British implementation as pre-existing agreements (PEAs), negotiated agreements (NAs), and standard or fall-back arrangements. PEAs are agreements existing on the date the Directive came into force (23 March 2005), as well as any subsequent renewals of such agreements. Negotiated agreements are those negotiated by management and labour, at the appropriate level including at undertaking or establishment level, setting out the practi-

---

[204] This was subject to transitional provisions in Art. 10 (introduced largely to benefit the UK).

[205] According to the Commission, this excludes 97 per cent of companies in the EU with salaried employees.

[206] Art. 1 of Dir. 2001/23 considered in Ch. 13.

[207] Art. 3(2). According to Art. 3(3), Member States may derogate from this Directive through particular provisions applicable to the crews of vessels plying the high seas.

cal arrangements for informing and consulting employees. Neither the PEAs nor the negotiated agreements are subject to the fall-back provisions.

Article 4 contains the fall-back position: it specifies the (minimal) rules which apply in the absence of the social partners having a PEA or entering an NA. In essence, Article 4 is the I&C Directive's equivalent to the standard rules in the ECS Directive. Article 4(2) specifies that information and consultation must cover:

(a) *information* on the recent and probable development of the undertaking's or the establishment's activities and economic situation;

(b) *information and consultation* on the situation, structure and probable development of employment within the undertaking or establishment and on any anticipatory measures envisaged, in particular where there is a threat to employment;

(c) *information and consultation* on decisions likely to lead to substantial changes in work organization or in contractual relations, including those covered by the Union provisions referred to in Article 9(1).

Thus, the Directive covers three subject areas: economic or strategic matters (paragraph (a)), employment trends within the undertaking and associated measures (paragraph (b)) and specific decisions concerning work organization or contractual relations (paragraph (c)). Since the matters referred to in paragraph (a) are generally outside the control of the employer, these are subject only to information. The Directive provides that '[i]nformation shall be given at such time, in such fashion and with such content as are appropriate to enable, in particular, employees' representatives to conduct an adequate study and, where necessary, prepare for consultation'.[208] And Article 4(4) provides that consultation shall take place:

(a) while ensuring that the timing, method, and content thereof are appropriate;

(b) at the relevant level of management and representation, depending on the subject under discussion;

(c) on the basis of information supplied by the employer[209] in accordance with Article 2(f) and of the opinion which the employees' representatives are entitled to formulate;

(d) in such a way as to enable employees' representatives to meet the employer and obtain a response, and the reasons for that response, to any opinion they might formulate; and

(e) *with a view to reaching an agreement* on decisions within the scope of the employer's powers referred to in paragraph 2(c).

Thus, the standard rules envisage the strong form of consultation (i.e. 'with a view to reaching an agreement'); where there is a PEA or an NA the consultation is the weak form.

---

[208] Art. 4(3).

[209] According to Art. 2(c), 'employer' means the natural or legal person party to employment contracts or employment relationships with employees, in accordance with national law and practice.

The only provisions which will apply regardless of whether it is the Member States or the social partners laying down the detail of the rules are those contained in Article 1. In particular Article 1(3) provides:

> When defining or implementing practical arrangements for information and consultation, the employer and the employees' representatives shall work in a spirit of cooperation and with due regard for their reciprocal rights and obligations, taking into account the interests both of the undertaking or establishment and of the employees.

2.3. Related provisions

Following the model of the EWC Directive, the Information and Consultation Directive lays down rules concerning the confidentiality of information,[210] the protection of employees' representatives[211] and a clause concerning the relation between this Directive and other Union and national measures.[212] The Directive also contains a non-regression clause[213] and, as with all Directives, a deadline for implementation. The question as to how a Member State might implement the Directive arose in *Holst*[214] where the Court ruled that the Directive could be transposed by way of a collective agreement which results in a group of employees being covered by the agreement, 'even though the employees in that group are not members of the union which is a party to that agreement and their field of activity is not represented by that union, provided that the collective agreement is such as to guarantee to the employees coming within its scope effective protection of the rights conferred on them by Directive 2002/14'.

The remedies clause, found in Article 8(1), requires Member States to provide for appropriate measures in the event of non-compliance with the Directive by the employer or the employees' representatives. In particular, Member States must ensure that adequate administrative or judicial procedures are available to enable the obligations deriving from the Directive to be enforced. Article 8(2) adds that Member States must provide for adequate sanctions to be applicable in the event of infringement of this Directive by the employer or the employees' representatives. These sanctions must be effective, proportionate, and dissuasive. The wording of the provision is broadly based on current Union law and the case law of the Court.[215] The Commission had also proposed a provision that restructuring decisions taken by employers in serious breach of

---

[210] Art. 6.   [211] Art. 7.

[212] Art. 9. The Directive 2002/14 is without prejudice to the specific information and consultation procedures set out in the Collective Redundancies Directive 98/59/EC, the Transfer of Undertakings Directive 2001/23/EC, the European Works Council Directive 94/45/EC and to any other rights to information, consultation and participation under national law.

[213] Art. 9(4).

[214] Case C-405/08 *Ingeniørforeningen i Danmark, acting on behalf of Bertram Holst* v. *Dansk Arbejdsgiverforening* [2010] ECR I-985, para. 45.

[215] See further esp. Ch. 13.

their information and consultation obligations would be suspended.[216] This ambitious provision was omitted from the final version of Directive 2002/14.

While the EWC, ECS, and I&C Directives are the principal Union measures on worker involvement, other Union instruments also require or permit varying forms of worker participation. In Chapter 11 we have already examined the worker involvement provisions in the Framework Directive 89/391 on health and safety. In the next section we look at certain other measures which also envisage a degree of worker voice in the course of procedures leading to some form of restructuring.

F. WORKER PARTICIPATION UNDER OTHER UNION INSTRUMENTS

1. THE MERGER REGULATION

Limited recognition of the collective interests of workers can be found in the Merger Regulation, initially Regulation 4064/89[217] now replaced by Regulation 139/2004.[218] According to this Regulation, concentrations with a Union dimension, as defined by the Regulation,[219] must be notified to the Commission which must then consider whether the merger is compatible with the Common Market.[220] In making this appraisal the Commission may take into account considerations of a social nature.[221]

The Preamble also states that the 'Regulation in no way detracts from the collective rights of employees, as recognised in the undertakings concerned, notably with regard

---

[216] 'Member States shall provide that in case of serious breach by the employer of the information and consultation obligations in respect of the decisions referred to in Article 4(1)(c) of this Directive, where such decisions would have direct and immediate consequences in terms of substantial change or termination of the employment contracts or employment relations, these decisions shall *have no legal effect* on the employment contracts or employment relationships of the employees affected. The non production of legal effects will continue until such time as the employer has fulfilled his obligations or, if this is no longer possible, adequate redress has been established, in accordance with the arrangements and procedures to be determined by the Member States.

The provision of the previous paragraph also applies to corresponding obligations under the agreements referred to in Article 3,

Within the meaning of the previous paragraphs, serious breaches are:

a) the total absence of information and/or consultation of the employees' representatives prior to a decision being taken or the public announcement of that decision; or

b) the withholding of important information or provision of false information rendering ineffective the exercise of the right to information and consultation' [emphasis added].

[217] OJ [1989] L395/1, as corrected and amended.
[218] OJ [2004] L24/22.   [219] Arts. 1 and 3 of the Regulation.   [220] Art. 2.
[221] This is confirmed by the 23rd recital of the Preamble which says: 'It is necessary to establish whether or not concentrations with a [Union] dimension are compatible with the common market in terms of the need to maintain and develop effective competition in the common market. In so doing, the Commission must place its appraisal within the general framework of the achievement of the fundamental objectives referred to in [Article 3 TEU]'. Cf. the thirteenth recital of the Preamble to Reg. 4064/89 which was more explicit about the social objectives. It provided: 'The Commission must place its appraisal within the general framework of the achievement referred to in Article 2 of the [EEC] Treaty, including that of strengthening the [Union's] economic and social cohesion, referred to in Article 130a [EEC]'.

to any obligation to inform or consult their recognised representatives under [Union] and national law'.[222] Article 18(4) entitles the Commission to hear the views of '[n]atural or legal persons showing a sufficient interest' and in particular 'the recognised representatives[223] of their employees shall be entitled, upon application, to be heard'.[224] As the Court explained in the *Grandes Sources* case,[225] the primacy given in the Merger Regulation to the establishment of a system of free competition could be reconciled, in the context of an assessment of whether a concentration is compatible with the Common Market, with the social effects of that operation if they are liable to affect adversely the social objectives referred to in Article 3 TEU (ex Article 2 EC). The GC continued that the Commission, therefore, might have to ascertain whether 'the concentration is liable to have consequences, even if only indirectly, for the position of the employees in the undertakings in question, such as to affect the level or conditions of employment in the [Union] or a substantial part of it'.

The *Grandes Sources* case concerned the Nestlé/Perrier merger.[226] Although the trade union representatives (CGT Perrier) had met with the Commission to express their concerns about the social consequences of the merger, the Commission nevertheless allowed the merger to proceed on condition that Nestlé complied with certain conditions, including selling the brand names and sources Vichy, Thonon, Pierval, and Saint-Yorre. This led to two sets of challenges. First, the trade union and the Perrier works council sought an Article 263 TFEU (ex 230 EC) judicial review of the Commission's Decision allowing the merger.[227] Under the then Article 230 EC natural or legal persons could challenge a Decision addressed to another provided it is of direct and individual concern to them. In this case the Court ruled that while the employee representatives were individually concerned by the Commission's Decision they were not directly concerned because the Decision did not prejudice either the rights of the organizations or the employees affected. However, the Court did say that the employee representatives had standing to bring proceedings to ensure that the procedural guarantees which they were entitled to assert during the administrative procedure under the Merger Control Regulation were satisfied.

The second proceedings were brought by the Vittel and Pierval works councils, challenging the transfer of the Pierval source which was operated by Vittel. Interim relief

---

[222] Recitals, para. 45.

[223] In Case T-96/92 *Comité Central d'Entreprise de la Société General des Grandes Sources* v. *Commission* [1995] ECR II-1213, para. 34, the Court said that it is for the Member States to define which organizations are competent to represent the collective interest of the employees and to determine their rights and prerogatives, subject to the adoption of harmonization measures such as the European Works Council Directive 2009/38.

[224] See additionally para. 19 of the Preamble. For the difficulties involved in invoking these provisions see Case T-96/92R *Comité Central d'Entreprise* v. *Commission* [1992] ECR II-2579 and Case T-12/93R *Comité Central d'entreprise de la société Anonyme Vittel and Comité d'establissement de Pierval* v. *Commission* [1993] ECR II-449, Order of the President of the Court of First Instance [1993] ECR II-449. S. Anderman, 'European Community Merger and Social Policy' (1993) 22 *ILJ* 318.

[225] Case T-96/92 *Comité Central d'Entreprise de la Société General des Grandes Sources* v. *Commission* [1995] ECR II-1213, para. 28. See further Case T-12/93 *Vittel* v. *Commission* [1995] ECR II-1247, para. 38.

[226] Case No. IV/M.190, *Nestlé/Perrier* (OJ [1992] L356/1).

[227] They also made a separate application of interim relief under Arts. 278 TFEU (ex 242 EC) and 279 TFEU (ex 243 EC), but this was dismissed (Case T-96/92R [1992] ECR I-2579).

was initially granted,[228] suspending the operation of the Commission Decision until certain obstacles relating to the transfer of the rights to exploit Vichy and Thonon had been removed and the Court had been informed of that fact by the Commission.[229] In the subsequent judicial review proceedings, the applicants, now supported by the Perrier trade union and works council, sought annulment of either the Commission's Decision as a whole or the imposition of conditions.[230] Once again the Court found that since the applicants were the recognized representatives of the employees concerned by the concentration and they were expressly mentioned in the Merger Regulation they were individually concerned. However, they were not directly concerned and so had no *locus standi* because the transfer of the Pierval plant 'did not in itself entail any direct consequences for the rights which the employees derived from their contract of employment'.[231] These rights were protected by Directive 2001/23 on transfers[232] and (now) Directive 98/59 on collective redundancies.[233]

2. STATE AID

While the Merger Regulation expressly grants procedural prerogatives to the recognized representatives of employees, this is not the case with the state aid provisions. Therefore, the General Court said in *SFP*[234] (decided before the Lisbon reforms under Article 263 TFEU) that employees' representatives were not individually concerned for the purposes of having locus to challenge a Commission decision declaring state aid to the industry to be incompatible with the Common Market and ordering its recovery. The General Court did, however, concede that bodies representing employees of the undertaking in receipt of aid might, *qua* parties concerned within the meaning of Article 108(2), submit comments to the Commission on considerations of a social nature which could be taken into account by the Commission.[235]

The Court of Justice upheld the GC's decision.[236] It said that the employee representatives' status as negotiators with regard to social aspects such as staffing and salary structure within the company did not suffice to distinguish them individually.[237] The Court admitted that when determining whether state aid was compatible with the Common Market, social aspects were liable to be taken into account by the Commission, 'but only as part of an overall assessment which includes a large number of considerations of various kinds, linked in particular to the protection of competition, regional development, the promotion of culture or again to the protection of the environment'.[238]

---

[228] Case T–12/93R *Comité Central d'entreprise de la société Anonyme Vittel and Comité d'establissement de Pierval v. Commission* [1993] ECR II–449.

[229] Following the communication of that information the applications for interim measures were dismissed by order of the President of the GC [1993] ECR II–785.

[230] Case T–12/93 *Vittel* [1995] ECR II–1247.

[231] Para. 58.   [232] OJ [1977] L61/26 as amended.   [233] OJ [1998] L225/16.

[234] Case T–189/97 *Comité d'entreprise de la société Française de production v. Commission* [1998] ECR II–335.

[235] Para. 41.

[236] Case C–106/98 *Comité d'entreprise de la société Française de production v. Commission* [2000] ECR I–3659.

[237] Para. 51.   [238] Para. 52.

However, on the facts, the status as negotiators with regard to the social aspects within SFP constituted only a 'tenuous link' with the actual subject-matter of that decision and so there was no locus.

By contrast, in *3F*[239] (also decided before the Lisbon reforms) the Court of Justice said that a trade union could be regarded as 'concerned' within the meaning of Article 108(2) TFEU if it could show that its interests or those of its members might be affected by the granting of aid. The trade union must, however, show to the requisite legal standard that the aid is likely to have a real effect on its situation or that of the members it represents. In addition, in order to benefit from locus standi, the trade union had to demonstrate that it enjoyed a particular status within the meaning of the *Plaumann* judgment,[240] namely that its 'market position is substantially affected by the aid which is the subject of the decision at issue'.

The case concerned a decision by Denmark to establish a Danish International Register of Shipping ('the DIS register') to supplement the ordinary Danish register of ships ('the DAS register'). The DIS register was intended to combat the flight from EU flags to flags of convenience. Shipowners whose vessels were registered in the DIS register were allowed to employ seafarers from non-member countries on those vessels and pay them wages on the basis of the laws of their home state. Further, the wages of all the seafarers employed on a DIS registered ship were not subject to income tax. 3F, the general trade union for workers in Denmark, complained to the Commission that these fiscal measures were contrary to the EU guidelines on state aid to the maritime sector (the objectives of which included preserving EU employment) and hence to Article 107 TFEU. The Court of Justice said that 3F was an economic operator which negotiated the terms and conditions on which labour was provided to undertakings. It said that the aid resulting from the fiscal measures affected the ability of its members to compete with non-Union seafarers in seeking employment with shipping companies, and 3F's market position was therefore affected as regards its ability to compete in the market for the supply of labour to those companies, and consequently its ability to recruit members.[241] It therefore had locus standi to challenge the Commission's decision which had said that the Danish fiscal measures were state aid but were compatible with the common market.

3. THE TAKEOVER DIRECTIVE

Finally, the Directive on Takeover Bids 2004/25/EC[242] makes provision for 'appropriate' information[243] (that a bid has been made and the offer document) to be given to the 'representatives' of the offeree and offeror company's employees, of failing that, to the employees directly.[244] The board of the offeree company must draw up and make public a document setting out its opinion of the bid and the reasons on which it is based, including its views on the effect of the implementation of the bid on the company's interest 'and specifically employment'. The board of the offeree company must at the

[239] Case C-319/07 *3F v. Commission* [2009] ECR I-5963.
[240] Case 25/62 *Plaumann v Commission* [1963] ECR 95.
[241] Para. 52.   [242] OJ [2004] L142/12.   [243] Preambular para. 13.
[244] Art. 6(1) and (2).

same time communicate that opinion to the representatives of its employees or, where there are no such representatives, to the employees themselves. Where the board of the offeree company receives in good time a separate opinion from the representatives of its employees on the effects of the bid on employment, that opinion must be appended to the document.[245] Article 14 adds that the Directive is without prejudice to the rules relating to information and to consultation of representatives of employees and, if Member States so provide, co-determination with the employees of the offeror and the offeree company governed by the relevant national provisions, and in particular those adopted pursuant to the EWC Directive, together with the Collective Redundancies, ECS, and I&C Directives. The 23rd preambular paragraph goes further still. It says that '[t]he disclosure of information to and the consultation of representatives of the employees of the offeror and the offeree company should be governed by the relevant national provisions', in particular those adopted pursuant to the European Directives on information and consultation. It continues that the employees of the companies concerned, or their representatives, should 'nevertheless be given an opportunity to state their views on the foreseeable effects of the bid on employment' and adds that Member States can always apply or introduce national provisions concerning the disclosure of information to, and the consultation of representatives of the employees of, the offeror before an offer is launched.

G. FINANCIAL PARTICIPATION OF EMPLOYEES IN A COMPANY

1. INTRODUCTION

The discussion so far has focused primarily on industrial democracy: employee participation in the processes of management and decision-making within the firm. Economic democracy, on the other hand, has enjoyed a renaissance in recent years. It covers a variety of forms of direct participation by employees in the ownership of the enterprise and in the distribution of economic rewards.[246] While in the case of a wholly owned workers co-operative, economic democracy can go hand in hand with industrial democracy, more usually economic rewards are designed to encourage, in an indirect way, 'identification' of employees with employers and to produce incentives for employees to increase the profitability of their employing company by allowing them to reap some of the benefits of that increase (generally through share ownership or profit-sharing).[247] This form of financial flexibility offers both macroeconomic and microeconomic benefits. The macro-economic effects relate to the flexibility of the job market: if workers accept a substantial proportion of their remuneration as a profit-related element, either in cash

---

[245] Art. 9(5).

[246] H. McLean, *Fair Shares—The Future of Employee Financial Participation in the UK* (IER, London, 1994) 3.

[247] Ibid., 3.

or shares in the company, then the company's wage bill increases only as it becomes more profitable. Consequently, the dangers of wage inflation are reduced. Companies can also deal with fluctuations in the economic cycle by reducing the profit-related pay element rather than dismissing workers.[248] At the microeconomic level profit-sharing can lead to increased effort and efficiency because employees with a financial stake in a company have an incentive to work more productively and co-operate more willingly with management.[249] This in turn leads to improved competitiveness and better industrial relations.

The Union has made various attempts to encourage the development of schemes for employee financial participation. For example, the Capital Directive on the formation of public limited liability companies and the maintenance and alteration of capital[250] permits Member States to derogate from certain provisions of the Directive on the grounds of the need to adopt or apply provisions designed to encourage the participation of employees in the capital of companies.[251] In 1979 the Commission published a memorandum on employee participation on asset formation[252] but despite a resolution by the Parliament in 1983 calling on the Commission to draw up a Recommendation and to consider whether a Directive might be necessary, little progress was made. However, in the Social Charter Action Programme 1989, the Commission said that employee participation in asset formation and productive capital formation helped bring about a fairer distribution of wealth and was a means of attaining an adequate level of non-inflationary growth. This, combined with the advantages of greater involvement of workers in the progress of their companies, precipitated the adoption of a non-legally-binding Recommendation concerning the promotion of employee participation in profits and enterprise results, known by the acronym PEPPER.[253]

2. PEPPER

The PEPPER Recommendation invites the Member States to acknowledge the potential benefits of a wider use of schemes to increase the participation of employees in the profits of the enterprise and to take account of the role and the responsibility of management and labour in this context. It recommends that the Member States ensure that legal structures are adequate to allow the introduction of such schemes, and to consider

---

[248] McLean, previously, at n. 246, 3 and 4, for a critique of this view.

[249] This model still allows room for 'free-riders' where an individual employee calculates that if other workers continue to perform optimally and he does not, the firm's productivity should be only marginally affected; the value of his ownership stake should not change and he can retain the gains from his self-serving behaviour. If most employees think this way the viability of the enterprise is threatened. Therefore managers are necessary to monitor the staff's performance. See Cheffins, previously, at n. 8, 559.

[250] Dir. 77/91/EEC (OJ [1977] L26/1) as amended.

[251] Art. 41(1). Moreover, Art. 41(2) provides that Member States may decide not to apply certain provisions of the Directive to companies incorporated under a special law which issue both capital shares and workers' shares, the latter being issued to the company's employees as a body, who are represented at general meetings of shareholders by delegates having the right to vote.

[252] Bull. Supp. 6/79.

[253] Council Recommendation 92/443/EEC (OJ [1992] L243/53).

the possibility of financial advantages to encourage their introduction. The Recommendation also lists key points in the preparation of such schemes or in reviewing existing schemes, including the regularity of bonus payments and the formula for calculating the payment to each employee. However, the Commission suggests that the existence of financial participation schemes should not stand in the way of normal negotiations dealing with wages and conditions of employment. It also recommends that the risks inherent in participation schemes, particularly if their investments are relatively undiversified, should be made clear to employees.

It seems that the Commission was not, at first, totally convinced by the benefits of these schemes. In the Preamble to the Recommendation, it said that the body of empirical research into the effects of PEPPER schemes 'does not yet provide overwhelming evidence of strong overall advantages'. This is because, although companies with extensive financial participation schemes do perform better on average than companies without them, this is as at least as likely to be due to the fact that they are better managed overall and have progressive employment policies. Research also suggests that employees tend to regard PEPPER schemes as a perk.[254]

The Commission's view is now changing.[255] In its Communication on Modernizing the Organization of Work,[256] it considered that the financial participation of employees was an important way of promoting workers' motivation and adaptability. It argues that there is some evidence that a 'sense of ownership' is an important 'intervening variable' between actual ownership and attitudinal change, although it has been found that opportunities for participating in decision-making are more important than ownership *per se* in generating feelings of ownership.[257] By 2002 the Commission was so committed to the idea of employee financial participation that it issued a further Communication[258] aimed at promoting greater use of employee financial participation schemes across Europe.[259] Yet research shows that financial participation is very low in most countries: only 12 per cent of European employees receive income from some form of profit sharing scheme and only 2.3 per cent from shares in the companies they work for.[260] And this debate is likely to be eclipsed by broader discussion of remuneration in financial institutions in the wake of the financial crisis.[261]

---

[254] McLean, previously, at n. 246, 4.

[255] See the Pepper II Report: COM(96) 697 which noted that financial participation schemes are associated with a number of important benefits, especially in terms of higher productivity levels, employment and workers' involvement.

[256] COM(98) 592, 5.

[257] A. Pendleton, N. Wilson, and M. Wright, 'The Perception and Effects of Share Ownership: Empirical Evidence from Employee Buy-outs' (1998) 36 *BJIR* 99 and A. Pendleton, 'Characteristics of Workplaces with Financial Participation: Evidence from the Workplace Industrial Relations Survey' (1997) 28 *IRJ* 103.

[258] COM(2002) 364.

[259] For further details, see <http://www.eurofound.europa.eu/areas/participationatwork/pepperreports.htm> (last accessed 29 January 2012).

[260] C. Welz and E. Fernàndez-Macías, 'Financial participation of Employees in the European Union: Much Ado about Nothing' (2008) 14 *EJIR* 479.

[261] See eg Commission, 'Green paper: Corporate Governance in financial institutions and remuneration policies': COM(2010) 284.

H. CONCLUSIONS

This chapter has considered a wide range of mechanisms introduced by Union law to encourage worker participation in the workplace in an attempt to foster greater trust between workers and their employers. The principal model relied on by the Union is the provision of information to workers or their representatives, and consultation. This approach envisages a co-operative/partnership style of worker/employer relationship rather than the more antagonistic relationship sometimes found between trade unions and employers. In the next chapter we move on to consider freedom of association more generally in the Union legal order, together with the Union's approach to industrial action.

16

FREEDOM OF ASSOCIATION, COLLECTIVE BARGAINING, AND COLLECTIVE ACTION

A. INTRODUCTION

So far we have considered the Union rights given to worker representatives. These representatives may well be trade unions or elected worker representatives. In this chapter we focus specifically on how the European Union protects both trade union rights and the rights of employers and their associations. It will become apparent that the Union competence in this field is limited and the recognition of collective labour rights takes place largely through fundamental rights,[1] now buttressed by the Charter. This chapter will concentrate on the various sources that inform the shape of these fundamental rights as recognized by the Union. We begin by considering freedom of association—the right to form and join trade unions—and then examine the extent to which the Union recognizes the rights related to freedom of association—the right to bargain collectively and the right to take industrial action.

B. FREEDOM OF ASSOCIATION

1. LEGAL SOURCES OF THE RIGHT

Freedom of association is recognized in a number of civil and political rights instruments as well as by economic and social rights documents as a fundamental right. This can be seen in, for example, the International Labour Organization (ILO) Conventions 87 and 98, the United Nations Universal Declaration of Human Rights,[2] and the accompanying

---

[1] See B. Ryan, 'The Charter and Collective Labour Law' in T. Hervey and J. Kenner (eds), *Economic and Social Rights under the EU Charter of Fundamental Rights* (Hart Publishing, Oxford, 2003) 67 on the paradox of the generous provision for collective rights at EU level in the Charter compared with the historical weakness of collective labour law at EU level.

[2] Art. 23(4): 'everyone has the right to form and join trade unions for the protection of his interests' but it also provides that 'no one may be compelled to belong to any association' (Art. 20(2)).

International Covenant on Economic, Social and Cultural Rights[3] and the International Covenant on Civil and Political Rights.[4] Significantly, for the EU's purposes,[5] freedom of association is recognized in the European Convention on Human Rights (ECHR) and the complementary European Social Charter (ESC) 1961 (revised in 1996). Article 11(1) of the European Convention talks of workers having the rights of freedom of association with others, 'including the right to form and to join trade unions for the protection of their interests'. The contents of Article 11(1) are largely repeated in Part I[6] of the European Social Charter 1961[7] but expanded in Part II, where Article 5 provides:

> with a view to ensuring or promoting the freedom of workers and employers to form local, national or international organisations for the protection of their economic and social interests and to join those organisations, the Contracting parties undertake that national law shall not be such as to impair, nor shall it be so applied as to impair, this freedom.

The EU itself has also recognized the right of freedom of association. Article 11 of the Community Social Charter 1989 provides:

> Employers and workers of the European [Union] shall have the right of association in order to constitute professional organisations or trade unions of their choice for the defence of their economic and social interests. Every employer and every worker shall have the freedom to join or not to join such organisations without any personal or occupational damage being thereby suffered by him.

The Social Charter Action Programme talks only of responsibility for the implementation of such policies resting with the Member States 'in accordance with their national traditions and policies'. Certainly the right to freedom of association, that is 'to join, without interference by the state, in associations to attain various ends',[8] exists in some form in all Member States of the Union. In a number of states the right of freedom of association is considered to be so fundamental that it is enshrined in the Constitution.

Most importantly, now, freedom of association is recognized in Article 12(1) of the Charter of Fundamental Rights:

---

[3] Art. 8(1). See generally B. Wedderburn, 'Freedom of Association or Right to Organise? The Common Law and International Sources', in B. Wedderburn, *Employment Rights in Britain and Europe: Selected Papers in Labour Law* (Lawrence & Wishart, London, 1991).

[4] Art. 22.

[5] The Preamble to the Single European Act 1986 recognized both the ECHR and the ESC 1961 as forming part of the foundations of the European Union. Art. 151 TFEU (ex 136 EC) refers to 'fundamental social rights such as those set out in the European Social Charter 1961...and in the 1989 Community Charter...'. The Praesidium explanation accompanying the Charter expressly refers to Art. 11 ECHR.

[6] Part I of the Charter takes the form of a declaration which lists those social and economic rights which all Contracting Parties must accept as the aim of their policies. Part II consists of the breakdown of those rights into their component parts which it then elaborates. States are then obliged to consider themselves bound by such articles or paragraphs of articles as they choose subject to certain fundamental provisions and an overall minimum selection.

[7] A new Protocol to the Social Charter was concluded in 1991 designed to improve the machinery of the Charter.

[8] Application 6094/73 *Association X v. Sweden* Dec. 6.7.77, D.R. 9, 5, at 7 in the context of the European Convention on Human Rights.

Everyone[9] has the right to freedom of peaceful assembly and to freedom of association at all levels, in particular in political, trade union and civic matters, which implies the right of everyone to form and to join trade unions for the protection of his or her interests.

2. THE CONTENT OF THE RIGHT

2.1. The right to establish unions

Both the ECHR and the EU's two Charters recognize two components to freedom of association. The first is the right to establish *unions*, which should be free to 'draw up their own rules, to administer their own affairs and to establish and join trade union federations'.[10] The use of the noun 'unions', in the plural, is important, because, as the Court of Human Rights indicated in *Young, James and Webster*,[11] it precludes the establishment of union monopolies and envisages the freedom to establish rival unions.

2.2. The right to join or not to join trade unions

The second right, and the corollary of the first, is for people to join—or not to join—those unions. The Community Social Charter 1989—but not the Charter of Fundamental Rights—expressly recognizes the negative freedom, i.e. the right of an individual *not* to join a union. Consequently, a closed shop contravenes a worker's fundamental right. There is evidence that when the ECHR was drafted the right not to join a trade union was expressly excluded.[12] Nevertheless, the organs of the ECHR have not been constrained by this and, in *Sigurjonsson*,[13] a case concerning a pre-entry closed shop, the Court of Human Rights pronounced conclusively that 'Article 11 must be viewed as encompassing a negative right of association' although it added, 'It is not necessary for the Court to determine in this instance whether this right is to be considered on an equal footing with the positive right'. In *Sørensen*[14] the European Court of Human Rights referred to the Community Social Charter 1989 and the EU Charter of Fundamental Rights to support its conclusion that 'there is little support in the contracting states for the maintenance of closed-shop agreements' and that the EU instruments indicate that their use in the labour market is not an indispensable tool for the effective enjoyment of trade-union freedoms. Denmark had therefore failed to protect the applicant workers' 'negative right to trade union freedom'.[15]

---

[9] Stressed by the Court of Human Rights in *Demir and Baykara*, Application No. 34503/97 [2008] ECHR 1345.

[10] Application No. 10550/83 *Cheall* v. *United Kingdom*, Dec. 13.5.85, D.R. 42, 178.

[11] *Young, James and Webster* v. *United Kingdom*, Eur. Ct. H.R, Series B, No. 39.

[12] Report of 19 June 1950 of the Conference of Senior Officials, in Vol. 4 Collected Edition of Travaux Preparatoires.

[13] *Sigurjonsson* v. *Ireland*, Eur. Ct. H.R, judgment of 30 June 1993, Series A, No. 264; see additionally *Sørensen and Rasmussen* v. *Denmark*, judgment of 11 January 2006, application nos. 52562/99 and 52620/99, para. 64 (pre-entry closed shop): the compulsion to join a trade union 'struck at the very substance of the freedom of association guaranteed by Article 11'. See too *Young, James and Webster* (post-entry closed shop), Eur. Ct. H.R., judgment of 13 August 1981, Series A, No. 44, 21, para. 52.

[14] See additionally *Sørensen and Rasmussen* v. *Denmark*, judgment of 11 January 2006, applications nos. 52562/99 and 52620/99, paras. 73–4.

[15] Paras. 75–6.

These cases do, however, point to an individualist—as opposed to a collectivist—conception of the right to freedom of association. Individualists see freedom of association as a right for individuals to use as they choose. The collective wishes of the group—to force the individual to join a trade union on the ground that a powerful union is better placed than a weak one to bargain with the employer—are subordinated to the individual's choices. By contrast, the collectivist view argues that groups are stronger if they are able to exercise some control over the individual: by forcing them to join a trade union or to go on strike. And a powerful union is better placed than a weak one to bargain with the employer.[16]

If an individual does decide to join a trade union, a case from the UK, *Wilson and Palmer*,[17] makes clear that trade union membership means not just holding a union card but being able to make use of the services offered by the trade union. The case concerned a decision by an employer to offer pay increases to employees who agreed to accept personal contracts in place of collectively agreed terms and conditions of employment. Employees who refused to agree, and consequently did not receive the increase, claimed that the employer had taken action short of dismissal against them on grounds of their union membership contrary to section 146 TULR(C)A 1992. According to the Court of Appeal, the right of an employee under section 146 was not only a right to union membership itself: Dillon LJ said there was no genuine distinction between membership of the union and making use of essential services of the union. By contrast, the (then) House of Lords held[18] that in the case of an omission (withholding from an employee a benefit which was conferred upon another employee) this could not amount to 'action', whatever the purpose of the omission, and hence the employers had not taken *action* short of dismissal against the employees. Consequently, the existing legal protection for trade union members under section 146 meant no more than the right to carry a union card. It did not mean that members could call on the assistance of their union for help in dealing with their employer.[19]

However, the UK was subsequently condemned by the European Court of Human Rights.[20] At paragraph 46, the Court made clear that:

> It is the essence of the right to join a trade union for the protection of their interests that employees should be free to instruct or permit the union to make representations to their

---

[16] In *Wilson and Palmer* v. *The United Kingdom*, Applications nos. 30668/96, 30671/96 and 30678/96, judgment of 2 July 2002 the ECtHR said the 'essential object of Article 11 is to protect *the individual* against arbitrary interference by public authorities with the exercise of the rights protected' (para. 41). See additionally *Sørensen and Rasmussen* v. *Denmark*, judgment of 11 January 2006, application nos. 52562/99 and 52620/99, para. 58: 'although individual interests must on occasion be subordinated to those of a group, democracy does not simply mean that the views of the majority must always prevail: a balance must be achieved which ensures the fair and proper treatment of minorities and avoids any abuse of a dominant position'.

[17] *Wilson and Palmer* v. *The United Kingdom*, Application nos. 30668/96, 30671/96 and 30678/96, judgment of 2 July 2002.

[18] [1995] IRLR 258.

[19] K. Ewing, 'The Implications of *Wilson and Palmer*' (2003) 32 *ILJ* 1.

[20] Applications nos. 30668/96, 30671/96 and 30678/96 *Wilson and NUJ* v. *UK*; *Palmer, Wyeth and National Union of Rail Maritime and Transport Workers* v. *UK*; *Doolan and others* v. *UK* [2002] IRLR 568.

employer or to take action in support of their interests on their behalf. If workers are prevented from so doing, their freedom to belong to a trade union, for the protection of their interests becomes illusory.

Ewing describes the paragraph 46 right as the 'weaker dimension' of the freedom of association right.[21] However, the Court then adds a stronger dimension: that it was the role of the state to ensure that trade union members are not prevented or restrained from using their union to represent them in attempts to regulate their relations with their employers.[22]

The Court therefore concluded in *Wilson and Palmer* that by permitting employers to use financial incentives to induce employees to surrender important union rights, the UK failed in its positive obligation to secure the enjoyment of the rights under Article 11 of the Convention, both in respect of the individual and, in a nod in the collectivist direction, to the applicant trade unions.[23]

2.3. Legal protection for those exercising their rights

The corollary of the right to establish and join trade unions is that, as the Community Social Charter 1989 expressly states, workers (or employers) must not suffer any 'personal or occupational damage' as a result of exercising their freedom of association.[24] This might include dismissal or action short of dismissal (the very issue in *Wilson and Palmer*), or pressure by an employer on an employee to give up a position in the union. While such action is not expressly proscribed by the ECHR, the Convention provides practical recourse: Article 13 says that 'everyone whose rights and freedoms as set forth in this Convention are violated shall have an effective remedy before a national authority'.

3. RESTRICTIONS ON THE RIGHT OF FREEDOM OF ASSOCIATION

There are, however, limits on the freedom of association. Most notably, Article 11(2) ECHR provides:

> No restriction shall be placed on the exercise of these rights other than such as are prescribed by law and are necessary in a democratic society in the interests of national security or public safety, for the prevention of disorder or crime, for the protection of health or morals or for the protection of the rights and freedoms of others.[25] This article shall not prevent the imposition of lawful restrictions on the exercise of these rights by members of the armed forces, of the police or of the administration of the state.

The question of what constitutes 'lawful restrictions' was at issue in the *GCHQ* case.[26] Here the European Commission of Human Rights considered a ban on unions and

---

[21] Previously, at n. 19, 6.   [22] Ibid.   [23] Para. 48.

[24] No express prohibition is made by the Charter against unions exploiting their dominant position by e.g. expelling members contrary to union rules.

[25] Para. 14 of the Community Social Charter 1989 merely states that 'the internal legal order of the Member states shall determine under which conditions and to what extent the rights provided for in Arts. 11–13 apply to the armed forces, the police and the civil service'.

[26] Application no. 11603/85 *Council of Civil Servant Unions* v. *United Kingdom*, Dec. 20.1.87, D.R. 50, 228.

union membership at a government intelligence-gathering centre to be lawful. However, the case fell at the admissibility stage and so did not get beyond the Commission to the Court. As Ewing points out, a more egregious form of anti-union activity is harder to contemplate, as both the Freedom of Association Committee[27] and the Committee of Experts of the ILO made abundantly clear, yet the *GCHQ* case provided a 'classic example of the failure of the Strasbourg system to protect trade union rights'.[28] However, this is beginning to change: as we shall see later, the Court of Human Rights was somewhat more rigorous in its application of the derogation in the *UNISON* case[29] and even more so in *Demir*,[30] a case concerning a refusal by Turkey to allow civil servants to join a trade union.

In *Demir* the Court found that there had been an interference with Article 11 and/or a failure by the State to comply with its positive obligation to secure the applicants' rights under Article 11. However, it continued:

> As to the necessity of such interference in a democratic society, the Court reiterates that lawful restrictions may be imposed on the exercise of trade-union rights by members of the armed forces, of the police or of the administration of the State. However, it must also be borne in mind that the exceptions set out in Article 11 are to be construed strictly; only convincing and compelling reasons can justify restrictions on such parties' freedom of association. In determining in such cases whether a 'necessity'—and therefore a 'pressing social need'—within the meaning of Article 11 § 2 exists, States have only a limited margin of appreciation, which goes hand in hand with rigorous European supervision embracing both the law and the decisions applying it, including those given by independent courts. ... The Court must also look at the interference complained of in the light of the case as a whole and determine whether it was 'proportionate to the legitimate aim pursued' and whether the reasons adduced by the national authorities to justify it were 'relevant and sufficient'.[31]

On the facts, the Grand Chamber found:

> ...it has not been shown before it that the absolute prohibition on forming trade unions imposed on civil servants... by Turkish law, as it applied at the material time, met a 'pressing social need'. The mere fact that the 'legislation did not provide for such a possibility' is not sufficient to warrant as radical a measure as the dissolution of a trade union.

The Court concluded that there had been a violation of Article 11 of the Convention on account of the failure to recognize the right of the applicants, as municipal civil servants, to form a trade union.[32] This conclusion prompted Ewing to make a fundamental—and more positive—assessment of the Court of Human Rights' position.[33]

---

[27] ILO's Freedom of Association Committee, 234th Report of the Committee on Freedom of Association, Case no. 1261.
[28] Ewing, previously, at n. 19.
[29] *UNISON* v. *United Kingdom*, judgment of 10 January 2002, [2002] IRLR 497.
[30] *Demir and Baykara* v. *Turkey*, Application no. 34503/97 [2008] ECHR 1345.
[31] Para. 119.   [32] Para. 127.
[33] K. Ewing and J. Hendy, 'The Dramatic Implications of *Demir* and *Baykara*' (2010) 39 *ILJ* 2.

4. FREEDOM OF ASSOCIATION AND UNION LAW

What effect do these rules have on Union law? The first point to note is that Article 153(5) TFEU (ex 137(5) EC) expressly excludes freedom of association from the Union's competence, at least under Article 153.[34] In other words, the Union has no power to legislate in the field of freedom of association under Article 153. However, the Court of Justice has recognized freedom of association to be a fundamental right which will bind (1) the Union institutions when they are legislating or adopting administrative measures, and (2) the Member States when they are implementing Union law, derogating from Union law or, more broadly, when acting in the field of Union law.[35] In this respect, the jurisprudence of the European Court of Human Rights interpreting this fundamental right is highly significant.

In respect of action by the *Union* institutions, the right to freedom of association was recognized in a staff case, *Kortner*,[36] where the Court said:

> Under the general principles of labour law the freedom of trade union activity recognised under Article 24a of the Staff Regulations means not only that officials and servants have the right to form associations of their own choosing, but also that these associations are free to do anything lawful to protect the interests of their members as employees.

Thus, as Advocate General Jacobs noted in *Albany*,[37] the Court recognized, first, the individual right to form and join an association and, second, the collective right to take action. In his view the fundamental nature of those two rights was confirmed in *Bosman*[38] with respect to freedom of association in general, and in *Maurissen* more specifically with regard to trade unions.[39] In the light of this line of case law, if the European Union tried to legislate in a way which interferes with freedom of association, it is likely that any such measure could be successfully challenged as being incompatible with freedom of association.

In addition, the Court has insisted that Union secondary legislation be interpreted in the light of freedom of association, as *Werhof*[40] demonstrates. In the context of a case about the Transfer of Undertakings Directive 2001/23[41] a question was raised whether a transferee was bound by a collective agreement subsequent to the one in force at the time of the transfer of the business, when the transferee was not party to the collective agreement. The Court began by recognizing that '[f]reedom of association, which also

---

[34] For a discussion on this point, see Case C–14/04 *Abdelkader Dellas and Others* v. *Premier ministre and Others* [2006] ECR I–10253, para. 39 considered in Ch. 2.

[35] Case C–260/89 *ERT* [1991] ECR I–2925 considered further in Ch. 1.

[36] Case 175/73 *Union Syndicale, Massa and Kortner* v. *Commission* [1974] ECR 917, para. 14.

[37] Case C–67/96 *Albany* [1999] ECR I–5751.

[38] Case C–415/93 *Bosman* [1995] ECR I–4921, paras. 79 and 80.

[39] Joined Cases C–193/87 and C–194/87 *Maurissen and European Public Service Union* v. *Court of Auditors* [1990] ECR I–95, paras. 11–16 and 21.

[40] Case C–499/04 *Werhof* [2006] ECR I–2397.

[41] OJ [2001] L82/16 considered further in Ch. 13. See additionally the Sex Equality Dir. 2006/54 (OJ [2006] L 204/23), 20th recital.

includes the right not to join an association or union,[42]... is one of the fundamental rights which, in accordance with the Court's settled case-law, are protected in the [Union] legal order'.[43] It then considered two approaches to the interpretation of the Directive. The first, the 'dynamic' interpretation, supported by the claimant employee, would mean that future collective agreements apply to a transferee who is not party to a collective agreement with the result that his fundamental right not to join an association could be affected.[44] The second, the 'static' interpretation, supported by the defendant transferee, makes it possible to avoid a situation in which the transferee of a business who is not party to a collective agreement is bound by future changes to that agreement.[45] This interpretation safeguards his right not to join an association and it was this approach that the Court chose.[46]

While fundamental rights are usually used to *limit* the powers of the Union (as in *Kortner*) or the Member States, they can also be used by the Member States to justify limiting other rights, in particular the free movement provisions. This can be seen most clearly in *Schmidberger*.[47] This case concerned not a trade union but an environmental association which organized a demonstration, blocking a stretch of the Brenner Motorway (the A13, the major transit route for trade between northern Europe and Italy) for 30 hours, to draw attention to the threat to the environment and public health posed by the constant increase in the movement of heavy goods vehicles on the motorway. Schmidberger, a German transport company, sought damages for the losses it suffered from its lorries not being able to use this route. The Court said that the fact that the competent authorities of a Member State did not ban this demonstration was capable of restricting intra-Union trade in goods and so breached Articles 34 and 35 TFEU (ex 28 and 29 EC) on free movement of goods, read together with Article 4(3) TEU (ex 10 EC) on the duty of co-operation.[48]

However, the Austrian authorities justified their (in)action on the grounds of the fundamental rights of the demonstrators to freedom of expression and freedom of assembly guaranteed by the ECHR and the national constitution, principles which, the Court said, it recognized formed an integral part of the general principles of EU law.[49] It continued that 'since both the [Union] and its Member States are required to respect fundamental rights, the protection of those rights is a legitimate interest which, in principle, justifies a restriction of the obligations imposed by [Union] law, even under a fundamental freedom guaranteed by the Treaty such as the free movement of goods'.[50] Thus, the Court saw the fundamental rights—including freedom of association—as a free-standing justification or public interest requirement[51] which could in principle take precedence over the free movement of goods.

---

[42] Citing Art. 11 of the European Convention and the Eur. Ct. H.R. cases: Eur. Ct. H.R., *Sigurjónsson* v. *Iceland*, judgment of 30 June 1993, Series A, No. 264, § 35, and *Gustafsson* v. *Sweden*, judgment of 25 April 1996, *Reports of Judgments and Decisions*, 1996-II, p. 637, § 45.

[43] Para. 33.   [44] Para. 34.   [45] Para. 35.   [46] Para. 36.

[47] Case C–112/00 *Eugen Schmidberger, Internationale Transporte und Planzüge* v. *Republic of Austria* [2003] ECR I–5659.

[48] Para. 64.   [49] Paras. 71–3.   [50] Para. 74.

[51] See further C. Barnard, *The Substantive Law of the EU: The Four Freedoms* (OUP, Oxford, 2010) Ch. 6.

However, since the two human rights at stake, described by the Court as 'fundamental pillars of a democratic society',[52] were not absolute, the Court recognized that their exercise could be restricted, provided that 'the restrictions in fact correspond to objectives of general interest and do not, taking account of the aim of the restrictions, constitute disproportionate and unacceptable interference, impairing the very substance of the rights guaranteed'.[53] The Court then determined whether a fair balance had been struck between the competing interests (the claimant's fundamental (economic) right to free movement of goods versus the protesters' fundamental (civil/social) right to freedom of association/assembly).[54] It noted that the demonstration took place following a request for authorization, as required by national law, and after the Austrian authorities had decided to allow it to go ahead;[55] the obstacle to free movement was limited (a single event, on a single route, lasting for 30 hours), the demonstrators were motivated by a desire to express their opinion on a matter of public importance and not by a desire to restrict trade in goods of a particular type or from a particular source;[56] and various administrative and supporting measures had been taken by the Austrian authorities to limit the disruption to road traffic, including an extensive publicity campaign launched well in advance by the media and the motoring organizations, both in Austria and in neighbouring countries,[57] as well as the designation of alternative routes. The Court therefore concluded that the fact that the authorities of a Member State did not ban the demonstration in these circumstances was compatible with Union law.[58]

Following the Court's ruling in an earlier case, *Commission* v. *France (Spanish Strawberries)*[59] which concerned a long history of violent attacks by French farmers directed against agricultural products from other Member States[60] to which France had failed to respond, leading the Court to find France in breach of Article 34 TFEU on the free movement of goods and Article 4(3) TEU on the duty of co-operation, the Council adopted Regulation 2679/98[61] which was designed to set up an intervention mechanism to safeguard free trade in the Single Market, the so-called Monti I Regulation.[62] This provides that State A can complain to the Commission about obstacles to the free movement of goods which are attributable to State B—either through action or inaction[63]—where the obstacles lead to serious disruption of the free movement of goods, cause serious loss to the individuals affected and require immediate action.[64] However,

---

[52] Para. 79.   [53] Para. 80.   [54] Para. 81.   [55] Para. 84.   [56] Para. 86.
[57] Para. 87.   [58] Para. 94.   [59] Case C–265/95 [1997] ECR I–6959.
[60] Para. 2.
[61] OJ [1998] L337/8. See additionally the Resolution of the Council and of the Representatives of the Governments of the Member States meeting within the Council of 7 December 1998 (OJ [1998] L337/10) which encourages the Court to adopt an expedited procedure in respect of cases arising under Reg. 2679/98. This is considered further in Ch. 5.
[62] See additionally the proposed Monti II Regulation (COM(2012) 130) considered in Ch. 5.
[63] 'Inaction' is defined in Art. 1(2) as covering the case when the competent authorities of a Member State, in the presence of an obstacle caused by actions taken by private individuals, fail to take all necessary and proportionate measures within their powers with a view to removing the obstacle and ensuring the free movement of goods in their territory.
[64] Art. 1(1).

this complaints procedure is subject to the fundamental rights recognized in Article 2 of the Regulation (the so-called Monti II clause):

> This Regulation may not be interpreted as affecting in any way the exercise of fundamental rights, as recognised in Member States, including the right or freedom to strike. These rights may also include the right or freedom to take other actions covered by the specific industrial relations systems in Member States.[65]

This Regulation demonstrates the importance of these fundamental rights as a defensive mechanism to claims against Member States for failing to prevent strikes and other forms of industrial action.

5. THE CREATION OF A EUROPEAN-WIDE TRADE UNION MOVEMENT?

Will the EU's recognition of freedom of association lead to the creation of a European wide trade union movement? At present this seems unlikely. Industrial relations in the Member States are characterized by significant diversity. In some Member States, such as the UK, Germany, Ireland, and Denmark, unions are 'unified'. In others, unions are politically ideological and confessional (i.e. religiously orientated).[66] In the Netherlands, for example, the three main trade union confederations comprise: a confederation (FNV) created from a merger between the socialist and most of the Catholic organizations; a Protestant Union federation (CNV) which includes some Catholic civil service unions who refused to join the socialists; and a federation of white-collar organizations (MHP).[67] Similarly, in Italy industrial relations reflect that nation's divisions in politics and ideology: Catholic and anti-Catholic; Communist and anti-Communist; collectivist and individualist.[68] This pattern is echoed in Belgium where the three main ideological pillars of society—Catholicism, Protestantism, and socialism—are cross-cut in industrial relations by the differences: between employer and employee, Catholic and non-Catholic, and French-speaking and Dutch-speaking communities.[69] The existence of such differences, combined with the lack of significant transnational power resources, suggest that worker representation will continue to take place primarily within the national or subnational context but with co-operation through the European trade union confederation.

---

[65] The Monti I Regulation formed the basis of the social provisions of the Services Dir. 2006/123 discussed in Ch. 5.

[66] See U. Zachert, 'Trade Unions in Europe: Dusk or a New Dawn?' (1993) 9 *IJCLLIR* 15, 16.

[67] J. Visser, 'The End of an Era and the End of a System' in A. Ferner and R. Hyman (eds.), *Industrial Relations in the New Europe* (Blackwell, Oxford, 1998) 328.

[68] A. Ferner and R. Hyman, 'Italy: Between Political Exchange and Micro-Corporatism', in Ferner and Hyman (eds.), previously, at n. 67, 524.

[69] See J. Vilrokx and J. Van Leemput, 'Belgium: A New Ability in Industrial Relations?', in Ferner and Hyman (eds.), previously, at n. 67, 363 and 367.

C. THE RIGHT TO ENGAGE IN COLLECTIVE BARGAINING

1. INTRODUCTION

As we saw in the previous chapter, Union legislation emphasizes information and consultation with worker representatives. This can be a far cry from collective bargaining since no agreement need be reached and ultimately the final decision rests with the employer. In the original Treaty of Rome the Social Partners had only a discreet presence—through the Economic and Social Committee (ECOSOC)[70] and as the subject of close co-operation which the Commission was obliged to promote between the Member States.[71] The situation has changed dramatically since 1957 and the Social Partners now have a potentially important role, as legislators and as partners of change in the European Employment Strategy. The Commission's discourse has changed dramatically too. It now focuses on the need to develop 'a strong partnership at all appropriate levels: at European, national, sectoral and enterprise level' to 'negotiate agreements to modernise the organisation of work'.[72] The question, then, is what is meant by collective bargaining and how is it protected at EU level?

2. COLLECTIVE BARGAINING AND COLLECTIVE AGREEMENTS

2.1. The meaning of collective bargaining

In its broad sense[73] collective bargaining is a process of interest accommodation which includes all sorts of bipartite or tripartite discussions relating to labour problems directly or indirectly affecting a group of workers. The discussions may take place in different fora, with or without the presence of governments, and aim at ascertaining the view of the other party, obtaining a concession or reaching a compromise. A narrower but more precise meaning of collective bargaining views it only in connection with the bipartite discussions leading to the conclusion of agreements. In this narrower sense, collective bargaining involves a process of negotiations between individual employers or representatives of employers' organizations and trade union representatives. As a rule, any agreement concluded is regarded as binding not only on its signatories but also on the groups they represent.

Collective bargaining offers a variety of benefits neatly summarized by Advocate General Jacobs in *Albany*:[74]

---

[70] Arts. 301–4 TFEU.

[71] Art. 156 TFEU (ex 140 EC) provides that the subject-matter of close co-operation includes 'the right of association, and collective bargaining between employers and workers'.

[72] COM(98) 592, 2.

[73] See E. Cordova, 'Collective Bargaining', in R. Blanpain (ed.), *Comparative Labour Law and Industrial Relations*, 3rd edn (Kluwer, Deventer, 1987). These definitions roughly correspond to what is called in France the informal and formal types of negotiation (*negociation officieuse* and *negociation officielle*).

[74] Case C–67/96 [1999] ECR I–5751, para. 181.

It is widely accepted that collective agreements between management and labour prevent costly labour conflicts, reduce transaction costs through a collective and rule-based negotiation process and promote predictability and transparency. A measure of equilibrium between the bargaining power on both sides helps to ensure a balanced outcome for both sides and for society as a whole.

2.2. The content of collective agreements

The content of collective agreements can be determined by the contracting parties but comprise principally of (1) normative clauses and (2) contractual or obligatory clauses. The normative stipulations refer to the terms and conditions of work which must be observed in all the individual employment contracts in the enterprise concerned. These include all aspects of working conditions, wages, fringe benefits, job classifications, working hours, time off, training, job security, and non-contributory benefit schemes. The collective agreement can also contain collective normative stipulations relating to informing and consulting workers, worker participation, and procedural rules.[75]

The contractual or obligatory clauses include all provisions spelling out the rights and duties of the parties. Often the main duty is the peace obligation which means that for the duration of the agreement neither of the parties is permitted to initiate industrial action against the other party with the intention of altering the conditions laid down in the collective agreement. Such an obligation is considered to be a natural consequence of collective bargaining, which is supposed to bring stability to labour relations. This obligation may be absolute, in which case the parties are obliged to refrain from all industrial action,[76] or relative, in which case neither of the parties is, for the duration of the collective agreement, permitted to initiate industrial action against the other party with the intention of altering conditions laid down in the agreement.[77] The relative peace obligation offers trade unions the advantage of safeguarding their right to formulate new demands if and when substantive changes in the socio-economic environment occur.[78]

Article 12(1) of the Community Social Charter 1989 provides that, 'Employers or employers' organisations, on the one hand, and workers' organisations on the other, shall have the right to negotiate and conclude collective agreements under the conditions laid down by national legislation and practice'. In most Member States collective bargaining has been used as a means of setting standards or improving upon standards laid down by contract or statute. However, between the Member States attitudes and approaches to collective bargaining vary considerably. At one end of the spectrum lies Denmark where collective agreements form the cornerstone of labour standards. At the other stands the UK where there is a statutory presumption that collective agreements are not legally binding between the parties.[79] Collective agreements do have legal effect in the UK if incorporated into the contract of employment, but equally, since collective agreements

---

[75] Commission, *Comparative Study on Rules Governing Working Conditions in the Member States: a Synopsis*, SEC(89) 1137.

[76] R. Birk, 'Industrial Conflict: The Law of Strikes and Lock-outs' in R. Blanpain (ed.) previously, at n. 73, 413.

[77] Commission, previously, at n. 75.   [78] Cordova, 'Collective Bargaining', previously, at n. 73, 28.

[79] S. 179 TULR(C)A 1992.

do not constitute a floor of rights, the individual contract can be used to derogate from its provisions. In between lie Romano-Germanic countries such as Belgium, France, and Germany where collectively agreed norms can be given by law an *erga omnes* or 'extended' effect. Thus, the law is used to ensure that the normative terms of collective agreements are applied more generally throughout the industry or sector. The original rationale for this procedure was the need to avoid unfair competition from non-unionized enterprises, but subsequently the extension mechanism has been justified by the need to promote collective bargaining and to pursue more egalitarian goals.[80]

3. COLLECTIVE BARGAINING AT EU LEVEL

3.1. The early days

The Commission has long aspired to develop European level collective bargaining[81] from the weak legal basis originally provided by Article 118 EEC. This said that the Commission should have the task of promoting close co-operation between Member States in the social field, especially in matters relating to, *inter alia*, 'the right of association, and collective bargaining between employers and workers'.

The Commission's drive towards establishing a European industrial relations area has been frustrated by the fact that traditionally trade unions and employers' associations are national in scope and collective bargaining is usually conducted within a national framework and/or at regional, sectoral or enterprise level rather than at a centralized European level. Despite this, the two sides of industry—the *intersectoral* Social Partners—have long co-operated at Union level, for example, by participating in consultation. Formal consultation occurs in the Economic and Social Committee (ECOSOC), in cross-industry advisory committees, such as the Tripartite Social Summit for Growth and Employment which meets ahead of the Spring European Council.[82] Most importantly, the Commission has sought the opinions of the EU-level Social Partners on its proposals for social legislation, an arrangement formalized by the Maastricht Treaty.[83]

In addition, management and labour have been meeting at a sectoral level since the establishment of joint committees with the Commission's assistance in the 1960s. These committees, with equal numbers of employers and employee representatives, covered a range of sectors including agriculture (1963), road transport (1965), transport by inland waterway (1967), sea fishing (1968), rail transport (1971), and more recently civil aviation and telecommunications (1990).[84] They produced a number of joint opinions and recommendations on employment, working conditions and health and safety, but did not enter

---

[80] Cordova, 'Collective Bargaining', in Blanpain (ed.), previously, at n. 73, 329.
[81] See generally B. Bercussion, *European Labour Law* (CUP, Cambridge, 2009), 2nd ed., Chs. 5, 17–19.
[82] Co. Dec. 2003/174/EC (OJ [2003] L70/31) and Art. 152 TFEU.
[83] Art. 154 TFEU (ex 138 EC). See further Ch. 2.
[84] For more details see *Social Europe* 2/95, 30.

into European-wide collective agreements, largely due to opposition by the employers.[85] The Commission intended these bodies to 'contribute to the construction of a European system of industrial relations and foster free collective bargaining'[86] but the reality fell far short. Although some committees were successful, particularly those with Union-level issues to discuss (the agriculture, fisheries, and transport committees), many participants felt that the committees were formal and bureaucratic and doubted both the usefulness of their work and the Commission's real interest in their activities.[87] Consequently, the Commission initiated an informal dialogue between the sectoral Social Partners with the aim of encouraging exchanges of views, consultation on EU policies and the organization of studies and seminars, designed to 'create a climate of confidence between employers and workers'.[88] In the late 1980s this led to a new form of sectoral dialogue: informal working groups with the role of carrying out studies on employment in their sector and providing the Commission with a forum to consult on specific proposals. These contacts were formalized with the establishment of new sectoral dialogue committees.[89]

3.2. The SEA 1986, the Maastricht Treaty 1992, and the Lisbon Treaty 2009

Calls for increased dialogue between employers, trade unions, and the Union continued, not just at the sectoral level but at the intersectoral level, as a means of dealing with both economic recession and resolving the impasse which had been reached by the mid-1980s in passing social policy initiatives. Jacques Delors, then the Commission President, seized on the idea of the social dialogue as a vehicle for formulating social policy. He told the European Parliament:

> Collective bargaining must remain one of the cornerstones of our economy, and efforts must be made to secure some harmonisation at [Union] level. That is why I raised the idea ... of European collective agreements to provide the framework which is essential for the achievement of a large market.[90]

This precipitated what has become known as the Val Duchesse intersectoral social dialogue in January 1985 between the European Trade Union Confederation (ETUC), representing employees, the Union of Industrial and Employers' Confederations of Europe (UNICE), representing private sector employers (now BusinessEurope), and the European Centre of Public Enterprises[91] (CEEP), for public sector employers. Two working parties were established, one looking at the implications of new technology and work, the other dealing with employment and macroeconomic policies. Both groups issued 'Joint Opinions',[92] so called because the employers refused to countenance

---

[85] See *The Sectoral Social Dialogue* 224 EIRR 14 and B. Hepple, *European Social Dialogue—Alibi or Opportunity?* (Institute of Employment Rights, London, 1993) 13.

[86] *Social Europe* 2/85.   [87] 224 EIRR 16.   [88] Ibid.

[89] Commission Communication, *Adapting and Promoting the Social Dialogue at Community Level* COM(98) 332 and Commission Decision 98/500/EC (OJ [1998] L225/27). See additionally <http://ec.europa.eu/social/main.jsp?catId=480&langId=en> (last accessed 28 January 2012).

[90] Cited in *The Social Dialogue—Euro-Bargaining in the Making?* 220 EIRR 25, 27.

[91] Now known as the European Centre of Enterprises with Public Participation and of Enterprises of General Economic Interest.

[92] E.g. 6 November 1986 for the macroeconomic committee, 6 March 1987 for the new technology committee.

the notion of European-level collective agreements. However, the impetus was soon lost, in part because the exact purpose of the social dialogue was never resolved.[93]

It was against this backcloth that Article 118b was introduced by the Single European Act 1986 (now the much amended Article 155 TFEU (ex 139 EC)). This provided that '[t]he Commission shall endeavour to develop the dialogue between management and labour at European level which could, if the two sides consider it desirable, lead to relations based on agreement'. This was reinforced by Article 12(2) of the Community Social Charter 1989 which provides that 'The dialogue between the two sides of industry at European level which *must* be developed, may, if the parties deem it desirable, result in contractual relations in particular at inter-occupational and sectoral level' (emphasis added). The Commission's view was that there should be 'complementarity between legislative initiatives on the part of the institutions and independent action by the two sides of industry'. The establishment of a balance between these two approaches would make it possible to manage 'the diversity of social practices and traditions specific to each Member State'.[94] However, since the Treaty prescribed no formal procedures for the organization of the dialogue under Article 118b and failed to specify the legal consequences of any such dialogue, it was difficult to regard Article 118b as more than a political gesture legitimating the Val Duchesse talks.[95] However, Article 118b did lead to a relaunch of the Val Duchesse dialogue, focusing this time on education and training and the problems surrounding the emergence of a European labour market.[96]

The Val Duchesse dialogue did send out the message that the two sides of industry could work together and this paved the way for consultation by the Social Partners in the drafting of the Community Social Charter 1989[97] and, more significantly the Social Partners concluded a joint agreement, on 31 October 1991, which was presented to the Maastricht intergovernmental conference and transposed almost verbatim into Articles 3 and 4 of the SPA (now Articles 154 and 155 TFEU). This Agreement entitled the Social Partners not only to be consulted about proposed legislation[98] but also to enter a dialogue which may lead to agreements[99] which can be implemented autonomously or by a Council 'decision'—in reality a Directive—on a proposal from the Commission.[100]

Finally, Article 152 TFEU was introduced by the Lisbon Treaty where the Constitutional position of the social partners was formally recognized. It provides that the EU recognizes and promotes the role of the social partners at its level, taking into account the diversity of national systems.

---

[93] 220 EIRR 27.   [94] *Social Europe* 1/88, 67.   [95] Hepple, previously, at n. 85, 16.

[96] Ibid., 28. The relaunched dialogue was more productive. The education and training group produced three joint opinions and the working party on the labour market one further opinion, but these opinions lacked specific application and there was no requirement for the signatory parties to apply them.

[97] Their involvement is reflected in the numerous references to collective agreements, particularly as a means of guaranteeing the fundamental social rights in the Charter (Art. 28) and 'the active involvement of the two sides of industry' (Preamble).

[98] Art. 154(2) TFEU.

[99] Art. 155(1) TFEU. See further Ch. 2.

[100] Art. 155(2) TFEU. The English language version of the Treaty provides for a 'decision'. This has been interpreted to mean any legally binding instrument, including Directives. See further Ch. 2. See further, B. Venziani, 'The Role of the Social Partners in the Lisbon Treaty' in N. Bruun *et al.* (eds), *The Lisbon Treaty and Social Europe* (Oxford, Hart Publishing, 2012).

3.3. Assessment

For a while, the SPA, EMU and subsequently the EES revitalized the transnational role of the Social Partners both at the intersectoral and now at the sectoral level. From small beginnings, the Social Partners now have the potential to enjoy significant influence at EU level and, in so doing, strengthen collective bargaining at national level. At EU level we see a form of tripartite or bipartite concertation—or Euro-corporatism—emerge. The role now envisaged for the Social Partners is one of partnership[101] and co-operation rather than adversarialism, a shift from industrial pluralism[102] to a more managerialist perspective.[103] At national level we also see how European-level collective bargaining is helping to steer national collective bargaining. Social policy Directives, such as the Directives on proof of the employment contract,[104] working time,[105] and young workers,[106] can be implemented by collective agreements. They contain a clause providing that the Member States must pass laws, regulations, or administrative provisions to adopt the Directive by a particular date or ensure 'that the employers' and workers' representatives introduce the required provisions by way of agreement'. This method of implementation has now been confirmed by Article 155(2) TFEU. Collective agreements or their equivalents can also be used to flesh out substantive standards in the Directives. For example, Article 4 of the Working Time Directive 2003/88[107] requires that rest breaks must be provided if the working day lasts longer than six hours but that details of breaks, 'including duration and the terms on which it is granted, shall be laid down in collective agreements or agreements between the two sides of industry or, *failing that*, by national legislation' (emphasis added). This is an example of what the Dutch and Germans call an opening clause, allowing greater flexibility of practices (notably over working time) at company level,[108] albeit that that flexibility comes at the price of allowing collective agreements to derogate from the legislative norms *in pejus*,[109] thereby allowing standards to deteriorate. These examples are, however taken from the 1990s/ early 2000s. Some would argue that this was the golden age of Euro-corporatism. Reforms to national systems of collective bargaining introduced, especially in Greece, at the behest of the troika, have severely undermined the effectiveness of collective bargaining, as the ILO has noted.[109A]

---

[101] See e.g. the Commission's Green Paper *Partnership for a New Organisation of Work* COM(97) 127.

[102] For a classic exposition of pluralism in labour law, see O. Kahn-Freund's *Labour and the Law* by P. Davies and M. Freedland, 3rd edn (Stevens, London, 1983).

[103] See the typology suggested in M. Terry, 'Systems of Collective Employee Representation in Non-union Firms in the UK' (1999) 30 *IRJ* 16, 17.

[104] Council Dir. 91/533/EEC (OJ [1991] L288/32).

[105] Council Dir. 93/104/EC (OJ [1993] L307/18).

[106] Council Dir. 94/33/EC (OJ [1994] L216/12).

[107] OJ [2003] L299/9 considered further in Ch. 12.

[108] Ferner and Hyman, previously. at n. 67, xvi.

[109] See generally B. Wedderburn, 'Collective Bargaining at European Level: the Inderogability Problem' (1992) 21 *ILJ* 245. For a further more recent example, see the Temporary Agency Work Dir. 2008/104 (OJ [2008] L327/9) where Art. 5(4) allows derogations from the principle of equal treatment provided they are negotiated at national level.

[109A] ILO, Report on the High Level Mission to Greece, 2011, para. 243.

4. IS THERE A FUNDAMENTAL RIGHT TO BARGAIN COLLECTIVELY?

Do these developments mean that there is a fundamental right not only to freedom of association but also to bargain collectively? Up until 2008 the answer was no. In *Wilson and Palmer* the European Court of Human Rights said that 'although collective bargaining may be one of the ways by which trade unions may be enabled to protect their members' interests, it is not indispensable for the effective enjoyment of trade union freedom'. It continued that compulsory collective bargaining would impose on employers an obligation to conduct negotiations with trade unions. The only right expressly recognized by the Court of Human Rights was to be 'heard' by the state.[110] A trade union had no right to be consulted by the state,[111] nor, as we saw above, was the state required to impose an obligation on employers to recognize a trade union or conclude collective agreements.[112] The Court also said that there was no obligation to recognize a trade union.[113] As a result, the Court of Human Rights in *Wilson* found that the absence under UK law of an obligation on employers to enter into collective bargaining, did not give rise to a violation of Article 11.[114] Likewise at EU level Advocate General Jacobs said in *Albany* that there was no fundamental right to bargain collectively, even though it was the freedom most fully articulated in the Union legal order. He said that only Article 6 of the European Social Charter 1961 expressly recognized the existence of a fundamental right to bargain.[115] He also pointed to Article 4 of 'the carefully drafted "Right to Organise and Collective Bargaining Convention" [which] imposes on the Contracting States an obligation to "encourage and promote" collective bargaining. No right is granted'.[116] He concluded that:

> . . . it cannot be said that there is sufficient convergence of national legal orders and international legal instruments on the recognition of a specific fundamental right to bargain collectively.[117]

Yet in *Demir*[118] the Court of Human Rights made a dramatic volte-face. Having reviewed the position under the ILO Conventions 98 and 151, under Article 6(2) of the Social Charter 1961, Article 28 of the EU Charter, and the 'practice of European states',[119] the Court considered that its case law needed to be reconsidered, 'so as to take account of

---

[110] Ibid., para. 39; *Swedish Engine Drivers' Union* v. *Sweden*, judgment of 6 February 1976, Eur. Ct HR Rep., Series A, No. 20 (1976), para. 40.

[111] *National Union of Belgian Police* v. *Belgium*, 27 October 1975, Eur. Ct HR Rep., Series A, No. 19 (1975), para. 38.

[112] *Swedish Engine Drivers' Union* v. *Sweden*, 6 February 1976, Eur. Ct HR Rep., Series A, No. 20 (1976), para. 39; *Wilson and Palmer* v. *The United Kingdom*, Applications nos. 30668/96, 30671/96 and 30678/96, judgment of 2 July 2002, para. 45.

[113] Para. 44. See additionally *UNISON* v. *United Kingdom*, judgment of 10 January 2002, [2002] IRLR 497, para. 42 where the Court of Human Rights said that the Union could not claim under the Convention a 'requirement that an employer enter into, or remain in, any particular collective bargaining arrangement or accede to its requests on behalf of its members'.

[114] Para. 45.   [115] Case C–67/96 *Albany* [1999] ECR I–5751, para. 146.

[116] Para. 147.   [117] Para. 160.

[118] Application no. 34503/97 [2008] ECHR 1345.   [119] Paras. 147–152.

the perceptible evolution in such matters, in both international law and domestic legal systems'.[120] It said:

> 154. Consequently, the Court considers that, having regard to the developments in labour law, both international and national, and to the practice of Contracting States in such matters, the right to bargain collectively with the employer has, in principle, become one of the essential elements of the 'right to form and to join trade unions for the protection of [one's] interests' set forth in Article 11 of the Convention, it being understood that States remain free to organise their system so as, if appropriate, to grant special status to representative trade unions. Like other workers, civil servants, except in very specific cases, should enjoy such rights, but without prejudice to the effects of any 'lawful restrictions' that may have to be imposed on 'members of the administration of the State' within the meaning of Article 11 § 2—a category to which the applicants in the present case do not, however, belong.

Ewing and Hendy note that this is 'a remarkable delegation to external standards and their dynamic application' and that 'in treating the ECHR as a living instrument, the Strasbourg court is also acknowledging that these other treaties are living instruments as well'.[121]

It seems likely that this decision has had an energizing effect on the Court of Justice as well. Article 28 of the Charter provides:

> Workers and employers, or their respective organisations, have, in accordance with Union law and national laws and practices, the right to negotiate and conclude collective agreements at the appropriate levels and, in cases of conflicts of interests, to take collective action to defend their interests, including strike action.

The coming into force of the Charter, together with the fact that the right to bargain collectively is 'recognised both by the provisions of various international instruments which the Member States have cooperated in or signed, such as Article 6 of the European Social Charter [1961]' led the Court to conclude in *Commission* v. *Germany (occupational pensions)*[122] that the right to bargain collectively is a fundamental right.[123] However, it is not an absolute right: it may be subject to certain restrictions including that fact that it must be exercised in accordance with EU law,[124] in particular the principle of equality.[125] The Court concluded:

> Exercise of the fundamental right to bargain collectively must therefore be reconciled with the requirements stemming from the freedoms protected by the FEU Treaty, which in the present instance the [public procurement] directives are intended to implement, and be in accordance with the principle of proportionality.[126]

There is a certain paradox in the case law. In the case of *Albany*,[127] decided at a time when the right to collective bargaining had not been recognized as a fundamental right,

---

[120] Para. 153.   [121] Previously, at n. 33, 7–8.   [122] Case C–271/08 [2010] E.C.R. I-000 discussed in Ch. 5.
[123] Para. 41. See additionally Trstenjak AG, para. 4.
[124] Ibid, para. 43. See further Case C–447/09 *Prigge* v. *Deutsche Lufthansa* [2011] ECR I–000, para. 47.
[125] Joined Cases C–297/10 and C–298/10 *Hennigs* v. *Eisenbahn-Bundesamt* [2011] ECR I–000, para. 78.
[126] Ibid, para. 44.   [127] Case C–67/96 [1999] ECR I–5751. This is discussed in detail in Ch. 5.

the Court was able to conclude that 'despite the restrictions of competition inherent in it, a collective agreement between the organisations representing employers and workers which sets up in a particular sector a supplementary pension scheme managed by a pension fund to which affiliation is compulsory does not fall within Article [101(1) TFEU]'.[128] Yet in *Commission v. Germany (occupational pensions)* when the Court had recognized the right to collective bargaining as a fundamental right, the Court merely saw this right as one right which had to be balanced against the economic right of freedom of establishment and freedom to provide services.[129] The Court found that because the service contracts in respect of occupational pensions were awarded directly, without a call for tenders in accordance with the EU public procurement Directives, to organizations identified in the relevant collective agreements Germany was in breach of EU law. Once again, as with *Viking* and *Laval*,[130] many commentators doubted whether the balance had truly been struck between the economic and the social rights. This issue is discussed in more detail in Chapter 5.

D. THE RIGHT TO TAKE COLLECTIVE ACTION

1. INTRODUCTION

So far this chapter has focused on collective bargaining. The corollary of collective bargaining is collective action: without the realistic threat of industrial action there is little incentive on employers to engage in collective bargaining, a point expressly recognized in the first Recital of the Monti II proposal.[131] Collective action can take a variety of forms. While strikes are the most obvious expression of conflict, industrial action can also include overtime bans, go-slows, a work-to-rule, withdrawal of co-operation, sit-ins, and picketing. Workers may also refuse to handle products made by a firm in a dispute (blacking) to support workers of that firm or they might go on strike to support workers in this firm (sympathy industrial action). Collective action is not necessarily one-sided: management can lock out workers, the reverse of a strike, dismiss workers or bring in others to do the strikers' jobs (blacklegging). These workers may be employed by a subsidiary or an agency[132] located elsewhere in the Union and, exercising their right of free movement, drafted in to assist the employer. More drastically, the employer may decide to close the plant and/or relocate the business.

---

[128] Ibid, para. 45.   [129] Ibid, para. 52.

[130] Case C-438/05 *Viking* [2007] ECR I-10779 and Case C-341/05 *Laval v. Svenska Byggnadsarbetareförbundet* [2007] ECR I-11767. For discussion, see S. Deakin, 'The Lisbon Treaty, the *Viking* and *Laval* judgments and the financial crisis: In Search of New Foundations for Europe's "Social Market Economy"' in Bruun (ed) previously, at n. 100.

[131] COM(2012) 130.

[132] Although cf. Recital 20 of the Agency Work Directive 2008/104 (OJ [2008] L327/9) considered in Ch. 9: 'The provisions of this Directive on restrictions or prohibitions on temporary agency work are without prejudice to national legislation or practices that prohibit workers on strike being replaced by temporary agency workers'.

2. THE RIGHT TO STRIKE

2.1. Recognizing the right to strike

The right to strike is recognized in a number of international economic and social rights instruments but it is not expressly recognized by Article 11(1) of the European Convention on Human Rights.[133] It has been only gradually that the Court of Human Rights has read a recognition of the right to strike into Article 11. In *National Union of Belgian Police*[134] the European Court of Human Rights relied on the phrase 'for the protection of his interests' in Article 11(1) to hold that freedom of association included the rights that were 'indispensable for the effective enjoyment' or 'necessarily inherent elements' of trade union freedom. It said that Article 11 therefore also 'safeguards the freedom to protect the occupational interests of trade union members by trade union action, the conduct and development of which the Contracting States must both permit and make possible'.[135]

However, the scope of collective action that can be taken to protect those interests under the European Convention was far from clear. Given the Court of Human Rights' sensitivity to the social and political issues involved in achieving a proper balance between the respective interests of labour and management, and given the wide degree of divergence between the domestic systems in this field, it has given the Contracting States a wide margin of appreciation.[136] That said, in *UNISON* v. *UK* the Court of Human Rights did expressly recognize the significance of strikes to trade unions,[137] albeit without actually declaring that Article 11 included a right to strike. It said that '[w]hile the ability to strike represents one of the most important means by which trade unions can fulfil [the function of protecting the occupational interests of their members], there are others'.[138] However, when, in *Wilson and Palmer*, the Court repeated this phrase, the language had changed to become '[t]he grant of the *right* to strike, while it may be subject to regulation, represents one of the most important of the means by which the State may secure a trade union's freedom to protect its members' occupational interests'.[139] This came very close to the European Court of Human Rights recognizing the right to strike.

In *UNISON* the trade union had called a strike by its members working in University College London Hospital (UCLH) to protest about the fact that, with the transfer of the hospital's staff to a Private Finance Initiative consortium, the hospital would not enter

---

[133] *UNISON* v. *United Kingdom*, judgment of 10 January 2002, [2002] IRLR 497, para. 35: 'There is no express inclusion of a right to strike or an obligation on employers to engage in collective bargaining. At most, Article 11 may be regarded as safeguarding the freedom of trade union members to protect the occupational interests of their members.'

[134] *National Union of Belgian Police* v. *Belgium*, 27 October 1975, Eur. Ct HR Rep., Series A, No. 19 (1975), para. 39.

[135] Ibid., para. 40.

[136] See, e.g. *Schettini* v. *Italy*, Application no. 29529/95, judgment of 9 November 2000, under heading 2.

[137] It expressed similar sentiments in *Schmidt and Dahlström*, judgment of 6 February 1976, Eur. Ct. H.R. Rep., Series A, No. 21 (1976), para. 36.

[138] Ibid.   [139] Para. 45.

into a contractual arrangement with the consortium guaranteeing the maintenance of the terms and conditions of employment of the transferred staff for 30 years on the same terms as the non-transferred staff. The employers successfully obtained an interlocutory injunction from the High Court restraining the strike, on the grounds that it was unlikely that the union would succeed at trial in establishing immunity from tort liability for the strike action. While the Court of Human Rights found that the prohibition on the strike was a restriction on UNISON's power to protect the occupational interests of its members and therefore disclosed a restriction on the freedom of association guaranteed by Article 11(1),[140] the restriction could be justified under Article 11(2) (considered above). The restriction was prescribed by law,[141] pursued the legitimate aim of protecting the 'rights of others' (i.e. the employer, UCLH, whose ability to carry out its functions effectively, including securing contracts with other bodies, would be interfered with),[142] and was proportionate (the union's members were not at any immediate risk of detriment or of being left defenceless against future attempts to downgrade pay or conditions).[143]

Most recently, the new dawn signalled by *Demir*, was confirmed in *Enerji Yapi-Yol Sen*.[144] Turkey prohibited public sector employees from taking part in a national one-day strike to persuade the government to engage in collective bargaining. Members of the trade union who ignored the prohibition were disciplined and the union brought the case to the European Court of Human Rights, alleging that the ban on strikes interfered with their right to form and join trade unions as guaranteed under Article 11. While the Court acknowledged that the right to strike was not absolute and could be subject to certain conditions and restrictions, it held that a ban applied to all public servants was too wide a restriction. The Court held that the disciplinary action was 'capable of discouraging trade union members and others from exercising their legitimate right to take part in such one-day strikes or other actions aimed at defending their members' interests' and amounted to a threat to rights guaranteed under Article 11. The strike ban was not in response to a 'pressing social need' and the Turkish government had thus failed to justify the need for the impugned restriction in a democratic society.

In some human rights instruments, such as Article 6 of the ESC 1961 and, more importantly for our purposes, Article 28 of the EU Charter of Fundamental Rights, the right to strike is expressly linked to collective bargaining. Article 28 provides that workers and employers have the right to negotiate and conclude collective agreements 'and, in cases of conflicts of interests, to take collective action to defend their interests, including strike action'. Linking collective bargaining and strikes in this way emphasizes that the primary purpose of a strike is to put pressure on the employer in the course of

---

[140] Paras. 36–7.   [141] Para. 38.   [142] Para. 39.   [143] Para. 42.

[144] *Enerji Yapi-Yol Sen* v. *Turkey*, Application no. 68959/01 [2009] ECHR 2251. This case concerned a complaint brought by a trade union; for the Court's position on the situation where the applicant is an individual, see e.g. *Danilenkov* v. *Russia*, application No. 67336/01, judgment of 30 July 2009 and *Saime Özcam* v. *Turkey*, application no 22943/04, judgment of 15 September 2009, discussed in Ewing and Hendy, previously, at n. 33.

negotiations over matters that can be collectively bargained, such as pay,[145] a link which was underlined by the facts of *Enerji Yapi-Yol Sen* and recognized by the Court in *Wilson and Palmer*. There the Court of Human Rights said:

> the essence of a voluntary system of collective bargaining is that it must be possible for a trade union which is not recognised by an employer to 'take steps including, if necessary industrial action, with a view to persuading the employer to enter into collective bargaining with it on those issues which the union believes are important for its members' interests.[146]

These observations highlight the structural imbalance in European-level collective bargaining where the ETUC cannot realistically threaten industrial action to persuade BusinessEurope/UEAPME and CEEP to engage in collective bargaining.

2.2. The 'right' or 'freedom' to strike

Article 13 of the Community Social Charter 1989 recognizes the 'right' to 'resort to *collective action* in the event of a conflict of interests' (emphasis added). This includes the '*right* to strike, subject to obligations arising under national regulations and collective agreements' (emphasis added).[147] In *Wilson and Palmer* the Court of Human Rights also emphasized the right to strike. It said that:

> The grant of the right to strike, while it may be subject to regulation, represents one of the most important of the means by which the state may secure a trade union's freedom to protect its members' commercial interests.[148]

Consistent with the Romano-Germanic tradition, the 1989 Community Social Charter, and less clearly, the EU Charter, recognize the *right* to strike, as opposed to the Anglo-Saxon *freedom* to strike.[149] Freedom to strike means that the strike is legally permitted but no special privileges are granted: the strike is tolerated, but not privileged, and the legal limits of the strike are dictated by the general legal order. The right to strike, by contrast, means that the legal order of the state must take precautions to ensure the exercise of the right and so the strike is privileged. This demonstrates that the legal order evaluates the pursuit of collective interests more highly than the individual obligations arising from the contract of employment. The importance of this right, and the recognition of the inequality of bargaining power between workers and employers, has meant that the right to strike is expressly recognized in the constitutions of many Member States.

In most countries the right to strike belongs to the employees who organize their interests collectively. Individual action is generally excluded. By contrast, in the UK the

---

[145] On the other hand, it also means that strikes not directly linked to collective bargaining, such as political strikes, are not permitted.

[146] Para. 46.

[147] For a full discussion of this issue, see T. Novitz, *International and European Protection of the Right to Strike: a Comparative Study of Standards set by the International Labour Organization, the Council of Europe and the European Union* (OUP, Oxford, 2003).

[148] Para. 45.

[149] R. Birk, previously, at n. 76. The discussion that follows draws on this chapter. See additionally B. Wedderburn, 'The Right to Strike: Is There a European Standard?', in Wedderburn, previously, at n. 3.

right to strike does not exist as such, but, subject to certain stringent conditions, trade unions are protected by immunities established by law when their members take certain forms of industrial action. These same immunities now do provide some protection for individual employees but they are likely to breach their individual employment contracts by taking any form of industrial action and can, in certain circumstances, be dismissed as a result. By contrast, in most Romano-Germanic countries, the contract of employment is suspended during the strike. Lock-outs do not enjoy the same protection as the right or freedom to strike.

2.3. The right to strike and Union law

Article 153(5) TFEU expressly excludes Union competence (at least under Article 153 TFEU) in respect of the right to strike or the right to impose lock-outs. Thus, the Union will not be legislating on this basis. On the other hand, as we have seen, Advocate General Jacobs suggested in his opinion in *Albany*[150] that the collective right to take action was a fundamental right.[151] Later he added: 'In my view, the right to take collective action in order to protect occupational interests in so far as it is indispensable for the enjoyment of freedom of association is also protected by [Union] law'.[152] He said this was significant because any impairment of the substance of the right, even in the public interest, might be unlawful.[153]

This issue was acknowledged in Council Regulation No. 2679/98[154] which, as we saw above, provided that the intervention mechanism to safeguard free trade in the single market was not to be 'interpreted as affecting in any way the exercise of fundamental rights, as recognised in Member States, including the right or freedom to strike'.[155] This Regulation also provided the justification for the European Parliament to insert into its revised proposal for a Directive on services an equivalent 'Monti' clause[156] and again in the Macro-economic Surveillance Regulation,[157] and now in the proposed Monti II Regulation.[158]

Most significantly for the EU was the express recognition for the first time in *Viking* and *Laval* of the right to strike as a general principle of EU law. The Court noted that 'the right to take collective action, including the right to strike, is recognised both by various international instruments which the Member States have signed or cooperated in, such as the European Social Charter, signed at Turin on 18 October 1961—to which, moreover, express reference is made in Article [151 TFEU (ex 136 EC)]—and Convention No 87 concerning Freedom of Association and Protection of the Right to Organise' and by instruments developed by those Member States at Union level or in the context

---

[150] Case C-67/96 [1999] ECR I-5751.   [151] Para. 139.   [152] Para. 159.
[153] Case C-280/93 *Germany* v. *Council* [1994] ECR I-4973, paras. 78 and 87; cf. paras. 162 and 163 in Case C-67/96 *Albany* [1999] ECR I-5751.   [154] OJ [1998] L337/8.
[155] Reg. 2679/98 was accompanied by a Resolution of the Council and representatives of the Member States of 7 December 1998 on the free movement of goods (OJ [1998] L337/10).
[156] Art 1(7) of Dir. 2006/123 OJ [2006] L376/36.
[157] Regulation 1176/2011 OJ [2011] L306/25.   [158] COM(2012) 130.

of the EU, such as the Social Charter 1989 and the Charter of Fundamental Rights.[159] It continued that:[160]

> Although the right to take collective action, including the right to strike, must therefore be recognised as a fundamental right which forms an integral part of the general principles of [Union] law the observance of which the Court ensures, the exercise of that right may none the less be subject to certain restrictions. As is reaffirmed by Article 28 of the Charter of Fundamental Rights of the European Union, those rights are to be protected in accordance with [Union] law and national law and practices.

Thus there is a right to strike at EU level but it is subject to the limitations laid down by (1) national law (e.g. balloting and notice requirements) and (2) EU law. Those EU limits are significant. As was discussed in Chapter 5, the Court has said the right to take collective action under Union law is justified only where jobs or conditions of employment are jeopardized or under serious threat, and collective action is the last resort. This prompts Ewing and Hendy to talk of the 'disembowelling' of the right to strike in *Viking*.[161] The limits also appear to rule out any possibility of the development of a transnational right to strike.

The tantalizing question is whether the decision in *Demir* and *Enerji Yapi-Yol Sen* will have any long-term consequences for the EU, particularly when it accedes to the European Convention. The answer may well be yes. The Court of Human Rights reached its decision based on a 'pure' human rights reading of the Convention. In other words, it was and is not operating under the potentially conflicting imperatives of creating a 'social market economy'. Thus the Court of Human Rights adopted a traditional 'human rights' reading of Article 11. It established that (1) prohibiting the strike breaches the fundamental (social) right, thereby requiring (2) the defendant (the employer/state) to justify the breach and show that any breach is proportionate. Thus, the starting point of Court of Human Right's approach is the legality of the strike action. By contrast, the Court of Justice's approach in *Viking*, while also couched in the language of rights, adopts a different starting point:[162] (1) the strike action constitutes a restriction on free movement which then has to be (2) justified by the trade union which also must show that the strike action is proportionate. The criticism of *Viking* is that, despite the talk of balancing of the economic rights with social rights, the one-sided *Säger* analysis adopted by the Court, starting from the premise of the illegality of the strike action, inevitably led to a finding that the economic right to freedom of establishment and free movement of services prevailed over the right to strike. This prompts Ewing and Hendy to conclude that:

> It is difficult then to see how the ECtHR could avoid upholding Article 11 and the right to collective bargaining and to strike over the business freedoms contained in what are now Articles 49 and 56 of the TFEU. And so issues would bat to and fro between the two courts in a titanic battle of the juristocrats, each vying for supremacy in the European legal order, one determined to impale trade union rights on the long lance of economic freedom and the other subordinating economic freedom to the modest demands of human rights and constitutionalism.

---

[159] Para. 43.   [160] Para. 44.   [161] Previously, at n. 33, 8.
[162] This is considered further in Ch. 5.

While, at first glance, the Monti II proposal[163] does not appear to offer a way out of this structural dilemma, it was argued in Chapter 5 that, in fact, a careful reading of the proposed Regulation, combined with the recitals and explanatory memorandum, provides scope for a pro-human rights understanding of the Regulation.

3. OTHER TYPES OF COLLECTIVE ACTIVITY

If primary industrial action (action taken employees against their employer (A) with whom they are in dispute) is, in principle, unlawful since it is a restriction on free movement, then secondary, or sympathy, industrial action (action taken by employees against their employer (B) with whom they are not in dispute but intended to put pressure on the employer (A)) is also likely to be a restriction on freedom of movement. This can be seen in *Viking*.[164] Not only did the Finnish Seaman's Union (FSU) threaten to take industrial action but so did ITF, as part of its campaign against flags of convenience (FOCs). The primary objectives of this policy were, on the one hand, to establish a genuine link between the flag of the ship and the nationality of the owner and, on the other, to protect and enhance the conditions of seafarers on FOC ships. ITF considered that a vessel is registered under a flag of convenience where the beneficial ownership and control of the vessel was found to lie in a State other than the State of the flag. In accordance with the ITF policy, only unions established in the State of beneficial ownership had the right to conclude collective agreements covering the vessel concerned. The FOC campaign was enforced by boycotts and other solidarity actions amongst workers.[165]

FSU sent an email to ITF which referred to the plan to reflag the *Rosella*. The email further stated that 'the *Rosella* was beneficially owned in Finland and that FSU therefore kept the right to negotiate with Viking'. FSU asked ITF to pass this information on to all affiliated unions and to request them not to enter into negotiations with Viking. ITF then sent a circular to its affiliates asking them to refrain from entering into negotiations with Viking. The affiliates were expected to follow this recommendation because of the principle of solidarity between trade unions and the sanctions which they could face if they failed to comply with that circular. The Court ruled that in relation to the collective action seeking to ensure the implementation of the policy pursued by ITF, where that policy resulted in shipowners being prevented from registering their vessels in a state other than that of which the beneficial owners of those vessels are nationals, the restrictions on freedom of establishment could not be objectively justified.[166] The Court then considered whether the policy could be justified on the grounds of improving seafarers' terms and conditions of employment, a point the Court accepted in principle.[167] However, the Court noted, with apparent approval, Viking's criticism that ITF's policy was undiscriminating: solidarity action was taken in respect of any FOC situation, even where the vessel was registered in a State which guaranteed workers a higher level of social protection than they would enjoy in the first State.[168] In such a situation, the Court hinted, the solidarity action would be disproportionate.[169]

---

[163] COM(2012) 130.   [164] Case C-438/05 *Viking* [2007] ECR I-10779.   [165] Para. 8.
[166] Para. 88.   [167] Para. 90.   [168] Para. 89.   [169] Para. 90.

The Court was also critical of the extent of the collective action taken in *Laval*[170] in order to persuade Laval to sign the collective agreement. The Court set it out in some detail:

- In November there was blockading ('blockad') of the Vaxholm building site consisting of preventing the delivery of goods onto the site, placing pickets and prohibiting Latvian workers and vehicles from entering the site (Laval asked the police for assistance but they explained that since the collective action was lawful under national law they were not allowed to intervene or to remove physical obstacles blocking access to the site[171]).

- In December the collective action directed against Laval intensified when Elektrikerna initiated sympathy action. That measure had the effect of preventing Swedish undertakings belonging to the organization of electricians' employers from providing services to Laval.

- In January other trade unions announced sympathy actions, consisting of a boycott of all Laval's sites in Sweden, with the result that Laval was no longer able to carry out its activities in Sweden.

While, as we saw in Chapter 5 most of the case turned on an interpretation of the Posted Workers Directive, the Court found that because the collective action could not be justified, the question of proportionality did not arise.

4. PREVENTION AND SETTLEMENT OF DISPUTES

Most Member States, with the exception of the UK and Ireland, draw a distinction between disputes over conflicts of interests and disputes over conflicts of rights.[172] While disputes over conflicts of rights concern the interpretation and application of existing contractual clauses, disputes over conflicts of interests relate to changes in the establishment of collective rules and require the conflicting economic interest to be reconciled with a view to reaching a solution on the basis of legal or collective procedures. In principle, strikes are permitted to resolve conflicts of interests between labour and management, but the courts, especially the labour courts, usually decide disputes concerning conflicts of rights.

---

[170] Case C–341/05 *Laval* [2007] ECR I–11767.

[171] Laval also spoke to the liaison office identified under the Posted Workers Directive to assist companies providing services. The Court noted that 'the liaison office's head of legal affairs informed Laval that it was required to apply the provisions to which the law on the posting of workers refers, that it was for management and labour to agree on wage issues, that the minimum requirements under the collective agreements also applied to foreign posted workers, and that, if a foreign employer was having to pay double contributions, the matter could be brought before the courts. In order to ascertain what provisions under the agreements were applicable, Laval had to speak to management and labour in the sector concerned'.

[172] See generally R. Blanpain, 'Prevention and Settlement of Collective Labour Disputes in the EEC Countries', Parts I and II (1972) 1 *ILJ* 74 and 143.

Article 13(2) of the Community Social Charter 1989 (but not the EU Charter of Fundamental Rights) encourages the use of alternative dispute resolution:

> In order to facilitate the settlement of industrial disputes the establishment and utilisation at the appropriate levels of conciliation, mediation and arbitration procedures should be encouraged in accordance with national practice.

Member States recognize both judicial and non-judicial mechanisms for preventing and resolving collective disputes. Conciliation, mediation, and arbitration are the most common forms of non-judicial or third party intervention. Conciliation is where a third party encourages the parties to reach their own agreement. By contrast, in mediation a third party hears the dispute and makes formal but non-binding recommendations for resolving it. Finally, in arbitration a third party hears the dispute and makes a binding decision.

Conciliation and mediation may arise from, and have their legal base in, the obligatory part of the collective agreement. This suggests that the parties themselves are primarily responsible for finding a solution to their conflicts. This is closely related to the principles behind the peace obligation. Government mediation and conciliation services are available in most Member States, but in most cases they perform a secondary role.[173] Arbitration, by contrast, imposes a solution on the parties from outside and so interferes with the autonomy of the Social Partners.[174] For this reason it is not permitted in some Member States.

E. CONCLUSIONS

The enormous difficulties faced by the EU in enacting measures relating to collective labour law bears testimony to Kahn-Freund's observation that 'individual labour law lends itself to transplantation very much more easily than...collective labour law. Standards of protection and rules on substantive terms of employment can be imitated—rules on collective bargaining, on the closed shop, on trade unions, on strikes, cannot'.[175] The experience of the ILO and the European Social Charter is similar: according to Kahn-Freund, 'nothing could more clearly demonstrate the knowledge of the draftsman that collective bargaining institutions and rules are untransplantable'.[176] This, he attributes to a different 'habitat of industrial relations' where the relations between management and labour are organized under the influence of strong political traditions, traditions connected with the role played by organizations on both sides as political pressure groups promoting legislation, and as rule-making agencies through the procedures of collective bargaining.[177]

---

[173] Commission, previously, at n. 75, SEC (89) 1137. See additionally Art. 3 of the Monti II proposal: COM(2012) 130.

[174] The right to 'autonomy' in collective bargaining was recognized by AG Trstenjak in Case C–155/10 *Williams v. British Airways* [2011] ECR I–000, para. 65.

[175] 'Uses and Misuses of Comparative Law' (1974) 37 *MLR* 1, 21.

[176] Ibid., 22.   [177] Ibid., 20.

That said, at EU level, intersectoral and sectoral collective bargaining has enjoyed some success, and the recognition of freedom of association and the right to strike as fundamental rights has helped to protect the integrity of national systems of labour law from the full rigours of competition law; the language of social rights has done much less to protect national rules on collective action against the force of supreme economic law. So long as the four freedoms remain benefit from the full force of the supremacy of EU law, national labour traditions remain vulnerable to attack.

INDEX

Omnibus Edition — Contents

THE CANADIANS
Biographies of a Nation

The making of a well-resourced documentary is difficult in the contemporary television world. Broadcasters are starving for revenue, so producers are usually obliged to negotiate with at least three of them in different countries in order to pay for the production. Each of those broadcasters will want a different approach, and sometimes the differences are irreconcilable. Even after securing a collective agreement on a treatment, the producer will often be given a bewildering bundle of contradictory notes when the first rough cut is shown to the broadcasters.[1] Many of the young men and women making program decisions at the new satellite and cable services have never written, produced, or directed anything themselves, and often they seem more interested in showing off their authority than in nourishing the vision of the filmmaker. For independent producers trying to make honest, responsible documentaries, this world of "international co-production" is often neither convivial nor creative.

What a heartening contrast, then, was the making of the sixty-five one-hour biographical documentaries from which this book is derived. *The Canadians* was commissioned by a single visionary broadcaster, History Television.[2] Its funding was secured by a substantial grant from Charles and Andrea Bronfman's CRB Foundation (later Historica). It was produced through one company, Great North Productions of Edmonton (now part of Alliance Atlantis), under one executive producer, Patricia Phillips, herself an able writer and director.

The series grew along a clear and definable path, a path mapped out over the past sixty years or so by the pioneers Robert Flaherty and

---

1 Ironically, although they are known as *co-producers*, in reality they are *co-purchasers*. The word *broadcaster* in Canada and the UK is often used to refer to newsreaders, hosts, and interviewers. In the US, and at the business level, the word refers to the proprietors of stations, networks, cable services, or other broadcasting undertakings. I use it here in that latter sense.

2 It was entitled *Faces of Canada* in its first year.

Humphrey Jennings in Britain, by Joris Ivens in Holland, and by Eisenstein, John Huston, Frank Capra, and all their progeny in this wonderful young form—the documentary film.[3] A great deal of the mapping was done here in Canada, at first by the National Film Board, which began as a wartime propaganda machine under the Scottish director John Grierson and then evolved into a world-renowned innovator and standard setter in independent documentary. The arrival of television in Canada in 1952 created a productive and competitive spirit between the young documentary makers at the NFB and those at the CBC, among them Allan King and Douglas Leiterman.

The CBC's filmmakers, not surprisingly, showed a more journalistic edge. They were less tolerant of the spirit of advocacy that is still an element in much of the NFB's important work. The NFB remained a haven for outrageous experiment, while the CBC's producers, both in-house and independent, had to be more concerned with intelligibility and engaging a wide audience. The two nourished each other. The whole craft is richer for that willingness of the NFB to encourage its filmmakers to reach out into the unknown, with such daring experiments as Norman McLaren's animation created by painting and scratching directly on the surface of the physical film.

As the American National Educational Television service evolved into PBS, Canadian documentary filmmakers and their broadcasters found a modest secondary market for their work.[4] Perhaps just as importantly, they now had some stimulating competition. Edward R. Murrow at CBS had already made enormous strides in current affairs and journalistic documentary. American pioneers, such as Leacock and Pennebaker[5] and the Maysles brothers,[6] soon pushed out into the far

3 Capra, Huston, and Eisenstein, renowned as feature film directors, all made distinguished documentaries, as did Lindsay Anderson. Capra's and Huston's films were sponsored by the US government as propaganda. This backfired in at least one case when one of Huston's films was accused of being "anti-war." There has often been a fairly narrow dividing line between disinterested documentary and propaganda. Flaherty's last and very beautiful film, *Louisiana Story*, was commissioned by the oil industry to calm public fears about environmental destruction. In the view of many modern critics, it is a reprehensible and dishonest piece of flackery.

4 The act creating The Corporation for Public Broadcasting was passed in 1967. NET held on until late 1970, but finally yielded to the pressure from Washington. PBS came into being soon after, starting with WNET, Channel 13 in New York.

5 *Don't Look Now*, a cinéma-vérité film about Bob Dylan, was their breakthrough.

6 They first attracted attention with a controversial and pioneering film on abortion. Their films on the artist Christo are classics.

reaches of cinéma-vérité, taking the camera unobtrusively into raw Life-As-It-Is-Being-Lived.

Although Vancouver director Allan King (*Skid Row, Warrendale, A Married Couple*) led the way in this kind of filmmaking, with NFB pioneers Roman Kroitor and Wolf Koenig[7] close behind, it was the Americans who aggressively spread the style and won international acclaim that helped and stimulated us all. Later, Ken Burns's series *Civil War* for PBS, and those on jazz and baseball, would set new stylistic traditions. Among other things, they confirmed the power of the still photograph as an element within a motion picture documentary.

Advances in style were often linked to technical change. When I made my first full-length documentary in the spring of 1958—a portrait of a maximum-security prison—the camera was a hefty Auricon with 1,200-foot reels of 16mm film. The massive construction of brown, pebble-grained aluminum needed a heavy tripod. Sound was recorded on 16mm magnetic tape, the recording machine was even bigger than the camera and hard-wired to the Auricon, and both were driven off the electric mains (the amplifier was still based on power-hungry incandescent tubes). The gear was virtually immovable unless put on a cart or mobile boom, and its range was still limited by having to be plugged into the wall.

Within a year or two, the NFB had built a quarter-inch sound recorder that still had sprocket holes but was much smaller than the 16mm machine. This yielded to the first Nagras, with ordinary quarter-inch tape (the first I used was hand-wound like an old Victrola). Then along came transistors. So you could get off the mains and go for a long time on a single battery charge. Those early transistors would die if you took them outdoors in temperatures much below freezing, but within months that was fixed. Bob Crone and John Foster in Toronto and Wolf Koenig at the NFB began stripping down the Auricon, replacing those bulky 1,200-foot rolls with 100- or 400-footers. Foster substituted balsa wood for metal in the body. Cameras and recorders became smaller and lighter and less obtrusive.

Soon there was a crystal like those that regulate watches. One in

7 Along with Graeme Ferguson, they would go on to invent the system now known as Imax.

the camera and an identical one in the sound recorder kept the two running at the same speed with no need for a connecting cable. I remember the excitement of driving up FDR Drive, the parkway that runs along the East River in Manhattan, with the cameraman in my car as we filmed a conversation taking place in a car beside us. The sound-man was crouched out of sight with the interviewer and the subject in the back seat of that car, and the two unconnected machines were perfectly in sync, thanks to those crystals.

By the time *The Canadians* got underway in 1996, the filmmakers and technicians that Great North assembled were working within a rich body of tradition and experiment. With decisive and consistent judgment and support from Norm Bolen and Sydney Suissa at History Television, we were able to quickly choose our subjects, get the outlines or treatments approved, and make maximum use of our modest budgets. We didn't have to reshoot or re-edit to respond to the daft and juvenile whims of some inexperienced broadcast executive who shrinks from such considerations as meaningfulness or engagement (these will "just lose us viewers") and wants everything to be dumb, loud, and fast-paced.

The result is a body of sixty-five one-hour television documentaries, at least fifty of which are "distinguished": several Columbus Awards; ribbon finalists in the CAB Awards; a finalist in the New York Festival; a bronze at Flagstaff; a special Jury Award at Yorkton; two golds at the Houston Worldfest; the 2002 Sovereign Award; three Gemini nominations; and seven AMPIA nominations and one win.[8] The documentaries have been seen by hundreds of thousands of Canadians, and they continue to occupy a substantial position in the History Television schedule in rebroadcast. Work is underway to distill these hours into six- to seven-minute classroom lesson starters, and there is growing interest in resuming production of the full-length documentaries.

Over the past three hundred years, novels have preserved and conveyed a vivid sense not so much of the great themes and issues of the societies that gave them birth, but of the texture of life that in the

8 The Alberta Motion Picture Industry Association.

4

end is what a culture is all about: the colour of the wallpaper and how people greet each other and blow their noses and make love and eat dinner. Similarly, biographies convey a richly woven fabric of their subjects' culture and mores. When *The Canadians* books began to come out, a fourth printing was needed within six months, and there are now 50,000 copies in print.

On the platform, I often say that the first and most important historical question is "Mommy, where did I come from?" That always gets a laugh, but it's not just a biological joke. It's the beginning of an expanding set of circular ripples of questioning: it's an interrogative way of exploring in order to understand our history, *to understand where we came from.* That's what these biographical documentaries do while telling immediate and compelling personal stories at the same time. And, as the numbers above suggest, Canadians are hungry for those stories and for that historical texture. The commonplace that holds that Canadians are both dull and uninterested in their own stories is no longer true, if ever it was.

Warm thanks as always to Patricia Phillips, who caused these documentaries to happen, and to Hugh Graham, who wrote much of the third volume: both are superb collaborators.

◄ T H E ►

CANADIANS

Biographies of a Nation

VOLUME I

Patrick Watson

PERCY WILLIAMS
Running Out of Time

On a grey afternoon in 1984, a frail man in dark pyjamas and bare feet walked into the bathroom of his apartment in West Vancouver. Painfully, slowly, he put first one foot then the other over the side of the empty bathtub, and stepped into it. A slight man, five-foot six, 125 pounds, moving slowly.

An old man with no family, no friends, no prospects; alone, sick, poor, out of luck, at the end of his road. In his right hand a six-shot .32 calibre revolver.

He had heard a lot of pistol shots in his life, this man. He had heard them in Vancouver, in Seattle, in Hamilton, Ontario, in New York, and perhaps best of all in Amsterdam, at the Olympic games there when he was only eighteen years old. For him those pistol shots had almost always signalled the start of a race he was going to win.

Not this one. There is reason — as you will see at the end of his story — to speculate whether just at the last moment he may have felt a twinge of irony, maybe even of some dark kind of humour, if he reflected on the fact that those shots in Amsterdam had started him on two brief runs, totalling less than thirty-three seconds — two runs that would earn him the title The Fastest Man in the World. But now he was quite slow in his movements. His shoulder hurt grievously as the hand came up. This pistol shot would be the last sound he would ever hear.

He was seventy-four years old.

His name was Percy Williams. He had grown up in a Vancouver that was mad for track and field. It was also a Vancouver where people who got married were expected to stay together, and if they did not they were expected not to talk about it. Percy's mother and father were Dorothy, known as Dot, who took tickets at the Capitol theatre, a vivacious good-looker who hung out with theatre people, and Fred, an electrical engineer who did not like theatre people.

Dot used to invite actors and their friends home for elaborate supper parties that drove Fred nuts. Perhaps Percy drove Fred a little bit nuts too, with his obsessive training for the 100-yard dash. But Dot liked Percy's running, and Fred probably quarrelled with her over that as well, and after a while they broke up. When they finally divorced, Percy of course stayed with Dot. In fact, Percy Williams would end up living most of his adult life with his mother. She kept on encouraging him to run.

Perhaps he associated the running with his family's coming apart, for it seems that Percy, even as he realized he was getting to be very good at it, didn't really like running very much. This is not uncommon with athletes. In many cases it is because, having had their talent discovered by a coach or a parent, they have been put under a lot of pressure to prove themselves — not because the young athlete wanted this kind of life, but because some adult wanted to bask in the glory of the kid's success. That kind of pressure was part of Percy Williams' problem with the running, and maybe the family disputes were another part. But there was one aspect of the track that he did like: winning, and he won a lot. And so he kept on at it. Once Bob Granger saw him run in a physical education class at the high school, it almost seemed that there would be no way out of it, even if he came to hate it completely. Bob Granger was that kind of coach.

He was not, however, a professional coach, not even a physical education teacher; he was the janitor in the high school. But he was an amateur coach. He loved coaching runners. As janitor he had the run of the school and he used to hang around the PE classes when they were doing track and field; nobody minded, he was just the janitor. He would watch out for talent he thought he could apply his theories to.

He had read a lot about how great athletes develop, and he had some theories, and he was looking out for the kind of runner who would allow him to turn his theories into practice: medal-winning practice.

Granger already had a young runner named Wally Scott who was good, really good, but not good enough to stop him looking for talent, visiting those PE classes, keeping his eyes peeled. And when he first saw Percy Williams run, this slight kid with the skinny arms and legs and the big Adam's apple and the intense, slightly pouting look as he knelt into the holes you used to dig for starting from, he must have said to himself, "This is the one."

And he would be right. Bob Granger and Percy Williams became a team that would astound the world.

Granger not only knew runners, he knew what they ran on. He thought about all the conditions of the track. Soft tracks, wet tracks. Grass, cinders, clay. Wind speed, air temperature, humidity, slopes and curves. Everything he did on the track was part of an integrated strategy. He did not work from hunches; he had strategy.

For example, the American coaches in those days were obsessed with the stopwatch, with record-setting times, because that was what made the headlines, a world's record for the 100 metres at the Olympics, say, of 11.1 seconds. But unlike the American coaches, Bob Granger didn't run his boys against the clock. He ran them against other runners.

He would tell his runners something like this: "You are there to beat the other men, beat them in the final. Don't try to take the lead out of the starting pits. Run beside them. Let them get tired setting the pace and worrying about you. Then put on the steam at the end and beat them in the final, on *that* day, in *those* conditions. Don't even think about the time. Let somebody else worry about the time. It's winning that counts, beating other runners, not beating the clock."

Percy Williams liked beating other runners, so he heard Bob Granger loud and clear. And they became a kind of couple. Bob Granger needed Percy to be the embodiment of his theories. And Percy Williams needed Bob Granger because Percy Williams really liked to win. There was no point running if you couldn't win. And Bob Granger was going to teach him how to win.

Granger would put him up against another very good runner, and set the other boy's starting blocks five yards ahead of Percy's, maybe even ten yards. They used yards in those days, not metres. A yard is just under a metre, .9144 metres to be exact. Percy would run races in metres a little later, in Europe, but here in Vancouver you ran in yards. So the other boy would be given a ten-yard advantage, and Bob

Granger would say, "You have to be ahead of him before you hit the hundred-yard mark. Pace him at first, and learn when it is you have to pull ahead. And then you beat him in the final."

And Percy would do just that.

Bob Granger had dropped Wally Scott by then; he would keep on coaching a number of runners, "My boys," he called them. But from now on, Percy was his Prime Boy.

Bob Granger was a reclusive, difficult man, and Percy Williams was not very comfortable with other people, except his mother. He was really uncomfortable with girls. If other male athletes were partly motivated by the opportunity to impress a girl, the only female whose admiration Percy sought was Dot Williams'. And Dot came through for him. But so did Bob Granger, and although the relationship was a difficult one, for neither the boy athlete nor the coach was good at relationships, in this case they recognized their need for each other.

Historians of the sport say that Percy would have stopped running after high school if it hadn't been for Bob Granger. But Granger knew he had found an authentic and maybe even unique talent. He put Percy in the Vancouver Grand Championships in 1927. Percy was just seventeen.

It is surprising, in a way, that he was running at all. They had told him when he was fifteen that he should definitely not engage in any strenuous activity. The doctors had diagnosed rheumatic fever. Anything that would strain his heart might kill him. But maybe the doctors were wrong, because under Bob Granger's demanding, constant presence, Percy just got stronger and faster, and more and more sure of himself.

That's what a coach does, more than anything else, by the way. He is present. He is a dynamic mirror in which the athlete can search for his strengths and weaknesses, and a constant source of the kind of human contact that says, often silently, "What we are doing together counts; it is meaningful; it will have consequences." Bob Granger was present, and with that presence there was always the strategy. And the object of the strategy was Percy Williams. To win. Not to place or show; to win.

Percy Williams won that Vancouver race, the 100 yards, in ten seconds flat, uphill on a grass track, and Bob Granger was pounding his hands on the fence where he watched, pounding his hands with delight. A few weeks later it was Seattle, the prestigious Seattle championships, and the small-boned, slightly muscled boy won again, 9.9 seconds.

And now it was time for Hamilton, Ontario, a kind of pre-Olympic year meet to take a look at the coming talent. Granger entered Percy, again for the 100 yards.

With Dot's help Percy managed to scrape together the money for train fare. But Bob Granger had no money, and no Dot; so he hired himself on as a dishwasher on the CPR dining car, and that is how he got to Hamilton.

There were tryout heats, just like the Olympics. You ran against other candidates in heat after heat and the winners of each heat would be candidates for the final race, the real race. There was a group of officials who would choose, from among the candidates, whoever they thought promising enough to go on to the finals. The officials were men in straw boaters. They wore blazers, and on the blazers were always badges. So the athletes called them the Badgers. Although the track had only five lanes, the Hamilton Badgers picked six finalists, and then decided to toss a coin to see which of the six would be dropped, and they dropped Percy Williams.

He was too good a sport to quarrel with the Badgers, but he hated them from then on.

The following year, 1928, was different — the real tryouts for the Olympics. Bob Granger knew his boy would qualify. It was Hamilton again. This time there was no nonsense about the number of lanes, and this time — with no surprise to Bob Granger or the increasingly confident young runner — Percy won the trials going home, beat them in the final, and Amsterdam beckoned.

The official coach of the Canadian men's track team was an ex-soldier and high-school teacher named Cap Cornelius. There was no room for the outsider, Bob Granger. Percy and Granger both knew that they had to be together, and Granger persuaded Percy to go on ahead, he, Bob, would find a way. He hired himself onto a cattle boat shovelling manure, the worst job he had ever had, he said; but he was able to get wireless messages, with training advice, to Percy on his boat during the ten-day transatlantic crossing. Bob Granger arrived in Amsterdam a few days after Cap Cornelius had started training the Canadian boys.

Percy was so grumpy, training under a strange coach and fretting about Bob Granger, that Cap Cornelius concluded that the skinny little British Columbian couldn't possibly win anything anywhere. And so when Granger turned up and said he would take over Percy's training, Cornelius was glad to be rid of the wimp.

The American athletes stayed on a luxury liner in the harbour. The European and British athletes mostly stayed in five-star hotels, and so did the Badgers. But the Canadian boys were sent to a crummy two-star hotel. It was down in the red-light district, noisy with traffic and night voices, no place for athletes to get the good, peaceful rest that Granger believed was a key to success. Granger would harass the Amsterdam police in the streets, asking them to try to quiet the crowd down. "We've got Olympic athletes sleeping in there!" Then he would get a blanket and a pillow and bunk down on the floor outside the door of Percy's room, and shush and shoo away anyone who came on the floor making the slightest noise that might wake up his candidate.

In the morning he would waken Percy, and then after breakfast they would go back up to the room and take the mattress off the bed, and put it up against the wall as a stopper. This way Percy could practise his starts in the little room and get up to speed in three or four paces and have something soft to bump into. Thump! Thump! Thump! It echoed throughout the little hotel.

Starts had been Percy's weak point. They couldn't get time on the track to practise as much as they needed, but here in the room, between the two of them they worked out all the tiny little fine-tunings and grace notes of that crucial first second of the race, and Percy's starts became spectacular.

The heats began. The Americans were sure to win, everybody knew that. The Americans would win and the Brits would come second, or third maybe, after the Germans. The Canadians? Well, who cares, really.

Bob Granger applied some more theory. He told Percy, "You don't have to win the heat, you know. If you come in second you go on to the next heat. Just pace your guy and size him up and keep moving up the heats and you'll be okay." And Percy did that, and the Americans always tried to win and some of them tired themselves and had to drop out but Percy did not tire himself, won some heats, came second in others, moved up and up.

And qualified.

The "final" was scheduled for four p.m., July 30. A hot day was forecast but it turned cold. While the other runners were down on the chilly track digging their starting pits, Granger kept Percy back in the tunnel wrapped in a thermal blanket until the very last second, then sent him down, still comfortably warm, to dig his starting pits just in time for the pistol, no shivering, warm and fit and ready to run.

There was a pistol shot that reverberated in memory a long time.

And 10.8 seconds later — this was metres, not yards, so it was equal to almost 110 yards, 109.36132 yards to be exact — 10.8 seconds later a young unknown Canadian had astounded the stadium, his country, the world, by beating them all — the Americans, the British, even the Germans. Almost a record but not quite; that would come later. He stood up there, slight and small, beside a tall powerful black man on one side and a tall powerful white European guy on the other side, and he was the world's champion.

He wrote in his diary, "Well well well I am the world's 100-metre champion. Crushed apples, no more fun running any more."

But in fact there was a lot of fun to come.

First it was Bob Granger who, watching the race from behind the link fence, had this time pounded his hands so hard on that fence that they were bleeding. He didn't seem to notice. He suddenly decided to enter Percy in the 200-metre, four days later. Percy had never run the 200; he was a sprinter. Cap Cornelius was totally against it and so was the Committee.

But it is hard to say no to a coach whose boy has just won gold. So

Percy began to train, and to run the qualifying heats. And a few days later, when the pistol went off, it took him exactly 21.8 seconds to beat them all again, and head for the podium to collect his second gold medal.

The Canadians in Amsterdam went wild. The women's team sent Percy flowers. Those women would set some records themselves that week, and the versatile Bobbie Rosenfeld (see *Part Fifteen*) would make her own gold-medalled mark as a heroine athlete. But it was Percy Williams who was the toast of Amsterdam. Even the British came over and lined up with the Canadians as the Empire against the Yanks. They all wanted to stand in the glow that radiated from The Fastest Man in the World. Then in London, Paris, Dublin, where he ran exhibition races before heading home, the crowds came to gawk and then to cheer.

And so, it seemed, did everybody in Canada. He was mobbed in Quebec City, Montreal, Toronto, Winnipeg. At last we had a national athletic hero, undisputably the best in the world. In the Vancouver Parade Dot and Bob Granger rode with him in the lead car, and even his father Fred showed up, but only in car number six.

The Vancouver sports officials knew that the young star would be wooed by American universities, which had already begun the practice of offering very substantial sports scholarships. There was no counterpart in Canada, so they pledged to raise $25,000 to send him to UBC, and even came up with a gift of $500 for Bob Granger. They also hired Granger to take Percy on the road doing exhibition meets in the States, to build the publicity they would need in order to raise that twenty-five grand. There was no television then, so people who hadn't been to the movies when the newsreels played hadn't seen Percy's win, and the gold medal races had not quite been world's records so the American press had not made much of Percy. The only way to really make him famous was to arrange for people to see him "live."

It was pretty audacious, what they did. They exposed him to almost certain defeat. Granger put him up against the best college athletes across the whole United States, twenty-one races in twenty-two days. He would get up, have lunch, run a race, get on a train, sleep, get up, have lunch, run another race. All of his opponents were fresh; he was running every day. He ran on concrete, which he had never done before, and he ran on boards, also for the first time. He ran one race that was 70 yards, so he had to pace himself radically differently against a champion who always ran 70 yards, and another at 80 yards. And he won and won. Twenty-one races and he won nineteen of them.

Sports historian Bill McNulty now says that the two Percy lost were "flyers," which means that the guys who beat him made false starts, were out of the blocks before the pistol shot but were not called back by the officials, who clearly did not want the Canadian kid to win. McNulty calls it the Tour of Guts.

That had been the summer of 1929. He came home in triumph. He publicly tore up the $25,000 scholarship an American university had just sent, and enrolled at UBC. But Vancouver never did raise their $25,000, only $14,000, which was a lot of money all right, but not what had been promised. And anyway Percy found that university life was not really for him, and at the end of the first year he dropped out. He went to business school and learned how to sell insurance, and got a job doing that, and kept on running.

In August of 1930 he finally set a world's record, the 100 metres in 10.3 seconds. That record would stand for eleven years. In late 1930 he went down to the first ever British Empire games in Hamilton, and told everyone that he was in the top of his form. Perhaps he was, but this time Bob Granger was not with him, and neither was Bob Granger's thermal blanket, and the weather was cold. As he came out of the blocks Percy was still cold. Something was wrong with his left leg. He could sense it coming, and at the 40-metre mark something went snap, a muscle had pulled. It hurt like hell but he kept going. The pain was almost overwhelming but this time he had uncharacteristically pulled into the lead early in the race. He held that lead and he won the race. But something was wrong. He was hurt. He would never win another race. He was the British Empire Victor, and that was a great triumph. But it was his last.

Nobody was ready to believe it was his last, not Granger, not Percy himself, certainly not Vancouver or the Canadian Olympic

Committee, and so of course off he went to Los Angeles for the brilliant, showy 1932 Olympics. Once again there was no money for Bob Granger's travel, and Granger came up with a scam, a kind of lottery, using some of his other athletes to sell the tickets. But the Olympic Committee is said to have found out about this and put the cops on him, and so he was disgraced and never made it to Los Angeles. Percy had to do without him, but even had Bob Granger been there the leg injury from the Hamilton British Empire Games was giving him so much trouble that he never even made it into the finals.

He never raced again.

Percy Williams was probably relieved to be done with it. That is what he said, anyway. He told people he was glad it was over. But not Bob Granger. Granger's nephew Frank, now an old man himself, says that for "Uncle Robbie," it was the end of a dream.

It was also the end of the relationship. They met only once more, on a bus, by accident, in 1948. But they had nothing to do with each other, ever again. Bob Granger could not make a living coaching his boys, so he drifted from menial job to menial job, sweeping parking lots, picking up bottles, living in a little room over a barber shop.

"A beautiful person had lost touch with himself," Frank Granger says. Bob started to drink, and died alone in 1970.

When World War II broke out, Percy had joined the air force and spent much of the war in Saskatchewan training navigators. He came to love airplanes and flying, and maintained that interest for years. He took up horseback riding again, which he had learned with his father. Later he fell in love with golf.

The Vancouver sports establishment had begun to show mixed feelings about the fastest man in the world when Percy came back into civilian life after the war. In 1953 when a local newspaper wanted them to name the new stadium they were building for the Commonwealth Games "The Percy Williams Stadium," the Committee said no. The Badgers again. "He didn't give anything back to track and field," they said. Whatever that meant. So they wouldn't use his name. In the 1960s a Vancouver physician and coach, Doug Clement, put together what would become an annual track meet and got Percy to agree to call it

The Percy Williams Invitational. But Percy disappointed Dr. Clement, showed very little interest in the meet, did not show up at the dinners and press conferences and other publicity events, and generally left a bit of a sour taste all around. So the next year they dropped the name.

George Parkes, who was Percy's chief in the little insurance company where he was now working very diligently and successfully, is inclined to excuse Percy saying that he was actually a very shy person. "Unusual for an insurance salesman," says Parkes, "but he was." You can see it in the photos. The smile of triumph after a win, or in a victory parade or at an awards ceremony, is a wide, appealing smile. It transforms the small, somewhat tight face. But it is not a cocky smile. It is the smile of a man who could, indeed, be quite shy.

Perhaps that had something to do with the drinking. He had discovered golf, and gradually golf replaced flying and horses, and became something of an obsession. He was soon playing three times a week. Although he often refused to have a drink with his boss, George Parkes, saying "I don't do that," in fact he was staying late at the prestigious Capilano Golf and Country Club, where he very much valued his membership, staying late and drinking at the bar. And, worse, drinking alone at home. A lot.

He still lived with and looked after his mother, until she died in her nineties in 1978. He briefly had a girlfriend. They were together a great deal until she despaired of Percy's drinking and told him that he had to make a choice: her or the bottle. Percy chose the latter. So now he had nobody to go home to.

Before long he had no golf club to go to either. He had taken to staying very late in the lounge, and was caught, as a friend kindly put it, "imbibing other people's liquor." They took away his membership in the Capilano, perhaps the only thing that he really cherished any more, besides the drink. He was disgraced. At that point Percy Williams more or less disappeared from view.

In 1982 he had two strokes. They left him weak and in pain. He had bad arthritis in his knees, indeed in all his joints. In 1950 a Canadian Press poll had chosen him the half-century's greatest track athlete, and in 1972 that was upgraded to "Canada's all-time greatest

Olympic athlete." But if that gave him comfort, it was not enough, and so he stepped into that bathtub with one of the guns from his considerable collection. He left no note. As was still occasionally a custom of kindness in the media of those times, no mention was made there of how he died. He had simply . . . died. There is a fine bronze statue of him at the Vancouver Airport. You can see it there.

There are two footnotes. One is that to celebrate his Amsterdam gold medals he had been presented with a symbolic pistol, which he kept all his life, in a collection of guns that in the end became quite big. The one he chose to kill himself with was the Amsterdam gold medal presentation pistol.

The other footnote is that he had donated those Olympic gold medals to the Vancouver Sports Hall of Fame, but within weeks after they went on display, they were stolen and never recovered. Bob Duncan wrote, at the end of his film biography of this great athlete, that Percy Williams "simply shrugged off the loss, and no replacements were ever ordered."

◆ ◆ ◆

Percy Williams: Running Out of Time was written by Robert Duncan and directed by Annie O'Donaghue.

• PART TWO •

RUBY KEELER
The Queen of Nostalgia

Sometimes in the story of a very ordinary person who accomplishes something extraordinary, it is difficult to tell whether circumstance and accident (or "fate," as we once would say) handed that person something which lifted them, all unconscious, to extraordinary heights . . . or if there was a special strength in that person, a strength that somehow remained hidden, even after her accomplishments made her famous and thus the object of great scrutiny and the asking of questions.

In the case of Ruby Keeler, it was so common as to be expected after a while that at the end of her extraordinary life people would say, "But she was really just like everybody else, you know." Here was this kid from Dartmouth, Nova Scotia, who went through New York to Hollywood, made a string of very successful movies, had a near-disastrous marriage to the most prominent entertainer in the world, left him, found her way into a homey marriage and children with a good and uncomplicated and very private man, eventually returning to Broadway and reaching a new level of stardom when she was a sixty-year-old grandmother. Yet people kept saying, "Well, she was really, you know, *ordinary*. There was nothing that *outstanding* about her."

Audiences did not think she was ordinary. When she put on the tap-dancing shoes and came downstage and launched into one of her staccato, thundering numbers, they were rapt, enchanted. They stood and applauded and yelled for more. And yet today the tap-dancing teacher our filmmakers consulted, trying to reach some understanding of this woman's astounding success, could say that, well, compared to say Fred Astaire and Ginger Rogers, with their incredible lightness and flair and *lift*, Ruby Keeler was, well, down-to-earth; there was not that much distance between her shoes and the stage. She had facility, she was "articulate," precise, clean, her whole body was dancing, not just

21

her feet, but measured against their almost faërie lightness and grace she was "down to the ground and earthy and loud."

She herself would say that she was not all that special as a dancer or singer or actress, did not do any of those things all that well.

But they loved her, the audiences. And perhaps it is partly because hers was the art that concealed art. Perhaps she did that thing that, like Bing Crosby's crooning, made everybody out there feel "I could do that, I could sing (dance, tap, act) like that." That must be partly what made guitar playing take off like a rocket with the advent of television in the 1940s and 50s. Suddenly millions of people saw what looked like a very easy way to make music: "I could do that," and guitar playing and, at first, the making and singing of folk songs, and then blues, and then later a genre that we used to call *rock and roll*, became something that just about everybody could do.

But if there was an aspect to the art of Ruby Keeler which demonstrated something like that seeming ease and accessibility, there was also a deep underpinning of something else we'll try to get at in this story of the long and extraordinary life of this Nova Scotian who never forgot her roots.

Like so many Canadians her Irish ancestors had actually intended to end up in the United States of America. But Ralph Hecter Keeler's mother and father had stopped off in Canada and tried to make a life here. Ralph became a butcher in Dartmouth, a successful one by all accounts, and in the early 1900s he married Elenora Nellie Lahey.

Nellie was the daughter of another Irish family, prominent in the Halifax/Dartmouth area. She was seriously Catholic, and she was stunningly beautiful. A photograph of Nellie at the time of her betrothal to Ralph is arresting in its serene grace and subtle sensuality. Ralph looks like a butcher; even in his formal photographs in a pinstriped suit with a watch chain, you can easily see him in his blood-spattered white apron, behind the counter, one hand comfortably up on the glass display case, another caressing a knife or a sharpening "steel," saying, "Sure now, Missus Callaghan, would ye be after tryin' a bit of the pork bellies today, fresh in, good as they come?" Broad shoulders, a broad man, altogether, with a broad smile, and his daughter Ethel Ruby would dote on him for the rest of her life.

Ralph and Nellie had a tiny house at 13 Oak Street, in Dartmouth, now a vacant lot. Their first child was a boy, William, and then on August 25, 1909, Ruby came along, and two years later sister Gertrude. Both Nellie and Ralph worked in a store in Halifax. It was not an easy life, with three young children. There were lots of stories of the great opportunities south of the border, the kind of legends that had brought so many Irish to these shores in the first place, and after a while Ralph and Nellie decided to give it a try.

Not surprisingly, the legend, at first, did not fit the reality. The only job Ralph could find was driving a truck. Their home was a run-down cold water tenement on the east side of Manhattan, where Bill and Ruby and Gertrude hung around in the streets, and soon were joined by Helen and then Anna May and Margie. There was never quite enough money and only barely enough to eat, and hand-me-downs for clothing. Everybody had to help out with everything, but somehow they got along.

One of the somehows was music: particularly singing and tap dancing. That old Irish love of simple music at home was part of the formation of the young Keeler family. Ruby showed such a natural feel for it, especially for rhythm, that one of the nuns who taught her at St. Catherine of Sienna's Catholic school on E. 68th Street, persuaded Nellie that the girl ought to have some training. Nellie scraped together the money to get both Ruby and Bill into Jack Blue's School of Rhythm and Tap. The teaching Sister was right: Ruby did have something special, and before long Jack Blue (there really was a Jack Blue) noticed it too.

Now Jack Blue was not one of your back-room failed stage performers trying to eke out a living teaching kids how to do what he had never really succeeded in; Jack was an impresario with a wide acquaintance in the world of stage musicals. He was Dancing Master to an actor/dancer/singer/producer named George M. Cohan who was, at the time, just about the biggest name on Broadway. People who do not know the Cohan story assume that the name is a variant of Cohen and that he was Jewish. In fact, George M. Cohan was an Irishman. On a foundation of his natural talent and the street sense of a kid who had gotten himself into a lot of trouble on the pavements of Manhattan's slums, he had built an understanding of what would play to the crowd and an outstanding ability to play it himself. He was a good songwriter, too; people are still singing his "Give My Regards to Broadway." If you want to get a sense of the Cohan blend of talent and guts, see if your video store can find you a copy of the movie *Yankee Doodle Dandy* (1942). It stars James Cagney, who much earlier on would, as it happened, co-star in one of Ruby Keeler's early great successes in the movie musicals.

George M. Cohan was in production with a new musical, *The Rise of Rosie O'Grady*. Jack Blue watched the slim adolescent kid with the amazing blue eyes and the "down-to-the-ground earthy and loud" tap-dancing style, and he said to himself, I think Mr. Cohan should see this. So he told Ruby that there was an opening in the chorus line for *Rosie O'Grady*, and if she wouldn't mind lying about her age she would have a good chance at it.

George M. Cohan agreed, doubtless with some prompting from his proud Dancing Master, and within days Ruby Keeler was bringing home more than her father earned, $45 a week. The show opened on Broadway at the Liberty Theatre, on the 22nd of December, 1922. Ruby was thirteen years old, though her photographs at the time might give her, say, seventeen or eighteen.

Herbert Goldman, the author of *Jolson: The Legend Comes to Life*, told us that

New York in the 1920s was probably the greatest city in the history of civilization. And its nightlife scene was certainly the greatest of all time.

You had the legitimate theatre. You had vaudeville, which was still flourishing.

You had the nightlife, nightclubs, which were called "speakeasies" at the time, because of prohibition. The speakeasies played host to Broadway celebrities, politicians, sports figures and gangsters, all melded together in one big entertainment and whisky pot.

Prohibition, an absurd attempt to legislate morality by making it illegal to drink alcohol, was one of the most destructive experiments ever tried in the still relatively young American democracy. It was such a boon to criminals that it has been seriously speculated that the legislative initiative was fuelled by campaign contributions from would-be bootleggers, and perhaps even from the liquor industry. But the campaign was carried by legions of men and women, many from the Protestant and evangelical right. Quite properly appalled at the wreckage booze was causing in working-class families, they wrongly thought that instead of education and the raising of incomes they could eliminate the scourge of alcohol by forbidding it. Prohibition did not last long (1920 to 1933), but in those few years it spawned a huge criminal industry, much as the present drug laws are doing today. Prohibition also created a mythology that is still alive and well, and a legacy of story and entertainment that had much of its genesis in the very Broadway where the adolescent dancer was on her way to stardom.

In fact the speakeasies changed Ruby Keeler's life. Nils Grunland had a "speak," a pretty notorious nightclub, called The El Fey. He not only ran the club, he also produced its entertainment, and when he came to see *Rosie O'Grady* there was something about the young dancer that caught his eye, so when the show closed he offered her a regular spot at the club.

One of Ruby's characteristics that struck people was an air of innocence in the midst of all this sophisticated and socially marginal life. Here was a girl — they probably assumed her to be in her late teens — a girl who *must* know the score, must know the facts of life, must have "been around" because, well, she was a showgirl after all; and yet there was a kind of *innocence* about her that struck everyone, a vestal virgin kicking up her heels in a seductive short-skirt tap-dancing routine. It is a combination that has turned many a hard male head soft, in the history of man/woman relationships. One man whose head was truly turned in this case was a gangster, "a *nice* gangster" according to Herbert Goldman, who has made an intense study of that scene, but a gangster all the same. He was an Italian named Johnny "Irish"

Costello. He watched her dancing in the El Frey and was enchanted by this combination of innocence and an earthy, rough and ready know-ingness. He began to suggest around town that it might be a good idea if some Broadway producers found her more roles in Broadway musicals. Producers did not like to say no to Johnny Costello, and Ruby began to get some very nice roles.

Since Johnny Costello was a kind of lieutenant for a not-very-nice gangster named Owney Madden, "Owney the Killer," you tended to pay attention to him. By the time Ruby really was seventeen, in 1926, it was understood all over the scene that Ruby Keeler was Johnny Costello's girl, and that if you did not want to get yourself into trouble, you would respect that fact.

Now there was a singer in the clubs and on the stages who had eclipsed the great George M. Cohan. The newcomer made his reputation by putting on black makeup and singing "minstrel songs" as a fake black man. Before he died, he was probably the most beloved and most powerful American entertainer of them all (although that kind of superlative is very hard to measure). The newcomer's name was Al Jolson.

Once again, if you want some sense of the power of this man rent a movie that hit the world like a thunderclap shortly after the end of the Second World War. It is called *The Jolson Story*. Its star is an actor who would otherwise have been forgotten, Larry Parks, lip-synching the great Jolson songs to Jolson's own recorded voice. Parks soon had a whole continent singing the songs all over again. This writer was in high school at the time; within months there was seldom a school musical in which some kid did not get up, *in blackface*, and do a Jolson song. Sometimes they lip-synched to the newly re-issued Jolson records (on hard wax 78 RPM disks then — this was pre-vinyl), and sometimes they worked at imitating the slightly hoarse, distinctive Jolson Voice, and got down on their knees holding their white-gloved hands out beseechingly and singing to their "Mammies." It was happening in just about every town and city all over the North American continent.

Twenty years earlier it had already happened when the real Al Jolson was singing. He found adoring crowds wherever he went. Here was a Jewish kid from Lithuania who had learned to sing under the cantor at his synagogue, who was now making his name disguised as a black man singing pseudo-black sentimental southern songs. "He gave every member of the audience the feeling that he was sharing a private joke with them," said his biographer Herbert Goldman. "I don't think there has ever been a performer who was able to do that to the extent that Jolson did."

He had a weakness for young girls with innocent looks. He saw Ruby Keeler in a show called *Sidewalks of New York* at the Woods Theater in Chicago, and he was smitten. Jolson was very powerful by then, very well-connected, very capable of getting good intelligence on people's comings and goings, very capable of finding out when this enchanting child would be in circumstances where he might be able to get to know her without interference from her handlers. When Ruby got off the train in Los Angeles one afternoon, where she had gone for a brief engagement, for once all on her own, there on the platform was one of the most famous men in America, calling out to her, to Ruby Keeler, "Hello Kid!"

Jolson knew he was living dangerously; this was Costello's girl. But he wanted her. He spared no expense. While Ruby was at first terrified, it is clear that if Jolson turned on the full power of his brilliantly contrived charm, he would eventually get what he wanted. Johnny Costello found out that they were secretly engaged. Apparently, instead of ordering the great man's assassination, he decided that *his* code demanded he act in Ruby's best interest. Perhaps he could understand that Ruby might really love the great entertainer. In any case, having heard that Jolson had abused a former wife, he let the singer know that his life was forfeit if he ever harmed Ruby, and that he had better make sure she was financially secure. On September 21, 1928, the couple got married and boarded a transatlantic ocean liner for their honeymoon in Europe. Costello had found out that some of his hoods were so offended they planned to take a shot at Jolson on his behalf. He threw an immense party down in Atlantic City for all of "his people," on the very night that Al and Ruby sailed from New York on the *Olympic*, and the story is that he did it to make sure they had a safe departure.

Al Jolson, as it turned out, was somewhat less chivalrous about the marriage than Costello had been. Jolson was forty-five, Ruby had just turned nineteen. Jolson was at the peak of his career. Ruby's was accelerating rapidly. Jolson seemed to adore her. But, knowing he was sterile, possibly from a venereal disease, he let her believe it was her fault that she wasn't getting pregnant. She desperately wanted children, but throughout the marriage she kept thinking it was *she* who was not fertile. In the meantime, while his career had peaked, hers kept climbing, and that added another element of stress to the relationship.

Ruby starred in Florenz Ziegfield's *Whoopee*, dancing with the young Jimmy Cagney, and choreographed by the famous Busby Berkeley. The next year there was a Gershwin musical, *Showgirls*. On opening night Jolson, in the audience, stood up and sang while she danced her star number. He came back and did it again. It might have been a publicity stunt. Audiences were entranced. Some of Ruby's friends and admirers thought he was doing it to upstage her, because he was jealous. He let on he was doing it to celebrate her, and that is credible too, as the marriage was still young and the bitter and unforgiving side of his resentment and jealousy had not become the dominant theme, not yet.

But he was a possessive, jealous man. He was embarrassed about her grief over their childlessness, but did not have the courage or the decency to tell her the truth about it. As the movies turned to sound, the clackety-clack of Ruby Keeler's down-to-earth loud tap dancing appealed to producers and before long she was a star in her first film, *42nd Street*. She played love scenes with Dick Powell. Producers were calling her all the time. Jolson hated it.

Something in her steadfast Catholic beliefs may have led her to think that a child might save the marriage, and Al agreed. They adopted Al Junior, "Sonny," in May 1935. Ruby was twenty-five. The boy was half-Irish, half-Jewish, which seemed to fit. But the fit did not save the marriage, and Ruby turned more and more to her own private friends, and to the Church, although the Church's prohibitions against divorce did not stop her from thinking in that direction.

One night she went out to play bridge with an old friend,

Madelyn Fiorito Jones. The game went on later than usual; perhaps Ruby found it easy to overlook the passage of time when the homecoming would not be something she looked forward to. But when she did get home Jolson was waiting, and he was angry, and that was the trigger. Next morning she met her friend Madelyn to go to Mass, and she said, That's it. I'm going to divorce him. Madelyn says that she asked for nothing, no support, no house, nothing but the custody of Sonny. And she took a tea set that her family had sent her as a wedding present. The divorce was made final in 1939. Ruby was thirty. She decided that she was through with show business. She wanted a happy life with a man who loved her. And, miraculously, she found it.

There was one last film, *Sweethearts of the Campus*. On a blind date she met a younger man, John Homer Lowe, who had actually dated her sister Gertrude earlier. John was handsome, wealthy, a solid, unpretentious character with strong opinions and a generous disposition. Both he and Ruby were saddened by the prospect of no children, but had come to love each other deeply and went ahead with the marriage. To their great joy and surprise she was soon pregnant. Before long there were two more sisters for Sonny, and then a brother. They still lived in North Hollywood, and the movies were still an important part of their life. But they were home movies now, some black and white, some in colour. They show the still lithe, slim, lovely woman, still with that touch of innocence and the huge engaging eyes, now carrying around one or more little kids, who keep getting bigger as the home movies unwind. Now they are clowning in the swimming pool, now the whole gang out on ponies, learning to ride. Now they are taking a trip back to the Nova Scotian roots and son John Junior recalls, when his mother had to produce her identification crossing the border into Canada, the pride with which she told them that her birthplace was "Halifax, Nova Scotia." Her son and her daughters remember her as a mother who was always there, always the number one car-pool driver, the mom in the front row at the yo-yo contest or the swimming meet. Her daughter Kathleen tells how there was one hint — only one — that there might have been something unusual in her past.

"She would occasionally do a little dance in the kitchen. We would comment on it and try it. And she was proud of the fact that she could do it and none of us could do it. Not just her children, my father as well. We all tried these little steps, from the sink to the refrigerator. That was . . . one of her moments, certainly."

But nostalgia for her time as a star of stage and screen was certainly *not* one of her moments. The children would grow up having no idea — for several years — that their mother had been a famous performer. Her daughter Theresa says,

> She would say, "Don't ever wear makeup." This is a woman who had been in showbusiness wearing lots and lots of makeup. "Because you don't need it; you're just much too beautiful." And that's a wonderful thing, you know, to hear.

But what they didn't hear about was the showbusiness part. Theresa says,

> She kept it from us because she wanted to be Mrs. John Lowe. And her stardom was not a part of her life any more. And it certainly was not a part of our lives. We did not know that she had been in the movies. And every once in a while as we were growing up she would make a television appearance, for instance on a variety show — Jackie Gleason or something like that. And honestly, we thought that probably everybody's mother did that once in a while. Isn't that remarkable?

Death began to mark her life, however. Her younger sister had died just as the marriage to Al Jolson was coming to an end, and perhaps helped precipitate the divorce. Ruby was a woman to whom family was a central value. As she became prosperous she had given everything she reasonably could to her parents and siblings, bought them houses, showered gifts and personal attention on them.

Her father died shortly after Theresa was born. Then in 1964 her mother Nellie died too. At about the same time she learned that her dear husband John had cancer. They kept the disease under control until 1969. But then she called all the children to come home, to be there at the end.

Those years in the late sixties, which so upset the moral and cultural tone of America and the world, may have been responsible for a wave of nostalgia that some cultural historians see as characteristic of America as the seventies loomed. The youth voice had become almost the loudest in the land, after the death of John F. Kennedy in 1963. There came the mounting anger at the war in Vietnam, and later the tragedy at Kent State University where American soldiers fired on and killed college students, their own neighbours, who were protesting the war.

Perhaps seeking some kind of balance to the turmoil, in Hollywood and on Broadway there was a lot of talk of revivals. They dreamed of bringing back the old light-hearted stuff that had grown up in the Roaring Twenties and then helped a nation make it through the dark misery of the 1930s and the worst depression ever. Producers talked among themselves about those lovely, innocent cheery musicals with Busby Berkeley and Dick Powell . . . and Ruby Keeler.

A producer named Harry Rigby dug out a 1925 musical, *No No Nanette*. He wanted his two idols, Busby Berkeley and Ruby Keeler, to get involved. Ruby at first said no, my God she was a grandmother, she was sixty years old for heaven's sake, do a tap-dance number in a Broadway musical! Had they all completely lost their senses? But her old friend Madelyn Jones, among others, said, "Ruby, what have you got to lose?"

So she thought about it for a while. She tried a few tentative little tap routines to the fridge when she thought nobody was looking. She talked it over with Rigby. The whole family knew what a wonderful medicine it would be for the grief of losing her husband, and urged her to go for it. And so she went to New York to start rehearsals. And it went marvellously.

They did the out-of-town opening in Boston. Ruby's son, John Lowe, Jr., now a man in his fifties, was there on opening night with his sisters.

And you could hear people in the audience whispering to each other.
They were trying to see if she had her tap shoes on. That's what they
were looking for, "this person who couldn't tap dance very well."
But the electricity in that room, and the murmur and the energy!
And it all had to do with the lady who was on stage. And the

feelings that were being evoked . . . And to be the son of that . . . not just part of it, but to have that be my mom, was probably the proudest thing I have ever experienced in my life.

The photographs from that musical show a fit, trim, and alert Ruby Keeler who is swinging onto the stage in her long pink pleated skirt, a skirt you just *know* will start to swirl right out horizontal once she starts into the fast turns, her eyes wide, her grin a curious combination of playfulness, serenity and excitement. And, yes, *innocence*. As if a little child had grown tall in the finding of herself, and had come out in front of the crowd to show them a great thing.

Madelyn Fiorito Jones says, in the documentary, the emotion flowing out of her, "She was beautiful."

She looked . . . twenty years old. And dancing like she did when she was twenty years old. And the audience just — when the show was over and the curtain time, and Ruby came out? The audience went wild. And of course I just sat there, I got up, and, but I was crying. And my mascara was all over my face. And I was just sobbing because of what . . . now I'm . . . and remembering it now, I'm sobbing. It was great.

The reviews were raves. After the Boston tryout and the fixes, they moved it down to New York, and it was sellout time. Ruby Keeler, the kid from Dartmouth, had come back to New York.

Kathleen, her daughter, says she went back and back.

My heart would always pound. No matter how many times I saw it, my heart would always pound. And, because I was nervous for her, and I knew she was nervous . . . But as soon as she would start tapping, it was spectacular. She started with the soft-shoe. She came downstairs and the audience, you'd start to hear the murmurs in the audience. And then she'd start with the soft-shoe. And then everyone just relaxed. Including Mom. It was a wonderful, wonderful moment.

She was sixty-one. She had left the stage more than thirty years earlier. She had not danced professionally for decades. She was a grandmother. She did not need to do this for money, or for self-esteem. It is certain that she knew there would be healing in doing it. But it is equally certain that she did it because there was an imperative in it, in the way all those things had come together, in America's need for that kind of gaiety just now, in the fact that Busby Berkeley was still around, and that Broadway wanted them back for what would almost certainly be a last visit. The ability to recognize that imperative, for a woman who had long ago left all that behind in order to be the mother whose role was more important than any fictive role she had ever played on the stage or before the cameras — that is not an ability that is given to everyone.

So it seems strange, now, that some of those close to her, who clearly admired her, were bewitched by her, loved her, would say that she was in any way "ordinary." An important part of the reason for their saying such an absurd thing is that here was a woman of immense strength, and talent, and determination, who apparently never needed to remind you of that strength, talent and determination. Whether or not it is true that her dancing was not especially good, part of its communicative power, the power that made people want to see and hear it over and over again, was that it seemed, not *easy*, exactly, but accessible.

She wasn't showing off something impossible; she was doin' sump'n that's neat to do.

They would say, "It made you feel that *I* could do that!" It made you feel that being up there on the stage conjuring a standing ovation from full houses night after night was something that moms did, just as they went on Jackie Gleason and the other talk shows. And if that is what moms do, then when we grow up we can do it too, and if we don't get around to it, well that's okay too because, hey, it's no big deal, see how ordinary she is.

And that, this writer would argue, is *really* extraordinary.

Four years after the greatest comeback in the history of the Broadway stage, visiting her family in Montana, Ruby Keeler was felled by a massive aneurism, a stroke that could have killed a person of less character. It left her unable to walk. She was determined not to let it keep her down, however. She undertook a heavy daily regime of physiotherapy, day after day, month after month. Getting out of the wheelchair was both a real and a symbolic achievement; next came the orthopaedic shoes, which she was determined to get out of too, and did. She was, her children say, still full of rhythm, as if she was about to start dancing again, even with the cane. She accepted gigs as a show host on cruise ships and TV specials. The audiences had not forgotten her.

The end came when she was eigthy-four. The children were all with her, at her Rancho Mirage in California, sleeping in her bedroom, on couches or cushions on the floor. They tell how there came a night when something woke them and they knew it was time. Then one by one they came close and said goodbye. When it was John Jr.'s turn, his sister Theresa says, he was the one who told her that it was "okay to go." And so she went.

Biographer Howard Goodman, himself a hard-boiled, savvy chronicler of the Broadway scene and of the life of one of its most hard-boiled great characters, Al Jolson, said simply, "She was one of the most fulfilled people that anybody would ever want to meet. Ruby Keeler's life was, one would have to say, a complete success."

◆ ◆ ◆

The Queen of Nostalgia was produced by F. Whitman Trecartin, written and directed by Chuck Stewart.

PART THREE

BIBLE BILL
The Story of William Aberhart

The man who came out onto the platform was overweight with puffy, almost pouting lips. His thick neck strained at the stiff collar and tie. His glasses seemed too small for the massive bald head, and the suit too small for his hefty frame. Yet when he opened his mouth and began to preach, he held them spellbound. He called on them to stand firm against the Antichrist, whose evil power was spreading drought and famine across the parched, dustblown prairie. He had that evangelical knack of reaching right into the deepest fears in the minds of his listeners. He showed them how the Gospel (his very special version of the Gospel) would save them not only from Satan and all his works, but also from the diabolical priests and ministers of the established, error-ridden churches, from the bankers, and from wicked governments.

His preaching would soon spread from the platform to the new electric medium of radio, and through that medium he would make himself powerful and famous. He left a mark on the province of Alberta that has never quite gone away, although almost every single one of his ideas has now been rejected. While his greatest fame came from his time as premier of the province, much of his influence grew out of a kind of religious cult that he founded, a sort of church that evolved from his Calgary Prophetic Bible Institute. The Institute's first graduate was Ernest C. Manning, who would also become premier of Alberta. Ernest Manning's son Preston would found and lead the Reform Party of Canada during its brief existence from 1987 to 1999, and, as its leader, would briefly be the Leader of the Opposition in the Parliament of Canada. The footprints of William Aberhart are still visible on Canadian soil.

He was born near Seaforth, Ontario, in 1887, one of the many children of a German immigrant, also named William, a remarkably progressive but alcoholic farmer. He himself would grow up detesting alcohol and all it stood for, preaching against it, and yet dying of cirrhosis of the liver, which normally affects only heavy drinkers. While his father could not read and write at all, the boy William would become a school principal as well as a Bible teacher, and an obsessive reader. He had a powerful memory, a hypnotic speaking style, and a prophetic vision that thousands rallied to. Others called him mad.

Family photographs show the father as an authoritarian, stern-looking man with a vast, spreading beard and fierce eyes. He is said to have discouraged his sons from any form of original thinking, demanding that they obey and not argue. He taught young William to plough, walking behind the team of horses and guiding the heavy blade through the stiff soil. One of the lessons that stayed with him, he would later say, was his father's instruction to keep his eyes on the tree at the end of the field, don't look down. Look up, into the distance, to your distant mark.

The young William became a solitary, isolated child when he was not obliged to work with his brothers in the fields or the cattle barns. He taught himself to play the violin, and, later, when they moved to a bigger farm, to play his mother's new piano.

Years later, as the head of a new political party he founded himself, he would win the largest majority ever registered in an election in Alberta, even though the press constantly ridiculed him, accused him of romantic nonsense and, worse, of fascism. He would propose legislation intended to bring the press completely under the control of the provincial government. One of his closest political colleagues would be sentenced to prison for counselling the murder of a number of prominent bankers. And yet when William Aberhart died in 1943 thousands of his supporters would gather to mourn the man who had briefly seemed to be saying to Alberta, and to the world, that there was a foolproof way of bringing prosperity to all. And ironically, while he never succeeded, even at the height of his power, in bringing any of his revolutionary economic theories into reality, the theoretical basis of what he proposed has never been completely rejected by economists, even though it works *only* in theory, or in a completely closed economy, a state that has no trade or commerce with other states.

The Aberhart boys had to get up at five o'clock in the morning, milk the forty or fifty cows and then load the heavy cans onto wagons and drive the horses into town to sell the milk. Sometimes his brothers would trade some of the day's production for beer, but not William. The few photographs of him in his youth and adolescence show a lean, athletic build. He became a good football player. But before long he would start to put on weight and lose his hair. The image the world has of him now is the puffy face and bulging eyes, which gave the political cartoonists so much fun later when he became premier.

While he was still in high school William went to a revival meeting and heard his first evangelical preacher, hypnotizing the crowd with passionate accounts of the Armageddon that would sweep away all the sinners and leave only the elect. William liked that idea, of being in a special group, the chosen ones whom the Lord would save at the last day. And he very much liked the role of that fire-breathing preacher who could bring the room to wide-eyed silence one moment, and then have them breathing out their ecstatic "Amens" the next. He went off in the fields, on his own, and preached to the trees and the stones. Critics would later point out that Adolf Hitler also polished his speaking skills by going alone into the countryside and speaking to the fence posts, but budding orators from the time of Demosthenes in ancient Greece have tested their skills in solitude, shouting to the sky, and are probably still doing it today.

He finished high school, got a teaching certificate and then a job in a one-room school near the farm. But within two years we find him in Brantford, Ontario, already pulsating with the life of a small but bustling town on the verge of becoming a city, even boasting a couple of these new-fangled electric tramcars, running on rails in the middle of the newly paved streets. In Brantford he falls in with a religious sect called the Plymouth Brethren. The Brethren believed that the Devil had the world under his control, and so they detested much of the world, certainly the part that *they* did not control. They were severe and exclusive, very hostile to the major churches, anti-Semitic of course, and not at all sociable.

Somehow during this period the young high-school teacher kept on playing football, and may have been something of a star on the Brantford team. The story is that it was watching him on the football field that won the heart of the lively young Jessie Flatt, who set out to win his heart in return, and did so. They were married in 1902 when the teacher was not quite twenty-three, but working hard enough to soon qualify for a principalship. This was helpful because Jessie was fond of jewellery and furs and entertaining, and not very much interested in the evangelical movement. So while they did manage to have two daughters, and it is reported that Aberhart was kind and attentive to the girls and read them Bible stories at night, it is also reported that there was not a great deal of common interest in the marriage.

He would, over the next few years, go deeper and deeper into his Bible studies. He taught Sunday School at the Presbyterian church, and began to try out his preaching skills. The Presbyterian elders became a bit nervous after a while. Aberhart's theology was pretty unconventional. He seemed to be saying that the Second Coming of Christ was just around the corner, instead of part of that Day of the Last Judgment which was, well, far enough in the future that we don't have to worry about it right now. This young evangelist seemed to be suggesting that we should do everything we could to prepare for it, here and now. And yet he wanted to stay within the comfortable family of the Presbyterians, while also spending time with the Plymouth Brethren who despised the traditional churches. Some historians, studying this increasingly strange and complex figure, have concluded that he must have had one of those "compartmentalized" minds that easily permits a person to believe several contradictory things at once, like the White Queen in *Alice in Wonderland*.

Perhaps it was criticism or even overt resistance from those elders that led Aberhart to start thinking about moving on. He had lived all his life in Ontario, but now the country was opening up to the west, and perhaps there was an opportunity there for these religious ideas that were taking over his life.

He applied for a teaching job in the newly established province of Alberta. Alberta had become part of the Canadian confederation only in 1905, and was booming as the new provincial government offered free land to attract a larger population. That population had nearly doubled by 1910 when the Aberhart family arrived from Brantford. Calgary was a boom town. There were actually houses — and even churches — built of brick and mortar instead of wood. While it did not have the elegant, quiet, tree-lined streets of Jessie's native Brantford, and she missed that, it did have some of those reassuring electric streetcars.

Jessie found the family a two-storey house that reminded her of Brantford, and an affluent church, Grace Presbyterian, where she could wear her furs to the Sunday service and feel at home. At Grace Presbyterian William became a communicant and an elder as well as a Sunday School teacher. At the same time he began to teach a Bible class down near the breweries and the stockyards in the east end, at Trinity Methodist, preaching his ideas about prophecy and the Second Coming, which would not have been very welcome at Grace Presbyterian. The Presbyterian authority was vested in the group, the elders who ran the church and determined its policies. The Methodists on the other hand responded to the authority and personal magnetism of a powerful individual, and William Aberhart liked that. He stayed on at Grace Presbyterian, officially. That was what Jessie wanted. But in 1912 the Elders had had enough of his unorthodox prophetic message, and they forced him to resign. When he moved over to Trinity Methodist, full time, a lot of his Bible class people from Grace moved over with him.

Now the Bible classes really took him away from Jessie and the girls. By 1913 his was the largest Bible class in Calgary. He led Bible studies at the YMCA and was invited to a number of different churches as guest preacher on Sunday. When war broke out in Europe it seemed to play into his prophetic hand. His sermons identified the German king, Kaiser Wilhelm, as the Antichrist one Sunday, and another Sunday it would be Kemal Pasha of Turkey who was this incarnation of the Great Evil. Larger and larger crowds came to hear him, and it seems that they simply ate this message up.

In the social atmosphere of the time it was necessary that the

Aberharts maintain at least the exterior impression of a real marriage. Although Jessie's furs and jewels were very much out of place among the cloth-coat, plain-hat congregations that the populist preacher now favoured, she came along from time to time, to maintain appearances. Aberhart kept working hard at his school job. He landed the principal-ship at Crescent Heights, Calgary's most important high school at the time. He moved to yet another church. Even the Methodists at Trinity had begun to dispute his right to preach those radical ideas. He learned that Westbourne Church was in financial trouble. He had not even been baptised, a sacrament central to the Baptist practice, so he arranged for that ceremony, by total immersion in the river. Then he took over Westbourne and made it his own. His prophetic message had never really fit in any of the mainstream churches. Now he was pastor of his own congregation. Aberhart had never been ordained into the ministry, but nobody seemed to mind that, certainly not the hundreds who came across with him to Westbourne, where the crowds kept growing larger and larger.

Like his father he was an authoritarian, both in his church and his school. As early as 1903 he had written a manual on the running of a school, in which he saw the principal (himself) as the general of an army, the staff and students bound in absolute obedience to his will. The attitude that underlay this was not unusual at the time. Heads of institutions were traditionally men who were expected to take total responsibility for running things, and thus had to have total authority. But William Aberhart's measure of authority went beyond the tradi-tions of the time. He was not interested in discussion or in differences of opinion. The teachers who worked under him at Crescent Heights were made to understand that their views did not count: they were there to teach what and how he told them to teach.

He was going more and more deeply into his own mystic decod-ing of what a later scholar, Northrop Frye, would call "The Great Code," the cryptic messages of the Bible. His sermons became violent-ly coloured with flames and demons who assaulted people sexually in their sleep. He sometimes seemed obsessed with the Sins of the Flesh. He banned school dances.

It is interesting to note that his immediate family paid no attention to this puritan absolutism. The photographs of the teenage girls, Ola and Khona, show a perky pair with bobbed hair (which must have outraged their father) and flirtatious grins. Now about the only congress he had with the family was the evening meal. After dinner he retired to a study he had fitted out in his garage. The garage was something new in Calgary, a mark of prosperity in a modern house as the automobile made its appearance alongside the horse and wagon, which was still the major form of transportation.

In the garage Aberhart began to develop a huge diagram of the world and the cosmos, both revealed and hidden. It looked like some mediaeval mystical chart of the hidden worlds. It was meticulously drawn with ruler and compass, a vast, layered portrayal of the world below and the world above, the past and the present and what is to come. Circles intersected circles, and the circles themselves were subdivided into sectors and segments, with carefully printed designations of the places of God and His Son, and of the Forces of Evil, the Antichrist, The Prophets, The Elect Who Will Be Saved.

Night after night, poring over the Bible, he continued his work on this great blueprint of God's intentions for the future of the human race and the vast extensions of eternity.

Does this all sound like a person who is not quite sane? He was certainly not impaired from successfully presiding over his important high school and running his church and preparing his lectures and his sermons. When the Great War was over, the troops came home and a wave of prosperity began to crest. Along with prosperity came striking changes in social behaviour. Sexually provocative dancing in public, like the Charleston, gave the evangelists, including Aberhart, a new target to deplore. Gin had become the popular drink, and as the popularity of alcohol spread and the new prosperity brought it more and more into the open, the prohibitionist movement grew in opposition. Aberhart was one of the most powerful voices against the demon drink.

But this is not a man whose evangelical obsession blinds him to how he is seen, or to what he must do to reach the sceptical. He is a calculated and knowing producer of his own communications package. The historian David Elliott told our filmmakers that, at Westbourne, he really knew how to build a show.

He puts on a good religious performance. There was lively singing. He had orchestrated music. He would give a lecture, and his voice would be a rising crescendo, and it would hit a sort of climax, and then there would be a kind of cooling-off period. . . . It was interpreted by some people as almost being a kind of emotional catharsis, even some saw it in sexual terms. It was a kind of release.

He began to realize that he needed a church, or something like a church, that was entirely his own; he really had no place among the existing congregations, even the very evangelical Baptists. But there was no money to build the kind of place he wanted to house his great evangelical spectacles. He kept on building his own congregation, trying hard to reach out more and more widely into the community at large. And when the next communications revolution arrived at his doorstep, he was ready for it.

The first public broadcast of the human voice had taken place in 1906, when a Canadian inventor, Reginald Fessenden, overcame the technical obstacle that had kept radio, until then, at the level of a wireless telegraph, able to transmit simple sound — a tone or click that could be converted into a code composed of "dots and dashes." Fessenden discovered a method of modulating the simple wave form of the radio signal so that the height or amplitude of the waves and valleys would change according to the pitch of the sound that was fed into the system: A.M. or Amplitude Modulation. By the early 1920s entrepreneurs had discovered the commercial potential of the new medium, and radio stations were springing up all over North America. In 1925 when the new medium was just nineteen years old and commercial radio even younger, William Aberhart realized that it would be a powerful new way for his preaching to reach out to the multitudes. He began to broadcast Sunday afternoon services. He was also quick to recognize that the numbers might become large enough that if he were able to persuade a fraction of his listening audience to send even a few pennies each he would be able to forget about the money problem and start a new centre to house his Bible Institute.

Radio was taking off all over the province. Muriel Manning, Preston Manning's mother, described going into some small towns and being able to hear Aberhart's voice as she walked down Main Street from one end of town to the other, because people would take their radios out onto the porches on a spring evening, to listen to what was becoming the most listened-to program in the region, "The Bible Hour." He asked his listeners for contributions, in the form of the purchase of bricks and mortar for the new Institute he was planning. You could buy a sod or a brick, or even a pew if you had a little more money, and if you could only afford 25 cents that would buy some of the sand and cement needed to bind the bricks together: a quarter's worth of mortar. By 1927, after only two years of campaigning like this, he was able to commission a $65,000 building, well over a million in today's dollars, and formally open the Calgary Prophetic Bible Institute.

Since 1923 he had been teaching night-school classes in theology in the basement of the Westbourne Baptist Church. He had been broadcasting Sunday afternoon services since 1925. Now he had his Institute. He taught many of its classes himself while still administering Westbourne, preparing and delivering his weekly broadcasts, and all the time still working as the principal of Crescent Heights High School. The energy of the man was prodigious. Now he had a school in which he could train ministers and missionaries for the furtherance of fundamentalism. With the Institute flourishing he now had enough supporters to take the next logical step and found his own sect, the Bible Institute Baptist Church.

Aberhart had his detractors, of course. By 1929 even the Westbourne congregation was drifting away from his increasingly demonic theology. The diagram in the garage was getting bigger and bigger, but his hold over the Baptists was shrinking. Then in October of that same year something happened that played into his hands — the stock market came crashing down. Its collapse precipitated the worst economic crisis the modern world had yet faced: the Great Depression.

It is likely that the turbulence and fears generated by the Great War of 1914–1918 had contributed to a popular spread of uncertainty about the old establishments among people who were struggling to make their way in an Alberta that would look to us now something like a Third World country. While fortunes were being made and lost, power and prosperity were in the hands of a very few. The expectation of most people was for a short life of hard work and deprivation. But here was a message preached by a galvanizing evangelist, who told people that if only they believed in the Great Dispensations available to us through a true reading of the Bible, then there would be a paradise of rest and plenty at the end of the path. This message had a powerful resonance. It was not hard for people to believe in and to wish for the end of a world in which there was nothing but struggle and failure.

When evangelists like Aberhart can convincingly "de-code" the message of the scriptures to "prove" that "the end of the world is just around the corner and you, my friends, are going to be among the ones who are lifted into salvation while the wretched bankers and merchants will roast on the spits of hell," desperate people may listen. After all, they have little reason to desire that the present world of poverty and disappointment should be preserved as it is.

So now, when even the meagre incomes of marginal farmers and workers were taken away by this mysterious Great Depression, and the soil of overfarmed and under-irrigated prairies began to blow away in great dark clouds as an unprecedented drought dried them to dust, it was easy for many to believe that these were signs of the coming of The End. The world was being seared by "The Branding Irons of the Anti-Christ," Aberhart and his right-hand man Ernest Manning wrote, in a jointly authored pamphlet. But true believers would be lifted out of all this misery, *there was no doubt of it*, while the wicked were cast into everlasting flames.

It was a time of terror. Once again, while the looming figure of the puffy-faced preacher with the little round spectacles might be seen today as the embodiment of evil, it may be that he had a streak of compassion too. Among the ideals and fantasies that streamed through his head as he pored over his blueprint of God's plan for the world and eternity, it is probable that he saw himself not only as the preacher of a paradise beyond the end of the world, but also as the hero who would bring his people up out of the dust and despair, into a new (and prosperous) Jerusalem within this present and very real physical world.

He went up to Edmonton in the summer of 1932 to mark high-school leaving exams, "The Departmentals." It is bizarre to think of this already far-overworked preacher and school principal continuing the summer work that he had begun years ago just to make a little extra money. But there he was, in that Dust Bowl prairie summer of '32, when a fellow teacher on the exam marker's board gave him a new book on economics, by a British engineer named Major C. H. Douglas. The friend suggested that Aberhart might be the man to take Major Douglas' radical ideas and save Alberta from the depression. Aberhart took the book back to his room at St. Stephen's College, read it overnight, and was converted.

Social Credit was born. Aberhart sanctified it in his broadcasts as "God's Great Economy," and began to preach it regularly. But he also began to believe that it held a practical solution to the economic miseries of Alberta, maybe of the world. And if you read it in the context of that Depression, and of a provincial, not a world economy, it is possible to see how desperate people could be captured by it.

What it said was, basically, that the people providing the goods and services that were sold in the capitalist market system would never be paid as much as the goods were worth. Therefore in a free market there would always be less money going to the workers than they needed to buy those goods. It is a formula that sounds like Marxist economics of Communism, but the solution that Major Douglas proposed was in fact quite different. Instead of the workers taking control, as Marx and the Communists proposed, the state would simply create enough credit for people to make up the difference between what they earned and what a reasonable supply of food, housing, clothes and other goods would cost them. Everyone would thus be able to buy everything they needed. The producers would be happy because they would sell everything they produced, and the people would no longer have to struggle for their basic needs.

It is a recipe for steadily mounting inflation. Government keeps putting more money into the system and the money keeps losing value, even as the markets are humming along.

But if you are not tied into an external world, where other currencies are keeping their value, then in theory it will work. There is no question that Aberhart, his mind demonstrably capable of believing several contradictory things at once, saw it as some kind of miraculous solution to the poverty of his world. He developed a political platform that would become the Social Credit Party. That platform, within three years, would bring him to the premier's office with the biggest parliamentary majority any political leader in Canada had ever had.

Although his language was careful and he never actually said he was going to give the citizens money (he called it a "credit"), in a way he had bought their votes. What they thought they heard was that as soon as he got into power every single citizen would suddenly be given $25 a month. In a world where you could put together a meagre meal for 25 cents. (Milk was about 8 cents a quart, for example.) That meant that a couple would get $50 a month, enough to live on.

Paradise was at hand.

The preaching now abandoned its flaming portrait of the End of the World and began to envision a new real and present world of prosperity.

Back in Britain the inventor of the idea, Major Douglas, whom many saw as some kind of fascist, said (perhaps correctly) that only a military coup could bring about the Social Credit world that Aberhart was offering, and called Aberhart's proposals "bogus." But that did not stop his Canadian disciple. Aberhart and Ernest Manning travelled the province with a public address system mounted on cars or pickup trucks. The $25 promise swept the province like a grass fire. When the *Calgary Herald* exposed the scheme as quackery, Aberhart started his own newspaper. He told his congregations that God was backing his campaign. He made comparisons between himself and Moses leading the Israelites to the Promised Land. Bake sales and socials helped to raise funds.

Some of his people began to grumble that he was behaving like a dictator, choosing all his candidates personally and tolerating no difference of opinion. The *Calgary Herald* began to call him a fascist dictator. Mussolini had attracted world attention to the idea of fascism, and it seemed to the *Herald*'s editors to be a label they could borrow and that people would recognize. Aberhart responded simply, "We should allow none of our fellow-citizens to suffer want, and if that is what you call a dictator, then I am one, and I'll be glad to take the title." He began to use the electoral tactics of the fascist parties in Europe, as well. Social Credit goon squads began to harass gatherings of the United Farmers party, and others opposed to social credit.

"Social Creditors would be banging on the walls outside the buildings," says historian David Elliott. "Or putting sugar in their gas tanks. And you'd have churches divided down the middle between those who were for Social Credit on one side of the Church and the non-Social Creditors on the other side. And it really was dividing the province."

Only three years after he first discovered Major Douglas and Social Credit, the 1935 vote was overwhelming. Polling stations were swamped. They ran out of ballots and they ran out of pencils. On election eve Aberhart knelt at the edge of the platform grasping hand after hand reaching up to him as though he were the Saviour himself (though never losing the expensive fedora clamped firmly on his large round head). They believed. The headlines on August 15, 1935, said,

MUSSOLINI THREATENS TO ENTER ETHIOPIA. ALBERTA
SOCIAL CREDIT SWEEPS THE POLLS.

The newspapers had seen it building, and were riveted. The major U.S. dailies sent their representatives to Edmonton. *Pravda* sent a man from Moscow. This was the most dramatic political experiment North America had ever seen. Let the Nazis take over Germany and the Fascists in Italy; this seemed far more exciting because people *believed* it, and it was happening democratically. In England the somewhat dippy and yet influential Dean of Canterbury, Hewlett Johnson, said that it was "the fulfillment of Christ's teaching. Here are the hungry. Let us feed them. Alberta will kindle a worldwide torch." In London an army of Social Credit supporters of Major Douglas put on their green shirts and marched in celebration around the Bank of England, saluting the crowd with the same straight arm salute that Adolf Hitler was turning into an icon in Germany.

Exhilarated by all this — who would not be (except, perhaps, a realist) — Aberhart turned to astrology and numerology to choose a cabinet, and took a suite for himself and Jessie at the Macdonald Hotel. He fired off a telegram to Major Douglas: "Well! Victorious! When can you come?"

It would appear that Aberhart had never thought through the practical implications of what he had sold the electorate. He must just have supposed, Douglas' book having so bewitched him, that once in power all he had to do was import the genius who had invented this miraculous scheme, and simply put it into practice.

Now in power at last, Aberhart had to deliver, but he could not. He himself was living very well in his government-paid suite in the Macdonald (which Jessie disliked and presently fled, going off to stay with Ola and Khona in B.C.). But he nonetheless had to face, on the one side, an electorate lining up for their promised $25 a month, and on the other a treasurer telling him that the province was almost bankrupt.

He went begging to Ottawa. Major Douglas, learning that Aberhart had thus "consorted with the enemy," refused to come over and put the Great Plan into effect. Aberhart pleaded for eighteen million dollars; Ottawa sent two and a half. The press lined up like tigers after the kill, and began to use the word "fraud."

Aberhart asked Ottawa for more money. A second loan arrived, but a third was refused. In April 1936 the province defaulted on its loans. Aberhart went off to Vancouver with Manning and his new wife, Muriel Preston, and a vacation on the beaches, and came back with a new scheme: they would print provincial "Prosperity Bonds" that looked quite a lot like actual currency.

He tried to pay the civil servants with what the press was quick to call "Funny Money," but nobody wanted it. A cartoon appeared in the *Herald* in which the Nazi swastika frame by frame morphed into the face of William Aberhart. Aberhart began to think seriously about muzzling the press. He was warned that the caucus was planning to oust him. His response was to throw a picnic for ten thousand people, with plenty of free food. A mix of supporters and protesters came to the picnic, but his party did not come round. When he tried to pass his next budget the caucus refused to support him.

But it was Aberhart the man they were trying to get rid of, not Social Credit. They still believed in the scheme. And so, when Aberhart refused their demand that he resign, they let him know they'd throw him out *unless he brought Major Douglas in with full power to implement Social Credit his way!* Douglas still refused to come. Instead, he sent two of his men. Aberhart's confidence was shaken. With the agreement of his caucus he turned the financial planning of the province of Alberta over to these two English fascists, who in turn were taking their orders from the Great Man, Major Douglas, in London.

"It is absolutely wild," says David Elliott. "A government is prepared to turn over its complete power to this eccentric Englishman . . . [and] one of the first dictates he sends them is to get rid of the Mounties, put in your own Social Credit police force." They also declared they would solve the financial crisis by simply declaring that Alberta would not honour its debts.

Not surprisingly, the federal government intervened and declared the financial proposal to be *ultra vires* (beyond the powers of the provincial government). As the federal government has the responsibility of protecting civil rights across Canada, Ottawa also overturned the Accurate News and Information Act, which would have given Edmonton the power to control the press, and stopped the proposed Party police as well. Aberhart was so furious when the Lieutenant-Governor, John Bowen, refused to sign the Accurate News and Information Act into law that he evicted Bowen from the Official Residence and took away his car.

It was becoming very nasty. Late in 1937, acting on a tip from some provincial Conservative MLAs, the RCMP raided the Social Credit Party headquarters, and discovered documents proposing the assassination of certain prominent bankers. One of Major Douglas' British agents was, as a result, charged, tried, and convicted of counselling to murder. He was sent to prison with hard labour.

When the Alberta newspapers were awarded the Pulitzer Prize for their fight against Aberhart's repressive legislation, the premier fled to Jessie on the west coast, to lick his wounds. In 1939 King Edward VI and Queen Elizabeth visited, partly to build support for the war against fascism that many now feared was coming. The Lieutenant-Governor, now working from a residence he had to rent for himself, kept his premier out of sight most of the time. Aberhart was invited to only one formal welcoming ceremony, outdoors, on the steps of the legislature, where the premier made a deferential speech.

But, although he was already talking with lugubrious self-pity as though he were finished, "prepared to be cast aside like an old shoe," World War II in fact gave him a brief reprieve. His government was returned with a small majority. He joined the voices rallying against Hitler and Nazism, but at the same time kept up his anti-Semitic tirades against the international Jewish financiers. He even accused the Jews of persecuting their own people in Holocaust-ridden Germany.

He looked old now. The once fat, shining face and puffy lips became ashen in colour and his skin shrank and sagged. He, who had never taken a drink in his life, was diagnosed with cirrhosis of the liver. Visiting the family again, in Vancouver in the spring of 1943, he was hospitalized and died a month later.

But they came out to the funeral, the old supporters, thousands of them. Perhaps they still believed that his dream had held some kind of reality, if only . . . . The family, however, having long ago repudiated Alberta, insisted on his being buried in B.C., where he lies in a simple grave, and where Jessie joined him in 1966.

Could there be another like him? There were his counterparts at the time, notably the similarly fascistic and corrupt governor Huey Long of Louisiana, who was murdered in the lobby of the state legislature. In a society with vigorous and watchful news media, and a general population whose education is vastly greater than what it was seventy-five years ago, and where politics is almost a national sport, it seems unthinkable that such crazy ideas could be taken seriously for five minutes. But Alberta has not forgotten Bible Bill.

A<small>N</small> A<small>FTERWORD</small>: The Social Credit fantasy attracted at least one other very prominent figure, the American poet Ezra Pound. Incarcerated in Washington D.C., at Saint Elizabeth's hospital for the insane after he had made anti-American, pro-Mussolini radio broadcasts from Pisa during the Second World War, the anti-Semitic genius had also discovered and been converted by Douglas' scheme. When the present writer wrote to Ezra Pound at Saint Elizabeth's, proposing to bring a camera down to Washington for a television interview in 1957, the poet wrote back, "Elementary my dear Watson; just get Grampa out of quad and then we can talk turkey." And then he added a whole page of notes about the great Major Douglas' world-saving economics, the work of genius, and urged us all to revive Social Credit.

◆ ◆ ◆

Bible Bill, the television biography of William Aberhart, was written, produced and directed by Patricia Phillips.

PART FOUR

DAI VERNON
The Spirit of Magic

The figure on the screen is at first slightly obscured by watermark damage to the film, and the black and white picture is grainy and faded. There is no sound. And yet this beguiling man, who is smiling straight at us with a mixture of aristocratic generosity and mischief, is a presence, a compelling presence.

He is thirty-five years old and looks absolutely in the prime of his life. His head is perfectly formed, his features almost too handsome, his hair impeccable and his thin moustache gallant. He is doing something with his hands, very slowly.

He holds a single playing card out for us, well forward of his face, but just low enough so we can still see his devastating smile. What he is about to do with this card will be seen very clearly, but it will be perceived as totally baffling. As he turns first one hand palm out, and then the other, v-e-r-y slowly, the card vanishes. It is simply gone. There are no sleeves it could have gone up. The man rotates for us the empty palms and backs of both those hands, and then, still moving slowly, as he turns one hand back again the card is quite simply . . . *there* again. And the man is so tickled, so boyishly pleased to be showing us this . . . this *miracle* of sleight-of-hand, of deception of the eye . . . that we are totally won over. We love the guy.

As did much of the world, at that point, a few years after World War I. Dai Vernon was by 1924 the toast of High Society New York, and among professional magicians he was becoming the most sought-after master craftsman in the world. Before long they would drive across the continent or take a ship across the Atlantic for the opportunity to sit at his feet and learn. They began to call him The Professor, and they still do, almost a decade after his death. The noted contemporary magician, mentalist and historian of magic Max Maven now says that Vernon had become to magic "what [James] Joyce was to the novel and Einstein to

52

physics: [someone who] comes along and just changes the way people approach that field."

It was a long way from Ottawa.

Dai Vernon was born in the Canadian capital city in 1894 and christened David Frederick Wingfield Verner. His father James was a successful senior civil servant, and his mother Helen something of a society *grande dame*. His uncle Frederick Verner was a much admired landscape artist whose work hangs in the National Gallery of Canada to this day. Young David would inherit Uncle Frederick's skill in the plastic arts. He was a gifted watercolourist as a child and, not yet in his teens, taught himself to cut superb portrait likenesses out of black paper. These silhouettes, an art that today has virtually disappeared, would be, throughout much of this really great magician's life, a reliable fallback as a source of income, and a way to flatter wealthy clients. He would leave behind arresting likenesses of society flappers and great industrialists. And of celebrities including novelist Scott Fitzgerald and dancer/actor Ray Bolger (The Scarecrow in *The Wizard of Oz*), and of the New Deal and wartime President of the United States, Franklin D. Roosevelt. Tiny cut-outs, some of these silhouettes now command impressive prices from collectors.

Young David's father, James Verner the civil servant, dabbled in conjuring, which he had learned from *his* like-minded father, a professor at Trinity College, Dublin. James, in turn, began to show his young son a few tricks when the boy was only four or five. David was enchanted. He begged to be taught how to do it. Ottawa was an important stop on the entertainment circuits in those days, too, and while the boy loved any kind of performance, music hall, vaudeville, legitimate theatre, it was the visiting magicians who held him rapt. He haunted Ottawa's new Carnegie Library and pored over all the books on magic he could find, discovering the secrets of those travelling conjurors and teaching himself tricks to dazzle his father with. James Verner had some influence in Ottawa, and when Howard Thurston, one of the best magicians in the world, came to town, young David's father got the seven-year-old backstage, where the boy confidently showed the Great Man a card trick, of his own devisal, and the Great Man said he was totally stumped.

It is perhaps not a bad idea, after all, to get a bit ahead of the story again right here, because there was another showing off to a great magician, an event that became and remains a legend among magicians, and gave Dai Vernon a label that stuck. He was in Chicago on February 6, 1922. Harry Houdini, by then world-famous more as an escape artist than a magician, was being fêted at the Great Northern Hotel by a gathering of magicians from all over the continent, celebrated and toasted for his lifetime contribution. The cocky Canadian was introduced to Houdini in the lobby by a mutual friend, Sam Margules. Vernon managed to persuade this Great Man to pause long enough to look at a card trick. Houdini had long boasted that he could never be fooled with a card trick if he could see it three times. Here is what Dai Vernon did, and nobody had ever seen anything like it before.

He got Houdini to put his initials, H.H., on the face of a playing card, which Vernon (he had changed his name by now, but would keep on changing back to Verner from time to time for years to follow) then inserted back into the deck underneath the top card. Then, without doing anything that anyone could see, no move, no covering the deck, nothing but softly stroking the top card for a moment, he then turned that top card over and it had become Houdini's card with Houdini's initials on it. "Again!" said Houdini. The challenge. *Show me three times and I'll know how it's done.*

So Dai Vernon did that trick not three but seven times. The Great Man admitted defeat. For the rest of his life Dai Vernon was known as The Man Who Fooled Houdini.

But we are getting ahead of our story; back up twenty years, to 1902. That year a little book appeared which would transform both gambling and card conjuring, and quite literally would also transform the life and destiny of David Verner. It was a book on how to cheat with cards. The eight-year-old boy started reading his father's copy, although James had told him it would be too difficult, too complicated and detailed for such a young mind. This proved not to be the case. He read it right through, then and there, and for the rest of his life he kept reading it, studying it, interpreting it, applying it.

In 1984 there appeared an annotated version, under the title *Revelations*. The author of this annotated version was Dai Vernon who was then ninety years old.

When it first appeared in 1902 this little volume was called *Ruse and Subterfuge at the Card Table,* with an intriguing paragraph in italics, under the title, which read:

> *Embracing the whole Calendar of Sleights that are employed by the Gambler and the Conjuror . . . every known expert move and stratagem of the Expert Card Handler.*

The author's name was given as S.W. Erdnase. Among magicians to this day there is controversy as bitter as the arguments about Shakespeare among literary folk, as to who Erdnase really was. The book was reissued later as *The Expert at the Card Table.* It is still in print under that title, but everybody simply refers to it as *Erdnase.* It became the young David's Bible. He said he had it memorized by the age of twelve. Many others have been fascinated or even obsessed by *Erdnase.* In the spring of 2000, when *The Wall Street Journal* did a nostalgic and humorous feature story on the controversy about "The man who was Erdnase," reprints of the old text soared onto the best-seller lists, ninety-eight years after being published. Very serious scholars have been taken with *Erdnase.* The Californian professor of mathematics Persi Diaconis lived and travelled with Vernon for a couple of years as Vernon's protégé when Vernon was about the age we first met him at the beginning of this film and Diaconis was fourteen. Much of what they did together was to track down stuff related to Erdnase.

Herb Zarrow is a gifted magician whose deceptive technique for fully shuffling a deck without changing the position of a single card bears his name, The Zarrow Shuffle. Zarrow says that when Vernon started hanging around the magic shops in New York in his late teens and early twenties he was showing card work out of Erdnase to grizzled old veteran professionals, and they were baffled. They knew Erdnase, they thought, but they didn't know *this* stuff. Vernon was on his way to becoming a legend.

Sometime between discovering Erdnase in Ottawa and those early New York days the Verner family went to Old Orchard Beach in Maine for a summer holiday. There, young David saw his first silhouette cutter working on the pier, the way charcoal artists work the sidewalks at Fifth Avenue and Central Park South, or Bloor and Yonge, today. Vernon said he went home and got a little pair of scissors and cut a couple of silhouette faces that his father praised as "better than the man on the pier." When he went back to New York a few years later he tried his luck on a pier at Coney Island, next to Larry Grey The Dizzy Wizard's little magic shop, and soon found he could make a living at it. Coney Island was a major middle-class holiday spot for New Yorkers then. Roller coasters and slides with big boats that carried a dozen passengers WHOOSH right down into the ocean, kewpie dolls and burlesque and sideshows; magic and sidewalk artists. Vernon had intended to study at the Art Students' League in New York; that was what his parents thought anyway. There is no record in the League's archives of his ever having enrolled. In fact he had by now, at the age of about nineteen or twenty, realized that magic was his life. Cutting silhouettes could be a livelihood to support the magic if need be. He was exactly where he wanted to be.

His personality was a contradictory blend of obsessive focus on a single subject: magic, and at the same time he was outgoing, humorous, a fine hockey player, a trained engineer and technical draftsman (skills learned at the Royal Military College at Kingston, Ontario). He was a writer and a social being. He served briefly in the Royal Flying Corps in World War One. In World War Two he went overseas with the rank of Captain in the United States Army's entertainment group as a volunteer, and gave himself to entertaining the troops with exemplary generosity.

But as a family man he often seemed to be not quite there. His son Derek now says, "As a father he was a fine magician." When Derek tells some of the details of family life when he was a boy, Dai Vernon's insensitivity to the two sons who were born in New York sounds almost incredible. He would allow his family to get evicted because he didn't get around to paying the rent. There was a bizarre afternoon once when young Derek came to him crying and bleeding from a beating he'd got from his drunken mother. She had confusedly picked up a souvenir Japanese bayonet to smack him with, and he was in desperate shape. But Vernon held up his hand to Derek for silence as he considered the move he was about to make in a chess game, called out "Check," and only then turned to attend to the boy's serious wounds.

A very strange man. And a very great magician.

There is an eccentric little magic shop tucked away in a back corridor on the fourth floor of an office building on New York's 42nd Street, Flosso's Magic Shop. The proprietor, Jackie Flosso, well into his seventies, only recently sold it after carrying on the business his father Al Flosso started early in the century. You could buy all the latest manufactured tricks there in those days, and a few books (though nothing like the thousands of magic titles you can buy now, on everything from simple card tricks to making a skyscraper disappear). But the place to be, in Al Flosso's magic shop, was the back room. And you got into the back room only if you were really good. Dai Vernon had not been long in New York before he was invited into the back room at Flosso's, which was called Martinka's when Vernon first went there. Even then, long before he was called The Professor, long before he decided that teaching and inspiring and studying were more rewarding than actually performing, even then he was showing them stuff they had never seen before.

Magicians like to say that Dai Vernon's great contribution to magic was naturalness. His son Derek says now that "it didn't look like magic, but magical things happened." What Derek means is that magic had traditionally been surrounded by, well, *hocus pocus*: much waving of hands, bizarre costumes up until the late nineteenth century (and still today, in some venues like Las Vegas), elaborate rituals with the hands, and wands, and inverted bowls and huge silk scarves. But Dai liked to keep it in close, to make things happen, as he had with the trick that fooled Houdini, in which, well, nothing actually *seemed* to happen at all.

It is not, however, true that this was Vernon's invention, not true that he was the one who brought naturalness to magic. His great predecessors, Max Malini and Nate Leipzig and others, had begun that motif. Max Malini would perform magic anywhere, with anything, and was booked by kings and emperors. He would produce a block of ice at a dinner table where he was a guest, or rip the buttons from a senator's waistcoat on the steps of the Senate Office Building and then restore them by magic. No formulas or spells or magic gestures, just natural movements and then magical things happened. Vernon admired that naturalness, and studied ways to make everything seem quite normal up to the point where the magical effect was to happen, but he didn't invent it. Perhaps his greatest contribution was to try to restore dignity and depth to magic.

Max Maven says, "The tragedy of magic in the twentieth century is that magicians have taken an art that is intrinsically profound, and trivialized it. For Vernon, magic was never trivial." He seems to have intended it to be a high art, subtle, profound, intensely refined, a matter of dignity and wonder. He would take any classic effect and refine it until he had found its quintessential centre, and then polish it until, when magicians saw *his* version of a trick, it seemed that there really could be no other way to do it. Max Maven says that Vernon set the pattern for the classic called the Cups and Balls. The Cups and Balls are often called the oldest trick in magic. There is what appears to be reference to them in Roman documents before the modern era. In at least one of the great outdoor country fair scenes of Breughel the Elder, in that gallery full of Breughels in the Kunstmuseum in Vienna, you can see a mountebank performing a version that looks almost exactly like the one this writer would perform today.

A senior British magician, Bob Read, has collected documents and drawings and etchings and paintings of hundreds of different takes on this wonderful old illusion. Any magician worth his salt has got to learn at least one version of the Cups and Balls. It was first unmistakeably described by Reginald Scot in his *The Discoverie of Witchcraft* (1584). The trick commonly uses three metal cups and three small balls the size of an olive or a grape. Some performers actually use olives or grapes. At a snap of the fingers or a wave of a wand, balls that have been clearly seen separately under each cup vanish and re-appear together under one cup, or move singly from one cup to another, or vanish and reappear on command, all in the most mystifying way. Often at the end of the routine the magician asks you where you think the balls are, but whichever cup you point to you are wrong. Because now, when he lifts the cups which you have only just now seen empty, under each one there is an orange or a lemon or a tennis ball. Paul Gertner does it with three impossibly large stainless-steel ball bearings.

So Dai Vernon studied the Cups and Balls and then refined it according to his principles of naturalness. He even introduced a segment in which he actually does reveal one of the key sleight-of-hand moves that makes the illusion work, while still leaving the audience delightfully mystified. The Vernon routine, when you see it, makes you feel for a moment that, well, there really is no other way to do it. And Max Maven says that if you go anywhere in the world today and find a magician performing the Cups and Balls, "ninety percent of the time it will be Vernon's routine, or there will be something of Vernon's routine in it."

In the early 1920s Vernon met a gifted and beautiful sculptor, Jean Hayes. Jean had been the assistant to a great stage performer, Horace Goldin, whom Vernon had met at Coney Island. Goldin made beautiful girls rise into the air and vanish, or sawed them in half. Jean was one of the latter. Dai Vernon was enchanted. They began to go out together, and would suddenly surprise everyone by getting married one day in 1924 at Manhattan's Church of the Transfiguration, known to New Yorkers as the Little Church Around the Corner.

His New York friends probably thought that Dai Vernon had been transfigured too because, while he was hugely fond of the company of women, nobody would ever have called him the marrying type. The marriage was, in fact, turbulent. Even though Jean had worked for an extremely capable practitioner, she did not like magicians very much. She distrusted them, found them intolerably vain and self-obsessed. And yet there was something about Dai that was very special.

Their first son Teddy was born in 1926 followed by Derek in 1932. While both men now speak with a mixture of admiration and dismay about their talented parents, both developed an interest in magic. Derek kept many of his father's props, playbills, letters and photos, and only recently turned them over to the Canadian magician and historian of magic, David Ben, for cataloguing and safekeeping.

Both of the Vernon sons have a huge catalogue of stories about their father's obsession with his art. Young Teddy, crying from his sense of neglect one day as his father characteristically practised some card sleight-of-hand over and over and over again, reported that Dai finally noticed him crying and said, "Come here, stop crying, I'll show you a card trick." Whereupon Jean intervened saying, "Stop torturing the boy! Can't you see he's had enough?"

Derek said, "If I weren't working on a magic trick or watching him work on a magic trick I don't think he knew I was there." Ted says that he entered a swimming competition once and Dai came to watch, and when the boy took third prize his father told him sternly that he must never again ask him to come and watch him race if he didn't come in first. And meant it.

It is curious, this obsession, and the way in which it kept orbiting around that one old book. Vernon's fascination and delight with Erdnase never left him. Gamblers often talked about the seemingly impossible "Centre Deal" Erdnase had referred to. It was a sleight that would make it possible for a cheat who had controlled some cards to the top of the deck as he shuffled, to imperceptibly retrieve those cards even after the other player had cut the deck so that they were now in the centre. Somehow you would deal them from the centre of the deck while it seemed you were dealing from the top in the normal way. Gamblers and magicians had long known how to deal from the bottom or to deal the second card while appearing to deal from the top, but the ability to deal from the centre seemed like a fairy tale, though a much desired fairy tale.

Some time in late 1931 Dai and a brilliant fellow-magician named Charlie Miller heard of a man in Wichita, Kansas, a farmer named Allan Kennedy, who could do this seemingly impossible feat. It is said that these two grown men immediately packed their bags and headed for Kansas. Dai Vernon is on record, on videotape (included in this documentary, by the way), saying that they searched in vain, asking everywhere, and had given up. Charlie Miller had gone back to New York, and Dai himself was about to go home too. And on the verge of heading back he passed an ice cream shop outside which a little girl was licking a cone. Vernon said that just on a mischievous impulse and not expecting an answer, he asked the little girl, "I don't suppose *you* know where a Mr. Allan Kennedy lives?" And the girl said, "Sure I do; in that house right there, up on the hill."

"I'm not a biblical scholar," Dai said later, "but I said to myself, 'And a little child shall lead them.'" It was January, 1932. He had found Kennedy. Kennedy showed him the Holy Grail, the Centre Deal, and Dai mastered it, which is something few cardmen have done since.

Visualize it. If you are watching the documentary, it is right there on the screen in front of you. The magician's hands are seen removing the four aces from the deck. The deck is cut in half. The four aces are placed on top of the lower half of the deck, and the top half is placed on top of them. The aces are clearly in the middle. The magician begins to deal four hands of poker smoothly and naturally. Each card comes off the top of the deck, as it should. At least that is certainly what it looks like, perfectly normal. Each time around he deals one card to you, one to me, one to our friend, and then one card face-up, to himself. Guess what his card is, four times in a row. It is totally deceptive. And while this writer has spent a lot of time mastering some sleight-of-hand with cards, he cannot imagine being able to perform this one.

Dai Vernon was doing all kinds of magic in those days, but cards were his first love, and cards remained his love all his life.

In 1924 he was approached by a theatrical and social-events entertainment agent named Frances Rockefeller King. While good magicians might get twenty-five or fifty dollars for an evening's entertainment in a society mansion, King guaranteed Vernon a minimum of $5,000 a month, and his minimums were soon several hundred dollars for a single evening. It was unheard-of. It was because her clients were all multi-millionaires is how he recalled it, decades later: "I only worked for the Astors and the Vanderbilts and the Schwabs. . . . 'Cause she had that kind of clientele."

For some time he had been musing about an elaborate stage presentation that would embody his ideas about the elevated art of magic.

Jean, who was a gifted sculptor and designer, would do masks and costumes, and together they would create something of elegance and grace and wonder. Perhaps he thought it might rehabilitate the faltering marriage, too. They worked it up together in 1938. He shaved the trademark moustache and wore a classical Harlequin loose-fitting suit and a black widow's peak hairdo. He perfected the Symphony of the Rings, and devised a number of gracefully mysterious effects with billiard balls, rope, salt, and a version of the classic Snowstorm in China. In the intimate atmosphere of the elegant and exclusive Rainbow Room, virtually surrounded by wealthy nightclub patrons, it played brilliantly.

He had allowed himself to imagine that this same show, which for all its elegance was really an intimate thing for a relatively small and attentive audience, would play on the stage of the six-thousand-seat Radio City Music Hall. It is a vast stage where people come for spectacle, for long chorus lines, brassy great orchestras and spectacular scenery. The audience simply could not see what he was doing with his hands. He was too far away from most of them, and it is pretty hard to see some of these small props from a hundred feet away. The show closed after the second night. Vernon was devastated. He began to think that maybe performing was not what he wanted to do any more.

There was one routine in the Harlequin Act that played almost as well on the big stage as it had at the Rainbow Room, Vernon's very special version of a classic known as the Chinese Linking Rings. Most published routines for this trick are based on a set of eight rings. Vernon had used twelve in the past, but for the new act he reduced the number to five. You can buy a version of the Linking Rings in any magic shop, in which one ring will have a gap in it that allows the other rings to appear to penetrate it and link to it, if you cleverly conceal the gap. Vernon's version made it patently clear to the audience that there could not possibly be a gap in *any* of his rings, and yet they mysteriously linked and separated again, musically, choreographed like a ballet.

He called it the Symphony of the Rings. This writer saw him do it on CBC television when Vernon was over eighty. He performed at Paul Soles' home-base desk on the late night show Soles was hosting then, right under Soles' nose, inches away. Soles gaped. His jaw quite literally dropped. Vernon, now a wizened and squeaky-voiced old man, didn't really appear to be doing anything at all, it was the rings that did it, gracefully and simply and mysteriously.

Performers today who use eight or five or even as few as three rings will often acknowledge that they have a debt to Vernon and the Symphony, a debt of style, or of manner. That is the Vernon effect; he left the art in a state where most performers feel they cannot do it as well as it should be done unless they take account of his way. Like physics and Einstein or hockey and Gretzky. Max Maven will go so far as to say that there is not one great performing magician anywhere whose work — of whatever genre — doesn't have some Vernon in it.

The same year he learned the Centre Deal he had published a little typewritten pamphlet, thirty pages or so just stapled together, ten card tricks. He liked writing up his discoveries and teaching them and putting them out for magicians to pick up. This modest little mimeographed manuscript sold for the unheard-of sum of $20, which is the equivalent of close to a thousand dollars today. Even at that price it sold out quickly, and Dai saw that there might be something for him to do as a teacher and an author. He still did silhouettes, too. He could go to Long Island and cut silhouettes for the Junior League convention and make a few dollars with his tiny shears and the fine black paper.

As he talked over the possible alternatives to performing, Jean began to get at him about how he had never really had a man's job. She had read that New York was at last building the East River Parkway and needed men with the engineering and drafting skills Vernon had learned at the Royal Military College. So he took an on-site job. Only days after he started he fell from a scaffolding into the East River, and broke both his arms.

A magician with broken arms is a sorry thing, and it got worse. The arms were in dreadful shape and the doctors wanted to amputate. Vernon refused, against their protestations that he might lose them anyway. Somehow they recovered, but not completely. His elbows never did function normally after that. His hands did, though, and he would continue to amaze people with those hands until shortly before he died.

For a while he worked the Caribbean cruise ships where the pay was good and the company fun. It was High Society again, which he'd gotten used to with Frances Rockefeller King. The women were attractive and compliant. His marriage was pretty well over by now, and he could hang out with the gamblers and con men he found so fascinating.

At the same time there was this other thing in his life, the Professor thing, the teaching. Nowadays almost every good magician of repute travels and lectures to other magicians. It is a modest source of income and, if they have props or publications of their own for sale, that brings in some extra revenue too. But in the middle of the twentieth century nobody had ever heard of magicians giving lectures. Vernon's first lecture, in New York in 1946, was a turning point both for him and for the profession.

Soon people were driving hundreds of miles to sit at his feet, and he liked that. He lectured in London and old magicians still talk about how the world changed that day. Ricky Jay, who the same year that Dai Vernon passed away would do a record-breaking sixteen weeks alone on the stage of a Broadway theatre with virtually nothing but cards, would later say, "Dai Vernon made happy pilgrims of us all." Ricky Jay's wonderful evening of card magic, called *Ricky Jay and His Fifty-Two Assistants*, rich in irony and often presented as a lecture rather than an entertainment, was by its very nature a kind of homage to Dai Vernon at whose feet Ricky Jay had been one of those happy pilgrims.

His friends and professional colleagues, however, worried about Vernon, because he never learned to put anything away. When he wasn't working he was often broke. People began to think about finding a kind of home for his Teaching Self, a place the Pilgrims could always find him, where he could be himself and do what he did best, study and teach and demonstrate, and occasionally perform if he felt like it. Suddenly the right place was there, staring them in the face.

The Larsen family had converted an old private mansion in Hollywood into a very special club for magicians called the Magic

Castle. They invited Vernon to come and make it his home base; they would look after him. Nothing to worry about from then on.

Some of the New York magicians were dismayed. They felt that, in a way, they *owned* Dai Vernon, or that New York owned him. He belonged there. But they had nothing to propose that could compete with the Castle. The East/West rivalry became both bitter and funny. It is partly reflected in the pronunciation of the nickname, Dai, which the guys on the swimming team at Ashbury College in Ottawa had invented for him, years earlier. In New York they still pronounce it "Day." On the West Coast it sounds like "Die." When someone asked him which he preferred he said, with a twinkle, "Eether or Eyether." At Ashbury, by the way, while he was an indifferent student (if you measured by exam results), he did some fine artwork and was an outstanding athlete. In 1912, Sir Sandford Fleming, the inventor of Standard Time and an architect of the Canadian railway system, gave the school a trophy in his own name for the best track and field athlete of the year. Vernon was its first recipient, receiving the trophy from the hands of Lady Fleming just before Sir Sandford delivered the convocation address. He may very well have spent that afternoon at one of his favourite activities, playing ragtime piano, for which he had a city-wide reputation. The records of this event were discovered in the Ashbury archives by Vernon's biographer, Toronto magician David Ben, in the autumn of 2000.

The Magic Castle is still there. In a corner of the lobby, near the bar, where you first come in after whispering "Open Sesame" to a magic door, there is a table with a brass plaque on the wall behind it marking the spot where from 1963 at the age of sixty-nine almost to his death Vernon would hold court. There were three small theatres and a glass-walled conservatory on the downslope side of the second floor looking out over the city, with eight or ten little round green baize tables where magicians would sit and show each other stuff. In the trade it is called "sessions." You still have to be a member to get in, or the guest of a member. Today it feels like just another restaurant with magic theatres. But in those days, guests as well as members could sit at those green baize-topped tables and watch the sessions, and they were, well, magical.

This writer's first visit to the Castle was in 1968. I remember Vernon's performance vividly. He did the classic Three Card Monte. It was elegant and funny, and contained a Vernon invention which lifted it from the excellent scam it always was to the level of the totally baffling.

For the next twenty years he would be there to receive people who wanted to sit at his feet, to pass on what he had learned, to drink, to flirt with beautiful women. He kept on studying Erdnase. He kept on inventing and refining. The mathematician and card aficionado Professor Persi Diaconis says that Vernon's most important contribution was the bridge he built to the long and richly carpeted past of magic. While some of the masters resented the way he took their material, even when he refined it — maybe even thought him a thief of ideas and techniques — Professor Diaconis says unequivocally that if Vernon had not studied and polished and written up what these pioneers did, the world would have lost that material, and that there is a lot of magic being performed today only because Vernon preserved it.

He was often crusty and difficult. Castle regulars love to tell how he would scold young hopefuls who came to show off a new trick. He would send them away and shout after them something like "Get out of here, go back to selling shoes, you're not a magician, that's the worst damn thing I ever saw."

But to others he was patiently generous and helpful. He left behind an impressive number of books and pamphlets, some of them dictated or "as told to" other magicians or writers. Many of the young magicians who hung out at the Castle — especially those who collaborated on the publishing projects — began to act as though they, like the New York magicians before, owned Dai Vernon, and many still seem to feel that today. But in fact he included the rights to his writings and some of his cards and coins and rings and cups and balls and other props in his estate, which his sons would inherit. After he broke his hip at the age of ninety-six he went to live with Ted, who looked after him generously until he died in 1992 at the age of ninety-eight.

All those years in the Castle he had been well looked after: fed and watered and adored. It would seem that the last almost quarter-century at the Castle was a golden time. A golden time for this, the most celebrated magician of the twentieth century, this graduate of Ashbury College, Ottawa, this young silhouette cutter from the piers of Coney Island. Dai Vernon. The Professor.

◆ ◆ ◆

Dai Vernon: The Spirit of Magic was produced by Patricia Phillips, written by Patricia Phillips, Richard Pereschitz and Daniel Zuckerbrot, and directed by Daniel Zuckerbrot.

PART FIVE

PAULINE JOHNSON
The Mohawk Princess Who Was Not

So many Canadians are really two different people that it could almost be called a national characteristic. Nation of immigrants that we are, the experience of living more or less at ease in more than one different culture is something that the majority of us have at least observed. It is conceivable that in these early years of the twenty-first century the number of people in Canada who have in fact lived in two cultures may be greater than those who have not.

Tens of thousands of Canadians — from coast to coast but especially in New Brunswick, Quebec and Ontario (and particularly people in the federal public service) — work in both French and English and move easily in and out of both languages and the social and cultural environments where they predominate.

Italian Canadians have, since the end of World War II, played a major role in helping to transform Toronto from a stiff, undemonstrative Anglo-Saxon fortress into a vibrant cosmopolitan metropolis, "the third largest Italian-speaking city in the world, after Rome and Milano." Like their immigrant or first, second, or even fourth and fifth generation counterparts who came from or whose forebears came from China or Vietnam, Poland, Germany, Nigeria, Ethiopia, Haiti, Jamaica, Japan, Bosnia, Ceylon, Pakistan, India . . . they are and speak of themselves both as Canadians and as something else. Italian, Indian . . .

When most of us say the word *Indian*, we mean our First Peoples. Many of them also call themselves Indian. But other titles, such as First Nations, Aboriginal — or the actual names of the Nations themselves, Nish'nabe, Mohawk, Oneida — are becoming more and more widely known to all Canadians. Belatedly, Canada is coming to terms with injustices done in the past and with new relationships to be forged. Whereas cultural wisdom and sharing were often a mark of the European/First Nations contact from the beginning, it was grievously lost as European greed and power set out to destroy what should have been one of the greatest Meetings of the Nations the world has ever seen. Systematically, but grievously slow, the country seems to be trying to heal those wounds.

Six years before Confederation, a woman was born on the Six Nations Reservation in Ontario who, in a dramatic and public way, exemplified this theme of being two persons, living comfortably in two worlds at once. She used the drama of that double heritage, with all its contradictions, to turn herself into the single most famous stage performer in the country. She was the author of a body of work which became mandatory reading (and for some of us memorization) from before her death in 1913 up to the beginning of World War II in 1939.

Her name: Pauline Johnson.

And she was two people. When you see the photograph of her parents, George Johnson and Emily Howells, staring confidently out of the screen in this intriguing biographical documentary, you have to look carefully to realize that their marriage represented the coming together of two worlds. George looks not unlike a black-haired Charlton Heston, but with an intelligence and focus much stronger than the actor's. Emily is strong-jawed, dark-eyed, brimming with irony and inner strength.

George Johnson was a Mohawk. His father, Smoke Johnson, a gifted orator, had married a Clan Mother. In the Mohawk nations it is the Clan Mothers who determine much of the national policy, and whose collective decision selects the chiefs. George Johnson, the son of Smoke Johnson and his wife the Clan Mother, became a chief.

He would also apparently inherit his father's linguistic skills, and spend an important part of his life as an interpreter for the Anglican Church. Through the church connection he met Emily Howells, a young Englishwoman who was visiting her brother-in-law, the Anglican priest.

George was living in the Anglican mission at the time. There was some opposition from both families when he and Emily announced that they were in love and wished to marry. But George Johnson was not a person to be easily dissuaded, and from the strength of character that shines out of that photograph, neither was Emily. George, as a prosperous and influential chief, was able to give his English bride a fine house as a wedding gift. It is called Chiefswood, and it still stands there, on the north bank of the Grand River, a few miles from the bustling modern town of Brantford. Brantford is named for a great Mohawk chief and warrior, Joseph Brant, who was also a gifted interpreter and in his later years, living at Burlington, Ontario, would translate part of the Bible into the Mohawk language.

But more people would learn the words of Pauline Johnson than of her gifted father or of Joseph Brant, the much admired founder of the Six Nations Reserve. Growing up at Chiefswood, with a rather splendid English lady as a mother, and a father who believed strongly in the importance of education, Pauline and her three siblings would be schooled in both traditions. While she understood some Mohawk, and in her travels would pick up some phrases in other Native languages, it was in English that Pauline Johnson found her voice.

She was a journalist to begin with, and later a poet and stage performer. And her timing was very good, because it was a time when the romantic idea of the "Noble Savage," that vanishing race of wise and passionate people, was so popular that it brought Pauline Johnson huge audiences, on both sides of the Atlantic. Pauline Johnson played to those audiences, brilliantly and quite consciously, as a woman of two worlds.

Even the house she grew up in bespeaks two worlds. It had two front entrances; one on the Grand River for the Iroquois people (Mohawk is one of the Iroquois nations) who would arrive by canoe, and one on the land side for the townsfolk who would come by wagon or carriage or on horseback.

Among the visitors to Chiefswood was the inventor and speech teacher Alexander Graham Bell. The man who invented the telephone built the first working model of that instrument in his Brantford house not far from Chiefswood. George Johnson, Pauline's father, helped string telegraph wires for some of Bell's experiments. Bell had himself formally photographed wearing George Johnson's ceremonial buckskin suit.

An important part of young Pauline's education took place on the river. Her Grandfather Smoke was still alive when she was young, and they spent hours together in a canoe, as Pauline learned to handle the supple elegant little craft, and absorbed her grandfather's stories of the Mohawk people. And so she knew that she was a Mohawk. But unlike most young Mohawks she had a mother who made sure she was also raised as an inheritor of the English tradition. By the time she was twelve it is said that she had read all of the standard classics that George Johnson's well-stocked library had to offer. She began, like many young English girls of "good families," to write poetry.

Because of her father's prominence both as a Chief at Six Nations and as an agent of the Anglican Church, she met a number of distinguished people who came as guests to the house. Chiefswood was a house of hospitality. One of the visitors was the then very young Prince Arthur, Duke of Connaught, whose mother Queen Victoria thought of herself as Empress of many great nations. Some of these nations were themselves led regally by such dignitaries as George Johnson. The Great Queen sent her young son — who was later to become Canada's Governor General — to Canada to meet the chiefs — among them Smoke and George Johnson. The young Prince made the Johnsons a gift of a fine red blanket.

But a shadow was to fall over this world of privilege and distinction. Suddenly and dramatically the girl had to take another, much more practical look at the two worlds within which she had so comfortably grown up. Pauline's father, as chief, was the guardian of the Reserves resources, a role that turned out to be perilous. George Beaver, a contemporary Six Nations historian, tells it this way.

The great forests [at Six Nations] were very valuable, and white people would come and steal the wood if they could. George Johnson went about keeping an eye on things in the forests and as a result he was caught and beaten very, very badly, almost killed. A similar thing happened to him because of his opposition to selling whisky. The whisky peddlers beat him. He was actually attacked twice. And the last time he was in ill health for about ten years until he died.

His death left the family almost destitute. Emily and her daughters had to put Chiefswood up for rent, move into a small house in town, and look for work. Eva found an office job. Pauline made a little money as a freelance journalist, discovered the community theatre, studied Shakespeare and began to think about turning her early love of storytelling and verse into a life. Since childhood she had performed recitations and playlets for the family. Now she joined the Brantford Amateurs, and found that she had a gift for the emotionally extravagant melodramas that were the heart and soul of popular theatre. Her name survives on the playbills and programs of dozens of those plays. The plays themselves have not survived on the stage, but they gave the young performer a taste of that most intoxicating experience: applause.

At some point, perhaps, she began to realize that her gifts were more theatrical than truly poetic. Looking at her poetry now, readers will find themselves wondering sometimes what all the fuss was about (and there would soon be plenty of fuss), sometimes how any of this could be taken seriously. This writer was required to memorize some of it in school. The teacher, who had actually *seen* Pauline Johnson on stage when she, the teacher, was an adolescent at the turn of the century, managed to convey the idea that this was pretty wonderful stuff, the outpouring of the soul of a Mohawk Princess, after all! That there was and is no such thing as a Mohawk Princess, and that Pauline herself never actually claimed the title, did not matter. Along with probably hundreds if not thousands of other ten-year-olds, I had to learn lines like these:

. . . Swirl, swirl!
How the ripples curl
In many a dangerous pool awhirl!
Dip, dip,
While the waters flip
In foam as over their breast we slip.

It is not that much more laughable than much of the poetry of the out of doors that the era produced. But it had a greater effect than most verse of its kind, because the author was a powerful performer. Wide-eyed audiences from British Columbia to Birmingham felt that they were in the presence of a Red Indian. And that Red Indian looked comfortably just like them. Audiences were taken, swept up by the soulful beauty, the daring exposure of bare arms and ankles, the passionate declamation, the buckskin and wampum, and the famous viceregal red blanket. The poetry took on the reputation of the performer, and that reputation survived for decades.

Pauline Johnson's biographer, Professor Carol Gerson, appearing in the documentary, pointed out that when Pauline began to write poetry she was doing what any other well-brought-up Anglo-Canadian society girl would do: write poetry about graceful nature, about conventional love; imitative poems. Not poems about the Mohawk experience. Nobody else was writing about that; why should she?

But in trying to make some money as a freelance journalist she discovered that her editors at the *Brantford Examiner*, and their readers, seemed to really enjoy what she had to say about life on the Grand River, and about the traditions of the Reservation. Now those themes would begin to manifest themselves in her poems as well. An early piece about Joseph Brant (1742–1807), while it celebrated the achievements of this extraordinary Mohawk leader, sounds today like a piece of British jingoism. We do not know what Pauline's contemporaries at Six Nations thought of it; a Mohawk warrior in the present day would likely be appalled.

Then meet we as one common brotherhood
In peace and love, with purpose understood
To lift a lasting tribute to the name
Of Brant, who linked his own with Britain's fame.

She first published in about 1884 or '85, when she was twenty-three or twenty-four. She had not yet quite put together the poetic and the dramatic strands of her professional life. But the convergence had begun. In the meantime, the *Examiner* was running pieces that sounded like this:

Ah, who would not know it was the Grand River, with its romantic forests, its legend-thronged hills, its wide and storied flats, its tradition-fraught valleys. This was the domain of that most powerful of North American Nations: the Iroquois.

And another, inspired by her father's death:

Cold had settled in all the broken places of his poor body, and he
slipped away from her, a sacrifice to his fight against evil, on the
altar of his Nation's good. And almost his last words were, "It must
be by my mother's side," meaning his resting place. So his valiant
spirit went fearlessly forth.

It was playing well, this kind of thing. Perhaps as the young country settled into some kind of stability, and confidence and prosperity brought a time for reflection on the circumstances of its birth, some white Canadians were beginning to sense the guilt of their suppression and exploitation of the indigenous people. If that was so, here was the very comforting appearance of a voice that could accuse us of our genocidal behaviour but at the same time forgive, and even say in effect: It's really all right, because that *most powerful of all the North American Nations, the Iroquois,* is still alive and well: I am the living proof of it.

In January of 1892 a man named Frank Yeigh invited Pauline to recite her own work to a gathering of the Young Liberals club, in Toronto. This was the chance to try how far she could go. She gave them "A Cry from an Indian Wife," regrettably not one of the texts we children were urged to memorize in the 1930s.

They but forget we Indians owned the land
From ocean unto ocean, that they stand
Upon a soil that centuries a-gone
Was our sole kingdom and our right alone.
They never think how they would feel today
If some great nation came from far away
Wresting their country from the hapless braves
Giving what they gave us, but wars and graves.

Imagine the scene. Ontario Hydro was still nearly fifteen years in the future, but electric lighting was an established and popular novelty on the urban scene. In the streets of the larger towns the horse-drawn trams plying along dozens of miles of tracks were being replaced with electric trams. The electric tram had a Belgian-invented trolley in which a tiny wheel at the end of a spring-loaded pole on the roof actually brought sparking electric power down to the wheels, which in turn completed the circuit through the electrified rails beneath. People were telling scare stories about how you mustn't step on both rails at once (they were four feet apart!) or you'd fry. But that was not stopping the city folk from jumping on the trams and heading downtown to the shops and the excitement. It was a revolution in city living. For another fifty years or so the horse and the electric tram were both important parts of the transportation scene, slowly being pushed aside by the automobile. On that January evening in 1892, no cars on the scene yet, as Pauline arrived at the Young Liberals gathering, the better-off members of her audience would be stepping out of horse-drawn carriages in their heavy fur coats, but dozens more would be arriving in the new electric trams with their little coal furnaces and uniformed motormen and conductors.

And here comes this smouldering beauty in a simple ball gown that showed off a classical figure, the dark pools of her brown eyes, the sensuous lips, a great English beauty. Then they learn that she is a Mohawk, an Indian! Who looks just like us. Who speaks to us of her pride and her anger, and yet . . . she *likes* us! She's one of us.

She was an instant hit.

Professor Gerson says,

The first performance in Toronto in January 1892 allowed Frank Yeigh to mythologize himself as the discoverer of Pauline Johnson. This shy little forest maiden who tip-toed out on stage and stood shivering before the audience and was completely taken by surprise when they applauded. Well, she was nothing of the sort. She was thirty-one years old. She'd been involved in amateur theatricals. She'd published dozens of poems in the Toronto papers. She was a known entity.

Sheila Johnston, of Brantford, has made a study of those early performances. She says:

People would go out to see jugglers juggle or bell-ringers ring bells or elocutionists speak. Pauline sweeps into town and she's got props and a costume and poetry and stories to tell. She would [first] come out on stage in an evening gown, and present herself as her mother would have wished . . . a very aristocratic, sophisticated, educated, articulate woman. And then later on in the bill she would come out and she would be the complete opposite to that image: a Mohawk woman with her hair unbound, wearing a buckskin dress, using a few props like her father's hunting knife and a bear-claw necklace. So the audience would go away thinking, 'Well, that was worth the price of admission. I got two Paulines for the price of one.'

And author Margaret Atwood:

Well first of all she made up the costume. That picture you see of her is not a real Indian, [not] anything a real tribe would have worn. It allowed her to write different kinds of poetry. She could write the contained, rather lady-like lyric poems, and do those first. And then she would come on in this other costume, and be another person, the Indian Princess . . . could do really blood-curdling, you know, violent poems.

His eyes aglow with hate and triumph as
He hisses through locked teeth.
An evil curse, a flash of steel, a leap,
A thrust above the heart, well-aimed and deep
Plunged to the very heart in blood and blade
While vengeance, gloating, yells "THE DEBT IS PAID!"

"She was a howling success," Margaret Atwood continues.

People were smitten . . . She had a very thrilling voice. And made quite an effect. She wrote in the nineteenth-century style. Possibly the biggest influence might have been Longfellow. And she wrote for performance. So it was rhetorical, it was dramatic. And they were intended, like Charles Dickens' recitations, to make you laugh or cry.

My hand crept up the buckskin of his belt.
His knife hilt in my burning palm I felt.
One hand caressed his cheek, the other drew
The weapon softly. "I love you, love you,"
I whispered. "Love you as my life."
And buried in his back his scalping knife.

George Beaver tells us that people would think nothing of travelling forty or fifty miles to see and hear her. The kind of publicity machinery that today manufactures celebrities overnight and by the dozens did not exist in the 1890s. And yet, within a couple of years Pauline Johnson was unquestionably a national celebrity. It would not be long before she began to think of a larger stage.

Today it is the conventional wisdom that Canadian performers and artists who want to succeed in a big way have to prove themselves in the USA. In the 1890s it was a British tour that they dreamed of. We were still in a colonial state of mind, we Canadians. And the way to demonstrate that you were as good as anyone else was to go and take London by storm. So that was Pauline Johnson's next target. She booked passage on a liner, and once again she hit the bull's eye. London was as smitten as Toronto and Montreal had been. In a sense it was easier. There was a romantic distance. Not many in London had actually seen a real Mohawk person. Londoners knew the romantic legends of the "noble savage," and had largely been spared the sight of desperate poverty and degradation of the authentic North American Indians. Pauline was a hit in the salons and on the stage. She was invited everywhere. She met the military, the aristocracy, the upper middle class, members of parliament, lords and justices. The Duke of Connaught sent to know what had happened to the famous red blanket. She pointed out that it was with her on the stage. Once again, secure in her comfortable persona, she was able to lecture them on their culpability.

Suppose we came over to England as a powerful people. Suppose you gave us welcome to English soil, worshipped us as Gods, as we worshipped you white people. And suppose we encroached upon your homeland, and drove you back and back, and then said, "We will present you with a few acres of your own dear land." What would you think of it all?

And her audiences would nod wisely and sadly, and think, Yes, we have done wrong, and isn't it comforting to see that she does not hate us for it. Because, of course, Mohawk though she may be, she is also one of us.

She was quite conscious of this. She marched into the Bodley

Head, a premium imprint for poetry, and talked them into publishing her. And the collection of poems she called *White Wampum,* openly reflecting the double identity of white and Indian. She openly spoke of being two persons. It was a strength, not a weakness. It allowed her a sexuality on stage that would have been unseemly for a proper English recital artist.

As an Indian she could let her hair flow free and show bare arms and calves. When she returned to Canada she had the cachet of a British success, and now she was selling out wherever she went. It was not just the concert halls in the cities. She went to Moose Jaw and Banff. She played the mining towns and the lumber towns and gave the rough guys and the ladies of the night a taste of her own lusty and blood-drenched drama. When she walked out on stage, she owned the house.

In 1897 she moved to Winnipeg and became engaged to Charles Drayton, a banker. But it did not last, and perhaps — as is often the case in showbusiness relationships — what he had fallen in love with was the image, not the person, and when it became clear that his fiancée was on the road most of the time, and *certainly* not about to settle down as a Winnipeg *grande dame,* to run a home and put on shows in it for him and his friends . . . but this is speculation. They did not get married.

Soon after this her mother died. Pauline felt forsaken. Her brother Beverly was dead. Her sister Eva was far away in the States. She would soon be forty. She had been on the road for eight years. She was a success, but she was tired. There is a mannered, stilted scene in a 1933 movie called *Shadow River*. A society couple is at dinner in a fancy restaurant. She asks, "Did you ever hear of Pauline Johnson?"

"Can't say I have. Does she live in these parts?"

"My dear, Pauline Johnson was a poetess."

"Ha! That explains everything."

"You know, I think perhaps she is my favourite Canadian writer. She died twenty years ago. She was part Indian, you know.

'Dream of tender gladness,

Of filmy sun and opal-tinted skies

And warm midsummer air that lightly lies
In mystic rings.'"

So twenty years after her death they still remembered her, the Double Person. The White Mohawk. The Indian Princess. Eighty years after her death and she is almost forgotten, but that is ironic, because the challenges that ring out from her poetry when she sounds like an authentic First Nations Poet can still be heard and admired, whereas her British jingoism simply sounds absurd.

Few of us have the blood of kings.
Few are of courtly birth.
But few are vagabonds or rogues
of doubtful name and worth.
And all have one credential
that entitles them to brag:
That we were born in Canada,
beneath the British flag!

Trite and conventional in their own time, most of us would find them silly, if not offensive now. But when she writes, "You have given us Bibles and stolen our land," her poems on genocide still ring with an authentic feeling:

You have killed him. But you shall not dare
To touch him now he's dead.
You have cursed and called him "cattle thief"
Though you robbed him first of bread—
Robbed him and robbed my people.
Look there at that shrunken face,
Starved with the hollow hunger
We owe to you and your race.
What have you left us of land?
What have you left of game?
What have you brought but evil
And curses since you came?

Squamish Elder Joe Mathias, great-grandson of Chief Joe Capilano who was her last close friend, says that such a voice was rare in Pauline's time. It is not that common today, either; so split personality or double identity though she undoubtedly had, in her most powerful voice Pauline Johnson may have helped set in motion some of those declarations of right and of entitlement that still importantly drive the First Nations in their ongoing search for a place in the North American sunshine even today.

By 1906 she was tired, and she had done the big work she set out to do. But she was not finished yet. Now forty-five years old, she tried Britain again. It was not quite the smash success of the earlier tour. But in London she met the Squamish chief, Joe Capilano, there to seek an audience with King Edward VI. Pauline was able to greet him in a few words of his own language. A rich friendship blossomed from this encounter. It would last the rest of her all too short life.

Back in Canada again she wrote stories for *Boys World*, and *Mother's Magazine*. She launched an exhausting tour of recitations in Canada and the USA, with her new and very loyal manager Walter McRaye. And then she had had enough. In 1909, perhaps already aware of the encroaching illness that would take her life, she just stopped. Exit. No fanfare. No farewell tour. She just stopped. She thought of Joe Capilano. She moved to Vancouver.

There would be one last great task, although she did not know that yet. Joe Capilano, according to his great-grandson Joe Mathias, was a man of few words but a far-reaching intellect and had a vision of the possibilities for his people, the Squamish.

> There had to be a deep spiritual connection [between them]. He was not about to share a lot of his intimate views of the universe with [just] anybody. And, well, I think they became such good friends that he was willing to share these stories, these myths, these legends that come from the Squamish people, that in a way explain who we are, why we're here, where we come from.

Pauline wrote these stories down in her own style, and with the Chief's permission she sent a couple off to the *Vancouver Province*, which serialized them. The stories of a coastal people, until now conveyed by word of mouth, and virtually unknown outside their own circle, proved intriguing to a wide readership, soon to become wider. They were assembled in a book, *Legends of Vancouver*. The first edition sold out. A *Collected Poems* was planned. When she published it under the title *Flint and Feather*, it was, like *Legends*, an instant success. She was a popular writer again.

And she needed the money. She had been diagnosed with breast cancer. The rest of her days were spent in hospital, and much of the revenue went to pay for what was a costly business in the days before a public health care system.

There is a footnote about Prince Arthur, Duke of Connaught. He had been appointed Governor General of Canada. His first contact with the Johnson family had been at Six Nations, more than forty years earlier; then there was the message about the blanket, in London (but no meeting).

But finally, in 1912, the Governor General came to the poet's bed-side. We do not know what they said to each other. But if you look at the title page of *Flint and Feather*, you will see that it is dedicated to him.

The Mohawk from Ontario had fallen deeply in love with her new home on the Pacific Coast; the grandeur of the mountains, the easy-going friendliness of the people, the bustle of the shops. She particularly cherished Stanley Park and the long ruminative walks she took there with Joe Capilano. She asked the city to bury her ashes in the Park, overlooking the ocean. There is no other tomb in the park that we know of. But Pauline is there. And from time to time, on her small marker, with a carved profile of the poet in stone, you will see a fresh bunch of flowers.

She died a few months after *Flint and Feather* was published. She was not yet fifty-two. Her books have been printed in many languages. There have been several biographies. Four schools are named for her, including a French-language school. She has had a commemorative postage stamp, and Chiefswood is a national historic site, open to the public. Although few Canadians now know who she is, she left a foot-print. Perhaps she was ahead of her time, in her passion to utter the passions and the stories of her native heritage, and at the same time build a bridge of understanding between the First Nations and the "Founding Nations." It is difficult to think of anyone since who has undertaken quite the same task. She represented, says biographer Carol Gerson, "a possibility in Canada that has not been reproduced."

♦ ♦ ♦

The Pauline Johnson biography was written by Simon Johnston and produced by Scott Calbeck and Morgan Earl, with line producer David Hoffert.

♦ PART SIX ♦

ANGUS WALTERS
The Captain and the Queen

One of our coins has not one but two queens on it. Take out a dime, heads or tails. If heads comes up first you'll see the familiar face of Her Majesty Elizabeth II, as she was in her late twenties, lean and graceful and every inch a Queen. Turn it over and you'll find the image of a ship under sail, also lean and graceful. And also every inch a queen, though not yet in her twenties as depicted there in chiselled silver metal.

She is a schooner. The age of sail being long gone, for many readers nowadays the word *schooner* just means a sailboat, perhaps a little bigger than the Lasers kids learn to race on, but, hey, schooner, sailboat, same thing.

Not so.

The schooner arrives fairly late on sailing's long horizon. She is the ultimate design of that last period of the world's history in which sailing vessels went to sea to work, to carry cargo or passengers or to fish, not primarily as the computer-designed playthings of wealthy sportmen and women sailing for glory. In the late eighteenth century and long into the nineteenth, the transoceanic record-breakers were the clippers, ships of four or five masts — or even more — bearing both square sails and fore-and-aft sails, huge loads of canvas that could drive them across an ocean faster than anything that had been seen before.

The fore-and-aft sail, a triangular canvas with its luff or forward edge laced to a pole or a line, allows a vessel to sail into the wind, within about 45 degrees of head-on to it. But the big traditional square work sails of the ocean-crossers and warships of the days before steam were a great way to sail before the wind. You could not sail closer to the wind than broadside under square sails; with a straight north wind you could head up as close to the wind as straight west or east, not into the wind on a northerly course. But running before the wind you could pile on great masses of sail, acres of billowing cloth, and fairly leap over the waves.

Then marine architects began to refine the shape and distribution of sails, and to come up with patterns that somehow drew the wind over the vessel in a way that gave her more speed over the long haul than any other rig. Their great achievement was called the schooner, a Dutch word originally. The schooner's mainmast, the tallest of her two or three masts, would be the one furthest aft, the foremast the smaller. And if there were a third, the mizzen, it would be in-between in size. There was something aerodynamically effective about that big collection of sails making up a huge triangle with the longest edge the furthest back that made for speed, but also made for difficult handling. With all that wind pressure far aft, there was a tricky balance of wind and water pressures on sails, rigging, hull and rudder. You really had to know what you were about. Many a young skipper who thought he knew sail would find himself in trouble the first time he took a schooner into a serious bit of wind.

Not Angus Walters. If you look at photographs of the Newfoundland and Nova Scotia fishing fleets going off after the cod towards the end of the 1800s and the beginning of the 1900s, bit by bit you see more of those tall mainmasts aft, the shorter foremast, bit by bit three masts reduce to two and the square sails vanish, bit by bit, until by the time Angus Walters was ready to take command of a vessel, his first command, at the age of twenty-three, *Captain* Angus Walters, there was little doubt in the minds of serious fishermen that the schooner was the rig. Angus Walters could really not remember much of a life before he went to sea, and when he went there it was in schooners, and their little dories in which the men went off for the cod and brought it back to the schooner for salting and packing.

Cod is a cold-water species, found mostly in the North Atlantic. Now, in the twenty-first century, stocks are grievously low. But when early explorers first entered our waters, they found so many that the myth was you could throw a basket over the side with a line on it and haul up the crew's dinner. Some even claimed that the fish on the surface were so thick they slowed the vessel down. When the Italian Giovanni Caboto reported back to the King of England who had commissioned him in 1495, he confidently reported that the waters off the New Found

Land were so rich in fish that Europe could be fed for the rest of time.

Cod would become a prize for which nations went to war. For centuries conflicts between France, Britain, the Scandinavian countries, and finally Canada and the United States, over cod, were in many ways as important, if not as bloody, as the conflicts over sovereignty and land. They are not over yet.

Angus Walters was born in Lunenburg, Nova Scotia, on June 9, 1881, one of twelve children born to a sea captain and his wife. Many a Nova Scotian kid would be off to the cod at the age of eight or nine, especially if his dad had been lost at sea and the kid was suddenly the man of the house. But Angus' dad wanted to make sure his kids got a good schooling, and Angus did not turn up working the cod, a "throater" cutting the heads off as the fish were gaffed up over the side of the schooner, from the dories, until he was thirteen. By the age of fifteen he was out in the dories himself, a doryman under the tutelage of an experienced fisherman, the dory skipper.

His first time out was almost his last. A thick fog came down on them, they could neither see nor hear the mother ship, night fell, the older man feared that their fate would be that of hundreds, maybe thousands of Nova Scotian men who went out in the dory into storms or fog and never came back. They were lucky that night. The fog lifted. In the distance the boy and the man could see lights, a red light and a green light, their schooner, and they rowed and yelled and rowed and yelled, and made it back safely.

A few years later, still in his teens, Angus was on deck one night with the captain, who was his older brother John. The sea was running very high, just the two brothers on deck, everyone else below. A wave washed right over the deck. Angus heard a cry from his brother, and when he could get the water out of his eyes, the young skipper was gone, washed overboard. It was fairly easy to get washed overboard. The rails were built low to permit the fish to be easily gaffed from above or thrown from below when the dories came back with their catch; the sea often washed over the deck. Men sometimes lashed themselves in place at the wheel but John wasn't tied on that night, and he was gone. Young Angus showed his natural flair for command, took over the ship, yelled for some men, and ordered a dory lowered over the side. Almost miraculously John caught a line hanging from the dory, and was saved. Angus had had his first taste of command.

It came to him not long after, with a vessel called the *Minnie M. Cook*. Although he was but twenty-three years old, he was already known as a veteran of the Atlantic cod fishery. Young Captain Angus Walters. He is still remembered as extraordinary by those who sailed with him.

His son Spike says, "He might have been small, but he was mighty. All you had to do was sail with him on a fishing trip . . . and you'd know that he had fight in him. If you fooled around he'd just as much say, 'We'll throw *you* overboard.'"

Sailors were a bit afraid of him. Authority then was taken seriously in every field and was often fearsome. But Angus' sailors loved him, and the survivors still do; you can hear it in the warm burr of their Nova Scotia voices. Clem Hilz sailed with him for years, and says, "There was no fear in him. And you didn't have too many men saying anything back to him or you know, that wasn't in the books. When he said 'We'll do such,' that Such — whatever it was — was done."

They remember him, even from those early days, as a "sail-dragger," a skipper who liked to pile on the sail and push the vessel as hard as she could be pushed. But not beyond reason. He impressed them even then, in his young twenties, as a captain who knew very well that he had the lives of his men in his hands. But he loved to push a vessel, to make her lift, to get the last one percent of a knot out of her.

The cod fishery had a strong racing tradition. It was not just racing for sport: the fastest vessels would be first in with a catch and would command the market. Nonetheless, whenever a pair of ships were on the last leg home, or even outward bound for the Grand Banks empty and fresh, and came within hailing distance, chances are one skipper or the other would pull up alongside the other man's ship and haul out a megaphone and cry "Let's have a Hook!" And that meant, let's see who'll be first at the fish, or first back in port. And then it would be pile on the sail and all hands on deck, and cheering and yelling taunts back and forth. They sailed dangerously close to each other, learning their vessel's quirks and quiddities, and looking for that tiny bit of added speed that would not seem very much from minute to minute, but overnight, say, or through a long day, could bring one skipper home to port a minute or two or even an hour or more ahead of the other.

So racing was a great sport and also a way to improve your profit margins.

When he was twenty-six Angus Walters fell in love with and married Maggie Tanner. Sons Gilbert and Spike and Stewart arrived over the next seven years, although their dad was at sea at least as much as he was home, building a reputation as a Highline skipper who brought home huge catches. He would take his new vessel the *Muriel B. Walters* (named after his mother) to the same grounds as another man, and come home with twice the catch. Substantial profits for his shareholders, and a comfortable income for his young family.

And a hell of a reputation whenever they went for a Hook, outbound or homebound.

You can see his picture from the high days of the schooner trade, on the 37-cent Canadian stamp issued in 1981. It is a lean-boned tidy face, with eyes that are always scanning the horizon and the weather and the set of the sails. The mouth usually had just a hint of an ironic pout, a turnup at the middle of the outer lip that made you wonder if he wasn't thinking of some stunt or some technique for making her sail just a bit faster. It was a face that would become famous. It is seldom seen, that calculating face, under a formal captain's peaked cap with an anchor, or over gold-braided shoulders. It's more often an old cloth cap like an Irish farmer's, and a tweed jacket, or oilskins. The old cloth cap is what he wore at the wheel, and almost everywhere else. It is hard to think of him without it.

In 1920 someone got the bright idea of turning the Hook into a formal international race. Many of the skippers from Lunenburg had gone up against their counterparts from Gloucester, Massachusetts, and other New England fishing ports, and there was a kind of international rivalry that was friendly and respectful but intense at the same time. So they put together the plans for a series, the International

Fishermen's race. This wasn't something for well-off sportsmen. The vessel in competition had to be a working fishing vessel, and the men sailing her had to be fishermen. The first race would be in September, and so Angus took the *Muriel B.* out against fellow Lunenburger Tom Himmelman in command of the *Delawanna*, in the qualifier off Halifax. And Angus piled on the sail — too much, as it turned out, for the *Muriel B.* He should not have done it. It was not necessary. He was well in the lead. But now he was carrying nine thousand square feet of sail five miles short of the finish line, and the *Muriel B.* couldn't take it. The foremast snapped, and the foredeck was a mess of splintered spruce, broken lines and tangled canvas. The *Delawanna* pulled ahead and crossed the line six minutes ahead of Angus and the *Muriel B.*

As if that wasn't bad enough, the *Esperanto* out of Gloucester, up against Tom Himmelman and the *Delawanna* in the finals, simply walked away with it. The *Esperanto*'s skipper Marty Welch sailed home with the $4,000 prize, the equivalent of $100,000 or more in today's money, dollars that the Nova Scotians had put up, confident that *their* man would win. But he didn't. It was shameful.

Nova Scotia Curator of Education Ralph Getson says he believes it was then that Angus began to think of building the greatest schooner ever, a vessel that would win that cup back from the New Englanders, the ship that would be the *Bluenose*. He stewed all winter about the strain it would put on his family life, with the three young boys and a wife whose health was not the best, but he knew it had to be done and sensed that he was the Lunenburger who could restore honour to the port. He talked it up with politicians and businessmen. The money was raised. They sought out a naval architect named William Roue and told him he had to build them a schooner that would beat the Gloucestermen.

There was never any question as to who would command her. Ralph Getson says that Angus "had a track record. He had proven he could handle a vessel. . . . They were still fishing. He was a fish killer. He could find a trip of fish. . . . Also he could handle a crowd of men."

He was passionately committed to the new project. Obsessed is probably the better word. He was down at the yards most days that winter. He even began to interfere with the design. That made for some hard feelings, for a while, with William Roue, according to Ralph Getson.

The tradition in designing accommodations for fishermen was that the men's needs did not matter as much as the design of the hull for cargo and speed. But Angus Walters was a sailors' skipper. He said, "My men are not midgets. They need more room in the fo'c'sle [fore-castle]." The fo'c'sle is where the sailors sleep. Angus wanted his crew well-rested. If you look at the photographs of the hull you can see what they call a "knuckle" at the bow, where they raised the deck above the forecastle, an eighteen inch add-on that Bill Roue always said slowed her down. Roue kept on saying it long after Bluenose *became the fastest sailing ship in the world.*

"No!" said Angus Walters, in an interview with J. Frank Willis, this writer's old colleague, a gravel-voiced CBC announcer and TV host who had sailed with Walters on her last great race, sending the race out live by radio.

"It didn't slow her down. He [Bill Roue] thinks that by raising her up, when you 'haul by,' . . . that there was much more wood higher up in the air. But on the other hand, when you were off [sailing before the wind], there was that much more wind up higher in the air in that. So I don't think it affected her one way or the other. . . . Raising her up forward still made her a drier boat. In bad weather or . . . a fairly good breeze. . . . If it had been down eighteen inches lower, more water was going to come over, and more come over it had to go back off the deck and run off of her. . . . (And) you never want water on deck when you are racing if you can help it!"

Ships in the Nova Scotia fleet often carried the name of a woman, the wife of an owner or master often as not. But this time the schooner that was going to be the pride of Nova Scotia and of Canada, a symbol of maritime pride known around the world, for twenty-one years the fastest of her kind afloat, would be named for her people, the Nova Scotians, the Bluenoses. She was launched from the Lunenburg yards on March 26, 1921. Her skipper was thirty-nine years old. He was at the height of his powers.

Clem Hilz says that Angus talked to her as if she were a person. *Honest to God. He always talked to that ship. . . . He could do more with that ship than he could do with any . . . I don't believe he could have done it with another ship. That ship and him were just like bosom pals. Wonderful!*

He could go up and take the wind out of the sails (of the competition) and sail by them. . . . "Luffing" they used to call it. Luffing. Get up windward of a guy and his sails would be going this way, and the Bluenose *would be going right along you know. Smooth sailing. Oh yes. Tricks in all trades. And he had 'em. . . . That's the beauty of it. And he knew he had a ship that could do the tricks if he put it to it. And he used to put it to it!*

Luffing works like this. You are slightly behind the other vessel, sailing just a bit upwind of her. That is, if the wind is coming from the starboard, your right hand, the other vessel is a few metres ahead of you and to port, to your left. It is desirable to be upwind of the other vessel. Presently you will have to make a turn in that direction to tack onto the next leg, and if you are upwind that means you are ahead as you turn. But there is this luffing trick that allows you to make it even better.

If you pull her too hard into the wind, trying to "haul" as Angus said, to get even further upwind, you will lose a little speed. You have this trade-off between getting a little more speed by falling off a little to port, just off the wind, or holding up into the wind, keeping upwind but a little slower.

Here is what Angus Walters (and generations of racing sailors after him, including this writer) would do. He would suddenly turn slightly to port, falling off the wind, picking up speed substantially but crossing right behind the other vessel where, for a moment, he would be blanketed by her sails as he pulled ahead but slightly downwind of her. It seems, the first time you try it, as though you have lost position, in relationship to the wind. But you are really fast now, and that momentary blanketing effect is so brief it hardly affects your speed at all. And so the next thing you know you are pulling ahead of the other guy, but slightly downwind. And there is a curious effect that takes place if you judge the positions of the two vessels very precisely. There is a backflow coming off your sails that disturbs the flow of air over the sails of the ship upwind of your starboard. You are "covering" her. And before he knows it the other skipper, who has everything set for this close-hauled course, close into the wind, is losing his wind, luffing, slowing down grievously.

He is in a kind of trap. He can't come much off the wind towards you to recover or he'll hit you. If you play it just right (and it *is* a high-risk manoeuvre, requiring a *very* nice judgment) you begin to pull ahead. Then you can position him dead behind you, the luffing gets worse in your slipstream, you pull away ahead and he never recovers.

Angus pulled that in the two qualifiers, and then sailed *Bluenose* down to Gloucester for the International, and of course brought home the cup and the money and the glory, to Lunenburg, where it belonged. And the next year he did it again.

Clem Hilz says, "They could build boats forever and a day over in Gloucester, they'd never build one to beat that *Bluenose*. In calm waters, yes, *maybe*. But you give her 25 knots of wind and the devil in hell couldn't catch her!"

Bluenose will never be forgotten. There will be a *Bluenose II*, we'll come to that. She'll be skippered by Angus Walters' grandson Wayne Walters. But even Wayne, proud as he was of *Bluenose II*, still speaks of the original and her skipper with a sense of wonder.

He knew how far to push it. . . . He knew the vessel. The vessel was part of him. He knew every inch of canvas and wood, and he knew the breaking point of everything, and I think he must have had that extra sense of being able to tell when there was going to be a slight change in the wind, or where the best position would be to take advantage of . . . ah . . . of "covering" the other vessel, so to speak.

Before long, Angus Walters, of Lunenburg, Nova Scotia, a town few west of New Brunswick could even find on the map, became not just a hometown hero, but a national hero. His schooner was now officially the fastest sailing vessel in the whole, wide, windy world. This seemed not to go to his head. He kept perspective. Work was what it was all about. Work to do as well as the other fellow, perhaps a little better. Work was best if you had a vessel you could talk to, who could listen to you. But there was a lot of luck that went with the work, and you depended critically upon the skills and support of the crew, all able sailors, each one knowing what he had to do at every moment.

Angus Walters radiated a quiet pride now (how could he not?) but he didn't wear it like medals or a flag. He was firm but soft spoken, apparently not interested in personal glory; just in doing the best that could be done. That is how they remember him.

There was another well-respected Atlantic coast cod fisherman. His name was Ben Pine. He fished out of Gloucester, Massachusetts. Now the Gloucestermen looked at Ben Pine, and they looked at *Bluenose*, and they said *Bluenose* was the ship to beat and Ben Pine was the man to beat her.

But they didn't have a ship. So they decided to do exactly what the Lunenburgers had done; they would build one. They hired the best marine architects they could find. Money was no object. They knew that the Lunenburg yards had produced something the world had never seen before. But maybe it was a fluke, and they had the science and the resources to do better than those fishermen in Nova Scotia; they were Americans, after all. And so they gathered it all together and got to work.

The result, the following year, was the *Columbia*; sleek, some secrets about the hull they wouldn't let anyone even look at, the latest in materials and fittings, the best craftsmen New England could provide. She was a beauty. Ben Pine looked on the *Columbia*, and saw that she was good. He hand-picked a crew. Every member of that crew was himself a Captain. The skipper and his captains set out for Halifax, for the next running of the International Fishermen's. The world was watching. The first race began. It was very close for a while. At one point the ships got too close to each other and as she came about for the next tack *Bluenose*'s boom raked the *Columbia* and caused some damage. Angus Walters said, "As soon as we got clear of him, it was just the same as saying goodbye to the *Columbia*, because from there in we still crossed the line between two and three minutes ahead of her . . . well, we come in . . . it's officially announced . . . *Bluenose* won, everybody felt happy, and no more about it."

But there *was* more about it. *Columbia* won the second race, and then the race committee changed the rules. *Bluenose* won the third race, but the committee declared that under the new rules, which had not been discussed with the competing captains, Bluenose had rounded a buoy the wrong way. So they awarded the race — and the cup — to Ben Pine and the *Columbia*.

Angus Walters said that he went to the chairman to protest, and said, "Can you give us a reason? Oh yes, he said, a protest entered and you did this and you did that. . . . Well, I said, we got our rules, I said, before the race started. And you and no other committee can do anything out of those rules without the consent of the two sailing masters."

And then one of those extraordinary events happened that gives grace to the world of high competition between people of character and integrity. The Gloucestermen heard of it. And Ben Pine and his crew of captains said to each other, Angus is right. And they told the committee they would not accept the prize under that unheard-of piece of flim-flammery where the rules had been changed without the captains' agreement. The committee had to find some way to save face. And the only way they could think of was to hold another race.

Pine and his captains agreed to this, but Angus Walters said, "No, not unless you put up another trophy and raise some more money. We're due to sail for Lunenburg in the morning." And that was the end of it. Bitterness all round. Ben Pine and the *Columbia* crew felt the same: too many rules, too much bureaucracy. The spirit had gone out of the thing. The International would not be held again for eight years.

As far as the world and the fishermen were concerned *Bluenose* was still undefeated and Angus Walters was simply one of the best skippers on the whole Atlantic coast. All his life at sea, and skipper of the world's fastest sailing vessel. And still fishing her, and still able to get a trip of fish where other men were just "fish peddlers," coming in with a skimpy catch while *Bluenose*'s holds were full.

There was a close call one night in August of 1926, when they were hit by a storm that most of the men at sea could not recall the likes of. Fifty Lunenburg sailors drowned that night. And while it may have been luck in part, there is no doubt that Angus Walters' extraordinary knowledge of his ship, of the sea and its weather, and of his men, were the main reasons why they all came through. Clem Hilz said they all prayed, and they said to each other if she went over they would all get up on the high side and hold hands and jump in the water together. If they had to go, they would go together.

Angus was anchored off Sable Island, "The Graveyard of the Atlantic." When the barometer dropped and the wind began to make up he was trapped right in the middle of one of the storms of the century. He put on just enough sail, all forward, to keep his beloved vessel ahead of the wind, stern to the towering seas but moving enough so she wouldn't be "pooped," that is, drowned by a following wave pouring over the ship from astern. Then he made sure he was going to steer her out of it.

Clem Hilz, who lived through it, said,

And you talk about blow! I never saw nothing like that in my life and never want to. . . . Heisted up what sail we could get on her, was the double reef foresail and a double reef jib and jumbo. That's all you could use. And he got lashed to the wheel. He stayed there for eight hours. Now you talk about a brave and courageous man. That he stood there knowing in his own mind and saying in his own words, "We'll never see Lunenburg again." But, good ship that she was, and brave . . . and capable man that he was, we sailed out of it and next morning we was out in plenty water.

In 1931 the International was held for one last time. Once again *Bluenose* sailed home well ahead of the competition. But it was almost over now. The age of the schooner was effectively gone. Diesel engines and steel hulls and factory ships with refrigerated hulls were moving in. *Bluenose* was only sixteen years old, but it began to look as though she was a museum piece. Angus considered retiring. Maggie had died. He was tired and dismayed as he saw the end of his era like a cloud blowing in from the east. There would be one more go at the International Fishermen's, against the Gloucestermen, and this time in their waters, off the coast of Massachusetts. It was 1938. *Bluenose* lost her mizzen topsail half-way through the final race, but Angus got the lads working together as well as ever they had worked, and got a line on her, and cleared the mess, and won the race.

In the *Heritage Minute* that celebrates that last race you can hear Angus Walters (and the actor who played him was at the actual wheel of the real *Bluenose*, brought into a movie studio for the making of the *Minute*), you can hear him whispering to his beloved schooner, "Just one more time, Old Girl, and then you can rest." That was a script-writer's invention, of course; we don't know what he actually said. But we do know that Angus talked to his great love, the ship he loved more than he loved his house. He would have saved his ship before his house if they both burned at once, the sailors said. So he *could* have said exactly that.

And we do know that she was going to her rest.

At least that was what Angus Walters hoped for her. They had put diesels in her for a while, but it wasn't the same. The old Skipper tried to get Nova Scotia to draw her up on land and make her a museum. He would stay with her and tell visitors the stories of her glory days. But the money didn't come, and Angus was broke. And so in 1942, when a couple of guys from the States offered him $25,000 cash for her, he had nowhere else to turn.

She was gone. Many of them said Angus was gone too, from that moment on. Oh, he married again. He started a dairy business. His grandson, who would skipper *Bluenose II* years later, remembers Angus rousing him at four a.m. when he worked for a summer on the milk truck. Angus Walters was eighty years old that summer, and hoisting sixty-five-pound cans of milk, one in each hand, onto the truck, maybe a hundred of them in a morning's round.

The last chapter in the book of the great schooner *Bluenose* was ugly. They took the masts off her and used her as a barge in the Caribbean, under tow. In January 1946 the old barge, with still a few marks of paint on her bow that once said *Bluenose, Lunenburg,* struck a reef off Haiti, and began to go down. The skipper of the tug said to hell with it and cut the line and let her sink.

Wayne Walters was at the curling rink with his grandfather when they got the news. "You might as well have put a knife in his heart," Wayne said.

But, curiously, just when it seemed that the story was over, the myth began to grow. People came to Lunenburg to seek out Angus Walters, to hear his stories of the *Bluenose*. The Lunenburg yards had built a replica of the *Bounty* for the MGM movie; so people said, If we can build a *Bounty* we can build another *Bluenose*. This time, the money was found and the keel was laid. In February of 1963 Angus Walters, *Captain* Angus Walters, drove the first spike for the laying of that keel. A replica of his Queen, and his own grandson to skipper her.

He died on August 12, 1969, at eighty-seven. But his story did not die. Take a look at your dime again.

◆　◆　◆

The Captain and the Queen was written by Ian MacLeod and Chuck Stewart, and directed by Chuck Stewart.

PART SEVEN

JUDITH JASMIN
Televising the Revolution

Now in the early years of the twenty-first century, when the Province of Quebec is noted for its advanced social legislation in education, justice, health and welfare, and for its vigorous popular culture and professional and commercial sophistication, it is easy to forget that early in the twentieth century it was comparatively poor and backward. Its French-speaking population was looked upon by official Canada as a source of cheap labour. Its educational standards were abysmal. Its politics and social standards were dominated by the Roman Catholic Church.

It is almost always wrong to ascribe important social changes to any single cause. But in the case of Quebec the arrival of Radio-Canada's first French-language television station in 1952 was swiftly followed by a torrent of social and cultural change. It would be difficult to argue that there was not a cause-and-effect relationship, however simplistic that might seem to some sociologists. The era had the marks of a genuine social revolution. It would bring to an end the Church's domination and the officially sanctioned suppression of the population's self-fulfillment in its own cultural terms.

The growth of an astonishingly widely viewed entertainment industry, with brilliantly produced variety shows, comedy, sports, and extended soap operas called *téléromans*, gave this French side of the CBC an early and powerful success that outstripped (and still does) the impact of CBC's English-language television. Home-grown television along with other forms of popular entertainment was, and remains, a vital element of modern Quebec's pride in its own culture. But at the beginning it was, above all, the journalists who brought to Quebecers a portrait of themselves as a special people of distinct character but with unacknowledged rights and unfulfilled potential. That portrait would contribute substantially to the rejection of old values, of the old compliance in the face of authority. Out of those changes grew the new

Quebec: vocal, demanding, confident, different, troublesome, rich, energetic, ambitious.

One of the most famous of the television journalists who helped transform Quebec was a gifted woman named Judith Jasmin. She was to take the standards of investigative journalism to heights not yet achieved anywhere in Canada. Jasmin was a woman of profound convictions about justice and humanity. She would be accused by some of allowing those convictions to colour her reporting and analysis, at a time when "objectivity" was supposed to be the watchword for journalists. It was an accusation she acknowledged with good humour, insisting that fairness and completeness were what really made for good journalism, and that it was simply unrealistic to pretend that a journalist's work should not be influenced by her values. When she began in television the medium was completely dominated by men, and the conservative and machismo management at Radio-Canada must have been surprised to find themselves, giving this . . . this *woman!* . . . such prominence.

But they couldn't refuse her; she was just that good.

Talented, brilliant, determined, energetic, wise in the ways of the world, Judith Jasmin had, however, a turbulent and often disastrous personal life. Somehow the men she loved — and there were many of them — could not give to her what she yearned for. And when late in her life she would say that it was her career that had prevented her from marrying and having children, you could sense a deep, melancholic wistfulness behind the radiant, resolute, confident, and (to Quebecers) comfortingly familiar strong eyes and knowing mouth.

Thirty years after her death, with a park named after her, as well as a building at the University of Montreal where students are taught to be journalists, few of those students know anything about this once most famous of Quebec women. Asked about the name on their building, present-day students will say, "Well, there is a journalistic prize in her name." A rare respondent will know that she was a broadcaster, and a few more know that there was some connection with René Lévesque.

But the old broadcasters know. Pierre Nadeau, now in his late sixties and in many ways the surviving dean of the television newsmen, remembers Judith Jasmin as "a fabulous reporter, a great journalist, a great human being, and a very joyful person." But that is partly, as he admits, what he wants to remember; it leaves out the melancholy side.

She was born in 1916 into an unusual family. Her mother was an ardent and premature feminist, with a huge laugh, a strong, country kind of face, and great energy. She learned to drive a car at the age of seventy, in a Quebec where women were still, on the whole, expected to stay in the kitchen and bear a child a year until they collapsed.

Judith's father Amédée was a socialist, which was unusual in Quebec then, and — even more unusual — a feminist like his wife Rosaria. Often he was the only man present at the meetings of the small pioneering group of feminists in the province. Women were not allowed to vote in provincial elections in Quebec until 1948, thirty years after they had received that right in federal elections.

In 1921, when Judith was five, the family moved to Paris. Monsieur Jasmin wanted to study co-operative work projects and expose his two little girls to an atmosphere richer in the oxygen of the human imagination than what he could find for them in the convent schools of Quebec.

Paris, in the 1920s! The booming, illusory prosperity of those post-war years, before the Great Crash of 1929, had turned Paris into a favoured destination for people from all over the globe who were seeking intellectual, artistic, and physical pleasures. The bookstalls along the river Seine, the presence of art and design almost everywhere you looked, the turbulence of the night life, the debates about life and meaning that overflowed the walls of the universities and penetrated the streets — all these had attracted people who would leave an indelible mark on the way in which the modern world looks at itself. Picasso, James Joyce, Gertrude Stein, before long Ernest Hemingway, musicians, philosophers . . . the vitality was breathtaking. And when Jasmin Père decided eight years later to take his adolescent girls back to Montreal where there seemed to be an irreversible surge of prosperity at last, he had on his hands a very rebellious thirteen-year-old named Judith.

You can see it in the family photographs, of which many survive. The confident tilt of the head, the frank gaze, comfortable with the camera. There are people in the world whom the camera loves. Judith Jasmin was one of them. That has a lot to do with why she became such an influence as a television journalist years later. And you can see it in the youthful photos and the odd moments of home movies that have come down to us. The relationship with the camera was one she seems to have trusted all her life.

She stuck it out in Montreal for two years in the convent schools and the stultifying role-determined world where girls were scarcely considered to be people, but rather instruments for the propagation of the race and of the Faith. After the stock market crash of October 1929 had generated the worst global economic depression ever, only months after their return, the spirited teenager suddenly realized that she was poor.

"For the past two years we have lived frugally," she wrote, in her clear angular hand in a diary she had begun to fill with youthful out-pourings of inspiration and desire. "Maman does all the chores and total-ly deprives herself. Papa too. [Me], I don't want . . . a life of poverty."

Somehow — it is not clear where the money came from — she managed to get two more years of school in Paris. And then it was back to Montreal and a college for girls, where she completed a degree and helped support her family by working in a bookstore.

In the bookstore there was time to listen to the radio. Judith Jasmin began to think that there might be a world out there that she could thrive in. She joined a theatre group and began to act. She discovered that she had a natural gift for the stage. Her reviews were glowing. A little more money coming in. And then, one day in 1937, her world shifted once again, when she auditioned for a role in a radio drama series, the forerunner of the television *téléromans* that would later bring Radio-Canada TV its most numerous and most loyal view-ers. The series was called *La Pension Veldor*. They gave her a starring role. Before long her photograph was in all the papers. She and the series were a big hit. She fell in love with a theatrical impresario named Paul Maugé, and moved in with him. Maugé was popular with the stars he booked into Montreal, partly because he was a great host. Night after night there was champagne and caviar. Maugé's little apartment would be packed with glittering people, artists from Russia and France and America. It became the glittering world of Judith Jasmin.

She stayed with Maugé for about twelve years, but her friends and admirers say now that she was not really all that happy. Maugé was separated but still legally married. To be with a married man was a genuine scandal in Quebec at that time, but he refused to get divorced, which at that time in Quebec required an official Act of the Senate of Canada, and was a long, difficult and expensive process. Restless, she tried a job as a radio producer, at first not thinking that it was a vocation, just something to do. Radio exposed her to a new world. She began to think about reporting, getting out in the world, bringing stories home to her people.

Judith would say later, in a television interview when she was fifty, that the theatre had never been her real craft. She had fallen into it by accident. She felt that there must be something else more meaningful. When she took her first steps as a radio reporter, she knew she had found that something.

But it is possible that she was at least partly wrong about the "accidental" attraction of the theatre, and that she had undervalued the importance of her theatrical ability. While she cut her journalistic teeth in radio, and there met and was encouraged and trained by another young and ambitious reporter named René Lévesque, it was in television that she would come into her own. The really strong television journalists have always had a strong sense of theatre, of using the body, the voice, gesture, the measured or dramatic rise and fall of the narration, to compel attention and convey meaning and a sense of importance. Think of the Canadian reporter Morley Safer in Vietnam, and the cigarette lighter sending the thatched roof of a suspected Vietcong village family up in flames. Think of Walter Cronkite and the persona of reliable Uncle Walt that he carefully cultivated. Jasmin knew what it was like to be in front of an audience, how to use that dancer's body, the light flick of the eyes or the tiny curl of the corner of the mouth. She understood the power of dropping the voice at the crucial moment, the moment when a non-theatre person might go loud to gain attention whereas Jasmin knew you went soft.

Whatever the relationship between theatre and television journalism (and this writer believes it to be very close), Jasmin's years in radio, in harness with the seasoned reporter that Lévesque already was, turned her into a shrewd field reporter, a populist with a sense of the streets. She and Lévesque are credited now with having effectively invented broadcast street journalism for Quebec, going out with equipment that was new to them but seems so primitive to us, such as wire recorders, and talking to ordinary people instead of officials and authorities.

The wire recorder preceded the tape recorder and changed journalism radically. Before the portable recording system, recordings could be made in the studio on huge machines that physically cut sonic grooves in huge wax discs. Reporters came back from the field with notes, wrote up their stories, and read them on the air live. Lévesque and Jasmin changed that and took the microphone into the streets. What they were doing is normal now; then it was a breakthrough.

Judith Jasmin and Lévesque moved over to television in 1952, and she realized she could go around the world with the 16mm film camera and bring that world back to her audience. The cameras were primitive, by today's standards. The sound was recorded on an optical track right on the film, and the quality was not very good. Equipment was cumbersome. But it was a heady time; journalists were at last able to bring back to their audiences a vivid, moving visual representation of the experiences they had formerly been able only to speak or write about. Some of them were becoming stars.

Judith Jasmin's name became a household word. In the view of some of her surviving colleagues such as Pierre Nadeau and Jasmin's biographer Collette Beauchamps, she became one of the most significant contributors to Quebec's new awakening to the world, and to Quebec's place in that world. Algeria, Israel, France, India, Haiti — there now came pouring out of our screens an ongoing visit with parts of the world that we had only dimly heard of before. And if we lived in Quebec and spoke French, Judith Jasmin would be there, night after night, making sense out of the chaos of poverty, revolution and global transformation.

When she went off to New York, as she did in 1967 to cover the Women's March on City Hall, it was undoubtedly part of her strategy to be conveying to the women of Quebec the news that there was something afoot in the world. There were changes in outlook and values, and possibilities; things that they ought to be part of. As a woman she was a pioneer, out there in the field with a cameraman and her wits and her courage. In those early days at Radio-Canada TV there were women with Ph.D.s working in the news department and the best they could get was a research job clipping newspapers. But Jasmin was reporting social change in Manhattan and social paralysis in Latin America, and everyone in Quebec was listening.

Her partner René Lévesque was another journalist who had quickly made a distinctive mark for himself in the television era. Later to be the first leader of the independence party known as Le Parti Québécois, and for nine dramatic years the premier of the province, Lévesque had honed his journalistic skills as a war correspondent in Europe during World War II. Now, with the advent of television, he started a television series, in which he simply lectured, with a blackboard, like a schoolteacher. Working without a script, he talked to his audience, not with the lofty, condescending attitude that was characteristic of many of his colleagues in the news business, but treating them as equals and as fellow citizens. He told them what was going on in the new post-war world, with a particular focus on issues of social justice, education, and politics. The program was *Point de Mire*, which means focal point, and it made Lévesque into a kind of journalistic hero.

René Lévesque and Judith Jasmin became one of the most powerful journalistic teams in the history of Canadian television. René Lévesque was more experienced than Judith Jasmin, though younger. He had been married shortly before they began to work together. Although the personal chemistry between them was an important element in the professional relationship, that relationship remained strictly professional until about a year and a half after the partnership began. They were in mining country in northern Quebec. They were looking for a location to film, and had stopped for a rest. And suddenly he grasped her in his arms and kissed her. She wrote later: "It was as if we had loved each other in another life."

So now she was travelling the world with the man she loved, doing the work she loved more than anything, and doing it better and better. They were in some respects an odd team. She was deliberate, thoughtful, careful, a demon for preparation and study and careful planning and scripting. Lévesque was an improviser. The veteran reporter, newscaster and news executive Knowlton Nash remembers Lévesque from much later, during the democratic presidential convention in Chicago in 1968. Nash himself would be in the studio for a good half-hour, polishing his report before reading live at airtime. Lévesque would come in fifteen seconds before airtime, his pockets bulging with notes, no script, and just stand there and tell it to his viewers, occasionally digging out a crumpled note to refresh his memory. Judith's style was to take time, think everything out methodically in advance, and deliver her reports with an air of authority and seriousness that was in marked contrast to Lévesque's playful improvisations.

But they were a team, professionally and personally, until that mysterious day four years later when he just left. One day he was there, the next day gone. Collette Beauchamps says, "It happened just like that. He stopped and he went to somebody else. Without any explanation or anything."

Judith Jasmin's life was shattered. In 1954 she pulled up stakes and left the country. She had reported from India and had sensed the intensely spiritual quality of life on that subcontinent, as so many visitors do. Although she was a thoughtful atheist, she was in anguish and in deep need and hoped she might find some kind of insight, and heal some wounds if she went back to India to stay for a while this time. She told her diary, "This trip is necessary to dissolve my last illusions. They will be washed away little by little by silence, by distance. It is as though I am under the effect of a drug that allows me to escape from myself. I am prepared for solitude."

When she came back to Montreal, in 1955, Lévesque still haunted her. She addressed him in that same diary: "I want to forget you, but I am more connected to you than ever. Six years of silently loving an unattainable man. . . . the thought of suicide has subtly been taking shape. . . ."

But she was a survivor. With the help of a therapist she fought off those thoughts of suicide. Like many professionals she found healing in her work. And then she fell in love again.

The torn, oppressive poverty-stricken Caribbean nation of Haiti had been one of her first foreign assignments as a television reporter. Now, back in that country on assignment, she met a tall, handsome black economist named Jo Chatelain, and would later say that he was her greatest love after René Lévesque. Chatelain was unmarried, a free man. Perhaps he wanted to keep it that way, because while they were together off and on for seven years, he lived in Washington or Paris and she in Montreal, and they met when they could. She decided Paris would be a better base: she would see more of Jo. So she decided to take her chances on the freelance life and return to the City of Light that had so enchanted her adolescence. It was tough. Unknown to the French-broadcasting community she found only a little work there. She made a meager living by sending pieces back, as a freelancer, to Radio-Canada, who paid her a disgraceful pittance, sustenance pay, a fraction of what staff reporters were making back home.

But she was free, working in Europe and North Africa, keeping that distinct voice and figure in front of her own people, bringing them an international perspective on her favourite issues of justice and liberty.

And those two themes were what would draw her back to Quebec as the long-simmering independence movement brought the so-called *Révolution Tranquille*, the Quiet Revolution, into louder and clearer focus, month by month as the 1960s began. It was a time when the rousing and energetic new culture of Quebec led more and more intellectuals and artists and young people of all backgrounds to interpret the Liberal Premier Jean Lesage's slogan, *Maîtres chez nous*, Masters in Our Own House, more and more literally.

And so back she came, once again. She had earlier been vice-president of a movement promoting secular schools. That had nearly cost her her job at Radio-Canada in those days, but now the mood was changing. There were even a few clergy whose view of the Christian message gave pride of place to justice and liberty, and Judith made sure that her work helped get that message out. She brought the most outspoken and famous of those young priests before an astonished television audience on *Premier Plan* ("Foreground"): he was Father Jean-Paul Desbiens. He had anonymously published *Les Insolences,* a book on Quebec and the Church, whose stance was so outrageous he had prudently signed it only "Frère Untel," Brother So-and-So. His superiors found out who "Frère Untel" really was and told Father Desbiens to shut up. But there was another radical priest, Paul-Émile Cardinal Léger. Léger would later renounce his own princely title and go to live among and serve the lepers and handicapped children in Cameroon. At the time of the Frère Untel controversy, Léger intervened as the principal Roman Catholic authority in Quebec, and allowed Desbiens to go on television. Judith Jasmin jumped at the chance, subduing her usual hard-edged questioning, and encouraging him to promote his cause.

"The cause . . . was dear to her heart," he would say later. "And she had no intention of putting that cause at risk by being too aggressive [with me]."

Some of her fellow journalists were scandalized at her apparent public support for a cause while she was supposed to be doing objective journalism. Some would say that even today you could not get away with it. They are probably wrong. If you review Jasmin's archived interview with Desbiens, while it seemed unusual at the time, that was likely because a conventional interview back then would have reflected some hostilty towards a seemingly rebellious priest — hardly an objective stance.

Long after she had been recognized as one of the truly great journalists, she would be challenged publicly on this issue. Interviewer Wilfred Lemoine asked, in 1966, "Being involved in certain social causes . . . doesn't it damage your credibility [as a journalist]?"

Jasmin's answer was that if you are doing your professional work with sincerity and good faith, the fact of your having personal views and commitments doesn't have to weaken your credibility. It is a valid answer, but the issue is one that still occupies journalists today, some still maintaining that you should try not to have opinions and if you have them, conceal them. Judith Jasmin would probably have thought that naïve and unreal.

"Reporting means sticking to the facts," she said. "And even if a journalist has private opinions, that's not important if he reports the facts."

She did support the independence of Quebec. Then, as now, it was not uncommon for journalists at Radio-Canada to hold separatist feelings. It is a tribute to their professionalism and to the policies, standards and management of that news service that those opinions have seldom contaminated the highly professional news service. Inquiry after official inquiry, especially after election campaigns, has consistently exonerated Radio-Canada journalists from charges of letting their biases distort their work.

In 1963 she wrote a letter to the editors of *Le Devoir*, a newspaper that was often sympathetic to the separatist cause. Some shadowy rebels calling themselves the FLQ (*Front de Liberation de Québec*) had blown up a couple of mailboxes. They would later kidnap a British diplomat, James Cross, and viciously murder a Quebec cabinet minister, Pierre Laporte. There really was no FLQ, no genuine movement as such, only a few isolated cells of romantic misfits. And Jasmin's public letter probably reflects the opinions of the majority of even the most dedicated separatists of the time.

She wrote it from Algeria, where she was on assignment:

Here, in this land bathed in the blood of a million victims of the war of liberation, I think about those of you who have adopted some of the combat methods employed by Algerian patriots. At the core, both are issues of independence. But the context here is very different. In the history of the conquest of Algeria in the 19th century there are countless pillages, rapes, massacres. What exists in our Quebec rebellion to compare in scale with the martyrs of Algeria?

*Aspiring heroes of Quebec's independence, lay down your arsenal
of violence. The work we must accomplish at home is more difficult
than you imagine.*

It would be interesting to know how the proponents of journalistic "objectivity" would view that letter now.

Judith Jasmin's career as a television reporter would take her into
the heart of some of the great stories of the era. She was in Dallas within hours after President John F. Kennedy was shot. Remembering that
the alleged assassin's mother was born in Canada she used her "Radio-
Canada" status to attract the bereaved woman's attention, and managed to get an interview with Mrs. Oswald, not long after Lee Harvey
Oswald was shot dead. Jasmin seemed at ease in hot-spots. She was
jailed at a demonstration against racism in New York. Pierre Nadeau
had to go down from Montreal and bail her out. At home the press
loved it, but in Washington, where she was then Radio-Canada's official correspondent, things were different. It had already been especially difficult for her as a woman, since women were not then admitted to
the National Press Club, where much of the real information passed
between politicians and the press. Now, as a result of her having been
jailed in New York, the White House took away her permanent pass,
and she had to apply for a day pass each time there was a press conference. Knowlton Nash, the CBC correspondent who worked out of
the same office and had come to have enormous admiration for Jasmin,
laughingly says, "I presume the security people felt [the President]
would be better protected if they didn't give her [the] pass!"

She could laugh at those little hardships; the big ones were still, as
always, the pain of loneliness and the loss of love. She would rational-
ize her childlessness by pointing to her career. But she felt the lack, and
took on the role of surrogate mother to her sister's son Christian, sometimes even taking him with her on her foreign assignments. Christian
is a man who now has a profound love of and admiration for his late
aunt and substitute mother.

And then there was the loss of a breast. Diagnosed with cancer,
she had a radical mastectomy. She told her close colleague Jean
LeTarte, who had been her cameraman in some of the toughest hot-

spots and still says that she was always much more courageous than he was, that she was "no longer the woman I used to be."

All this time her reportorial style got stronger and stronger. At Radio-Canada headquarters in Montreal the management decreed that she was not to do live reports or commentary any more. It was too risky. Record her stuff and then if she was too outspoken something could be cut. And yet those journalism students at the University of Montreal, the same ones who couldn't tell us exactly who Judith Jasmin was and what she did, once they had been shown some of her work and told the main outlines of her life expressed envy for the way it was, back then, for this pioneering reporter.

But more importantly, for these young journalists who are just starting out but are already very critical of if not sceptical about contemporary television news with its fads and formulas and ten-second sound bites, the work that Judith Jasmin was able to turn out seems almost like paradise. Yes, she was a pioneer: the first woman to be made official foreign correspondent. She broadcast long thoughtful reports. She had time to prepare them thoroughly, to think about them, to edit with care. She had room to add interpretive tags, to make her reports mean more than just a quick flash with a few pictures of people yelling or being beaten or a cliché background shot of a landmark like the Eiffel Tower or the White House. Journalism has changed, since Jasmin. She was there when television news editors expected meaningful stories, not just entertainment in the form of a few hits of random information or the faces and flavours of the month.

All that time the cancer that had cost her a breast was still lurking. When she came home in 1968, just fifty-two years old, it had spread to her bones. Old friends gathered around. René Lévesque was close and affectionate and more supportive than he had been since those early days working together. But her old employers at Radio-Canada were not so kind. Where once she had been their first choice to interview world leaders, now that she was not able to fly off to the danger spots she was assigned to local stories about fires and fashion shows. Her friend Francine Bastien, still bitter, says, "Even her, who had been such an outstanding person . . . who brought so much quality to what CBC was about, and put CBC on the map so to speak . . . was treated very shabbily towards the end of her life. She was very ill, and not much attention was paid to try to treat her decently or with respect."

For some, having put up with insults and injuries from such an employer all her life, it might have been possible to just accept that as one of the ironies with which one lived. Not so for Judith Jasmin. "[It] hurt her a lot," her nephew Christian says now; "I remember her crying about that."

She needed Jo Chatelain then, badly. But Jo seldom came; he was all over the world. Her mother was still alive, and would visit her in the hospital, and bring her flowers, and say, "Oh, these are from Jo. Jo sent you these lovely flowers." But she knew.

Her old cameraman comrade, Jean LeTarte, would come and sit by her bedside. He remembers one phone call, when he said he was on his way over, but Judith said, "No, don't come any more. I'm not the Judith you knew. Let's keep on speaking only on the telephone."

She died on October 20, 1972. She was fifty-six. As a young television producer in Toronto, helping to start *Close-Up*, in 1957, the first Sunday night current affairs magazine program in English-Canadian television, I had heard a lot about Judith Jasmin and her program *Premier Plan*, which was the counterpart to ours, though we seldom got to see it as there was no French television in Toronto then. Jasmin was already a legend in 1957. Her reputation would grow steadily. The men and women who helped bring Quebec into the modern age in those decades now give her credit for a major contribution to that amazingly peaceful revolution.

In one of her last interviews, asked what her life as a reporter had meant to her, she said, with feeling and humour, "It was marvellous; it was the kind of life you'd expect to pay for the privilege of having."

◆ ◆ ◆

The biography of Judith Jasmin was written by Maureen Marovitch and directed by Maureen Marovitch and David Finch. Carrie Madue was line producer.

PART EIGHT

THE RELUCTANT WARRIOR
The Story of Ben Dunkelman

One of the well-entrenched ideas that Canadians seem to have about the character of the nation is that we are a peaceable people whose armed forces are primarily intended to be sent to trouble spots around the world in order to help keep the peace. But this is a relatively recent image. Canada became Canada out of warfare. Its capital is placed in a totally unlikely part of the country to keep it safe from invasion. Soldiers from Canada marched on Washington and set fire to the presidential residence, whereupon it was painted white to cover the scorch marks and remains the White House still. An Iroquois unit under the command of the great Tecumseh crossed the river from Windsor during the War of 1812 and conquered Fort Detroit. Canada sent soldiers to the Boer War in Africa at the turn of the century. In World War I the per-capita (of the national population) count of Canadian soldiers killed far exceeded that of our American neighbour. In World War II Canadian troops conducted the almost suicidal dress rehearsal for the invasion of France, on a blood-soaked beach called Dieppe, and later, when the real thing happened in June 1944, successfully captured and held their assigned Normandy beaches.

Anyone who lived through that last world war, here in Canada, remembers vividly the way in which the country pulled together around the war effort. The words "we" and "us," that have long since been dropped by our political leaders as they try to win the country with tax cuts or spending, resonated then with a passionate, cohesive power as millions of us collected scrap metal, put our savings into War Bonds, hand-knit socks and toques for soldiers and sailors and airmen, and lined up at recruiting depots faster than we could be enlisted.

War divided us, too: French Canadians in Quebec found it difficult to believe that they had a responsibility to help Britain with a war that nobody really wanted, both in 1914 and again in 1939. The conscriptive solutions arrived at by governments who, themselves, had been pretty equivocal about going to war, left scars that are not yet healed.

So we have had our experience of the costs of war, and of its glories, if that is still a valid word. And some historians believe that we have been too ready to forget the sacrifices and the courage that our men and women have shown in battle and behind the scenes of battle, despite the war memorials in the civic squares of big cities and of little towns. And we are perhaps too ready to forget some of the outstanding individuals who fought in those battles.

One of them was vividly remembered in episode number 39 of *The Canadians*. His name was Ben Dunkelman, a big, broad-shouldered, soft-spoken man whom this writer met just a few months before his death in 1997. We were planning a film on his extraordinary life and exploits and hoping to find a way to do it while he was still able to participate.

We called this episode "The Reluctant Warrior," not because Ben Dunkelman was in any way slow to offer himself for duty when the country went to war, but because he really saw himself as a peaceable guy who joined up because that is what you did when your people needed you. But when his spectacular ability as a battlefront soldier and commanding officer brought him an offer to take command of the entire armed forces of a small but powerful nation, he refused: it was time to get back home and do what he was supposed to do in the beginning, namely run the family business.

That was quite a business. If you lived in Toronto in the 1930s and after, you could not fail to be impressed by a big building down on Front Street, just west of the old Maple Leaf Baseball stadium at the corner of Bathurst Street, with a tall sign at roof level: TIP TOP TAILORS. Ben's father David had arrived as a penniless immigrant from Poland. He started this mass-produced men's clothing business soon after, and made a huge success of it. By the time Ben was born in 1913 the family was very well off. The present Sunnybrook Medical Centre on Bayview Avenue, just north of Eglinton in what was at the time deep countryside, was originally the Dunkelman family estate,

Sunnybrook Farm. Ben grew up in an atmosphere of luxury and play. He had his own sailboat from the time he was in his teens, and was a prominent figure at the Queen City Yacht Club. Jews were not allowed in the Royal Canadian Yacht Club at that time, but Ben always said that while he knew there was an anti-Semitic substratum in Toronto in those days, he was not really aware of it, it didn't affect his life. He had a naturally sunny disposition that went with his imposing stature and prodigious natural athletic capacity, and perhaps if anyone ever felt like putting him down for being Jewish, any such notion vanished upon actual contact. From the time of his adolescence his was a big, winning, even commanding presence.

Another permanent reminder, however, of the extent to which Ontario's Jews were excluded from the mainstream is Balfour Beach on Lake Simcoe, a forty-minute drive north of Toronto. A cottage culture had bloomed on Lake Simcoe early in the century (and has left most of its shores now almost saturated with summer dwellings), but it was difficult for Jews to buy a cottage in the developed areas. Ben's mother Rose simply saw to it that the family bought up thirty acres of excellent shorefront and turned it into a club where Jews and only Jews were welcome. She named it for Sir Arthur Balfour, the British politician whose Balfour Declaration had paved the way for the creation of the State of Israel. A street in Balfour Beach is named after The Czarina, as they called her, but misspelled as Dunkleman.

Israel did not exist when Ben Dunkelman was a boy, but hundreds of young Jews from other parts of the world were already building towards it by wresting productive farmland out of the stony desert on collective or communitarian farms called *kibbutzim*. Young Ben would hear tales of the *kibbutzim* from the Zionist leaders whom his mother often entertained at Sunnybrook or at their Balfour Beach house. He said that he often sat staring into the flames of the cottage fireplace, dreaming about taking part in the building of the New Israel. He had passed an adolescence of parties and sailing and girlfriends, and now he was beginning to think about the *why* of it all, and that *why* kept coming up Israel. On his seventeenth birthday his parents gave him passage to Palestine and five hundred dollars in cash, and off he went.

He said that he found it intoxicating, a kind of homecoming, and decided to stay and work on a *kibbutz* at Tel Asher, a tiny settlement surrounded by not very friendly Arab villages. It was a long way from Sunnybrook Farm, Ben wrote later.

That experience changed his life. Sometimes he referred to it as a "trial by *turiya*," the Hebrew word for the hoe with which he was assigned to try to cultivate the parched stony fields of the *kibbutz*. He confessed to having been overweight and soft when he arrived. Before long the fat was gone, the muscles were hardening, and the adolescent was turning into a tough and idealistic young man. He said that it was an early short-wave broadcast from Germany that alerted him to the alarming new phenomenon in Germany called the Nazi party, and that it chilled him. But he went back to Toronto in 1932, to work unhappily at Tip Top Tailors. Those were not good years. He drank too much bootleg liquor, but would clear his head and find some solace afloat on his much loved sailboat. It was a schooner whose design he had commissioned from a celebrated naval architect named Hand, built by Cecil Schramm, in Port Dover, and sailed on Georgian Bay, out of Midland. He called her *The Dinny*.

Seven years went by like this.

When Ben Dunkelman was five years old he had stood in the streets of downtown Toronto waving a Union Jack and cheering the return of soldiers from the Great War. He said that the experience marked him with a sense of patriotism and of the nobility of soldiering. So when the Second World War broke out in the autumn of 1939, he not only saw it as a way of escaping what then seemed the vacuous routines of the men's clothing business, but also a way to demonstrate his pride in his country, and to do something about that horror he had first learned about on the short-wave radio in Palestine.

He wanted the Navy. Later he would say that it may have been his Jewishness that got him rejected, but in fact the Navy was not accepting recruits in those first months of the war: the government was trying to steer young men into the infantry. Ben found himself in the Second Battalion of the Queen's Own Rifles. Perhaps because of connections and a good education, but certainly aided by his stature and presence and natural gift for leadership, he was soon commissioned as an officer and headed overseas.

Ben Dunkelman knew how to party, and his first months in England saw plenty of drinking and brawls and rowdiness. But he discovered that he was a natural soldier, and he found that a stubby little weapon called the mortar was right up his alley. The World War I mortar was a huge, squat, heavy kind of cannon firing an explosive shell on a high trajectory. By the time Ben was training, it had shrunk to a small tube about five centimetres in diameter (the calibre) and less than half a metre long, propped up by two small legs (the bipod) and aiming into the sky at an angle of about 60 to 80 degrees. At the bottom of this smooth-bore tube was a central firing pin, really just a hard little knob that would strike the cap of a cartridge that was dropped on it. You dropped a small bomb in the mouth of the tube and got your hand out of the way in a hurry. The bomb was shaped like an elongated pear, with fins on the narrow end, and in a tube at the centre of the fins was a shell that looked exactly like a shotgun shell. When that shell hit the pin it was exactly as if you had pulled the trigger on the shotgun. The shell had enough cordite in it to propel the bomb high into the air, over the heads of your own forward troops if necessary, and down into your target. You could use it against tanks or a fortified position, but the target was often enemy troops, perhaps out of sight of your riflemen but vulnerable to something looping down out of the sky.

Ben Dunkelman seems to have rapidly mastered the mortar. If you could concentrate the fire of several of these tubes on a target, and get a trained group of mortarmen working together so that you could have a lot of bombs in the air at the same time, the effect on your enemy would be terrifying and devastating.

The Canadians, Americans, British, Free French, Free Polish, Australian, New Zealand and South African troops mustered in England all knew that sooner or later there would be an invasion of Europe; that was what they were there for. It was a long wait. A lot of beer was drunk and a lot of hangovers slept off. Many English girls became pregnant and some even got married. Rumours were all over the camps. Some of the rumours foresaw a Nazi invasion of Britain. But bit by bit the strategists were putting together a plan that Prime Minister Winston Churchill called *Operation Overlord*, and then, early in June 1944 the orders came to move out. D-Day was on them. Seasick men tumbled out of their landing craft on the beaches of Normandy at dawn the next morning, and waded ashore with their weapons held high over their heads to keep them dry. Lieutenant Ben Dunkelman of the Queen's Own was in the second wave. He was thirty-one years old.

Hundreds of our men were cut down by machine-gun fire as they came ashore. Ben saw a close friend's body crumpled on the sand as he ran dripping up the beach. But the first wave had cleared the closest German positions with astounding success, and Ben's career as a mortar specialist began in earnest. The big guy from Toronto, with the easy smile and the confident manner, soon attracted the attention of the war correspondents:

> *The Toronto Star. With the Canadian Army. December 14th, 1944.*
> *Big Benny Dunkelman of the Canadian Army is a mortar man. In fact he is Mr. Mortar of the Canadian Army. Ever since D-Day Benny has been making music with those mortars of his . . . using his observation post as a sort of podium to direct his fire, like an embattled Toscanini. He likes to pull out all the stops and make big music. He is not happy until each mortar crew has 22 bombs in the air [all at once].*

One of the most decisive battles was in the thirty-kilometre zone from Caen to Falaise. The Canadians ran into some still very strong Panzer and SS divisions of the German army, and a badly planned opening assault led to a terrible casualty rate among the Canadians. It would have been even worse, according to the Queen's Own official history, "had not Lt. Dunkelman detected German tanks hidden in the haystacks" around the target. His mortar unit went to work. Dozens of bombs were in the air, all at once. The Germans were pinned down and the Allied retreat well protected. Ben was blown off his jeep by an exploding shell and his seatmate killed outright. His steel helmet was snapped down on his head by the explosion and he lost consciousness momentarily. When he came around he threw away the helmet and refused to wear one from then on. It was called *Operation Totalize*. While

Ben would later blame the Americans for not properly closing the Allied pincer movement, and allowing a considerable German retreat through the famous gap, nonetheless the operation killed or wounded an astounding four hundred thousand of the enemy. "We crushed a whole damn army," he wrote.

1945 found him in the mud of the Scheldt estuary, trying to clear the way into the crucial Belgian port of Antwerp. Mud and the stench of death. Ben now was Acting Major. A young war artist from Amherst Nova Scotia, Lieutenant Alex Colville, was on that campaign and recorded its horrors in some powerful paintings.

A reporter wrote, "The bitter five-day fighting in the Hochwald ended Sunday when Toronto soldiers drove the last of the Germans out. Though the Germans were still mortaring and machine-gunning the area, Canadian troops, unshaven and dirty, enjoyed their first rest in four days. The enemy was stubborn, but Major Ben Dunkelman confirmed that they surrendered readily when hemmed in."

Ben wrote later, in his autobiography, the single modest line, "For my part in the Hochwald action, I was awarded the Distinguished Service Order." A newspaper put it this way:

The Distinguished Service Order goes to Major Ben Dunkelman of 53 Russell Hill Road, Toronto. Under murderous fire, the Major picked up a gun whose crew had been killed. He then rushed forward killing ten Germans with his pistol and bare hands. All the time shouting to his men to press forward and the enemy to come out and fight.

Ben Dunkelman was not an especially modest man, but his friends did not hear him talk about that episode afterwards. There was nothing in his account of himself to suggest that he took any pleasure from the killing. He seems to have been a soldier because that is what you were expected to do. He didn't wear or show off the medal. His friend Barney Danson, who fought in the same war and would become Minister of National Defence years later, said, "I recall seeing it only once when we had a special ceremony up at Meaford and Ben was the guest speaker, which he didn't want to be, he hated to be. Everybody else had beautifully polished and mounted medals, and Ben's looked as if he had fished it out of some bottom drawer somewhere, where it had been lying since the war."

When he came home after it was all over, after *three hundred* days of combat from the beaches of Normandy to the banks of the Rhine, he had had it. They offered him the command of the Queen's Own. He was thrilled at the honour but he turned it down, and went back to the family business. The post-war prosperity was dazzling, but Ben was soon preoccupied with the struggle for Israel. "He was a super Zionist," Barney Danson says. "And before I knew it he was gone, and over there fighting again."

And soon the Canadian Press was reporting (June 2, 1948):

A distinguished officer with The Queen's Own Rifles overseas in the Second World War, Major Ben Dunkelman, is reported to have gone to Palestine to be second-in-command of the Jewish army in their fight against the Arabs.

Shimon Peres, who later became prime minister of Israel, knew Ben in those early days.

[David] Ben-Gurion (Israel's first president) was very anxious to have a group of professional soldiers in an organization that was more of a movement than a disciplined army. Now Ben came in. You know he was a very imposing person. Tall and heavy and talkative and charismatic. And he brought this authority of experience, of a commander. . . . I would like to have him as my friend, not my opponent, if I have a choice, and secondly, my second impression, would be that beyond his toughness he was a very soft person. As much as he put on the air of a great commander, he was a very emotional man, I believe.

Ben developed a close relationship with Ben-Gurion, whom he came to respect enormously. He tried to organize an all-Canadian unit in the Mahal, the technical elite of the Israeli forces. But Ben-Gurion assigned him to the Palmach, an assault group for *Operation Nachson*, to open up the Jerusalem road. Ben was struck by the quiet personal power of the twenty-six-year-old commander, the young, blond, Yitzakh Rabin (later to be assassinated when he was Labour prime minister); a youth with the fate of a hundred thousand people in his hands.

That was the big tactical challenge, the road from the coast to Jerusalem, cut off since the beginning of hostilities, depriving the Holy City of water and food as well as military supplies. Tackling the relief of that siege put Ben back in the line of fire. They assembled a motley collection of trucks and cars, rigged with metal plates that they hoped would be some protection against the fire they knew would come. You can see the remains of those vehicles now, on that road. They have been mounted up on the hills as a monument to the battle that soon came. Ben later said it looked to him like a kind of mass Armada, a mass suicide. At one point he switched places to take over as driver of a second car. The man he switched with was shot dead with a bullet through the head. The situation looked dreadful, but somehow they turned it around, and later carved out a permanent, protected route that Ben-Gurion would eventually name the Road of Valour.

The new State of Israel was proclaimed on May 14. The fighting went on. An Arab stronghold at Latrun was a key strategic target. They brought in new immigrants, scarcely trained but passionate for the defence of the new state. "That is our secret weapon," Rabin said. "They have nowhere else to go."

They took Latrun. Ben was put in command of the Seventh Brigade, the Latrun Veterans, and was ordered to move north. He took Tel Kissam, then Shafa Amir, where Ben found an undefended "back door" that could be taken by night if you kept your nerve, and they took Shafa by night. Again and again he deployed the surprise attack by night. The Israelis were outnumbered and outgunned, at least in theory. But at night the enemy could not see how little force was actually coming against them. The Israelis kept on winning.

And now it was the biggest target of all: Nazareth, both symbolically and strategically of enormous importance. Most of the Nazarenes were Arabs, and its religious significance was more Christian and Muslim than Jewish. But Ben said he fell in love with Nazareth. He said its rocky, pine-covered slopes reminded him of home, of the Canadian Shield, of granite and pine. Militarily it was delicate: harming the alleged birthplace of Christ would alienate a lot of friends whom Israel needed, especially in the United States, which had been quick to recognize the fledgling state, and was now watching the war with intense scrutiny. Ben-Gurion signalled, "I would just like you to remember that Nazareth is a holy place for the Christians, and don't hurt any holy Christian place, nor Muslim holy place." Ben could respect that order, but Professor David Bercuson says that there was another order that he disobeyed.

"Nazareth was a place where Dunkelman was definitely given the order to drive out the Arab population, and refused to do it. He was going to fight a clean war, as far as he was concerned. But he was not going to fight a war against civilians."

And at eight-forty, local time, the morning of December 17, he sent Ben-Gurion a simple two-word signal: NAZARETH CAPTURED.

The war had been an exhilarating series of unexpected successes. But Ben was tired now, and racked with malaria. He had to rest. During a lull he met a young female corporal named Yael Lifshitz. He was short-tempered with his illness and fatigue, and would later ruefully recall how rude he had been to her at first. But a relationship was forming. The delicately beautiful young soldier was not as delicate as she perhaps looked at first. She had a fine sense of humour and a strong intelligence. As the days went by the initial rough spots were worn smooth, and before long they decided to get married, with the Seventh Brigade standing by. The marriage would last until his death, in 1997.

Ben Dunkelman could have stayed in Israel for the rest of his life. By the end of that war he had built a solid reputation for courage, inventiveness, tactics and strategy. But he had gone out there to do a definable job, to help get the struggling young nation on its feet. He was not a soldier by vocation. He spoke of himself as a reluctant warrior. When this writer sat with him over dinner, a year and a half before his death, his warm voice and expressive hands could still conjure up vivid pictures of some of the adventures he had lived through, and he was proud of his contribution. But he said that he was always eager to get home. Toronto and the family and the business were his real responsibility. The government of Israel was prepared to offer him a position of high command for as long as he wanted it. A professional soldier would not have hesitated to accept: Ben did not hesitate to turn it down and call it a day, for his career as a soldier.

There is a tradition in the Canadian military of the vital role of the non-professional soldiers. Our standing army has always been small. When there has been a war it has been fought primarily by volunteers like Ben Dunkelman. Many of them joined up not because they saw themselves as soldiers, not for a career, but just because the country needed help in a crisis, and they hoped it would be over soon. Sir Arthur Currie, the brilliant commanding officer of the Canadian Expeditionary Forces in World War I, was an "amateur" whose successful strategies, some historians argue, were made possible precisely because he was not saddled with the traditions of the professional army, whose officers always seemed to be fighting the previous war rather than this one.

Ironically, for many, those war experiences turned out to be the most meaningful time of their lives, and they talked about them wistfully for the rest of their lives. We were planning a different kind of television biography with Ben; one in which he would take an active part. He could summon enthusiasm for the stories, but they were the stories of a man whose heart had always tugged him homewards. He died before we could bring together the resources to make that documentary, but Yael and his family and friends were generously helpful in the making of this one, and I cannot finish this section without a word of thanks to them, and to Ben himself, the reluctant warrior.

◆　◆　◆

The Reluctant Warrior was written and directed by Bruce Yaccato, with Carrie Madu as line producer.

PART NINE

BEHIND THE RED DOOR
The Story of Elizabeth Arden

The door to a handsome if modest brown-brick building at 691 Fifth Avenue, New York City, corner of 54th Street, is enamelled a bright red. During business hours, which last till well into the evening, a uniformed doorman swings the red door open with a flourish when customers arrive. The customers are mostly women. The dignified stone lettering across the façade of the building proclaims: ELIZABETH ARDEN INC., for this is the headquarters and principal salon of the world-famous cosmetics company founded in this city more than seventy years ago.

Elizabeth Arden is a name known throughout the western world, and still epitomizes high-quality cosmetics despite a growing number of competitors. Unlike Betty Crocker and many other brands based on a fictitious person, there was a real Elizabeth Arden, and in the 1930s and 1940s she was a North American celebrity. It was not, however, her real name, and she was not an American.

She was a Canadian woman from Woodbridge, Ontario, where she was born in 1878, on her father's precarious "truck farm," the common phrase at the time for a market garden farm. She was christened Florence Nightingale Graham, because, it is thought, her mother was dismayed at her own descent from an upper middle-class British family to what her daughter Flo would call a "farm drudge" by the time this fourth child was born. Susan Graham, née Tadd, Flo's mother, feared that without a little extra help the new girl child would suffer the same fate as most working-class or farm girls: drudgery, invisibility, toil, exhausting non-stop child-bearing, and something more like servitude than a free and creative life. The most famous female "doer" in the British Empire at that time was the heroine of the Crimean War, the nurse Florence Nightingale. Susan Tadd Graham is said to have hoped something of that energy and determination and maybe even fame and accomplishment would come to her own little Florence Nightingale along with the name. Whatever the influence of the name itself, the young namesake would, after her first three decades of relatively undistinguished endeavour, suddenly find what it was she was meant to do in life, and would indeed demonstrate the energy, determination and accomplishment, that Susan Tadd Graham had hoped for her. But Susan never knew it; by that time she was long dead, at thirty-nine, from tuberculosis, which was so common at the time that it was assumed, when someone died young, that TB was probably the cause.

Flo was only six when her mother died. She had to take on farm chores *and* the care of her younger sister Gladys. That relationship would remain central, one of mutual love amounting almost to adoration, for the rest of their lives. The other task they gave the young Flo, just as soon as she could manage it, was the care of the horses.

In the year 2001 the chances of a child seeing a horse on the streets of Woodbridge, Ontario, are pretty slim, and in downtown Toronto next to nil except for those rare moments when the Police Department sends out one or two of its fine mounts for ceremonial occasions. The horse at the beginning of the twenty-first century is an animal associated with leisure and prosperity. Fairly well-off people in Ontario, if they retire to a country, often take up riding, but it is a costly sport. The wealthy raise horses, some for racing, although horse racing going into the twenty-first century was losing its fans so rapidly that the desperate race-track operators started installing slot machines at the track, thinking somehow that might stanch the haemorrhage.

But in the 1880s, when her father Willie sent her to work in the stable, horses were the principal form of transportation. They pulled carriages with people in them and wagons carrying goods. There were no automobiles and in a village the size of Woodbridge the electric tram, making its first appearance in the larger centres, was still unknown. Horses were a necessity, and caring for them an art. And the little girl seemed to have inherited something else from her famous namesake: healing hands. Horses need to be rubbed down and when their legs get sore, as they often do, a good horse person will spend a great deal of time on her knees rubbing the horse's knees. Flo was good at that, and liked it.

A lifelong connection with horses was started, which would, in a completely unexpected way, have a lot to do with rubbing their knees, too, even after Flo Graham had become the rich and famous Elizabeth Arden.

Willie, her father, wasted a lot of money buying horses that he hoped would win at the races, which they seldom did. His real business was selling vegetables at the market in town, and Flo had to help out there as well. It is possible that some of her early ideas about the role of women were formed in that Woodbridge marketplace. It was a time when women were coming out in public more than they had in the earlier part of the Victorian era. Some had a little disposable income, as we would say now, and were spending it on clothes that would give them a modest elegance. Some of them — probably in secret — were applying substances to their skin to make them look younger, more attractive, more . . . *distinct.*

The writer Alfred Allen Lewis, author of *Miss Elizabeth Arden: An Unretouched Portrait,* is a biographer who, as he appears in this television documentary account of Elizabeth Arden/Flo Graham's life, demonstrates a more than academic curiosity about his subject; his warm (and sometimes magisterial) observations about her life and her personality are always coloured by a sense of affection. And at this point in her life he sees her as soaking up the experiences that would lead her on to the amazing success that *seemed* to come upon her so rapidly, more than a decade later. He says that those days in the market place, watching the newly elegant women, were important to her.

All of her life Elizabeth Arden was a sponge. She was a quick study. She saw things, and she absorbed them, acquired them. . . . She would pick up their manner of speech. . . . She obviously could not pick up the clothes, but she would take on their airs and graces.

Not very admiring of Willie Graham, the father, biographer Lewis says that he spoke flirtatiously with those women as he tried to interest them in buying his vegetables, and that young Flo disliked that; and especially disliked the way he became deferential to them, subservient, lowering himself. But, Lewis suggests, what remained with the now nearly adult girl was a sense that she would rather be the woman who induced that deference, and that perhaps the idea began to form right there in the Woodbridge market.

She began to think that money was the secret to life. It was money that allowed those women to humiliate her deplorable father. She is said to have answered, when asked what she would be when she grew up, "The richest little girl in the world."

It certainly seems likely, in light of what happened later, that she was studying the faces of those market-going women, as well as their clothes and their voices. Women had been painting their faces for centuries. From what we can tell of the ancient Egyptians in the great treasures of sculptured and painted portraiture that survive, they appear to have used makeup in a highly formalized way, especially around the eyes. Shakespeare talks about makeup: "Let her paint an inch thick, she must come to this." Queen Elizabeth the First, powerfully played by Cate Blanchett in the 1998 film about that monarch, established a chalk-white face with a startling red mouth as a sort of icon with the power to summon a sense of her power and her brilliance. In the eighteenth century there was a torrent of satire against the extravagant painting and coifing and gowning of women. But in the Victorian era makeup had become something unseemly. Painting your face meant falsehood, and cosmetics, if they were to be applied at all, tended to be done in secret. It was an injustice against women. The conventions of the time still meant that it was the pretty woman with the smooth complexion who was likeliest to marry well and thus live well. However, if she were known to have done anything artful in order to *achieve* that complexion, she risked the rejection of those same male arbitrators upon whose approval she depended. We are told that women began to use "secret ingredients," ranging from the healthy use of lemon, through slightly more risky whiteners such as hydrogen peroxide, to creams compounded with lead, which could be deadly. The aim was to appear to have a "natural complexion" in the achievement of which there had been no artifice.

But then towards the end of the 1800s there seems to have come — along with the prosperity and bustle of the times, with the bicycle (which women were riding with abandon) and the tramcar and the softening of the old Victorian disapproval of being seen in public — a new commercial venture, the Beauty Culturist. This began in the form of small, discreet, commercial hair salons.

In the meantime, since Willie Graham could not afford to keep his girls in school (Flo never finished high school), and the life of a stable hand and a weekend vegetable stand attendant were clearly not leading her anywhere, Flo went to Toronto and enrolled in nursing school. Perhaps her healing hands would find a more dignified employment there. But she did not feel the same sense of calling as her famous namesake, and in fact she did not like nursing at all. The squalor and smell of the hospital and the indignity of illness offended her. The filth and the blood were as bad as the dirt of the stables, no, worse: because they came from human beings. She thought of her mother's tragic illness. She found illness ugly.

There is a lovely photograph of her at about this time, and she was strikingly beautiful. Photographs of her throughout her long life appear in this television biography. This one of the eighteen- or twenty-year-old shows her contemplating the camera in a slightly challenging way, as if to say, "Guess what I am thinking!" And it is conceivable that she was thinking about cosmetics. During her brief spell at nursing school she worked for a while with a hospital chemist who was experimenting with skin-healing creams. She thought perhaps it could help make the skin look better. She quit nursing school and went home to Woodbridge and tried cooking up some kind of cosmetic "cream" on the kitchen stove, with rendered fat and lemon juice, rosewater from the drugstore, a little lye and perhaps some lanolin, and herbs from the vegetable garden. We know only that she made a stink, and that her father was furious. Soon after, she had had her fill of him and of Woodbridge, and, for the time, of concocting creams. So back she went to Toronto.

She knocked around at this and that for several years — shopgirl, secretary, whatever she could get, nothing permanent, nothing productive, nothing interesting. One of the few amusements was the Nickelodeon, "High Class Motion Picture Theatre: Admission Five

Cents." A bit later she would be seeing the early pictures of another Toronto girl, Gladys Smith, who was out in California making three or four short dramatic pictures a week, and already known by her movie name Mary Pickford. The new phenomenon of the movie star was just around the corner. Already, at these "High Class Motion Picture Theatres," Florence Nightingale Graham, nearing thirty, no prospects, no way she was going back to Woodbridge though she missed her sister Gladys a lot, was seeing painted women in positions of power. Fictions, perhaps. But they suggested something to her, and part of what they suggested was that she had better get out of Toronto and get herself a lot closer to where, it seemed, women were at least within arm's reach of something like power. As luck would have it, her brother Bill had gone to New York. He was doing well as a salesman. She got on a train and changed her life suddenly and dramatically.

Later she would say that after she stepped out of Grand Central Station and began to walk along Fifth Avenue, she just *knew* that it was going to be her street. Shops of undreamed-of luxury and elegance, "a flow," as biographer Allan Lewis says, a whole area downtown called Women's Mile. There was a salon for women, something more advanced than the early Beauty Culturists, but grown from the same root. Flo began to think about cosmetic creams again, and took her healing hands to a Beauty Culturist salon called the Adair, moderately famous at the time. She studied a facial procedure called the Strapping Treatment, and learned massage. She learned how to gently rub creams into the sagging skins of the wives of wealthy New Yorkers. Allan Lewis says that not long afterwards Flo "met a woman named Elizabeth Hubbard. . . . [who] had a better cream than [what they used at] Adair." But she had no gift for massage. Florence had no cream and a great gift for massage. And so they got together and they opened a little salon on Fifth Avenue near 42nd Street.

The nerve of it! Here she was, only months into her new life as a New Yorker, and she takes the long chance and opens a business. Her brother Bill was an important anchor for her, he had a bit of money, and could borrow more, and he admired and encouraged Flo to "go for it." When he heard that she wanted to borrow $6,000, which is more like a hundred thousand in today's money, he balked for a moment. But she said firmly, "You have to spend money to make money," and Bill believed that too, so he came up with the cash.

And it was at this time that she hit on the idea of the brilliant red door, which is still the Elizabeth Arden Salon signature, and gave its name to this episode of *The Canadians*.

Wherever it came from, Florence Nightingale Graham had brought to New York an extraordinary confidence, a readiness to take a chance, and an almost uncanny sense of what was waiting for her out there in the great marketplace. The colour red was prophetic: red, in lipstick especially, would be more than just a colour for her for the rest of her life; it would be a symbol and a confirmation of her power and her skill. She loved red; she would experiment with hundreds, maybe thousands of different reds, and invent names to make each one of them special in the eyes of the women for whom she was going to make going out in public an adventure where they would win.

And that was explicitly another component of the many complex forces that were converging in this woman: the drive to make women strong. It does not matter a great deal, and in any case is impossible to determine, whether this concern was generous or cynical. Most likely it was both, as in the good works of most of us. But she certainly knew that what she was setting out to do would grow in the way she wanted it to grow only if her creams and other cosmetics gave something like her own confidence to other women. She joined the suffragette movement. That fit the motif, and it also brought her directly into contact with a lot of women who had time and money and who were very much interested in how they looked when they appeared in public.

She needed a name. The image of the wartime nurse, Florence Nightingale, going through the tents of the wounded with a storm lantern did not quite fit. She took the Elizabeth from her former colleague (the partnership with Ms. Hubbard did not last long). Elizabeth was nice; she would use that. At the time she was reading a classic by Alfred Lord Tennyson, *Enoch Arden*, and the Arden had a ring to it. How to test it? Was it a marketable name? Who had a better sense of the market than she herself? She had to see it in print, or something like that. In a frame. In a formal, official kind of presentation. So she wrote herself a letter, addressed to Elizabeth Arden at her Fifth Avenue address. It looked pretty good on the envelope, better with a stamp on it, but it would be still better when the postman handed it in and it had a postmark on it, making it an official kind of a thing. So she mailed it. And there was something fine about the look of it when it came back in the next day's mail. She said, "That's it." And from then on, when she was doing business she was Elizabeth Arden. Among those who watched her reinvent herself over the next few years there is some speculation that Flo never really went away from her interior life (how could she?). But officially, Elizabeth Arden was here to stay.

She was still trying to come up with a cream that would outsell the others. She put on a white lab coat at night and experimented. Elizabeth Hubbard accused her of stealing the Hubbard formula, but in fact almost all the creams that the salons used were made of the same basic ingredients; it was the scent, the name, and the packaging that made the real difference then and still does today. Elizabeth Hubbard had called her concoctions Grecian Creams. Arden decided that Venetian Cream sounded better and would lead women to think they were buying something substantially different from what Elizabeth Hubbard was selling.

That was the beginning of the Elizabeth Arden Line. The now omnipresent craft of packaging was in its infancy in those years before the First World War, but Flo — or perhaps we should refer to her by her professional name, because she is firmly established in that new life now — Elizabeth Arden was one of the packaging pioneers. Her eye-catching containers had to work in the elegant department stores, not just in the Fifth Avenue salon. She had to get them out across the United States, and she knew already that her real market was the world.

By 1914 makeup was establishing itself as a norm for the modern woman. The historian Kathy Peiss has written a whole book about it, *Hope in a Jar*. She says, in the documentary, "They [women] needed to create a social image of themselves. And they do that in part through the use of makeup. Makeup implies putting on products to help you realize who you are. You make up for a show. You make up for a public performance . . . that is the modern connotation of makeup."

Robert Goldman, who has also written on the sociology of makeup, said that this woman had seen her lovely, almost aristocratic mother descend into drudgery and fatigue and ultimately death because, as Arden saw it, the woman who had been Susan Tadd allowed herself to fall into a role instead of taking control. Elizabeth Arden was obsessed with control. Goldman says of her, "She became very much aware of the nuance of *action* in everyday life. From observing the women in the [Woodbridge] market, and how they could use their beauty to gain control, to her recognition of what she could do in a male world to wrestle control away . . . just by putting on a particular outfit or by putting on a particular face."

Arden was now mixing her own colours to help women achieve this kind of control. Her colours were brilliant, not subdued. She understood them as a way of making a statement about yourself. Her clients began to recognize that when you went to the Arden salon, you entered with one face and left with another, and they liked the other. They told their friends. The old taboos about the unseemliness of makeup were evaporating, and Arden was doing her best to accelerate the process. The business prospered.

While pioneering in the concoction and marketing of cosmetics, she was also fastidious about the safety of her ingredients. There was a history of women poisoning themselves with cosmetics. Kathy Peiss told us, "Women who worked as ballet dancers, or secretaries, [had used] lead-based powders [and developed] symptoms of lead poisoning. . . . The doctor keeps asking them, Are you using lead powders because I can't understand where you are getting the lead from . . . They are keeping it a secret because they are ashamed [of using makeup]. They don't want their cosmetic use to be known."

By 1914 that attitude would be waning. That was the year when *Vogue* magazine, THE authoritative voice of fashion, would declare in favour of makeup ". . . a discreet application of colour will enhance a woman's appearance." That was still a couple of years ahead, but Arden was preparing the way for it, and with colours that were not all that discreet. She wore the white lab coat in the salon now, to emphasize the scientific care she took in developing her materials, and her own complexion was still miraculously childlike. At thirty-five she looked twenty-five. She was her own best advertisement. She was selling *control*, and, as she knew very well, she was selling desire.

But Florence Graham, according to biographer Allen Lewis, was still there inside the aggressive, confident Elizabeth Arden, and Florence Graham was not yielding to her own desires; they were too dangerous. Eloping with a handsome young ne'er-do-well had meant that her mother's desire led to a kind of imprisonment that she, Flo, wearing her Arden mask, was determined to avoid. Sex was dangerous; it could kill you. "Elizabeth Arden wanted to be the safest woman in the world, and there was only one way to be safe if you were a woman," said Allen Lewis, "and that was to be independently wealthy."

But men were smitten by her, all the same. And one of them, a banker named Thomas Jenkins Lewis, authorized a substantial loan for the expansion of the Arden business, and let it be known that he was very, very interested in her as a woman. Elizabeth Arden was courteous but cool. She held him at bay but he kept calling. She went to Paris. She wanted to see what the French women were putting on their faces. She was struck by the eye makeup she saw in the fashionable cafés. There and then she started experimenting, enlisting the hotel maids as subjects for her experiments. She went from salon to salon, buying samples of creams and colours and perfumes to take back to New York, and analyse, and improve upon. She had to cut the visit short. War was imminent. She crossed to England, and boarded the *Lusitania* for New York.

The *Lusitania* had been built to challenge what was then the German mastery of the seas, in terms of fast transatlantic crossings. The great ship *Kaiser Wilhelm der Grosse* had won the Blue Riband in 1897 and Germany had held on to it ever since. The Cunard Lines, with massive financial support from the British treasury, had built the *Lusitania* and her sister ship the *Mauritania* to win that mastery back from Germany. At 31,500 tons and almost 800 feet long, the *Lusitania* was a winner. She had won the Riband back with her second crossing, in

October of 1907, completing the westbound voyage in just under 116 hours. Arden did not know that her banker admirer, Tommy Lewis, would be on board. She was annoyed at first, but accepted his invitation to join his party for dinner, and learned that there were advantages to having a male companion during a sea voyage; she would be right in the middle of the first-class passenger society. These were people who could be useful to her. Tommy Lewis may have misinterpreted her enthusiasm, and on the voyage he proposed marriage. She was thirty-six but looked twenty-six, and he was, by now, totally enchanted.

But Elizabeth was not, and she let him know that while she would like to see him from time to time, she was not interested in a relationship; business drove her life. Back in New York she threw herself into the work, moved to a larger building, hired a chemist to analyse the samples from Paris and develop lighter creams and stronger colours. She moved to a much bigger apartment. If there was a Flo inside her, a Flo who wanted relationships and comfort and affection, that person would have to wait. She was on the crest of a wave. She coined a new slogan for the salon: "Where everything is so refreshingly different and the spirit of youth is so pervading that you cannot leave without catching some of it." If that seems long-winded today, it worked then. Her profits kept going up.

But now, in an oblique way, the *Lusitania* came into her life again. On May 1, 1915, the great ship cast off from New York, bound for London with nearly two thousand people on board. None of the passengers knew that she was also carrying tons of munitions, bound for Britain. But German spies, prowling the New York docks, did know, and that may have had something to do with the submarine U-2's intercepting the *Lusitania* off the coast of Ireland a few days later, and sinking her with a single torpedo. She went down in twenty minutes, and nearly 1,200 people died. The controversy about that sinking is still debated today, with one faction claiming that she was callously used as a way of bringing America into the war, that Winston Churchill, then First Lord of the Admiralty, had arranged that it would go into waters where the German submarines were known to be on patrol, and others arguing that it was purely an accident.

The sinking of a passenger ship shocked the world. For Tommy Lewis the banker it was also a reminder of his relationship with Elizabeth Arden, and he sought her out and proposed again, and for reasons that are not clear she accepted. They were married soon after, and the moment the ceremony was over she went back to work. Tommy joined the army and went off to war. Elizabeth acted as though she scarcely noticed, but in fact she was lonely, and asked Gladys to come down from Toronto to work with her. She had her own war to fight, the cosmetics war. Helena Rubinstein had opened a competing business and set her sights on the wealthy and glamorous movie stars. The competition between Arden and Rubinstein was ruthless. Arden staked out the high-society market. While she talked about the democ-ratizing effects of makeup ("Beauty is every woman's right"), her prices were aimed at the elite class.

"She threw around her products an aura of exclusivity," Kathy Peiss says, "so that any woman who bought an Arden product would know . . . that ordinary women could not have purchased it."

Tommy Lewis came back from the war, and Arden gave him a job in the company. Before long he began to see other women. Arden would put up with that as long as he was discreet about it. Her biog-raphers say that she seemed not to have wanted a sex life, at least not with him. Whatever the truth of that, it is clear that she didn't want anyone to see any cracks in her domestic life. She kept Tommy intense-ly involved in the business, perhaps hoping that this would keep him faithful.

Within a few years the giant companies Ponds and Colgate became stiff competition to Elizabeth Arden and Helena Rubinstein, mass-marketing cheap cosmetics of reasonable quality and high safety standards, and Arden was tempted to compete with them on their own ground. But Gladys and Tommy, who had become close colleagues in the business, persuaded her to stay on the elite upscale exclusive side of the marketplace. They would sell less but they would charge a lot more. They opened a salon in London and then one in Paris. Instant success. Soon there were forty salons. Profits kept rising.

Despite the success, Elizabeth Arden seemed to be very unhappy.

She would fly into rages at employees, screaming at people in front of both customers and staff, then later regretting her outbursts and sending huge bouquets of conciliatory flowers to the offending, or offended, employee. Perhaps it was because she knew that her husband was sleeping around, but had no idea how to deal with that profound insult to her person. Her biographer, Alfred Allen Lewis, says that it had something to do with a sense of frustration at the fact that with all this wealth she still was not accepted as an equal among those New York High Society women whom she pampered and creamed and coloured, and admired and envied but could not join.

This was about to change. She met Elizabeth Marbury. Bessie Marbury was Old New York, Old Money, and a prominent member of what they called the Sapphic Circle, a homosexual circle of wealthy New Yorkers in the arts and society crowd. She was a successful theatrical agent and producer. She was friends with the Morgans and the Vanderbilts, and her friendship with Elizabeth Arden, which may or may not have had a sexual side to it, as Bessie was certainly a lesbian, was a spectacular display of contrasts.

Bessie Marbury, in one photograph, looks something like a sumo wrestler, massive, an almost Asian lift to the corner of her eyes as she confronts the camera aggressively, glowering under the upswept hair that is also in the sumo style. Muscle and heft and confidence. Beside the slim, graceful, almost petite and certainly not visibly aggressive Arden, she loomed like a fortress.

They became inseparable. Elizabeth went up to Bessie's farm at Lakeside, Maine, and soon built her own house there, which Bessie named Maine Chance. They bought horses. She would leave Tommy in charge of the business in New York and go off for days to Maine with Bessie. She looked great. She was fifty-one in 1929 when the Depression hit, but she looked thirty-eight and said that was her real age. The Depression did not much hurt the business; women still needed lipstick, perhaps more than ever as the gloom of the Great Crash spread around the world; while a lipstick still cost 75 cents, and that was a lot of money for ordinary folk, people kept buying. In 1930 Elizabeth refused an offer of $15 million for the company, something in the order of $200 million in today's money. By now her husband's infidelities were more than she could bear, and when she found out that her brother Bill was covering for Tommy's adventures, she fired both of them. Bill died not long after. Biographer Alfred Allen Lewis says that, bitter and unforgiving, she acted as though she scarcely noticed.

"Her only statement . . . was, 'My sister's brother died today. It's going to be a hard day at the office.'"

Through Bessie's connections she had joined the racing set and now had a new hobby, buying and breeding thoroughbreds. But then Bessie died. In her grief Arden turned Maine Chance into a kind of shrine in memory of the only really close friend she had ever had. The house became the first real beauty spa in America, according to Lewis:

> *The food was excellent but it was diet food. Women dressed for dinner. There were exercises, there was swimming, there were parties. It was a woman's world but a very upper-class woman's world. . . . She developed what many called the greatest treatment cream ever devised. . . . It was Elizabeth Arden's Eight Hour Cream. What had first been thought the whimsical dream of this crazy woman from the cosmetics business became a part of treating horses all through the late thirties. Everybody was using her eight-hour cream on their horses as well as their faces.*

Her motto became "Treat a horse like a lady, and a lady like a horse." She would go out to the stables herself, and get down on her knees as she had in her father's stable back in Woodbridge, and rub a horse's sore legs with her own cream.

Sister Gladys had moved to Paris and married a wealthy French count. Now it was 1939 and another world war had broken out. When Paris was occupied, Gladys courageously helped allied troops to escape. She was caught by the Nazis, and her aristocratic husband revealed himself to be a collaborator, did nothing to help her, and allowed her to be sent off to a concentration camp. Arden was devastated, but there was nothing she could do. She began to use the business as a contribution to the War Effort, devising a "Victory Red" lipstick, and featuring women in uniform in her advertising. She met a powerful Hearst Corporation executive, another Tom, Tom White.

Inexplicably she seems to have fallen in love, but he was married, Catholic, and very correct. She could not have him. On the rebound, she married an exiled Russian Prince, Evlanoff, seventeen years younger than she. It was a disaster. When she found out that he was homosexual and insisted on travelling with a male lover, she divorced him.

In 1944 Gladys was released from prison, but not long after that Elizabeth's relief over her sister's rescue was scarred by the loss of a number of her favourite horses when a fire destroyed her stables at Arlington. Then, in a way, horse racing came to her rescue. She became the first woman in history to win the famous Kentucky Derby, with a thoroughbred called Jet Pilot. Her still youthful face appeared on the cover of *Time* magazine. Her business was better than ever. But, according to A.A. Lewis, this preoccupation with age was building within her a serious level of stress. She would say, "Father Time, you don't bother me and I won't bother you." But in fact they were bothering each other. Lewis said, "As Florence Graham aged, Elizabeth Arden was remaining young. She was Dorian Grey."

There is an ironic touch about those last days. She was a friend of the designer Oscar de la Renta, and he made an extraordinary gold lamé gown for her, but she never wore it. De la Renta appears in the documentary, talking about that dress. "I said, Miss Arden, I made a tea gown for you. It took me a lot of time to do. It cost me a lot of money. And you never wear it. She would always say, 'No, no, I am saving it for a special occasion.'"

That special occasion was Elizabeth Arden's funeral. She died in 1966. She was eighty-nine, and even she could no longer avoid seeing that she was really old. No tape or cream or puffs or colours could hide the drying skin, the sad eyes, the wasting figure. She was heard to say to the mirror, "I am old. I am really old. I will not be here much longer."

The rich and famous came to say goodbye, as she lay in her casket. Oscar de la Renta was shocked, he said, when he saw that at last she was wearing the tea gown.

Feminist, suffragette, industrial pioneer, innovative marketer and manager, Elizabeth Arden had built a business that at her death was worth millions. She may not have been "the richest little girl in the world," but she was able to leave legacies of $11 million. Four million went to Gladys, one million to John, two million to her niece Patricia Young, and four million to the employees of her company. She had not protected the business, though, and it was the subject of ongoing wrangles. Millions were spent in legal fees before the company finally ended up in the hands of Eli Lilly and Company, who soon set about to make things more efficient, less exclusive, more profitable.

But she had achieved her ambition. She had conceived the idea of a revolutionary business, brought it into existence, made herself rich, and left the world with a name that still stands for elegance, beauty and power.

She also left a mischievous a poem.

DAUGHTERS OF EVE
You don't really wish to start
A seven years war
But
It's nice to know that
You've got that kind
Of face.
you don't really wish
men
to break their hearts
for love of you
but it's nice to know they feel
that way.
you don't really wish
to twist
monarchs
round your little finger
but it's nice to know
you could.
you don't really wish
other women to envy
the beauty that
Elizabeth Arden gave you

but it's nice to know
they do.
Elizabeth doesn't wish you to be
a menace
you don't wish to be
a menace
but it's nice to know
you are!

◆ ◆ ◆

Behind The Red Door was written and directed by Patricia Phillips.

PART TEN

NORTHROP FRYE
A Love Story

Northrop Frye
What a guy
Read more books
Than you or I.

Some time in the mid 1970s, a hearing of the Canadian Radio-television and Telecommunications Commission was receiving submissions from a citizens' group concerned about violence on television. Among the commissioners was a small man in his early sixties, a man with a huge mop of unruly waved hair that had once been a spectacular yellow colour but was now grizzled. He was a famous scholar, a university professor who served on this government body because he felt it was his duty to undertake a public responsibility when asked.

His expression suggested puzzlement and amusement at the same time. The slight humour of his characteristically pursed lips was more than balanced by a narrowing of the eyes — almost to invisibility sometimes — which people often interpreted as more sinister than it really was.

On the floor, an intervenor was expressing earnest outrage at what she characterized as an almost uninterrupted flow of violence on our home screens. When she said that this violence was worse than anything the world had ever seen, or something to that effect, the quizzical professor signalled to the chairman of the meeting that he would like to comment.

He said, "Madame, have you read the *Old Testament*?"

This was Northrop Frye, who had read the *Old Testament* more carefully than most of us. At the time of his death early in 1991, if it had been suggested that a documentary film on his life should be subtitled "A Love Story," most Canadians who knew the name would have been puzzled. With a million copies of his books having been sold around the world, he is indisputably the widest-read Canadian scholar, well ahead of Marshall McLuhan and Harold Innis. Scholarship and literary criticism were the fields that made Frye famous. His achievement in the understanding of the eighteenth-century genius William Blake initiated a whole new era in the study of literature. As a teacher he had the capacity to send students reeling from his lectures, almost overwhelmed with the power of his ideas and of the questions he raised.

Frye had other personae, among them the broadcast regulator, a commissioner on the CRTC, helping decide on television licence applications and even on the rates the telephone company can charge. He was also an administrator, principal and later Chancellor of Victoria University in the University of Toronto; and he was a clergyman, an ordained minister in the United Church of Canada.

So why did we call his television biography "A Love Story"?

A few years after his death his letters and notebooks began to be published. Columnist Robert Fulford, in the Toronto *Globe and Mail*, reported with apparent delight that this prim-looking scholar we had gotten to know over the years was prepared to write to his wife such surprising sentences as "We are fucked and far from home." But what these papers revealed more importantly was a passionate, lyrical, playful (and sometimes wittily obscene) spirit. Frye honoured — at the very centre of his being — the primacy of sexual love as "the gateway through which most of us enter the life of the creative imagination." He said that religion, love, poetry, music and indeed all art, are intimately involved with each other, perhaps even aspects of the same human gift. When he spoke of love he very often meant love between the sexes, a passion that at its best lifts the human experience to the highest realms.

Herman Northrop Frye said he felt he had come close to something that teases and seduces every single human being who ever stops to reflect on life: its meaning. During his lifetime he would experience several sudden, clarifying moments. Taking decades to work out the language with which he felt he could express what those revelations had contained, he began to feel that he had uncovered the secret to some of the most profound and puzzling questions. He wrote about the nature of sex, of God, of beauty, truth, science, art, politics and society. Reading Frye, we sometimes feel that if he had lived long enough he would have written about every single thing in life that is worth thinking about, and that he would have had something disturbing and fresh to say about each one of them.

When the actors Don Harron and his wife Catherine McKinnon began to read those letters, between Northrop Frye and his wife Helen Kemp, they almost immediately saw them as the text for a stage presentation. Daniel Zuckerbrot, the writer/director of this episode of *The Canadians*, chose to begin the documentary at one of those readings with:

> *Saturday night, Spring, 1932. I would have given anything to come to you. I wanted to spend about a day lying on the floor in front of you, with my arms around your ankles and my head on your feet. But of course I didn't do anything as silly, or even try to. I had my institutional dignity to think of! What would the English and History course say if they saw their Norrie Frye making a fool of himself in front of a female?*
>
> *It's one o'clock. You're sleeping now. My lips have brushed your forehead and my hand has smoothed down your hair.*
>
> *But you don't know that.*
>
> *You're asleep.*

Frye himself said he thought his life had not been very interesting. On his sixtieth birthday, in one of the tens of thousands of journal entries that scholars are now poring over, searching for what is ultimately close to a mystery embedded in the huge range of this man's mind, Frye wrote:

> *I notice that at the age of sixty I have arranged my life so that nothing has ever happened to me, and no biographer could possibly have taken the smallest interest in me.*

But this is simply not true, as the documentary quickly set out to demonstrate. The camera moves along a set of corridors, descending into the lower regions of a climate-controlled section of the Pratt Library at the University of Toronto. It is a long walk to the Frye collection, which is kept in a locked section accessible only to qualified scholars. Men and women sit in their tiny cubicles a few buildings away, transferring and indexing material from pages and pages of handwritten words in that collection. They are sorting through thousands of journal entries and letters, cataloguing and analysing the vast outpouring of ideas and speculations about everything from God to the motor car. It is becoming clear to the Frye scholars (who come together from time to time, to international conventions where men and women from all the continents meet to discuss his work) that at the heart of that work is a series of sudden flashes of what seemed to Frye to be profound and intricate insights that would require a vast amount of rigorous thinking to explore and to make comprehensible both to himself and to others.

They had begun when he was still in his teens. Like many adolescents he was struggling to make sense out of a world that was dominated by a version of Christianity that seemed to him to deny his own sexuality, his liberty, his imagination, in short: his humanity. This was a fifteen-year-old boy from New Brunswick, the son of a travelling hardware salesman, who one day on his way home from school was struck by a sort of spiritual and intellectual searchlight beam. He said that he had known at the time it would take him years to find out what the sudden clarity meant, but he also knew right then and there that it would change his life.

"Just then suddenly," he wrote later, "that whole shitty and smelly garment of fundamentalist teaching I'd had all my life dropped off into the sewers and stayed there."

That does not sound like a boy who will in a few years be ordained as a minister in the United Church. But it is the opening chapter in a series of spectacular and sudden insights that will lead him to see the whole of human life — that part of our life, that is distinctly human, is different from all other creatures — as being shaped by the combined forces of love, the imagination, and the divine. In the end these three powers, in the mind of Northrop Frye, seem to be different expressions of what is really one distinctly human power or capacity.

Herman Northrop Frye was born in Sherbrooke, Quebec, on Bastille Day, July 14, 1912. His grandfather was a Methodist preacher.

Methodism, which had begun as a humanizing protest against the politics and theology of the Church of England, had by then become a rather severe fundamentalist movement, and Frye's mother Catherine was a serious Methodist. For Catherine and Herman Frye life had seemed a solid, reliable path along which we are clearly guided by the precepts of the faith. Then this illusion of assurance and safety was shaken up badly in 1918, when young Norrie was six; first by the death of his brother Howard, a soldier overseas in the Great War, and then by the failure of the family business. Herman took the family to Moncton, New Brunswick, and Frye grew up there, shy, somewhat solitary, an intense student of the piano at which he himself said he was "infernally precocious," and of literature.

"I read all of [George Bernard] Shaw at fifteen," he would say later, "and he turned me from a precocious child into an adolescent fool."

There would be very few besides Frye himself who would ever refer to him as a fool.

A couple of years later, the agile fingers that were already flashing prodigy-like up and down the piano keyboard turned out to be what was needed to get him out of Moncton and into a world where his powerful imagination and eccentric personality would be an asset, rather than a reason for him to hide away at home: he learned to type. He became very good at it. There was a national typing competition. Frye won the local playoffs, and that got him a railway ticket to Toronto for the grand championships. Somehow that led to his taking a look at the university, and deciding to enroll in what was then called Victoria College (now Victoria University). There he met another young man who was destined for the ministry, Kingsley Joblin. They would remain friends for life, and Joblin says that he vividly remembers an early demonstration of an unexpected talent.

He was pale in complexion. He was slight in build. He had this mop of yellow hair. He had been all through high school what the kids would call a nerd. . . . In those days of initiation he and I were walking through [the famous Vic archway on Charles Street] and we were met by three sophomores. You remember that great mop of yellow hair. The first said, "Good morning Butter-cup." And the second said, "Does your mommy know you're out?" Well Frye let loose a stream of profanity that curled their toes and mine too. Nobody ever called him that to his face again.

But one student would give him a nickname based on that yellow mop, and get away with it. She was Helen Kemp, also a gifted pianist and a fine artist. They met at the Drama Club. Out of that love those hundreds of pages of letters would flourish, along with a marriage that lasted more than fifty years.

At the University he was finally among people who found him fascinating. The apparently shy exterior mixed with a dazzling intellect and plenty of raw personal courage was daunting but intriguing. It was a world where brilliance was recognized and respected. That was new to Frye. Soon he was editing the college literary magazine and making his mark on the debating team.

Helen wrote to him while he was visiting the family in the summer break, "Having decided that I will not improve my mind or do anything the least uplifting or educational this summer, I shall be very interested in seeing how *your* muse develops, Feathertop."

Apparently pleased, and not at all offended, he replied,

You ask about my muse. It's still stubborn. I have a good idea but no technique. I have a conception for a really good poem, I am pretty sure. But what I put down is flat and dry as the Great Sahara. I guess I'm essentially prosaic. I can work myself up into a state of maudlin sentimentality, put down about ten lines of the most villainous doggerel imaginable, and then kick myself and tear the filthy stuff up. However, I got a book of twentieth-century American poetry at the library, and that cheered me up. There are bigger fools in the world!

Before very long Frye's teachers at Victoria College realized that among that small group of very bright young people who stayed after the lecture to ask the questions there didn't seem to be time for during class, who could be found in the library late at night and early in the morning, and who were turning in witty and perceptive essays, this Frye was really something special. One day his Romantics professor, a well-known academic named Pelham Edgar, told him, "I think you're the guy to write on Blake in this class."

Blake is a poet who has baffled both scholars and lovers of poetry. He has created some of the most durable and powerful images in the history of English literature. All serious readers of English — and thousands not so serious — have read or heard:

Tyger, Tyger, burning bright
In the forests of the night
What immortal hand or eye
Could frame thy fearful symmetry.

Perhaps not quite so many, but still enormous numbers, have felt the delight of the apparently simple lines:

To see a world in a grain of sand
And a heaven in a wild flower
Hold infinity in the palm of your hand
And eternity in an hour.

In churches and on choral concert stages all over the English-speaking world, the great hymn "Jerusalem," set to music by Charles H. Parry, is Blake's preface to his epic poem *Milton*. It begins,

And did those feet in ancient times
Walk upon England's mountains green?

And continues,

Bring me my bow of burning gold
Bring me my arrows of desire

And ends,

I will not cease from Mental Fight
Nor will my sword sleep in my hand
Till we have built Jerusalem
In England's green and pleasant land.

It is not hard to see the young scholar being swept away by those resonant lines. However, very few, none but serious scholars these days, have ventured into Blake's long, complicated mythic epics about the origins of the world and the titanic struggle of huge mythic figures with names such as Orc and Urizen. But all who read Blake are struck by two things at once: the power of the words, and the sense that they convey something far more profound than you would expect from their seemingly simple form.

What happened to Frye when he tackled Blake for the first time went far beyond the sense of delight and even mystery that many feel when they first encounter this daunting writer. Like many students he had put off writing the essay until the last possible moment, in this case the night before it was due. He had to work late into that night. Suddenly he had another vision:

> Around about three in the morning the universe broke open, and I've never been, as they say, the same man since. It was just a feeling of enormous numbers of things making sense that never did before; a vision of coherence. Things began to form patterns and make sense. It was a mythological frame taking hold. I've had two or three nights where I've had sudden visions like that. They were visions of what I might be able to do.

What would those things turn out to be? Professor Michael Dolzani, who spent years in close association with Frye as his research assistant, said that Frye envisioned a coherent single body of work, composed of eight great separate but related pieces:

> . . . a set, an interlocking set that he called The Ogdoad: sort of an old word for a set of eight gods. These were not even necessarily to be books. They were going to be . . . eight great symphonies or something. They were to be . . . the eight elements of the total vision that he had come into the world to say. It was only towards the end of this life that the notebooks start to say, "I'm coming to see that this vision, this ogdoad total pattern, is not only something to see, let alone something to write: it is something to see by. Like a lens, rather than something that is projected out into the world."

And central to this projection was the *act* of literature. "He calls literature a power of meditation," says Professor Dolzani. "And it's available to anybody. You don't have to do drugs. You don't have to get into arcane things. Literature itself can be . . . an expansion of consciousness."

Much later in his life, Northrop Frye would write two very provocative books about the Bible: *The Great Code*, and *Words With Power*. These books, of which the subtitled theme is "The Bible and

Literature" (*not* "The Bible *As* Literature"), examine the Bible as the Western world's prime source of all of the great stories that we use to make sense out of our lives. Frye shows how those stories keep turning up: in Shakespeare, in movies, even in comic strips. One of the striking things about these two books is that, while they are focused on the Bible, they discover reflections of its myths and legends in just about every aspect of modern life. One of the contributors to this film biography, Phillip Marchand, the literary critic of the *Toronto Star*, even finds the role of the umpire in a baseball game embedded in the same set of ancient myths about the Scapegoat that Frye said was the soil from which grew the story of Christ.

This was a view of the Bible very different from the one that Frye felt he had been saddled with, and an uncomfortable saddle at that, in his Methodist upbringing. That Bible was a set of rules and threats of punishment for those who broke the rules. The Bible that suddenly broke free of those rules, as Frye plunged into the strange and powerful poetry of William Blake, was a radical document. It was not an authoritarian prescription for a way of life that would get you into some creamy place up in the sky if you did what you were told. It was in fact a revolutionary call to arms, spiritual arms.

Frye said, "The Bible to Blake was really the *Magna Carta* of the human imagination. It was a book that told man he had the power to create and imagine. And the power to create and imagine *was ultimately the divine in man.*" For the rest of his life he would condemn the way in which the traditional churches had allowed themselves to be used throughout history as a political instrument to keep people in their places so that the powerful could rule in comfort. This was a form of tyranny, he said baldly. It contradicted the real message of the Bible, which was God is everywhere, including inside each one of us. The creative imagination is an expression of the divine in man, he said. Its purpose is not to keep us in line but to free us so that we can realize our divinity, escape the tyranny of rulers and of our own blindness. Religion is about love and liberty, not about doing what you're supposed to do so that you'll get into some place called Heaven — where there is nothing left to do.

But that doesn't mean that Northrop Frye himself was as suddenly freed from the grip of his traditional religious upbringing as he perhaps hoped, or imagined. He wrote to Helen, from Moncton, in 1932:

*The Ministry is my "vocation." I have been "called" to it just as
much as any blaspheming fool of an evangelist that ever bragged
about what a sinner he was before he was converted. But that does-
n't mean that I am fitted for it, necessarily. It doesn't mean that I
am not deadly afraid of it and would rather do a hundred other
things.*

*Above all it doesn't mean that my friends ever imagine I'll be a
minister. "Minister," snorts the janitor at Gate House. "You'd
make a damned good hypocrite, that's what you'd make!" My communist friend Norm Knight says, "My dear boy, you can't be a
minister, you've got brains!" And so they go.*

*They are absolutely and devastatingly right, of course. I wonder
what those writers who talk about . . . fate would say to a man who
had two Fates, pulling in opposite directions. The trouble is, I can't
figure out which one is God.*

It was about that time, in a letter, that Helen confessed that she
was in love with him. Another student, a man named Robert, had been
teasing her, moving in on her perhaps, and asking her if she was in love
with anybody. "Well," she wrote, "I did mention you, Norrie. Do you
mind very much?"

*You frighten me a little [he replied]. Love may mean anything from
a quiet friendship to an overwhelming passion. It may be anything
from a purely sexual impulse to a declaration of honourable intentions based upon a close survey of the economic field. It acts like a
tonic upon me to hear you say you love me, certainly. But it does
make me nervous to be carrying such a warm, pulsating heart
around in my pockets. I'm afraid it might drop out and break.*

One of the puzzles about the life of this undoubted genius is this:
Given his absolutely radical take on the real meaning of the Bible and
the Christian message, and his contempt for almost the entire traditional baggage and politics of the traditional organized churches, why
did he go ahead with his "vocation" to the Ministry?

By the summer of 1933, Helen had gone to study in Britain, and he was in Saskatchewan. He got saddle sores riding the circuit as a student minister, and visiting farmhouses where he was incapable of the expected small talk.

Gull Lake, Saskatchewan, May 1934. There's nothing to say about the trip, pet, except that I made it . . . or most of it. If I were a mystic this past week . . . would register as the Dark Night of the Soul. . . . I can't figure out this damn country. . . . Twenty more Sundays. I don't quite know how I'll survive. . . . I am horribly homesick and thoroughly miserable. Yet I can't think I made a mistake in coming out here. Everything, horse, country life, standards of living, moral attitudes, conversation, interests . . . are so absolutely different from anything I've been accustomed to. If I thought I should have to stay out here all my life I would commit suicide without the slightest hesitation.

By the time he had done the apprenticeship in the field that being ordained required, he had decided firmly that teaching, not the Ministry, was his real vocation. He enrolled at Oxford, to round out his studies. And yet, before he left, he went ahead with the ordination, and became the Reverend Northrop Frye, brains or no brains.

Now it was 1936. In Europe fascism was growing like a diabolical weed. It had already spawned the Nazi party and would soon bring the greatest war in the history of the world, and the Holocaust: the massacre of the Jews of Europe. Frye's tutor at Oxford was the renowned literary scholar Edmund Blunden. Frye was shocked to find that Blunden, like the poets T.S. Eliot, W.B. Yeats, and a number of other intellectuals, seemed to think that fascism might contain a ray of hope for a confused world. Moreover, Blunden had trouble with Frye's ideas.

Blunden returned my Blake paper with the remark that it was pretty stiff going for him as he wasn't much accustomed to thinking in philosophical terms. I could have told him that there was a little girl in Toronto who could follow it all right . . .

He was twenty-four. Helen was in Canada.

Merton College, Oxford. 1936. There are very few moments, if any, when you are out of my mind. I think at least half of you must be inside me. I feel as though I had only to turn around three times to turn into Helen. Nobody can talk to me five minutes without hearing about you somehow, and without realizing that I am prouder of my attachment to you than anything else. I love you all day long. And if you would mind stepping across the Atlantic a minute, I would soon prove it.

It was during this time that his undergraduate lightning flash about Blake was beginning to mature as he found words for Blake's revolutionary images of liberty and love and the divinity within the human mind, not in some God-in-the-Sky whom Blake (a devout Christian) dismissed as an

Old Nobodaddy aloft
Who farted and belched and coughed.

As the spectre of fascism, with its sanctification of blood and authority, grew stronger and stronger, so too did Frye's conviction that there was a vision of liberty in Blake that had to do with basic human needs and values. He, Northrop Frye, could bring these metaphors to the attention of the world, or at least to the world of scholars. It was a challenge to explore the creative experience as the starting point for a larger life and a better world.

I propose spending the rest of my life, apart from living with you, on various problems connected with religion and art. Now religion and art are the two most important phenomena, for they are basically the same thing. They constitute, in fact, the only reality of existence. Atheism is an impossible religious position for me, just as materialism is an impossible philosophical position. And I am unable to solve the problem of art by ignoring the first and distorting the second. Read Blake or go to Hell; that's my message for the modern world.

He came home to Helen. *The Toronto Daily Star, August 24, 1937: In Emmanuel College Chapel, Reverend Arthur Cragg, a classmate of the groom, performed the marriage of Herman Northrop Frye and Helen G. Kemp. The matrimonial pair will honeymoon at the bride's parents' cottage, Gordon Bay, Muskoka, after which they will reside at the University Apartments, 6 St. Thomas Street, adjacent to Victoria College.*

As World War II raged across Europe and through the Pacific, Frye, medically unfit for military service, threw himself into the book on Blake. He was a popular lecturer at Vic, often testing his ideas in the classroom where his students were sometimes shocked and often provoked to the point where they started digging into Blake themselves. The Blake book was still in the works. Northrop Frye's view of life began to converge so closely with that of the difficult and brilliant genius he was studying that, in chapter after chapter of the book he was still labouring on, it was increasingly difficult to discern whose voice the reader was hearing, Frye's or Blake's. The message was not one you would expect from a soft-spoken, apparently retiring United Church minister:

Tyranny requires a priesthood and a God. Religion has been called the Opiate of the People. But religion in its conventionally accepted and socially established form is far more dangerous than any opiate, whose effects are transitory.

The book was called *Fearful Symmetry*, from the poem beginning "Tyger, Tyger," quoted above. Frye finished it at last, in 1945. That date is a dividing line in Blake studies: before Frye and after Frye. Scholars, poets and students are still reading *Fearful Symmetry*, putting it down in astonishment, picking it up and starting all over again. From 1945 on, if there was ever any doubt that the world of literary criticism had a new giant to contend with, that doubt vanished. What scholars and lovers of literature found in *Fearful Symmetry* was an argument for the power of myths and metaphors that brutally tested the conventional scientific and materialistic view of the nature of reality.

Michael Dolzani:

Blake thinks almost purely in terms of myths and metaphors: the units that poets think in . . . a different way of thinking . . . a different mode of perception. They're native to all of us, because the deeper layers of our mind do think metaphorically, do think mythically. Our dreams are evidence of that. . . . The thing is to bring it up into daylight, and integrate that into consciousness. We live at

about a tenth of the level of consciousness and being that we could
. . . Blake . . . says that if the doors of perception were cleansed we
would see much much more than we do now.

From now on, for the next quarter-century, when Frye wrote, the literary world read, and paid attention. His next major work would be an original theory of literary criticism published in 1957: *Anatomy of Criticism*. Writers and scholars talk of it as a book that changed their lives. There had not been a theory of literary criticism before Frye. He argued that criticism was not a matter of saying whether a work was good or not, but of identifying the myths and metaphors it contained, telling the reader where they came from and why they were powerful and what they were connected to, so that the work could be seen as part of a whole.

That was the radical idea. What Shakespeare, William Styron, Montaigne, Li Po, and the many authors of the books of the Bible (who often disagreed with each other), and Walt Kelly, Walt Disney and Stephen Spielberg were all doing was a part of one comprehensive world vision. Whether or not they knew it, they were all working out of the same body of myths whose great expression in the Western world begins with Greek mythology and the books of the Bible. You could not understand, Frye argued, what you were doing here if you didn't know about Greek myth and the great formative stories of the Christians and the Jews.

He took his own prescription to heart, adding Greek to the Latin he already knew from high school, and then going on to Hebrew and Sanskrit. He was at ease with French and could make his way in German, and pretty well in Italian and Spanish too. Armed with these tools he would penetrate deeper and deeper into the stories, myths and metaphors in which he was convinced were buried the meaning of the human experience.

Poet and novelist Margaret Atwood, who received one of her many honorary doctorates from Frye's hands, said,
Norrie . . . said essentially the comic book and the Jane Austen novel
and the Greek myth have the same structure. What are we talking
about? Human desire. What is one of the greatest human desires?

To fly about without an airplane and to be all-powerful. Captain Marvel? Zeus? Take your pick.

And Michael Dolzani, again:

[Frye] did not read the Bible as history, because the Bible is not history. . . . Blake said that the Bible is the "Great Code" of art, and art is the great key to human behaviour. Then you get a sense of the patterns we all live out. Jung said that he began his career by asking himself What myth am I living? And that's the moment when we wake up; when we ask ourselves that question. . . . We do live out myths in our daily life. I mean long before Frye came around, Freud and Jung and the early depth psychologists were very articulate about how we're always playing out myths. The Oedipus Complex is only a stock example, but even if you don't like that one, [try] scapegoating. Anyone who was ever on a playground in an elementary school knows [about scapegoats]. Why do we pick out one kid and beat him up and bond as a group? That's mythical. It's a primitive sacrificial ritual that binds the group together.

The Canadian poet and playwright James Reaney adds, "The Nazis . . . took the whole thing [about the scapegoat] and turned it into a Jew, and started slaughtering them."

All this seems to convey the impression of a scholar whose preoccupation is with evil. But in fact Frye's excitement with the work of Blake, and with the vision he felt he had received about the almost identical qualities of the idea of God and the idea of the human imagination, was joyful. Sometimes the language he used to make his points was quite playful, and young people, fascinated with his legitimization of sex, joy, play and wit, flocked to his lectures by the hundreds, to hear things like this:

Blake suggests that eternal joy is a positive thing, an achievement in a world of gratified desire. [Now] a world where the lion is said to lie down with the lamb is a world of stuffed lions. Sexual love, however, is the door through which most of us enter the imaginative world. Mating and copulating may be "animal," but imaginative love is part of our divine birthright.

Frye's was a long, productive and rewarding scholarly life. He

153

would give guest lectures in other universities, in Canada and abroad, and his lectures would be made into books. Unlike many senior academics, who find teaching a chore and undergraduates a nuisance, Frye seemed to understand what every really great teacher knows deeply: that the joy of bringing a young mind to the edge of discovery is among the greatest joys that life has to offer. He never stopped meeting with undergraduates, challenging them, making them laugh, making them see life afresh. Impatient with careless thinking he sometimes humiliated them when they asked dull questions. Later he regretted his cruelty.

Music, which had informed his life as a gifted young pianist, was never absent from his study of all forms of art. He said that great writers know that if you get the sound right, the sense will take care of itself. He talked about the Order of Words. *Anatomy of Criticism* contains powerful arguments about the way in which certain structural combinations of verbs and nouns and adjectives are so embedded in the consciousness that they seem a response to inherited patterns in the brain. Rhythm and meter, waltz and mazurka, melody and rhyme, shape and colour: for Frye these were intimately connected, and partook of the experience of love.

Love brought him grief, too. Helen was stricken, and he had to contemplate this closest of all his imaginative accomplices deprived of her memory. When she died his old pal Kingsley Joblin conducted the funeral just a few metres from where he had stood agape with Norrie outside that famous Victoria College arch half a century earlier as Norrie curled the toes of the sophomores with his colourful obscenities. Joblin said that he asked Norrie to write a few words about Helen, but that the Old Professor could not bear to read them at the funeral; so the Old Clergyman read them in his stead:

> *The dark shadow of Alzheimer's disease fell across the last years of our life together. And I watched helplessly the gradual shrinking of her energies and personal resources. She was a generous and very pure spirit, no matter how amused or embarrassed she might be to hear herself so described. She died at 3:10 p.m. The medical attendant said 3:30. But I happen to know what time she left me.*

And that is why we called our documentary film "A Love Story."

Herman Northrop Frye died on January 23, 1991. He was seventy-eight years old. For some time his pioneering work had gone out of fashion as the hip scholars discovered something called deconstruction and forgot about myths and meaning in life and literature. But now he is coming back almost as if he had not gone. And when Frye scholars gather, the outside observer might wonder whether the Old Professor would be happy to see how much they defer to his authority. If he listens closely he will find it is not deference; it is a spellbound attempt to unravel, to understand. For if Frye felt that his work was to make his strange visions clear to the world, he should be gratified to find that scholars are carrying on that work; not in abject agreement but in fascination and intrigue.

So: two last words on the life of this most famous of all the Canadian scholars: first from Professor Dolzani:

Literature is hypothetical, Frye said. All of these myths and metaphors are human creations. They are fictions. But . . . the moment of finding something whether in literature or in the Bible or any text, and saying, "That's for me: that is the guide for me, for my life and my quest": that is the moment you step from the fictions of literature into a more existential view of things. And that is a religious step: whether you believe in . . . God, or not.

And the very last word to the Old Professor himself, an obituary he left for us to find, in his notebooks, characteristically witty, but not really a joke.

The 20th century saw an amazing development of scholarship and criticism in the humanities, carried out by people who were more intelligent, better trained, had more languages, had a better sense of proportion, and were infinitely more accurate scholars and competent professional men than I.

I had genius.

No one else in the field known to me had that.

◆ ◆ ◆

Northrop Frye: A Love Story was written and directed by Daniel Zuckerbrot.

PART ELEVEN

DISTANT SKIES
The Story of Wop May

"They say you have angels on your shoulder; [well] Wop must have had a whole squadron of them."
—Marie Wright, pioneer ferry pilot and friend of Wop May.

It is a nickname that would be considered politically incorrect today, having been used to insult Italian immigrants to North America in times when that was considered acceptable. His real name was Wilfrid, his father having been a fan of Prime Minister Sir Wilfrid Laurier when the boy was born. When he was six his three-year-old cousin Mary came to visit. She couldn't say "Wilfrid"; it came out as "Woppie," stuck somehow, as such accidental nicknames often do, became "Wop" before long, and stayed there. In the old photos you can see it painted in block letters three feet high on the upper wing of the Curtis Jenny he was barnstorming in during the 1920s. But barnstorming was not what made him famous. For years he was known, not quite correctly, as "the man who helped shoot down the Red Baron."

Here is how the legend developed. Young Wilfrid and his brother Court had grown up thinking about airplanes and of learning to fly. It was an idea that was beginning to infect the whole continent; just beginning to change from a mythical dream into a real and present possibility. In 1903 Wilbur and Orville Wright had become world-famous overnight with the first-ever flight of a self-powered heavier-than-air machine. By means of another new technology called the motion picture the boys had seen images of that historic event. They now knew, for sure; that was for them. They made a pact that, together, they would fly. Somehow, some day.

The brothers had grown up around machines. They felt comfortable with them. Machines were not just to use, they were to take apart, to find out how they worked, to fix, to put back together again. The

May family had found its way from England to Scotland to Ireland to Canada. Alexander May had a successful farm implements business in Carberry, Manitoba, when his son Wilfrid was born there in 1896. Cockshutt ploughs, reapers and steam-powered threshing machines, and — before long — the early gasoline-powered tractors with huge metal lugs on their wheels. Those rusting hulks can still be seen around small agricultural villages or out behind a barn or, even today, parked in the back lots of the present-day versions of implement businesses like Alexander May's.

Alexander had a well-stocked library: mostly military history and books about machines. The boys devoured those books. When the family moved to Edmonton, Alex May opened a service station, selling gasoline and tires and repairing these newfangled automobile things, which broke down a lot. By the time they were in their early teens the boys had developed a taste for speed and risk, and for working around gasoline engines where they came to love the smell of hot metal and oily rags.

They would race anything. There is a photo of young Wilfrid at the tiller of what appears to be an Aykroyd dinghy — in a race almost certainly. The Aykroyd was a fat, stable fourteen-foot clinker-built gaff-rigged catboat, designed and built on Toronto Island in the early part of the century. Thousands of kids across Canada learned to sail and to race in the handy little craft.

The first airplane Court and Wop actually saw came to Edmonton for demonstration flights in 1910. It was a Curtiss Pusher, not much of an advance over the Wright Flyer of seven years earlier. The elevators, movable horizontal surfaces that control the up or down attitude of the machine, were stuck out in front of the pilot on a sort of frame. The control wheel was very much like an old automobile wheel, big and ungainly. The heavy, not very powerful liquid-cooled engine, with a big radiator like a car, was behind the pilot and the propeller behind the engine, hence the name "Pusher."

On the Wright Flyer the wings were kept level or put into a bank by a set of wires that actually bent the shape of the flexible, cloth-covered bamboo frames that made up those wings. It may have been

Curtiss who invented the movable winglets called ailerons that became the standard control surface before long, and the Curtiss Pusher the May brothers saw would probably have been so equipped. There may or may not have been a safety belt in Hugh Robinson's pusher when he had it shipped from town to town across the west that summer to do his demonstrations. The idea of strapping the pilot into his seat came only after somebody actually fell out.

At Victoria High School Wop met another student who was mad for airplanes. That boy's name was Roy Brown. Their knowing each other would later have a big impact on Wop's life.

War had come to Europe. The boys heard that some Canadians who went over as foot-soldiers had managed to transfer to the Royal Flying Corps. There was no air force in Canada yet. They decided to try getting into the air by way of the infantry.

However, Court had suffered from poliomyelitis as a child, and the army would not take him. Polio was a common disease then, striking children more than adults and often called "infantile paralysis." Many died of it when their chest muscles failed. Others carried a paralysed leg or arm — or worse — for the rest of their lives. Court's paralysis left him with a serious limp, which ruled him out for active service and would tragically shorten his life. Wop joined the 202nd Infantry Battalion, known as "The Edmonton Sportsman's," and soon found himself on the way to England.

It took some time to get into the Flying Corps. Many young men saw air combat as a way to stay in the war but get out of the trenches. War in the air had glamour; war on the ground had mud and rats and almost certain death. So there was a waiting list. It was not until late in 1917 that Wop was accepted. By March of 1918 he graduated from 94 Training Squadron, at Acton. He had flown a total of five and a half hours.

To put that in perspective: it would be unusual for a student pilot today to even take his first solo with less than ten hours. Fifteen is a likelier number, and you will be pretty impressive if you get your private licence with less than forty hours at the controls. In the two weeks after he left 94 squadron the young man would build up another thirty-some hours, with gunnery and formation flying to prepare him for combat. But then, with no more time in the air than a newly minted private pilot of today, he was sent off to combat squadron number 209. Now promoted to Lieutenant, he was twenty-two.

The aircraft they trained on initially were not much like the fighters they would fly in combat. Some of those trainers were pushers, not much of an advance over that Curtiss, the first airplane that Wop and his brother had seen back in Edmonton. They were slow, underpowered and ungainly. Today they look just plain ugly and impossible. Once at the front lines the new fighter pilots were given the very latest machines, but even they were often awkward and, by today's standards, terrifying.

The machine Wop May flew in 209 squadron was considered the best yet: a British fighter called the Sopwith Camel. The Camel not only flew in France and Flanders, but were bought for the British Navy as well, and flew off the new aircraft carriers, as well as from improvised launching arrangements on cruisers and battleships. It was considered to be the summit of fighter design at the time. There were several versions, and Wop's was the top of the line. Powered by a British-built Bentley rotary engine of about 130 horsepower, it climbed well and could work effectively up to 12,000 feet. But it was difficult to fly. It often spun out of control in tight turns, and the problem was that *rotary* engine.

Most people even in the jet age know what a *radial* engine looks like, and a rotary looks like a radial but has one crucial difference. Radials powered the legendary DC 3, the De Havilland Beaver and most of the famous World War Two heavy bombers like the Flying Fortress B-17, the Liberator B-24, and the Mitchell B-25. The radial had five or seven or nine cylinders radiating out from the hub of the propeller like the petals of a flower. Some had two such "flowers" back to back, with as many as eighteen cylinders. The rotary also has the cylinders radiating out from the hub, exactly like a radial. But instead of the engine being fixed to the firewall (the flat plate forward of the cockpit), with the turning crankshaft sticking out ahead with a propeller bolted to it, in the rotary the engine was turned backwards, the crankshaft was bolted to the firewall, the propeller was actually fastened to the engine, *and the whole engine revolved!*

This meant that out at the front end of a wood and canvas aircraft that weighed (without armament) less than a thousand pounds, there would be three or four hundred pounds of metal rotating at 900 to 1200 revolutions per minute. A rotating solid object, like a flywheel or a planet — or a rotary engine — resists any attempt to change its attitude, to make its axis point in a different direction. Huge ocean liners were equipped with such big heavy wheels to help keep them from tossing about in storms and making the passengers ill. You can experience the effect by going to a toy store or a science store and buying a small gyroscope. Wind the string around the shaft and get the wheel spinning. Hold the wheel by the ends of the axle, so that it is spinning on a horizontal axis, as if it were a rotary engine with a propeller fixed to it. Now try to turn it, to left or to right. Depending on which direction you've got it spinning, it will not only resist your turning it, it will quite strongly either dip down or tilt up, in response to your attempts to turn it. That is what happened when a pilot tried to turn the Sopwith Camel. Pilots had to completely relearn how to turn in flight, if they had been trained in aircraft that did not have a rotary engine. Although the Sopwith Camel shot down more enemy aircraft than any other fighter in that war, more pilots died learning to fly in it than died in combat.

The rotary engine was lubricated by castor oil. The oil was not burned; helped by centrifugal force to spray out from the crankshaft to the ends of the rotating cylinders, it percolated through the engine and came out in the exhaust. At the end of every flight the fuselage of the aircraft would be glistening with a film of oil. There was always oil on your clothes and goggles, and on your face. If you hadn't been warned, or if in the heat of combat you forgot yourself and licked your lips, you could ingest quite a bit of it. Castor oil is a powerful emetic and laxative. It takes effect suddenly and explosively. Many a new Camel pilot, even though warned, would come back from a mission not only terrified by the experience, but with his flight suit sodden, inside and out, with the odorous results of swallowing castor oil. His plane's cockpit would have to be flushed out before anyone could fly it again.

But the pilots — those who survived their training — liked the eighteen-foot long machine, all the same. If you were a Camel-driver you were good. It was faster than what they'd been used to (115 miles an hour), and was the first fighter to be equipped with two .303 Vickers machine guns. Unlike some of the earlier machines, you didn't have to aim the guns or even touch them. They were fixed to the fuselage and fired forward, through the propeller, with two firing buttons on the spade-grip of the joystick and a synchronizing mechanism that kept the bullets from hitting the prop. Some were equipped with guns firing straight down through the floor and were flown over enemy trenches to strafe the soldiers below.

So that was the plane which the brand-new fighter pilot, Wilfrid Reid May, nourished by what was probably an inappropriate level of confidence, would be flying into combat when he got to 209 squadron. The Flying Corps had a partying tradition. Pilots at the front used to joke about coming back from a mission and heading for the Officers' Mess, which meant the bar, and staying there so determinedly that the routine next morning would be "Get up; suit up; throw up; start up." Wop May got a head start with some sort of party en route to the squadron, and as a result arrived late and perhaps not in very good shape. The Major fired him from the squadron before he even got started. But the high-school friendship with Roy Brown saved him, as it would save him more dramatically only a few days later.

Roy Brown was a Flight Commander. He ran into the disconsolate and hung-over lieutenant, interceded on his behalf with the Major, and got Wop re-instated. Then he took him under his wing.

Roy Brown counselled Wop May to stay out of the action during the first few sorties, and just watch the patterns of combat from a distance. They would be up against German pilots who had been fighting for months, some for years. It would be suicidal to tangle with them until he had observed war in the air from a close, but not engaged position, for at least a couple of missions. Indeed there was a possibility that the top German ace, the legendary Baron von Richthofen, the "Red

Baron," would turn up; he was known to be flying in their sector. Richthofen had already tallied eighty kills. So stay out of it, was Roy Brown's advice.

Wop May was, however, and remained for the rest of his long career, impulsive, a risk-taker, a man who tended to be deaf to prudent warnings. The first two flights with 209 were uneventful. But on the third, the new boy, with zero hours of combat experience, suddenly saw an enemy airplane he thought he could handle. Into the fray he went. Before long he found himself with a red triplane on his tail. A Fokker triplane with black crosses on its wings that was firing machine-gun bullets at him.

May headed for the ground and zigged and zagged between trees and buildings, heading towards the river Somme. Roy Brown saw what was happening, and while he had no idea then that it was Richthofen on the tail of his inexperienced friend, he knew it was serious trouble. He dived after the Fokker, out of the sun, firing as soon as he got within range.

It has never been established exactly what happened next. Roy Brown got the official credit for downing the Red Baron that morning. The credit was also claimed by a group of Australian riflemen on the ground. There were at least half a dozen ground-based machine guns and hundreds of rifles firing up at the low-flying red triplane as it followed Wop May along the Somme. The chase was now across the lines, in Allied territory.

Baron Manfred Albrecht von Richthofen, pride of the Imperial German Air Force, had been urged to quit flying. He had done enough, they told him; he was more use to the war effort as a living hero than he would be dead. He had been shot down and survived twice, once in March and once in July 1917. The second time a head wound left him with agonizing headaches thereafter. And yet, he kept on flying and fighting, and his score kept mounting. But this time the Red Baron went down for good. Amazingly, after all that firepower they had thrown at him, from the ground and the air, he actually flew his plane to a landing that would have probably been successful had the ground not been rough enough to break off the landing gear. But he was mortally wounded. A British soldier ran up excitedly. Von Richthofen looked at him grimly, muttered something that included the word "Kaput," and closed his eyes forever.

They found only one bullet hole in the wrecked aircraft. The bullet that caused it had passed through Von Richtofen's body and fallen into his flight jacket. The bullet was lost; so who fired it is not known. Von Richthofen was twenty-five years old.

Those were still days of chivalry in the air war. The German ace was given a hero's funeral, full military honours, a twenty-one-gun salute from the Australians. Wop May and another pilot took a set of photographs of the ceremony and dropped them over a German aerodrome. Rich-thofen himself was said to have lavishly entertained at least one downed and survived Allied pilot, sending him off to Prisoner of War Camp with champagne in his kit.

Wop became a skilled combat pilot in the last few months of the war. It takes three kills to earn the title "Ace"; May had thirteen before it was over. It was not fun. Here are actual excerpts from his log book.

May 14. I lost formation for about 10 minutes. Samie Taylor took my place. Bell took Samie's place and was hit by a direct hit by archie [anti-aircraft fire], spun down. Fenton crashed & Harker crashed & Brettorious nearly crashed, none of the last were hurt. Bell I think has gone he was a friend of Stover's just came back off leave.

May 15. Escort and H.O.P. escorted D.H.4's over met 2 Hun Scouts on a French Spad's tail, chased them off. Capt. Redgate got one, went in with D.H.4's tail. We chased them off and strafed with them. Capt Redgate and Brettorious and Wilson pushed off. Taylor and I stayed and scrapped with them for about 15 minutes he got one and I got one. Both my guns jammed and I came home. Taylor joined the formation they ran into a bunch of triplanes. Wilson and Brettorious were shot down, one was thrown out of his seat and the other spun to the ground. Capt. Redgate was wounded in the leg got home OK. 3 Bristol fighters also brought down.

The final entry reads "Taylor and I are all that's left in flight A." After that he stopped keeping a log. What was the point if you were going to die tomorrow?

But then came that day in November when the great guns went silent. Wop took the Sopwith Camel up for a last flight. He had the Distinguished Flying Cross now; he was a decorated hero. He went home with his medals and an odd kind of fame: five minutes of running for his life had written him into the history books. Back in Alberta his career would write a lot more aviation history: less glamorous, perhaps, but far more significant.

Court was waiting for him. They were going to open a flying business, remember? Court had lined up a Toronto-built Curtiss Canuck, the Canadian version of the Jenny, the standard trainer in American Army Air Corps training bases, had posted a bond for it and leased it from the city of Edmonton for $25 a month. There are still a few of these aircraft around. They don't look their age. In Edmonton a retired airline pilot named Jack Johnson still flies a rebuilt Canuck/Jenny out of the same field that Wop May used over eighty years ago.

"It's pretty slow," Johnson says, a bit ruefully. "I wouldn't say on the ragged edge of a stall but sometimes you're close to it. They spin nice and fly real nice on a nice smooth day. But on a gusty day they aren't too much fun."

So this was the machine they hoped to turn into a business. It did not work out very well, at first. There was some barnstorming, of course. You flew your clattering machine to a fairground and made a deal with the promoters to attract visitors to the fair by putting on stunts. Then you flew a few loops and rolls, and perhaps you got somebody to stand on the top of the wing holding on with a strap, and perhaps you took people up for a ride over the city for a couple of minutes, at 50 cents a pop. There was only one passenger seat in the Jenny.

Wop flew the mayor of Edmonton over the ball park, in the passenger seat of the Jenny, from which His Honour threw out the opening ball of the season. He would fly low over the city so that people would look up and see the big EDMONTON painted on the fuselage. If they were curious enough to find their way out to the airfield, they would see "MAY AIRPLANES LTD." painted on the tail. But the business was not coming in, and indeed they did not have a lot to offer, with one little passenger seat and almost no freight-carrying capacity.

Wop became friends with the American barnstormers. But while that was fun it was not the business he and Court had in mind. They wanted passengers and freight and enough money coming in to buy a serious machine. In 1927 Wop founded the Edmonton Flying Club, and was Chief Pilot and Manager.

He got a contract to ferry two big Junkers JL6 aircraft from New York to Edmonton, for Imperial Oil, and hired a friend named George Gorman to fly the second machine. Six years before Lindbergh would fly the Atlantic, these two flew the Junkers six thousand kilometres from New York in the dead of winter, and made some news and a bit of money. But the flying business was so far proving unprofitable. And then a disaster struck: Court's leg gave way on a flight of stairs. He had a terrible fall and died from his injuries. That was it, for Wop. He couldn't take it any more. He was lonely, and when he met Vi Bode, a woman as mad for horses as he was for airplanes, he felt that at last there might be some sunshine somewhere in his life. And there was. They got married. Now he had to have a job. He found one as a machinist for the National Cash Register Company in Dayton, Ohio. It was 1924 and he was twenty-eight years old.

In that factory he had an accident worse than anything that had happened to him in the war. He was working a lathe when a fragment of metal flew into his right eye and partially blinded him. When he came back to Canada a year later he had to cheat on his aviation medical tests. The doctor would say, "Cover one eye and read the chart." He would raise his right hand and cover his right eye. Then the doctor would say, "The other one now," and Wop would raise his left hand and cover the right eye again. Sometimes he just memorized the chart. Pilots who have not tried flying with only one good eye will tell you — and it seems logical — that since depth perception depends on your having two eyes, it would be really tough to judge height and distance with only one. But that is not so; such judgments in flying are concerned with distances that are too great for the binocular function to be much good, and angle judgment is much more important. If you have only one eye, you have to develop a flexible neck for looking out the bad side. Wop seems never to have had any trouble, at least not with the flying. But the eye would cause him enormous grief a few years later.

By the late 1920s Canadians had begun to realize what a boon the airplane was in a land where communities were so widely separated, and where there was so much exploration and prospecting going on hundreds of miles away from any kind of settlement. Wop began to get work flying prospectors and supplies into the North. A few years later his experience in those vast barren lands would earn him another reputation as a hero.

It was 1929. Six hundred miles north of Edmonton, the settlement at Little Red River had been devastated by diphtheria, and there was a desperate search for a way to get anti-toxin serum to the tiny community. The Alberta Deputy Minister of Health, Dr. Malcolm Bow, asked Wop if it would be possible to fly the serum there. It was thirty below zero and the whole area was deep in snow. The only machine available was Wop's Avro Avian. There was no protection from the weather. The Avian was an open cockpit cloth-covered biplane on wheels, not skis. But Wop's son Denny May, now the custodian of the family history, says that Dr. Bow told him that characteristically Wop did not hesitate for a moment: "Of course! Let's go."

They wrapped the five hundred units of anti-toxin in woollen rugs around a little charcoal burner on the floor of the Avian to keep them from freezing, and off they went, Wop and his friend and fellow-pilot Vic Horner.

When the news reached Edmonton that the boys had made it and were on their way home, a welcoming party gathered. The whole city seemed to realize that something both heroic and historic had just happened, and it was an Edmonton boy who had made it happen. People began to gather at the airfield, but the little plane was long overdue, and anxious murmurs began to ripple through the thousands of people now gathered to welcome it home. Retired pilot Doug Matheson was there.

"I can still see that old train," he said, "chuffing down from Calder, down to the downtown area with this plume of smoke. Then suddenly out of the smoke came this little Avro Avian, and dropped down into the field and taxied in. The crowd all gathered around and shouldered them and carried them into town."

Wop's wife Vi was the first. When she unwound the silk scarf covering his face, the skin on his lips was frozen to it. You can see the raw patches in the photograph where bits of skin came away from his lips. The story of the flight made it into newspapers around the world.

This time Wop's fame brought him opportunity. A new company, Commercial Airways, had decided to buy a state-of-the-art Lockheed Vega (the same machine that the famed aviator Wiley Post was flying when he and comedian Will Rogers were killed in Alaska). Cy Becker, at Commercial, enticed Wop by asking him to go to Los Angeles and pick up the Vega, and then to fly it for Commercial.

In California the legendary Howard Hughes, with the famous *Frankenstein* director James Whale, was making a monumental 135-minute War In The Air film called *Hell's Angels*. The combat sequences were loosely based on the Red Baron story. When Hughes heard that the heroic pilot of Little Red River was in town — *and was the same guy the Red Baron had been chasing on that fateful April day in 1918!* — he asked Wop to come over and consult about combat flying. Wop and Vic actually flew some scenes in the movie. But a little bit of the movie business was enough for Wop. He and Vic fired up the Vega and headed north.

Soon, working with Becker, they established a base at Fort McMurray which was then on the north edge of the Frontier. Commercial bid against Western Canada Airways for the airmail contract, and won it, and now there was a steady revenue stream, reliable airplanes with enclosed cockpits and substantial cargo capacity. With the mail as the bread-and-butter of the business, and Cy Becker looking after the office, Wop was flying all the time now, the sound of his engine penetrating parts of the planet where no such sound had ever been heard. He joked that he was the first to bring ice cream north of the Arctic Circle. Prospecting was still an important part of the business, although the accountants would probably not have agreed. Denny May says of his father:

He grubstaked, I think, every prospector in the north. He probably

outfitted them, gave them a tent and food, flew them into their site.
They'd park the aircraft. They'd set up camp for the night on the
shore and they'd sit around talking . . . it's absolutely spectacular
country. He would pick them up at the end of the season. They [paid
him with] shares in their gold mine, none of which ever panned out.
I have an envelope full of shares that are totally [worthless] . . . If
you . . . broke down you can't just run to the nearest airport . . . you
land on a lake and you fix your aircraft, you put it back together
and you carry on.

Stories abound of the ingenuity of downed pilots in that era, like rebuilding a busted propeller out of dogsled runners and boiled leather straps; escaping through a zipper in the cloth roof after the plane went through the ice, improvising a crane and block and tackle out of tree trunks and spare rope to haul the drowned plane up out of its watery grave and reviving it; draining the oil at night into a pail to keep you warm in your tent, and then, about midnight, it's your body heat that starts to return the favour; keeping the oil fluid so you can pour it back into the subzero engine in the morning before you hang your tent over the cowling, light up a glow pot which you hope won't ignite the fuel line, and warm the frigid cylinders up so you can start it up again.

When Canadian Airways bought out Commercial, in 1931, Wop went to Canadian as well. It was about that time that the RCMP assigned him to try to find the Mad Trapper, a murderer on the run, on snowshoes, who had killed a Mountie. Wop's mechanic Jack Bowen took photos during the chase. In the few hours of decent flying weather they could get, up the Eagle River in a wet, snowy May, they followed the elusive fugitive's tracks from the air and finally found him. Wop directed the police to the scene. From the air he and Jack Bowen observed the final gunfight between Johnson and the police, and landed at the scene to take the body back to Aklavik (along with another man who was wounded in the gun fight). When it was over, a photograph of the dead killer was printed in every newspaper in the country and once again Wop May became a household name.

But it was the depth of the Depression all the same. Life in Fort McMurray was tough. Denny was born in 1935, so there was an added responsibility. Work was undependable. There was a bright moment when Wop was awarded the Order of the British Empire. But then there came a dark moment, the darkest that can happen to a pilot for whom flying airplanes is what life was meant for, as it seems to have been for Wilfrid Reid May. They took away his licence to fly.

It would not happen today. The Transport Canada officials responsible for assessing a pilot's ability to fly do not proceed simply by arbitrary rules: they test you. If you can do it, you get your licence renewed. If not, down you go. Of course if you have a heart condition that predictably could strike any time, then you don't get a licence. But if it is a physical disability, such as an impaired limb, you go for a test flight and if you can pass the stringent but fair exercises you are instructed to fly, you get your licence. Since the 1950s more than seven hundred Canadian pilots with monocular vision have had their licences renewed.

Wop did not. The damaged eye had gone bad and had to be removed. There was no more faking the vision test in the medical. He only had one eye. That did not meet the standards. The standards were made by an international commission and controlled by the RCAF in those days. Our Civil Aviation Branch hadn't been formed yet (though it would be launched only months later). Perhaps Canada was still in a slightly colonial state of mind, still doing its best to respond to standards that were set by the Important Countries, by some commission, distant, bureaucratic.

The present writer, learning to fly in 1966 with an above-the-knee-amputation, was told quite simply by the Civil Aviation inspectors, "Show us. If you can fly it, you get the licence," and became a commercial pilot, and an instructor. Had Wop May's eye troubles happened today, to such a demonstrably skilled, able, successful pilot, an inspector would simply have put him through his paces, rigorously. Then (as would almost surely have been the case with Wop May) when he flew as certainly and deftly as he had always flown, he would have his licence back the same day. But in 1936 they took his paper away; he was grounded.

His goddaughter and close friend Marie Wright, the ferry pilot, says, "It's like telling a person to stop breathing, tell him, a man like Wop May, tell him you're grounded? I mean, all pilots know they're going to be grounded at one point in their lives. But it's never going to happen to you. It's always the other fella."

Wop and Vi left the North and moved back to Edmonton where they adopted a second child, Joyce. Wop got a desk job. At least he would have more time for Vi and the kids. But imagine the blow to the spirit, of having to give up the air, when you were a pilot who had practically *invented* bush flying in Northern Canada, had flown that incredible adventure in the gunsights of the Red Baron, had advised Howard Hughes, flown the first great Mercy Flight, found the Mad Trapper. . . . It could scar the soul of a lesser man, and it probably scarred Wop May's soul too; but there was a family to raise and a life to be lived, and he got on with it.

When World War II broke out, it was decided that Canada was the place to train pilots from the Commonwealth countries. Young men and women arrived from all over the world, from Britain, Australia, New Zealand, South Africa, the Free French, the Polish kids in exile, and quite a few Americans in the sixteen months of that war before the United States came into it — American boys who wanted part of the action. Edmonton became a major training centre. Soon the runways were crowded with De Havilland Tiger Moth primary trainers, and the lumbering Avro Ansons for training bomber pilots, observers and navigators. When the question arose as to whom to put in charge of the Edmonton training establishment, Wop May was the obvious choice.

Imagine the cachet that would go with it, for a young pilot who could say — as a lot of them probably said (pilots having been known to exaggerate occasionally) — *I was trained under the man who shot down the Red Baron*. But May's concern was to put in place a training regime that would equip those kids *not* to get shot down, to bring them back alive. And he did what he was asked to do, always around flying, but not flying any more. Later, Canadian Pacific would hire him to help expand their overseas markets. And he was good at that. While his ports of call were once Snowdrift and Rat River and Aklavik, now they would be Hong Kong, Bangkok, Tokyo. But someone else was flying the planes; Wop was a passenger, an administrator, and still as always a man who pushed himself and expected others to push themselves too.

But one day in 1952 he said to Denny, who was seventeen then, "Look, I need a holiday," and off they went to Utah to explore the Timpanogos Caves, near Provo, just a few miles northeast of Utah Lake. Denny May recalls the day they went there.

We headed off down there and started hiking the trail. And it was quite a steep trail up to the cave. About half-way up he said, "I can't go any further." He said, "I'll walk back to the car and wait for you there." I started up the trail, and he called me back and he said, "Take my picture to show people I got this far." And I didn't think anything of that so I took his picture, and then I headed back up the trail. And came back about half an hour later, walking on the trail, and very close to the top of the trail there was Daddy, lying dead on the trail, a fellow guarding him . . .

The funeral was huge. Standing room only. The people of Edmonton loved Wop May. They had not forgotten what he did. Max Ward, another great pioneer, would later name three successive airliners after him. One of them, a 310 Air-bus, C-GKWD, is a personnel transport for the RCAF, which seems appropriate. He is, of course, in Canada's Aviation Hall of Fame.

But a pilot, now, looking back on the story of Wilfrid Reid May, has to think to himself: How devastating was that day when he was forty, only forty years old, and they said he could never fly again? This was a man who had pushed the limits of possibility in the air.

He had lived moments which, once lived, cannot be eradicated from the soul. Every pilot who has done it seriously for any length of time has had those moments. You are at seven thousand feet, say, at night. The weather is closing in ahead. It could be clear if you go higher, and you can check your compass against the stars. Or you could go down, beneath the clouds. Perhaps there are five or six hundred feet of clearance above the ground, although it will be turbulent down there, and very, very dark. Up here, at least, there is starlight, and even in the thin clouds there is a faint luminescence from those stars.

You go up. Eight, nine thousand. At 9,500 you're well above the clouds, but you go on to 10,000 anyway. There is old Polaris, the North Star, hanging out there where it is supposed to be, exactly seven bowl-widths off the dipper bowl. And your compass checked against that star and the known deviation says you are almost exactly on the right heading. As you check your watch, you judge that at this height the wind will have veered about five degrees more, because you know about winds. You kick in another five degrees to starboard, no maybe that is too much, let's do *two* degrees . . . and the old cylinders are still thunking away, the way they are supposed to do.

You are alone. And yet the whole universe and everyone who ever lived in it is there with you, including all those who worked out the metallurgy, the chemistry of fuels, the maps, the aerodynamics of pro-pellers, the tensile strength of cables, they are all there with you. There is a sense of celebration of the human adventure in reaching out. The engine may be producing sixty decibels, who knows, but you are in utter silence with the stars.

You check your watch. *If* you have guessed right at that veering of the wind, and *if* all your other guesses — not *guesses* really, you have done this many times — if the forces of the sky have held still for you the way they mostly do, then in exactly nine minutes you will be over-head Fort Charles. Right now you could start down gently, hold your course, maybe come out right overhead, on time, that would be ele-gant. But it is very fine up here, in the starlight, the still air, no bumps, the clouds a milky cushion just below your wings.

You stay at ten thousand for five minutes, eight minutes, eight minutes-thirty, nine minutes. You bank left (you always bank left, not right, why is that?) and pull the throttle back, and start a slow, circling descent. Lots of fuel, all the gauges saying what they're supposed to say. Seven thousand feet, five thousand. It is warming up to the point where moisture in the cloud is beginning to make a little ice on your cold wings. Never mind, you will be out of it shortly. Three thousand, slowly circling to the left, throttle right back, carburettor heat ON so you don't make any ice in *there!*, hold it just above the stall so it's sort of whooshing softly down, scarcely flying at all, a leaf falling gently. One thousand feet. Should be seeing some thinning in the cloud now, uhmm, ahh, what is the height above sea level right here? I should remember, oh yeah. A little power on now, slow your descent, seven hundred feet, shoot! Should be seeing something now, have to do sumpn soon if I don't! . . .

Suddenly dark wisps the size of elephants stream by as the cloud breaks up. The black beneath is *very* black, no light penetrating from above, but we are out in the clear, and where the hell is Fort Charles, it *should be right there*, keep the wings almost level now, slow circle to the left, scan . . . the horizon . . . which you cannot see, only an impenetrable black soup.

And then, three-quarters of the way through that 360-degree turn, about three miles off to your left, a little cluster of lights. There can be only one cluster of lights, out here, in the middle of the distant barren. So the sky has met the ground, and you know that you have made your voyage, and your compact with the Gods, and with your passengers for tomorrow's journey home.

When you have spent just one night like that, even just one, and then they tell you that you will never spend another, it must leave a wound that will shorten your life.

Wilfrid Reid May, DFC. 1896–1952.

Canadian Pilots Licence number 49, June 1919.

◆ ◆ ◆

Distant Skies, the television biography of Wop May, was written and directed by Tom Radford and produced by Carrie Madu.

• PART TWELVE •

ALEXANDER MACKENZIE
From Canada by Land

Vancouver is a sprawling city of some four million people if you count all the municipalities and suburbs that go to make it up. For an eastern inland city dweller used to a regular grid of streets and some reliable indicators of where north and south are to be found, this hilly, meandering collection of spectacular buildings with majestic mountains reflected off the acres of glass-walled buildings and the various incursions of the Pacific Ocean right into the downtown area, it can be a disorienting experience for the first few days. But the city seems solid, at ease with its ocean and its mountains. Despite the adventurous modern architecture it almost seems to have been there forever, so well does it reflect and connect with its breathtaking landscapes. Bridges are an important part of it, and thinking about Vancouver always brings to mind the crossing of water, by way of soaring arches and the demonstration of the engineer's craft.

For most eastern Canadians the first visit to Vancouver, whether by air, train or car, is an eye-opener. The part of the journey that crosses the mountain ranges, for those who have never seen real mountains, is unforgettable. From Montreal by air it is a little more than five hours. The lucky traveller who has clear skies below will have moved from urban congestion over eastern woodlands, the largest freshwater lakes in the world, an apparently dead flat prairie that seems to have no limits in any direction, and then those mountains, followed by the world's largest ocean.

Eastern Canadians tend to think they live in the centre of the universe, but that centre tends to shift its position after a trip through the Rockies, and that can mean a radical change in their attitude towards the rest of the country. "That's mine?" people have been heard to say. "That's all part of Canada? I own that?"

The native peoples who have lived on the west coast for at least three thousand years are not inclined to respond positively to that rhetorical question. Quite apart from their having been on the land and fishing the waters for more than two millennia, they traditionally say that people do not own land at all, but have the use of it by the beneficence of the Great Spirit who made it, and expects his human tenants to look after it lovingly. And there are still some Indians in British Columbia who express regret that they were so helpful to the first Europeans to arrive on these shores, by water or by land, men with guns and metal who destroyed a way of life.

The first European settlement at Fort Taylor was established in 1827, and then New Westminster in 1859. The railroad would be the major influence on the development of cities here. Port Moody was established as the western terminus of the Canadian Pacific Railroad, in 1883. But CPR chief William Van Horne was soon persuaded that there was a better harbour twenty miles west, and Vancouver replaced Port Moody in 1886. Until the railroad, most of the newcomers had arrived by sea.

The first European visitors of whom we have any records began sailing up this picturesque coast in the late 1700s. The British explorer James Cook anchored off Vancouver Island in 1778, just months before he was killed in a dispute with local people in the Sandwich Islands. Captain George Vancouver had sailed with Cook and helped him chart part of the northwest coast. He decided to come back and continue that work, and met the Spanish explorers Galiano and Valdes off Point Grey in 1792. Those charts fascinated the British and the settlers in Eastern Canada, particularly the business pioneers who had long realized that this huge land mass held resources that would make them all rich. But although the French, British and Spanish had already explored hundreds of thousands of square miles, had found and crossed the Mississippi River and the deserts of the southwest, no European had yet crossed the continent by land north of Mexico.

It was the fur trade that spurred the first crossing. The French had pioneered it, pushing up the Ottawa River and into and beyond the Great Lakes. French explorers had found the headwaters of the Mississippi and left French place names all over what is now the

Canadian and American West. Some of them believed that if they could get to the Western Sea they would be staring at the east coast of Asia. One explorer even took oriental silk robes with him in his birch bark canoes so that he would be able to dress appropriately when he met the Emperor of China. Bit by bit the traders had pushed west and north, some of them mapping meticulously as they went. But there were still vast areas of *terra incognita*, and while the Rocky Mountains seemed an immense barrier to the Pacific, they were also a challenge and an invitation.

A young Scottish fur trader picked up the gauntlet. His name was Alexander Mackenzie. He was born on the stony island of Lewis in the outer Hebrides, in 1764. The Mackenzie clan owned the island then, and Alexander's branch of the family were closely related to the clan chieftain, Lord Seaforth. It was a troubled time in the Highlands of Scotland. Scottish Nationalists, determined to protect the Gaelic culture from the expansive English, had rebelled against the King. The rebellion was brutally crushed in a slaughter culminating at the terrible battle of Culloden in 1746, where the young Mackenzie's father Kenneth had fought on the side of the King of England. There followed a crushing of the thousand-year-old Gaelic nation, a crushing that today would probably be called ethnic cleansing. The old tribal ways, where land was shared on a tribal basis among the members of a clan, and disputes were settled with the sword, were over. It was the entrepreneurial class in the ascendancy now. And the Mackenzie family was part of that class. They lived in reasonable prosperity in the port of Stornaway, and the young Alexander was given an excellent private education. But in 1774, when the economy had been worsening for a while, and his wife Isabella had died, Kenneth Mackenzie took the young Alexander with him and set out for the New World.

He had left a Scotland that was still wounded from warfare and social upheaval, and he was not to find much peace on the Eastern Seaboard, where the American Revolution was brewing. Mackenzie, of course, enlisted in the British Army, and sent young Alexander up to Montreal, which seemed safer than Philadelphia or New York. Montreal was the hub of the fur trade. As the deepest inland port, it was the logical place for the traders to return from inland with their piles of beaver skins, and for the trade goods to offload from ships from Europe; to be put into wagons or canoes and moved inland for the new settlers and as trade goods for the furs. Young Mackenzie smelled opportunity here, and a couple of years after America declared its independence, he declared his as well and moved into a job at the Scottish fur traders, Gregory and MacLeod. It was those men and their French predecessors who had laid out the routes to the west. When Mackenzie decided to try for the Pacific, about two-thirds of the distance was already mapped and established as a known route. Although the fur traders would pass through native communities, and often enlisted the natives to travel with them as helpers and interpreters — and sexual partners — the settled communities were few and far between, and the men had to live off the land as they went. Fish were plentiful. They would paddle or carry their canoes twelve or fourteen hours a day, often trailing a fishing line as they went.

Game was plentiful as well, most of the time, but the weapons were still fairly primitive and you had to be a patient man to be a successful hunter. The rifle had not yet been invented. A musket was loaded from the muzzle of the barrel, each load consisting of, first, a carefully measured quantity of black gunpowder (which had to be carried in a waterproof container, often a cow's horn with a close-fitting metal lid). The powder was packed down into the smooth barrel with a ramrod, carefully, as a too vigorous push could detonate the explosive mixture and turn the ramrod into a projectile. Next came the wadding of paper or bits of rag, followed by the bullet, a single round ball or a spoonful of small buckshot, depending on the game. Buckshot for birds, a single solid lead ball for deer. When Mackenzie set out on his historic journeys the musket of choice was probably a heavy British product called a Brown Bess. It fired a very large ball, and if your aim was reasonably good you could bring down anything in the woods you were lucky to get really close to. The musket was pretty useless at a range of more than thirty or forty feet, and a single shot was all you would have a chance for, because loading the weapon took at least two minutes and one shot would scare away all the game for miles around.

Trapping was more reliable, unless you had experienced native archers with you. A man skilled with the bow could hunt silently, shoot a deer a hundred feet away, and get off five or six arrows a minute.

Curiously, the native peoples loved the musket despite its cumbersomeness and inaccuracy. Perhaps it symbolized the strange power of the newcomers. Perhaps there was a quality of mystery to it. In any case, it was one of the most seductive trade goods the Europeans had to offer. It was said that a musket would fetch a pile of skins as tall as the musket itself. By the end of the eighteenth century the native peoples of North America had far more firearms per capita than the whites.

It was the boat-building skills of the native peoples that made all this exploration possible. Archaeologists say that the birch bark canoe may have evolved to virtually the form it has today as long as three thousand years ago. Certainly by the time the Europeans arrived it was a piece of sophisticated design and construction that would not be improved upon for more than a century. And some canoe builders will tell you today that the architecture of those hulls made a better shape to be paddled through the water than anything that would be built since, until the evolution of computer-assisted design.

Even the large freight canoes were light enough to be carried by two or four men. If you crashed into a rock, you could usually make repairs overnight with materials you found growing close by. The oily, waterproof bark of the silver birch, tough stringy spruce roots for stitching the sheets of bark together, spruce gum boiled with fat and charcoal to make a tarry waterproof seal for the seams, and lightweight, springy, easily bent strips of white cedar to replace broken ribs or stringers. If you lost or broke your paddle, a good craftsman could take his razor-sharp axe and carve a serviceable paddle out of a piece of dry spruce in a couple of hours. As late as the 1950s this writer worked with an Irish immigrant named Alex Culhane who still worked in the bush, well into his eighties, and would still use his axe to make a paddle at least once a year, "Jist to keep in practice," and perhaps to show off what was after all a remarkable skill.

Of course you had to have water. Canada has such an abundance of surface water that it really is possible to paddle and carry your canoes from Montreal to the Pacific Ocean. In 1967 a group of hardy young Canadians decided to mark Canada's hundredth birthday by testing that possibility again. They built a large freight canoe, and re-traced the same journey that Alexander Mackenzie had first made in 1793. The longest portage they had to make was just a few kilometres.

Shawn Patterson, the curator of the museum at Old Fort William at Thunder Bay, Ontario, told us that

> If you . . . throw two darts anywhere on the map of Canada, you could put a canoe in at one place and paddle to the other and you would never have to carry that canoe more than thirteen miles. That's the longest portage across the country. . . . From your Montreal shipyard you can take those [trade] goods all the way up to Great Slave Lake, all the way through the Rocky Mountains to the Pacific Ocean, and you would never have to walk more than thirteen miles.

Eighty percent of the trade goods we are talking about were tex-tiles. Steel axes, knives, muskets, ammunition and copper pots were prized, of course, and would revolutionize the lives of the native peo-ples, who had no metals technology. The great totem poles, which we think of as the hallmark of the northwest native culture, the Salish, Haida, Kwakiutl and others, came into existence only after the arrival of steel tools in the nineteenth century. But in terms of quantity it was wool from the Oxfordshire mills, Indian cotton woven in southern England, and even Cantonese silk, that were the really hot items in those trading camps and at the forts. Now, instead of having to kill large animals and process the skins, the native peoples could trap the plentiful beaver and exchange them for colourful and easily handled fabrics that saved an immense amount of labour. The native peoples began to make themselves a large variety of colourful clothing which their own technology had not yet made possible. Textiles, like metals technology, had a considerable effect on the life and culture of the native peoples, not always to their benefit in the long run.

But the killer trade item was not textiles or guns, it was rum. Fifty years after Mackenzie's explorations, a young naval Captain named

John Franklin made an astounding fifty-five-hundred-mile trek from the shores of Hudson Bay to the Arctic Ocean, via Great Slave Lake, and back. He recorded in his journals heartbreaking accounts of native communities that had been demoralized and almost destroyed by the cruel and cynical trade in rum that so many of the fur traders were exploiting.

But that is another story.

The bright young Scotsman, unlike many of his high-handed predecessors, went out of his way to get to know the native peoples, to be courteous and respectful to them, and to patiently win their confidence. Had he not done that, we would not be reading about him today. Mackenzie recognized that he had a great deal to learn from them and seemed to understand that their traditions and memories would be a vital resource for anyone trying to find his way across the continent.

And finding your way in the days before the invention of reliable portable clocks was hard. Why clocks? An instrument called a sextant could reliably establish your latitude — how far north of the equator you were — by measuring the angular height of the sun above the horizon at noon. You had to know the date, and you could tell when it was noon when the sun was at its highest, or was due south if you had noted the position of the North Star the night before. The North Star itself would give you your latitude on a clear night.

But to know your longitude — to tell how far east or west you had travelled, you needed to know what time it was at your starting point, or at any fixed point you wanted to measure this distance from. If, for example, you saw the sun at its highest point overhead, noon wherever you were just then, and your reliable portable timepiece, which you had set at Montreal when you departed, informed you that it was two p.m. in that port city, you would know that you were exactly 30 degrees of latitude west of your starting point. The sun's apparent position travels west at exactly 15 degrees every hour. Thirty degrees is something in the order of twelve hundred miles in the Canadian prairies, and that twelve hundred miles you could refine to a precision of less than one mile once you checked your latitude.

The timepiece that would make this possible had finally, in fact, been invented. The Royal Society in London had offered a large cash prize to anyone who could demonstrate a genuinely reliable chronometer that would keep accurate time at sea or travelling by horseback, whatever motion it was subjected to. A genius named Johnson, after decades of painstaking labour, had finally produced one. Mackenzie did not know this, yet. All he had was a timepiece that was very accurate as long as it stood still, but it gained or lost badly whenever it was moved, so it had to be reset by the sun every day. This gave him the local time, but there was no way to know what time it was in the London suburb of Greenwich, where the zero longitude line lies now, by international convention. There was no such convention then and even had there been Mackenzie, with his unreliable instruments, would still have had to do his best by dead reckoning. This meant primarily estimating the exact distance traversed every day, an uncertain affair. His not having certain knowledge of his longitude would give Alexander Mackenzie some very bad days, indeed, as he tried to find his way by land to the Pacific.

In 1780 Lake Athabasca was the end of the mapped world, so to speak. It was called the Lake of the Hills then. An American fur trader named Peter Pond had found his way there in that year. He spent the winter on the lake, collecting from the Chipewyans twice as many furs as his canoes could carry. Muskrat was still a desired fur then, and the area was so rich in muskrat that a Chipewyan was said to be able to take a hundred a day. That could bring him the equivalent of a thousand dollars in today's currency. John Rigney, a guide who works that territory today, told us that taking muskrat two hundred years ago was "like picking carrots in your garden."

Peter Pond had put together some oral geographical information he got from the Chipewyan and Cree peoples he met, and had come up with a kind of a map of the as yet unexplored territory to the northwest. Pond had read Captain Cook's account of his voyage up the northwest coast and had been struck by Cook's description of an inlet that he believed to be the mouth of a great river. If he could just find the headwaters of that river, Pond thought!

181

By now Mackenzie's company, Gregory and McLeod, had gone into partnership with the much larger Northwest Company. The management of the newly merged companies decided to appoint Pond as the manager of the Athabasca trading centre. Peter Pond had been implicated in the murder of a couple of men who had died in a dispute when the two companies were at each other's throats, before the merger. It was only a rumour, but it affected management's assessment of Pond's eccentric behaviour, so they decided to appoint the twenty-three-year-old Mackenzie to replace him. It was a recipe for conflict, but instead of quarrelling the two men seem to have taken to each other. Mackenzie was impressed with Pond's energy, experience and optimism. Pond shared his dream of a river route to the ocean. He had concluded, quite mistakenly, that the river flowing west from Great Slave Lake was the very inlet that Captain Cook had written about.

Listening to Pond, Mackenzie conceived an ambition that would drive him relentlessly until he realized it. This bright young lad from Lewis, kinsman to the Chief of the Clan Mackenzie, decided that he would be the first to chart a route by land all the way to the Pacific. It became his obsession. With the diplomatic and psychological skills for which he was already well known in the Company, he persuaded Pond that he was the one to carry out the dream that Pond had been nursing for so long.

He was in charge now, so he left Pond to run the trading centre, and in June of 1789, still only twenty-four years old, he left Lake Athabasca through the confused delta where the Peace comes in from the west and the Slave flows north to Great Slave Lake. That delta is kind of a mess. John Rigney says, "The delta changes from year to year, from season to season. In a century a river channel can disappear and a new one open up." There is no way today to chart exactly where Mackenzie went, because the route he followed then has disappeared with the constantly changing sands and currents of the delta.

He had to make a crucial decision now. To turn west would have taken him towards the Pacific, but of course he had no way of knowing that. Because the northbound river was flowing out of Lake Athabasca, and Captain Cook's inlet was a "river mouth," he followed the river northward and was, in fact, on his way not to the Pacific but to the Arctic Ocean.

He had one big freight canoe and three smaller ones, and a group of voyageurs and native guides. The interpreter was a Chipewyan leader, Nestabeck, whom Mackenzie called "The English Chief." They turned west in Great Slave Lake and sure enough found an outlet. This must be it! The Dene people called it *Deh Cho*, the Great River.

Here is Mackenzie's diary entry for Sunday, July 5, 1789:

At three quarters past seven o'clock we perceived several smokes which we made for with all great speed. We soon saw the Natives run about in great confusion, some making for the woods, and others to their canoes. Our hunters landed before us and spoke to the people who had not run away.

Another Dene man whom Mackenzie persuaded to come with him seemed to believe he would never see home again. Mackenzie wrote:

He cut a lock of his hair, separated it into three parts, one of which he fastened to the hair of the crown of his wife's head, blowing on it three times as hard as he could and repeating some words. The other two he fastened to with the same ceremony to the heads of his children.

The present-day Dene chief Greg Nyali finds the story of Mackenzie perplexing in more than one way.

He was one of the first European people to come into contact with our people, the Dene. I guess at that time our people didn't know what Mackenzie was up to . . . or even in fact who he was. I think they were a little bit startled by the fact that he was of quite lighter complexion from our people. . . . From what I understand . . . they probably thought he was pretty sick and needed a little bit of help.

And they gave him that help. Chief Nyali, with only a trace of humour, says that turned out to have been a bad idea.

Our people must have helped him . . . [by] providing such things as whitefish and coney (rabbit). Moose were in abundance way back then and we even had bison. [But] I think . . . if our people might have seen into the future, and . . . really see what type of impact meeting Mackenzie and helping him out . . . I think that our people would have thought twice. I think that if they had seen all of the oppression and destruction as a result of it, I think they probably would have took him as an enemy and they probably should have killed him. And then we probably wouldn't have all the problems that we have today.

But they did not see into the future. Nor would it have done them any good to kill Mackenzie; if it had not been him, it would have been someone else before long. Mackenzie, in fact, while some historians say he would use any means he could to secure the services of the native people, seems on the whole to have treated them with respect and to have earned their admiration. The Dene women were especially helpful. They hauled the freight, put up the tents, brought in the firewood, skinned the game, cooked the meat, and made the moccasins. The men were the guides. And within a hundred kilometres, this new river, this great hope for the Pacific route, turned north, paralleling the Rocky Mountains.

Now they were crossing into Inuit territory, the enemies of the Dene. His guides began pleading to turn back.

The information that they gave us respecting the river seems to me so very fabulous. They would wish to make us believe that we would be several Winters getting to the Sea, and that we should all be old men by the time we would return. That we would encounter many monsters, which exist only in their own imaginations.

Curator Shawn Patterson says, "The Dene guides became more and more anxious . . . that they are going to meet with an end similar to the slaughter that Samuel Hearne describes, with the Inuit butchering everyone in the camp. . . . It's quite impressive to think that they continue. . . . There are local people telling them that they're going into a very dangerous place. And they continue."

In fact the Inuit encampments they came to were deserted.

Our conductor says they are gone to where they fish for whales, and kill reindeer.

They had reached the delta of the Great River, where billions of litres of freshwater flow into the ocean. The delta was rising and falling with the rhythm of the tides. It was the Arctic Ocean. And after all this hardship and the overcoming of obstacles, it was the wrong ocean; not the dreamed-of Pacific. He knew now that there would be no easy route. He would have to cross the Rockies.

It turned out to be a much longer journey than he had expected. When he came back to Lake Athabasca just in time to beat the freeze-up, he met Philip Turnor, a surveyor from the Hudson's Bay Company. Turnor actually had one of those new-fangled, dead-accurate chronometers with which he could find the exact longitude. He was able to demonstrate that Mackenzie had probably been seven hundred miles short of the position that his dead reckoning had produced. This was disappointing but it did not cool Mackenzie's obsession. He called that northern river that had led him astray the River of Disappointment. He would not be disappointed again, he said. Mackenzie decided he needed to know more about navigation and he needed a chronometer like Turnor's. He went to London. He sought out the best navigators in London and acquired the latest instruments. The dream had taken over his life. He would make it to the Pacific by land, or die in the attempt.

Four years later, in May 1793, he set out once more, this time taking the Peace River westward, even though he was going up river, against the current. West. The Peace split in two. His guides told him to take the southern branch. As he followed the sinuous path of the flood plain, on what was what we now call the Parsnip River, he could see the land rising ahead of him.

June 11th, 1793. The lake is about two miles in length, East by South, and from three to five hundred yards wide. We landed and unloaded where we found a beaten path leading over a low ridge of land to another small lake. We embarked on this lake which is of the same course and about the same size as that which we had just left and from whence we passed into a small river that was so full of fallen wood, as to employ some time and require some exertion to force a passage.

But soon there was another river, a major river. It flowed west. He had crossed the height of land. He did not know that this river flowed into the Ocean he sought, but the hopeful thing was that it flowed west, southwest in fact. It was the river we now know as the Fraser. The guides told him that it was dangerous water, and that he would be better from now on to take an overland route called the Grease Trail, which the Carrier people had used for generations to trade with the coast.

These people describe the distance . . . as very short to the Western Ocean, and, according to my own idea, it cannot be above five or six degrees.

This would mean some two hundred miles at that latitude.

Sunday, 23rd June, 1793. I was very much surprised by the following question from one of the Indians. "What," demanded he, "can be the reason that you are so particular and anxious in your inquiries of us respecting a knowledge of this country? Do not you white men know everything in the world?"

I replied that we certainly were acquainted with the principal circumstances of every part of the world; that I knew where the sea is, and where I myself then was, but that I did not exactly understand what obstacles might interrupt me in getting to it. . . . Thus fortunately I preserved the impression in their minds, of the superiority of white people over themselves.

It is probable that by now a fur trade route was no longer Mackenzie's concern; he was simply possessed by the goal; the ocean; by whatever route and means. They followed that Grease Trail, west across the lava flow to a high plateau and a pass that bears Mackenzie's name today.

Before us appeared a stupendous mountain, whose snow-clad summit was lost in the clouds. The Indians informed us that it was at no great distance. We continued . . . We arrived at the bottom where there is a conflux of two rivers that issue from the mountains. They are both very rapid and continue so until they unite their currents, forming a stream of about twelve yards in breadth. The water of this river is the colour of asses' milk.

Now there was unmistakable evidence that they were getting somewhere. They encountered people who spoke a language none of the interpreters had ever heard. They communicated by signs. The new people received the strangers courteously. Mackenzie asked for the loan of a canoe. They provided one and a young chief offered to come with them down the river. Now he was in what could only be an inlet of the sea. It was not over yet.

> *21st July, 1793. I began to fear that I should fail . . . our provisions were at a very low ebb. . . Ten half-starved men in a leaky vessel and on a barbarous coast. Under the land we met with three canoes with fifteen men in them. They manifested no kind of mistrust or fear of us. . . . They then examined everything we had in our canoe with an air of indifference and disdain.*

These disdainful men were fur traders from the coast, native fur traders. By an extraordinary coincidence just a few weeks earlier they had seen another vessel, they told Mackenzie's guides. It was, they said, very large and carried sails, and much grander than this "leaky vessel on a barbarous coast." Mackenzie had just missed what would have been a dramatic encounter with another famous explorer. These natives had seen Captain George Vancouver who, that same summer of 1793, had made a second voyage up the inlet he had first discovered a few years earlier.

> *One of them made me understand, with an air of insolence, that a large canoe had lately been in this bay, with people in her like me, and that one of them whom he called "Macubah" had fired on him and his friends . . . he wanted to see everything we had, particularly my instruments. While I was taking a meridian two canoes of a larger size, and well-manned, appeared. . . . My people were panic struck and asked if it was my determination to remain there to be sacrificed. My reply was . . . that I would not stir until I had accomplished my object.*

"Macubah," of course, is a pretty good approximation of "Vancouver."

The new arrivals proved friendly after all. They were also fascinated by the instruments. Having taken his sights and determined his latitude at last, Mackenzie knew his mission was complete. The inlet was, in fact, an arm of the Pacific Ocean. He was twenty-eight years old.

I now mixed up some vermilion in melted grease, and inscribed in large characters on the southeast face of the rock on which we had slept last night, this brief memorial — Alexander Mackenzie from Canada by land, the twenty-second of July, Seventeen Ninety Three. I took five altitudes. The mean of these observations is equal to 128 degrees, 2 minutes, west of Greenwich.

Well, he was off by about forty kilometres. But he had made it. The vermilion and grease are long gone but you can still see the rock, marked with a plaque. It is a good-sized boulder, with a fairly flat sloping face on which Mackenzie painted his famous words "From Canada by Land."

The ambition had been satisfied. Perhaps he was tired. He said that he was thinking of staying on in trade in Canada, perhaps starting a great new company. But he went to England, got married, was made a knight, and somehow never came back to the land of his sometime obsession.

He died in Scotland in 1820, at the age of fifty-six The rock is his monument, a national monument to a great adventure and a great spirit.

◆ ◆ ◆

From Canada by Land, the Alexander Mackenzie television biography, was a Canada/Scotland co-production written by David Halliday and Finlay Macleod. It was produced by Brian Dooley and Sam Maynard, directed by David Halliday.

PART THIRTEEN

SAM HUGHES
The Enigma

Of all the really puzzling figures in this country's recent history —
people about whom we have extensive records and know a great deal,
yet still find them difficult to understand — not many are as baffling as
this boy from Darlington. He became a famous and troublesome politician, a controversial military leader, and a man whose record still has
our most prominent historians almost at verbal fisticuffs over the balance of good and evil in his heritage. We know that he was genuinely
crazy in the last years of his career as a cabinet minister (although he
would continue to sit in the House of Commons for another three
years). But whether those who say he was mad from the start are right,
or those who say he was simply outspoken, determined, vain and
maddeningly successful are right — that is part of the riddle.

If you stop people on the street in any Canadian city today and ask
them who Sir Sam Hughes was, unless you are on Parliament Hill and
maybe even then, you will draw blank stares. During the first two
decades of the twentieth century, Sam Hughes was a household name,
but often as not that name was spoken with contempt if not with hatred.

The many photographs we have, and the magnificent oil portrait
at the War Museum in Ottawa, all show a powerfully handsome face
on a proudly erect body, an aristocratic bearing, a penetrating brown-
eyed gaze, a determined jaw, the mouth characteristically downturned.
The lower lip is often pushed forward defiantly or perhaps just confidently. Scores of raucous political cartoons of the period from about
1910 to the end of World War One show dark bushy eyebrows, a cruelly caricatured square jaw and a trap-door mouth.

It seems that he was not someone to whom painter, cartoonist, or
even the camera could be indifferent. Who was he, and where did he
come from?

His gravestone says Sam, not Samuel, and gives no middle name.

He was born into a family of Irish immigrants in a part of rural Ontario that is only a few hours by car from Toronto today, but then was on the edge of the wilderness. In the mid-nineteenth century Canada was a hoped-for salvation for thousands of Irish people who fled grinding poverty and the cruel indifference of their British rulers. From 1848 to 1852 what pitiful viability their world offered was devastated by a potato blight that led to a famine that killed tens of thousands. While the British and Anglo-Irish landlords continued to export milk and butter to England, few ever lifted a hand to help their starving tenant farmers. Canada's rich heritage of Irish names and mythology, especially in Ontario and Quebec, stems from that period, and it was just at the end of the peak immigration spurred by the famine that young Sam saw the light of day at Solina, near Darlington.

Like other farm kids he was used by his struggling father as cheap and controllable labour. But the five a.m. daily call to shovel out the stables or the cowbarns, or head for the hayfields or the plough still left the brilliant, tough and wiry youngster with the energy to get himself enough education so that, by the age of sixteen, he was teaching on a temporary permit in a local primary school.

Within a few years he had earned a regular teaching certificate. Then, still a young man, Sam wrote and published two school textbooks. He got himself appointed as an Ontario school inspector. *Mens sana in corpore sano*, "a healthy mind in a healthy body," was one of the favourite slogans of educators in those days, and Sam Hughes exemplified that motto superbly. He played outstanding lacrosse, was a champion long-distance runner, and a tough and enthusiastic wrestler.

He had an appetite for fame that would endanger his later career. He loved to win and to be seen to win, and he loved the very idea of glory on the field of combat. He had fed on tales of soldiering and adventure from his early years, and he revelled in his prowess on the playing field, as if it were a rehearsal for the battlefield. His appetite for victory and recognition drove him hard. He tried his hand as an inventor, and got a patent for a railway-car ventilation system. He quit teaching at the age of thirty-two and moved to Lindsay, Ontario, where he bought a newspaper, *The Victoria Warder*. Here too he succeeded. As an influential local editor/proprietor he played to the prejudices and values of his readers, and built himself a reputation along with his very satisfying subscription list.

Lindsay was Orange country. The Orange Lodge, based upon Irish Protestantism, loyalty to the King and a hatred of Catholicism, has dwindled almost to invisibility in Canada (though not in Northern Ireland). As recently as the 1960s many Ontario communities still held their July 12 Orangemen's parades, with the British flag, banners for each local chapter, and grown men wearing outlandish bowler hats. In Hughes' young days it was shiny top hats. The men and the boys marched to loud band music that was meant to let Catholics know they had better keep discreetly in their places if they didn't want trouble. That trouble frequently meant violence.

The Ontario Orangemen hated the French Canadians, too. In *The Warder* Sam Hughes would write:

> *The unfortunate French-Canadians are very little better than brutes. The poor creatures have for ages been kept in darkness, ignorance and superstition till now; they are dulled and blinded as to be insensible to the ordinary feelings of humanity.*

It was, of course, the priests who put them there; every Orangemen knew that. So it is not surprising that at least one Canadian historian accuses Hughes of being one of those responsible (in this land of extraordinary tolerance) for making religion a source of serious division. Author Jack Granatstein says that Hughes helped make Canadian politics "in the 1890s in particular, revolve around religion. What are the rights of Catholics [to publicly supported sectarian schooling]? What are the rights of French-speaking Catholics to be? People like Sam Hughes are . . . making those strains real, turning them into fissures in our public life."

But another distinguished historian, Professor Desmond Morton, who directs the McGill Centre for the Study of Canada, argues that in this regard Hughes was not far from the mainstream liberal tradition in Canada. To support his view, Morton looks ahead to the time when Hughes was in government in Ottawa, as Minister of Militia, roughly the equivalent of today's Minister of National Defence.

Professor Morton says that Hughes

believed, like many Canadians, that Church and State were sepa-rate, so that when he found . . . that Quebec militia units partici-pated proudly and actively in religious ceremonies he put a stop to it. When . . . Archbishop Bégin [was made] Cardinal, the militia vied for the honour of welcoming him home with guards of honour, Hughes put a stop to it. Why should some Romish potentate have Her Majesty's Soldiers — even if they were the militia of Lévis — on parade. This was stupid on his part, but . . . many liberal Canadians might think he was right.

Professors Morton and Granatstein differ even more sharply on the question of Sam Hughes' mental stability. For Granatstein Hughes was "certifiably mad . . . probably schizophrenic, probably should have been institutionalized. . . ."

For Professor Morton, "he was that fatal phenomenon; an honest politician who did what he set out do. Thank God we haven't had very many."

Professor Ronald Haycock, at the Royal Military College in Kingston, Ontario, agreeing that Hughes was "wrong-headed and wrong — a lot!" adds that "there is more about this very complicated man that deserves analysis."

So let us try to do some of that.

The old-fashioned view of war as heroic and glorious is not in vogue these days. Machine guns and poison gas in the so-called Great War made it possible for tens of thousands of hapless kids to be killed before breakfast. Aerial bombing put an end to the old principle that it was the brave military who got killed in a war; now whole civilian populations can be wiped out in a single raid. But it was not simply the geometric multiplication of the numbers of the dead that changed the world's view of war; it was also media. Before the American Civil War that began in 1860 there had been no photography on the battlefield. But now the citizens at home could begin to see the horrors of war. For about a century the propaganda offices kept the worst of it from them while the war was actually in progress. But at the end of World War One, the Great War, the photographs of thousands of rotting corpses —

men and horses — of the stinking, mud-soaked horror of the slaughter began to lay the ground for a new view of war. Television would be the medium that would make that view so strong that it would bring a major war — Vietnam — to an end.

But in the 1890s when Canada was asked to raise troops to go off to fight for the Empire in South Africa, most Canadians thought that was grand and noble. They turned out in the streets not to mourn but to celebrate. Commanders hoped to be given cavalry, for a glorious troop of lancers on horseback would strike fear into the boldest adversary. This stupid attitude would send thousands of riders and their mounts to almost instant death under the relentless fire of German machine guns in August 1914, before the lofty British High Command finally caught on. But when this country sent troops out to South Africa, the cavalry myth was still in force, as was the notion that war was glorious.

Sam Hughes was by then a Member of Parliament. He was completely ingrained with that romantic view of war. And, like the Israeli view of its army today (which does not much include the glory part any more), and indeed like the attitude of that first Greek democracy 2,500 years ago, he saw militia service as a noble and appropriate extension of citizenship itself.

Jack Granatstein says, "Hughes was a great believer in the idea that every Canadian was a natural soldier. Just give a Canadian a rifle and he was immediately an expert marksman. Make someone a Lieutenant and he would automatically become a Field Marshall, just by virtue of the innate skill that resided in every Canadian."

The mirror of that was Sam Hughes' view of the professional soldiers. Men who joined up for a career were not to be trusted, he said. They had abandoned the civic responsibilities of civilian life in order to live off the state and wear a uniform and swagger around whether there was a war or not. "Layabouts," he said. "Parasites. A drain on the state when you didn't really need them."

Professor Haycock says that Hughes saw the Militia as a kind of social and moral force that would permeate the whole fabric of the country and help build a healthy society. It seems that he also thought that a Canada strengthened by its Militia would help save the British

Empire, which suffered not from being an Empire, but from the English who controlled it. They lacked the decency and courage and other social and moral qualities that Sam Hughes believed were part of the real imperialist way, and were to be found in Canada more than anywhere else in the world. Canadians were superior human beings; it was as simple as that.

So the new MP was not your average rookie. He was forty years old. He had been running a very political newspaper for seven years. He knew everybody in his Ontario community. He had made a mark in the militia. He had thought about things, a lot; he had what almost amounts to a theory of society and a theory of politics. His energy was legendary. He was an indefatigable worker, with a playful side and — at least at the beginning — the ability to laugh at himself. This, unfortunately, he would soon lose.

But as he arrived in Ottawa he felt himself poised to take a position of power. He was very much interested in power. He understood that the Militia could help his political career, and soon learned that politics could advance his position in there too.

When the South African War broke out, late in the 1890s, Hughes was quick to ring the bells of national pride, and the honourable citizen role of the Militia. He stood up in Parliament and said that it simply would not do to let the Australians send a larger contingent to South Africa than Canada was sending: Canada must take the lead among the Dominions. It was an impressive speech and it worked, though not as completely as he had intended.

Hughes had hoped that the Militia in its gratitude for his intervention would give him a command in the war, which the Imperial forces were bound to win, no doubt about that, everybody knew. But perhaps he overstepped the bounds. His aggressiveness in Parliament, and around Militia headquarters, began to irritate people. And already some were inclined to see him as too eccentric, unpredictable, troublesome. He had no experience in combat or training for command in the field. The Militia chiefs, supported by the Government, refused to give him a command. He went off to Africa anyway, as a junior officer. Once there, when the hostilities got hotter and there were not enough British officers to go around, he was put at the head of a scouting platoon south of the Orange River.

Before long, letters describing his heroic adventures began to appear in the press. In one, his most famous, he took a detachment of cavalry out against a town called Uppington, which was held by an enemy garrison far bigger than his own little troop. We have the story only from Hughes himself. He wrote that he and six others galloped ahead of the wagons, impatient for the fray, and rode hard as they approached the enemy to drive up as much dust as possible so that Uppington would think the attackers to be greater in number than this gallant handful of seven men.

According to Hughes it worked. The Boer garrison surrendered, but because he did not have enough men to effectively guard his captives it seems they slipped away in the night and disappeared into the grasslands. But he had taken Uppington. Or had he?

Jack Granatstein is not sure. "To the best of my knowledge he plays no major role [in the Boer War] except in his own mind. And his own mind was such that he could convince himself that he had done great things."

Professor Granatstein is careful not to accuse Sam Hughes of lying: his portrait of Hughes is that of a man who was not only unstable, but capable of believing his own fabrications. He also made a lot of enemies.

Desmond Morton says, "He broke all kinds of gentlemanly and military behaviour by writing frank and insulting comments about his superior officers in the British Army, and sending them to the Capetown newspapers. This is not done . . . and it was for that specifically that he was sent home."

At home the people of Canada knew nothing about this. They had read only the glory stories. And when Hughes came home he was a hero, and poised for another run at Parliament. Then a curious thing happened.

Hughes was a Conservative. The Liberals, under Sir Wilfrid Laurier, were in power. Hughes was the opposition Militia critic, and seen as an asset by the government, as he was a bit of a loose cannon in the eyes of his own colleagues. And with his particular brand of partisan cunning, Laurier named Hughes to a parliamentary committee looking into the possibility of a Canadian-made rifle for the Canadian army, which until then had always used British weapons.

Laurier's own Minister of Militia had found it difficult to get his men enough small arms in the Boer campaign. A British industrialist, Sir Charles Ross, proposed building a weapons factory in Canada, to build a rifle named for himself, the Ross Rifle.

The Ross Rifle would end up shooting down Sam Hughes himself. It was not he who had accepted Sir Charles Ross' proposal, but he would become the rifle's staunch advocate at a time when Canadian soldiers in the field were cursing it and throwing it away even during battle. Hughes would keep on saying that it was the most accurate firearm ever made. That would earn him the undying contempt of thousands of the poor mud-soaked foot sloggers who had to fight with it and try to keep it from jamming on the imprecisely machined British-made ammunition they had been given. But that happened a few years later.

In 1911 the government of Sir Wilfrid Laurier was defeated over Free Trade. When the Conservative leader Robert Borden began to put together a cabinet, the experienced militiaman and much celebrated African Wars veteran seemed the logical choice for that ministry. But there were already enemies within the party itself, who warned the new Prime Minister about Hughes' eccentricities and, as Borden wrote in a letter summoning Hughes to a showdown in Ottawa, his "erratic temperament and immense vanity."

It seems that Hughes contritely admitted his faults, promised solemnly to mend his ways, shook hands on the commitment, and was made Minister of Militia. Then within a few years we were at war again, and it was Hughes' responsibility to raise the armies Canada had undertaken to send to Europe.

As a Dominion of the British Empire, Canada still considered the military support of Britain to be a responsibility and had kept a mobilization plan in force. But Hughes said that all he would need to raise an army was determination, energy and patriotism, and a direct call to his old comrades-in-arms. He sent out a direct appeal, in the form of personal telegrams, to all the heads of militia units across the country, asking for volunteers. He even swallowed his contempt for the Quebecers and designed recruiting posters that he hoped would appeal to their sense of being members of a special fighting unit.

Then he decided to build a big new army base at Valcartier, Quebec, on an unused tract of land north of Quebec City. There the expected recruits would be assembled and trained for combat before shipping out to England. The order to build went out on August 7. By early September the four hundred workmen on the job had installed water mains, sewers, tent platforms, administrative buildings, and even a special rail link to Quebec City. Hughes' critics, who had scorned the extravagance of his recruiting and training initiatives, were effectively silenced as the twenty thousand men Hughes had asked for grew to twenty-five and then almost thirty thousand, as the Valcartier Base materialized almost by magic.

Hughes was in his element. He would drive up in front of the parading recruits and make patriotic speeches to them from the back of his car. He took the Prime Minister with him once, and Borden led the men in cheers for the Militia Minister. Hughes would parade the training grounds like a Field Marshall, upbrading slackers, heaping praise on the diligent, demoting an officer here and creating one there, as if the Canadian Army were his personal fiefdom. And it is likely that in his heart he believed it to be so. If the men laughed at him behind his back when he came out on the range to show them how to shoot or to fight with the bayonet, or to demonstrate his own favourite wrestling holds for man-to-man combat, they didn't let Sam Hughes know they were laughing. And it is likely that he very soon began to believe in his own legend, the single-handed creator of a great fighting force.

The legend persists. Even his great-grandson Samuel G.S. Hughes will tell you today that when the Canadians arrived in Britain, and the British wanted to distribute them in the British Army under British Command, Sam Hughes went straight to Lord Kitchener, the Commander-in-Chief, and said firmly that the Canadians would serve together, in Canadian units under Canadian commanders, or he would ship them home. Professional historians say that they can find no evidence for this very attractive legend, but it keeps on getting repeated.

And there are professional historians, such as Jack Granatstein, who decry Valcartier and dismiss it as only part of the legend. "Sam Hughes screwed up," Professor Granatstein insists. "There had been a mobilization plan in place that called for the rational calm way of mobilizing a Canadian Expeditionary Force. . . . Hughes threw it out. . . . He 'miraculously' created a camp that didn't have to be created, mixed up historic regiments. . . . It was, I think, totally disorganized chaos."

But Valcartier was a huge public relations success. It made Canadians proud, and it made Hughes, once again, a national hero. And yet it was done by a man who had completely ignored the vital separation of the civilian government from the military machine it creates in order to carry out the political intentions of that government. For Sam Hughes, it seems, there really was no distinction. It was all for Canada, his great Canada. And not only was he the man who created the army, he now decided he would lead that army into battle; glory was only an ocean away.

Now this was all fiction. While he knew that he did not have the confidence of the government or the senior officers (even though he appointed those officers), and must have recognized that he did not have the experience to lead an army at war, yet he went ahead and announced that he was going to do just that. He put out a story about an assassination attempt — against himself — that was false and later seen to be only another publicity stunt. When the first troops shipped out from Halifax he went down to see them off, made a long patriotic speech at dockside with a patriotic song at the end of it, did not seem to notice or mind that they laughed at him, and went off to New York to catch a fast ship that would get him to Britain in time to welcome the lads when they landed.

Once there, he put out a story that he had received secret German strategic information from a beautiful woman on board his ship who was actually an espionage agent of some mysterious origin, and that he had personally taken this information to the King, George V.

It was all made up. Fantasy and reality may have been so closely intertwined in the Hughes narrative of himself that they could never be separated. And the fantasy led him into experiments in weaponry.

Perhaps the most bizarre of these, though not in the long run as damaging to his reputation as the Ross Rifle, was the shovel shield. A secretary, it is said, suggested that if the shovels the infantrymen were issued to dig trenches with had a small hole in the blade, they could be stood on the ground convex side to the enemy while the soldier fired his rifle through the hole and lay behind the shovel, protected from enemy fire.

They did not work, either as a shovel (a shovel with a hole in it?) or as a shield. But Hughes ordered fifty tons of those idiotic things, the taxpayers paid for them, and they were eventually all sold at a loss for scrap.

And yet even Sam Hughes' most severe critics agree that he was a seasoned politician, a diligent and often brilliant student of military matters, and a leader capable of daring decisions. Jack Granatstein, who never met Hughes but still seems angry at him eighty years after his death, said that when Hughes' son Garnet, an officer in the British Columbia Militia, recommended to his father that Arthur Currie be made commander, a great service was done to Canada. "Hughes listens to his son," Professor Granatstein tells us, "and appoints Arthur Currie as one of the brigadiers in the first Canadian contingent that goes overseas, and Currie turns into the most skilled soldier of the Canadians in the First World War, and arguably the most skilled general this country has ever produced."

But many of his appointments were less felicitous. When Hughes tried to redirect the haemorrhage of Canadian dollars that were leaving the country to buy munitions in the USA, he appointed friends and at least one relative to the Shell Committee, and they weren't appointed for their competence. "Buffoons and fools," says Professor Granatstein. "Corrupt friends. To run our war effort! I don't think Hughes himself was corrupt, but he didn't pay much attention to what his friends were doing."

Even after one of those friends was revealed to be on the take, Hughes defended him. Sir Joseph Flavelle would call Hughes "a degenerate, without moral sense," and then Flavelle himself would be accused of profiteering from the wartime sale of bacon to the armed forces, and although an inquiry exonerated him, his reputation was badly damaged.

So perhaps it was a time when Canadians suspected a degree of corruption amongst their politicians — Sir John A. Macdonald having been exposed in his corrupt dealings with the Canadian Pacific Railway with scarcely a scar to his enormous popularity.

It was also an era when Canadians received honours from the British Crown. Flavelle himself would be given a baronetcy, the last hereditary title awarded to a Canadian. And Hughes undoubtedly began to agitate with the Prime Minister for a Knighthood. It was normal to reward political loyalty in that way. A Prime Minister of one of the Dominions had simply to send his annual list to London, and with relatively few exceptions the honours would be agreed to. Prime Ministers themselves were routinely knighted. But the process was troublesome. Sir Wilfrid Laurier, delighted to receive his own knighthood, nonetheless found preparing the annual honours list troubling. He probably knew the saying of the great French minister Talleyrand, that bestowing an honour created a hundred enemies and one ingrate. The subject was much in debate by the time Borden became Prime Minister, and by 1935 knighthoods for Canadians were abolished.

But this was 1915, and maybe Borden thought it might calm Hughes down, and so his name went on the list and he became Sir Sam. It seems not to have calmed him down; in Professor Granatstein's view it "tended to increase the madness."

Now the Great War was getting worse. Terrible tales of slaughter in the mud were making their way homeward. The casualty lists were appalling. In four years Canada would lose more than sixty thousand men, and thousands more were wounded in body and in spirit. And it began to be said that one of the reasons for our losses was the Ross Rifle, which Sam Hughes continued to champion. It was Canadian. It was made here, and it was, undoubtedly, very accurate. But part of its accuracy was due to its weight, almost ten pounds, which kept it steady in your hands but was a terrible burden for a soldier who was already carrying a heavy kit into the field. And another part of its accuracy was its very precise machining, which demanded perfectly made ammunition if it were not to jam. The British munitions industry was turning out bullets by the tens of millions; the standards of precision the Ross needed did not apply to the British Lee-Enfield rifle; and the Ross was jamming, and — worse — sometimes "blowing back." Thousands of soldiers just threw it away and picked up Lee-Enfields from fallen British comrades or German weapons from fallen enemy soldiers.

At the battle of Ypres, where we lost six thousand men in just a few days, a third of the Canadian troops threw down their Ross Rifles.

Sir Sam Hughes had not developed the Ross. But he kept insisting on its excellence, against all the evidence, and thousands of Canadian soldiers (this writer's father included) came to loathe his very name.

When General Alderson, the commander of the Canadian Expeditionary force, persuaded the government to let him switch to the British Lee-Enfield, Hughes accused Alderson of cowardice and sent a copy of the accusation to Lord Kitchener. Kitchener was shocked, the King was angry, and the Duke of Connaught called for "that conceited lunatic" to be court-martialled. In fact by now, despite his very real accomplishments, almost nobody could be found to have a good word for him, and his whole organization came under increasing scrutiny. His personal appointees — and he had three or four senior military men in England each of whom thought *he* had exclusive power delegated to him by Hughes — began to quarrel. The Canadian High Commissioner in London, Sir George Perley, who despised Hughes and thought him totally vain and incompetent, took over as Minister of the Overseas Forces.

By this time Hughes really was losing his bearings. He wrote a letter to his own Prime Minister, the man upon whom he depended utterly for his position in government, accusing him of lying and of conspiracy. Borden had no choice. He fired Hughes. This time the public, on the whole, approved. The halo of heroism had been shot to ribbons by the Ross. A soldier serving in the Canadian Field Artillery wrote home, "The Mad Mullah of Canada is deposed. . . . I do not like to kick a man when he is down, but I would break nine toes in kicking Sir Sam in the stomach or the face or anywhere else."

Perhaps the worst thing Hughes did, in the end, was to try to destroy his own best General, Sir Arthur Currie, by accusing him of wasting Canadian lives at Mons, the last battle of the war, which ended only with the armistice on November 11, 1918. Perhaps it was because Currie had refused to promote Garnet Hughes, Sam's son, who had recommended Currie in the first place. That story is told in Volume III. It is a sordid story, and Hughes' actions helped fuel a scandal that nearly killed a great, great general. There was, as it turns out, no evidence to support Hughes accusations. Perhaps he knew that. Perhaps it was just the last lashing out of a failed hero, a deeply disappointed man whose stability of mind, never one of his great strengths, had deserted him utterly. This man of enormous capacity and drive, of energy and invention and courage, and a deep passionate love of his country, was finished; a shell; going through the motions.

He stayed on in Parliament for almost three more years. When he knew he was dying they arranged a private train to take him back to Lindsay. He had long ago planned a huge funeral, and in the event twenty thousand people would turn out for the procession. But it was on that train, heading back to Lindsay, that the last words are recorded that seem to speak for the man. Once he was installed in his chair, and the train had pulled out of the Ottawa station, the engineer came back to the car and asked the frail old man, "Sir Sam, what speed should I go?"

"Go like hell," said Hughes.

◆ ◆ ◆

The Enigma of Sam Hughes was written and directed by Daniel Zuckerbrot.

PART FOURTEEN

GREY OWL
The Fraudulent Environmentalist

On a soggy April day in 1938 two Canada Parks rangers in Prince Albert National Park, about two hundred kilometres north of Saskatoon, trudged through the heavy snow around the edge of Lake Ajawaan dragging a sled long enough to carry a human body. They had not heard for several days from the resident of a lonely cabin on that lake, who worked for the Parks Department. They knew he had been sick, and they were worried. While he was a real pain in the neck, this contract employee, with his heavy drinking and erratic behaviour, was also probably the most famous Canadian in the world, and unquestionably the most famous North American Indian.

Those rangers had read the sensational reports about his recent appearance at Buckingham Palace where he had shocked the protocol officers but kept King George VI and his family (including the nine-year-old future Queen Elizabeth) spellbound with his tales of the Canadian wilderness. He had talked to the young princesses passionately about his woodcraft and of the beavers whom he had befriended and written very successful books about. And he had — as he did everywhere he went — made a passionate plea for the protection of the wilderness and its inhabitants; for this man was a pioneer conservationist who had changed attitudes towards wilderness, on both sides of the Atlantic.

The rangers found his cabin a stinking mess, bottles everywhere, including a cache of dozens of bottles of extract of vanilla, which some people used to drink when the liquor stores wouldn't serve them any more. The man in the bed was racked with coughing and almost too weak to move. They bundled him up warmly and put him on the sled, and took the shivering wreck back to hospital in Prince Albert. Three days later, on April 13 he was dead.

And it was only then that those Park Rangers and indeed the rest of a very shocked world — for Grey Owl was known worldwide —

would discover that he was not an Indian at all, he was not even a Canadian. He was an impostor, a very successful impostor. His son John used to call him Archie Baloney. His real name was Archie Belaney. He was a superb woodsman, a fine writer, and an accomplished naturalist. He was also a drunk and a bigamist.

Archie Belaney was the son of an unsuccessful, alcoholic Englishman who had gone to America to make his fortune, failed, and returned bankrupt to his seaside home town of Hastings (where William of Normandy had conquered the English and killed their King, Harold, eight hundred years earlier).

George Belaney had married a seventeen-year-old American girl, and brought her with him, pregnant, when he slunk back to the Sussex summer resort town. Archie was born in 1888 at a house that still stands: number 32 St. James Road, Hastings. Neither of the parents wanted the boy. They soon turned him over to George's unmarried sisters, and then disappeared.

It is not surprising that the imaginative young boy asked a lot of questions about who his parents were. The aunts were trying to raise him as a young English gent, and put him off with vague answers. Somehow the idea of his father's being in America stuck, and later he would tell his friends that his dad was travelling with Buffalo Bill Cody's Wild West Show.

That might have had a touch of credibility to it, because Buffalo Bill had, in fact, brought his show to Hastings when Archie was about fifteen. The boy had been devouring books about Indians and the American Frontier, and suddenly there was a whole troupe of honest-to-god Indians in eagle-feather headdresses riding bareback pinto ponies and shouting war cries. Archie began to dream a dream.

For a while it did not very much impede his education. He was a very bright boy, tall, good-looking in an angular way with a strong, straight nose and deep-set brooding eyes. He loved to read and began to do a little writing. He studied the piano and played more than passably. The aunts wanted him to study medicine, but Archie pleaded with them to let him go to Canada. He did not tell them that he wanted to become an Indian. The aunts, however, were not about to send him off across the Atlantic, and it is not clear whether his subsequent erratic behaviour was just the way he was, or whether he was trying to make his continued presence in Hastings uncomfortable for the maiden ladies. In any case the turning point came one summer day when he lowered a package of fireworks, with a lit fuse, down the chimney of his boss's office, where he had a summer job at the lumber works. When the fireworks exploded in the office grate the job was abruptly terminated, and apparently that was when the sisters decided that Canada might be worth a try, after all.

He got off the boat in Halifax in the spring of 1906, not quite eighteen years old. The first record we have of his finding a job is in the kitchen at the then new Temagami Inn in Northern Ontario. Before long he was volunteering to help the guides and trappers, and learning to handle a canoe. The dream was taking concrete shape.

It received considerable impetus two years later when he fell in love with Angele Egwuna, an Ojibwa girl. The Ojibwa had become one of the largest of the Algonkian-speaking peoples in North America by that time, having spread out widely from their original territorial centre near the present-day Sault Ste. Marie (they were earlier called *Les Saulteaux*, by the French). Further south they were called Chippewa, and to the west sometimes Bungi. Angele spoke Ojibwa fluently and offered to teach it to Archie. She was also an accomplished trapper and canoeist, and taught him what she knew about those disciplines as well. Perhaps jokingly Archie said that he would make a white woman out of Angele, or perhaps he thought that was what *she* wanted. But she said, no, she would make an Indian out of him. And it may have been at that point that the dream he had been harbouring, in some shapeless, undirected way, suddenly came into focus. They married, he moved in with her traditional Ojibwa family. They soon had a daughter, Agnes. Archie grew his hair long, tied behind in a long tail, and took an Ojibwa name.

Scholars translate the name, *Washa Quon Asin*, as White Beaked Owl. It is easy to see where the white might have come from, and the Belaney nose was indeed an impressive beak. Archie liked to tell white people later that the name meant "He Who Walks By Night," and then, after a while, he just settled on Grey Owl, the name by which he became famous around the world.

If he felt the least bit indebted to Angele for having transformed him into something approaching the heroic figure he had been aspiring to since childhood, he did not show it very well. Within three years he simply walked out on his wife and child, and headed west.

Biscotasing, Ontario, has a population of less than fifty now, but before World War I it was a busy little town, and Archie Belaney settled into the life of the trappers and rivermen, and tried to let on that he was an Indian. He became close to an Ojibwa named Alex Espaniel and his family, who more or less adopted him and continued his education in the ways of the wild, and let him practise the language. Alex's daughter Jane would remain a friend for most of Belaney's life. She told her grandson Armand Ruffo, a poet who wrote a book called *The Mystery of Archie Belaney*, that the tall Englishman's masquerade hadn't fooled them, but in their adoptive way they "just let him go on . . . didn't pay him any mind." If the man wanted to be native, then they would help him be native.

"Native people have always adopted non-natives into their tribe," Armand Ruffo says, "into their communty . . . it wasn't anything out of the ordinary."

Gradually the English voice was edged and sculpted into the sounds of the voices of Biscotasing, the skin darkened, perhaps with some chemical help, the hair too. Archie called himself Grey Owl from time to time, but didn't insist on it with his Bisco friends. Like them he drank a lot; that was what you did in Bisco. He worked as a fire ranger in the summertime, or on the railroad, and did a bit of trapping in the winter. He moved in with Marie Gerard, a Métis woman. They had a son, John. And then, just as he had with Angele at Temagami, he walked out on them and disappeared.

It was 1915. The War that was going to be over by Christmas, 1914, had settled down to the horrible carnage that was to continue for four slaughterous years in the mud-filled trenches of Belgium and France. Archie told the enlisting officers that he was an Indian and a crack shot. They put him in a uniform and trained him and sent him off to the

Western Front as a sniper. It didn't last very long. He was wounded in the foot — some said later he did it to himself when he discovered just how dreadful trench life really was — and they shipped him back to convalesce in a military hospital in England.

By chance that hospital was on the east coast, at a Sussex town called Hastings. One day he ran into Ivy Holmes in the street. Ivy was a dancer, the daughter of friends of Archie's aunts. They renewed their friendship. Before long it had become something rather more than that, and they got married. Archie did not mention to anyone that he had a wife named Angele in Temagami and a daughter named Agnes, and a four-year relationship with a Métis woman in Biscotasing. He told Ivy Holmes that he would go back to Canada and prepare a home for her and send for her. And indeed he did go back to Canada, but that was the last he saw of Ivy, or she of him.

It was 1917. Marie Gerard had died of tuberculosis. Their son John was living with another family, and would grow up as Johnny Jero. Archie never even went to see him. This was the boy who would later call his father "Archie Baloney." Archie stayed on in Bisco, picking up odd jobs here and there, trapping, drinking with the trappers, and learning to throw knives. That skill fascinated him, and would later get him into trouble. For now it was part of "the Indian thing," as he saw it. The Ojibwa and Cree of Bisco didn't find his "Indian thing" very endearing, especially when he started doing what he declared to be an authentic war dance. He did not know how to play the drums; the music must have been something he heard in the Buffalo Bill show or just made up. It was all wrong, offensive even. But they were tolerant people and "didn't pay him any mind."

The police did, though. Some time in 1925 he was seen throwing knives at passing trains, drunk and erratic, and they issued a warrant for his arrest, and once again Archie disappeared.

It does not, until now, seem to be shaping up as the story of a visionary conservationist who would, even after the imposture was exposed when he died, still be blessed by millions of people for his contribution to the industrialized world's awareness of the dangers of the disappearing wilderness. He just seemed, to the people among whom he lived, another drunken trapper who liked to play at being an Indian.

He went back to Temagami and moved in with Angele again, and in 1926 they had another daughter. Well, Angele had the daughter; Archie had vanished again when he discovered the pregnancy. This time he left for good. In 1925 the Ontario Government had banned trapping to non-natives. Archie was too well known to the Ontario Lands and Forests officials to try pulling his I Am An Indian stunt on them, and trapping was the one economically viable skill he had. He moved over to the Quebec side of Lake Temagami.

There was a lovely girl working as a waitress in the local hotel. Her name was Gertrude Bernard. They called her Pony, nineteen years old and strikingly good looking. She was Iroquois but had lost touch with her people's culture and was trying to make a life for herself in the white world. A pair of wealthy American tourists had been struck with her grace and beauty and natural intelligence, and had offered to finance her education at an expensive boarding school in Toronto. She had jumped at the chance.

But fate and Archie Belaney intervened. Perhaps his story up to now makes this man seem very unattractive. But a photograph of him in his forties, just a few years later reveals a tall, seriously handsome man with a kind of nobility in his face, especially when he was acting the part of Grey Owl. That part would soon completely take over his life. From his other adventures we know that women were quickly attracted to him. When we see him in the many films he would later star in for the Parks Department we can sense the charisma. When he utters the poetry, the mystic connection with the great trees and the wild things that he communicated so powerfully, then it is not possible to think that he was cynical about *that*.

When Pony first saw him he was wearing a red sash and a tall fedora pulled down over his eyes, just so, and a silk scarf. And on his hip he wore a silver-plated revolver. He was a *presence*. She had no reason to doubt that he was what he said he was: a trapper, part native. He found out she was Iroquois and told her that he would bring her back to the great wisdom and treasures of her Indian heritage. He gave her a name to go with it. Gertrude Bernard became Anahareo, and was so smitten with this soft-spoken veteran of the traplines and the woods and rivers that she gave up her chance at an education, and stayed that winter in Temagami.

In the archives of the National Film Board of Canada there is film we were able to use in the documentary, of Pony talking about her famous lover long after his death. In her sixties she was still a wonderfully attractive woman, and although she had been hurt and disappointed, there was a wistfulness about her when she spoke about the man.

"He told me that his mother was Apache and his father a Scotsman, and that they lived in Mexico. If I had ever suspected . . . his being an Englishman, I would have tumbled to a lot of things."

But instead she tumbled into his bed, and if Archie Belaney ever really loved any of the women he was involved with, those who have studied the mystery of this brilliant impostor's life agree it was Anahareo. He abandoned the other women he'd lived with; Anahareo would change his life forever.

She had never been on a trapline. She pleaded with him to take her out trapping, and struggled with the awkward, unfamiliar snowshoes, and was eager and excited as a teenager, which she still almost was, until she saw him kill a beaver.

It disgusted her. The animals would be caught by the leg in a powerful spring trap with sharp pointed jaws. The trapper would take a hatchet out of his belt and club it to death, pry open the trap and set it again and move on to the next one. She couldn't take it. Somehow she persuaded him to let her bring home two helpless kits whose parents he had killed, and she raised them in the cabin that winter. Soon Archie began to see beaver in a different way. They named the kits McGinnis and McGinty. It was a kind of love affair. In one of the early films he made for the Parks Department he talks about that time in a tone that seems to us today a touch theatrical, a little over-earnest and contrived, but at the time seems to have mesmerized his viewers:

I began to have a faint distaste for my bloody occupation. These beasts had feelings and could express themselves very well. They could talk. They had affection. They knew what it was to be happy, to be lonely. Why, they were like little people! And they must all be like that! To kill such creatures seemed monstrous. I would do no more of it.

How would they live then? As a wounded veteran he had a small army pension, but that was his only regular income. They set up a tent and charged people ten cents to see him play with the beavers. He wrote proudly to his aunts in Hastings about "my wife Anahareo" and said she was the daughter of a chief. The aunts were now in touch with Kitty Belaney, Archie's mother. After a silence and absence of some thirty-five years, mother and son began to correspond.

Kitty Belaney was enchanted with the letters she received from her son. Perhaps the idea of writing had always been in his mind since his schooldays. He kept notes and journals and a record of times and temperatures, and descriptions of people they met and animals and landscape and the quality of the water. Those descriptions he sent off to his mother were so lyrical that she forwarded them to the hugely popular British monthly, *Country Life Magazine*, asking wouldn't they like to publish them? Better than that, the editors commissioned an article. He sent them an essay called "The Men of the Last Frontier." The editors loved it.

Archie knew his readership, of course. He had grown up on *Country Life*. He correctly guessed that there was a romantic curiosity about Indians in the English countryside, and he decided he would be their Indian, an Indian with a message. It would revolve around the beaver, with whom he had so suddenly and revolutionarily identified. He would use the beaver as the symbol of this new vision he had of himself as the saviour of the wilderness. He told his editors that he had spoken "nothing but Indian" for fifteen years, that he had been adopted by the Ojibwa, and soon he was saying that he wrote solely as an Indian, whatever that meant.

McGinty and McGinnis, the two kits whom Anahareo had rescued on a whim, had become the focal point of their lives. And suddenly, they disappeared. Trappers had been seen in the area, and perhaps that is what happened to them. Or perhaps they had reached the wander year that all young beaver come to. But they were gone. Signing himself Grey Owl, he wrote:

At last we knew that they were gone forever into the darkness from whence they came. And they left behind them no sign, no trace. And the aged trees whose great drooping crowns loomed high above our heads, omniscient in the wisdom of the ages, seemed to brood and whisper and look down upon our useless vigil in a mighty and compassionate comprehension. For they were of the wild, as we were, the wild to which, in our desolation, we turned for a solace and a refuge, that ageless wilderness that had ever been and would, somewhere, always be, long after we had followed our little lost companions and were gone.

He actually spoke this way in public. People drank it in. They felt illuminated, even blessed. If the words sounded much more like a well-educated Englishman who was intimately acquainted with the King James Bible than like a native Canadian who had "spoken nothing but Indian" most of his life, no one remarked upon it, at least not out loud. The editors at *Country Life*, having observed the transition, may have been amused. For many whose concept of the native Canadian still bore traces of the French philosopher Jean-Jacques Rousseau and his notion of the Noble Savage, it was probably comforting to feel that under the buckskin jacket and the long hair dyed black he was "just like us."

It was now that the Parks Department got interested. They had started producing short films to promote their work, and here was the perfect spokesman. They gave him and Anahareo a cabin in Riding Mountain National Park. Five hundred metres above the Manitoba Plains, on a rolling escarpment of mixed forest and grasslands rich in lakes and swamplands, the park has plenty of beaver and about sixty other mammals, including bison and black bear. The Cree and Assiniboine peoples had first hunted there about twelve hundred years ago. It had just been established as a National Park in 1929, and the Parks Department wanted to bring in tourists from all over the world to camp and explore its miles of wilderness hiking and riding trails. Grey Owl would draw them in. He was paid as a ranger, but his real job was starring in their films. Those films were sent to Canadian embassies all over the world.

There had to be beaver, of course. The new pair were called Jelly Roll and Rawhide. Grey Owl called Jelly Roll "King of the Beaver" until she got pregnant, and then it became "Queen of the Beaver." She and Rawhide would be seen by international audiences sitting up to drink milk, nuzzling Grey Owl and his "Iroquois Princess," mewing and paddling about, climbing in and out of the canoe, stealing scenes from their human friends.

Grey Owl was becoming famous.

Country Life now commissioned a book. Archie gave it the same title as that first essay, *The Men of the Last Frontier*. *The Times Literary Supplement*, as hard a marker as you can find in the world of book reviewing, said that it would be difficult to recall another record of the Great North that was so brilliantly and lovingly handled. *The Canadian Historical Review* said it was "extraordinarily vivid."

It was 1931. The Great Depression had the world in its grip, but Archie and Anahareo were doing just fine. He was invited to go lecturing with the films. That boosted the sales of the book. He discovered that he really loved writing. The next year the Parks Department moved him up to Prince Albert National Park, to Lake Ajawaan, and built him a special cabin with an entrance for the beaver who came and went like members of the family. There was plenty of money for booze now, and they both got into it with gusto. Margaret Connibear, who lived in the vicinity, remembers hearing a woman who had a cabin near them talk about some of the goings-on.

She was out in the summer kitchen and she could hear shots being fired out in the woods. It wasn't hunting season. This was strange, so she decided to go and investigate. She was about four foot ten, I think. Anyway, she went tromping out to the bush to find out what these shots were about, and came across . . . Pony, who was Anahareo, sitting on a tree stump with a rifle taking pot shots at Grey Owl's heels, chasing him, shooting just behind his heels, chasing him from tree to tree. . . . And they were both drunk as skunks. She must have been a wonderful shot!

A daughter, Dawn, was born in Prince Albert. Grey Owl and Anahareo went back to the lake, and Dawn was left in Prince Albert

with a foster family named Winters. But it was not like the rude abandonment that the other three children, John and Agnes and Flora, had
suffered. Dawn's foster sister Margaret Winters later got to know
Archie very well when he hired her to type his manuscripts, and she
remembers him fairly kindly.

> *He always said he wanted Dawn to be brought up . . . to be like me.*
> *I was the only girl. He saw her whenever he could, and being at our*
> *place, anytime he was in Prince Albert he knew he could be with*
> *her. And Anahareo used to take her to Wascasu where he could see*
> *her there, and even up to the cabin, so he was in contact with her as*
> *much as he could, living where he did. It was no place for a child.*

But the fights were becoming bitter now. Maybe the drunken pot
shots were a game, but it was a dangerous game. Anahareo was an
active young woman; sitting around for days when he did nothing but
drink and write made her restless and resentful. "She wanted more in
life than being connected to a pen," says his biographer Don Smith, of
the University of Calgary. When Archie announced a speaking tour of
England where he would dress as an Indian chief and unequivocally
declare himself to be an Indian, she was embarrassed and angry. In her
words, in that archival film:

> *I said, why not go as the woodsman that he was? He says, "They*
> *expect me to be an Indian. I'd stand on my head if I knew that peo-*
> *ple would listen. And besides, if the lecture was a flop I'd at least*
> *have given them a show for their money."*

When Dawn was a year old, Anahareo left Archie. Armand Ruffo
says that Grey Owl wrote to a friend, "'We are finally broken up, as
Anahareo tried to choke me for forty minutes,' or something like that."

Nursing his wounds he went off to England. They had heard
about him, and read his pieces in *Country Life*. His book, *Pilgrims of the
Wild*, an account of his conversion by Anahareo, was in all the libraries.
His Indian act was an outstanding success. The industrial towns of
northern England were desperately bleak in the middle of the
Depression, and when this beautifully dressed, beautifully spoken,
desperately handsome Noble Savage stepped out on the stage with a
maple leaf in his hand and said, "I bring you a green leaf," there was a

breath of hope in it from the new world. He would show the films of Jelly Roll and Rawhide, and himself and Anahareo as they had been, and people would forget the cold nights and the locked mills and the breadlines and the fear.

Grey Owl was now Canada's greatest celebrity, perhaps the greatest we had ever had. The publishers were ready for another book. So back he went to Ajawaan and an empty cabin. That would be the title of the next book, he decided: *Tales from an Empty Cabin*. Margaret Winters and her brother moved into a neighbouring cabin where she typed up the pages from Archie's terrible handwriting. He would stay up all night with the night-loving beaver as company, and a bottle. In the morning Margaret would tiptoe in and pick up the scattered barely legible pages. The writing would be worse towards the end of the session as the lamp burned lower and the bottle got emptier. Margaret said that perhaps Archie had been left-handed as a child, and had been forced to change to the right.

The vision was authentic though, clouded as it may have been by loneliness and drink and the masquerade. A genuine ecology pioneer, he lobbied the Parks Department to hire native Canadians as game wardens, because they would understand. He fought the development that he saw poised to contaminate and maybe destroy the wilderness that he now so deeply identified with. In a way he was his own wilderness. All around him they were measuring progress in terms of trees cut down and dams built, while he was angrily calling upon them to preserve, to treasure, to cherish. Trees spoke to him, he said. He is not the only one to have said that.

Lonely without Anahareo, he married yet again, and then again, without bothering to divorce either of his other two wives. In Ottawa he had met yet another woman, a French Canadian named Yvonne Perrier. He told her the story about the Apache mother and the Scottish father, but this time he had to be careful because there were legal records in two countries of the marriage of a man named Archibald Belaney. He invented a family of some distinction, the McNeils of Barra. He took his oath on the marriage licence that his name was Archie McNeil, and under that name he married Yvonne Perrier.

Whatever the triplicate word is for bigamist, he had become that. But it did not seem to help; his life was unravelling now, in many ways. His latest film had been shot in northern Quebec, and the producers had told the Department that he came to work drunk every morning; so they began to think it was time to bring that contract to an end.

Other things were coming to an end. His health was failing under the enormous stress, part of it from the constant watchfulness required to keep up the imposture. He was too far into Grey Owl now to tell the truth. He must have known how risky it was to be drunk so much of the time. He could not confide in Yvonne. He had created a fictional rocket that was travelling so fast now there was no way to jump off.

A year after his return from England a very curious thing happened. A reporter for the *North Bay Nugget* found Angele, and Angele spilled the beans about who Grey Owl really was. The reporter took the story to his editor, and they talked it out; the scoop of the decade, it would get the *Nugget* into every major paper on the continent, in Britain too, hell, all over the world. And they made a very strange decision. They suppressed it. They so admired what Grey Owl was saying to the world about the need to save the wilderness that they decided to protect him and his message by silence. Was it a good journalistic decision? Perhaps not; it would certainly not happen today. But the moral fibre of those two journalists is impressive. In any case, when Archie planned another British tour, for 1937, he was still safe. Or, the imposture was safe; he was in terrible shape.

Like other showmen he pulled it together brilliantly. Pushing the limits he decided to put Hastings on the itinerary, perhaps to see if anyone twigged. That is what Armand Ruffo says the motivation was. And he wanted to show off to the aunts, whom he could trust. In the event another woman, a friend from his youth, decided that Grey Owl looked an awful lot like the Archie Belaney she had gone to school with. She asked the aunts about it. They told her everything. She agreed to keep the secret.

He himself went to see the aunts on the morning of December 15, 1937, and took tea with them, and perhaps he even played on the old piano. They promised their discretion. They came to the White Rock

Pavilion to hear him speak (that was where the other woman had recognized him). Then he bade them farewell and never saw them again.

Buckingham Palace was the high point of that last tour. The King had asked especially that the great Indian visionary come and meet his daughters. Protocol demanded that the guests be in place before the Royal Personages entered the room, but Grey Owl was feeling his oats and insisted that he come in last. Apparently the King agreed. Yvonne was introduced as the Mohawk Princess Silver Moon.

He may have begun, as he often did, by saying, "On my buckskin shirt I wear a beadwork pattern of the maple leaf, Canada's national emblem, and the emblem of a beaver, my patron beast." For three hours he held them, rapt, with his tales and his soaring rhetoric. He told them, as he told us all and we still remember, "You belong to nature; it does not belong to you." At the end of his presentation, although he had been firmly instructed to bow and to wait until Their Majesties had left, he ignored the instructions, bowed for applause, stepped quickly forward, and then stunned the stiff and correct Palace officials there present by actually touching the Royal Person. Grey Owl put his hand affectionately on the shoulder of George VI, King of England, Scotland and Ireland, and of the Dominions Beyond the Seas, Emperor of India, and said, "I guess I'll be seeing you, brother!" Then he swept out of the room leaving everyone speechless.

Even knowing as we now do about the drunkenness and the bigamy, the violence, the abandoning of children, the lies and the masquerade, it is hard not to be charmed by the balls of it, the chutzpah, the effrontery. There is a Grey Owl Society in Hastings today, and perhaps the *North Bay Nugget*'s men had not really needed to be so protective. In Hastings and anywhere else where Grey Owl is still read or otherwise remembered, it is mostly as a prophet of the wilderness and not as a fraud. Colin and Betty Taylor, who are the curators of that Grey Owl Society in Hastings, talk over each other, interrupting in their enthusiasm as they tell the Buckingham Palace story on camera.

"'I'll be seeing you!' He was a pretty easy-going fellow. I don't think he was overawed by anybody. He was pretty sure of his ground. He probably had a good stiff drink before he went to the palace."

216

Probably. In those last weeks, he was living on whisky and two raw eggs a day. He survived the brilliant British tour long enough to follow it up with another, in North America, where the publicity from England helped him play to huge audiences. That went on until early April. When they arrived back in Saskatchewan they were both totally worn out. Yvonne was admitted to hospital for exhaustion. Archie insisted on going back to the cabin.

Then there was silence. The rangers began to worry.

"Archie Belaney is dead," Robert Duncan wrote, at the end of his film. "But the legend and the spirit of Grey Owl live on."

The legend does indeed live on. Fraud he may have been, but it is beyond question that without Grey Owl we would be far less ready, today, to understand and respond to that authentically North American native message he left with the King: "You belong to nature; it does not belong to you."

◆ ◆ ◆

This episode of *The Canadians* was written and directed by Robert Duncan, with co-producers Barbara Shearer and Jonathan Desbarats.

PART FIFTEEN

BOBBIE ROSENFELD
The Natural Athlete

There were fifty thousand people in the stadium in Amsterdam that day, for the women's 800 metres. They knew they were in for a dramatic race. The Canadian women had already done spectacularly well in the 100 metres, and were thought to be very strong contenders for the relay. Their star 800-metre runner, Jean Thompson, was looking very good to the insiders, but then so was the American Betty Robinson, the sixteen-year-old who had taken the gold from the Canadians a couple of days earlier, after a very controversial decision by the judges. The Japanese runner Kito was a third strong contender. The Canadian Jean Thompson was said to have injured herself, but she was still in the race so the injury could not really be serious.

It was going to be an outstanding race, all right. But not one of those fifty thousand people could have anticipated the heroic act that would transform the race into something more than a contest, and provide a display of athletic generosity virtually unheard-of in the annals of competitive sport.

It was 1928 and the first time women had been allowed to compete in track and field at the Olympics. De Coubertin, the old-school chair of the International Olympics Committee, had said that if women were to be at the Games at all, it should be just to place the laurels on the brows of the men who had won. But de Coubertin had retired. The twentieth century was taking hold. The rules had been changed, and Canada had sent a women's team. There were only six of them, compared to forty-nine male athletes, but those six women made history.

The women were Ethel Catherwood, Ethel Smith, Jane Bell, Myrtle Bell, Jean Thompson, and a funny, rangy, outspoken long-nosed Jewish kid from Barrie, Ontario, an immigrant girl of twenty-four named Rosenfeld. Her real name was Fannie, but after she had bobbed her hair when that became fashionable just a few years earlier, the flapper thing, they started to call her Bobbie and Bobbie stuck.

It was true that Jean Thompson had hurt herself. It was not serious enough to keep her out of the 800; she and the coach and the other girls knew she could run all right, and had the stuff to win. But they were worried about her morale and her confidence, and so was Jean. The spiritual and mental state of an athlete are at least as important as her physical condition, and Jean's teammates felt she needed a little extra moral support for this very demanding race. Some of them went to Bobbie Rosenfeld, who had won silver in the 100 metres against that sixteen-year-old from the States, and they said to her, "Look, it's not your distance, 800 metres, you're a sprinter, we know that. But look, you are so good at everything and it would be a boost for Jean Thompson's morale and confidence if you would enter the 800 with her, just run beside her till the final when she would do her characteristic pulling ahead thing and try to go for a medal." Bobbie was a good sport and a real team member, and of course she agreed.

In addition to the coaches and athletes, there was a solid contingent of Canadian fans at the games that summer. Post-war prosperity was at an all-time high. Except for a few gloomy economists, to whom no right thinking people paid any attention, nobody was worried at all that the financial bubble might be getting too big to last. People had money to spend and lots of them had come to the games. They were already pointing with justifiable pride at young Percy Williams from Vancouver, about to go home with not one but two gold medals, and the label The Fastest Man in the World (see *Part One*).

Percy Williams would be in the stand to watch the women's 800 metres that July day in 1928, along with his coach Bob Granger. The women's team had sent him flowers when he won his second gold; he wanted to be there to watch them and to cheer them on to a win as well.

The race started for the two Canadian women more or less as they had strategized. Jean Thompson moved into the fifth position early on, where she could run comfortably until her tactical sense told her it was time to put on the steam as they moved into the final 100 metres or so. Bobbie Rosenfeld kept a couple of places back, close enough to be able to call out an encouraging word, not so close as to throw Jean off her stride; Bobbie wasn't there to win anything, just to be moral support for Jean. Jean stayed solidly in fourth place, running easily, greatly reassured by Bobbie's being right behind her. It didn't mean anything in a practical sense, but the moral effect was palpable.

Now it was time, the last 200 metres. Jean sucked in her breath and gauged her position and where everyone else was running. Then she made her break to pull ahead. At exactly the same moment the Japanese runner, Kito, broke as well. Suddenly they bumped into each other, and Jean veered off into another lane.

Nobody was hurt. But Bobbie Rosenfeld could tell from, well, from what? From the rhythms of the other runner's limbs? From posture? From how *she* would have felt about being thrown off her stride? She sensed that Jean was fading slightly. She pulled up from sixth to fifth, a close fifth, right beside Jean, inches behind, and she hissed, "Keep going! You can do it."

And Jean Thompson recovered her morale, and her stride, and kept going.

Teammate Jane Bell, watching from the sidelines, knew that she was witness to a heroic act of giving. She said afterwards that Bobbie could easily have beaten Jean Thompson that day. But it was Jean's race, not Bobbie's; Bobbie had gone in to give her moral support, and that is what she did.

And even if she was thinking, I could pull ahead of Jean now, Jane Bell thought afterwards, *even if she was thinking Hell I could* win *this thing, I could get that gold that Betty Robinson stole from me in the 100 metres . . . even if she was thinking that . . .* she stayed back!

She stayed back, right at Jean Thompson's shoulder, at her ear. She kept saying, "Keep going. You can do it." And Jean kept going, she made fourth, a good fourth place, and Bobbie came in fifth. But it wasn't only Jane Bell who said to herself, Bobbie Rosenfeld could have won that race. People are still saying it, seven decades later. Nobody had seen anything like it before, and a lot of eyes filled with tears at the generosity of it.

Bobbie Rosenfeld was born in Russia in 1904, a time when being

Jewish in that country was even worse than being Jewish in most countries at the turn of the century. Russian Jews were in constant danger of harassment, destruction of their property, and even loss of life as vandals and thugs started pogroms in the Jewish quarters at the drop of a hat, with no interference from the police and often tacit encouragement from officials. Bobbie's father went ahead to Canada and sent for his wife and the two little girls, Gertie and Fanny, as soon as he could, and over they came, little Fanny seasick all the way, and worse, with an almost fatal dose of smallpox.

They settled in Barrie, Ontario. Ontario was a pretty anti-Semitic place to live in those days, in fact. There was nothing like the overt violence of Russia, but Jews were expected to "know their place." Many professions were either closed to them or difficult to enter. There was a quota at the medical school of the University of Toronto, limiting the number of Jewish students coming in each year, but it was never referred to openly. As late as the early years after World War II, despite the transforming lessons of Nazi Germany, Jewish kids were still insulted in the streets, and young Jews wanting to get into the teaching profession would have a tough time if they had no friends in influential positions.

Max Rosenfeld opened a shop with one door on the streetside and another in the lane at the back. The sign at the front said "Antiques Sold Here," and the one at the back said "Junk Bought Here." Despite the fact that Jews, and especially immigrant Jews from Russia, were unfamiliar to most of the pretty conservative inhabitants of the small Lake Simcoe town, the business thrived and the kids made friends at school and life was a lot better than it had been back in Russia.

Fanny was not yet known as Bobbie; that would come later. Her sister Ethel Berman tells how her interest in track and field came about more or less by accident.

My sister Gertie and Bobbie went to a fairground and took their lunch, and they lost their lunch. And there was a race on and the prize was a box lunch. So Bobbie took my sister Gertie and they entered the race. And Bobbie won and dragged my sister across; so she came second. And they had two box lunches.

And young Fanny Rosenfeld realized that she was pretty fast on her feet, and that she *really liked winning*. So for the next few years she went in every race she could, and almost always won. The year she entered First Form (what we now call Grade Nine) of high school, the word got around that she was as fast as a boy. So somebody decided to put *that* silly rumour to bed. The Simcoe County Archivist Bruce Beacock tells the story with a real sense of relish.

As she became a little older and she pretty much exhausted the competition among the girls, it was not unusual for her to run against boys. And there's a famous story where the year she entered Barrie Collegiate she ran against the three top male sprinters. They graciously gave her a three-yard head start, which turned out to be a bit of a mistake because she extended the head start a little bit by the time she won the race. So, I think after a while, the male ego being what it is, she had trouble getting competition against male runners as well.

The whole school applauded when she beat those three boys. She was on the way to a new career that would be flooded with applause.

"She loved applause," Ron Hotchkiss says. Hotchkiss is a member of a pretty small specialist profession: he is a sports historian. And he believes that Bobbie Rosenfeld was perhaps the greatest athlete Canada ever produced; not the greatest woman athlete of the half-century, which she was formally declared to be in 1950, but simply . . . The Greatest.

She loved applause. She was a performer. She took strength and satisfaction from the response of the crowd. Hotchkiss says that sports helped move the outsider inside. What he means is that, for all the relative peace and prosperity of her early years in Barrie, the girl felt very strongly that she was . . . different. She was a woman in a world where women didn't do much more than marry and have kids or teach school or work in a shop. And she was a Jew and an immigrant. And she wanted to really be part of this Canadian world. Sports would make that happen.

And, adds her sister Ethel, "She was one of those people for whom, well, to win is great, but *to compete is imperative*."

Well, there would be a lot more competition in Toronto, already a real city in 1920 when Bobbie turned sixteen and bobbed her hair in the flapper style and earned the nickname that everyone called her from then on. More competition, bigger audiences, more fun, and somehow the teenager persuaded her parents to let her go to Toronto.

She had already become interested in baseball. Before long she would move into track and field, including the shot put and the javelin. She was an outstanding lacrosse player by then. And hockey. She played for the City of Toronto's women's team, and they won the Championship two years in a row. Years later she would tell Foster Hewitt, in a radio interview, that it was a pretty rough kind of hockey.

"We played outdoors, of course, on the cushions (rinks) at Trinity Park and places like that. And we were really rugged. I remember one game, it was about 15 below zero [Fahrenheit: the equivalent of –26° Celsius], and none of us realized how cold it was until I shot the puck and it hit the goalpost, and the doggone puck splintered in about 29,000 pieces."

After a while she joined the Young Women's Hebrew Association (YWHA) and played basketball with them until 1926. She would take up lawn tennis at about that time, and after less than a year at it she entered the Toronto Lawn Tennis City Championships and won the singles.

But in a way it was baseball that brought her back into serious track and field competition. In 1926 she was playing shortstop in one of those commercially sponsored little teams that were just beginning to be a popular way for small businesses to get a little publicity, Hind and Docked it was called. The manager of the team, Elwood Hughes, arranged for them to play an exhibition game in a Northern Ontario town, and as a publicity stunt put on an exhibition track meet. On the other team was the city champion sprinter Rosa Grosse. So he put up a prize for a "Hundred Yard Invitational," all comers welcome, try to beat Rosa Grosse. They would run it off before the ball game, bring a lot more spectators in, who would then stay and watch his girls play ball and see the company name on their uniforms.

He entered his outstanding shortstop, Bobbie Rosenfeld, in the

Invitational, in her baseball uniform, with, as Bobbie would say, "the pup-tent bloomers." Bobbie not only beat Rosa Grosse, who was a close second, but she also came within two-fifths of a second of the women's world record for the 100 yards.

Then the famous University of Chicago team came to the CNE, and Toronto put up four girls against Chicago: Myrtle Cook, Grace Conacher, Rosa Grosse and, of course, Bobbie. The Canadians beat Chicago in the relay, and in the 100-yard dash Rosa and Bobbie were first and second.

Now the papers really began to pay attention to this incredible all-rounder. For some of the sports writers it appeared a bit unseemly that she should be so good at so many things. They began to urge her, in print, to specialize. And if there was to be a specialty, that two-fifths of a second off the 100-yard dash World's Record seemed to point to what it should be. But all the same, she was so good at baseball, for example, that people would come down to the old Sunnyside Stadium (where the Boulevard Club is now, on Lakeshore Boulevard), just to watch Bobbie Rosenfeld play baseball. Two miles east there would be men's pro ball teams playing in the old Maple Leaf Stadium, down by the ferry to the Toronto Island Airport, but there would be 1,500 to 2,000 people out at Sunnyside watching Bobbie; she was outdrawing the pros.

However, she got to thinking about that close approach to a World's Record, what it might mean. And so although she didn't give up on the hockey and the basketball — or indeed the javelin or the shot put — she really settled down to polishing the run. The starts needed work. There were really no coaches for women's track in those days, so she had to solve her problems on her own, but it would help to be in some kind of team, to have pals who were running too, trying out different rhythms and strategies and exercises. So when her boss at Paterson's Candy, realizing he had a budding star working for him, proposed forming Paterson's Athletic Club, she readily agreed to be part of it. Soon they were giving her time off to practise — and to compete — and Mr. Paterson's company name was getting a lot of ink because Bobbie just kept on winning and winning and winning.

According to sports activist Phyllis Berck, Bobbie became "as famous in her day as any pro athlete today, and as good a team player as she was an individual competitor."

And greater fame was yet to come. But the city knew Bobbie Rosenfeld now, and wasn't Mr. Paterson pleased. For Paterson's Athletic Club the long-faced girl from Barrie took five firsts for Ontario in that first year, and a trophy as best all-round woman athlete of the year. And Papa Rosenfeld would come down from Barrie to watch her run or play hockey, and when the crowd leapt to its feet to cheer for Bobbie he would shout, Ethel recalls with a grin, "Dot's mein goil!"

They ran on cinder tracks in those days. Today the tracks are all synthetics. Bruce Kidd, the first Canadian to break the four-minute mile, laughingly calls it "the fastest cinder track in the world," as he talks, with wonder on his face, about the Rosenfeld versatility and style. Like Hotchkiss and Berck he sees her as being in a class by herself, unique in her capacity not just to play but to be better than anyone else in sight at all those different sports.

And the next cinder track that would beckon would be the one they were planning for Amsterdam, in the summer of 1928. The first Olympics for women runners. So the Canadian officials had to hustle to put together a women's team, and all the hopefuls who could somehow rustle up the train fare went off to Halifax to show their stuff. The judges hit their stopwatches and checked out the styles and the endurance and picked six women. Ethel Catherwood and Ethel Smith; Jane Bell and Jean Thompson (she of the 800 metres, at the start of this story); Myrtle Cook, and of course Bobbie Rosenfeld, who, in those Halifax trials, set a couple of Canadian records and a world's record as well.

Remember that although there was no television then, and radio had not yet found a way to make sports the big item it would later become, everybody read the paper, and Bobbie's face was always in the paper. People stopped her in the street to tell her how great she was. And so when the papers said that she was off to Amsterdam, while there would have been a good crowd of well-wishers to see off the women's team, our first, whoever they were, the fact that Bobbie was on it meant that thousands turned out at Union Station.

The Canadian men's team, forty-nine of them, were given rooms in a shabby little hotel, and the women in a rooming house. Those six girls went running in the streets, chasing streetcars. The mailboxes were on the backs of streetcars in Amsterdam then, and it was more fun to post your postcards on the run than it was to decorously wait for the tram to stop. And while they were seriously training and qualifying, they were going to have fun too. A popular tourist's way to see Amsterdam then was by horse and carriage. Bobbie, who still spoke Yiddish well enough to get along, found a Yiddish-speaking cabbie. She talked him into letting her take the reins and the whip while he sat back with the rest of the girls as Bobbie drove them up and down the canals and over the bridges of the famous old city.

She was entered in the 100 metres, the shot put, and the four-person relay. But there was a scheduling conflict that forced her out of the shot put; so the first event was the 100 metres. Her serious competition was a sixteen-year-old American girl named Betty Robinson. Myrtle Cook and Ethel Smith also made it to the 100-metre finals, which Bobbie won to become the official Canadian entrant for the Olympics.

Bobbie was not as fast out of the blocks as Robinson, but she paced herself well against the flying little American, and began to pull ahead in the final as she liked to do. Her teammates all believed she had won. It looked to them as though Robinson had touched the tape with her arms, which was a disqualifier. But the judges gave the race to Robinson. When the coach started over to the judges' stand with a written protest, the head of the Amateur Athletic Union of Canada, who was also an Olympic Committee official, Dr. A.S. Lamb, put a stop to it. Decorum demanded respect for the judges' decision, he declared; there would be no protest.

The athletes and historians interviewed in the documentary still sound angry at the injustice of that decision, and the failure of the Canadian officials to protest it. The photograph of the two young women hitting the tape is not perfectly clear. Are Robinson's arms touching the tape? Or just above it? The Canadian historians still say it should have gone to Bobbie Rosenfeld, but Betty Robinson, remembering her gold with satisfaction seventy years later, said simply, "No. I won it. I was the fastest." Bobbie said at the time that it was too bad,

226

because if she had won gold they would have given her a synagogue when she got back to Toronto; now all she would get was a pew. That was typical of her humour.

There was one more race to run. Myrtle Cook and Ethel Smith and Bobbie had run the relay together at the Canadian National Exhibition in Toronto, the CNE; here at the Amsterdam Olympics they would get a new fourth member, Jane Bell. Myrtle wanted to be the finisher, and Jane said she always liked chasing someone, could she run third? That left first and second, and since Bobbie was clearly the fastest she would go first, to set a lead and discourage the other teams, and that left Ethel in second place.

Historian Ron Hotchkiss tells the story with so much excitement you would think he had been there, even though it took place more than twenty years before he was even born.

The gun goes off and there was no false start and away they went. When Bobbie handed the baton to Ethel Smith, she had given the Canadians a good two-yard lead. Smith puts up the baton and extends the lead somewhat and hands it over to Jane Bell, and Jane Bell takes it and runs around the curve as she did so well and perhaps probably of the four runners she ran the best leg of the relay, but she got the baton to Myrtle just before Myrtle stepped out of the passing zone, and Myrtle grabbed the baton and sped away with Betty Robinson close on her heels. But Cook crossed the line ahead of the United States, and jumped up and down, the other runners you can see the videotape of them jumping up and down as they ran to Myrtle to embrace one another.

And Bobbie's sister Ethel Berman says, "When we heard how well she did in the relay, well of course we all needed bigger bra sizes."

And then there was that amazing act of generosity and spirit in the 800 metres; by the time they got on the boat for Montreal the Canadians were national heroes and Bobbie Rosenfeld was a living legend. The Canadian women had racked up a total of 26 points, well ahead of the Americans, and of those 26 points Bobbie Rosenfeld had 13.

Toronto went mad. Ron Hotchkiss says that there were two hundred thousand people waiting to meet the women when they got off the train at Union Station, and another hundred thousand at Sunnyside Stadium for the speeches and presentations. Crowds lined Lakeshore Boulevard all along the route to the stadium. People ran into the road to touch the athletes as they went by, slowing down the parade. When Ethel Catherwood complained about the slowdown, Bobbie, who was uncharacteristically silent, said that it was all right with her, it could last forever as far as she was concerned.

There were fireworks and speeches and the Jewish Community gave Bobbie a car. Her father built a special cabinet for all her medals and trophies, and her mother polished them "as if they were her best silver," says Ethel Berman.

But if it looked as though a lifetime of triumph lay before Bobbie Rosenfeld, tragically it was not to be. She had noticed some pain in her ankles, even before she got home from Amsterdam. For a while she probably thought it was from all that running, but it was not. Deep inside her system nature had played her a nasty trick. White blood cells, which are one of the great defences against injury and disease, had started to act perversely. They invaded the tissues around the joints in her ankles and feet in a way that caused an enzymatic reaction, in which a kind of detergent began to demolish the cartilage that cushions bone from bone. When they had finished with the cartilage, they began to eat away at the bones themselves.

And then the doctors said they would have to amputate a foot. The foot of the most spectacular female athlete the country had ever seen. The foot of a runner. Bobbie Rosenfeld was twenty-five years old.

She refused the amputation; she could not believe she wouldn't heal. She had always beat the competition, she wasn't going to give in to this one. The pain was tremendous. The medical profession did not then have the immense armamentarium of benign analgesics, anti-inflammatories or cortisone, and if she was going to keep that foot it would mean bed rest, continuous bed rest, and ice packs; and that would go on for nine months. Her mother looked after her throughout the whole anguished time.

With her indomitable spirit she was soon up again and out in the world on crutches. Her old hockey teammates invited her to come

228

down and watch a game. When it became clear that the team was losing, Bobbie went back to the dressing room to see them all before the last period, and decided that there were worse things than the pain in her ankles. She dressed, put on a pair of skates, left her crutches in the dressing room, and went out on the ice and scored the winning goal.

Once again nobody had ever seen anything like it, and sports physician Ed Keystone, looking back on that day, says it "is what I call nothing short of a miracle."

But Bobbie Rosenfeld's days as a sprinter were done. She made a try at baseball, but she couldn't do it. She saw the dream of the next Olympics, 1932 in Los Angeles, fade like a cloud in a brilliant sky. As an athlete she was done. What had been a time in the sun that could be called nothing less than incandescent, was now a huge black hole. *National Post* columnist Robert Fulford, who had joined the staff of the *Globe and Mail* a few years later, when Bobbie was doing a sports column there, and came to think of her as a big, loud, emphatic woman, says now that there was a melancholy about her too, a constant. "It never left the room. It was her partner."

But it did not stop Bobbie Rosenfeld. She put together the Toronto Pals, a girls' hockey team, coached them and got them to Madison Square Gardens in New York to play against the New York Wolverettes. She was still signing autographs, they still recognized her in the street, and for some reason she began to sign herself "Just a Natural: Bobbie." And her old friends say that was appropriate. Because Bobbie Rosenfeld was a natural athlete.

She moved to Montreal for a while and wrote a column for the *Montreal Gazette*, and then the *Globe and Mail* called her back to Toronto. For this writer, growing up on that newspaper, her column "Sports Reel," with her photo in curled hair and heavy lipstick, seems, in memory, to have always been there.

In the year 2000 it is not easy to conceive of a time when the idea of a famous female athlete was, well, strange. But sportswriters, historians, athletic officials and professionals looking back on those last few years of the 1920s give Bobbie Rosenfeld a substantial part of the credit for bringing women into the foreground in sports, for showing the world that women can compete just as well as men. And perhaps — although the Toronto that this writer remembers as a child was still carelessly anti-Semitic — perhaps she really did make an important dent in that shameful part of our growing up as a nation. Because everybody loved Bobbie Rosenfeld. And there was no doubt that Bobbie Rosenfeld was a Jew. And it is not really possible to be a committed anti-Semite when you are in love with a Jewish girl.

In 1950, when they named her Woman Athlete of the Half-Century, there were some who thought it should have been simply Athlete of the Half-Century. And most of the people who contributed to this fine film biography by Martin Harbury talk as though she should have been Athlete of the Century too. Bruce Beacock, in Barrie (now a city), where they still feel they *own* Bobbie Rosenfeld, says flatly, "I would challenge anybody to look objectively at the facts, and talk to people who were active at the time, to look at the number of sports she played, and played well, and *dominated* . . . and tell me that there has ever been an athlete in her class. Anywhere."

If people fell in love with her, did she fall in love? This is not entirely clear. Her sister talks of a boyfriend, another Olympic athlete, whom Bobbie might have married if he had been Jewish, but she would not marry out of the faith while her mother lived. Others talk about her living with a woman companion.

But in the end she was alone. One day when she had not answered her phone for more than twenty-four hours her sister Ethel called the super at the apartment building, and the super came back to the phone to say that Bobbie's newspaper was still outside the door.

She had died in her sleep. She was sixty-five. Today, Jane Bell, who ran that third position in the relay at Amsterdam seventy-two years ago, said at the time that a part of herself had died too. They were no longer a team. Bobbie had been the glue that held the team together. The Natural Athlete.

◆ ◆ ◆

The Natural Athlete was written and directed by Martin Harbury, with Carrie Madu as line producer.

PART SIXTEEN

TOM THOMSON
The Real Mystery

On a chilly spring day in 1913 a man stepped off the train at a tiny station called Joe Lake carrying a backpack, a small wooden case and a fishing rod. It was his first visit to a part of Ontario that would not only change his life, but also affect ever since the way in which Canadians see their own country.

Almost three hundred kilometres north of Toronto there is a largely uninhabited tract of land nearly eight thousand square kilometres in area. Its rolling topography ranges across the southern limits of the Canadian Shield between Georgian Bay and the Ottawa River. It is mostly Precambrian granite — some of the oldest rock in the world — granite that was polished in some places, pitted and scarred in others, when the ice sheet that once covered it receded about ten thousand years ago. It is called Algonquin Provincial Park.

There are some 2,500 lakes in the park, many of them linked by river, which give paddlers 1,500 kilometres of canoeing and portaging. Hunting is forbidden. Logging is controlled in 90 per cent of the Park, although in the twenty-first century that control has become far too lenient for most conservationists.

From the time of its founding in 1893 until the end of World War II, it was almost pure wilderness, though by no means in a pristine state of nature. Logging operations had left it with thin, poor soil, and a harsh climate, and many forest fires gave the Park a varied and changing second growth forest: red and white pine, spruces, birch and poplar. Wolves patrol throughout. Canoe trippers around their campfire at night will, if they are lucky, be treated to the spectral symphony of a wolf howl that is picked up by another voice from another direction and then another, until sometimes the whole sky seems to resonate with the long, eerie wails.

Deer and bear are common. Driving the road that cuts through the southern sector, providing a route from Huntsville to Ottawa, travellers can stop and watch moose calmly grazing by the roadside, apparently confident that they will not be shot.

By 1945 the few Fire Rangers' towers and their accompanying cabins were decaying, as the fire patrol had gone airborne out of a floatplane base on Smoke Lake, in the southern sector of the park. The Park was served by rail until about 1960. There was a hotel and a store at Joe Lake, a few kilometres inside the east boundary, and another at Smoke Lake about ten kilometres further along. There are a few commercially operated summer camps for children. One of them, Camp Ahmek on Canoe Lake, has been host to a number of boys who later became prominent in Canadian public life. Our Prime Minister for close to fifteen years, the late Pierre Trudeau, was seen by millions of Canadians in a television biography that was rebroadcast after his death in 2000, paddling with the distinctive Ahmek Stroke, the upper hand never rising above the chin line, pushing straight ahead on the stroke, the boat heeled sharply to the paddling side, the gunwale only a couple of inches above the water.

On a couple of the roadside lakes there are a few cottages now, mostly with fixed-time leases from the province. Apart from that it is a wilderness that has given Canada some of its most defining images. A painter named Tom Thomson brought those images into focus more than anyone else — first for other painters, then for the world.

There are two mysteries about Tom Thomson. In the summer of 1917 his body was found in Canoe Lake with his feet trussed in copper fishing line and a wound on his head. Inexplicably, the coroner called it drowning. But people have not stopped speculating about what really happened.

The mystery of his death, however, is overshadowed by the mystery of his life. Until the last five years of that life he seemed unremarkable, a journeyman commercial artist and engraver, whose work was skilled but undistinguished. Yet in those last five years, between the ages of thirty-five and forty, it was suddenly clear to his fellow artists that they were in the company of genius. And then he was gone, leaving us with a vision of our land that has legendary power.

Tom's British grandparents immigrated to Canada in the 1830s, and eventually moved to a 150-acre farm near Claremont, Ontario. The farmhouse today looks much as it did when Tom's father John Thomson was born in it in 1840, and when Tom himself was born in it in 1877.

Joan Murray, an art historian and Director Emerita of the Robert McLaughlin Gallery, wrote the Tom Thomson Entry for the new edition of the *Canadian Encyclopaedia*, and has published a book entitled *Tom Thomson's Trees*. She has been fascinated for years with the Tom Thomson story.

When Thomson was only a few months old he and his family moved to the Leith area. His father was rather a character. Apparently he carried money from the sale of the house in Claremont, with him in a sack. And when he saw a farm that he thought appropriate, he stopped the carriage, got out with his sack of money, and bought the farm for cash.

That old farm is still there. The house still stands on a rise just north of Owen Sound, on the shores of Georgian Bay. The present-day picture we see of that house in the documentary is easily recognizable as the house in the family photos from the late nineteenth century.

Tom's childhood there was a happy one. There is a treasury of early photographs in the documentary. As a boy he had a smooth, round, almost angelic face but with a touch of curiosity and humour peeping out. The eyes in those photos are almost always contemplating the lens, and they are powerful, almost spiritual eyes. There is a lock of hair hanging down over the right side of his forehead.

He was the sixth of nine children, all of them talented to some degree, and almost all of them musical. Tom himself played cornet and violin, and his favourite, the mandolin. His father liked to sketch, and Tom soon began to do puzzle caricatures, meaning that they were designed to get people to guess who they represented.

Although he had weak lungs from childhood, he developed a profound love of the out-of-doors, and in this he was strongly encouraged, Joan Murray told us, *by a distinguished relative.*

There was one great man in the family, Dr. William Brodie, that's Tom's cousin. A true, truly great biologist of the period. Before Dr. Brodie died he was ... head of the biological section at The Royal Ontario Museum. He died in 1909, and he was the most distinguished biologist of his day ... a true scientist and a wonderful man. He used to take the children on Saturday morning walks which extended for miles, and he would name the plants, and speak of philosophy and speak of poetry. .... Our Tom Thomson ... collected specimens for Dr. Brodie.

For a while Tom even considered becoming a professional naturalist. He gave his parents a drawing he called *Nature's Peace*. He wrote on it: "Be glad of life because it gives you the chance to love, to work and to play, and to look up at the stars. Spend as much time as possible, with body and with spirit, in God's out-of-doors."

In 1899 at the age of twenty-two he volunteered for the expeditionary force going off to South Africa to fight in the Boer War. His lungs were not up to the training and although he tried three times to enlist he never made it. He tried apprenticing as a machinist at the Kennedy Foundry in Owen Sound, but was often late, did not get along with the boss, and was fired after less than a year. According to Joan Murray, despite the apparently vigorous cultural life at home, Tom's school days had been as unsuccessful as his industrial apprenticeship.

He actually never completed grade school. He never went to high school. [He went to] a little business college in Chatham ... Canada Business College ... and Thomson was good at penmanship. .... His brother George [who had also gone there] went ahead to Seattle and started his own business college, and [Tom] went there too.

Brothers Henry and Ralph were also in Seattle when Tom arrived in 1901. His first job was elevator operator at the Hotel Diller. Then he did design work for George's business school, a poster, a newspaper advertisement and a business card. These he took around to commercial art firms in Seattle as samples of his work, and began to get some assignments. Evenings he and George would go to the theatre or to a concert, or visit friends with the mandolin for an evening of homemade music. The Seattle photographs show an almost overwhelmingly handsome young man, his nose now much sharper than in the boyhood photographs, the eyes still dark and compelling, the lock of hair over the forehead almost a trademark. Sometime in 1903 or 1904 he met Alice Lambert, a woman eight or nine years his junior. Joan Murray tells what happened next.

> *He decided to marry her and he proposed . . . outside the boarding house, and he said the words [and] she was so nervous — it's the stuff of movies — she was so nervous she giggled. Now Tom Thomson had a very thin shell. . . . He was shocked. . . . He turned on his heel, went back to the boarding house where he roomed, packed his bag and left Seattle. And he never wrote her or spoke to her again.*

Joan Murray showed us her copy of a book by Alice Elinor Lambert, who became a successful writer. Two of her novels are still available via the Internet. In *Women Are Like That* (1934) she wrote of a fictional character:

> *For one disturbing year she had been desperately in love with a tall dark boy named Tom, a commercial artist who in the summer used to take her on streetcar rides to Alki Point. . . . He had gone East. The girl, unversed as she was in the art of pursuit, had let him go, powerless to hold him, or call him back. . . . Years later, when she learned that he had been drowned while on a sketching trip in the North, a section of her heart had sealed up, never again to open.*

When he came back to Toronto in 1905 the tall dark boy went to work as a senior designer for Legge Brothers. He was twenty-eight. From time to time he jumped on the train on a Friday afternoon and went to visit his parents in Owen Sound. He began seriously sketching in the out-of-doors too, particularly up the shallow reaches of the Humber River just west of the city.

> *That's when he decided to become an artist* (Joan Murray recounts). *He had no thought of it earlier. . . He went to school at night and he learned to draw . . . in a painting class by a wonderful teacher named Cruikshank . . . One of his early works . . . is just like an amateur sketch, but . . . Cruikshank . . . the great man, spoke to him and said, "Did you do that?" and Thomson said he did. And Cruikshank said, "Well, you better keep on."*

That was 1906. A.Y. Jackson, one of the founders of the Group of Seven, said that Cruikshank was "a cantankerous old snorter" when Tom was studying with him at the Ontario College of Art.

A painting of a man with a pair of horses, the man's back to us, survives from that period. While it is competent it is completely without interest and foreshadows nothing of what was to come. Soon he moved over to Grip Limited, a design firm whose name survived into the late twentieth century as part of Rapid Grip and Batten. They were typesetters, an industry that vanished overnight a decade ago, when the computer age made obsolete the setting of type by pouring hot lead into molds.

At Grip Limited Tom met a group of artists who would change his life, as he would theirs. Arthur Lismer was at Grip then, and so were Frederik Horsman Varley, Franklin Carmichael, Franz Johnson, and J.E.H. MacDonald, four of the seven painters who would form the famous Group of Seven in 1920. He appears to have lost some of the impatience and erratic behaviour that had often brought him trouble in earlier jobs. He seemed to feel at home here. The artists at Grip liked him immediately, and later talked of him as a quiet man, easy company. They praised his landscape painting too, and encouraged him to keep on working at it. Lismer and Varley made some playful pen-and-ink sketches of their new friend, which survive. They encouraged him to take a look at the wilderness north of Toronto, as a stimulus for the landscape painting. And so he boarded that train in July 1912, for the Joe Lake Station, just above the dam at the north end of Canoe Lake.

Eighty-eight years later the director of our biographical documentary invited Toronto artist John Fraser to go to Canoe Lake, to see that landscape today through the eyes of the Tom Thomson of 1912. John Fraser is a versatile artist who works on computer images more than with paint these days. He has an impressive ability to paint like other painters, and on an afternoon in the autumn of 2000, he set up an easel on the shore of Canoe Lake and demonstrated the Thomson technique and style. John Fraser knows the lake well, and is a skilled paddler, like the man whose work he was reproducing with uncanny verisimilitude.

He said, as he painted for the camera,

Tom's work has a very strong sense of the subject, a very strong sense of the environment he's in moving through him and onto the canvas. It was a moving, active process. It was definitely . . . the painting was a verb, it was not a noun. He tended to work on a birch panel. It would be pre-oiled . . . so that the paint would ride really nicely over the surface. . . .The colours I'm working with here are the same ones that he would have had back then. And this is a conventional oil palette. Some of the colours we have today didn't exist back then. I have enough paint on the brush where the paint is actually delivering itself. I'm really not letting the brush influence. As much as I can I'm just trying to keep enough paint on the brush that the paint will just sort of onload itself on the existing wet paint underneath, and that's what keeps it fairly alive.

As Fraser works, what appears to be a Tom Thomson painting takes shape on the panel in front of him.

He worked overhand, a good distance from the painting. He didn't get caught up in details. He . . . was involved with the colour, the play of the light. I'm now going to go with the burnt umber and the ultramarine blue which was the classic way in which the Group of Seven and Tom Thomson . . . made black. They never used black [from the tube], black was absolutely a no-no. The colours themselves were not mixed too heavily together, they were sort of loosely folded together so that the original quality of the colour would be able to come through. . . . The idea is to have a folding together of the complementary colours so that they work together and [convey] a sort of light and a shadow at the same time.

Tom was seen by his artist friends at Grip Limited as a kind of natural, according to Dennis Reid, Chief Curator of the Art Gallery of Ontario:

He was understood by his contemporaries to be somebody who was essentially untrained and who responded in a very natural way to the Canadian landscape . . . somebody who essentially sprang from the soil. . . . And they saw this as being the essence of genuineness. So he was authentic. . . .

Joan Murray adds:

They all liked Thomson and they lent him the studio on the weekend,

Grip premises . . . because he had no place to paint. And everyone took a hand in teaching him. . . . Varley apparently took the brush from his hand to help him show certain areas in a painting.

That painting may have been a canvas based on sketches he made that first wilderness summer of 1912. He had gone from Algonquin Park along the Spanish River to the Mississagi Forest Reserve between July and September, with a painter named William Broadhead. When he came back one of the sketches, *Northern Lake,* so impressed his artist friends that they persuaded him to work it up into a full-size canvas. The Province of Ontario bought the work for $250. As Tom was earning 75 cents an hour at Grip Limited, that was the equivalent of about two months' salary.

In the fall of 1913 Lawren Harris, a painter who became famous both for stark paintings of the north country and for homey views of Toronto streets, was developing studio and living quarters for artists to share in, The Studio Building, at 25 Severn Street. Their sponsor was Dr. James MacCallum, who would also become Tom's sponsor. The Studio Building was soon full, and Tom set up a combination studio and living space in what had been a construction shack. In the fall of 1914, Dennis Reid says, the other artists were beginning to look on Tom's work as something *they* could learn from.

They all went up to Algonquin Park and there was very much a sense of Tom introducing them to the Park. They were all there together. [A.Y.] Jackson wrote back to Dr. MacCallum, who was patron to all of them . . . "Tom's making great strides." . . . I think each one of them felt that they had a hand in directing him along, in bringing him out. So it's an unusual relationship . . . they felt like the parents in a certain sense, but then they somehow ended up feeling like progeny.

Now he would go to the Park every year. Another "Northern" painting, *Northern River,* one of his most famous, its foreground laced with the naked branches of swamp spruce, sold for $500 in 1914. His confidence was soaring. James Marsh, who wrote about Thomson for the *Canadian Encyclopaedia,* said, "His work now had the smash and stab of passion without thought." The big canvases are the traditional form that makes a painter's name. But Dennis Reid says he is convinced that the sketches were more important than those forty canvases.

I mean there are aspects of The West Wind, *that great icon, that are clearly unresolved. So I don't think he was . . . right there . . . in terms of his canvases. But his oil sketches, he was entirely comfortable with them as a vehicle. There was a strong sense of development in them, every time he went out. I think people sense that when they confront them. I think people also sense that these were very direct responses to a moment, to a place, a time. And so there is a sense of actuality, a sense of being there that is magical . . .*

Important though they were, he often gave them away or sold them for a few dollars. If he liked a motif in one, he would take it into the studio and develop a canvas from it; he was responding to that tradition. It is possible that he himself did not recognize the power of those birch panels.

There are emotionally powerful photographs of him from those days in the Park, not painting but paddling or fishing or showing off his catch. Nearing forty his always good-looking face had become intensely handsome. There is a serenity in the strong eyes when they gaze at you, and in the comfortable angles of the body as he stands on the river bank contemplating something we cannot see. The strong forelock is still hanging down like a slash over the right side of the forehead. He is usually clean-shaven, sometime smoking a pipe.

He was perfectly at home in the canoe. The theory was circulated later that he had fallen out of his canoe while standing up to haul in a fish, which got him all tangled up in the copper fishing line. It is an absurd idea, as any paddler knows who has half Tom Thomson's skill and experience. Perhaps somebody was trying to justify the "Death by Drowning" verdict from the Coroner, but it rings false. Thomson was in his canoe for months at a time. When he was paddling, it almost looked as if the small craft were an extension of his tall, capable frame.

In Europe and America, in the years leading up to the Great War, there had been a yeasty ferment of painterly innovation. Tom Thomson was only fleetingly interested. The cubists, the post-impressionists, and the non-objectivists, were redefining the art world, it seemed, almost every year. Tom was redefining the world inside his head and out there in the wilderness. While he may have lost an opportunity to grow and prosper artistically from the stimulus of these European and American movements, critics now say that it was that very freedom from any of the demands of artistic fashion that allowed him to develop the style that now speaks to most Canadians as if it were *the* Canadian style.

Joan Murray said, "He seemed to see around the edges of the land . . . the land kind of extends beyond the painting."

When war broke out in the summer of 1914 Tom tried again to enlist and again was refused. A.Y. Jackson and Fred Varley would go overseas as War Artists; Tom would head back up to the Park with his knapsack, fishing rod and paint kit. The tree that served as the model for *Jack Pine* is pointed out today as an almost bare-branched wreck, still there on the shores of Canoe Lake. Whether or not it is the actual tree, visitors still come to stare at it. The spirit of Tom Thomson is palpable on that lake. There is a cairn to his memory at the north end, on a point thrusting out into the water, with an inscription by his friend Jim MacDonald:

He lived humbly but passionately with the wild and it revealed itself to him. It sent him out from the woods only to show these revelations through his art, and it took him to itself at last.

This writer met a professional guide on Canoe Lake in the summer of 1949 who quite seriously told about portaging into the Oxtongue River, just south of Canoe Lake, from a day's fishing in Drummer Lake, two or three miles west of the river. He said he was carrying his canoe at night with a storm lantern hanging from a thwart to light his way. He saw a man carrying a grey canoe coming towards him on his way into Drummer, and stepped aside to let the man pass. At that moment, Hopkins swore, the man and the grey canoe vanished. "I know who it was," Hoppy Hopkins said. Somewhat spooked by that story, a few weeks later, when I was paddling up the lake at five o'clock in the morning, I was terrified for a moment to see out of the corner of my eye a man paddling beside me, matching me stroke for stroke, in absolute silence. For a moment *I knew who it was, too.* But then I realized it was my moonshadow on the wall of fog rolling out of the bay that bisects Camp Ahmek, where I was working at the time. I used that story to open my novel *Ahmek,* in which Tom Thomson plays a major role. Almost everyone I ever met on Canoe Lake had some kind of story about Tom Thomson. Mark Robinson, who had been the Park's Chief Ranger when Tom was painting there, almost ninety when I knew him, loved to tell the boys at Ahmek about the time Tom asked him where he could find "a buncha birches, shaped just so," that he wanted to paint and did not want to invent. The boys sniggered a bit about Old Mark and his Buncha Birches, but they were excited all the same to have met a man who actually knew Tom Thomson.

Much of the power of that *presence* on Canoe Lake flows from the belief that Tom Thomson was murdered, and the mystery attached to that murder since he was so liked and admired. There was talk about a ferocious argument the night before he vanished, an argument about the war with a German named Martin Bletcher. There was talk about a fight with another man, Shannon Fraser, over money, or perhaps over a woman.

Here are the bare bones of the story. He had been seeing a woman named Winnifred Trainor whose family had a nearby cottage. Winnifred is said to have said there was a reason they should get married, and Joan Murray, among others, has speculated that Winnifred may have been pregnant. At about this time, on July 8, 1917, Tom went off alone on a fishing trip. The next day Martin Bletcher told neighbours that he had seen an overturned canoe on the lake, and when found two days later it was identified as the Thomson canoe. It was a week before they found the body, the feet tangled in fishing line, the head badly bruised.

Joan Murray tells another story about Thomson's last night, which he had spent at a hotel called Mowat Lodge.

We may imagine that Thomson had a few drinks. And his friends did. And somehow he approached one of the friends he'd lent money to. . . . And he must have appeared threatening to this man because apparently this man punched him and Thomson fell backwards and hit his head on the grate.

The Coroner's report said later that he had a four-inch bruise on his right temple. So that man panicked. His name was Shannon Fraser. He was the postmaster of Algonquin Park and he was the owner of the Mowat Lodge, which was the hotel where Thomson stayed during inclement weather. And that man panicked and asked his wife to help him. Her name was Annie. They packed the canoe apparently with Thomson's body. They tied fishing line around his wrists and feet, and put him overboard in Canoe Lake. And that is Annie's story. She told a girlfriend named Daphne Crombie. And Annie told this story a second time on her death-bed, made a death-bed confession to a friend.

Our documentary crew found and filmed the cross that marks where Tom Thomson was buried in the small cemetery on the west side of Canoe Lake. After a few months the family had the coffin disinterred and shipped home. There was a rumour that the coffin contained stones, not a body. Dennis Reid shares the puzzlement that every student of the Thomson story feels.

In fact what happened, it is just all speculation. Other than the fact that he certainly seems to have died suddenly and at the hands of another. The family had the body disinterred from the grave at Algonquin Park in which it was first placed, and brought back to . . . Leith and buried there. A curious Justice of the Peace, Judge Little, took it upon himself to probe the grave at Algonquin Park, and found remains in the grave still. Because of his connections he was able to take them to the forensic clinic in Toronto here and they were examined and it was determined that the head was probably a Cree.

That skull, as shown in the documentary, also appears to have a fracture in the temple. What had killed this native Canadian, if indeed he was a Cree? And how did he end up in Tom Thomson's grave? The family have refused to have the body exhumed from the family plot for forensic tests. The mystery may never be resolved.

And the mystery about the late surfacing of the brilliant and innovative painter, whose artist friends found suddenly that instead of teaching him they were learning from him? It is not an unheard-of change of direction. Every great artist has been an apprentice who almost always outshone his or her teachers. The great Artemisia

Gentileschi, heroine of *The Obstacle Course,* Germaine Greer's pioneering work on women painters, was a student of her very successful portrait-painting father. By the time she was a young adult all of Rome was seeking her out for portraits, instead of commissioning the father who had taught her. Rembrandt had his teachers and exemplars, and so did De Kooning and Lucian Freud. What is different in the case of Tom Thomson is that the great ability took so long to surface — perhaps it was just hiding there, waiting for the teachers he should have had twenty-five years earlier. There were about five hundred of the little birch panel sketches when he died, but only forty canvases. While a canvas sold in 1914 for $500, you would be lucky to get it today for a million dollars. The sketches, on the rare occasion when one is sold, are valued at well over $100,000.

J.E.H. MacDonald wrote once that "Tom was never very proud of his painting, but he was very cocky about his fishing." But, "Without Tom the North Country seems a desolation of brush and rock." A.Y. Jackson wrote "My debt to him is almost that of a new world."

That seems to be what most feel who study this man's legacy, that he helped us to see our land with new eyes. He brought to Canadians a vision of our own skies and lakes, our rocks and trees, a vision that had little to do with the heritage of another culture. It was not the European visitor, sophisticated and wise in the ways of paint on canvas. It was not the powerful vision of the West Coast native sculptors with their magical merging of the animal and the human, or of the Eastern woodland native painters with their brilliant mythic panels. It was the view of the newcomers to Canada, the children of immigrants still feeling a bit fresh and amazed at the vastness and still fascinated with the pure unmediated *surfaces* of a land that their First Nations' predecessors had long since transformed into a vision that goes far below the surface into deep spiritual meanings.

◆ ◆ ◆

The Mystery of Tom Thomson was written and directed by Daniel Zuckerbrot.

VOLUME II

Patrick Watson

PART ONE

MONA PARSONS
The Role of a Lifetime

Imagine a *Heritage Minute* produced from the following script.[1] While the Mona Parsons story seems too close to a romantic movie script to be anything more than a highly contrived version of what really happened, it is in fact, except for a great deal of compression as required by the format, very close to the true story of a truly extraordinary Nova Scotian woman.

• • •

MONA PARSONS
A Heritage Minute

(1) EXT. DUTCH COUNTRYSIDE. DAY. The aftermath of war. In the distance, puffs of smoke and the rumble of gunfire. Two fighter aircraft scream overhead. Jeeps and walking soldiers proceed away from the camera. Coming towards us, a small platoon of sad, exhausted German prisoners is being herded along the road by Canadian soldiers. SUPER: *THE DUTCH/GERMAN BORDER, 1945*

MONA, an emaciated, slightly dazed forty-five-year-old woman, is being escorted by a young Canadian SERGEANT, towards the camera, as three or four OFFICERS come into frame from the opposite direction.

MONA
I'm telling you it IS true! I've been in a Nazi prison camp for four years. Look at me! I'm half starved! I . . .

---

1. This is an actual script that, as of October 2001, was in the queue for production in the *HISTOR!CA* heritage project. Continuing the work begun in 1988 by Charles Bronfman's CRB Foundation, the *Heritage Minutes* are a series of (as of this date) almost seventy "micro-movies": dramatic slightly fictionalized films of sixty seconds' duration that are seen on more than a thousand movie screens across Canada when first released, and then given as gifts to every television broadcaster and cable service in Canada.

Clearly seen in the foreground as the OFFICERS meet MONA and the SERGEANT is an officer's shoulder patch or other insignia: The Nova Scotia Highlanders.

> LIEUTENANT
> *What's going on here, Sergeant?*

> SERGEANT (cont.)
> *Claims she's a Canadian, sir.*

> SERGEANT (cont.)
> (sotto voce) *I think she's a German spy, sir.*

> LIEUTENANT
> *What's your name, lady?*

> MONA
> *Mona Parsons, sir.*

FOSTER, an older officer, with general's shoulder markings, pushes forward.

> FOSTER
> *Mona Parsons!! From Wolfville? Mona! It's me! Harry Foster.*
> *My God, what's happened to you?*

> MONA
> (still dazed)
> *Well . . . you see . . . I . . .*

> DISSOLVE TO

(2) INT. NAZI COURT MARTIAL. HOLLAND, 1941. DAY. A Nazi flag, a mix of uniformed and civilian officials. MONA in the dock. The dialogue is in German, with subtitles. SUPER: *AMSTERDAM, 1941*

The judge is a uniformed officer, monocled, dignified, a scar on his cheek.

JUDGE
(in German)
. . . and you are convicted of hiding enemy airmen in your
Amsterdam home, and aiding their escape to Britain. The penalty
for treason is death by firing squad.

MONA
(under her breath)
Firing squad!

JUDGE, PROSECUTOR, UNIFORMED GUARDS and others watch her with cool cynicism; they expect her to break down. Instead, after a cool beat, she bows courteously to the court, speaks with real dignity.

MONA
Meine Herren: Guten Morgen.

The JUDGE, others, are surprised, impressed.

(3) EXT. AMSTERDAM STREET. DAY. Two soldiers escort MONA to a vehicle. The JUDGE is standing near it in a leather trench coat, attended by two junior OFFICERS. He bows courteously as she is brought to the vehicle.

JUDGE
(in German)
Dear Lady: you have great courage. I recommend you appeal the
sentence. You may use my name.

They lock eyes.

(4) INT. A WOLFVILLE LIVING ROOM. DAY. As the camera gently prospects the room, plants, piano, many photos of Mona, at several ages, including at the piano, we hear, with the accompaniment of appropriate music:

NARRATOR
Mona Parsons and her Dutch husband had saved dozens of

downed Allied airmen. Escaping from a German prison in 1945,
she walked several hundred kilometres across Germany to
Holland. Widowed, she came home to Wolfville, married again,
and died in 1976.

During this narration we DISSOLVE TO

(5) EXT. WOLFVILLE CEMETERY. DAY. Mona Parsons' actual tomb-
stone. The inscription reads simply: Mona Louise Parsons, 1901–1976,
Wife of Major General Harry Foster CBE DSO.

END

♦ ♦ ♦

The story came to this writer's attention almost by accident. A
short article about Mona had appeared in *The Beaver*, a small historical
monthly published by The Bay, in the October/November edition of
1998. I had barely skimmed that edition, being preoccupied with a documentary in production at the time, and had left it in the out-
basket. Caroline Bamford, my wife, business partner, and the in-house
editor at our small concern, put the magazine back on my desk a few
days later with an imperious note scrawled on it in black marker-pen:

"Heritage Minute in Here: Page 16!"

I re-read the piece.
The author, actress Andria Hill, was a graduate student at Acadia
University, in Wolfville, Nova Scotia. She was doing research for a
Master's thesis on the history of the Acadia Ladies' Seminary in
Wolfville, an institution that had, early in the century, a very active the-
atre program. She came across a brief note saying that one of the 1920
graduates of that program had been found safe in Holland at the end
of World War II after spending nearly four years in Nazi prisons.
Andria Hill set off on a quest.
Her research began in Middleton, Nova Scotia, in the heart of the
Annapolis Valley, where Mona Louise Parsons was born at 370 Main

Street, on February 17, 1901. Her father Norval was the eponymous head of Parsons and Elliott Home Furnishings on Commercial Street, just around the corner from the family home. Mona was the youngest of Norval and his wife Mary Parsons' three children, with older brothers Ross and Quinn. The business was prosperous, as was the town of Middleton, in the years leading up to the Great War. Norval was a patriot as well as a successful merchant. He wore the uniform of an officer in the local militia, and his photos show a confident, genial man with a sense of position and of the obligations of that position. This morality he seems to have communicated to his adored youngest child, Mona.

A class photograph at the new MacDonald Consolidated school, taken in 1910, shows an already graceful, womanly Mona, glancing at the camera with what might have been a shy look, but knowing what we know about her as she matured may well have been an early example of her skill as an actress.

The turn of the year, from 1910 to 1911, was expected by the Parsons family to be the opening of another decade of prosperity. But disaster struck a month after Christmas. Downtown Middleton — like many Nova Scotia towns built almost entirely of wood — caught fire on January 26. Parsons Elliott Home Furnishings was completely destroyed, along with most of the downtown area, and photographs of the smouldering town a day later show it almost flattened.

Norval Parsons was not only a successful merchant but also a prudent one, and the insurance on the furniture business allowed him to move the family sixty kilometres up the tracks to Wolfville, where he decided to become a stockbroker, having done pretty well in the market during his home furnishing days. Wolfville was already a lively university town. There was some old money. The colonial sense of class and position was still alive and well in those pre-war days, and we have to suppose that Lieutenant Colonel Norval Parsons did not find that aspect of the community's social life difficult to live with.

Norval and his sons would go off to war in 1914, and survive it (Norval coming home with the crown and pip of a lieutenant colonel on his epaulettes), and while they were away the little girl transformed into a tall, lithe, elegant young woman with a modestly theatrical manner and a bewitchingly sultry voice. After graduation, she studied voice in Boston, and then taught drama in Arkansas between visits home. By 1929, she knew she wanted a career on stage and that she should go where the theatre was the centre of the universe instead of a casual amusement for the better families of a small provincial town. When Mona announced her intention of going to New York to try her luck on the stage there, her mother Mary was not pleased. Mona and Mary had spent the war closely together while the men were away in the army, and Mary found the prospect of losing her great companion difficult to contemplate. But Norval was enchanted: his daughter on the stage? In New York! He quietly let Mona know that it was all right with him. Anything that was all right with Norval, it seems, was all right with Mona too. So off she went.

New York in the 1920s presents a series of old black-and-white newsreel and movie images that keep turning up in historical documentaries and studies of the social evolution of the United States, almost like icons. It was a euphoric time for a while after the horrors of The War To End All Wars had died down, and the world was at peace and would always be at peace for the rest of time, as everyone knew. The prosperity that had boomed with America's wartime production of armaments kept on booming. In 1920 the "manufacturing, sale, or transportation" of alcoholic beverages had been made illegal by the Eighteenth Amendment to the Constitution. This ill-conceived and destructive legislation, supported by the *Volstead Act*, which added a powerful enforcement mechanism and was intended to strike the fear of the law into drinkers and merchants of drink, in fact so dramatically produced the opposite of what its promoters had intended that a best-selling novel a few years later was based entirely — and quite credibly — on the premise that the anti-alcohol movement had been started and funded by the distillers.

What happened was that flouting the law by drinking became a kind of national sport. Respect for the law and its officers was a laughing matter. Thousands of people died from drinking cheap bootleg liquor. Distillers in Canada and the United States became rich while no alcohol-based tax revenue flowed into the national coffers. For hundreds of thousands of Americans organized crime became glamorous and flourished as never before.

New York was peppered with illicit drinking spots called speakeasies. Disdain for the law was reflected in widespread public dismissal of proprieties of all kinds. Dress became flamboyant. Sexual adventuring was open and glamorized. The automobile, still in its youth and still competing with horses (and their droppings) in the streets of all North American cities, grew exponentially as a favourite location for sexual adventure and a favoured mechanism for showing off flamboyant clothes and wild behaviour. This was the New York where Mona Parsons came to make her mark on the stage.

It did not go well — at least, not in the way she had expected. Instead of stardom in the latest Noel Coward or Sherwood Anderson play on Broadway, she auditioned for a bread-and-butter job as a chorus girl in the Ziegfeld Follies. This was a series of stage reviews produced by the flamboyant Florenz Ziegfeld in imitation of Paris's famous *Folies Bergères*. They were splashy, naughty, expensive, popular: a stage reflection of the genially outrageous tone of the age. The chorus-line dancers were trained to a mechanical perfection, and cast for their legs and their faces almost as much as for their dancing abilities. It is probable that many of the girls dancing alongside Mona Louise Parsons thought they had reached some kind of professional pinnacle to be doing the high kick in the Follies, but not Mona. She liked the glamour and the attention, all right; there was no shortage of lively dates and brilliant parties. The pay was adequate. But the artistic rewards were not what she had come to New York to find.

Remember, this is a woman in her late twenties to whom the universe has been very good. She carries herself with a combination of regality, confidence, and grace that bring people to a dead stop just to watch her pass. When her eyes light on yours as she sweeps the room, you hope that she really sees what a fine and desirable person you are; you can't help a surge of something like desire. There is a combination of appraisal, delight, and quizzicality in that glance from which you cannot look away.

There are people who love the camera and people whom the camera loves: Mona Parsons was both. Had she grown up in the early days of television she would have set new benchmarks, perhaps as an actor, but more likely as a program host. We know from the thousands of photos and the few moments of home movie footage that you could not take your eyes off her, and from what her friends said and wrote we know that her voice held you in thrall.

But New York is New York: the best and the brightest in the world of theatre still come there for the main chance, and many end up working in drug stores or offices — or head for home. The competition is so vast and the decisions of casting directors and producers so whimsical and ultimately private that there simply is no guarantee that rockets will ignite as designed. Mona Parsons kept on pounding the streets auditioning for serious roles and for a while she kept on hoping. But what happened next suggests that the New York exhilaration had exhausted itself. While she seems to have fallen in love with Manhattan like so many who come to try it out and end up staying forever, after a while that dream of triumph on the stage began to seem more like a fantasy than a strategy.

It is probably not necessary to say that up to this point there is nothing in the Mona Parsons story that in any conceivable way points to her finding herself in the dock in a Nazi court in Amsterdam, accused of the capital crime of treason, just a little more than ten years down the road. What did happen next was a call from home: Mary Parsons had been felled by a stroke. She was calling for Mona. She needed constant care. Mona gave her notice to the Ziegfeld people, gathered her stuff together, said good-bye to her pals, and took the train for Canada. It was just a few days before her twenty-ninth birthday, February 17. A day after that birthday Mary Parsons had a second stroke and died.

It is at this point that Mona Parsons makes one of the relatively few conventional decisions of these first few decades of her life. It seems that the sudden death of her mother led her to stand back and reconsider the romantic role of the New York star of stage (and screen?), and to conclude that it was either less glamorous or less possible than she had hoped. Probably influenced by her father's practical business and career outlook, in the midst of an economic depression that left millions starving and walking the streets, she knew that she had better find something to do that was solid, predictable, useful, not likely to be made less viable by the Depression. She chose something that — at a time when careers were very limited for independent-minded women — was seen as normal: nursing.

We next find her in New Jersey, at the Jersey City Medical Center. When she finished training there she made use of family contacts and landed a job with a Nova-Scotian expatriate, Dr. Ross Faulkner, who had a fashionable clinic in Manhattan, on Park Avenue. So there she was, professionally established in a city she adored, well placed to find a husband should she choose to do that, among the medical professionals or the fashionable clientele of Dr. Faulkner's clinic. And if it had not been for a phone call from her brother Ross, it seems likely that she would have done exactly that.

Ross had come to know a wealthy Dutchman named Willem Leonhardt, who was travelling in North America to develop outlets for his family's plumbing fixture business. He was coming to New York and needed someone who knew the town well, and was socially gifted, to show him around. At first, when she learned that Willem was divorced from a woman who had born a son he had not fathered, Mona hesitated to respond to the millionaire's playful charm and his obvious infatuation with the willowy, throaty-voiced, dark-eyed beauty from Nova Scotia. But the relationship blossomed pretty rapidly, all the same. In the summer of 1937 the two of them went to Wolfville to visit Norval (who had remarried), and then got on a liner bound for Holland. She had agreed to marry him.

Mona was a hit in Holland. Willem Leonhardt's nephew Kristoph told Andria Hill when the author arrived in Amsterdam to track down that part of Mona's story that when he first met the compellingly beautiful Mona he said to himself, "My God! My uncle is marrying an American film star!"

Willem was the centre of a lively social circle. Mona had to start from scratch learning Nederlands, not the easiest of the Germanic languages, but despite that handicap she played her new hostess role like a trooper, and soon won over the initially suspicious Leonhardt parents (after all, their son was a millionaire, so of course they would be suspicious). And — ironically as it would turn out — she also won over Willem's close friend the horse breeder Piet Houtapell and his very young wife Pam.

The documentary film of Mona's story is rich with photographs of that period, most in black and white but some in a faded colour that still seems very immediate and present almost sixty-five years later. There are photos of the family gatherings, of the smiling faces of Piet and Pam Houtapell, with their arms around Mona and Willem, of the wedding with its luxurious outdoor reception, Mona reigning queen-like and confident over the legions of the Amsterdam upper crust who came to celebrate Willem's latest. Mona's brother Ross is in those pictures too, with his wife Mary. The champagne bottles and the wedding cake and the mountains of food and the extravagant dresses, the monocles, the top hats, the Amsterdam *savoir-faire*, the nonchalance, the luxury, all recorded by the omnipresent camera.

As was much of the honeymoon that followed. Six months of it, in the swellest resort spots of Europe. Money was not a problem for Willem Leonhardt. They drove fast cars, lounged on yachts and danced in glamorous ballrooms. If they were conscious of the rumblings from Germany, it did not show. When they got back to Holland early in 1938 they found a piece of land at Laren about half an hour from downtown Amsterdam, and built a house there, and called it *Ingleside*. They hired staff, and planted hedges and gardens which are still there and were photographed by Andria Hill when she went to see *Ingleside* for her book on Mona.

Willem was away in Amsterdam a lot, commuting in a series of expensive cars. Soon *Ingleside* and its glamorous couple were the talk of the town. Willem had a pale oak August Förster grand piano specially built for her. She would play classical favourites for her guests and preside over those glittering evenings as if she were a stage queen, in gorgeous costume and careful makeup. It was a role, and by God she was going to play it really well.

Before long, she would be caught up in the role that would bring her the biggest challenge of her acting career. The Second World War was moving in on them.

The Germans crossed into Holland in the small hours of the morning, and in five days, despite a brave but ill-prepared resistance by the tiny army of Holland, it was all over. Some of the survivors will tell you now that the defences had been concentrated on the coast for so long, because of the historic rivalry and difficulties with England, that they were not ready for invasion from the East. As unlikely as that seems (since the war had been raging for eight months when the Germans crossed the border) wherever the Dutch had concentrated their defences there would be, by May 10, 1940, no way for that small country to stop the *Blitzkrieg*.[2]

The historian Hans DeVries who helped guide us through the Holland part of the Mona Parsons story says that for many people life went on much as it had, at least for the first few months of the German occupation. "The Germans sort of pussy-footed their way in," De Vries said, describing their early attempts to relax and even make friends with their new Dutch "citizens." But by late 1941 the colour of that occupation had changed. Rigid rationing had been introduced, there was a nine o'clock curfew. A resistance movement had been organized. Arrests were frequent, and so were executions. People disappeared. The pretence of normalcy was gone.

Now as the war gathered momentum the traffic of warplanes across the English Channel, in both directions, became heavier week by week. In 1941 the Battle of Britain began with the nightly pounding of London and other industrial targets, the flattening of the city of Coventry, the brilliant defence by teenage pilots in Spitfires and Hurricanes that would lead Winston Churchill to say that "never in the field of human conflict was so much owed by so many to so few." But it was not just Britain that felt the rain of bombs. She was vigorously retaliating against Germany, and morning after morning, as the exhausted and often wounded bomber crews returned over Holland from their raids deep into German territory, pilots sometimes decided that they were out of luck, or fuel, or altitude, and decided to bail out

2. *Blitzkrieg* literally means "lightning war."

over land rather than over the dark seas where they would never be found alive. Dutch citizens began to take them in.

This was perfect for the brilliant, wealthy socialite proprietors of *Ingleside*. They built a secret room up under the eaves. Downed Allied pilots and crews, protected by the farmers who found them hiding by the dikes or windmills, could be brought to the Leonhardt house for their few nights of hiding before transport could be arranged to Leiden, on the coast, and thence by fishing boat to waiting British submarines. This was a great adventure for Mona and Willem, a cool adventure, a feeling of invulnerability in face of the risk of death, of pulling it off under the noses of the hated enemy, of Nothing Can Happen To Us, we're the Leonhardts. There was a kind of cell of conspirators, trusted old friends mostly, deeply pleased with themselves to be — in the midst of the seeming impotence of an occupied people — to be actually *doing something*.

However, one of the trusted friends at the Leiden end of the underground railroad was in fact a Nazi informer. The *Ingleside* safe house had been used only four times before the Leiden cell was infected. In September 1941, Willem and Mona gave shelter to two Allied airmen, Richard Pape and William Moir, for an unprecedented six days — unable to move them because of the increasingly tight net of Nazi intelligence. A couple of days later, when Pape and Moir arrived at Leiden, the Nazis moved. Now *Ingleside* was on their map. An architect named Dirk Brouwer was arrested and shot. He had brought fliers to *Ingleside*. Mona and Willem thought that if they fled it would be evidence of guilt, but if they stayed they would be sitting victims.

Willem was well known as a fishing enthusiast; so, assuming that only the male members of the cell would be of interest to the Germans, they decided that Mona would continue to entertain at *Ingleside*, as usual, and just say — if they came after him — that Willem was on a fishing trip, she didn't know when he would be back. When two Gestapo agents appeared at her door she invited them in and offered them drinks.[3] They were not fooled. Before long she was in Weteringschane Prison in Amsterdam, awaiting trial.

3. *Gestapo*: a contraction of *Geheimestaatspolizei* meaning "state secret police."

In a way, you already know the rest. But it is a story that keeps unfolding its amazing chapters. The Gestapo were holding Mona as bait to help catch Willem. It took three months. Then they caught him; December 21, 1941. On December 22 Mona's cell door opened, and she was told to dress; she was going to trial.

It would be a military court. Military courts did not convict women. But they convicted Mona. The trial was in a ballroom where Mona had often danced the night away, at the Carlton Hotel, in Amsterdam. Mona's comprehension of German was not very good, but she did understand the phrases *Todestraffe*, and *Exekutionskommando*, "death sentence," and "firing squad." She blanched but stayed erect. She offered a cool, dignified bow to the court. She said, in the best German she could muster, *"Meine Herren: Guten Morgen,"* and walked with dignity between her escorts towards the waiting van.

The judge must have been a man of character. He had clearly been struck by her courage and dignity. He crossed the court and stopped the escorts. He complimented her, and recommended that she appeal, and said he would forward the appeal to the highest-ranking officer in Holland, with a recommendation of clemency.

The first of the many prisons Mona would live in for the next few years was at Krefeld, in the German Rhineland. She was put to knitting socks for soldiers, and concealed a painful blister knot in each sole. They found her out. Eventually she was moved to a prison at Vechta, in Northern Germany south of Bremen, and thrust into solitary confinement. But after a while she was put back to work again, this time in the kitchen, as a cleaner, and here is where the next part of the story begins.

A young Dutch Baroness was also in a solitary cell in the Vechta prison, having shown her German captors that she was an incorrigible escape artist. Somehow the two women got to know each other, and Mona began to smuggle a few potatoes, in her apron pocket, to the hungry twenty-two-year-old aristocrat, the Baroness Wendelien van Boetzelaer. Now that she had an ally, the Baroness began to devise another escape plan. Interviewed in Amsterdam for our television program, she told us that not only were they very hungry in Vechta, but that there was no heat on that top floor where the solitary cells were, and that, oddly, the prison governess took sufficient pity on the two women to respond to their pleas for some warm clothes to help them survive the winter of 1944. This, Wendelien pointed out to Mona, would give them cover for their prison drabs when the opportunity came for them to slip away. She was sure, she said, that such an opportunity would come. When it did it was spectacular and dramatic.

To help them keep up their morale, Wendelien told us, "[w]e exchanged recipes, which was a great thing in the camps because everybody was so hungry. And Mona was fond of delicious recipes. Also she had a great repertoire of songs . . . military songs, happy songs, naughty songs, whatever." Before long there was an opportunity that would shut the songs down, but get them out of Vechta.

Vechta had an airfield and rail yards. The two prisons, one for women and one for men, flanked the runway. The Allies, in the early months of 1945, were systematically destroying airfields and rail facilities all over Germany, and one day they hit Vechta. The first bomb missed the runway and blew the men's prison to fragments, killing hundreds of inmates. Wendelien still does not understand why she had been allowed to come down to the ground floor that day, but she was there and watched with horror as the other prison building burst into flames and began to collapse. Suddenly the head of the women's prison ordered her charges out into the yard, under guard, in case her building was going to be a target for the Allied bombs as well.

"All these German women threw themselves on the floor shouting 'Ich will nicht sterben!' (I don't want to die!)," Wendelien recounts, at seventy-nine, still crinkling with what looks exactly like mischievous delight at the memory. "So Mona and I . . . we took each other by the hand and we [just walked] out. No one even looked at us. All these guards were [distracted] by the bombs . . . and we just ran along the airfield. So. On and on we ran."

Vechta is some 160 kilometres from the Dutch border. So "on and on" would be the condition of life for the forty-four-year-old Canadian and the twenty-two-year-old Dutch girl for quite a few days. Eighteen kilometres the first day. They had nothing to eat. They drank water out of ditches. They shivered in the cold, even under their extra clothes. As night came down they came to a farm where the barn was well separated from the house. There were lights in the house but the barn was dark. Exhausted, they took the chance, slipped into the dark old building, found some straw, bundled themselves up under it, and slept.

In the morning they were starving, and decided to take the chance. They walked boldly up to the farmhouse.

"Of course Mona didn't speak . . . German,"Wendelien told us. *And we were supposed to be Germans. We were not supposed to be an English (sic) woman and a Dutch woman evading from prison. So my German happened to be quite good, but Mona absolutely had to keep her mouth shut. So we had to pretend that she was a little . . . ga ga. A little, you know, addled. Which she was very good at! Because she was an actress. She had trained as an actress. She was fantastic. They were sorry for that condition, they were sorry for me! And she played that up so naturally that even I thought she was not quite well in the head!*

It took them two weeks. They did farm chores in exchange for food. As they came closer to the Dutch border they began to find people they felt they could trust. At a village near the border with Holland they took the risk of confiding in the mayor, who gave them false papers. And from then on, billeted in different homes, they did not see each other again until they met for dinner — at *Ingleside* — a year after the war.

The first troops across the border in the sector that Mona and Wendelien had found themselves in were Poles. Right behind the Poles were the Canadians. Battalion commanders were very careful about German civilians trying to cross the border. They had been warned that the Germans might use women as decoys or subversives, plant booby-trap bombs on them or give them weapons they could use to kill senior officers they got close to. So when Mona was picked up walking out of Germany, despite her fluent English and exhausted appearance, they were not going to take any chances. The first encounter was not precisely the way we depict it in the *Heritage Minute* script; that is dramatic licence. But the encounter with the North Novies in a later interrogation was every bit as dramatic in its essence.

The Nova Scotia Highlanders are headquartered in Amherst and have been since the unit was formed to fight in the Great War, in 1914. Captain Robbins Elliott, a Highlanders veteran, was a young logistics officer at the time, and knew a young soldier who was the third or fourth to question her.

"And she said, 'I am a Canadian.' And he said, 'If you are a Canadian where are you from?' And she said, 'My name is Mona Parsons and I come from a little tiny village in Nova Scotia called Wolfville.' And apparently he nearly dropped the box he was holding. He said, 'Dear God! My name is Clarence Leonard. I'm from Halifax, and you've just encountered the North Nova Scotia Highlanders!'"

The unit surgeon was Kelly MacLean. Mona had acted on the Acadia stage with him. And there were two other friends from her Acadia days: Captains Vincent White and Ralph Shaw. She also met an old childhood chum, Harry Foster, now a major general. Mona's amazing story got her a ride home to *Ingleside*, and a good long rest among friends.

Young Captain Robbins Elliott, whom she had met with the North Novies, came and visited her at *Ingleside*. So did Lie Van Oldenburg, a neighbour who had managed to grab some of her possessions when she was arrested, and keep them out of the hands of the Germans who had taken over her house for an officers' billet, and left schnapps glass stains all over the oak surface of the beautiful August Förster, which was, miraculously, still there and still playable. There was no sign of Willem.

In fact he was alive but not well. The three years of starvation and brutal prison conditions had worsened an inherited kidney disease, and when American forces liberated his concentration camp they put him into hospital for ten weeks, during which time he was able to get word to Mona. Relieved that he would be coming home after all, Mona sought the healing touch of plants and flowers, and began to restore her gardens. When Willem did get home, finally, he sold his part of the family business to his brother, and — between bouts of hospitalization and immobility — he and Mona travelled, at first in Europe, and then to Canada. Mona's brother Ross organized a Nova Scotia–style fishing trip for Willem, and Mona tried to persuade him to stay in Canada. But as his body and spirit deteriorated, he wanted to be home and with doctors and surroundings he knew and trusted.

Now Mona who had always suffered from lung problems and bronchitis began to have more frequent and more serious bouts of illness. Willem sent her to the Birchel Benner Clinic in Switzerland, and while she was resting there in 1953 she got the news that he was permanently bedridden. When she got home to *Ingleside*, she was surprised to find that Piet Houtapell's young wife Pam had taken over as the principal caregiver. This made Mona a little uneasy, and for good reason. When Willem died in April 1956, she discovered that he had left one-quarter of his estate to Pam, and that they had been carrying on a secret affair for years.

Then, in the midst of that devastating news, the estranged son from Willem's first marriage, a man who was not even Willem's natural son, launched legal action to claim three-quarters of the remaining estate. The legal battle continued until 1961. By that time there was little left of the estate, and Mona had lost. That struggle finished Holland for Mona, for all time. She took what was left, including her beloved August Förster piano, and headed back to Canada.

When she had first come back to Nova Scotia in 1957, she stayed in Halifax's elegant Lord Nelson Hotel, and then moved to a flat at 56 Inglis Street. Norval was dead; her two brothers Ross and Gwynne, and her stepmother Alma, were the only family left. One day she ran into her old chum, Major General Harry Foster, retired, and as they chatted about that extraordinary encounter on the Dutch/German border more than a decade before, a sense of the affection that grows out of shared adventure and adversity grew up between them, and in 1959 they were married. It was a good, comfortable marriage. They lived for a while in the Chester Basin in a tranquil house at Lobster Point. Friends came to visit, and life was good for a while, until Harry was diagnosed with a cancer, and died just five years after their wedding. Now Mona said it was time to go home to Wolfville.

The August Förster piano is still there, you can go and see it if you make friends with its new owner. Mona kept it in Wolfville for a few years, and invited young people to come and play it. She took a course or two at the university, went to the theatre, developed a reputation for amiable eccentricity, managed to cope with the encroachments of old age, and, oddly, did not say much about her wartime adventures. After a while, to pay for the extra health care she needed, she began to sell her possessions, including the piano with its schnapps-stained lid, and to give away her silverware to friends. She refused to have it refinished; it had memories. She let her friends know about the family plot at the Willowbank Cemetery, just off Ridge Road in Wolfville, and wrote to her old comrade Wendelien that "at least when it's my turn to go they won't have to cart me from anywhere."

And among her things, when she died in November of 1976, they discovered two certificates of commendation for her contribution to the Allied War Effort. One is signed by British Air Chief Marshall Lord Arthur Tedder. The second bears the signature of the Supreme Commander of the Allied Forces in Europe, and later President of the United States, Dwight D. Eisenhower. Her photograph is on the wall of Branch 74, of the Royal Canadian Legion in Wolfville, just behind the dyke that keeps Wolfville from being flooded by the giant tides of the Bay of Fundy. If you get invited to the Legion on one of the great anniversaries, D-Day, say (the invasion of Normandy), or VE-Day (the end of the war in Europe), you'll probably be with the grizzled old veterans there when they stand and raise their glasses to that photograph, and call out a toast "To Mona Parsons, a brave and beautiful lady."

But if you stroll over to Willowbank, to the Parsons family plot, you will not find on the fine big stone that marks her place anything that even hints at the courage and fortitude and wartime experience of this valiant and luminous woman. The marker says simply:

MONA LOUISE PARSONS
1901–1976

WIFE OF MAJOR GENERAL HARRY FOSTER
CBE DSO

◆ ◆ ◆

The original documentary was produced and directed by F. Whitman Trecartin.

PART TWO

JOSHUA SLOCUM
A New World Columbus

The great challenge to the biographer, whether on film or video or in print, is first of all to find an imaginative way into not only the narrative line of his subject's life, the list of events and people and places, but also into that life's texture, its buzz, its little manners and asides and apparently trivial details. A writer trying to put together a meaningful account of the life of someone who has been dead for a hundred years should read not only whatever documents have survived, and pore over photographs, he should also walk the streets and touch, if he can, the physical objects that were touched by his subject: the books, clothes, furniture, the cups, and plates. To be true to the subject, if that subject climbed a mountain, the biographer should climb it too. If it is a painter we are dealing with, the biographer should at least know the smell and texture of wet paint, and the feel of its going onto canvas; if a magician, the writer who takes the trouble to find out what it is like to perform some sleight of hand will get further into that magician's mind than the writer who only sees a performance.

Filmmaker Peter Rowe, himself an experienced single-handed deepwater sailor, set out to make this documentary on the life of Joshua Slocum. He found he was in the company of many other sailors who, in trying to reproduce the Fundyman's extraordinary feat of sailing alone around the world, had to become partial biographers themselves. Some of these sailor/disciples provided our writer-director with the very kind of physical texture I am talking about. Many of the sailors who set out to emulate the Slocum circumnavigation have chosen to do so in replicas of Slocum's own vessel, the *Spray*, a decaying wreck that Slocum found at Fairhaven, Massachusetts, and rebuilt, plank by plank, until she was a totally new boat. Director Peter Rowe concluded that the *Spray* has been copied more than any other vessel in the history of sailing, perhaps as many as eight hundred times. Burl

Ives had a *Spray* and when it began to decline and fail, another would-be Slocum imitator named David Dunn not only acquired the famous folksinger's replica, but also followed the pattern of Slocum's own reconstruction of his *Spray*, building a steam box to bend the new planks in, and replacing everything that needed to be replaced. Many others have started from scratch, using the drawings and descriptions that the pioneering circumnavigator published in his classic of narrative writing, *Sailing Alone Around the World*. David Dunn is an Idaho school-teacher who dropped his career for a complex ten-year project on the ancient mariner. He told us,

> We are going to recreate Slocum's voyage in its entirety. Again, we'll enter and exit the ports at the same time Slocum did. Our vessel is the largest copy of the Spray ever made. We have totally rebuilt her and systems are set up as an expedition vessel. And then teams of teachers will join me in teams of three. They will teach via satellite into the Internet and the lessons will be distributed around the world.

We will meet and hear from several other Slocum pilgrims and emulators, but it is time to step back and review some of those narrative signposts of place and people and events upon which the texture of a life story is arranged.

Joshua Slocum was born on the shores of Nova Scotia's famous Bay of Fundy, on (he wrote) "a cold spot on coldest North Mountain, on a cold February 20, 1844." He was the fifth child of John Slocum, of a loyalist New England family. John Slocum was a not very successful farmer, and by his son's account a tyrannical father. In 1852 he gave up the failing farm and moved the family out to Brier Island where he started a boot factory. Joshua was set to work there when he still just a boy. Pew 13 in the Westport Baptist Church is marked with a plaque to show where the Slocum family worshipped every Sunday. The building that housed the boot factory is still there too. The ferry that takes you out to the island bears the name *JOSHUA SLOCUM* on the plate across the wheelhouse, both fore and aft, the young bootmaker and later master mariner being the island's most famous son, perhaps its only famous son.

He used to muse about the sea as he watched the sails pass out-side the boot shop window. When he cobbled together a miniature clip-per ship out of scraps of wood and canvas — almost certainly a metic-ulous model given what we know of his skills at make-and-mend when he finally did go to sea — the father saw the little vessel as a sign of frivolity. "The handiwork of the devil," he said — and smashed it under foot. That was probably the moment when young Joshua saw unequivocally that he did not belong in that boot shop with that man. He soon ran away to sea, first as a cook on a schooner, and then as an ordinary seaman on a *deal drogher* sailing for Liverpool. *Deal* is a very old word for slices of timber (nine inches wide, three inches thick, at least six feet long) rough sawn from a log. *Drogher* (or *droger*) is a not very complimentary word, originally for slow and awkward coastal vessels in the West Indies. Later the word was applied to the rough craft that sailed the millions of tons of Nova Scotia pine and spruce that for a couple of centuries constituted the colony's principal export to Britain.

Young Slocum had only a few years in school, but books and words caught him young, and there is a natural cadence to his writing, never more winning than when he is dealing with the passion that guided his life.

The wonderful sea charmed me from the first. I was born in the breezes, and I studied the sea as perhaps few have, neglecting all else.

That study rewarded him well. Almost entirely self-taught, he rap-idly acquired the complex mathematical skills needed to navigate by sun, stars, and compass. He impressed his superiors with his confident handling of rope and canvas, the repairing of broken spars, and his command of the respect of others. Throughout the 1860s and the 1870s he sailed the Atlantic, the Caribbean, the Pacific, and the South China Sea. He also tried boat building, fishing, and for a season, hunting sea otters off the coast of British Columbia. By 1869 he had won command of his first ship, a coasting schooner. He was twenty-five years old.

Two years later he was commanding a barque bound for Australia. The barque, with its main and foremast billowing with classic square sails, a cloud of triangular jibs and staysails forward and a mizzenmast aft, also fore-and-aft rigged, was *the* ship for the merchant skipper of the period. Sail had less than a quarter century left before steam overtook it as the motive force of maritime commerce. But to be in command of a transoceanic barque at the age of twenty-seven was to have arrived.

Ashore at a dance in Sydney he met the beautiful, confident Virginia Albertina Walker. As captain of a vessel he had private quarters and the right to bring his wife along on voyages. Within weeks Virginia was Mrs. Joshua Slocum, and had gone to sea with her new husband. This courageous woman would, in her tragically short life, bear all of her children at sea, often with only her husband to help. She would save his life during a mutiny, much later, coming on deck with a pistol at the crucial moment. And she would leave him bereft when she died, during a voyage, after only thirteen years of marriage.

But before that blow to the young skipper's life, he rapidly climbed about as high as it was possible to climb. The *Northern Light*, his next command, was said by many to be the finest American merchant vessel afloat. Her owners had been impressed by the young Nova Scotian with the reputation for firm command, sure navigation, and rapid crossings. The command of the *Northern Light* was not all they had to offer: they gave him shares in the ownership of the magnificent ship. He fitted out the captain's cabin so that Virginia could live in comfortable elegance. Before long he owned the ship outright. He had been five times around the world, had skippered some of the finest ships afloat, and now was part owner of the best of them all. He was just forty years old.

But there was not much time for him to enjoy it. Things began to sour, rapidly, but it is hard to discern exactly why. On a sixth voyage around the world, the captain with the reputation for firm and successful command found himself faced with mutiny, his wife having to take up a weapon to help him. He regained control and put the mutineers in irons. Later a mate whom Slocum had imprisoned brought criminal charges against him, and the principals were able to confiscate Slocum's shares in the ship. So he had lost the *Northern Light*. He took over a smaller vessel, the *Aquidneck*, running to Argentina and Bolivia. It was on *Aquidneck*, anchored off Buenos Aires, that he lost his beloved Virginia.

His second marriage, to a distant cousin, was a disaster. He took *Aquidneck* to Brazil with a cargo of poorly stowed pianos that were destroyed in a storm. Disease was rife on the ship, and when she was wrecked, finally, off the coast of Brazil, and Slocum had paid off the crew, he was left with almost no money, a very unhappy wife and two sons, and no way to get home.

It was at that point that Joshua Slocum seems to have begun to look at himself in a new light. He was, at first, appalled at the loss of his ship.

I'll wager that since man first took to the oceans, there have been literally millions of ships sunk on the edges or the bottom of the seas, but hefty precedent doesn't make you feel any better when you hear that terrible sound of keel striking bottom, or feel the awful sensation as your ship cuts her way, not through water, but into granite.

He looked at the wreck. He still owned it, what was left of it. He had experience as a boat builder. He had two sons to help him. We do not know enough of what was going through his mind to tell exactly how the notion came to him, but somehow he decided to build a seagoing canoe, the *Liberdade*, and take his young family home to New England in it. And he did that. The vessel was thirty-six feet long, rigged with slat-ribbed sails, like a Chinese junk. The *Liberdade* voyage, 5,800 miles from Brazil to Washington, DC, was quite remarkable just as a feat of seamanship. When they reached American waters Slocum decided to take the little craft north through the swamps and wetlands of the Carolinas, thus becoming one of the first blue water boats to navigate what is now called the intracoastal waterway. Slocum would later turn that adventure into his first book, *The Voyage of the Liberdade*.

This book has also generated at least one imitator. More than a century later, one of the many Slocum followers, who had also lost his own ship (to a storm in the Irish Sea), decided that his next challenge should be to reproduce that part of the great old Captain's life as well, and he too built a *Liberdade*. He also wrote a book about it, and sailed it across oceans to relive the experience of his hero. This was a Welshman named David Sinnett Jones. His career as a professional racing driver had been wrecked when he lost a lung to cancer. His first boat, a replica of Slocum's *Spray*, lay at the bottom of the Irish Sea. Like Slocum on a beach in Brazil, David Sinnett Jones set about to rebuild his life.

I said to Suzanne, "That's what I should do, if I can get sponsorship
to build Liberdade, *because I'm shipwrecked, so I haven't got a ship.*
So this is what I should do, the same as Joshua did. He built the
Liberdade *when he was shipwrecked in southern Brazil."*

So he built a replica, the first ever, of the thirty-six-foot sailing canoe that Slocum had built with his family on the Brazilian beach. This seventy-one-year-old with one lung sailed his *Liberdade* alone from Wales to Brazil, then recreated Slocum's route, sailing from Paranagua to Martha's Vineyard.

Slocum's new wife, after the terrors of the shipwreck and the terrors of the *Liberdade* voyage, would never sail again. She took the children by rail to live with her inland relatives. Slocum's marriage was crumbling, and so, it seemed, was his life at sea. Steamships, "filthy, stinking steamships" he called them, were replacing the great winged sailing ships. When the Brooklyn Bridge was built in the 1880s it was made too low for the tall ships to pass beneath. Electric trams were replacing horses. Railways were replacing ships on the coastal runs. Slocum tried contracting himself out to that disagreeable new coal-fired world. He undertook to deliver a warship, the *Destroyer*, to a civil war–torn Brazil. The wrong faction — from Slocum's point of interest — intercepted him and sank the *Destroyer*. The contract was not fulfilled; so the backers did not pay their captain, and he slunk home broke in pocket and broken in his soul. Within five years Slocum had lost virtually everything: his wife, his home, his money, his family, and his profession. He had run aground.

One day he heard that the great Herman Melville was coming to a Massachusetts hall to read from a new novel. Melville, Robert Louis Stevenson, and a few others had found the decline of the age of sail a literary goldmine. As the world began to feel the disappearance of a great commercial and cultural set of images, some novelists discovered the poetic and fictional power of accounts of a vanishing craft. Slocum went to hear Melville. The novel was *Typee*. Always a great reader, and with one fairly successful book already in print, he began to think that perhaps the prime task of the next part of his life would be to translate into print his own adventures across the oceans and among the islands that so beckoned readers' imaginations away from the dark Satanic mills. If there was going to be no more need for traditional sailing captains in command of great vessels with great crews, what about making a major voyage in a smaller boat, and then, like Melville and Stevenson turning the adventure into literature, and making the voyage pay by telling others about it.

But he *would* need a ship. In a Boston shipyard a chance meeting with an old whaler would put his life back on course. Captain Eben Pierce was a whaling captain who had made his fortune (and contributed to the reduction of the world's whale population) by inventing the power harpoon. He listened to the tale of Captain Slocum's declining fortunes. "You want a ship?" he asked. "Come down to Fairhaven. I'll give you a ship."

The ship Pierce was offering was a rotting, 100-year-old oyster smack sitting in a field with a tree growing through it. Slocum sat on a log and stared at the derelict. It was called the *Spray*. The name was attractive, and so were its lines. Despite the smell of rotting wood and the sunlight filtering between the shrunken planks, there was something about the thirty-nine-foot sloop. She was broad of beam, fourteen feet, squat, clinker built, a broad flat transom, good cabin space below. To the Captain's eye she just felt right.

Like his follower David Dunn, Joshua Slocum built a steam box and began to rip the old planks off the frame of the derelict. As sunlight penetrated the dank interior, with the removal of each plank the oak framing began to look pretty questionable too. From the amused farmers in the neighbourhood Slocum got permission to cut a few oak trees. Always at ease with wood and cutting tools, he seems to have found himself exactly where he wanted to be, and while another builder might have been dismayed at the unfolding revelation of decay, Slocum, realizing that he would finish with an entirely new ship, with nothing left of the original *Spray*, wrote of the enterprise with relish.

But why call it *Spray*, when it was done, if it were to be an entirely new boat? The old master mariner knew his marine insurance regulations. Lloyds of London had set it down quite explicitly, in the case of a vessel named the *Jane*. "A vessel repaired all out of the old, until she is entirely new, is still the *Jane*." And, wrote Slocum later, the reality was that even he could not say with precision "at what point the old died or the new took birth." Another Slocum disciple, Len Pearson, helped us with our biographical need for texture by describing his own restoration of a derelict *Spray* in British Columbia 120 years later. Except for the local references and a few phrases unlikely to have been used by Slocum himself, in Pearson's account you can almost hear the voice of his nineteenth-century mentor:

It was a lot of work and a pretty rough looking project, but the bare essentials were there in aces, and it was very, very good. I did a lot of scrounging. Most of the teak came from old steamer doors from an abandoned shipyard. And I chased old demolition companies around to scrounge the best material out of the houses that were being torn down in Victoria back in the 70s. So every piece of wood on this boat has a history.

Len Pearson would spend years on his replica. Joshua Slocum finished his reborn *Spray* in thirteen months. He took odd jobs as a fitter on whalers, and probably was able to "scrounge" some bits and pieces from those ships as well as feed himself and pay for the few articles he actually bought. He claimed that the total cost was $553.62, which would put it in the $50,000 range in today's money, modest enough for a boat built of prime oak frames and beams, and planked with 1 1/2-inch-thick Georgia pine. He fitted her out with comfortable bunks and a good set of bookshelves — for he never went to sea without a library if he could help it — and confidently launched the *Spray* in the spring of 1894.

Now it was time to test her mettle. Joshua Slocum came from a world of Nova Scotia fishermen; fishing could bring a reliable livelihood in those days if you owned your own boat and knew what you were doing. He deferred some of the below-decks finishing and took

Spray out off the coast of New England. There he fished her for a year. He was able to put a little cash aside, but more importantly he got the feel of the craft in which he now *knew*, with almost religious certainty, that he was going to sail alone around the world and be the first person in history to do so. To his delight he discovered that once he had set the sails to their optimum for any course, off or into the wind, he could lash down the wheel and *Spray* would hold whatever course he had set for her, until the wind changed. This reduced the burdens of the day for the single-handed fisherman, of course; but on the voyage he was about to undertake it would save his life by allowing him to keep well-rested below as the stout little sloop ploughed through the oceans all night long with no one at the wheel.

I have called her a sloop — a single-masted fore-and-aft rigged boat with a four-sided mainsail topped by a wooden gaff running out at an angle from the mast, and one or two triangular sails, jibs, forward of the mast, varying in size depending on the strength and direction of the wind. The mainsail could be shortened by reefing. It carried two lines of reef points, short cords embedded in the canvas a foot or two apart in a line parallel to the boom (the wooden spar at the foot of the sail). There are two halyards, lines fastened to the gaff, and used to haul up the sail till it was trim and straight along the luff (the line of sail parallel to the mast). By slacking off the halyards the sailor can bind those reef points around the boom thus reducing the size of the sail by the amount of canvas tucked in under the reef points. Slocum always called the *Spray* a sloop too, although many of the drawings in his book, and many photographs of *Spray* replicas show a small second mast mounted on a tiny half-moon shaped ledge fastened to the flat stern (the transom). A sailboat with a second mast stepped abaft the wheel or tiller is properly called a yawl, and when the *Spray* was so rigged (Slocum called this short mast a jigger) she was technically a yawl. Sailors are tiresomely punctilious about language in this respect. "But I called her a sloop all the same," he wrote in *Sailing Alone Around the World*, "the jigger being merely a temporary affair."

Although the world voyage would officially begin at that Fairhaven launch point (on April 24, 1895), and conclude there three years, two months, and three days later, Slocum had a few ports of call to make before he left the sight of land. He stopped off in Boston. There he met a vivacious and optimistic young heiress, Mabel Wagnall of the giant Funk and Wagnall publishing empire. Whatever the relationship became, Mabel Wagnall told Slocum that she had no reservations or qualms about his improbable adventure, and that she would help with the book he intended to write about it. Others might tell him he was crazy; Mabel Wagnall was an enthusiast. She was one of the pioneer promoters of the artificial language Esperanto, and her archives contain a lot of documentation on the development of that movement. She became personally involved in some of the company's projects, such as the life of Franz Liszt by Carl Lachmund whose archives contain the author's letters to Mabel. When she looked at the lean, grizzled, fifty-one-year-old Bluenoser from the Bay of Fundy, she saw that mariner's look of infinite horizons that we can still see in his portrait by the famous Civil War photographer Matthew Brady. She listened to his story, and she told him to follow his dream. "The *Spray* will come back," she said flatly, and that was that.

He headed north for Nova Scotia. Phil Shea, in his nineties now, lives on Brier Island in a Westport not that much changed since its famous navigator dropped in that time for a last visit. Shea's great aunt had told him stories about the Captain's having an eye for the ladies. Her father didn't like that very much, and disappointed her by saying no when Joshua invited her to come out on the *Spray* for a sail around Brier Island. He did succeed in hosting some other young ladies for a few such trips, and then headed for Halifax and the open sea. In Westport our documentary crew found a letter of Slocum's that contradicts the traditional accounts of the Slocum circumnavigation, which all give Yarmouth as the departure point. In this letter, mailed from Gibraltar a few months later, Slocum says he had a score to settle in Halifax, but changed his mind at the last minute, sailed around George's Island, and headed out into the Atlantic.

The first day out, he reported, he trawled a line astern and caught "one cod, two haddock and one hake." He had a barrel of good potatoes and lots of butter. Was the butter tinned? How could it keep? He does not say. There are dozens of provocative little puzzles like that in his book. His sister gave him a big fruitcake before he left Westport. He writes that it lasted forty-two days! One newspaper account of his return to Fairhaven years later says this:

Fairhaven Star, July 9, 1898
Voyage Around the World

Captain Joshua Slocum, the intrepid navigator, who in April, 1895, started from Boston in the 33 foot yawl *Spray* on a trip around the world, dropped anchor above the bridge, within a short distance from the spot where the *Spray* was built, Sunday. Captain Slocum has sailed something like 46,000 miles since leaving Boston, and during the entire trip he was entirely alone. The captain came to Fairhaven for a little rest, to put the *Spray* back in condition, and renew his acquaintance with his many friends in Fairhaven. The hold of the *Spray* is filled with all kinds of curiosities gathered from various parts of the world. Judging from the books of newspaper clippings in the captain's possession, he is considered an excellent lecturer and has been honored by high officials everywhere. He has a stereopticon and 300 excellent slides which he uses to illustrate his lectures. Captain Slocum said he intends to remain around here a few days and will then go cruising with his wife and son. He intends to go to London before long. Among the mementos brought home by Captain Slocum is a big bamboo stick given him by the widow of Robert Louis Stevenson. The bamboo was grown by the novelist. Captain Slocum also received several books from the library of the late novelist.

This takes us some distance ahead of our story, but I insert it here because it is characteristic of those textual puzzles. Slocum himself writes of giving lectures with the "stereopticon" in Australia. A stereopticon was a pair of "magic lanterns" projecting superimposed images taken from different positions to produce the illusion of three dimensions, and usually viewed with spectacles of different colours to filter out one image for each eye. Did Slocum carry a supply of such spectacles? Were they standard issue in lecture halls? Where did he get the slides, and what did they represent? Slocum makes no mention of his carrying a camera with him. Making the double image photography needed for these stereoscopic images is not a casual affair and requires a special and rather challenging setup. Given the Captain's curiosity about everything, and his delight in the details of his daily round, it is not believable that he would have been taking these demanding photographs but not writing about the process. So what did the slides depict, that he could lecture knowingly about? Were they slides he acquired at different ports-of-call? We will probably never know. We will probably never know whether the ship that reported his patched together mainsail in the Pacific, after Tierra del Fuego storms had blown the original to shreds, and said that "Captain Slocum was evidently using a patented sail of some very modern design" was Slocum's invention, or just an exception to his later statement that in his entire voyage across the Pacific he did not see another ship.

I insert this observation here, because the tale that follows is full of wonders. Joshua Slocum was a sailor. Sailors tell stories. There is probably a good deal of invention in Slocum's. But there is also no doubt that the broad lines of his great adventure are what he claimed them to be. He can have appeared in the ports he appeared in only by actually traversing the seas he said he traversed. There is ample written evidence of his being where he said he was on the dates he reported. The modern reader of his engaging account of that adventure cannot help pausing from time to time over some of the details, but this writer will not much pause on them further, having given this caution, as the story unfolds.

He was lonely at first. For a while he called out commands to an imaginary crew, but gave it up because "my voice sounded hollow." He regretted that the press of commerce upon the passing steamers — much as he detested them — had done away with the tradition of ships "speaking" to each other. "No poetry-enshrined freighters on the sea

277

now," he wrote, ". . . it is a prosy life when we have no time to bid one another good-morning."

His first landfall on the east side of the Atlantic, as it is for many a sport sailor today, was the Azores. Like hundreds who follow in his wake he painted on the seawall his name and the date and the ship's name as a memento of his visit; it has been carefully preserved. He attended services for the appropriate guardian saints and angels. Somebody gave him some plums and white cheese, and a day or two out of the Azores he ate them and then developed painful cramps that sent him below in agony. He awoke after a troubled night to find a bearded figure in fifteenth-century garb beaming down at him from the wheel above the aft companionway. This person identified himself as a pilot on Columbus's ship the *Pinta*, and, according to Slocum, assured the sick man that the ship was in good hands. He was chewing black twist tobacco, somewhat anachronistically, and, writes Slocum, the apparition again turned up several times further along in the voyage, at times when the Captain was feeling out of sorts.

He sailed north to the Straits of Gibraltar where he was welcomed by the British Navy, who knew he was coming, towed him in, dry-docked and checked out the hull of the *Spray*, entertained him royally, warned him about the danger of pirates if he proceeded east through the Mediterranean to the 171-kilometre-long Suez Canal, which had opened for business more than twenty years earlier, and sent him on his way back out into the Atlantic. He boasted that he beat everything across the Atlantic, both ways, except steamers. He was appropriately proud of his navigation by dead reckoning. Dead reckoning usually requires not only a compass, but also an accurate timepiece and a way of measuring your daily run. Slocum ran a "patent log," a kind of four-bladed propellerlike rotor towed astern and reading out on a counter. But his time-keeping was not state-of-the-art.

My old chronometer, which was a good one, had been long in disuse. I tried to get it cleaned and rated, but they wanted $15 for it. $15! They may as well have asked for the moon. I travelled with nothing until I got to Nova Scotia, but once I got to Yarmouth, I got my famous tin clock, the only timepiece I carried on the whole

voyage. The price of it was a dollar and a half, but on account of the
face being smashed, the merchant let me have it for a dollar.

He had long ago mastered the now largely forgotten lunar
method of determining latitude and longitude, a fairly accurate but
laborious system that does not depend on a timepiece. Whatever the
method, his landfalls were sure and his crossings rapid. Taking the
advice of the British Navy he headed back across the Atlantic towards
South America. He describes a near encounter with a felucca, off the
African coast, which may or may not have been a pirate vessel but
from which he was saved by a freak wave sweeping over the approaching marauder. He grounded on the coast of Uruguay and was nearly
drowned (like most Nova Scotia fishermen of the time he did not
swim), and later had to struggle to retrieve both the *Spray* and its tender from Gauchos who hitched horses to them and tried to tow them
inshore. But later, news of his adventure always preceding him, he ran
into old mariner friends who gave him money ("an advance" he called
it) and in Montevideo the British steamship agents drydocked the ship,
overhauled it for him at their own expense, and gave him 20 pounds
sterling to help him on his way.

Leaving Brazil, he rigged the jigger, wanting the increased directional stability of the balanced rig when he entered the legendarily difficult waters of the Magellan straits at the very southern tip of the continent. This was the most challenging part of the whole amazing voyage.
Nobody had tried it alone before, and few have since. To get a feeling for
this mysteriously beautiful and difficult passage, director Peter Rowe
contacted Larry Tyler, a British filmmaker and singlehanded sailor, who
took a camera with him through the straits, and talked to it, against the
background of looming mountains and luminous snowstorms. In the
documentary we see one of these video diary entries at a moment of
uncharacteristic calm, for those waters.

The three most important voyagers who came down here, the first
was Magellan. He discovered the straits and they have been named
after him. And secondly was Sir Francis Drake, who sailed
through the straits from the Atlantic through to the Pacific in six-
teen days without any chart. And thirdly, and probably the most

remarkable in terms of seamanship, would be Joshua Slocum.

Following in the wake of Joshua Slocum on the Spray, *the* Dove *and I, we sailed a similar route from Montevideo to Buenos Aires and then from Buenos Aires out into the sea, encountering the same kind of conditions that he had, horrible head winds. And we beat out two days and two nights with nasty, sharp seas. The whole place is like a graveyard to ships. Then once we were out at sea, we headed south down the Patagonian coast, a wild and forbidding country. The winds just howl and howl and howl. Today you could say it's the calm before the storm. It's one of these dead, dead calm days, hardly any wind. We're hardly making any headway. But within an hour we could start having a snowstorm. In the evening it could be hailing or heavy, heavy rain. It's a very dramatic and wild corner of the earth. It's a challenge for sailing boats to come down here nowadays. But think of it a hundred years ago when Joshua Slocum was here. It was even more of a challenge. A most remarkable man.*

As Tyler talks of the snow, he cut in for us shots of the soaring ridge above his passage, with wings of snow sweeping over it almost as if they were alive. We see the hailstones bouncing off his deck, and the whipping spray rising off the turbulent water like animated beings as the convoluted passage sends twisted ropes of aerial turbulence whistling along its dramatic corridors. Slocum was blown out of the straits and then back into them. Some say he did part of his navigation by echoes off the land at night. David Dunn, planning his own GPS- and Internet-guided passage told us, as he contemplated his approach to a section of the straits called the Milky Way,

that it is considered to be the most treacherous water on the earth. The story goes is that only two vessels have ever, in that time anyway, have ever made it through the Milky Way. One was the Beagle *with Darwin and a full crew, and they made it during the daytime. And Slocum made it through the Milky Way by himself, tacking by sound at night. It just — it boggles my mind to think about it. But I believe five attempts to get it through. I remember one time he lost forty days he said, and he said he just turned the boat around and whistled a new tune and started to tack it all over again.*

The passage took Slocum several weeks. Nothing in his account of it suggests that he even approached the threshold of despair. He wrote, in *Sailing Alone*:

> It's a fact that in Magellan, I let pass many ducks that would have made a good stew, for in this lonesome, wild strait, I really had no mind to take the life of any living thing.

And then he was out. A last burst of steady but powerful wind brought him clear of the west coast. The winds continued favourable all the way across the Pacific, bringing him by Juan Fernandez Island where Alexander Selkirk's marooning gave Daniel Dafoe the story that would become *Robinson Crusoe*. Slocum climbed to Selkirk's cave, pronounced himself moved, and sailed on. He didn't stop again until Samoa, where, as noted above in the Fairhaven Star, he visited the widow of one his literary mentors and heroes, Robert Louis Stevenson, and slept in Stevenson's house. Then it was on to Australia.

How did he pass the time? Reading, much of it. He fished. Often flying fish would crash into the sails at night and fall on the deck; he would feast on them in the morning. Old friends and new admirers in his many stops made sure he went away with fresh provisions. When the day's chores were done and his belly full, he stretched out on the bunk below, his back comfortably propped on pillows against the bulkhead under the bookcase, and he read his Hackluyt's *Voyages*, his Drake, and his Hawkins. He wrote his diary. He made sure he was well rested except when storms forbade it. Much of the time he let the *Spray*, with its extraordinary directional stability, steer itself, the wheel lashed down, often finishing the day (according to his never diffident account of his navigational skills and the *Spray*'s steady heading) within a mile or two of his predicted day's run.

Much of the power of this spellbinding book is Joshua Slocum's account of putting the *Spray* back into operating condition after she had been damaged in a storm. Rescuing broken spars before they were swept overboard, getting out his sailor's palm[4] and heavy needle, and (and here is a part of the story that is difficult to grasp in an age where

---

4. The sailor's palm is a kind of open leather glove. Fixed into its palm is a large pitted lead dome like the working end of a giant thimble. This allows the craftsman to push a heavy needle and thick, tarred twine through a thick piece of sailcloth or canvas.

the loss of a few seconds drives professional people to the point of rage, never mind the loss of days) Slocum would spend two or three days, or a week, rebuilding a sail out of scraps of cloth that a storm had left him with when the previous sail disintegrated in an explosive gust. Nothing seemed to discourage him. Irritated as some readers may be at the self-congratulatory tone, if that was the state of mind that kept him at it, we have to end up in thrall to his skill and his determination.

In Australia he hauled the boat out for repairs and began to give lectures with the stereopticon we have already met. Mariners like David Sinnett Jones are still continuing the tradition, in Sinnett Jones's case telling his tale and retelling Slocum's in the same village hall where Slocum himself had spoken a hundred years earlier.

From Australia, with a new set of sails given to him in Sydney, he sailed to Cocos Keeling Island in the Indian Ocean, a passage of 2,700 miles, in twenty-three days, of which, Slocum says, he spent less than three hours at the wheel. Many scoffed at this claim, indeed, scoffed at his entire voyage. They didn't believe he could sail alone, that the boat would steer itself; but the modern replicas, built as exactly to the old *Spray* plans as their obsessed Slocum acolytes can make them, demonstrate the same true tracking.

He met President Kruger in South Africa and argued with him about Kruger's fundamentalist conviction that the earth was flat. In the South Atlantic, east of the African coast, he visited St. Helena where Napoleon Bonaparte had lived out his last dreary years of exile. They gave him a goat at St. Helena, so that he could have some fresh meat on the upcoming third Atlantic crossing of the voyage. The goat got into the charts and ate the Caribbean. Slocum knew the Caribbean as well as he knew the deck of the *Spray*, and didn't even bother trying to find a replacement chart when he made his landfall after a three-week crossing. And then it was a straight run up a familiar coastline, easing into Harbour in Massachusetts where many had assumed him long dead. June 27, 1898. Three years, two months, three days.

What next?

What does a fifty-four-year-old former merchant captain do, who has achieved something no other sailor in the history of the world has ever achieved, but has nothing much to show for it but memories? He writes a book. Mabel Wagnall helped him get it published. His return to his home port had been overshadowed by the Spanish-American War, but when *Sailing Alone Around the World* appeared it was immediately admired and has been reprinted and translated hundreds of times since. Two years later, and by now a celebrity though still impecunious, he took the *Spray* up the new Erie Canal to Buffalo for an extraordinary exposition. Director Peter Rowe uncovered some very early motion picture footage of that now somewhat-nondescript bustling upstate New York border city, which had been fantastically transformed in 1901. He wrote these words for me to narrate over the last few minutes of the documentary, and this is exactly how they are heard in that film.

In 1901, Joshua Slocum, late of Brier Island, Nova Scotia, was invited to bring his boat to Buffalo, New York, to the great Pan American Exposition, the biggest ever held. He towed the Spray *by horse up the Erie Canal. The canal, built and expanded throughout the nineteenth century, played a vital role in opening up the midwest of America. Now again Slocum cut a new swath, being one of the very first non-commercial boats to use the canal in the way it is used today — a passage for adventurers between the Great Lakes and the Atlantic, and then the South Seas.*

As can still be seen in this early motion picture tour shot by Thomas Edison, the Exposition was a fantastical recreation of Venetian canals, and along their sides electric towers and Eskimo villages, and Slocum's Spray. *While Slocum was moored in Buffalo, he printed and sold a small souvenir pamphlet describing his voyage, with an autographed piece cut from the tattered mainsail he'd used until Australia. For a Slocum aficionado to find a copy today and touch the sail that took Slocum around the world is a rare and almost awesome moment.*

Slocum traded yarns here with Buffalo Bill Cody who'd brought his Wild West show to the Exposition. In September, President William McKinley visited the Exposition, boarded the Spray, *and signed Slocum's logbook. An hour later McKinley was shot to death by an anarchist. Slocum was at the swearing-in of the new presi-*

dent, Theodore Roosevelt, and became a good friend of the energetic and adventurous new chief.

The Exposition is long gone, but this lake and the very wall that Slocum tied to are still there. He left Buffalo for Martha's Vineyard, mooring the Spray here in this harbour, just like this replica a hundred years later. Martha's Vineyard is a place of grand yachts, grand hotels, and grand houses. Slocum is still remembered today, though with one of the world's most overgrown and neglected memorials.

In Slocum's day the Vineyard was a sleepy farming and fishing community. Slocum tried his hand at growing hops. But it was a dismal attempt to "toss in the anchor." It didn't work. Within a year he was back at sea, sailing for the Bahamas, Jamaica, and the Caymans.

But now the Spray was beginning to look as weather-beaten as her skipper. In 1908 he told President Roosevelt of his plan to sail to Venezuela, up the Orinoco and on to the headwaters of the Amazon. He took off into a November gale and was never seen again. He may have foundered in that gale. He may have fallen overboard. Perhaps the old girl sprung a plank. But most likely, one of his hated steamships had finally caught up with him.

His most recent biographer, Anne Spencer, has found evidence identifying a particular Caribbean mail steamer as the ship that ran old Slocum down. Whatever really happened, it seems appropriate that the old seadog who loved the sea and did so much to share that love with the world, should still be in and of it.

Less appropriate to those who love his memory is the dry language of the Dukes County court official statement: "The court finds that Joshua Slocum disappeared, absconded, and absented himself on the 14th day of November, A.D., 1909, disappearing under the following circumstances. He sailed from Tisbury, Massachusetts in the sloop Spray of nine tons burden and has never been seen since, and therefore the court declares that the aforementioned be declared lost at sea and legally dead."

There is not another story quite like it. No one who has gone down to the sea in ships, in ships that are moved through the waves by the wind filling out one sail or twenty sails, can fail to be taken by it, to be in some measure in love with the *idea* of this man and his adventure. Hard-minded sceptics may flinch a bit at some of the tall tales, although even the tallest of them are probably somewhere rooted in fact. He loved to tell how a certain Captain Pedro Samblich gave him a box of tacks to sprinkle on the deck at night if he had to sleep moored or anchored during the Patagonian passage (the Straits of Magellan), in territory where there were tribal peoples with a reputation for local piracy. Slocum says the tacks saved his life several times. His revelling in that story will make some readers uncomfortable. In the long run it does not matter. Whatever the cultural and moral currents he carried out of his childhood in Westport, Brier Island, Nova Scotia, first among them were courage, patience, indomitable confidence.

And a love of his element. Give him the last word:

The sea is in its grandest mood. You must then know the sea, and know that you know it, and remember that it was meant to be sailed upon.

Note: In May of 2001 this documentary television biography, in competition in Houston, Texas, with more than a thousand other documentaries from around the world, was awarded the Gold Special Jury Award at the 34th Annual Houston International Film Festival.

◆　◆　◆

The original documentary was written and directed by Peter Rowe, with producer F. Whitman Trecartin.

PART THREE

JACQUES PLANTE
The Man Behind *the Mask*

"There are good goalies and there are important goalies — and he was an important goalie." —Ken Dryden

"Will I ever see a goalie who will play better than Plante did? I have my doubts." —Red Fisher

He was the eldest of eleven children, born Joseph Jacques Omer Plante, in a farmhouse near Mt. Carmel, Quebec, on January 17, 1929. His sister Thérèse said that while it was a family typical of the times and the region, where everyone helped out with every aspect of the household economy and there was never enough money, that her brother Jacques was unquestionably the leader, right from the start. "First in everything," she said. "And we followed him."

Soon after Jacques' birth, their father abandoned the farm and went to work as a machinist at the aluminum company in Shawinigan. He held onto his job despite the wreckage of the economy in the stock market crash when Jacques was nine months old. His sister thinks that Jacques began to play hockey (without skates — who could afford skates?) when he was three years old, and that his mother taught him to knit at about the same time, toques, hockey socks. "You're going to learn because I can't knit for everyone," the mother would say. "He was very fast and he never dropped a stitch," according to his sister. Writer-director Andy Thompson, who said he made this documentary because he had grown up in Montreal in the 1950s when "Plante was the greatest goalie ever, playing for the greatest team ever. And besides, he was my mother's favourite player, probably because of the knitting."

He must have decided that he was a goalie pretty early on because people remember him haunting the doors of the arena — he seldom had the ten cents you needed to go in and skate — and saying to the other boys as they arrived, "If you need a goalie for your team, I'm ready to play." They took him up on it fairly often; the crease was not a popular position in those days. Even Jacques did not especially want it, not at first; but it was a way of getting to play when you had no money. More importantly, while he had started as a defenceman, he found that his asthma left him on the boards after a few minutes of play. Since he just could not sustain continual high-speed skating, he settled for net-tending. Most would agree that Jacques Plante's asthma led to a better game.

By the age of twelve he was obsessed. When they sent him to bed before the hockey broadcasts started on Saturday night, he would slip into Thérèse's room. The room above was rented to a man who played his radio loud enough that if young Jacques stood on the bureau with his ear near the ceiling he could follow the game.

Hockey was his life. Before he hung up his skates he would play almost fifty thousand minutes on the ice in more than eight hundred games, with a remarkable goals-against average of 2.34, and a shared record (with Clint Benedict) for playoff shutouts (15), that would hold until 2001 when Patrick Roy pulled ahead of them. His first paid game was back at that Shawinigan arena where, by the time he was fifteen, he was playing for the factory team. When his father found out he was not being paid he insisted he do something about it. Jacques approached the coach in his typically straightforward way. The coach said, All right, 50 cents a game, but don't tell the other boys.

In the National League he would play for the Edmonton Oilers, the California Golden Seals, the Boston Bruins, the New York Rangers, the Saint Louis Blues, the Toronto Maple Leafs and, of course, the team that he had set his heart on from childhood and for whom he was playing in 1959 when he changed the look of professional hockey forever: *Les Canadiens de Montréal*, "the Habs." He earned the Vezina trophy for best NHL goaltender seven times (once shared with Glenn Hall), played on several All-Star teams, and was inducted into the Hockey Hall of Fame in 1978.

In 1947 he finished high school and signed up with the Quebec Citadels. Up to that time the goaltender always stayed in his net and did his best to stop the pucks that were fired at him. Jacques Plante's first important innovation changed that. He decided that it was perfectly acceptable, and within the rules as established, for the goalie to do a little traffic management *before* the puck was fired, and that meant coming out of the net. People said, "It's impossible! Goalies don't leave the net." But Plante left the net. He said that he surveyed what was going on during one game, and realized he had a group of incompetents out in front of him.

Ahead of me were four defencemen with assorted flaws. One couldn't skate backwards. One couldn't shoot the puck up to the blue line. One of the other two could only turn one way. Somebody had to clear loose pucks, and I began to do the job myself. It worked so well that I kept right on doing it. Right up to the NHL.

By the end of the 1948 season he was the man to beat, and one man who played against him, Dickie Moore, says he was assigned to swing his stick in front of Plante's face to try to make him blink. The whole league was still perplexed at the way he was coming out of the net to clean up the mess just in front of the crease, and they said that years later the great Toe Blake would still grit his teeth with anxiety when the masked man left the gaping net back there behind him as he came down the ice to create order out of disorder.

Despite his demonstrated talent, breaking into the National League proved difficult for Jacques Plante. The Montréal Canadiens, his dream destination, had bought up the rights to a substantial number of strong players, and already had a goalie, Bill Durnan, who some said was the best in the league. Durnan was not about to be replaced by some teenaged newcomer. In May of 1949 the Montréal Royals took Plante on and that same year he got married to Jacqueline Gagné. Dickie Moore, the man who used to swing his stick in his face, was a teammate on the Royals. Moore says that another difference with Jacques, right from the start was that "he played the game like a first baseman, with his glove. I would say — even in today's hockey — no one — no one catches the puck like Jacques Plante did."

In 1951 his first son Michel was born, and he bought a home movie camera. Those films show a man whose family life was becoming as vital a part of his life as hockey had been until then. Hockey was also beginning to acknowledge that this was a pretty outstanding player. Bill Durnan retired and was replaced by Gerry McNeill. McNeill broke his jaw in a Toronto game on November 1, 1952, and coach Dick Irvin brought Plante in for what he was told would be a three-game tryout, starting against the New York Rangers. McNeill said his chagrin at having to be replaced was somewhat tempered by the new kid's spectacular ability.

I thought he was very good. You know, I keep saying that to myself today. I needed a good goalkeeper to replace me. . . . If it was a guy that wasn't so good, I wouldn't feel so good.

Jacques still wore one of those toques his mother had taught him to knit; it had become a trademark. In his first practice sessions the coach assumed that he just wore it for fun; it certainly was not part of the uniform. But Dickie Moore was there.

We would try to pull it off with our sticks sometimes, from behind the net. But I mean he went through hell to wear that toque. I was there when the coach says, "You don't play if you wear it!" And that's hard. For a kid that's coming out of nowhere and be strong enough to say, "I want to wear it!" . . . You have to be proud of him for standing up for his rights.

It made Dick Irvin very nervous, that toque. First of all it would bring ridicule, some on Plante for wearing it and some onto the coach for not being able to control his rookie. Plante said — perhaps with a touch of the tongue in the cheek — that it was for his health.

When I was young we played on outdoor skating rinks, and because it was cold we had to wear toques to cover our ears. When I began to play on indoor rinks, that weren't heated, it was cold. I'm asthmatic and I didn't want to catch a cold. So I kept my toque. Well, I kept right on up until those three games that I played in '52 with the Canadiens. I was preparing to go play, but my toque — my toques (I always had two or three) had disappeared. I asked the coach, "What's going on?" And he says, "I don't know. They disappeared."

That sartorial argument he would lose. But not the next one.

In the meantime he beat the Rangers 4 to 1 in that first game for Montréal, tied the next, and then beat Toronto 3 to 1. Pretty good for a rookie, everyone said, and a couple of months later Montréal signed him for $9,100 a year and sent him to their farm club, the Buffalo Bisons, to get him worked up. The local press began to call him Jake the Snake.

The Bisons did not make it into the American Hockey League finals that spring, but if that bothered Plante the bother did not last. Irvin brought him back to the Canadiens as a back-up for Gerry McNeill in the Stanley Cup Playoffs. On April 3, 1953, it is said that there were shock waves when Dick Irvin sent Plante out instead of McNeill, when Chicago was leading 3 games to 2. It was seven p.m. at the hotel, just as they were leaving for the Chicago Stadium for the sixth game. With no warning,

> *Dick Irvin calls me. He says, "Jacques, you are going to be the goalie tonight." I had no idea . . . since Gerry McNeill was in good health and all that. So I started to tremble. In the dressing room. I tried to lace up my skates, but it was impossible. I couldn't do it. Maurice Richard came to see me and said, "Jacques, in a game like this one, everyone's nervous." And he held out his hand, like that, and it was shaking too.*

But Plante got over the shakes, scored a shutout in that game, and three days later led his team to a 4 to 1 victory in the playoffs. They were off to the finals. He won one and lost one against Boston, but the Habs took the championship, and so in that spring of 1923 when he was twenty-four years old Jacques Plante's name was, for the first time, incised into the ever-expanding metallic rounds of the Stanley Cup.

McNeill admits to letting Irvin know that he, the *real* goalie, was not very happy about being arbitrarily replaced by Plante, and the new kid was sent back to the Bisons for the '53 to '54 season. Then, when Irvin put him out as first-string goaltender at the start of the '54 to '55, McNeill said to hell with it, and retired. "I wasn't the type that could handle that," he says. Towards the end of that season Jacqueline gave birth to a second son, Richard, and Jacques was leading the Canadiens into the Stanley Cup finals again, when St. Patrick's Day arrived and all hell broke loose in Montréal.

In a game in Boston on March 13 a nasty brawl had broken out. When the smoke cleared, NHL Commissioner Clarence Campbell announced that the luminous Maurice "The Rocket" Richard, some say the greatest player ever, had been suspended for the rest of the season because of his role in the fights. In Montréal the fans were outraged. When Campbell came into the Forum on the night of March 17 he was physically attacked, a tear gas bomb went off, the game was forfeited to Detroit, the building was cleared, and a major riot began to spread along Ste Catherine Street. There were hundreds of arrests. Maurice Richard was not allowed back on the ice that season, and Detroit took the cup.

This is all part of the mythology of hockey in this country. Today, with the Forum no longer there and the great Rocket and Jake the Snake both gone too, the details of the story have faded somewhat, but the entire era is vividly recalled by someone who started the next season as a new young sportswriter at the *Montréal Star*, Red Fisher.

I first saw him when I started covering the Canadiens in 1955, '56. He was different. He was a splendid goaltender. He's certainly the best goaltender that I ever saw and I've seen a few over the years. But, I got to tell you this about Jacques Plante: he played for Toe Blake for eight years, and Toe Blake hated Jacques Plante.

I mean really hated the guy because Toe liked to be in control, that's what made him a great coach. He controlled the players; he told them what to do. But, he just couldn't move Plante around the way he did the other players. And I'm talking about guys like the two Richards and Béliveau and Geoffrion and Moore. But I still remember him telling me, in the five years that the Canadiens won the Stanley Cup, Jacques Plante was the best goaltender he's ever seen. You have to know Toe Blake to understand how great an admission that is because when Toe Blake didn't like somebody everything was bad about the guy. So when he says Jacques Plante was the best he's ever seen, for those five years, you know it's coming from the right guy. . . . I've never met anybody who studied the game as much, who knew more about the game, who knew more about the job that he had to do, who was more proud of the job he did.

With Toe Blake at the helm, the Canadiens would go on to become perhaps the finest hockey team in the history of the league (and some say in the history of hockey). They won five Stanley Cups in a row. Dickie Moore says Plante had a lot to do with that.

> Jacques was a big instrumental player; he kept us in the game. Like, I can go and talk about Boston, it's like yesterday, when they'd hold us in our zone for ten minutes — ten minutes! And Jacques Plante would keep us in the game, and wouldn't let them score. We needed that goaltending and he was the guy that did the job. He used to sleep thinking hockey. He would wake up playing the game. I mean this guy — believe me! — knew hockey inside out. He studied every hockey player that played against him. He knew if they slapshot or if they deeked or what have you. He knew all their shifts on the ice.

Sometimes a teammate would feel that Jacques was doing more than sharing his knowledge, when he pronounced upon an aspect of the game that was not exactly within his field of expertise. Jean Beliveau said that he once got a bit irritated when Plante started instructing him on *his* part of the game, and told Plante a bit sharply, "You take care of your net and I'll take care of the face-off." Others will recall that he was a bit slow to put his hand in his pocket when it was time to pay for the drinks, or for being more of a loner than is the norm in a sports team. But in the end the affection and respect that both opponents and allies had for him is the dominant theme of all the interviews that were given to the producers of our documentary. His son Michel confirmed that his father was something of a solitary figure

> even at home when he wasn't playing with us, or when there was nobody around him. He liked to be on his own. He would read all kinds of books, listen to classical music, taking pictures of birds and filming some birds. The bird that he had was a singing bird. It was making life in the house, it was maybe creating for him a different scene — a different environment — than to concentrate always on hockey.

In the late 1950s, as the new curved sticks made it possible to scoop up the puck more decisively than the old straight sticks and gave the slapshot its murderous potential, a man named Bill Burchmore suggested that Plante wear a fibreglass mask in practice. He offered to mould one to the shape of his face. Michel Plante says that Burchmore came to the Plante house and that the two men worked on it together on the basement workbench. Toe Blake tolerated the mask in practice, but then there came that turning point game in New York in November 1959 when Plante and Blake nearly came to a parting of the ways. Red Fisher said,

I was in New York, the night he first put it on. Andy Bathgate of the Rangers comes down and lets go a short backhand, and I thought it was deliberate, right into Plante's face. And there was a cut from the corner of his mouth that ran right up through his nostril. I was the only guy in there with him. And he's standing in front of the mirror and he's spreading the cut apart and it looks pretty ugly and even he agrees that he and it look pretty damn ugly. And then he went over to the table, where the doctor waited. He stitched him up — no anaesthetic. A whole pile of stitches. And then he came out of the clinic, skated across the ice, and then went to the Canadiens' dressing room and put on the mask.

Toe Blake threatened to fire him if he went out on the ice wearing that mask. Blake swore it would hurt his game, make it hard for him to see what he had to see. Plante insisted, the other players thought it was a blessing, and young fans today have never seen a league game with a barefaced goalie. Jacques said that playing catcher in baseball had helped him think about the value of the face-protector.

I had been a catcher in baseball as well as a goalie in lacrosse and in both those sports I wore a mask. And in hockey I was perhaps more unlucky. My nose was broken four times, the two bones in my cheek got broken, my jaw twice, and so on. So, I said to myself, for crying out loud if I was going to be injured as often as this, I had better protect myself. We had a good club; we kept winning and in '59 when I began to wear the mask, in the spring of that year, we won the Stanley Cup in eight consecutive games. So, no one could say that the mask prevented me from playing well. So, thanks to the Canadiens and their strength, the mask was introduced early and eventually the mask was accepted.

But the courage of standing up to a bullying, powerful coach was what the world admired as much as the innovation. And as it turns out, Blake was wrong about the mask's detracting from the goalie's alertness. Another eminent goalie, Ken Dryden, says that the mask in fact helps do the job.

Playing goal is always at least an unconscious compromise between safety and effectiveness. And part of that compromise is if you get hit in the head it hurts or worse. And so you try to keep your head as far away from the action as you possibly can. Now if you're wearing a mask you don't need to do it quite as much. So you know the impact doesn't stop with safety, it bleeds over — nice word — into effectiveness, you know, and how you play.

The following season, ironically, was a disappointing one for the Canadiens, and Plante did not get his name on any more trophies that year. Rocket Richard retired. Toe Blake was probably muttering "The Mask, The Mask," as Plante's goals-against statistics got worse and worse. The Canadiens made it into the playoffs, in fact were top team for the season, but were quickly eliminated by Chicago who went on to win the cup. When the season was over Plante went in for a surgical repair to a torn ligament in his knee, which might have weakened his goaltending a little during the season, and then into intensive physiotherapy to get the leg back into shape. But the next season, 1961 to 1962, he was superb. Red Fisher was concerned at first because Plante's most reliable defenceman, Doug Harvey, was gone.

When Harvey was traded to the New York Rangers, of course the big question that everybody asked Plante: "How are you going to do without Doug Harvey on defence?" Plante said, "Listen, we all know what a great defenceman Doug Harvey has been and is, but I'll tell you what: I'm going to win the Vezina trophy this year without Doug Harvey." And sure enough, he won the Vezina trophy without Doug Harvey. Not only did he win the Vezina trophy; he also won the Hart trophy as the most valuable player in the league.

The Hart was to be his last trophy with Montréal. His asthma was getting worse, and so was his relationship with the coach. Red Fisher was witness to one encounter, between the two when they were playing against the Maple Leafs.

[Jacques] didn't want to stay at the Royal York Hotel because he said that the bedding in the room brought on asthma attacks. He wanted to

*stay at another hotel by himself and Toe Blake eventually let him do
that. But just for one game. Because, you know Toe and I went to
Maple Leaf Gardens one morning to watch the Maple Leafs practise
and we were walking up the steps and coming around the bend is
Jacques Plante with three young ladies on his arm. Toe Blake said,
"Good morning, Jacques!" and Jacques said, "Good morning, Toe!"
and Plante kept walking and Toe and I kept walking with Toe swearing under his breath saying: "That so and so, he'll be back at the Royal
York before he can blink."*

*And that night on the train, Plante said: "I want you to know,
Toe, that those three girls, they were my cousins." Toe said, "Fine!
Your cousins can come and visit you at the Royal York Hotel, next
time we're in town." And that was the end of that.*

It was not long afterwards that Toe Blake had apparently had
enough of his war with Plante. The goalie wasn't winning the games the
way he used to, Blake thought. The coach was fed up, he said, with
what he called Plante's "act." But his behaviour was reprehensible
when he made the decision to move. He negotiated a seven-player trade
with the New York Rangers. One of the players was Jacques Plante.
Blake did not even have the courtesy to tell Plante what he had done;
the goalie heard about it for the first time on his car radio. He went off
to New York grieving for his real team, the team he belonged to, he
always thought, missing Montréal, missing his kids. After a strong first
game where he shut out the Detroit Red Wings, the rest of his two seasons with the Rangers was undistinguished. He was thirty-five. He
announced that he was retiring.

He had done pretty well for himself financially. Molson's gave
him a "representative's" job. He bought a beauty parlour and three
small apartment buildings. Radio-Canada brought him in as an analyst
for some of the televised games, and he enjoyed that in a wistful kind
of way. He spent a lot of time with his sons, coached them at baseball,
and stopped talking about the hockey wars.

But hockey had not stopped talking about him. In 1965 when the
young coach Scotty Bowman was asked to field a Canadian team
against the world and Olympic champion Russians, Bowman talked

Plante into the net for that one game, and after only a couple of weeks of practice with those Junior Canadiens, against the genuinely superior opponent, Plante shocked the Russians by letting in only one goal. The Junior Canadiens scored twice.

Three years later, professional hockey expanded suddenly when six new teams were added to the NHL. Scotty Bowman was hired to build a team for St. Louis, and brought in not one but two retired goalies, Glenn Hall and Jacques Plante. The two somehow worked it out and were able to play together. Given the mythology that sportswriters nurture, in this case a legendary enmity between two high-level stars, their playing together on the same team was puzzling to some of the fans. But Jean Beliveau said that anyone who had played in that collegial atmosphere of the old Canadiens would understand.

I suppose that after his first retirement he found that he was still enjoying the game. You miss the action on the ice but you miss . . . I know in my case — and I can speak for many of my former teammates — we missed that great atmosphere we had in the room, the great atmosphere we had together travelling on the train. So, I'm not surprised.

What was a surprise was the grace demonstrated by the two old rivals, Hall and Plante, who played such a great season that they were jointly awarded the Vezina trophy, making it number seven for Jacques Plante. Then came a bigger surprise, when he went up to Toronto to play for his old arch enemies, the Maple Leafs. At about that time he started a new business, Fibrosport, making goaltenders' masks. He brought his son Michel in as a partner. It looked as though he had found something to do that was as rewarding as being on the ice. A soon as the season was over he would give all his time to Fibrosport. Soon he was making enough money manufacturing masks that he could take his Maple Leafs salary and put it in the bank. He was also playing very, very well. His 1971 goals-against average was 1.88, the lowest since his record 1.86 in 1956. The next year he was invited to Sweden to teach his goaltending methods there. He brought out a book, *Devant le Filet* (Before the Net), and in the Series of the Century between Canada and the USSR, he was Radio-Canada's principal analyst.

For a while it seemed as though his temporary retirement had been some kind of aberration. He was forty-four years old when he went to the Boston Bruins for the 1973 playoffs, and then negotiated a ten-year, one-million-dollar contract as coach and general manager of the Quebec Nordiques in the newly formed World Hockey Association.

But his personal life was in some disarray. His marriage with Jacqueline was over, after twenty-three years. His son Richard committed suicide. There were bad times at the fibreglass plant. Perhaps all that anguish rendered him especially vulnerable to a proposal to return to the ice. In any case, he made headlines on the sports pages when Bill Hunter brought him to the Edmonton Oilers. One day, in a practice session in Edmonton, he took a slapshot in the side of his head and severely damaged his right ear. A serious loss of balance followed, as well as sudden deafness with all the disorientation and grief that that can cause. And so now he really did retire, finally and irrevocably. He married again and went to live in Sierre, in Switzerland. He came back briefly for his induction into the Hockey Hall of Fame (in 1978). But although he would die of cancer regrettably young — he was only fifty-seven — Jacques Plante seemed to have come to terms gracefully and cheerfully with the fact that the rich and productive life he had led on the ice was done now, and he could play a new role: the Swiss Retiree.

He went to the same coffee shop every morning and did the grocery shopping. He coached hockey a few hours a week with local kids. He would come back to Canada for the playoffs, and sometimes would be seen at a training camp in September, chatting with the old pals.

And then he was gone, leaving behind a game to which he had given his life, and given an entirely different face.

♦ ♦ ♦

The original documentary was written and directed by Andy Thompson.

PART FOUR

RATTENBURY
A Tale of Murder and Genius

When the television series upon which these books are based was first proposed, Executive Producers Patricia Phillips and Andy Thompson, of Great North Productions in Edmonton, commissioned a brilliant, crusty, inventive filmmaker from Vancouver, Bob Duncan, to make the pilot. When the CRB Foundation, Historica's predecessor, was invited to consider helping to fund *The Canadians* — this was two years before I became commissioning editor — I was asked to keep an eye on the development of this pilot, and advise as to whether or not it was an appropriate venue for the Foundation's Heritage Project.

I was fascinated from the beginning. Here was a sprawling creative life story revolving around a vicious and almost bungled murder. In the late evening of a spring day in 1935, an eighteen-year-old chauffeur and general servant, a semiliterate boy named George Stoner, stood nervously behind the drunken, slumbering form of the sixty-seven-year-old retired architect Frances Rattenbury. Stoner was drunk and high on cocaine. He was also enraged because he thought that he had heard his lover, the young and voluptuous Mrs. Alma Rattenbury, having sex with her husband, the boy's employer, the semiconscious old architect in the big armchair. Stoner carried a big wooden mallet he had taken that morning from his grandmother's house. He struck the dozing old man three times over the head, and then broke down and raced upstairs to his mistress's bedroom, undressed, climbed into bed with her, and said, "I've hurt Ratz."

The trial, at London's Old Bailey, was a sensation. People slept in lineups in the street to get a place. The papers were full of the salacious and bloody details of the bizarre household and the murder that had taken place there. But curiously they said nothing about the rich, productive, memorable career of the architectural genius who had just been bludgeoned to death.

Of all the provincial capitals in Canada it is Victoria that most vividly strikes the visitor with the harmony of the architecture of its great traditional public buildings: the legislature, the ferry terminal, the Bank of Montreal, and perhaps more than anything else, because for those who arrive at the harbour by ferry or by air it is the first building they see, the Empress Hotel. She presides over that landfall like a true empress, and declares unequivocally that one has arrived in a city to be taken seriously, at a palace of elegance that Will Not Let You Down. Some will say that, in fact, the hotel does let you down, it is really all show, "like a cardboard cutout against the sky," but Victorians and visitors alike generally find the building awesome, at least from the outside. And there are few city arrivals in the world quite like stepping off the commuter seaplane from Vancouver onto the stone wharf at sea level, and then climbing those stairs at either end while the Old Empress reveals herself to you, step by step, in all her splendour.

It is a bit jarring to discover that the soaring imagination that gave Victoria these buildings and set the style for this most distinctive of provincial capitals belonged to a man who was not only a genius, but also an embezzler, a fraud, a liar on a huge professional scale, an unconcealed adulterer in a time when such things Were Not Done and Were Not Spoken Of, ending as a battered and bloody corpse in his own living room in London.

Frances Mawson Rattenbury emigrated from Yorkshire to Vancouver in the booming summer of 1892, looking for work and waving an impressive resumé. It declared that he had worked on some of the most eminent public buildings of both Bradford and Leeds. "Ratz," as his friends called him, apparently submitted his spectacular *curriculum vitae* in a way that did not require him to be in the same room with it when it was being read. Had he been present during its reading even the more credulous public officials might have noticed that among the specific projects therein noted was one (on which Rattenbury was listed as senior architect no less) that was finished when he was only six years old, and another built before he was born.

As far as we know, Frances Rattenbury had not in fact built anything before he came to Canada, although he had worked on the design of the ugly Town Hall of Cleckheaton, Yorkshire. This is not to take away from his genius, which was remarkable, nor from his ability to turn out, at lightning speed, the most compelling drawings. Both his preliminaries and his developed work were not only overwhelmingly beautiful and seductive, but also thoroughly practical and professional. But he had not, in fact, supervised the actual *building* of anything in Britain. His first commission in Canada, for a printer named Gustav Roedde, was a house intended to remind the nostalgic Roedde of his native Germany. When finished, however, it looked rather more like an English Queen Anne cottage, with a crenelated tower added on for a touch of grandeur.

Rattenbury demonstrated a flair for publicity from the beginning. When he first came to Vancouver in those balmy days of July 1892 he managed to get a spectacular report of his arrival published in the *Vancouver Daily World*, which apparently did not check out any of the above fraudulent information. (He did not mention the Roedde house caper.) His sense of timing was that of a showman, for in the same edition of the *Daily World* that introduced that amazing twenty-five-year old to the Vancouver public, there was announced an anonymous competition organized by the provincial government, to replace the old colonial legislative buildings (known as the "Birdcages") with new parliament buildings. British Columbia wanted something appropriate to the grandeur of the great mountainous Pacific Coast territory that had been a part of Confederation for twenty-one years, but only five years earlier had at last been connected to the rest of the country by the completion of the transcontinental railway. The citizens felt it was time to show off, and so they put out a call for architects to submit proposals in an anonymous competition. The entries had to be signed pseudonymously, so that established reputations would not count, at least on the first round.

Some of the entries were signed with cute names. One hopeful called himself "Patience," while another signed his drawings "Tah-Ra-Ra-Boom-De-Yay." But one set of drawings bore the simple designation, "B.C. Architect." Rattenbury, a bit presumptuously since he had been there only a few months, correctly supposed that a British

Columbian would be preferred over an outsider, all other things being equal. Things were not, as turned out, all that equal. Rattenbury's drawings were brilliant, exceptionally well executed. They proposed a dazzling building complex that strongly impressed the commissioners, and it is likely that the B.C. Architect pseudonym also helped. In any case, he made it into the finals, which were also pseudonymous. This time he signed his submission "FOR OUR QUEEN AND PROVINCE," the spirit of the time being both royalist and locally patriotic.

A few months later it was publicly announced that "Vancouver Architect" Frances Rattenbury had won the competition and would direct the building of the largest government project in the history of British Columbia. He took the steamer to Victoria to present himself to the authorities. They found themselves congratulating a confident, good-looking, red-headed man with a neatly trimmed full moustache, who appeared to be and actually was all of twenty-five years old. If they had cross-examined him on his actual building experience to date, they might have discovered that it consisted of the building of Herr Roedde's Queen Anne cottage.

The builder assigned to the project was, however, a very experienced local man named Frederick Adams. Adams had stationery printed — CONTRACTOR TO THE PARLIAMENT BUILDINGS — and proudly set out to make his reputation and his fortune. But things did not go well between Adams and his young architect.

Rattenbury wanted thousands of square feet of marble, sheet after sheet of the very best. As supervising architect he had the right and responsibility to approve the quarry and sign off on the choice before the stone was mined, and with Adams he looked at samples from all the best sources, and agreed on one. But when the marble arrived, a huge order, paid for by Adams, Rattenbury realized he'd made a mistake; it was not the right colour. To save face he declared that the stone as delivered was inferior to what he had approved, not acceptable. He tried to dump the problem on Adams' shoulders.

The terms of the contract were such that Adams the contractor was responsible for delivering materials that would satisfy the architect's demands and standards. If Rattenbury won this one, Adams would go bankrupt. It dragged on for months, through a series of meetings with lawyers and officials. Rattenbury and the builder yelled at each other during some of these meetings, in a manner that was most unseemly for the project heads of an assignment for queen and province. Rattenbury billed his client, the provincial government, $3,000 for attending at those meetings. This would be the equivalent of close to a quarter of a million in today's money. Historian Tony Barrett at the University of British Columbia said that this was typical of the architect throughout his career, and that Rattenbury had

> an idea of how you should handle all the contracts, and he didn't really feel himself bound by the rules, when it came to that, that [he thought that those who did respect the rules] were . . . petty minded, and lacked vision.

Trying to figure a way to avoid ruin, Fred Adams decided to visit another island quarry where there was marble he knew would do the job. He went over in a small steamer one afternoon, on a day when prudent mariners would have stayed home. A storm destroyed the boat, and the unfortunate builder was drowned. Ironically, a later steamship disaster would almost ruin Rattenbury, but this time his luck was holding.

When some bureaucrats in Victoria began to complain of cost overruns, Rattenbury made mincemeat of them. Magnificence was the watchword of the day, and his appeals to the senior officials' sense of the moment, of the significance of this work in the eyes of destiny and the world, seems to have carried the day. When a bureaucrat suggested that perhaps a lesser stone would be quite satisfactory for the interior of the legislative hall (and would substantially reduce the overruns), Rattenbury sent an indignant letter, which prevailed. He wrote:

> The grandeur of the whole scheme would be absolutely ruined should the legislative hall be poor and commonplace, and it would be if the marble is omitted. The whole character depends entirely on the rich and massive marble columns, and we cannot in any adequate way replace these with cheaper imitation.

For a while the bureaucrats and perhaps even some of the politicians worried and fumed about delays and costs. It began to look as though the $600,000 cost that the architect had agreed to might easily double (it nearly did). But as the great structure began to rise, to gleam in its cladding and rejoice in its columns, it soon was seen to be so splendid, so fine, so far beyond the glory anyone had dreamed of, that there was no going back and no way to even seem publicly regretful. It was, quite simply, magnificent. At least, on the outside. Once it was in use the MPPs discovered that the acoustics in the legislative assembly were so hopeless that they had to hang fishing nets from the ceiling to cut down the reverberation. The lieutenant governor, given a splendid third-floor suite of rooms for entertaining, was embarrassed the first time he tried them to discover that there were no washroom facilities and he had to send out for buckets.

Furthermore, there was nothing really original about the buildings. They were probably a direct copy of a "Chateau Style" failed proposal that his employers back in Britain had earlier developed for Bradford City Hall. Indeed that firm, Mawson and Mawson, tried to make Rattenbury turn over part of his Victoria fees to them as the traditional architect's due, on a first assignment, to the firm that had trained him. He ignored them, even though he would continue to claim, dishonestly, that he had been a major architect on some of their most famous projects.

Professor Barrett says that Rattenbury himself was convinced that the splendour of his work excused him from paying attention to normal professional obligations, to interior details, or to the other ordinary concerns of ordinary, responsible architects, and that he had absolutely no qualms or conscience about such trivial things as doubling the costs over what he had "committed" to, especially when the client was the government. He was also somewhat less than correct about his business practices. At about the time he started work on the main drawings for the parliament buildings, he saw a competition advertised for a state capitol in Olympia, Washington, and entered it. Apparently he was concerned neither with the impossibility of guiding two such gigantic tasks at the same time if he won, nor with the damage to his reputation if he lost. When he did not get the Washington State contract, a story began to go around that he had in fact won the competition but refused the commission out of moral indignation when the Washington State commissioners asked for a bribe. The commissioners of course declared this to be an outright lie, and Rattenbury himself said that somebody must have made it all up, he had not submitted a proposal at all, what were they talking about? Then he added privately that the reason he had refused to enter the competition in the first place was that the corruption of the Washington commissioners was of course well known.

His own fee for the parliament buildings was $40,000, quite enough for a man of even substantial appetites to retire on, or at least to rest on his laurels for a while, reflect, and consider what next. His reputation was made. He could have sat back and chosen the best commissions. When the buildings opened officially the press called them a marble palace, and the people came in droves to admire the detail and gape at the grandeur of their new parliament.

But Frances Mawson Rattenbury was not at that opening. He was back in England trying to raise money for a greed-driven boat-building scheme connected to the Yukon gold rush. It was 1898. He had already invested in cattle for the Klondike, at great risk, buying a thousand head and shipping them off to Dawson where a steak could cost you your life savings and cattle with any flesh on them, which you might have bought out of Seattle for sixty dollars, were selling for a thousand dollars a head. Ratz had heard about the huge crowds of prospector hopefuls willing to pay absurd prices for the trip across Bennett Lake on their way to the goldfields. Combined with the continuing appetite for high-priced beef in the north, it seemed to call for steamer service across Bennett Lake, cattleboats with plenty of accommodation for passengers as well. With his spellbinding rhetoric he tried to raise a substantial amount from gold-bedazzled Londoners for this not entirely crazy scheme.

His prudence was less than his rhetoric, however. He did not do well before the investors in The City. Ambition overcame judgment, and he made the classical promoter's mistake, investing his own capital in the project. But it was too late. By the time the company was up and running, the gold rush had exhausted itself and he lost his entire investment.

By this time he had married. Florence Lenora Nunn was a not very attractive girl who was pregnant when they tied the knot. She had gone up to the Yukon with him to christen and launch two of the steamers that had actually been built. The three boats, the *Flora*, the *Ora*, and the *Nora* had all been named for this rather lumpy, unattractive woman. They took the time while there to climb the Chilkoot Pass — which they claimed was easy, just a charming scenic walk, all the hysteria was invented. Rattenbury built them a house in elegant Oak Bay, and went back to work in Victoria, picking up on his still solid reputation as an architect in the Grand Manner. They had two children, Frank, who had badly deformed feet, and Mary, a nervous, erratic girl who would nonetheless become one of the great beauties of the city. Much later Rattenbury would disown both these unfortunate offspring, but for the time being he puttered about the garden in the early and apparently fairly sunny days of the marriage, and went on with his work. He sketched plans for more monumental projects and set about trying to sell them.

When one project looked as though it might go to competition, Rattenbury wrote an eloquent letter to the appropriate official pointing out that a competition was unlikely to produce the kind of elegant results the project merited (despite his success in the parliament buildings competition). He did the same thing a second time, arguing eloquently that the public interest would be best served by engaging an architect of proven record in the field of magnificent public structures. Somehow, he managed to pull this stuff off, but his rival architects did not forgive and forget, and bit by bit stored up resentment and, as they thought, evidence that might one day be used to bring him to grief.

Rattenbury's offices in the Five Sisters block burned down in 1910, and records of some of those key periods of his life are incomplete. But from the early days of his marriage a letter to his mother survives, in which he wrote:

Somehow the mornings creep on, dodging about the garden, in the woods, and along the beach. Then I get away downtown for a little tiffin. Florrie has a marvellously good temper — a jolly good thing for me because mine is rather short, especially when rushed for work. So we pull along well together.

On the evidence of people who actually knew the Rattenburys this letter seems to be more in aid of keeping his mother from worrying than an authentic description of what was going on. In fact, Rattenbury soon came to despise Florrie, although he doted on and was very good to Mary and seems to have been admired by the crippled Frank long after the boy would have been pardoned for giving up on his father.

He did not have to wait long for new commissions. Tourists and corporate chiefs were coming from far and wide to admire the parliament buildings, and before long the Bank of Montreal took him on as its principal western architect. His reputation flourished. The bank let it be known that they had secured the services of The Best. The rich of Victoria and Vancouver commissioned elaborate private homes. When the architect designing a new official residence for the lieutenant governor began to go way over budget, the government, showing not a great deal of diligent memory either for overruns or bathrooms, engaged Ratz as consultant.

Ratz looked at the residence proposal and told the premier it was almost certainly going to go 50 per cent over budget; they should hire a new architect. But who? Seemliness and perhaps protocol prevented Frances Rattenbury from recommending Frances Rattenbury; he suggested one Samuel Maclure. Perhaps he did not mention that he shared offices with Maclure and had partnered with him on a number of projects. The government admired Maclure's work and made him an offer. Maclure said he was not well, and could not take on a project of such importance just now, not all by himself, he would bring in a partner. The partner was Rattenbury. Who went over budget by 50 per cent.

In addition to the overruns, there was a buzz of rumour about some materials that had gone missing. Rattenbury's biographer, Terry Reksten, said:

In particular . . . a rather large quantity of marble, sheets of marble. And, certainly, there was marble in Government House, but not to the degree that had been paid for. And anybody who had visited Rattenbury's home and seen his recent renovations realized that his kitchen was lined with marble from floor to ceiling, and also that a very special fireplace, that was similar to one missing from Government House, now graced his dining room.

Rattenbury's many rivals and enemies in the architectural community, incensed that he seemed to be getting all the good commissions despite breaking all the rules and sullying the profession with his constant overspending and his open contempt for his fellow professionals, now knew they had him on the ropes. They wrote an indictment to the provincial government calling for a public inquiry. Rattenbury responded in character.

I emphatically deny the charges. They are slanders, maliciously and knowingly made for the purpose of discrediting me in the eyes of the Government and the people of British Columbia.

He accompanied his letter with a formal notice of intent to file charges of libel and slander. The government did not want a fuss. One of the two firms who had called for the inquiry decided, upon reflection, that their participation in such a public event would reflect badly on them. The whole profession was, in fact, stained by kickbacks from suppliers, inappropriate gifts to officials and other practices that at the very least verged on corruption. Rattenbury was known to be a gifted, relentless opponent. The firm withdrew. The remaining individual architect, who actually took the stand to testify against Rattenbury, could not have been a better witness from his opponent's point of view. He vigorously objected to being sworn, as if it were an attack on his integrity and credibility. He was pompous, evasive, abusive, and forgetful. Rattenbury was cleared. It was December 29, 1923. His club threw a great party for him. As they lustily sang "For He's a Jolly Good Fellow," a twenty-seven-year-old widow, passing through the lobby of the hotel after playing piano at a reception that night, heard that song sung with what struck her as unusual fervour, and lingered to see for whom all this affection was being expressed. Alma Pakenham, who had lost one husband to the Great War and divorced a second, was a lusty, rich-voiced, pouty musical prodigy very much in demand as a pianist at classy social functions. The man who had aroused her interest was Rattenbury. He was polite at first, then curious, then more than friendly. By then his marriage with Florrie had degenerated into mutual contempt. They lived in separate parts of the house. Rattenbury had begun to drink heavily, but recent splendid commissions had sobered him up, brought a glint back to his still lush red hair, and trimmed off some of the pudginess that he had accumulated during some of the bad days.

He and Alma started a fairly open affair.

The single most important commission in that period was the CPR's Empress Hotel. Sir Thomas Shaughnessy, the railway's president, had done a brilliant job of seducing the city into giving the CPR free land and water and no municipal taxation for fifteen years, in order to overcome the railway's official posture of indifference to a tourist hotel in the capital. It was decided that the stinking old mud-flats behind the causeway across the foot of the harbour would be reclaimed. On the evidence of drawings that emerged later, proving that Rattenbury had designed a hotel for the mudflats at a time when a different vacant lot near the parliament buildings was commonly understood to be the site that would be chosen, it is clear that here, as in many other cases, Rattenbury had some inside knowledge which he used to invest in ways that would today land him in court with a criminal charge. The Empress Hotel sealed his grip on the harbour and his stamp on the city. He would design and supervise the building of many important public and private structures in British Columbia — the renovations of the Hotel Vancouver, the Vancouver and Nelson courthouses, a vast amusement centre with three ocean-water heated swimming pools — sixty years ahead of the West Edmonton Mall — (Rattenbury's amusement centre did not get built as such but metamorphosed into his version of the Crystal Palace, known as the Crystal Gardens).

The parliament buildings, predicted by the naysayers to be so big it would take five hundred years to fill them, were by now too small for the burgeoning government and an addition would be needed. Rattenbury was clearly the only man to do the work, despite the whiffs of scandal and the overruns. The results (about 35 per cent over budget) were — once again — magnificent (the single word most often applied to this man's work). Queen Victoria's son the Duke of

Connaught, by then governor general of Canada, presided over a grand official opening.

Along with these successes Rattenbury did make some bad financial decisions, again based on what would now be deemed the criminal use of insider information. Before the war he had been wooed and won by the new Grand Trunk Pacific railway, whose chief Charles Melville Hays had conceived the idea of making Prince Rupert a kind of San Francisco of the North West. Rattenbury drew preliminary sketches for Grand Trunk Pacific hotels from Alberta to the coast. Grand Trunk Pacific bought a clutch of coastal steamers, and commissioned the architect to redecorate their interiors. By the end of the decade it looked as though travellers from Calgary to Vancouver Island would sleep in Rattenbury-designed hotels throughout their journey, and cross to Victoria in a Rattenbury-decorated ship. He actually completed the work on one of those vessels. Hays went to Britain, successfully raised the capital he needed to push the GTP line through to the coast, convincing investors that it would displace the CPR as the principal east-west carrier in Canada if not the continent as a whole, and boarded his ship for home in triumph.

That ship was RMS *Titanic*. Charles Hays did not survive her sinking. His successor, E.J. Chambers, was a cautious man, not at all convinced of the viability of Prince Rupert as a great commercial and tourist centre. He dithered and delayed. Rattenbury waited patiently. The GTP would, in the end, have to make good on its commitments to its shareholders. Rattenbury had bought up relatively worthless land that would, as the project got underway, make him a millionaire. But 1912 turned into 1913, and then 1914, and January turned into August, and the guns broke out in Europe. No settlers were coming west any more; the GTP plans were put on hold. The hold became permanent. Prince Rupert was finished. Rattenbury lost all that investment, took what he had left from the hotels and the courthouses and the mansions, and began to look for another way to live.

If Rattenbury's marriage to Florence Nunn had been forced by the accidental pregnancy of a woman with whom he was only dallying, it had by now deteriorated into something worse than a sham. He bought a silk-lined cape and wore it with a flourish as he took his mistress Alma to the opera. Before long everyone knew that while he nominally still lived in the Oak Bay home he had designed and built and enlarged into a mansion, he was really living with Alma. He asked for a divorce. The undenied adultery would have made it easy for Florrie, and divorce would have brought her a comfortable settlement, but she refused.

Rattenbury, now openly moved in with Alma, cut off power and water to the Oak Bay house to try forcing Florrie to leave. When that didn't work he brought Alma there and had her play the piano in the parlour while poor Florrie hid her head under the pillows upstairs. When Mary came down to complain that this was all making her mother ill, Alma loudly played the "Funeral March."

In 1929 Alma gave birth to a son, John, and when Rattenbury rewrote his will John and Christopher, Alma's son by an earlier marriage, were the beneficiaries: Frank and Mary were cut off. It is strange that when Rattenbury and Alma, who legally married on Florrie's death, turned their backs on Canada forever and sailed for England, the only person who came to see them off was poor, crippled Frank. They settled in Bournemouth, perhaps the closest they could come to a town that felt a bit like Victoria, and rented the *Villa Madeira*, at 5 Manor Road. This second marriage had disintegrated too, at least sexually. Rattenbury, who had started drinking fairly heavily to help himself over some of the rough spots in Canada, was back at it again, almost a bottle of whisky a day. Alma tried to get him interested in developing new projects, and for a while he brightened up and met with one or two fellow architects whom Alma had gotten to know in London, but these discussions never led to anything.

Rattenbury had been a major figure in Victoria for almost forty years. In Bournemouth he was just another overweight, boozy, retired bloke in his sixties who had once been in some profession or other. He was probably sexually incapacitated. But Alma, at thirty-five, was passionate and lonely. She went up to London often, much in demand as a pianist, and soon began to write songs for a popular tenor named Frank Titterton, whom she accompanied for his Sunday night concerts on BBC radio. Ratz was now sleeping downstairs next to his study, and

Alma upstairs. In 1934, they hired a slow, bow-legged, strong seventeen-year-old named George Stoner as a driver and general helper. Alma gave the good-looking fair-haired boy the small bedroom just down the hall from her own. It was not long before she had overcome any reticence Stoner might have felt, and he was spending most nights in her room. She was disarmingly open about it all at the trial. The judge and the lawyers found it intriguing but puzzling. Here was a sophisticated, worldly woman, thrice married, with two children, who had taken up with someone young enough to be her son, a quiet, withdrawn, late-adolescent person: it had to be purely animal. In that court, at that time, this was not a recommendation.

Rattenbury had become very close with his money. Alma took to lying to him about household and personal finances. He let her pay all the bills and manage the servants, and seems not to have found her occasional demands for large sums unreasonable, although his monthly allowance to her was only a few pounds. Stoner was uneasy about his double life as lover at night and common servant in the daytime, and complained to Alma. In fact, while he was nominally a common servant with a salary of 4 pounds a month, he was given very few tasks apart from driving. He often played cards all afternoon with Rattenbury, and took to swaggering, lording it over the other servants, and wearing a small dagger as an ostentatious mark of distinction.

Alma, however, was worried that her young bed partner might do something erratic, perhaps reveal to her husband what was really going on, or even act violently, as he sometimes seemed to be about to do. She told Rattenbury that she needed 250 pounds "for a woman's operation" in London, and had Stoner drive her to Kensington. They went shopping at Harrod's and checked into the Kensington Palace Hotel as "Mrs. Rattenbury and brother." She bought him fine suits and silk pyjamas, and gave him money so that he could buy her a diamond ring. They spent the week there, dining, drinking, shopping, and going to bed. When they returned Rattenbury was "jolly," as Alma described his inebriated state, and amiable. He did not even ask about the alleged operation. Alma, guiltily relieved, feeling some trace of her old affection for her husband, and mellow herself after an uninterrupted week of satisfying all of her appetites, helped the old drunk out of his chair and into his bedroom. She made the mistake of closing the door.

George Stoner's barrister claimed at the trial that his client, allegedly addicted to cocaine, was hallucinating on the drug that night and had imagined that the sounds he heard coming through the closed bedroom door meant that Alma and her husband had gone to bed together. His slow brain found only one way to deal with this. He resolved to kill the old man. The next day, on a routine home visit, he found a heavy wooden carpenter's mallet in his grandmother's house, and brought it back to 5 Manor Road when he returned that evening. He found the architect dozing, drunk, in the usual armchair, went up behind him, and brought down the mallet, three times, on Frances Rattenbury's now balding head.

Alma had been out for the evening. When she came home, late, she chatted briefly with her personal servant Irene, assumed that her husband was safely asleep in his own room, and went upstairs to hers. After a while Stoner came up and climbed into bed beside her. She testified afterwards that he seemed very agitated, but that she thought it had something to do with the drugs he was taking. Suddenly she heard a loud groan from below, the voice unmistakably her husband's.

"What's that!" she asked Stoner. "I've hurt Ratz," he said, blubbering. She ran downstairs.

By the time the police got there she was very drunk. At first she insisted that some intruder had come in through the French doors, but when it was shown that those doors were locked from the inside, she tried to bribe and then to seduce the investigating constable. He remained very correct and quietly kept questioning her. She was, in her confused state, trying to protect George Stoner. She declared that she had finally lost all hope for the marriage, had decided to kill Rattenbury, had bludgeoned him with a mallet, which she had hidden outdoors and would try to find in the morning. When she was sober the next day she stuck to this latter story, admitting that there had been no intruder. The police were confused, and when Rattenbury died in hospital a few days later they ended up charging both of them with murder — to which Stoner also confessed.

At the trial, which started on May 27, 1935, Alma decided to tell the truth and seems to have convinced the jury that she was doing so. Stoner did not withdraw his confession, but tried to plead insanity due to his addiction to cocaine. He described the drug as being a flaky brown colour with dark flecks. Medical experts disagreed as to whether his known symptoms might reflect a cocaine addiction, but not on the actual colour of cocaine of any quality. The trial lasted five days, and the jury were out for only forty-seven minutes before acquitting Alma and convicting George Stoner.

Stoner was sentenced to hang, but Alma would die before him. She had gone to a nursing home, guilty, despondent, badly needing rest and perhaps to dry out, as she had been a heavy drinker since before they came to England. One afternoon, after a Dr. Bathurst had seen her and agreed that she was now much better, she told the matron that she was feeling well enough to go walking. In fact, she took the train to Bournemouth and there was a witness to what happened after that. A farmer driving his cows back to the barn saw a handsome young woman standing by the riverbank, smoking a cigarette, and scribbling in a notebook. Suddenly, as he strode along after the cattle staring at the well-dressed stranger, she threw the coat back off her shoulders, brought out a small dagger, and plunged it into her chest. As the farmer rushed towards her, not having seen the dagger but aware that she had done something sudden and perhaps violent, Alma pitched headlong into the water, which reddened around her. The man could not swim. He ran for help. It was too late.

The police found a tin of cigarettes, a fountain pen, an empty dagger sheath, and some scribbled notes.

If only I thought it would help Stoner, I would stay on, but it has been pointed out to me all too vividly that I cannot help him. That is my death sentence. . . . It is beautiful here. What a lovely world we are in. It must be easier to be hanged than to have to do the job oneself, especially in these circumstances, being watched all the while. Pray God nothing stops me. . . . I tried to throw myself under a train at Oxford Circus. Too many people about. Then a bus. Still too many people. One must be bold to do a thing like this. It is beautiful here.

313

. . . Thank God for peace at last.

Alma and Frances Rattenbury's son John was five years old when his parents died. When Robert Duncan and his production team found him, he had become one of the United States' more senior and respected architects. He was quietly philosophical about the jungle from which he had emerged, scarred but not impaired.

I was playing once with some children my age, and you know how children are . . . incredibly cruel without really meaning to . . . and one of them just suddenly turned to me and told me, "Your father was murdered and your mother took her own life." . . . It was a terrible shock to me. I would be sitting in class years later, you know? Suddenly I would start to cry and the teacher would look over: "What's the matter with this person?" [But] I've never held it against anybody, not even the chauffeur who fell in love with my mother. Those sorts of things happen. And the fact that it developed into a tragedy . . .

Here Mr. Rattenbury's voice trailed off.

As did the life of his father's killer, in the end. There was a huge public protest against the proposed hanging of George Stoner, part of it driven by a growing anti-capital punishment movement in Britain, part by a widespread conviction that he was, as he had said in court, not entirely compos mentis at the time of the killing, whether deranged by jealousy, or by drugs, or by both. Although the mallet seemed evidence of premeditation, in the end the home secretary acknowledged the half million signatures on petitions to save him and commuted the sentence to life in prison. He was released on parole, to join the army when World War II began in 1939. He returned to Bournemouth in 1945, then still only twenty-eight years old. He married, and apparently lived a very ordinary life. He was in the public eye briefly in 1990 when, an old age pensioner, he was arrested wearing only socks and a beret, for sexually assaulting a young boy in a public toilet. He would never discuss the Rattenbury case. He died in a Bournemouth nursing home.

Vancouver writer-director Robert Duncan wrote at the end of his documentary on the life of Frances Rattenbury:

In Victoria, Rattenbury's Empress Hotel still dominates centre stage. His legislature building, a hundred years later, still houses the provincial government. But the stately ferry terminal has been converted to a wax museum. Government House, which almost caused his downfall, was destroyed again by fire in 1957. His house in Oak Bay is a private school, the Crystal Gardens an aviary and botanical garden. In Vancouver his majestic law courts are now home to the city's art gallery.

The man who built monuments has no monument of his own. He's buried here in an unmarked plot in the Bournemouth cemetery. Alma's grave, just a few feet away, is identified only with a cemetery spike, to remind the attendants that the space below is occupied.

◆ ◆ ◆

The original documentary was written, directed and narrated by Robert Duncan.

PART FIVE

NELL SHIPMAN
"Aw Gee. Forgetting Me."

The credit for performing the first nude scene in a movie is traditionally accorded to the Czech star Hedy Lamarr, in a 1933 film entitled
Ecstasy. The twenty-year-old was photographed totally immersed,
decorously breast-stroking through a brief scene that became some
kind of international scandal in the days when sexual behaviour was a
Hollywood obsession. For hundreds of thousands of film enthusiasts
the only way to see those delectable few seconds of naughtiness in an
otherwise profoundly dull and forgettable film was to belong to a university film society where the usual censorship strictures did not apply.

But there is an earlier and more daring nude scene in a movie, performed by the Canadian producer-director-screenwriter-star Nell
Shipman of Victoria, BC, who had herself provocatively filmed disrob-
ing by the edge of a mountain pool, plunging in, and partially emerging as she sensually exposed herself to the spray of a cascade falling
into the pool. The film was called *Back to God's Country*. It was produced in Alberta in 1919. Shipman had based her script on a novel by
the then popular James Oliver Curwood. The picture was produced by
Shipman's husband Ernie Shipman, and starred the writer herself. The
distributors tried to turn the nude scene into a market-boosting scandal by means of a mildly salacious advertising campaign ("Please do
not ban this film!"). The movie was a great success but the nude scene
generated almost no comment, and Shipman went on to build a movie
career that peaked when she was in her late thirties, and then slowly
declined into a final couple of decades of poverty and obloquy.

The Shipman films did not find their way into the university film
societies. Perhaps the reason her pictures disappeared after flashing
briefly and successfully onto North American screens was largely
Shipman's own impulsive and erratic business methods and romantic
idealism. But it was at least partly — some say mostly — because this

pioneer filmmaker's stubborn independence was a way of declaring war on the big studio movement as it blossomed in the 1930s, a movement that ruthlessly set out to grind down and destroy the Independents, of which proud company Nell Shipman was an exemplary member.

Whatever the reason, disappear they did, until the archivist D.J. Turner began the long process of tracking down and acquiring the lost footage, and Bill O'Farrell, a former production executive for another Canadian film pioneer named Budge Crawley, began the process of physically restoring the few badly decayed prints of Shipman's work that Turner had been able to find. Their most important acquisition and most challenging restoration was Shipman's great 1919 success *Back to God's Country*. These films had been shot on a film stock known as acetate, a transparent forerunner of celluloid. Acetate film was unstable, decaying with a distinctly vinegary odour. Its cousin nitrate film was explosive and caused a number of serious fires before they both were superseded by celluloid, which became and still is the preferred material for both still and motion pictures.[5]

The very word *archives* suggests the smell of dust in narrow corridors, old stone and sunlight slanting through narrow windows. But the National Archives of Canada are housed in an almost futuristic glass-and-steel building in the nation's capital, and in the basement of that building is a cold storage room where film is kept at zero degrees Fahrenheit (minus 18 degrees Celsius). Archivists dress in parkas and gloves to visit it.

Dozens of reels of Shipman originals are in those vaults. When the film restorers began to work through them, the task was daunting. The film had turned a dark orange-brown colour and was giving off the characteristic vinegar odour of decaying acetate. Whole sections were physically falling apart, frame after frame looking as though moths or mice had been at them. D.J. Turner kept scouring the world's repositories of old films, however, and over time acquired a sufficient number

---

5. This will probably change before long. Digital imaging with its ability to be stored in tiny solid-state chips is coming up fast, although even digital's staunchest enthusiasts agree that celluloid film will, for some time, remain the preferred medium for projection in theatres.

of copies, some of them in versions quite different from the one the restorers had begun with, to assemble a *Back to God's Country* painstakingly transferred frame by frame onto modern celluloid (and archived in electronic digital format as well), until they had a projectable finished copy. This movie is really the centrepiece of our story of Nell Shipman, as it was in so many ways the centrepiece of her life; so it is worthwhile hearing a few more words about the task of rescuing it from its very close brush with annihilation. Bill O'Farrell says,

> *Back to God's Country* . . . *remains one of the most complex restorations we have ever undertaken. One of the issues we had to deal with . . . was . . . restoration ethics. By that I mean you're faced with some interesting subjective choices, because of the fact that we had literally two versions of the film to work with, from two different camera angles. There was one shot where Nell is walking along the ravine. And in one version she is walking . . . [only] up to a certain point. And in the other version she walks the rest of the way. . . . There were probably two cameras rolling but only one camera got that entire shot.*

The restorers were faced with the question of trying to determine which shot, or combination of shots, would be most faithful to the intentions of the original producers. In the end they had to guess — or often to just go with the only version that was sufficiently intact to be copied onto a fresh roll of celluloid.

One of the things that writer-director Patricia Phillips discovered as she began to assemble this television biography of Nell Shipman is that in *Back to God's Country*, and in other Shipman films, there are striking parallels to Shipman's own life, enough of them to make director Phillips' documentary a running set of images drawn from these old movies, and interwoven with the story of a real life.

That life began in Victoria, about as dramatically as anything the child once grown would ever conceive for her dozens of novels and films: she died almost immediately after she was born. At least that was what seemed to happen, so unequivocally that the baby's despairing mother ran out into the night, to the edge of the forest, with the inert little body in her arms, holding it up to the sky, when suddenly the tiny limbs began to twitch and grope, and the baby came back to life. They named her Helen, Helen Barham.

It was at about the time that the little survivor was taking her first faltering steps in British Columbia, that in Paris the brothers Lumière helped a new industry and a new art form take their first faltering steps. For the first time in the world, in December of 1895, they projected onto a screen in front of a paying audience the image of a passenger train puffing its way grandly into a suburban Paris station. The power of that moving image was so great that as the locomotive grew unstoppably larger and closer on the screen some members of the audience ran screaming from the theatre, convinced that they were about to be crushed under the wheels.

As we begin to look at the new industrial and artistic world upon which Nell Shipman had such an impact, it would richly repay the film enthusiast to rent a video entitled simply *Lumière*, a brilliantly conceived centennial project (1995). For it, an original wooden-box Lumière brothers camera called the *Cinématographe* was put back into working order, reels of the special film were manufactured, and a couple of dozen famous contemporary directors were invited to make a movie each, within the space of the available single reel running time — which was only fifty seconds! They had to stick to the techniques of the day, which meant little editing and no synchronous sound. Spike Lee, Agnes Varda, John Boorman, Liv Ullman, and some twenty other well-known directors had a go at it. The first of the productions in this eccentric and sometimes brilliant collection took the camera back to that same suburban station for the arrival of an express, with predictable and hilarious results. An hour and a half with this inspired work will give any viewer a whole film course's worth of insight into the demands and strictures of early filmmaking.

Helen Barham had not yet acquired the nickname Nell; that would come with her first marriage, more than a dozen years later. But she had acquired a taste for public entertainments. It is likely that she saw her first motion picture in a vaudeville house when she was still pretty young. She was precocious, and her father gave her more freedom than most girls would have had growing up on the West Coast at the end of the nineteenth century. It seems likely that he took her to the popular vaudeville theatres to see this new phenomenon, the motion picture. Movies in those days were often travelling shows. An enterprising fellow with a projector and a bag or box full of short films, completely silent of course, would go from town to town and make a deal to split the receipts with the management of a local hall. He might hire a local pianist to provide an accompaniment. Because of the entertainment level of many of the early films — five- or six-minute simple scenarios of a bank robbery and chase and apprehension, for example — there was a natural affinity for the vaudeville theatres with their tradition of short snappy acts. Bit by bit the vaudeville companies began to install their own projectors, order their films directly from the distributors, and even use the movie shows to promote upcoming live events. The bank robber would be shot to death in the street, and then up would come some rudimentarily animated graphics of stars and moons, and words would spread across the screen:

SEE THE GREAT MANDRAKE THE MAGICIAN
LIVE ON THIS STAGE
NEXT THURSDAY AND FRIDAY ONLY AT 7 PM
LIVING MYSTERY TO THRILL AND *AMAZE!*[6]

Barham *père* was a remittance man, one of those younger sons of traditional British families who was not going to inherit, was a bit of an embarrassment to the family, and was shipped off to the colonies with a small allowance just to get him out of the way. Nell's father drank to comfort himself with his misfortune, which probably included a substantial dose of contempt from his neighbours — the remittance men were looked down upon as ne'er-do-well snobs. And it may be that the adolescent girl's acting ambitions seemed to her father to be some kind of opportunity. He had moved the family to Seattle, and in Seattle there was an acting teacher of reputation, Frank Egan. Nell gave up on school, enrolled with Egan, and by the age of thirteen was on the road with a repertory theatre, travelling up and down the West Coast. This was a trial by fire. You were not paid very much, and you had to cover

6. See Part Twelve for the role of film announcements like this in the life of the real Mandrake the Magician, another notable British Columbian.

your own hotel and meals and even make your own costumes. Nell's mother went on the road with the adventurous adolescent, primarily to protect her virtue, as they used to say, but also to comfort her, advise her on wardrobe, and give her moral support. The life was hard on both of them, but Nell refused to quit until she too got tired of eating inadequate meals in dirty rooms in horrid little fleabag hotels, and came home exhausted but experienced. She was sixteen years old.

She tried a stint in Alaska with another Seattle repertory company, managed by a man named Charles Taylor, who had hoped to make his fortune with a vaudeville company playing to the gold rush guys. But it was too late; the gold rush was over. Taylor's company went broke, and Nell came home.

Something about the North had grasped her imagination, and would not lie dormant for long. Back from Alaska, broke, but still confident that the theatre was her proper place in the world, she walked into Seattle's Pantages Theatre and met a man who was to radically change her life. His name was Ernie Shipman — "Ten Percent Ernie" — because as an agent, manager, and promoter he lived on that percentage of the earnings of all the talents he took under his wing. He was thirty-eight, pot-bellied, a rake with a reputation and an improbable and unattractive red hunting cap. She was eighteen, big-bosomed, voluptuous, with seductive eyes and the confidence of a road warrior. Improbably, they clicked.

They talked together about this new moving picture thing. The new moving picture thing was in California. So they got married and went to California. She began to think about writing; a book was taking shape in her mind. A collection of short stories called *Under the Crescent*, it would be tales of love and intrigue in an exotic Turkish environment. Ernie Shipman, for all his harebrained schemes and unsavoury ways, must have been an effective promoter, because before long he sold the film rights to *Under the Crescent*, landed Nell a contract to write a two-reeler based on it (some sources say a series), and launched the career of a screenwriter who would soon become a star.

Her ability to turn out screenplays quickly made them if not rich at least sufficiently well-off to take a gracious Victorian house in

Glendale, which is still there and still lovely. Stories of this svelte and seductive young woman sliding into a production executive's office with one new screenplay and out with a contract for another began to attract a lot of attention in Los Angeles. A company called Vitagraph decided to contract her as an actress in one of the then famous James Oliver Curwood's outdoor adventure stories. She was by now a recognized writer, at the age of twenty-three. Nell got the screenwriting contract for the Curwood project, as well as the principal role, and then talked her way into both producing and directing her own script.

The picture was a full-length feature, *God's Country and the Woman*. It put Nell Shipman back into the northern wilderness she had come to love in Alaska. And it gave her a name. For the rest of her career, the girl from Victoria would be known as the Girl from God's Country.

Sam Goldwyn, then still working under his original name of Samuel Goldfish, tried to secure the glamorous newcomer with a seven-year contract, the maximum allowed by law in those days. Nell came in for a test and a costume fitting. When she found that they were trying to force her big-breasted, wide-hipped long-limbed outdoors woman body into the then fashionable mould of a tiny delicate starlet, she went back to Vitagraph and another Curwood story, *Baree, Son of Kazan* (1917). Now she was getting cockily independent. She insisted on doing her own stunts in *Baree*. She was good at them, and perhaps it would save the cost of a salary to a stunt artist. But it was insubordinate, and Vitagraph decided they had to show who was boss. Her next few acting assignments were secondary roles. Nell went to Ten Percent Ernie and complained.

In the overall profile of the life of Nell Shipman *née* Helen Barham, the role of her first husband is mixed and not always savoury. But he did know how to make a deal. He went around by the side door, straight to Curwood who was a great deal more valuable to those Vitagraph pictures than Vitagraph was to Curwood. Curwood liked what Nell had done to *God's Country and the Woman*. He presciently saw the value of the same approach that years later would give us Rocky from I to V, and he proposed to go *Back to God's Country*. Nell Shipman would be star and co-writer with Curwood. Ernie was not only a full partner in the new production company, Shipman-Curwood productions, but also the producer of the seventy-three-minute feature.

As they began work on *Back to God's Country*, the Great War was just winding down in Europe. Much of the Western world had been hit by a severe epidemic of influenza. Nell and her mother Rose were both stricken. As Nell lay in a coma in an upstairs room, Rose died in the room below her. Before she was fully recovered from her illness, and in the midst of her grief at the loss of her mother, Nell had to start shooting some incidental scenes in California, while Ernie headed north to Alberta, where most of the film was to be produced, to line up financing.

It was probably one of the earliest instances of what has become a mainstay of feature-film production funding in this country: persuading governments, citizens, and businesses in the region where you are going to produce that they should put up the money for the production. Ernie Shipman met with the Edmonton board of trade. They all knew *God's Country and the Woman*. They didn't all know that Nell was a Victoria girl and were probably charmed to learn that little detail. They were told that it was going to be a great movie, much greater than its predecessor, so of course it was a huge investment opportunity. And they bought it.

The actual production, on the shores of Lesser Slave Lake, went less smoothly. When Curwood himself turned up on the set he found a script that had inverted the intentions of his original story, in which a hero — according to the convention of the genre — rescues an enchanting but vulnerable heroine. This latter was not a character that appealed to Nell Shipman, who had to play the role. So by the time Curwood arrived in Northern Alberta, with shooting too far advanced to make major changes, Nell's character (Dolores LeBeau) had become the prime focus of the narrative. The film historian Peter Morris told us, "She is the one who defeats the villain in the end. She is the one who protects her husband. She is the one who develops the very sensitive rapport with the dog . . ." And Curwood was distressed by all these changes until Nell got hold of him and buttered him up and told him how wonderful *his* concept was and how little she had had to alter it for film purposes . . . and doubtless other things that contemporary directors and screenwriters find themselves using to soothe the novelist who has arrived on the set. On the *Back to God's Country* set, although Shipman had no official role other than co-screenwriter and star, it is clear from the many accounts of that production that it was she who chose the key scenes and gave the film its natural look. It was she who discarded the flesh-coloured leotards to play the swimming scene described earlier. The leotards looked like leotards, she said, not like skin. So she would play it naturally.

It was a shoot with a lot of drama that was not all caught on camera. Another interesting man on set who turns up in the official cast list of some later films though not, it seems, in *Back to God's Country* — so it is not clear exactly what he was doing on that set — is Bert Van Tuyle, with whom Nell began to have an affair when Ernie went back to California in search of more financing.

Then the weather turned ferociously cold. The carpenters quit. Bert got severe frostbite, which turned to gangrene. The romantic lead, Ronald Byron, a handsome young Australian, developed pneumonia after a few days of shooting and soon died. When you examine the film closely, you find that the leading man in some scenes looks oddly different from the supposedly same man in other scenes.

This was the beginning of a whole series of films in which Nell Shipman would develop important relationships with animals. She was fiercely loyal to her animals. She would not permit cruel restraints like nose rings and genital rings, nor would she allow stun guns on the set. "They can sense it, you know," she insisted. No whips, no lassoes, no drugs.

In *Back to God's Country* they used two different Great Danes to play "Wapi the Walrus," a key role (and the title of the Curwood story on which the screenplay was based). One of them, Rex, was a soft and easygoing sweetheart dog. The other, Trésor, was a trained killer who could be counted on to be fierce when required, but you wouldn't want to get too close to him when he wasn't muzzled or when his trainer was not at hand.

The dogs got mixed up once, when Nell was supposed to play a close and affectionate scene with Rex. Shortly after they started to roll camera on the scene someone realized that a switch had taken place and whispered to director David Hartford that this was really the killer dog. Hartford said quietly, Keep 'em rolling. Nobody told Nell. Nell caressed and hugged the killer dog, which appeared to return her affection, and the scene went off perfectly. They cut. Someone told Nell, who did not seem very surprised. The director David Hartford came over to them laughing and said sarcastically something like "Some killer dog!" Trésor then leapt for Hartford's throat and they had to rush in and pull the dog off the terrified director.

Back to God's Country was possibly the most successful film in Canadian cinema history. It earned some 300 per cent profit for its investors. Nell does not seem to have shared that profit. It seems likely that she was cheated out of her share as a participant in several of the companies involved. The fading marriage may have played a part. Ernie was having his own affair in California while Nell and Bert Van Tuyle were keeping each other warm at Lesser Slave Lake. Nell was paid as star and screenwriter, but when it was all over she broke away from Shipman-Curwood productions, divorced Ernie, and set out on a road of stubborn independence that would be, for a while, exhilarating.

She founded Nell Shipman Productions, of Los Angeles. Bert Van Tuyle was her front man and business partner. Joseph Walker, a cinematographer who had worked on *Back to God's Country* and would go on to a brilliant career shooting for Frank Capra, helped her with an insignificant little two-reeler, *Trail of the Arrow*, and with *Something New*. She wrote, directed, and starred in *Something New*, a Maxwell Automobile promotional film that was supposed to be a two-reeler but grew into a hilarious feature-length film, set this time not in ice and snow but in the Mojave Desert. She found an "angel," a man named William Clune. Even though there were signs that the future of film was in the hands of the growing big studios like Universal, he took a chance on this brave new independent woman and financed what was going to be her really great film. This one was "take three" so to speak of the God's Country theme. They called it *The Girl from God's Country*.

The maximum length of a feature until then was nine reels, about an hour and a half. *The Girl from God's Country* finished up at thirteen reels. Nell's contract gave her editing control, but Clune believed that exhibitors wouldn't touch a two-hour film. He seized it, recut it, and put out a standard length version. That was the end of Clune. Historian Tom Trusky at Idaho's Boise University (where a centre of Shipman archives and studies has been created) told us that Nell took out trade paper ads saying, "That's what they do to women in China. They bind their feet and produce malformed beings. And that's what happened to my film. Do not book the 9 reel version of *The Girl from God's Country*."

"You can imagine how popular that makes her in the industry," Professor Trusky said. "The word is out that she is . . . blackballed in Hollywood. . . .The decision to start her own company was wonderful, but . . . wrong-headed. The industry is starting to centralize. [That's] going to be the pattern for the next forty years or so. [But now] Nell's going to try to do what Ernie did in Canada . . . go out and get local investors, the sort of people who had invested in *Back to God's Country*, and repeat that success."

Her former director, David Hartford, joined the blackball bandwagon and wrote to the newspapers warning potential investors, but the investors chose to stick with Nell.

Nell had not only started a new company, she had begun to assemble what soon became the largest private zoo in North America, a substantial menagerie that she intended to ship to Priest Lake, Idaho, for the location shoot on her next big project, *The Grubstake*. The studio scenes were shot in Spokane, Washington, at the Minnehaha studios, with a roof that rolled back to let in sunlight and equipment that was as up-to-date as anything in Hollywood.

Then, when it was time to move the cast and crew — and the menagerie — to Idaho for the location shooting, dozens of animals, including a cougar and several bears, had to be crated and barged up Priest Lake to Forest Lodge, a resort they rented from a man called Sam Byars. The shoot went overschedule and overbudget. Labs were pursuing Nell for the costs of processing the film. She was afraid they might impound the footage, and set up secret editing rooms, sometimes in the homes of friends. Actors who hadn't been paid for their work at Minnehaha Studios were making trouble, and actors at Forest Lodge were getting pretty touchy. Whether or not the picture would ever get finished was a cliff-hanger, and, like many of the events in Nell's life, had its parallel in the film itself, with a genuine cliff-hanger ending. Tom Trusky said,

> *Nell takes that word literally. We have one of the most dramatic finales . . . ever. . . in* The Grubstake. *We see Nell hanging by one hand to . . . a twisted, gnarled tree root on a huge cliff. And she spliced together a scene of Lookout Mountain, over at Priest Lake, with some [fake] cliffs at Minnehaha which are only maybe ten or twenty feet high but spliced together so this woman [appears to be] hanging on for dear life, about . . . to fall from the cliff, thousands of feet to a dreadful death below.*

Somehow, holding the creditors at bay and keeping the actors and crew from mutiny, she finished the film, took a train to New York and started screening for releasing companies. The first one seemed indifferent. The next day American Releasing offered her about $75,000. She accepted, only to have the first company call her later that day with a much better offer. It was too late.

Perhaps Nell Shipman was trying to do too much: conceive and write the story, raise the money, direct and act, and then try to market it herself. Perhaps a more realistic businesswoman would have recognized the changing world, and changed with it. But a more realistic businesswoman might not have made the breakthroughs and created the work that Nell achieved. Who knows? In any case it was not just the producers and distributors who were growing into huge corporations: the small independent exhibitors were leaving the scene as well. Film historian Kay Armatage at the University of Toronto told us:

> *The studios started buying up . . . the . . . independently owned vaudeville houses and making their own circuit. And of course there are all kinds of rumours about organized crime. If an independent vaudeville owner, for example, didn't want to sell, he might find his equipment smashed, his theatre burned down, his being knee-capped, whatever. Gradually they all fell.*

With the money she got from American Releasing, Nell went back to Idaho only to find that Sam Byars had tripled the rent on Forest Lodge. She brought in the barges again, cut leads through the thin ice, and moved the zoo and the gear down the lake to Lionhead Lodge where she built a studio and started producing a series of outdoor shorts for the Selznick organization. To make ends meet she did a vaudeville show, and to avoid the difficulties with the Hollywood actors who were, by now, doubtful about getting paid, she hired locals and tried to train them. She even put her twelve-year-old son Barry to work as an actor on the project.

In one scene Barry was to drive his mother across the lake on a sled. A patch of ice had been cracked open with axes so that it would break under the weight of the sled and Barry would fall in, only to be saved by the dauntless woman who jumps in after him. This was no studio tank with Styrofoam ice; it was Priest Lake, Idaho, in January. The moment Barry felt the freezing water penetrate to his skin he grabbed at the solid part of the surrounding ice and began to pull himself out. But that would have weakened the suspense, and close scrutiny of the restored footage reveals that Barry's later account, of how Nell grabbed his belt under water and held him back as he thrashed against the cold, while doing her best to appear as though she were trying to rescue him, is accurate. "Her priorities were . . . for the movie," said Barry's surviving daughter Nina.

The Selznick projects moved ahead quite well, as it turned out. Nell decided to celebrate with a Fourth of July Party. The former landlord Sam Byars, apparently seeking revenge for his having lost a lucrative contract, slipped ashore by canoe that night while the cast and crew were partying, and tossed a cyanide-laced piece of meat on the ground in front of the Great Dane Trésor, who by now was Nell's favourite and had been posted as a guard. Trésor knew Byars from Forest Lodge, accepted the delicacy, and died. Nell was trying to deal with that grief when she learned that American Releasing, who was also distributing the Selznick shorts, had gone bankrupt.

Now winter was coming on again, 1923 to 1924. Nell's relationship with Bert Van Tuyle was not surviving the financial strain. Bert's gangrene returned. Nell wrote in her autobiography that you could see a toe bone emerging through his diseased flesh. The lake was frozen again. Van Tuyle became emotionally unstable. Without telling Nell, he staggered out, hitched up the dogs, and tried to drive himself across the lake to get medical help. Nell saw him go and, with more cinematic sense than prudence, decided to follow at a distance so that he would not be humiliated. Once again her life imitates her art because it is almost exactly a scene from *Back to God's Country* (with the two different actors after one died), and filmmaker Phillips was able to illustrate this episode in the actress's real life with footage from that earlier film that parallels the actual lives of the actors and crew. An account of that whole winter — although it is about a group of real people struggling with real life-and-death issues — reads like melodrama. Nell began to spend time with a good-looking young local actor. Bert, now at least partly recovered from the gangrene, found out about his rival. One night, drunk and raging, he started threatening to kill somebody. Young Barry, having lived most of his life around cinematic melodrama, picked up a gun and stood at the window with his sights on Van Tuyle, thinking he would heroically save his mother if things got violent. Nell appears to have lost all sense of perspective at that point. She broke from the party, ran out across the lake, and seemed suddenly, madly, bent on suicide, heading for the open water at the edge of the ice. Barry dropped the rifle, tore after his mother, and forcibly brought the broken, deranged woman back to camp.

As historian Tom Trusky talks about the Priest Lake winter of 1923 to 1924 it sounds as though almost all the people in that settlement were constantly confusing their fictional stories with real life. But the reality was closing in on the play-acting. Soon the money was gone, there was not enough food for the animals, people were leaving, and Nell, finally, had had enough.

She never went back to Priest Lake. Trying to pull herself together she went to New York where she met a gentle, aspiring painter, Charles Ayers, who fell in love with her and took her off to Europe. It seems as though she was, by then, quite content to say good-bye to the world of film. In Spain she had two children, Daphne and Charles Junior. She rested and got herself back into shape, and when Charles

Ayers decided to go home to America, Nell began to think about performing again.

Florida, 1928. America is riding an illusory economic boom. Nell gets a job. It is not the movies, but it is show business. Ringling Brothers cast her as queen of the circus, with silver dress and silver shoes — well, painted cardboard — and the glamour of her career takes on a different tone. She starts to write again.

She was a prolific writer, banging away at her old typewriter turning out articles for women's magazines, novels, trying more film scripts. She sold a serialized novel to *McCall's* magazine, then turned it into a screenplay (to star Nell Shipman), and tried it out on the studios. But whether her bad name was lingering on, or the studios had decided they now preferred male screenwriters, or both — nobody bought. The marriage with Charles ended. Charles Jr. seems to have become estranged from his mother, and Daphne's mental health was precarious. Once more Nell was alone.

In New York she met a fraudulent sometime director who was on contract to the British company, Fox, in England. He was passing himself off as an Italian count, "Amerigo Serrao." They started to live together. Nell worked on a screenplay for Paramount, which was produced with Myrna Loy and Cary Grant. For a while this looked as though it might be the launching pad for a renewed career: the fame of a script for those two great stars was bound to open doors. But somehow, when the movie was released, there was no screen credit for Nell. She and Amerigo tried scheme after scheme.

"There are a series of letters," historian Kay Armatage says, "where Nell writes to Barry and says, 'They're going to rent a studio for us; the money will be in the bank by Friday.'"

But it was probably all fiction. In fact they were sometimes sneaking out of hotels to avoid paying. Her typewriter, bought on time, was repossessed. They were constantly dodging bill collectors. In Virginia they managed once more to intrigue local investors. Nell wrote and directed *Mr. Hobbs*, a twangy Virginian country love story. It was never released. She wrote an autobiography. She left Amerigo in New York and, now sixty and not well, tried her luck in California once again. She never saw Amerigo again. He died in a New York flophouse. Hollywood acted as if she were an unknown old bag lady. She was not far from it. She was destitute.

There is a comfortable seniors' Hollywood home for aging and indigent members of the profession, funded by the Motion Picture Relief Fund. Nell swallowed her pride and applied for a room. She was told that there was no record of her ever having been a member of the profession. The ranks that had closed against her in her proud and independent days stayed closed. She was saved from the streets by an old friend name Dick Diaz who had a dude ranch for dogs in the small town of Cabazon, and there she lived out the last few years of her life. You can hear her voice, in the documentary, sending a grandmotherly Christmas message to Barry's children.

Film historian Peter Morris said, "You know, when I think the last words of her autobiography . . . if I'm remembering correctly she ended up saying, 'Aw Gee. There they go. Forgetting me. So what?' Like . . . I had my moment in the sun and it was great, you know, when I was sort of a star. And then it didn't work."

"Pan. Well, okay."

When she died in 1970, thieves broke into the little house in Cabazon during the funeral; her four big theatre trunks of costumes, scripts, and other memorabilia were stolen and never recovered. As these prodigiously original early films begin to surface and are restored and screened, they show the pioneering work of a Canadian who made blockbusters in Alberta half a century before Telefilm Canada was even thought of and who then vanished. It has been a difficult time for the historians and archivists — and documentary biographers — to piece together the Nell Shipman story. But it has clearly been a labour of love, and that love shows through on the screen.

Note: This writer was able to locate one copy of her novel *Under the Crescent*. It is offered for sale via the Internet for $225 (US). It does seem as though there are some people who remember.

◆　◆　◆

The original documentary was written, produced, and directed by
Patricia Phillips.

PART SIX

BILL MINER
The Truth about the Grey Fox

It has to be confessed from the start that including the life of Bill Miner in a book of Canadian biography is, as Huckleberry Finn might have said, a bit of a stretch. Miner was born in Michigan and died in jail in Georgia, and the only place he could ever have called home for any length of time was the famous San Quentin prison in California. But the man they called the Grey Fox, Last of the Old Time Bandits, did become a hero in western Canada. He did humiliate one of the more detested of the great Canadian institutions of the time, the Canadian Pacific Railroad. And he seems to have negotiated with that same powerful Canadian corporation, a deal involving the equivalent of hundreds of millions of dollars in today's money. The deal appears nowhere in the record books, but it is historic in every sense of the word. And — we argued at History Television — that part of the story more than justifies giving Old Bill Miner a place in our gallery of Canadian rogues and heroes.

San Quentin is the oldest (1852) maximum-security prison in California. You can get there easily by bus from San Francisco, look at the virtual reality display by the gate, visit the museum for $2 or half that if you are a child or a senior. If you are a journalist or sociologist or have other credentials, and call well in advance, you might even get to interview the warden, Jeanne Woodford. Her annual budget of $120 million pays a staff of more than 1,500 people to look after more than six thousand inmates in an institution designed to house about three thousand. About six hundred of those men (women were moved to another prison in 1933) are on death row, and the prison houses California's only gas chamber.

Billy Miner spent thirty-three of his sixty-seven years in San Quentin. He went there as a teenager, convicted of his first robbery, when the United States was riven by the consequences of a bloody civil war and the murder of a great president. None of these events seems to have left any mark on the kid. He had chosen the way of the outlaw, and it seems that from then on the outlaw life is all he really thought about. California was, in any case, a long way from the war and relatively untouched by it. If Lincoln's death had seared the consciousness of the East and the South, California then as now had its own agenda and its own preoccupations, one of which was the out-of-control crime that had spiralled up out of the gold rush after 1849. That was why they had made San Quentin.

The prison still had the system of boss cons in those days. This let the toughest convicts actually control the discipline in the prison yard. If other prisoners didn't say good morning to a boss con, they could be beaten for disrespect, and if they did say good morning, they could be beaten for insolence. There was an average of ten whippings a day. Prisoners were routinely and savagely beaten and tortured. Sexual assault was routine.

The new boy was slight of figure, rather girlish in appearance, not effeminate but somebody who would be quickly seized on by the aggressive "wolves" among the inmates. Miner was probably sodomized on his first day. Later he became a wolf himself, was well known to inmates and staff, and, ironic though it sounds, was well liked by most of them.

This legendary bandit began his career of crime as a stagecoach robber in the great old tradition of the Western movies, pulled off the first train robbery ever committed in Canada, and was sentenced to life in prison as a result. Two years later he slipped away from the prison brickyard with two other cons one afternoon, under circumstances that only recently have focused on the strange role of the bandit's greatest victim, the CPR.

That set of events, around the CPR heist, was the most spectacular and the most successful of his many capers, many of which were hilariously bungled. But Bill Miner is remembered not so much for what he did, or even for his dramatic and comical ineptitude ("a very *bad* bandit," says historian Mark Dugan, meaning incompetent, not nasty). It was his character that struck people, perhaps his skill as a storyteller, weaving his own tales of derring-do and failures into a lasting legend. To the San Francisco historian John Boessenakker, the durability of that legend has little to do with Miner's one big multi-million-dollar success:

He's remembered today for a number of reasons. One is the longevity of his career, almost fifty years as an outlaw. He had the personality of a man who just refused to give up. He was able to adapt very quickly to new environments, new geographical areas, new societies, new technology. And he was a charming man, he was funny, he was bright, he was educated, and he was somebody who revelled in his reputation. At the time of his death, he had a national reputation as a criminal. We don't know much about his mother, Harriet Miner. She was definitely an educated woman. Bill in later years always said that she'd been a schoolteacher. We couldn't find any proof that in fact she was a schoolteacher. However, the evidence of his handwriting makes it appear that he was well educated. He certainly was literate; he could read and write. He was very well spoken and very gentlemanly and obviously had a very good upbringing.

The one photograph we have of Harriet Miner shows a serene and lovely woman of thirty or less, in an elegant heavy silk dress, looking dreamily off into infinity with a book in her hand. She had brought her two boys out to California from their hometown of Onondaga, Michigan, six years before Billy's first failed robbery and subsequent imprisonment. They had settled in a gold rush town called Yankee Jim where the reigning values were get-rich-quick and violence. John Boessenakker said,

What you had in California, was something historians call the bachelor cult of masculinity. This was a real culture that existed among young men in the nineteenth century whether it was on the east coast or in the frontier regions, where young men congregated in political clubs, volunteer fire companies, saloons, and they engaged in the favourite pastime, which was bare-knuckle fighting, and this is the kind of community that existed on the east coast and in the California gold rush. That's the kind of community that Bill Miner grew up in.

The prison records showed him convicted of robbery, and he served six years in San Quentin for that one, where he made friends with a professional stagecoach robber named Alkali Jim Harrington. They got out together in 1871, and before long had held up a stagecoach near San Andreas. Billy was apprenticed to Alkali Jim, but according to historian Boessenakker he was also already asserting himself as a kind of leader.

> *They robbed this stagecoach, and the driver, Cutler, was ordered to take his boots off and he complained about that and he said, "This is pretty rough on a guy to make me drive back in my stocking feet." And then they took his watch, and he said, "You can't take . . ." — the driver, Cutler, said, "Listen, you can't take my watch. It's a gift from my dead mother," and Miner said, "We respect men's mothers," and gave him the watch back.*

Cutler was also able to identify the men when they were arrested not long after the robbery. Before their cell bunks had cooled off, so to speak, they were both back in San Quentin sentenced to fourteen years with hard labour.

Billy Miner was twenty-five years old. In his prison photo that year he looks forty and he looks sad and bitter. The babyfaced kid look of the teenage years has been replaced by the trademark long inverted V of a moustache. The eyes are crinkled and sad, the expression distant. His sidekick Alkali Jim would die in San Quentin, but Billy was beginning to think about escaping. The rock quarry seemed an opportune take-off point, but it is probable that he did not seek as much advice as he should have when he made his break about three years into the term. Escapes from the quarry were enough of a natural temptation that the custodial staff was used to them. Tracking down the escapees was almost routine. They got him within hours, gave him twenty lashes, and threw him into the Dungeon.

If you get to San Quentin and visit the museum, the museum director Dick Nelson can tell you, as he told us, about the conditions Miner lived in there in the 1870s. How long and how badly you were punished would depend not only on your behaviour, but also on how you got along with the Captain:

*And then [he] probably would have, for a period of time, been sen-
tenced to the ball and chain, to preclude any further escapes — in
the immediate future, anyway. It doesn't take very long to assimilate into the prison society, because there's nothing else to do. The
morning would start at about 6:00, and they'd be served a breakfast,
probably in those days just a mush. Then they'd have to report to
work. They'd come back in about 4:00, and they'd be counted,
locked up, and then go to their evening meal. There's no record . . .
of any nighttime activities. They were locked up from dusk to dawn.*

Photographs of the prison yard show those afternoon lineups for
the count, several hundred gaunt men, drooping with fatigue, many of
them chained to a heavy cast-iron ball, all dressed in the long coarse
cotton prison jacket and pants, with broad black stripes running horizontally across the chest and back and around the legs and arms. There
was no concept of prisoners' rights. But as any inmate will tell you,
there was a moral code and a highly structured society. Study after
study of long-term inmates show that while they learned to live and
conform effectively inside, life on the outside is often so baffling to
them that after ten or fifteen years of prison it is almost a relief to be
caught and to come back "home."

Was that part of the Miner story? With almost forty of his sixty-
seven years of life passed behind bars, and so casual and unplanned
an approach to each of the jobs he pulled that it almost seems as
though he wanted to be caught, there is a temptation to think so. And
yet it doesn't seem to fit the character. Miner had a self-confidence
and a social ability that would not have left him ill at ease in the outside world. A later episode back in Onondaga, Michigan, attests to
that. He was not unintelligent, but there may have been an almost
pathological inability to distinguish myth from reality, a need to map
his life out according to a romantic notion, a need so compelling that
it overcame any training he might have received from mother about
planning ahead and considering the consequences of your actions.
Part of the romance was the partnership model — the James Brothers,
Butch Cassidy and the Sundance Kid. Billy Miner ultimately paired
up with a succession of very unpleasant people whose one attractive

feature was their dedication to the criminal life.

The next one of these guys was Billy Leroy. Miner had earned four years off his sentence for good behaviour and an apparently convincing promise to leave California. He said he would go to live with his sister in the state of Washington and turn his prison training in shoemaking into an honest living. He had no intention of doing this, although it does appear that his sister held out hopes for a while, and that he did in fact spend some time with her. But he kept looking out for the next accomplice, and he met Billy Leroy on a train.

The American historian Mark Dugan specializes in the study of rogues and rascals of this period, and has become an expert on Billy Leroy. It does seem an unusual subject for a historian to specialize in: Dugan himself finds little to admire in the little crook.

> Well, he's just kind of a brash, cocky kid from Iowa who got tired of working, and he gets on a train and Miner's sitting next to him, and Miner's — what? — thirty-something at that point? And they start talking on the train.

We can be pretty sure that the talk — from Miner's end — was well-embroidered storytelling, an account of a daring and successful life of crime that would easily turn a boy's head. Dugan went on:

> And the kid jumped at the chance to work with him. But in this case, I do not think there was any sexual relationship between the two. Billy Leroy, he turned out to be kind of a tough kid. In fact, in the end, he takes over control of the robberies. He takes Miner's place and puts Miner in a secondary role . . . in their last robbery. . . . I don't think Miner cared much for that at all. I think that really irritated him.

Irritated or not, Miner found Leroy an effective fellow bandit. For the first time in a long and undistinguished career he was actually a success. He was robbing stagecoaches and getting away with it. But in the end he couldn't stand not being in control, not being number one, unable to control Billy Leroy. They soon split up. Leroy formed a new gang and kept on robbing stages in Colorado until he and his partners were caught and put in jail in the town of Del Norte. While they were there, the good citizens of the small town paid them a visit, and there is a photograph of the two of them, in suits and ties, with bowler hats — they hadn't even gone to trial yet — hanging from a couple of trees on the Del Norte main street. So Miner's decision to break off that relationship was fortunate in a way, although without Leroy to keep things disciplined he went back to his bungling ways when he next turned to crime.

But that was not for a while. He took the considerable haul that was his share from the Leroy partnership, and inexplicably headed back to Onondaga, the Michigan town he had not seen since he was twelve years old. Nobody there remembered him as the adolescent kid who left with his serene-faced mother almost twenty years before. He told the townspeople his name was William Morgan and that he owned gold mines in California. He flashed a lot of money around, and for the first time in his life he fell in with local society. A portrait taken in Onondaga shows an elegantly trimmed moustache and goatee, a serious cigar (not lit, in the photograph), and a kind of soft bowler hat with a very tall round crown. His look at the camera still has that careful, appraising look, but there is a bit of a twinkle this time. Let John Boessenakker and Mark Dugan pick up the tale here.

John Boessenakker:

He met the mayor of Onondaga, and, more importantly, he met the mayor's daughter, young Jenny Willis, who was a very attractive young woman about twenty years old, and he was extremely well dressed, handsome, debonair, and Jenny Willis fell madly in love with him.

Mark Dugan:

Well, Bill got there and he played like a hotshot mining man from California, and he's got all these mines in South America and California and all over the place, and he's got all this money and whatever, and he starts squiring one of the local belles.

John Boessenakker:

They were engaged to be married. Bill Miner was the toast of the town. There was an engagement dinner in which Jenny's father toasted Bill . . . and this romance went on for a number of months.

But it is now that the power of that confusion between myth and reality kicks in again and sabotages Bill Miner's capacity to make a workable plan and carry it out. He has been spending unrestrainedly, and he is almost broke. It is time to pull another caper. Were he a man who can learn from experience he would have sought out a successful partner again, someone with "management skills." But no. He invented a story for Jenny. His mother was ill in California and he must take her on a cruise for her health.

John Boessenakker:

[His] elderly mother was back in California. She was living in poverty in Sacramento, and he needed to go back to California to do another robbery . . . to be able to continue this romance in Michigan.

So he hit another stagecoach in November of 1881, just outside Sonora, and got away with $3,700. That is the equivalent of about a quarter of a million dollars in today's money. There was no reason not to speed back to Michigan and get on with life. Bill Miner stayed in California. A few days before Christmas of that year they got him, in Sacramento. He was sentenced to twenty-five years.

John Boessenakker:

Jenny Willis was certainly heartbroken, but she eventually recovered and she had a long, happy, and productive life. She died in 1945 at the age of eighty-five, and she told her children of her romance with Bill Miner. She wasn't ashamed of it in the least. She was proud . . . of this romantic adventure she'd had as a young woman.

We do not know much detail of the next few prison years, which would bring his San Quentin total to just over thirty-three. The Spanish-American War had come and gone. The Boer War was winding down. Queen Victoria had celebrated her diamond Jubilee. McKinley had been shot to death in Buffalo, and Theodore Roosevelt was about to enter the White House. Just as he seems not to have noticed the Civil War forty years earlier, there is no reason to think that Bill Miner took any interest in these matters.

He was almost fifty-five when he got out of jail. There weren't any stagecoaches any more. In the new-fangled moviehouses of California

they were showing *The Great Train Robbery* in 1903. Billy Miner probably saw it. Perhaps he took notes. He did have the good sense to get out of California, and head up towards Canada. He stopped off in Oregon on the way north, and had a go at this new drama, the train robbery, although he found it a whole lot harder in real life than it had looked in the movie. He had enlisted two accomplices this time, one of them only seventeen years old. They put up a set of red signals to stop the oncoming train, but they put them on the wrong side of the tracks, for trains coming in the opposite direction, so the engineer of the train they wanted to rob didn't even see them and the train didn't even slow down. Four days later they decided to simply board the Oregon Express as passengers when it stopped at a station. Then they put on their masks and clambered over the coal tender to the engine where, with guns drawn, they told the engineer to stop, which he did. They knew the money was kept in the express car, but they didn't know that it was guarded by an armed agent. The guard shot at them and hit one of the bandits in the head. Miner and the boy, Charles Hoehn, ran away empty-handed. Police picked up the injured man, who squealed, and soon they had Hoehn, but this time Billy managed to stay out of sight.

By now the famous Pinkerton Detective Agency was half a century old. Its first major assignments had been with the railroads, and they were building a file on Bill Miner. Our crew visited the Pinkerton archivist Jane Adler, who showed us stacks of photographs of the man who would soon earn the soubriquet, the Grey Fox. She told us about the founder, Alan Pinkerton, and those early railroad contracts.

Five railroads building northwest out of Chicago hired him for $10,000 a year — which was a very sizeable sum in those days — to protect their lines, because they were building out into construction camps, and there were Indians and there were robbers on the trains, and their own employees were cheating them and taking the money. So there was a lot of embezzlement going on. . . . The Central Illinois Railroad was the principal line that Pinkerton first worked for. Later, his commissions or his engagements were with the major trunk lines in America, and occasionally, he did have to go out west to deal with somebody like Bill Miner.

341

THE CANADIANS: VOLUME II

Jane Adler showed us the reward poster Pinkerton put out on Billy Miner, which not only reviewed his career, showed his photograph, and listed all his prison sentences, it also added that Miner was "said to be a sodomist." They were very frustrated by his unusual invisibility this time, according to Mark Dugan:

> *They were so mad at him, they were hot. I mean, they were going to put everything they could get in there. Look, he robbed . . . he tried to rob that train in Oregon. They knew he did that. Then he went up to Canada. They knew he did that. And then in 1905 he hits the one in Washington . . . above Seattle. They knew he did that. And they're hot, you know, they can't catch him, they can't find him. . . . Here he has spent twenty years in prison, they let him out and boom, he starts this!*

He began to look for another partner, and this time he came up with a very experienced thug he had met during those last twenty years in San Quentin. Jake Terry was as naturally violent as Miner was courteous. His prison picture resembles a lean, bald Robert Duvall in a sinister role. Terry was a gunfight man. Why Miner picked him is not entirely clear from the record: Terry on his own had been as inept at keeping clear of the police as Miner himself was, and that should have been a warning. But in fact they worked well together, better than they ever had on their own. Jake Terry would eventually die in a gunfight, but not before he helped Bill Miner turn himself into the Grey Fox, become a hero to British Columbians, and take the Canadian Pacific Railway Company for a staggering sum in bearer bonds.

They picked up a third small-time crook named Shorty Dunn, and set out for Mission, BC, in the fall of 1907. There was no fumbling with badly placed signals this time. The hard-faced Jake Terry may have been a killer but he had also been a railroad man and he knew something about the technology. He figured out that if you had a telegraph key (which he knew how to operate) you could climb a pole and wire your key into the line and send a message that would look official because it came in on the company line. The message he sent was simple: COMBINATION LOST. LEAVE SAFE OPEN ON TRAIN.

Unbelievably, it worked. When the CPR express stopped for water near Mission, the three men went aboard and in five minutes were off again with $1,000 in cash, about $6,000 worth of gold dust, and a package of Australian Bearer Bonds worth some 50,000 pounds sterling. Added up in today's money we are talking about half a million dollars or so in cash and gold, and more than a hundred million in those redeemable bonds. Miner and his pals apparently did not understand exactly what the bonds were; nonetheless Billy buried them in a safe and secret place.

The railroad was not insured; it was responsible to their owners for the value of the bonds and would have to make good. The gang divided the money and went their separate ways, and this time Billy Miner acted more or less rationally for a while, perhaps thinking that in time he would find someone through whom he could make something out of those buried bonds. He went to Princeton, in the BC interior, and by John Boessenakker's account seems to have had a reasonably normal kind of life for a while.

He was able to ingratiate himself with people. The evidence is pretty clear that he loved children. He certainly loved women. Women were one of the driving influences of his life. . . . There are numerous stories of Miner's kindness and the things that he did while he was hiding out from the authorities. He would generally go by an alias, William Morgan being the most common one [and the one he used here].

So "William Morgan" got a job with a rancher, and simply smiled when he heard local people chortling over the train robbery. The CPR was not exactly the most loved of Canadian corporations. The Montreal historian Bob Stewart said:

Miner was perceived as a hero by many, many people in the area because, simply because he robbed the CPR, because of his victim, really, being so unpopular. I recall reading a quote from an old resident of BC who said, you know, "Hell, Bill Miner ain't so bad. He only robs the CPR once every two years, and the CPR robs us every day."

Ironically, Miner and his gang were never charged with the first train robbery in the history of Canada, the one that involved the CPR in what turns out to have been a bizarre manipulation of the justice system. After a decent interval, and feeling pretty cocky about the big one, Miner and Shorty Dunn and a twenty-eight-year-old drifter named Louis Colquhoun (whose prison ID photograph has a Russell Crowe look to it) decided to rob yet another CPR train just east of Kamloops. Without Jake Terry in the gang, Miner lapsed back to his sloppy old techniques, and made about all the mistakes it was possible to make. The biggest being that while they had intended to hit an express car full of registered mail and gold, they got the wrong train. This one didn't even have an express car. Miner ran off with a paltry $15.50 and a bottle of pills.

At about this time his admirers began to refer to the elusive hold-up artist as the Grey Fox. When the North West Mounted Police joined forces with the BC provincial force and brought in a group of native trackers, they were soon posing for their photographs as the men who had captured the Grey Fox. This time Miner gave his name as George Edwards, but before long he was identified and went to trial in Kamloops. John Boessenakker said that even though the robbery for which he was charged was trivial, the law acted almost as if they were nailing Miner for the Big One.

> They saw this man as a very dangerous threat to transportation, to commerce. Here's a single outlaw who managed to steal the equivalent of millions of dollars in bonds and securities. This is something that the Canadian Pacific Railroad is very angry about. They were a common carrier, and under Canadian and American law, they're responsible for making good a loss like that, and that has a lot to do with the stiff sentence.

Well, it was armed robbery after all, whatever the size of the haul. But it does add to the comic dimension of the Miner saga that, for stealing $15.50 and a bottle of catarrh pills, Louis Colquhoun got twenty-five years, while Shorty Dunn and Billy Miner were sentenced to life in the BC penitentiary. As the sentence was pronounced, and Miner was asked if he had anything to say, he smiled at the judge and replied, "No walls can hold *me*, sir." It was sheer showmanship. But in this case it proved to be true.

The boss con system that characterized Billy Miner's early years in San Quentin did not operate in British Columbia, and here the concept of the inmates' rights — while limited — somewhat eased the pain of confinement. The inmate had five declared rights: a cell of his own, adequate food, adequate clothing, adequate health care, and an hour's exercise each day. The definition of adequate was determined by the "joint," and the food was pretty bad, pea soup and burnt pea coffee and seldom enough of anything. The work was hard and the cells were cold in the winter. But Bill Miner's time there was made a little easier by a series of visits from a detective who worked for the CPR.

His name was Bullock. He had been charged with recovering those securities, and he was bound and determined to do that. The talks went on for more than a year. Bullock said that he was authorized to offer the Grey Fox a pardon in return for his showing them where the bonds were. Miner — more prudent than usual — demanded to see it in writing, which the detective could not of course provide. But in the meantime life in prison began to seem a little easier. Every other prisoner was shaved, face and head. The Grey Fox was allowed to keep his hair long and his long inverted V of a moustache just the way we know it from the movies. He asked to be assigned to the brickyard, which was not only thought to be an easy assignment, but was also easy of access from the outside, or, more importantly from the inside to the outside. One day in August the newspapers reported that the Grey Fox and three other inmates had tunnelled a hole under the wall, from a corner of the brickyard where they could not be seen from the gun towers, and had walked away.

There were, however, a number of contradictions. Reporters invited to examine the getaway site were shown a hole, all right, but it looked far too small for a man to have wriggled through. They concluded that it was simply not possible for four men or even one to spend an afternoon digging the said hole, in full view of the rest of the yard, without their being seen. Tony Martin spent most of his working life on the custodial staff of that penitentiary. He has made a study of the institution's history, and has a theory about the Miner escape:

My guess is somebody was bribed, and not necessarily the warden. After this whole thing was over, the warden was allowed to retire and get his superannuation, and prior to that, the guy could be fired for inattention on duty. Even in my time, I saw . . . I used to collect fines. An officer was fined if he fell asleep or missed something he should have done. So a warden losing a guy like Miner [and then] being allowed to retire and get his pension, it had to be organized by somebody with great political power. And there's absolutely no doubt that the CPR had tremendous political power.

There is indeed no question that the CPR did have substantial political power, and that influential politicians, at every level, owed their electoral success to the support of that company. Does this mean what it seems to mean? For historian Mark Dugan there is simply no doubt that the escape was engineered by the CPR. Jane Adler, at Pinkerton's, agrees.

It would not have been at all difficult. It's not difficult to imagine. Certainly it would have happened in America, easy as pie. In Canada, it's probably a bit of a shock to people, and certainly . . . and they didn't do a very good job of it. I mean, the men were supposed to have escaped. Somebody went and examined the hole where they were supposed to have burrowed out of the brickyard where they were working. Apparently, it wasn't big enough for, you know, a small boy to get out of, let alone three adult men. So the effort was made to cover up what was happening, which I'm sure everybody was well aware. And the people made a fuss about it in the House in Ottawa. . . . It had been arranged. That was it.

The fuss in Parliament died down after a few days. There were bigger things to worry about than an escaped train robber, particularly when — by coincidence it was said — the railway detectives stopped looking for the bonds once Miner was gone.

And gone he was. The Grey Fox had slipped over the border and back into the States. He lived quietly for a couple of years and it seemed that he'd finally retired. But in 1911 the sixty-four-year-old incorrigible was in the state of Georgia preparing to rob another train. There were, once more, two younger accomplices. On February 11, 1911, at Sulphur

Springs, they had the distinction of committing that state's first train robbery. The take was $2,200, which was a very good year's salary for a professional man at the time. The public were enchanted with the image of this "Old Man," a former friend of Jesse James it was said again and again, hitting the trail again — in "the best traditions of the Wild West," said the press. When they put him away — for twenty-five years once more (remember he was nearly sixty-five), reporters came long distances to interview him. The warden let him sit on the porch and tell his story.

Although the nearest he ever came to doing anything remotely Robin Hood-like had been to return the stagecoach driver's watch four decades earlier, the public imagination turned him into a good guy. Milledgeville Pen was new, state-of-the-art, when they put the Grey Fox there. It was a tough joint. Cons were chained to their beds at night and chained to a ball by day when they went out to work. But the warden took it easy on Old Bill, and let him sit there and tell the reporters about his diamond mines in the Transvaal and his days with Jesse James, and they wrote it down, and the people of Georgia lapped it up. Mark Dugan says that by now he was lying most of the time.

I think he lied; he had lied so much, even at the end, I don't think he knew truth from a lie. He didn't know one thing from another. He couldn't have told the truth in the end, I don't think, if he'd wanted to, because he had lied so much through his lifetime.

That does seem a bit harsh. And yet when, on October 17, 1911, the chairman of the prison board, one Robert E. Davidson, visited the prison and asked Bill Miner to keep his promise not to escape, the Grey Fox is reported to have replied, "Old Bill keeps his word. I am going to stay right here as promised."

He escaped at 2 a.m. the next morning. Tony Wilson tells it like this:

A guard had fallen asleep, and there was a large peephole where the guards could watch the prisoners. Apparently, one of the prisoners got out of his bunk and looked through the peephole, the other direction, could see the guard was asleep. The fellow in question was small. He squeezed through the peephole, took the keys off the sleeping guard and got back in, and he and two other fellows — Bill Miner . . . I can't remember the second guy . . . Tom Moore was the third fellow — opened the door, up over the walls, and they escaped, much to everybody's embarrassment, as you might imagine. I think part of the appeal, in that sense, of Bill Miner, was that sort of appeal of the rebel against the establishment, because the South was suffering in those years. The cotton economy was on the decline [and] the sense that large corporations were [the cause of it], particularly the railroad companies, the freight rates they charged for shipping cotton were so outrageous that you could barely make a profit. Well, here's somebody that's robbing the trains, that's standing up to the Georgia Railway. . . . He played on this, you know. "I never robbed poor people or innocent people," which wasn't true, but he said that. "I just robbed trains."

They got him a couple of weeks later, and put him back in Milledgeville. Somehow — he was after all about to turn sixty-six — the custodial staff let their guard down, and this time two of them sawed through the bars in the window — in Approved Wild West style — made ropes out of their blankets, lowered themselves to the ground and got over the wall and away. They waded downriver — to throw the dogs off the scent — and then got lost in the swamps for four days, and were so wrecked with dysentery from drinking swamp water that they gave themselves up. When the car brought them back to the prison there was a crowd outside; the cops feared that a lynching was about to take place; but in fact the Georgians were there to cheer the Grey Fox. They gave him cigars and let him know he was an OK Guy.

But Billy never recovered from his time in the swamps. He was taken to the prison hospital suffering from acute gastroenteritis, and on September 2, 1913, in his sixty-seventh year, the last of the old-style Western bandits died. The citizens of Milledgeville had a collection to pay for his funeral, and he was laid out in what was then the local funeral parlour for four days while people paid their last respects. "And he gets headlines," Mark Dugan told us: "'HE WILL GO HURTLING THROUGH GEORGIA HISTORY!' . . . His picture when he died was . . . the President's picture was in the same edition, and his was bigger than the President's."

They buried him there, with mistaken dates on the stone. Writer-director Robert Duncan wrote, at the end of his biographical documentary of the old escape artist, a kind of filmmaker's epitaph:

BILLY MINER, THE GREY FOX,
THE LAST OF THE OLD WESTERN BANDITS, REMAINS IN
MILLEDGEVILLE, GEORGIA
—AS FAR AS WE KNOW

◆ ◆ ◆

The original documentary was written and directed by Robert Duncan.

PART SEVEN

KATHERINE RYAN
The Saga of Klondike Kate

From the archival records of the Klondike gold rush of '98 it is easy to get the impression that there were more photographers per square mile in the Yukon Territory than in any other part of the world. Photographs come tumbling out of the files (and nowadays the hard drives and the CDs) by the thousands. The shots of departure points, where romantic hopefuls tried to board the steamers out of Seattle or Vancouver for Wrangell and Skagway, and the trains out of Skagway for Whitehorse, are reminiscent of railway history pictures from India at the turn of the century. People hang from ledges and railings, scrambling to board a boat or train that is already bursting with humanity, crowded onto docks and station platforms as if they were escaping from the latest maraudings of Godzilla.

You also have the impression that *style* was a prime consideration for entry into the ranks of the hopeful. They almost *had to* be wearing a tall hat with a round crown, a walrus moustache, yellow-tanned calf-high boots with pointed toes or else foot soldier–style laced boots with double thick soles. The famous panoramic photographs of the Chilkoot Pass with spider-sized men bent over under their murderously heavy packs ("like hairpins," Pierre Berton famously said) has become an icon of the period. Less familiar are these grainy, water-stained images packed with hundreds more people than could ever board the packets or the stern-wheelers or the trains that already look as though they will sink or collapse from their human burden. But after only a few minutes with those archival files, the researcher realizes that the Chilkoot Pass picture, while it eloquently speaks of the challenge and the difficulties, is nowhere near as powerful as these mob scenes. They are the depiction of a tragic madness that seized what looks like a whole generation of adventurers, few of whom would find any gold, many of whom would starve or freeze to death, and most of whom were miserable most of the time that they spent in the territory.

Whole sequences of these photographs compose a fascinating majority of the historic images in this documentary, the motion picture having been invented only three years earlier, and not having much penetrated into the frozen Canadian north. One of the reasons for the misery is that there are virtually no female faces in these acres of packed humanity. No mothers, no girlfriends, no wives, sisters, nurses, cooks. The men range in age from adolescence upwards. Some of the early arrivals will head into the wilderness woefully underequipped and undersupplied, and when the North West Mounted Police get on the case after the initial confusion and disasters, one of the first things they will establish is a Proving-Up procedure whereby you don't even get into the territory unless you can demonstrate that you have brought enough grub to keep yourself alive for months and enough warm clothing to get you through the winter without freezing to death. The few women who did make the trek to the Yukon would have to Prove Up — if they trekked in — just as the men did. Among the requirements for one leg of the journey were 400 pounds of flour, 150 pounds of bacon and the same of split peas, tinned milk, beans, a sleeping bag, a rifle, and a Bible.

This is the story of an adventuress from New Brunswick who did all that, proved up, trekked, mushed her Huskies, and drove her pack horses, went into business, acted as vicarious mom, real nurse and real cook, girlfriend perhaps, never a wife, came away with a modest fortune and a great reputation, lost her fortune in the crash of twenty-nine, died poor, but left a name and a mark on the Yukon that have not been forgotten.

Along the way she would build, run, and sell at a profit some half a dozen restaurants. A trained nurse, she would be the first and only woman engaged by the Royal North West Mounted Police as a special constable and a "gold inspector." She would become a pal of Robert W. Service, and used to say that she gave him some of the stories that turn up later in the famous *Songs of Sourdough* and *Ballads of the Yukon*. She was also a close friend of a dynamic entrepreneurial north country butcher named Dominic Burns who was one of the few who would stick with her right to the end. She was, in her late teens, plump, comely as a girl, and then towering, solid and daunting as a mature woman. She was smart, determined, tough. Her name was Katherine Ryan, and they called her Klondike Kate.

She was not the only woman on the gold rush, of course. There were the dance hall girls, famously so up in Dawson, which at the height of the madness was said to be the biggest North American city north of San Francisco and west of Winnipeg. The Dawson dance hall girls worked long nights, sometimes as many as 150 dances a night. Part of the deal with the proprietors was that, on commission at so much a shot, you drank watered whisky with the men in order to encourage them to buy as much as possible. There was an active white slave traffic, the young prostitutes largely recruited — or kidnapped — in Seattle, Washington. It was a trip to that city to heal a broken heart and work as a housekeeper that would launch Kate Ryan on the road to Whitehorse.

A few years ago the historian T. Ann Brennan, who lives in the Johnville region of New Brunswick where Kate Ryan was born, realized that the round pile of field stones wrested from the stony soil by a pioneer ploughman and still there near her own family homestead, had to be the Ryan place. It is just down the road from the Brennan place near the top of Campbell hill, surrounded by a coppice of lilacs and weeds, a familiar sight on old farm properties throughout the eastern woodlands. Anne Brennan was able to find the well and the site of the original orchard on the farm settled by Pat Ryan and his wife Anne Holden early in the 1860s, before Canada was a country, and when you could get a hundred acres for next to nothing if you undertook to clear it and farm it.

Katherine was born there two years after Confederation, one of five children, two girls and three boys. The boys were favoured. Katherine's sister Nora eloped with an actor, to Bangor, Maine, when Katherine was fourteen. The parents were disgusted and disowned the impudent thing. Katherine missed her sister, but seems to have accepted her duties as labour hand on the family farm, and got on with life. She was already over six feet tall and embarrassed at her size. She may have felt more at ease out in the field or the barns than she would have in town, and for the next several years, long after most girls in her circumstances would have married, she stayed on at home lending a hand with the farm and helping her brothers with their children.

Ann Brennan discovered that there were people still living in the region, seventy years after Katherine Ryan's death, for whom the saga of Klondike Kate was still so much part of the gossip and texture of their young lives that they talked as if they could remember the woman herself. Ann Brennan decided there was a biography to be written here, and set to work on it. One of her early contacts was a neighbour, Frances Cullen, herself well into her fourth quarter-century, who talked, as if it was just a few years ago that Katherine — disappointed in love — left home

> *broken-hearted. And I would suspect in her young days, her dream would have been to marry that man, settle here like people were doing, the pioneers at that time, but I think she was destined for something else. And I think there are people that no matter what their plans are, I think that their plans are, you know, I think a greater power changed their plans.*

The man in question was Simon Gallagher, whose family owned the big general store and whose mother wore expensive furs and looked down on farm people. Simon and Katherine stepped out together for several years, and it is said that he was the only real love of her life. It may be that Simon's mother was the cause of it, but whatever the real nature of the break-up, Simon did briefly enter a seminary. Brennan speculates that it was a device — invented by the mother, by which she could engineer his split with Katherine. He then later came back to the family business and married someone else. By then Katherine was long gone from the Johnville homestead.

Mary Healey, a friend (and a cousin of Simon Gallagher), had married and gone to live in Seattle. She invited Katherine to visit. Katherine turned the visit into a job when she found Mary Healey overwhelmed by a fragile constitution and too many children, and took over as housekeeper and nanny.

It seems that she supplemented her income here by making the first move towards what would become a calling: the restaurant business. She helped run the dining room in the Crifton Hotel in Seattle, at least for a few months. She also enrolled in a nursing school run by nuns at nearby Nahomish. In two years she had earned her nurse's certificate.

One of the difficulties in producing a biography of a person who leaves as few written records as Kate did is that the recollections of those who knew her (or knew someone who knew her and had told stories about her) often contradict the recollections of the next witness. In Katherine Ryan's case there is a curiously validating second stream of evidence: the photograph. There are photographs from Johnville when she was just a girl and photographs taken there at the Ryan farm when she came home for a visit, famous and prosperous a quarter of a century later, photographs in Vancouver, in Alaska, on shipboard, in front of her makeshift wilderness restaurants, in the little tent she lived in on the trail, in Whitehorse, in Stewart, BC.

So as our television team assembles the story from oral accounts on the one hand (with their evident fragility) and the solid reassurance of the photographs on the other, they are often in the position of having to conjecture, in building the links between fragmentary bits of evidence. "Well, it must have been *something* like this." A great deal of history is written that way, of course, and the amount of judgment and speculation that goes into any account of the past will vary both with the inclinations and experience of the historian, and the amount of incontrovertible documentation there is to work with.

Katherine's grandniece Kit McKernan is one of those witnesses who was not really *there*, but so vivid is the Kate Ryan legend that she seems to feel almost as though she had witnessed it.

The difficulty in getting there was the fact that it was very very hard to get passage on the boats, they were all booked very very quickly. And there were no women that really wanted to go. It was all the men going. So she had to find men and the only ones she knew and happened to find out were going were Danny Gillis and Peter Stokes. She always called Danny, Sandy. Sandy Gillis was his name. And they had an in. They were importers/exporters. They were going to Wrangell, and, ah . . .

Here Kit McKernan's voice drops to a conspiratorial whisper, as she confides that "they were taking liquor into Alaska, *which was dry!*"

Wrangell is a port on the Alaska Panhandle, named for Ferdinand Petrovich Wrangel, who was the first governor of Russian America. It was founded in 1835 by Russian fur traders, as a fortification against the Hudson's Bay Company. That didn't work; The Bay just moved in and occupied the place in 1840. It seems odd today to think that Russia had a substantial piece of North America a century and a half ago, with settlements as far south as Northern California. The United States bought Alaska from the Russians (for $7.2 million) in the same year that Canada became a country, 1867. The Russians had introduced agriculture and logging into the territory, and left behind some churches and place-names, including this ragged little town.

There is a clipping from a Seattle newspaper in August 1897, announcing the impending arrival of the steamer *Portland* bringing men back from those first gold-hungry forays into the Klondike, before it had become a rush. The paper says the ship's arrival is anticipated with increasing interest each day because there are rumours of "GOLD PILED ON THE DECKS LIKE CORDWOOD." That was a headline writer's invention, we can suppose. In one version of the Klondike Kate story it was those men gobbling up the steaming dinners at Katherine's Crifton House tables whose exciting stories about nuggets like slabs of cheese and fortunes being made overnight that got Katherine thinking about opportunities in the Yukon. However, Ann Brennan's book finds that when the spectacular reports of the Yukon gold strikes began to make their way south, Katherine was already in Vancouver, visiting more New Brunswick friends, and once again running a small restaurant.

In any case, it was reports of this kind that drew her towards the north, and on February 28, 1898, with her two bootlegger friends, Katherine was one of the very few women to board a Canadian steamer, the *Tees*, out of Vancouver for Wrangell. The preparation that she undertook, with no experience of this kind of thing, is staggering. She went to the Hudson Bay Company's special top-floor wilderness supply section, found a sympathetic salesman, and spent almost everything she had on the best clothes and equipment. In addition to the necessary gear and supplies she had acquired a dogsled and a team of five good huskies, in Vancouver, and loaded them onto the *Tees*. The dogs travelled on a lower deck with an odorous company of cattle and mules, in the care of a group of not very happy deckhands who had to spend a good part of the day shovelling cowpats, horse manure, and dog droppings overboard, and hosing down the filthy decks.

The records show that she had also acquired a Canadian "free miner's pass." That would allow her to travel into the Klondike, and to prospect and stake claims. We have to assume that the actual mining or panning for gold was something she at least considered as an option, although there is no evidence that she ever actually did either of these things. She certainly could have. Being out on the creeks with all those men was not likely to distress a farm girl from New Brunswick, used to working alongside boys and men, with little of the privacy and gender distinction that a town girl of the period would have expected. So to be at sea or on the trail or in a mining camp where she was the only woman or one of few seems never to have struck her as daunting.

She was twenty-nine years old now, but photographs of that year show a woman who seems much older, seeming close to early middle age. She is big, wide-jawed, solid, with a huge bosom and a daunting expression. If she was worried about being the only woman in that crowd, she left no record of it. Throughout the many and often dramatic tales that make up the legend, there is no suggestion that she was ever sexually harassed. It is likely that the prospector hopefuls assumed at first that her turning up there at all meant that she was a prostitute, but even more likely that it did not take long to disillusion them. As a serious Catholic with what appears to have been a Protestant touch of the puritan, it may be that she simply never recounted any of the encounters she had. But looking at the photographs of this square-jawed, broad-shouldered, over-six-foot, two-hundred-pound woman suggests that her sheer *presence* may have kept predators at bay. It is history's loss that she did not keep a journal, nor, in her letters, say very much about the day-to-day challenges she met as she made her way into the wilderness.

She begins to be called Kate at about this time. It was four days from Vancouver to Wrangell. There Kate learned that up the frozen Stikine River there was a staging point called Glenora, nominally a village but in reality not much more than a collection of tents and huts. It was said that the Canadian government intended to build a rail line from Glenora to the goldfields, trains to take the prospectors and miners in, and bring the gold out. The British Columbia government was also promising a wagon road. If governments were taking the gold rush that seriously, it must be a reality.

Whether or not she was ever serious about getting her hands on a miner's pick and shovel, Katherine Ryan was one of those fortunate people who assume that anything they set out to do they will succeed in. Whatever she had in mind when she applied for the free miner's pass, everything points to her having two primary objectives: to be a part of a great adventure, and, more importantly, to make money out of it by running a restaurant. She was now experienced and adept at the trade, and she enjoyed the social buzz and the whirr of gossip that swirled around her tables.

She knew that with all that money flowing into the Yukon in the form of the miners' stakes, and about to flow out in the form of gold dust and bullion, there would be no time for people to settle down and make homes for themselves with kitchens in them. There would be hungry men with money to spend. She could deal with that. Kate knew a business opportunity when she saw one: Glenora was going to need restaurants, a trade she knew a lot better than mining. But it was not going to be easy to get there. There were no roads, Wrangell was on an island and there was at least one more boat trip to the mainland. The rivers were frozen.

Kate made friends with a contingent of Royal North West Mounted Policemen who were staging through Wrangell to Glenora. When she visited their encampment, the first young constable she met complained to her that their cook had not turned up and he, who knew nothing about a kitchen, had been saddled with the job. Kate made the obvious bargain, provided the young cops with the first decent food they had had for a while, and when they set off for Glenora, along the

Stikine River she went with them as company cook. If there was some risk of exploitation (from steamboat operators and packers) that she would have encountered as a woman on her own, her temporary job with the police force would serve her well.

The NWMP contingent was under the command of Inspector Phillip Primrose, who would be a good friend to Kate for the rest of her years in the north. Primrose's surveyor, Jim Callbreath, told his commander that he believed that the rumoured Ottawa government-sponsored railroad was a fantasy, impossible to build in that territory, and that they should be pressing the BC government to make good on its more practicable wagon road.

Kate appears to have left the slower-moving police contingent at some point on this journey up the frozen river, and headed off on her own with the dogs. On the first or second night on her own, she was just setting up camp when another traveller turned up, a Presbyterian clergyman named Pringle, on his way to set up a mission. Pringle travelled with her the rest of the way to Glenora and they would be friends for the rest of her life.

In Glenora Kate found that the surveyor Callbreath had transformed his surveyor's warehouse, a sixteen-by-twenty-four-foot frame shack, into a rough little two-storey hotel. Kate tacked a tent onto the side of the building and opened a canvas-covered restaurant. Soon she would not be the only woman in Glenora. Helen Dobrowolsky, a historian specializing in the story of the North West Mounted Police, set the scene for us.

> There were thousands and thousands of people pouring into the territory. There was a very small force of mounted police that were expected to collect customs, to ensure that all these greenhorns who knew nothing about living on the country had enough supplies that they wouldn't starve to death. They were trying to patrol the entire waterway, between the mountain passes and Dawson, and just generally keep law and order. So to deal with this, the government of the day decided to put together a special force of 200 soldiers of what became known as the Yukon Field Force.

When the Yukon Field Force arrived in their totally inappropriate tall white pith helmets and a great deal of brass to polish, they were escorting a group of very dignified ladies. The government at Ottawa had recognized that in addition to maintaining law and order — and dealing with what would become a serious disagreement between the United States and Canada — there would be humanitarian needs to be met. Ottawa had financed a contingent of women from the Victorian Order of Nurses, under the sponsorship of Lady Aberdeen, the wife of the governor general and founder of the order. A Toronto newspaperwoman named Faith Fenton was also travelling with the nurses, and her accounts of Glenora for the Toronto *Globe* give us some of the little narrative documentation we have of that hastily built town.

Their presence was at least in part an international political move on the part of Prime Minister Wilfrid Laurier. With the US–Canada borderline in dispute, a military unit in the Yukon, Laurier hoped, would help him demonstrate Canadian sovereignty in the territory. If there was going to be a boom in gold there would be revenues for the national coffers, and Ottawa was going to establish a presence.

More stories were coming in about new discoveries of gold, and Jim Callbreath decided that he had better ride north towards Teslin to check out the route and see what the conditions would be like for men who wanted to head up towards the goldfields before any road or rail line was a reality. He was away two weeks. The river had thawed and there was steamer service now, all the way from Wrangell. In the two weeks Callbreath was away on his survey, the miners pouring into Glenora in response to the flood of gold rumours had swelled the little settlement from a village of about a hundred people when Callbreath left, to a town of more than three thousand. By the time he got back people were setting up three more hotels, a smithy, several outfitters, a barbershop, a newspaper, and even a brewery.

In the end the BC government's promised wagon road north out of Glenora never materialized. In Ottawa Sir Clifford Sifton, Laurier's minister of the interior, was spectacularly successful in getting Parliament to agree to finance a rail line, but in the Senate the Tories — who had a majority in the upper house — shot it down. A lot of hopes were dashed with it. The terrain between that staging village, Glenora, and the actual goldfields was desperately difficult. Some gave up and went home. One young man shot himself when the news came about the government's abandoning the rail line. The toughest and most determined swallowed their frustration, bought packhorses, learned how to tie the diamond hitch (without which you could not, it was said, really claim to be able to run a pack train) and headed north across the muskeg and the hills. The people — and the money — were moving out of Glenora, towards Teslin. If the money was migrating that way, the need for restaurants was too. Kate decided to sell the dogs, buy some horses, and pack herself north, alone.

Tom Radford, our documentary's director, sought out a modern-day pack train outfitter, Rob Touhey, to demonstrate on camera the famous diamond hitch and to comment on just what Kate would have been up against, as she followed each stream, the Thaltan, the Nahlin, the Twoya, and the Teslin Rivers, up to their headwaters, over the passes, down into another mosquito-infested valley and up another river. Touhey said that for an experienced team of packhorse men in prime condition it would have been a daunting trip; for a lone, inexperienced woman of thirty it was quite simply an astounding achievement.

First of all five horses is a handful in any kind of situation. I mean you can certainly take more, if you're experienced, but five horses is a handful for anybody. Now if you're on a trail with a lot of bogs and windfall and you know wasps and all those lovely things that wreck horses, and you're by yourself and you've never been over the trail, that's a hell of an accomplishment!

By the time Kate arrived in Teslin, still a long way from the goldfields, it was late fall. Freeze-up came early in 1898. She set aside her plan to reach the goldfields by Christmas. She heard that a settlement at Aitlin, back south in British Columbia, needed a nurse. The cook/restaurant-manager/packhorse woman was a trained nurse. She traded her horses for another dog team and joined a party of prospectors from Quebec. The Klondike historian Mack Swackhammer describes the conditions of a trip like that in winter.

Just imagine yourself walking, you're a woman that has maybe thirty-five pounds of clothes on — it's all wool and leather — and you're carrying perhaps forty-five to sixty-five pounds of gear and you're going to do that thirty times in six weeks, and it's bloody cold and you can't have trousers on.

Ladies don't wear trousers, and Katherine Ryan would not relinquish her status as a lady. The whole of that winter, the lady worked as a nurse, travelling out to tiny settlements by dogsled. In the spring she went over to Bennett City, on Bennett Lake at the headwaters of the Yukon River, with still about three hundred miles to go to Dawson, the centre of the goldfield action. In Bennett she began to hear vivid and discouraging tales of the squalor and viciousness of life in Dawson. At the same time they were talking about what a great place Whitehorse was turning out to be. She was tired of living in a tent. As she thought it over, the lure of the goldfields began to fade. With a new restaurant in a stable, civil town, she would have steady business and lots of company; she could keep warm. When a boating company started rafting people across Bennett Lake, she went with a party who were willing to let her off at Whitehorse.

If this were a movie, it is here that the subplot would be introduced by a couple of puzzling scenes, their central figure a much younger woman. It is not clear whether or not Kate ever met a dance hall girl in Bennett, an eighteen-year-old opportunist from Seattle named Kitty Rockwell. But Kitty Rockwell heard a great deal about Kate over the years, and will come back into the story a little later on. Kate got off the barge at Whitehorse, and Whitehorse, as Helen Dobrowolsky told us, was booming.

The railway from Skagway [on the Pacific coast, in the Alaska panhandle] had been recently completed. Just over here by the train station, this was the head of navigation for the Yukon River, so tons of goods and hundreds and thousands of people were coming over that train, offloading on to all these ships. All along here was all shipyards and docks, and stern wheelers tied up as well as all kinds of various more eccentric craft. It was a bustling little community.

A butcher named Dominic Burns helped her get a restaurant started and gave it its famous name, *KLONDIKE KATE'S*. Kate Ryan had decided she was finished with dog teams and pack trains; it was time to settle down. "I built my first home, a twelve-by-sixteen-foot log cabin, and finally put my first log on the fire," she wrote to her sister in Bangor.

(In the meantime, our subplot heroine, Kitty Rockwell, had gone the other direction, north to Dawson, and was building herself a hell of a reputation with something called the flame dance. "I'm here to make as much money as I can," she said.)

Down in Whitehorse, Katherine Ryan, restaurateur, added yet another set of skills to her already considerable repertory: police work. She had been helping the Whitehorse NWMP detachment in an informal way, coming around to some of the rowdier drinking spots on a Saturday night with a cartload of pies, which distracted the guys from their obsessive pursuit of oblivion. Soon she would have them all gathered around her table wolfing down pie dished out by a now rather stout, motherly-looking big person, the kind of person many of them missed or thought they missed and certainly sentimentalized about a lot when they were in their cups.

So she was well liked by the constabulary, and when they suddenly were directed to enlist a Special Woman Constable it is not surprising that they turned to Kate. The Women's Christian Temperance Union, as well as campaigning for the prohibition of alcohol, was also working on women's rights, including the vote and the rights of women in prison. Those dance hall girls and the prostitutes were getting jailed pretty frequently, and while their employers usually paid their fines and got them out again in short order, to get back to work, they were entirely in the custody of men while in jail, and the WCTU convinced Ottawa that this would not do. Kate was sworn in. Now she put in a few hours a week as a warder, and that inevitably meant counsellor and advocate. Later, when the NWMP had to start searching people for contraband gold, she was sworn in to a second police function, the first (and only) female gold inspector in the history of the force.

As the gold was shipped out of the Yukon there was sometimes as much as $400,000 a day moving through Whitehorse. This was a Canadian resource. Canadian taxpayers had footed the bill for policing and other services. The feds were determined to have a share of the proceeds, in the form of an export tax on gold leaving the country. Not surprisingly the smuggler's art was being practised with considerable ingenuity. NWMP historian Helen Dobrowolsky explained what that meant to Kate.

> *There were two routes out of the territory. Downriver by ship from Dawson, or you could come up the river, take the train from Whitehorse to Skagway and go out in relative comfort. And of course you couldn't expect a male police constable to be frisking these dignified female passengers. You needed a woman of tact and force of character to handle this. And this became Kate's job. There's one story of a woman who she asked if she had any gold. And the woman wouldn't say anything and the woman was wearing a particularly elaborate upswept hairdo. And amazingly enough she had this little cache of gold nuggets right in the middle of it.*

That particular smuggler was the wife of a general in the United States Army.

Still a practising Catholic, Kate Ryan had something less than a deferential attitude towards the clergy. Her grandniece Kit McKernan likes to tell of a priest, new to the territory, who got into Kate's bad books.

> *They had great missions up there, that the young priests used to come in for, the mission. And all of the Native people would come, all dressed up in their great costumes with buckskin and their moccasins on. And this young priest got up and said that the Natives' ways were so pagan, and that if you come into the house of God you don't come dressed in skins and moccasins. . . . Kate Ryan got up and walked out on him. Took the train over to Skagway, took the boat down to Rupert and talked to the Bishop because it was such an insult to the Native people.*

Katherine Ryan had never completely lost interest in mining. It was, after all, the motive power of her restaurant business and the economic engine of her territorial world. She invested a substantial part of her profits from the restaurant business in the claims of a number of prospectors and start-up mining companies. In a few years, as the gold rush began to wind down and Whitehorse to settle down, she had some money put away.

By 1904 she was a pillar of the community, a member of the

Catholic Women's League, the Hospital Committee, the North Star Athletic Club, the Yukon Liberal Association and the Yukon Women's Protective League. She became friends with a literary-minded young Scottish bank clerk who had come to work for the Whitehorse branch of the Bank of Commerce. Kate would later laugh and tell people that when she first peeked through the bank window to get a glimpse of the new clerk people were talking about, she thought, Well, *he* doesn't look as though he knew enough about the North to write anything about it! And it is said that she would later complain that the tales she told Robert W. Service about life among the sourdoughs got very badly distorted when he retold them in verse. This, like a lot of the Klondike Kate folklore, is pretty doubtful since he did not begin to publish until 1907, long after Service and Kate are supposed to have met. And if Kate did so complain, she was almost certainly only one of many who would, as Service's reputation blew into flame, declare that they were the ones who had told him the story of The Lady That's Known as Lou, or The Cremation of Sam McGee.

Now here comes the subplot again. There is an archive newspaper photo of Service and Klondike Kate together. It has been considerably retouched, apparently with the picture of a different woman pasted in where Kate was in the original, posing in front of *KLONDIKE KATE'S* restaurant. The woman pasted in is Kitty Rockwell.

Now a touch of the subplot again, still not clearly attached to the main story. As the high life in Dawson City wound down, Kitty Rockwell had gone back to Seattle to seek out Alexander Pantages, whom she had known in the North. The story of Kitty and Pantages is clouded by the myths that both of them created about themselves, but it is likely that they were lovers in the Yukon, where Pantages worked as a bartender, learning how to pick up tiny bits of gold dust that collected on the bar, and slowly accumulating the capital that would buy him his first theatre, the Orpheum, in Nome, Alaska. It seems probable that Kitty Rockwell, who was already prosperous when the young Pantages arrived in the north after losing his shirt to gamblers on the boat from San Francisco to Skagway, had lent him money and never got it back.

Pantages had worked as a waiter for a while in Skagway, then persuaded a party of innocents that he was an experienced guide, and somehow managed to get them all the way to Dawson, where he met Kitty and then abandoned her. When he became the successful proprietor of a movie house in Seattle, and married a Seattle girl, Kitty sued him for breach of promise. She had a publicity sense, and perhaps thinking it might help her suit, she passed herself off as "the Real Klondike Kate." Now the Kitty Rockwell story comes into contact with the Kate Ryan story. The lawsuit with its deliciously scandalous echoes of Dawson dance halls, gold, and immoral behaviour, became a national news story. *KLONDIKE KATE SUES PANTAGES*. So the real "Real Klondike Kate" had some explaining to do to family and friends. The embarrassment of it bothered her for the rest of her life.

The last years of Kate Ryan's life take her far from those adventurous beginnings in the late 1890s. During a home visit to New Brunswick in 1903, her brother John asked her to take one of his sons back to Whitehorse; his wife was frail, and pregnant again. Later she would die in childbirth with their fifth son. While it is not clear whether their father just dumped the four boys on his sister Katherine, or perhaps brought them out to her in Whitehorse, we soon find her back in Whitehorse raising the boys as her foster children. The photographs of them as slight, winsome boys give way to a quartet of heavy-set, serious-looking men, and then that quartet is reduced to a trio in the later photos, by the death of Kate's favourite, Leo, who wanted to lie about his age and join the army during the last days of the Great War. Kate would have nothing of it, and sent him back to New Brunswick, the trip starting by train down to Skagway and then by steamer, the *Princess Sophia*, down to Vancouver and the train back east. The *Princess Sophia* never made it to Vancouver; she ran aground on the Vanderbilt reef during a storm, and broke up. More than three hundred passengers and crew died, among them Leo Ryan.

Kate associated Leo's death with Whitehorse; that was where she had become deeply fond of him, where she had found real family at last, with her four handsome nephews. Now that she had lost Leo, she wanted no more of Whitehorse. She could afford to pick up and go; she had put away enough of her profits from KLONDIKE KATE'S that she did not have to run restaurants any more, or nurse the sick. She tried Stewart, BC, for a while, and even dabbled briefly in politics. They wanted her to run for office now that women had the vote, but she was afraid that the Kitty Rockwell/Pantages scandal would be raised all over again by her opponents, and declined. Kate, in her fifties now, poses in formal, bustled gowns and heavy hats, broad-beamed and broad-chinned and broad-smiled, grandmotherly, settled. The girl who packed five horses up the frozen Stikine is nowhere to be seen, except perhaps in the dreaming eyes. She tells people who ask, that she just wants to be left alone, once the boys are grown and gone. A reporter from *Maclean's* magazine says, "Why did you never marry?" "No man ever proposed to me," is her published answer, "And I don't really understand why!"

But it doesn't seem to matter any more. She goes back to Johnville for another visit, in 1923, and there is a photograph of her with her now very elderly parents in front of what has become a huge, sprawling frame farmhouse of several buildings growing out of each other. She makes friends with a Great War hero, Colonel George Pearkes, VC. This gives this writer "three degrees of separation" from Kate Ryan, as George Pearkes was my father's commanding officer in the 116th Battalion in that war.

Kate leaves Stewart and moves in to Vancouver. She is comfortably off and buys a house on Robson Street. Vancouver is growing at an exponential rate. She hears a lot of talk about what a wonderful thing the stock market is. Friends are making fortunes. This looks pretty interesting to a woman who, after a life of risk and adventure, is quietly clipping coupons and living on her investments. She puts virtually everything she has into the market. It is the autumn of 1929.

It is all gone now, the stories, the dreams, the gold, the restaurants, even the legend. The title *Klondyke Kate* has appeared on movie screens and the covers of hit songs that you buy at the sheet music stores, and serialized tales in the short story magazines, but they are all falsified — thefts from her own once very authentic adventures. They have brought some momentary glory and wealth to Kitty Rockwell, formerly of Seattle. But Katherine Ryan doesn't care about any of that now. Weakened by cancer and by the despair that hit her when the market crashed and all that KLONDIKE KATE'S had earned for her is gone, Katherine Ryan is close to the end. It is 1932. She is sixty-three.

Dominic Burns, the butcher from Whitehorse who had told her to call the place KLONDIKE KATE'S in the first place, shows up, right at the end, and so does the youngest of her four foster-sons, Charlie. She was in Saint Paul's hospital, Kit McKernan told us.

But no one I think expected her to die. She died on a men's ward. It was the only private room that was available at St. Paul's at that time. And she said, "I lived my whole life with men so I might just as well die among the men, too." It didn't bother her one bit.

It was a grand funeral procession, they say. She had made many friends in Vancouver, and despite her reclusive last years she was, after all, a celebrity. The cortege wound its way out to Ocean View Burial Park, where her body was interred.

There is no marker.

◆   ◆   ◆

The original documentary was written and directed by Tom Radford, in collaboration with Dave Cunningham, who also edited the program.

PART EIGHT

SIMON GUNANOOT
Chasing Shadows

This is the story of a man whose life was suddenly put in jeopardy by a double murder, and then saved by the power of the land he lived on — the land that he was *of* — and by the ancient culture in which his view of life was nurtured.

The Cassiar country north of Hazelton in northwest British Columbia was some of the last wilderness to be explored in North America. It is a vast, sprawling land of picture-book mountains reflected in mirror lakes, rich vegetation in summer and cutting snows that slant down the precipitous slopes in winter. A bald eagle perches motionless in a tree far below you, and below the eagle, down in the marshy flatland, a many-pointed elk picks his aristocratic way through the deep grasses, across a wide, shallow river, and up the far shore.

British Columbia patriots may tell you that this country is so huge that you could plop the whole of England down in the middle of it and come back next week and not be able to find it. Clouds come down to the ground and hang on the shoulders of the mountains and foothills so that a photograph can look like an ancient Chinese painting, with only a line or two emerging from the soft white envelope to suggest the outlines of a landscape. Early European adventurers getting lost in that territory would often stay lost. As distinctive as some of those mountain silhouettes can be to the knowing eye, after a few days trekking up the vertical canyons floored by shouting rapids, and passing through one meadow after another only to find yourself back in canyons again and confronting another breathtaking panorama, can lead to a deep disorientation in the brains of all but the most sanguine or experienced.

The Gitskan[7] of the Cassiar region say that their people came into being at Temlehan, in the shadow of Mount Roche Deboule. Their proud, brooding totem poles and gate poles were, according to one

7. Say "GISS-kan."

modern European cultural anthropologist,[8] part of the greatest art the world has ever seen, more powerful than Ancient Egypt or Ancient Greece or the European Renaissance. Ironically, the apex of that art was achieved after the arrival of the Europeans, who brought the steel-cutting tools that made it possible to easily and elegantly work the great cedars. Museum visitors at Toronto's ROM, Vancouver's Museum of Civilization, or the national Museum of Civilization at Ottawa or the Museum of Natural History in New York cannot escape a skin-tingling sense of ages immemorial, as they stand in the shadow of those immense North West Coast poles, but the truth is that their growth to meet the sun was brief. It crested in the 1880s, began to fade under the oppressive cultural genocide of the ruling population early in the twentieth century, and then flowered again in a renaissance in the hands of young artists from the many nations of that region. To some extent inspired by the sculptural adventures of the great Bill Reid, their work *feels* like ancient work.[9] It reaches back into the deepest cultural consciousness of peoples who felt such an affinity with the animal kingdom that in their art it is often difficult to know where the animal stops and the human begins. You can see the artists who made them in the turn-of-the century photographs and motion pictures of Edward Curtis, assembled in both a book and a film entitled *The Shadow Catcher* by Terri McLuhan. Curtis found them still going to sea in their whaling canoes carved out of a single immense log, the paddlers dressed ceremonially to go and greet the killer whales. And they are there among the stupendous poles, unlike any other national culture in the world.

Some of those weathered old giants of the early period still stand in the Cassiar country, cracked, tilted, fading into the undergrowth, but most are gone. The photographs of Kispiox village that were unearthed for our documentary show forests of them, taller than the tallest tree in a mixed eastern forest, gracefully watching over the spiritual life of their villages, watching for enemies, watching for danger, watching for the touch of life.

In the 1960s the renaissance of the old arts and the old values led

8. Claude Levi-Strauss, in an interview with the author, Ottawa, 1971.
9. Bill Reid was a Haida sculptor: b.1920; d. 1998.

to the building of 'Ksan, a replica Gitskan village on the Skeena near Hazelton. 'Ksan became a major training centre for Northwest coast native peoples who wanted to learn the styles and skills of their ancestors. Cultural anthropologists use the term *Tsimshian* as a collective name for the Tsimshian, Nishga, and Gitskan peoples. But the 'Ksan style is distinctive, clear of line and sharply detailed, positive, using the traditional U-forms and split U-forms in elongated or truncated versions, often outside the figure depicted. 'Ksan has brought thousands of summer visitors to the region to feel the power, through dance and mask and silkscreen works growing out of these rich ancient cultures.

And it was in that rich mix of nature, art, and a turbulent encounter of conflicting cultures, that a baby was born to two Gitskan chiefs, in 1874. His mother was a hereditary chief of the Fireweed clan, and his father a hereditary chief of the Frog clan. His childhood at his father's side prepared him for the great drama of his life. His father was a trapper and hunter who knew the land and its creatures and its ways, and how to survive in it, as deeply as millennia of tradition could provide. And Simon Peter Gunanoot, the child, would need all of that when he was thirty-five. He would be suspected of a double murder, made the object of one of the longest and most famous manhunts in Canadian history, and survive on the run with his family, in that fearsome landscape, for nearly a decade and a half.

The then active British Columbia Provincial Police, the RCMP, and even the legendary American Pinkerton Agency would pursue him, fruitlessly and at enormous cost. Rewards offered for his capture were the equivalent, in today's money, of hundreds of thousands of dollars. Yet nobody turned him in. He was seen in a number of the towns and villages of the region, whither he would glide like a shadow out of the mountainscape, to pick up a little salt, a bottle of whisky perhaps, leave word for his friends that he and his family — for his father, wife, and children were with him and two children would be born during his exile — that they were all right, and that the friends were doing a good job of throwing the pursuers off the scent and warning the Gunanoot family of who was hunting them and where. For thirteen years nobody turned him in.

Violent death was not a stranger to that family. Some years earlier Simon's older brother Din had accidentally shot and killed a companion when the boys were playing with guns not far from Hazelton. Din disappeared into the bush. His parents hunted for him for days, but before they found him he had hanged himself.

Simon took up ranching. There was a place on the Skeena River where the packhorse trains taking prospectors and explorers into the Big Country could cross over in the shallows. Simon married Sarah, a woman from the village of Kitsegas, and together they developed a horse-breeding ranch on prime bottomland near that ford on the Skeena, calling the farm *Anlaw*, which meant River Crossing in their tongue. Simon Gunanoot appears to have been able to live comfortably in both the Gitskan and the white cultures. He was educated in a church school, spoke an accented English fluently, and wrote in a clear, cursive hand, samples of which appear in the documentary, legible and elegant. Competent and at ease living off the land, both in the bush and on the ranch, he was also a successful businessman, running a general store in Kispiox village and travelling into town to buy supplies for his business. He bought and sold furs.

In the spring of 1906 Sarah heard that there was a good catch of fish for sale at a village a few miles away. Photographs of the river fishermen of the period show magnificently precarious log platforms slung out on beams over the gorges, and men standing on them casting nets down into the teeming rush of water a dizzying distance below. Salmon were so plentiful that workers on the CPR as it pushed through into British Columbia in the 1880s complained of having to eat it every day. Simon set off on foot, over the infamous wooden suspension called the Terror Bridge and down through the semi-outlaw community of 2-Mile, where he stopped in for a drink. The town council in Hazelton, then just a few muddy streets and wooden buildings clad in unpainted cedar bevel siding, were determined that their little frontier community be a "respectable" place; so they outlawed such popular but unseemly institutions as brothels and taverns anywhere closer than two miles from the town centre. 2-Mile had its supply of both services and did a regular and successful business although nobody lived there except the practitioners themselves. The big saloon was well furnished with brass spittoons and hand towels hanging under the lip of the bar every two feet along the polished mahogany panels. We have to guess what the towels were for. But that was where Simon stopped in for a shot of something, and then, apparently, another, in the company of numerous other well-lubricated packers, trappers, and prospectors.

The bartender's name was Cameron. From the evidence given at the inquest it seems that Cameron was already too drunk to work by the time Simon Gunanoot came in, and a dock labourer named Macintosh had taken over behind the bar. Macintosh was a big, powerful brawler fresh out of jail, probably for assault, under orders to leave the region within twenty-four hours, and making the best of a last night in 2-Mile. Witnesses said he baited Gunanoot with racist remarks and hints that he, Macintosh, had been "close to" Gunanoot's wife Sarah. When the inevitable fight broke out Simon was no match for Macintosh, who threw him out in the street badly beaten and bloodied with a ragged wound on his face that left him with a long scar for the rest of his life.

Somebody told the police they had heard Simon say that he would be back with a gun and Macintosh had better watch out.

But Macintosh was in bad shape too. There must have been broken bottles involved, for the pinch-hitting bartender's hand was bleeding so badly that the trail boss of his pack train sent him over to the hospital in Hazelton to get it treated. He never arrived. In the morning he was found dead on the trail with a single bullet neatly centred in his back. People still point out the place. The soaring mountains loom in the distance, and there on the trail wild lilies are growing.

It was Constable James Kirby of the BC provincial police who opened the investigation, with his rangy handlebar moustache and heavily lashed walrus eyes. "After investigating the grounds all around," his report reads, "I went back to the 2-Mile Tavern and discovered the circumstances of the night before," much of which has been related above. There was no morgue. The body was laid out at the police station. Kirby was sitting down to lunch when word came that a second body had been found on the trail, that of a farmer named Max

LeClair, a newcomer to the valley with no connection to Macintosh. He too had been shot neatly in the middle of the back with a single bullet.

It must have seemed pretty clear to Constable Kirby that Gunanoot was his man. As soon as Doctor Wrinch completed the obligatory autopsy, they got out a warrant for the Gitskan rancher, and the long search was under way.

Kirby swore in a posse. They lined up on the porch of the court-house and had their photo taken. The photo still exists, and in it the posse look as though, well, this will all be over pretty soon. They sad-dled up and rode out to *Anlaw*. Sarah and the children stared at them mutely, and just shook their heads when Kirby tried to question them.

"Searching around the house," he wrote, "we discovered three horses had been shot, a fourth killed by a pick, which we found with bloodstains on it. We searched the grounds thoroughly, but no sign of the accused."

And indeed it would be thirteen years before he saw his prey, thir-teen years of confusion, not without its humour, but based upon the desperate run for his life of an Indian in the days when Indians were still considered less than human by many whites, certainly less than civilized by most, and no more likely to be acquitted by an all-white jury — as it would inevitably be — than a black man in Mississippi in the 1930s. Gunanoot knew perfectly well, and so did his friends, that the likeliest outcome were he ever found would be a round of gunfire on the pretext of self-defence, and a clutch of Gitskan corpses left for the relatives to claim. He had no choice. The many photographs of this man show a watchful, appraising gaze, strong eyes that turn up sharply at the outer corners and always seem to have an exceptional glint. Sometimes he is in the ceremonial robes and bear-claw headdress of his national culture, and sometimes in the suit, vest, and tie of the white world. However he is dressed we do not see him smiling much. Perhaps it is just because we already know a great deal of his story, but this looks like a man who will not readily be surprised.

Indeed, Constable Kirby never got close enough to pull a gun. He found tracks on the trail heading north towards Sarah's home village, Kitsegas. That seemed a likely lead, so Kirby and the posse rode north.

Somehow, as they were interrogating the Kitsegas villagers, the posse's horses got loose and disappeared. Kirby and his men had to walk the forty kilometres back to Hazelton. There they learned that while they had been looking for him in Kitsegas, Simon had come back to the ranch, collected supplies and his family, including a brother-in-law named Peter Himadam, and once more vanished. Simon's father Nah Gun was rounded up. Perhaps Kirby hoped that when Gunanoot learned his father was in jail he would come out of hiding. Instead the old man escaped on his own, and before long word was going around the valley that he was with Gunanoot and the rest of the family-in-exile. A local historian, Bob Henderson, wryly narrates the next phase, which is not distinguished by a high degree of admiration for Constable Kirby.

> He wrote to Superintendent Hussey, who was chief Counsel of Victoria, and said that it was very difficult to chase Simon and Peter because they had access to horses and he didn't. And he really needed a horse. So it was allowed that he could go out and buy a horse. And eventually he writes back to Hussey and says, "I have found a very gentle mare, and she's going to cost $100, and then I'll need the upkeep." So it was decided that he would get $100 and $15 a month as the upkeep. [But] these horses were mythical. The province [sent] them $15 a month to feed these mythical horses, and . . . he . . . actually asked for a barn to be built for the mythical horse.

Hussey, in his bowler hat and greatcoat, superbly sculpted great bush of a moustache and eyes that glowered with deep civic menace (reminding one of Sherlock Holmes's pompous rival at Scotland Yard, Inspector Lestrade), was not long taken in by the bumbling Constable Kirby. He pulled Kirby off the case and sent in another moustache, Constable Berryman. Berryman got as far as Kitsegas and reported back that he needed more supplies. When Hussey learned that Berryman had been seen actually talking to Gunanoot, interrogating him without knowing who he was, he pulled Berryman off the case and sent a couple of real professionals out from the capital, Constables Munro and Wilkie. *The Victoria Daily Colonist* reported:

> By canoe and trail the constables are vigorously pushing their

quarry into a corner of the country where they will certainly in time round him up. Both Munro and Wilkie are hard, sinewy, tough men, and the task is to their liking. That they will be able to stand the tire of the trail, with its packing of grub, carrying of canoe, lining through rapids and resting at nights with the round boulders of the gravel bar under their heads for pillows, is no less certain than they will bring the bad Indian to civilization and justice.

But this was just a lot of romantic gush. The man they were up against was far less likely to tire on the trail than were his pursuers. They went all the way up to Dawson City chasing rumours of Gunanoot along the Yukon Telegraph line. Native workers on that line kept Gunanoot well informed. That winter of 1906 to 1907 was a killer. The mercury dropped to minus 45 degrees Celsius. Wilkie and his partner reported confidently that nobody could have survived that kind of a winter, and that the Gunanoot family had certainly frozen to death. They went back to Victoria. Spring came, and with it unequivocal reports that the Gunanoots were alive and well, and on the way to becoming heroes among the tribal peoples. The natives might, Hussey feared, use the symbolic figure of the fugitive as the rallying-point for an uprising or some other form of resistance to provincial authority. When a prospector named McPhail gave a statement to the police, in the fall of 1907, that he had met and talked with Gunanoot, Hussey sent Wilkie back on the trail. Wilkie's telegram to Hussey is still in the archives:

We constructed a raft to go down the lake and put our effects on board and started, but had an accident, the raft running onto a sunken snag and throwing everything into the water.

Another man, Haggard, went out with three juniors. They fell out over cooking duty and the juniors quit. Haggard hid his food and other supplies in a cache and went back in for orders. Gunanoot and his family rifled the cache and disappeared again. By now Premier McBride had given up on his own police and sent for the Mounties. The Mounties insisted on travelling in uniform, so everyone, including Gunanoot, always knew about their movements. By 1909 Hussey and McBride decided they needed something special, and went for the Pinkerton Agency.

The Pinkerton posters of the time show a great engraved single eye, with the motto *We Never Sleep*. The agency had become world famous; it even figures in a Sherlock Holmes story. Pinkerton men had hunted down Jesse James and Butch Cassidy and the famous but incompetent Canadian bank robber Billy Miner, the Grey Fox (see Part Six of this book). They specialized in undercover work. Their two agents took on the role of coal prospectors in the Groundhog Mountains, where Gunanoot was last seen. They were told to sign their telegraphed reports to Hussey with numbers (#8 and #26) instead of names. Sometime that fall they met a packing contractor up the telegraph line, and sent in the first report to suggest that maybe they were getting somewhere:

"We spent nearly all day with George Beirnes, [who] told us . . . that Simon had a special hunting ground, and that he had met Gunanoot there."

In the provincial archives there is a dirty watermarked slip of paper with a pencilled map that Beirnes drew for the Pinkerton men, believing them to be legitimate prospectors whom Gunanoot would help, although he warned them that Gunanoot would know they were coming long before they got close, and would decide whether or not to meet with them. Gunanoot decided not to. They came back, in the spring, as empty-handed as their predecessors.

And so Hussey called off the search. It was costing a fortune, earning the law only ridicule, leading nowhere. He announced a reward for information leading to the arrest of Gunanoot and Peter Himadam. Perhaps he hoped that bounty hunters would achieve what the lawmen could not. The reward was at first $300. This was raised to $1,000 and then to an unprecedented $2,300. Stories began to go around among the Gitskan that people were coming all the way from Europe to go on the hunt. But it was hopeless: not only did Gunanoot and his family know the land and how to live on it, but also they had become heroes to their people. They could slip into a village for supplies, a friendly word, and information about where the police were, or who the newest hopefuls were on the bounty trail, and there was simply no way that they would ever be caught. Gunanoot's son David, who was born on the trail, gave an interview much later in which he told of being at the head of the Skeena, and hearing of someone coming there to find them. The children were packed on the sled with the best dogs in the country, and, with Simon and Peter both perfectly fit within twenty-four hours they were miles away. That was family life for the Gunanoots, for thirteen years.

It was not without hardship and loss. Whether it was revenge or accident, Gunanoot's store in Kispiox along with all its inventory was destroyed by fire. His father Nah Gun died on the trail; consistent with tradition, Gunanoot carried the body to the old man's chosen resting place at Bowser Lake and buried him there. At least one of Sarah's babies died at birth. Peter Himadam's wife died and was buried in the Spatzi wilderness.

One evening Simon slipped into the town where he was most likely to be recognized, and was. A fur trader named Dick Sergeant had decided to try his luck as a motion picture exhibitor, and had bought a projector and hung up a sheet and put out a poster. Half of Hazelton came along one night to see their very first movie. Dick Sergeant later said that he had recognized a figure standing in the shadows at the back of the hall. And Gunanoot later told how he had gone back to his family in their tent in the bush and made shadows on the tent wall, with his hands and a lamp, to try to tell them about the moving picture marvel he had seen in town.

There is a significant political context within which this adventure unfolded:

Historian Tom Buri:

There was a great deal of . . . unrest with the native people. Alliances were being formed between the tribes. Declarations of rights were being promulgated. A delegation was led to England by Squamish Chief Joe Capilano to see King Edward. All of this while railroads were getting put in, trap lines were being taken away, land was being alienated. It was an extremely volatile political situation, when Gunanoot disappeared.

The weapon of conquest that seemed most visible to the Gitskan was the surveyor's transit. That was the seemingly innocent, but more and more powerful tool that opened the way for those steel invaders, the tracks — the tracks and the grade, connecting Prince Rupert on the Pacific coast with the inland wealth and markets of Eastern Canada. Those lines of steel, with the flat gravelled grades that supported them and changed the land forever: those were seen as scars on the territorial flesh of the Northwest native peoples.

Gunanoot was too busy staying ahead of the law to be actively involved in land claims issues as they began to take shape, but he became a symbol of the new assertiveness of his people. When an uprising was rumoured to be forming in the Hazelton area, even though Gunanoot had no possible way of being involved in it, his name turned the rumour into an event.

There was a big Irish constable at Hazelton, named Deane. Deane was new to the job and to the region, a guy who, by reputation, liked to "fight first and investigate later." Deane heard that the influential Squamish Chief Joe Capilano was visiting the local Gitskan leaders. He became seized with the notion (which he may have invented), that the Gitskan were going to lay siege to the town. The *Omenica Herald* ran a story saying that Gunanoot was ready to lead the Kispiox in battle, if that was what was needed to achieve their land claims. Deane organized a defence and rounded up a task force of bewildered residents. These people had been getting along just fine with the Gitskan; and just that day the Indians had helped with a major packhorse crossing of the Skeena. Nonetheless Deane somehow bulldozed the white residents into starting to dig a defence trench. He even brought out a forced labour gang from the town jail to help with the shovels. It was all a fantasy, but it brought Gunanoot back into the limelight, and at this point Premier McBride told the attorney general he wanted the hunt to be re-activated: "Bring in Gunanoot at all costs."

That packhorse man, George Beirnes, now becomes the crucial figure.

"[He] came here about 1908, and he packed for the Yukon Telegraph Line, and he was also a good friend of Gunanoot," Dorothy Allen told us. She knew him when she was a girl, and lives now on the very ranch that Beirnes had settled when he first came to the valley.

Beirnes knew where [Gunanoot] was most of the time. . . . In the
summertime he used to come in and hay for George Beirnes. And
George would bring him groceries and all that. And then in winter-
time when Gunanoot was trapping, George would take his fur and
sell it to the Hudson Bay, and bring groceries for his winter supply.
George Beirnes talked Gunanoot into giving himself up.

Gunanoot trusted Beirnes. Beirnes told him that he had become
such a hero, not only to the Indians, that he could count on a fair trial.
There was enough money from the furs to hire a top lawyer. The
lawyer's name was Stuart Henderson, one of the top criminal lawyers
in the country. When Gunanoot came out of the bush, he walked
between Beirnes and Henderson.

The newspapers of the time used to stack subheads over a story,
two or three or even four, above the column where the story began. The
Victoria Colonist wrote, in its edition of June 25, 1919:

Indian Whom Authorities Had Sought For Years
Gives Himself Up

Is Accused of Killing Two Packers in 1906

Came in under Direction of G. Beirnes and
Stuart Henderson

By the time he came in out of the cold on that June day in 1919 the
Western world had come through and had been transformed by a cataclysm. When Gunanoot and his family went into the bush they were
in hiding all through the war that killed tens of millions and exhausted the treasuries of Europe. The federal government had come up with
the idea of special university subsidies for returning veterans. The airplane had come to British Columbia, and so had the now world-
famous "Mohawk Princess" the renowned Six Nations poet and stage
performer Pauline Johnson.[10] Women had won the right to vote. New
notions of equality and social justice seem to have been born out of the
horrors of war. Not only had that Gitskan nemesis the Grand Trunk
Railroad been completed, but also — in the year that Simon Gunanoot
gave himself up — the Grand Trunk declared bankruptcy.

10. See *The Canadians: Biographies of a Nation*, Volume I, for an account of Pauline Johnson and her
relationship with Chief Joe Capilano.

Some dim beginnings of a sense of the greatness of the native culture, and the injustice of their segregated and oppressed life had begun to form in the minds of a few members of the dominant white population, and not so dimly in the minds of people like George Beirnes and Stuart Henderson. "The Bad Indian," as a 1906 newspaper had called him, was now being lionized. Chief Inspector Parsons of the provincial police came over from Victoria to be photographed with the famous fugitive. The *Colonist*, which had once called him "that murdering Indian," wrote,

> *Many stories are told by his fellow Indians of his prowess, of his ability to fell an ox with a blow of his fist, of his ability as a hunter and trapper and his fidelity to his friends. His escape and successful eluding of capture for so many years has made him a species of hero.*

He was a quixotic figure who had defied authorities, overcome immense adversity, saved his family, and found his freedom in the hills. Now he was exposing himself to the ultimate penalty of death by hanging should the jury find against him. This had to be the act of an innocent and much wronged man. It was a profile that must have had many saying, "I wish I had done that."

When he left for Vancouver by train, for the trial, they all came out to see him off. Peter Muldon, a Gitskan man from Hazelton, was nine years old that year, and remembers that Simon Peter Gunanoot had a rose in his lapel when he got on the train.

The prosecutor was also named Henderson, Alexander Henderson. He was up against a man who had become a myth, and he had little to work with. The luckless Constable Kirby was one of the first to testify, and everybody knew his story and knew that it was nothing more than circumstantial evidence and hearsay. There was no weapon, no witness, nothing but a coincidence in time and the hearsay account of a drunken threat. There was one witness whose appearance made defence counsel Stuart Henderson anxious. That prospector, McPhail, who claimed to have talked with Gunanoot thirteen years earlier just after he disappeared, had given police a signed statement, in which he said:

> *Simon had acted strangely. He came to our camp. . . . [He] said he*

had killed a white man at Hazelton a short time before he came to Bear Lake. He thought his name was Macintosh. The white man had treated him badly, he said, and had said something bad about his wife, too.

Strangely, that statement was not offered as evidence in court, and all that the dapper, goateed little prospector would testify to on the stand was that Gunanoot had said, "I killed a white man."

"Could have been the other white man," the judge said sourly, directing the jury. Gunanoot had not been charged with the other murder.

The only possible case that prosecutor Alexander Henderson might make would have to come from his cross-examination of the accused. The one question that troubled even some of Gunanoot's loyal supporters was, if he were innocent, why did he run away? "Even Moses fled," his lawyer said. "There's two different worlds out there." Here is how the *Colonist* reported the testimony of the accused:

After the fight my face swelled up. I was ashamed. I never fight before. I went into the bush. Not wanting to see anybody until all better. I would have come back in three or four days. But I hear shooting and see them kill all my dogs. And my father comes and tells me they are after me. So I go behind Glen Vowell for a few days, and then when my father got away we crossed the Skeena and started up the trail to Kitsegash.

That seemed reasonable to the jury. The judge took pains to warn them that they might convict only if they were certain of Gunanoot's guilt beyond a reasonable doubt, and of course there was all kinds of reasonable doubt available, even to a white jury, in the case of a fugitive whose story had climbed such legendary heights. They took just thirteen minutes to deliberate, one year for each of those years in the wild. Not guilty!

"As far as this court is concerned," the judge said, "you are entirely innocent." The courtroom dissolved into cheering and the shaking of hands. Gunanoot smiled. Friends and strangers pressed in to shake his hand and wish him well.

Perhaps those thirteen years had taken it out of him, or perhaps they had brought him a more tranquil sense of what life was for. In any case he gave up the store in Kispiox, leaving it in Sarah's hands, and went back to the ranch and did a little trapping and prospecting with George Beirnes and Stuart Henderson, who had become a good friend.

Simon Peter Gunanoot lived fourteen more years, and when he died in 1933 his son David carried him to the gravesite at Bowser Lake where Simon had carried his father years before, when they were still on the run.

"Because that was his father's wish," says cousin Gilbert Johnson. *In the old days, the . . . High Chiefs chose where they wanted to be rested. It was an honour for the other person to deliver that person to where he wanted to rest, and bury him there. That's his favourite ground.*

The Gitskan say that Gunanoot's courage and example inspired and re-inforced their determination to campaign for their rights in the succeeding years. David would later be a principal witness in a major case about tribal boundaries, the Delganote Land Claim. In 1997, the Supreme Court of Canada ruled in favour of the Gitskan claims and found that West Coast aboriginal rights had never been extinguished, despite what their opponents had claimed.

There is, of course, one question that still troubles students of the story: Was Simon Gunanoot *really* innocent of the murder of Macintosh? In the Cassiar country today, you can hear both yes and no.

◆ ◆ ◆

The original documentary was written and directed by Monty Bassett.

PART NINE

KIT COLEMAN
Kit of the Mail

Violet: I cannot see why you should feel it necessary to sacrifice yourself to "comfort" a man for whom you do not care. You say, "He kisses me, and I kiss him, and tell him I love him because he pleads so hard to hear it. But I do not love him." ... You need a cold douche; you have no right to go on like that. The young fellow will have every right to call you a jilt and a flirt. You think you'll marry him to "comfort" him. Some comfort you'd be!

    Kit.

In the Hamilton Cemetery in Hamilton, Ontario, there is a handsome, classical Celtic cross over the grave of a journalist named Kathleen Coleman who died in that city on May 26, 1915. Born in Castleblakeney, Ireland, in 1856, Katherine Ferguson, sometimes Kathleen Willis, Kathleen Blake, and Kathleen Watkins, was known to tens of thousands of newspaper readers simply as Kit. She was a successful pioneer women's page columnist, a widely travelled special events reporter, and the world's first female war correspondent.

If the Fergusons of Castleblakeney were indeed "tenant farmers," as the family history says, they certainly did not fit the famine-driven image of the shoeless starving agricultural indentured labourers who fled the stricken island in those dreadful years between 1848 and 1852. There appear to have been several layers to the tenant farmer class, and the Fergusons, with their comfortable house and seventy-five productive acres of land, were well up towards the top of those layers. They may even have owned a pub, and there is speculation that, indeed, they may have done well out of the dreadful famine, perhaps acquiring some land that in prosperous times they would never have been able to afford. Dr. Carla King, a historian at St. Patrick's College Dublin, says that they were part of a rising Catholic middle class whose economic and even political influence were on the upswing in those years. They had farm hands working for them on the land, and domestic servants in the house. They were able to give young Katherine and her sister Margaret riding lessons, and send them to a finishing school in Belgium.

The young girl was devouring the books in her father's extensive library from a very early age as well as doing her formal studies at Loretto Abbey, where her uncle, Father Thomas Burke, was the boarding school's popular chaplain as well as spiritual advisor to the nuns who ran the school. Katherine adored the independent-minded cleric, who once took his niece (now calling herself Kathleen), disguised as a boy, to walk the streets of Dickensian London with him, and see whether or not the famous novelist had got it right.

An unfortunate aspect of all this prosperity was that family, property, social position, and public status had a lot to do with whom you married, and whom you married was not a matter upon which the bride was always consulted. This is an unfortunate part of the social picture of aristocratic Europe that invaded the lower classes as they moved upwards. It is said of the brilliant French minister and diplomat Talleyrand that when his daughter came to him on the eve of her wedding to a certain duke and complained that she detested the prospective groom and did not want to marry him, her father replied brusquely and formally, "*Mélez-vous de vos affaires!*" If the twenty-year-old Katherine Ferguson returning from her Belgian school with refined manners and a modest fluency in French ever expressed any demurral when she discovered that she was engaged to a middle-aged merchant named Willis, the best she could have expected was a "There there, dear."

The marriage was a disaster for Kathleen, but probably brought her husband the equivalent in today's money of hundreds of thousands of dollars in dowry money. The husband, Thomas Willis, already wealthy, rode to the hounds, slept around profligately and cursed his bride when their first child turned out not to be a male.

The little girl died at the age of two. Kathleen became deeply depressed, and her philandering husband was not even interested in helping her. Not long after, he fell from his horse during a foxhunt and died from his injuries. Because there was no male heir there was no inheritance for Kathleen, either. Her beloved uncle Father Tom had died a year earlier. Somehow the determined young widow managed to establish her rights to part of the dowry, namely, the furniture she had brought into the marriage. Relieved to no longer be the domestic property of the noxious Mr. Willis, she sold everything and left for London, where she quickly found work as a governess. It was through her London employer that she met a Canadian government official, a Miss Richardson, who had been assigned to encourage educated women to emigrate to Canada. Kathleen Ferguson Willis began to save her money.

In 1884 she boarded a ship for Quebec City, symbolically erasing at least part of her eight hideous years of marriage by registering as "A Lady: Aged 19." She was really twenty-eight. From Quebec she took the train to Toronto, quickly found work as a governess, and married a flamboyant travelling salesman named Edward Watkins, who took them off to Winnipeg to try their luck there. He appears not to have been very good at his job, and, like her first husband, was a drinker and a philanderer. Watkins was a remittance man, a younger son whose British parents had sent him out to the colonies to keep him from agitating for part of the succession, and "remitted" a small allowance to keep him from coming home to England. Remittance men were figures of fun in Canada (see Part Ten on Calgary Bob Edwards) and it is clear that after the excitement of the first months together, the marriage fairly soon began to come apart. Kathleen taught French and music to help pay the rent. They had two children, Edward and Patricia, "Taddy and Patty," but before long, Watkin's irrepressible behaviour in other people's bedrooms gave Kathleen a legal opportunity for divorce, for which she may have applied. There is no record of a divorce having been granted, but the family legend is that Watkins was discovered to already have a wife in England, so that Kathleen would have automatic cause for annulment.

In any case, Kathleen is on her own again, has taken the distinguished County Galway surname of Blake, returned to Toronto with her daughter (Taddy stayed with his father), found a cheap apartment, re-established her teaching career, and enrolled Patricia in a boarding school.

Toronto was beginning to feel like a genuine literary city in the late nineteenth century. Magazines sprang up and flourished and died, and others replaced them. Newspapers were prosperous. On a whim Kathleen wrote a couple of stories, signed them "Kit," and to her delight sold both of them to the *Daily Mail*. A new weekly newspaper called *Saturday Night* had just started up in 1887 under editor E.E. Sheppard. It actually went on sale sharp at six p.m. on Saturday night. Kit sold three articles to *Saturday Night*, also signed simply "Kit." Suddenly the *Daily Mail* became interested in her as a regular. Christopher Bunting, the *Mail's* editor, had decided it was time to launch a woman's weekly page. He liked the energetic, confident, handsome, red-headed Irish woman and asked her if she would take charge of the new page.

The column, entitled "Woman's World," was a hit from the start. Author Ted Ferguson, whose book on Kit contains samples of a good deal of her writing, said,

> There were lineups outside the newspaper, to buy the column, every Saturday. . . . I don't think that . . . ever happened in Canadian journalism before or afterwards. People just absolutely loved everything she did.

And Mick Lowe, a Sudbury journalist who has also written a book on Kit, said,

> The modern newspaper columnist that most newspaper readers would be familiar with, whose work would fill one linear column of a newspaper — that's eight hundred words. Standard length. . . . An average "Woman's Kingdom" — I did a count — would run from six to seven thousand words. And it was in three parts. The first part would be an essay that . . . might run, say, two thousand words. The second part was called "Pot-Pourri." And it was kind of a collection, a mish-mash of things. Sometimes reprints, but often just . . . observations [or] news of the day . . . that she would be commenting on. And the third part was correspondence.

She started a lovelorn column, of which the quote at the head of this chapter is a sample. God knows she had had some experience in that department. Biographer Barbara Freeman said,

> *This became an incredibly popular feature. . . . "Oh Kit, I've met this wonderful man. But you know, he seems to have a drinking problem. What do you say, Kit? Should I marry him?" And Kit would write back and say, "No. You can't save a man from drink by marrying him."*

Not exactly a head turner in the era of Dear Abbie and her sexually explicit television progeny. But in a time when discussion of such matters was simply not done in public, this appears to have taken off instantly. There was a striking directness about it:

> *You are jealous of your husband's first love, jealous of his musings, his silence on occasion. [But] every human being . . . has a secret garden . . . each human soul is absolutely alone. . . . Respect the individuality of the man you love. His past does not belong to you. Let him walk in his garden.*

She was even-handed in her support and her criticism, to men and women alike:

> *Harry P: You have made a little tin god of yourself and, mounted on a little tin bicycle, you are careering around, watching the public and thinking it has eyes only for you. Dismount, little god, and be a sensible little human worm, wriggling along like the rest of us.*

At first, because of the gender ambivalence of her nom de plume, there was some uncertainty as to whether "Kit's" columns were the work of a woman or a man. There were not many women journalists working then. Photos of the *Mail* newsroom show an all-male collection of suits and ties. There may have been a slight stigma attached to the idea of a woman working in that environment. When she wrote a column once about riding to hounds she admitted to swearing at her horse when it got cranky. A reader wrote to say, "Well you must be a man, because ladies don't swear." For a few years she was able to maintain some uncertainty as to what sex she was. At one point the *Mail* ran a cartoon featuring four possible Kit characters, each one depicted as both a man and a woman.

The correspondence ranged far beyond the usual pangs of

unrequited love, and Kit dispensed advice on everything from diet to how to react when a man does not give you his seat on the streetcar.

You were a very foolish woman to have had a fit of crying over so small a thing. I have often been left hanging on my strap in the street-car while gentlemen have got up and made room for nice-looking young girls. One has not forgotten the time when such attentions were paid to oneself. They will be paid again, you know, when one's hair is white and one's back bent. . . .You and I and the rest of us ought to be glad of the humble crumbs.

People eventually figured out that she must work at the newspaper, and she began to get visitors there. One angry reader came to the office and attacked her verbally over an article he said was outrageous. Kit grabbed a pair of scissors and went for his beard. The man fled, but later wrote a letter demanding she apologize for trying to cut off his beard. She published a reply that said, "I did not try to take off your beard, I was trying to take off your nose because you were sticking it in someone else's affairs."

She was working sixteen hours a day now, and when Patricia was away at school she kept a pet white rat for company. She had become sufficiently important to the circulation of the *Mail* that she felt she could ask for some special assignments. Perhaps recalling her visit to London with Father Burke some twenty years earlier, she persuaded Bunting to send her back to Britain to walk those streets again and write about the disappearing London that Dickens had recorded. She visited the Whitechapel district where tourists and would-be sleuths still came to see where the notorious Jack the Ripper had committed his crimes. She interviewed a woman who claimed to have overheard one of the assaults, and saw an apartment where there were still bloodstains on the wall. This visit produced four weeks' material for the *Mail*.

In 1893 she covered the Chicago World's Fair, and wrote of a technological marvel that was apparently used outdoors there for the first time: "At night, when the vast buildings are flooded with electric light, that is past description."

In February 1895, as she was about to turn forty-one, the *Daily Mail* merged with another Toronto paper, the *Empire*, to become the

Mail and Empire (still published under that title into the 1930s when it merged with the *Globe* to become the *Globe and Mail*). On assignment for the *Mail and Empire* in Ottawa, having heard gossip that the prime minister was a steady reader, she introduced herself to him in the hallway of the House of Commons and asked him straight out if it were true. Wilfrid Laurier replied courteously that he liked the unpredictability. He seems to have indicated that he would be glad to hear from her, and Kit took advantage of this cordiality to ask Laurier to open a few doors for her at Queen Victoria's Diamond Jubilee later that year, where the PM was going to be knighted. When the *Mail and Empire* assigned her to the Jubilee story, the newly knighted Sir Wilfrid arranged for her to have a front seat for the procession, and even invited her to join him and Lady Laurier for a visit to H. M. the Queen. She wrote about the procession, and the figure of the "benignant" monarch in the carriage, with all the patriotic fervour that people expected of her, but she did not lose her sense of proportion, and sent this back to the *Mail and Empire* as well as the glory pieces:

> *The Royal Family has dreadful taste in furnishing their palaces. The Queen's drawing room at Balmoral is absolutely frightful. . . . Can you imagine anything more hideous than walls and windows hung with tartan?*

While in London she also took time to visit a famous fortune-teller, the White Mahatma, whom Kit hoped to expose as a fraud.

> *A door behind me opened and a limp, faded little creature walked slowly in. . . . She brought me a blank card, told me to write on it my name, age, profession and one question. [I wrote] Name: Jinkins. Age: Sweet twenty-two. Profession: Journalism. Question: Does he love me? Madam took the card (written side face down) and sealed it in an envelope. She sat down and laid the envelope, the fastened side up, before her.*

> *"Your name is Jinkins. I cannot tell your first name, it is not given to my mind to see. I see you surrounded by paper and pen — writing, writing — you do a lot of this work." She looked at me shrewdly. "You are younger than you look . . . about twenty — two, but you look many years older."*

"Would you mind letting me have that envelope," I said gently. She changed colour. "I cannot do that. I would lose my impressions."

"The back of the envelope is transparent. I know it madam. But don't worry. I'll pay your fee."

Kit's reportage on the Jubilee demonstrated to her host of readers that this was a journalist of consequence, but Kit never gave up her touches of playfulness in her column. She still called her readers "the paper people," and their domestic animals, about which she was consulted along with the love affairs and the wayward children, were "the jungle people." All the same, London had given her an appetite for larger stuff, and she kept her eyes open for the next big foreign assignment.

In the meantime, with a little more security and time for some social life, she had begun to "walk out" with a physician named Theobald Coleman, from Seaforth, Ontario. Kit had been scarred by her earlier marriages, but she was a passionate and social creature; devoting hours of writing time every week to matters of the heart was not merely a professional device. Coleman was a quiet, decent, humorous, and successful doctor, but Kit had been forced into one nightmare of a marriage and had allowed infatuation to rocket her into another. This time she was going to make sure.

In April of 1895 revolution broke out in Cuba, which was then a Spanish colony. Quite unlike their behaviour in a subsequent Cuban revolution sixty years later, this time both American business interests and popular opinion backed the rebels. Spanish rule had been harsh in Cuba. That is really where concentration camps were first used. The Spanish called them "strategic hamlets." Thousands of rebels real and suspected died in them. It was to become a very special war for newspapers, partly because printing techniques had been developed that made it easy to rapidly get photographs onto the printed page. The American president, William McKinley, appeared to be vacillating about Cuba, and the media, which meant primarily the newspaper empires of Joseph Pulitzer and William Randolph Hearst, had a field day stirring up outrage against the atrocities of the colonial government of Spain. Hearst sent the famous illustrator Frederick Remington to do provocative paintings of the turmoil. When Remington cabled that all was quiet in Havana, could he come home, please, Hearst told him to stay, and added a phrase that has become famous in the history of journalism: "You furnish the pictures and I'll furnish the war."

Kit had no illusions about Hearst. She had written, years earlier, that he was

neither an honest nor a great journalist. His newspaper methods are Standard Oil methods. Libel suits are settled privately for cash, no public apology is printed. . . . Mr. Hearst maintains that since the magazines use fiction, newspapers have the same right. [He] has bought up the maddest imaginations in the market today.

But those papers were what she had to turn to when she wanted to read about the Cuban rebellion, and she felt she could do better. As the tension built, Kate watched in fascination from Toronto. She became convinced that a real war was going to break out, and that she would go to it. Americans owned some fifty million dollars' worth of Cuban property, in sugar, tobacco, and iron. One politician, Senator Thurston of Nebraska, said openly,

War with Spain would increase the business and earnings of every American railroad . . . every American factory . . . every branch of industry. J.C. Breckenridge, the American Major-General of Volunteers, said, "Our policy should be always to support the weaker against the stronger, until we have obtained the extermination of them both, in order to annex [Cuba]."

It didn't require the journalistic sophistication of a Kathleen Willis Blake Watkins to see that it was just a matter of time, and in 1898 when the USS *Maine*, a battleship on a "friendly visit," was sunk by a mine in Havana Harbour, the war was on.

The invading Amerian forces were ill trained and ill equipped. The Spanish were even worse. Spain sent her fleet, but the US Navy bottled it up in Santiago Bay, at the east end of the island, and virtually destroyed it. Kit got herself assigned. There was no response to her telegrams to Washington for permission to go to the island. She got on the train. In Washington, if the Secretary of War, General Russell Alger, thought he could politely turn her away, he soon found out he could not, and ended up giving her a pass. In Florida the army's command-ers said quite rightly that they, not the secretary of war, were in charge in the field and they had no way to protect a woman in or on the way to Cuba. Kit tried the Navy, out of Key West.

It was a short war, and by the time Kit finally persuaded the Navy to take her across the less than a hundred miles of Gulf Stream that sep-arate Cuba from Florida, hostilities were over. That did not stop Kit from writing affectingly from the hospitals, the battlegrounds, the site of the sunken Spanish fleet.

A ghastly ship with torn sides and battered decks. Half a mile fur-ther on, at Juan Gomalez, the Almirante Oquendo *lay half upon the beach like some dying monster that had tried to crawl out of the sea and died in the attempt. We . . . crept as best we could from beam to beam of the torn deck, and peered into what had been the cabin of the Spanish Admiral, Cervera. We saw a charred and battered little room.*

It was stuff that had not been reported on by a woman before. Kit had the clarity and the skills to wring everything she could out of "the human angle." The international press picked up her reports. She had become a world famous journalist.

The awful cruelty of war, the pitilessness of men when set as foe one against the other — crying out there, dumb things as they are, against man's inhumanity to man, against the breaking of the great covenant of the Brotherhood of Man. And yet necessary, say the gentlemen [who] from Senate houses and Parliaments guide the destinies of nations. Perhaps . . .

In the end, what America wanted out of the Cuban conflict America largely got. Spain was out of the way as a military power in the Caribbean; so the area was secured for the next big US project, the building of the Panama Canal. It was a war that brought America out of a century of isolationism; she had become an international player. When it was over, official America downplayed the role of the Cuban rebels, and trumpeted an American military success. Cuban forces were not even allowed to attend the surrender ceremonies, and Cuban represen-tatives were not invited to the signing of the peace treaty in Paris. Even the American soldiers were not very well dealt with. Kit came back to Florida on a troop ship with the returning wounded. She wrote heart-wrenchingly about the appalling conditions, oppressive heat, insufficient water, food, and medicine, terrible crowding. Back in port in Florida neither the troops nor the correspondents were allowed off the ship for days, until they had completed quarantine for yellow fever. By the time Kit got ashore she was exhausted and sick.

She rested for a few days, and took the train to Washington, where Dr. Coleman met her. He proposed marriage. Kit thought about what she had been through, and about Coleman's patience and kindness in the year or so they had known each other. She accepted. They married then and there.

Her son Edward came to live with them now, and Patricia came home from boarding school. They had help in the house. Kit — now very happily Kit Coleman — could take it easy for a while, perhaps start writing that novel she had been daydreaming about. She went to concerts and began to include comment on the arts in "Woman's World."

An artist, giving a concert, should not demand an entrance fee but should ask the public to pay just before leaving, as much as they would like. From the sum he would be able to judge what the world thinks of him — and we would have fewer mediocre concerts.

And, "Literature would pay better if there were not so many dead men still in the business, hogging the customers."

It was also in 1898 that the great Sarah Bernhardt played Montreal. Kit decided it was time to see something better than what Toronto had to offer.

Why can't we have better plays in Toronto? For the past two seasons we have been no better off than the merest village. Burlesques . . . we have had in plenty, but plays — good plays and good actors — have been as rare as oases in the Sahara. . . . Caesar with a Scotch accent — by the Gods!

Her reputation got her backstage in Montreal and right into the Divine Sarah's dressing room. The two women looked at each other in shock. It was like looking in a mirror, so striking was the resemblance. "My God!" the great actor exclaimed, "We are like sisters!" She invited the journalist to stay as she dressed and made up.

Then she drew dark violet lines about her eyes that elongated and narrowed them, touched her ears with rouge, her lips, her cheeks, slightly, very slightly. And then she bolted the door for a moment, and taking a little phial, poured from it a drop in each eye. It was belladonna. Afterwards I noticed the effect of the blinding fluid. The pupils large, black, were dilated to their fullest effect.

Kit watched the play backstage.

I saw this woman who had been so particular as to her appearance a moment before change in an awful way as . . . the role forced itself upon her. . . . The face grew gaunt, haggard, old. Every line showed. She grew pallid, drawn. It was an old woman who faced the people.

But Kit's next move would take her far away from that world. In 1899 her husband got a well-paid commission with a mining company, and they moved to Copper Cliff, a desolate, sulphur-contaminated bleak landscape that destroyed Kit's images of the romantic north and set her down in a smoke-stained frame house where she had to carry water in from a well and make her own fires. From time to time, when there was an accident at the mine, her husband asked her to come and nurse the wounded. She continued to write the "Woman's Kingdom," and she was happy with her husband, but it was a bleak life. She missed the buzz of the city. She got her correspondence as before, and enjoyed writing her goofy or helpful replies; but it all seemed terribly far away.

On Valentine's Day in 1901 Theobald Coleman diagnosed a case of smallpox in Copper Cliff. Only six years earlier Montreal had been closed down by an epidemic of the disease, the port closed, the railways stopped, the last great smallpox epidemic in a Western industrial city. The Copper Cliff city officials were slow to respond, but Kit wrote a series of articles in which she urged a municipal quarantine, and finally the city built a quarantine centre, which probably prevented the outbreak from turning into a real epidemic. Both she and her husband felt that they had had quite enough of Copper Cliff, and so when the mining company cancelled Dr. Coleman's contract they were both relieved, moved back south, and settled in Hamilton, Ontario. It was a short train ride over to The City, to see her old pals and gossip with the guys at the paper, take in some theatre, get back into the swing of things.

There was one field of journalism that Kate had not yet tried: crime. It was becoming big stuff on the front pages, and she was fascinated. She was handed an opportunity when Cassie Chadwick was arrested in Cleveland for defrauding a number of American banks. It was a matter of millions of dollars, Chadwick was a woman, and she was from Ontario. An obvious assignment for this veteran of the Diamond Jubilee, the World's Fair, and the Spanish-American War. Her editors agreed. Ted Ferguson tells how she made out:

> *Kit went down to Cleveland. And when she went to the prison to try and interview Cassie Chadwick, there were so many other journalists that crammed into the cell that she really couldn't talk to her one-on-one. So she left her gloves behind. And then she went to the front desk and said oh, I left my gloves behind. And the police woman took her back there. And it was just her and Cassie Chadwick in the cell. And she got a world exclusive.*

So now she could add crime reporter to her resumé. The *Mail and Empire* was not displeased. It had a real star on its hands now. She was only a woman, of course, and before long the paper would get a shock when it made the mistake of refusing her a raise in pay. But for now, if she wanted a special assignment, she was likely to get it.

Readers of E.L. Doctorow's novel *Ragtime* may remember a sensational murder story that somehow gets woven into the middle of it. A spoiled young rich kid named Harry K. Thaw had married a showgirl named Evelyn Nesbitt. Nesbitt had been seduced at the age of sixteen by the architect of Madison Square Garden, a notorious roué named Stanford White. White was part of a kind of club of prominent New Yorkers who got together to see how many beautiful young virgins they could debauch.

Milos Forman made a film of it in 1981 — James Cagney's last appearance ever, with Norman Mailer playing Stanford White. Thaw, a man given to violent rages, apparently found out about his young wife's earlier arrangement with Stanford White some time after they were married. He had already taken to beating her with whips, so it wasn't much of a marriage anyway, but when he learned about Stanford White, he began to carry a gun. One night White had been watching showgirls doing a pistol-duelling number, on the stage of the Roof Garden Theatre at Madison Square Garden, when Thaw walked up with a pistol, put it between White's eyes, and fired three times.

The sensational details about the seduction club and the strange marriage that came out after Thaw murdered White made for sensational reading, and once more it seemed obvious to the *Mail and Empire* that Kit Coleman should go to New York.

Kit covered the trial, at which Thaw was declared insane and put into an institution where he spent just over twelve years. His mother paid Evelyn Nesbitt a million dollars to shut up and forget it all, while Thaw gave the press a statement that went:

> *The agony of Evelyn in the years of her girlhood formed the prelude*
> *to a long continuous drama of sorrow, the murk and gloom of which*
> *was never illuminated by a ray of sunshine until what occurred on*
> *the roof of Madison Square Garden and Stanford White fell dead.*
> *After ten years during which a crew of moneyed libertines had made*
> *life almost as unsafe for virgins as did the Minotaur, a revolver made*
> *New York safer for other girls. They are safe.*

This was all very apt grist for the Kit Coleman mill. The *Mail and Empire* presses worked overtime to meet the demand for her reports. She was famous. Her work sold papers. She had become almost an icon among journalists, although the word was not used in that sense in those days. She must have supposed now that whatever she wanted to do next she would get to do.

But that was then, and this is now, and Kit Coleman was a woman. She was never, not once, invited to the *Mail and Empire*'s annual dinners. She could not have covered the proceedings of Parliament even if Sir Wilfrid and her editors had both wanted her to do so, because only members of the Parliamentary Press Gallery could do that, and women were barred from membership in the Press Gallery. The gender equity clause in the Charter of Rights and Freedoms was still seventy years in the future. It is not so long ago that another great Canadian reporter, Judith Jasmin, was kept away from an important number of her contacts when she was CBC correspondent in Washington, and women were not allowed in the Washington Press Club.[11] It is easy for people who did not live through that era to forget that this kind of discrimination still functioned in the years after World War Two, but it most effectively did. Few professional men objected.

Kit started a women's press club. She then asked the *Mail and Empire* for a five-dollar-a-week raise. The newspaper said no. Kit resigned. She was fifty-five years old, at the height of her reputation and her powers. She seems to have taken the end of her relationship with the *Mail and Empire* in her stride. Now she added another first to a long list and became the first syndicated columnist in Canada. For a while she was making more money than she had earned at the *Mail*. That changed when war broke out in the summer of 1914. Kit thought war futile and foolish. She found it hard to be a rabid anti-German. She said to a colleague, "When the years of your life are slipping fast, it makes you wonderfully kind." Her readers were not so kind. When she began to write pieces that suggested perhaps they should feel compassion for women on both sides of the battlefront, editors began to cancel her column. Ted Ferguson said,

> She was very prickly and she was very feisty. And she was a very difficult woman in many ways. But ... I fell in love with her, reading her columns, because she had courage. She had wit. She had intelligence. She also was supposed to have had the most beautiful sherry brown eyes in the whole of the Dominion of Canada.

Everyone who encounters Kit Coleman's work and her person seems to fall under her spell. Biographer Barbara Freeman said,

> There were things that she did that caught the headlines, like going to Cuba. And everybody would say, well that was her great contribution because she did something that a man would do. But I think her greatest contribution was [carrying on] a career for twenty-five years, and by doing that, carving a new niche for women in journalism who were coming after her. Kit, really, I think was depressed [by] the struggle of trying to balance a career and motherhood.

11. See *The Canadians: Biographies of a Nation*, Volume I, for the story of this trailblazing television journalist.

Because there was even less support for that in her time than there would be now. She wasn't a prude . . . she hinted that she knew what sexual passion was, and that was pretty daring [back then] even to hint at that.

Ted Ferguson said,

She was a full-blown flesh and bones human being. But underneath she was a conservative person. She believed that marriage was the most important role that a woman should have. At one point, a Member of Parliament asked her if she'd be interested in running in a federal election. She said, "The idea interests me, but I'm afraid I'm no good at lying and stealing. So I have to say no."

Mick Lowe is a Sudbury journalist who practises the trade just a few miles down the road from where Kit helped her husband with a smallpox epidemic. He is writing a Dickens-like serialized novel about Kit's time in Northern Ontario. He said, at the end of our documentary:

I am not sure that her contribution has been fully made yet. She is someone whose writings should be revisited and studied. I really wish that would happen. Boy! It's all there. She really left it on the page.

To help make his point Mick Lowe sent me the following passage, from a New York visit Kit made during the Copper Cliff period. It is partly about journalism: we'll give her the last word.

Woman's Kingdom, May 11th, 1901
— "A Gossip of Gotham"

Away from this unsavoury neighbourhood and out to the middle of the Brooklyn Bridge only to look down on the big city at night. How far down, how pygmy the houses! How narrow and mean those lanes we call streets. Lights everywhere. Burning brightly on the tops of tall buildings, quivering in electric streams over shop and theatre, glimmering faintly in top storey windows, where perhaps one lay a-dying.

To be Asmodeus for one hour! Why should not the Devil Upon Two Sticks alight upon this parapet and bidding us to take hold of one end of his cloak flit with us to yon pinnacle and unroof to our view the houses of this big city! What things one would see. What crimes are being committed this very moment!

Accidents are occurring in the streets. Children are being born, men and women are dying. There is song and laughter and music, beauty and wealth and power, and set over and against all these — what an ocean of misery, what terrible poverty and hunger and nakedness, what desolation and disappointments and despair of soul! Even now some poor abandoned wretch is lifting his hand against his life. Even now the forger is signing his own death warrant, as his pen steals over the paper.

At this moment in one of those dark corners down below, black murder is being done, and looking backward to whence the tall newspaper buildings stand, one can well fancy their glittering eyes of light piercing those dark and forlorn places and dancing with delight in the thoughts of the stories they will fling into the greedy maw of the public in the morning.

A chill wind blows from the river. Come away.

◆ ◆ ◆

The original documentary was written and produced by F. Whitman Trecartin, and directed by Chuck Stewart and F. Whitman Trecartin.

◆ PART TEN ◆

CALGARY BOB EDWARDS
The Eye Opener

When Bob Edwards died in Calgary in 1922 the outrageous, challenging, humorous journalism he had given to this country almost died with him and was not revived for decades. His pallbearers were police officers in full dress uniform. Beside him in the coffin were a copy of his first newspaper, the *Wetaskiwin Free Lance*, the last issue of his great, nationally read paper, the *Calgary Eye Opener*, and a pocket flask full of good whisky. Calgary historian Max Foran says that when the *Eye Opener* was in business, the whole of Calgary's high society dreaded its every appearance because they could be in it, and if they were in it they would be subjected to some kind of ridicule. Catherine Ford, a columnist now at the *Calgary Herald,* said that Edwards "was a public scold because he could be, he put his money where his mouth was, he put his money where his typewriter was, and he had fun doing it."

"Fun," however, while it is a word that many use in talking about Edwards' work, more accurately describes *their* response to that work than the state of mind of the man they are talking of. He was a serious alcoholic, a lonely bachelor until the last three years of his life, a man who could dish it out — even against himself in his own columns — but was terribly wounded when they dished it out to him. In short, a complex, troubled, brilliant, original and provocative journalist, both tough-minded and vulnerable. He left a legacy of journalistic "attitude" which has never totally vanished. Year after year the legacy of Calgary Bob Edwards is celebrated in that city when his admirers gather to present an annual award in his name.

Robert Charles Edwards was born in Edinburgh on September 24, 1864, orphaned at the age of five, raised by rigidly moralistic aunts in Glasgow, graduated from the university in that city, and roamed around Europe doing odd jobs for a few years. Before he set out for the New World, his first newspaper experience was in France, as the youthful editor of a short-lived English-language tourist magazine, the *Traveller*. He was self-deprecatory about his university experience, saying sardonically that he emerged a "total ignoramus." However, this may indicate nothing more than the early development of a sardonic voice, a gift for a well-turned sarcastic *bon mot* ("A hypocrite is a man who is not himself on Sundays") — and a reflexive contempt for establishment institutions rather than any genuine diffidence about his own intelligence or knowledge.

This dismissive attitude towards convention — *'tude*, it might be called today — appeared early as a kind of editorial currency in his newspaper work. He used it to genuine effect as a device for raising public awareness and discomfiting the comfortable, but it may have been more a rhetorical device than a seriously considered view of either social institutions or powerful people.

He and his brother Jack headed for Idaho in 1892, where they hired on as ranch hands and moved around the American West for a while. Edwards would later say that it was witnessing the lynching of a thief that changed his mind about the Land of Liberty, and started him thinking about Canada. In any case he turned up in Calgary in 1894, virtually broke, and for some reason moved on to Wetaskiwin, a small town south of Edmonton, where he found work as a handyman and part-time bartender in the town's small hotel. Jerry Boyce was the hotelkeeper. Boyce took a liking to Edwards and Edwards took a liking to Boyce's bar. "Some men are hard drinkers," he wrote. "Others find it absurdly easy."

Bob Edwards was one of those others. For the rest of his much too short life (he would die at fifty-eight) booze was a support and a scourge, a subject around which he would build some of his more boisterous humorous writings, and the object of his bitterest scorn and invective. He was seldom able to stay dry for more than a few days, and among his loyal present-day fans there are those who say that self-contempt — linked somehow to the drinking — was an essential part of his makeup.

He would hang around hotel bars a lot for most of his life. When his brother Jack died three years after he arrived in Alberta, he seems to have made a very sudden life decision, left the Wetaskiwin Hotel (at least as an employee), and started a small weekly newspaper, the *Wetaskiwin Free Lance*. In its opening number he declared that its purpose would be "simply and entirely to amuse." But amusement was not, for Bob Edwards, a trivial matter. Alberta historian Hugh Dempsey said that Edwards

> used humour as a tool. He was a social activist. He was . . . for the little man, so to speak, and felt that there were everything from real estate agents to loan sharks to speculators who were constantly causing trouble, causing hardship and grief. So . . . his humour would be used as a very, very sharp sword to whittle that person down to size.

The thirty-three-year-old editor-publisher and sole correspondent aimed his blade at personalities and institutions alike. He included his own mistakes and drinking habits in his catalogue of lampoons, a device often used by satirists so they don't appear morally superior to their subjects. But if his public self-criticism was ever meant to reconcile the subjects to Edwards' ridiculing them, it certainly did not work in Wetaskiwin, where a committee of churchwomen let it be known that the town would be better off without him. He picked up and moved on, not settling anywhere at first, and perhaps — as Hugh Dempsey speculates — influenced more than was good for him by his friend the hotelkeeper.

> I believe he moved first to Leduc and then later moved to Strathcona. And I think . . . he was following Jerry Boyce, the hotelkeeper. He was a very close friend of his, and as Jerry Boyce left one hotel and bought another or built another, [Bob Edwards] followed him.

In 1899 he arrived in High River, southwest of Calgary, and a couple of years later the enterprise that had begun in Wetaskiwin as the *Free Lance*, became the *Eye Opener*. Max Foran speculates that it was during these years that Edwards first began to look on the newspaper as something more than an entertaining way to skewer pompous people.

> I think these stints in these smaller towns honed his journalistic skills. I think they gave him an eye for story and probably forced

him to go deeper into finding good stories and pertinent stories,
instead of relying on outside information.

He did, however, launch the *Eye Opener* off with characteristic
sarcasm, some of it levelled at himself. The paper's reputation — as
it grew and grew until it became a national institution — was at least
as much built upon the lampooning style as it was upon some of the
very solid polemical journalism that he pioneered in the west. This is
how the opening communiqué to the *Eye Opener*'s readers went:

Clothed in righteousness, a bland smile and a lovely jag, the editor of
this publication struck town two weeks ago. The management has
decided on the name Eye Opener *because few people will resist tak-*
ing it. It will be run on a strictly moral basis at $1.00 a year. If an
immoral paper is the local preference we can supply that too, but it
will cost $1.50.

It was here that he began his tirades against the hypocrisy of
churchgoers (he was one himself) who characteristically took the
opportunity of the Sabbath traditions to clothe themselves in righteousness one day a week. Max Foran said,

I don't think he had any trouble with the Sabbath [as such]. It was
the way it was compromised in the name of self-righteousness. You
go to church and you sing songs and you come home and you might
beat your wife or your dog or you might screw someone out of a
house you were trying to sell, and then go to church and sing about
how good you are. Sunday didn't make you a better man. And he
would argue that a lot of these people . . . were much different peo-
ple on Monday than they were on Sunday, and he didn't like it.

Whether it was the hostility towards him of his Methodist targets
in High River, or (more likely) a growing confidence that he had something that would sell in a bigger city, he soon moved on again. In 1904
he moved the *Eye Opener* to Calgary. "These small towns are awful," he
wrote, as he was leaving High River:

Wetaskiwin threw us down. Leduc threw us down. Strathcona,
being dead anyway, shook its shriveled finger at us. High River is
passing us up. Ye gods! That we should have lived in such places!

An Alberta social phenomenon that he had found especially

entertaining in High River, the remittance man, had led to the development of a fictional component in the *Eye Opener*, and there would be times later on when it became very difficult to distinguish Edwards' fictions from his reporting or his jokes from his diatribes. When he wrote that the three biggest liars in Alberta were "Robert Edwards, Gentleman, Honourable A.L. Sifton, Premier, and Bob Edwards, Editor of the *Eye Opener*," the premier did not get the joke, and launched a libel suit that he later withdrew when Edwards himself filed a similar action on behalf of "Robert Edwards, Gentleman, and Bob Edwards, Editor."

The remittance man theme was a far more elaborate gag. Hugh Dempsey described it in detail:

The remittance man was usually a younger son of a fairly well-to-do family in England. Very often the eldest son inherited the estate, the second son went into the ministry and the younger son was kind of left footloose and fancy-free. And it was often the younger son that was in the local bars and taverns and getting the local barmaid knocked up and so on. So, as a result they would send the youngest son off to the colonies and every six months they would send him a remittance, enough money to last him for the next six months so that he wouldn't go home.

So he developed this series of letters that this Buzzard Chumley, who was a remittance man, wrote home to his parents, with all these different schemes of getting more money out of [them]. And some of them were absolutely hilarious. One of them was that he had married this Native girl and that he wanted her to share in the family estate, so he wanted to bring her home to meet the family. But on the other hand, he had a chance to buy a ranch. But if he got this ranch he wouldn't be able to come home . . . and kind of left it at that, hoping that the parents would send him the money. And it was very believable because it paralleled the actual kind of situations that were occurring. Buzzard Chumley became a real favourite of the readers of The Eye Opener.

Calgary had gone through a few slow years, but now it was going into a boom. When Edwards arrived there the population was only five or six thousand and descriptions of the city recall Mordecai Richler's later joke that "Calgary will be a very nice city once they get it out of the crate." Jennifer Bobrovitz, the history librarian at the Calgary public library, said that as Edwards settled in,

> *the economy was rolling along fairly well. There were lots of oppor-*
> *tunities and in many ways it was a frontier town in every respect:*
> *independence was appreciated. Characters were appreciated. And*
> *Bob must have sensed that perhaps he would have an opportunity*
> *to succeed in Calgary. Calgary was very much a conservative town.*
> *It was centered around the Canadian Pacific railway station on 9th*
> *Avenue and generated out a few block radius from there. So the*
> *busiest corner in Calgary in 1904 was the corner where the Alberta*
> *Hotel stood.*

The Alberta hotel building is still at the corner of 8th Avenue SW and 1st Street SW, now overshadowed by the Pan Canadian Office Tower and the needle shape of the Calgary Tower. Bob Edwards got a room there in 1904 for a dollar a week. He made friends with a socially prominent lawyer, Paddy Nolan, who like Edwards was a man who loved a joke and loved a drink. They made a pair of satirically minded raconteurs. Nolan helped Edwards put together the necessaries to start up his newspaper again, and he kept the title he had invented in High River. "It is said the editor has never drawn a sober breath in his life," he wrote when he launched the Calgary version of the *Eye Opener*. "His rag will probably go bust inside six months." They laughed at that and began to buy the paper in gratifying numbers. "Come to Calgary," he wrote, "the Aquarium City. Full of sharks! Boozorium Park!" And that too was taken by the Calgarians as a good joke.

But before long there were people in high places who did not find it funny to open their copy of the *Eye Opener* and find a haranguing banner like this:

> *If Exhibits bore you to death, and you don't give a damn for*
> *horse races, COME TO CALGARY ANYWAY! And have a*
> *look at the Province whose GOVERNMENT GIVES AWAY*
> *ITS FATTEST CONTRACTS to New York City.*

He engaged a brilliant cartoonist named Forrester, and encouraged the artist to depict politicians as apes and hooligans. When Sir Clifford Sifton, the federal minister of the interior, turned up in Calgary, Edwards ran a front-page drawing announcing the visit, showing a man in a white hood and robe looking almost exactly like a member of the Ku Klux Klan. Sifton was a Liberal; Bob Edwards was a Tory. He was a pretty far-left Tory, who campaigned for free public health care, social justice, the rights of women and of all those who were downtrodden. But he was a Tory all the same, and he made the Liberals mad as hell. He would sit at his table in the Alberta Hotel, where it is said that half the deals and most of the money in Alberta were made, and look around him, and gather energy and material for the paper. The Alberta Establishment at some of the other tables would wonder if he was looking at them, and what outrage he would insult them with next.

That hotel was his domain. Much of the copy for the *Eye Opener* was written at his table. It was thought a grand place, with seventy-five rooms and a great dining room. There were far more men than women in Calgary then, and few of those women would be found at the Alberta. It was not easy to find a good meal anywhere else in the city, and the Alberta's dining room was always full. It was a ritual in the morning to stop in at the basement barbershop for a shave before heading off to work, and, if you liked, a start-up drink as well. Bob Edwards was only one of several prominent citizens who had their own regular tables. R.B. Bennett, the future prime minister of Canada, was another. Bennett was a teetotaller, so it was odd in a way that they should become friends, and it did not start out that way.

Bennett was a lawyer for the CPR. Edwards took the side of those who believed the CPR was a diabolical Enemy of the People. Whenever there was a train wreck he would put big photographs on the front page. The railway retaliated by refusing to carry the *Eye Opener* on the trains. Edwards ran a headline to celebrate a whole week without a wreck at the 9th Street crossing. When another train went off the rails, his caption would say, "Another CPR Wreck," as if they happened all the time. He once said to Paddy Nolan that he hoped he was doing something to give the West a social and political individuality.

But to many of his targets he just seemed to be an intolerant bully. Certainly R.B. Bennett must have thought something of the kind when Edwards ran Bennett's photo with the caption, "Another CPR Wreck."

Soon the portly editor with the bushy moustache and eyes that always seemed slightly startled about something became an institution. There were those who adored him and those who hated him, and almost nobody who did not have an opinion about his character. He promoted himself cheerfully, with, among other things, cartoons that showed him as a good-looking, relaxed big guy leaning back in his editor's armchair and thinking up new ways to annoy the pompous. He did not just write about politics and rascals. He did thoughtful pieces on what was then called "The Negro Question," and intelligent pieces about fattening hens and marketing eggs. He championed the Pig Lady, Mother Fullum, a filthy local street person who fed her pigs from garbage collected outside the Alberta Hotel and other restaurants. And then, on the subject of dirt, would write that "the [City] Council should appoint a civic laundryman to handle the dirty linen."

"His job was to irritate people," says Jennifer Bobrovitz, "and he took it very seriously. It was his way of keeping them honest."

In that prosperous, optimistic decade before the Great War there was one political phenomenon that has not changed much since: the Liberals in Ottawa were, then as now, constantly trying to think of ways to gain some ground in traditionally conservative Alberta. They had two mountainous enemies in Calgary: the *Calgary Herald*, which was a Tory paper, and the *Eye Opener*, which was Bob Edwards. So the Liberals funded a new paper, the *Calgary Daily News*, under editor Daniel McGillicuddy. McGillicuddy set out to destroy Bob Edwards.

Edwards went after McGillicuddy through an invented comic character named Peter McGonigle, editor of the *Midnapore Gazette*. He reported that McGonigle, who had been jailed for stealing horses, was given a huge banquet in Edmonton when they let him out. At that banquet a congratulatory telegram was read out, from Lord Strathcona. Strathcona, the former Donald Smith of the Hudson's Bay Company, had helped finance the CPR. He is the bearded figure driving the Last Spike in the famous photograph. Edwards fictitiously reported

Strathcona as saying, in the telegram, how glad he was that Peter McGonigle was back, and that if the CPR stocks had gone down instead of up he, Strathcona, might also have gone to jail.

Lord Strathcona was not amused. According to Jennifer Bobrovitz, he

> was livid and he phoned his good friend in Calgary, Senator James Alexander Lougheed, who was also a lawyer, and said: "I want this guy for breakfast. I want to sue him both in civil and criminal actions." Lougheed said: "You know, ultimately if you take Edwards to court in Calgary, it will turn into a huge farce and you will wish you'd never heard his name." Lougheed finally convinced Strathcona to let it go, but it wasn't without a lot of effort.[12]

Over at the *Daily News*, McGillicuddy had also been less than amused by the adventures of the satirical Peter McGonigle. He decided that he would serve his Liberal masters well if he could undermine Edwards' credibility in the weeks leading up to the next election. So he wrote and published a vicious personal attack on the satirist, which he signed pseudonymously.

> I intend to show that he is a libeler, a character thief, a coward, a liar, a drunkard, a dope fiend and a degenerate, A . . . journalistic bully, . . . a "four-flusher," a "tin horn" and a welcher . . . make-believe journalism . . . the contents of which were smut and slander.
>
> (Signed) "Nemesis"

Hugh Dempsey told us that Edwards "went deep into the bottle" when this piece appeared in the *Daily News*. The *Eye Opener* did not reappear for weeks. To his admirers it was troubling that the tough political critic and satirist could be so wounded by an obviously unfair and slanderous attack. Columnist Catherine Ford says, "It's there, take it, it rolls off your back. So what? You know, there is an old saying: Never pick a fight with someone who buys ink by the barrel."

Editors across the country came to his defence. The *Lethbridge News* said,

> If there were more editors with the independence and fearlessness of

---

12. Sir James Lougheed was Conservative leader in the Senate, and grandfather of Peter Lougheed, the much admired premier of Alberta from 1971 to 1985.

Mr. Edwards . . . and fewer prostituted journalists like the editor of the Calgary Daily News, *the country would be infinitely better off.*

Paddy Nolan took the matter to court, in a libel action against McGillicuddy. The judge found for Edwards, but took the occasion to scold Edwards for the *Eye Opener*'s "debasing and demoralizing content." Edwards came out of the trial thoroughly fed up and decided he'd had enough of Calgary. It was 1909. He tried Toronto for a while. He published the *Eye Opener* in both Port Arthur[13] and later in Winnipeg. By 1911 McGillicuddy and the *Calgary Daily News* were out of business, and when his friends convinced Calgary Bob that he was needed, he realized that Calgary was where he belonged, and back he came.

When Paddy Nolan died two years later, in 1913, it was weeks before Edwards could bring himself to write about the loss of his best friend.

Well might it be said of Paddy that in life he always left them laughing when he said good-bye. In this last good-bye of all, tears take the place of laughter.

In 1914 there were dramatic changes on the horizon. Edwards tried to enlist when World War I broke out, but he was too old, and his chronic drinking was well known. The gathering Prohibition movement would have seemed a likely subject for his scorn and ridicule, but it did not turn out to be so. Hugh Dempsey argues that this might have been foreseen.

When he missed two or three editions of his paper because he was on an extended drunk, he knew he was letting his subscribers and his followers down. At a time like that he would dry out. Actually there were some occasions when his friends came to him when he was in this drunk state, and said, "You know, Bob, you need help." And they would actually take him to his favourite place, the Banff Sanatorium. And he would come out and seemingly stay sober for a while and [soon] drift back to his friends at the bar.

13. Now Thunder Bay.

"No man," he wrote, "can appreciate the best of it until he has got the worst of it a few times. And don't we, the writer, know it!" He was talking about the drinking. "When a man is driven to drink," he added, "he usually has to walk back." As the Woman's Christian Temperance Movement gathered on the Prohibition front, he began to support them. He ran a cartoon of a stout man with surprised eyes and a bushy moustache collapsing helplessly into bed clutching a whisky bottle, and captioned it "Why the *Eye Opener* does not come out more often."

When Paddy Nolan reminded him that the teetotal R.B. Bennett was a Tory who hated the Liberals as much as he did, and that he might be an ally in the fight for Prohibition, Edwards agreed to come to a dinner that Nolan would host, and the boozy editor and abstemious future prime minister of Canada became good friends after all. "That man would annoy a saint at times," Edwards wrote, "but he has a fine intellect and I'm fascinated."

In 1915 the province was preparing for a referendum on Prohibition. Hugh Dempsey speculates that

Bob Edwards initially felt that this was the answer, maybe not for him. I think he'd liked to have thought it was for him, but certainly for the people of the West. And he saw the bars as being very, very destructive to the western Canadian family and western Canadian society.

Jennifer Bobrovitz, convinced like many of Edwards' fans that his support of the Prohibition movement was part of his personal struggle, said that his old friends the hotelkeepers decided they could bring him around to a more practical posture.

Foolishly, they went to Bob Edwards and offered him, I think it was, $15,000 — some ridiculous amount of money — to stop supporting Prohibition and to come out on their side. And that was their mistake, because Edwards was not the person to be . . . you couldn't buy him; and so the fact that you wanted to, offended him so deeply.

Jennifer Bobrovitz added poignantly, "In many ways, the very poignant narratives that he wrote about [alcohol] were about himself." Edwards wrote, "There is death in the cup, and if this Act [banning the sale of drink] is likely to have the effect of dashing the cup from the drunkard's hand, for God's sake let us vote for it." The Act passed. As in other parts of North America the immediate result was an increase in the criminal purveying of drink and no discernible positive effect. Edwards was dismayed. Perhaps it is a measure of the depth of his own alcoholic anguish that he had expected so much from a simple draconian solution to a profoundly complex social and behavioural problem. But now his journalistic and realistic side came to the fore, and he began to depict bootleggers as monsters, and to rethink the whole Prohibition issue. But he was still publicly scolding drink and drinkers. He wrote, as Calgary was preparing to send a battalion to France, that there should be a battalion of bartenders:

The bartenders have shown such success in killing off men at home, they ought to be able to kill off at least an equal number of the enemy abroad.

But the evidence against Prohibition was too strong to ignore and in the end he came totally around to the other side, and campaigned for its repeal. He also campaigned for votes for women. "Here's to women," he wrote,

once our superiors, now our equals. It is our firm conviction that blending of women's ideas with those of reasonably thoughtful men will someday bring about an era of common sense.

At fifty-four he was a bachelor, and most supposed him to be sexually neutral, or at least indifferent. About marriage he had written,

The saddest and funniest thing on earth is to hear two people promising at the altar with perfectly straight faces . . . to feel, think and believe for the rest of their lives exactly as they do at that minute.

So when a notice appeared one day in the *Eye Opener*, saying that "a certain newspaperman in Calgary got married the other day. . . . When a man is in love for the first time, he thinks he invented it," even his close friends were astounded. His bride, Kate Penman, was twenty years old. He published another cartoon of himself leaning back in the famous armchair, puffing cigar smoke at the ceiling, and thinking up the next surprise, with a caption that read, "Ho Hum! I wonder how they'll like the second reel."

The second reel turned out to be another surprise. Having sensed the excitement of campaigning for social reform, he finally gave in to the persuasion of some Conservative Party friends, including R.B. Bennett, and ran for a seat in the provincial legislature. In the end he decided that he would run not as a party man, but as an independent. "I'll go in clean and I'll come out clean," he said. His campaign consisted of a single one-minute speech. He hadn't really needed even that. He was ahead in the polls from the moment he announced, and he won handily. To nobody's surprise, while he served diligently and advanced some of the social justice issues that were dear to him, the disciplines of party politics he found burdensome, and at the end of only one session of conscientious attendance in the legislature, he stepped down.

There was still no shortage of issues to be addressed. His scope had become more national. He advocated old age pensions, minimum wage laws, public hospitals, schoolbooks with Canadian stories, and the abolition of the Senate. He applauded the earnest courage and humility of social activists like Nellie McClung. By now the *Eye Opener* was being read from Halifax to Vancouver, but there would be only a few more issues. Just about a year after he resigned from the legislature, a lifetime of neglecting his health caught up with him. A nasty flu laid him low, and his heart could not take the stress. On November 14, 1922, the wire services flashed the word across Canada: "Bob Edwards is dead."

But his spirit is not. For example, until about thirty-five years ago, parliamentary reporting in the nation's capital tended to be deferential, most correspondents allying themselves to one or the other of the major parties, and very few seriously challenging the statements of Important People like Ministers of the Crown — at least not in person. My colleague Douglas Leiterman, a Press Gallery reporter for Southam Press before he came to CBC Television, used to laugh about the times when he would challenge a minister during a press conference, saying something like, "But Mr. Minister that's a contradiction of what you said two weeks ago," whereupon his Press Gallery colleagues would frown and nudge him and suggest that he should cool it or they might lose access. This seems absurd now, given the aggressiveness of the "scrum" in the halls of Parliament. But that aggressiveness represents a relatively recent change of style in parliamentary journalism, one that Bob Edwards would have admired.

About fifty years after his death, a group of Calgarians decided to revive the memory of his puncturing the pompous, and created a foundation that presents a Bob Edwards award for journalism at an annual Bob Edwards luncheon. Here the premier of the day can expect to be skewered ("Neither Mr. Klein nor Mr. Woloshyn could be here today. They didn't want to lose their place in line for their MRIs," said the actor playing Bob Edwards at a recent Edwards lunch). The Bob Edwards award is for uncompromising journalism or commentary, and a succession of well-known reporters and commentators have been so honoured. The recipients treasure the accolade sufficiently that many of them reconvened in Calgary, from all over the country, when the twenty-fifth anniversary lunch was celebrated two years ago.

It is appropriate to give the last word to Edwards himself:

Lord, let me keep a straight face in the presence of solemn asses. Keep me sane but not too sane. Let me condemn no man because of his grammar and no woman on account of her morals, neither being responsible for either. Let me be healthy while I live, but not live too long. Which is about all for today, Lord. Amen.

The recipients of the Eye Opener Award, since its inception in 1977, have been the following:

Grant MacEwan 1977
W.O. Mitchell 1978
James Gray 1979
Jack Peach 1980
James MacGregor 1981
Hugh Dempsey 1982
Pierre Berton 1983
Andy Russell 1984
Margaret Atwood 1985
René Lévesque 1986

David Suzuki 1987
Patrick Watson 1988
Peter C. Newman 1989
Allan Fotheringham 1990
June Callwood 1991
Jack Webster 1992
Knowlton Nash 1993
Mordecai Richler 1994
Lise Bissonnette 1995
John Ralston Saul 1996
Peter Gzowski 1997
Carol Shields 1998
Guy Vanderhaeghe 2000
Timothy Findley 2001

◆ ◆ ◆

The original documentary was written and directed by Brian Dooley.

PART ELEVEN

BILLY HUNT
The Great Farini

A drive down the main street of Port Hope, Ontario, leaves the visitor in little doubt as to what part of Canada this is. The solid brick public buildings, the side streets with a mix of frame and brick houses, spreading trees, a touch of the old United Empire Loyalist architecture here and there, and you sense: Southern Ontario. No question. You would have to dig a little deeper to find the extraordinary number of distinguished and creative people associated with what looks on the surface to be a good solid commercial and slightly touristy town — a small city technically — with its yacht and tennis clubs, a retirement town for a fair number of Toronto folk (it's just over an hour east of Metro), busy but not driven, easy-going, you would guess. The author Farley Mowat has made his home close by for forty years or so. The pioneer television director R.J. (Paddy) Sampson retired here. David Lloyd Blackwood, the Newfoundland-born artist, has been teaching art here at Trinity College School for almost forty years. Canada's first native-born governor general, Vincent Massey, was born in Port Hope in 1887, and Joseph Scriven, who wrote the words to the world's best-known and most sung Christian hymn, "What a Friend We Have in Jesus," preached in its streets and died by drowning in a local stream.

It was a town that seemed secure, stable, conservative, to its nineteenth-century immigrants, which is what Thomas Hunt was looking for when he arrived from England in the early 1830s to take up farming and start a family. In Port Hope he met Hannah Soper. They married in 1835 in St. Mark's Anglican Church, and three years later, on their farm not far from town, she gave birth to William, an infant whose energy was astounding from the moment he opened his lungs for that first breath and first ear-splitting yell.

Playwright and theatrical producer Shane Peacock, author of a biography of William Hunt, concluded that the boy made life difficult for his rather stern and inflexible father, because from his earliest days he demonstrated a reckless adventurousness that seemed alien to the father, as if this were a child out of a different nest.[14] Young Billy was not only a daring and successful athlete from his first days in school, but also a brilliant student. When a circus came to town, parading down the then dusty and unpaved main street with eight Indian elephants leading the way, young Billy Hunt had been told in no uncertain terms that he would not be attending the event under the Big Top. We have to suppose that there was a blind spot somewhere in Thomas Hunt's understanding of his wilful son — or that he knew very well there was no way of keeping Billy out of the circus, but that he had to attach at least a modicum of guilt to this unseemly entertainment.

It was 1852. Bill Hunt had just turned fourteen. The travelling troupe was Pentland's Equestrian Circus. It was a classical three-ring, big tent affair with wild animals, clowns and acrobats; William Hunt, years later, would claim that before the day was over he knew what he wanted to do with his life.

He went home and set up a short tight wire near the barn, just a few inches off the ground to begin with. He discovered to his delight that walking on it, without even a balancing pole to steady him, was surprisingly easy. He made a little trapeze as well, and practised on it until he felt he had it under control. But it was the image of a slim young man in tights, seemingly hundreds of feet up in the air above the crowd, that he could not get out of his mind, and he simply had to find a way to put up a high wire.

When Thomas Hunt drove his buggy into the yard and saw Bill walking on a wire fixed to the roof of the barn, a line so thin it almost looked as though the boy were suspended in mid-air, the dour farmer was outraged. This was no way for an intelligent young man to behave; it was sheer folly. There were words. But young Bill had a way with words too. Before long Thomas Hunt found himself agreeing to a compromise. The boy would be allowed to continue fooling around with this high-wire nonsense if he would also commit to completing

14. For Shane Peacock's prolific work on Farini and other southern Ontario figures, check the various web sites that turn up by entering the name Farini in any good search engine.

school and then apprentice to the local doctor and work towards becoming a professional physician. A deal was struck. The father may have supposed that ambition and good sense would prevail in time. This seems to be further evidence that he did not understand his son as well as he thought he did, but he was doing his duty as he understood, trying to give the boy a respectable way to make a living.

In the summer of 1859 Bill Hunt was twenty-one. He had kept the high wire rigged up on the barn, and practised on it diligently, but he had kept his word about the medical career too — so far — and would soon write his first formal medical examinations. Thomas Hunt felt that things were sufficiently settled for him to turn his attention to other matters, and left for England on a business trip. He was scarcely out of sight when the young man was approached by a committee from Port Hope who were busy organizing the coming agricultural fair. They had heard about the aerial adventures, and thought that something like that might add a bit of thrill to the usual strawberry jam contests and cattle judging. So out they went to the Hunt farm to see what he could do. They found more than they had expected. The rope angling up from the ground became almost invisible at the point where it stretched along the peak of the barn roof, so that it was like a man walking in the sky. Author Shane Peacock said:

> I don't think they were quite prepared for what they saw the day that they went out to the Hunt barn in Hope Township and watched him, because he got on his little rope and went up from the ground to the top of the barn, carried a friend of his on his back, stood on his head and they were just astounded at what they saw.

They proposed that he walk across the Ganaraska River in the centre of Port Hope. He had read about an Italian daredevil named Signor Farini, and decided to adopt that name for the stunt. He put up his rope at night from one four-storey building to another seventy feet above the Ganaraska River. A fall would be crippling, even fatal. *The Tri-Weekly Guide* announced the event in the October 1 edition.

> This afternoon at 4 o'clock, Signor Farini will make a grand ascension, as the phrase runs, on a tightrope, stretched across the creek

from the brick buildings on either side of the stream, north of Walton Street Bridge.

To give the documentary viewer a concrete example of what this meant, the producers went with a contemporary high-wire man, Jay Cochrane, and videotaped his successful attempt to duplicate that long-ago performance of "Signor Farini." Cochrane says that his own career as an aerialist began in much the same way as his predecessor's.

When I was about seven or eight years old, my mother took me to my first circus and I saw a man by the name of Helldosana. It was in Sudbury, Ontario. He did a somersault on a wire about twenty-five feet high, a backward somersault, and I said to my mother, I said, "Mother, that's what I'm gonna do when I grow up." And she said, "Oh no, you're not." I said, "Yes, I am, that's what I'm gonna do." I think it's a God-given talent, I do, but it also takes hard work. If you have the love for it, that is part of the talent and it'll follow, you know you just follow your dream. It's what I've always wanted to do and I'm living out a little boy's dream.

Our television director mounted a tiny pencil-camera on Cochrane's chest, so that we could see what the Great Farini would have seen, looking down as he made the crossing reported next day in the *Tri-Weekly Guide*:

Pursuant to announcement, Signor Farini, on Saturday afternoon, walked on a tight rope stretched across the creek. The ascension was advertised to take place at 4 o'clock but so great was public curiosity, that as early as 3 o'clock, a crowd began to collect on the Walton Street Bridge and in every place from which a view of the rope could be obtained. At five minutes to 4 o'clock, Signor Farini made his appearance at the western end of his rope. He was attired in silk tights and the other usual clothing of acrobats. Grasping his balancing pole firmly in his hands, he stepped confidently out upon the rope and commenced his journey. He walked slowly, but steadily, reaching the building on the east side in safety and amid the cheers of the assembled crowds.

The members of the agricultural fair committee were more than satisfied. Farini had stood on his head, hung by his heels, and walked the high wire with and without his balancing pole. It was the largest crowd in the town's history. While most of the crowd believed they had been visited by a famous Italian daredevil, the aerialist's real identity was somehow conveyed to his father in England, and when Thomas stepped off the train at the Port Hope station a few weeks later, the son met him, hoping that the spectacular success of his adventure might win him paternal approval at last. It did not. Farini wrote about it later:

> *My father said, "I am grieved by what you had done. The news was a great shock to me and now, instead of being penitent for the shameful manner in which you have repaid my kindness and care, you delight in having disgraced your family by becoming a low common mountebank!" Scalding tears of anger started from my eyes as I went forth into the open air. I would not darken my father's doors again. Mountebank though I was, the world lay before me.*[15]

The young man must have had superb self-confidence. A few months later, learning that the famed French acrobat Blondin was going to string a wire across the gorge at Niagara Falls, Bill Hunt, now and for the rest of his life Farini, decided to turn it into a contest. He arrived at the Falls in July, 1860. Blondin promoted himself by saying that nobody else in the world could ever perform such a stupendous feat as walking a wire across the Niagara Gorge. Farini was offended by the hyperbole. He knew, as all tightrope walkers do, that the actual physical skill is something that most healthy young people can master. If you string a line thirty centimetres off the ground you can very soon learn to walk along it quite smoothly, even without a pole. A century and a quarter later, when she discovered who her famous forebear was, Farini's great-great-great-grandniece, Rashmi Baird of Port Hope, got *her* father to set up a line for her, in the garage. She speaks of the sport as if it were, well, something pretty well *anyone* could do.

> *The first time I realized I, I had maybe a chance or that maybe it was in the blood or something, was when I was probably about nine. So, that's when the research started for me and I became interested. I was — wanted to do what he did. I love it and that's one of those*

---

15. Today he might have said "snake oil salesman." *The Shorter Oxford English Dictionary*, 1933, gives, for *mountebank*: "An itinerant quack who appealed to his audience by means of stories, tricks, juggling and the like, often with the assistance of a professional clown."

things that surges up the middle and I'm sure I'm supposed to be doing it. It feels natural.

That 1860 Niagara Falls affair was a return engagement for Blondin, whose crossing point was actually about a mile downstream where the gorge was 800 feet wide. Farini believed he could do much better, and chose one of the widest parts of the gorge, just below the Falls, a stretch of about 1,800 feet. Nobody would ever walk a longer rope across that gorge. Author Shane Peacock says that the French acrobat was taken by surprise:

[He] was absolutely stunned to see that this guy, this twenty-two-year-old guy who had been practising on a high rope for ten months and really was only like a semi-pro, was actually going to take him on.

The Niagara Falls historian Bruce Aikin took us to where Farini's rope was positioned, not far from the site of Clifton House, and pointed to a clearing on the American side where he believes the other end, the starting point, was secured. The two rivals had agreed to do their walks on the same day, supposing that the double event would draw bigger crowds. And so the self-taught kid from Port Hope and the world's most storied acrobat of the age squared off against each other, on August 15. At ten minutes to four in the afternoon Farini got into a horse-drawn carriage at the American Hotel in Niagara Falls, New York, and was taken to the wooden platform next to his long, drooping, 1,800-foot cable. Shane Peacock describes the next phase:

So he started out holding this enormous balancing pole and he went down, of course he starts descending immediately as he went down on his rope, probably a little bit frightened although he claimed that he wasn't. Now then he went out a little bit further and I think he knew he had to do something spectacular at this point to really show them that he was capable, so when he got out about 100 feet . . . he put his head down to the rope and stood on his head.

But that was just to get the motor running — and perhaps send some runners over to the Blondin site to lure audiences back to this spectacular newcomer. He next hung by his hands, then by one hand, then by his feet, and of course by one foot. He had carried a separate coil of rope around his waist, and as he began to work his way back towards the American side, when he came directly above the tourist steamer *The Maid of The Mist*, he tied the second rope onto the main line, lowered it to the boat, climbed down that line to the deck, drank a ceremonial glass of wine, and then started back up. The return climb was almost too much. He was trembling with fatigue — or at least that is what everyone saw — when he finally pulled himself, agonizingly slowly, onto the main line.

When he stepped ashore, the applause was deafening, from both sides of the river. In the meantime, a couple of miles downstream, Blondin made a flawless crossing on his taut 800-foot cable. Critics said that Farini was more terrifying to watch on his unstable slack wire, but reported that the French aerialist was more elegant. The audiences, however, voted with their feet and their pocketbooks. Farini's crowds were substantially bigger than Blondin's and he made more money when the hat was passed. It was the greatest slack-wire performance on record, said the *Niagara Falls Gazette*: "But we never wish to see another such performance by any rope walker. For however the performer may consider himself, there is no pleasure to the beholder." Farini was delighted; now the crowds would have to come. Blondin must have been outraged at the upstart's success.

For the rest of the season they had a high-wire duel. Blondin on his taut 800-foot cable; Farini on his 1,800-foot slack rope. When Blondin carried a stove on his back and cooked eggs, Farini carried out a washing machine and did his laundry. When Blondin took a man on his back, Farini carried a taller and a heavier man. Farini began pushing the duel into truly dangerous territory. Blondin made a crossing with a sack over his head. Farini cut armholes in a full-length glazed cambric bag and started down the initial sloping part of his slack wire, slipped, almost went into the gorge, recovered, made it to the centre, and did a headstand with the sack blowing in the wind. A reporter wrote, "He looked like a small sail spread to the breeze."

In September, the Prince of Wales visited the Falls, saw a Blondin performance, and was quoted as saying, "Thank God, it's over," when it ended. He did not see Farini. As they drove by the Canadian end of the slack wire, it is said that he asked the head of his party, the Duke of Newcastle, what that was, *that* the duke replied, "A pathway for another fool." Farini supporters said that was pretty unfair to Farini — he was, after all, a Canadian and the prince should have taken the time to see him too. But fools or not, Prince of Wales or no Prince of Wales, while Blondin had again proved himself a legendary performer, Farini had consistently drawn larger crowds and made more money.

He went back to Port Hope for a visit. He offended his father once again by going around in the clothes of a dandy — the "mountebank." He met a young woman and fell in love. Her name was Mary Osborne. She is cryptically referred to as "an unconventional woman," and that could simply refer to her decision to run off with the mountebank, and marry him, or could also reflect the fact that before long she was part of the mountebank's act. The following summer they both turn up in Niagara Falls, Farini announcing that he will carry his bride across the Falls and back. It never happened. Niagara Falls was having a dreadful season; a depression was keeping tourists away; *The Maid of the Mist* was not operating. Clearly there was no money to be made there that season. Why they chose their next destination is not known, but they headed for Cuba.

Havana then had a bullring that seated 30,000, an ideal venue for the wire-walker. They stretched the rope between masts, over the heads of the crowd and all the way across the stadium. Biographer Shane Peacock described what happened next:

> *Mary was on his back. They started to cross, they performed all their routines and when he got to the end, for some reason, Mary Osborne acknowledged the applause of the audience and turned and waved to them. And that is a cardinal sin for somebody being carried on a high-wire walker's back. And at that instant, she slipped and fell from his back. And as she started to fall, he allowed himself to go with her and he hooked one of his legs around the wire, reached down and grabbed the hem of her dress, caught her and was actually at that point, saving her. But slowly the dress ripped out of his hands and she fell down to the seats and he watched her spiral all the way down and crashed, headfirst, into the seats.*

Five days later she died. Farini had her buried in a prominent Catholic cemetery. Her funeral was a major social event. In his grief Farini converted to the Catholic faith, had himself baptized as Guillermo, the Spanish equivalent of his given name. The Cuban who stood in for him as godfather was a man named Antonio; Farini added that name to his new christening.

A rumour began to be whispered about: that he and Mary had had a little son. For a while Farini disappeared from sight, but in the early summer of 1864, he surfaced in New York City and played one of P.T. Barnum's theatres, the Hypotriathon. He added a trapeze number to the act, and some strongman feats. He called himself — his own coinage, perhaps to fit the Greek theme of Barnum's theatre — a "Pangymnastikon Aerostationist." Later that summer he was back at Niagara Falls, trying to walk across the shallow brim of the American Falls, just above the cataract, on stilts. On August 8 he climbed up on the stilts, stepped into the rapids, and started out. Less than halfway across, one of the stilts got stuck in an underwater crevice. Farini could not free it. Whether he fell into the water or jumped for it is not clear, but the crowd watched as he was swept towards the brink, reached out for the trailing branch of a tree on one of the tiny outcrop islands, and pulled himself up onto the rocks.

He was marooned on that island long enough for the *New York Times* to print a story about it, and crowds came to see what they thought would be a man starving to death. There seemed no way to get him ashore, until someone thought to float a rope to him somehow, and he was pulled safely on land.

He next turns up in London performing with El Niño, whom he claimed was a street kid he had found in Boston. The act is now called the Flying Farinis. There was speculation that the child might be the natural son of Farini and the late Mary Osborne. Farini formally adopted the boy, gave him his name and a prominent role in his life from then on. El Niño was beautiful, with silky blond curls. On stage, he seemed as daring as his adopted father. He flew forty feet through the air from trapeze to trapeze. His photograph sold by the thousands, and a reporter for the *Daily Telegraph* was captivated.

A boy scarcely eight years old went a height which it would be painful to contemplate, takes some astounding flights, and plays a remarkable solo on the drum while swinging through the air with his head bent back over the bar of a trapeze. The gracefulness of the child does much to lessen the feeling of peril attached to the performance. But there is a general sense of relief in witnessing his descent in safety.

In August, the Flying Farinis were booked into the Royal Alhambra Palace, and their success was sensational. A popular composer, Robert Coote, put out a new waltz entitled "The Farini." The act toured England and Ireland for the next few years. When they came to the legendary Crystal Palace in 1867, they played to 22,000 people at a time.

Early in 1870, about to turn thirty-two and financially very successful, Farini went into seclusion for a few weeks, to consider whether he should, at that ripe old age, continue with these on-the-edge stunts. He took El Niño with him to Marseilles, grew a theatrically cultured black beard, stayed out of sight, and planned the next incarnation. It was not long in coming.

Lu Lu, "The Eighth Wonder of the World," first appeared on stage on July 29, 1870, at the 4,000-seat Imperatrice Theatre on the Champs Elysées. When Farini's newest partner, this blond, blue-eyed, allegedly sixteen-year-old beauty, came forward and suddenly leapt twenty-five feet into the air, there was a moment of stunned silence before the house came to its feet applauding. *How had she done it!* She settled lightly onto the carpeted seat of a trapeze. *L'Avenir National* wrote that she was like *un vase de crystal*, that her graceful, inexplicable faërie ascent was something from a dream. Lu Lu had her London debut a few months later at the Royal Holborn Amphitheatre. This time the Prince of Wales did come. The act toured England for a while, then crossed back to North America and played New York, Chicago, Philadelphia — everywhere to the same astonishment and delight as this graceful girl rose so mysteriously into the air. Did she leap? Did she fly? There were no wires, that was clear. And she was so beautiful. Men lined up at the stage door with flowers, but after the performances Lu Lu seemed to disappear.

When they came back to England in 1872, Farini married, in Portsmouth, a grocer's daughter named Alice Carpenter (with whom he would have two sons, William Jr. and Harry). The best man at the wedding was the performer the world had come to know as Lu Lu, who was in fact the same person earlier known to audiences as El Niño. This, however, was a family affair, and the world did not learn the truth about Lu Lu until she was nearly killed in Ireland, in 1876, and had to be examined by doctors at the Trinity College Hospital. That day in Dublin Lu Lu missed the trapeze bar at the zenith of that amazing leap, and crashed to the floor. There was pandemonium in the theatre, and then something of a scandal in the press after the doctor's discovery was reported.

But Lu Lu recovered, and, impudently playing the new gender ambiguity theme, they kept the act going for a few years more. In the 1880s Niño/Lu Lu played a New York date wearing glasses, a moustache, and a fetching female costume. He would later marry and raise a daughter.

The Royal Westminster Aquarium, a huge entertainment palace in the centre of London, had begun as an institution to educate the masses, but ran into financial difficulties. The managers asked Farini to see what could be done to keep it going, and it was here that he tried out his next innovation: the human cannonball. This time his projectile would be a real girl, Rosa Matilda Ricktor. They called her Zazel, and, like Lu Lu before her, she became a reliable audience draw, bursting out of the cloud of smoke as the cannon went off, and soaring across the stadium floor to land safely in a net amid roars from the delighted crowds. Today the act still fools some spectators into thinking that the acrobat has been fired into the air by an explosive charge.

In reality what Farini had invented was an elaboration of the technique that had propelled the Eighth Wonder of the World up to her carpeted trapeze: a powerful spring-activated catapult. In Lu Lu's case, as she walked to her take-off point in the ring she was masked from the knees down by a low curtain wall or skirt that concealed the tiny sprung platform. When Farini released a concealed catch a burst of smoke and a roll of the drums and crashing of cymbals effectively masked the spring's discharge, and what the audience *saw* — and completely believed, was the graceful young acrobat lightly bending her knees, as if for a normal balletic leap of two or three feet, only to keep on her skyward track all the way up to that trapeze. This time it would be a much longer travel — several feet along the inside of the barrel of what looked like a huge cannon — building up enough speed to send the daring Zazel along a parabolic path of more than a hundred feet, wreathed in smoke as a spectacular smoke charge of no propulsive value whatsoever was released just before she emerged from the muzzle of the "cannon."

They began to call Farini the "Father of the Big Thrill Acts." His working drawings for that cannon have survived in the patent office. Zazel became as big a star as Lu Lu; she was even the subject of a comic opera. Soon it was rumoured that the black-bearded Farini had a whole stable of Zazels — in case one lost her nerve or got killed.

Not everyone was delighted by the mysterious signor. In March 1880, a British MP named Edward Jenkins proposed to Parliament the *Dangerous Performances Act*, intended to stop the growing and scandalous evil of Farini's thrilling shows. The Act was never passed, but England began to seem less hospitable. Farini went through a messy divorce from Alice. It seemed a good time to leave. He gathered up his best acts, went to America and joined P.T. Barnum in "The Greatest Show on Earth."

The Greatest Show on Earth was arguably pretty well what it said it was, and Zazel was its star. She packed them in for a long run in New York and then played to as many as ten thousand a night in the big travelling tent.

And then it was time for that restless imagination to try something else. The next stunt seems to suddenly transform him from a showman into a charlatan. He found a young dwarf almost as hirsute as an ape, and billed her as Darwin's Missing Link. He had become a freak-show man. When the Zulu wars became front-page news, he staged Zulu war dances. He seemed to have sunk to the level that his father had feared, but at the same time he became genuinely fascinated with Africa, and it was that continent that generated the last (and some say still unsolved) mystery of Farini's career: the Lost City.

In 1885 Lu Lu/El Niño, was the proprietor of Farini Photographs in Bridgeport, Connecticut, when his father showed up and proposed a trip to the Kalahari Desert. They were there for six months, and Farini produced a book about it, *Through the Kalahari Desert*. In that book he claimed he had found the ruins of an ancient civilization. There are stories about people going out into the desert and falling asleep and waking up and seeing Farini's lost city and falling asleep again, never to see it again. The lost city is probably as fraudulent as Farini's missing link, but an American named Lee Haldeman has tried nineteen times to find it. He told our camera that the lost city is still lost, but that

> you are always in a situation that you believe it's just over the next sand dune. The area is vast, you're looking at hundreds of thousands of square kilometres that have to be searched and you're trying to translate ox-wagon miles into today's terms, and you're using these vague descriptions of, say, "for three days they travelled west." Now that might be northwest or southwest — and you sort of have to guess in which direction the lost city might be.

The Kalahari's secrets are (some would say "Alas!") open to the penetrating eye of the satellites today; if there were a walled city there it would have been mapped by now. There is a famous ancient walled city, Great Zimbabwe, a couple of hundred miles north of the Kalahari, which Farini may have heard about and allowed his fancy to play with. But Lee Haldeman is not satisfied with any of the reasonable explanations: He says:

> Now, if you are the type of showman that Farini appears to have been, you would have made it much more spectacular, maybe pyramids or underground caverns and gold and diamonds and things like that — rather than just a rock wall, which also lends credence to Farini's explanation of the lost city.

Invention or discovery, Farini returned to England, published his book, and went on to other things. He married again, a German woman of aristocratic bearing, Anna Muller. Fifteen years his junior, and said to be a relative of Wagner and a student of Franz Liszt, she was also alleged to have been raised in the court of the kaiser. Farini began to settle down and to focus on business, investing in railways and other stocks. He bought a genteel house south of London, and became co-owner of one of the world's most successful theatrical agencies, Richard Warners.

The Big Thrill Acts were still a field in which he was as clever and experienced as the best. In 1888 he brought an American aeronaut named Thomas Baldwin to the Alexander Palace, north of London, to jump out of a hot air balloon at 3,000 feet. Baldwin descended to earth wearing a device that, while it had been successfully used in Paris a century earlier, was still little known: the parachute. Baldwin seems to have been the first to use silk for the canopy, and had been demonstrating it in the United States before Farini brought him to London. He made fifteen exhibition jumps that season, and the stunt drew hundreds of thousands of spectators. It is possible that Farini tried to take some credit for the parachute's design, and conceivable that he had in fact made a contribution; he had been inventing things since childhood. In 1890, the profession he gave to the census takers was "inventor." He has been given credit for creating the circus safety net. He actually patented not only the human cannonball, but also the Lu Lu Leap. He invented folding theatre chairs, improvements in firearms, and machines to pack bottles into cartons. He tried botany and developed new strains of begonias. But the Baldwin parachute stunts marked the end of his life as a showman.

Perhaps it was just the passage of time. Harry, one of his two sons with Alice, had died. Britain's charms had run dry. It was time to go home. The Farinis left England for good and moved to Toronto. Here he became involved in one of the strangest inventions in the history of Canadian innovation. He had exchanged notes and design sketches for a revolutionary boat, the roller boat, with a man named Fred Knapp. The idea was that a vessel that rolled along the surface of the water instead of having to plough through it would not have to deal with all that resistance that keeps a displacement hull from exceeding a certain speed. It was — to say the least — a complicated design and engineering challenge, since the passenger and freight compartments of the boat would have to be suspended within the rolling cylinder without themselves rolling. Who deserves the credit for this preposterous idea, Knapp or Farini, is a matter of some dispute. Knapp actually built one, and both he and Farini took out patents in 1906. The thing was a dismal failure, although the idea has been revived in various forms since — including an aerial version — but never successfully. On its first sea trials, the Knapp/Farini prototype ran aground not far from Port Hope and lay there until it fell to pieces. Farini probably lost some money on it, and it was his last fling at invention. Now he turned to painting. Port Hope sculptor Ron Baird said that he was pretty bad at it.

The astonishing thing about Farini's painting is that he was a very worldly man. He was sophisticated, and yet he never learned anything about painting. His series of sixty or so paintings based on ethnic costumes — it never gets any better, just one painting after another, after another and they are all the same quality, exactly. I think his painting was pretty well consistently dreadful.

In 1910, the seventy-two-year-old dreadful painter and his wife moved again, this time to Europe, to be closer to her family. Farini painted and sculpted, soaked up the atmosphere, and somehow managed to weather the war as a Canadian alien living in the kaiser's Germany. In 1920, he and Anna left Germany. Now, after a lifetime of wandering, an aging Billy Hunt really did go home to Hope Township where he still owned some property with a house on it. Moving into it turned out to be difficult. Farini's living niece, Thelma Saunders, told us:

My cousin Lucia was in the house and she wouldn't have Anna and Farini. She said she'd be a servant to them and she didn't want that, so they stayed out in the tent. But of course, with the colder weather coming, they moved into Port Hope.

One of Farini's neighbours in Port Hope was the then ten-year-old Norman Strong, who still remembered, almost eighty years later:

I used to see him ever so many times and I was surprised and astounded. He looked so small and so slight, and he found time, when I would be out cutting grass, to stop and talk to me. And he'd keep complimenting me on doing such a good job. . . . He was a very human being in spite of his notoriety. At my age, we thought it was wonderful, but apparently some of the old people thought that he was too famous.

William Leonard Hunt, *The Great Farini*, Guillermo Antonio Farini, exercised every day and rode his bicycle all around Port Hope. He worked outdoors till he was ninety. They said he was fit as a boy. If he missed the high life and the old times, he didn't show it, although he would tell great tales and always had time for children. In January of 1929, in his ninety-first year, he caught pneumonia and was taken to the Port Hope Hospital. His great-grandnephew, Ted Hunt, said,

> *I don't think until Shane [Peacock] started to research, I'd ever heard the story about my uncle Ted and my father going to see him the day before he died and him sitting, you know, bolt upright and steady in his bed reading a newspaper, and saying that an old gypsy woman told him that he would live to be a hundred. And this . . . was the day before he died.*

His funeral took place on a rainy winter day. The procession moved up Walton Street, past the place he had first performed on the high wire, three-quarters of a century before. Shane Peacock said,

> *In those days . . . people around Port Hope believed that children were to be seen and not heard. Farini didn't believe that. . . . He always had time for children. And who could resist an old gentleman who could tell you what it was like to stand on a high wire over Niagara Falls or to be shot out of a cannon. . . . And the story goes that when Farini died in Port Hope in 1929, and the children saw the casket going up Walton Street, they took off their hats as he went by.*

◆　◆　◆

The original documentary was written by Shane Peacock and Andy Thompson and directed by Andy Thompson.

- PART TWELVE -

LEON GIGLIO
Mandrake the Magician

The man on stage appears to be about seventy years old, erect, gracious, lean but not thin, a handsome grey moustache, a twinkle in his eye. He is standing behind a table, on which are a one-gallon glass jug and a white silk handkerchief which has been draped into a cone, with a knot tied at the point of the cone so that it looks vaguely like a tiny dancer in a white robe with her head wrapped in a towel. The distinguished-looking man, who appears quite sane, is speaking to the handkerchief figure. There appears to be some tension between them.

"Come on, Katie. . ."

He pauses. The handkerchief has not responded.

But we now know that it is about to do so.

"Come on."

The handkerchief-figure suddenly "looks up" at the magician, and then takes a faltering step towards him.

"Ahhh. That's better. You're back with us."

The tiny handkerchief person takes a more few tentative "steps" along the table. The magician picks up a steel hoop, about eight inches in diameter, and dangles it from his right finger, above and to our left of the dancing handkerchief like an acrobat's swinging hoop, and invites the handkerchief to jump through it.

The thing is that we *do know better! We are not children!* But under the charming spell of this lovely man, for a while we are children, and it is more comfortable to believe he is talking to the dancing handkerchief, and she listening to him, than it is to be rational, doubtful adults who know that it is only a trick.

"Come on, Katie. All right. Let's jump through the hoop."

The handkerchief makes a tentative leap towards the dangling hoop, but the steel ring is pretty high, after all, higher than the top of her head, and she doesn't quite make it.

431

"You're not doing at all well, Katie. Nice big jump now."

The hanky crouches, leaps, sits decorously on the hoop, then begins to swing euphorically on it, we almost think we can see her grinning, she jumps up and down on the hoop, begins to get a little indecorous.

"Well, now, don't knock yourself out, Katie. You're too old for that sort of thing. Come back over the hoop. That's the girl. There."

We are not only watching a fine magic trick, indeed a classic, but also a relationship. For decades now this man has been touring North America out of his homebase in Vancouver, enchanting small groups like this — kids and their parents — with small, intimate, believable little narratives about a princesslike handkerchief who dances and sulks, jumps into the gallon jug when she gets feeling provocative, escapes from it when he stuffs a cork in the neck of the jug to keep her in her place, and finally — the appearance of a conflict or contest between them being, well, you know, just *show* — she comes and sits on his wrist and takes her applause with him. This — for those of us who prefer our magic up-close and intimate — is Mandrake at his best. And yet this man considered himself a stage magician first and foremost, played the big theatres, had his name in lights on the marquee, swirled onstage in his silk-lined cape and stunned the house with huge illusions and clouds of smoke and scantily clad showgirls vanishing and reappearing.

On the other hand, you could also find him sitting quietly in a seniors' home in a small town, on the edge of somebody's chair, with nothing but a few coins and a deck of cards, chatting away as though he were one of the residents, but doing charming, amazing things with his few simple props. His real name was Leon Giglio. His professional name: Mandrake the Magician.

Everyone in North America over sixty will remember the comic strip. For about twenty years Mandrake the Magician was a popular syndicated feature whose hero in dapper evening clothes had a compelling eye and a hypnotic gesture that could compel evil criminals to think that their hands and arms had turned into giant poisonous snakes. The heroic magician travelled with a beautiful assistant named

Narda and a gigantic, bald, silent man of colour, Lothar. Lothar, should Mandrake's powers ever fail, would use his prodigious strength to defeat the bad guys and protect his great master. The comic-strip magician had a sharp, narrow moustache and a cloak, and was seldom far from his top hat. He was syndicated in hundreds of newspapers across North America, the brainchild of Lee Falk, who brought the character to life in 1934, and sublet the actual drawing to Phil Davis who drew it for thirty years. Lee Falk died two years ago, but the comic strip is still syndicated by King. An artist named Fred Fredericks now draws Mandrake, and you can see the daily episodes on the King Features Syndicate's web site.

Some of Phil Davis's original artwork for Mandrake is offered for sale via the Internet for as high as $350 (US) per drawing. King Features Syndicate are the people who also brought us Popeye, Prince Valiant, Mary Worth, the Phantom, Rex Morgan M.D., and even the contemporary Sally Forth. King Features Syndicate has played a signal role in the formation of North American fantasy life.

Since the Mandrake comic strip has been in syndication for nearly seventy years, more people know the comic-strip character than ever saw the live magician who took his name. But at the height of his career his billboards advertised this man as America's Greatest Magician, although he grew up and indeed lived much of his life in British Columbia, where he died in 1993. He was born John Arthur Leon Giglio, at Dolphin Bay, Orcas Island, Washington, in 1911. His mother Harriet Jackson took him and his older half-brother brother Carl back to her hometown of New Westminster, BC, when Leon was still an infant. He said that his first great magician, the man who inspired him with a love of the craft, was a candy man at a circus midway who took a coin out of his ear and then made it disappear. The seven-year-old Leon got the bug. He worked for that candy man for a while, and was sent out to the ballpark to sell peanuts. He said that was where he learned to project his voice.

An aunt gave him a boxed set of magic tricks for kids, and he started practising in his room. The records show that he was first hired to perform on the stage of the old Edison Theatre in 1922, when he was eleven. He joked later that he was shaking so much during that first show that his knees were bruised from knocking together. He dropped stuff, and screwed up here and there, but there was a smattering of applause, so he went home moderately encouraged and continued to practise, practise, practise. For a while a rival theatre hired him, clumsiness and all, to compete with the Edison, and he would tell self-deprecating stories — after he was famous — about how the audiences would groan when he came on with the same old patter and the same awkward tricks. There wasn't a living in it, however, and young Leon had to start making a living. He hired on at a shingle mill.

When the carnival came to town that seemed closer than the shingle mill to where he wanted to be in life, so off he went and got a job in the midway. That was where his apprenticeship took place. Thirteen years old, and learning to *work* the crowd, picking up whatever the carnies would teach him, a bit of ventriloquism here, fire-eating there, card tricks, illusions. Among the junk and the trunks he found the wrecked remains of a mirror-based illusion, a "sword box." He dressed an old school chum in a blond wig and a false bosom and high heels (only at night, as the mirrors were in very bad shape) and called her Princess Thora (remember that name). Every once in a while some kid in the audience would call out, "That's not Princess Thora! That's Jackie Giles!"

The important part was that he learned to work the crowd, not lose your nerve, trust your patter. Although he left school after grade six, he used public libraries for the rest of his life, often visiting the local branch in a new town as soon as he had checked into his hotel. In later life he sometimes encouraged young magicians to meet him at the library; that was where he had done his research, he told them, and looked for ideas.

He went to every vaudeville show he could find. Years later, in Hollywood's Magic Castle, it was the vaudeville shows that he recalled as being the turning point, the intimation of a way of life that the adolescent found irresistible. This is from a 1972 interview videotaped with Peter Pit, then the programmer at the Magic Castle:

Oh, the polish. Four shows a day every day and oohhh. And you're looking . . . it's a world of wonder and the girls are all beautiful and they're wearing red diamonds. You find out later they're called brilliants and they're a little cheaper than the real, real thing. But it doesn't matter. You know, it was a wonderland. And it's like you went through the looking glass, like Alice. So you sit there in your overalls and you paid a dime to get in, you know, you can sit through two or three shows. You don't see backstage, you don't see the travel, the thing, the business, nothing, you just see it and say, "Gee, that's for me."

Downtown in Vancouver the Orpheum was beginning to attract the really big names in magic, Thurston, Alexander the Man Who Knows, then Blackstone and Dante. Leon would scrape together the busfare and sit there in the dark lusting, lusting to *do that*. To *be those guys*. When he was about sixteen he got backstage at the Orpheum to meet a man named Ralph Richards, who billed himself as the Wizard. This performer's name was really Ralph Ennis, and he is said to have been a relative of the actor Sir Ralph Richardson. Leon talked himself into a job and went on the road with the Wizard's show for six months, but then the show folded, and the teenaged boy came home and enrolled in business school. He had realized that being slick on stage with a bunch of billiard balls and a fan was all very well, but you'd better know something about keeping books, paying bills, and setting something aside for emergencies. As wiz of a wiz as you wuz, you wouldn't keep on wizzing very long when the creditors came calling.

Bit by bit Leon Giglio assembled an act, some props, a tuxedo, a line of patter, a style, and enough confidence in the dreary woodwork of road shows that he could book a house, find the accommodations he could afford, get local kids to help on and off stage for free — for the glory — and keep out of trouble. He revelled in what he was getting to be really good at: charming the starch out of people with his apparently unstudied and spontaneous approach to the material, while in reality polishing, polishing, polishing, so that all that memorized patter would sound as spontaneous and natural as though he had only that moment thought of it. He prepared alternatives and attitudes for those moments when things went wrong. That is the test of a fine magician:

that he can get himself out of trouble even when a prop has not been loaded or a sleight fails.

In 1935, not long after the first appearance of the Mandrake the Magician comic strip, Leon and a few other local entertainers took over the lease of a little joint on E. Hastings Street, the Green Lantern, in return for picking up the $6 a month neon sign rental. He did magic, some ventriloquism, even a bit of dancing, and for a while he and his pals were able to pay the rent. Now the twenty-four-year-old began to feel he was a genuine professional, but he was on the threshold of the first of a series of disasters that would periodically assault his life. About a year after starting at the Green Lantern, he nearly died. He was thrown from a car in a collision, the car rolled over on him. He lost a kidney, and suffered such messy fractures to his left hip and leg that the doctors wanted to amputate. He refused. For a while he had to walk with a brace, and when he recovered he walked with a slight limp for the rest of his life. He had to give up the dancing, but he developed a more elaborate ventriloquist act, which allowed him to work sitting down.

The Green Lantern went broke and closed. Once recovered sufficiently to perform, Leon decided Vancouver was too small a stage, and went out on his own to build a career as a travelling entertainer. Over the next few years he would put together a little show, take it on the road as long as it was earning (and, at first, sometimes too much longer than that) and then come home to Vancouver and get a day job for a while if he had to. Then he would practise and plan some more until he could get another road show together. Getting a road show together and taking it out and making it work became his life. By all accounts he was never happier than when moving out a new show, whether it was one of the enormously elaborate later illusion shows, with tons of props and staging and a troupe of twenty or so dancers, assistants and roustabouts — or just a little intimate piece, with himself and (later) his wife/assistant, and Katie the Dancing Hank. If, to make ends meet, he had to sell soap door to door or bus tables for a while in the hotel where he was playing the current act, then so be it. Once he was taken on as a maître d'hotel, not because he had any experience but because he owned a tuxedo.

A magician friend, Dick Newton, who met him in those grubby days, said:

Working in cabarets, beer halls, with audiences that had been drinking a lot and were even likely to toss something at you if they didn't like you, was great training. And if you could do well with those audiences, you could play anywhere.

It was a chimerical, unreal kind of life. A different town every night, perhaps too much to drink, a constant watchfulness for scoundrels, few people whom you could trust. He began to feel that his family was disintegrating. His brother had committed suicide and his father died of a heart attack. He was in need of some stabilizing human contact, and he found it in the person of another performer.

Bernard Abrams, who spent years as Mandrake's tour manager, was a magician playing those same circuits when they met. They stayed friends for the rest of Leon's life. When they were working the speakeasies and grubby little nightclubs together, Abrams says that Leon was

so versatile that he could take the place of two acts. In those days when you were working in a nightclub and if you were the master of ceremonies you went out and stayed there for a half hour. And he would do master of ceremonies and magic and then he would do the ventriloquist act, and then he could go on for hours because he was sitting down. We got along fine because I was impressed with his tricks, and he was impressed that I had a rabbit.

Packing along his cards and silks, his billiard balls and ropes, his "vent" dummies, and a couple of small "boxes" (as magicians call the kind of illusion where the girl steps into the closet and vanishes), he built enough confidence working the northwest circuit to start branching out, so he headed south. But then another disaster struck. In a club in Arizona a fire destroyed his dummies.

Vents can get pretty attached to those articulated dolls. The vent invests the dummy with a personality, and night after night exchanges jokes and insults with this person in what, at its best, is really almost credible. Leon was in grief when his Sammy, Gerry, and Charlie died. He did not have enough money to buy replacements, and he was somewhat impaired in his ability to get work, since part of his act had gone up in smoke.

He needed a "box jumper" (the girl who disappears from the magic chest or closet), and hired a dancer named Lola Wilson. She soon became his general assistant, and, as often happens in this trade, they married. It is not clear how or why he began to think that the comic-strip character might be his to bring to life on the stage. It is difficult to understand how King Features Syndicate allowed him to get away with it, but sometime before World War II, when vaudeville theatres regularly offered movies as well as stage shows, audiences began to see a short black-and-white animated screen announcement:

Coming on stage in this theatre —-
America's Mandrake the Magician !!

The producers of our documentary found a number of these cinema/vaudeville relics.

Coming ... on the stage of this theatre ...
a magical musical, starring in person ...
America's Mandrake the Magician. Don't Miss It!
It's a Once Seen, Never Forgotten Program!

So now he was coming out in a top hat, with a scarlet-lined cloak, pencilled eyebrows, a pointed moustache, a hypnotic gleam in his eye, a wave of the hand that seemed very familiar to comic-strip readers. A recognizable figure from the Funny Pages had come to life on the stage.

For a while he worked the same circuit under different names, to double his bookings. "So as to work solid," he said in an interview, "I'd go down the coast as Leon the Ventriloquist and come back up as Mandrake the Magician."

Journalists who tried to pin him down about using the comic-strip name had little success. The only occasion we know of that he came close to admitting that he had appropriated the Mandrake name and image with something less than a perfect right to do so was the Peter Pit interview at the Magic Castle in 1972.

Peter Pit: *Where'd you get the name Mandrake? You weren't born with that name, were you? Were you born with it?*
Mandrake: *Does it matter?*

Pit: *No, I just wanted to know. How'd you hit upon it? I mean, what was it that fascinated you . . .?*

Mandrake: *Who am I to explain the accident of fate.*

Pit: *I don't know, tell us.*

Mandrake: *I said who am I? Almost every person that made it in our business started out under one name, didn't do too well, bombed a little, changed their name and went in and said, "Um, Brad just came into town." And they had a different name. And along the line somewhere they went over real well. And somebody said, "I want that act." And that's the name you are stuck with from there on.*

Pit: *That has to do with the cartoon?*

Mandrake: *Got a lot to do with a lot of things.*

Pit: *Got a lot to do with a lot of things? It's one of those things?*

Mandrake: *Peter, everything is a commercial, in a sense, so you make any tie-ups you can and try to get established.*

This is unsatisfactory on two counts, the first being the obvious evasion, and the second that it does not seem to fit the usually generous and open personality of the man as we see him in almost every other environment. Court records in Los Angeles show that in 1944 he legally changed his name to Leon Mandrake. He often gave the impression in interviews that he had taken the name long before he had actually started using it, and that in fact he was the first. According to friends he started to bill himself as Mandrake in late 1941 or 1942. As far as we can tell, the Peter Pit interview is the closest he ever came to talking frankly about it. Artist Phil Davis always said that the comic strip and the live performer were mutually beneficial. If King Features Syndicate ever threatened to sue, the documentary producers could find no record of it. In his publicity he used Leon Mandrake the Magician for a time but then went back to Mandrake the Magician. If you check out the Mandrake web site you may find, in the old strips, a character called Thora, the name young Leon said he gave to his school chum in the carnival sword box illusion.

As Leon and Lola polished the act, they refined and slightly modified an illusion that Harry Houdini and his wife had made famous, the substitution trunk. Lola (now named Narda, after the comic-strip

Mandrake's companion) would be tied up in a mail sack and nailed into a large crate. The magician would stand on top of the crate, raise his cloak in front of him until he was concealed, at which point, almost instantly, the cloak would drop, and Narda would be standing there instead of Mandrake. Then, when the crate was laboriously opened (by a committee of audience members who had been on stage with them the whole time) Leon would be in the mail sack, in a different costume from the one we had just seen, smoking a lighted cigarette. It is a great trick, still widely and sometimes superbly performed.[16] Admirers said that Mandrake's "sub trunk" was the fastest ever, and Leon himself claimed to have originated the cigarette and the change of costume.

Peter Pit asked him to explain how it was done.

Pit: *We didn't have Velcro at those times. How did you make such a fast change?*

Mandrake: *That is one of the hardest secrets.*

Pit: *Is it really?*

Mandrake: *This is — look, you can go to a public library and find out almost any principle in magic but just try to find out about quick change. Oh, that's a hard one, Peter. Those secrets are not written. If they are I can't . . .*

Pit: *You're not going to tell us?*

Mandrake: *Yes, I'd be happy to explain it.*

Pit: *I'd love to hear.*

Mandrake: *Well, first you take the efferdan and tantifraz then you put them with the fabersham which will collidrig and puzzle. The incandescent frill, if the weather's proper, now you've got to take the phase of the moon into this or you're lost. Then the molidig remains fallified and the . . .*

Pit: *. . . You're not going to tell us, are you?*

Mandrake: *I just told you. What do you mean? You answer the man's question right away and he says, "Huh, they never tell you nothing." What do you want me to do? Tell you to practise?*

By 1945 they had a big travelling show with a costly troupe of

16. Notably by David Copperfield and the Pendragons, among others.

dancers, assistants, and wagonloads of props and equipment. They played Chicago, Vancouver, Los Angeles, in big theatres for a substantial ticket. The billings said MANDRAKE AND NARDA, but in fact the marriage was winding down, and 1946 was the last year they played together. When the marriage ended the magician lost his highly trained and popular assistant. He let it be known that he was looking for someone to replace her, and another dancer who had worked a number of magic shows applied for the job. Her name was Louise Solarno, a showbusiness kid who had grown up on the road.

I was in Chicago and I had just come off of a stock company so I decided to go to this agent Paul Saunders and I'd never been to him before and Leon was there. When [Paul] heard that I had worked for Blackstone he suggested that I go with Leon and I said, "Gee I was hoping for some small part in a musical or something." So he said, "Well you take this two weeks and I'll find another show for you," and he said to Leon, "You take her and I'll find another girl for you." So I signed up for two weeks and stayed forty-seven years.

They agreed on a stage name, Velvet, which she still uses as his widow. They married after six weeks.

It was simple all right, we got married at six o'clock at night and at eight o'clock we were doing the first show. We used to do two shows a night and when we were in the Midwest the clubs were open seven days a week. On closing night we would have to pack as we did the last show, travel all night and then get into the next town, which was usually 200 or 250 miles away and open that same night. You got so much practice because you were always doing your show and you had to get smooth, because you did it all the time.

By now television was making inroads in the American entertainment world. Big theatrical shows like Mandrake's cost too much. Ticket prices were too high for people who could get free entertainment at home. Many magicians turned to the nightclub scene. This was a very different relationship with the audience. In the theatre you had people seated out in front of you and you controlled the lighting. In a club you often had people sitting on three sides of the playing area, your lighting was sometimes rudimentary, people were being served, eating, drinking — often too much. Some magicians hated it, among them Blackstone. Mandrake seemed to thrive on it. It was in that environment that he took the classic Dancing Hank, combined with another classic, The Spook in the Bottle, and developed the enchanting presentation with which this chapter opens.

Leon and Velvet had three children, all the while touring, the South, the West Coast, and the Midwest. Their first son, Lon, was born in Chicago, Ron in Miami, and Kimball in Dayton, Ohio. Bernard Abrams says he knew that Leon was worried about keeping bread on the table, but that he never shared those worries with the troupe, that he seldom fired anybody. "You have to spread the blanket," he would say. But it was getting tougher all the time, despite his established reputation. "The real magic," says Bernard Abrams, "was that he kept the show on the road when all the rest of them folded up. The real magic the audience never saw."

Although Leon never stopped performing, for a while the audience stopped seeing Mandrake altogether. Charles Dunninger's mind-reading act had moved from the stage to radio and then to network television after 1944, and had made "Mind Reading" hugely popular. Another mentalist billed himself as Alexander: The Man Who Knows, and had enjoyed a successful touring career. Alexander died, and Leon bought his props, methods, and the rights to his show. "I'm not a mind-reader," he said. "I'm a people reader." Good magicians, those who work an intimate show, must be people readers. Many, like Alexander, combine mentalism and conventional magic. Leon had done a bit of the former, and now decided his career might get a boost from Alexander's reputation and that Mandrake might take a strategic vacation.

It is conceivable that there was some pressure from King Features Syndicate at this time (1951) about the use of the name Mandrake, and that the new identity was partly a way of riding out the storm. The strategy does not seem to have worked very well. Television had become an immense rival. A few TV impresarios — notably Ed Sullivan — booked magic acts from time to time, but the competition was fierce. Leon went back to being Mandrake and got a few bookings on TV, where he looks ill at ease with the illusions. He kept on touring. In 1955 their daughter Geelia ("Jill") was born in Portland, Oregon. It became more and more difficult to keep the family together. For a while they packed the kids off to their grandmother in Chicago. Lon says he woke up one night after a nightmare and told his grandmother that there had been a terrible fire, whereupon the phone rang from Anchorage where a club that Velvet and Leon had worked many times, and loved, had burned to the ground with all their props and costumes. The catalogue of disasters in the magician's life kept growing.

For a while they lived in Hawaii, and then came home to Vancouver, bought a house, and put the children into school, which Lon says they hated. Leon and Velvet did their best to book shows that involved less travel. They played fairs in the summer, including the British Columbia Provincial Exposition, home shows, conventions, gradually easing out of the nightclubs. Velvet got cut in half with a buzz saw and shot through the chest with an arrow on a ribbon.

On the surface Mandrake's career looks like the life of a journeyman who is doing what he is good at because that is how you earn a living. But the testimony of Mandrake himself, and of Velvet and the children, makes it clear that there was a conscious sacrifice in being a professional magician. He could have done better in real estate, he was a hell of a salesman, a people-reader like all good salesmen. Talk to a hundred magicians; at least fifty will tell you a similar story. Few are as diligent or adroit with the business side of their business as they are with the endless practice you have to maintain if your sleight of hand is going to be flawless, or with the people-reading and other elements of the performing scene. The great Dai Vernon (see *The Canadians: Biographies of a Nation*, Volume I, Part Four), acknowledged worldwide as an all-time master, was never able to save any money and was, to all intents and purposes, supported by the Magic Castle and friends and admirers for the last quarter-century of his hugely productive life. Performing magic is a consuming, obsessive craft for many. Leon Mandrake at least seems to have found it a source of deep and continuing joy. "You don't care if you have to eat beans," he said,

and sleep in the car because you know what you want and you're

*going to do it and nobody's going to stop you. But if you expect lux-
ury, if you expect the arts to keep you like . . . after all, we're very dis-
pensable you know. We are a luxury, we're easy to do without. You
can't expect to be — play and have fun and have everything else
showered on you too — you've got to give up something to get what
you like.*

As Ron moved into his teens he began to replace Velvet on the
road from time to time, so that she could stay home with the kids. They
all remember their father as a man who was full of surprises, not just
new magic (although he seems to have constantly been learning and
trying out new tricks). "He came up to my room one day when I was
practising," Kim said,

*and he took my guitar and played some really hip little finger pick-
ing thing. I never knew that he could play at all, and that was the
one and only time he did that. He never played it again.*

Mandrake had, in fact, composed complex orchestrations of his
own original themes for some of his more elaborate stage shows, but it
is not clear whether he ever formally studied music.

He began to do a little more steady television in the 1970s on a
CBC series called *The Manipulators*, and played himself in a dramatic
role on the long-running Vancouver CBC production *The Beachcombers*,
with Bruno Gerussi. The Magic Castle recognized his contribution with
their prestigious Performing Fellowship. He was generous with his
time to institutions for old people and children. Velvet says that he
never really gave up the dream of going on the road again with a big
show and a real troupe and, now well into his seventies, in 1985 he did
mount a major show. But he discovered a very compelling reason for it
to be his last. His son Lon was backstage. "He came out and he did a
wonderful thirty minutes," Lon told us.

*Then he said, "Thank you very much, ladies and gentlemen, for
coming" and he closed the show after [only] thirty minutes. And I
think now he might have had a little bit of a stroke, because, you
know, afterwards I said, "What happened?" And he said, "You
know, I thought that we'd completed the show." That was the last
show.*

"He couldn't not work," his son Ron said.

If he . . . thought his career was over or when he thought his career was over he ah . . . he became much older. . . . My dad's whole life was a show, and I think . . . his whole life, he was the entertainer and he wouldn't allow anybody to, to not be happy, you know. He wouldn't allow them not to be happy.

Bernard Abrams said that right up to the end his friend kept talking as though he might get a new show together, take it on the road next spring. When Mandrake died in 1993, his friends went back to the place where he had got his start as a stage performer, seventy-one years earlier: the old Edison Theatre in New Westminster. They say he would have got a laugh out of the fact that it's now a strip club. And that during that very last Mandrake show, the funeral, things didn't quite go according to plan. "The furnace went off," Velvet said.

And I said, "Leon would have loved this." No matter how much you planned, something always goes wrong, and it was the furnace, he would have really laughed. He's probably up there or down here laughing at the whole thing. Anyway, that was that.

As an epilogue, on a slightly personal note from this writer, who has from time to time sailed close enough to the wind of that obsession with performing magic to think he knows something about magicians: There is something odd about Canada and magicians — Dai Vernon, Stewart James, Doug Henning, Mandrake — names that resonate among magicians around the world. But not one of them turns up in *The Canadian Encyclopaedia*. That's what I mean when I say there is something odd about Canada and magicians. But maybe there is just something odd about magicians.

◆ ◆ ◆

The original documentary was written by Lynn Booth and Mary Ungerleider and produced by Lynn Booth. It was directed and edited by Mary Ungerleider.

PART THIRTEEN

JAY SILVERHEELS
The Man Beside *the Mask*

The first native North American to star in a television series was a Mohawk from the Six Nations Reserve at Brantford, Ontario. His name was Harry Jay Smith, but the film world remembers him as Jay Silverheels, and so do millions of fans of *The Lone Ranger*.

The Lone Ranger made its way into the legends and language of North American kids with the radio series that first went to air in 1933 and was broadcast continually for twenty-one years.

In all media the Lone Ranger story starts with the same fictional events. A man named John Reid, born in 1850, was the only survivor of a group of Texas Rangers who were ambushed by outlaws. Five rangers were killed, including Reid's older brother, Daniel. The Indian Tonto found him and nursed him to health. Reid then donned a black mask made from his dead brother's vest, mounted his stallion, Silver, and roamed the West as the Lone Ranger to aid those in need, to fight evil, and to fight for justice.

The character was created in the Lone Ranger radio program written and produced by George W. Trendle and Fran Striker. It began on a single radio station, WXYZ in Detroit, Michigan, on January 30, 1933. In less than ten years, more than four hundred stations were carrying it. It is probably fair to say that more people think The *Lone Ranger's* theme music was created for that program than know it as Rossini's *William Tell Overture*.

The radio programs got off to a rough start, with three different actors in the title role during the first three months. The original Ranger was a man named George Stenius who left after two and a half months to pursue a career as a writer in New York. As George Seaton, he would go on to a career in Hollywood as a screenwriter-director-producer, winning two Academy Awards for his screenplays along the way. He was replaced by one Jack Deeds, who was fired within days.

The station's dramatic director played one show, and then they found Earle Graser, who became the Lone Ranger on April 18, 1933.

Graser found the voice and the manner that raised the Lone Ranger from a character in a radio serial to something close to archetype. He played the part for the next eight years, until the morning of April 8, 1941, when he fell asleep at the wheel of his car and was killed when it slammed into a parked trailer. Graser's death presented two immediate problems to the Lone Ranger's producers: a new actor had to be found fast (the show was broadcast live three days a week; no reruns and no pre-recorded broadcasts) and the transition had to be handled smoothly without an abrupt and obvious change in actors. Moreover, the many adolescents in the listening audience had to be reassured that it was not the Lone Ranger himself who had died.

The part was filled by Brace Beemer, an announcer and studio manager who had at times narrated *The Lone Ranger* program, had been making personal appearances as the Lone Ranger (because he was much more physically impressive than Graser), and was currently playing the lead in *Challenge of the Yukon*, a popular television series later renamed *Sgt. Preston of the Yukon*. Beemer's voice was noticeably deeper than Graser's. They had to find a gimmick to ease him into the role. The gimmick used was to have the Lone Ranger shot and wounded at the beginning of the next script, an injury that left him unable to speak for several days as he struggled to recover. The transition helped convince children that, despite what they may have heard on the news, the Lone Ranger was not dead, as well as providing a bridge to Beemer's deep-voiced playing of the hero.

Brace Beemer was the Lone Ranger for the next thirteen years, until the radio series ended with its last live broadcast on September 3, 1954.

This may seem a long road to travel on the way to a story about the life of Jay Silverheels, but that life itself cannot be fully appreciated without understanding that *The Lone Ranger* was not just another radio serial; it was an extended morality play that worked out simplistic but powerfully presented issues of good and evil and was listened to by millions and millions of American and Canadian kids. Millions of them are still alive; for them the image of a great white stallion rising up on its hind legs as its masked rider pointed off towards the next adventure is still vivid. That image and the characters connected to it became cultural icons so *present* that it is difficult for the people who lived through that period to realize that the Masked Man and Tonto, and "Hi-Yo, Silver, Away" (the hero's call to the white stallion as they set off to vanquish evil) . . . to realize that they are gone. The *Seinfeld* and *This Hour Has 22 Minutes* generation — who may know of the Masked Man and Tonto as quaint symbols — never had the experience of being enthralled by them, and of believing that they were real.

The moral centre to the Lone Ranger stories makes the subservient, illiterate Tonto role played by Jay Silverheels seem ironic to us today. It did to Silverheels then — both ironic and demeaning. Nonetheless it did move the Mohawk actor into the Hollywood mainstream. Once there, he diligently used his reputation to advance First Nations actors out of their largely wordless stereotypical roles — howling, raiding white settlers, and getting shot and dying. Jay Silverheels prepared the ground for artists such as Chief Dan George, Graham Greene, Tom Jackson, Tantoo Cardinal, and Tina Keeper, who have been able to build serious careers and soar far above the clichéed confines of their Native predecessors.

Harry Jay Smith was born on Canada's largest reserve, the Six Nations, near Brantford, Ontario, on May 26, 1912. He was the third in a family of eleven children, eight boys and three girls. The large family grew up in a rambling Victorian house, on land that was given to the Six Nations in 1784. The house was a tall, imposing brick structure with an eccentric central section that towered above the ridge of the main roof, and decorative brickwork up the corners and on the valances. Harry's father went off to World War I and came back with a commission and a chest full of medals. Major George Smith had more decorations on his tunic than any other Native Canadian soldier in that war. He also came back deaf from a shell that exploded in a nearby trench and nearly killed him. And so young Harry had little conversation with his father as he helped him work the hundred-acre farm near the reserve. Most of his instruction, encouragement, and guidance in life came from his mother.

He went to a racially mixed school in Brantford, but there was little mixing between the kids from the reserve and the kids from town. His brothers Steve and Cecil remember him as a slight kid who was fascinated with the bodybuilding ads in *Popular Mechanics* and *Liberty* and the other five-cent magazines. Charles Atlas offered to turn every "97 pound weakling" into a muscular, confident giant who could reduce the nasty bullies on the beach to snivelling wrecks. Jay Silverheel's brother Steve Smith says:

> *My dad bought him these wrestling books on holds and all that, and the other people would be out mowing hay or cutting wood, and he'd be in the barn punching a punching bag. He used to get these magazines that were on bodybuilding. He used to look at all the barbells but he could never afford them. And so he would make his own out of steel rods and cement blocks and he would weight-lift.*

Then he started playing lacrosse and discovered that he was a natural. When he was sixteen he joined the Mohawk Stars, a field lacrosse team, and soon became one of their best players. The team's goalie was a man named Judy — Judy "Punch" Garlow. Garlow says he was there when Harry got the name "Silverheels."

> *When we played a good game, so our manager says, "I'm gonna buy all you guys new running shoes." So he bought us all white running shoes. And then after a while we started playing and Tonto would run down the field. All you could see is white feet flying. Says that we can't call him "White Heels" cause he's an Indian so we says "Silverheels." So that's how they call him Jay Silverheels.*

A lot of the young men from Six Nations went down to Buffalo, NY, during the Depression to look for work, and Jay went too. He played semipro lacrosse there, and photographs in the sports sections from that period sometimes call him H. Smith, and sometimes Jay Silverheels. He heard that some of the other guys were winning modest amounts of money at amateur boxing events. So he joined a local gym — you could become a club member for a quarter — and met a really good boxer at his club, a young man named Jack Donovan. Donovan invited the penniless Mohawk kid from Canada to come home with him and get a good feed. There is a photo of Donovan's mother serving out a huge platter of bacon and eggs to the two boys,

Jay grinning broadly as he digs in. His grin and his demeanour evidently charmed the Donovan family; Jay moved in and lived with them for some time. The Buffalo Boxing Museum has an extensive collection of records from that period. Ed Cudney, the curator, showed us photographs of Jay in the ring in those days, and talked about the Donovan relationship.

And she did all the cooking for him and put him up for the three or four weeks he was training for the New York State Championships. And they [Jack Donovan and Jay] both went to New York City to fight and they both won the Championships. And after winning it, they took them to Jack Dempsey's restaurant and they took pictures with Jack Dempsey. I don't think boxing was his primary love but he took it up and he just . . . he won at everything, I guess, that he ever played in.

The Dempsey/Silverheels/Donovan photographs are now in Cudney's collection at the Buffalo Boxing Museum.

Jay Silverheels was building a reputation. He began a relationship with Edna Lickers, a sixteen-year-old from the Six Nations reserve. Edna became pregnant. Her son Ron was born in Buffalo and took the name Smith. But Edna and Jay were both too young to really know what they were doing and the relationship did not last. Jay went back to lacrosse and was soon playing with a popular "All-Indian" team. It seems from some of the photographs and the memories of the players that part of the fun for the white spectators was to get tanked up on beer and yell "Kill the Indians!" But the team was very successful, and in the midst of the Depression Jay was beginning to earn a decent living, which he supplemented by modelling for local advertisers. He was still working with the barbells and the punching bag. A beefcake photograph that survives bears this caption:

He's one of those V-man jobs — broad of shoulder, narrow at the hips and with rippling muscles. He's a perfect specimen — wavy, jet black hair and sharply chiselled features set off the frame magnificently, and qualify him for matinee idol honors should he ever take a whirl at that industry.

That was from the *Buffalo Evening News*, December 14, 1936; he was now twenty-four. He married a woman named Bobbi, and they had a daughter, Sharon. When Jay's team played an exhibition game in Los Angeles, the comedian Joe E. Brown (*Some Like It Hot*) was in the crowd, and came back to the dressing rooms to meet the team. Brown took a liking to Jay. Like the *Buffalo Evening News*, Joe E. Brown wondered if the good-looking athletic kid shouldn't have a career in the movies. He arranged for Jay to get an extra's acting card. Bobbi did not like the idea of leaving home for California, but she liked even less being left alone in Buffalo with a new baby; so she came west with Jay and got a job as a waitress. They needed her small salary; the acting jobs at first were few and far between. When he began to do better, Bobbi was able to quit waitressing. But she was uncomfortable watching him being photographed with starlets. Perhaps she was right to be suspicious. His daughter Sharon says that he became very self-centred, that there were affairs outside the marriage, that she seldom saw him.

Before long Bobbi had had enough. She went back to Buffalo, sued for divorce, and remarried. Sharon would not see her father again for fourteen years. Jay's brother Cecil says the divorce made Jay stand back and take a more thoughtful look at things than he had before. It was too late for his marriage with Bobbi, but it may have helped him settle down to a more professional and more disciplined life.

Better roles began to come his way. He got a Screen Actors' Guild "A" card, and played an Inca prince in *Captain from Castille*. Then they cast him as the Osceola brother in Humphrey Bogart's *Key Largo*. Before he was finished he would play in fifty-five feature films, including *The Man Who Loved Cat Dancing* and *Cat Ballou*. He was always an Indian: that had not changed. In fact, for a long time Indian actors were not given principal roles even when the lead character was an Indian. Actor Peter Kelly Gaudreault, of the successful Canadian series *North of Sixty*, says, "The . . . parts which had reputations which transcended generations . . . characters like Geronimo and Crazy Horse from American Native history, they were always played by white actors."

Jay later starred in *Santee*, a thoughtful, articulate, sophisticated role as a breeder of quarter horses. Horses were a great love. When Jay was about fifteen, his brothers remember him on his father's farm gracefully riding a difficult black stallion, a stallion that nobody else had been able to stay on. Later in his career he would have a ranch of his own, take up driving a sulky in trotting races, and marry a Los Angeles woman who shared his love of horses and the track. But it was another kind of involvement with riding horses that was about to turn him from a successful actor into a star, shortly after he finished his film with Bogart in 1948. It was a movie called *The Cowboy and the Indians*. There he met an actor named Clayton Moore, who played the cowboy. They became friends, and Moore admired Jay's work enough to suggest that he audition for a television series that Moore would star in. This was, of course, *The Lone Ranger*.

Jay Silverheels had to compete with thirty-five other actors for the Tonto role. We don't know the names of all the others, but probably many of them were not Indians. The first Tonto on radio had been a white man, Jack Todd, who dressed in Native costume for publicity photographs. There was a 1937 movie serial of the Lone Ranger that played in the Saturday afternoon double features in ten-minute (one-reel) instalments. Its Tonto was also a white man, Victor Daniels. There had never been an Indian star; Jay was breaking a colour barrier. He and Clayton Moore became a partnership. He had steady work now, and within months he was famous.

The actual making of the television series sounds like a nightmare. Each episode was shot in two days. Much of the work was done in studio, but from time to time they would take a week out in the desert, at some of the spectacular rocky mesa sites that Hollywood has made so familiar. In that week they'd shoot all the exterior action scenes needed for a whole season.

Film historian Frank Thompson says that the company would rent a stagecoach for one day and use it from dawn to dark:

All day long they would have a bunch of bad guys chasing the stagecoach, the Lone Ranger and Tonto intercepting the stagecoach. And those scenes would be interspersed among five, six different episodes of the film. But they would have to do it all in one day. They worked very, very hard for very low pay. No star of a TV show would work for what they worked for.

The actor John Hart, who played the Lone Ranger for one season, replacing Clayton Moore during a contract dispute, said:

Guild minimum in those days was $125 a week — and that's a six-day week. And I didn't get much more than that, and I think he'd got a bit more than that because he'd done all those previous shows. If he had any kind of an agent, they'd have bumped him up. Because he was just as valuable an asset to the show as the Lone Ranger. And you couldn't be bringing in a new Tonto all the time.

Frank Thompson recounts an episode that seems to show a dawning political and social sense, which would later become directly focused on the status of First Nations actors in the movie capital. John Hart had finished out his one season as the Masked Man. Clayton Moore had settled his contract differences and was back in the saddle on the big white stallion.

When they shot up here at Iverson's Ranch, they would have to stop at a gas station down at the bottom of the hill and change their clothes in the men's room. One day Jay Silverheels refused to change his clothes. And they got to the set, everybody was set up and Jay Silverheels was nowhere to be seen. And Clayton knew that he would often come out to a big rock, perhaps that rock. He followed him up and said, "What's wrong?" And Jay said, "We're the leading actors in a hit TV show and we don't even have dressing rooms. They shouldn't be treating us this way. We have to change in a men's room. This is not right." Clayton said, "Yeah, you're right, but we do have the whole crew waiting for us and we should probably get back to work." I think it's . . . to Jay Silverheels' credit that he did get back to work. And the next day they had dressing rooms.

And there was another aspect to the daily grind as Tonto that Silverheels knew he had to swallow, but also knew that he had to do something about, someday.

Here is some sample dialogue.

TONTO
Him sent men to ambush me, but me take care of him. You find Cavendish?

LONE RANGER

Tonto, what happened?

TONTO

Nelson, he hit me. But me all right now. That not make sense. Me not understand.

Even his adoring relatives back at the reserve, who would gather at a neighbour's house to watch Cousin Jay star on the box, were embarrassed to hear the literate, intelligent man they knew talk in grunting monosyllables. John Hart, who had played that one season of *The Lone Ranger* and stayed close to Jay for the rest of his life, recalled his own unease when Jay talked about trying to get more challenging roles.

> *He thought he was being a dumb Indian a lot of the time, creeping around and someone hitting him on the head, and he'd fall over. He wasn't too happy with that. But it was a job and he did it, you know gracefully, with good spirit. He was [actually] capable of doing all kinds of things, but he was just Tonto to all these dumb producers that wouldn't see him any other way. He got that one part in* Santee *and it was a nice part, he was wonderful, very good in it. Well, I think it really frustrated Jay a lot to be Tonto to everybody, trying to get other jobs with other producers and they'd say, "Oh yeah, he's great, he's Tonto!" Well, so he's Tonto but he's a good actor, too. He can do other things.*

Always proud of his physical strength and agility, Jay insisted on doing his own stunts. But in 1955, after a rough brawl, something went terribly wrong. A sharp pain brought him to his knees. He was taken to the hospital with a heart attack. He was off the set for two months, replaced by the Lone Ranger's nephew. He came back to work with nitroglycerine tablets, a low-fat diet, and doctor's orders to stop the stunts.

Soon *The Lone Ranger* was cancelled, overtaken by more sophisticated Western series with more complex characters and situations: *Gunsmoke*, *The Rifleman*, *Bonanza*. Although he played in two more Lone Ranger movies, in 1956 and 1959, things were slowing down. He and Mary di Roma had married in 1954. With her love of horses and his new "career" as a sulky driver, it seemed to make sense that they start raising racehorses themselves on the ranch they shared. He went back to Brantford once, in 1957, to a hero's welcome and a slightly uneasy but excited reunion with his daughter Sharon, then seventeen. But the connection with Six Nations and family was now more symbolic than real. His ties were to Mary, the ranch, the horses, the track, and the community of Native actors in California.

The Lone Ranger had vanished from all but the Saturday morning rerun screens, but Jay and Clayton Moore occasionally still went on well-paid tours for advertisers who knew very well which generation would remember the Masked Man and his Faithful Sidekick. They were able to keep this up well into the sixties.

A joke entered the culture about then. Tonto and the Lone Ranger are cornered in the arroyo by a crowd of Sioux warriors who are galloping in for the kill. The Lone Ranger says, "Tonto, we're in serious trouble." Tonto rejoins, "What do you mean 'We,' Paleface!"

Jay was spending time with younger Native actors in Hollywood. In the mid-sixties, amid the social ferment that was activating — and perhaps creating — radicals all over the Western world, Jay Silverheels' political awareness matured. With the veteran actor Will Sampson he formed the Indian Actors' Workshop.

It would be difficult for a bright kid growing up Mohawk to avoid being at least slightly affected by the bug of First Nations politics. Of all the Iroquois nations, the Mohawks have the reputation for being the most determined. It was Warriors from the Caughnawagha community who met Laura Secord after her famous walk during the War of 1812; they were a fighting unit under the command of Colonel Fitzgibbon and turned the tide in the subsequent battle with the invading American forces. When the Iroquois nations (five at first and a sixth later) were united in confederacy by a Huron prophet remembered as Dekanawidha, it was the Mohawk leader Ayonwhatha who spoke to the once warring nations on behalf of this speech-impaired visionary. Ayonwhatha is remembered in later retellings of the story as "Hiawatha."

Dekanawidha declared the Mohawk chiefs to be Heads of the Confederacy and the Great Lords of the Peace. Dekanawidha had paddled across Lake Ontario in a magical stone canoe and demonstrated his prophetic role by surviving a leap or fall from a tall pine — the Tree of Peace — into a deep river gorge below. The Iroquois confederacy was assembled out of a group of linguistically related but traditionally warring separate cultures — Mohawk, Onandaga, Oneida, Cayuga, Seneca (and later the Tuscarora). It was a triumph of civilizing politics over tribal rivalries. The constitution, symbolically embedded in a superb belt of wampum, may date from as far back as the fifteenth century. It is almost certainly the first example of a code of laws in North America. It recognized women as persons and as a special repository of political wisdom. The version published by the University of Oklahoma's law school declares in its article 44:

Lineal descent shall run in the female line. Women shall be considered the progenitors of the Nations. They shall own the land and the soil. Men and women shall follow the status of the mother.

It is said that Benjamin Franklin, as he considered the challenge of putting together a constitution for the newly independent United States of America, studied the constitution of the Iroquois confederacy. Every kid raised in a Six Nations community hears these stories, and it seems to be the Mohawks who carry them with the most aggressive pride.

So when Jay Silverheels helped put together the Workshop, he was acting like a Mohawk. Although he had made a reputation and a modest fortune playing a sidekick, now it was time to help Native performers escape the racist clichés.

Actors Frank Salsedo and Michael Horse talk with affection of how Jay brought the young First Nations hopefuls in California together, trained them, watched out for parts for them, and kept arguing with producers. These talented people *must* be considered for non-stereotyped roles, for roles outside the racially determined ones that had been their only venue since the beginning of movies. Michael Horse said, "He fought a lot of the fight for us. I didn't realize again until I got into the movie business, talking to a few of the Indian actors who were around at that time, what a hard time they had, what trailblazers they were, what battles." The Workshop was a cheery, companionable place. It did find work for the members, but still always playing Indians. For a while it seemed as though those hidebound racist attitudes of the producers were immutable.

When he was not at the Workshop Jay spent a lot of time at the track. He was recognized as an outstanding harness racer. When he won at the Meadows in 1974 it was a national racing event, and suddenly he was in demand for television interviews. Perhaps it was that new prominence that allowed some Hollywood producers to see the actor in a new light. In any case it was shortly afterwards that his agent brought Jay a number of offers, and suggested that he had better convince the producers that he was physically up to a major commitment — it would be in the contracts anyway — and get a thorough set of medicals even before the negotiations began. It was then that calamity struck, just as he was on the threshold of yet another breakthrough.

He went in for an angiogram. This was a routine and mandatory part of an exhaustive medical examination, and nobody told him that there was any risk entailed (perhaps there was not). But during the procedure he was stricken with massive pain. It was a stroke, and when the pain receded he could hardly speak, his left leg trailed when he walked, his face was badly twisted, and his mind was far from clear.

Jay Silverheels was nothing if not courageous. He tried to fight that stroke, but it was bigger than he was. He sued the angiogram doctors for malpractice on the grounds that he had not been adequately advised of the dangers in the procedure, but it is likely that he was even less well advised in the bringing of the suit, which he could not have won. He sat stiffly in the courtroom, tears rolling down his face as he listened to witness after witness describe how he was merely a shadow of the physical man he'd so recently been. His defeat there discouraged him painfully. He tried one race in the sulky, but it was clearly too dangerous for a person as severely disabled as he had become. He had to give up the Indian Actors' Workshop. Without him at the helm it soon disintegrated. Now none of the old roads was there for him to walk down. In the film and photographs of those last five years he appears to shrink, bit by bit, day by day. There was a celebration when his star was laid down in the Hollywood Walk of Fame, but he was unable to even speak to reporters that day, and in the news clips of the event he looks sad, lost and helpless.

Not long after that he vanished. John Hart, who had done that one season as the Lone Ranger and stayed friends with Jay, says that he found him in "a dinky little hospital in South Pasadena. How in hell he got there, I don't know. He was down to a hundred pounds. I cared about him a lot." Hart's eyes welled with tears remembering Jay Silverheels, who died in hospital in 1980, at the age of sixty-eight.

The distinguished Cree actor Tom Jackson, born on the One Arrow Reserve near Batoche, said,

I don't remember the guy who said, "Hey Silver, come here." What was that guy's name? I don't remember him. I do remember the guy who went, "Get 'um up, Scout. Uhm. Kemo Sabe. Uhm." I remember him.

His name was Jay Silverheels.

◆　◆　◆

The original documentary was written by Maureen Marovitch, and directed by David Finch and Maureen Marovitch.

• PART FOURTEEN •

WILF CARTER AND MONTANA SLIM
The Yodelling Cowboy

When they have a Wilf Carter night in Canning, Nova Scotia, the Annapolis Valley town where the singer used to haul apples as a boy, there isn't an empty seat in the house, and most of those seats are filled with senior citizens. Wilf was born over in Port Hilford on December 18, 1904, and even though he became identified with the Prairies and the Rockies and Western cowboys, his fellow Nova Scotians still know where he really hailed from. But singers also come from as far away as Alberta to "do" Wilf Carter here, in his hometown. In the opening scene of Tom Radford's documentary life of Carter, as the yodelling Carter imitators stand up on that little stage in Canning, and wind out the old familiar prairie laments ("Oh how my lonely heart is aching tonight, for a home I long to see . . ."), you can see lips moving all over the hall as the fans silently mouth the words to the songs they know so well.

Wilf was one of seven kids. The family photographs show a lean, good-looking gang of lookalikes, all contemplating the camera with the same appraising expression. The father was a Baptist minister. It seems likely that the tall, handsome, presentable boy was intended to follow in the reverend's footsteps. Emotionally powerful hymns are an important part of Baptist worship. Wilf knew and sang them with gusto every Sunday at the compulsory services. There are echoes of them in his own music. Back in about 1916, after a Saturday night concert in that same Canning community centre had featured somebody called the Yodelling Fool, young Wilf took to yodelling his way through his barnyard chores and probably up and down the echoing valley roads. His father the preacher was not pleased. "That was not a very nice noise for a minister's son to be making."

This was a strict traditional Protestant minister's home. Reverend

Carter gathered the children each morning, had them kneel on the floor as he prayed for them, and then made each of them read aloud a chapter of the Bible before they set out on the long walk to school. Young Wilf started working for local farmers when he was twelve, harvesting, packing, and hauling to market the potatoes and apples that were the mainstay crops. If the father, as the legend has it, let him know that yodelling was an unseemly practice for a minister's son, Wilf wouldn't give it up. It is not difficult to imagine the tension in the Baptist home if the boy was slipping out of his early baritone into the yodeller's falsetto hour after hour, in house and out. Whatever the accumulated reasons for it were, when he was fifteen the conflicts became intolerable and the boy was asked, or told, to leave.

He walked the roads for a while, sleeping in ditches at first, until he found a job on John Tingley's dairy farm, milking cows and cleaning stables for 25 cents a day. That first winter he started to work the New Brunswick lumber camps. He later said that this was where he first encountered 10-cent paperback cowboy novels, which built a romantic image of the Prairies in his adolescent mind. When he saw a poster in the Canning railway station offering free transportation west for young men willing to work on the grain harvest, the lure of the prairie was irresistible, and off he went.

A boy from the Annapolis Valley would have been amazed by his first sight of an Alberta wheat farm. In the valley there were trees and hills everywhere, and until you went down to the shore and gazed out to sea — a vista that somehow never caught this boy's imagination — you wouldn't have seen anything like these endless miles of waving grain. Before long he began to work with horses, and the horse and Carter seemed made for each other. People will still tell you that Wilf Carter was a horse-whisperer long before anyone thought of the name, and it began here on the Alberta grain farms as the tall, long-boned, good-looking kid showed an aptitude for driving the horse-drawn machinery and looking after the big animals as if he had always lived among them. If the sound of the falsetto yodel bouncing off the hills of the Annapolis Valley or the walls of the parental parsonage had been irritating at home, it seems to have been at least tolerated out here on the prairies. Maybe it was even welcomed when the kid with the big, capable hands got his first guitar and began to twang away on it. He would croon the traditional "Come-all-ya's" to the guys at night, and soon put together his own rudimentary more-or-less original variants. Almost always with a refrain that let loose the gurgling high-pitched yodel that would become his trademark.

Soon he was living in a bunkhouse and riding the range on cattle farms, the wheat fields abandoned for something closer to his dime novel imaginings. Riding cattle did not pay as much as wheat farming, but it was closer to the dream. The songs he made began to tell the stories and yearn the yearnings of the guys he worked and bunked with. They were probably Alberta's very first own cowboy songs.

Tommy Hunter, who much later would build an impressive television audience for his weekly country music show on the CBC, got to know Wilf Carter well, and talks about him with a kind of affectionate reverence, well-salted with humorous observations on some of the pioneer country singer's idiosyncrasies. Hunter says,

He had the heart of a cowboy and the heart of a westerner. [But] he never forgot his roots. He had a tremendous love of the East Coast, but he was . . . a cowboy. Wilf used to have the old thumb pick. Like I said, he had powerful hands. You'd hear Wilf getting ready there, and he would start a song: "Now here's one that goes back to the early days of my recording career," and he would give a couple whacks on the strings. And he'd hit this and if it got out of tune, boy! You'd hear that. You'd see that thumb whomping those strings. And I'm not sure whether it was to blame the guitar for going out of tune, or see if he could hit it hard enough to bring it back. . . .

When he started going to the Calgary Stampede in 1927, it was both to ride broncos and to sing. This was a performer who, while he loved his music and loved to sing and to play the guitar, did not set his sights on a performing career until fairly late in the game. Unlike, say, a Bob Dylan, who seems to have wanted to be a star from the time he began to think about anything, and bent all his efforts in that direction, Wilf Carter's songwriting and his ultimate move to the professional stage grew out of the working contours and paths of his life. As he wandered from one job to another, the idea formed gradually that he might actually earn money by singing about this itinerant life with its joys and its loneliness.

Edmonton is home to the first ever public broadcaster in Canada, radio station CKUA, which went on the air from a studio at the University of Alberta in 1927 (and was privatized by the Alberta government in 1994). Its veteran programmer Brian Dunsmore said in the documentary:

> I think it is significant that Wilf Carter the entertainer didn't come about for a number of years after he hit Alberta. It took him a few years of becoming himself, becoming this man that we talk about. He's sleeping in a bunkhouse with a bunch of rough and ready men, and he's up at the crack of dawn riding horses, this Wilf Carter who was very deeply grounded in his own being. And then he starts to think about doing other things. And one of these other things is becoming an entertainer.

He would go into town on weekends and sing at community dances, just trying it out. Now it was time to test himself in a larger venue, the Stampede. He would get himself thrown off a bronc a few times, sometimes collect a modest amount of prize money, sometimes break a bone, and then, evenings, if he was in shape for it, he would seek out a dance or a beer hall, get out the guitar, give it a few whacks with that great big thumb, and sing them one of his new creations. There were lots of guys trying out their cowboy songs on the Stampede crowd. Few if any of them were really cowboys. This tall, big-boned guy was real. Even the love songs seemed real.

> Ay – yii yii yii,
> Beautiful girl on the prairies
> With eyes so blue
> And a heart so true
> She's the girl I'm going to marry.

Both the lyrics and the tunes were often pretty derivative, a characteristic of country songs that doesn't bother its fans. It was not just the songs they were coming to hear: it was the man. The Alberta disk jockey Jack Fox told us that this particular song somehow rang a bell for him when he was just a kid. "My introduction to Wilf Carter was at the age of five. That song just turned me on to country music. I've never forgotten the song. I can [still] recite . . . the first verse of it." (Which he does: *Ay – yii yii yii . . .*)

Wilf Carter began to record the stories of the living legends of Alberta. Pete Knight was a world champion bronc rider. There are dramatic photographs of him lifting off the horse as if he was being shot into outer space, one hand high in the air for balance, the other gripping the reins, the mouth wide open in a triumphant yell, the wide leather chaps ballooning out from the calves of his legs, with the word P E T E in huge white leather appliqué on each side. Knight watched Wilf doing his best in the bronco ring, and then came to hear him sing at night. He told Wilf to give up riding the broncs and concentrate on his songs, which would not kill you, after all. When Pete Knight was killed, by a horse called Duster, his funeral was one of the biggest Calgary had ever seen. Wilf Carter put it all into a song.

The musician David Wilkie, who travelled the country with Wilf years later, when he was making his "Last Roundup Tour," says, "He was singing songs about Crossfield, Pete Knight, the Calgary Stampede, and the Yoho Valley. Wilf was really putting all of that down on record. I think someday people are going to realize that is really our only Alberta folk music."

> *Come all ya young boys and lean over the rail*
> *I'll tell you the story of the dynamite trail.*
> *In Calgary Alberta . . .*

The song might become a panoramic portrait of the Stampede, with a catalogue of all the familiar elements of that annual event making up the texture of a narrative song about danger and daring. Gordon Lightfoot says that Carter had a strong influence on his own work as a balladeer, telling the mythic stories of his own land. And as Calgary theatres began to pay Carter five dollars a week to come and sing on their stages between movies, an interesting new device called the microphone began to show up. Radio was making its way across the land, perhaps nowhere more effectively than on the Prairies. Vast distances

electronically disappeared when people gathered around the huge bat-
tery-powered black-boxed ponderously dialled early sets and made
their way through the squeals and static of what sounded like the whole
universe clashing out there in the cosmic waves, until they found a
human voice or the sound of fiddles. One of the voices, Wilf Carter's,
made its way not just across the prairie spaces but also right across
Canada, where the romantic idea of the cowboy was almost a universal.

> There's a love knot in my lariat
> And it's waiting for a blue-eyed gal you bet. . . .
> When I swing my lasso
> You'll hear my yodel-ay-ee-whoo!
> There's a love knot in my lariat.

When he got a regular Friday night spot on CFCN radio the pay
was now five dollars a show. CFCN advertised itself on billboards, celebrating its amazing ten-thousand-watt signal and the fact that it was
"Locally made, Nationally known."

David Leonard, the official historian for Alberta Historic Sites,
sees that as a turning point both for Carter and also for Canada's sense
of itself.

> It was the biggest radio and most powerful broadcast station on the
> prairies. And when Wilf Carter began to broadcast over FCN this
> was one of our own. This was a western Canadian cowboy singing
> music that relates to us, about us, to us. . . . Western Canadians . . .
> saying to Eastern Canadians, "We aren't a pale imitation of you.
> We are Western Canadians. With our own . . . culture and our own
> music. And . . . the ethos of the cowboy became the most dramatic
> symbol of that.

The Trail Riders of the Canadian Rockies was a tourist organization operating out of Banff. Adventurous and well-off Americans
would pay twenty dollars a day to ride the breathtaking mountain
trails, bathe in icy streams, eat camp meals around a campfire, and
sleep in tents. Early film footage of those rides through the spectacular
scenery shows the excited, wide-eyed faces of these visitors. The Trail
Riders had heard him on the radio. Dennis Orr is a past president of
that company. He told us,

The original sponsorship of the Trail Riders . . . was done by the CPR. They needed people both to entertain and to be cowboys, and Wilf Carter fit both those categories. . . . A tremendous number of his original songs (the only ones that he did) were actually written in those trail ride camps, to entertain the people.

Photographs from the 1930 season, taken around the campfire in the evening, show many of those people holding song sheets and singing along with a tall good-looking guy in a cowboy hat, a guitar in his big, spreading hands.

Oh how my lonely heart is aching tonight

For a home I long to see . . .

In my Blue — OOO Canadian Rockies . . .

People who are too young to have heard the long, yearning wail of a steam train whistle in the night as they drift off to sleep in a sleeping bag are missing a sound remembered in many of the Carter songs. The painful longing for home and loving arms, always central to country music, is the theme of dozens of songs.

He was bo-o-orn in Crawwwssfield Alberta

And he rode on a strawberry Roan.

I remember my own older brother John, sometime in the late 1930s, bringing home a ukulele and sitting on his bed with mournful eyes, twanging away and crooning out cowboy songs, and trying a yodel or two. I did not know it then but I do now; they were the songs of Wilf Carter.

There was only one summer of that Trail Riders idyll for Wilf. By the time he was back in town and the snow began to dust the foothills, the Depression had made itself cruelly felt all across the Prairies. David Leonard said that grain prices were down to 35 cents a bushel

for number one wheat! Too low to make it viable for most western farmers to ship their grain to the Lakehead. The railway was seen to be maybe the culprit in all this, as the freight rates were just a little too high. By the same token the railways seemed to be a sort of lifeline to freedom. You knew things were terrible where you were right now, they may not be much better in the next community, but it couldn't be any worse.

465

But it did get worse. Suddenly there was no work for Wilf in Alberta. He tried fishing on the west coast and farming in Saskatchewan. He learned that his father had died, and if he had dreamed of reconciliation, as the songs sometimes suggest, now it was too late. His daughter Sheila Dukarm says that he just sat on the street corner in Calgary and sang with his hat out on the pavement. Like Woody Guthrie and Jimmie Rogers in the United States, he was singing of the lost generation, the lost dreams. People who only had a few cents for a cup of coffee were putting five or ten of those desperate cents into Wilf Carter's hat. He said he would go into a restaurant and get some crackers and a cup of hot water and put ketchup into the cup to make a free soup. Foxy John at Radio D says he thinks that tough as things were, Carter may have been better off than a bricklayer or a carpenter, because "people would always throw a nickel in your hat."

In 1933 you could buy a hamburger on a bun for 10 cents.

Somebody at RCA Victor Records in Montreal heard Wilf on the radio, tracked him down where he was doing odd jobs on a ranch somewhere in the foothills, and asked him to come to Montreal for a meeting. There was a first-class ticket, the meals were paid for, the beds were warm and comfortable. He had probably — like so many out-of-work men all over the continent — ridden trains by climbing up to the roof of a cattle car somewhere out in the yards, or hanging on underneath "riding the rods." Now he was going in style. When he got to Montreal they showed him into a recording studio. This would be Canada's first cowboy song on disk. He recorded "Swiss Moonlight Lullaby," and "The Capture of Albert Johnson," a narrative ballad about the "Mad Trapper" who had recently been shot to death in the snow by the Mounties.[17] Then Canadian Pacific sent him to New York to perform on a two-week inaugural cruise of their huge new liner the *Empress of Britain*. Wilf cracked that the ship was so big it took him three days to find his stateroom, and he had to camp out in the dining hall. While he was at sea "Swiss Moonlight Lullaby" was released in the United States

17. For an account of the manhunt and shooting of the "Mad Trapper" see *The Canadians: Biographies of a Nation*, Volume I, Part Eleven, "Distant Skies." It's the story of pioneer bush pilot Wop May who found the fleeing killer from the air.

as well as Canada and was an instant hit. Tommy Hunter's eyes crinkled with delight when he recounted what happened next.

This record was so popular, somebody from RCA ran down to meet the boat and they had this great big limousine for him. Wilf kept looking at him and he said, "Get in," and Wilf looked back at him and walked away. . . . "We're from RCA!" And he said, "I don't care where you're from, get out of here," and kept right on walking by them.

RCA signed him to a contract and told him to go back to the Rockies *and* keep on writing songs. Now both those brittle ten-inch wax 78-RPM disks, and the increasingly popular and necessary radio were bringing Wilf Carter's voice into the lives of Canadians from coast to coast. In 1937 CBS radio called from New York. They signed him up with Lucky Strike Cigarettes, and the newspaper ads for the regular morning radio program show him puffing a Lucky, something he did only for the photographer. Something else he did, and does not seem to have been troubled by, was to change his name. Why some CBS executive would think that Montana Slim would play any better than Wilf Carter who had already made a continental hit with "Swiss Moonlight Lullaby" is not clear, but Wilf went along with it, and so there are millions of Americans who know that haunting tenor twang as the voice of Montana Slim while the same songs for Canadians are unmistakably Wilf Carter's.

Oh what I'd give if I could be home tonight
With the sweetheart who's waiting for me.

Tommy Hunter says he believes that it was Carter records that kept RCA Victor's Canadian company from going broke during the Depression. Important as recording had become for him, David Wilkie, who played with Carter's road show towards the end, says that Wilf refused to fuss over the process.

Nowadays they spend millions of dollars and they have overdubs and thirty-four tracks where they have the banjo player come in at noon and the steel guitar player at three. Wilf . . . just hated that. He didn't like to rehearse. He'd just go in and say, "I got twelve songs, turn on the tape machine. I'm gonna be here for as long as it

*takes me to do them once, and you'd better get them down 'cause
that's my new album." So it was like bronc riding for Wilf, recording was. Like getting it on for eight seconds and riding it . . . and
going home. That's the way he was.*

Recording had made Wilf Carter prosperous in the midst of a
Depression that had dropped land prices to the floor. He came back to
Alberta in 1939 and bought a substantial ranch to bring his new wife
to, a New Yorker named Bobbie Bryan. They agreed that it was time to
start a family and settle down, but it must have been a shock for a professional woman from Manhattan (Bobbie was a registered nurse) to
suddenly find herself helping to run a grain farm, with the threshing
team showing up at five o'clock in the morning ready for the big breakfast that would send them out to the fields. Wilf got a broadcasting contract that would take him into Calgary once a week for a show; Bobbie
could get her hair done, take in a movie, get at least a faint touch of the
city life that she missed.

But the worst thing was the car crash. Driving in Montana they
had a head-on collision with a truck that had crossed the centre line,
and after several operations Wilf still had to walk with a brace and live
with constant pain. For years he couldn't face up to recording. But
there were two new elements in his life that seem to have been the
determining factors in getting him and Bobbie through that rough
period — their daughters Sheila and Carol. The Carters were in good
shape financially. Even though Wilf was not recording, his records kept
selling. In 1947 they hit two million. Wilf began to feel well enough to
think about going back on the road. The girls were learning the songs
around the fireplace at night. A handsome pair of bright-eyed blond
kids, they could belt out the lines with gusto as their dad's big thumb
whacked the guitar. In 1949, when it was time to let the world know
that Montana Slim and Wilf Carter were both back on stage, he took the
girls with him as part of the show.

They started with a cross-Canada tour, playing towns of any size,
from Vancouver Island, up to Whitehorse and Yellowknife, back down
through Alberta, across the prairies and the woodlands, right out to
the east coast and then by boat over to the newest province,

Newfoundland, which had joined Confederation just that year.

Carol Cooper, Wilf's younger daughter, said,

I must have been maybe five or six years old and we were on the stage. Daddy was singing a song and I pulled at his pant leg. He stopped singing and said, "What's the matter?" I said, "You made a mistake." He said, "Okay. We'll just have to start right over again." So we started from the beginning, and . . . everybody laughed, and of course I didn't realize that I was causing a commotion, but that was part of us being together as a family on the stage.

There are plenty of showbusiness stories about the terrible tensions of being on the road with the family in tow, but from the geniality of the photographs and the chuckled memories of the surviving members of what Wilf Carter called "The Family Show With Folks You Know," it appears that this was as happy and productive a time — for all of them — as they would ever have.

They played some stops that looked like a crossroads in the middle of nowhere. Ken Reynolds, the Ottawa promoter who put the tour together, talked about pulling into Minden, in the Haliburton Highlands of Ontario:

Wilf noticed a sign, "Population 260." And he [said] what was I trying to do to him! Even if everybody came there wouldn't be enough — even though I was paying, it was coming out of my pocket.

They needn't have worried. The rural population for miles around turned up that night in Minden, as they did in similar small towns across the country. Ken Reynolds said that they had to stop the show several times as the people kept crowding in by the hundreds, to reposition the loudspeakers so that everyone could hear. Wilf's daughter Sheila Dukarm said,

By six o'clock at night this town had thousands of people coming in and you were just wondering where do all these people hide! I can remember Mom is trying to take tickets, tear off tickets and take money, and there's money everywhere, and she looks up at these Mounties and says, "I've got to have some help down here." And he says, "You don't ever have to worry here, nobody will ever touch one of those dollar bills." He says, "Let them fall on the floor. No one will ever pick them up." And nobody ever did.

Singer Bobby Wright, who toured with the family, said,

I always looked forward to it because it was like working with an encyclopaedia. He had . . . stories about every town you would go into. One place in Ontario, we'd pull in there and he said, "I remember working a rodeo here once. They didn't have a stage set up. There was so many people . . . I had to climb up the telephone pole and hook a belt around of me and hang off of the pole and sing to the people."

He tried a few other things. Perhaps it was Bobbie who said, after a few years of this touring, Look, you're getting on. Maybe we could settle down — but to something a little less demanding than a ranch. They bought property in a Florida orange grove and built a big motel, with TV in the rooms and a huge sign across the building, THE WILF CARTER MOTOR HOTEL. Not Montana Slim; there were lots of retired Canadians in Florida.

Television had come to Canada, and Tommy Hunter soon had a regular show of his own. Wilf was one of the first of the early performers to make a guest appearance. For the hip young television producers, he was already somewhere back there in the past — even though the Hunter production team was turning out a country music show. "None of the producers, frankly, wanted him on the show," Hunter says now, with a puzzled look. Had he gone on too long?

"He never became . . . hip," says musicologist Richard Flohil:

Wilf was the old geezer, you know, who came on and smiled and sang the old songs. . . . The young kids never got onto him in the way they got on to Stompin' Tom Connors. Who would tell you to your face that Wilf Carter was the greatest thing that ever happened to country music. . . . Maybe [Wilf's] music was just what it was for its time.

Another famous country and folk singer, Ian Tyson, suggested to us that Wilf had, in fact, gone on too long. "As a senior citizen," Tyson said, "I'm allowed to voice that." But the reality is that wherever he went, they came. The people. As he got older, so did they. They were coming to hear a man who had sung to them when they didn't have enough to eat and didn't know how they were going to clothe the kids. But if they were coming to hear a memory, they stayed to listen to a friend. How could he stop doing that? It was nourishment for him. It is clear from the bits of film and video that survive, and from the thousands of photographs, that going among the crowd and shaking hands, and signing autographs, was not a chore. He is beaming in those photographs. He answered all his mail by hand. We found people who had written to him regularly, over the years, and said they could always count on a reply. In 1985, when he was eighty-one, the CBC broadcast his inauguration into the Canadian Music Hall of Fame. At the awards shows they were introducing him as a surprising survivor out of the past, almost as if a dinosaur had unexpectedly come to life and was still among us. There is a video clip of him performing in a seniors' home. Like those Nova Scotian oldtimers listening to Wilf Carter imitators in the community hall in Canning, Nova Scotia, the audience knows the words. Wilf tells them a story. He had been playing at another seniors' home:

> *I looks over and there's this little guy in a wheelchair. "Come here," he says. So I got up real close to him, and he says, "How long have you been in here?" And I said, "Not very long." And he says, "I ain't seen you around." I said, "No." He says, "I don't like your singing." And I said, "I'm sorry sir." "I don't like it," he says. "I'll tell you something. I don't know if you know him or not, but that Wilf Carter can sing." I looked at him and I said, "You know him?" And he said, "No, but I've got lots of his records and we play the dickens out of them. You never met him?" And I said, "No." And he said, "I don't think you're going to go far in singing."*

Tommy Hunter went to see him do some of those seniors' shows, when he was now past eighty.

> *He was getting very hard of hearing. That bothered him. . . . There were people that . . . just loved to come and sit and talk to him. They would be . . . pouring out their soul, about the first time I met you, you were so kind to me, you signed my autograph and I've carried it around with me. And they'd pull out an autograph signature. And it used to bother Wilf because he couldn't hear.*

There had to be an end. He decided on a final concert. He chose Alberta, of course. Trochu, Alberta, population 907. It was May 30, 1994. Wilf Carter would be ninety later that year. He had never learned to read a note of music, but he had written the words and music to six hundred songs and sold most of them. He was in the Music Hall of Fame in both Canada and the United States. He had sold millions and millions of records. There were people all over the continent who knew his songs, often without knowing they were his, they had always been there, they were part of the country music landscape. At Trochu he introduced his daughter Carol's daughter Bobbie, his youngest grandchild, who had never seen him in concert. He brought her up on the stage with him. People who were there say that while the applause was deafening and never seemed to stop, the tears in everyone's eyes are what they remember most vividly.

Brian Edwards, tour manager for that last concert, said he sobbed along with everyone else. "He put his hands up on the guitar, like this, and he said, 'Well folks. Me and the old girl are gonna have one last tune. And here it is.' It was called 'Have a Nice Day.'"

And at the end Wilf said, "I'm gonna unstring my guitar." He never played it again.

The Calgary Herald. *December 17, 1996*
Wilf Carter, the yodelling cowboy, who was Canada's first cowboy star, died Thursday night in Scottsdale, Arizona, at the age of 91.

♦   ♦   ♦

The original documentary was written and directed by Tom Radford.

PART FIFTEEN

GRANT MacEWAN
A People's Prince

It was one night sometime in the mid 1970s. Henry the vice-regal chauffeur was driving the lieutenant governor back to Edmonton from an official ceremony somewhere or other, he doesn't remember *that* detail any more, when his honour said, "Henry, pull over." He wanted to get out and look at the stars. They were spectacular that night, as they so often are in a clear Alberta sky.

The lieutenant governor and the official chauffeur stood there in the cool summer night and looked at the display together. After a while his honour asked the chauffeur to get the sleeping bags out of the trunk, he wanted to lie down and *really* look at those brilliant lights in the sky. And that night the Queen's representative in Alberta, and his official chauffeur, slept on the open ground under the stars.

What kind of man, wearing the official trappings of vice-regal office, would do that? Not new to public office and public note, he had been an alderman for the city of Calgary, and later mayor of that city. He'd been head of the Alberta Liberal Party, an unsuccessful candidate for the federal Parliament, a professor of agronomy, and a broadcaster. Before he died, he would have published fifty-five books, novels, biographies, textbooks on agriculture, and histories of a dozen different aspects of his beloved West. Where did he come from?

His name was Grant MacEwan, and he began and ended almost precisely with the beginning and end of the twentieth century, a farm boy from Brandon, Manitoba. A farm boy who kept a diary. Almost from the beginning words and the making of them on paper began to take him into orbits away out beyond the fence lines. But his feet and his hands never lost the feel of the soil, and his spirit never left it for a moment. Animals great and small, plants of every kind and especially trees, were a spiritual necessity. He started a conservation movement on the Canadian prairies at a time when many laughed at the idea. He planted trees where they were not supposed to grow. There are people today who will show you a tree that came out of the trunk of Grant MacEwan's car one day, not much more than a seedling, and they will say, as they stand in the shade of its spreading branches, "This is Dr. MacEwan."

He was born before the first airplane flew, and he died long after the computer had become entrenched as a way of life. He grew up amongst cattle and hogs and fields of grain; before he died he would preside over the deliberations of governments, teach generations of university students, and softly leave a world that scarcely resembled the one he had been born into. His dazzlingly beautiful and mischievously humorous granddaughter, Fiona Foran, chuckled at the camera as she said of her beloved grandfather in those last years (and in saying it set the tone for this biographical documentary), "A lot of those [new technological] things he found . . . incomprehensible. Things he couldn't really understand, and why should he? You know, when he was nearly 100, at the turn of . . . the millennium, [well, he'd say] 'Bugger it!'"

His mother Bertha Grant was a serious Presbyterian from Brandon, in fact from six generations of hard, determined Nova Scotia Scots lately arrived in Manitoba. She was strong-willed, judgmental, radiantly beautiful. She had just graduated from Brandon Nursing College the year before she met Alex MacEwan, a tall rangy hired hand with big ideas who had come to work on her father's farm. This was also a determined, confident man. *His* granddaughter — and there is a remarkable sense of cohesive family about this clan — Alex MacEwan's granddaughter Heather MacEwan Foran, tells a story about Alex, a "family story" which you know, as you hear it, is a MacEwan way of telling you what the family values are based on.

"He was coming back across the country by train," she said. "And the train was stuck . . . in the snow, and they didn't know when they were going to . . . get out of this snowbank. And my grandfather walked the hundred miles home. . . . He had only the clothes on his back . . . dress-up clothes and his little satchel . . . I think he had a sandwich . . . in the satchel."

So Alex and Bertha got married, Grant was born, and Alex got a farm of his own. Times were good and he liked to experiment. His son grew up in a universe that prized risk and innovation. It seems that Grant caught his love of animals from his father, and learned that how you cared for a horse was as important (because of the relationship) as was the labour the animal provided. They had prize Clydesdale horses and Black Angus cattle. Every year they would show at the Winnipeg Fair, and check out the amazing new machinery, *some of it actually self-powered — by gasoline-burning engines!* — that was changing the face of agriculture.

Alex MacEwan had a business drive in him, and when the Great War in Europe began to drive grain prices up, he seized the financial moment, took his unexpected profits, invested them in a fire-extinguisher business in Brandon, and left the farm.

Bad call, as it turned out. During a demonstration of the new products, the building that housed his business and his inventory caught fire, and for all the dozens of fire extinguishers lying around Alex could not get the blaze under control. The building and its contents were destroyed, and so was the business. There was no insurance.

There were still homesteads in Saskatchewan to be picked up just for the asking. The MacEwans took up an empty piece of land near Melfort, dug a well, lived in a neighbour's barn while they built their own place, and started all over again. Grant would later recall how his mother frugally turned down the flame in the lamp when the family knelt for their evening devotions. There was no point burning up kerosene when everyone's eyes were closed in prayer. That's what things were like in those early days in Saskatchewan. The frugality was a characteristic Grant MacEwan would inherit, and later be accused of penny pinching. When he was mayor of Calgary he walked or took the bus to work, leaving the official car in the official garage because it was just, well, *extravagant*, to use a car when the bus service was good and walking was good.

But that was much later.

They did rebuild a life on that Melfort farm, but there was a painful sacrifice in it for the bright, inquisitive, book-hungry boy.

Needed in the barns and on the fields, Grant had to quit school at the end of grade eight. About then he started keeping a diary.

We still have some of those early journals. They record the weight of cattle he took to the fair or the auctions; the breeding of a prize steer; the sinking of a great ocean liner; the boy's craving for a dish of ice cream; the barn-raising bees where the whole neighbourhood would gather to pole up into position the sides of a huge barn and get the roof on, all in a single weekend; the time when a neighbour was so sick he had to be taken to hospital, and the neighbours carried him the whole way (Grant said it was fifty miles) in a litter.

Now he was well into his teens. He began to discover girls. He told his biographer, Donna van Hauff, about Mamie Argyll, whom he met at a box lunch social. The boys would prospect the box lunches on display and bid on them. The lunch you bought brought with it the girl who had made it, and she became your date for the evening. Grant and Mamie went for a sleigh ride that night under the buffalo skins. Grant would later say with a grin, according to Donna van Hauff, "Everything I needed to know about women I learned from Mamie Argyll."

Another young woman, his cousin Willa from Ontario, came for a visit and changed his life in a different way. Willa was from Guelph. There was a new institution of learning there, the Ontario Agricultural College (OAC), and they were teaching a new kind of science called agronomy. Grant did not want to leave the farm, exactly, says his son-in-law Alberta historian Max Foran, "But [he wanted] to go beyond the farm." He sensed that farming was just as susceptible to the great advances wrought by science as were the more spectacular fields of weapons, transportation, and energy, and became convinced his future lay in bringing science and farming together.

It was the fall of 1921. The country was relatively tranquil, prosperous, and optimistic with the Great War nearly three years behind it, the boys back from the front, the myth of permanent peace very much in the air, and a widespread assumption of new possibilities and horizons. Grant MacEwan emptied out his small bank account, took the $63 the college required for registration (several thousand dollars in today's money), and enrolled in the Bachelor of Science program at Guelph. The amiable idiosyncrasies for which he is fondly remembered produced at least one story about the train trip east. Grant slept in the nude, did not own the pyjamas he would later need for a college initiation parade, and often walked in his sleep. You can see it coming. The story says that partway to Toronto he woke up in the middle of the sleeping car corridor, naked as a jaybird, the object of inquisitive glances from behind the curtains of neighbouring bunks. He was obliged to climb the awkward little ladder in front of all this scrutiny to regain his upper bunk. If it is true it seems likely, from what we learn of Grant MacEwan as his life story unfolds, that he would have been as amused by it as everyone else. It is also conceivable that he made it up to entertain his friends, although he was known to be a truthful man. But the most significant thing about the story is that his friends and relatives love to tell it, and tell it with affection, not derision.

He was a striking kid, six and a half feet tall, a glistening head of rich dark hair, lots of it, and blue eyes, people said, that "cut through a room." He was in love with horses and they said he could drive a team with scarcely a tug on the reins. He was a quick student. He thought for himself and spoke his mind. This may have irritated some of his teachers but seems to have won the respect of most because there was no hint of hypocrisy or falseness. The cockiness and self-assurance were authentic, not, as in many young men, a mask for insecurities and inadequacies. He played an outstanding game of basketball. Years later the basketball coach, by then an old man, came to visit him in Edmonton, and said to Grant's son-in-law Max Foran, "Did you know that 'Shorty' here was the best centre in Canada?"

In the summers during his long stay at the Ontario Agricultural College he went down to Toronto in the summer breaks and sold farm produce out of the back of an old Model T Ford. He began to understand the demands of the small entrepreneur and to respect that trade. In 1925 he was awarded a position on the college livestock judging team, and that winter, at the Royal Winter Fair in Toronto, his team won the Canadian intercollegiate championship.

Another young man might have been lured to stay close to the lights and the excitement of the big city. He loved theatre and acted in comedies, and found the cultural life of the city very attractive. But the Manitoba boy had become a son of Saskatchewan, and Saskatchewan for all its severity and challenge — or perhaps because of it — seems to inspire unquenchable loyalties in many of its children. When he got his Master of Science degree — the first degree of any kind in seven generations of farm families — he headed for home.

The next few years were hard work and career building. He took up a post in the University of Saskatchewan's extension department, and set about establishing and spreading scientific and verifiable agricultural methods in a society built on old traditions and not inclined to experiment. This is not a kid any more. He was twenty-six when he started the university job, and while he was far from socially inept or withdrawn, he seems not to have felt any pressing interest in marriage or starting a family. But after a few years he met Phyllis Klein, from Churchbridge, who was in the cast with him in a goofy slapstick show called The Pickle King. Grant played the eponymous lead. When they were married in Saskatoon in June of 1935, the federal minister of agriculture was a guest at the wedding. This was thought to be a mark of distinction.

As he went around the province spreading ideas and offering counsel, he built a reputation for intolerance of sloppy or careless husbandry. Son-in-law Max Foran recalls going with Grant to visit a farmer friend "and the hay was on the ground, and the guy was inside watching a baseball game. . . . 'That hay is on the ground, it's not raining . . . how dare he!' . . . 'Well,' I said, 'maybe there's a good game on.' He said that didn't matter. This guy had no *right* to leave the hay on the ground!"

This illustrates some of the attitudes, not untouched by the Presbyterian part of his background, that Grant MacEwan brought to his profession. The farmer was not just taking a living out of the land, he was a *custodian*, a *warder*. He had rights as an individual, but they were balanced by obligations, not just towards other citizens and the law, but also to the land and to what it produced. Anyone who did not respect those rights and act accordingly lost the respect of Grant

MacEwan. He knew that the university was seen as an elitist institu-tion, and the farmers distrusted it because of the academic disdain for the judgment and opinions of the hands-on guy in the barn. He believed that by beating up and down the province month after month, bringing to farmers ideas they could use, ideas that would improve their production (and their custodial roles) that he could build a bridge between science and tradition. And he felt that he gained ground in that respect. The farmers began to listen to the scientific ideas, his col-leagues' respect for the knowledge of the working farmer rose sub-stantially, and the university was able to learn from their experience. Each side was listening to the other more openly.

In the mid 1930s the heady prosperity of the postwar decade was forgotten. The Depression that was crushing North America and the world was literally terrifying in Saskatchewan where a sustained drought was causing whole farms to blow away in clouds of dust. Livestock was starving to death, farmers were dying of despair, and there was year after year of crop failure, with wheat yields averaging less than three bushels an acre. Grant put his agronomical research training to work and researched drought-resistant wild plants. Russian thistle not only survived, but it had also helped hold the soil in place. This weed (*Salsola pestifera* or *S. tragi* or *S. iberni*) is popularly known as tumbleweed because it breaks off at ground level and rolls in the wind, sometimes for miles. Farmers and ranchers hate it, as it sharply reduces crop yields. But in this cropless landscape it was surviving, and, amaz-ingly, hungry cattle could eat it, metabolize it. The Russian thistle pro-gram was a lifesaver.

A second experiment was less so. Grant MacEwan loved horses, but horses were dying and being slaughtered compassionately — and the people were out of meat. Grant knew that there would be terrific resistance from horse-loving Saskatchewanians to the very idea of eat-ing horsemeat, so he concocted an uncharacteristically devious scheme. He brought sandwiches to a university cocktail party, and did not tell anyone that half of them were made with horsemeat. He kept this quiet until the sandwiches had all been consumed. Then, still with-out saying why, he took a poll as to which sandwiches people liked best. It is not recorded how he distinguished between the two, but when the poll declared the two types of sandwich to be equally popular, he revealed the secret. And, says Calgary history librarian Jennifer Bobrovitz, "There were people who never, ever forgave him for that."

He began diligently to preach the interaction and interdependence of living things, the way in which vegetation secured the soil, bacteria fed the plants, decayed matter fed the bacteria, trees cleansed the air. Even "noxious" animals were dear to him. His daughter Heather said that when she was a kid her parents acquired a pair of baby skunks: someone had killed the mother and brought her two babies to Grant out of curiosity. Grant got out his scalpel and some anaesthetic from his veterinarian studies kit, descented the kits, and named them This and That.

Grant adored trees. "He loved tiny things," Heather's daughter Fiona says, her eyes gleaming. "Guinea pigs, gerbils, mice . . . animals like that are often maligned, you know . . . they're vermin, they're pests. . . . Little creatures were . . . the underdogs of the animal world; so Grant was their special friend. . . . There was the romantic aspect of trees and how lovely they were; but then there was the very practical . . . you know, on a farm you plant trees for windbreaks . . . for food, apples, berries. . . Trees were necessary for oxygen exchange. . . . So Grant was always a voice for animals and for trees and the environment, long before it was in vogue to be that way."

It was right in the blackest part of this prairie disaster period that he became poignantly aware that not only were land and farms and livelihoods being ruined, but also that the preoccupation with disaster was leading people to forget their stories, their legacy. On June 10, 1937, he went to Eaton's and bought a typewriter. He would write the story of the Canadian West as he knew and loved it. He went to the CBC and sold pieces to the old radio Department of Talks and Public Affairs. His first one was called "How Horses Came to Western Canada." Then he did a very popular series of essays, "Sodbusters," very personal pieces about his boyhood on the homesteading frontier. One of the most heroic characters in these sketches was his father, Alex MacEwan.

But Alex and Bertha were dead now; within a year of leaving the farm they were both gone.

By the end of World War II he had a prairie-wide reputation, and his daughter Heather had just started to school when he got a call from Winnipeg. They offered him the position of dean of agriculture at the University of Manitoba. It was too good to resist, and even if he was leaving Saskatchewan, well, he *had* been born in the adjoining province, so in a way he was going home. Not long after he took up his new post, the worst flood in Canadian history hit Winnipeg. There are photographs in the papers of Grant MacEwan saving the university's pigs and sheep. He spent night after night up on the dikes with the citizens, piling up sandbags, patrolling for breaks, taking the midnight to six a.m. shift and then putting in a day's work before he caught a short nap and headed back to the floodwaters for the midnight watch.

A man whose view of his own integrity and rightness is as serene and confident as this man's appears to have been does not escape envy and even hostility. The citizens may have admired Grant's pictures in the papers during the flood, but some eyebrows at the university were raised, not with admiration. Some colleagues thought that it looked as though MacEwan was actually *seeking* the publicity.

He began to realize that he had better watch his back, and it was probably at that point that he began to think of the importance of politics, negotiation, compromise, and the need to take time, to plod, to not expect everyone to instantly see your truth. Now he was better known than the president of the University of Manitoba. He recognized that there was a risky imbalance of reputations. But if these rumblings of disapproval were sharpening his political sensibility, they may also have caused him enough unrest and dissatisfaction with the university authorities to start him thinking about alternatives to an academic career. When a by-election came up in his old hometown of Brandon, he somewhat imprudently dived in. Imprudently because his opponent was a native son and a skilled campaigner, Walter Dinsdale, later to be a prominent and popular minister in the Diefenbaker Conservative governments of 1957 to 1963. Walter Dinsdale just ploughed poor MacEwan into the dirt.

So it was another turning point. The university had let him know that his political candidacy was not acceptable. There was no career protection then for parliamentary candidates, as there is now. Even before the election they brusquely told him he would not be welcome back in the dean's office. And so the day after he was defeated he packed his bags, headed out to Alberta, and took a public relations job with the Canadian Beef Producers' Association. A bit ironic for a vegetarian whose motto was "You don't eat your friends."

He and Phyllis bought land along the slopes rising to the Rockies, at Priddis. He would say that he intended to farm there, but Phyllis knew better; she knew he had caught the disease called Public Life, endemic wherever democracy is practised, and that he couldn't keep away from that public, from the attention, the limelight, the society, the argument, the turmoil, the chance to make a difference.

She was right. In 1953 Grant went after a seat on the Calgary city council, as alderman, and won it. He was almost immediately a source of confusion and dismay to many of his new colleagues at city hall. When a petition came around to ban prostitutes in the neighbourhood where he lived, he said, "These people are my friends!" He would meet them late at night when he walked home from the office and they were working the streets. He had no difficulty with the profession they pursued. They were citizens. He thought the petitioners stuffy and constipated. What they thought of him is not difficult to guess.

Now the provincial Liberals came after him. They supposed he was one of them, at least in spirit; he had after all run as a Liberal in the Brandon by-election. Would he consider leading the not very healthy party? It had long been in the Alberta political shade of the Social Credit Party, the bizarrely successful invention of the evangelist William Aberhart.[18] Founded ostensibly to carry out the economic fantasies of a British fascist named Major C.W. Douglas, the party had somehow survived the hostility of the local press (which it had tried to legislate into silence), and its failure to deliver anything resembling rational policies. It had grasped the anxiety of prairie Albertans in those dark days of the thirties, appealing to their superstitions and

18. See Part Three, "Bible Bill," in *The Canadians: Biographies of a Nation*, Volume I.

promising divine intervention. Aberhart's successor as party leader and premier, Ernest Manning, a balanced and far more attractive politician, was still seen by some Albertans as having a pipeline to the Lord. The Social Credit Party had brought great prosperity to Alberta, said one farmer. New Liberal leader Grant MacEwan asked if it weren't possible that the discovery of oil and gas had a lot to do with that prosperity. To which the farmer is said to have rejoined that the Good Lord put the oil and gas in the ground in answer to Mr. Manning's prayers. Once again there is some difficulty in distinguishing between legend and reality when Grant MacEwan's friends and family are talking about this extraordinary teacher, writer, and politician. Max Foran says that MacEwan, when he began to write the stories of The West, consciously and deliberately began to build myth. Myth was needed; there was not enough Canadian myth. Myths were what held a people together, said MacEwan.

"We as a nation are not myth builders," Foran said to us. "And that's part of our problem with identity, I think. See, he built the myth, the Western Canada myth . . . through his writings and his love of the land. . . . He built the myth . . . and he *was* the myth."

For all the human encounter and bustle and attention of the political game in mid-century Alberta, it is possible that during this period (and perhaps even constitutionally) Grant MacEwan was a lonely man. His biographer Donna van Hauff says so. She attributes it to his being out there in public, responding to groups and pressures and policies eighteen hours a day instead of playing with his daughters or spending time with Phyllis. His son-in-law and adoring granddaughters don't talk that way, however; and it will not be possible to write or talk objectively about a man of such presence until those personal connections and memories have receded a bit.

And perhaps it does not matter. Lonely or not, he gave of himself, hugely. In return he was loved and hated, admired and despised. When Harry Hayes relinquished the mayor's chain of office to go into federal politics in 1963, he campaigned successfully to move Grant into the empty office. "Hayseed Wins Mayoralty" is what the *Calgary Herald* wrote, and when the official press release described the new chief magistrate as "lean and lanky," one reporter said it should have read "mean and cranky." They said he was a penny pincher. He left the city's black Chrysler limousine in the garage and walked to work or took the bus. Walking into town before sunrise one day he was stopped by a suspicious cop, who looked at the ID and gasped something like "Holy God, I've just pinched the mayor!" The thrift of the bus appealed to him, and so did the company. He talked to everyone, and reported on his gleanings to his colleagues.

And he started writing again. Out of this period came books on the Blood Chief Tatanga Manni, Louis Riel's pioneering grandmother Maria Ann Gaboury, Nigger John Ware the Black Cowboy, *Eye Opener* Bob Edwards the journalist,[19] a clutch of characters whose individuality and slightly contrary Alberta spirits he found companionable and worthy of recounting. He loved to read aloud. Fiona talks about his reading poetry with tears streaming down his cheeks. It was not just the myths of his own making that moved him deeply.

Heather went off to Australia to teach, and came back with Max Foran in tow, and in the spring of 1963 they married. Soon Fiona and then Lynwynn were born, and the Gramp doted on them. He still worked dawn to dusk. A few years later, at the age of seventy, he decided that the house needed an addition, and that he would build it himself, by hand.

"Of course he had done this," Heather told the camera, "many times, on the prairie, with his dad. So we started by digging the foundation with a shovel, putting all the dirt in the back of my truck, hauling the dirt up into the field, dumping it, coming back for another load. And this went on, of course, for months. Because this was a big . . . eight hundred square feet . . . and we were eight feet down!"

Soon after this a phone call came that would, in a way, bring us back to the start of this chapter. In 1963 the Progressive Conservatives under Prime Minister John Diefenbaker lost their grip on the national confidence, and the Liberal leader Lester B. Pearson squeaked into power with a fragile minority government. Alberta has always been a tough sell for the Liberals. Pearson needed a popular and attention-

19. See Part Ten of this volume.

getting appointment. He phoned Grant MacEwan. Be our lieutenant governor, he proposed. It was a pretty surprising appointment to most; but probably not to the appointee, who always took everything in his stride.

So now this stoic-looking tall Scots Canadian with the stiff little bit of a moustache and the straight back and the thrifty habits is the Queen's representative. How would he be? The stories began to circulate. He was soon going around switching off lights in Government House to save money, and Phyllis went around after him turning them on again. People outside saw this processional dance of lights in the windows of the official residence.

"He pushed the office to the limit," Max Foran told us in his engaging Aussie twang. "He set a pace that no one [could] keep up . . . he showed how an elitist position that is window dressing could be translated into a viable political function. . . . He does for the lieutenant governorship what he had done for the university. He takes that bloody thing to the people like no one ever could."

He opened the New Year's levy to women. It is hard to believe that in the second half of the twentieth century there was a public function like this, in the populist province of Alberta, from which women were excluded. But Grant MacEwan put an end to that absurdity. When Phyllis was not well enough to attend public functions, he took Heather with him instead. He brought his granddaughters into the legislative building's cafeteria and bought them every cake and goodie they pointed to. He kept cookies in a jar on his desk and pressed them on people, including Pat Halligan-Baker, his new secretary.

As she remembers it, "He would say, 'Now Miss Pat, have a cookie.' And I would say, 'Your honour, I can't spend [all] day coming into your office having two or three cookies.' And he would say, 'Woman! Have a cookie!'"

Party leader Peter Lougheed's Alberta Conservatives finally beat out the long-reigning Social Credit government in 1971, but the new young premier forgot that he had an obligation to the vice-regal office.

"I heard his voice as he came into my office. He said, 'Is he in?' And . . . I thought, Oh my gosh, I've forgotten. It's my responsibility . . .

to review the cabinet with . . . the representative of Her Majesty. He said, 'You know, I'm supposed to see your list before tomorrow.' And I said, 'Oh I know, your honour, and I'm really embarrassed about that.' And he looked at the list."

Remember this is a Tory premier meeting a long-committed Liberal, who by one of the elegant quirks of our parliamentary tradition stays in office at the pleasure of the federal government, and has the power to name a new premier should death or any other misadventure remove the existing premier.

"He didn't make any suggestions for change," Premier Lougheed told us. "But he made comments about it that were helpful to me then and in the future. . . . He was a good mentor . . . we would have our periodic meetings where the leader of the government can go down the hall and consult with the representative of Her Majesty, and I was very very fortunate to have a Grant MacEwan down the hall."

The graciousness and wisdom went hand in hand with the idiosyncrasies, and perhaps, in that tall personality, they were the same thing. He still loved to work with his hands, especially in wood. For the librarian, Jennifer Bobrovitz, he carved a beaver and a maple leaf out of a piece of a beavered log complete with the tooth marks where the animal had felled the tree. He offered to build coffins for Heather and Max, and when Max expostulated, "What do we do with them in the meantime!" the practical-minded lieutenant governor said, "Use 'em as blanket boxes."

He carried a shovel in the trunk of the official car and planted trees at many schools, hospitals, and other institutions.

When the Queen invited him, as her official representative, to fly to the coast and dine with her on the royal yacht *Britannia*, he turned it down because he had already accepted an invitation to a Boy Scout supper on the same day and he wouldn't let them down for royalty. When he finished his term in 1981, the province gave him a high-end Jeep as a farewell gift. MacEwan traded the glossy machine in on a smaller, more efficient model, and gave the difference back to the provincial treasury. A new community college in Edmonton was named after him, and he agreed to conduct informal seminars with the students. He was still doing that at the age of ninety, taking the bus into Edmonton, often to be greeted by the drivers with "Well, Grant, you going to drive the bus to Edmonton for us today?" to the consternation of those passengers who didn't know the joke and feared perhaps the bus driver meant to turn the wheel over to this ancient, blinking creature.

Grant MacEwan's century was drawing to a close. Phyllis was gone now. He moved into a seniors' home. He needed care most of the time.

"Bugger it," he said sometimes, when he fell off a chair or suddenly found that there was some once simple task he could no longer perform. His family tried to tell him that he should stop trying to do everything, but "you could not tell Father not to do anything," Heather said. "You could tell him, but he wouldn't listen."

Fiona went to see him in the hospital after he had broken a hip. "I smuggled my guinea pig into the hospital to show him, and . . . I'm blithely walking into the room in the hospital and I could hear this 'oink, oink, oink' from . . . my purse. . . . I opened my purse and out came that little black head, and Gramp was just overjoyed. . . . There was a sort of childlike quality that never left him. Never."

He decided to make one last trip to see the students.

"We thought, well, he can't; he's slowed so much," his granddaughter Lynwynn said. "He's tired if he makes the trip to the dining room and back, you know? That's a long haul for him. And if he has a visitor for half an hour he's tired at the end. How can he possibly make the trip?"

Paul Byrne, the college president, went to the seniors' home to see if the old man was really fit for a trip. Grant was not in his room and the roommate didn't know where he had gone. He was not in the bathroom. Somebody at the nursing station said, "Oh, he's decided to take lunch in the cafeteria." That was a long haul. "It was during the walk back that I knew, now he *is* serious," Paul Byrne told us. "Just as an Olympic competitor, he was in training, and wanted to make sure he had the strength and the stamina to take on a day of visiting our campuses and speaking to our students."

Greyhound had named a bus the Grant MacEwan. They brought it back from the coast for this last trip. It had to be the bus; Grant would not agree to go in a car. When they lifted his wheelchair down from that bus, he was surrounded; some were weeping, some were laughing, and many came to kiss him and shake his hand. Grant MacEwan just grinned and said, "Let's go." He made it to every event they had planned for him.

When Grant MacEwan died, Max Foran delivered the eulogy in his rangy, compelling Australian voice.

When I went to say good-bye, and I saw those hands, those big gentle hands that had written a million words, hands that had assisted in a birth of many an animal, hands that had reached across three provinces to touch people, hands that could carve wood beautifully, that could use an axe like you and I would use a toothpick. Yet hands that had never raised in anger and never raised in threat to any human being or animal.

And I could see those great big hands. And I kind of lost it. And I said, "Good-bye, Mate."

Director Tom Radford, who made the documentary biography on which this chapter is based, chose one more image with which to follow that farewell. It is a wide shot of the prairie, with foothills in the distance, an empty shot: and into the frame there comes a lone fox, its ears up. It stops briefly, in the middle of the frame, and looks towards us. And then it turns and lopes off, easily, confidently, gracefully. It seems tall, somehow. And then it is gone.

◆　◆　◆

The original documentary was written and directed by Tom Radford.

PART SIXTEEN

RUTH LOWE
I'll Never Smile Again

Between the one-hour biographical documentaries in the History Television series on which this book is based, and many of the Historica Foundation's *Heritage Minutes*, there is a natural affinity. I opened the Mona Parsons chapter of this book with its related *Heritage Minute*, and it seems appropriate to do this again for Ruth Lowe. Here is the script of a *Minute* that, at the time of writing this chapter, is in the queue waiting for production.

◆ ◆ ◆

LOMBARDI
A Heritage Minute

EXT. NIGHT. A stretch of war-torn battlefield on the edge of a Normandy beach, a day or two after the D-Day Landings of June 6, 1944. Close-ups of Canadian soldiers in battle gear, dug into slit trenches in the sandy soil. Distant flares as artillery shells go off. SUPER: NORMANDY, 1944

In a lull in the distant gunfire, a very British voice, considerably exaggerated in its pompous formality:

VOICE
This is the BBC. . .

We see that it is actually a helmeted Canadian SOLDIER, his face blackened, crouching in his foxhole, speaking with exaggerated tones into an imaginary microphone.

SOLDIER
Dauntless Canadian troops beat back hitherto invincible German
forces on their Normandy beachhead today.

Other soldiers' faces in other slit trenches grin nervously, all look up as two Pathfinder Mosquito bombers roar overhead and fade off rapidly to the east. Now another "radio voice" is heard.

LOMBARDI

And this is Canadian Armed Forces Radio . . .

We see this other soldier, also speaking into an imaginary microphone, his free hand digging a battered, tarnished old cornet out of his pack. His nametag says LOMBARDI.

LOMBARDI (cont.)

*. . . with sump'n that **really** matters, that great, great hit, "I'll Never Cry Again," by Toronto's own Ruth Lowe.*

He puts the cornet to his lips and plays the familiar first four bars. As he hits the last note another pair of Pathfinders roar by, and LOMBARDI instinctively ducks, pauses in his playing. As the noise of the Mosquito bombers fades we hear a spattering of applause, see a few hands, faces, in foxholes, as a voice calls out,

VOICE

Play it again, Johnny!

Other voices echo, *"Yeah! Encore!"* etc. with spatterings of applause, as the cornet picks up again, this time with "Put Your Dreams Away."

NARRATOR

Musician and broadcaster Johnny Lombardi would continue to play a prominent role in our popular culture for another half century, and . . .

DISSOLVE

STILL PHOTO: RUTH LOWE, PULL BACK INTO THE HERITAGE MINUTE GRAPHIC. LOON CALL.

NARRATOR (cont.)

. . . his Toronto composer friend, Ruth Lowe, would be named to the American Music Hall of Fame.

◆ ◆ ◆

This chapter is about that same Ruth Lowe. Her song was indeed "a great big hit," a sensational hit. All the radio stations were playing it. I vividly recall my sister Mary bringing home the sheet music, spreading it out on the piano, and singing the words. That was probably in 1940. I remember my brother John saying, "Did you know that song was written by a Toronto girl?" That seemed very special, a song that was being heard all over the continent, written by a Toronto girl? We knew nothing about her, but we all felt proud anyway.

She was born in 1914, and left us twenty years ago, in 1981. But as the production crew began to prepare this biography, they found no shortage of people who wanted to talk about "Ruthie." First among them, Ruth's younger sister Micky Cohen.

My mother was born in England, my father was New York born, where they met I don't know. . . . We were born in Toronto actually, Ruth and I, and then we moved to California when I was about two years old.

Bert Lowe, Ruth's and Micky's father, was a butcher who had been brought up in an orphanage in New York. After a few successful years in Toronto he yielded to the luxurious descriptions of California life in letters from his two brothers there, and decided to try his luck in his native country. Photographs of Bert show a ready smile and an outgoing personality, plump, genial, a touch of playfulness around the eyes and mouth.

"He had a wonderful sense of humour," Micky Cohen says. "He liked to entertain a lot at family gatherings. He sang. He could always improvise and make everybody laugh."

In his butcher shops, it is said, Bert was likely to be singing when a customer came in, would start up again as he made up the order, and break off in the middle of "Gee But It's Great After Being Out Late," and hand over the string-wrapped parcel with "Pound and a half of veal, Mrs. Green, twenty-five cents, thank you" and go right on with "Walkin' My Baby Back Home." He was seriously overweight.

There was always a piano in the house. In middle- and working-class homes of the pre-television age a piano was often the entertainment centre of gravity. Tens of thousands of unwilling kids were forced into piano lessons. To get a teaching certificate in Ontario schools, a candidate had to have a certificate of proficiency in piano from the Royal Ontario Conservatory of Music. There was a piano in almost every classroom, and music was a fundamental component of the public education system. By grade three kids were being taught to read music by what was called the Sol Fa system (*do, re, mi, fa, so, la, ti, do*); long green-and-beige charts hung from windowblind rollers on every blackboard in the junior grades.

Micky Lowe was one of those kids who did not find the piano lessons very rewarding, and soon gave them up. But Ruth loved the piano from the start, and her Los Angeles teacher ("Professor Zimmerman" he called himself) predicted a future for her as a classical concert artist. Ruth had other plans: jazz and popular songs had taken over her creative imagination, and would never leave.

"Ruthie's jazz was really of her own invention. She was never *taught* jazz," Micky says.

We always had a piano. We could be poor as church mice but we had a piano, always. Family days were picnic days, going to a big park on a Sunday afternoon, taking big picnic lunches. . . . There was always a lovely bandstand with music playing, and that was our Sunday afternoons. Ruth and I got along extremely well. We didn't quarrel although there was six years' difference. [But then] due to bad circumstances things go really tough and my father decided to come back to Toronto to my mother's family. And the only thing he shipped [back to Toronto] was the piano.

This was the Depression that followed the stock market crash in October 1929. And if Bert Lowe was determined to keep music alive in his house, he certainly was not alone. Songs kept pouring out of America. "If You Knew Susie," "Don't Bring Lulu," "These Foolish Things Remind Me of You," the whole Al Jolson canon because Jolson was everybody's favourite, "Mammy," "Alabammy Bound," and a seemingly endless stream of love songs, most of them soppy, some of them sublime. Irving Berlin and the Gershwins were as well known in Canada as they were in the States.

In the dozens of family photographs that have survived you can see the affection Micky speaks of. The two girls always seem to be together, more often than not hugging each other or holding hands or looking affectionately at each other as the parents beam at them, Depression or no Depression. The Lowe family came back to a Toronto that pretty well ended at St. Clair Avenue to the north. Nobody in downtown Toronto had even heard the word Mississauga, and a kid could get on a bike and be out in the country within ten minutes from just about anywhere in the city you cared to name. A fine new building was going up on King Street, the Canadian Bank of Commerce, and Torontonians boasted (correctly) that it would be the tallest building in the British Empire. The Royal Ontario Museum, which had opened on Bloor Street just before Ruth was born, was now overflowing with visitors who could afford little other entertainment but would spend a happy family afternoon browsing the mummy cases, the arms and armour, and the dramatic glass-cased First Nations and wildlife dioramas.

There were lots of cars left over from the pre-Depression days, the early Chevrolets, the Model T Fords, and a long spoke-wheeled monster called a Hupmobile with two spare wheels tucked into wells in the front mudguards and a real steel and leather-strapped trunk mounted on the back end. Horses were still everywhere, drawing the milk and bread and ice wagons and delivering for Eaton's and Simpsons, the two big rival department stores. On the east side of Yonge Street near Shuter there was an archway that opened into a tunnel running right through to Victoria Street. It was called the Yonge Street Arcade. As you strolled through on the sidewalk level, looking in the windows of Doc Jones' Clothing and Furnishings, or Harry Smith's ARCADE MAGIC AND NOVELTY SHOP, you could also look skyward towards the arched glass roof and see the second and third levels with their cast-iron balconies and staircases running up from the ground level. A few doors further along you would come to Anne Foster's Song Shop, the *Song Shop* for short. Within a few years after the Lowe family returned to Toronto that's where you would find Ruth Lowe almost every afternoon.

Bandleader Johnny Lombardi went into the Song Shop all the time. "Our band would play one parish hall after another," he says. "We were very popular because we played for less than anybody else. We found our material . . . on Yonge Street . . . and particularly in the Arcade. . . . It seemed to be the Tin Pan Alley of Toronto."

When she was about sixteen, Micky says, Ruth quit school to work full-time at the Song Shop. There were sheet music shops like that all over the continent. That was what George Gershwin did for a living before he became famous as a composer. Good young sight-readers would sit at the piano all day. You came in and said, "What've you got that I'd like?" or "Gee, I heard a new Irving Berlin song on the radio today, something about dancing cheek to cheek? Have you got it yet?" and the song-plugger would pull it down off the shelf and put it on the music rack on the piano and play it by sight. And if she played it well and you liked it you took it home for the Saturday night party and started to learn it. Ruth was a superb sight-reader.

"She had to be," says conductor Howard Cable, who was long a mainstay of CBC Radio in the days when radio concerts were still a big programming item. "Because the music would come up from New York and it would be lined up in the shop and she'd have to play it by sight if she hadn't seen it before. . . . I always understood that she was pretty well self-taught. But she was certainly an exceptional pianist and she could . . . also personify the song. She didn't actually sing the song, she wouldn't sing it but she would say, 'This is the way the song goes and these are the lyrics . . .' Of course, the idea was to sell the [sheet music.] We got almost all of our repertoire, our library, from Anne Foster's Song Shop."

And Johnny Lombardi adds, "When we talked about certain hits of the day . . . we would always mention, 'This is what Ruthie Lowe suggested.' . . . And she was always giving you advice, especially new-comers in the business, people like myself that were just starting up a band. Musicians are a hard sell. They just don't buy anything. They've got to be sold on the idea. And she sold everybody that listened to her piano playing."

In addition to plugging sheet music for Anne Foster, Ruth got some work at a local radio station. She was playing and listening to songs all day long. It was inevitable that she start creating some of her own. One of her early pieces, which appears to come from that period, when she was about nineteen, is "My Dreams Will Soon Be Gathering Dust, But I'll Get Along." It is a mature, well-thought-out and quietly witty romantic lyric with a comfortable and original tune.

Ruth's family was dealt a heavy blow at about this time. Maybe it was the overweight problem or maybe it was just bad luck, but Bert Lowe died of a sudden heart attack, and didn't leave much of anything. Now Ruth would have to be the family breadwinner. She was working close to full-time as a studio accompanist at CKCL radio. That paid more than the Song Shop, but she kept on part-time at the Song Shop too, and so the family kept going.

In the famous Marilyn Monroe movie *Some Like It Hot*, there is an all-woman dance band. It is, in fact, modelled after a real band, led by a dynamic blond conductor and arranger named Ina Rae Hutton. Toronto was an important venue for all the big American bands. Duke Ellington, Cab Calloway, Tommy Dorsey, Glenn Miller: they all played Toronto. Sometimes they performed at the Casino Theatre on Queen west of Bay, which was a vaudeville and striptease theatre that booked good swing and big band jazz from time to time, sometimes at the huge Shea's Hippodrome on Bay Street just north of Queen. The Shea's stage could accommodate the biggest of the big bands. Ina Rae Hutton was playing Shea's. When the pianist got sick someone told Ina Rae Hutton to check out this young girl name Ruth Lowe, at the Song Shop.

Not only was Ruth a fine sight-reader able to learn new music by heart in the beat of an eyelid, but she also could write out arrangements on the suggestions of the conductor-arranger. Ina Rae Hutton was dazzled. By the end of that week at Shea's Ruth was invited to join the band and go on the road.

"I think the sales of music sheets went down considerably when Ruthie Lowe left town," says Johnny Lombardi.

It was 1934, so Ruth was about twenty. And when this natural brunette turns up in her first photograph with the Hutton band, she is suddenly a blond. They toured by bus. They would sometimes strike the setup at one town and get on the bus to the next, find a hotel, stretch out for a few hours, and then be on the bandstand again for two or even three shows the next night. If the band stayed in town for several days there could be up to five shows a day. Ruth loved it. The photographs show a very happy woman who is maturing rapidly, has put on a modest and healthy few pounds, and seems to have found her place in the universe. She is sending home a substantial amount of her salary to her mother and sister, and she is seeing New York and Pittsburgh; Minneapolis/Saint Paul; Kokomo, Indiana; St. Louis, Missouri; San Francisco; Boston; and all roads in between. And Chicago, where she met Harold.

In every city there was no shortage of good-looking men who wanted to rub shoulders or better with the women in Ina Rae Hutton's glamorous band. Harold Cohen was a song-plugger in Chicago, so he and Ruth had a lot to talk about. Although she was soon on the road again and a long way from Chicago, Harold burned up the telephone lines night after night, and Ruthie wrote home to Momma about this great guy she had met. Before long they were married.

But it didn't last. By all accounts, and from his photographs, Harold Cohen was a strong, optimistic, capable, athletic, extremely good-looking man. But Micky recalls a very difficult moment, not two years after Ruth and Harold married. The phone rang; it was Ruth. Harold had gone in to hospital for a routine operation and had died.

Ruth came home to Toronto. Her photograph from that period shows a pinched face, exhausted eyes, the comfortable roundness of her figure from the pictures of only a year earlier now gone, the frame thin, the shoulders stooped.

Seeking consolation in her music, she began to work on a song that would become, almost overnight, part of the repertoire of just about every band and singer on the continent, the song that Johnny Lombardi plays in the *Heritage Minute* script at the beginning of this chapter, the song that she addressed to her dead husband, "I'll Never Smile Again (Until I Smile at You)." It is melodically and harmonically sophisticated, three different chords for each of the three notes on "I'll ne-ver," right at the beginning, with a yearning and even slightly sexy augmented fifth on the last of those three, and a clear and authoritative melodic line all the way through the piece.

Ruth soon found her way back into the radio studios as an accompanist. One day, she was playing her new composition in the then only six-year-old CBC station in the Canada Carbon Building at Davenport and Bathurst. The CBC's elegant and famous composer-conductor-arranger Percy Faith stopped by, listened to the plaintive melody and lyric, and asked if he could use it in his big-band live CBC concert. He did a rich arrangement with lush strings and brass polish. In those days there were no tape recorders, but whole shows were sometimes recorded for archive purposes on big fourteen-inch disks called "soft cuts." These were cut directly into an acetate plastic that would not survive more than a few plays with a phonograph needle. Percy Faith gave Ruth a soft cut of her song from that show. The family still has a copy of it, with a faded typewritten label dated November 22, 1939, and marked "Dub." So it is not the original, which must have been made not later than August of that year. We know that because in August the Tommy Dorsey Band was booked to play the Canadian National Exhibition in the huge tent where ten thousand people could dance to the visiting orchestras. Ruth decided to take the big acetate disk down to the musician's entrance at the tent and wait until Tommy Dorsey showed up, and then give it to him.

"You see," she said much later, in a radio interview, "I knew his guitar player very well. And Tommy Dorsey thought it was a marvellous song. He asked if he could publish it. He also thought Percy Faith was . . . wonderful . . . and wanted to hire both of us at the time!"

It is not surprising that Dorsey was impressed. Big name bandleaders were flooded with manuscripts of new songs from hopefuls, but here was a recording, with a big band (and strings, no less!) and a name conductor, by a virtually unknown composer-lyricist, and a young girl at that, a girl with a real romantic tragedy behind the song. He apparently thought it was a song worthy of a well-strategized launch. In 1940 a promising young singer joined the Dorsey band, a kid named Frank Sinatra, and Tommy Dorsey gave him "I'll Never Smile Again" to work on. Howard Cable speculates that Dorsey believed that

America was soon going to war and the song was meant for those going away and for those who were left behind, "I'll never smile again, until I smile at you."

"And I think in 1940 [Sinatra] left Harry James and he went over to Dorsey, and I think Dorsey's idea was that . . . this . . . would be part of that whole nostalgic emotional aspect of wartime music."

Johnny Lombardi adds, "They'd hear Sinatra singing that song, and they'd say, 'Gee . . . I'm thinking about my girlfriend and my family, and that's the song I remember more than any.'"

Dorsey used the song to launch his new singer. Sinatra's brilliant technique, with phrasing which mined out of those simple, straightforward words the maximum impact they could convey, turned it into an instant hit. Glen Miller was one of the first of the other big bandleaders to pick it up, and then pretty soon it was everywhere. Dorsey recognized the marketing power of Ruth's personal story, the story behind the song. He brought her to New York and made sure she was interviewed by newspapers and radio at every opportunity. Photographs of the Paramount Theatre, where the band was presenting the song, show RUTH LOWE in two-foot-high letters, bigger than Sinatra and bigger than Dorsey himself.

Before long Ruth felt overwhelmed by the demand for public appearances, and brought Micky down from Toronto to act as her secretary. "Frank [Sinatra] was performing with . . . the band at the Paramount," Micky remembers. "That was when all the people were lined up outside and screaming and screaming. And after the performance that night Frank came back to our room in the Astor to say Hi and everything, and I . . . I just about died. . . . I *met him!*"

When Frank Sinatra got his first network radio show he called Ruth and said, "I need a closing theme." She was thrilled, and agreed to start on it right away. Sinatra said that was good, because he needed it tomorrow morning. Ruth said that she had a melody shaping up in her mind almost before the phone call was over, but she had trouble with the lyrics. So she called two songwriting friends, and the three of them stayed up all night and delivered the song on time, the next morning. It was "Put Your Dreams Away for Another Day."

For a while Ruth had been half of a double-piano act in New York with a popular and gifted pianist and singer named Sair Lee. Sair and Ruth had met in the Ina Rae Hutton days. There is a recording extant of a goofy song they sent Harold in Chicago during the courtship period. Sair and Ruth had stayed friends, and now they became very close again, playing New York clubs, according to Howard Cable, until Ruth went back to Toronto. Sair Lee died very young. Ruth had lost two of the people with whom she was closest. Her songs often reflect a dreamy and slightly sad sense, and Ruth herself used to say, "Audiences enjoy a good cry sometimes."

But a blind date brought new sunshine to Ruth's life. Her brother-in-law, Mickey with an "e," had arranged for her to go dancing with a businessman named Nat Sandler, and Nat Sandler kept putting it off. Perhaps he felt he was being set up with a nice widow, but that wasn't exactly on *his* road map, and so he would say yes and then change his mind. The first time he actually agreed to meet Ruth he did not show. So when they finally met and Ruth realized that this was the rude man who had stood her up she was pretty cold at first.

But not Nat Sandler. He was, it seems, smitten.

"He just couldn't keep his eyes off her, and from that moment on," said Johnny Lombardi, "he just knocked on her door until they married."

They were married two months later and soon had a son, Stephen, followed not long after by Tommy. From the photographs of those first days, photographs in which someone is always embracing someone else, much like the albums of Ruth and Micky and Momma and Poppa, it looks as though all the threads had come together at last.

Nat was probably a little uncertain about the entertainment world from which Ruth had come, but he was fascinated at the same time — sufficiently so that one night after a few too many whiskies with an old friend he actually agreed to buy an old Toronto nightclub. At around that time the film director Vincent Minelli approached them about making a movie based on Ruth's life, to star Minelli's wife Judy Garland. It was a pretty heady proposition: both Minelli and Garland were names you saw in lights at that time. But Nat Sandler was very cautious about the business side of the entertainment world. When he had finished examining the terms of the Minelli deal he advised Ruth to turn it down, and she turned it down.

The nightclub at 12 Adelaide Street West had been operating as the Club Norman. Nat and his partner changed the name to the Club One Two, and Johnny Lombardi remembers it as "the nicest club in Toronto."

Stephen Sandler remembers going there. "It was black tie. They had live dancing, live bands. I don't know how he got out of that, the transition between that and the brokerage business . . . [but] when he started his own firm in 1962 or 1963 . . . he was probably the first or second Jewish member of the Toronto Stock Exchange."

It seems strange, in 2001, to think that anti-Semitism was still such a functional part of Toronto society only forty years ago. But for the most part Ruth's life had taken on a social and familial tranquillity and stability that was welcome and comforting; restful after all those years of travel and glamour and the excitement and demands of the band circuit. Tom Sandler describes it from the child's point of view.

It was . . . a typical 1950s kind of an upbringing where that's basically what the roles were, the man would go out and work, and the woman, the wife, stayed home sort of thing. But she really didn't stay home, and do baking and cooking, kind of. She did that too, but, she had a lot of fun, she liked to have nice things and she would like to go shopping, she was involved with a lot of charity work and stuff like that. And then of course she was always writing or re-writing or playing music or, you know, speaking to somebody, going somewhere like New York to talk to somebody about her music.

I remember her playing every day. She would sit down at the piano, and play, and she had a number of songs that she really loved. The music was . . . totally powerful, all-encompassing.

And Cookie Sandler, Stephen's wife, adds, "Whenever there was a party we'd always get her to sit at the piano and play. We used to do May long weekends at the cottage, and we'd have fireworks and I can just remember her sitting there pounding away at the piano and everybody singing. . . . Everybody loved her."

She was an avid card player. The room service bills and other notes all scribbled over with game scores on the back — which Ruth

saved from her honeymoon with Nat — show that even at the beginning of their marriage they were spending hours playing gin rummy.
One of her great pleasures was to go off to Buffalo with some women
friends, hole up in a suite in a hotel, and play cards non-stop, for
money, for a whole weekend. She went to the races and bet on them
too. Tom Sandler remembers the all-day card parties at the house at 1
Manitou Boulevard.

> *And I would come home from school sometimes and the house
> would be like . . . you needed a gas mask to walk into the house
> because there was so much smoke in the air you couldn't breathe,
> they were all smoking cigarettes, they were all screaming at each
> other, there was no booze, nobody drank, thank God, or they would
> have burned the house to the ground probably. The card games
> [were] always in the basement. There were at least twelve to fifteen
> women, all my "aunts." My sister-in law Cookie reminded me that
> as well as the smoking and the screaming, some of them would be
> sitting playing in their brassieres. Mom would aways make me her
> partner, but only if she was winning.*

Life had settled into comfortable patterns. Ruth may have thought
that the world was beginning to forget about her, although in Toronto,
whenever they went to a clubby restaurant like the Imperial Room at
the Royal York Hotel, where there was an orchestra, they would always
strike up "I'll Never Smile Again" when she walked into the room. The
Mills Brothers played that room and would come and sit at Ruth's table
between sets. Oscar Peterson was a friend. Lena Horne brought a show
to town and Ruth took the family backstage to meet her afterwards and
they all sat around the dressing room and talked about the old days.

There was a woman songwriters' convention of some kind in New
York to which Ruth invited her daughter-in-law Cookie.

> *We stayed at the Waldorf Astoria. And as we were walking around
> the corner to the hotel . . . she yelled, "There's Frank!" She started
> moving very quickly forward to catch him, and we walked into the
> lobby and she yelled, "Frankie!" and he turned around and said
> "Ruthie!" And I kind of stood there . . . and she introduced me, and
> we chatted for a while, and . . . I mean . . . it was as if he'd seen her*

the day before!. . . . She did tell me that she [had thrown] Frank
Sinatra out of her room [once, and that] she kind of regretted it at
times. She'd say, Maybe she shouldn't have. . . . It would have been
a nice story for her.

It is clear that the life of family and friends completely overshadowed her showbusiness career. Of course there would be moments
when the stage beckoned, and sometimes in a club Ruth would begin
to make signs that she might like to go up there and maybe do a number or two at the piano, the bandleaders would have loved it. But Nat
valued his privacy and discouraged that. Ruth was really happy with
Nat; so she complied for the sake of the marriage: that was where the
real values lay.

One day in 1955 she was asked to go to California, to discuss the
possible publication of one of her older songs. She did not for a
moment suspect that she was being set up. Her sister Micky had been
enlisted to help ensure her unwitting compliance. It would be fun to
spend a few days in Los Angeles, maybe look up some of the old music
pals, maybe have a drink with Frank Sinatra, take in a show. She had
no idea what was really in store.

It is difficult now for people of the cable and satellite era to sense
what the television world was like when there were only four or five
channels, and the most popular programs were known to virtually
everybody in North America. One of those shows was called *This Is
Your Life*, and its smooth and charming host, Ralph Edwards, was as
well known in America as the president of the United States. The program brought both celebrities and relatively unknown local heroes (a
street cop beloved in his town, for example) out to Los Angeles on
some pretext or other. Their secrecy was almost watertight. They were
very inventive in helping a conspiring friend or relative devise reasons
why the unsuspecting Guest of the Week should suddenly pick up and
get on a plane or the train for the West Coast. Very few of the subjects
ever guessed the real reason behind the sudden suggestion from the
kid brother or the cousin in Milwaukee that they take a few days and
go have some fun in LA. In the meantime the program's research staff
would have contacted as many relatives and close friends as they could

manage and invited them to the live broadcast, sworn to secrecy. In the case of media celebrities they would secure some film footage or sound recordings to play during the show. And then, expecting that you were going to the theatre for an afternoon's entertainment, you would be led out onto the stage, and told "Joe Smith, This Is Your Life!" And there would be people you might not have seen for decades, the evidence and footprints of your life across the years, your accomplishments, your loves, sometimes your losses and dismays. Tears were a necessary part of the emotional armamentarium of that experience. Millions tuned in every week.

Micky Cohen was the prime conspirator this time, and says that she easily persuaded Ruth that the fake cover story was true. There was to be a press conference — still not that unusual when Ruth made one of her visits to the States — in a downtown theatre, which was also fairly ordinary.

Ralph Edwards is seen in the old kinescope recording of that show (no videotape in those days) whispering conspiratorially to the live audience in the theatre, "She's a Canadian. So she doesn't know anything about *This Is Your Life* being from this theatre."[20] Ruth was suitably emotional. The boys, then five and ten years old, were flown out and brought on for their hugs and kisses. Ruth is seen saying, "If I'd known I'd've had a bleach!" People who remember the television of that period will know that, even for a mature and already well-recognized artist such as Ruth Lowe, appearing on that program was tantamount to having some kind of Global Seal of Approval stamped on your life. Ruth took it in stride; the family still light up with smiles and excitement when they talk about it. You had arrived, if you were on *This Is Your Life*.

The American Academy of Recording Arts, the people who organize the Grammy Awards, sponsor an American Music Hall of Fame. When they learned of Ruth's death in 1981, Tommy Dorsey and Frank

20. The kinescope recording was a sixteen-millimetre-film camera focused on a television screen, with a shutter adapted to eliminate the problems caused by the difference between film's twenty-four frames per second and television's thirty frames. It was really just a black-and-white motion picture of the television image as it appeared on the screen. It was low on contrast and resolution, but a perfectly usable archive or analysis recording, and still employed as late as 1966, six or seven years after videotape was in common use. It is the only format in which many programs from as recently as the late 1960s were recorded.

Sinatra signed the nomination for her inclusion in the Hall of Fame, and the same year saw her awarded a Grammy posthumously. There is, to this writer's knowledge, no such honour for the prophet in her native land, nothing for the brilliant composer and lyricist who sent a song into the hearts of millions, and stayed home in Toronto to play poker with the girls.

If Ruth Lowe's head had been turned by her success, if celebrity had been the driving force in her life, she could, like many a "star," have put together a publicity machine to make sure her name was always in print and up for nomination to every award going. Celebrity is a well-understood business, and most of its practitioners are obsessed with it. But this was a creative artist whose authentic life currents were as rooted in the core values of family and friends as they were in her music. She was too wise in the joys of simple human intercourse over a dinner table or a hand of gin rummy among the laughter and affection of old friends — too wise to be taken in by the glitter. Agreeable and entertaining though it was — to be sought after by the columnists and hailed as a friend by the great and famous — it never became a need for Ruth Lowe, and so it never threatened to destroy her as it has destroyed so many.

When Frank Sinatra died in 1998, his family chose one song to be played at the funeral. It was "Put Your Dreams Away for Another Day," the piece Sinatra had commissioned from Ruth Lowe for his radio series so many years before. The stories about Ruth Lowe just keep on coming. My favourite is Johnny Lombardi's, who said that as he lay in a slit trench under the artillery barrages during the invasion of Normandy, he reached into his kit and pulled out a battered German soldier's cornet he had "captured," and put it to his lips, and inspired the brief drama with which I opened this chapter.

And the boys called out from the other trenches, amid the clamour of war, *"Play it again, Johnny. Play it again."*

◆ ◆ ◆

The original documentary was written and directed by Martin Harbury.

THE
CANADIANS
Biographies of a Nation

VOLUME III

Patrick Watson
and Hugh Graham

PART ONE

MARION DE CHASTELAIN
Family Secrets

In April 2002, a small group of Canadians gathered around a television set, drinks in hand, in a private salon on the second floor of the Slieve Donard Hotel, Newcastle, County Down, Northern Ireland, to look at the documentary on which this chapter is based. Many of them had contributed to the making of the film, most importantly the Irish-born writer/director Patricia Phillips, who is also executive producer of the series *The Canadians*. But the key person in the room that evening was General John de Chastelain, a Canadian soldier of impeccable integrity and credentials, who for nine long years had been a key negotiator in the international effort to persuade the combatants in Northern Ireland to decommission their weapons as a prerequisite to establishing the peace.

General de Chastelain is the only person ever twice appointed CDS, chief of the defence staff, first by Pierre Trudeau, and later by Brian Mulroney who called de Chastelain back from his then post as Canadian ambassador to Washington, to once more take over as commander-in-chief of the Canadian armed forces. He had come to this screening at our invitation, to give us his assessment of the biography's accuracy and relevance. The film's principal subject — in this case it is not excessive to use the word heroine — was the general's late mother Marion de Chastelain.

General de Chastelain has a reputation for honesty and candour, and yet he was raised in a family that dwelt in the twilight world of spies, where lies are routinely conveyed as truths, where people you think you know turn out to be someone else, and where deeds of valour must often be buried, concealed, forgotten, in order to protect the lives of those who carried them out or those who benefited from them. Much of the biography of Marion de Chastelain is just such a story of buried valour, of dangerous unpredictability, unusual characters and connections, deception and war.

Her story contains a famous secret coding machine and the Canadian who helped crack its secrets, an aristocratic saboteur, a female spy who employs the classical tool of sexual seduction to get secrets from men who should know better, and Marion de Chastelain's two children, one of them a Calgary woman named Jacquie Brewster and the other Canada's best-known soldier.

Marion de Chastelain lived her last years quietly with her daughter Jacquie in the foothills of the Rockies, where she died as the twentieth century ended. While our research has been able to piece together a good deal of the story of her wartime service, almost none of it ever came from her lips. As has been the case with many in the spy trade her secrets were buried with her. Even to her closest relatives she had revealed almost nothing. That evening in Northern Ireland her son the General watched the documentary intently, with a half smile on his face most of the time, once shaking his head and muttering over an error (we had given him a birthday a year later than the real one), and then he joined the production group for dinner. "I learned a lot about my family that I never knew before," he said with a grin. In the documentary he had said,

> One thing that always struck me was her reticence about herself. I mean she loved talking about her family and other people, and what they had achieved, but not herself. She was very proud of my father of course, and I think she felt that what she had done was much less than what he had done in terms of the war effort.

The war he referred to was World War II, from 1939–45. But our story begins shortly after the 1918 armistice. The story is composed of a number of at first seemingly unconnected subplots, some set in Germany, some in Romania, and some in Britain and Canada. As we began to assemble the documentary film, to set this intricate life story in motion we first opened a number of those subplots.

William Stephenson, who would become famous as The Man Called Intrepid, had started as an engineer in World War I. He transferred to the Royal Flying Corps in 1917 and shot down twelve enemy aircraft before he was shot down himself in July 1918. After the war, the twenty-three-year-old adventurer came home to Winnipeg, intending to become a millionaire by patenting a can opener he had liberated from a guard while he was a prisoner of war in Germany.

At about the same time a nine-year-old girl, Marion Walsh, daughter of an Irish-born New York accountant, found herself in Romania living in luxury. Germany had controlled Romania's huge and lucrative oil fields, but with defeat she lost that control, and companies from America, Holland, France, and Britain poured into the country, bringing with them educated young men like Marion's father, Jack Walsh. He was alert to the opportunity in Europe for moving his family socially upwards, and so he put his daughter into the best schools he could find, which were in Switzerland. She became competent in seven languages, including Romanian, French and German. She was small in stature, but athletic and courageous, crazy about winter sports and fearless in her specialty, the luge, hurtling down those breathtaking iced troughs with striking assurance. She revelled in risk.

So the first pieces of our story are found in a world of success and privilege, full of optimism and prosperity, whose denizens were carelessly insensitive to the dark forces building up in the devastation that was postwar Germany. Demoralized by defeat and then beaten into the ground by the overwhelmingly punitive financial reparations the victors had imposed in the Treaty of Versailles, there were hundreds of thousands of desperate, resentful Germans ripe for the rallying cry of someone who could show them a way out of their penury and humiliation. The one who would do this was the young Adolf Hitler. In 1924, serving time in prison for an attempted coup, Hitler wrote a long boring book, *Mein Kampf (My Struggle)*, which, astonishingly, became a kind of blueprint for the New Germany. Hitler smuggled the manuscript out of his cell, got it published, and found eager readers who saw in it not only hope for a renaissance of the Fatherland, perhaps even for the conquest of the world, but also the person who would lead them to that glorious end, *Der Führer*, The Leader.

That same year, William Stephenson, the working-class kid from Winnipeg, former World War I pilot and prisoner of war, by now a successful London-based businessman, had come across a "secret writing machine" that was being offered to commercial companies. Whatever was typed into it was so cryptically scrambled that only if you bought the deciphering key — which meant buying the machine — could you return the meaningless characters to their original sense. Stephenson did not, at the time, catch on to the military potential of the Secret Writing Machine. As a business tool it was amusing but cumbersome to use. Stephenson fiddled with it for a while, and then forgot about it.

In 1930, Marion Walsh turned twenty. She had a degree in international law from the Sorbonne, but when she returned home she was at first somewhat overwhelmed by ambitions that had nothing to do with her own, namely, her dictatorial mother's vision of a daughter's place in high society. Marion's daughter Jacquie said,

My mother was actually married in 1931, I believe, to a Count. It was an arranged marriage by her mother. My grandmother was a schoolteacher. Her name was Mary Mulligan from New Jersey. She reminded me very much of Queen Mary, ramrod straight, very tiny, about 4' 11," but when she was there, you knew she was there. And, I think [even] I might have had problems standing up to her — about anything. (Laughs)

But if Mrs. Walsh had counted on her daughter's continuing dutiful rise into the upper levels of European snobbery, she was soon to be disappointed. Jacquie said,

She did not want the marriage in the first place but her mother did, so she complied to that point and then did her own thing and had it annulled.

Shortly after this, she met the man who would become the above-mentioned saboteur, Alfred Gardyne de Chastelain. He had a pretty aristocratic-sounding name too, but it was the character not the family crest that brought them together. De Chastelain, known to his friends as Chas, had been born in London, studied industrial engineering, and went straight to those Romanian oil fields as soon as he had a degree. "He rode a horse and looked very romantic," Jacquie said. Marion's close Romanian friend Lady Joan Roderic Gordon, who was the daughter of the then Romanian minister of the national economy, watched from her own romantic perspective as the relationship blossomed. "He was very dashing and very good-looking," she told us, waving a slim, heavily jewelled hand, "and very charming I would say, and she was very beautiful. So it was a natural thing that they should meet and get married."

They were married in 1933. Alfred Gardyne de Chastelain was twenty-seven; Marion was twenty-three. She was now the wife of an oil executive, in an environment where oil was *the* field to be in, and at a time when postwar false optimism put a premium on the pursuit of pleasure. The de Chastelains' pleasures were not quite as sybaritic as some. "My father was a racing car driver," the General said, in the film.

Both rally and racing, and he and my mother took part in a number of those kind of events, which involved them with a structure of society in business, and even the royal family. He got to know Prince Michael at the time. They raced cars together. I think it was a vibrant society and largely because of the international nature of the people that made it up.

Marion was Chas's navigator in the rallies. They rode horses together, belonged to the golf club, and enjoyed the nightlife of "The Paris of the Balkans," the General said.

It was a very cosmopolitan city . . . a city in which the arts flourished. My parents lived a fairly affluent lifestyle in comparison to many people in Romania. . . . . It was a period of great excitement, great interest, great intellectual challenge and great enjoyment. Now, for people who were reasonably close to the top of the totem pole, that was nice. For those who were struggling at the bottom it wasn't, but I think by and large life in Romania at the time was enjoyable and that's why so many people stayed there.

But in 1933 the smell of smoke was already beginning to drift across Europe from Germany. Hitler's *Mein Kampf* had become the Bible of German recovery, a recovery nourished by a hatred of everyone and everything not "Aryan," especially Jews. Under Hitler's eloquent leadership the National Socialist Party, Nazi for short, was growing exponentially. The swastika and the straight-arm salute were

511

becoming the symbols for the new optimism and for the restoration of the racially pure glory of the *Heimat*, the German homeland. Fascism, the power-based, violence-enforced rule by self-appointed elites rather than by the rule of law, was the new religion. Hitler, the former prison inmate, became the Chancellor of all Germany. German Jews were feeling the brutality of the Nazi thugs, and so was the whole brilliant world of German culture. The yeasty mix that had given rise to Bach, Beethoven, Mozart, Hegel, and Goethe was now in danger. At the University of Berlin, young Nazis built a huge bonfire to burn hundreds of copies of the world's greatest books, books incompatible with the new doctrine of racial superiority. Germany was predominantly a devoutly Christian country, the birthplace of Protestantism, but with a large and committed Roman Catholic community as well. While it seems contradictory on the surface, the Bible and the whole Christian vocabulary of God, redemption, and salvation were appropriated by the Nazis (who wooed the Vatican but privately distrusted all the Church authorities). "I was sent by Providence," Hitler told the cheering mobs. "The Nazi Party is Adolf Hitler, and Adolf Hitler is Germany," his deputy führer yelled at them, and they yelled back, "Heil Hitler! Heil Hitler! Heil Hitler!"

And that was when the Secret Writing Machine that William Stephenson had fiddled with years before surfaced again. Stephenson was now a millionaire in London. Part of his fortune was made in currency trading, but much of it came from his having invented the wirephoto while still a student at the University of Manitoba, and then a wireless system for the transmission of text and images. It was this invention that brought him to London, where he cannily marketed it to the newspaper companies and built his reputation both as an innovator and a businessman. One of his companies supplied electronics to the International Telephone and Telegraph Company, which was making armaments for Germany. From IT&T Stephenson learned that Hitler was using the Special Writing Machine to code Nazi party communiqués, and that the Japanese military was also using it. Now he recognized the threat. His wide, high-level connections in London snaked through the political and military elite as well as the commercial and social, and he began to compile his own operating list of people he could count on being anti-Nazi. Many Britons were admirers of Hitler and his fascism, among them some who would deeply regret it later, including the poets W.B. Yeats and T.S. Eliot. One of Stephenson's anti-Nazi friends was a man named Desmond Morton (not the Canadian historian), and Morton was a friend and neighbour of Winston Churchill. Churchill had been warning Britain about both Hitler and Stalin for years, had often been called a warmonger for his stance, and had lost much of his influence in the government. However, in 1935, he discreetly assigned Desmond Morton to gather intelligence about German rearmament, and to start quietly putting together an unofficial and clandestine group of specialists in espionage, sabotage, and assassination. Morton brought Stephenson into that group.

In 1936, the Germans were deporting undesirables and declaring that they were going to purify the Master Race. Marion de Chastelain saw an aspect of it first-hand. Pregnant, on a visit to Berlin she was overcome by nausea in the street and had to vomit in public, holding onto a railing. A matronly middle-aged German woman stopped solicitously, patted her on the back, and said: "It's okay, dear, you're doing it for the führer." The child-to-come was Jacquie, who was born in Bucharest soon after. Her brother John was born in 1937. The following year Hitler occupied the Rhineland and took over Austria. The de Chastelains should probably have left Romania then — it was an obvious target for German expansion — but they hung on. Both Romania and Czechoslovakia looked to Britain for support but none came. Churchill urged those he trusted in British intelligence to convince Prime Minister Neville Chamberlain to take action. Chamberlain did that. He visited Hitler in Munich for a friendly talk.

In light of what happened next, Chamberlain's search for accommodation with Hitler — his critics called it "appeasement" — seems almost criminally wrong. But Britain was only twenty years away from the hideousness of the First World War, still scarred by the waste of it, its meaninglessness, and the cynicism that had led to it. The British — and the French, and probably even the majority of Germans, although they no longer had a voice in national policy — did not want to go through all that again. When Chamberlain announced that his agreement with Hitler meant "Peace in Our Time," he was cheered. But in October 1938 Hitler's *Wehrmacht* marched into the Sudetenland. Czechoslovakia, Romania, and Poland pleaded with Britain to act. Britain stuck to its guns, or rather its rejection of guns. Churchill said bitterly but with characteristic elegance, "Britain and France had to choose between war and dishonour. They chose dishonour. They will have war."

Not only was Britain not arming itself, just in case, but there was also almost no budget for intelligence. The intelligence service had little more to work with than reports from the military attachés in their embassies. The Bucharest legation reported that there had been a secret meeting of Romanian officials to discuss oil with Hitler's *Reichsmarschall* Hermann Goering. Hitler had more than a business relationship in mind, however; he and Stalin were quietly plotting to occupy both Poland and Romania. In March, Hitler took Prague. Marion and Chas went to Germany ostensibly to buy a car, but Chas was already more than idly curious. They saw tanks in the streets, and thousands of soldiers being trucked down the autobahn. "Both my parents realized that the writing was on the wall," General de Chastelain told us,

> [They realized] that Romania would in fact become involved and that they both decided we should leave. And [my mother] took my sister and me out of Romania by train and took us to England.

Chas booked them on the Orient Express, and kissed them goodbye at the station. Marion could navigate a road rally, luge down a polished trough of ice at eighty miles an hour, and speak seven languages, but after a life of servants and luxury, finding herself on a train to Paris without the children's nurse was too much. Jacquie remembers that vividly.

> She was absolutely, totally . . . just didn't know what to do with us. So, my brother ate his way through a box of chocolates and . . . a lady returning to England who was a nanny realized what was going on and offered to help, and she took over and we were in good hands at that point.

And Jacquie's son Ian Denton, who would become very close to Marion in her later years, told us,

My grandmother was not what one would call the maternal type. She never seemed to have that sort of stereotypical motherly or grandmotherly attitude. My grandmother would sit in her chair and have her Scotch and cigarette while other people cooked and prepared.

"We had a cook and maid," Jacquie added, "so she didn't have to cook. . . . She could do it if she had to but she hated it."

The destination of that train trip was London, where William Stephenson had just got a tip from an American source that Germany was now mass-producing the Secret Writing Machine near the Czech-Polish border. Code-named "ENIGMA," and far superior to the original commercial model, it had been developed into a device able to instantly encipher messages that stumped even the most experienced cryptologists. Churchill wanted one of these things, and Stephenson had a plan. Not even the Prime Minister was told about the secret mission, which is said to have involved a bit of sabotage and a suitcase switch in Warsaw. The machine arrived in England in late August 1939, without the key. The British found it baffling. A research unit of crack cipher people took over a vast country estate called Bletchley Park. They called the project "ULTRA." At the height of the Bletchley Park operation there were some 12,000 personnel involved, only a small number of whom actually knew what the ULTRA project was about. There was an ULTRA list of insiders: Stephenson and the other key people. Being on that list was to be a member of the most exclusive club of the war effort.

It was September 1, 1939, when the German invasion of Poland finally pulled Chamberlain to his feet. Britain and France declared war on September 3. Largely isolated from the mainstream of policy and executive decision for most of the decade, Winston Churchill's take on Germany was now vindicated, and Chamberlain asked him to resume his old First World War position: First Lord of the Admiralty.

On September 17, Hitler and Stalin divided Poland up between them. Polish refugees started streaming down the roads towards Romania. "And then they'd arrive in Bucharest," Lady Joan Roderic

Gordon says, "and we looked after them, took them into our homes." But Romania's neutrality was precarious now that Poland was no longer a buffer between Russia and Germany. The Romanian Prime Minister was assassinated by pro-Nazis. Romanian trade with Britain was nearly cut off. There had been a secret agreement with Britain to destroy the oil installations if the country were invaded. The British began to prepare for this, contacted Chas through the Bucharest legation, and persuaded him to secretly accept a commission in the British army. With his knowledge of the Romanian geography, language, and especially of the oil fields, he would be a prime candidate to lead a sabotage program to destroy the oil installations so the Germans could not use them.

Late in 1939 ULTRA was making some headway with the ENIGMA codes, and had decoded a German message revealing something about Hitler's plan for a *Blitzkrieg*, a Lightning War, which would be a massive, high-speed mechanized attack on Western Europe. Chamberlain had received identical information that official intelligence had gotten out of a downed German pilot but had chosen not to believe it. Churchill considered showing him ULTRA's version, but the ULTRA list people persuaded him that the project should still be kept from the PM.

Despite the danger after Germany attacked Norway and Denmark in April 1940, and not saying what she was up to, Marion de Chastelain left her children with their grandparents and, travelling on a British passport, set out to meet Chas in Bucharest. She was en route through France on May 10 when Hitler began the *Blitzkrieg*. Not long after Marion arrived in Romania, the German war machine would sweep through Belgium, France, and the Netherlands. Chamberlain resigned, asking the sixty-six-year-old Churchill to take over as Prime Minister. Almost immediately, Churchill created an instrument to manage all available intelligence through one agency, the BSC, British Security Coordination. The man he assigned to run BSC was William Stephenson, and Stephenson set up shop in Washington, DC, not as an intelligence official but as a distinguished and wealthy businessman. The United States had not come into the war yet, and an open military intelligence operation on American territory would have been impossible.

Stephenson's covert assignment now was to convince the American government to start collaborating with the BSC. He was able to persuade Canada to send to Washington some of the RCMP's best intelligence people, both men and women. Stephenson believed women to be especially adept at the intelligence game.

Back in England, Churchill had added sabotage to the intelligence machine, setting up the SOE, the Secret Operations Executive. Alfred de Chastelain, Chas, was given the Romanian team. "He knew the oil business," his son told us. "It was his life. He knew what were effective targets." Hitler had reminded Romania that Britain was also occupied on the Western front and wouldn't help in the inevitability of a Russian land grab. "We signed our last treaty with England in 1939," Lady Joan told us.

It was signed in our house between my father among some of the British delegation, some of them. And after that the Germans walked in and they said, "You are no more friends of the British, you must be our friends, you see. We can help you, [but] the British, oh they're finished, they've got nothing."

When Stalin made his pact with Hitler in June 1940, Romania was given twenty-four hours to cede them some oil-rich northern lands. As the Germans had predicted, Britain did not interfere. Romania, still technically neutral, was effectively occupied. By September, Hitler had moved in a whole division of the German army, allegedly to train the Romanian army but really to protect the oil installations and to prepare a push against the Russians. "Anybody with a British or American antecedence had to leave," Lady Joan said. "The Germans, although they didn't bother the Romanians, they said, 'Oh, we're here to defend you from the Russians.' But the people who were in the know, they just left."

Chas was suddenly instructed by SOE headquarters to get his team out of Bucharest and take them to safety in Istanbul for the time being. Marion went back to England to be with the children. John de Chastelain said that at this point his mother had had enough. "And she was quite clear, I think, once she came back. She had decided with my father that we should go to the States and live with her parents."

She was not, however, allowed to drop out completely. When Marion and the children arrived in New York in the fall, William Stephenson knew she was coming. John de Chastelain again:

So after we'd been in New York for some time — we were living in Forest Hills with my grandparents — she got a call from somebody from the British embassy saying, "Would you like to do something for your king and country?" and she said, "Yes." Because of my father's background, my mother's circumstance was known to the intelligence people in London and therefore to the intelligence people working for Sir William Stephenson in Washington. And it was known that she was a linguist.

Stephenson needed a French speaker who could be trusted. Marion fit the bill. The assignment was top secret. She was going to run a spy in Washington, Betty Thorpe Pack, who was an adventurous and gorgeous woman code-named "Cynthia." Originally from Minneapolis, Cynthia was the daughter of diplomats, had married a British diplomat twenty years her senior, had been initiated into the undercover game in Poland and loved it, and now was about to graduate into that classic combination of espionage and the oldest profession.

Cynthia spoke fluent French. France, nominally a separate nation but in fact run by the Nazi-directed Vichy Government, still had an embassy in Washington. In May 1941, Cynthia was assigned to penetrate the Vichy French embassy, and Stephenson had decided to put Marion de Chastelain in charge of the operation. She had the language, she was a woman, she could get along with Cynthia, and she had a much broader experience of the world than anybody of similar skills in Stephenson's BSC.

It may begin to sound a bit comic book or television sitcom about now. Cynthia, in her Washington home, seduces a Vichy French attaché, Charles Brousse, and somehow — blackmail? a romantic appeal to old loyalties? — somehow persuades him to give her copies of secret documents. Her personal risk was huge. Since the US was not in the war, should her life be threatened, for example, there was no way she could turn to the American police for protection. What she was doing was completely illegal and official America would have been furious. And this was a highly emotional adventurer. She swung from extreme highs to desperate lows. She would come back from one of her assignations and report to Marion in moral tatters, and at other times be sailing high, giddy with risk and success. Marion was the straight one, the stabilizer, a functional link between the romantic adventurer and the serious work.

Marion often travelled six times a week between New York and Washington, rarely getting home to see John and Jacquie or to get some sleep. But December 7, 1941, was different. She had been working sixteen-hour days for some time, and that weekend she told the BSC people not to bother her. But in the middle of the night the phone began to ring and did not stop. She finally got up in a very bad humour, and a voice said, "Marion. Get in here right away. Pearl Harbor's been bombed."

So America was at last in the war, and by that time William Stephenson had so effectively developed his covert co-operative relationships between the American and British intelligence agencies that they were ready to swing into full-scale action together. Stephenson had accomplished his mission, and Marion de Chastelain was one of the key people who had helped him do it.

Stephenson's next assignment brought him home to Canada for a while. The decision had been made to establish a secret Canadian training base for saboteurs and spies, Camp X, on the north shore of Lake Ontario near the small city of Oshawa. They set up a state-of-the-art communications centre, with a soaring radio tower, the HYDRA Wireless Station that linked Washington, London, and Ottawa and relayed some of the most sensitive information of the war. Of course, they needed a powerful encryption system. A Canadian electronic genius named Benjamin de Forest Bayley designed an encoding machine called Rock X, a central component of the whole HYDRA operation, and as far as we know, the enemy cipher specialists never broke it.

Marion de Chastelain was still running Cynthia in Washington, and was soon reporting back to Stephenson through HYDRA, sending him, among other documents, Vichy naval materials coded by ENIGMA. In May 1942 Cynthia had moved into the Wardman Park Hotel where Brousse lived in Washington. While it was more convenient to slip into her apartment for a passionate embrace, it was also more dangerous. His wife lived at the hotel too, and it was a favourite residence for other foreign operatives. Marion would take an early morning flight over from New York, and meet with Cynthia at the Wardman Park, using different entrances and exits in case she was followed.

An Allied operation along the coast of French North Africa was being developed as a stepping-stone into Europe. The code name for the plan was TORCH. The planners needed to know the movement of the German-controlled Vichy French fleet in the Mediterranean, and so Marion was assigned to get Cynthia to try for the Vichy ciphers and codebooks. Her chance came in June. She arranged to meet Brousse in the embassy at night to pick up the documents. At a crucial moment they heard a guard coming. Cynthia told Marion that at this point she just whipped off all her clothes and when the guard came upon a steamy love scene in the corridor he discreetly turned away and left them alone. "Boy, what a night I had," Cynthia told Marion, and Marion laughed, and headed back to New York and the HYDRA transmission station. The ciphers and other materials made their way, via Camp X and HYDRA, to Bletchley Park in time to be incorporated into TORCH.

Now Chas got involved in Camp X. He had been assigned to enlist a team of Romanians to be parachuted into Europe. They would be trained at Camp X. The SOE said, "Well, you speak Romanian, you'd better go with them." And so when he came to visit Marion in New York, it was to tell her that he was about to do a little drop into their former European home country. "The mission was in fact to try and make a separate peace with Romania before the end of the war," Lady Joan told us. Chas's assignment was at the request of King Michael himself, Chas's old friend. Marion was frightened, but she agreed: he had to go.

By late 1943, the Wardman Park Hotel Caper was finished. Now BSC gave Marion an assignment in England, dealing with the Balkans.

We don't know what this one entailed, and characteristically Marion never discussed it. Once again, the children were uprooted, this time travelling across the Atlantic and into the heart of the war. At least she would be with Chas, who was back in London preparing his team of Romanians for the parachute jump. Marion and the children sailed from New York in a convoy of artillery freighters. Jacquie was seven and John only six, but he says he remembers the trip very clearly.

She felt that my sister and me were being spoilt rotten by our grandparents, which may have been the case. Anyway, she felt that we should be back in Britain, over the objections of her parents, who thought this was absolutely crazy. This was not the time to be going to Britain, you know there were still U-boats in the Atlantic. . . . It was an important convoy and it was a big convoy and there was a great deal of concern I found amongst the crew about their own safety. I mean they had been doing this a number of times, but I think the impatience with me making a nuisance of myself was partly the fact that this was deadly serious, and a torpedo at any moment could make life very difficult.

Jacquie said, "My brother loved it and drove everyone crazy blowing the little whistle on his life vest. But I was sick as a dog and I hated it." Arriving in Liverpool just after an air raid they took the train to London. The worst of the Battle of Britain was over, but some bombs were still falling, and from time to time Marion had to take kids into a tube station to sleep. She wanted to get them out of that kind of danger, and sent them off to a boarding school in the north of England. "I remember twice she came up," Jacquie said, laughing. "And I was really embarrassed because she had long, red nails and none of the other moms up in northern England had long, red nails. And, I just wished she would sit on her hands."

On December 21, 1943, Chas and his team parachuted into Romania. They were to radio Istanbul on their arrival at the safe house, but the signal never came. A few days later Marion got a telegram from a Romanian friend. Chas was a prisoner. She assumed the Germans had him. She had shared with him what she knew about ULTRA — which was quite a bit — and was sick with terror thinking that he would be tortured, that he would give something away, that all that work would be destroyed and so would her beloved husband. But then the good news arrived; it was not the Germans who had Chas, it was the Romanians. The Germans wanted him, but the Romanians would not give him up. Lady Joan said,

> Chas was very cunning in that way. He pretended he was just a playboy and he didn't know why they parachuted him and he, oh, he liked to drink and smoke and all this sort of thing. He told the soldiers, who looked after them, "Come on and let's have a drink, bring some cigarettes and bring this," and nobody thought of tormenting him.

The pro-Nazi government had allowed King Michael to live on at the palace, and he secretly began to organize a coup. With Germany preoccupied in France after the invasion of June 1944, the young king successfully overthrew the puppet government, and one of his first triumphant acts was to release the political prisoners, including his friend Alfred de Chastelain. His son told us,

> The operation my father [had led in Romania], Operation Autonomous, was bitterly criticized by Stalin and as a result, after my father was released and King Michael had taken over the government, he sent him to Istanbul to reopen communications with the Allies. My father had given a commitment to Michael that he would come back [to Romania], but he wasn't allowed to, and he was brought back to Britain, and I think that really ended his SOE operation as far as action in the Balkans.

When Chas and Marion and the children got back together, the experience of walking down a London street together may have changed John's life. He said,

> He was wearing a uniform, he was a Lieutenant Colonel, and everywhere we walked around Richmond he was getting saluted because there were troops all over the place. And finally, in disgust, he took his uniform off so he didn't have to be saluting all the time. So I knew he was quite important.

But that was classy stuff, all the same, and the rank, and the salutes, and the stories that came with them stayed in the boy's mind.

And then came May 1945, and the war in Europe was over. Chas and Marion would have loved to go back to Bucharest; in most ways it was still Their City. They had a house full of furniture there. But the Communists had taken over by then, King Michael had been forced to abdicate, the de Chastelains were able to recover a small shipment of photographs and other personal stuff, but everything else was lost.

Spying is often said to be a kind of aphrodisiac. Once you've entered the secret world of intelligence, once you've had access to secrets, once you've handled intelligence, it's a world that is difficult to leave behind. Chas found it so. He had loved the excitement of a saboteur's life. Marion set about creating the impression that the world of secrets was past, and that getting the family together was the future. But she may have been complicit, with her husband, in continuing the game. Jacquie told us,

When my mother finally found a house for us, it was in Kensington, sort of backing onto the Russian embassy. It never really seemed odd to me until later on, and it just struck me one day, I wonder if that was by design that we backed onto the embassy, or if it was just pure chance.

Pure chance or not, it will never be known. They acted like any other family trying to recover from the war, and if there was something else going on, Marion never talked about it. John de Chastelain said,

My father started a business, a multifaceted business dealing with imports and exports and a particular chemical process dealing with film. He became a city man, pinstripe trousers, umbrella, briefcase. Eventually, of course, the business didn't work out and he went back into the oil business, which brought him to Canada.

In 1954, the family began a new life in Calgary, but without John. Perhaps it was the memory of his father in uniform that made him choose to study for a military career in Edinburgh. But his father wanted the family together.

My father suggested that I join him in Canada, and mentioned that there was a place called the Royal Military College that would allow me to do my military service and get my degree at the same time. So I came to Canada and went to RMC and joined the army.

Chas and Marion became part of Calgary society. They joined the golf club and the Ranchmen's Club. Calgary seemed an unlikely place to run into fellow spies. Lady Joan said,

> I was in Calgary already, having lunch with my husband and suddenly I feel somebody coming from behind me and putting his hands over my eyes. He said, "Guess who?" And I thought that it was a pretty silly joke . . . my husband didn't like those kind of jokes. I turned around and it was Chas, and of course we hugged and embraced, because you know you get very fond of the people who lay their life down.

Twenty years later, John de Chastelain was well on his way to becoming a Canadian general. His father died proud in the knowledge that his son was commanding a battalion in Winnipeg and his daughter had her dream, a family. On his death, friends remembered all he had done. Romania's King Michael sent a bouquet and a letter of condolence. The Man Called Intrepid came to the funeral, and said obliquely to young John that his father's work had "had an impact," but he never explained what that impact had been, the commitment to secrecy surviving the man in the coffin.

Marion took a job with a Calgary company and kept it until well into her seventies. Every day she lunched at Oliver's. Today the restaurant is called Quincy's, but nothing else has changed, not even the tables. Marion had her own, and it is still there. Few dining at Oliver's would have had the faintest idea what she carried in that secret head. She was just a nice lady who worked across the street, and apparently that's the way she wanted it. The secrets stayed secret.

Her grandson Ian got to know her over those lunches, and found some common ground.

> With her sort of car fascination — and I really loved cars — we kind of connected, on sort of a guy level. . . . And, as I said, my grandfather and her used to do rallies through Europe and they collected all these little badges. We talked about that kind of thing a lot and we decided that, why not get together and go on a road trip. So we went to Freehold, New Jersey, where she was born, and we spent a day there and we saw the house where she was born, and were just

sort of reminiscing about it and just wanted to see how her life started, basically.

But neither the grandson, nor the son, nor the daughter, ever got her to talk much about exactly what she had done in the war. William Stephenson, now Sir William, had retired to Bermuda, and once a year Marion went to visit him there. "I sure would have liked to be a fly on the wall when those two got together," Jacquie said.

But if there were any flies on those walls, they're not talking.

◆　◆　◆

The History Television documentary was written and directed by Patricia Phillips.

Part Two

ROBERT MARKLE
An Investigation

Unlike the other chapters in this Volume III of The Canadians: Biographies of a Nation, *in which the collaborating authors Patrick Watson and Hugh Graham would be at a loss to say exactly which sentences were written by which of them, the following chapter is entirely a first-person narrative from Patrick Watson, for reasons that will be almost immediately clear.*

In May 1965, my colleagues and I in the CBC production offices of the current affairs television magazine program *This Hour Has Seven Days* were surprised to learn that the Toronto police had raided a small local art gallery and confiscated a few pieces, charging the gallery owner with having exhibited obscene objects. The show in which these works had been hung was a major event for the small but popular Dorothy Cameron gallery. It was called *EROS 65*. The opening was very much a gala affair, and many Toronto celebrities had been invited. Pierre Berton conducted the "official" opening, and all of the works hung, by Harold Town, Dennis Burton, and Robert Markle, were in one way or another celebrations of sexuality.

The five Markles that had been impounded — Marlene Markle likes to say that they were put in jail — were highly stylized nudes, two women in each, and the women appeared to be making love to each other. It would later be whispered around town that the person who laid the absurd charge had been rebuffed as a lover by the gallery owner, Dorothy Cameron, and was exacting some kind of eccentric vengeance. The only reason to give that rumour any kind of credence is that the works, while lyrically erotic and intriguing, seem so inno-cent today that it is not credible that they could have seriously offend-ed anyone, even in the Toronto of four decades ago.

The *Seven Days* editorial group was unanimous in thinking that there was a story here for us, and I was assigned to interview the twenty-eight-year-old artist, Robert Markle, whom I had not heard of before. The interview went well, but it was not long enough to satisfy me, and I invited him across the street to the Celebrity Club for a beer. One beer led to quite a few more, but more importantly the conversation that began that May afternoon was picked up again over a few more beers a few days later, and became an extended exploration of ideas and experiences between Robert and me that grew into a close and profoundly affectionate relationship. You could say that the conversation begun in that basement bar that May afternoon never really ended until Robert's life ended, and long before that he had become my closest male friend.

So it was with some hesitation that I proposed his biography to History Television for this series, and I sought verification of the idea from producer/director Daniel Zuckerbrot — who knew Robert only as a friend of mine and through the half-dozen canvasses in my house. Zuckerbrot soon came back to say that he was intrigued, that I should not worry about my closeness with the subject, and that the story was eminently worth an hour of prime-time television.

It began in Hamilton, Ontario, where Robert was born in 1936, the son of steelworker Bruce Maracle and his wife Kathleen. Maracle is a common name in the Mohawk reserves at Deseronto and at Tyendinaga where Bruce was born. Kathleen used the spelling Markle — we don't know why — and although he was listed in the Ontario Births Registry as Robert Maracle, Robert always used his mother's version. He had the characteristic features of an Ontario Mohawk, but his personality and intellect were so compelling that it had never occurred to me to wonder about or inquire into his origins. In those first months of our rapidly burgeoning and turbulent friendship, he never brought it up, and when he made some offhand remark about "us Indians," he was surprised that I was surprised.

It was not that he wanted to conceal or suppress his Native origins; in a sense his mother had preferred to be quiet about their Iroquois beginnings, finding that in Hamilton, Ontario, in the 1940s life was a little easier if you were not identified as an Indian. Not until his mid-forties did Robert's curiosity about his origins begin to stir, hesitantly at first, but later strongly enough to take him to the Tyendinaga reserve near Deseronto, which he had never seen, a reserve dotted with mailboxes with Maracle painted on them. It was an experience that transformed both the man and his art.

But that was much later. In 1954 he enrolled in OCA, the Ontario College of Art in downtown Toronto, and there met Paul Young, another artist who became a close friend, and who now teaches at OCA. Young says that the college was very conservative in the '50s and '60s, and that guys like him and Robert had come there to learn the now-established traditions of landscape painting in Canada. Professor Young told us,

> Most of the faculty were either realistic painters of the old school or sort of semi-abstract painters of a slightly lower grade. So we weren't terribly impressed with their relevance to modern society as it was in 1955. But as students, of course, we weren't all that hip ourselves. When Robert and I used to go out painting, I mean we were trying to do Tom Thomson and Arthur Lismer, and so on. So we didn't really know what was going on. That passion for landscape eventually left him and I think be began to realize that in a sense it was history and there was no sense repeating history.

But even in those early days, when landscape painting was still the prime focus, Robert Markle, Young says, had a streak of difference, originality, and universally vectored curiosity about him that was noticeable from the start.

> The first time we ever went painting together, we were actually drawing. We had brushes and we had ink and everything, and we were down in the Humber Valley. And I got bored with my picture and I went over to see what he was doing. And do you know what he was painting with? He was painting with dirt, and it was the black sludgy muddy stuff and there was another kind of dirt and some other kind of dirt. He had them all sorted out in front of him like a palette and he had his brush and he was painting with dirt. And his picture was better than mine!

From later in his life there is quite a lot of video and film footage of Robert at work and at play that has survived. In some of those moving pictures you can see the tactile, sensual, skin-sensitive curiosity of the mud-painter. The artist bends down, bringing his thick glasses so close to the work that you fear they'll be spattered, and he spreads a thick crescent of wet black ink on the thick toothy paper. He follows up instantly with a piece of wadded facial tissue that he pushes thoughtfully into the wet black, and moves it about almost as if it too were mud that he was shaping as well as painting.

That inked crescent in the old black-and-white film is shadow on the thigh of a naked woman. Nudes in ink, paint, plywood, pencil — who knows, perhaps even in mud — are by far the dominant image in the large legacy of his surviving work (much of it now being collected by the Art Gallery of Ontario, and some as far abroad as the British Museum). Paul Young said,

> *He loved the strippers. He used to go to strip joints all the time,*
> *especially burlesque. It wasn't so much the girls in the bars. It was*
> *burlesque that he was really crazy about because the girls were so*
> *exotic and so bizarre. They all had enormous breasts and strange*
> *acts with snakes and balloons and everything, and he loved all that.*
> *He loved the showbiz part.*

And while many of his nudes are decorated with the pasties and G-strings of the striptease performer's repertory, the vast majority of these naked bodies are really one body, that of Marlene Shuster. Robert met her when she was in first year at OCA and he in second, and he almost instantly fell in love with her. He persuaded her to pose for him while they were still students. She had never posed in the nude before. She says,

> *I was going off to art school. Here's a nice little Jewish girl going off*
> *to art school. Wasn't supposed to do that in those days. He was the*
> *first person and I did it without even thinking. I mean he just drew*
> *that out of me. I became, I just became enamoured of him.*

Their studies at OCA stopped abruptly when Robert lost his temper over something so trivial he later could never remember what it had been. His reaction was not trivial; it was dangerously furious. Paul Young couldn't remember what caused it either, but the event is still vivid in his memory.

He got into some kind of a hissy fit. I don't know what it was about. But he picked up a bottle and threw it against a wall in a rage. And it turned out that it was a bottle of acid for etching plates. And whatever damage it did to the wall, which I'm sure was considerable, and it probably splattered on other people's work or perhaps somewhere else, I don't know. But the man who ran the print shop would not put up with that kind of stuff. So he was just summarily dismissed from the college and that was it. I don't think he put up much of a fight.

The painter Gordon Rayner, who was not at the college with Robert, says that

Marlene apparently went down to the boss man and said, "You kick him out and I'm leaving too." So they both did. Robert left. The school wouldn't give in. And so Marlene went with him. It was really a great happy ending because it's how Robert and Marlene got together and stayed together all those years.

They soon got married — November of 1958 — and then both had to look for work. The man who would make his reputation as a provocative painter of the nude female body could then be found lettering cardboard signs for Goodbaum's grocery store on College Street, including elegantly correct Hebrew script for the High Holidays. But that almost instant fascination with the contours and light and shadow on Marlene's body kept its hold on him. He photographed her with a simple stills camera, and then borrowed a 16mm motion picture camera and shot a few exquisitely framed sequences of Marlene posing nude by a rushing stream, supine in the long grass, slipping mysteriously through the shaded trunks of the forest. The film itself is visually gripping — Marlene generously made it available for the History Television documentary on Robert's life — but his primary purpose in filming these scenes was to have her available for his easel and his brush while the real person was out earning their living.

He did so much in the early years that he could draw a line without my being there and it would be the line of my body. He knew my body so intimately that he was able to put a line on the paper of a

*rib cage or a breast resting on the rib cage or the calf being extend-
ed. He always said, "It's yours, because that's how I learned and
that's what I draw." . . . Sometimes he'd say to me (chuckles), "I
wish I could do something else, you know. But I can't."*

She knows, and he knew, that this was a joke: Robert Markle could
paint anything he set out to paint. But it was a meaningful joke, for
Robert never lost his almost obsessive fascination with Marlene, her
body, her conversation, her spirit. She is there in the thick impasto
images of him with a saxophone and a glass of beer and she with high
heels and pointed nipples at a table in some imagined bar; or in the bed
in their farmhouse at Holstein, he watching television (he was a television nut, I thought) and she gazing at the ceiling; or in the next panel of
that same brilliant, funny, profoundly affectionate little triptych, she in
the bath (there are hundreds of bathtub paintings) and he on the toilet;
and in the third panel they are both in the kitchen, at the table, eating
and once again watching television.

He called her "The Muse." There is a canvas on the only wall in
our house big enough to take it — it is about 200 centimetres by 150
centimetres — of the two of them in the water, a lake presumably, she
standing, he apparently sitting for only his ponytailed plump head is
out of the water. It is entitled *The Muse Home for the Holidays*.

Robert Markle had an immense sense of humour and an infectious
lilting laugh that lit up a room. He was also an arresting writer: essays,
narrative journalism of an intense poetic and gossipy character — brief
flashes of imagery. Here is a short piece he titled *Statement: The Painter
and His Model*.

*Into the topless taverns and the gritty bars where the regulars have
puke on their shoes and the cleaning lady is a fire hose, the artist
goes, searching for his model. The model is his Muse, and he finds
her modeling in the raw night of these places, explaining her body
the way the artist might explain his art. She writhes under the
watchful eye of the artist. She dances to rock and roll, silently
mouthing the words as though they had the power to justify. She
moves with an amazing and splendid fury, fighting, in that bleak
interior, not to win a point but to preserve her very existence. The*

artist understands the event, he makes it his own by entering into her celebration, by leaving his.

"The real only exist in the mind of the artist strong enough to contain them and give them form." Lawrence Durrell had one of his Alexandrian Quartet *characters say that.*

Art is not art unless it threatens your very existence.

He was still painting his Muse the year he died.

The strippers he painted were not always Marlene, but Marlene often went with him to the Victory Burlesque on Spadina Avenue just north of Dundas, to legitimize his request as an artist to come backstage and meet and talk with the performers. She would study the G-strings and the pasties and come home and make copies of them and get herself up in the makeup and the tiny slips of fabric and the high heels . . . and he would paint her.

He wanted some of this stuff duplicated at home so that he could work more closely from it. So I'd be sewing costumes and that's how I learned how to make G-strings and stuff, was watching these women and how to move. Robert was kind enough to go out and buy me a record about how to do burlesque and little books, you know. How to do [it] books, how to do the moves and all that. Oh yes, we studied. We studied.

He experimented from time to time with lithographs. There is a 1987 documentary film, *Priceville Prints,* that shows him at work on the stones. His earlier (1975) five-part series of black-and-white lithos, *The Victory Burlesque Series,* changes hands these days at substantial prices — in the rare cases when its owners will part with one of the only fifteen sets that exist. Anna Hudson, the assistant curator of Canadian art at the Art Gallery of Ontario, said,

The nude in Robert's early works from the sixties, his burlesque dancers and even his movie star series — when you place these images together, the woman sort of begins to dance. She turns and moves. It's rhythmic. It's hard to take one of these paintings all by themselves and see it in isolation because it's part of a woman danc-

ing or a performance. So each of these images captures just seconds or just a moment. So it's like there's constantly a cinema in Robert Markle's head.

In the spring of 1960 Marlene went to work in the Isaacs Gallery. Avrom Isaacs had started buying and selling paintings when he was scarcely out of college. He was not that knowledgeable, he says, but he sensed a new energy radiating from the canvasses of this group of young Toronto painters, Markle and Rayner, Graham Coughtry, Nobuo Kubota, Dennis Burton, Michael Snow, and Snow's wife Joyce Wieland, and he began to round them up for his gallery. Marlene was working there before Isaacs took Robert on as one of "his" painters. He says that Robert hung around a lot because of Marlene. Robert would try to persuade her to leave work and come over to the Pilot Tavern. Sometimes he'd have a folio under his arm, and when Av eventually asked to look at some pieces, he found them pretty interesting.

Years later, after Robert was gone and Avrom retired, it was through the large Isaacs collection of Markles that a couple of pieces found their way into the British Museum.

In addition to painting, music, talk, beer, and his Muse, he loved his 250 cc Honda motorcycle, and pined for a bigger one. When that Dorothy Cameron scandal broke in the papers in 1965, he and Marlene had jumped on the little bike and driven off to New York together, motoring back just in time to discover that he was famous.

On July 9, 1969, now riding a 650 cc candy-apple red Triumph, Robert was hit by a car and terribly smashed up, most especially, and seriously for an artist, his arms. He was in intensive care for a week. During the months of recovery, his muse became his nurse. She told us,

When he was able to start to work again, get the use of his hands again, it was still in black and white but it was a different kind of imagery because he had to use a big shaving brush. . . . He couldn't close his hand around anything finer. So the image became really bold and broad stroked, not the finesse that he had. But still, very rhythmic — big broad lines covering the page.

As they talk about Markle now — often as if he were just out of the room for a few moments — his friends and colleagues and former students are as eager to tell you about Robert the talker, Robert the jazz enthusiast, and Robert the philosopher and teacher, as they are about Robert the artist. Not just teacher of art, either: he had a natural gift, almost a compulsion to teach, and a gift for philosophic inquiry and clarity that would have propelled him to academic stardom had he ever chosen to study in those often dismally obscure environs. Instead he taught in bars and taverns, or at the little dining table in the kitchen at the Holstein place (where this writer spent many enchanted hours being guided through the elusive craft of painting in watercolours). Not long after settling down in Egremont Township he joined a hockey team, most of whose members spent much of the winter living on their Unemployment Insurance Commission cheques. The team was called the UIC Flyers. Robert designed the logo and cap and sweater badges. You can see some of the boys — most of them getting on a bit now — wearing the badges in their caps, in the documentary, as they talk over a few beers about how life has not been the same since he left them. This was in the Mount Royal Hotel in Mount Forest, where they'd go for a few after a session on the ice, and the few would get to be quite a few, and by closing time Robert would not be in very good shape to drive the eight miles back to the Holstein house. So if Marlene was not with him, the boys would find somebody sober to drive Robert's vehicle and someone else would follow in another car — or more likely a pickup — to bring that driver back, and they would get him home safely. Teaching — and those evenings in the pub are remembered by the guys as being laden with the most intriguing kind of teaching — was not a one-way matter. As he tried to engage them in the stuff that engaged him, he was being nourished in return. Marlene remembers that

> he came home after an evening with the guys and he said, "You know, Tim said something really interesting to me. He'd seen me working on something and he said, 'Do you really see all those colours in the trunk of a tree?'" He was really grateful for that question because that meant that Tim was really looking and it just sort of opened the floodgate for conversations about art.

It was the same with his friends in the art world. Av Isaacs says, "A lot of people became very attached to him because he had a very special mind and it didn't flow along normal predictable lines. He could cause you to really dig when you were talking to him."

As an art teacher he combined an almost evangelical eagerness to lead people to find joy in the investigation that line and form and colour constituted for him, and at the same time to provoke and tease and upset any predisposition they might have to take themselves and their work too seriously.

There is film from his days at the New School of Art, part of the Three Schools started by John Brown, of *Warrendale* fame. This was a school where the instructors were all young contemporary artists whose work was being shown in the city, and you didn't need a high school certificate to get in: if they liked your portfolio, that's all it took. A lot of the sometimes very intense teaching took place around the corner at the Brunswick Tavern. In the film, Robert is working with a young woman, telling her in that soft, crooning voice he dropped into when he wasn't barking at the students, that she was

> *trying to make the colour do something in terms of form. And also you're trying to design on the page. With one brush full of paint you're trying to do all those things.*

Woman's Voice:
That's right. . . . Yeah, all those at once . . .

Markle:
You can't do it.

Rae Johnson, now on the faculty of OCA, was one of those early students.

> *I met Robert Markle when I started at the New School of Art in Toronto and it was a different kind of an art school run by artists. These were like the real McCoy. These were like the guys, the Isaacs guys. . . . I [still] hear him talking to me sometimes. I still remember the things he said just as if it was yesterday. And when I'm teaching my own class, I'm constantly reminiscing and coming up with Robert stories to tell people.*
>
> *The very first class, we had the nude model. Robert walked in*

and said, "Okay, draw the model," and he left. And you know, he came back hours later and he stood up and he said to everybody, "Okay, I want you guys to take your drawings home tonight and look at them and try to figure out why they're all so shitty!" And he walked out and that was it.

His language was often rough, the F word popping up as often as ums and ahhs and other pause words and with not much more intent. "Asshole" might sound like a distressing dig at you, when he probably thought he was being affectionately critical. Rae Johnson says she almost slips into those modes sometimes, Robert being so much present when she teaches. But you can't get away with casual "sexual" references in this time of Political Correctness, she says.

The way it is now it's all kind of, you know, you have to be very namby-pamby and make nice and everything. Once in a while, a little bit of Robert kind of creeps in there and then I kind of hope nobody is going to go hire a lawyer or something.

But beneath the playful, verbally rough edges, there was the constant inquiry. Paul Young again,

We went to New York [together] several times. We were standing in the Metropolitan in the roomful of Rembrandts. We were looking at one of his self-portraits. I was looking at it thinking, that's a nice picture. I like that, I like that. And I asked Robert, "What do you think?" And he said, "Hmm, I'm trying to figure out what the fourth last mark is." I thought, what? He said, "Well you can see the last mark and then you can see the mark before the last mark and then you can see the marks that came before that. But what's the one before that?" He was literally taking the picture apart backwards. And most people, even artists, stand in front of something like a Rembrandt and they're just awestruck. But nobody ever actually takes one apart and tries to figure out what makes it go. And that's the way Markle thought about art.

Rembrandt's own life work he had interpreted as investigation, one he was intensely eager to share as far as he could. In 1974, when I was making my television series *Witness to Yesterday* (for Global, which in those days was trying to demonstrate a commitment to original

Canadian programming), Robert called one day and proposed that he play Rembrandt — we wouldn't need a script; he knew Rembrandt's life story so intimately all I had to do was ask the questions a scholar or a journalist would ask the real person. His proposal had an imperative tone. I knew I would refuse at peril, but in fact it was an appealing idea, and I had no difficulty persuading my producer-director (and the series' originator) Arthur Voronka.

He had never acted, although he was certainly a performer, as his music and storytelling revealed, and his dancing — astonishingly light and graceful for a man who had become so heavy that one of his closest friends always referred to him as "The Fat Man," an echo from the dialogue of the Humphrey Bogart film *The Maltese Falcon*.[1] But if he was not a professional actor he was certainly a performer, and I was also counting on the drama of watching that probing, playfully inventive intelligence at work.

We partied irresponsibly the night before the shoot, and Robert was fearfully hung over when we got to the studio for his character makeup, which he mostly slept through as the makeup artist transformed him into an arresting version of one of the famous self-portraits. He walked painfully into the studio two hours later, waved away a proffered coffee and said plaintively, "Anybody got any speed?" — not as shocking a remark in those days as it might be now.

One of the stagehands said he was pretty sure he could get some nearby, and came back with it in minutes. Robert popped a couple and leaned back in his chair on the set with a dreary sigh. Arthur Voronka came over looking not inappropriately very anxious. "Uhmm . . . is this going to be all right . . . ahh, should we ahh . . .?" Robert waved at him irritably and said, "Get on with it, man, get on with it." Voronka looked beseechingly at me. I gave him a wave that was more reassuring than I felt, he called the set to order, and we began.

We were shooting 16mm colour film in those days, 400-foot rolls, so there was a pause at least every ten minutes. The slate went up, the call for silence, the "Roll 'em" command — the clapper boy put in the slate, and I put the first question.

1. The Fat Man in the film was played by Sydney Greenstreet.

There was a pause. Robert leaned forward, frowned, and said, "I don't think that's a very interesting question. Listen. In my time . . ." and he was off, a Flemish painter struggling to make a name for himself four hundred years ago. He was looking for the issues basic to his work, and in a strong metaphorical and dramatic sense we all believed we were listening to Rembrandt van Rijn. At the first ten-minute pause the whole studio burst into spontaneous and sustained applause. Robert blinked, smiled a shy smile, and said, "I could take that coffee now." That episode of *Witness to Yesterday* remains one of the best in the whole canon of more than sixty programs. Paul Young said,

> *In terms of his own work, I think that's really what it was about. He was looking for the basic issue — why am I an artist in the first place and why do I care about this and why should I take all this trouble? What does it all mean?*

"What does it mean?" was the question he asked more often than any other, and he expected answers from Marlene, from the priest who dropped in at the gallery, from the drunk at the bar, from his hockey mates at the Mount Royal — leading all of them, through his own radiant intensity about the central nature of *investigation* in the process of living, to feel the importance of that search in their own lives. It was, indeed, a question he often put in a despairing voice, sometimes overwhelmed by its elusiveness. At other times, over a just-completed painting or even just a stroke of the brush, he evinced a quiet sense of triumph: the investigation had arrived somewhere.

Another mode of investigation was music. Robert learned and played the tenor saxophone with highly individualistic gusto, and once said that anyone can criticize his art but "if they criticize my music I'll kill them." He had taken only a few lessons and had only a vague intellectual grasp of harmony, or chord and melodic structure. But he was — characteristically — a profound student. Jazz was his first taste, his tastes were wide-ranging, and he had great tolerance for experiment and the edges of the envelope. Where an Ornette Coleman would leave me wincing at what I heard only as resentful screeching, he would discern aural probings. And he too was always probing. Once, I came into the house to hear his great McIntosh sound system, cranked up high enough to make the windows shimmer, swarming with the rich viola and 'cello sonorities of some hypnotic medieval French music that he'd just discovered and was transported by. That particular music remained an almost daily favourite, and when I play the copy he made for me, he is suddenly sitting there in the room, nodding softly with a look of distant and profound understanding.

Gordon Rayner says unequivocally that music was even more important to Robert Markle than was his painting. They both played in the AJB, the Artists' Jazz Band: Rayner was a gifted natural on the drums and Coughtry (also untaught) was on trombone; what might have been acoustical chaos was given a spine and a coherence by the piano work of Michael Snow. Snow would later become famous for his *Walking Woman,* for his slow, sculptural, dreamy, prodigiously original films, for his flying geese at Toronto's Eaton Centre, and even more famous for the huge comic heads of baseball fans that decorate SkyDome's outside walls. Snow said,

> None of them had any basic technical knowledge at all really. They just got instruments and started playing. So it's an interesting kind of representation of what they liked in the jazz that they admired. They didn't have the harmonic understanding or the chops to make exact imitations, but out of having a kind of aesthetic formal sense and just out of a pure passion and the substances, some truly amazing things would happen. The music was very, very good.

When he came to the Artists' Jazz Band, Michael Snow was already an accomplished painter, sculptor, and filmmaker and the only professional musician among them.

> It was Christmas time and everybody decided to play — or it was suggested that we play a Christmas carol. And somebody said, "How about Joy to the World?" It's just a scale. Da da da-da, da da da da. So we got all these guys, Graham on trombone and we started to play it. And nobody could play it. So you have this wonderful thing of going . . . (sound effects). It does descend sort of . . . (sound effects). It's amazing. The funny thing about that is that incompetence in a certain sense is a kind of way of making variations, because it's better than playing it right, in fact, what they did.

In June 1978, the AJB was invited to play at the Canadian Cultural Centre in Paris, and to bring an exhibit of their art to be hung in that institution. Robert said he didn't want to go. "When I get more than twenty miles away from my studio my nose starts to bleed." Caroline, my wife-to-be, was living in Paris then and I was planning to spend most of the month there as well, so I more or less forced him to get a passport.

Gordon Rayner says that Robert tried to walk off the plane at Montreal. When he got to Paris, Caroline took a week off work to look after him. While he was still muttering, "Get me on the next plane home," she started to drive him around the city, just quietly letting him see all the stuff she knew would fascinate him visually — the ornate Metro stairway arches, the huge seventeenth-century buildings, the painted cast iron street urinals, the bars.

They stopped in a few bars she knew, including the one her mother ran, Casey's Irish Bar. He was wearing the denim suit that he had, for an Art Gallery of Ontario contest, decorated with exquisite needlework — nudes, of course — which had taken him a year to complete. The Parisians made a great fuss over him and the suit, and bought him drinks.

He withdrew his plea to be put back on the next plane, went off to Ibiza with the lads for a few days, came back in great spirits, and allowed himself to be bamboozled by Caroline and me into visiting the Louvre for which he had expressed a lofty contempt: "They're all tourists." Once in, we couldn't get him out till closing time at nine that night, and our photographs show him sometimes with his nose right up against the brush strokes of a ten-foot-high Géricault, sometimes posing beside a standing mummy case whose profile matched his, always staring with that look of penetrating inquiry.

The AJB concert at the Cultural Centre was a great success, and he felt by the end of the trip that it had all been glorious, crowned by making music for strangers in one of the world's greatest cities. "When he came back," Marlene says now,

he looked so young and smooth and — transported is the only word
I can think to describe how he looked. It sort of reminded me of how
he described his feelings when he first went to the reserve — that

he'd just been so moved and thrilled and his eyes opened. His heart
and his spirit opened to something he never suspected was there.

Making and listening to music were a constant part of the Markle investigation of meaning and of life. The central element of that catalogue of investigations was the sexual mystery. But in his forties another theme, almost as powerful, at first crept up him on like a hardly known visitor from his youth, and later became a motif that transformed the last years of his life: his Mohawk heritage.

I suspect he was drawn back to his roots in part by a new sense of the importance of heritage that this very urban-formed man had found when he and Marlene moved to the country northeast of Mount Forest, Ontario, in 1970. Somehow in those conversations at the pub the idea flowered of his doing something for the community of Mount Forest. Bill Koehler, then the manager of Freiburger's supermarket (now an IGA store), offered the eighty-foot-long stuccoed storefront as a surface Robert might work on. "He drew a sketch," Bill Koehler says, "and we seen this sketch. But I'll tell ya, it'd scare the hell out of you, okay . . . (chuckle). But anyway, he says, 'That's what I'll do.'"

It scared the hell out of them because it filled that whole eighty-foot wall, eight feet high, and would turn out to be one of the most intricate public murals in any small town in Canada. It is still there; you can't miss it if you drive down Main Street, although it is a bit faded and perhaps in need of a local philanthropist to provide the modest funds to restore and protect it. It is an intricate, narrative depiction of the woods and rivers, streets and birds, farms, old buildings on Main Street, and legends of the area, and it already contains hints of this next chapter in the artist's investigation of heritage.

It was soon after finishing the mural that Robert made the transforming visit to his parents' reserve at Tyendinaga. It was an opportunity to investigate another part of himself. "When he came back," Marlene says,

he was really, really quiet, very, very still. And slowly it came out
what the experience had been like. He walked onto the reserve, and
not like there's a line there, but suddenly you're on the reserve. And
he said, all the post boxes and all the signs on the stores were Maracle.

He told his sister Susan, "I saw people that looked like me and people that looked like you." And he said, "And it was such a good feeling." And he told Marlene that he suddenly felt at home and peaceful. "He wanted to move onto the reserve. If it had been possible, I think that's the direction we would have gone."

He took me down to Brantford and the Six Nations Woodland Cultural Centre to meet its director, a fellow Iroquois, the Onondaga teacher and curator Tom Hill. Tom Hill was helping Robert with a script for my *Heritage Minutes* dramatizing the creation of the Iroquois Confederacy.[2] The script was a daunting challenge, and he was still struggling with it when he died.

He also wanted to honour his township with a Mohawk theme; so, using traditional cedar split-rail fencing, he built a snaking structure in front of his and Marlene's house. The work is still there, seventy feet long and twelve or fourteen feet high. "You can only see it [properly] from an airplane," he said with a laugh (when we were shooting that pilot). "It's called the Great Horned Serpent of Egremont."

Around 1982, when Metro Toronto called for proposals for a mural in the then new Metro Convention Centre, he proposed a Mohawk-inspired piece, to be made of untraditional materials: coloured neon tubes, mirrored stainless steel. Some of it was painted, and every shape was drawn from the forms and traditions that had taken on such significance in his life. His proposal was accepted. The fee was substantial, but he kept little for himself, spending almost every cent on materials and on the specialized crafts he had to engage to form the stainless steel and to bend the neon tubes into his Mohawk shapes. He called the work *Mohawk: Meeting.* It is an astonishing 160 feet long. You'll see it immediately as you begin to descend the escalator from the main entrance to the lower level at the Convention Centre, and you may want to stay and be with it for some time. He signed it Maracle.

2. Originally the League of Five Nations (also known as the Iroquois Confederacy) included the linguistically related Cayuga, Onondaga, Mohawk, Oneida, and Seneca. It became the Six Nations when the Tuscarora joined the confederacy in the early eighteenth century. The original confederacy, whose constitution is one of the worlds's oldest, may have been formed as early as the fifteenth century.

◆ ◆ ◆

My wife Caroline Bamford and I saw a lot of Robert in the last months of his life. Together the three of us developed a television series in which he would ride a Harley (the company provided the bike) from town to town seeking out the microbreweries that were springing up. Robert had discovered Creemore Springs Lager, in the Dufferin County town of that name, and that was the brewery we chose for the pilot of the series that was to be called *Something Brewing*. CBC Television liked the proposal well enough to invest a crew and an editing suite for that pilot, and we went up to Creemore in June to shoot it.

With Caroline producing and me directing, Robert would ride the Hog into the microbrewery town. He'd spend as much time sketching the local architecture and chatting on camera with the weekly newspaper editor or a group of teachers in the local middle school as he did investigating the brewery and its products. And then the idea was that he'd stack his drawings on the back of the bike and ride off to the next episode and the next microbrewery town. Sadly, he died only days after we finished editing the pilot.

It was a July evening in 1990. Robert had a beer with the Flyers at the Mount Royal, and set off for home on his own. He was fine, no need for anyone to drive him. Doug Kerr, known to the lads as Suds, was the last person to speak to him. "He said, 'See you tomorrow, Man,'" Suds recalled in the documentary, at a table at the Mount Royal, his eyes welling. But somehow, inexplicably, in that clear starry, moonlit night, Robert drove hard into the back of a tractor on the road, and that was it.

One of his friends said, "There is a big black hole in the universe now."

There is.

◆ ◆ ◆

The History Television documentary was written and directed by Daniel Zuckerbrot.

• Part Three •

FRED ROSE
The Member for Treason

Sometime in 1946 Soviet espionage agents working the Montreal area set up a meeting with a thirty-nine-year-old Canadian named Fred Rose. Rose was sympathetic to the Soviet cause. He was a card-carrying member of the Canadian Communist Party, and, like many Canadians in those first years after World War II, he still saw Stalin's Soviet Union as the great friend from the East who had helped bring down the Nazis. That was one reason he was proud to be a Communist. Probably the majority of Canadians then, whatever their political outlook, still thought of Stalin as the "Uncle Joe" they'd been taught about in school during the war, the benevolent head of an allied nation without whose help the democracies would almost certainly have lost. Some cooler heads had not lost sight of the dark essential centre of Soviet power; Winston Churchill had made his famous "Iron Curtain" speech on March 6 of that same year, but the phrase had not yet entered the popular vocabulary as the prime metaphor for the closed and cruel Soviet dictatorship. The Cold War had not really started.

It was about to do so.

The Russian agents wanted something from Fred Rose, of course, and they were very good at their job. They flattered him, but not too much. They responded with almost shy courtesy and dismissive gestures to his praise of their country's role in defeating Hitler. The gifts they proffered were pleasant but not extravagant. They had heard about a new explosive formula developed by a Canadian chemist, something called RDX. They were able to persuade Fred Rose that it was in the interests of International Socialism and World Peace that Russia have this RDX, about which their Canadian allies were being unreasonably secretive. Rose was able to find a chemist who knew RDX, and to pass the required information to the engaging Russian who, in his low-key but authoritative way, was clearly someone close to the levers of power, an insider.

The Soviet embassy in Ottawa had brought this man in as a "military attaché" from Mongolia. His name was Colonel Nikolai Zabotin, and Rose was pleased to be brought into the inner circle. He was excited when Zabotin gave him a code name and secret instructions for communicating with him. Zabotin was, in the parlance of the espionage professionals, "running" Fred Rose: Rose was his agent.

What makes this story much more extraordinary than it would have seemed had Rose been just another seducible member of the CCP, is that he was also the Member of Parliament for Montreal-Cartier. He was the first and only Communist ever elected to the Canadian Parliament, and even in the eyes of some of his political opponents, a pretty darn good MP.

Rose was Jewish. The Montreal community had been badly divided between Jewish anglophones and Catholic francophones in the years leading up to and well into the war. In those years there was, among some Quebecers, what now seems an incomprehensible sympathy for the Nazi movement. Anti-Semitism was a normal undercurrent of the times, not only in Quebec but also across Canada and throughout the United States. Jews did not get elected to public office. It was hard to get into medical school if you were Jewish: there was a quota on Jewish admissions at McGill in Montreal and at the University of Toronto, never publicly acknowledged, but quietly firm and effective. If you wanted to teach in a public school in Ontario and were Jewish you'd just better forget about it. There were eminent Jewish law firms, as there are now, but in those days it was hard to get into such a firm if you were not Jewish, and hard for the Jewish firms to attract Gentile clients, next to impossible for a Jew to get into a non-Jewish firm.

But in Montreal for a while, layered on top of that "normal" undercurrent of anti-Semitism was a sympathy for the Nazis not unrelated to the fact that during World War I the issue of conscription had set off a huge conflict in Quebec. Most Quebecers felt that they had no obligation to fight the British Empire's wars for them. Their reluctance to be roped into another seemingly irrelevant war allowed Fascism to take hold in Quebec more strongly than most places in prewar Canada. There were brown shirt marches in the streets of Montreal, with the famous straight-arm salute. The producer of our documentary on Fred Rose, Francine Pelletier, found a photograph of a Montreal mother tucking her baby into a cradle decorated with a swastika, beneath a photograph of a benign, avuncular-looking Adolf Hitler.

Montreal's Jews were, not surprisingly, very fearful about all this. They had heard the stories coming out of Germany. For many of them, the far left was the natural opposition to Fascism, and in those days a great many members of the CCP, the Canadian Communist Party, were Jewish.

But even fellow Communists close to Rose were deeply disturbed by what he did. For many, an important part of Fred's getting elected to Parliament had been the legitimization of the Party as a part of the Canadian democratic system. Probably very few members of the Party, even the deeply committed and ideological ones, had any idea how profoundly undemocratic the "Parent Company" was. When they went for visits to Moscow they didn't see the gulags, or the dissidents being tortured and shot in the head; they saw happy smiling faces and well-fed kids who had been paraded for their benefit. It was a good show, and they were taken in by it, as were many non-Communists — the British philosopher Bertrand Russell among them.

But this! This was a guy committing out-and-out treason, and not just any guy, but an MP who had taken a special oath of loyalty. It would hurt the country, and more important it would hurt the Party. Yet Rose was not alone. A younger Canadian Communist, Harry Gulkin, had also considered committing sabotage on behalf of the Soviet Union. In our documentary he tells the story, looking elderly and benign, with long flowing white hair and moustache. It is hard to believe that this is the same Harry Gulkin who once planned to blow up a freighter in Montreal Harbour, the SS *Cliffside*, which was known to be carrying munitions to the Chiang Kai-shek's nationalist, anti-Communist Chinese. Chiang Kai-shek was technically an ally of the West in the war against Japan.

Gulkin says now that his pals had warned him: if his scheme was discovered it could destroy the hopes of Canadian labour. In the end, Harry Gulkin's commitment was to the workers more than it was to International Communism, so he did not go down to the SS *Cliffside* after all.

"We didn't think about the consequences through," Gulkin mused on camera. "I think Freddy could not have thought through the possible consequences of . . . that act."

Those consequences began to gather momentum. A man named Igor Gouzenko, a cipher clerk in the Soviet embassy in Ottawa, defected and went to the RCMP. Gouzenko was so terrified of what might happen if he were caught by his former bosses after he appeared in public to testify, or to be interviewed on television (once by Laurier Lapierre and me, for *This Hour Has Seven Days*) that he wore a pillowcase over his head with cutouts for his eyes. This gave an unfortunately comic colour to what was the extremely serious message Gouzenko had to convey.

He told the police and later the media about the enormous extent to which Russia had been spying not just on Ottawa but also on all its Western so-called allies. The news exploded. The Western world was scandalized. Canada was at the centre of the scandal, Russia went from friend to enemy, and the Cold War was on with a vengeance.

Colonel Zabotin's spy ring, Gouzenko revealed, included military men, high-ranking bureaucrats, and scientists. Rose had been working Gordon Lunan, a captain in the Canadian army and a CCP member, and had tried to get him to bring Canadian scientists into the net.

All told there were twenty other CCP members nailed for collaborating with the Communists. Nineteen of them were, after all, "only Communists"; you could expect mischief from them. But Fred Rose was a Member of the Canadian Parliament, and what he did was explosive. There was a widespread demand to declare the Party illegal again, as it had been for a while in the 1930s. Captain Gordon Lunan, an officer of His Majesty's Armed Forces, was tried for treason, convicted, and given the surprisingly short sentence of five years. He would later write a very readable book about his experiences, *The Making of a Spy: A Political Odyssey* (1995), trying — with a measure of success — to exonerate or at least explain himself. Fred Rose also claimed innocence; cocky to the end, he said to reporters when he was charged, "If I was guilty, do you think I would have stuck around?" He never testified in his own defence. He got six years, which also seems surprisingly little.

The Party was not declared illegal, but the Rose case did lead to the RCMP's decision to set up Canada's first separate elite intelligence unit, the Security Service. And if Official Canada began to isolate Canadian Communists, the Canadian Communist Party also took steps to isolate the convicted members from the rest of the Party. Ironically, that was Fred Rose's idea. He insisted that none of the convicted group say anything to incriminate the CCP: they had acted on their own, that would be the myth. Rose may have been foolhardy, but he was steadfastly loyal to the party — more so, as it turned out, than they would be to him.

In 1951, on his release from prison at the age of forty-four, Fred Rose died — not physically, but spiritually. The rest of his life was lived in a weird twilight, a state hard to reconcile with the irrepressible street fighter and outspoken parliamentarian he had once been, who had carried the banner for social justice, for universal tolerance, and for the rights of the downtrodden. Now he was just a shabby little traitor, and outside his family nobody wanted anything to do with him. When he got out of jail, his old comrades in the Party set him up in a small business selling lamps, and then told him to stay well away from them.

After RCMP agents began to appear, all wanting to buy lamps, the Party proposed that Fred think about moving abroad "to look after his health." Poland would be a good choice, they said. Poland was Fred's birthplace. He and his parents had immigrated to Canada when he was thirteen. Returning now, in his mid-forties, he could find little there to make it seem like home. His home was Canada, and he was an exile. The Polish Communists gave him and his wife and daughter a comfortable existence. The apartment near the *Staromiejski* (town square), once a grand bourgeois residence stripped and partitioned to make tiny workers' flats, was now restored to its original splendour and nicknamed "the movie set." The Party even provided tropical vacations. But for Rose it was still limbo. He had refused Polish citizenship and Canada had revoked his Canadian citizenship, so not only was he nowhere; he was, in a way, no one. Polish Party members might tell him what a hero he was, risking his life to spy for the cause, but it seemed to Fred as though they had put him in a case, in some kind of museum.

The ironies became more painful now. From his "museum case" he witnessed the beginnings of the collapse of Communism. It began with what seemed a roar to the West but was perhaps not much more than the whispering of what had been tacit but common knowledge inside the Soviet Union: Khrushchev's denunciation of Stalin. When the plump, humorous, gap-toothed Khrushchev made his way to the top position, he seemed to be ready to open some doors and strip away some of that absolute power that Lenin had established and Stalin had entrenched. Khrushchev said he would not agree to be "General Secretary," only "First Secretary," first among a small group of equals. He said that too much power invested in one leader led to problems, and he openly denounced in the twenty-first congress of the party the blood-soaked excesses by which Stalin had murdered so many millions of his own people and imprisoned millions more.

Bold though this seemed to the West, where the monolithic loyalty within Russia had seemed unbreachable, in fact, Stalin had already begun to appear as the monster he really was and the exposure of his regime as a black comedy made it easy to dissociate the dictator from "real Communism."

Rose was also a witness to Poland's growing rebellion against the authoritarian heart of Communism. In Canada his old friends had fallen away from the old Party one by one, but Fred had not. In Poland, even as food was rationed and martial law imposed, even as he and his wife watched in fear through the windows as riot police gassed the demonstrators, they kept the faith. What a sad picture it is in retrospect, the countryless little guy, once influential and applauded. He'd a big name in what he thought of as his real hometown, Montreal, and he was on his way to be a somebody in his adopted country. And now he was a nobody — a citizen of nowhere. He could dream and watch TV. One of his few pleasures was television, especially the broadcasts of big Soviet military parades. Those, he loved; they bespoke the old dream that he still clung to.

His nephew, one of the few who visited them in Poland, said that Rose was "trying to show that he was quite comfortable and quite on top of things." But of course things were not as they appeared. He was desperately lonely; all he had left were his memories. He treasured a recorded message from Paul Robeson, a recording he would play over and over, as if to keep him in another age. It was Robeson's endorsement of Rose's campaign for a seat in the Parliament of Canada, as a Communist.

By the time he turned sixty he was almost bald, and what was left of his hair was wispy and white: he looked naked and helpless. The old twinkle was gone from his eye. His daughter Laura tried without success to get permission from Ottawa for her parents to return. "He was so harmless by that time," Laura said. "How could they not allow him to go back?"

How could she not understand?

He turned seventy-six in 1969. Everything got slower and slower. His heart stopped. The historian Pierre Anctil wrote, "He rode the wave to power and when the waters receded, he just drowned and was never seen again."

And indeed today, Fred Rose, once a name on the front pages of every newspaper across the country, is forgotten. When the story was proposed to History Television, almost nobody among that very historically alert group of programmers had heard the name. Our crew, canvassing Montreal streets with that device familiar in the biographical documentary — "Have you ever heard of a man called Fred Rose?" — found only one elderly francophone who had, in a working-class coffee shop: "A Communist, wasn't he? Didn't he go to jail or something?"

Of course, there may be more to that story than we know even now. The RCMP files on Rose, three bankers' boxes, mostly of newspaper clippings, are still unavailable to historians. Maybe they contain the memoirs he left, which seem to have disappeared, unread, unpublished.

What is solidly documented is that Fred was born Fishel

Rosenburg in Poland about 1907, the son of Jacob and Rachel Rosenburg. The family arrived in Montreal about 1920. They were part of the great influx of Eastern European Jews, a fact that would be decisive in Fred's political future. His daughter Laura said that the new life in Canada, even for their parents, was the real life. It was the first sense of security and the possibility of some kind of future that they had known.

The Rosenburgs settled in the Jewish neighbourhood around "The Main": Boulevard St. Laurent. And they probably had no idea that they would become part of a three-way political and cultural struggle. The old, deep-rooted conflict between the minority English-Canadian establishment and the French-Canadian majority was becoming tense again as the war fanned some old, never-quite-cooled embers. The largely Protestant anglophones had the money that ran the province, politically and industrially, and the francophone majority trusted too much in its true royalty, the hierarchy of Quebec's Roman Catholic clergy, who were grandiose, powerful, reactionary, and quietly in league with the powers in Ottawa to keep the Quebec French Canadians ignorant and in their place. "The white niggers of America," one writer would call them, a cheap supply of labour. Ripe for a revolution which, amazingly, when it came thirty-odd years later, was carried through almost without bloodshed, The Quiet Revolution it would be known as, *La révolution tranquille.*

But when Fred Rose was a young man in Quebec there were no professions open to the French Canadians except the law, whose Napoleonic Code was different from the English Common Law that prevailed in the rest of Canada; there were no schools of engineering, little chance of medical school at McGill — the best in the country, no chance on the upper floors of the business community unless you assimilated almost to the point of disguising your francophone origins.

If, in the midst of this ancient stress, the Jews were to become a new force of dissent, that was bound to send the temperature up. The Jews, many of whom had reached maturity in Europe, had lived through the revolutionary violence of 1917; many were intellectually inclined and most were on the political left. It was a recipe for conflict.

The most radical elements among the Anglos and the French were hard right and xenophobic. Lots of young Jews joined the Communist Party, many of them hardly out of their adolescence. They felt it was part of their history, in their blood. Harry Gulkin was only eight years old when he signed up, Fred Rose seventeen. That youth brigade, The Young Pioneers, an enlistment device in Communist countries around the world, marched out in trademark caps and red neckerchiefs, proudly chanting, "One, two, three, pioneers are we. We're fighting for the working class, against the bourgeoisie." It was a world struggle; they sang it in several languages. Some of them, Rose and Gulkin among them, would get free trips to Russia and come back feeling elevated, justified, confirmed: they had seen paradise, and it worked.

When Rose was in his twenties the Communist Party was outlawed in Canada, and for a while in his early married years Rose was harassed by the government, occasionally jailed, and often publicly booed. He spent much of the time in hiding. His wife Fanny called him "the little man who wasn't there." Their daughter Laura had repeatedly to change schools as she and her mother moved from shabby rented room to shabby rented room.

By the time Rose was thirty the Spanish Civil war had begun to change some of these attitudes. It was the Communists who spearheaded the international volunteers in the fight against Franco's Fascists in Spain. Rose, now working as an electrician, was one of the organizers of the 1200-strong Mackenzie-Papineau Battalion, the Canadian contingent assembling itself to go to Spain and fight the republican Franco. Rose helped to set up the system of blood supplies for the wounded anti-Franco forces. He worked on the organization of a ten thousand-strong rally in Mount Royal Arena for the Canadian Communist hero Norman Bethune. The charismatic surgeon was just back from the Spanish front. The mood at the rally was euphoric, and the threat of fascism had begun to return some respectability to the Canadian Communists.

The social values of our present age are so profoundly coloured, if not determined, by that motif of the advertising stranglehold on our culture whose prime message is that the good life is achieved by buying things and that shopping is a duty. It may be hard for people raised in this world devoid of appeals to common purpose and shared values, to understand what it meant to be a marching Communist. To those zealots, some scarcely bearded, others whose dark eyes remembered a dark Europe, the world seemed as though it could just be on the verge of a revolution, a glorious, long-dreamt-of revolution. The empty-spirited, socially purposeless bourgeoisie would be trampled by the unavoidable march of history, and the working class would finally come to its rightful heritage where real social justice would be universal.

It was only a matter of time — that seemed so clear, so inevitable — only a matter of time now, before a few gentle pushes in the right place would bring the whole rotten structure crashing down. One of those gentle pushes was getting someone elected to Parliament, to show the whole country that a Communist is a serious player. Join the party, help the Bolsheviks, destroy fascism, and infiltrate the bourgeois political structure. You argue it, and you hear it, and you believe it on the street corners, at the poulterer's, in the bakery, at home over dinner. This kind of faith is not easily distinguished from religious conversion.

And when Marxist Messianism was married to a messianic Jewish culture, you had something more than belief. It became indisputable knowledge, certainty. For many it was like a drug that carried you through each day, because the end was at last in sight, as it was for the evangelists who gathered on the hilltops every few years to hail the apocalyptic blaze of light that would signal the end of the world, the Millennium, the Apocalypse.

The Revolution, the Millennium, the Messiah, it was all the same. And it was already embodied in the Soviet Union, a massive working-class country, where everyone lived in contented equality, in perfect freedom. That's quite possibly the roseate illusion that drove Fred Rose. He'd been there; he'd seen and possibly believed the show (although there was a part of him that seemed more of a realist). It was certainly that kind of evangelical fervour that fired hundreds of his young comrades in the Party.

By the late 1930s, Fred Rose had developed formidable organizational skills, more than ever in demand as the conflicting forces coalesced around their ideologies. Quebec's hard-drinking premier and demagogue, Maurice Duplessis, had declared war on Communism. He brought in the infamous Padlock Law by which the possession of Communist literature was made a criminal offence, and he used it to attack the Jehovah's Witnesses. The attack turns out in the long run to be a mistake for Duplessis and a move forward in Canadian civil liberties when the poet and civil libertarian lawyer F.R. Scott wins the case for the Witnesses.

But in the meantime, the police, instructed to be suspicious of anything in a red cover — it could be Communist literature — confiscated, among other things, Bibles and a copy of George Eliot's *The Mill on the Floss*. This brought ridicule down on the traditional authorities, and it certainly did not hurt the Communists.

With the Great Depression into its seventh or eighth year, the class war seemed to the Communists to be arriving right on schedule. Now imagine this multisided nest of animosities in which anti-Communist populism mixes with Jewish Communism, Anglo-Protestantism, and French Catholicism, and then Nazism emerges on the eastern horizon, dark and angry and atavistic.

Nazism's Quebec counterpart, Adrien Arcand's Fascist Party, began to move against the Jews of Boulevard St. Laurent. The photos show the young converts crowded into a room with their dark shirts and slicked-down hair and a sea of arms in the Nazi salute. Anti-Semitic cartoons of the period show dark, big-nosed Jews leering over showers of gold coins. An old woman now recalls that it was better not to shop too far from St. Laurent or storekeepers might peg her as Jewish and give her trouble. Harry Gulkin remembers a mob of students from the university moving down the boulevard, shouting *"A bas les Juifs! Et les Communistes!"* (Down with the Jews and the Communists!). He remembers his father rounded up local Jewish storekeepers and set out after that same mob. Later, his father came home victorious, crowing with delight, with blood on his shirt. The formula for this animosity was as volatile as the RDX that would soon send Rose to jail. Catholicism, not least the French-Canadian kind, has a history of anti-Semitism. The compliance — or silence — of the Anglos did not help. It was born of the massive power of English Canada in Quebec: it was easy to just ignore the Jews. Meanwhile, the French Canadians — a useful majority, kept in their place by the Church — were on the same lower level as the Jews, and they often lost out in commercial competition with Jewish merchants and professionals. The Jews, after all, were not long out of the *Shtetl* where talents were honed and children disciplined with uncommon intensity. Marxists in the Jewish minority looked on the French majority as class enemies. And finally it was anti-Semitism that helped bring Rose to prominence. As he appealed to all these groups to fight it, he would be in the lead, and while the Gentile anglophones were the despised bourgeoisie, you could deal with them, perhaps even get close to them, get them to trust you even if you could obviously not trust them.

In 1941 the hero of the hour was Uncle Joe Stalin. The Stalin-Hitler pact, which had given pause to many a Communist, had finally been broken. Hitler had launched his disastrous march on Leningrad. Sustaining unthinkable losses, the Russians stood fast around the starving, beleaguered city, the Nazis retreated into a winter that killed almost as many of their soldiers as the Red Army had, and from now on that Red Army would beat the Germans in victory after victory.

For the time being, Uncle Joe, benign, moustached, with a thick head of hair, a pipe, and a twinkle in his eye was adored on both sides of the world as a champion of freedom from Nazi oppression. In Canada, the Communist Party acquired a new legitimacy by changing its name to the Labour Progressive Party. Fred Rose was their number one organizer. The dream of World Revolution had now been replaced by the practical promise of better housing and wages for the working class, be it Jewish, French, or even English.

You only have to see the pictures of the wretched poverty in Quebec in those years — children nearly naked, in filthy slums — to get a sense of Labour Progressive's appeal. Out from under the stigma of the outlaw, they went vigorously public in an open, familiar, legitimate political campaign complete with glossy brochures. Fred Rose looked very much the man of his time, with an elegant pencil moustache. Everyone wore suits and hats: Fred's suit and fedora were unusually sharp. Fundraising was suddenly a piece of cake. Party members gave a percentage of their income; donations came from middle-class supporters moved by guilt or by the Party's announced humanism. The popularity of Stalin didn't hurt. Even Jacques Parizeau (destined, in half a century, to lead the Parti Québécois as premier of Quebec) lent help and advice, and met from time to time with Fred Rose.

In April 1942, Michel Chartrand and other Quebec nationalists who opposed the national policy of military conscription formed the Bloc Populaire. It was made up of people who were outraged that Ottawa broke its post–World War I promise to never again introduce compulsory military service. Their leader was the journalist Andre Laurendeau, who later became a commissioner on the Royal Commission on Bilingualism and Biculturalism, which would change the face of Canada. A fair-minded and rigorous journalist — long the editor of *Le Devoir* — his time in the Bloc would inevitably trouble him with that Party's taint of racism. One friend of Rose's said the Bloc Populaire was "not just anti-English, anti-American (and) anti-Canadian — (it was) anti-Semitic."

On the eve of the federal election of 1943, the riding of Montreal-Cartier was evenly split between French-Canadian and Jewish voters. The issues were explosive, calculated to set the two head to head. Foremost for the Jews was anti-Semitism. It faced them every day in Montreal and in the dreadful stories out of Europe. For the French Canadians, it was the newly announced policy of conscription and they were in a fury: Why should they sacrifice their lives in a war they didn't want, a war on behalf of the colonizer who had stripped them of their dignity? Why should they fight for a colonizer in whose language they'd had to live day to day, where all signs had to be English, where all transactions, business deals, and even the call-up notices were printed in English?

The Bloc Populaire blamed the anti-Semitism on street bullies, although they did observe that Jews had taken a dim view of the refusal of French Canadians to participate in the pro-war Berlin parade. The

Jews wanted a united front against Nazism; Quebec did not. Sadly, many Québécois were still quietly sympathetic to Arcand's Fascists.

In that Montreal-Cartier by-election, the Liberals were primed to fight to the death for their long-held seat, but they hadn't a chance: the real battle was between the French-Canadian Paul Masse and the anglophone Jewish Communist Fred Rose. The fight became pretty sordid. One of Rose's acquaintances saw thugs rolling metal rods into newspapers to attack the drivers taking Rose's constituents to the polls. At election headquarters at 5 Mount Royal, Jack Shaw, a seaman's organizer, leaned out the window shouting out the results as they came in. He referred to Masse as "The Fascist." Rose won by the narrow majority of a hundred-odd votes. His mother's response seems almost prescient. When her son came home jubilant she said quietly, "My son, I hope some good will come of this."

By 1946 the rough style of the streetwise, subversive Jewish immigrant had worn off. Fred Rose had joined the mainstream of Canadian society as a Member of Parliament. To many, even passionate enemies of Communism, perhaps he represented a hoped-for end of the war between the working class and the ruling class: perhaps it was a sign of hope that one day there could be a government that would care about them. Rose built a reputation as an indefatigable worker and a politician who never forgot that he was a man of his constituency. He was a good MP who chatted with his parliamentary colleagues on both sides of the house, nodded wisely, and put in an appealing good word for the working people.

And that was when Colonel Zabotin made his move. It is likely that Fred Rose's guard was down, and his confidence up. Russia still had the affection of the public, and he was in a position of privilege. What could go wrong?

And yet he was not a stupid man: he must have known something of the risk. So why did he do it? Why did Fred Rose throw away the best years of his political life? Why did he do something that many, if not most, of those in the CCP would condemn?

Oddly, perhaps, Rose was sentimental, not a quality we commonly associate with the disciples of the Karl Marx who condemned sentimentality as a vice of the bourgeoisie. Rose tried to hide his sadness during his exile in Communist Poland, the land of his birth. But he longed for Canada and Quebec. He heard the song about the wandering Canadian, "*Un Canadien errant,*" and when the singer came to the words *Si tu vois mon pays, mon pays malheureux* he cried. When his mother died, he wept easily and he wept long. He loved schmaltzy music and waxed grateful when someone sent him records of love songs by Dinah Shore.

A complex little guy, our spy, our condemned traitor. An irrepressible charmer. Short but rakishly handsome, he had brilliant blue eyes, with a faintly distant look. He was a ladies' man and a flirt. He loved action and the lure of power. Altogether, he had a charisma that attracted even people like Jacques Parizeau.

But there is, along with this charm, a sense of Rose not having time for ordinary people or ordinary things. One contemporary remembers him as being abrupt. Another speaks of an oversized ego: "a little man . . . who would like to be a big man." And there seems to have been little doubt, among those who knew him, that he enjoyed power and publicity. He sang songs too, but his were always Communist songs with a theme for every occasion. His daughter Laura remembers that as sometimes grating — never a song just for the fun of it — a kind of relentless political moralizing.

She also speaks of the bitterness she felt as a girl in need of a father and a family life while Fred Rose devoted everything to the Party or to hiding from his persecutors. Ironically, it was only during their exile in Poland that family life took on some elements of the traditional. "It was the first time in my life, at the age of seventeen, that I lived in a house with my mother and my father, and my father went to work and my mother did the shopping and the cooking."

The life stories of many famous spies get a little elusive when it comes to explaining their betrayal. Ideology is rarely the reason. Some, such as Kim Philby, were merely arrogant. They wanted to be sort of daring supermen. Indeed, many British spies were from the aristocracy; Oxford was a KGB recruiting pool. Few if any British spies came from the working class. American spies, such as Aldrich Ames, were seduced by money. Some Russian spies must have done it from boredom and a hunger to get out of their interminably drab home country. In many cases and in many countries, the act of treachery was the most colourful and the most decisive thing a spy ever did.

Perhaps we can even say that Rose was more sincere than most. Of course he would claim a transcendent loyalty to the Revolution and its progenitor, the Soviet Union. He would call what he did an act of principle, a supreme gesture of loyalty. But you can't help feeling that behind it all there was something vainglorious. Something of the ladies' man and the charmer, the hero who had little time for his daughter but all the time in the world for the Revolution. Maybe that's what his mother was thinking about when she said ironically, "My son, I hope some good will come of this."

◆ ◆ ◆

The History Television documentary was written and directed by Francine Pelletier.

‹ Part Four ›

BROTHER XII
Prophet or Fraud?

This is the bizarre story of Edward Arthur Wilson. It is a story that has been difficult to piece together. Wilson himself took elaborate steps to disguise, conceal, and erase his history. There are few living witnesses, and not much documentation, so there are gaps that invite a good deal of speculation. But there is enough evidence to considerably frustrate Wilson's intention to disappear without a trace. The story is layered with appearances and disappearances: an intriguing labyrinth out of which emerges a portrait of a man who seems to have been one of the most unlikely scoundrels ever to tread the Canadian scene.

For much of his life Wilson was a British sea captain. He was small of build, soft-spoken, but with a commanding presence. For purely narrative or dramatic reasons it is tempting to jump in at the point where Captain Wilson was personally going to choose the next vice-president of the United States of America. He told his followers it was time to strike. There would be a presidential election in 1928, and Wilson declared that the election would set off a war between Protestants and Catholics. He would travel to Washington, DC, from the Aquarian Foundation headquarters in the Gulf Islands of British Columbia, to make contact with James Heflin, the Washington spokesman for the Ku Klux Klan and also the US Senator from Alabama. Heflin led a strong anti-Catholic faction in Congress. Wilson would convince Heflin of the equally dangerous threat revealed in the book *The Protocols of the Elders of Zion*, and that these two evil forces would have their way paved for them by what he predicted would be a massive financial crisis triggered by an imminent crash of the stock market. He said the stock market was on the edge of collapse because of insane margins, dangerously overinflated stock values, and out-of-control speculators. The ensuing depression, he said, compounded with the inevitable religious wars, would lead to a worldwide cataclysm. He, Wilson, would be the world's saviour.

He announced all of this in the November 1927 inaugural edition of *The Chalice*. Published out of Nanaimo, British Columbia, *The Chalice* was the newsletter of Wilson's newly formed organization. It was no ordinary newsletter, nor was the Aquarian Foundation just another charitable institution or service club like the Rotary or the Lion's. It was an instrument of Wilson's own version of Theosophy, the movement founded in New York in 1875 by — among others — Madame Blavatsky. Helena Petrovna Blavatsky — H.P.B., as her followers often called her — said that she was in touch with the Accredited Masters, who did not apparently live in the same world as the rest of us, though there was something about a secret place in the Himalayas to which H.P.B. was able to travel by some kind of spiritual means.

We know that E.A. Wilson joined the Theosophical Society in 1912, giving an address in California, and that he stayed with it for several years. The movement is still active. There are thousands of enthusiastic pages to be found on the Web that describe it in language like that of one of Blavatsky's co-founders, W.Q. Judge:

> [An] ocean of knowledge which spreads from shore to shore of the evolution of sentient beings; unfathomable in its deepest parts, it gives the greatest minds their fullest scope, yet, shallow enough at its shores, it will not overwhelm the understanding of a child. . . .
> Embracing both the scientific and the religious, Theosophy is a scientific religion and a religious science.

A tough-minded investigative journalist named Colonel Henry Steel Olcott had gone to one of Madame Blavatsky's seances with the intention of exposing her, and was so impressed with her apparent ability to contact the spirits of the dead that he moved in with her and helped found and finance the movement. Despite reams of scientific material exposing the fraudulence of Blavatsky's occultism, the movement survives today, although Wilson's Aquarian Foundation, inspired by Blavatsky, is long since defunct.

Wilson also declared his belief in the theory, then much in circulation, of an international Jewish conspiracy. This theory held that world finance, elections, executive decisions and government, whether monarchy or republican, were all secretly controlled by a small, shadowy group of Jewish financiers. The proof lay in a viciously anti-Semitic book entitled *The Protocols of the Elders of Zion*. It has long ago been demonstrated to be a hoax as fraudulent as Blavatsky's interviews with spirits, but it is still quoted by anti-Semites. In Wilson's time it had not yet been exposed, and was credited by a surprising number of influential people. Wilson said that the Jewish conspiracy in fact intended to so control the whole of the world's governance and capital that it would achieve its goal of a world dictatorship led from Paris by a member of the Rothschild family. Wilson's views of Catholics, Jews, and others whose beliefs he deplored, were, in addition to being focused and nourished by such works as *The Protocols*, a rich and educated mixture of an enormous range of the world's religions, ancient and modern. He was a diligent student of the legends of the Egyptian gods Horus and Osiris, and other exotic texts including the *Bhagavad-Gita*, and the *Upanishads*. He talked with apparently great understanding and conviction about Karma, the Great Christian mysteries, and the unity of all things. And even when he carried out his final disappearing act (if indeed he did carry it out), it still seemed possible that in some measure he believed in his own extravagantly self-aggrandizing sermons, and in the reality of the special role in the history of the world that he believed he would play.

By the fall of that year, 1927, the most promising candidate for the leadership of the American Democratic Party was a Roman Catholic named Al Smith. If Smith ever won a federal election, Wilson said, it would be the end of Protestantism. He said that since the Republican candidate, Herbert Hoover, was under the control of World Jewry, there would have to be a third party. As an agent and founder of that third party, Wilson would save Protestantism, which meant saving the world. He said he had been told by the voices of his spiritual masters that he had to slip into the White House by acting as a sort of elder advisor; and thence, by controlling the choice of both the next president and the vice-president, to save the world from perdition.

Curiously, his failure to penetrate the White House as announced, and thus to save the world, like the unfulfilment of most of his prophecies, did not seem to disenchant his followers. The man, like his inspiration Madame Blavatsky, had charisma.

In July 1928, the year of the election, Wilson convened a gathering of Aquarians from all over North America at Cedar-by-the-Sea, a few miles from Nanaimo. He then left by train for Chicago via Seattle. Travelling with him was an Ontario-born woman named Myrtle Baumgartner from Clifton Springs, New York, where her husband had been practising medicine. A few years earlier Dr. Baumgartner had been permanently disabled in a car accident, and the marriage had begun to disintegrate. In her distress Myrtle had a dream that seemed to point to a new direction for her life. In the dream she was crossing a dangerous, fragile bridge and on the other side of it a man stood waiting for her, a saviour. Later she had another version of the same dream, this one set in ancient Egypt. When she met Wilson, she recognized him from the dreams. It was later alleged by his enemies in the Aquarian Foundation that he told her she was the reincarnation of the Egyptian goddess Isis, and he of Osiris. He said they would have a child who would be the Horus of the New Age, that they had worked together in past ages and on "inner planes," and that the time had come when they must work as one in the real and outward world. By the time they got to Chicago, she was pregnant.

It was clear now that she had to wind things up with her husband Ed and move to Cedar-by-the-Sea. She headed East to settle her affairs. Meanwhile, in Chicago, Wilson was organizing the founding convention of that messianic Third Party. This was a gathering of a number of formerly separate fringe parties, who, realizing that they had a common bond in their militant Protestantism, were now trying to become the political saviours of America. The idea of a mystical Protestant crusade had come to Wilson in the form of a spiritually communicated instruction from a group of wise ones. Like H.P.B's mentors, Wilson's were known as the "Masters," were also hidden somewhere in the Himalayas, and were, perhaps, not exactly human. It was the Masters who had given Wilson his predictions. None of those predictions came true, except for the stock market crash and the Great Depression that followed. By then, the Third Party had been dismissed by the press as a national joke, and the movement had fallen apart.

E.A. Wilson was born in England in 1878. His father had built a metal bedstead manufactory into a substantial enterprise, thanked the Good Lord for his success, and took his family into an evangelical Protestant sect called the Catholic Apostolic Church. This was a millennial church whose members believed in the imminent Second Coming and required children to study the Bible and memorize vast passages to help insure their salvation.

Wilson would later say that as a child he not only knew the Bible inside out, but he had also had direct contact with the world of seraphim and angels. But the sect's evangelical fervour did not at first seem to be able to maintain its hold on him, nor did his father's authority, and in his teens he went off to sea as a trainee on a British Navy windjammer. He then took his skills into the merchant navy, worked hard, and acquired a command at an early age. In fact, although he had abandoned his family and his active membership in the Catholic Apostolic Church, that early training was always quietly at work in his inner being, as he travelled the world, and stood alone at the wheel during the long night watches. The author Colin Wilson[3] (no relation) specializes in self-styled prophets like E.A. Wilson[3] — spiritual frauds and other misfits and criminals. He finds that many prophetically inclined people often feel like outsiders, reject the tribal magnetism of family and sect, and characteristically go through a long wandering period. Wilson tried to settle down in New Zealand, and even married and started a family. But he later abandoned them and they never saw him again. His later letters to colleagues and followers reflect on the almost continual sense of spiritual quest that accompanied his years at sea.

Wilson's uneven course, which included a lot of serious illness, continued for much of his life. But the bumps in the road seldom slowed him down. Colin Wilson's studies suggest to him that this continual sense of being on the outside can lead to despair, suicide, even a fatal wasting away with this lack of direction, which can come to be,

---

3. *The Outsider, The Spider World Trilogy, The Strange Story of Modern Philosophy*

effectively, a lack of the will to live. But if the outsiders begin to feel they understand the reason for their spiritual or existential hunger, that's when destiny may appear.

It happened to Wilson in October 1924 when he was in the south of France. He said that he was sick in bed one night, lit a candle, and got up to get a glass of milk. But before he could move from his bedside, a cross with the head in the form of a loop, appeared to him. He recognized it: the Ankh, the Egyptian symbol of life. Then the room seemed to dissolve in an explosion of light. An Egyptian temple materialized before him, he wrote later. Wilson himself was standing in a colonnade whose pillars went on for infinity. A great echoing voice addressed him as the Pharaoh: "Thou who hast worn the crown of Upper and Lower Egypt."

Certain that he was in touch with one of the Masters or Brothers of the Great White Lodge, a hidden spiritual committee which, in Theosophy, controlled the world, he took the name of the invisible brother to whom he had spoken, Brother XII. A generous assessment of his legacy might credit him with inventing the Age of Aquarius and with developing much of the semi-evangelical and occult theory and practice that we now call New Age. True to his Catholic Apostolic education, he preached that the millennium, a great spiritual and cataclysmic revolution, was at hand and that everyone had to prepare for it. The chosen, he said, would pass into the New Age, namely the Age of Aquarius, which would reach fulfillment in the year 2000. We are saying he was "certain," and that he "believed" these things, as a convenient way for recounting the next part of the story. To the student critical of this man's strange career, it is not clear how much he believed and how much was an invention convenient to his plans and ambitions. As the story unfolds there does appear to have been a period of genuine seeking and inspiration, which may have been contaminated — even destroyed — by the wealth and power that suddenly came within his grasp.

The First World War and the great influenza epidemic of 1918–19 was followed in Britain, America, and much of Europe, by an economic boom and a new spirit of excess. The flapper girls, the automobile, the rage for dance, drink, and sexual adventure among the affluent young — these phenomena had disillusioned conservative-minded

people who had felt there were real lessons of moral and social consequence to take from the War and from the epidemic. It was to those
people that Brother XII came with his message about the New Age. The
Masters had told him to begin in England, where his leadership would
be eagerly welcomed; and so, in England, he wrote and published *A
Message from the Masters of the Wisdom in 1926*. With a table of contents
framed in a classical arch supported by two Doric columns, the work
purported to be an epistle from the Brothers of the Great White Lodge,
addressed to all those alienated by twentieth-century materialism. It
invited them to reject self-indulgence in favour of the wisdom of a universal brotherhood. The work had a strong millennarian flavour, pre-
dicting the collapse of the social order:

> *In the near future, existing institutions will be destroyed and
> practically all religious and philosophical teachings will be blotted
> out. Therefore the Masters, foreseeing these things which are soon
> to come on the earth, have prepared the present work. The message
> is everything; the personality of the messenger is nothing.*

The messenger, of course, was Brother XII. Soon another article of
his appeared in *The Occult Review*, over the pseudonym Chaylor. *Chela*
is the Theosophical word for a special messenger of the Masters, and in
British speech the two words can sound exactly alike. "Chaylor" wrote
that there was an unusual centrifugal pressure from astral forces, or
beings, pushing out into the normal world. Some of this pressure was
benign, and some was composed of unprecedented evil. *The Occult
Review*'s editor praised the author to his readers. Wilson began to
receive masses of correspondence, and soon was signing up members
for his Aquarian Foundation. Among them was a soft-spoken, fairly
prosperous middle-class couple, Alfred and Annie Barley, who were
astrologers. When they came to visit the Messenger in Southampton he
read them a letter that he said had been dictated by the Brothers of the
Great White Lodge:

> *This people is shortly to pass through a great tribulation, and
> warning is given so that those who heed it may remove to a place of
> safety. A small settlement is to be prepared in British Columbia.
> You should act now and save what you can. Remember that the*

existing order is about to disappear. You and yours . . . will almost
certainly disappear with it.

British Columbia would be the centre not only of the new Spiritual Age, but also the development of a "sixth sub-race." Money would be needed, of course, and the Barleys began selling their possessions. Brother XII allegedly became friends with some very influential Britons: Oliver Lodge, Arthur Eddington, Neville Chamberlain, and others. He was soon able to write to all of his new Aquarian members to say that he was about to fulfill the command of the Brothers of the Great White Lodge by building the Aquarian Foundation colony in North America.

Early in 1927, Brother XII took passage across the Atlantic and up the St. Lawrence, and proceeded forthwith to visit the Theosophical lodges of eastern Canada on a mission of proselytization and recruitment. Most of the members had read *A Message* and were breathless with anticipation at seeing the great Brother XII in the flesh.

They were not disappointed. His photograph shows a good-looking man always in a shirt and tie, with a rakish goatee and intense black eyes at once foreboding and mischievous. He was more articulate, persuasive, and inspiring than they had imagined. A good number of these Theosophists began to sign up with the Aquarian Foundation, many offering to establish chapters in their home communities. These were not the innocent or the despairing so often seduced by cults: on the whole they were intelligent and sophisticated. Many were quite well off. They had already accepted the idea of the extraordinary spiritual accomplishments of Madame Blavatsky; now they were face to face with the one who might just be her successor.

Certainly there is ambivalence here: beliefs developed over fifty years, esoteric ideas and yet allied with a sort of hucksterism. G.K. Chesterton wrote that there was definitely an extraordinary power involved in the movement, but — diabolic or celestial — it did tell lies about matters of the spirit. At this stage, however, it would have been hard for anyone to see exactly where the lies were. To the disciples it seemed as though the entire future was theirs, promised by the — up to now — totally credible and powerfully charismatic Brother XII. People began to head for Cedar-by-the-Sea, on Vancouver Island, seven miles from Nanaimo, which was already a prosperous coal town, with its curving, busy, and crowded main street. The Masters had instructed Brother XII that this was one of the few parts of the world in which it would be possible for believers to survive the coming millennial cataclysms.

Brother XII got an eminent Vancouver lawyer by the name of Ed Lucas to incorporate the colony under the Societies Act of British Columbia. This was concluded in May 1927. The group arrived — Brother XII, his common-law wife Elma, the Barleys, and two more Englishmen who had also sold everything for the Aquarian life. They created a board of governors that took on added weight when the German-American novelist, astrologer, and wealthy entrepreneur Will Levington Comfort became a member at Brother XII's invitation. A distinguished Vancouver publisher also joined the group. There was more than enough money from donations to buy the land at Cedar-by-the-Sea. Then as today it was a surprisingly tame wilderness, a flat serene coastline, intensely verdant, forested with old cedar and backed by distant, misted purple mountains. Then as today its waters were often still as glass.

It all seemed to happen overnight. Ten months before, Brother XII had been unknown. Now, on the wilds of the British Columbia coast, he held the first meeting of the board of governors under a large tree. And you can see them still in the group photograph: a gathering of middle-class patriarchs, elderly and middle-aged, mostly in shirts, ties, and vests, standing and seated in the shade of a great cedar. It was Brother XII's forty-ninth birthday.

The place seemed to grow under its own power. First, as the colonists cleared the land, there were only tents. Then they began to build houses exactly like the trim, clapboard cottages of the 1920s that are all across Canada. The houses were spread out a mile apart, perhaps to ensure privacy, perhaps because Brother XII felt he could control things if people were not close together.

Lumber and supplies came from the co-op in Nanaimo; the father of one member, Mervyn Wilkinson, was the treasurer of the co-op. Construction went on day and night. In a matter of months it was done.

A picture of about eight or ten colonists shows them looking like farmers of the period in overalls and dungarees, broad grins on their sunburned faces. Brother XII is in the background lounging on a veranda in hat and tie, separate in space and in style.

Soon, as if the settlement had always been there, there were social evenings. There is still no sign of the devious, whimsically cruel person who will so enrage his once-devoted followers that the whole enterprise will soon break down. In his recollection of the colony, Wilkinson's son Mervyn, lively today and in his eighties, gives us an insight into the personality of Brother XII who, in the following exchange, isn't quite the demagogue one might imagine. Not yet thirteen, Mervyn was doing his homework when Brother XII was visiting. The visionary asked if he could watch Mervyn and after doing so, remarked, "It's very good. You're doing well. You keep at it." And then he added, "One thing, Mervyn, yeah, remember that there is so much to learn that none of us have the time to know it all." And before leaving, he said, "Carry on, you're doing well . . ." And then what Mervyn felt: "That was my first meeting with Brother XII, which for a boy of twelve, he talked *to* me. He didn't talk down." Brother XII, as we will have to remind ourselves, was a very likeable, appealing, sensitive man. At this point.

Before long the Aquarian Foundation had about 125 chapters of ten members each around North America. It was also now that Brother XII revealed the bigotry at the heart of his mystical teachings and attempted to apply it to politics in the Third Party movement.

As we have suggested, the spectacular failure of the Third Party only revealed another side to this driven personality. After the founding convention in Chicago (which was after the Isis-Osiris generative train trip with Myrtle Baumgartner), Brother XII went to Toronto to meet Mary Connally, a wealthy woman from Asheville, North Carolina. She had written him to ask for the meeting, and the letter was particularly appealing since it contained a cheque for $2000. Somewhat softened and spoiled by her wealthy family, Connally was twice divorced. She had almost lost her only son to pneumonia at the age of thirteen. Connally was likely as desperate as she was unquestioning:

perfect material for Brother XII. In any case, she — like so many others — had found sudden meaning and hope in his writings, and had been smitten with the idea that she had a role to play in The Work.

> *I was convinced (she later wrote) that this was The Work which I was going to do in the world. It was as if different architects had offered you a plan for a great building or a temple. I accepted his drawings. . . . I then realized that he was to be the contractor as well as the architect, and that he, alone, could carry out these plans.*

When she met Brother XII in the lobby of the King Edward Hotel, his electric presence confirmed to her that The Message and The Work were indeed the meaningful directions she was so in need of. She wrote him out a second cheque, this time for $25,000, the biggest single donation the Foundation had yet received.

Back at Cedar-by-the-Sea, when the other new female adept, Myrtle Baumgartner, arrived she was not made very welcome by the colonists, including the board of directors. Not surprisingly, Brother XII's common-law wife Elma was outraged, and many of the colonists were on her side; what was this outrageous flouting of fidelity. Wilson/XII elaborated a complex proposition about the divine imperative of certain unions, which had no element of sexual gratification within them but were solely intended to bring into the world a new life to carry on The Work. Some members who were, like Brother XII, familiar with the Egyptian legends, were prepared to accept that the begetting of a Horus was only a metaphor for Brother XII's successor. Brother XII said that the divinely appointed child would begin his work in 1975, and would lead the Aquarians into the new millennium. But others speculated about an extension of that metaphor, which they thought was displayed in the central hieroglyphs of the Osiris story. In that schema, while Osiris actually faces toward Isis, his body is turned toward Nephthys, the Goddess who ultimately causes his death. Who then, they wondered, would Nephthys be?

The colony was no hit-and-miss do-your-own-thing sixties commune. The board of governors looked like a group of 1920s bankers on vacation. As they considered the Myrtle Baumgartner incident, with Brother XII's convenient explanations about the spiritual imperative of

The Succession and his contradictory abandonment of Elma, they began to wonder aloud whether or not The Messenger was, in fact, losing his mind.

When they confronted him he continued to insist that this was the sacred but temporary union of two higher natures. When Myrtle had a miscarriage, some took it as evidence against him. One said, "It seems Horus has slipped his moorings."

Then there was an incident involving Mary Connally. The board found out that Wilson had deposited her $25,000 cheque to his own personal account instead of to the Foundation's. "Enough!" they said, called the lawyers, and formally had him charged with misappropriating the money for his personal use. The preliminary hearing was a circus. The trial proper unfolded like a plot. At its crisis, reporter Bruce McKelvie wrote in the *Province*,

> *The dingy courtroom of Magistrate C.H. Beevor-Potts Thursday would have made an admirable setting for a movie drama or a scene for one of the old-time plays of the coal-oil circuit where, at the crucial moment of the trial of the hero, the heroine, blonde and blue-eyed, bursts into the group of serious-faced officials, lawyers and spectators, to proclaim the innocence of the accused.*

Remarkably, the judge believed her, and the accused was acquitted. But his troubles were not over. News came that the provincial government intended to investigate the Aquarian Foundation. In the meantime, Brother XII — who by now was beginning to quite dictatorially tell members of the colony what they could and could not do — confined Myrtle to the "House of Mystery," his place of meditation. She had a second miscarriage and then a nervous breakdown. He decided to send her home. Her dream of being consort to the Egyptian God Osiris was at an end. She sent a pathetic telegram to her paralyzed husband: "If you will have me back, may I come, heart sore and weary?" Dr. Baumgartner saw no reason to forgive his ex-wife for what must have appeared to him to be demented wanderings, and so Myrtle's story ended with a final plea to the doctor to expedite the divorce.

At the end of 1929, it might have seemed that the tragicomedies of the Third Party and the scandals of Myrtle, Mary, and the trial would have finished Brother XII. But we have to remember he was widely known to Aquarian groups scattered all over, people who knew little first-hand of the squalid goings-on. Immediately after the trial, Brother XII sent out letters inviting yet more Aquarians to the colony to be the next generation. And indeed they came.

Now, using Mary Connally's money, Brother XII bought the De Courcy group of three islands totalling close to seven hundred acres. Suitably lined with rock cliffs, De Courcy Island was to be the "inner sanctum" of the colony. Before long, an elite of the most zealous and still loyal colonists arrived to take up residence off the mainland. A couple named Herbert and Dora Jefferson converted their life's savings into gold and handed it all over to Brother XII. The preferred currency for donations was the gold American Eagle. The splendid coins were packed into mason jars, and hot wax was poured over them, as if they were preserves. The jars were then packed forty-three to a box and hidden on De Courcy Island. This would keep the gold safe from intruders, Brother XII told the colonists. But then secretly, at night, he would dig up the boxes and move them to different hiding places. And then compulsively, like some sweating miser, he would move them to discourage theft.

In early 1929, things got stranger yet. A peculiar woman named Mabel Skottowe arrived with the man whose mistress she was, the wild, bearded Roger Painter. He was the Poultry King of Florida and had made a contribution of $90,000. Brother XII was fascinated with Mabel, the sense of power in that cold, forbidding eye, her mouth stern with decision and hostility. Perhaps this was Osiris's other woman, Nephthys, his dark destroyer of the hieroglyphics. The god dressed as a pharaoh has his body turned to his right but his face is directed towards a second goddess on his left.

Roger Painter was named Brother IX. Mabel became Brother III. But Mabel had another name as well; they called her "Madame Zee." Madame Zee, with a lofty disdain for conjugal prudence, left Mr. Painter and went to live with Brother XII in his new house on a promontory overlooking the De Courcy Island anchorage. At this point we do not hear anything more about poor Elma. Mabel's new status as Madame Zee gave her an authority that she seemed to relish. She issued commands to the disciples, berating them, once even using a horsewhip. Snapshots were popular at the colony, but not with Madame Zee. It was speculated that she was on the run from the police.

But even then, there was a measure of harmony. The colonists were hard at work clearing and cultivating the land on De Courcy to grow enough food to make the island and the colony at Cedar self-sufficient. They succeeded. The ground was lush, the weather benign, the trees bore fruit and nuts, and there was a healthy dairy herd. Perhaps, some hoped, the unbalanced behaviour of Brother XII and the ranting of his mistress would pass. There seemed to be some promise that the colony could indeed spawn the New Age.

But Brother XII got worse. When the police came out to De Courcy to investigate some of the bizarre stories about buried gold and strange practices, The Messenger got the message: it was time to think about writing another chapter in this long, complicated novel that was his life. He and Mabel decided they needed time away from the colony. They spent part of the year in England, in Brixham, a pretty south coastal town of almost Mediterranean aspect, its crooked streets of bright buildings crowding down a steep incline to the water. He put his seamanship to work and bought a yacht that had once been a fishing trawler — a long, low, sleek seaworthy vessel with many doors and windows. They called it the *Lady Royal*. Together they sailed her to the Caribbean and there they docked for repairs. Brother XII had a fight with the shipyard owner and sailed away without paying. Much later, Wilson would discover that a huge steel bar had been driven through the keel, the shipyard owner's revenge presumably. The bar gathered kelp, and the boat mysteriously got more and more sluggish; they went ponderously through the Panama Canal and up the coast of Mexico where they were hit by a hurricane. Taken far out to sea, they ended up becalmed and out of drinking water, parched, close to death (and wishing for it, they said afterwards) until a passing ship heard their dog bark in the night, and they were saved.

When Wilson returned to De Courcy in December 1930, the disciples gathered to watch him remove packets wrapped in black oilskin, all the time muttering wildly to himself. He began to bury the packets around the island, as he had buried the colonists' gold years before. Because of Brother XII's erratic behaviour and the subsequent strange business of headlights flashing from the mainland and secret boat trips back and forth, the colonists began to talk about drugs.

Things deteriorated fast. When Mary Connally's money dried up, she was put to work at exhausting manual tasks and completely cut off from the man to whom she had been so dramatically loyal. It was her money — yet another donation, $10,000 this time — that had bought De Courcy, but now she had to chop wood and carry heavy loads on her back. "It is a test," he said and when in his judgment she failed, she was given another, ploughing and cultivating a three-acre field, a test she also failed.

The colony was now arranged in a distinct hierarchy with De Courcy at the top and Valdes Island at the bottom. Mary Connally was sent to Valdes. Brother XII forced everyone into a game of "musical houses" by which residents were moved from house to house. Soon they were freezing cold and eating poorly as they worked to exhaustion, terrorized and submitted to new extremes of humiliation at the hands of Madame Zee. As Roger Painter put it later, "We thought we were in the brotherhood of love. We found out we were in the brotherhood of hell."

There is no doubt that total control was at the heart of the cruelty. And by this time it probably wasn't even a means of enforcing the faith. Colin Wilson suggests that Brother XII had grown tired of his religion and his only real goal was to eliminate any possibility of anyone contacting the authorities or looking for the hidden wealth. When all was under control, he might escape with Madame Zee, a free and a rich man. But there is another explanation, and that is that he was syphilitic — which would explain his weekly trips to Nanaimo. A couple of doctors from a clinic there would claim in the future that a certain Dr. Hall had treated Brother XII for syphilis.

Sometime in 1931 the names of Edward A. Wilson and Mabel

Skottowe were legally changed, his to Amiel de Valdes and hers to Zura de Valdes.

When immigration officers turned up one day in 1932 to investigate a reported violation, Brother XII began to talk paranoically about attacks by government agents. He set about stocking firearms and fortifying the De Courcy area. You can still see the sniper nests, small, one-person forts of boulders rolled together where the sentries — exclusively women — watched out for interlopers. They did four-hour shifts, moving from nest to nest. Sometimes they fired shots in the air when boats came too close.

Then came the breaking point. Madame Zee ordered a seventy-eight-year-old schoolteacher to drown herself so that she could attain everlasting life. When the old woman tried several times and failed to carry out the order, Madame Zee terrorized her until the woman broke down. The De Courcy colonists were not yet so brainwashed that they could accept such an outrage. They confronted Brother XII. He responded coolly and systematically, ignoring the complaint, by quietly getting them off the island in twos and threes until everyone except for two determined loyalists was moved to Cedar. Only then did they realize what he was doing to them. They launched a legal action.

Mary Connally and Alfred Barley were the ones who brought that suit, technically to recover some of the money they had put into the colony. In a sensational deposition, the betrayed lover Roger Painter, once the Poultry King of Florida, declared that Brother XII and Madame Zee had tried to kill their enemies in the colony with black magic rituals held at midnight in the cabin of the *Lady Royal.*

In the end the judgment went against Brother XII, but not in time to stop his escape. He and Madame Zee moved quickly, destroying many of the buildings on De Courcy. They sank the yacht, dug up the gold — maybe half a million dollars' worth — and disappeared. The courts awarded the De Courcy property to Mary Connally.

The fugitives reappeared briefly in Devonshire, where Brother XII made out his will, leaving all his wealth to Madame Zee. In 1934, they move abruptly to Neuchâtel in Switzerland. Brother XII had heart problems (perhaps a cover for syphilis) and was treated at the luxurious Clinique du Chanet, with its *Deuxième Empire* Mansard roofs and gallery verandas on every floor. At sunset on November 7 of that year, in the idyllic setting of an apartment with a wrought-iron balcony overlooking the lake, Brother XII died, perhaps of a heart attack.

Or did he? Colin Wilson offers another version. The one-time visionary had been reduced to the empty, bitter, and evil-tempered Mr. Wilson. Mabel, bored and fed up, deliberately terrorized him to bring about an end by which she could only profit. Perhaps it was a subtle and undetectable murder. In any case, she had him quickly cremated, and disappeared with an amount equal, in today's money, to at least ten million dollars.

And then there is another version, and in this atmosphere of paranoia it has a hell of an appeal. Did Brother XII, or E.A. Wilson, perhaps fake his death? Donald Cunliffe, the son of Wilson's Nanaimo lawyer Frank Cunliffe, says that in 1936 he travelled to California with his father. He saw Frank meet a mysterious man on a yacht in San Francisco Bay and hand him a briefcase full of money. The man was all in white — shoes, hat, everything. He had gleaming eyes and a powerful presence. Colin Wilson dismisses this, and says he thinks murder is much more likely. But in 1937, Donald Cunliffe said, his father got a call from Gibraltar from a man the operator called Mr. Wilson, and the lawyer afterwards confirmed to his son that it was the man on the yacht, Edward Arthur Wilson.

Whatever the truth, the wildest speculation only inflates the myth. Even the embittered colonists were not so alienated as to leave De Courcy Island despite the horrible associations. They stayed on for several years. Mary Connally, once forced to be a beast of burden, was the last to leave, in 1944. She told her lawyer: "For the old Brother I'd give that much money again, if I had it to give." Even journalists and historians are ambivalent about the man, some inclined to read in his early writings a deep and sincere inquiry into the human condition, an inspired if romantic vision of how that condition might be transformed, and then a transformation of the man himself from a benign leader into a crazed despot. The speculation about syphilis contributes to this almost forgiving view.

Hundreds of people have combed the island looking for gold that might have been forgotten or left behind in that hasty final departure, but the old caches have turned up nothing, except one hidden vault in the basement of a colony bunkhouse, empty but for a handwritten note: "For fools and traitors, nothing!"

If there is a Brother XII spirit looking down on it all, he must love the story about the man in white on a yacht in San Francisco Bay.

◆　◆　◆

The History Television documentary was written and directed by David Cherniak.

Part Five

JOHN WARE
The Fame of a Good Man

During the dreadful winter of 1882–83 an American cowboy named John Ware came north with the drive, and hired on with the Alberta rancher to whom he had helped deliver the cattle. That winter was brutal even for Alberta. Ware had never seen anything like it; where he came from all that happened after November was that some leaves fell off the sycamores, and the nights got a little cooler. But that first winter in Alberta, one day when the herd disappeared and the boys had to ride out looking for them, there were places out on the range, far from the few trees around the ranch house, where it felt like — and probably was — 40 degrees below zero.

The other cowboys gave it up and beat it for the bunkhouse, but John Ware had somehow determined he would find that missing herd — he had, after all, driven them all the way from Montana. The wind brought tears to his eyes; he later said he thought they had frozen. He lost his hat. He said that he'd been afraid to move his fingers in his thin woollen gloves for fear they'd break off. He went so far into that white hell looking for those cattle that he had to go four nights without sleep before he got back. He knew that if he and his horse stopped moving they would die, and in fact when he reappeared at the ranch he had been given up for dead.

His boss found the man's stamina uncanny. Not only had he seen few if any come through an ordeal like that, but once warmed up the cowboy appeared to be in great spirits: "Happy as a woman with a new hat," the boss said.

But he had not found any of the cattle, and no one else had either. When the wind stopped a few days later, and they all went out on the search, eight thousand head lay piled in the river bottoms, hard as rocks. But for all that, as we will see, there were good reasons for John Ware to be happy in this barren land, this white hell, as he called it.

You do not hear a lot about Canadian cowboys, but John went on to live most of his working life as a Canadian cattle hand and then as a rancher, and earned such renown and admiration that his funeral in Calgary in 1905 was the largest the town had ever seen. And when they began to write about him, it was not so much his achievements as his character that shaped what became the John Ware legend. Not so much because of what he did as what he was, and to know how that character was shaped we have to back up a bit. There had been a lot of adversity, in the shaping of that character, and some of it was very recent.

In Montana, that summer of 1882, John Ware had been hired on as night herder, the lowest and most trying position on a drive of three thousand cattle. The destination was Highwood, up in the territory of Alberta, which was still twenty-three years away from becoming a province. That would happen the year that John Ware died.

The Montana stockman was a man called Tom Lynch, and it seems that he had not wanted to hire Ware. Perhaps Ware's size — over six feet and 230 pounds — had something to do with it, a lot to feed and heavy on a horse. Lynch liked his boys lithe and light. But there was probably another reason, a reason that has a little bit to do with Ware's fame, which we will come to later.

The hand whom Tom Lynch really wanted for that drive was a good-natured cowboy named Bill Moodie. But Moodie was a close friend of John Ware. He told Lynch that he'd come only if Ware came too. The blackmail worked. Ware was hired on. But there may have been a residue of resentment in Lynch's mind.

In any case, from the beginning Ware sensed that he'd better conceal his own resentment at being the low man on the drive. He was, and he knew it, a better cowboy than the others. But life up till then had given him a lot of practice at lying low, and had given him a talent for irony and modest indirection. When he wanted a better horse than the old nag they'd fobbed off on him, he would say something like "I wouldn't mind a worse horse . . . if you got one." The gang decided there might be some fun here, so they brought out the worst-tempered horse they had. It may have been a routine initiation, or it may have been part of that other aspect of Ware's life that we'll come to presently.

At any rate they put him on this mean critter, and the horse bucked, reared, jounced, jolted and swung the cowboy's massive bulk around the fence-line for twenty minutes, while John Ware hung on spectacularly, and the other cowboys had to concede that the guy they'd been trying to humiliate was a gifted bronco rider. The unassuming, slow-spoken, ruefully smiling John Ware had won their respect, a reluctant respect perhaps, but genuine; the guy was really good.

He went onto the day crew, and things began to get better.

They were driving those three thousand head north for Fred Stimson, the manager of the Bar U Ranch in Alberta, the same man for whom Ware would endure the blizzard later that same year. After the three thousand head and their drivers had crossed into Canada and signed off the herd, Stimson hired Ware at twenty dollars a month. It was on the recommendation of Lynch, the man who had not wanted Ware in the first place.

It is true that some people would not have hired Ware on sight, but Alberta was virgin cattle country, there was a huge demand for cowhands, and Stimson didn't look twice when he found a man who could do the job and came with a top recommendation from Tom Lynch. Winter arrived; the blizzard came and went. Stimson lost the cattle, but by then he knew that Ware was a man he wouldn't want to see the back of.

The hands liked Ware too, and thought they knew him well, but after a while they began to notice some idiosyncrasies. Cowboys were not an educated lot; they tended to have certain odd beliefs and rituals. But by comparison with the profoundly superstitious John Ware the others were models of rationality. He could brave blizzards and stampedes, but he believed — among other things — that snakes were inhabited by Satan. One night the other members of the crew coiled up a rope and placed it in the foot of his bedroll so that it was just like a sleeping rattler. What they expected to happen, happened. Ware lost control and went into a monumental rage. Whether or not the big man actually hurt any of his mates is not recorded, and maybe it was, again, a matter of character that when he calmed down he regretted his display of temper and left the Bar U ranch.

Here we ask the reader to forgive the "we'll-get-to-that-later" device above; it seemed to be a way of communicating some of the surprise that accompanies the John Ware legend, without giving it away all at once. It is sometimes hard to believe this whole story because this was the 1880s and John Ware was not white; he was black. He was a black cowboy. Because he was good at what he did and lived in a cut-and-dried world of casual manners and unending work, it is difficult to tell whether or not there was an element of racism in his treatment in Alberta. We are not told. In Montana it may have been the reason for Lynch's reluctance to hire him, or for the low position they gave him when he started. The legend doesn't say. But it does seem unlikely that it could have been absent from the practical jokes with the bronco and the rope snake.

John Ware had survived a lot of horrors in his young life, and surmounted most of them. His fear of snakes came from his childhood and adolescence as a slave in South Carolina. He said that a dead snake had been used to whip him when he was young. On the range, his memories travelled with him:

> I have often been awakened by the most heart-rending shrieks of an aunt of mine. The slave holder used to tie her up to a joist . . . and whip upon her naked back till she was literally covered with blood. He would whip her to make her scream and whip her to make her hush . . . and not until overcome with fatigue, would he cease to swing the blood-clotted cow skin.

That plantation was near Georgetown, South Carolina. In the documentary, the slaves do not look as different and separate from the white world as we might imagine. The ancient photographs usually show them in the cast-off clothes of their employers, dark and tattered shadows of the larger society. Even at work in the cotton, they are in the same breeches and doublets and vests, the long dresses and shawls, the frock coats, although now these old garments are filthy and ragged. Pictures taken outside of work hours show men, women, and children anonymous in their grimy surroundings with nothing to do. The black faces seem to hide something, perhaps the last shreds of dreams, or hopes that their children at least might still make something of themselves. Or maybe there were no dreams at all, just numb habits of concealment, hidden rage, and grief.

For Ware, the time came — as it must have come for every slave at least once — when he got fed up. One day he saw Chauncey, his overseer, beating his sister. Ware spoke out, and for his trouble he too was whipped without mercy. It was at this time that the American Civil War broke out and wore on four long years. There was not much change to the slaves' lives during the war, but at its end, General Sherman's march had, in a great firestorm, wrecked the whole plantation system that had held slavery in place. Ware couldn't leave without having a last word with Chauncey. He found him not far from the whipping tree. He pinned Chauncey to it and told him he could finish with him then and there, but just to show his spirit was nobler than that of his ex-overseer, he let him go. He was lucky not to be shot in the back.

The slaves left the plantations in groups to pursue a future in a world that was only nominally free and probably more dangerous than the plantation, where they had at least held the status of valuable property. Even if they had ever been allowed to know anything about the world outside, they must still have wanted to get away from plantation territory, and about fifty thousand did manage to leave the South. But the majority stayed on, south of the Mason-Dixon line, as hired labour, often itinerant, still in poverty, still in cast-offs from their former owners now "employers," still barred from participating in the re-invigorated Republic that had freed them.

John Ware travelled farther than most. He worked his way south and west to Texas and then back into Oklahoma where he came upon the legendary Chisholm Trail. James Horan and Paul Sann, in their *Pictorial History of the American West*, tell how the defeated confederate veterans came back to Texas after the civil war and "found their ranches in ruins, and the entire state running wild with unbranded longhorns, the tough, ugly-tempered steers descended from the herds imported earlier from England and Ireland."

They would not have been steers, which are castrated. So when these authors tell us that a steer got five bucks a head in Texas and fifty dollars in Chicago, they probably mean cows as well. In any case the saying was that any Texan with a pencil and paper knew where his future lay. So instead of trying to reconstitute the old cattle ranches, they drove north with the first 260,000 head in 1866. The first big drive. By the time John Ware got there the three-and-a-half million wild cattle that had been grazing all over central and west Texas were slowly being gathered up. They must have looked like a walking gold mine. The idea was to claim and brand as many as you could and drive them north along the Chisholm Trail from Fort Worth to Abilene, Kansas, and eventually to the rail head whence they would be shipped up to the stock yards of Chicago.

At that point John Ware was no cowboy. The only beast he had ever ridden, as he put it, "was a buckin' mule." But when he saw the open range, something slipped into place in his mind. He never looked back. He neither saw nor heard from any of his family ever again.

John Ware's decision here was uncommon, and what made him different from so many of his fellow former slaves is not clear. Like Ware, most ex-slaves had the mobility that went with their transient labour. But the majority of them seemed to be locked in a kind of paradox. Fear caused them to stay in the place where there was, in fact, the most to fear: in the reconstructed South, or in the confinement of factories and farms in the north. They had drifted into other forms of bondage, perhaps less inhumane than what they had known as slaves on the plantations, but virtually as inescapable.

We know there were blacks who drifted into roping and handling and herding, but mostly in groups, in a few all-black cowboy outfits. The lone black freelance cowboy was a rarity.

But John Ware moved on alone working his way around the Southwest until he had picked up enough of the craft to be able to handle cattle on horseback. And now he kept moving until he found a life better than the one he would have had back across the Mississippi or in a Chicago sweatshop. Somehow he was able to climb out of whatever it was that had immobilized so many of his people. To them what he decided to go for might have seemed wildly improbable, but he thought it was just common sense, plain logic. It would actually be better for a black man to go where there were fewer people, more money, and such a rush to hire able bodies that colour didn't matter. All you needed was ambition and a steady eye on the horizon.

You can see it in the few and extraordinary photographs of him that survive. Above the closed lapels of an old flannel suit jacket there is a big and pleasant face with a thick goatee. But the eyes are startling. In each picture they have a light in them: the gaze is unmistakably distant and yet burning with reproach, of pride, as if to say, "Nobody can stop me."

Cattle trails branched out and spread quickly like a pattern of veins on the skin, until, by the late 1870s, there wasn't enough grass left in the southwestern states. Now it was the grasslands of Wyoming and Montana that beckoned, and there was word of a growing cattle business up north in some place called Canada. By 1879, pressure from the ranchers persuaded the government to open the northwest to the cattlemen.

It was this spreading growth of the trails that gave John Ware his opportunity. Somewhere, probably in Texas, he signed on as drag man to a herd of twenty-four hundred Texas Longhorns headed for Montana. Ware couldn't read or write, his horsemanship was still only half-developed, but he was strong and willing, and the stockmen needed anyone they could get.

As drag man, Ware was slotted at the "back end push." The job was considered to be a notch above night herder. Nobody wanted to be night herder. It was boring; you had to sing the cattle to sleep. You had to watch for rustlers and you had to keep things quiet. A sudden noise could waken the cattle and start a stampede that could kill you or anyone else, and — worse from the stockman's point of view — kill some cattle as well.

Drag man was a better job than that, but it was the dirtiest job. The drag men rode behind the herd and got all the dust day after day for maybe a thousand miles. It was in that slot that Ware met Moodie, the man who would stick up for him, later, with Tom Lynch. Ware and Moodie were both new, both drag men. You rose in the hierarchy as you moved forward in the herd. There were men on the flanks and two men at the front and finally the man ahead of them who "rode point" and was the most experienced of all. Ware rode back there with Moodie, and dreamed of moving forward in the herd, and then moving forward beyond the herd, and then beyond the horizon and beyond that too. Moving as far as he humanly could from the past.

Whether being black was any obstacle to his moving forward, Ware doesn't tell us. Perhaps on the frontier there actually was a greater respect for individuals and for talent, just as the myths and the movies suggest. Ware survived all the physical hazards of the ride. He got to the other side of the dangerous Brazo River in Texas where cow pokes often drowned during the crossings. He survived the outrage of the Indian tribes whose grasslands the herds crossed, and he was lucky to miss out on the gun-slinging thieves who sometimes ambushed a lone rider, after his pay if he was carrying any, or his watch if he had one, or even a few cattle.

Ware travelled through the middle of the Wild West just before 1880. It was at its height and at its dirtiest. The herd no doubt rested at the notorious Dodge City, marshalled by Wyatt Earp and Bat Masterson. They provided order in a world where there was almost none. Maybe Ware and another hand walked down its streets to get provisions, or maybe the entire crew felt it best to stay clear and stop somewhere else.

The myths and the movies have not, in fact, captured much of that West, the real one that John Ware saw. The old still photographs convey more of the tone of that life, the spirit, the mood. You sense a too-fast, impatient adventure over a huge distance in an extremely short time. The vistas are flat, blasted, and bleak. Almost everything built on that land-scape ends up small, ugly, and quick, little more than an infrastructure minimally needed for the movement of beasts and money, more a construction site than a building. Nothing seems finished. Stores and hotels are half tents, half rough boards. Everything is dirty. What looks like faded cloth or wood in the old photographs of dresses, old coats and trousers, saloon floors and coaches, is really the bleached look of mud and filth dried to dust. Genuinely bad men seemed to rise out of that dirt, like Orcs in a fantasy film, stupid-looking, gaunt, underfed, instinctively brutal. It is all freakish; neither city nor country, its habits are neither east nor west. Even in the few faded shots of Ware facing the camera or at work, there is no cowboy wear, in Western Movie terms, no chaps or bandannas or Stetsons. Like everyone else on the crew, he wears city clothes — or their remnants. Like everything else in this makeshift, short-lived world, the wardrobe is mixed and in flux and unexpected, a sort of shabby variety. And perhaps, in this free and chaotic confusion, a solitary black cowhand like Ware, passing through on a big drive, would not look at all out of place, since everything was out of place.

When the heaving ocean of grass that was Montana appeared ahead in the distance over the dusty backs of those thousands of cattle, it must have seemed nearly primeval, virgin, a good place to stop and create a new life. But Ware's old drag-mate Moodie wanted to go farther. He persuaded Ware that they should go on, to Canada. He had heard about the Canada thing, even more untouched than Montana, a sort of Promised Land for American cattlemen who had begun to settle southern Alberta when there were still only a handful of non-native Canadians there.

The Hudson's Bay Company, moving in from the East, had collided with some of those northern-bound pistol-toting Americans. The Native peoples, whose lands these were, were in between. The whisky trade, the systematic depredation of the Native peoples, and the mad slaughter of the buffalo were threatening such chaos and lawlessness that in 1874 the government of the seven-year-old Confederation created the Royal Northwest Mounted Police.

Some historians say that one reason there is less violence in Canada than in the United States, despite the commonality of the two countries' origins, is that the Canadians put the law on the land before the people got there. The RNWMP moved into southern Alberta from their base at Fort McLeod. The white settlement followed the Mounties, and soon there was a market for ranchers and cattlemen.

In Montana, what Ware and Moodie had probably heard about was the heart of this paradise, the Alberta foothills: well watered, sheltered, and kept relatively free of snow by the warm westerly chinooks. They had to get there some way, and Lynch's drive seemed to be the way. They crossed the border and henceforward Canada would be

Ware's home. Some time afterward, after the blizzard and after the prank with the coiled rope, he decided that he wanted to be on his own again, at least away from trail gangs, running things, not being run.

That was when life began to look up for Ware. A serene reward for his adventure was in sight. So far he had had no trouble making a living. His skill was already getting known. And for someone so long on the trail, he was remarkably obliging. What he wanted more than anything was the chance to do a thing that was primordial and universal, a thing which, in the world that he had come from, he couldn't hope to do. He began to think of owning a piece of land, and some cattle, and a house to settle down in, and maybe even a family. A disciplined man, he saved every cent he could, and by the mid 1880s he had enough money to go into the land registry office in Calgary to sign for a property.

And things continued to go well, although there were some surprises. Calgary was a surprise. Calgary was young and wild but it was also a city. In Canada, it was the city that was more likely to harbour racial prejudice than was the country. There had already been a murder or two, and the latest one was traced to a culprit who happened to be black; so all black males were under suspicion. On his way into town, to that registry office, he saw how they were looking at him. Somebody must have told him what it was about, but all we really know is that he never made it to the registry office that day, he just turned around and left town. He planned to winter that year, at Stimson's Bar U Ranch, and perhaps the racial tension eased off, or perhaps Fred Stimson took the application in for him. In any case he got his land that same autumn, and he cut and squared timbers for a cabin, and dragged them three miles by hand by tying them to a rope around his waist. But he didn't have enough time to finish building before the snow flew, and Stimson gladly took him in.

While Ware was at the Bar U, Stimson signed him up in the rancher's own local militia. The experience and the contacts would be useful in the future, and the pay would get him back to his half-built cabin. One can only speculate on his feelings, if any, at being something like an Indian scout for the white man. There had been trouble in the northern territory. The Second Rebellion of Louis Riel's Métis had sent alarming rumours through the hills. There had been the now famous battles at Batoche and Duck Lake. Soldiers and cowboys were mobilized to defend the settlements. Now no one knew what the Blackfoot would do, whether or not they might join Riel and substantially change the balance of power. What Ware and the other militiamen had been assigned to do was watch their movements on the plains.

Did Ware see in the Métis people a situation similar to that of his own people — free but with few effective rights? What was more, many of the ranchers commanding the militia had an upper-class British or Canadian military background. From what can be pieced together out of the slim documentation, it seems that Ware understood himself in no special way as a black man with a mission in a white world, nor indeed was he assimilated to the larger white world. He referred to himself as a man who had made his own destiny and had a duty to continue to do so — beholden to no one except by his own good will.

The rebellion didn't last, and the peaceful spring brought with it opportunities for raising cattle. We know that on May 25, 1885, John Ware walked into the office of CED Wood, recorder of brands, and registered the number 9. It was just a practical thing: 9 was the number of cattle he could afford to start with, and with a flourish he stamped it on each of them four times: Brand 9999. This was exuberance, but it was not a legal brand. A few years later, when he finally had the money, he officially bought brand 999 and settled for three nines instead of four.

He had his house up by now, rough and unfinished but livable, in that Sheep Creek area in the foothills. We are told that when he moved in, his neighbours were at first uncomfortable with this "nigger in the neighborhood," but he won their acceptance before long. He would walk right up to people and ask if they needed a hand. They'd seen him handling cattle with as much deftness, speed, and horsemanship as the best. He took part in the local roundup and its communal spirit, and the way the story is still told in Alberta, if there had been any tetchiness about that "nigger in the neighbourhood," John Ware soon put it to sleep and was accepted as a citizen. He had adapted to Canada in three years and risen to the top of his trade in five.

All the same, John Ware's small farm and few cattle were not enough for a living and not enough to fill his time. He went to see John J. Barter, previously of the Hudson's Bay Company, who now had the Quorn horse ranch, raising thoroughbreds for the English gentry of the Leicestershire Hunt Club. Barter tried him out and made him foreman in charge of the ranch's saddle ponies. It was a step up, and it was serious business. Thoroughbreds were a kind of power centre in the colonial hierarchy. The Quorn Ranch set out to supply mounts for the British cavalry; in return various earls and marquises seem to have invested in the ranch while their sons worked there. If Ware was a foreman, Ware had their respect.

Now he had a position, but for all his work, little he could call his own. The unfinished hill cabin and the herd, now grown to seventy-five head, were still not enough. He needed land that would produce what he needed to make him fully independent. Then he would be ready to marry. It was 1886; he was thirty-seven. It would be hard enough to find a wife.

Another bad winter tested everyone on the prairie. The round hooves of horses could paw through the ice and snow for stubble pasture, but the cloven hooves of cattle could not. John Ware lost half his herd. He needed a better job. When Fred Stimson and John Barter decided to put the two best men in the region against each other in a round of bronco riding, they put John Ware against a man called Frank Ricks, and gave them the deadliest unbroken beasts they had. Ware easily won, and the High River Horse Ranch people were impressed and took him on at a better salary than Barter had paid: fifty-five dollars a month. He would be able to finish his cabin and set up properly on Sheep Creek, but he was still alone. It had become clear that citizen or not, champion bronco rider, admired professional, all the friends and admirers notwithstanding, the colour bar had never really vanished, and he was never going to marry a white woman.

So when John Barter told him that a Negro family by the name of Lewis had moved into Calgary and that they had a daughter named Mildred who was not yet twenty, he obviously had to see her. He must also have been embarrassed, even angry that all eyes were on him and presuming a match just because they were both black. He was a man who made up his own mind; this might be an opportunity, but he would not have people think it simply inevitable. Nonetheless, he walked with dignity into the dry goods store where the meeting had been set up, and Mildred liked him. He was invited to Sunday dinner with her family. Soon he and Mildred settled down to a careful round of what was for John Ware an all-too-public courtship.

By the spring of 1891, John Ware was a rancher. He had finished the house. It had a fine front porch and several rooms. There were two hundred cattle branded with the now legal 999. But his land was unfenced, and crop farmers started to trickle in buying up land, encroaching on the ranchers. Had he thought about it, he might have sensed danger, but he seems not to have foreseen what was coming. Fall had come and he was thinking about marriage. For the first time he had what he needed to support a family and the prospect of another hard winter alone was not attractive. He had to propose, now or never. He spent Christmas with the Lewises. The story is that he finally showed her a photograph of the house, and said, "It's an awful nice house and if you ever think you'd like to be an old cowman's missus and have that house, I'd sure like to know." She must already have made up her mind because she answered, "Yes John." They were married on February 29, 1892.

When the newlyweds went up to John Ware's house that night they paused; there was candlelight in the window. The trespassers turned out to be the neighbours, gathered to bid the new couple a happy future. For a while that seemed to be finally possible. Ware's lucky number 9 turned up again. On March 9, 1893, Mildred gave birth to a baby girl whom they named Jeanette. All he needed now was for everything to stay as it was. That would prove to be the hardest part of all.

The early 1890s were dry. Instead of riding out the droughts like most ranchers — or being ridden down by them — John dug an irrigation ditch that led in from the creek and watered the meadow where he was growing hay for the winter. The farming was going well, but Mildred hated John's long absences out on the range. She hated the cold and the hard work. But the bonds were still stronger than the differences and in November 1894, Mildred gave birth to a son Robert.

So often the beginning of the end of something remains imperceptible. For John Ware that beginning seems to have been a mild discomfort at the arrival of an unexpected burgeoning population where he had always counted on open space and the long divides that make good neighbours. The crop farmers were finally getting their way. The government was selling the good grazing land right up to the back-country. Encouraged by good land prices and the search for larger pastures, the ranchers were moving out. Ware drove his three hundred cattle eastward to better grazing. He sold Sheep Creek, and then he and Mildred loaded the children and everything they had into a wagon and moved ninety miles east to cheaper land on the Red Deer River.

From there things took a different course that must have seemed relentless and without cause. The landscape itself seemed a kind of warning: low, marshy, dreary, melancholy. Mildred's next child died shortly after birth. The labour had been difficult and left her permanently weakened. Cattle mange swept across the territory like a plague. The sores ate ruinously into the hides of the cattle, herds were quarantined, and the entire trade came to a stop.

For John Ware everything became a fight now. He tried to fight Mildred's increasing illnesses, to fight the vicissitudes of raising cattle, to fight the inhospitable land. He tried to raise his children at the same time. His daughter Jeanette recalled a stream over which her father had placed a hut where he kept the milk fresh and cool. And in that stream they were not allowed to play. She said her father caught young Robert playing there, seized him by the ankle, and dipped the boy into the chilling water several times just to scare him a little and teach him.

But this was only a moment in a train of sorrows that seemed to increase. In 1902, the river, of which that creek was a tributary, burst its banks and carried off the Wares' entire house (ironically, the tributary is now named Ware Creek). When winter arrived, Mildred came down with pneumonia. Ware rode off to get medicine but his return was slowed down for hours by a blizzard. He must have remembered the futility of his search for Fred Stimson's cattle in that blizzard years before. When he finally got home, Mildred was all but gone. It was

March 1905. When she died he sent the children away to their grand-mother and stayed alone for a while, in the desperately empty cabin.

Freedom at its best is a condition of possibility, not of perfection. The dreamed-of destination of his life, of honourable self-sufficiency, work, and marriage turned out to be a place of hardship and heart-break. Floods, disease, and death are as indifferent to freedom as they are to talent and hard work. Still, he said, it was better to suffer in lib-erty than to be born without hope. And indeed he kept the facts of his past from his own children.

Five months after Mildred's death, when his son Robert was ten and Ware himself only fifty-six, they were out riding together when his horse stepped into a gopher hole, threw John Ware, and killed him. He had ridden half a million miles, up to then.

His epitaph said that the purity and fineness of his colour reflect-ed the purity of his soul. His story came down to us in the tales of aged ranchers and cowboys, and those few photographs, and a couple of newspaper accounts. The ranchers and the cowboys told it because they recognized it. In a way it was about them, and — like them — both ordi-nary and remarkable. They told it because he was a man who rose out of a nightmare they could only guess at, came to their land, did the kind of work they did, and did it with courage, skill, and honesty beyond what was required. What they did not talk about so much, although they knew it with that kind of unspoken social common sense of people of the open spaces, is that one person of a different colour is more like-ly to be accepted than is an entire community. When you are alone, the colour of your skin is a pigment and nothing else, and your abilities are free to develop so that you can show yourself for who you really are.

In the end, in those tales from those ranchers and cowboys, John Ware's fame is of a rare and amazing kind; it is for being a good man.

◆　◆　◆

The History Television documentary was written and directed by Brian Dooley.

Part Six

SAMUEL CUNARD
The Man Who Invented the Atlantic

In the minds of millions of people around the globe, the image of the classic ocean liner used to conjure up the romance of a sophisticated passage between New York and Southampton, dressing for dinner, dancing with a handsome stranger to the strains of a white-coated orchestra, flirtations and more on the starlit afterdeck. Hundreds of movies — most spectacularly the 1998 *Titanic* — have entrenched all these clichés, perhaps to the point where they have become archetypes. The great liner also bespeaks another kind of romance, one sometimes triggered by desperation, sometimes by great hopes: in the darker lower levels and crowded decks there travelled millions of players in the great drama of immigration to the New World.

For most of us the prototype for the classic age of transatlantic travel, roughly from 1900 until 1950, is the Cunard Line's first *Queen Elizabeth*. Launched not long before the start of World War II, she seems to us now almost timeless, not especially modern, not old-fashioned, simply *the* ocean liner, inheritor of her predecessor's style, the *Queen Mary*. It is not easy to imagine a world without those *Queens*, as big as floating cities, yet with a regal grace in their soaring prows, the black hulls and towering funnels over the white superstructure, the bright red strip of the waterline. The three erect funnels of *Queen Mary* become a swept-back pair on the *QE One*, then a graceful single stack on *QE II*. When *Queen Mary II* comes down the ways on which she is taking shape in France, she too will have a single stack, broad as a wing and utterly distinctive, but she'll still be unmistakably a member of the same royal family.

Although the preposterous, towering, pregnant bulges of the Mediterranean and Caribbean cruise ships may have overtaken the *Queens* according to purely commercial criteria, the great liners still bespeak a vision, and the first incarnation of that vision was built by a man from Nova Scotia named Samuel Cunard.

He was born in Halifax in 1787. Halifax is a city created by wars, a major mustering and supply centre for British naval strategy from the moment of its founding in 1749 by Colonel Edward Cornwallis. The Seven Years' War (1756–63) established the port's strategic importance. Towards the end of the eighteenth century when George III's son Prince Edward,[4] the Duke of Kent, moved there as Commander in Chief of the British forces in North America, he built parts of it to resemble a tony aristocratic British city. When Charles Dickens visited in 1842 he said that looking at Halifax was a bit like looking at Westminster through the wrong end of a telescope.

Samuel Cunard's father had been a successful shipbuilder in Pennsylvania, but his loyalty to the British cause, which brought him to Canada after the 1776 American War of Independence, also forced him to abandon everything he owned, and he arrived penniless in Nova Scotia. When his son Samuel was born, Abraham was working as a foreman-carpenter for the British Naval garrison in Halifax. The boy would show a sharp entrepreneurial sense early on, would go on to build a substantial industrial empire, and die Sir Samuel Cunard, in London, in 1865, by then the owner and builder of the great and seminal Cunard Steamship Lines. Long before that company would bring into being the above-mentioned archetypes, its founder would have made and lost millions, and set his name in stone, wood, and paint all over Halifax, to mark his many and various enterprises.

Much admired today by those historians of business for whom competition and private enterprise are the great values in life, Samuel Cunard was, in fact, one of the first great industrial beneficiaries of massive state subsidies. His steamship line exploded from a modest coastal enterprise into the world's greatest transoceanic service when he tapped into the British Treasury by persuading the British admiralty that his ships would be at the disposal of the Empire in time of war.

And indeed they did serve in times of conflict, carrying troops

4. The colony called The Island of St. John was re-named Prince Edward Island for him in 1798.

overseas in all of Britain's subsequent wars. It was a Cunarder, the *Lusitania*, whose sinking helped propel America into World War I. On May 1, 1915, the *Lusitania* left New York for Southampton, carrying a good number of Americans, including the famous millionaire Alfred Vanderbilt and the noted theatre producer Charles Frohman. On May 7, with the coast of Ireland in sight, a German submarine, the U-20, torpedoed the *Lusitania*. She sank in eighteen minutes taking 1,195 lives — 123 of them American. Although America did not actually declare war until April 1917, it is generally agreed that the *Lusitania*'s sinking contributed to the turning of the tide of American public opinion against Germany and led the United States to join the Allied cause. The outrageous suggestion that British officials, including Winston Churchill, were complicit in setting the ship up for this disaster in order to arouse America has been taken seriously by many historians, challenged by others, and is still not completely dead.

At a cursory glance, Samuel Cunard is remarkable for an apparently unending string of successes, each greater than the last. But when you look at it closely, the successes are interspersed with an almost equal number of failures, bankruptcies, and staggering periods of seemingly ineradicable debt. Samuel Cunard's failures tell you something about the man: he seems to have learned little from them, except to try harder.

He is a little like Napoleon in that way. As a military strategist, Napoleon was nicknamed "the scrambler." Cunard, too, always seemed to begin in chaos and then formulate some rapid, almost too-clever head-on plan that would get him out of it. Like Napoleon, he was a small man. He had a reputation for rushing everywhere as if he could never quite pause long enough to organize his day. He was a devout Christian. His last communication — a letter written from his deathbed — is a glad exclamation of thanks to God for a full and satisfying life.

As a young man during the War of 1812, he was beginning to succeed as a merchant when peace came, and with it a recession that all but wiped him out. A few years later he decided to invest in whaling. Some whaling outfits were making huge fortunes, but those old prints of whaling skiffs being tossed in the air by angry blunt-nosed sperm whales give you some idea of the prodigious risks. With characteristic haste, Cunard appears to have greedily overlooked the need to keep his investors happy, and proceeded to build and outfit the big ships at a speed that suggests he had either forgotten or ignored the certainty that there would be no return on the investment for at least three years. All he seemed to know was that when it paid, it paid in showers of gold.

But when three improvident whaling trips drove him deep into debt he had to quit. It should be remembered that the idea of a public company of limited liability was a new-fangled American idea at that time; it had not caught on in Canada. Sam Cunard, both legally and by the standards of honour of the time, was personally liable to his investors, and his whaling caper looked as though it was going to wreck him permanently. This does not seem a promising start for a man who is going to build a maritime empire.

In the 1830s he embarked on the fulfillment of a Nova Scotia dream that must have been as old as it seemed impossible. It took a week to sail around Nova Scotia. The logical thing, people had said for years as they studied their maps, would be to build a thirty-mile canal right across the colony, linking the Dartmouth Lakes to the east end of the Bay of Fundy along the old Mi'kmaq Indian trail. Cunard got some partners together and decided to actually do what had long been speculated. They put the locks in first, great stone walls with heavy wooden doors. But soon after they began the actual digging and dredging, the tidal bore of the Shubenacadie River drove in with such force that it washed out the locks, and an eighty-five-thousand-pound investment was washed away with them. Cunard's canal company was bankrupt. The canal was actually finished, almost half a century later, not long before Cunard's death. It ran for about a decade, but could not compete with the railways. Ironically, it was Samuel Cunard who financed the first railway in Nova Scotia.[5]

Astoundingly, given the outcome of the first venture, the man had another go at whaling, this time in the South Pacific. And with it came something that would become a motif in his life: a hint of conflict of

5. It was Sandford Fleming who built it for him (see Part Fourteen in this volume).

interest. The South Pacific adventure was started with a government subsidy arranged by a politician who just happened to be a good pal of Cunard's. It was no more successful than the first. Within a few months, although the event was never satisfactorily explained, it appeared that his crew had inexplicably deserted ship off New Zealand.

Then, around the same time, this apparently luckless but indefatigably persuasive man managed to borrow enough to invest in the Halifax and Quebec Steam Navigation Company which sent the very first paddle steamer, the *Royal William*, across the Atlantic. It was to be the start of a new kind of shipping, but the other investors were not impressed with that first voyage, and pulled out, and once again Sam Cunard was up to his ears in debt.

We have been a bit unfair to Cunard so far, stressing this one theme, the almost continual failures, and the growing mountains of debt. He obviously had his share of good luck too, and added to that driving, restless enterprise were his indisputable brilliance, an ability to argue compellingly for his visions, the good ones as well as the feckless ones, and talent for making and keeping influential friends.

One of these was Lord Dalhousie, the lieutenant-governor. Around 1815 Cunard had persuaded Dalhousie to give him an exclusive contract for the vice-regal official boat tours around the colony. A few years later he got out of the whaling fiasco by landing a maritime mail contract. Then he was saved from the canal project by his shipping company. When the South Pacific Whaling project's demise was followed hard by the cancellation of the Atlantic steamer service, Cunard used the latter's technology to start local steamboat and ferry runs. He survived a much later financial crisis — in 1842 — by marshalling family, in-laws, and a grudging bank into working with him.

So Samuel Cunard's life is more than just being knocked down and getting up again. There was a generous helping of good luck in it, and there were some simply stupendous, inventive, and genuine accomplishments, nourished by zeal, diligence, and daring.

Samuel Cunard's father, Abraham, had been an enterprising and successful shipbuilder in Philadelphia. Loyal to the cause of the

Crown, he fled Philadelphia after the thirteen colonies declared their independence, and arrived in Halifax with nothing. Abraham's ancestors may have been Huguenots, business-minded Protestant refugees who had fled persecution in Catholic France, some heading for America. Now, ironically, Abraham himself became a refugee, fleeing Republican America for the Royalist Canadian colonies.

Much as his son would have to do time and again, Abraham Cunard had to start all over when he got to Nova Scotia, at first as a foreman carpenter in a shipyard. He married Margaret Murphy, a young woman he had met on his way north from Philadelphia, to whom he proposed as soon as he had established himself securely in Halifax. They had nine children; Sam was the second. A childhood portrait shows little Sam with a sly expression; a later photograph shows the short and energetic man with bushy sideburns, high collar, and that bright gaze that led someone to say he had the look of a furiously energetic rodent.

Period prints show most of Halifax as little more than a village, although with a few stern and somewhat grander houses, men in knee breeches and tricornes, an uneasy mixture of small luxury and much shabbiness that seemed part of the city until after World War II. The sea was a constant presence. From the big windows of his father's tall Brunswick Street house, the wharves, the forests of square-rigged cargo boats, the ships-of-the-line, and the provenance of trade and naval and military business were seldom out of sight as the boy grew up. Scarcely past puberty, Sam found his entrepreneurial feet, and took advantage of the busy port by buying spices and coffee right off the ships and carrying them up to the town where he sold them door-to-door. He peddled vegetables, ran errands for anybody who'd give him a penny, and carried messages as well.

He was haunted by an urge to regain his father's fortune, and so when Abraham decided to build a wharf at the foot of Brunswick Street and go into business for himself, Sam dropped everything else and put himself at the disposal of what soon became A. Cunard and Son. Before long they were doing very well, primarily shipping fish, salt, and timber to the West Indies and to Europe. Sam's craft and cunning got them through the boom and bust of the War of 1812. Much of it was a cash business. There were no banks. Sam carried so much currency on his person that he took to walking around Halifax with a guard armed with a club.

On February 4, 1815, he married Susan Duffus, the daughter of a tailor who had the Halifax contract for British military uniforms. With the marriage and the Dalhousie connections he now had a substantial social position. The children began to arrive. He built a fine house next door to his parents' house, and took a respectable family pew in St. George's Anglican Church. The pew is still there, marked by a discreet brass plaque. Samuel Cunard had entered the Halifax establishment.

Misfortune and good fortune are often coupled in the story of Samuel Cunard. It was the recession after the war that brought him the first of his powerful British contacts. The lieutenant-governor, Lord Dalhousie, had asked him to set up a soup kitchen for Halifax's sudden crowd of destitute men, women, and children. His reward would be that contract to take Dalhousie on official tours. He used his hundred-ton brig, the *Chebucto*.

When Abraham died, Samuel changed the name of the company to S. Cunard and Sons. He had already been given control by his father. The company negotiated an international tea contract that soon began to write down the debt. The man he beat out for that contract, Enos Collins (who would be known as the richest man in Canada when he died) was angry at Cunard as a result and shunned him for a while. But this was a small world where it did not pay to make long-term enemies. Cunard and Collins buried the hatchet and, among other things, decided to eliminate the need for armed guards by founding the Halifax Banking Company. The original building is still there, and the company would grow, acquire, spread, and finally turn into the Canadian Imperial Bank of Commerce. By 1827, Samuel Cunard was a millionaire. His company had forty ships. He was quietly invited to join "the Club," the compact that ran Nova Scotia. He became a close friend of the editor and future statesman Joseph Howe, who helped him open offices in London, Glasgow, and Liverpool. S. Cunard and Sons was on its way to becoming one of the first vertically integrated multinational corporations, its enterprise diversifying as it grew.

Samuel Cunard's wife, Susan, died in 1828, and for years afterwards Haligonians who had attended the funeral at St. George's spoke of the devastation in the small man's face that day. But he was soon energetically back at work, perhaps displacing his grief with hard work.

By 1835 his vision, this time correctly, had led him to embrace the newest shipping technology and launch the first of what would become a whole fleet of steamships. Steam needed coal; Cunard took over most of the Nova Scotia mining industry. He acquired a huge piece of Prince Edward Island to ensure a steady supply of lumber. He retailed the surplus coal out of Halifax, delivering it from the S. Cunard Coal Company in horse-drawn wagons. He started a coast-to-coast pony express mail service across Nova Scotia and up into Quebec. He bought the first steam locomotive in the colony, and built a railway in Pictou.

His fifty-first year was marked by his crowning achievement. In 1838 Cunard's friend Joseph Howe happened to be in London with Judge Haliburton (the author of the popular Sam Slick stories) when they learned that the admiralty was inviting tenders for a transatlantic mail contract. Ocean travel was still painfully slow, and it took two and a half months for Cunard's friends to get the news back to him in Halifax, but as soon as they did Cunard commandeered one of his own ships, made his first steam crossing, and arrived after the deadline had passed. He went straight to the admiralty and found a sympathetic contact, a senior officer whom he convinced that with his sources of coal and lumber he could make the most attractive bid, and he successfully secured an extension of the deadline.

That admiralty contact promised to help, but Cunard knew he was fighting some highly placed competition. He needed contacts, and set out on a round of socializing that led to a certain Caroline Norton who found the irrepressibly optimistic Canadian completely charming. He told her about his scheme for the transatlantic mail, and how his resources and experience made him the very best of all the contenders if Britain seriously wanted an effective and secure service, better than those Milords and Sirs who might have many friends at court but nothing like Cunard's own hardware, supplies, and track record.

Caroline Norton said that she quite agreed, and would do what she could. Cunard would say later that he had no idea at the time that she was Prime Minister Melbourne's mistress, a connection that led to the biggest single coup of his career.

S. Cunard and Sons began to build steamships in Scotland. First the *Britannia* slid down the ways, to make her maiden Liverpool-Halifax-Boston mail crossing in 1840. *Britannia* was followed by the *Acadia*, the *Colombia,* and then the *Caledonia*. All the ships' names, Cunard decided, would end in "ia" — it would become the brand. Compared to their queenly liner descendants they were an odd-looking hybrid kind of a vessel, but to Samuel Cunard they were jewels of undeniable beauty. Their hulls, long and low in the water, were roughly interrupted by the hub and cowling of the paddle wheel. They still had three masts with both square-rigged and fore-and-aft sails, but they *were* steamers nonetheless. They made the crossing faster than had ever been possible, and reliably on schedule. Soon, with more ships coming out of Boston as well, Cunard was delivering millions of letters on each vessel, on both sides of the Atlantic in a steady stream of literally tons of mail.

The effect of this traffic on both Halifax and Boston was marked: both cities had fought to be chosen the North American destination. Halifax encouraged the building of several hotels to accommodate the expected Cunard Line passengers. Boston did better, putting on a huge parade in his honour and bringing an impressive cohort of dignitaries to persuade Cunard, successfully, that their city was the better business opportunity. The next year was spectacular. In the depths of the winter Boston cut a seven-mile channel through the harbour ice to get the Cunard ships into port. In that single year Boston's take from international trade doubled. They gave Cunard a massive silver trophy in his honour, and it is said that he received two thousand dinner invitations.

There were to be more financial ups and downs, but the mail service and the rapidly growing passenger traffic soon produced a cash flow strong enough to discharge all the loans and mortgages, and the steamship service continued to grow.

He was a pioneer in transnational finance. In a way, the Atlantic

Ocean was more his home than anywhere on land. He was one of the first to recognize the Atlantic as a self-contained unit of trade, a kind of continent with terminals on either side in which there were fortunes to be made. And as other enterprising colonials began to set their sights on transatlantic business opportunities, this seemingly hit-and-miss guy was always a bit ahead of them. When he heard that his fellow Haligonian Enos Collins was planning a trip to England to negotiate what would be, in effect, a monopoly in the tea trade, Cunard did not hesitate or plan. He just took the fastest ship he could find, beat Collins to London, and got his foot in the door with the famous East India Company, which effectively controlled the world's tea trade. Soon he was delivering the first ever shipload of tea to arrive in Halifax from China.

He played the intrigues of the British aristocracy as if he had written the scripts. To secure those Nova Scotia coalmines that he needed for his steamships, he had to get the coal-mining rights in the colony, which were a royal prerogative. Cunard learned that the King had rescued the Prince of Wales from his gambling debts by selling those mining rights to the jewellers to the Crown, Rundle and Rundle. Cunard understood that a London jeweller wouldn't have the faintest idea of what to do with mining rights in Nova Scotia, wherever the hell that was, and he knew from his gossip connections that the Rundles themselves were serious gamblers and seriously short of cash. He simply made them an offer, and the relieved jewellers were happy to accept.

Now he had to find the money. He had started building ships in Scotland, and wrote to his daughter Mary: "I had to go to Scotland to contract the building of my steamboats and so have to pay another visit to see how they are progressing." It was here, oddly enough, in the land of canny thrift and caution, that Cunard found people willing to make up the balance after he had invested his own money. The Scots shipbuilders saw that coal and steamships were a perfect fit. They had already been interested in railroads. It was a Scot after all, James Watt, who had seen the promise of steam to begin with. Cunard told his Scottish friends that the Atlantic was better than a railroad, because "we have no tunnels to drive, no cuttings to make. No roadbeds to prepare. We need only build our ships and start them to work." The base for his new company would not be Halifax or Boston, but the busy port of Liverpool.

With the heavy penalties imposed by the Royal Mail for failure to adhere to the timetable, it would not have been surprising had Cunard made fast crossings his top priority, but he did not. He was convinced that reliability was the better virtue, and reliability meant safety. A reputation for safe crossings would help put more passengers in the tiny cabins on his mail ships.

His decision was dramatically justified by the activities of his first major American competitor, another Collins, Edward this time, who went to the US government when he heard of Cunard's fat 275,000 pounds sterling subsidy from the British admiralty. Edward Collins persuaded Washington that the US could become the prime mail carrier because he would build ships that were bigger and faster than anything on the Atlantic, and — like Cunard's — would be an asset in time of war. He got an initial $350,000 subsidy, which grew to nearly a million dollars before he was through. While Cunard was skimping on his furnishings and hammering home to his captains that safety was everything, Collins built colossal ships twice the size of Cunard's. He supplied heated private cabins, made the interiors of his vessels like Bavarian palaces, and had one dining room designed to look like an opera house.

Collins told his captains that breaking the speed records was what it was all about, and for a while he stole a lot of business from the Cunard line. Then, in 1854, off the coast of Newfoundland, Collins' flagship the *Arctic* collided with another vessel. Three hundred and twenty-two lives were lost, among them Collins' wife and children. Ships of other careless and aggressive Cunard competitors met similar misfortunes. For Edward Collins, the vicissitudes of haste included mechanical failure and a disenchanted US government, who, after the Newfoundland tragedy, soon decided that the annual $875,000 subsidy was not helping the country, and stopped it. Collins filed for bankruptcy in 1858.

Cunard had laughed at Collins' gimmicks, which he dismissed as "trying to break our windows by throwing sovereigns at us." His fleet grew to eight ships, each built for simplicity. What was lost in luxury and speed was made up for in safety and punctuality. Passengers grumbled about the accommodations. Charles Dickens described his Cunard passenger cabin as a hearse with windows. "Retired to my bed," he wrote, "somewhat smaller than a coffin, read to this day I know not what. Reeled on deck. Drank cold brandy with unspeakable disgust. And ate hard biscuits perseveringly. Not ill, but going to be. The cow bellowing moodily in the fog." But Dickens had chosen Cunard, and so did tens of thousands more, because they felt safe.

When a Cunard vessel ran aground near Seal Island off the Nova Scotia coast — the only accident of substance during his whole career — Cunard personally took charge, sailing out to the wreck, and supervising the successful rescue of every passenger.

It may have been an earlier shipwreck that had set the issue of maritime safety firmly in the young Cunard's mind. There were no lighthouses around Nova Scotia when he was a boy, and one night the frigate La Tribune sailed blindly into the harbour and was wrecked with the loss of 240 men, women, and children. Young Samuel saw the funeral and the masses of coffins and never forgot them. In the 1830s he was on his way to being a magnate when he became commissioner of lighthouses, and erected the towers with their warning lamps along the dangerous shoreline. And collected their fees as well.

The present-day Michigan Institute for Public Policy, a hard-nosed centre for free-enterprise rhetoric, scolds Edward Collins for his subsidies and praises Cunard for his private enterprise, apparently forgetting that his spartanly furnished mail ships not only collected $200 from each passenger — roughly equivalent to about $10,000 today (although those comparisons are fraught with irrelevancies), plus 24 cents per letter (say $10, with the same proviso), but that he also had that 275,000 pounds sterling annual subsidy from the admiralty, and kept on collecting it because he did indeed deliver on his promise of safety and punctuality.

But it was not all diligence, luck, prudence, virtue, and hard work. There are traces in the story of "sharp practice," that nineteenth-century euphemism for dealings not quite above board. What, for example, was this special permit, early in his career, for trading with the New England States during the War of 1812? Working from a British colony, surely Cunard was, at least technically, trading with the enemy. The money from his 1831 tea contract enabled him to buy up a seventh of Prince Edward Island for lumber. That land grab and his Nova Scotia coal rights amounted to sole possession, and Cunard's flair for cornering markets and developing monopolies was not quite in tune with the best traditions of fair and free competition.

His lucrative position as commissioner of lighthouses came from political connections. When he went after a government subsidy for his second whaling expedition even his friend Joseph Howe accused him of corruption. How indeed did he get the contact with the king's jeweller to secure the mining rights? It was not just his gossipy London connections: he had already persuaded Lieutenant-Governor Lord Dalhousie to make him Nova Scotia's commissioner of mines, a position that facilitated what we might now call insider trading.

And who was the man in the Admiralty Office in London who actually stretched the deadline that day in 1838, so that Cunard could put in his own tender for the transatlantic mail? He was Sir Edward Perry, a one-time Nova Scotia midshipman, an old family friend who had been a regular at Cunard parties in Halifax. And are we to believe the story that the socially alert Cunard really had *no idea* that Caroline Norton was the Prime Minister's mistress? He seemed to know everything else that was going on in London.

In 1842, when he learned that the British banks decided to foreclose on their Cunard loans, he was working out of his Liverpool offices. To buy time he skipped town, had himself secretly rowed out to one of his own ships, raced back to Nova Scotia for help, and got it. The Bank of Nova Scotia, which just happened to have his brother-in-law on its board, guaranteed the needed loan. Connections, connections, connections.

The family connection was the strongest of all. Samuel's son Edward went to England to manage the shipping trade so that Cunard himself could put matters in order at home, the bank having bound him to stay in Nova Scotia until the loan was discharged. The family had backed him in his times of need, and now he showed that he would give as good as he got. His brother Joseph, a lumber baron on the Miramichi River, came to Cunard in desperation: he was nearly broke. Sam took on his debts, and spent twenty years paying them off. When he finally returned to England to handle investment matters and contracts, he put his younger son William in charge of the entire concern, S. Cunard and Company, and then, when he turned seventy-four in 1861, he made his elder son Edward the senior partner in the company, and retired.

As with the city of Halifax itself, war has a lot to do with the Cunard story. In 1811 Cunard was all of twenty-four when he sensed hostilities coming between Britain and America and obtained a special permit to trade essential goods to the New England states. He captured his first fortune in the boom that followed. In mid-century, troops and supplies had to be rushed to the Crimea. Once there was a whole shipload of army boots, all for the left foot. True to his promise to the Admiralty, Cunard volunteered his vessels to be "STUFT": Ships Taken Up From Trade. Among the more tragic passengers his fourteen STUFT ships were to carry, were those doomed cavalrymen destined to be immortalized by Alfred Lord Tennyson in his poem *The Charge of the Light Brigade*.

In time Samuel Cunard beat out every one of his competitors. In 1863 he retired as Sir Samuel Cunard with a mansion in Halifax and a fine address in Kensington, Number 26 Princess Garden. In April, two years later, he came down with bronchitis on a cold trip back from Canada (he kept up this vigorous transatlantic mobility to the end). He took Holy Communion a few hours before he died, going off happily, his son reported to the family, "trusting in Jesus Christ and him alone."

Throughout that long and productive life — and the age of seventy-eight was very old a century and a half ago — not only was there the almost constant dance of success and failure, huge revenues and huge debts, but there were two apparently similar contradictory aspects of his character: an almost obsessive concern for safety, and a love of risk. Again Napoleon comes to mind; flagrantly ambitious designs for campaigns bristling with risk, and the insurance of an enormous army with high morale and crack training. With Cunard it was a willingness to move far afield in search of contacts and investment, always mediated by a scrupulous concern for the physical safety of his ships and passengers.

By the time of the next war, the First World War, and with Sam long dead, Sam's grandson Ernest was running the company, and Cunard ships were once more being STUFT. The line bore its share of losses. Ten were sunk by the Germans, including the Cunard flagship the *Lusitania*. Winston Churchill said that the great twentieth-century Cunarders, the *Queen Mary* and the *Queen Elizabeth*, shortened World War II by a year. The *Queen Mary* was stripped of all her trimmings, until she was nearly an empty shell of compartments. In one aerial photograph the decks and superstructure are almost invisible. The topsides look like a teeming ant colony — solid humanity. On one crossing the *Queen Mary* carried more than sixteen thousand soldiers, the greatest number of passengers ever carried by a sea-going vessel. Forty years later a Cunard vessel assisted in the Falklands War. In about eight days it too was stripped down and converted into an armed floating barracks, with helicopter pads placed fore and aft.

It was Cunard ships that brought the masses of immigrants to Canada early in the twenty-first century. If we include the US immigration of both centuries, Cunard vessels delivered over two and a half million immigrants to North America.

The company was characterized by resilience, adventure, and mobility, always tempered by that commitment to safety rather than speed. They built an empire on land and at sea. But no enterprise, no empire, no work of genius can ever quite outlast its founder. The elder Cunard son, Sir Edward, was less astute than his father, and in the late nineteenth century the keystone of the company, its mail service, lost business. When Edward died, his younger brother William took over a company that was now up against powerful competitors who had learned a lot both from Cunard and its earlier failed rivals. William finally took it public and put it on the London stock exchange.

It was Samuel Cunard's grandson Ernest who took the Cunard

Lines into World War I, and by then the ships began to resemble the ships of today, their hulls high in the water, smooth stretches of riveted steel, the white above, the black below, the four tall funnels that would become three, then two, then one.

Ernest's death in 1922 marked the end of the Cunard family as directors of the Cunard Steamship Lines. The great twentieth-century liners were launched. The first of the great liners was to be called the *Victoria*. Her keel was laid at the John Brown shipyards in Glasgow in 1930 as "Hull #534." When the Cunard chairman went to see King George V to seek the royal permission necessary to use His Majesty's grandmother's name in this way, he neglected to tell the king in advance what it was about.

When the opening formalities were over, the chairman said, so the story goes, "Sir, we are about to launch the greatest ocean liner the world has ever seen, and we have come to ask your permission to name it after England's most remarkable Queen." To which His Majesty replied, "My wife will be so pleased." And so that was the end of Samuel Cunard's brand-name "ia" endings. In 1934 Queen Mary swung the champagne bottle against the prow of Hull #534, launched her, and named her after herself. A few years later the *Queen Mary* would be followed by the *Queen Elizabeth*.

Although most of Samuel Cunard's papers were burned in a dockside fire at the turn of the century, his great-great-grandson Hugh Paton still has a few of the original letters. They include the one to his daughter about the shipyards in Glasgow, the one from son William about the old man's devout last hours, and the founder's original leather-bound passport. You can see the writing kit on which he signed the admiralty mail contract on display in the Cunard museum in the original *Queen Mary*, which no longer sails, and is a dockside hotel and tourist attraction in California.

But there is still a Cunard heritage on the Atlantic. The conventional wisdom now says that the jetliner spelled the end of transoceanic travel as a commercial norm. But for those who see that ocean not as an obstacle to be overflown but as a splendid part of the world to be enjoyed for its raw beauty, the liner is still the way to go. The new

Queen Mary demonstrates that the founder's vision, though much modified, is not dead. The real presence of Samuel Cunard's hand is in that mastery of the Atlantic, the drawing together of Europe and America, and in the millions of immigrants who came to the New World in Cunard ships.

◆　◆　◆

The History Television documentary was written and directed by Peter Rowe.

Part Seven

SIR WILLIAM OSLER
The Enlightener

In the fall of 1919, at Oxford, Sir William Osler was stricken, along with millions more around the world, by the great influenza epidemic. Before long he knew he was dying. The attending doctor tried to be encouraging, but Osler said, "You lunatic, I've been watching this case for over two months and I'm sorry I shan't see the post-mortem." A few weeks later on December 28 he was dead.

Osler's death seemed not to interest him much, nor did death in general. But life certainly did. And this is a clue, if a small one, to his enigma. He founded no great institution; he made no startling scientific discoveries. Yet he stands with Paracelsus, Hippocrates, Galen, and Pasteur as one of the giants of Western medicine. To say that he was not much taken by death will at first seem contradictory as the images unfold in a documentary film, so many stained, grainy old black-and-white photographs of him gesturing over a cadaver on a table, to a crowd of intrigued students. The cadavers often seem more than dead with their skin partially flayed and what remains blackening with time, with parts missing, tendons and organs exposed, manifestly much handled. But it was not the death in the corpse that intrigued Osler; it was the implication of life and the suggestions for healing and the relief of suffering that teased at him from every fibre, every fragment of diseased tissue, every sign of where something had gone wrong that might have been prevented or healed.

In the end he became famous for something discreet and rather surprising, and it is interesting that as significant an authority as the *Dictionary of Canadian Biography* isn't much help in getting to know this monumental figure. It says, simply, "He published numerous monographs and essays on medical subjects," and proceeds with a list of rather uninteresting titles. Nothing much on the reason for the reverence with which he is still held by the profession. Nothing on the interesting speculations we could easily make about what this great generalist's views of medicine might be now, were he to see it from the grave. Would he shudder at our specialization and industrialization, at the shortage of general practitioners, the obsolescence of house calls and other humane elements of the practice of medicine to which he devoted his life?

Or perhaps he would just shrug it off, and get on with whatever he was doing: he wasn't really a moral or social critic. Perhaps it is best to look at what he did in terms of the state of medicine around the time of his birth in the mid-nineteenth century. Medical practice was a loose and quiet anarchy, full of speculation and quackery, fatalism, and vain and damaging remedies. Patients were treated like broken machines. The causes of disease were largely unknown. Louis Pasteur was only then discovering that bacteria lay at the root of so many of them, but his drastically important discovery had not yet persuaded surgeons to wash their hands before operating.

Cell theory and microbiology did not exist. Surgical patients were strapped to the table so they wouldn't writhe too much, and the only anesthesia in common use was still a bottle of whisky, although Queen Victoria was pioneering and would soon help popularize the use of "Twilight Sleep" — nitrous oxide or laughing gas — in childbirth. That was a practice many disapproved of, as the pain of childbirth was thought to be morally improving.

Theory still eclipsed practice. In medical schools, everything was done in the classroom; a student almost never saw a patient until he graduated and actually went to work. House calls were not a significant element of the practice. The emotional state of patients was still decades from being understood as a critical component of disease and healing.

Death — we begin with death. Death was not simply the cessation of vital processes, it was encased in religious and mythic baggage, a sacrosanct and desired release from the miseries of life, and at the same time a mysterious terror to be resisted until the end. Life after death was taken for granted and generally thought to be a desired and wondrous state, and the terminally ill were often tendered respect and deference.

The actual study of dead bodies as a way of understanding disease was little used. There was no general consensus on therapeutic techniques. The practice of medicine had, to a large extent, developed haphazardly, and on the whole it was still a poorly defined somewhat mysterious profession.

And here is where we find the essence of Osler's contribution to medicine, and the reason why he is still honoured around the world. While it is true in a strictly technical sense that he did not, as we said at the outset, make any great scientific discoveries, what he did accomplish, working out of the heart of this chaotic, unsystematized, and largely intuitive or even guess-based profession, was to *invent* medical practice as we know it in the modern world, a set of methods organized around commonly agreed principles, like engineering — or indeed, like science itself. The British scientist, historian, and popularizer of science, John Ziman, argues convincingly in his definitive book *Real Science* that at the heart of it is a social or communitarian principle of consensus about what constitutes science, a social convention that is more important than mathematics, experiment, theorizing, rationality, or any of the other elements commonly seen as central to science. Osler brought the same idea to medicine, and to do so he worked from a base of humanitarian common sense, in which seeing patients and examining the fabric of the human body was right at the centre of things. Everyone in the profession would agree.

He committed his learning and his ideas and principles to print. His seminal thousand-page *The Principles and Practice of Medicine* has gone through countless editions. Written out of his own experience, it summarized the proven and agreed-on knowledge of the day and also rigorously listed all that was obsolete.

His own collection of medical works, the *Bibliotheca Osleriana*, is his largest material legacy to the world. It is a massive collection of books and other documents on the history of medicine that fills several rooms. Osler had read them all and written many of them.

What he accomplished seems to have grown out of an attitude, perhaps an attitude to the whole question of existence, in which he saw life, as the poet said, "steadily and saw it whole." In an age when doc-

tor, patient, disease and sufferer, student and hospital were seen as separate entities, Osler realized that in fact they were all just aspects of a
single, interdependent organ. He conceptualized that which had been
haphazard, made it into a system. And in doing so he made medicine
humane, simply by making it into a single, agreed-on system. It was no
longer detached, its problems isolated like auto mechanics. He said,
"Treat the patient not the disease" only to take it further, expounding
above all on the doctor-patient relationship. And then of course the
medical student had to learn from a real live — or even dead — patient
as well. Osler gave the Americans the idea of interns and internships
for novice doctors. He gave Canada's first course in histology, the
microscopic study of the body. He gave North America's first course on
post-mortems. At the Medical School of Philadelphia he used his own
money to set up an autopsy lab since no one in America took autopsies
seriously. His classes were so crowded that some students attended by
looking through the skylight. His humour made people desperate to
perform autopsies. When a student blundered, he congratulated him
roundly; he praised mistakes because they were the way people
learned.

In the process of defining what it was the profession could agree
on, Osler also raised what had often been a thankless study, its practitioners often the butt of contemptuous humour, into a rewarding art.

Attitude appears to be the key to this man's character. As important as system and agreement were to him, so was the emotional
bearing and deportment of the practitioner. While defeat in the face of
unconquerable death had traditionally produced either panic or resignation, Osler saw a better way. Metaphysical panic, hair-tearing, or
sleeplessness were not, after all, going to help. Nor was throwing up
your hands in resignation and trusting in the Almighty. If there was
anything approaching a Bible in the armamentarium of this utterly
practical and undoctrinaire man, it would have been Thomas Browne's
Religio Medici (1643) on the pragmatic reconciliation of religious
belief with reason. With Browne in hand, Osler seemed to say, "You can
have nothing before you but the problem." And out of this attitude
grew the principle that is still attached to his name, still cited as the

deportmental and even spiritual aim of the best practitioner, the resolute calm in the face of other people's storms, which Osler called *Aequanimitas*.

So Osler is theory, practice, and *attitude*. If he is not the Descartes or the Leibnitz of medicine, he is very much like the age that followed them. He opened up, systematized, and criticized; he removed superstition and prejudice. He procured agreement. Osler was an Enlightenment.

But as with all rich and complex personalities, there is still a world of contradiction and enigma in the compact frame of William Osler. There is no *gravitas*. There is not much of the stormy impatience we might expect from a man who saw early and saw clearly that the profession he had chosen needed an overhaul so prodigious that one lifetime might be insufficient. And there is a certain lack of dignity for one so universally acknowledged to be a Great Man.

In fact, he was — all his life — as much a prankster as a serious professional and a teacher. That part of him shows up early. At the age of eight he locked all his fellow students' desks in an attic and filled the classroom with geese. At nineteen he barricaded an unpopular teacher in her classroom, and then fed in the fumes of burning sulphur and molasses. (Was this intended as an admonitory metaphor? Sulphur and molasses were a common spring tonic and mythic remedy for constipation.)

When he was twenty and studying to be an Anglican priest (a brief digression before he settled on the field that apparently already intrigued him), he swiped a fetus from the school of medicine and left it in the divinity school. The joke became a parting gesture, since he was expelled for it.

Later, when he was at McGill and visiting his Montreal cousins Marian and Jeannette and their family, he brought all the children over to a friend's house. The friend was William Molson, son of the great brewer. Molson was giving a big party that night and when the main course had been served and taken away, the servants were flabbergasted to find that all the desserts had disappeared. Osler had given them to his cousins' children.

As he matured, so did the style and character of his irrepressible mischief. On the threshold of fame he took a prodigious risk by posing as the non-existent "Dr. Egerton Y. Davis," the author of a deadpan letter to the editor of the pompous *Medical News*. The letter was about the phenomenon known as "Vaginismus," the entrapment of the male's penis by constriction in a vagina, popularly said to be common among dogs. Osler invented a fictitious human case that ended in a laborious separation by a surgeon, during which the man sustained some serious injury. Of course it was all to embarrass the self-important and, Osler thought, slow-nodding fools who ran the *Medical News*. The jape worked. They published it, whereupon he unmasked himself — and somehow got away with it.

But another joke was so broad and so profane, that even today it would separate the literal-minded majority from the rest. It was 1905. In his farewell address to Johns Hopkins — of which institution much more later — he offered, for the university's consideration, some thoughts about how long a professional person should continue with this moving on from one post to another, as he was about to do. Perhaps, he suggested, in order to open things up for new people and new ideas . . . perhaps, in the medical profession where people were no longer superstitious about death . . . perhaps, we could deploy euthanasia as a form of retirement. After all, old age was not only an obstacle to the advance of society — it was also a dreadful burden to the old themselves. They should be chloroformed.

Scandalized, people took it seriously as a cruel proposal for the extermination of the aged. Of course he had only been making fun of useless hand-wringing about old age. Many discerning editorialists got the joke and exposed it, but somehow the world did not, and the tremors lasted for years. Osler was asked again and again if he had been serious. The thing even turned up in James Joyce's *Finnegan's Wake* with "The ogry Osler will oxmaul us all," an environment where it was probably understood as the joke that it was meant to be.

Perhaps genius can never be entirely serious. It takes a talent for mischief to break rules and make connections that no one else would. Certainly there is nothing in Osler of the unsmiling moral mission. In his early education he became enamoured of the classics. His instincts were artistic and literary — which we take to be a good sign in anyone, including mechanics.

And so we are tempted to draw a picture of a man producing inner synaptic fireworks while doing handstands on the street corner, or booby-trapping doorways with cans of water while conceiving the idea of internships, or realizing the true value of cadavers at a production of Aristophanes' comedy *The Clouds*. And then — in what *may* have been a very different state of mind — Osler proposed the idea of the "day-tight compartment," a mental work space in which, having only the problem before you, you were supposed to rigorously exclude regrets for past mistakes — and perhaps rejoice in successes — and certainly exclude anxieties about the future. You would have only the problem before you. This was not a neurotic or psychologically self-defensive withdrawal; it was a technique for achieving that essential *Aequanimitas*. But it is doubtful that the compartment was really watertight, even as he practised it. He always had his mischief and his art with him, in whatever space he was working. They were part of the *Aequanimitas*.

And could he work! When Grace Revere Gross refused his proposal of marriage as long as he was lost in the composition of what was to become his thousand-page *Principles and Practice of Medicine,* he cranked up the pressure on himself and finished the book in seven months.

The marriage was superbly happy and Grace's first pregnancy a blessing. Osler's fondness for his young son knew no bounds. They swam and fished together. When the boy was sick, Osler found it hard to treat him; he lost the equanimity for which the outside world knew him. Again, when the child needed discipline, the doctor was something of a softy. In many ways he preferred the company of children to that of adults. He entertained them. It was his capacity to entertain that made him loved by strangers.

It seems likely that some of his humour was connected to his dry sense of practicality. For example, at the time when Osler was just beginning to teach at Johns Hopkins, the medical school found itself

strapped for funds. It needed a benefactor. There appeared a committee of women in Baltimore who undertook to raise the necessary
money, on condition that Johns Hopkins would open its doors to
women. The male directors were red in the face. At first Osler shared
their prejudice, but it must have been a sense of the ridiculous that
made him see the idiotic pomposity of sticking to the principle at the
cost of an entire medical school.

And anyway, he couldn't see any practical reason to deny women
the study of medicine. Surely this was also an example of *Aequanimitas*,
and he said so, and publicly agreed with the women. But the other men
held out. They raised the target from a hundred thousand to a whopping
five hundred thousand dollars — probably more to block female enrol-
ment than to build the wing. Of course the women called their bluff and
raised the half million. Due to Osler, if only in part, Johns Hopkins
became one of the first medical schools in the world to admit women.

This sort of leavened genius had uncertain beginnings. He was
born in the bush, in Ontario, in 1849. His first school was the grammar
school in Dundas, Ontario, the one where, at age eight he had filled a
classroom with geese. For that he was expelled. He was sent to Trinity
College School up in Weston, where, despite the usual colourful behaviour he began to apply himself and was made prefect. In that school
there was a microscope, a rarity even in a university in those days, an
instrument that transformed the commonplace world into an entirely
different sort of universe. It was the headmaster who had blessed his
students with this treasure: in the half-cleared bush it was a piece of
technology that would have been far ahead of its time in many a city
school. And that particular microscope, for all its scratches, may have
changed history when the young Osler saw the minute moving structures that lay within what had seemed to be the clear and empty water
of ponds, the familiar surface of a leaf. He saw the miraculous components of blood, and was enchanted.

That enlightened headmaster, W.A. Johnson, introduced the
young Osler to Dr. James Bovell, who taught at the Toronto School of
Medicine. Still a student, Osler walked with Bovell and Johnson
through the bush and river valleys as Johnson sketched and Bovell

collected specimens of insects and plants. Johnson spoke little but demonstrated much: the motion of the heavens alongside the micro cosmos of a drop of pond water.

It was 1867, Osler was eighteen, and surprisingly, given the path his life would soon take, his first choice for advanced study was divinity, at Trinity College in Toronto. We have to speculate here, since he did not leave us an account of what happened. But the maturing mind would soon move far away from the authoritative mythology of the Bible, and it may have been the smug, self-satisfied dogmatism of his ecclesiastical teachers that helped him turn the corner. While those divines were vesting everything in the authority of scripture and of the hierarchies, Dr. Bovell was inviting him to look into Browne's *Religio Medici*, a book of inquiry in which the author, himself a physician, was struggling to reconcile faith and reason. This was more appealing than doctrine; it seemed to touch a real world; the givens of the divinity school mentality began to smell like superstition. Only someone deeply contemptuous of the institution he was enrolled in could have played that genuinely tasteless and offensive joke with the fetus, and he got his hands on that fetus only because a teacher very different from the Trinity clerics — Dr. Bovell — had been quietly and unofficially opening the labs at the medical school to his young friend.

This is not to suggest that Bovell's inquiring and experimental mind was characteristic of the institution in which he taught. Bovell, like his young apprentice, was an exception at the Medical School of Toronto where Osler now moved, and where he spent the next two disappointing years. The faculty doctors taught by lecturing. The students saw no patients, no corpses, no diseases in action. They were not allowed professional access to the Toronto General Hospital. This at a time when Pasteur was studying harmful bacteria, Rudolf Vierchow was exploring the complex world of putrefaction, and cell theory and microbiology had made it into the scientific curricula at last. Toronto was not an advanced school, but it was not so backward that his teachers didn't recognize that the young man had genuine talent, and someone suggested that he turn to what had become one of the premier medical schools in North America.

The McGill University Medical School, in Montreal, gave him the luxury of studying the dead. He trained at the Montreal General Hospital, which he said had two great advantages. It was old and full of infection, disease, and rats; and it had talented teachers.

At the time autopsies were still at the frontier of medical practice and not taken entirely seriously. But young Osler seemed almost obsessed, and some of his fellow students thought him genuinely eccentric with his endless dissecting, extracting specimens, fragments of diseased livers, collapsed hearts. Some of his specimens are still on view, almost unidentifiable cloudy and diaphanous tissues, grey or salmon-coloured lobes of organs waving gently in their great jars of formaldehyde. He became, literally, the pioneer of the dead house. Pathology, the study of the causes of disease and death, usually from dissected corpses, was his prowess. He had the genius to grasp its full significance. It was a talent rare enough to bring him fame.

This knack for the practical, for getting straight to the heart of the matter, for turning medicine towards root causes, culminated in a brilliant dissertation that earned him his MD and Master of Surgery at the precocious age of twenty-two. Well ahead of provincial Canada now, he was able to finish his studies in London, Berlin, and Vienna.

It has been said that when he returned to McGill, where his obsession with the microscope and minute organisms and the process of infection and decay were still a curiosity, he next had to bring the university up to his own standards. McGill had been wise and generous enough to teach him but not quick enough to catch up to him. Autopsies were still marginal, and this premier medical school, like the prep school back in the bush in Ontario, still had only a few microscopes. And so Osler and the medical dons George Ross and Francis Shepherd set about something that now seems laughably obvious: they decided to bring more science into the curriculum, beginning with more microscopes.

But in those days at McGill a skyrocketing reputation as a teacher and prolific writer were not enough to pay the bills. He still had to trudge over to the Montreal General Hospital to earn a decent salary. What might have been a fatal stroke of bad luck only brought him closer to the medical concerns that would become his major field of endeavour. It was 1878, the year of Montreal's first dreadful epidemic of smallpox. It is difficult to give an idea of what the young pathologist had to face. That smallpox could exterminate entire peoples among North American Natives was bad enough. It was also a spectacularly raging disaster to which the grand and powerful courts of seventeenth- and eighteenth-century Europe had been as vulnerable as a peasant village or an urban slum. Contemporary descriptions of the appearance of ailing kings and queens only hint at the almost indescribably repulsive expression of the disease in its advanced stages.

We have almost forgotten smallpox. It occasionally surfaces in the public awareness with news stories about the risk of its use now by bio-terrorists, and the proposal by some politicians, discouraged by scientists, that we return to mass vaccination of the population. Mass vaccination is the reason we no longer know what smallpox is. The virtually universal vaccination program is one of the world's great success stories. The last "natural" case of the disease was in 1976, and while mass vaccination now would almost certainly kill more people than a terrorist attack (the virus is very difficult to spread artificially), the result of the vaccination program is that the only known stores of the virus are in laboratories in Florida and Siberia.

The disease began with headaches and pains in the belly. After three or four days those pains became excruciating. The rash of encrusted sores would start to appear around the tenth day, and death could follow any time in the next two weeks, often sooner rather than later. Once the rash appeared, death was more likely than recovery.

It was not just the patient's cheeks or arms or forehead that showed sores, but rather the whole head. In the worst cases the entire body became a pustular, undifferentiated mass of sores. For a physician to venture onto the ground and try to treat this contagion was to play Russian roulette with his own life. And here we must stop abruptly. Because Osler too must at least have paused. He must have realized he had to concentrate on the problem, not its effects — which might well include his own infection. Perhaps he just concentrated on the patient as a person, and not simply the pathology. Or maybe he did not; maybe that's what he learned in the course of treating eighty-one appalling cases. For this focus on the person came to be the central point of what he taught.

He must certainly have applied the principle of detachment to himself; he had to because he caught the disease and got over it. Ironically, at almost the same time smallpox killed Osler's much-loved mentor, the schoolmaster W.A. Johnson, who probably was infected by a sick student.

When he recovered, Osler was rewarded with the position of attending physician at the hospital. But in the late nineteenth century the medical doctor was not, as he is today in most countries in the West, one of the best paid of all professionals. Here was a man with great good looks and superb professional prestige, but at this time he was simply not earning enough to marry and raise a family. He doggedly kept on though, deciding to take some time away from teaching, visit some of his old colleagues abroad, see what he could learn in Berlin and Leipzig and London. While he was in Britain his name somehow came to the attention of the medical school at the University of Pennsylvania. That was the largest training ground for doctors in the whole United States. It needed a professor of clinical medicine. The faculty heads liked what they had heard about Osler's methods at McGill, and sent him an offer. McGill heard about it and sent a counteroffer. Osler is said to have flipped a coin, and taken a ship for Pennsylvania.

Before long that institution found itself with its first autopsy lab. For five years he lectured on, and popularized the use of cadavers. He became admired, even loved, and certainly listened to, as he had been at McGill. He published without stop.

Not far away, in Baltimore, Maryland, there was a new university, Johns Hopkins, that would before long become one of the most important educational institutions in the United States. Johns Hopkins needed a physician-in-chief and professor of medicine. The university and medical school were all new; the medical school itself was already the most advanced in America. Osler made his decision; before long he delivered his farewell speech at Pennsylvania. This was the speech in which he first publicly developed the idea of the doctor's *Aequanimitas*.

We have said that William Osler made no spectacular scientific discoveries, but perhaps that's not quite true. Strange as it seems now, the idea of teaching at the hospital bedside of a real, live patient instead of in a lecture room was sufficiently revolutionary to deserve the term *scientific discovery*. At the new university in Baltimore, Osler took American medical students to the hospital wards for the first time. He had introduced internships to the United States. It was at Johns Hopkins that he wrote and published *The Principles and Practice of Medicine*. Here again he was innovative, for Osler gave credit where it was due when he could easily have claimed certain discoveries for himself. Plagiarism of that kind was not unknown in the profession; the rigours of publication in the scientific society had not made that practice as impossible as it is now, and Osler's honesty was exemplary.

In Johns Hopkins, Osler found an institution his own equal if only because he and the new university actually made one another into what they became. Married, prestigious, well paid, and generally loved, he could not go much further than this. It was his apogee. At forty-five he became a father and began a semi-retirement by increasing the proportion of speeches, articles, and addresses to classroom and laboratory work. His private practice blossomed. It was said you couldn't die respectably unless Osler had gently sent you on your way.

It was at Hopkins that he gained his worldwide renown. His practical philosophy for approaching medicine became a world standard. It was still an age when doctors from San Francisco to Berlin went into the field knowing anatomy and perhaps even what they wanted to achieve, but they did not know how to achieve it or how to question what they were doing. With the teachings of Doctor Osler there now stood beside them a spectral figure who provided a relation between themselves and their craft, between doctor and patient.

What was there left to do? Where could he go but to some position more august, more serene, but also less demanding and better for his health? Seldom short of luck, he was offered the Regius Chair of Medicine at Oxford. Fully confident but a little jaded, perhaps, by the eager worship of his vast audience, it was in his farewell address to

Johns Hopkins that he offered the notorious "euthanasia" proposal.

In 1905 he took his family to England. As Regius professor at Oxford, even though he was now in a position of unchallenged authority and prestige, there was little change in the routine of his days. At the "Open Arms," which he called his house, he received visitors and carried on his profession as before. He maintained an enormous practice, and his hospital routine wore out the young interns. He was fifty-six. Life has rarely been so good to anyone for so long. Wealthy, serene, balanced. Presently a Knighthood. An age of equanimity.

That period between the Boer War and the Great War was perhaps the closest to a "normal" time the Western world has ever known: neither hectic boom nor frantic bust; no war, no insane progress, no revolutions, social or otherwise. Blissfully unaware, it lay in the shadow of doom. As did Osler himself. Britain's declaration of war on August 4, 1914, startled him.

He must have had very mixed feelings when his only son, Revere Osler, enlisted at nineteen. At first Osler managed to keep him away from the action by getting him placed in the McGill Hospital unit. But young Revere wanted to be at the front, and got himself transferred to a field unit. At twenty-one he wrote to his family from the muddy squalor of the trenches that he was gambling on getting a "blighty": a wound just grave enough to send him home. But on August 29, 1917, in the middle of the terrible Passchendaele campaign, Revere Osler was splattered with shrapnel from an exploding shell. They carried him a couple of miles by stretcher to a dressing station. A friend of his father's from the McGill days was on duty there and tried his best to save him, but Revere died a day later, and was buried on the devastated, shell-pitted field.

Who knows how Osler felt during his last two years, as he busied himself building the *Bibliotheca Osleriana*? Some say his son's death crushed him, that the Oslers had felt its approach from the beginning of the war, as the world began to fall apart. Others say his resort to building a library was only a living demonstration of his principle of *Aequanimitas*.

Beneath the exterior near cliché of The Good Doctor, there was certainly this rich combination of determination and humour, and a confidence in his own capacities that he certainly shared with his siblings. Inherited or learned? That is one of those continuing vexations in the scientific world: nature versus nurture. But certainly that Osler family was spectacular. The boy grew up with the unsubtleties of the frontier bush, but in an atmosphere of religion and learning. His father, Featherstone Osler, had once been a naval officer but had become an Anglican priest and circuit preacher. William Osler's mother, Ellen Picton Osler, bore William, their last son, in 1849. They lived in a leaky, drafty house in the hamlet of Bond Head, now a sleeper suburb of Toronto. He was the youngest of eight children. His brothers became masters in their professions, one a great judge, one a great lawyer, another a great financier. As far as we know, William's sense of mischief that, so strangely for a man of such sensitivity and compassion, could descend to demeaning pranks and genuinely hurtful jokes was not shared.

His death from influenza in 1919 was mercifully speedy, and not particularly different from the millions of such deaths that swept around the world that year and the year before, his particular case in no way instructive. Sir William would probably have been quite disappointed in the post-mortem.

◆　◆　◆

The History Television documentary was written and directed by Roberto Verdecchia.

Part Eight

MA MURRAY
The Fastest Pen in the Yukon

The state of politics in Canada is as low as a snake's belly in Arkansas.
But a snake there would never go so low that he didn't have a pit to hiss in.
– Margaret (Ma) Murray

In the town of Lillooet, British Columbia, in the 1930s, there was a weekly newspaper called the *Bridge River-Lillooet News*. Lillooet was a mining and lumber town, big enough to have some delicate issues and small enough to have a few local egos. That was normal. But as soon as a woman by the name of Margaret Murray took over the editorship of *The News*, the complaints — both from the egos and about the delicacies — came unusually fast, many of them on lawyers' letterheads: "Dear Mrs. Murray, I would like to advise you that my client is not a crooked horse trader and he is not a gypsy." Or, "Madam, I have been instructed by my client to demand a full apology — and a retraction." And one that almost looks as though she'd written herself, as a spoof: "I have the highest regard for our volunteer fire department, and must point out they are not all wet."

In 1935, Margaret Murray, or just plain "Ma" as she was by then known, had been left to run the paper while her husband, the editor, George Murray, took his seat in the BC legislature down in Victoria. Ma Murray had her way of doing things. She had only a grade three education, a pretty raunchy approach to self-expression, a lot of strong opinions, many of them unpopular, and only a dim notion of the concept of libel. Although she had nominally replaced her husband when he left for the legislature, being The Editor meant that she would write the paper most of the time and nobody would edit what she had written. The traditional restraints and cautions of George's blue pencil may have gone to Victoria with her husband; they certainly didn't show up much at *The News* any more, once he'd left it in her hands.

Libellous, bawdy, plebeian, infuriating, and colourful, Margaret Murray was, in fact, a very good fit for a rollicking frontier town. Lillooet was not the sort of place that would care a whole lot about spelling, punctuation, and grammar. When some complaints did arrive about the absence of periods and commas in *The News*, Ma ran a front-page box in the next issue completely filled with punctuation marks and told her readers they could put them in themselves if they felt the need.

While much of Margaret Murray's style was wisdom in the rough, sometimes she was just plain indecipherable. Most of her readers loved it; perhaps it made them feel part of things. And once she got her children working for her, she didn't object when they followed her style. Her daughter Georgina wrote about a fire reported by a miner named Ollie. And it proceeded: "Ollie had just completed the first two hours of his afternoon shit." "Shift" was the intended word, but as we've said the blue pencil was not getting much use. The readers were delighted. Ollie was known to spend quite a bit of his work time in the privy, and Georgina also noted that he was said to have evacuated the town as well.

That story about Ollie helped cement the paper's *succès de scandale* and the issue that it appeared in became sufficiently notorious that it sold for five dollars apiece — the price of a year's subscription. By then the *Bridge River-Lillooet News* was selling almost 2000 copies a week, although "selling" is not quite the right word, Ma being not very much focused on money matters. She would barter the paper to those who couldn't pay cash — for an issue or subscription. One small enterprise paid for the paper with raisin pies, of which the Murray kids later said, "We had them coming out of our ears." Chickens, vegetables, before long the newspaper was bringing in pretty well all their groceries without the usual intervention of cash.

Ma was a supporter of her husband George's political career and she was tireless in attacking other politicians, not just his opponents, but also his superiors in the Liberal Party. In one editorial she called

George's boss, the premier, a "paragon of senile decay." George would write home, "In the name of reason, what are you trying to do to me?" But Ma didn't care. Embarrassing her husband had become an old habit which for her didn't mean much since, as we will see, she loved him more than she loved anything and she thought he ought to be able to put up with a bit of fun.

But this playful and mischievous journalist was nonetheless a powerful presence. In her photographs she seems imperious, even menacing, despite the huge smile adorned with fairly irregular teeth. It is a smile declaring that she has something great to offer and doesn't give a damn what anyone thinks.

Once someone made the mistake of asking Ma to introduce George at a political event; she accepted with enthusiasm and opened by saying that the north was filled with good men, "none better than my husband. . . . And as you all know, when a good woman gets under a man he moves." The characteristic dour probity in Depression British Columbia hadn't a chance. The room collapsed in howls of laughter.

"Well," she continued, "we like to grow 'em big up north." Whereupon she puffed out her great forty-four-inch bust. A button popped and ricocheted with a ping off a wineglass and the decorum of the house was destroyed for good. Now it was George's turn. He stepped up and took, quite appropriately, a long pause. He said that he now understood why the American President Franklin Roosevelt was reputed to pray that his wife Eleanor would wake up more tired than when she'd gone to sleep.

Ma's wordplay would not even be roped in by the protocols surrounding royalty. The Murrays had been invited to meet the King and Queen on the royal prewar tour of Canada. Ma wrote afterward in her lead editorial that she hadn't known whether to curtsey to the king or give him a big kiss. She told them in a later issue that what she finally did was to hold his hand "'til his little sword rattled."

Behind that perfectly genuine façade of playfulness there was a woman of great practicality. In 1937, George was sent to China on a trade mission. A photograph shows the two of them in Shanghai looking like a rich Western couple in a rickshaw. When a Japanese battleship began bombarding the city, they had to make their way through the chaotic streets, strewn with mangled corpses, to the British troop ship that was to evacuate them. The refugee-laden ship was teeming with chaos and desperation. The Murrays had an elegant suite of state-rooms since Ma had managed to let people think George was the pre-mier of BC. She could easily have sought refuge in those staterooms and disappeared and rested up after the ordeal of escaping from a city under siege. Instead, when she learned that another refugee was in labour, and there was no doctor or midwife to be found, Ma delivered the baby.

But there was a contradictory and sometimes hateful side to this uncommonly generous-spirited woman. During World War II thou-sands of Japanese-Canadians were moved from their coastal homes lest they help their Japanese relatives carry out an invasion of Canada — it was one of the major injustices of the war. Lillooet was far enough inland that the authorities considered it a safe stopping point for some 4000 of these internees, and most of Lillooet thought the sudden increase in the population both good for business and a useful supply of low-cost labour. Not Ma Murray. Her editorials bristled with racist vituperation. Perhaps she was surprised to find out how unpopular these editorials were; she made herself unpopular with everyone, Japanese-Canadian or not. The Murrays left Lillooet. Ma said it was because the town was getting overcrowded.

By this time Ma's pictures show her on the far side of middle age, more formidable-looking than ever. Scouting for a town that needed a paper, she looked almost as far east as Edmonton and finally settled for Fort St. John where there were wooden sidewalks and weather that got to sixty-below. Ma and George and the family moved into a log house. Ten thousand US troops were building the 450-mile Alcan Military Road from Edmonton to the Yukon. George had long championed such a road and decided it was time to start a new paper, *The Alaska Highway News,* and try to keep the Lillooet paper running from a distance. *The Highway News* wasn't going to sell many copies; the Lillooet paper would have to subsidize it for a while. Ma didn't think much about that side. She had a new paper to help run and that kept her going.

Now if Ma Murray had little financial ambition for herself, she was completely against any sort of welfare for anyone else. In the documentary we see her in a late interview polemically declaring, "Nothing is worth a damn in this world unless you've earned it. And that's the reason why your socialism won't work. It won't work for anybody, because something you get for nothing isn't worth any more than you paid for it." She was not one for the velvet glove; you can hear the hostility, the finger-shaking menace in her voice. Curiously, the only political party she could stand was Social Credit, which had been founded on the principle of giving a subsistence income to every citizen. However, by the time Ma Murray became involved with it, it had become *the* right-wing party in Western Canada. When her husband George's Liberals formed a coalition with the provincial Conservatives, George disliked the Tories so much that he ran as a lone independent. Ma ran for Social Credit, against her husband. Her son Dan, then editing the Lillooet paper, used the front page to warn readers that Margaret Murray was related to the family only by blood.

Ma may have had strong opinions but she wasn't big on details. It was doubtful that such a dogged individualist could ever have really been a party person, and in any case she didn't seem to care what policies her party stood for: this was just an opportunity for some more polemical fun and a chance to play at George's game. Campaigning she would just duck questions about policy. Her son Dan, unlike her husband, was not amused. Rebelliously serious and fastidious, Dan wrote another *Highway News* editorial that said, "Mrs. Margaret Murray has nothing whatsoever to do with the editorial policy of this newspaper." The election was a disaster for both Ma and her husband. They both lost, miserably.

Dan's editorials against his mother are characteristic of family life among the Murrays. They all fought among themselves and the battle lines were usually around Ma. Dan himself had his own family now and the family wars hadn't abated. It is not clear whether Ma's robust delight in conflict and mayhem made her oblivious to what people outside the circle might feel, like Ma's daughter-in-law, Dan's wife. Dan's daughter Bridget said of her mother,

Mom would be so upset when they'd come for . . . Christmas. This was when we'd always have the big arguments, and there'd be a great hoo-ha over something or other — great, great debate. And Mom would be just destroyed because there would be, you know, foul language and shouting and raging and a lot of unhappiness. And yet I'd say, "Mom, it's just the way they relax, the Murrays. It's just how they go through this Gethsemane of arguments and discussions."

Ma's daughter-in-law would simply never understand how a disagreement about Canada's new maple leaf flag versus the old red ensign could ignite an outright screaming quarrel full of personal invective. Even less could she comprehend the speed at which they returned to normal before they left, and maybe young Bridget was right, maybe the whole thing really was just some form of family pastime.

In any case, all that receded for a while when George went into federal politics, got himself elected federal MP for Cariboo, and he and Ma went off to Ottawa. Left with both the *Lillooet* and the *Highway News*, Dan worked to make them solvent, serious, grammatical, efficient, and businesslike, exactly the sort of papers his mother hated. But even at a distance Ma managed to interfere, and in the end Dan gave up, sold the Lillooet paper, and left. Ma came back to Fort St. John and took over, doing what she had always wanted to do.

Within a few issues, *The Alaska Highway News* was back to its old, raucous, faintly scatological self. There was a water shortage. Ma quite reasonably determined that the single most extravagant use of water in the town was the flush toilet. She wrote an editorial about it, saying that it was simple: "Never flush for number one, just for number two."

"Only flush for number two" was the phrase that would stick to Ma Murray for the rest of her life. At the time it was delightfully picked up by newspapers and broadcasts all over North America. It made Ma Murray famous. It may not have had the sonorous glory of "Ask not what your country can do for you . . ." or "The lights are going out all over Europe . . ." but it said a great deal about a persistent ecological issue and about a crusty, determined, and practical-minded interventionist editor. And it stuck and spread and endured. In Whitehorse today, half a century later, they still say, "If it's yellow, let it mellow; if it's brown, flush it down."

In 1959 Ma had had enough of Fort St. John. The *Bridge River-Lillooet News* had been idle since Dan dropped it, and Ma decided to get it going again. She was past seventy, amazingly high-spirited, and unsinkable as ever, but she would soon have to draw on all the character and experience that had carried her this far, and it is probably appropriate here that we back up a little to look at how that character was formed and what those experiences had brought her.

The woman we remember as Ma Murray grew up poor in rural Kansas; she had been christened Margaret Lally in Kansas City in 1888, the seventh of nine children. Her mother and father had been Irish immigrants, poor enough that one winter the family had nothing to eat but turnips. She was working as a housemaid at the age of thirteen. Then she got some office training that led to a job in a saddle factory that supplied cowboys in Alberta. That's where she conceived her first dream: to marry an Alberta cowboy. Cowboys she knew only in their romanticized incarnation by Zane Grey and the other dime novelists of the era. She and the other girls who worked in the saddle factory used to slip notes into the finished saddles with their names and addresses. Nobody ever wrote back, but the lure of the Northwest was still strong; so Margaret and her sister Bess decided to work their way west, arriving in Vancouver via Seattle sometime in 1912. By then they had run out of money. Margaret was twenty-four.

Around the same time, George Murray was using some family money to start a newspaper in South Vancouver, a new suburb being hacked out of the forest. The big Vancouver papers like the *Daily World*, were put together in varnished offices downtown — you've seen them in old photographs: six or seven stories of West Coast rococo, massive and hazy from the dusty streets. A new man with some new ideas, Murray took rooms at 30th and Main out in the sticks, and announced his new venture, *The Chinook,* which he declared would advertise neither tobacco nor liquor.

As soon as two days' worth of papers had been sold, Murray

advertised for a bookkeeper at twelve dollars a week. Margaret Lally applied. On the way to her interview she stumbled badly on the crude plank sidewalk, breaking her heel. But she limped on painfully to the *Chinook* office, and said, "George Murray, you live at the end of the line." George said, "Margaret, I like to think of it as the beginning of the line." And she was hired.

Margaret, as we have already seen, was not one to beat around the bush and no sooner did she walk in the door for her first day than she asked for a raise to fifteen dollars a week. All it took was a little verbal bluff to convince George Murray that Margaret Lally was worth it. She got the increase, and she got down to work.

It did not take this down-to-earth, hard-nosed practical woman long to realize that her employer often had his head in the clouds, and that much of what he did was backwards and impractical. She wrote home that his *Chinook* was the "dinkiest little paper that you ever saw." But already she felt herself falling for the distracted, muddling, occasionally infuriating George Murray, cowboy though he definitely was not. His photographs show a man of middling good looks with a bit of a distant narrowing of the eyes, nothing that looks like vanity, a sense of stolidity. But still, even though she was intrigued, and had a pretty good time keeping him laughing at her earthy language and sharp observations, George remained hard to figure out.

If George Murray was the type who delayed or failed to notice or maybe was just too dumbstruck by a woman who was as subtle as a locomotive, Margaret was the kind to run out of patience. She hadn't entirely given up on the romantic notion of an Alberta cowboy. So she submitted her resignation. George, more than a little taken aback, nonetheless gave her a fine fountain pen as a parting gift. "You take it," he said. "Think about us and write us some time."

Whether Margaret Lally actually ever met any Alberta cowboys is not recorded. But it seems that she soon found herself missing the *Chinook,* and it is not unlikely that she was even playing a bit of a game anyway, taking a risk in order to let George see what he'd be missing. In any case, she was back to Vancouver five days later, and the scheme, if it was a scheme, seemed to have worked because George was there to meet her at the train. And George even managed to keep focused long enough to say right out that it hadn't been the same without her and would she marry him. Having finally got the question she wanted, Margaret gave the answer she'd been saving. They were married before the week was out.

He consented to be wed by a Catholic priest and knew enough not to invite his Protestant family. For a while they didn't speak to him, but they soon relented. An uncle of George's let them have an apartment in a building he owned, and before Margaret knew it, she, a poor, Kansas, Irish-Catholic girl, had become a member of the Vancouver middle class.

Perhaps it was some of those differences that made the marriage so rewarding. He came from an established, well-heeled Presbyterian family and she from a poor brood of Irish Roman Catholics. In the photographs, he's modest, quietly cheerful, and well dressed but sombre. In almost all her photos, from youth onwards, she has a grin and wears hats, often sombrero-like and wide enough to be pretentious. Both were dutifully observant, she going to early mass, George going at a more reasonable hour to the United Church service (after the Presbyterians and Methodists merged in June 1925 to create that uniquely Canadian almost secular denomination).

That early leap upward was followed by a couple of dips, although still well within the middle class. The *Chinook* was struggling at best. Margaret had given birth to their first child, and financial difficulties drove them to look for new ways to pay the rent. George learned that the government was handing out free land an hour and a half by boat up the Burrard Inlet. He borrowed the ten-dollar registration fee and suggested to Margaret that country life would be good for their new young family.

But the face of Burrard Inlet was not much like what we see today: it was high country, clothed in dense conifer forest descending steeply to the water. They found what someone called a stump ranch — a dark, wet, and dreary landscape made up of what the lumber companies had left behind. You get a sense from the letters that, disappointed as Margaret may have been, she was undaunted. Some of the stumps were gigantic. In one photograph lumberjacks are posing in front of one as big as two Volkswagens. George and Margaret set about burning and blasting them to open up some land for cultivation.

The prewar depression of 1913 didn't help, but coming from the poverty she had known as a kid, Margaret was less affected by it than George or probably most other people. All her life she took pleasure from simple things. She said once, "We had bread lines . . . we had soup kitchens, we did everything to get along, but my goodness alive, beans were the nicest thing that there ever was. I'd even trade a good plate of beans for the best porterhouse steak you ever had." They were saved from the far-reaching family tragedies of World War I. Since Margaret was on the way to giving birth to their second child, the Dan we've already met, George was exempted from military service.

But it was a tough time. They lived by subsistence work, both at the newspaper and their small ventures into agriculture. George did the writing, and Margaret tended a vegetable garden. Together they raised chickens and bought a cow and a couple of goats. It was Margaret who cut the heads off the chickens and coaxed a crop of vegetables out of what had been stump-strewn, rocky, weed-laden soil. George would dream, and Margaret would get on with it.

After the war the economy improved spectacularly. George was able to sell the *Chinook* and move into the position of managing editor at the *Vancouver Sun*. But he and his wife shared a dislike of working for someone else and he only lasted a year at the *Sun*. Nevertheless, he used his new connections to keep moving. Modest and conservative George may have appeared, but he also had the nerves of a gambler. It is said that he invested his last ten dollars in a lunch meeting with the lumber magnate, H.R. MacMillan, and soon had the money to start up two new journals — the *Western Lumberman* and *Country Life in B.C.* Patrician though the name might sound, Margaret got involved in *Country Life*, and made sure it was a magazine for pioneering farm women. Instead of hunt club news there were instructions for salting and preserving. She got George to publish the club reports for the BC Women's Institute, an institution that was helping farm women to find some sense of common purpose and solidarity. Now her rough-hewn practicality found fertile soil, and from the start her stuff was marked with a kind of cheerful country-style eccentricity. In one column she explained how to make a yellow dye that worked well in wool. It was composed of goldenrod flowers steeped in horse urine. Margaret made a wool suit to try it out, and modelled it herself.

And so almost without thinking about it much she had become a newspaperwoman. She would hammer all this out non-stop on the typewriter without regard for the conformities of punctuation, capitalization, and accepted spellings. George would do his best with the blue pencil, when he could find the time, but it seems likely that Margaret enjoyed the teasing her typographical eccentricities earned her. In any case, she never did conform and apparently he did not insist.

And so the twenties rolled on pretty happily. There would never be another war; everybody knew that. Margaret had time to take the kids to the beach and George began to think about being in the legislature instead of just telling it what to do in his papers. There are photos of her in those summer days in a black dress with an enormous black hat (still bigger than a sombrero); maybe she's telling the kids their father was "on the verge of the verge of getting into politics."

But before George had made up his mind, they were hit by the Depression and their advertising revenue dried up. Once again they were back to something close to the subsistence level, and the garden and livestock were essential. One of the daughters was at St. Anne's Boarding School, and they didn't want to have to give that up. One day the girl saw her father coming across the St. Anne's courtyard with her tuition payment on his back, in the form of a pig. But through those hard times, indeed fuelled by them, George kept his sights set firmly on politics. In 1933 the Liberal Party asked him to run provincially. That's when he and Margaret first heard of Lillooet, 250 miles away, which was having a by-election. The party gave George three hundred dollars for three months of campaigning, and the family packed up and headed north.

Lillooet was a rough little frontier town, mining and logging. Everything was primitive from the hand-cranked telephones to the mud streets, the omnipresence of horse-drawn wagons and buggies and the near-absence of law and order.

The Murrays arrived on a Saturday evening. The miners had just got off work and were headed for wherever they get something to drink. There are photographs of that Lillooet, and of those men, dirty under vests, suspenders, vast unruly moustaches, and seemingly very long arms and big hands. That first night, as George and Margaret were talking in a room they had rented above a tavern, there was a terrible snarling down below where a gang of these guys were pounding the hell out of each other, staggering, falling into the muddy road and making a huge row.

Margaret opened the window, stepped out onto a ledge, and bellowed down, "Will you stop making so much damn noise!" They did not. She came back inside for the washstand's pitcher of water, went back out, and dowsed as many as she could. Her reputation was getting under way.

This was not a place she very much wanted to stay in, but she stuck it. George hit the road with the official Liberal platform modified by his own somewhat visionary and less-than-well-thought-out proposals. He told the voters that if he were elected the farmers in the Peace River country would get wealth and commerce from an extension of the Eastern Pacific Railway. He probably honestly believed in the outlandish idea that a highway to Alaska, for trucks and motor cars, could be built with enough votes and goodwill, and he promised to do what he could to make it happen. And he topped it off with a promise to fight the expansion of bureaucracy. Visionary though they may have been, impractical and imprudent though George Murray often was, he kept his promises when he could, and the one about the bureaucracy was the only promise of the three that wasn't kept.

Margaret, meanwhile, ran a parallel campaign in support of George and her promise was to move the family permanently to Lillooet — and to start a town newspaper if he won the election. And if that happened, she told them, "This town will never be the same again."

She was getting stronger, more confident, certainly not mellower. Photos of the time show a woman in early middle age. The rather homely Kansas girl with large opaque eyes and rimless spectacles had grown into an imposing iron-jawed, no-nonsense matriarch, the kind you might be a bit afraid of, even in a photo, if she weren't always smiling.

George won Lillooet, and Margaret launched the newspaper. There wasn't a printing press to be found within two hundred miles; so she got a Vancouver printer to do the production, sold the ads, and wrote the stuff herself, and got her first advertising revenue in from the local Chinese businesses.

She cheerfully used the *Bridge River-Lillooet News* to boost her husband's reputation. Again and again the lead editorial and even the news would feature George Murray stories. She unabashedly promoted his plan for shipping Lillooet pears to Vancouver and his fairly advanced ideas for trade with Asia.

It's hard to say with precision exactly when it was that she became "Ma Murray." But her soon-to-become-famous editorial style was established almost from the start, and before long they were able to order a printing press shipped up from the city, and buy a building on the Main Street, where Ma ran the paper while George was more and more over in Victoria at the legislature.

At the beginning of this narrative, we followed this unlikely and intriguing couple up to their leaving Fort St. John and the *Alaska Highway News*, and making their way back to Lillooet again, in 1959. They were both hugely enjoying the rough and tumble of it all, and Ma was a woman who could carry her curmudgeonly style as well as anyone. She'd been through a lot, and now she was where she wanted to be, and things were just fine. And then George Murray, seldom sick in his life, died painlessly of natural causes.

It was 1961. Ma was stopped in her tracks. George was gone. He had whispered near the end that he wanted to convert, finally; so she was able to have him buried in consecrated ground, which gave her some comfort. As their children later observed, they had not appeared on the surface to be an especially close couple. There were lots of rows, and he was away a great deal. But those two may have been spiritually closer than anyone knew. For a long time after his death she was still running upstairs to call out, "George, I've got to tell you something." George's hat and coat remained hanging where they had always been, and Ma didn't want to hear anyone say anything about that.

One of her daughters saw her do something after George died that she had never done before, as far as anyone knew. As she was writing her husband's obituary she picked up a dictionary, something George had been after her about for years.

Like many, Ma countered grief with work, probably working even harder than she had at any time since George Murray had hired her forty-eight years before. There is a poignant photo from this time, taken through the windows of the editorial office at night, and Ma Murray is in there alone, typing, typing, typing. She hired her kids as reporters and columnists, rewrote a lot of their copy with an ironic eye, and made sure that they were not "overpaid or underworked."

She was politically active too. Once she was speaking at a meeting in the BC interior, now attacking Social Credit and especially the Social Credit premier, W.A.C. Bennett. Ridiculing the famous premier's shameless oratorical style she said, "You know, at the right time, if you can just jerk a little tear and have it trickle down, that's when you know that you've really got things going your way." Upon which the audience gave her a standing ovation. Then suddenly Bennett himself appeared and jumped up on the stage and kissed her. The crowd cheered all the louder.

Not long afterward, Ma remarked, "Did you see that? He's a smart politician. I had them right in the palm of my hand and that old son of a B, he jumped up and gave me a hug and a kiss and he swung them all back just like that. It was all for naught." In her editorial she was quick to say that he may have kissed her but she had not kissed him back.

By now, Ma was a national figure. There is really no twilight to her story: it just seems to get bigger as she gets older. The wonderfully comic Eric Nicol wrote a very successful play about her, starring the irrepressible Joy Coghill. It toured all across the West. When the tour got to Lillooet, a special performance was given for Ma, and she arrived in the theatre, all dressed up with her hair done, and there was a standing ovation. Afterwards she went backstage and sat and held the actress's hand for a while, and she said, "You know, you're good. I can't hear a goddamned thing, you know, but I could see them all laughing around me. We should form a company, and we'll go East. We'll go to Toronto and all those places and we'll make a lot of money."

In the world that Ma lived in, of newspapers and barn-burning outdoor speeches, it is hard to remember that this had been the age of radio and was now the golden age of television. Elderly as she was, television seemed made for her. Her big smile and steadfast iron jaw had become a trademark. Assertive glasses with heavy black rims replaced the old rimless spectacles. She and the networks were an excellent fit: they knew exactly how to use one another: one minute she'd be interviewed and knocking over the audience with one of her famous slips: "Well, women — women hold men right in the palm of their hand. I always held my husband right in the palm of his hand." And the next she'd be alongside Sophia Loren or appearing as the mystery guest on a game show. Or sitting on a panel beside Gordon Sinclair who's covering his face and shuddering. And then — it seemed a bit of a stretch, but a stretch that people loved — she'd be up there on a university's convocation platform, in the great gown and cap, accepting an honorary doctorate.

Throughout, she never stopped gathering news. One storekeeper remembers her style very clearly. She came into the store one day and wanted his opinion on a few of things. She suggested a chat by the fire. They went down to his house and sat down and she asked for some brandy to warm things up. She talked for an hour or two until she realized she was late for an appointment, thanked the man for his ideas, and left. And the storekeeper realized he had not said a word.

She finally sold the *Lillooet News*. The new owners gave her a weekly column on condition that she not interfere with the business. Unable to change, unable to stop, she kept on butting in and almost certainly scolding. There is television footage of her striding among the massive presses, and gesturing and saying something to the typesetters, who appear ill at ease. The new owners fired her. She was eighty-five. She said, "I've had a wonderful life, really, and every day of it has been fun. I told you I wouldn't want to live one day of it over, for fear

I'd miss some of the good things. Mind you, it ain't all been beer and skittles. There's been lots of ups and downs." And indeed there had.

Ma Murray's death in 1982, at the age of ninety-four, was a national event. She probably would have liked the funeral. The coffin was hot pink. She had chosen powder blue for George, twenty-one years earlier. She was buried beside him in the Catholic cemetery at Fort St. John. The best picture to remember is a simple image from television: She is old, and she is moving down the sidewalk — fast. As she herself might well have put it, "She is dead and gone. . . and we haven't seen her since."

◆ ◆ ◆

The History Television documentary was written by Robert Duncan and directed by Annie O'Donaghue.

Part Nine

J.B. TYRRELL
Dinosaur Hunter

In the pictures taken in the 1940s and '50s he looks frail, posing in his suit or in shirt and suspenders, sometimes beside his aged wife. By then he was a figure very different from the lean, pale-eyed, buck-skinned nineteenth-century explorer of the Canadian frontier who shows up in the earliest photographs. When Joseph Burr Tyrrell retired, the Canadian geologist, prospector, and surveyor of the Northwest Territories moved to a farm on the Rouge River, not far from the little town where he had grown up. His marriage, which had been buffeted by the prodigious professional obligations that had taken him away from home so much, was finally settling down; his wife Dolly kept a garden, Tyrrell looked after the orchard, and from time to time he told extraordinary tales about a very long and very adventurous life.

He was born in 1858, in Weston, which then was way out in the bush northwest of Toronto. In his childhood, there are some discernible conditions that may have influenced his life choices, given him the taste to spend weeks paddling the whole length of the Kazan and Athabaska Rivers, or to venture alone into some of the most forbidding places in Canada. Defects in his sight and hearing that had cursed his youth also gave him a kind of comfort with solitude, and a definite preference for the bush lands of the Humber rather than the streets of the city. By the time he was twelve the solitary, self-sufficient kid had become an indefatigable collector with a very unboyish fastidiousness about precisely annotating and cataloguing the detailed results of his scavenging through the countryside. He gathered every grasshopper and spider he could find in the Humber Valley where it ran through his parents' farm. Mud turtles and crayfish crawled across his bedroom floor. He had a strong sense of and fascination with the texture and heft of physical things. Although he was demonstrably bright, words were not his best medium. He never even completed the autobiography that the scientific community urged upon him in his later years. But back then, in Weston, his fascination with the life in that river valley, and in the river bed itself, were beginning to turn him towards a vocation.

As so often with unusually talented children, Tyrrell's parents had a hard time trying to understand him. They were gentry; they thought of science as something close to manual labour. The boy's fascination with what he found in the dirt was unseemly, and a life work informed by that kind of curiosity was certainly not something for a Tyrrell. At one point they invited John A. Macdonald to lunch to investigate the possibility of getting the boy into law school.

In 1867, the year of Confederation, Canada started to appear in atlases as an independent nation, strung out along the St. Lawrence and the Great Lakes and across the prairies and the mountains to the Pacific. Tyrrell was nine years old. He began staying late at school, fascinated by those areas in his atlas that were largely empty. He would "explore" them with his pencil, filling in guessed-at details of forestation, rivers and lakes, and geological features.

In Upper Canada College and later at the University of Toronto he compensated for the problems with his eyes and ears with a defensive assertiveness and aggression, and by living high and fast until exhaustion brought him down with tuberculosis. The doctors told him that if he wanted to live any length of time he should find something to do that kept him working outdoors. The photographs of this period do not look like a young man who was having problems with self-assurance. He looks serene, tall, fair-haired with budding side-whiskers, moustache, and spectacles. Once again his father contacted John A. Macdonald, now Prime Minister of the new nation, and within weeks the young Tyrrell had an indoor job with the Geological Survey of Canada, based in Ottawa. They started him off literally in the cellar, unpacking the crates of fossils sent back from the explorers out on the survey. It was familiar stuff, calling on that fastidious taxonomy that he had taught himself as a boy in the Humber Valley.

But the bureaucratic politics of the Survey establishment were very different from the comfortable solitude and silence of his basement crates and catalogues. It was hierarchical and competitive, and when the men gathered for a group photograph in their dark suits and severe expressions they looked like a collection of bankers about to foreclose on a mortgage. They were obsessed by credentials, and another young talent in the Survey, one George Dawson, told his chiefs that he thought Tyrrell's credentials were not very impressive. Perhaps aware that Tyrrell was a protégé of the Prime Minister, the Survey's white-bearded director Joseph Selwyn adroitly gave Dawson the task of smartening up the new boy by taking him out into the field. So the job did turn into an outdoor assignment after all, and would remain so for much of the next two decades.

It was not, however, an agreeable assignment at first, going into the field under a man who would have preferred to sack you, and who definitely resented having to not only drag you along but also to teach you the trade. The expedition of 1883 took them into genuinely unmapped territory. There is a picture of them taken at a place called Maple Creek (there must be fifty Maple Creeks in Canada; this one is in southwest Saskatchewan in the Cypress Hills). A picture of the crew posing against their wagon shows most of the men in their frontier-fashionable (and contrived) battered upturned hats. Tyrrell is a bespec-tacled dandy in long-fringed buckskin and large, floppy-brimmed pale hat. Dawson is short, slightly hunchbacked, with a scruffy beard, flinty eyes, and a sly and amused expression. On his head is an ancient top hat that makes him look like a cross between the Artful Dodger and the Mad Hatter.

Tyrrell's granddaughter, Katherine Tyrrell Stewart, says that Dawson "seemed to make lots of friends, but he also seemed to make a few enemies." He was an old hand, having been in the survey that mapped our border with the United States. He did not suffer fools gladly, and neither did his apprentice, Tyrrell. At times they took one another for fools and the tension was palpable. Dawson put Tyrrell in a position where he would be the last to see anything, walking behind the team, measuring the distances they covered. At night it was Tyrrell who had to stay up and keep watch over the horses; Dawson was said to care more for animals than for his men.

But it was great to be out of doors. He was used to being alone, and content to see as little as he could of his chief. The long active days were toughening him. His lungs felt clear and his determination to make something out of himself in the Survey just got tougher and tougher. In spite of his poor eyesight, he became the best shot on the survey. The men found it entertaining, the diligence and precision with which he collected stuff. He even studied the fleas on the horses and wrote them up. Dawson did not find this as amusing as the other men did, but they were soon treating him with affection and calling him "J.B."

The 1883 expedition eventually took them west into the Rockies. Tyrrell's eye was caught by something that still puzzled him. The massive U-shaped valleys had been scraped out by glaciers, which he estimated to have been a half-mile in thickness; but the markings that must have been made by the ice were an enigma. Those markings would later bring Tyrrell an indisputable victory over his difficult survey boss.

Tyrrell spent the following winter back in Ottawa, writing up the summer's findings, relieved to be away from George Dawson. Arthur Selwyn recognized that Tyrrell had more than proven himself, decided to protect him if necessary from the carnivorous bureaucracy, and find opportunities to put in his way. He put Tyrrell in charge of a new expedition. This was the survey that would make his name in the summer of 1884. The area northeast of Calgary was vast, bleak, much of it steep and devoid of vegetation, a stark desert in the summer and a snow-covered moonscape in winter. Forty-five thousand square miles of what is now Alberta, and Tyrrell was to geologically map it, fix elevations, collect fossils, and record mineral deposits. He would be responsible for recruiting a team and purchasing the horses. "The Geological Cavalry," he called them. And he was in charge of the whole enterprise. He was twenty-five years old.

There were few maps of any practical value. David Thompson's two-hundred-year-old survey did not extend to the deep, impassable canyons of the Red Deer River. The pack horses soon looked nothing like cavalry chargers, often bogged down under their loads as they struggled across the swiftly flowing gorges. Photographs show the whole crew sometimes half submerged. The rivers were the only navigable highway, and Tyrrell began to think that slicing through the aeons of rock layers as they did, they were more revealing than any other single feature. He would get a canoe. Then he could really study what were essentially the earth's paleolithic graphics, mineral diagrams laid out before your eyes in the endlessly layered strata in the rock.

It is one of the world's most eerie landscapes. There are palisades bigger than anything conceived by man, curious pillars capped with huge flat boulders, and in the most colossal formations, melted and twisted by millions of years of fire, wind, and water into strangely beautiful forms. Local Native people told Tyrrell about the Serpent People, whose spirits still roamed in the creeks and coulees. They warned Tyrrell to go no further. But the party continued, and what they found was not ghosts but gold, black gold, not real gold, gold you could burn. With a geologist's hammer you could pick it out of the stratum before your eyes.

On the seventh and eighth of June he discovered, noted, and mapped part of what would turn out to be one of the largest coal deposits ever found. These huge coal deposits in the Red Deer Valley would be a political plum for his boss Selwyn to present to his minister, and their discovery would give Tyrrell another sudden career boost.

It was to be a productive week, a productive three days, in fact.

On the ninth of June he was high on the crumbling ridges, just about to get out of the noonday heat, when he saw a kind of fossil he had never seen before. At first it was just an odd, dark, pointed ovoid, no, a series of them in a line, protruding out of the pale flaked layer of shale like, well, like what? They looked like some kind of gigantic teeth. He took out his trowel and brush and began to clear away the flaked stone. The teeth were set in an immense jawbone. Mapping the location, he found other bones, vertebrae scattered down the hillside. Then another tooth, different this time, sharp-edged, serrated, the creature had eaten meat. Carefully he uncovered it. When he told his granddaughter about it years later he said, "Here was this great ugly face looking out of the cliff at me!"

It was wonderfully preserved, grinning below its huge arched empty eyes, with a great snout, massive teeth, and black nostrils. Maybe this was where the Native people had got the idea about the serpent spirit, some ancestor lost, stumbling upon the apparition, racing away terrified, magnifying what he found, in his terror, investing it with life and menace.

J.B. Tyrrell could not know immediately that what he had uncovered was sixty-four million years old; or that it was the head of what would be the first complete carnivorous dinosaur skeleton in Canada: *Albertosaurus sacophagus*.

Eventually that bit of luck and skill would lead to the richest field of dinosaur remains in the world and the foundation nearby of the Royal Tyrrell Museum of Palaeontology. The jealously competitive George Dawson had ten years before found the very first dinosaur bones to be discovered in Canada and there were bound to be repercussions when he learned that this . . . this *upstart* . . . upstaged him. It struck J.B. that in Canada's Geographical and Geological Survey good news often led to bad feelings.

In the spring of 1885, the peace of the prairie was broken by civil war: the Riel Rebellion had got under way and John A. Macdonald was sending regiments into the area to force the rebels into submission. The survey was suspended, and to Tyrrell's disappointment, so was his work in the dinosaur beds of the Red Deer River. As the war rattled on and J.B. waited for news in Calgary he had accepted the fact that the summer was a write-off, when one morning Ottawa telegraphed permission to explore as long as he avoided the war zone. Tyrrell went straight to a Native village on the edge of town, the Stoney Camp, and hired a guide. A snapshot shows the grave, powerful, nearly black profile of a Native man from the Prairies. He had adopted the name William to avoid the hostility that all First Nations people were feeling from whites angered over the war with Riel's Métis, and who were not much interested in the difference between the Métis and the full-bloods. William and Tyrrell headed west, moving slowly along the eastern slopes of the Rockies, living off the land as they went, and exploring the watersheds of the Clearwater and Saskatchewan Rivers.

It was now that Tyrrell made a very different kind of discovery, a discovery that in some ways would affect his life as much as his spectacular successes of the previous summer, perhaps even more so, for the young Stoney Indian seems to have put the young scientist and explorer in touch with his spiritual side. William talked of how the land, from its great canyons to its grains of sand, from the gigantic skeletons to the fleas on the horses, the leaves, the crickets, and birds were all possessed of spirits. Tyrrell sensed a kind of wisdom in the young man and found himself listening with a calmness that was new to him. He had not thought before about the idea that the land and its living burden were not simply resources to be exploited, but rather gifts towards which we have a custodial responsibility, an obligation to protect and pass on. To whatever extent such ideas had been approached in his Christian upbringing, they had meant little more than the pious mouthings of elders for whom he had little respect. As William talked, Tyrrell felt he had found a mentor he could trust. He had been brought up in a culture that spoke with contempt of the Native people; now his feelings for his young teacher led him to a new respect for them. The aggressiveness and swank that he had used to deal with his deafness had kept him away from close relationships; now he felt a new hunger for companionship, and even began to think what had been unthinkable: that he might meet a woman whom he could love and even marry. William died young, of tuberculosis, the same disease that Tyrrell had survived. The loss was grievous, but he felt that his soul had been tempered.

Back in Ottawa that winter of '85 to '86, some of the brashness came back again as he moved among the bureaucrats. He now sported a substantial blond walrus moustache. His colleagues probably still thought him too single-minded to pull away from the niceties of differentiating paleolithic strata in order to go to a party, but that was the old Tyrrell. The new man began to move out in society, a bit tentatively at first, the tentativeness soon mediated by his meeting with Edith Carey, nicknamed Dolly, a serious Baptist whose father was a local clergyman. Dolly was struck by the explorer's rugged physique and newly tender manner. Her father was very much impressed when Tyrrell expounded a geological discussion of the probable nature of the bones in the Old Testament story of Ezekiel. Dolly and Joseph came to love each other unreservedly, a love that would last for a very long time. "There was a kind of gentleness when they were together," Katherine Tyrrell Stewart said. They could not seriously contemplate marriage yet. Tyrrell's salary was only eight hundred dollars a year, and despite his successes many of his colleagues still thought him a lightweight. The Geological Survey was underfunded. He might lose his job.

However, they found him another assignment, so he would be employed at least through the summer. Not a promising enough situation to give him the confidence to propose marriage but, better than nothing. The 1886 trip to Manitoba would not be nearly as dramatic as the Rockies and the Alberta Badlands had been, but he had hopes of turning up something exciting, of extending his earlier run of good luck. He bid Dolly farewell, and got on the train for Winnipeg.

He had a newfangled device with him on this expedition, a Kodak Hawkeye camera. He traced the shoreline of Lake Manitoba in his boat, the *Pterodactyl*, and photographed almost every mile. He learned about the old fur trade from what he could, detective-like, narrate out of the remains of the old fortified log trading posts. He thought about Dolly a lot. He worried away at the edges of David Thompson's two-hun-dred-year-old survey maps and just knew that he should be surveying the uncharted land beyond those edges. Maybe Arthur Selwyn would extend his employment with the Survey long enough to at least make a start. He wrote to Selwyn. Selwyn agreed. He was secure for a bit longer; time to stop dithering about Dolly. He proposed by mail. Dolly accepted, but he still had to carry out that survey before he could come back to Ottawa for the wedding. He began to assemble his team and resources.

The plan was to cross Lake Athabaska and then move north by river to the watershed that divided the boreal forest from the tundra. His time with William had convinced him that wilderness exploration needed the instincts and experience of Native people, and he tried to enlist men from the Dene Nation. But the Dene told him that they believed the Inuit whom they would meet in the north were cannibals, and they wanted nothing to do with them. Tyrrell sent for a group of Mohawk paddlers from the Kahnawake reserve near Montreal, and hired his brother James as interpreter. In addition to the big canoes, they had a number of flat-bottomed freight barges with upturned prows to deal with the expected whitewater sections of the Athabaska River. In the photographs, their baggage train seems big enough for a small army. The paddle across Lake Athabaska was straightforward and exhilarating, but once over the watershed both the land and the river became more forbidding. The distances accomplished each day diminished steadily. The low riverbanks stretched out into melancholy fields of stones. It was so bleak that Tyrrell found it hard to imagine human habitation would be possible. But on July 25 the expedition came upon a small tent camp and a group of Inuit, who were apparently terrified by the aspect of the unwashed, sun-blackened explorers, and fled leaving their fires smoking and their few possessions in simple skin tents. Tyrrell left packets of steel needles and tobacco in the tents: tokens of friendship.

He thought of Dolly hourly. He had sent her one last letter before he reached the end of the known world. A blue flower was pressed into it, and Dolly told her granddaughter that the scent filled the room, dried and faded as it was. That letter would be the last for six months. The snows came early. The great dark river ran endlessly northward, taking them with it, their supplies of food and fuel shrinking day by day. Tyrrell had expected the river to turn east toward Hudson Bay where they would be able to return by boat rather than spend the winter in that murderous emptiness. But the river kept going north and soon a life or death decision faced them: should they retreat back south, upriver; or should they cross the divide into the tundra where they might find caribou, maybe a coastline with seals and fish, maybe even people whom they would be careful not to frighten this time, who might guide them, help them find food?

All the while, Tyrrell had to keep making observations; particularly about glaciation that was still little understood. The striations in the rock had suggested a massive concentration of glaciers in a single area. George Dawson had made something of a geological splash by demonstrating, conclusively as he thought, that the glaciation of this part of the continent had all flowed in from a single source. The Survey had instructed Tyrrell to look for that source.

He wrote a lot while they were on the river. It was sometimes calm enough that he called it "my writing desk"; and sometimes turbulent enough that they all had to hold on for their lives as the barges were sent flying over rocks and then plunging into the whitewater and its bone-chilling clouds of spray.

They were moving against time and against the weather, trading off the delay that a stop for hunting would entail, and the subsequent risk of being overtaken by the snows before they could make it to the more congenial tundra they were sure they would find. They pressed on, sometimes close to starvation. And then the breezes in the morning began to bring in a new smell, of something alive. The endless fields of stone blended into sparse, stunted vegetation and then to grass.

One afternoon they suddenly felt the earth vibrating, drumming all around them. Tyrrell wrote in his journal, "When we came around this bend there was a grassy meadow right over there, and we saw these caribou and they leapt up and kept coming and coming. . . . It was a beautiful sight." The half-starved explorers leapt from the boats with their rifles. They feasted that afternoon, and in a few days they had a month's supply of dried meat.

The snows began in August. Sleet at first, and fast-dropping temperatures, but at least they were now heading east again, towards Hudson Bay. They reached it a month later than planned, and pitched their sad-looking vulnerable little tents along the brutal shore. The sextant, however, showed them not far from Fort Churchill. A day's rest, and then the walking began. They had been out of touch with Ottawa for months. Speculation there was gloomy. By October Dolly was sure he was dead and she abandoned.

But, in fact, the team had made it to Fort Churchill after all, having travelled 1400 miles. Tyrrell had lost fifty pounds. You can see him in a group picture taken in the snow, smoking a pipe as if nothing had happened, his skeletal frame hidden in a huge fur coat. They went by snowshoe from Churchill to Winnipeg, and warm beds and cooked food. Then, they took a train back to Ottawa and Dolly. He brought her the snowshoes as a memento.

The wedding was February 14, 1887. Afterwards they dined with Governor General Lord Aberdeen and his wife, and made an influential friend. Lord Aberdeen became a kind of patron. Tyrrell would soon need support.

To the government who had to pay the bills — some seven thousand dollars for those 1400 miles — it seemed as though the Athabaska expedition had not produced very much. There was a debate in the House of Commons, and one MP said derisively, "They even starved on that money! Imagine what it would have cost if they'd eaten well!" For a while it looked as though Tyrrell's exploring days were over. Then his new patron stepped in. Lord Aberdeen persuaded a wealthy fellow Scot, Munroe Ferguson, to fund another expedition. Dolly would have to be patient once again. It would not be the last time.

Just north of the point where the new territory of Nunavut meets the provinces of Manitoba and Saskatchewan, two connected lakes give rise to the Kazan River. The river then zigzags northeast through more lakes and finally flows into Baker Lake, which issues eastward into Chesterfield Inlet which in turn leads to Hudson Bay. Tyrrell's assignment was to navigate the Kazan from its source to Hudson Bay before the onset of winter. Giving themselves the better part of the year, the team set out in spring. The black flies were appalling. Ferguson had supplied the expedition with tar oil as an insect deterrent, but Tyrrell reported that the bugs seemed to love the stuff, and the men were better off without it. So they covered as much of their bodies as they could, and forged on sweating and slapping and still dripping with blood from the bites.

One day in the silent motionless wilderness, small boats in groups of two or three appeared from behind several points of land. The river had been empty, and then suddenly the boats were there. They were Inuit, who remembered an offering of needles and tobacco from a year before, and somehow made the connection. They gave the travellers food and firewood, and Tyrrell's Hawkeye recorded the poignant image of a line of kayaks with their generous paddlers, who had asked for nothing in return. It more than confirmed Tyrrell's affection and admiration for the First Nations people of the North.

For all of the hardship, and his yearning for home and Dolly, Tyrrell often felt a deep sense of peace in the North. Returning home to warmth and comfort and affection carried the price of going back to the Survey offices and Dawson and the rest of the bureaucracy. During the next few years his time in Ottawa was characterized by a growing, warm domestic scene. Their first son would be born in 1897. The trust and affection between the couple deepened year by year, but the atmosphere was somewhat clouded by financial anxiety and bureaucratic tensions. Dawson was still on his case, and may well have been the one who made sure that Tyrrell's salary never met his family's needs.

We know that Tyrrell had asked for an increase after Dawson succeeded Selwyn as director of the Survey, in 1895. The next year gold was discovered in the Yukon, and the collection of tents and huts from which the prospectors streamed out to the gold fields was named Dawson City, after the new Survey chief, who seems to have taken some credit for the discovery of the gold. Dawson refused Tyrrell's raise. Things between them were not helped when Tyrrell brought out his paper on the glaciation issue, which was published by the British Association for the Advancement of Science. It persuasively contradicted Dawson's theory of a single source, Tyrrell demonstrating that the ice that had once covered North America had radiated not from one but from several epicentres. Tyrrell's theory won the acceptance of the international community of geologists, and Dawson was furious.

In the spring of 1898, Dawson gave Tyrrell an assignment in the midst of what had become the anarchy of the gold-mad Yukon. Tyrrell was forty, and despite his prodigiously important discoveries, especially during those amazing three days in the Alberta badlands fifteen years earlier, he was no more secure than he had ever been. Landing in Skagway he got his first taste of the gold-driven madness that infested that dark town. The mere act of asking directions from some men in a bar nearly cost him the thousand dollars Dawson had given him to finance his project. He had escaped, he later found out, from a saloon known as "the slaughter house" while the town itself bragged of a murder rate of three per week. The day he arrived at the pass over the mountains twelve men were killed in an avalanche. That caused no break, he noted in his journal, in the continuous trail of humanity that moved upwards day and night in search of wealth. He pressed on past the skeletons of overburdened and beaten horses that lined the way. It may have been on the sailing barge loaded with hopeful prospectors that the idea came to him: with his finely tuned geological antennae he might just make one hell of a prospector himself.

When he landed at the city named after his detested boss, there were an estimated hundred thousand prospectors, gamblers, entrepreneurs, criminals, confidence men, and other parasites stumbling around the frozen slough. The town was in constant change, building, expanding, thriving, being corrupted, by the power of gold. Its cheery symbol was a picture of a woman raising her dress to show her underwear for money.

But when J.B. Tyrrell followed his keen geological nose that summer, and found himself at a place called Ben Low's Fraction, and said to himself that it might just be the richest little piece of ground in the world. He looked around and saw people sometimes finding the equivalent of his whole year's salary in a few minutes' panning in the creeks, and he knew what he was going to do next.

It took a few months, but he made a strike, finally, "below Hunter Creek, a valley over from Bonanza." He got a loan from the bank, told George Dawson to shove it, quit the Survey, and began to develop his find. It took six years. Dolly came to stay with him twice, but most of their intercourse was on paper for the next few years, until he finally had extracted everything he could from the Yukon, and it was, at last, really and truly time to come home.

George Dawson died in 1901 at the age of fifty-four. Tyrrell said he felt a little sad that their old battles were over, but it did not mean very much anymore. He and Dolly had moved into a fine house in Toronto. He became the residential agent for a London-based investing syndicate, Anglo-French Explorations, and had his photograph taken in a pinstriped banker's suit with the syndicate's board of directors. Two more children arrived — three sons altogether. And when he was asked to take a look at the abandoned mines at Kirkland Lake, to see whether there was anything left to do with them, the boys were old enough to be left at home with paid help for the time it took J.B. and Dolly to get up there to the Northern Ontario town and take a look. It did not take him long. He quickly determined that the veins were far from exhausted. It did take long — almost ten years — to convince investors that the gold mine was a gold mine, but it was worth it in the end. He was comfortably busy in the meantime, and when Kirkland Lake reopened he became chairman of the board and a millionaire.

And the rest is serenity, with a little nostalgia thrown in, an elderly adventurer's fond memories of some times that were tough, at an age when you could handle tough. Katherine Tyrrell Stewart was there from time to time when he would hang a sheet at the end of the hall and get out his old black-and-white slides and project scenes of the North that he had crossed with such courage and determination, and tell some of the stories again. He settled into a routine of comfortable predictability, occasionally brightened by a family visit. "If dinner was at 6:30," remembers his granddaughter, "dinner was at 6:30, and you went into the dining room precisely at 6:30."

She also recalls venturing into her grandfather's study, and discovering that there was something about the grand old gentleman that was still a little boy:

> I would sneak into the sunroom . . . just so I could be there in the same room with him and hear him writing. Every so often he'd get up and he'd go and take a book out of his bookshelves and then later I'd go and sneak and see what the books were. They were all sorts of geological survey reports, journals of this and journals of that, and then mixed with them, there were a whole series of Tarzan books . . .

The first of the Tarzan stories was published in 1931, so the great geologist could not have read them before he was in his mid-fifties.

Having survived tuberculosis, the wilderness, near starvation, and corrosive years of professional rivalry, he survived Dolly, who died in 1945, and lived on twelve more years at the farm. He survived his sons. He watched colleagues and friends vanish from his horizons one by one. At the end he was alone, a grand, faded monument to the map of Canada, sparkling with blue rivers and lakes he had paddled, veined with minerals he had identified with such assurance, home to those mysterious bones he had stumbled upon, and gazed at with a wild surmise when he was twenty-five. In 1957, J.B. Tyrrell died, one year short of his century.

◆ ◆ ◆

The History Television documentary was written and directed by Tom Radford.

SIR ARTHUR CURRIE
An Extraordinary Ordinary General

In small towns all across Canada, there is almost always a public feature that is at once a little strange and a little reassuring. The town will
have, usually near its main intersection, a stone, sometimes a large
plaque, sometimes a four-sided pillar, with between four and twenty
names inscribed on it. The names are of townspeople, usually young
men, killed or missing in action in France and Belgium between 1914
and 1918. There will often be names from the '39 to '45 war too, but the
list from the First War is longer.

How many Canadians pause to ask why those World War I numbers were so great? General Sir Arthur Currie, field commander of the
Canadian Army, wrote to his brother: "We have never been called upon
to perform a harder task. The obstacles to be overcome in the way of
hostile defences, bad roads, bad communication, difficulties of assembling, were greater than any we had ever encountered."

Currie was a general and as such he listed the most immediate
and practical problems. The summer of 1917, the fourth hideous summer of the war, was the wettest on record. There lay before him, in the
area of Passchendaele, a sea of mud stretching to the horizon. It was
inescapable. It was in your food, you slept in it, it seeped through your
clothes, it rotted your feet. The wounded disappeared in it, the living
lived in it, and even the able-bodied men moving forward on an
assault could drown in it, or in the stinking, murky water that filled
craters called shell holes.

By 1915 there were four million men living in trenches. There are
millions of photographs. The camera was newly cheap and relatively
portable, and hundreds of soldiers — those lucky ones who survived
— brought home numbing pictures of unbelievable misery. They show
the mud and the shell holes and shattered trees as a backdrop to the
staring, pale, stunned faces of Canadian soldiers in the remains of

trenches. In one famous shot there is a putteed leg and booted foot pro-truding from the mud wall of a blasted trench.

Sometimes on the horizon we can see a few shattered walls of the houses that once formed a village. The rest is a single black-brown mass. On this ground, throughout that hideous, cynically directed and spectacularly useless war, advancing troops, of either side, if they achieved anything at all would measure their day's success in yards, not miles, of ground.

Today on that piece of otherwise unremarkable Belgian country-side, there are three cemeteries containing the bodies of the thousands of Canadian men who died there eighty-five years ago in the Battle of Passchendaele. Many if not most are marked "unknown," a brief and neutralized reference to what was so often the indescribable condition of the remains that his comrades had to gather up for burial.

And behind all that wasted sacrifice, coolly ordering it to happen, day after blood-soaked day, was an arrogant, distant, glory-maddened, cowardly and spectacularly incompetent commander-in-chief of the British forces (to whom the Canadians were attached), Field Marshall Sir Douglas Haig.

Haig told his masters at Westminster that he could "gloriously" win this boggy, cruel, and motionless war simply by throwing thou-sands upon thousands of "gallant" men across the impassable land and into the shell and machine-gun fire. And in the old newsreel footage (some of it faked in Canada for propaganda purposes as we would find out decades later) you can seem them moving towards their deaths, not running, not charging or yelling, but great broken lines and knots of them walking slowly, tediously forward. It was almost as if death had become an acceptable routine, which, to Haig, it certainly was: not just acceptable, but glorious and gallant.

General Arthur Currie detested much of what Haig sent him to do. But he had eagerly sought this command, and, despite this hopeless supreme commander, despite the hopeless field, Currie actually won the mud-and-blood-bath of Passchendaele, April through November 1917, taking the strategic objective from the Kaiser's grey-coated army at the cost of sixteen thousand Canadian casualties.

Here, from its web site, is the 28th Canadian Battalion's own historians' account of a November day close to the end of the Passchendaele campaign:

Clear skies, turning to cloudy but no rain. Pastor van Walleghem observed an enormous artillery barrage by several thousand cannons firing explosive and shrapnel shells with red and white rockets intermixed is opened up on the German positions from Wytschaete to Vrijboch at 6:00 a.m. The Battalion moved forward as the barrage began. They came under heavy machine-gun fire as the men struggled in the deep mud of the Ravebeek valley. The 6th Brigade report records that the men "being knee deep, and in places waist deep, in mud and water."

When the 28th entered Passchendaele, the buildings had been smashed flat and mixed with the earth. Corporal H.C. Baker recounted that shell-exploded bodies from previous attacks were scattered everywhere so that you could not avoid stepping on them and the Germans fought a tough rearguard battle that was murderous for both sides. Men of the 28th were "falling like ninepins" but it was worse for the Germans. If they stood to surrender, they would be caught in the machine-gun fire from their rear and killed; if they tried to move back, they were caught in the Allied artillery barrage. The advancing men moved from shell hole to shell hole and crouched in the cellars of destroyed buildings. By 7:10 a.m., the Canadians were streaming through the village, and bayoneting the Germans in the rubble along the main street. When they encountered pillboxes, especially at the north exit of the village, the soldiers laid down covering fire with Lewis guns and rifle grenades and then outflanked them. By 8:45 a.m., the village had been taken.

Corporal Baker's own note says:

I went up the trench and called out "Hi there." There was no answer but I could make out blurred figures below, so I slithered down in, thinking they were sleeping. I shall never forget what I found. Down that stretch of trench the boys were sitting in grotesque positions, and every one was dead. The trench was only shell holes joined up, and it was open to overhead shrapnel fire from both sides.

And Private Jacques Lapointe of the 22nd described the scene he saw when he arrived in relief:

In a flooded trench, the bloated bodies of some German soldiers are floating. Here and there, too, arms and legs of dead men stick out from the mud, and awful faces appear, blackened by days and weeks under the beating sun. I try to turn from these dreadful sights, but everywhere I look bodies emerge, shapelessly, from their shroud of mud.

General Haig who had seen nothing of this, spending the day comfortably in the safety of his distant chateau, wrote in his diary that that day was "a very important success."

If Passchendaele had seemed impossible, Canal du Nord was absurd. On the field, Currie had sixty thousand Canadians and Haig wanted them hurled at the Germans over territory not unlike Passchendaele, except that a canal lay straight across it. What was more, the Germans were dug in along a ridge and not a single one of their units was without a full view of the twenty-foot-deep water-filled ditch. If the Canadians moved over this field against the heavily fortified German line, with their tanks and light artillery far behind them blocked by the canal, they would have been facing nothing less than a mass execution.

But that was the kind of attack Haig wanted. Currie refused, rightly. Still, this was war, and the deadlock had to be broken. Currie decided to attack at night, somehow moving all of his sixty thousand men across the canal in the dark to silently form a new line under cover of darkness, and then to surprise the Germans when the light came back into the sky.

Haig, to whom the regular suicidal, frontal attack seemed a matter of plain logic and gallant tradition, said that he found Currie's subtle and plausible manoeuvre impossible, but agreed to send over General Julian Byng (later Governor General of Canada) to assess the plan. Byng said to Currie, "If you really think this is going to work, I'll recommend it to Haig. But if there's a disaster, then all that's going to happen is you're going to lose your job and your career." Practically before the man had finished, Currie said, "Okay, let's go."

Among the long catalogue of Haig's failures of comprehension was his ignorance of the engineering skills of Currie's Canadians, and of the importance of those skills. In his nineteenth-century mind you didn't fight battles with engineers, you sent men out to get killed. But Currie's men carried out seemingly impossible reconnaissance missions, and in the dark, the engineers got prefabricated bridges set up all along the canal, where they could be thrown across the water in minutes at first light. They did practice sessions at first, in the dark, got the construction time down to half an hour, and took the bridges down before morning so the Germans would see nothing. On a strategic road, they found and dug out three hundred anti-tank mines, again, with no light. Finally, when everything was ready, they set up those prefab bridges in the dark, threw them across the canal at first light, attacked moments later, surprised the Germans, and smashed their line.

There seems little doubt that Currie's manoeuvre at Canal du Nord was one of the actions that brought about the beginning of the end for Germany. In the last three months of the war, he and his Canadians ploughed through German defences in victory after victory. The British and the French had both tried for two years to dislodge the apparently impregnable German installations at Vimy Ridge. Currie's repeated successes now earned him a shot at it. He planned meticulously. Once again, night work was essential, and Currie is sometimes credited with inventing the stealthy patrols of two or three men, creeping silently to the edge of the enemy trenches sometimes only a few hundred feet away, slipping silently over the edge to capture a sleeping sentry and bring him back for interrogation. When his Vimy plan was ready, Currie calculated that he would hold the ridge by midday. They went over the top at first light on an April morning in 1917. By 1 p.m. as planned, they had secured the first of the key German positions, and by the afternoon of the third day, again as planned, they controlled the ridge. That battle convinced all the combatants that the Canadians were a force to contend with. It had an electrifying effect on Canada's self-confidence as a nation newly emerged from its colonial origins.

But as Currie neared that final triumph, there was another war brewing. This was a civilian contest at home, a contest that would prove, in a way, tougher than anything he had faced in Europe. A younger man named Garnet Hughes had asked Currie for a chance to command. Currie thought him not capable, and had refused, and in doing so put himself in very hot water with Hughes's father. That father, Sam Hughes, was the powerful, flamboyant, eccentric minister of the militia (whose story we told in Volume I of *The Canadians*). Sam Hughes already had some unfinished business with Currie, and Currie's refusal of his son wouldn't make things any better for the General when he returned. As the subsequent mess developed, for a lot of the men who had fought in that war and were fiercely proud of serving under Currie, like the father of one of the writers of this book, it seemed that there was no achievement so great, no military record so stellar, that vindictive rivals would not try to destroy it.

In late nineteenth-century Ontario, there were not many ways to escape the farm, but Arthur William Currie had found one. The third of seven children born in 1875 to Jane and William Currie of Napperton, Ontario, he completed normal school and then went to teach in nearby Strathroy. There was a lot of talk about opportunity in the fast-growing British Columbia, and around the turn of the century Currie got on the train, and then the boat, and found a job in a high school in Victoria, population twenty thousand. He tried his hand at insurance on the side, and that led to real estate, and before long he was a senior partner in a major Victoria real estate firm.

Currie was a complex man and displayed many contradictions. And one of those was the co-existence of a strong sense of his own honour with a discreet tendency to social climb. One way to climb was through the army. British Columbians thought of themselves as the defending bulwark of Canada's Pacific coast. The militia in the provincial capital was more or less a gentleman's club, and if you could get in there you were usually set for life. Currie joined a regiment called "The Dandy Fifth." Before long he had a commission and a fiancée, Lucy Sophia Chaworth-Masters, who lived in the same boarding house, a discreet and elegant place run by Currie's aunt. People found them a great match, her tireless high spirits providing some mediation of Currie's tendency to stuffy self-importance.

Whether through ambition or through a sense of duty, Currie was at the armoury 150 nights a year, when most militiamen were giving maybe two hours a week. He was desperate for action, but the type of action he got was probably not what he had in mind. A hard-fought strike by coalminers had resulted in six deaths. Currie and the Dandy Fifth were called in to bring order.

That was when Currie became friends with Garnet Hughes, the man he was to turn down some six years later, during the final offensive at Vimy, the man whose father Sam Hughes was to start a campaign against Currie. But in these early days they were friends and fellow officers, and the younger Hughes asked the elder, Sam Hughes, minister of the militia, to keep an eye out on behalf of his pal Arthur.

About then the first signs of trouble showed up. Most of Currie's money was in real estate, and the market went desperately flat. In his desperation — and this still seems strange set against what we know of the cool and confident commander at Passchendaele and Vimy — he did something much worse than foolhardy. He embezzled money that had been allotted to his new regiment, the Fiftieth Gordon Highlanders, to pay for uniforms made by Moore Taggart of Glasgow, regimental outfitters. In one photograph Currie himself is wearing such a uniform. The white fur sporran, the kilt, the plaid, the doublet, the ostrich feather bonnet, and a host of trimmings look embarrassingly costly. The allotment was ten thousand dollars. In those days before the war, working women made less than a dollar a day, men in menial jobs only a little more, the Prime Minister earned eight thousand a year, and if you take it against any other measure — the price of eggs or a train ticket or a new Bible — the comparison with today's dollar has got to be in the vicinity of twenty to one. Those ten thousand dollars Currie had been given for uniforms were worth not far off what a quarter of a million would buy today.

He quietly took the money for himself. Officially the crime would have been called "fraudulent conversion." It could have brought a convicted man three years in penitentiary. For Currie it could mean instant cashiering from the army and the loss of that precious social standing.

He was saved by the outbreak of war in August 1914. Before anyone noticed that a huge sum had gone missing, the officer in charge of the Gordon Highlanders had been tapped by his friend Garnet's father, given a brigade of nearly five thousand men, and was on his way to France.

His behaviour now became more and more curious. He left his family abruptly and only occasionally kept in touch in spite of longing and affectionate letters from his daughter. He did nothing about the money.

When Arthur Currie got to the front the French were already taking a beating. In April 1915, the Germans had surprised everyone with poison gas at the battle known as Second Ypres — 5700 canisters of chlorine gas, released through holes punched in the parapets just ahead of the German troops, and just ahead of a light wind from behind them. A *New York Times* correspondent wrote that the "vapor settled to the ground like a swamp mist and drifted toward the French trenches on a brisk wind. Its effect on the French was a violent nausea and a faintness, followed by utter collapse." The poet Wilfred Owen saw it through a gas mask, which gave the seer the aspect of an enormous insect, no less inhuman than what the seer saw:

"Dim, through the misty panes and thick green light/
As under a green sea, I saw him drowning."

It was early in the fighting at Second Ypres that Currie witnessed the weaknesses that would later lead him to refuse a command to his friend Garnet Hughes. In the St. Julien sector, a part of that battle when poison gas was used for the first time in history, Hughes's misunderstanding of an order had led Hughes's commander, General Richard Turner, to call for a disastrous retreat. Currie's brigade was left alone, against a much larger enemy force. Instead of responding traditionally, Currie outraged his British superiors by personally leaving his position, and his men dug in, and finding his way alone to another brigade whom he brought back as reinforcements. Had he followed orders or tradition, and stuck to his position un-reinforced, he and his men would almost certainly have been wiped out. He was not a "chateau general," the type of commander who lived with his batman and his aides, receiving news and giving orders in the comfort of a fine chateau far from the front, untroubled by the fall of enemy shells or the rattle of machine guns, insulated from the muddy stench of his grimy troops; that was Haig's style, not Currie's. Even young Winston Churchill, still an MP when he arrived at the front with a command, would get himself flown back to Britain when he felt like it, to go to a debate in the House of Commons or spend a convivial evening with his beloved Clemmie. But Currie stayed with his men every night during that St. Julien episode, and that became his trademark as a commander, to expose himself to what the troops were getting hit with.

And yet they did not admire him much, and certainly they did not like him, those soldiers. After the war, after the victory at Vimy had been analyzed and shown to be the extraordinary tactical event that it was, even those who had disdained him in the field came around and admitted that the facts showed him to have been a great commander, but not a loved commander.

Pompous, distant, he was a man who, a private noted, "didn't have the trick of rubbing fur the right way." Another reported angrily that Currie had with prodigious insensitivity tried to give his brigade's morale a shot in the arm by saying, "Soldiers, your mothers will not lament your death. You'll step into immortality." The men jeered him from the trenches. Even after the war and out of uniform he kept this air of self-importance, insisted on being called "Arthur," and admonished his family when they called him "Art."

The historian Desmond Morton argues that Currie's extraordinary successes prove him not to have been some kind of military genius, but in fact a man who benefited from ignorance of the rules and traditions. Unlike Haig and his wrong-headed, confident general staff, Currie was a civilian, an amateur soldier. He had not been to officers' training. He didn't know and didn't care how it had been done at Amritsar or anywhere else in the Empire where the great successes had built such blind confidence in, for example, the cavalry charge, that long after this new weapon the machine gun had demonstrated the complete ineffectiveness of men on horses, the old generals were still sending those mounted boys out to their certain (gallant) destruction.

Currie was just an Ontario farm kid, a practical guy, looking for advantage. That's what led him to those night patrols at Vimy, and some other innovations we'll come to shortly. He was totally unencumbered by the old rules, codes, routines, and dusty habits that were sending thousands of men to die under fire before the generals had taken their morning tea. Currie wanted to find ways around the rules, simple tricks and manoeuvres that did not come from staff college and in the end probably weren't much more complex than a plumbing problem, a blocked drain, a wet supply of firewood, a cow gone missing. Few of his British superiors, most of them from wealthy families, many who had bought their commissions, would have had the faintest idea what to do if confronted by blocked drains.

They did have dash and bearing, though, those high-born Brits, and hard as he may have tried to seem superior, dash and bearing were not part of the Currie personal armamentarium. He was tall, six-foot-four to be exact, but he had a soft, clean-shaven baby-face in contrast to the angular moustaches of many of the other allied commanders, the almost clichéd indicators that their wearers were men of authority. At over two hundred pounds, Arthur Currie was heavy around the lower middle and had a large posterior; he was so pear-shaped that his belt rode up over his stomach. Mounted, he looked as if he might break the back of his horse. They tagged him "The Old Man" and it was neither a respectful nor an affectionate epithet.

But the brain inside that mushy-looking head was a serious piece of work, and a close look at the photographs — perhaps only because we now know a lot of what was going on in there — seem to reveal a feral seriousness in the eyes; the seriousness, perhaps, of a man who — unlike so many of his British fellow officers — knew that his social class was not going to save him if he made a mistake.

Currie had no confidence in the virtues of endurance and attrition that guided the tactics of the generals on both sides. He was interested in winning, not in mere survival. He nagged his junior officers and drove them to hone their own skills and the skills of their men. He was constantly thinking about communications and never distracted by The Way To Do It. If the phones broke down or the lines were cut, if it took too long to reel them out again on the old bicycle wheels they used,

Currie knew that the safest way to move messages around a dark, messy battlefield was to entrust them to the hands of courageous running men.

When he found that the maps young British officers were making on makeshift tables in the field were often wrong — and the archives show some with mistaken names, and even one with the compass rose reversed — he made sure his men understood, as at Vimy, that under this bleak field, as it began to dissolve into an unfigured, monochromatic quagmire, there were actually the remains of roads, there were villages, there was a theatre of combat with features you could find if you looked more carefully. You could find them and frame them, and build a plan on them. But you had to know where they were. He wanted this understood at the molecular level so that his men would know where they were over every foot of the ground. He wanted them to know where they were going and precisely what and where the objective was. He wanted them to understand that, even amidst the chaos described in those reports above at Passchendaele, or in what the young Lieutenant H.L. Scott of the Canadian Engineers wrote home about: "The whole earth in the air. Hundreds blinded, arms and legs blown off. One man without any arms and legs still living."

In the midst of this horror, Currie didn't merely hope for the best or trust in God, or in the valour of his men. He made objective plans designed to ensure that he would win, and without which he would not give the order to advance, however much Haig would babble about gallant lads. At Vimy when he found his properly mapped terrain to be, in the end, impossible to advance across, he ordered the men to dig a network of tunnels. He went into those tunnels and spent serious time there, watching how his men reacted to the dim confusion of the half-lit warren. He made sure the tunnels were tall enough to move through, rapidly and upright with your heavy kit of weapons, ammunition, rations, and a groundsheet. The walls were damp chalk and it was freezing down there, but the tunnels got them closer to the enemy. When they told him there was no way men could carry enough water through those tunnels, for themselves or for the fifty thousand horses they would have to bring up, he built a pipeline.

In that winter of 1917–18 Currie came up with another innovation that he believed would help him deal with the massed German troops that faced his men. Between the two armies lay not only a plain of half-frozen mud, but also an endless channel of barbed wire a hundred yards deep. On the German side of that wire, thousands of machine guns and artillery pieces awaited anyone who might try to cross. Currie had no desire to continue Haig's policy of sending unprotected soldiers out against those guns. He invented his own form of "creeping barrage," a moving wall of artillery shells, coming from cannon whose trajectory started so low that the first line of shells fell just far enough ahead of his advancing men that they themselves would not be hit. But nobody could see them coming through the clouded chaos of that line of exploding shells. Then, as the troops moved forward, the gunners raised their sights, and the line of exploding shells moved forward at the measured rate of the advancing infantrymen, masking them, shielding them, taking out those great coils of barbed wire, vaporizing them, showering the German machine-gun positions with their deadly fragments of shrapnel, as the Canadians came invisibly onward behind the creeping barrage.

Currie and his men took Vimy Ridge in a few hours. The men to whom he gave this and other victories respected him. But they could still not love him. And yet, he achieved something that no other Canadian commander — or politician for that matter — had ever done. By leading regiments from Halifax and Toronto and Montreal and Dryden, from St. Boniface, Moose Jaw, Red Deer, and Penticton up the smoking ridge, shoulder to shoulder, he made them aware that they were Canadians in a way that no Canadian had ever felt before. Their signatures are still there on Vimy Ridge. Their presence is still vivid today in the Vimy tunnels, now preserved as a museum. It looks like an endless horizontal mineshaft buttressed with timbers. All the detritus, the rusted metal and equipment, the great rot of war, has been left where it lay. The cold tedium and the heroism that came from it remain in the intricate graffiti, here a heart, there the tracing of a gun, here the name and date carved by a soldier into the chalk wall of a passage.

Arthur Currie was taken back to London to be knighted by King

George V, and this winner of unwinnable battles was promoted to corps commander.

But there was other business that he had neglected. He now had a respectable income. He could with little difficulty have acknowledged his "mistake" about the uniform allotment. He could have arranged to pay it back. He did nothing. In the same year of his knighthood, 1917, Moore Taggart, Glasgow outfitters, sent the letter that had to come sooner or later.

The Prime Minister of Canada swallowed hard, decided that the country should not have to bear the disgrace of a war hero, and persuaded two well-heeled political cronies to come up with the ten thousand dollars; he would deal with the general later. When Currie was briefed, he quickly said no, he would look after it himself and found two well-off younger officers to advance the money. Now he was clear at last. The money was not, as it turned out, in the clear. The then colonel of the Gordon Highlanders seems to have gotten his hands on it and vanished. What has famously come to be known as "the clothing file" has remained open. The regiment is still short of that ten thousand dollars.

But Currie's war continued, undisturbed by scandal. There were the victories of Passchendaele and Canal du Nord. And then came the fateful time when Currie refused to let Garnet Hughes command, remembering his incompetence at St. Julien.

Here and there, in the fall of 1918, the last hundred days of the war, the German line began to dissolve. In November, Currie advanced on Mons, Belgium, not sixty kilometres east of Vimy Ridge. His troops arrived, as you see them in the photographs, ghosts of men, their aged battle dress caked with mud. The Germans put up a solid, skillful resistance. The fighting was brisk right to the end. At the very moment that Currie took the city of Mons, two things happened: at 10:58 a.m. a certain Private George Price of Nova Scotia became the last Canadian to die in the war, killed by the last bullet of a German sniper. In Mons today a plaque to George Price serves as a goalpost for kids playing football in the street. Two minutes after Price fell dead, at the stroke of eleven, the armistice came into effect. The hostilities were over. It was November 11. As Currie put his troops on parade before a grateful crowd of Belgians, in the vast, cobbled square and main thoroughfare of Mons, he could not have guessed that this simple, final victory would almost be transformed into his greatest defeat.

It took ten years. It happened in 1928. By then Currie would, on ceremonial occasions, pin on his chestful of medals for an appearance at McGill University, in Montreal, where he was now Principal. Old-school academics had protested this appointment of an unlettered mere soldier to an academic post. Even his friend the economist and humorist Stephen Leacock had said it wasn't right, but that did not bother the general. There was, indeed, not much from day to day that did. Until that afternoon when Sir Sam Hughes, father of the slighted Garnet Hughes, declared in the House of Commons under parliamentary privilege that "you cannot find one Canadian soldier returning from France who will not curse the name of the officer who ordered the attack on Mons. . . . Gallant fellows butchered!"

Not long after, an Ontario newspaper, the *Port Hope Evening Guide*, expanded on the story that Sam Hughes had been the first to broach. The paper's story said this:

> *It was the last hour and almost the last minute when, to glorify the Canadian headquarters staff the Commander-in-Chief conceived the mad idea that it would be a fine thing to say that the Canadians had fired the last shot in the Great War.*

Thirteen million soldiers had been killed in that war, and thirteen million civilians. Even the Americans, who had not come in until 1917, lost 320,000. On a per capita basis, Canada's 232,000 casualties, including our 59,544 dead, all those names on all those village memorials, were huge. It was an allegation of the very gravest consequence to charge that a Canadian general had, for his own glory, led men needlessly to their deaths. The story dominated the front pages. Even Babe Ruth was shoved to the back of the paper.

Principal Currie sued the *Evening Guide* and its editor, William Preston, for libel. Stephen Leacock tried to persuade him to withdraw, but Currie said no, it was untrue, his honour was at stake, he was claiming damages of fifty thousand dollars. The trial would be sensational.

The courthouse in Cobourg has been meticulously preserved, the fly-in-amber metaphor appropriate for its colours at least, its beautiful mid-nineteenth-century interior just as it was. The painted coat of arms in meticulous detail sits enormous over the judge's bench. In 1928, this was a terrain to which Currie was unaccustomed, a field that may as well have been as covered in fog as the battlefields on which he'd made his name.

A telegram came from the father of that last man killed at Mons. The contents were astonishing, but reassuring:

> As the father of George Lawrence Price, the only Canadian killed on Armistice Day, I wish to convey to you, Sir, my humble hope you will succeed in bringing to justice those responsible for bringing this case before the public, because all this simply renews old wounds that are better forgotten.

But some people very much wanted to open those wounds. The *Evening Guide*'s editor Preston engaged as his defence counsel a man named Frank Regan who set out to save his client by ruining Currie. He brought into the courtroom a gruesome imaginary painting showing the streets of Mons littered with dead Canadians. He claimed he had a hundred witnesses — simple infantrymen who had survived. He brought in respected officers who actually had served with him and had documented the whole campaign. When he stood face-to-face with Regan, the counsel for the defence declared flatly that since the war had been virtually over, the general could have spared the lives of his men. Currie said simply that two days before victory was not victory, but that in any case there had been no Canadian casualties at Mons, except poor Price. He should have waited to see if the war was ending, Regan scolded, and Currie replied that that would be treason, he had sworn to obey orders and he was obeying orders.

Regan, in his summary, said, "I therefore impeach Arthur Currie before this bar on behalf of the widows who lost their husbands and mothers who lost their sons for a needless, heedless, frightful loss of human life in this useless attack on Mons."

It took three and a half hours for the jury to file in with its verdict, and it seems that most of that time was arguing over the size of the settlement. They found *The Port Hope Evening Guide* guilty of libel, but reduced the damages from fifty thousand dollars to five hundred dollars. When Arthur Currie got back to McGill the students gathered by the hundreds and yelled, "Arthur C . . . Arthur C . . . Don't take guff from anyone."

It seems likely that Currie's defence of his honour had damaged his health. The emotional strain had been prodigious: the libel had been uttered by the father of a friend, once a very close friend. Currie was a man who, for all his carelessness about money and his arrogance and his stuffiness, had striven to do everything he could to protect the lives of his soldiers, but for weeks his fellow citizens had been told that he had thrown their lives away for glory. It was a shameful calumny; winning the case could not heal the wounds.

For all that, he still had his soldiers' welfare at heart, even though they found him distant and offensive. He launched a campaign to lobby the government for better pensions for the veterans. He was at that work in 1933, on Armistice Day, November 11, an appropriate day for a soldier to die, when the strain hit him with one last blow. His heart gave out, and he collapsed. It was fifteen years to the day since he had captured Mons. He was fifty-eight years old.

Sir Arthur Currie's honours included Knight Commander of the Bath, the *Légion d'Honneur*, Knight Commander of the Order of St. Michael and St. George, *Le Croix de Guerre*, and the US Distinguished Service Medal. Heroic in military matters, he remained, even after his death, puzzling about matters involving money. In his will he had provided his wife with a pittance, only eight hundred dollars a year. It was the government who saved her from humiliation and penury, with a capital fund of fifty thousand dollars, an endowment in the order of a million dollars in today's money. And the official statement from Parliament said, "The day will come when veterans of the grand army of Canada will be proud to say to their children, 'I served with Currie.'"

◆ ◆ ◆

The History Television documentary was written and directed by
Roxana Spicer.

Part Eleven

GEORGES PHILIAS VANIER
Soldier, Statesman — Saint?

Canadians like to speak of their country as a mosaic, not a melting pot, meaning that while another country might work hard to assimilate its immigrants into the dominant culture, we have established laws, institutions, and traditions that honour and nourish the cultural riches that the newcomers bring with them. We hold as central to our values at least the toleration of difference and at best a rejoicing in diversity.

It was not always so. The first European settlers brought with them much of the religious and political division that had troubled their homelands, divisions that had often, especially in the later centuries, been the propelling force that led them to choose the New World. These ancient essentially tribal attitudes would lead in some cases at their worst to the genocide of many of our aboriginal people, and there are more than traces of that racism active today. The anti-Semitism and other strains of xenophobia that were common in Canada as late as the mid-twentieth century are shameful to recall. Young people today will find it hard to believe that only sixty years ago a Canadian judge would send a young white woman to jail as an "incorrigible" because she had been found in bed with a Chinese-Canadian man, and that her pregnancy, which she revealed in order to beg the mercy of the courts, was instead taken as proof of her criminal behaviour.

The French and English streams of our national culture have had their periods of violence and injustice too. In comparison with nationalist struggles in other parts of the world, that rough seam in the fabric of our civilization seems pretty tame most of the time. Neither in terms of violence nor duration can it be compared with other tales of countries divided. But these two hearts are beating in *our* breast, not in some distant latitude, and those old metaphors of Two Nations and Two Solitudes do not seem likely to disappear soon from the cultural landscape.

A soldier and statesman named Georges Philias Vanier, very much driven by his deep religious convictions, is one who is honoured to the point of reverence for his lifetime insistence that those two cultures would be stronger together than apart, had much to give each other, and in harmonious co-existence could give Canada a significant role in international affairs far greater than she could achieve were they divided.

Contributing to the History Television biography of General Vanier, military historian Jack Granatstein said simply, "Was he the exemplar of a kind of Canadian that we should venerate? Well, yes." If veneration seems an unusual word in the context of national development and French-English relations, another contributor's observation goes even further and explains the reason for the provocative title of this chapter. The Jesuit historian Fr. Jacques Monet said,

> There was a dimension to him that really was remarkable and that was the spiritual dimension and that deserved recognition. And I think for Catholics that would mean that he should become a saint.

Georges Vanier was born in Montreal on the 23rd of April, 1888. His mother, Margaret Maloney, was Irish. His father Philias's French forebears came to Canada in the seventeenth century. Raised in Montreal, he grew up in a home where the usual language wasEnglish; Margaret was more comfortable with it than with French, and Philias found it useful for business.

Georges and his brothers were sent to the Jesuit-run Loyola College where Georges became president of the literary and debating society. Fluently and elegantly bilingual, he was a serious boy, studious and romantic. He enjoyed writing and, while still a high school student, was able to get some essays published in local newspapers. There was a religious society at Loyola called The Savality of Our Lady. The Virgin Mary's day is Saturday, and the members of the Savality — "The Savalities" they called themselves — would start that day with an early mass and then go out into the community to work with the poor and the sick, "a concern," Fr. Monet says, that was also "a devotion, a practical one but also a prayerful one."

While his home had tended to favour the English-Canadian side of Quebec's cultural life, at Loyola Vanier seems to have made a conscious decision to embrace his French-Canadian identity. He had not yet thought about the military career that would become an important stage for the playing out of his nationalism. After Loyola he took his bar exams — law, medicine, and the Church were effectively the only professions open to French Canadians. He was practising law in Montreal when war broke out in August 1914.

He was twenty-six. Posters began to appear urging young men to sign up "For King and Country." But most of Vanier's young friends were hostile or at best indifferent to Canada's involvement in a meaningless foreign war that was being played out by ancient empires on the other side of the world. Before the war was over Ottawa would enact conscription legislation, and the province would be riven with riots whose scars are not completely healed. Jack Granatstein said,

> For a French-speaking Canadian to decide to go to war was an act
> of will in a very real sense. For English Canadians it was the thing
> to do and it took an act of will not to go. For French-speaking
> Canadians, it required a conscious decision of duty, service and a
> willingness to fight.

Fr. Monet said that Vanier's decision was motivated by his religious conviction. He saw the German attack on Belgium and the atrocities against women and children that British propaganda gruesomely (and falsely) reported, not only as inhuman but also as hideously un-Christian. As in almost all the major decisions of his life he explicitly explained this one in terms of his faith, and off he went to war. Because he was a university man he was automatically a candidate for an officers' commission. Professor Desmond Morton of McGill University describes what Vanier found as his training began:

> The expeditionary force is formed up at Val Cartier outside Quebec
> City and there are French Canadians represented there. What is
> missing in this organization is a French-Canadian battalion. So
> noticing this, the relatively few military minded Quebeckers said
> we better do something. The Vandoos, the 22nd, is authorized and
> formed.[6] And Georges Vanier was one of the young officers, totally
> inexperienced and untrained, who joined and who proceeded to try

6. "Vandoos" is the colloquial anglicization of *vingt-deux*.

to learn the business. Easier for him because his English was pret-
ty good, but having to learn it with English-language textbooks and
manuals, from English-speaking instructors for the most part in an
English-speaking kind of military organization.

In fact, some 50,000 francophones served in that war, and while that figure is less than one-tenth of the 650,000-strong Canadian army, from a community who had for almost two centuries been systematically told by their anglophone rulers that they, the French Canadians, were not welcome to the full fruits of the increasingly prosperous young nation, that 50,000 is a very substantial figure.

Many of those men were poor and this was at least a job. The same was true for tens of thousands of anglophone recruits. Many, like their English-Canadian counterparts, were just looking for adventure. In both communities Georges Vanier was a standout "right from the start," historian Jack Granatstein says, "because of his pan-Canadian, his imperial sense of duty and service." He enlisted with the rank of lieutenant and soon became actively involved in recruiting for the Royal 22nd Regiment. In March 1915 they set off for Nova Scotia for more training. At times this simply meant marching twenty miles in the snow "to toughen them up." Later that summer the Vandoos were shipped off to France with Vanier as their machine-gun officer. He wrote:

Never in my wildest flights of imagination could I have foretold
that one day I would march through the country I loved so much in
order to fight in its defence. Perhaps I should not say "in its
defence" because it is really in defence of human rights, not solely
of French rights.

Vanier's letters from the front at first downplayed the drudgery, despair, and horrors of the battlefield. He wrote home to his mother,

At night the effect is faerie-like, fireworks illuminating the German
lines, shells exploding in a burst of light which is fantastic and pic-
turesque. One gets so quickly accustomed to the most abnormal sort
of life. The trenches are relatively safe. If a chap keeps his head well
down, he's not likely to be hit. This of course applies to rifle and
machine gun fire. Shell fire is harder to avoid. And whether you're

hit or not is largely a matter of chance. The game is worth the candle. I would not exchange the marvellous experiences I have gone through for five years of life. The weather has been very favourable and the trenches have been very dry. But as soon as the wet weather sets in, we shall probably be ankle deep in mud.

He wrote almost daily. His words demonstrate that his sense of family was a sustaining force for the ordeal that soon became very different from what he had described in his cheerful letter about the relative safety of the trenches. As he had forecast, the November rains changed things drastically; the tone of his letters home changed too.

A dismal morning, low clouds. Everything is heavy. You feel oppressed and stifled. You paddle in a foot of mud and water. These are appropriate conditions for the month of the dead.

He had found the challenges and the comradeship of the army stimulating and rewarding, and trench life in those first weeks an adventure. It was an adventure that soon became filthy and depressing, but he had enlisted for the long term, not for a good time, and he stuck with it. In June 1916, Vanier, already decorated for bravery, was knocked out when a German shell exploded close by. He said it was only the fact that the ground had been softened by all that rain that saved his life. The injuries were serious enough to land him in the hospital and then in a convalescent centre back in England. Jack Granatstein told us that Vanier was badly shell-shocked, the name given to the prodigious damage to the nervous system that is committed by a combination of the explosion itself and the pervasive fear that a conscious act of courage can keep at bay. But after an immense explosion has blasted you into unconsciousness and you awake covered in your own blood, shell shock can invade the spirit and destroy the will to live.

Shell shock [usually] finished people. Or if they came back after a bad period in the trenches, they weren't much good afterwards. People probably have only so much courage and after a time the well runs dry. Well, Vanier clearly was able to pump up the level again and to continue to serve and to sound optimistic to his parents, to persuade his troops that they were doing something important and to persuade himself that what he was doing was important.

After his time in the convalescence centre, he volunteered to go back to the battlefield but was offered a support post well back from the frontlines. He refused. "I feel it's my duty to see this sacred war through," he wrote.

> *I don't mean that I revel in the noise of bursting steel. There's the tremendous consolation of being in the thick of it, of the biggest fight that has ever taken place for the triumph of liberty. That sometime or other, we have all wished that we had lived in Napoleonic days. But the present days are fuller of romance, of high deeds and of noble sacrifices.*

The elevated language is characteristic. His biographer Deborah Cowley said, in the documentary, that he was

> *passionate about poetry and he carried a little copy of Shelley's poems in his breast pocket throughout most of the war, together with a picture of his mother and his favourite sister, Frances. So he's sort of Georges Vanier the romantic, as well.*

It was not uncommon for soldiers in that war to carry poems into battle; many of those men were university students or graduates. A pocket book popular among the British university lads, who had all studied the classics, was *The Odes of Horace*. Stories circulated about how books of poetry or of prayer carried in a breast pocket had stopped a bullet and saved a life. But poetry and prayer, while they comforted the men in the trenches, did not mediate the life and death decisions of every day nor stay the hand of even the devout and gentle Georges Vanier when it came to exercising the traditional authority of a wartime commander. Jack Granatstein told us about one aspect of the maintenance of discipline that now seems sufficiently extreme to have, in 2001, led a group of parliamentarians in Ottawa to publicly apologize to the families concerned.

> *There was a sense on the part of the officers and certainly on the part of the men as well that it would be disastrous if [The Royal 22nd] should be seen as anything other than the equal or the superior of any of the English-speaking battalions and discipline therefore was a matter of French-Canadian pride. Discipline was a matter of showing the English that we could do it just as well as they*

could. And there were something like twenty-five Canadians execut-
ed by firing squads in the First World War for cowardice or desertion
or other military crimes. Vanier himself presided at at least one exe-
cution of a deserter. This was extraordinary, except that it was
deemed necessary by the commander of the unit, Colonel Tremblay,
because he believed, as Vanier did, that we had to demonstrate that
we were the best disciplined, the best battalion, the one that would do
anything to achieve the objective. And if it meant shooting your own
men who broke down or deserted, well then so be it.

The 22nd fought effectively at some of the most decisive battles of
World War I, including the blood bath at Ypres, which the soldiers
called "Wipers." Then, at 5:30 a.m. in the morning on the 9th of April,
1917, the attack on Vimy Ridge began.[7] The French and the English had
already failed to take the ridge, and Canada had inherited this seemingly impossible task. It would be a turning point for our armies'
reputation in Europe, and for the country's sense of self-esteem and
independence.

Vanier wrote home about how the infantry leapt out of the shell
holes and trenches and emerged from secret tunnels right up against
the enemy lines in a hail of bullets and a bitter northwest wind. The
leading battalions gained their objectives quickly and the 22nd followed through, capturing machine guns, trench mortars, and hundreds of prisoners. The troops' morale was high and Georges wrote
about the wonderful consolation to be driving the *Boches* out of France.
But there was another battle that ended Georges Vanier's war, and
came within a hair's breadth of taking his life.

It was a German offensive at a place called Cherisy. The machine-
gun fire was ferocious, and in the first few minutes two bullets ripped
into Vanier, one of them smashing some ribs. His wounds were serious
but not life-threatening, but as the medics were dressing them a shell
exploded right beside them. He wrote restrainedly that "this final
explosion caused rather unpleasant shrapnel wounds to my right and
left legs." In fact the right knee was shattered, and the leg was ampu-
tated the next day. Many of the 22nd's officers were killed at Cherisy,

7. For an account of the Vimy campaign, see Part Ten of this volume.

and not a single one survived unwounded. Once again Vanier would draw on his faith. Deborah Cowley said,

> *Even though when he'd had his leg amputated, he rarely said anything that gave any indication of the pain, the suffering. The only word of complaint I ever read in his letters was "Oh, God, how the nights are long!"*

And Jack Granatstein added,

> *The extraordinary thing is that he decides he wants to stay in the army. There he is, with one leg, a wooden leg in effect, and he is convinced that he can continue to serve. And Arthur Currie, the commander of the Canadian Corps during the war, says to him, it's impossible.[8] You can't serve, you've only got one leg. And Vanier says, do you want people with brains or do you want people with legs? It's a good line.*

Among the many changes that World War I wrought in Canada was that now the French Canadians had their own regular force regiment, the Vandoos, the Royal 22nd, a regiment of the highest distinction after Vimy. Vimy had brought Georges Vanier the *Légion d'Honneur*, pinned on him personally by France's minister of war; he had also been awarded the Military Cross and Bar, and the Distinguished Service Order. And now the Vandoos were home, based at the Citadel in Quebec City, and Vanier was the regiment's second-in-command.

One day in 1919 his old friend and sometime commanding officer, Tommy Tremblay, took a striking young woman for lunch to Montreal's Ritz Hotel. Vanier was at a nearby table. Tremblay pointed him out to the woman, saying, "That's the man for you."

Pauline Archer was the only child of Quebec Superior Court Judge Charles Archer and his wife Thérèse. Pauline had grown up in a large house on Sherbrooke Street where she had an entire floor to herself. When she met Georges Vanier she was twenty-two. A few months later, he proposed. On September 29, 1921, they were married at Montreal's Basilica. His brother came along on the honeymoon as the chauffeur, Georges being uneasy about driving with his artificial leg.

8. The story of Sir Arthur Currie is the subject of Part Ten of this volume.

But it wasn't long before Georges slipped his brother five dollars and told him to get lost. Professor Morton said,

It was a very good marriage. She was very intelligent, very able . . . a very supportive kind of person. I mean not exactly in the modern style of equal partner, because I think she had great strengths that he didn't have, particularly her awareness of the realities of culture and what was current and interested in music and so on, probably much more than he was, I think. But she has her strengths, he has his and they worked together.

The postwar governor general of Canada, Lord Byng, had been the British Commander of the Canadian Corps in Europe, and in the optimistic atmosphere of the early 1920s Byng and Vanier cemented a friendship that had begun in the trenches. Byng had "no side, as the British would say," according to Professor Morton.

He wasn't an arrogant guy in any way. He was very friendly, a bit scruffy-looking, didn't go in for spit and polish. Perhaps that was pretty good for the Canadians because they didn't either. And he kind of got to know and like the Canadians and they kind of got to know and like him. And after the war, he becomes the governor general. And for the first time, instead of bringing out a British officer to help guide his affairs in Canada, he invites his old friend and admirer, junior friend, Georges Vanier, to come to Government House [as Aide de Camp].

There are odd bits of gossip that emerge from the story, some seemingly inconsistent with the image of propriety that attaches to vice-regality, though certainly not to the rich sense of humour that the Vaniers shared. Pauline was said to have remarked to a visiting British aristocrat that he should not hesitate to take advantage of a Rideau Hall chambermaid, but perhaps the story says more about the colour of the inner circle they moved in than it does about the real person. The Byngs and the Vaniers became close. Byng arranged for Vanier to spend some time at the British Staff College at Camberley, near London, and it was there in 1923 that their first child, Thérèse Marie Cherisy, was born. In 1924 he was promoted Lieutenant Colonel. Back in Canada, probably with a word from the governor general to open the door, Vanier was invited by External Affairs to be the Canadian military representative at the League of Nations in Geneva, working on the Disarmament Convention. When their fourth child and third son Jean was born in 1928, Lord Byng sent a note saying that perhaps Pauline was thinking of starting a league of nations of her own.

It is worth pausing at this point to note that while it seems natural enough today that a distinguished and much-decorated soldier should become a highly placed diplomat, such a sequence of events was not at all natural in the 1920s if the soldier in question happened to be a French Canadian. Jack Granatstein told us that this was

a time when a French-speaking officer in the Department of External Affairs writes a memorandum in French to the Prime Minister and the Prime Minister says, this man has gone mad. Literally says that he's crazy because he sent this memorandum in French. Vanier would know not to send a memorandum in French. But he's a French Canadian who understands that at this point in Canada the anglophones rule and French Canadians have to go along to get along.

Lord Byng died in 1935, and within a few years a number of old friends and relatives were also gone. Vanier began to reflect on death in a way that was different from those dramatic years in Flanders. He became more diligent than ever in his religious observance, going to mass almost every day, and taking half an hour for private prayer. Busyness was never an excuse for overlooking his acts of devotion. Professor Morton said that "for him the Catholic faith was a living entity."

It guided his life. He believed profoundly, but not superstitiously. He was a remarkable Christian because his brain never got in the way of his faith. He could reconcile them, which is not a common or universal achievement. And he made people feel, certainly I did in his presence, that this was something I too should explore.

In December 1938 Vanier was posted to the embassy in Paris. The events that would build the launch pad for World War II were in rapid motion. In July, Germany and Russia signed a Non-Aggression Pact, and in September the uneasy peace that northern Europe had known

681

for scarcely two decades ended with the Nazi invasion of Poland. By May of 1940 it was clear that France could not hold out. Georges sent the family to London. A month later, among the last foreign diplomats to do so, he made his way to the coast where a Canadian destroyer, HMCS *Fraser*, brought him to England and the family.

When Hitler conquered France he found some powerful officials willing to collaborate, including, ironically, a distinguished World War I soldier, Marshall Pétain, who set up a puppet government in Vichy. The resistance movement, and the "Free French" in exile, looked to General Georges de Gaulle for leadership. "De Gaulle saw himself as the embodiment of Free France," Desmond Morton said, and

> *Vanier saw de Gaulle in much the same way. [He] was dismayed to find his country, Canada, had continued to keep diplomatic relations with the Vichy regime. Why did Canada do that? For two reasons. One was that Quebec thought that the Vichy regime was just about the right government for France. The [Vichy] slogan of "travail, famille, patrie" would have been a good slogan for Quebec society. A Catholic presence in the government — [which] Pétain insisted on — looked pretty good to Quebecers. What was wrong with all of this?*

So the Ottawa government did that for Quebec reasons and also for Allied reasons. Somebody should stay in touch with France. Maybe Vichy would be a good listening post, at least that was the polite explanation given to English Canada. "Our Allies want this from us." Well! Vanier wasn't buying either line.

He wrote a letter to Prime Minister Mackenzie King asking to be relieved of his duties. The letter was ignored. He was instructed to take command of the military district of Quebec, a tough job in a province that had not forgotten the conscription riots of World War I. He persuaded the High Command to bring more Quebeckers into command and strategic planning, and was moderately successful in increasing the numbers of volunteers from Quebec over what had been expected.

Their fifth and last child, Michel Paul, was born in July 1941. That same year, their thirteen-year-old son Jean announced that he was joining the navy. Pauline and Georges recognized that Jean was serious.

Volunteers that young were much a part of British naval tradition, and here was a bright young Quebecer bucking the tide that was holding back so many of his friends. They signed the consent forms, and he went on to become the youngest executive officer on any warship in the history of Britain or Canada.

In 1942 the Canadian government withdrew its recognition of Vichy, Vanier was in favour again, and was promoted major general. A year later he was appointed ambassador to the Free French. De Gaulle set up the exiled capital in Algiers, and Vanier got on a military flight to North Africa. Jack Granatstein told us that the British and Americans found de Gaulle a very difficult ally.

> *You know Churchill's story that he had many crosses to bear during the war but the cross of Lorraine [the double cross-barred emblem of Free France] was the heaviest cross of all. De Gaulle acts as if he's the leader of a great power and demands that his concerns, his status, his role, his nation's role be respected in everything.*
>
> *This drove Churchill crazy. It certainly upset Franklin Roosevelt. And the Canadian government — which is a minor player in this, to be fair — isn't going to take the initiative, isn't going to step out in front and urge the British and the Americans to recognize de Gaulle. But there's no doubt that such support as de Gaulle has in Canada is led by Vanier and de Gaulle knows it. . . . [And yet] de Gaulle will eventually betray them.*

Pauline wrote that it was impossible to describe the atmosphere in Algiers, a mixture of heroism and decadence that would make the film *Casablanca* seem a masterpiece of understatement. A long line of guests came and went from their new home. Among the regulars were ambassadors, resistance fighters, and of course, de Gaulle and his entourage, who wanted recognition by the Americans and knew that Vanier was his first advocate. It would be difficult, maybe impossible, to evaluate the extent of Vanier's influence in Washington, but in 1944, President Roosevelt did beat the other allies to the punch and declared American recognition of de Gaulle as the leader of the government of liberated France.

Meanwhile the Royal 22nd Regiment distinguished itself brilliantly again, in the Italian campaign, and as its former commander in chief, Vanier was invited to the Vatican to meet Pope Pius XII. Vanier had been outraged at the Vatican's refusal to allow priests in Vichy France to administer the sacraments to resistance fighters, and according to Fr. Monet, he took the opportunity to speak out.

Georges Vanier was increasingly shocked at how many of the Catholics and the Catholic hierarchy in France were much more sympathetic to Vichy and to the Pétainists than they were to the Free French and said to the Pope that this was going to be a great scandal for the church. A few weeks after that, the French bishops started allowing the French priests to be chaplains to the Underground.

With the German surrender of Paris on August 26, 1944, the Vaniers prepared to return to their old posting there. But France was still far from safe, and Georges was advised to return without Pauline. He said, "You try to stop her. I can't." Someone suggested that she might be safer in uniform. She borrowed one from a Red Cross worker on leave, and entered Paris with Georges on the 8th of September as the Canadian Red Cross Representative to France.

With the liberation, minor collaborators faced humiliations and the court of public opinion, but more serious offenders were in danger of prison or worse. Vanier's loyalty to the church may have skewed his judgment at this point. Historian Jack Granatstein says that some of these dubious characters were actually helped into Canada by the Vaniers — at the request of the church.

He becomes a conduit to get into Canada a number of French fascists who were fleeing de Gaulle's regime. Quite extraordinary that this gallant soldier who understood the horrors of fascism would still nonetheless be prepared to turn his gaze away from someone's undoubtedly monstrous record. It's a blind spot in him. It suggests to me that a recommendation from a priest was worth more than the good judgment of his own common sense.

As ambassador to France he accompanied de Gaulle on the French President's visit to Ottawa in 1945. It would be years before Vanier had any reason to doubt de Gaulle's friendship. Hadn't the general written to him that "from the very first day you were the faithful friend of the

Free French and the evident defender of their cause. Every fresh proof that France gives of her vitality is homage to your clear-sightedness."

When Colonel Tremblay died in 1950, Georges was named honorary colonel of the Royal 22nd. In April the Vaniers sailed to Canada for the ceremony and to see their son Byngsy enter the priesthood. The country was approaching another step in the long weaning away from its past as a British colony: we were now ready, for the first time, to advise the Queen that the next governor general, HM's official representative and the titular head of state, should actually be a Canadian not another Brit. Vanier's name came up, but since Canada already had a French-Canadian head of government, Prime Minister Louis St. Laurent, it was thought impossible to appoint a French-Canadian head of state. Vanier went into retirement, and began to spend time at the old family retreat at Lake Memphremagog. Perhaps he had even put any future public service out of mind, but he had, in fact, not been forgotten in Ottawa. It was in 1959, "perhaps to his surprise," according to Professor Granatstein, that

> John Diefenbaker, as Prime Minister, approaches him and asks him to be governor general. His surprise I say, because he is a Liberal. But Diefenbaker decided it would be a good thing to have a francophone as governor general and shore up some support in Quebec.
> And so Vanier is asked, and being a man of duty he says yes.

The appointment was decided officially at a special cabinet meeting in Halifax, over which the Queen herself formally presided. His installation speech began, "My first words are a prayer that God will give me the strength to carry on this responsibility. I am very weak and it is only out of my weakness that I can get God's strength." They moved into Rideau Hall and began remaking both the building and the role of governor general. Biographer Deborah Cowley said in our film,

> The first thing he and his wife did when they entered Rideau Hall was to transform one of the upstairs bedrooms into a chapel and he visited the chapel briefly every morning of his life in Rideau Hall. And if he was travelling, he made clear that he had that time for prayer. They inspired people. They brought an inspiration to Canadians that I don't think has been matched since. They travelled

to little villages, to large cities non-stop, even though they were both in their seventies, late sixties by that point, sharing their passionate belief in both parts of Canada, French and English. And since they both were completely bilingual and bicultural they could do this so beautifully.

Some of our French-Canadian statesmen and women, among them Louis St. Laurent and Jeanne Sauvé, have had a patrician presence seldom if ever seen among their anglophone counterparts. In this regard Georges Vanier was striking. Tall, his bearing was always stately despite the limp. The full-swept white moustaches flowed out from beneath a pair of sharp eyes that always seemed to have a humorous twinkle at their corners. Even when he was dressed in the plainest of civilian clothes you could almost see the gold braid on his cuffs and the gleaming row of medals across his chest. The Queen appointed him to the Imperial Privy Council in 1963.

Every Sunday they went to mass in a different local church, to meet citizens on their own ground. Only Pauline knew how difficult it was becoming for Georges to be a public person, but on April 8, 1963, when he suffered a mild heart attack, it was time to stop. He would stay in harness long enough to say an official farewell to John Diefenbaker, the man who had appointed him governor general, and to swear in Lester Pearson as Prime Minister. He was surprised when despite his heart attack Pearson asked him if he'd stay on beyond September 1964, when his term as governor general would end. Georges agreed so long as his health and the Lord allowed him to. In the spring he attended the annual press gallery dinner, a traditionally rowdy affair whose principal speakers vie with each other in rough language and outrageous jokes, and the hottest ticket in town to which non-members of the gallery, if invited, are made to feel that they have been accorded one of the great privileges of life. On that occasion, which this writer attended, it felt like such a privilege: General Vanier's speech as guest of honour so far outstripped the others in both laughter and wisdom that everyone felt agreeably humbled. His theme was the occupational options open to an unemployed governor general.

It was a period in our history when those old wounds and divisions that began this chapter began to grow very nasty once more. The generally relative calm of Quebec's Quiet Revolution was punctuated by a couple of bombs. "The temperature is getting hotter," Jack Granatstein said,

> *and Vanier probably is seen by many in Quebec as a sell-out, a vendu, not a Vandoo . . . but a vendu, a sell-out. And he I'm sure must have found this excruciating. Here he was, someone who believed in Canada, believed in a pan-Canadian vision of the country, being damned in his own province by his own people.*

During the St-Jean Baptiste Day Parade in 1964, both Vanier and members of the Royal 22nd were booed while a small plane cruised overhead dropping separatist pamphlets. The majority of the crowd shouted down the separatists, but Vanier was furious. Later he would laugh about it, saying, "What would you like separatists to do? To give you an ovation?"

A few months later, despite the Quebec situation, the Queen herself paid a visit to Canada. Hers was soon followed by one from an old friend of the Vaniers. Professor Granatstein said,.

> *De Gaulle seems to, by the 1960s, seems to be supporting what Vanier sees as the destructive elements in Quebec, supporting the separatists. Thinking of Canada as an anglo country only, thinking of Canada as part of the United States almost and therefore a nation that is not really able to play a part in the world. To Vanier this is a betrayal by a man that he had revered, a betrayal of the country that he believed in and it's shattering to him.*

Georges Vanier died two months before that betrayal culminated with de Gaulle idiotically shouting a separatist rallying-cry from the balcony of Montreal City Hall. But "I don't think it was a surprise to Madam Vanier," Deborah Cowley said,

> *what he did in Montreal . . . shouting "Vive le Quebec libre." She knew ahead of time, and she had a devastating meeting with him and his wife in Paris at which General de Gaulle indicated that this was his feeling about Quebec. And all she said was: "I am so glad my husband is not alive to hear this."*

On Saturday night, March 4, 1967, he had watched his hockey team, the *Canadiens*, beat Detroit, and the next morning he was dead. "The outpouring of affection . . . was absolutely incredible," Deborah Cowley said.

> *Messages that came in by the thousands, poured into Government House and it was very heart-warming. And even more so was the funeral that I remember very well on a wintry March day in Ottawa. First of all he lay in state in the Senate chamber for quite a long time as people thronged to pay tribute to him. Heads of state from all over the world came to pay tribute. Then after that, the casket was put on a train and travelled to Montreal and on to Quebec City and he was buried in a chapel on the grounds of the Citadel.*

That chapel, where our documentary of George Vanier's life comes to an end, was constructed under his order when he had lived at the Citadel, the home of his beloved Royal 22nd. Pauline would live another twenty-four years, be appointed to the Privy Council, and serve as Chancellor of the University of Ottawa. She spent her last days in France at *L'Arche*, the community for handicapped adults that her son Jean had founded. In 1991 at the age of ninety-two, she died and was buried next to her husband in the chapel at the Citadel.

Of the many honours and acts of recognition that came to them both, the last is the most striking testimony to the central role of their Christian faith in those two extraordinary lives: their nomination by the Vatican for beatification, which could pave the way, as Fr. Monet thinks it should, to sainthood.

◆　◆　◆

Deborah Cowley is the author of *Georges Vanier: Soldier*. The History Television documentary was written and directed by Daniel Zuckerbrot.

• PART TWELVE •

VLADIMIR VALENTA
Of Truth and Comedy

When he first came to Canada, we didn't see clearly enough what
he had to offer; he was struggling to learn English, and had a hard
time getting his ideas across. But I came to see that he had the great-
est integrity of anyone I ever met. He lived by his principles. He
could not bend his principles.
– Patricia Phillips, Producer

CBC Edmonton television host and interviewer Colin MacLean remembers his feeling of astonishment: "The phone rang and someone said,
'There's this Academy Award winner washing cars down here at this
car wash.' I said, 'No, give me a break.' He said, 'No, no, it's true; I think
his name is Valenta.' And I said 'Uh, Vladimir Valenta?' Well I was
thunderstruck. I took our cameras down there and then we sat down
and talked about why he was here, why he had come to Canada, why
he was in Edmonton."

Vladimir Valenta had played a major role in the Czechoslovakian
movie *Closely Watched Trains* that won the Academy Award for Best
Foreign Film in 1967, and at that point in his life he was famous in the
acting and movie community, but he was broke. But that was only the
surface of a story that went much further underground, and in an
important part of it, quite literally so.

Valenta, who came to Canada from Czechoslovakia in 1968, had
done time in Shebram Prison, a brutal holding pen for the slave labourers who were sent down to work the uranium mines there. At forty-
two stories beneath the surface it was said to be the deepest mine in the
world. Valenta had indeed earned his living as an actor, and a comic
actor at that. But both his comedy and his life were driven by a profound commitment to human rights, not a popular motif in the
Communist-ruled Czechoslovakia of the postwar period. And while

some of his friends afterwards said that Vlad did not like to talk about his time as a political prisoner, in 1990 not long after the Berlin Wall came down he went back there with a group of his fellow former prisoners for a kind of reunion at Shebram.

It was not a sentimental reunion: Vladimir Valenta was on a quest for justice, a constant motif in this plump comic actor's dramatic life. He and his fellow prisoners had been tortured, some of them to the point of death. They had been starved, tormented, often driven mad by their Communist captors who were trying to get confessions out of them and break their wills in order to put them back into the community as penitents, loyal to the great Soviet Cause after all. Valenta was furious when he discovered that in the new Czechoslovakia, among the thousands of former officials who had run the old oppressive regime and sent hundreds of thousands into forced labour camps, torture, and death, only nine had been sentenced for their crimes.

Vladimir Valenta and the other veteran prisoners were filmed by the CBC[9] visiting the abandoned Shebram gulag, where they found the underground cell where he had been kept in solitary for three weeks because he insisted on singing the Czech national anthem on the traditional National Day. With the cameras rolling he went down the crumbling weed-grown steps, bent, crept into the tiny square concrete box, looked back at the camera and said,

> [I told them] "It's a pig house, but you cannot make me a pig too. I will not eat here." So every day they brought, you know, food, and put it here, hoping that I will touch it, I will give up. I drank only water, I had to leave coffee and the food untouched."

As he looks around the squalor of this low-ceilinged memorial of a nightmare, you can hear a voice off-camera saying, "Watch your head," and Valenta snaps back, "You forget that I was a miner, you idiot."

This was the abrasive man who had returned to postwar Czechoslovakia, to a delicate situation where freedom fighters and the collaborators they detested were trying to work out some kind of co-existence. Valenta was impatient with process, with trying to

9. This was for a CBC Edmonton project entitled "Closely Watched Freedom."

work things out. He always wanted action now, results now. He didn't mind if his candour and his insistence embarrassed anybody, or made them nervous; that kind of consequence he shrugged off; the consequences he was after were much bigger: to punish the bastards.

When he arrived in Canada in 1968, a big man with a huge belly, a broad, bald head, wide grim face and heavy, black-rimmed glasses, his role in *Closely Watched Trains* brought him small roles in a number of television projects and a few larger films. One who cast him in those early days, the pioneer Canadian director Allan King, describes him as "stern, imposing, authoritative." Voices of people who had known him float through the soundtrack of our documentary. "He had one of those kinds of amazing faces that would look sad even if it was joyful" and "It's hard to imagine . . . Vladimir as a romantic guy because he wasn't. He was grumpy and gruff and that's what he appeared but I mean, he was a romantic at heart."

Nelu Ghiran, another director and believe it or not admirer, said, "He was a prick . . . he didn't care if he hurt your feelings. He didn't mean to."

It was speaking out without regard for the consequences that had put him behind bars in the first place. They threw him into the Pankratz Prison in Prague in 1949 and sentenced him to twelve years for treason against the state. With its nineteenth-century walls and rows of windows it looked like a traditional insane asylum, but inside there were so many highly educated men that they were able to turn the jail into a sort of institution of higher learning, and share their minds with their fellow prisoners. Part of the captor's strategy was to give the prisoner the impression that release was only a month or two away and then just stretch it out, move you to another prison and then another prison and another and so on. This transient incarceration was intended to prevent any effective conspiracies among the prisoners, and bit by bit to morally break them down with one disappointment after another.

One cruel punishment you discovered only after your release. Wives were commonly told that their imprisoned husbands were enemies of the state, imperialist agents, and that they would never see their men again anyway and should divorce them. A man would race home, free at last, to find that he had no home.

One of Valenta's companions, Lumir Salivar, said about the prisons in winter:

> You came here to die. It was very cold. The average temperature at that time was around twenty, minus twenty degrees Celsius. We were hungry. It was not enough food. Some people, they committed suicides or some people were killed. The walls were not insulated. The water from the air condensated on the walls. So they were licking the walls just to [get something to drink].

The teaching sessions were permitted as long as they did not get expressly political. Valenta's "higher education" group — perhaps courting a certain amount of emotional danger — tried to keep themselves going by meeting every afternoon to describe to one another the best meal they had ever eaten. If it drove them crazy, they said afterwards, it still gave them marvellous dreams of liberty. Oddly, they were given a film to watch from time to time. Once, Valenta was astonished to see a title come up in the darkness: *Svirdomi (Conscience)*, and then the credit, *A Film by Vladimir Valenta*. And there he was, "In a bloody concentration camp for God's sake!" watching one of his own films, a film about personal responsibility and justice.

The mine at Shebram sent raw uranium to Russia for nuclear weapons and the electrical power generators. Before dawn the prisoners were packed into a small elevator and sent down the forty-two-floor shaft to the chosen working level. They had no protective clothing, just a work jacket, shirt, trousers, and a soft-brimmed hat. Day after day, by hand, they dragged wagonloads of uranium sludge along a gloomily lit tunnel with a single endless track. At twelve hours a day, seven days a week, one prisoner logged his time in the mines at 3658 days.

Valenta's anger and resolve were apparently never eroded. He had enormous mental discipline, and a reverence for the power of words. Another fellow ex-inmate said, "You will discover what a word means and how many times a single word can save you, not your life but your soul." After Valenta's release, another prisoner found dozens of poems he had left behind, scribbled on toilet paper, about life in the camp and the spiritual struggle to retain your sanity and will. His irrepressible anger at injustice and total inability to keep his mouth tactically shut drove him to take terrible risks by provoking his guards with challenges to their humanity, their sense of fairness, their intelligence. The day he went too far was October 28, Independence Day for the old republic of Czechoslovakia, traditionally a day of marching and singing and banners and drinking. But under the Communists the day was silent, the churches closed, public gatherings forbidden, and the national anthem itself outlawed.

One of Valenta's fellow prisoners remembers: "During roll call, (Vladimir) stepped forward. He began to sing the National Anthem. Twenty-five-hundred inmates stood at attention and began to sing with him." Another remembers, "The guards did not dare do anything. We finished the anthem. Vladimir suffered the consequences . . ." A third adds: "They put him into the bunker. There was nothing inside, no washroom, no bed, no chair, absolutely nothing." That was the cell he was filmed revisiting, at the Shebram reunion, a windowless eight-by-eight underground concrete room, with a rusty pair of handcuffs lying in wreckage outside it.

When Valenta began his hunger strike in that cell, soon the whole camp knew that he was living on water and nothing else. After twenty-three days, perhaps fearing that his death would trigger an uncontrollable uprising, the authorities allowed him back into the general prison population. Not, however, without exacting their own petty revenge: they told him his wife had deserted him to marry a Communist party official. He grew very dispirited. He was down to half his weight. He was beginning to think that he would be a prisoner for the rest of this life, when, without any discussion with officials, a letter came announcing his release in 1956. There had been a retrial and he had been found innocent of the charges against him. It had been seven years.

Vladimir Valenta was born in Prague in 1923, four years after Czechoslovakia had become an independent republic. In the national legend, centuries of struggle by artists, farmers, towns-people, and their leaders against foreign occupation had finally led to triumph. He told a friend once that wherever it came from, his commitment to the idea of truth made it hard for him to tell lies even as a kid when a few white lies here and there could have smoothed the way with a difficult parent or teacher. A snapshot shows him on a rocking horse, a little boy with a man's face, a dark earnestness. Much of his childhood was spent in the Stromofka Park, where he would later take his daughter Eva to learn to ride a bicycle, secretly removing the training wheels, after she had climbed aboard. She remembers him saying, "Don't worry, I'll hold you," pushing her into the independence that for him was so primary a value he was prepared to risk her hurting herself. She stayed upright, and was pleased in the end, and perhaps he had in fact been right there, sure she could make it but ready to catch her.

In 1938 Hitler's armies invaded Czechoslovakia announcing the start of World War II. The fantastic misted city of Prague, a many-spired movie set of medieval buildings, beckoning galleries, and lanes, resounded with the sound of jackboots. The new government cancelled the freedoms to which the Czechs had become accustomed. A survivor said, "We did hate the Nazis because they behaved like slave drivers, they behaved like you are nothing and we are everything, we are the supermen of the world."

The Gestapo arrested people for listening to the BBC, their only source of reliable information. There is a photo of Vlad and his younger brother Jiri, both looking profoundly grave. They trusted each other well enough to join the resistance together when Vladimir was seventeen. Once, when he and a friend were delivering a message, they were stopped by a German soldier. As the man approached, Vladimir whispered to his friend to step to the curb and take a pee. When he did, the guard turned away and the boys ran to safety.

When their father was jailed for listening to foreign broadcasts, he found on the walls of the holding cell the signatures of hundreds of Czechs who over the years had also been jailed for defying authority. "It was like the side of a monument," he told the family later. And among all those names he found his own father's signature.

But they survived that most terrible war in their history, and at first the liberation of 1945 was full of hope. The citizens of Prague tossed bouquets to the soldiers clustered like flies on the Soviet tanks rolling in triumph through the beautiful old city, the heroes, the liberators. But within two years any hopes for the return of democracy had been shattered. A venal Czech variant on the Soviet oppressive ideology had replaced the Nazi tyranny. The liberators became an army of occupation. There was a substantial Czech Communist Party, dating back decades, and Stalin's men had no difficulty setting up a puppet government of officials who would do Moscow's bidding disguised as a legitimate government of Czechoslovakia. The formal date of the new occupation had been marked with a veritable ocean of humanity massed around the statue of one of Czechoslovakia's oldest heroes, Jan Hus. To understand the determination of Vladimir Valenta, who lived five and a half centuries later, it is useful to take a brief look at the Hus story, and at the Hus legacy.

Jan Hus (1371–1415) became rector of Charles University in Prague in 1402, and as the various claimants to the Vatican throne (there were three at one point) were snarling at each other over who should be the next Pope, Hus began to attack what he saw as a whole catalogue of serious abuses of clerical authority. His sermons had a distinctly democratic flavour to them. He argued for the right of all communicants, not just the celebrating priest, to drink the sacramental wine, and most importantly for the patriots who over the following centuries rallied around his name (and later his statue) he called for the scriptures to be translated into and the mass to be celebrated in the Czech language. When one of the papal claimants proposed selling indulgences (the forgiveness of sins for money) in order to finance a war, he raged against it, and probably sealed his own fate by declaring that there was no holy ordinance establishing the papacy in the first place.

He was charged with heresy, really just to control his insubordination. He would not recant as demanded, and was burned alive on July 6, 1415. For Czech patriots Jan Hus became the personal symbol of their national aspirations. His story strongly affected Vladimir Valenta, who saw himself as carrying forward the national hero's commitment to the people and to the culture. He decided to deploy the most modern of media and went into film.

His first film, *Conscience*, has been acclaimed as one of the best of Czechoslovakia's postwar period. It is the story of a man who accidentally runs his car over a baby carriage, killing the baby, and driving off without looking back. But while Valenta's aim was a hard-edged moral lesson about the nature of personal responsibility, it was characteristic of the man that he never let it all sink into a swamp of polemical seriousness; he would never abandon his sense of humour and his sensuality. In one scene in *Conscience* he has a bureaucrat sensually remove a young woman's underwear in order to apply an official stamp to her buttocks, while she closes her eyes and smiles. All of this in the face of Communist Puritanism and correctness.

Eventually life under the Stalinists got difficult not just for artists and rebels, but also for everyone. Now you had to watch what you said, even in ordinary conversation. People discovered that they could not trust friends or workmates. People began to disappear for speaking out, and, what was worse, sometimes for speaking privately. Many were killed; most went to the camps. Valenta, perhaps foolhardy, just never shut up. With a group of kindred spirits at the studio, he wrote for and helped put out a magazine of reviews and features, ostensibly on film and theatre, but carrying enough thorny comment about the regime to get them all into trouble, It was a piece of Valenta's, in that magazine, that got him charged, convicted, and jailed for treason.

Those seven unspeakable years in the prisons and uranium mines did not break him; they intensified his loathing of the regime and his determination to do something about it. After he was released, abandoned by his first wife, he married a pharmacist named Eva Francova. They moved into Vladimir's father's apartment, and for a while it was a good time to be on the stage and screen. A long-time Communist, Alexander Dubcek, was rising in the ranks of the party and encouraging his colleagues to allow a little more artistic freedom. The anti-Nazi film *Closely Watched Trains* went into production early in 1966, with Valenta superbly cast in the subtly comic role of the stationmaster, and as we have noted it won the Academy Award for Best Foreign Film the following year. The Canadian writer and film director David Cherniak says of it,

> *That was a marvellous film and the first film, the first Czech film that I'd ever seen and probably one of the, one of the dominant influences which made me want to go study film then. There are some images in that film that stick with you and one of them is Vladimir with the pigeons on his shoulders, talking to them like they're his children. It's a very powerful image.*

At that time Valenta was not an experienced actor. The director of *Trains*, Jiri Menzel, said that he had trouble with his lines, but that the face and the natural charisma made it impossible not to watch him with fascination and delight. The film is about resistance to dictatorial authority, its hero a young railway employee who smuggles bombs aboard German munitions trains during the Nazi occupation. Although both the citizens and their Communist rulers detested the Nazis, the Czech-Canadian novelist Josef Skvorecky said, in our documentary, that *Trains* was, all the same, a very courageous movie to make under Communist rule. Although its story was set in the time of the Nazi occupation, it was in fact an indictment of the very kind of brutal authority with which the Communists themselves ruled the country.

We encountered a parallel in Bucharest, filming there for *The Struggle for Democracy*, in the early spring of 1992 just after the fall of the Ceausescu tyranny. The minister of culture in the interim government was Ion Caramitru, a classical actor and theatrical director. When we filmed an interview with him he told us about directing an uncut version of *Hamlet*, in Romanian, during the Ceausescu years, when the theatres were on short rations of heating gas, and people came to the production wearing heavy winter coats and hats and mittens. He told us that after the production the audience would meet the actors at the stage door to talk about their interpretation of the play, and the issues it raises about conscience and personal responsibility that Prince Hamlet faced under the tyranny of his patricidal uncle, and that only the thought-police failed to understand that what they were really discussing was life under the Ceausescus.

In *Closely Watched Trains* a group of citizens in a small Czech town sets about dynamiting German munitions trains. The movie would go on to inspire filmmakers in the free world, probably more for its comedy and its characters than for its politics. Certain sequences became emblematic: there was Valenta as the station-master, feeding and talking to pigeons; and then a woman conductor at the railing of the last car in the train bending and kissing her soldier lover as the kiss is slowly broken by the train pulling away.

In the early months of 1968 Dubcek came to power. Dubcek had joined the Communist Party in 1938 when it was illegal, had opposed the Nazis both as a guerilla fighter and organizer of the national resistance movement, and had been appointed a member of the powerful Central Committee soon after the formation of the postwar Communist government. In 1967, encouraged by what seemed like widespread public unrest, he had begun to move against the arbitrary and unpopular party chief, Novotny. Moscow, under Brezhnev, was preoccupied with its own problems and did not support Novotny. The Party made Dubcek first secretary, whereupon he announced that he was sweeping away the old instruments of repression, that Czechoslovakia's Communism would become what he called "socialism with a human face," a true people's government. Freedom of speech, open discussion, and even dissent would be not tolerated but encouraged. Czechs could travel; a new wind was blowing. The world called it the Prague

Spring; Valenta was doubtful. Prison, the camps, and all the worst aspects of Communism had taught him that liberties handed down from above are not real liberties. And he was right. At eleven o'clock on the night of August 19, 1968, Soviet tanks rolled across the Czech border. August 21 became Czechoslovakia's day of infamy as Soviet armour filled the streets of Prague.

This time the people were not protesting local Communist rulers. It was the Soviets they were talking to now, the Soviet commanders and soldiers in the streets. Under the statue of Jan Hus — whom they had blindfolded as if to save him the sight of another occupation of his country — the Czechs, many of whom spoke workable Russian, asked the soldiers why they were there: "We are your friends. What are you doing here?" The soldiers said, Well, they didn't know exactly. Some of them weren't even sure where they were. Some said they thought they were putting down a German uprising.

For a while a group of citizens held the radio station and tried to keep the people informed about what was happening. A permanent watch was set up around the statue of Jan Hus. Crowds coalesced around the tanks in the streets, as if their sheer moral courage could stop those tons of armoured force; they could not. Many were killed, crushed under the grinding tracks. All the while, at the dreary, dirty steel-and-glass Communist-era broadcast centre, the Prague station played *"Ma Vlast"* (*My Homeland*). When the Russians forced their way into the studio, the Czechs fought them with bare hands until the studio floor was awash in blood.

Vladimir Valenta was abroad in London to promote *Closely Watched Trains* when the news of this new Soviet occupation broke. A difficult decision lay before him. He and Eva had children now, and for Valenta to go back and fight the Soviets would be to put his family in danger. He decided to emigrate. As a boy he had read Jack London. For him, as for so many Europeans, Canada had a romantic appeal. A friend said he closed his eyes and put his finger on a map. Within a week they were on their way to Edmonton.

If a lot of Canadians think of Edmonton as just another prairie capital on a cold, endless flat plain with nothing but cattle, wheat, and oil, for Vladimir Valenta it was an adventure in a snow-covered movie set where you could do and say and write whatever you wanted: wide-open spaces, wilderness, freedom, independence, privacy. He told people that he was going to be a lumberjack.

The Czechoslovakian lumberjack living with his family in a remote cabin in the bush, howling like a wolf (like a character he would later play in a Canadian made-for-TV movie) didn't quite materialize. At the beginning he bore the immigrant's cross with dignity. In Colin MacLean's footage you can see him, bald, with his great stomach and heavy dark glasses washing a car at the Edmonton car wash with the vigour of a man half his age, or strolling with his stiff rolling walk among the pines on the outskirts of town, his eyes roving happily over the snowy landscape.

Producers cast him in clichéd fat-man heavy-accent immigrant semicomic parts, never a principal, never a hero. He wanted to play something meaningful, dignified, mature, but they often made him a clown.

His blunt, uncompromising discourse did not help; he was restless with, perhaps even contemptuous of, Canadian tact and concern for image. He felt that he was being taken for granted as the available guy with a funny accent. After thirty or so television shows and a couple of tax-shelter unwatchable films he had had enough. He approached both the University of Alberta and the National Film Board to see if his film and stage experience could be put to use in teaching. They both gave him contracts. Valenta was an uncompromising idealist; for him the theatre was a temple and film an instrument of social awareness. But the mainstream of Canadian film and television had long since abandoned such ideas, vigorous as they had been in the early days of CBC Television. As the pioneer Canadian director Allan King said, "We have an industrial manufacturing approach to making films, even more so for television, which is simply a vehicle for advertising." Valenta found that disgusting. Students found him blunt to the point of rudeness. He was always correcting them. But many said later that while he was more charismatic than comprehensible, there was a power in his polemic and in his person, and they found themselves using what he had taught them, imitating his style, and reproducing his passion.

Eva found a good job as a pharmacist at the University of Alberta hospital, and Valenta could easily have retired. He gave up teaching, and for five years he financed, edited, and published *The Telegram*, a newspaper monitoring Communist regimes around the world, largely written by freelance expatriate Czechs. There was even a children's page. *The Telegram*'s voice joined others like Josef Skvorecky and the poet and playwright Vaclav Havel, crying out for freedom and justice in Czechoslovakia. He was warned that he had better not try to visit Czechoslovakia, as he would be thrown in jail for treason once again. And yet his sense of the rightness, even the nobility, of his cause was marred by a reaction from the homeland that hurt him deeply: some of the very people in Czechoslovakia whose treatment he had protested and exposed now shunned him. They felt that by emigrating he had avoided the real battle at home.

Then, in 1989, the old Communist regime began to crumble in Russia and its protectorates, along with the Berlin Wall. During that almost completely unexpected change in the axis of the world, that winter of '89 to'90, Valenta was online on the Internet, and as these spectacular events came over the newswires and airwaves of the Western world, he was sending out messages just as fast as he was able to type, brimming with the latest news. Censorship kept most of the Western press out of the Soviet-ruled countries at first, but Valenta's computer gave him access to all the newspapers he had time to read, and he was able to provide his Czech friends on both sides of the Atlantic with an international summary of everything that was happening.

In Czechoslovakia Vaclav Havel became the leader of a blood-less transformation they called the Velvet Revolution, and his peo-ple asked him to take over as president of the republic: the Czechs made a poet and playwright their head of government. Next they would bring Dubcek back from exile to cheers in the streets and to a National Assembly that would unanimously vote him their chairman.[10]

It may seem a little odd that out of this journalistic initiative in newly hopeful change in the greater world, Valenta would emerge with a new and irrepressible enthusiasm: he would star in a cooking show on TV. The goofy premise was that he was the long-lost relative of the female co-host, and he had just arrived in Canada with a suitcase full of sausages. Valenta was massive and had a sort of sad comedy about him, while that co-host was a sprightly, small, funny, and provocative Irish woman. It got a little wild and confused for a cooking show. There were frequent arguments between the two cooks. Valenta and the director would get into shouting matches after thirteen takes, in each of which he drove the crew nuts because he did something they weren't ready for.

Perhaps it was a brilliant idea that failed, or even a show before its time, given the proliferation of oddball cooking shows in the new universe of specialized cable and satellite channels that was in place within the decade.

That Irish woman, the co-host, was Patricia Phillips, an actor and writer and later the executive producer of *The Canadians*. Phillips had first met Valenta in about 1987 when she was invited to Edmonton as a script editor to help producer Tom Radford and this Czech immigrant named Valenta polish up an earlier proposal for a television series on the early days of Alberta. She says that she found

> *this big huge bear of a guy who had a Tandy 100 laptop computer*
> *and his one hand completely covered the keyboard. He was totally*
> *intimidating. I said, "What have I gotten myself into?" He had the*
> *most extreme views on everything. On the first day we worked*
> *together it just all fell apart towards the end of the afternoon. We*
> *had a huge fight, and I went back to the hotel saying, "That's it. It's*
> *all over." But next day he turns up with a big cardboard box, and*
> *he brings out all this food, sausages, containers of soup, and he says,*
> *"Now we eat." We started to eat and talk over the stuff from the*

10. Alexander Dubcek died in 1992 of injuries sustained in a car crash.

previous afternoon, and it was a great day. And at the end of the day
I loved him.

They developed the cooking show *Too Many Cooks* around 1992, after Phillips had moved to Edmonton to start a production company with her husband Andy Thomson. It was probably a good thing that it did not last, because that was when the idea bloomed of going back to Czechoslovakia to try bringing to justice the officials who had put him and his colleagues through such misery and pain.

The film of that visit shows him shambling gloomily across one of Prague's many bridges, then with a group of fellow ex-inmates pushing open the rusted, barred gate of the Shebram mines; and with the same companions in the cruel low-ceilinged bunker where he had lived in solitary confinement without eating. And finally in the countryside where he had been raised, outside the Church of the Dissident Brethren, we see twin cypress trees that once stood as a secret sign of the outlawed faith, from the time when Rome was killing its heretics. Inside, in the gentle gloom Valenta looks in total absorption at the words of Hus's sermons inscribed into the walls by Jan Hus himself.

There was even a reunion for the people who made *Closely Watched Trains*, held in the train station where it had been shot. Cast and crew welcomed home the big, gruff man who thirty-three years before had played the stationmaster, who had fed and talked to pigeons. The villagers who were served by the station turned out as well, and let the filmmakers know that they, the local citizens, considered that the movie really belonged to them.

So there were some warm and rewarding aspects to that journey, but it was not, he felt, really a journey home, nor was he any more inclined to forget and forgive than he had been when he set out. This was a man who was almost brutally obsessed with what he took to be the meaningful truths, the truths that mattered—a man whose candour punished his enemies but also often embarrassed his friends. Everywhere he saw the transforming greed and corruption of power. He saw Nazis who had become Communists and now those same Communists holding power as capitalists. He had no intention of staying: "No," he had said to a friend who asked, before he left Canada, if he would renounce his new citizenship and return to live in Prague, "I will go and get my business done. I will go and visit my friends, I am Canadian." Not surprisingly, he did not succeed in finding the justice he had hoped for. He visited his friends, and he went home.

During his last years he was blessed with a granddaughter, Dashenka. In a snapshot he lies holding her in his large round arms: one of those rare moments that filled his face with innocence and made him smile. "It's unfortunate that he wasn't around for more of her life," his daughter Eva said,

> they were really starting to understand each other, and you know, it clicked between them. I remember at one point there was even a children's page [in The Telegram]. He wanted to make sure that the children would, you know . . . he wanted somehow to keep the Czech spirit alive even though, you know, people went to Canada or Australia or, you know, Western Europe.

He died on May 13, 2001. Five months later, Czechoslovakia celebrated its Independence Day, and the trim ranks of her very own briskly marching soldiers in dress uniform centred the celebration not on the statue of Jan Hus but on that of a modern dissident and founder of the republic, Thomas Masaryk, the statue newly restored and remounted after having been found in a Communist-era warehouse. There were among the celebrants many more than he would perhaps have guessed who knew about and valued Vladimir Valenta's commitment to justice and liberty. Happily, before he died they had awarded him the Masaryk Medal for service to his country.

In some ways he was an unlikely hero, but those rough edges, the rudeness and impatience with compromise, unquestionably contributed to the big man's credibility, and to the love he engendered among those able to overlook the prickly parts. A friend said, "He's like some big shabby cathedral . . . you know, that had this huge history behind it; that had a kind of beauty and grace about it and this shabby kind of human skin." A living monument of a man

who always insisted: "Go back to your heart, go back to your soul . . . go back to your kitchen to find the truth."
Vladimir Valenta, 1923–1991.

◆ ◆ ◆

The History Television documentary was written and directed by Tom Radford.

Part Thirteen

MOSES COADY
Beyond the Mountain

The world calls loudly for a real democratic formula to bring life to all its people. It is not going to be done by guns, making armies or bombs, but by a program in which the people themselves will participate. This is democracy not only in the political sense but it is participation by the people in economic, social, and educational forces which condition their lives.
– Michael Moses Coady

As risky as it is to propose any part of this country as the possessor of landscape that is uniquely memorable, few who have spent time on Nova Scotia's Cape Breton Island would begrudge that blest territory some such encomium. Almost no matter which way the wind comes from, it carries the scent of the sea, and that briny freshness blows across green fields and hills of an Irish intensity, and up the slopes of ancient mountains that the millennia have rounded off but left looming and majestic. Like the Great Lakes, the Prairies, the Tundra, and the Rockies, Cape Breton often gives people who were born and grew up there an inclination to attribute the best parts of their character to the inspiring beauty of the Island that nourished them. Moses Coady was one of those. Coady was a Cape Breton boy who walked out of the Margaree Valley and into the pages of history, and when people asked him whence came the poetic spirit, the insistent creativity and the irresistible confidence, he would point to the hills. Ellen Arsenault who worked for him in his later years said, "He thought there was no place like [the] Margaree. He loved where he was born and brought up, and it was beautiful, there's no question." And Father MacDonnell, a former president of St. Francis Xavier University, told us,

> Oh, he had the soul of a poet. Going down, driving along the shore road to Halifax, one day he came into some marvellous rock faces.

And oh, he took off. "How Mother Earth must have shuddered when she delivered these marvellous things unto us," he says. He loved this country. There's no question about it.

This poetic spirit was not attached to the person of a dreamy and idealistic preacher, although he did his share of preaching, and both dreams and idealism were very much part of the man. Moses Coady was a hands-on, down-to-earth activist. His ideas and energy — and above all his *presence* — stimulated thousands of men and women to free themselves from economic feudalism. His practical approach to community self-help was an alternative to both the insidious devious-ness of communism and the cowboy capitalism of America, but he was not a politician, an economist, or an industrialist. He was a Roman Catholic priest.

Moses Michael Coady was born on January 3, 1882, high up on the mountain overlooking the Margaree Valley. Throughout his life he came back to the Margaree when he needed to straighten things out, recharge his batteries, or stiffen his resolve.

Moses was the second of eleven children born to Michael J. Coady, known as "Whistling Mick," and Sarah J. Coady, who was born a Tompkins. He was baptized Moses after the progenitor of a founding Margaree family, the Doyles. His grandfather had fought England for Irish economic independence. It is likely that young Moses's Irish her-itage contributed to his poetic sensibility. The Tompkins and the Coady families lived together in a frame house you can still see up on the mountainside, and as the babies kept on coming and the few small rooms kept shrinking, Michael Coady found some farmland down near Margaree Forks and began building a house. There are still Coadys living in the house today.

Most Margaree families worked the land, raised livestock, fished, and cut timber. The children would be out in the fields as soon as they could handle a rake or a hoe. Young Moses would often look up from the soil he was working, and wonder what might lie beyond those beautiful hills, and whether whatever it was might hold something for him. His older cousin Jimmy Tompkins (a "double cousin" — two Tompkins married two Coadys) had already left the valley to become a teacher. Moses found that intriguing, what it might be like to go and live among other people, and teach them. The teaching he himself received as a child was often interrupted by the endless demands of the land and seasons. It was not until he was fifteen and the farm more settled and prosperous, that Mick Coady realized he had to give the boy a bit of room, a bit of time to see what that ravenous young mind might do for itself if it had a chance. Moses started attending the Margaree Forks School full-time.

That was 1897, the year that Moses's cousin Jimmy went to Rome to study for the priesthood. He wrote to Moses frequently, sending pamphlets, an old rosary, a pocket Bible, and a great variety of other books. Moses's imagination was fired up by the idea of the great and legendary city whence all these kindnesses had come. Historian Jim Lotz said that this correspondence opened things up for the teenaged boy:

> It showed Coady there was a world beyond this small rural community in which he lived. I mean it was accustomed rounds in these communities. It was a healthy life. It was a good life. You were surrounded by your family and friends and your kin. But Coady was always dreaming beyond the mountain. He was always seeing beyond. And then these packages and these parcels and these letters coming from Rome, and this feeling, Hey, there's a bigger world out there. And I want to go out there and I want to see it.

At the turn of the century, Moses Coady received his high school graduation certificate. Cousin Jimmy was his model. He would go into teaching now, he said, and set out for the normal school in Truro. He did all right — intellectually, spiritually, and physically (he was now tall, massive, commanding of presence) — and was a great deal better than "fair." What did they know down at Truro? City folks. So when Moses Coady came back to Margaree for the summer, a small delegation came around to the house to chat about the normal school experience and ended up doing what they had planned to do in the first place, namely, ask him to take over the Principalship of the Margaree Forks School he had graduated from only a year before.

He accepted and began his teaching career in August 1901. Jimmy Tompkins came home from Rome the next year an ordained priest with a professorship of Greek and algebra at St. Francis Xavier University (St. Francis Xavier College at that time) in Antigonish, about halfway between Sydney and Halifax and twenty-five miles west of the Canso Strait that separates Cape Breton Island from the mainland.

Father Jimmy was twelve years Coady's senior, but throughout their lives there was a strong bond between them. Tompkins told Moses that normal school and a rural high school were very nice but that he, Moses, was ready for more challenging stuff now, and kept on badgering and encouraging the young teacher to go for a university degree. No doubt he made sure that St. F.X. would make room for him when he inevitably applied for admission.

When Moses applied for admission to St. F.X. in 1903, Father Jimmy's confidence proved well founded. It only took the young student two years to finish a bachelor's degree, complete with medals in Greek, philosophy, and history. He came out of college with a nickname too, Mighty Moses of Margaree, which had more to do with his athletic achievements than his academics. He had been a star on the football team and a champion at the hammer throw. That was okay with Father Jimmy, who liked an all-round guy. But he had been quietly nursing his ultimate ambition for the kid he was mentoring, and came down to Margaree to talk things over with him during the summer evenings when Moses would come into the house all bronzed after a day of pitching hay and still wondering what might be out there for him on the other side of the mountains. Jimmy Tompkins knew what it was, and seeded the idea quite explicitly at last. Moses would later say that it was waking up to the sound of a distant church bell, which seemed like some sort of message, that finally decided the issue. He would become a priest.

In those days in Nova Scotia the Church was one of the few ways in which a person from a relatively poor family could find a solid career. Teaching was not bad but the priesthood was really something. The diocese of Antigonish would be sending a couple of students to Rome that year, and Father Jimmy Tompkins was not at all reluctant to let them know who one of those students should be.

Rome! He had already formed a picture; he had the smells, the sounds, the music of the place in his head before he even got off the boat. The Bishop of Antigonish encouraged him to do a Ph.D. in philosophy and theology, and that was fine with Moses. But what he wrote home about, and talked about when he finally came back, was the city, the streets, the people, the smells, the food, the opera, the language (in which he had become fluent). He was in Rome for five years. His family began to wonder whether they would see him again, the letters about life in Rome were so rhapsodic. What could possibly bring him back to Margaree?

But he was a Margaree boy. He missed those hills. And he was a teacher, after all. He missed his people, and he wanted to share what he had feasted on, and lift their spirits, of his people back home, and give them a taste for a larger world of the spirit and the intellect. Father Jimmy got him a post at St. F.X., teaching Latin and mathematics. He was a natural teacher, a spellbinder. Physically imposing, with massive shoulders and head, coal-black eyes, and a striking demeanour, he had a rhetorical style that was homey and poetic all at once. He drew them in whether they were registered for his courses or not. He was a star. He didn't mind the crowds. They would sit on the floors and the windowsills. "It was a question of what the windowsills would hold," said Father MacDonnell.

After five years he felt the need for more study, and spent a year at the Catholic University of America, in Washington, DC. He worked on his rhetoric, on speaking to crowds, which he had begun to enjoy a lot. When he came back to Antigonish in 1916 the bishop made him Principal of the St. F.X. High School. The war was on now. It had transformed the port of Halifax, a major departure point for troops and supplies and munitions. Moses was thirty-four, beyond the call-up age. He and Father Jimmy began to spend evenings together talking about what they ought to do next. Father Jimmy had already begun to promote the idea of adult education as a way of helping Nova Scotians out of their almost feudalistic lives. The fishermen then were virtually the indentured servants of the packing industry, and the farmers not much better off. He had been "nagging the hell out of the university," Jim Lotz told us, saying

"Take the noise to the people. Go to the pitheads. Go down in the

mines. Go to the wharf, etcetera. Go to the places where people are.
Take the knowledge to the people. Don't expect the best and the
brightest to come to the university."

He called his plan the Antigonish Forward Movement, but it was
not moving forward very rapidly. As he would sit there by the fire listening to Moses talk about where he'd been and what he hoped for,
Father Jimmy was aware that the very impressive man had acquired a
new sort of glow. Father Jimmy was, Jim Lotz said, "the size of a pile
of dimes," and Moses was almost a giant. Jimmy had a squeaky little
voice and not much presence in a crowd. He was very persuasive with
one or two people, speaking quietly but urgently in a farm or fisherman's kitchen about how they had to get some learning so that they
could take charge of their lives more effectively. But he couldn't work
the crowds. The message had to get to crowds, and this towering
charismatic cousin of his, he realized, was the guy who could do it. Jim
Lotz said of Father Jimmy that

> *he wouldn't put the cat out for you. He'd spend the whole night sit-*
> *ting up with you, nagging you to put the cat out. Now, Coady was*
> *the guy who would have put the cat out. So that's it. Let's get on*
> *with the next thing. It's the impressive physical presence and the*
> *way in which he put these simple words forward with passion. . . .*
> *Once you heard him speak, you could never be the same again.*

When Father Coady got involved, the Antigonish Movement
would ultimately become the foundation of a genuine new social order
in Nova Scotia. But in the meantime the war had drained able young
men from the already faltering primary production-based economy of
eastern Canada. The priorities and preoccupations of the war made it
difficult, for the time being, to get anyone's attention for proposals
about adult education, or the Antigonish Movement. So for now Moses
Coady kept on running the high school and planning with Father
Jimmy what they would do when the world came back to something
like normal after the war.

Father Jimmy also began to promote the idea of merging all the
small educational institutions in the province into one big University
of Nova Scotia. The many Nova Scotia universities and colleges were

too small for big ideas, said Father Jimmy; their resources should be combined to form a united secular university in Halifax, following the American model. What happened next was a very complex episode in Church politics. It involved — indirectly — the Carnegie Foundation, which Father Jimmy had been pretty successful in interesting in some of his proposals, and a number of other clerics on both sides of the amalgamation debate. St. F.X. had been a pioneer institution in bringing working men in for adult classes and had established a "People's School" in 1921, something that Father Jimmy was very enthusiastic about. But Father Jimmy was a man who often pushed too hard and did not know when his agitation was counterproductive. Tompkins just kept pushing Bishop Morrison until he could not listen to him anymore. Those senior clerics who opposed the amalgamation scheme held the upper hand, and both Father Jimmy (who had never worked as a parish priest) and a Father Boyle, who was supporting him in the amalgamation issue, were in effect exiled to small rural parishes.

Both Father Jimmy and Father Moses Coady were stunned by this, but that negative response of the ecclesiastical authorities had at least alerted them to the need for a more adroitly political approach to getting the Antigonish Movement to move. Coady himself had already made one move in a secular direction that the Church authorities could not openly object to: he had become head of the Nova Scotia Teacher's Union. When he spoke in public now it was to stress the importance of education in the future prosperity of the province, a message that seemed innocuous enough before the authorities realized what he really meant. He was also teaching part-time on campus, and still running the high school as well as leading the teachers' union. Imagine a Principal leading a teachers' union anywhere in Canada today.

Now he got an idea for a new enterprise, and found the time to go over to Margaree to help build a school there — literally and physically, digging and hammering, as someone said, "down in the trenches." He enlisted the Sisters of Saint Martha, an order he admired very much, which had been established at St. F.X. in the late 1890s. They would teach in the Margaree School, and he would help them start a convent there. He would later help them establish their independence from St. F.X., and they still express their gratitude for that. "If I had fifty Marthas I could save the world," he once said.

The postwar world of rural Nova Scotia was certainly in need of saving. In June 1925, the Glace Bay miners struck the oppressive British Empire Steel and Coal Company. The company broke the strike with scab workers from as far away as Scandinavia. And then, calling the strikers Communists, they simply cut off the striking miners and their families, forcing some of them literally into starvation.

The fishing industry was also in a lamentable state. Beginning in the late 1800s, large fish companies had moved into the coastal areas. They bought fish and sold the fishermen the hardware and groceries and other goods the fishermen needed, setting the price for both. It was a time of poverty and despair in fishing communities throughout eastern Canada. Canso, where they had sent Father Jimmy for his sins, was as badly hit as any. Father Jimmy saw it all, and became newly energized about the movement. Jim Lotz said that he was telling the fishermen to "raise hell and get the government to do something about it." Father MacDonnell said,

> He was obsessed with doing something for the fishermen, the poor
> fishermen, who were being done in by entrepreneurs from away.
> And he finally managed to get government people, schoolteachers,
> the clergy, together for a meeting. And he harangued them. Told
> them they simply had to do something about this situation.

But it was not just a blind lashing out this time. With Moses Coady's help, Father Jimmy's haranguing had begun to take on political shape and energy. They got to the press, and the editors loved the story. The movement, now usually referred to as the Antigonish Movement, began showing up on the front pages, and now there was real public debate. The federal government saw an opportunity and convoked a commission of enquiry, which called 823 witnesses. Not surprisingly, one of the most impressive was a priest named Moses Coady. Coady outlined for them a simple, cost-free way to improve the lives of the fishermen: they should be encouraged to form, and protected in the doing of it, producer and consumer co-operatives. The commission agreed, and decided that the very man to go about the province helping to spread the idea and enlist the fishermen was the big charismatic guy from Margaree. The government could easily pay the salary of one man. It was time to give up the teaching job and go on the road.

And so over the next ten months, Moses Coady travelled a thousand miles around the province, sometimes exhilarated, sometimes exhausted, but day after day, without let-up, preaching to and teaching the fishermen and their families how they could throw off the lethargy and desperation of near slavery by uniting as a single voice. In June 1930, 208 delegates met to found the United Maritime Fishermen. The world was changing, and the fish companies could not stop it because the government of Canada had given its blessing, and the press were watching closely.

Of course in the long run, the whole province would become more prosperous, but it would take the bosses a while to realize this.

Father Moses Coady now had a profile in the province. Now he seemed the ideal man to help realize a project that many had been agitating about for a long time. The alumni, the Scottish Catholic Society, and the industrial conferences had been urging the governors to start an extension department. Once again there was a complex political situation here, among those for and those against, but in the end the governors invited Coady to set up an extension department and to head it. At that time he was totally taken up with his organizing of the fishermen and could not begin work on the extension department right away, but he knew that extension would be another powerful instrument to help realize the dreams that he and Father Jimmy had for helping people get the good and abundant life. In 1930 he set to work.

He went back on the road to tell the fishermen that they should not just settle for their co-ops; they needed more education. He knew where they could get it, and he was ready to persuade the university to help bring it to their doors. Canon Russell Elliot, an Anglican friend, told us,

> *His technique was to get people to talk. People had very little education in most cases. But that didn't mean they weren't wise or that they didn't have good minds. And so as they sat around in little*

groups looking at things together, he could toss in a little bit, ask a question or two. Inevitably they came from the meeting having learned something.

And Dougald MacDougall, who got to know Moses well through the co-ops, added,

He used to say, "I'd like to take the nut out of your head and pour in some knowledge. Because with knowledge will come hope. And with hope will come a better life. And people will become masters of their own destiny." Those are the things that I learned from him.

That was the way he talked. He used language as a tool. He would tell them, "You can get the good life. You're poor enough to want it and smart enough to get it." His voice was being heard across the Maritimes. Ironically today, the sound of that voice exists in just a handful of archived sound clips. On one hissing old tape you can hear him saying,

You start work. Get the people interested where they are. Find their interests. Lead them up. And when they see that thinking pays, they'll put in some, they'll put in some . . . The most exciting and thrilling of all things . . . in this world, is creative thinking, you see. To know life is ahead of you. And life is there. And if you're smart enough to find the techniques by which you can siphon it down to yourself. That's, that's our philosophy. Our formula for social progress is the complete mobilization of the adults of this country. The workers, the farmers, fishermen, lumbermen. To get the knowledge and the social techniques that will give them the good and abundant life. That's the story. That's what the Antigonish Movement is.

Sometimes the philosophy became a bit unrealistic, but it always sounded as though it were grounded. Father MacDonnell told us about driving down with him once to the community of Judique, a hundred and twenty miles or so southwest of Sydney, on the west coast of Cape Breton.

On his way down there one evening, he happened to notice these vast stretches of wonderful land, all the way down to the ocean as he came in. And nothing in particular going on. So he started out

by picturing an incredible development of a cabbage industry in the community of Judique. And the cabbage would be so wonderful and so plentiful that no one with any sense of palate at all would dream of having any other cabbage but what came from Judique. They knew perfectly well that they weren't going to do this. But they were enthused. And then in would come people like A.B. Macdonald and other good workers who would do a lot of the organizational work.

With Coady goading them into working together, the Judique community pooled its resources to not a cabbage industry but a lobster-canning factory. Another group formed a marketing co-operative to sell the product. These were among the first producer and marketing co-ops in the country. The idea took hold. Within three years, Maritime fishermen could look around them and see and touch the new prosperity that had come from their elimination of the middlemen and the cod lords. Soon, with the guidance of Coady and his workers, the idea spread to farming communities. Sheep farmers started butchering, processing, and selling their own animals. Then the people of Cole Harbour and Port Felix opened co-op stores to sell the increasing number of co-op produced products. By 1935, this network of producer, marketing, and consumer co-ops was threatening the established business community and returning substantial profits to co-op members. And then along came a new co-op idea, the credit union, which had been invented by the Quebec Hansard reporter Alphonse Desjardins at the turn of the century, and now made its way up into Nova Scotia from Massachusetts and Maine. The fishermen said at first that they had enough difficulty making a few pennies, let alone putting anything aside, but Coady kept at them, and before long taking your savings to the co-op, however small they were, became something everyone did. Dougal MacDougall told us,

[When] I was a youngster going to school . . . we had those, I don't know if many of you remember, those big black pennies. They were big ones. Twice as big as a little penny. And we used to save those and put them in the credit union in Antigonish. And [Father Coady] always believed that people could do much, much more than

what they were doing. If they could work together, gain knowledge, because with knowledge came hope. And with hope came a better way of life. That people could walk with their heads held high and dream a bit. And look into the hearts of their fellow brothers and sisters. And to be able to share in a good and abundant life which is throughout the world for all to have.

The Nova Scotia newspapers began to refer to Antigonish as "The New Jerusalem" and to Coady as "The New Moses," as if it was going backwards to a simpler time. Indeed his vision always took him back to Margaree. "It was his Shangri-La," Jim Lotz said. And he unquestionably found the virtues of the simple rural life to be way ahead of that grubby oppressed wharfside life the fishermen had lived before the co-ops. But he saw all this as a road to Rome, in a way; not Rome meaning the Vatican and his theological studies, which now seemed so far away, but Rome meaning the full life of the intellect and the senses, music, language. "We're going to bring them to Shakespeare," he used to say, with a big laugh, "open up their minds, their imaginations. That's what it's for, finally."

Moses Coady was not just a solo act. His brilliant rhetoric made him look like a star, but it was always in the service of getting people working together, and much of the time that meant working with him. He was a team leader and always tried to find people smarter than he was. Father MacDonnell said,

He surrounded himself with a group of very good people, and I think particularly of the women who worked for him. Creative people. Being on the Coady team was an exhilarating experience for people.

And Jim Lotz again,

Hey, it must have been fun to be around these people, because you never knew what was going to happen. You never knew when his book was going to be thrust at you, and he'd say, "Read this by tomorrow." Or you know, when Coady would say, "Let's go up to the Margaree and pick strawberries." So it was a wonderful time. I mean this is the great thing about talking to the people involved in the movement. It was a wonderful time in their lives. They didn't feel they were doing good works among the poor. They didn't even think, I think they were doing development. They were just learning, having fun, and working with like-minded people to alleviate some of the prevalent miseries of the time.

Ellen Arsenault was living in Prince Edward Island when Coady advertised for a secretary. She said,

Dr. Coady himself told me that he had about fifteen or twenty applications for this job of secretary. But they were all teachers. And I had been a teacher, but I had also worked in a bank. He told me later, anybody that can work in a bank can do anything. That's how I got the job.

One of her tasks was to help publish *The Maritime Co-operator*, a monthly newsletter about the movement, which had built a growing readership. Another woman who got involved was Irene Doyle, a Cape Breton girl who came to Coady to see if she could drive over to Antigonish with him one day.

And he says, "You're going to join the Marthas?" And I said, "Yes." And he said to me, he said, "Did you ever drive sixty miles an hour?" I said, "No." "Well," he said, "you're going to do it this afternoon." So on those twisty roads, you know, we got here in a very short time. But I mean that was what, the impression you got about him was energy.

He loved to drive fast and hard. He spent thousands of hours in the car, tearing around the province from one project to another, lining up other drivers to give him a break when he could. He used everyone as a helper, a referee, a testing ground. Every colleague, employee, or friend. Father MacDonnell told us that Coady turned to his staff — most of them women — not just to do his bidding, but to help guide his hand, as a staff is supposed to do.

He could toss an idea at them and they could come up with an essay or a letter very quickly. He'd want to try out his speeches on them. And he knew he had a marvellous speech. And he'd come down with great enthusiasm and he'd gather the circle around. And he'd deliver the speech, only to find that quite occasionally heads would start shaking. No, you haven't got the right emphasis here. That idea should be downplayed. You should emphasize this more. And for a few moments he'd look like a spanked boy in the classroom. But then the battle would be on as they debated. But he'd take their counsel. He listened to them. He never heard of the term feminism. *But he certainly appreciated the talent of women.*

Sister Irene Doyle was often there, one of two Marthas who came to work in the extension department.

[We] were having a little meeting. And I said, "What's 'Little Mosey' think of this?" "Oh," he said, "she's calling me 'Little Mosey.'" Now he liked that. He would like that far better than for somebody to cower in front of him. He wouldn't mind arguing with them. So I think that in that way he was a big man, he was.

Resolute and confident in his faith, he was, however, in no way a complacent servant of the institution. In a way it was the reverse. Coady "stood on the Church," Canon Elliot told us,

[in order] to be able to jump into society and help it out. So it was not really a Church movement in one sense. But it was using the Church, motivated by the Church to do things for the community at large. So it was not a Roman Catholic movement in itself at all.

One day in a conference someone said to Father Jimmy, "Well, you know, you Catholics are doing very well," and Father Jimmy's acerbic rejoinder was "There's no Catholic or Protestant way of catching fish." But critics among the businesspeople who felt they had been hurt by the Antigonish Movement — and elsewhere — could not shake the idea that there was some kind of sectarian thrust to the movement. Canon Elliot said,

People who were in the financial world didn't like what was going on. . . . [N]ot being a Roman Catholic, they would say oh, you're just falling in the hands of the Roman Catholic Church, you see. That was their way of doing it. Roman Catholics who were in business or whatever and didn't like the co-operative movement would use another way of criticizing.

This meant, according to Father MacDonnell, himself a senior Catholic cleric, that

In some quarters he was considered a Communist. Certainly a Red-

eyed socialist. He was not welcome in some dioceses in Canada at all. Because these were the days when we saw a Communist Red behind every bush. It's hard for people to understand today how apprehensive people were about this menace. Coady's work was regarded by a lot of people as not being very suitable church work. Here is Coady's own voice:

Now we, we admit to the accusation of materialism. We want to explain right away that that's not our ultimate objective. Our aim is Shakespeare and grand opera. And we think that's the road to it. And they say, how long are you going to be in this messy materialism? And I don't know. But I think it'll be several decades. It'll be my lifetime. But I hope there will be enough idealism implanted simultaneously with this thing, that the boys who succeed us will carry on to the higher place we have in our mind.

But the hierarchy of the Church had seen the blessings embedded in this good man's work, despite the secular criticism, despite his "standing on the Church," as Canon Elliot put it, using the institution as a base from which to pursue his social programs, the authorities recognized that the priest was doing what they saw as God's work. When they elevated Coady to monsignor, Coady claimed to be displeased. Jim Lotz quotes him as saying, "The sons of bitches, they can't do that to me." Lotz says that the priest believed deeply that he was

"primus inter pares," first among equals. I think that's how he saw himself. [And] I think internally there was an awful lot of struggle in this, in this man's mind about whether he was really sort of bringing his people forward, or taking them back into an imagined past.

Father Jimmy Tompkins suffered no such conflict. They had exiled him but they hadn't stopped him. When the Reserve Mines of Cape Breton co-operatively built a settlement of seventeen modern homes they called it Tompkinsville. By now, the Antigonish Movement was widely hailed as a plausible educational co-operative process for achieving a new economic and social order. Antigonish had become an international centre for social reformers. They had enlisted A.B. Macdonald to take over the management side of things, and this allowed Coady more time to travel and spread the word. In 1936, the Carnegie Foundation sponsored him on an international tour. Ellen Arsenault told us that the staff began to worry about his stamina:

> *He spoke in so many different places. But somehow we always missed him when he was gone, you know. You'd always know when, it seemed to me that everybody perked up when Dr. Coady would come back from a trip. Because they could hear his voice and that would, I don't know, there was something about his voice that brought us all to the alert, you know, and realize he was back home again, thank God, you know.*

In 1937, the Rockefeller Foundation invited Moses Coady to use their retreat centre in South Carolina to write a book about the Antigonish Forward Movement. He accepted the invitation, but even as he boarded the train to head south he complained that he was not feeling well. The staff at the Extension Department were used to hearing him complain; he was a noisy hypochondriac. But by now, knowing the incredible demands he was making on himself, they were probably beginning to worry. As they should have. Arriving at the Rockefeller Retreat Center he started on the book, but before long he was so run down and racked with chest pain that they sent him up to Boston for tests. After a month in hospital there, he went back to Antigonish, where the St. F.X. extension staff worked through Christmas to help him complete the writing. He felt well enough to take the finished manuscript down to New York for discussions with the publishers, but once more had to be hospitalized.

The book about the movement, *Masters of Their Own Destiny*, was published in the fall of 1939. A few weeks later he had a severe heart attack, and when he came home from the hospital this time it was with firm and unequivocal instructions to rest for at least a year. In fact it was two years before he felt strong enough to begin again. He had been terribly restless during his down time, thinking about all the ways in which he could have been helping the movement to profit from its new respectability, bring more people into it, spread the word further and further. He had the sense to know he had to give up the cigars and the fast driving, but he was determined to get back on the road. "He was very fussy who drove him," Dougald MacDougall said. "He would not sit in the back seat . . . and he would check you out about a week before you were going somewhere with him."

Canon Elliot was one of the drivers who passed the checkout, just in time for a trip to Halifax.

It sort of just happened to be my privilege, I guess, to be the driver for Dr. Coady. We started down this grade late at night, pitch dark. And my car lights went out. As I did on many other occasions, I aimed for the centre of the road as much as I could in the dark. And with the other hand I reached under the dash to find and fumble with the fuse for the lights. And sometimes by wiggling that, the lights would come on. And they did. And we were still in the centre of the road. And I turned apologetically to Dr. Coady sitting beside me. And he was fanning his face with his felt hat. And he was saying, "My God, and me with a heart condition."

By the time World War II broke out in September 1939, Moses Coady and the Antigonish Movement were known to social reformers all over the Western world. But while the war demanded more time from his volunteer workers and drained the financial resources of government, it also eliminated unemployment and put a lot more money in the pockets of workers and fishermen and their families. Some were beginning to think more conventionally about their financial affairs, and to be nervous about their mates in the credit unions knowing much about what they had and what they were doing with it. They began to turn to the established banks. After a few years Coady began to think about a Canada-wide co-op movement. But in February 1952 he had another heart attack, came to terms with the fact that at sixty-nine he really had to slow down drastically, and asked the bishop to let him retire. " I think he was kind of disappointed that the bishop did accept his resignation," Ellen Arsenault told us.

I think he'd like to have carried on. The bishop said that he could keep his office, but he would retire from, you know, actual working. And he would be named as director emeritus of the Extension Department.

In an interview with Ken Homer at the new CBC Television station in Halifax, he said,

> *I retired five years ago, but I still stay here in my quarters at St. F.X., which has been my home for forty-seven years. I take a hand in some phases of the extension. I make the odd speech. I teach some-times in the short courses. I do some writing.*

He kept his room at the university and ate his meals with the other priests in the dining room. Father MacDonnell was one of them. He told us how they particularly enjoyed

> *the evening get-together around nine o'clock. . . . Coady would appear on the scene, and we were a captive audience. And we were to be enlightened. He enjoyed company. And we enjoyed him. And he could be very, very encouraging to anyone who did something worthwhile. Time and again he'd single out some of the priests who had given a good talk somewhere or done something that he rather had fancied.*

There was a continuing stream of American and overseas visitors coming to study the movement and to meet the founder. Careful to husband his time and his strength, he found these encounters good for his morale and he gave them as much time as he could.

From the time his retirement was announced, accolades poured in to the university. The old priest wrote to his niece Mary Coady, "a fellow never knows how popular he is until he is about to die," adding, "This year the extension has come to the point where there is not much possibility of it ever failing."

When A.B. Macdonald died of cancer in 1953, of the three pillars of the Antigonish Movement, there remained only Coady and his cousin, Father Jimmy Tompkins. Father Jimmy's physical and mental decline had hospitalized him at St. Martha's Hospital in Antigonish. Coady went to see him, and when he came back to St. F.X. he told Ellen Arsenault, "I never want to see him again like that. I don't want to remember him like that." Father Jimmy died in St. Martha's, in May 1953. One of the men who carried him to his grave in the Tompkinsville Cemetery said to a reporter, "By heavens, there was one hell of a man."

Against advice, Coady still accepted a few speaking engagements, and collapsed during one of them, in Madison, Wisconsin, in 1958. Father MacDonnell visited him in the Halifax infirmary.

He was great, even on his deathbed. He, oh he assured me that the world was just beginning to be interesting. And he would have enjoyed . . . all the technology development and that sort of thing. He had the imagination to see what effect it could have. He wanted to get people free time to develop themselves culturally, into music, into arts, into the finer things of life.

On Tuesday July 28, Monsignor Moses Michael Coady quietly passed away. The following Friday morning, a steelworker, a miner, two farmers, and two fishermen carried him to his simple grave in the cemetery across the road from St. F.X. Obituary writers had a field day with metaphors about his broad shoulders fitted for carrying the little people through adversity. Canon Elliot said, "His heart condition, as far as I'm concerned, is only because his heart was in people. And he gave his heart for everybody."

A year later, and within sight of his grave, the university began to build the Coady International Institute to house and train community development workers from less developed countries. The Institute, now directed by Mary Coyle, is the big man's big footprint on the surface of the planet. It has become a centre for extension work around the world. Dougald MacDougall told us that the Institute

used to borrow me for seminars, out-of-country seminars. There were a group who graduated from the Coady from West Africa, and they went home to their own native places in order to work the programs. And [The Institute] felt that now was the time to get them together so they could share and help [The Institute] improve their courses. I spent six weeks over there. And we had people from six different countries of West Africa represented there. Each and every one of them were graduates. . . . Now, that's twenty-five years ago. And the Coady program has been improving every year since. They've graduated thousands of students now working throughout the world. To make the world a little better and more human for people.

"I think that's still a good philosophy," is what Moses Coady would say. That was one of his favourite phrases: "That's a good philosophy."

◆　◆　◆

The History Television documentary was written by Whitman Trecartin and directed by Whitman and Matthew Trecartin.

◆ Part Fourteen ◆

SIR SANDFORD FLEMING
Making the World Run on Time

> *He was the greatest man who ever concerned himself with engineering. . . . His hands were clean, his eye was single, his heart was pure.*
>
> – Sir Andrew Macphail, a man of letters at McGill University, speaking of Sir Sandford Fleming

The man who (more than any other individual) is responsible for the massive engineering project that knit this country together with a ribbon of steel rails was born in Kirkcaldy, a small town just above Edinburgh on the Firth of Forth, in 1827. His name was Sandford Fleming. One of the six children of Andrew Fleming, a cabinetmaker, Sandford spent much of his childhood helping out in his father's Glaswyn Road workshop where tidiness was a prime virtue and simplicity of motion in the achievement of ends was the mark of competence. Nothing out of place, moving parts and cutting edges oiled, messes cleared away as they were formed.

Sandford's clever mother, Elizabeth, kept the accounts. Historian Alan Wilson said,

> *Andrew could not have persisted being the* pater familias *without a very strong lieutenant. And indeed, in many ways she also ruled the roost. Andrew had a very good reputation in the Kirkcaldy district. He was a first-class cabinetmaker and a respected man in many ways. And he was ambitious for his son. He was apprenticed, therefore, as early as fourteen to John Sang [whose] reputation went well beyond Kirkcaldy. He was acknowledged as an outstanding civil engineer. Also a surveyor. But as a civil engineer, and as an experimental one.*

John Sang thought of his profession not just in terms of its

726

mechanical products, but as a way of also contributing to the public good, to the larger community. So the boy's apprenticeship would give him a deep love of the transformation that good design and math, and metals and wood and stone, can creatively wreak upon the underpinnings of a nation. From his father, young Sandford had inherited order and system, and a thirst for adventure from his mother; her brothers worked overseas and wrote home intriguing letters about the opportunities that lay in the new world.

The boy had a big head of sandy hair, confidence to match, tall, feisty, inexhaustible supplies of energy, and to go with all that, big ideas. He would find a new country, make influential friends there, and his name would become a household word in his lifetime. A wit once said that Canada was a railroad in search of a country, but when Sandford Fleming arrived here there was not much of a country and no railroads at all. By the time he left us, the country was vast, railroads criss-crossed its length and breadth, and Fleming had played a role in the development of most of them.

His mother was not the only one with overseas contacts. His father, Andrew, corresponded regularly with a cousin, Dr. John Hutchison, who had settled in the town of Peterborough, in what they then called Upper Canada. That part of Ontario is increasingly urbanized today, but in the middle of the nineteenth century it was covered with huge stands of ancient white pine, some trunks more than a metre in diameter. Peterborough was still being carved out of that forest but it was developing quickly, and Dr. Hutchison urged the Flemings to come and share the promise of all this marvellous white pine. The lumber and the other natural resources of the area were already being exploited by a group of entrepreneurial Scots who ruled from Scotstown across the river.

When Andrew wrote back to his cousin expressing anxiety about the weather and the perils of the ocean voyage, Dr. Hutchison replied that "if it were not for the nights, I have seen far colder weather at home in June." But the boys had to wait two years for their father's permission to make the feared crossing. As they discussed that Upper Canadian opportunity, the idea began to form that they would all go, together. The boys would be the family's advance scouting party. On April 24, 1845, David, twenty, Sandford, eighteen, and Cousin Henry, twenty-five, stood excitedly at the stern of the ship, *Brilliant*. Andrew gave them three uneasy cheers from the quay, but the boys could see that their mother was weeping.

The voyage was stormy and the dreadful stories they had heard about cholera in the St. Lawrence ports loomed over them throughout the voyage, but they debarked safely and in good health. Ascending the Ottawa River to Bytown,[11] they travelled down the Rideau Canal to Lake Ontario, took ship for Cobourg, and fifty-five days after leaving Scotland they arrived at Dr. Hutchison's door. The boys knew that they would find relatives in Peterborough, but they had not been prepared for the town itself. Peterborough today seems flat when you drive through it, but it was all peaks and valleys when the Fleming boys arrived, and the main intersection, George and Hunter Streets, was a swamp. Sandford wrote home about his surprise at finding not a real town but a poor little place with stumps still in the muddy streets, a wooden house here and there, and a few villas on some of the better surrounding farms. The Hutchisons' stone house was an exception, as was Sheriff Hall's brick house.

Cousin Henry set out for Toronto almost immediately, and David, who wanted to study wood carving, was not far behind. Sandford — it was one of the few times in his life that he demonstrated uncertainty — was not sure what he should do. For a while he stayed on with the Hutchisons, working at surveys and collecting the doctor's accounts. But when he learned that David had found a steady job with a Scots furnituremaker, and digs that they could share, he went to Toronto to join his brother. He had an introduction to another outstanding engineer, Sir Casimir Gzowski, the great-great-grandfather of broadcaster Peter Gzowski. Fleming perhaps hoped that Sir Casimir would be a kind of Canadian John Strang, but he was disappointed. Gzowski, he wrote to his father, said, "Why don't you go back to Scotland? There's no future for you here."[12]

11. Bytown is the original name of what is now our capital city.
12. I am sometimes corrected when I refer to Toronto in the early nineteenth century, by people who say, "Ah, but it was called York then, wasn't it?" In fact, the name first appears officially as Fort

He went back to Peterborough instead; at least he was getting a reputation there as a surveyor, and he loved the outdoor life. He was a very good draughtsman, and he began to get commissions for lithographs of outstanding buildings and to draw up plans for the expansion of Peterborough and the development of new towns in the region. By the time he was commissioned to design a spire for Peterborough's Catholic Church, Fleming had developed a considerable estimate of his own worth, and he and the commissioning priest, Father Butler, fell out over his fee. When it got acrimonious he went to law, and Fleming was eventually able to write to his father, "with Dr. Hutchison's advice, I sued him and gained. He had to pay the costs and all. Think of Sand Fleming having a lawsuit with a Catholic priest. It's not everyone has the honours."

Meantime, David was doing very well in Toronto. He wrote to his father describing Canadian mass production techniques and praising the quality of the factory-made furniture. "Not like our clumsy old-fashioneds," he wrote. "A Scottish cabinetmaker has to come here to learn, not to teach. And whether we farm or go into business, we're quite a colony by ourselves, capable of everything."

The historian Alan Wilson said,

David foresees a vertically integrated operation that starts in the forests and ends in the shops, for the whole family. But it is amusing that Sandford finds other reasons for the family succeeding if they come out. "My name is middling well known about this part of the country. You will excuse my flattering myself a little." He's twenty years old, and he's already caught that confidence in the country and in himself.

And he was now a big man, six-foot-two of hearty spirits and self-importance. He wanted to challenge people, he said, and set them an outdoors manly model. Soon his confidence and his skills made him feel ready to invite the family to join him. For all the ego, family was always his rock, his anchor, and the most important mirror for his

Toronto in 1720, shortened to Toronto twenty or thirty years later, and then changed to York in 1790, because Governor John Graves Simcoe disliked aboriginal names and wanted to honour the Duke of York. Council did not wait long after Simcoe was out of the way and re-established the original name in 1834.

self-esteem. On April 16, 1847, their father, Andrew, wrote to David: "I write you, and most probably for the last time from this side of the Atlantic." Still fearing the St. Lawrence plague ports, Andrew and Elizabeth boarded the ship *Mary* in Glasgow, bound for Montreal. They had a much easier trip than did the boys; they did not get sick, and were thankful for a safe landing and a quick escort to Canada West, as the Toronto area was then called.

Sandford recognized from the start that railways would play an enormous role in Canada's development, and he wanted to be part of that. He had moved to Weston, northwest of Toronto, to study under a well-known surveyor named Stoughton Dennis. Surveying was heavy work then. There was no such thing as a transit from which you could take sights across long distances; you had to walk every foot of the territory and measure your distances with a chain. To measure one mile, that chain had to be spread nearly twenty-seven times. Surveyors would be lugging those cumbersome hundred-link chains from the Atlantic to the Pacific before long, and Sandford's surveying certificate would be his way of getting into railway engineering.

When the parents arrived David met them at the boat and brought them out to a farmstead near Weston that Sandford had surveyed before buying it for the family. For seven years they all worked that land, young and old alike. They ploughed and sowed and harvested, built barns, raised some livestock, managed woodlots, leased a sawmill on the Humber, and cut and sold thousands of board feet of gleaming white pine. Andrew Fleming resumed cabinet-making and became a consultant to the firm that David had joined, Jacques and Hay, the colony's leading furniture manufacturer. David Fleming became one of their most respected carvers.

There was more and more talk about the need for railroads. Sanford looked for every possible commission that might build him the reputation he wanted to establish when the money started to flow. He was not, however, doggedly single-minded. He sketched buildings and designs for bridges, and designed and had constructed a pair of in-line roller skates, a century and a half before they would become the commonplace they now are.

He was also very good at what people now call "networking," constantly expanding his contacts, particularly in the world of engineering, finance, and building. One good friend was a temperamental and ambitious engineer named Collingwood Schreiber, who landed a commission to design Toronto's Palace of Industry and brought the young Fleming in as his partner on the project. Schreiber admired the younger man's breadth of vision and his promotional ingenuity. Not all the promotions were successful; he had campaigned for a railway down Southern Ontario's spine, with Peterborough as its hub, but no one bought into it. Nonetheless that campaign did, as he might have said, help his name to become middling well known in railway circles across Canada West. In 1849, he was the leading spirit in founding the Canadian Institute, a professional association for surveyors, engineers, and architects. More contacts, at least that was the hope. At first they met irregularly, and it took Sandford some time to get the Institute going. One Saturday night there were just two of them at the meeting. But Fleming persevered, and out of a slow beginning there grew the Royal Canadian Institute, which still meets on Saturday nights. He also started the Institute's *Canadian Journal*, which would become an invaluable medium for scientific and technical information. His draughtsman's hand kept busy too, and in 1851, he won a contest by designing the first Canadian postage stamp, the three-penny Beaver. Today one of those stamps in good condition will fetch several hundred dollars in the collectors' market — more than ten thousand times its face value.

When the *Toronto Globe* announced that there was to be a rail link between Toronto and Lake Huron in anticipation of a further bold leap along the Great Lakes to the northwest, Sandford Fleming sensed that his time had come. He applied successfully to Chief Engineer Frederic Cumberland to be his assistant. "He got up there," Alan Wilson told us,

> *and started building the railway up to Collingwood, and discovered that Cumberland, the man he was to work with, had so many irons in other fires that he, Sandford, was left doing most of the day-to-day stuff.*

But he characteristically took it all on his own shoulders and stuck with it, and won the admiration of the communities through which the line passed. The people at Saugeen were particularly pleased with his decision to put a stop at their tiny community, and, he wrote in his diary, they "decided to found a library, to be called the Fleming Library, a great mark of respect to me." Adding, in good Scots Presbyterian style, "Must not be too vain, too sanguine, an evil day may come. An important week to me. How will it end?"

While he was using the project to teach himself the skills of the railway builder, and being none too modest about it, Cumberland's jealousy was aroused and he fired Fleming. Fleming shot back, telling the board of directors pointedly about Cumberland's absences and delinquencies. The board responded by naming him the Northern Railway's chief engineer. Meanwhile, he began to look for a permanent family homestead, something a bit grander than the Weston farm, and settled on a property just beyond the railway's terminus at Collingwood on Georgian Bay. It reminded him of Scotland. He named it Craigleith, and the family moved again. They all worked on the building of the house, David carving elaborate clusters of grapes around the eaves and constructing an ornate circular staircase. Now beginning to imagine a railway plan of considerably greater dimensions than the Northern's, Fleming declared that from Craigleith he could almost see the prairies.

In the meantime, always alert to opportunity, he bought more forest land, a huge acreage this time, which he gave to his father who had become Jacques and Hay's chief supplier. His brother David developed a lumber business, and would go on to build some of the finest homes in the growing town of Collingwood. Not long after they settled in at Craigleith, the Flemings announced plans for a new village.

For sale. Valuable town and villa lots, beautifully situated at the foot of the Blue Mountains with frontage on the Georgian Bay. A quarry of the finest building stone, and an excellent place for a fishery. From its salubrity and picturesque beauty, it must become a favourite summering resort and watering place. A healthful summer retreat for capitalists, merchants, and mechanics.

They developed the waterfront for shipping, and, with an abundance of wood, limestone and water power, they opened a mill and a quarry, and then a general store, and gave the community both land and materials for a school and railway station.

In his diary on New Year's Eve, 1853, Sandford Fleming wrote,

An intimacy has grown up with Miss Hall of Peterborough. How it may terminate, I do not know. An amiable well-bred woman with her peculiarities.

Jeannie was several years his junior, graceful, vivacious, as headstrong as Sandford and with a touch of the tomboy that he admired. He sent her a love poem illustrated with his own watercolour painting of a bluebird. Peterborough historian Jean Cole told us,

They were somewhere near Lindsay and driving a little cutter,[13] I think it was. At any rate, it crashed and he was flung out and injured. Well, when he came to, there was Jeannie hanging over him all anxious and whatnot. And she got a neighbouring farmer to take them in. Sandford was a number of days recuperating at this . . . stranger's house. And then when he got back to Toronto, he wrote to her and asked her if she would marry him. The very next mail came back with the answer, yes she would. One feels that that little episode outside of Lindsay pushed it on a bit there.

On New Year's Day, 1855, Sandford wrote in his diary,

At Cobourg on the way to marry Jeannie Hall, woke up at the Globe Hotel, a great big Canadianized Scotsman with rather an ungainly figure, large head, red or sand coloured beard and mustache. Such is my house of clay.

It was a happy and bountiful marriage: five sons and four daughters, though three would die in infancy. Sandford encouraged in his own home all of the team energy of his birth family.

In 1862, a vengeful Frederic Cumberland talked his way back into favour with the Northern Railway's board, was named general manager, and immediately fired Fleming for the second time. It really did not matter. His marriage to Jeannie had opened a new door for him in the east. Jeannie's mother came from Halifax's establishment, and on his visits to Halifax, Sandford worked the busy port's social scene with

13. A cutter is a horse-drawn sleigh.

his now well-practised charm. He became friends with Samuel Cunard,[14] and with the great democrat and then premier of Nova Scotia, Joseph Howe. Fleming knew that Howe had once brought a Halifax audience to its feet by declaring,

I believe that many in this room will live to hear the whistle of the steam engine in the passes of the Rockies, and to take the journey from Halifax to the Pacific in five to six days.

Howe liked this confident cocky Sandford Fleming, and he was genuinely convinced about railways. He named Fleming chief engineer of railways for Nova Scotia. Samuel Cunard, who in addition to his shipping interests had an effective monopoly on coal in Nova Scotia, ordered a locomotive and began to promote the development of a line from Truro to Pictou. Sandford and Jeannie moved the family to Halifax and bought a fine house on fashionable Brunswick Street near the Cunards. His closest friend in Halifax, however, was not a business contact or a Nova Scotia blueblood, but a clergyman. Alan Wilson said,

Being a devout man, he would go to the appropriate church, which was St. Matthew's. Here's this young twenty-five-year-old livewire, George Grant, in the pulpit there at one of the churches of the town. And so he's caught up in the life of Halifax very quickly.

St. Matthew's was originally the Christian Dissenters' Church, but more and more Presbyterians had joined, and had ultimately taken over, with some Dissenters staying on and others leaving angrily. By the time Fleming got to Halifax, it was where the Halifax establishment worshipped and went to see and to be seen. The friendship with Grant was solid and it would be lasting.

With Fleming's advice as chief engineer, Joseph Howe let out contracts for Samuel Cunard's rail line between Truro and Pictou. But when Charles Tupper's Tories beat out Howe's Liberals in the next election, Tupper discovered that there were serious delays and cost overruns on the Pictou line. Sensing the political change, Sandford had already shrewdly courted Tupper, who asked him what they should do about the railway's problems. At that, Sandford made his boldest proposal yet. It was outrageous. When they found out about it, the

14. See Part Six in this volume.

press screamed patronage and collusion, and called Tupper and Fleming the "Sinister Siamese Twins."

What Tupper did was to accept Fleming's brazen proposal to cancel all the existing contracts, and turn the project over to him, Sandford Fleming, the former chief railway engineer of Nova Scotia. Alan Wilson said,

> *Well, he did come in on time and under budget. We don't know how*
> *far under budget. But I think an awful lot. For example, when he*
> *ballasted, he voluntarily put 25 percent more ballast* [15] *into that line*
> *than the contract called for. You don't do that unless you anticipate*
> *a pretty comfortable profit.*

All Halifax was gossiping and guessing about those profits, particularly when Fleming acquired a substantial acreage on Halifax's fashionable Northwest Arm, not far from Tupper. But there was no denying the fact that the Pictou line was a success. He had learned a tremendous amount, and had made some innovations that were hailed by American, Canadian, and British railway engineers. Many of these would become standard railway procedures. He used steel rails, not iron. He had learned about embankments and stone bridge approaches from John Sang. He used iron not wood for bridges and laid track with the finished ballast. He did all the work that would lead to his being the natural choice as the guiding genius of the great transcontinental railways of Canada.

The 1867 Act of Confederation promised that the new federal government at Ottawa would build a railway between Eastern and Central Canada. One of the men competing with Fleming for the railway job was Charles Bridges of the Grand Trunk company. Bridges advocated building railroads quickly and cheaply, and then repairing and upgrading from operating revenues, sure that this would appeal to the new cash-poor federal government. But Sandford knew that along the Intercolonial's underpopulated and underdeveloped route any profit would be a long time in coming, perhaps generations away. Better to do it right in the first place. He stuck to his guns and won the commis-

---

15. Ballast is broken stone or gravel of a consistent size that beds down firmly, drains well to avoid heaving with frost, and thus provides a firm and unshifting base on which to lay the rails.

sion. Then he fought to get iron bridges instead of wooden bridges, so trains of the day wouldn't set them on fire, and he won that battle only after the line was started and a couple of the wooden bridges did what he had predicted they would do and burned down.

The government had created a railway board to oversee the project and had appointed Charles Bridges to sit on it. There were frequent disputes between Bridges and Fleming, but when his old Siamese twin Charles Tupper became minister of railways and canals, Fleming seldom lost an appeal. When we made a *Heritage Minute* about him in 1992, I had the Fleming character climb flamboyantly onto a handcar, calling out to the board members who could scarcely keep up with him, "We're not just building a railroad, gentlemen, we are building a country." Alan Wilson said that for the most part Fleming

was revered on the line. But the trouble was in some cases, and he came under heavy fire from Bridges and others later on, for the fact that he let his people get away with too much. [But in fact] he did, and no one else had ever done it this carefully. He created a form wherein the engineers had to report on a very, very frequent basis. So he rode herd on them. But on the other hand, that other warm side of him often drew him close to people.

But while he readily won friends and admirers, that strong and decisive personality also attracted critics and sometimes dedicated enemies. The work was difficult; he met strong criticism. But he was getting track laid. And then he was shaken by a message from Ottawa. Alan Wilson again:

He was asked to take on yet another responsibility. To bring British Columbia into Confederation, Macdonald had offered to build a transcontinental line. Fleming was asked to be its chief construction engineer, too. Now that's a huge burden, and he hesitated.

George Grant may have helped him decide, Alan Wilson says, by proposing that they go west together to see exactly what the territory would demand.

A Pacific railway would be a vital link in an imperial global chain. And since Sandford had dreams of developing a cable link to New Zealand and Australia, surely this was part of a grand design. And remember, they're both Presbyterians. The whole idea of predesti-narianism is very amusing. And in the summer of 1872, with his son Frank, and with Grant and a couple of others, he set out on the first of two exploratory journeys across the Prairies to the Rockies and beyond. And this was a pretty daring venture. Because Sandford, although he's only, he's still only forty-five, and Grant's only thirty-seven, they loved the outdoor life. But it was a demanding trip. And yet Sandford sat and sketched and did watercolours in the evening while Grant wrote notes for a book that would become a Canadian classic, Ocean to Ocean. And that was matched by a serialized version lavishly illustrated, sold in chapter lengths, and priced for a popular audience.

And so Fleming took it on. Grant said, "It's manly work, moving mountains." Fleming liked that, but the job's demands, the political wrangling, and then the death of his beloved father, were hard on his health; the next decade was a tough one. With Charles Bridges still harassing in Ottawa, he seemed to dither about the right route through the Rockies. This time his insistence on getting it right the first time was not well received. Parliament was impatient, and Tupper's loyalty to Fleming was splitting the Tory party. Tupper needed a decision, and Sandford seemed lost in the passes of the Rockies. He'd become a political liability. In May 1880, Tupper abruptly dismissed his old Siamese twin.

The settlement of thirty thousand dollars and the promise of a Pacific cable contract eased their separation, but at fifty-three, Sandford Fleming was out. For the first time in his life he seemed face-to-face with an uncertain future. When they had commissioned him to take on that first railway job, from Eastern to Central Canada, Fleming had moved the family to Ottawa and built an imposing mansion called Winter Home, whose tropical arboretum became his hobby. It was now a retreat and a solace. And his old pal from St. Matthew's in Halifax came up with a proposal that would, he hoped, be of some comfort.

In 1879, George Grant had been named Principal of Queen's University in Kingston, Ontario. Now he persuaded the governors to install his old friend Sandford Fleming as Chancellor. Fleming had confessed to Grant a certain diffidence about his lack of a formal, classical education; but Grant knew, rightly, that his friend would be a superb figurehead and advocate for the university. Fleming's inaugural address was a hymn to scientific learning. He worked his contacts to champion Queen's in its rivalry with McGill. He stayed on as Chancellor for thirty-five productive years.

He invested heavily in Hudson's Bay Company stock, and became a close friend of the company's largest shareholder, Donald Smith. Smith and Fleming knew that the Hudson's Bay Company held huge tracts of land in the West, land that might be of interest to the transcontinental railway. Smith got Fleming into the Montreal syndicate that had taken over the development of the transcontinental railway — the Canadian Pacific Railway Company under William Van Horne. Fleming liked this bluff engineering giant, who once told a doubting investor, "Go sell your boots, man, and buy CPR stock." Fleming did not have to sell *his* boots, obviously, but he did buy a lot of CPR stock, and in the famous photograph in which Van Horne drives the Last Spike, the tall figure at Van Horne's shoulder is that of Sandford Fleming.

His energy and his confidence had flooded back as they finished the railway. Now he turned to the submarine telegraph cable that would link Canada to the South Pacific colonies in the west and Britain to the east. He thought he had a promise from Tupper about this, but if he did, Tupper broke it. Fleming set out to raise the money on his own. He knocked on doors in England, New Zealand, and Australia. Eager as he was to see the project financed, he refused the offer from a group of British monopolists whom he felt had nothing but profit in mind. If the railway had been a way to build a country, the cable would be the way to build an empire. When it finally became a reality, it was New Zealand and Australia who showered the Canadian with the greatest praise for this modern link to the ancient world.

Then a not very uncommon incident in Ireland prompted him to take up what was certainly the most world-changing cause in his whole career. Missing a train in Ireland because of a confusion in schedules, he also missed his boat to England. He began to reflect on chaos in transportation that was caused by cities and towns setting their municipal clocks by the sun, more or less. And with the scores of different departure and arrival times for the railways across the continent, there was a prodigious safety problem: What time do you expect this train to be on this section of track? If two trains travelling in opposite directions are using different clocks, and the engineers driving them are not aware of those differences, something a lot more serious than missing the next boat is bound to happen, and to happen with mortal frequency.

Rail travel had made the industrialized world aware that the time issue was urgent. The American Society of Engineers liked Sandford Fleming's approach, and appointed him chairman of their official Committee on Time. What he proposed was a series of equal-width time zones, twenty-four of them around the world. In our *Heritage Minute*, we dramatize his invention through a conversation with a younger engineer in a construction shack during the building of the CPR.

FLEMING:

Between Halifax and Toronto, there are five different time zones. It's ridiculous. After the railway and the electric telegraph, what the world really needs is a system of standard time zones.

ENGINEER:

But sir, cities set their own time by the sun. They'd never agree.

FLEMING:

Well, we'll have to make them agree. Even if it takes years.

It did take years. He published his first papers on the issue, in the journal of the Institute, in 1878. The idea caught on in North America first, and by 1883 every railroad in North America had built its schedules on the time zones that we still use on this continent. Fleming had to work on all the political establishments, of course, among other things dealing with national rivalries over who would be home to the prime meridian, the line of Zero Longitude from which the whole world's time system would start. He won it, in the end. In 1884 he was able to convene the international Prime Meridian Conference in Washington, DC, and by 1885 it was all done. His mark was now on the whole globe.

He had persuaded all those competing national interests to shake hands and establish Greenwich, just outside London, as the marker for the prime meridian. There is a plaque there marking the zero point with astronomic precision. But Fleming's name is not on that plaque and sadly nowhere in Greenwich can you find any mention of Sandford Fleming.

But under a Canadian maple tree in the town where he was born, in the front garden of the Kirkcaldy Museum, there's a small plaque commemorating Sandford Fleming, and a few metres away local and international travellers board trains that connect with services around the world — and all those services run on Sandford Fleming's Standard Time.

The pain of his father's death had receded by the time he had thus changed the world. But within a brutally short space of time his brother David, then his wife, and then his mother all died. The family, that old anchor, that rock, that mirror — and in a sense the legitimation of all his invention and accomplishment — was suddenly fractured, crumbling, sliding away from him. Alan Wilson says that he "went haywire" for several years, keeping up some work by mail and telegram, seldom leaving home, even his business correspondence tinged with grief.

He spent a good deal of time developing the property in Halifax, Alan Wilson told us.

He built a chapel. And he built a cottage. And he built stone walls across the front. He gave ninety-three acres of it to the city of Halifax to be used as a park. The whole property was known as The Dingle. He determined to rally as much support as he could (of course, he had friends worldwide) to build a commemorative tower in that public park.

What Sandford Fleming set out to do he usually finished. The support was found and the tower built. It celebrates the 150th anniversary of the establishment of representative government in Nova Scotia, the

740

earliest such achievement in the British empire. Opened by the Duke and Duchess of Kent with great ceremony in 1912, its walls are embedded with plaques and carvings contributed by Commonwealth members, universities, societies, and governments. The park is called Fleming Park.

Although that name is most importantly attached to the prophetic work of the 1870s and 1880s that culminated in Standard Time, just to list his other accomplishments is to wonder how one person could do so much. Sandford Fleming had surveyed new towns, designed buildings (and a prophetic set of roller skates), set standards for and steered the building of thousands of miles of railway, and guided and inspired a fine institution of higher learning. He had loved and encouraged, and gathered around him, a great extended family. He helped found the Northwest Mounted Police and the Royal Military College. He set professional standards for the new Engineering Society of Canada, and helped found the Royal Society with a Science Division, reminiscent of his old Canadian Institute. He was an apostle of Canadian nationalism and science, and a staunch imperialist. He had honorary degrees from Canadian, American, and Scottish universities. In 1897 he became, by Royal Decree, Sir Sandford Fleming.

Through personal and professional adversity he had piled success upon success, and he was really not in any hurry to leave the world in which he'd played such a dramatic role. Jeannie was no longer there to be the gracious hostess that she had been for so many years, but he regularly welcomed his children, grandchildren, nieces, and nephews to Winter Home, where he held a number of modest galas. As the guests bundled up for their carriages at the end of these afternoons or evenings, he would take each by the hand and look at them with affection, saying a philosophical word or two.

It was, one said, a kind of extended leave-taking. He wrote once, *How grateful I am for my birth into this marvellous world, and how anxious I have been to justify it. It has been my great fortune to have my lot cast in this goodly land, and to have been associated with its educational and material prosperity. To strive for the advancement of Canada.*

He died in Halifax, on July 22, 1915, aged eighty-eight.

◆ ◆ ◆

The History Television documentary was written by Whitman Trecartin and Alan Wilson, and directed by Whitman and Matthew Trecartin.

MARION ORR
A Life in the Sky

In Montreal in the winter of 1995 we produced a *Heritage Minute* about a pioneer Canadian aviator named Marion Orr. It was shot in the studio, though it very convincingly looks like the outdoor scene it represents, at an English RAF airfield during World War II. It shows the RAF controllers at a country fighter base, dense fog swirling around, and the unlikely sound of an aircraft engine in the distance, in weather that no sensible pilot would venture out in. We see the Spitfire flash by the control tower, half-veiled in mist, and when it lands and the pilot climbs stiffly out of the cramped cockpit, to be greeted by the ground crew, the young sergeant calls up, "Great landing, Sir!" and then has to amend his greeting with "I mean, Ma'am," as Marion takes off her helmet and a cascade of dark and very feminine hair falls out.

I had been writing the script the previous spring, and when I had a draft ready I had a preliminary telephone conversation with the pioneer pilot, in which we agreed to meet and go over the story together when she got back from her upcoming Florida vacation. A few months later I saw an item in the newspaper one morning: "Pioneer Woman Pilot Dies." Sadly it was Marion Orr. She had become confused at a traffic intersection, driven ahead when she should have stopped, and been hit by another car.

Marion Orr was born Marion Powell, in Toronto, on June 25, probably in 1916, although this was sometimes put into question because Marion late in life occasionally said that she had come into the world just when the Great War was going out, in 1918. And on some documents related to flying she has given the date as 1920. She was distressed at aging, not for the usual reasons but because she was afraid that a day would come when "they" wouldn't let her fly any more. Since she saw her first airplane when she was just a little girl she had told everyone that this was what she was going to do in life, fly airplanes. Before she was finally grounded she would have put in more than twenty thousand hours, many of them as an instructor and many as a wartime ferry pilot in Britain. She had flown nearly seventy different kinds of aircraft, including helicopters.

She was the youngest of four girls in the Powell family. Her father died when Marion was two, and her mother tried unsuccessfully to support the family by running a store, then took in boarders and got the children to help her as much as they could with the boarding house, cooking, making beds, cleaning house, doing laundry. Her friends from that time said that Marion was a pretty rebellious kid. Lillian Powell married again when Marion was an adolescent, and sent the girls out looking for jobs before they finished school.

Marion used to go up on the roof to watch for planes flying over. When she moved out of the house with her sister Marge, they shared digs and got jobs together in a perfume factory or a bakery. Marge said that on their days off Marion would often walk all the way up to Barker Field, at Dufferin and Lawrence, to watch the planes take off and land. Dufferin and Lawrence was raw countryside then. The farms started before you got to Eglinton.

Violet Milstead was a major contributor to the biographical documentary in the History Television series. She is a flying instructor who years later would teach the famous Canadian journalist June Callwood to fly, and she was an early professional colleague of Marion's. Milstead is another woman for whom a life in the air was an early dream and a continuing need, like food or breathing, and even she speaks of Marion's desire as something more intense and more profound than anyone's.

Aviation was and remains primarily the domain of males. In those early days they were mostly wealthy males and virtually all white. But Amelia Earhart would become a symbol and a beacon for women like Violet Milstead and Marion Orr: if Earhart could fly solo across the Atlantic, there was certainly no reason why they couldn't get into the air.

After one of those six-mile walks to watch the planes at Barker Field — more than an hour from her downtown shared rooms — Marion got up the nerve to approach Pat Patterson, the owner of Fliers

Limited, and ask him about lessons. It was six dollars an hour then; Marion was earning ten dollars a week. She said later that she would go without lunches and makeup and do anything she could to get even twenty minutes of instruction. That walk, from Queen Street, was about six miles. When the twelve-mile round trip wore holes through the soles of her shoes, she put cardboard in them. She did go without lunches, and her weight dropped to ninety-five pounds. But she kept at it.

It was not by any means all six-mile walks with cardboard in your shoes and partial flying lessons and going without lunch. The sisters had a lively sense of a good time, too. Eileen Hobbs, Marge's daughter, said,

Marion and my mom, they dated a lot and loved dancing. Of course, the two of them were in the high kickers, dancing at the Royal York and Maple Leaf Gardens. So they loved just going to the pier, the Palais Royale. Always had lots of dates and sometimes someone would come to the door and they were expecting another person to go out with. At that point in time they looked very similar and if my mom didn't want to go out with him, then she would get Marion to take him out. But he didn't know that it wasn't my mom, that it was Marion. And my mother would be dashing out the back door. They used to do crazy things like that. But they had a great time together. They were like one.

Violet Milstead was training at Fliers Limited at the same time. The training planes were the earliest Piper Cubs, two-seaters with forty- or fifty-horsepower engines. The instructor sat in the back and the student pilot in front. They took off at about forty miles an hour, climbed at fifty-something, and cruised not much over seventy-five. But they were real airplanes, a delight to handle. Marion was ready for her flying test in 1939. "Taking flying tests was a little different than it is today," Violet Milstead said.

The inspector sat in his car facing the runway, and one had to do X number of landings and you had to roll to a stop within so many yards of the car. And then you had to go up and do spins and from the spin you had to come and land and do the same thing — land in front of the car.

On Marion's test flight her engine quit. She had been taught procedures for dealing with this, which usually meant keeping on straight ahead to the nearest available flat patch of land — you could land a cub in a little more than a hundred feet of grass — but Marion was not about to abort her test if she could help it, and with extraordinary aplomb she turned back just at the right time to be able to make a dead-stick landing within a few feet of the inspector's car. He was very much impressed by both the skill and the cool-headedness, and of course she got her private licence. "And then after you have X number of hours, you're allowed to take passengers," Violet Milstead said.

Well, that was the best revenue you've ever had, you know, under the table, or under the, you know. Because you could take your brother or your sister or something and they all knew that you needed a little bit of money to continue flying. So you didn't refuse. And I think likely she did the same thing. I assume that we all did. I know I did.

Marion took the risk of being caught at this illegal commerce because she was now determined to get her commercial licence. The assigned instructor for this next phase was Deke Orr, a good-looking, rather domineering guy. Perhaps Marion's judgment was a bit bent by spending so much time in a small airplane with him. She accepted his proposal of marriage. "Not my particular type," Violet Milstead said.

Marion and I had been asked by Pat to go down to Windsor in a Cub to pick up a Stinson. So we set out, but you know, December gets to be a fairly short day. So anyhow, we got down to Windsor and picked up the airplane. Quickly turned around and it was getting dark and we thought, "Well, should we or shouldn't we?" At least I did, and I'm sure she did. But I thought, "Oh, hang," and we made it. It was dark when we got around in the circuit. But the local custom is if an airplane is out after dark and you think they're coming in, why the boys get their cars out on the runway and do their thing the best they can to tell you which runway to use and it worked just fine. And Marion came in behind me, not too far behind. So everybody rushed up . . . and said, "We'll get you along and so on." And all I can remember is Deke sort of coming along to

*Marion and just sort of saying, "Get out of that airplane," and just
really upset. So, I don't know. Men! — that's all I have to say.*

The marriage was soon over. World War II had begun, and fuel
was getting short. Private and small commercial aviation was restricted. Marion was taken on as a controller in the tower at the Goderich
RCAF base. In the meantime, Violet found out that the British Overseas
Airways Corporation was contributing to the war effort by setting up
an Air Transport Auxiliary, the ATA, and was hiring women to relieve
combat pilots from the task of ferrying aircraft from the factories to the
bases. She went off to Montreal to check it out, came back with a contract in her pocket and a booking for England, told Marion to check it
out as well, and within a couple of weeks she too was told to come
down for her test flight. Historian Shirley Render said,

*The check-out plane was a Harvard. So to go from say a Piper Cub,
sixty horsepower into a Harvard which was a six hundred horsepower, retractable gear, and to be able to fly this big plane. And a
person saying, "Hey, you can handle that plane, and if you can
handle the Harvard . . . we can train you to fly Spitfires and
Hurricanes and Typhoons and Beaufighters and all of these others."
So right there, the adrenalin starts flying. The whole idea of women
being able to fly military aircraft must have been so exciting for
Marion.*

The test went well, she got the job, and booked passage on the
same boat as Violet. Marion's estranged husband Deke found out and
was furious. He was actually in the Air Force, and here they were keeping him at home to train young idiots and his uppity wife was going
off to the war. And off she did go, and before long she was, indeed, flying Spitfires and Hurricanes.

The training took place at a BOAC facility at Waltham. It was
expected that six flights would suffice to familiarize the trainees with a
new type of aircraft. Many of the women were much shorter than the
male pilots for whom the fighters had been designed, and had to stuff
an overnight bag under the parachute they normally sat on, in order to
see over the forward cowling, and then had to pull the seat all the way
forward to reach the rudder pedals, or stuff another bag or a folded

towel behind them if the seat would not come forward as far as they needed.

When their basic training was completed Marion and Vi were assigned together to an all-female ferry pool at Cosford. They were expected to fly any machines in the same category as their training craft. Each type had its *Blue Book*, a detailed operating manual written in English perhaps slightly more comprehensible than today's software manuals. The ferry pilots would turn up at a factory — at Coventry, say, to fly a new type or an updated model of an older machine up to a fighter base in Scotland or Essex — and the first thing was always to pore over the *Blue Book* to make sure they knew what the take-off speed was, and that they would be able to find the undercarriage lever and the fuel-tank selectors.

Some of the aircraft were very eccentric. The *Supermarine Spitfire*, the most famous fighter of that war and some would say of all time, used a shotgun shell to start the engine. You had to prime the massive Rolls-Royce Merlin's twelve cylinders with just the right amount of raw fuel. When you pressed the starter the shotgun shell fired into a cylinder that had a piston that whammed downwards and turned over the big crankshaft just enough to send a couple of the twelve pistons up to the compression and firing position — enough to lurch the Merlin into that coughing, hesitant start we've seen in the movies and the newsreels. You had two chances, a second shell being available if you overprimed or underprimed on the first shot. Pilots got the hang of it. The superb engines were beautifully tuned and seldom failed. But it was all pretty daunting at first. There were no training Spitfires equipped with a second seat for the instructor; you just got in and did it. Marion said in a television interview once that her first circuit in a Spitfire nearly overwhelmed her.

The first one I ever had was a real shock. Because I got in it, opened up the power, and everything went numb. That thing just shot right off the ground and up in the air. I was five thousand feet before I even sort of shook my head and thought, good heavens, what was that?

But after they came to terms with a couple of thousand horsepower instead of the forty or fifty they were used to, and learned to decipher the language of the operating manuals, the women began to feel pretty cocky about these warplanes.

"We'd just take it in our lap like this," Marion said in a 1991 television interview, showing an old copy of a Spitfire *Blue Book*. "After we got on the airplane, we checked on here and we looked for everything that was going on down here until we got it started. And then just did what the book said."

"And then you'd taxi out," Violet Milstead said, in the documentary about Marion,

and it's an airplane, you know. Like it's got an engine and a frame
and it's got a little more power and you know it's going to do this
because you've talked to people who've flown them. So you get into
it and you go down to the end of the runway and you turn around.
And you'd get a green light, because no radio control, of course, and
off you went.

And when they got to their destination, they'd say, "Okay now, what's my letdown speed, what's my landing speed? Well, I'll look in my *Blue Book*." Once when Violet Milstead delivered a Spitfire, she was told when she landed that there was a Beaufighter that had to be ferried to another base.

So this chap came up to me, a flight lieutenant or something, and
said: Did you just bring in the Spitfire? And I said yes. He said,
"You're getting in the Beaufighter? Have you ever flown one
before?" And I said no. And he said, "Well, what gives you the idea
that you can fly one of those?" And I said, "Well, I carry my little
book around with me." And he said, "How can you fly an airplane by
the book?" And I said, "Oh, it's easy. You know, you just get all your
information and know where your knobs and taps are on the airplane
before you start it up, and away you go." . . . When I talk easily about
taking off and landing a Spitfire and then people will say to me, well
how long does it take to train a Spitfire pilot just on Spitfires. And
I'll say to them that the only expertise I needed was to get up and get
down. And all the expertise that they need is beyond measure.
They're fighting for their lives most of the time.

Historian Shirley Render retailed a story she had from Marion, the story that in fact served as the plot for the *Heritage Minute*.

She was ferrying, I think it was a Spitfire, from Scotland to England and she was flying along the coast. And again, the weather came down. It was a priority one aircraft and when ferry pilots were given the task of taking a priority one aircraft they felt a real pressure on them in taking off and getting that aircraft to the squadron that needed it. And she said she took off in crummy weather and the weather just proceeded to get worse and worse. She said she was just about ready to ditch that aircraft when all of a sudden she saw runway lights and she was able to slip through to safety.

And that was the way it went. Pretty heady times for people in their mid-twenties, especially so for women. "I can remember one morning that we got up," Violet Milstead tells,

I was getting dressed and she was over at the window saying, "They can't make me fly this morning." And I thought to myself, "Oh my." And I said, "Marion, you can't see as far as the backyard." That's not 800 feet and it's not so many yards, no one could — they're not going to make anyone even — they're not going to put chits out this morning, let alone make you fly. But then I said, "We're supposed to drive to the airport. Now get busy and get dressed."

We lost a number of pilots and one in particular, a girl, Jane Winston. Jane was from New Zealand. And we had a Spitfire assembly plant right on Cosford and so this day I guess most of the pool of pilots were taking their first delivery of the day out of the factory and Jane got one that had a problem. Jane took off in hers and had engine trouble. And it would stop and start, you know, it was intermittent. And she tried to turn back to the airport and didn't make it and went straight in and she was killed. Well, that upset of course all of us at the airport, and it was really a shock. That was the only one that we had right in our own pool while I was there.

Now Marion began to hear from Deke again, long tender letters full of regret for their break-up and contrition for his behaviour. It seems that he had been playing around even while they were still together, but now he promised to be faithful, and careful, an attentive husband, respectful of her career and her needs. The old feelings that had been so powerful when the two of them had pounded the circuit together doing her commercial pilot's licence apparently flared up again. She went home on leave, and listened to his proposal that they patch it up again, and then came back to England and her Spitfires, to think it over.

A few weeks after the Normandy invasion, in the summer of 1944, she gave that all up and came home for good. It did not work out. Deke did not stay faithful. Once again they separated, and Marion went back to Barker Field with her eight hundred hours of wartime flying and her radiant confidence and good looks, and started instructing for the Henderson Brothers at an outfit called Aero Activities. When Vi Milstead came home she signed on with a competing flight school at Barker, Leavens Brothers, and the two veteran ferry pilots would meet for coffee at Mrs. Ward's Diner right on the field.

When Marion was offered the chance to buy Aero Activities, she knew that she would have to be able to do virtually everything herself if the place was going to ever get in the black, and so she took an Aero Mechanics' course, and soon she had yet another licence to post up on the wall. Not that Aero Activities actually had a wall. She was operating out of a tent at first. Students came in gratifying numbers though. They found her a warm and personable instructor — inclined to suddenly take the controls from time to time and show off a bit, perhaps throw a bit of a scare into the poor student with a sudden wingover or a surprise cutting of power. But they kept coming. She gave parties in that tent, and scrimped and saved. When Leavens Brothers decided to sell Barker Field as Toronto pushed northward, Marion had saved enough to buy land farther north at Maple, where she set out to develop her own airfield and flying school.

In conventional financial terms it was a totally marginal enterprise. Her pals and colleagues from Barker Field, and many of her students, pitched in to help cut trees and dynamite the roots, dig ditches, lay drainage tiles, seed out the grass runway, set tie-downs, and build a rudimentary clubhouse and office. The Department of Transport regulations required a minimum of 1800 feet for the runway, but there was only 1600 feet available. So when the officials came to check it out, a helpful club member discreetly pulled the hundred-foot tape backwards, step by step, until the measure was correct.

As soon as the runway was approved, there was another setback. A petition by concerned Maple citizens resulted in a new bylaw to stop the airport from opening. Marion decided she needed some high-level support at this point, borrowed a car, drove to Ottawa, found her way to the Prime Minister's office and talked her way in to see him. As anyone who ever met Louis St. Laurent will testify, once you got by the protective wall, this Prime Minister was courteous and direct in his quiet, patrician way. He listened carefully to her account of her wartime career, her commitment to teach flying, and her having put her life savings into Maple. We do not know how the strings were subsequently pulled, but the bylaw was withdrawn. The pals put on an air show for the opening, De Havilland sent over their new Otter, the Air Force flew a formation of jet fighters overhead (CF 100s), and Maple was — however precariously — in business. You can still see it today as you drive north on Highway 400, about fifteen minutes north of Toronto; it's much more elaborate now, with a small control tower and an imposing brick building — which largely masks that original grass runway, still in service.

What happened next indicates an aspect of Marion Orr's character that had not yet revealed itself, even to her. Her ambition from childhood had been to fly. She had achieved that. The thing had taken on the specific form of running her own flying school, and the effort to achieve that had been prodigious. But now that she had it, there came a sense of letdown, of no more horizons. So after a few years, she decided to pull back for a while and consider whether there was anything left to achieve. She put the Maple operation up for sale and went off to Florida to stay with her sister Marge. She dyed her hair blond, spent a lot of time at the beach, and occasionally went over to the local airport, Opalaka, to see what was going on.

Early in 1961 she found herself in conversation with a helicopter

pilot, and realized suddenly that here was a very challenging kind of
flying about which she knew almost nothing. The difference between
flying a fixed-wing airplane and flying a helicopter is largely mechanical and physical. A regular airplane's controls constantly feed back to
the pilot a muscular indication of what you are trying to do — climb,
descend, bank, turn, hold steady. In normal straight-ahead flight, with
everything properly trimmed, you can take your hands and feet off the
stick and rudder and the airplane will just keep going the way it has
been set to go. But when you move the controls to change course by
turning or climbing or descending, the controls resist you, letting you
know very precisely that you are asking the machine to do something
it is not trimmed to do. The greater the change, the more muscle
required to control it.

Not so with a helicopter. The control column is limp, "the wet
noodle," they used to call it. There is no muscular information. You are
almost totally dependent on your eyes to tell you what's going on.
Some fixed-wing pilots find the transition so difficult that they give it
up. Marion Orr never gave up on anything, except perhaps her marriage. She hurled her formidable energy into the helicopter challenge,
and in a matter of weeks had mastered the new craft sufficiently well
to earn an instructor's licence.

But they say that you are not really safe in a helicopter until you
have flown a thousand hours. Marion had a hundred hours, if that.
One day, with a student at the controls, the engine failed. The Canadian
poet Karen Solie wrote of the sensation

> . . . *that first engine stutter lifts a hand*
> *to collarbone. In concussive measures*
> *of the blade the chance*
> *of a guttering pause . . .*
> *. . . Movements*
> *of each pilot's arm look much like*
> *our own, panic the soft spot*
> *we are all born to.**

*Excerpt from "Why I Dream of Helicopter Crashes" from *Short Haul Engine,* by Karen Solie, published by Brick Books, 2001.

There is an altitude below which — unless your forward speed is considerable — you cannot recover. Hovering at less than about four hundred feet you are in deep trouble. Marion was in deep trouble. It is doubtful that she felt the panicky soft spot we are all born to — Marion Orr was not a panic person — but she was not able to stop the machine from falling out of the sky.

Marge's daughter Eileen Hobbs told us that she and her mother, Marion's sister, were in the car on the way to California

when I was seven or eight. And as we were driving along, my mother became violently ill and we stopped the car. And when she got back into the car, she said, "We have to get to a phone." She goes, "There's something wrong with Marion." And that's when we found out that Marion had had the helicopter accident. So the same time she got very sick was when she had had the accident. My mother just knew instantaneously it had happened.

The impact had broken her back. She came out of the hospital in a brace and with a lot of pain. She stayed on with Marge and got a job as a bookkeeper at the Opalaka Airport. At least she was still around planes and aviators. Marge tried to set her up with eligible men. That did not work, but the sisters remained very close, and Marion became very fond of Marge's daughter Eileen, from whom we had much of this story. Sitting there at Opalaka with her ledgers and invoices, and watching the planes rise and descend, and the young aviators eagerly telling each other war stories and moving their hands about like flying objects as they came and went from the office, Marion began to feel that her time as an instructor in real airplanes had been pretty rewarding after all. She decided to come home and get back to what she was really good at.

The little airport at Buttonville, Ontario, a few miles east of Maple, was expanding in the early 1970s. Its new owners, Michael and Heather Sifton, had decided to turn it into a serious player in the Greater Toronto aviation scene. The northwest-southeast runway, a grass strip when this writer started flying there a decade earlier, was now paved, and the airport was the only privately owned facility in Canada to have a D.O.T. control tower, integrated into the national air traffic control system. The

Siftons' flying school was big and growing, and an instructor with Marion Orr's experience, qualifications, and personality was just what they needed. Now in her mid-fifties she was authoritative, distinctive, diligent, energetic . . . and unconventional. Peter Muehlegg, a sixteen-year-old boy who had been hopelessly infected with the flying bug and had saved barely enough to pay for the minimum thirty-five hours of flying time plus ground school, was sent to her to be assessed as a candidate. He asked her if it was really possible to complete his licence with those minimum hours.

> *Before she answered she said, "Are you really dedicated and is this something you really want to do?" And obviously the answer was yes. "Are you willing to work hard and put your mind into this?" I said, "Oh, absolutely," again without hesitation. And, "Well you may not enjoy it. I'm going to work you real hard and it's a little bit tough sometimes getting [through the course] on minimum hours, but as long as you're willing to work, I'll do it."*
>
> *On a few occasions if there was a couple of parts of lessons that required a little extra work, there was numerous occasions where we were flying and she would look at her watch and say our hour is up. We'd probably best head back towards the airport. She would look at her watch and realize it was still an hour before her next student and she would pretty much shut off her clock and we would train for another fifteen or twenty minutes and stay in the air that much longer. And we did that on maybe a dozen or more occasions just to get in that little extra flight time and training. And then when we landed and went back in the office, she walked up to the dispatch office and handed him a time sheet that only had one hour written on it.*

She was a meticulous person with a sensitive nose. If students were careless about bathing, she let them know it. She carried a packet of breath mints and often pressed one on a student when they got into the cockpit and she got a whiff of the slightest unpleasantness. One of the students who turned out to be problematic — for quite different reasons — was Marion's favourite niece Eileen Hobbs.

> *I called Marion. I said, "Do you think I could come stay with you*

and learn to fly with you?" And she said, sure, no problem. So we went up in the end of September or October and on my first flight we did attitudes and movements. So when we got up in the air, she was showing me how by pulling the control column back you go up in the air, and push it down and you go down. Then she looked at me and she said, and this is what happens when you students over-control the aircraft. And she reached back the control column and we were just standing straight up. And then she pushed it forward and you could feel your body just came up out of the seat and we were just diving down. And then she pulled the aircraft level. And then she looked at me and she said, "Aren't the trees beautiful down there this time of the year, so much gorgeous colour." I was petri-fied in my seat because I thought we were going to die. (laughter) That's pretty well how we ended up the first flight lesson and then we landed and she got out of the plane as if nothing happened and that was that.

After a few more lessons, Buttonville's chief instructor Gordon Craig had become concerned that Marion was being unusually tough on her niece. He proposed that someone else take over Eileen's train-ing. Marion became uncharacteristically angry, and said that if she couldn't teach her niece to fly then nobody would. Eileen decided on a discretionary retreat, and went over to Maple to continue her training. Marion didn't speak to Eileen for the next fifteen years. Then, just after Eileen's father died, and without a word of explanation, Marion called her. They were to remain close for the rest of Marion's life.

The next few years were rich in satisfaction, and teaching people to fly, as it turned out, was in many ways the most rewarding part of this pioneer's long and productive life. Of the nearly 21,000 hours she logged in the air, almost 17,000 of them were while instructing. In 1982 she was inducted into the Canadian Aviation Hall of Fame. "I'll fly till I'm ninety," she said, "as long as I don't lose my licence."

But she did lose it. Friends had begun to notice what at first seemed a slightly distracted air from time to time, and then a more alarming level of forgetfulness. Memory is a pilot's single most essen-tial protective device. There is a constant list of conditions that must be

reviewed as you fly, ranging from the simple and obvious such as altitude and speed, fuel quantity, engine temperature and oil pressure
(which are constantly displayed on the panel) as well as the condition
of switches for the electric supply and the landing gear and other crucial matters that are not displayed and the pilot must remember to
check.

There are, of course, checklists. In a light aircraft of the kind in
which Marion did much of her instructing the list would have a dozen
or twenty items on it. In an airliner there may be hundreds. The more
sophisticated aircraft have mechanical devices to record the pilot's
review of those checklists, but the pilot does have to remember to *use*
the checklist in the first place; must remember to check fuel levels and
the exterior mechanical condition before even climbing into the cockpit; must remember to flick the tabs on the checklist's mechanical
reminders if the airplane has such a thing; must constantly remember
to check, check, check.

Pilots who do so live a long time; pilots who do not, die. Marion
was beginning to show signs of forgetting things.

A friend called her doctor, suggesting that he check it out. And the
next time her licence renewal was supposed to arrive in the mail, it
never came. Marion was stricken. In 1993 when she was inducted into
the Order of Canada, she forgot where she was sitting, and had to be
helped back to her seat after the Governor General had placed the
medal's ribbon around her neck.

When we spoke to her a couple of years later, about developing
the script for our *Heritage Minute,* she sounded alert and pleased at the
prospect of the dramatization of her ferry pilot days. She would call as
soon as she got back from Florida, she said cheerfully. A few days after
she returned she drove to Peterborough to see a friend who had been
helping her with her taxes. Ironically she had said in an interview once,
when asked about the dangers of flying,

> *I feel a lot more secure in an aircraft than I do in my car. I feel that
> in an aircraft that if anything was to happen I could, you know, get
> out. But in a car, I don't know, you've got so many other people
> around you that you're driving everybody's car, plus your own, eh?*

Coming back from Peterborough she seems to have become confused. One of her friends said that perhaps in her mind she was airborne in the circuit at the Peterborough Airport, and just didn't see the stop sign. It was April 4, 1995. She was seventy-nine years old. Or perhaps seventy-five. Who's counting?

◆   ◆   ◆

The History Television documentary was written and directed by Martin Harbury.

Part Sixteen

NORTHERN DANCER
Little Horse, Big Heart

When we approached History Television with the proposal to step out of the frame, so to speak, and produce one episode about an animal instead of a person, in this television series *The Canadians, Biographies of a Nation,* the initial response was a kind of tolerant "Wha-a-at?" until we named the animal. We then discovered an interesting phenomenon, as writer/producer/director Martin Harbury began to develop the documentary. Virtually everyone to whom we mentioned that we had initiated this slightly unorthodox venture in Canadian biography immediately responded with enthusiasm: "Northern Dancer! Of course! What a brilliant idea!" And yet, when asked, few of these respondents could say anything more about The Dancer than that it was a famous Canadian racehorse.

"Well, was this horse a stallion?" we would ask. "A mare? A gelding?" Few knew. Yet this little guy had set himself, icon-like, in their minds as a feature of the Canadian celebrity landscape. So radiant was his fame, at the height of his career, that you would have to be fairly young today not to recognize the name, and even very young people we've talked to, if they are horse people, will say, "Oh yeah, Northern Dancer, great horse."

The little stallion's name is a large part of the legend of E.P. Taylor, himself one of those iconic names for the generations growing up in the 1930s, '40s, and '50s. Born in Ottawa in 1901, Edward Plunkett Taylor would become the biggest brewing magnate in the country, O'Keefe's being the prime brand, and in the popular mind thought of as the richest man in Canada. But important as his managerial, financial, and technical contributions to Canadian beer certainly were, his most enduring legacy was his dramatic rescue of the track from its messy decline and potential collapse. The fears, preoccupations, and economic focus of World War II had deeply hurt racing throughout North

America. But Taylor and others recognized that the postwar euphoria and prosperity were a whole new scene.

And to this scene Taylor and his colleagues and counterparts brought a new tone of adroit marketing, insistence on high standards of safety, cleanliness, honesty, and comfort, and a revival of the old glory around horses who ran clean and brave, and the shared delights among the men and women who shared that passion and worked with the great animals and their housing and facilities to give racing that quality of the regal that it historically has always had.

Taylor was not at first driven by those mythic appetites: he had started in racing as a way to make O'Keefe's famous and sell more beer. Then in 1946, his horse Epic (out of Fairy Imp by Bunty Lawless) won the Queen's Plate, an annual 1 1/4-mile race for four-year-olds foaled in Canada. That win is said to have instantly inoculated him with a life-long passion if not an obsession.

E.P. Taylor had shown from his youth a quick, inventive streak. As a toolmaker's apprentice in 1918 (he was seventeen), he invented an electric toaster, built a prototype, and sold the rights to a Montreal company for one dollar. If this does not sound like an impressively entrepreneurial transaction, note that he also secured royalties of 40 cents per toaster sold, and these royalties put him through university. He studied mechanical engineering at McGill. He also was away ahead of the crowd with a primitive propeller-driven snowmobile. He and a friend mounted a motorbike engine on skis, the propeller behind and a seat on top. The noise complaints slowed that one down, and then we don't hear more of E.P. the innovator until he reappears in the brewing industry.

Our documentary begins, appropriately, at the track, the jockeys settling tensely into the stirrups behind the closed white bars of the starting gate, the starter raising his hand, the jangling of the bells, the white bars swinging open and the horses bursting out, straight towards the camera. And as they do, in this film we begin to hear voic-es talking with affection and in some cases with wonder, about Northern Dancer:

"Northern Dancer had more heart than most." "He epitomized this

*little guy who no one thought was going to do anything, doing it
all . . ." "His running style made you want to admire him . . ." "He
was almost invincible up to a mile and a quarter . . ." "He was
Canada's horse, and they were proud of him." "For the first time
Canadians had a horse that could win the Kentucky Derby . . ."*

Let's pick up the thread from the owners of those voices, for our
story of this endearing little stallion — and he was disconcertingly
small, even for E.P. Taylor — is embedded in the minds of the men and
women who raised him, trained him, rode him, and, in the end, cared
for him until the end and then buried him with love and honour.

Here's Bernard McCormack, the general manager of the Taylor
family's now famous Windfields Farms:

*E.P. Taylor was building Canadian racing. At the time he became
more heavily involved in breeding. In the late 1940s he was buying
the best-bred fillies at the sales in Kentucky. He had asked the blood-
stock agent George Blackwell to buy the best mare he could in the
Newmarket December sales in 1952, and that mare turned out to be
Lady Angela. And to give credit to E.P. Taylor, he insisted on buying the mare but he had the opportunity to breed back the mare
before she was imported to Canada one more time to Nearco, who
was the greatest stallion of his time.*

And Noreen Taylor, E.P.'s daughter-in-law, who is now vice-president of Windfields:

*You don't usually breed a mare back to the same stallion twice in a
row, and the first breeding wasn't tremendously successful from
our point of view but the second one produced Nearctic.*

Nearctic looked like a winner, and Taylor entered him in a dollar-
laden race in Chicago, which he won. With those winnings in hand he
then went to the annual auction at Saratoga, Florida, and was very much
taken with and acquired a handsome filly named Natalma, who had
raced for two years and was in prime shape to be bred. And why not to
the stallion whose winnings had brought her to Windfields Farms?

But Natalma was still a pretty attractive candidate for the track,
and her trainer, Horatio Luro, wanted to run her in the Kentucky Oaks.
The Kentucky Oaks is the number one race in the world for three-year-

old fillies, just as the Kentucky Derby, always run the day after the Oaks, is *the* race for three-year-old colts. It is said that a filly who wins the Kentucky Oaks is one of the premier females of her age — good stuff for breeding of course, but Luro thought, Couldn't he get one more splendid win out of her? However, a few days before the Oaks was to be run, the beautiful thoroughbred injured her knee on the training track, and Luro and his vet, Alex Harthill, had to think hard about what to do. Dr. Harthill said,

> *She would have been a strong favourite, she would have been six to five or even money had she ran. And Horatio wanted to ice her and juice her up and run her and she would have probably won. Anyhow, this was Horatio's thought, and I thought differently. I thought if we ran her she could very well have broken down and we'd be bringing her home in the meat wagon so to speak, and I prevailed upon him not to do it, and I said, "Gee Horatio, we can send her home and get her bred right away."*

It might be appropriate here to say a word about exactly what constitutes a thoroughbred. *The English Jockey Club's Stud Book* of 1949 said:

> *Any animal claiming admission to the* General Stud Book *(which registers all Thoroughbreds) from now on must be able to prove satisfactorily some eight or nine crosses of pure blood, to trace back for at least a century, and to show such performances of its immediate family on the turf as to warrant the belief in the purity of its blood.*

Half a century earlier an American definition said a thoroughbred must be "of Oriental extraction and an animal developed through centuries of cultivation by enlightened nations (Merry, 15)." In both definitions, the ancestry of a horse and the purity of its family tree are primary. In fact every contemporary registered thoroughbred's genes can be traced to one of three eighteenth-century stallions.

Most thoroughbreds have strong, muscular hindquarters, and a high withers, but those don't make a thoroughbred, and they are found in other breeds. A thoroughbred can be any colour from black through chestnut to roan. So in the end it is ancestry. And Natalma would, as it turns out, make a memorable contribution in that regard.

The American Race Museum's account of the breed says this:

To complement the speed of native Galloway horses, [English] breeders in the late seventeenth and early eighteenth centuries began importing stallions from both the Near East and from Spain. Andalusian horses, native to Spain, were imported heavily in the seventeenth century. The height, size, and agility of these horses made them ideal for inbreeding with the speed of the small, heavy English mares. Stallions imported from Eastern countries, in particular Arabia, Turkey, and the Barbary Coast, offered still more to the mix. Races in England were held over long distances, and were often run in heats. Heats, usually one to four miles each, were repeated until one horse had won twice and proven himself the best of the field. In this system of racing, a horse could be expected to run up to twenty miles in one day. Imported stallions from the East were known for their incredible stamina and strength, two traits essential in the heat style of racing. Eastern stallions, too, were purebred horses. Unlike English breeds, which were indiscriminately mixed by constant cross breeding, Eastern horses were carefully bred to maintain the same characteristics in each new generation. This purity of breeding would add genetic stability to the new breed being developed.

In this century the names of some racing thoroughbreds became household words, known to millions who weren't even interested in racing: Man O'War, Secretariat, Nashua. Before long, Natalma's first foal would become one of those household words.

Peter Poole, then general manager at Windfields Farms:
Northern Dancer was born fairly early in the evening, everything went well, and he was a good little individual, he was up on his feet fairly quickly, and he wasn't big, but then a mare's first foals usually are a little smaller, but he was very robust, and he was a cocky little guy.

Always careful not to be seen keeping the best of his new colts for himself, E.P. Taylor almost always offered all of his yearlings for a set price — Dancer's was $25,000 — at an annual sale. Everyone who saw him liked him, but, as vet Rolph de Gannes told us, "they were mostly looking for big, good-looking horses that in their opinion would become stakes winners and good race horses." And this colt was very good-looking, but he was, well, small.

Bruce Walker, the former publicity director of the Ontario Jockey Club, says,

He wasn't the top horse in the sale, but there was a lot of interest in him and I recall him, especially because Carl Chapman who trained horses for Larkin Maloney was very interested in the colt and he kept taking me over to the stall door and saying, "Look at this horse, what do you think?" And I said, "Well, he's a little on the small side, don't you think?" And he said, "Yeah, but I really like the breeding." Here was . . . this little runtish-looking [colt] . . . and Chappy said, "I really like that horse, I'd like to get him. But," he said, "the boss wants to get the big colt."

And another potential buyer, Jim Boylen:

Well, my brother and I both liked him and so did the trainer but he didn't like his size. He said he was too small, would take too long to come around.

When the intermission bell went off and the crowd headed for the bar, half of the colts and fillies had still not been sold, and when everybody headed for the bar the sale seemed effectively over, so — as usual — the unsold colts went back to Windfields. Northern Dancer was, happily as it turned out for Taylor and the Windfields gang, too small to have made his proposed $25,000, and back he went to the Taylor acres.

Windfields' yearlings manager then was a man who, when he first appears on the screen in our documentary, almost makes the viewer wonder whether we've accidentally wandered into a ventriloquist's studio. His heavily sculptured eyebrows and almost immobile features above a cartoon-like grin and rigid torso are powerfully reminiscent of some of the great ventriloquists' wooden partners — until he speaks, when the animation and excitement of his recollections are instantly engaging, even though the man scarcely moves as he talks. His name is André Blaettler. He told us:

Northern Dancer I got after the yearling sale in sixty-one, so he wasn't a yearling yet of course, he was a weanling. When he was a

yearling you never saw him fly around like some of the other ones.
He went more like a . . . he galloped but looked more like a hackney
pony than a thoroughbred to be honest about it. But you really
couldn't push him around too much or he would start fighting.

Fortunately for us and for the history of the breed, Taylor's people
captured the colt on film almost from his earliest days, the tossing head
and distinctively marked forelegs, and the unmistakable action of a
creature that rejoices in being alive. Even at normal speed, as the colt
moves across screen before the camera he seems to be moving in slow
motion, the four legs coming off the ground at once as if he were airborne. Peter Poole says,

You can look at a horse, and see what's obvious, see the confirma-
tion he's got, whether he's going to be able to move well, whether he
should stay sound which there's no guarantee. But you can't see
what's inside, and I think it's the heart that's the unknown thing.
. . . After the sale he left and went to our racing stable, which was
just across the road at the old Windfields, and they broke him there.
He was quite a handful to break. In fact, I think he bucked about
everybody off that got on him at the start. Breaking is a very hard
time for a horse to go through, he's into something completely
different, and it's not a natural instinct for a horse to have some-
body on top of him, so they have a difficult time depending on who's
riding them, who's looking after them.

In the film you can see the breaking jockey lying across the saddle,
crossways, holding on for dear life. They are in the stable and a strong
woman trainer has the colt firmly by his bridle, leading him as quietly
as possible in small circles about the straw-floored stall, and the jockey
is not having an easy time of it. Even André Blaettler, who was fond of
the little guy from the start, didn't think he would amount to much.
E.P. Taylor kept hoping he'd grow, and asking the staff if he were getting any bigger, and they were tempted to add an inch or two to their
reports because they all liked him so well too and didn't want him to
be sold. But they knew they couldn't get away with fabricating that
increased stature. Yet, somehow when it was time to start serious
training, E.P. Taylor decided to put him into the best hands available,

so off he went to Horatio Luro, the same man who had wanted to race the colt's dam with an injured knee.

Luro was a star. They called him "The Latin Lover." He would say things like "Six days I train horses; the seventh is for making love." About the latter activity not much is reported, but as a man who trained horses for almost fifty years, he is talked about throughout the trade. "Hard to ride for," the jockeys would say. Although a big man, far too tall and heavy to race professionally, the handsome Argentinian had spent so much time in the saddle that nobody could pull any excuses on him. His wealthy family in Argentina had owned thoroughbreds for years. As a young man, he had been a real Argentinian playboy and his life was polo, fast cars, travel, women, and the good life. But when his father died in 1937 and the family called him home to run the stables, he found his real vocation. They called him *El Gran Señor*. He trained professionally for forty-seven years, retiring in 1984. The frivolous playboy had been replaced by a focused professional for whom patience and care were the central instruments of his work. "You mustn't squeeze the lemon dry," he used to say of his charges. In 1980 the Racing Museum inducted him into the hall of fame. For all his experience and insight, Horatio Luro found The Dancer hard to handle, and suggested to E.P. Taylor that he be gelded to make him more manageable, quite possibly one of the most regrettable decisions he had ever made in his long and illustrious career. Taylor detested the very idea of gelding and would not hear of it. He "almost bit his pipe in half when it was suggested they were gonna geld him," Bruce Walker said,

> because Mr. Taylor not only liked the pedigree and thought the horse had some chance to be something, but he was a personal favourite of Mrs. Taylor because she had often gone into the fields at Bayview and she had picked this little colt out as one of her favourites, and used to feed him peppermints through the fence.

Billy Reeves, the exercise boy for Pete McCann who broke The Dancer, had been raving about the colt's speed, and everyone was talking about how well the training was going. And so — perhaps because of all those comments about his size — they decided to get him into a race pretty early: August 1963, a 5 1/2-furlong maiden race at Fort Erie. Horatio Luro's vet, Dr. Harthill, said,

Horatio was a fellow who always wanted to prepare his horses for longer races and he didn't want them used up early because it was his thought that they would last so much longer if they were allowed to settle in stride and not be hoop-de-doo and scrambling out of the gate.

But André Blaettler was there, and saw the little guy get out of the gate, his head and ears straight up, his first time ever. "He just ran!" Blaettler said, still enjoying it. "He just kept flying and he won by eight lengths or something."

On his back in that first race was the legendary Canadian jockey, Ron Turcotte:

Mr. Luro never wanted a jockey to hit his horse first time out. When I rode him I was moving up head in head with the second horse which I'd say was Brockston Boy, and he just did not want to leave him, he was just doggin' it with him, and I switched my stick, and just sneaked my whip to the left-hand side, and just brought it down slowly and tapped him. And when I tapped him we were down to past the eight pole and he just took off.

In his fourth race, the Cup and Saucer Stakes at Woodbine, 1 1/8 miles on turf, when you went up to the pari-mutuel wickets to place your bet, Northern Dancer was the clear favourite, but was beaten at the wire by a 40 to 1 outsider. But of his first nine races, he had seven wins, including four stakes races. In the other two he finished second. Taylor and his people decided it was time for New York, and the colt did not let them down. He won the Remsen Stakes, his first time out on a New York track.

He was two years old, and the sun was really shining on him, they said, but a bit of a cloud moved over that sun, a bit bigger than a man's hand, when they found out that he had a quarter crack. That is a split up the side of the hoof, very painful and potentially very dangerous. Dr. Harthill met with Horatio Luro, and they decided to anesthetize the foot, with a local, and then with a farrier's knife parallel the crack on either side, and draw the diseased portion down to the bottom, and then immobilize the area as much as possible with a bar shoe. A vet named Bane in California had developed what was called a patch technique. Once again they anesthetized the foot against the high heat levels entailed in applying the patch, gave the colt small doses of tranquillizer, and hoped for the best but worried a lot about the worst.

But the patch held. Let's hear about the next phase from those of the principal players who are still here to recall it. First Dr. Harthill:

[Horatio] wanted to get him ready for the fall races in New York and the winter racing in Florida to prepare him for the Kentucky Derby. He had high hopes from the moment he got him.

Bruce Walker:

Bill Shoemaker rode him in the early classics in Florida and they thought they had Bill wrapped up for the Kentucky Derby.

Milt Dunnell:

The fact that Bill Shoemaker was riding him added considerable prestige. If he was good enough for Bill Shoemaker he was good enough for everybody else.

Dr. Harthill:

[Shoemaker] rode Northern Dancer in the Florida Derby and just the day before the race, in the training procedure, Horatio had told the jockey to go 5/16 of a mile, just a little over a quarter, as a blow out. The exercise boy misunderstood him and went 5/8 of a mile, which is twice as far. And he went in 59 seconds for the 5/8 and galloped out 3/4 in 11, which is racehorse time. So when Shoe rode him the next day he won, but it was just because he was such a great horse. And before we could get to him and tell him what had happened, Horatio hadn't told him prior to the race, and after the race [Shoemaker] had taken a plane, somebody had invited him to go to Cuba, and there was no way to communicate with him. He was out of touch, so he announced to the world in a press release that he was gonna ride Hill Rise [in The Derby.]

Bruce Walker:

[Shoemaker] rode a lot for Mesh Teddy who was the trainer of Hill Rise and so politically, and for business reasons, he had to pretty well jump to Hill Rise. So they were scrambling for a rider. But Horatio had always had a love/hate relationship with Billy Hartack, they had a lot of success together, and it was decided that they would go with the experience of Hartack. He had won the Kentucky Derby a couple of times before that and they felt that having that experienced a rider on the colt would be an advantage.

But enough of an advantage to win? Milt Dunnell wondered aloud about it.

He'd beaten the best horses in the east, if he beats the best horses in the west, why shouldn't he win the Triple Crown? Two days before the race I talked to Horatio Luro and I told him that Hill Rise was going to be the favourite, the morning line favourite, and Northern Dancer would be second. I said, "What do you think of it?" He said, "Well, if they beat us," he said, "it means they beat two minutes."

You would have to be a race historian to know that no horse had ever run the Derby in two minutes, the time that Luro was now sure The Dancer could make. But you don't even have to be a race fan to know that the Kentucky Derby is an event of mythic dimensions; the media are all over it, fortunes and reputations are made and lost. Owners, trainers, riders, journalists, fans — they all speak of it as a once-in-a-lifetime matter, and for the majority of all of the above, it is exactly and only that. The costs of entry, of preparing the horse for it, and hiring a name jockey, and even for fans — they can pay up to $4500 (for a clubhouse package ticket) just to watch the race — mean that it is never to be taken lightly. Not that its almost sacred resonance would ever allow such negligence.

Some might argue that the great French and British races have longer pedigrees, but few will try to designate any other as more important or better known. Horse folk will tell you that the horses know that they are in the midst of extraordinary tension, long before they get near the track itself and the deafening blare of the bands. Ron

Turcotte says, "When we step on the racetrack, and they play 'My Old Kentucky Home' and your horse is prancing to it and all that, it's something to behold, I'll tell ya."

Dr. Harthill, the vet, said he was sure despite the superb training that The Dancer had had "training to the minute" and improving all the time, the race would be extremely close. After all, the best horses in North America would be lining up behind those white bars, and every single owner and trainer felt that once-in-a-lifetime urgency.

Hill Rise, as predicted, was the favourite, at two-to-one. The bells clanged and the gates swung open, and the first quarter of a mile took the lead horse twenty-two and two-fifths seconds, with Northern Dancer and Hill Rise just apparently coasting along easily around the fourth or fifth position. The reporters and the fans and the owners could see, it was obvious, that Shoemaker on Hill Rise was watching Hartack on The Dancer "to see he didn't make a move on him," as Milt Dunnell put it. Even Ron Turcotte thought that Shoemaker had Hartack boxed in right where he wanted him, and knew it. But Hartack, as it turns out, also knew that he had a horse he could manoeuvre, a horse that could get him out of Shoemaker's box like a puppet on a spring. Harthill says he is convinced that Hartack outrode the more famous Shoemaker, "beat him to the punch up the backside," he says, and "I believe that's where the race was won." The journalist Milt Dunnell says,

> I waited until they got to the mile pole and I took a look to see what the time then was and he had run the mile in 1:36 and then that told me that he had to run that last quarter [mile] in twenty-four seconds. He opened up about two lengths on Shoemaker, before Shoemaker made a move.

As they came down the stretch, those who were there remember that the whole place erupted like a volcano, everyone screaming and jumping about. It was that dramatic. Even in the press box, they said, just the way Northern Dancer came battling through that stretch had all the hard-nosed old reporters up on their feet cheering him on. Bruce Walker says his running style made you want to admire him: "He just, like he grabbed the bit in his teeth and . . . 'You're not going by me, Hill Rise, that's it, I don't care how far we run, you're not going to get by me on this day.'"

Hill Rise seemed to make a terrific run at The Dancer, right at the end, but they could all see that he would never make it, and that even at the end the little three-year-old from Canada was still "digging in."

When they flashed the time, two minutes flat, all the old hands immediately knew: it was a record. You can see in the news film the quiet look of triumph on E.P. Taylor's face as he leads his little champion into the winner's circle and they put on the blanket of fresh red roses.

Three American races — the Derby, the Preakness at Baltimore's Pimlico track, and the Belmont Stakes at Belmont Park, New York — are called the Triple Crown races, and it is a dream seldom even tried for by owners: to have a horse who wins all three. And to the surprise of some observers the shouting and the tumult had scarcely subsided after the Derby when they heard E.P. Taylor's people talking about Baltimore — just two weeks away — and the phrase the Triple Crown. It is not common to run a horse that hard. Many bettors would anticipate the possibility of the horse's not being up to it that soon, maybe even fall apart. And so despite his win in the Derby, he did not come up as the favourite in Baltimore. Preakness bettors and odds-makers made him, once again, the number two. The too-soon argument did not seem to apply to Hill Rise, though, who had a solid record, and Horatio Luro became furious when the majority of the American sports writers seemed to be putting The Dancer down as a one-trick-pony, a fluke, and saying that this time Hill Rise would just run right over him; he'd only won by a neck, albeit a long one, in Kentucky; he'd get nailed at Pimlico. But Horatio said they were wrong, certainly wrong, they didn't know the horse: the distance was less (1 3/16th of a mile) and the little horse's tactical abilities were perfectly suited to anything up to a mile and a quarter.

Horatio was right. The Dancer won by two-and-a-half lengths. This time the blanket was made of black-eyed Susans. "They traditionally send over a case of champagne on ice," Bruce Walker said,

and Mrs. Taylor was in the tack room and she spread her fur coat over the tack trunks and said, "Come on in, boys, and have some champagne." And then Horatio was standing at the door like a

*bouncer and said, "No, he can't come in," and "He can't come in,"
and "He can't come in." Because he remembered all the writers who
had put Northern Dancer down and this was personal to him.*

Horatio also had reservations about moving on to the Belmont,
after two heavy-duty races in a row. But the pressure must have been
irresistible: two legs of the Triple Crown down and one to go. The
Dancer had earned his shot at it. Luro said, Yes, but maybe the
Belmont's mile and a half is too much so soon after the Preakness. Over
the next couple of days he scrutinized the horse's gait, his wind, his
attitude, his eyes, his smell. Northern Dancer came bouncing back.
They decided to go for it. To this day there is bitterness about how the
race was run. Not about the decision to go; The Dancer was apparently in great shape, dying to take the lead, an easy win in Peter Poole's
view, who was Windfields's general manager then. But it seems that
Bill Hartack inexplicably held him back, right from the start. "Throttled
him," Bruce Walker would say later. A questionable ride, others say
now. Not so questionable that Horatio would fire him, but a source of
grief, when the little horse came third after Quadrangle and Roman
Brother, a sore that for The Dancer's "family" has still not healed.

Well, the Queen's Plate was still ahead. And in the meantime, back
in Canada Northern Dancer had become a national hero. People wrote
letters to him. Not to E.P. Taylor or Ron Turcotte or Horatio Luro, but
to the horse himself. Among them was one that was very special. Bruce
Walker tells the story. The letter, he said, was

*from a boy at the Brantford School for the Blind, saying that he had
listened to all of the races and that he would like to meet Northern
Dancer. And Mrs. Taylor arranged transportation and she met the
boy at the track. Just prior to the arrival of Mrs. Taylor and her
special guest, Horatio had had the horse cleaned up and he went into
the stall to put the halter on Northern Dancer. And just as he reached
for the horse, Northern Dancer turned on a dime and was up on his
hind legs and he was flailing at Horatio. He didn't want to be bothered, just leave me alone, and Horatio had to dive under the webbing,
and the stall door out into the shed row. And Northern Dancer was
right behind, and he was intent on doing some damage to Horatio.*

*Just after Horatio escaped, Mrs. Taylor started walking down
the shed row and she said, "Where's my baby, where's Northern
Dancer?" And the horse stopped, and he pricked his ears and
looked, and he started to nicker, because he knew that he knew the
voice, and he knew that he was going to get some mints from Mrs.
Taylor, because she had been feeding him mints from the time he
was a baby. And the horse was a perfect gentleman. She walked
right up, gave him a mint, patted him, and was almost nuzzling
with him. And then she brought the boy over from the school for the
blind and she guided his hand to the horse's head. He just stood
there, and slowly patted the horse's head. And Northern Dancer
never moved. Never moved a muscle. It was amazing.*

When they got to Woodbine for the Queen's Plate, Luro and
Hartack had arrived at an understanding, and Hartack said later that
there was no way he could not win that race unless he fell off the horse.
He apparently decided it was time to redeem his reputation and that
this would be his show, Billy Hartack's show, not Northern Dancer's.
And when they came out of the gate The Dancer's fans were appalled
to see Hartack holding him back again, reining him in. Was he going to
make the same mistake all over again, do another Belmont and humiliate not just the horse and the trainer and the owner now, but the whole
darn country? Peter Poole described it:

*Hartack finally let the horse run and the horse cruised down the back-
stretch, and coming into the stretch Langcrest was on the lead and
Northern Dancer went by him like he was standing still. And he won
very easily and in hand, but I'm still convinced that that ride in the
Plate hurt the horse. And it wasn't announced that the horse had
bowed a tendon or injured his tendon until after the horse had gone
back to New York, and they said he injured himself training there.
But I'm convinced that he left here with a slight knot on his tendon.*

Milt Dunnell is convinced that The Dancer could have broken the
track record that day, but that Hartack was right to hold him back.

*He said, "I wasn't asked for a track record. If I had been, I would
have tried to provide it. All I was asked to do was win the race and
that's what we did. We won by seven lengths." So of course he won*

773

the race, but after the race was over I was talking to Hartack. I said, "Bill, eight horses in the race, you've got seven in front of you, you've got the Kentucky Derby horse underneath you. Weren't you a little bit concerned that you might run into a little traffic here and get the hero beaten on his homecoming?" And he looked at me and said, "Are you out of your goddamn mind? I'm sitting on the Derby winner and I'm going to get beaten by a bunch of damn Canadian breds?" I said, "What did you think you were on, Bill an Egyptian bred?" He said, "Well, I was on Northern Dancer, he's different."

That tendon was bowed, however, and, at three years old, it was time to retire him to stud, where he would leave an even greater mark on the sport than he had from the track. Ron Turcotte was on his back the first time he appeared on a racetrack, and rode him out again when they retired him, to a clamorous demonstration from the fans at Woodbine in June 1964.

Although he had outstanding records in speed (the two minutes at the Derby) and impressive cash returns for both his owners and those who bet on him, his real contribution was as a sire. A "prepotent sire," Dr. Harthill said, a sire of sires and a sire of fine broodmares, whose progeny are still selling at prime prices and still winning races.

From his own loins were sold 174 yearlings, averaging almost a million dollars a yearling. A world's record sale was established when one of his progeny, My Charmer, son of The Dancer's son Nijinsky (whose dam was Flaming Page), sold for thirteen million dollars.

It is getting to the point now where there are so many superb thoroughbreds with his genes that every time you see a great winner the chances are very good — perhaps as high as 75 percent according to Peter Poole — that he can be traced back to The Dancer. Bernard McCormack, Windfields' general manager, said,

There's only one horse that has ever run faster than him in the Kentucky Derby and that was Secretariat. [Northern Dancer] was the most dominant stallion of the thoroughbred breed in the last hundred years. And he will fulfill, going into the fourth and fifth generation of some very, very good race horses, a role where at some point, if we haven't reached it already, that 50, 60, 70 percent of all thoroughbreds will trace to him. That's a legacy that perhaps no other stallion has left.

He is the only horse ever inducted into Canada's Sports Hall of Fame, and according to Allan Stewart there, nine of the fourteen starters at the 1999 Kentucky Derby had bloodlines that trace back to The Dancer, thirty-five years after his own Kentucky Derby.

He was so small that as a stud he had difficulty mounting the mare. He got very frisky and rough with his first mare, Flaming Page, and she just turned around and kicked him in the ribs. When he finally did get her in foal it was the legendary Nijinsky. To get over the mounting problem, at Windfields they dug a shallow pit for the mare to stand in. Later, when the aging stud was moved to Chesapeake City, Maryland, they built him a "pitcher's mound" instead. At first his stud fee was a modest ten thousand dollars. Before he was finished it was up to a million dollars a time. The mares are usually at least equally important to or more so than the stud in determining the major characteristics and behavioural tendencies of the foals, but Northern Dancer's offspring tended to look and behave much more like their sire than their dam. "Prepotent" was what they called it. He continued to get pretty excited when a mare was presented. One stud manager still has a horseshoe-shaped scar from being pawed. He would get very rambunctious in his stall when a mare was near. "He couldn't quite understand that anybody else could have mares. . . . He wanted [them all]," said Peter Poole.

He was still breeding mares at the age of twenty-six. Noreen Taylor told us,

> *There's a thrill that comes off a good stallion. . . . Oh, it's like being a girl at the dance and saying "That boy sure is good-looking." And they had that kind of presence and they would just say, "Look at me," and you did. He had a warm, sensitive eye and I think people would say "the look of eagles," but he had it, a wonderful warm eye. But there'd be glints of fire in it, just fire and magic and charisma. And he demanded attention, and he usually got it.*

Peter Poole recalled going to see him in Maryland, when he was pretty old,

> *and he came charging at the fence and his eyes quite startling like*

he was looking right through you. The good horses have that look of eagles and they look at you and they don't look at you like they're seeing you, they're seeing whatever's going on through you.

They knew they were managing a legend. There was pressure to bring him home to Canada when he retired from stud, but they told people he was an old man for a horse, and not up to travel. And his last trip was only after he came to the end. He was twenty-eight, and very sick and in a lot of pain, and it was only a mercy to put him down. E.P. was gone now, too. His son, the distinguished foreign correspondent Charles Taylor, and Noreen's husband, took charge. He went to the border to meet this almost unheard-of cortege to do the paperwork and deal with the border officials. They dug a grave at Windfields. The cortege arrived at about midnight, and around two in the morning there were more than thirty people there, family and staff, the Windfields community and The Dancer's family, gathering to say a quiet goodbye. Noreen Taylor, fighting tears, said, "You don't stay up until midnight to throw roses in the grave of a horse you haven't . . . seen for, what, twenty years."

But they did that.

"Heart" was the word they all used about him, the men and women who contributed to this film, their voices still saying softly over the final seemingly slow motion filmic reprise of that gracefully running body and the tossing mane, things like,

Northern Dancer had more heart than most horses on the racetrack.

. . . A racehorse cannot perform at the highest level, consistently, without a huge heart. "Heart" is what one always says, on a great racehorse, that he had that competitive desire, that instinctive character, that he would not, that he wasn't willing to lose easily.

And they like to tell a story about his statue at Woodbine, that as the horses circle the paddock there, they look over at the statue and they whinny.

◆　◆　◆

The History Television documentary was written and directed by Martin Harbury.